T0396410

Judicial Review of Competition Law Enforcement in the EU Member States and the UK

International Competition Law Series

VOLUME 91

Editor

In its series editor, Alastair Sutton, Kluwer is fortunate to engage and benefit from the experience and expertise of one of the world's outstanding authorities on European Union and international economic law.

Introduction

In their efforts to regulate competition in an increasingly complex business environment, competition authorities face a daunting task. The European Commission and Courts, as well as national courts and legislatures, policymakers, and regulators, are constantly proposing, enacting, reviewing, and enforcing new legal measures, often addressing novel situations. Every industry and service is affected.

Contents/Subjects

With many titles currently available and new ones appearing regularly, the series' coverage includes detailed analyses of relevant legislation and case law in major global trading jurisdictions, defences used in cases involving the digital network economy, state aid cases, enforcement methodologies and a great deal more.

Objective & Readership

The purpose of Kluwer's International Competition Law Series is to follow the ever-changing contours of this dynamic area of the law, keeping the practice in sharp focus so that practising lawyers (including in-house counsel) and academics can be assured of the most up-to-date guidance and sources, in the widest possible range of applications.

The titles published in this series are listed at the end of this volume.

Judicial Review of Competition Law Enforcement in the EU Member States and the UK

Edited by

Barry Rodger and Or Brook

Maciej Bernatt
Francisco Marcos
Annalies Outhuijse

Published by:
Kluwer Law International B.V.
PO Box 316
2400 AH Alphen aan den Rijn
The Netherlands
E-mail: lrs-sales@wolterskluwer.com
Website: www.wolterskluwer.com/en/solutions/kluwerlawinternational

Sold and distributed by:
Wolters Kluwer Legal & Regulatory U.S.
920 Links Avenue
Landisville, PA 17538
United States of America
E-mail: customer.service@wolterskluwer.com

The empirical database, coding, coding book, and additional information about this project are available online. Please scan the QR code to access them.

ISBN 978-94-035-0238-0

e-Book: ISBN 978-94-035-0248-9
web-PDF: ISBN 978-94-035-0258-8

© 2024 Barry Rodger, Or Brook, Maciej Bernatt, Francisco Marcos & Annalies Outhuijse

All rights reserved. No part of this publication may be reproduced, stored in a retrieval system, or transmitted in any form or by any means, electronic, mechanical, photocopying, recording, or otherwise, without written permission from the publisher.

Permission to use this content must be obtained from the copyright owner. More information can be found at: www.wolterskluwer.com/en/solutions/legal-regulatory/permissions-reprints-and-licensing

Printed in the Netherlands.

Editorial Team

Co-Editors

Barry Rodger is a professor at Strathclyde Law School, Glasgow and has published widely in competition law. His co-authored textbook (with A MacCulloch) *Competition Law and Policy in the EU and UK* (Routledge) is in its 6th edition, and he has published numerous articles in journals such as the European Competition Law Review, the Journal of Antitrust Enforcement and Antitrust Law Journal. Many of his publications have focused on private enforcement, including his comprehensive studies of all competition-related litigation in the UK courts (ECLR 2006, GCLR 2009) and *Competition Law and Article 234: An Analysis* (Kluwer, 2008), which focused on all competition law Article 234 preliminary rulings. He coordinated an AHRC-funded project into comparative private enforcement and collective redress in the EU (www.clcpecreu.co.uk and *Competition Law Comparative Private Enforcement and Collective Redress Across the EU*, (Kluwer Law International, 2014) B Rodger (ed)). He has considerable experience in leading EU-wide research projects and is co-editor of *The EU Antitrust Damages Directive, Transposition in the Member States*, published by OUP in December 2018. His recent publications include: co-edited with A MacCulloch and P. Whelan, *Twenty Years of UK Competition Law: a Retrospective* (OUP 2021); co-ed with Prof A Stephan, *Brexit and UK Competition Law* (Routledge, 2022) and *Research Handbook on Private Enforcement of Competition law in the EU* (co-eds M Sousa Ferro and F Marcos, Edward Elgar, 2023)

Professor Rodger is the Chair of the Competition Law Scholars' Forum (www.clasf.org) and co-editor of the Competition Law Review.

Or Brook is an associate professor of Competition Law and Policy and the deputy director of the Centre for Business Law and Practice (CBLP) at the Law School of the University of Leeds. She specialises in international, EU and comparative competition law and regulation and empirical legal research (particularly systematic content analysis of legal text). Her main research focus has been the boundaries of competition law and its interface with other public policy considerations (e.g., sustainability, digital platforms, financial stability, and workers' rights), how competition authorities and other economic regulators set their enforcement priorities, and how procedural and institutional aspects of the enforcement inform the substantive scope of the law. She also explores the use of research methods more generally, and the law and politics behind empirical legal research. Dr Brook published a book titled *Non-Competition Interests in EU Antitrust Law: An Empirical Study of Article 101 TFEU* (Cambridge University Press, 2022), in which she systematically examined the role of public policy considerations in the enforcement of Article 101 TFEU on the basis of a large database of 3,100 cases. She has published articles in leading journals, such as the Modern Law Review, Common Market Law Review, and the Journal of Competition Law and Economics, making use of novel empirical methodologies. She is coordinating the Priority Setting Project, which studies enforcement priorities rules and practices of competition authorities, for which she has received funding from the UK's Economic and Social Research Council (ESRC) Impact Acceleration Accounts and the Michael Beverley Innovation Fellowship, and is supported by the United Nations Conference on Trade and Development Research Partnership Project.

Dr Brook acts as the director of the UK's branch of the International Academic Society for Competition Law (ASCOLA).

Maciej Bernatt is a professor at the University of Warsaw. He holds a habilitation, PhD and MA in Law and MA in International Relations (Political Sciences). He is the director of the Centre of Antitrust and Regulatory Studies and the head of the Department of European Economic Law, Faculty of Management, University of Warsaw (Poland). He is also the editor-in-chief of the Yearbook of Antitrust and Regulatory Studies as well as the director of ASCOLA Central Europe Chapter. He held visiting fellow appointments at the University of Melbourne, the Max Planck Institute for Innovation and Competition (Munich), the UNSW (Sydney), and the Loyola University Chicago. He has received scholarships and research grants from several institutions, including the Polish-US Fulbright Commission, the Max Planck Institute for Innovation and Competition, the Polish Minister of Science and Higher Education, and the Polish National Science Centre. His publications appeared in, *inter alia*, the Common Market Law Review, the European Law Review, the Journal of Antitrust Enforcement, the Columbia Journal of European Law, and the World Competition. He is also the author of two monographs as well as a co-author of two leading commentaries on the Polish Competition Act and the Polish Unfair Competition Act. In the past, he worked as a référendaire in the Polish Supreme Court and in the Constitutional Tribunal of Poland, as well as in the Helsinki Foundation for Human Rights, where he coordinated the Strategic Litigation Program. His litigation experience involves cases before the European Court of Human Rights and Polish courts.

Francisco Marcos is a professor of law at IE Law School (Spain), where he teaches business law, competition law, and law & economics. He holds a law degree from Universidad de Oviedo, an LLM from Berkeley [Fulbright scholar (1994-1995)] and a PhD from the University of Bologna. He is a member of the Editorial Board of World Competition (Kluwer), the European Business Organization Law Review (TMC Asser) and of European Company Law (Kluwer). Author of numerous academic works, including four books, he also has written more than one hundred contributions to collective books or law-review publications. He serves on the Boards of the Academic Society for Competition Law (ASCOLA) and the Competition Law Scholars Forum (CLaSF). He has worked all over the world as an independent consultant for the Asian Development Bank, the Centro American Bank for Economic Integration, the European Commission and the World Bank, advising governments, companies and firms on different matters in the area of market regulation and antitrust law. He served as the Client and Users' Ombudsman at SGAE, the main copyright-collecting society for composers and music publishers in Spain, and as General Director of Competition Policy at the Regional Antitrust Authority in Madrid. Nowadays, he is the academic consultant of CCS.

Annalies Outhuijse is an associate at Stibbe Amsterdam in the area of Administrative law. Here, she specialises in environmental law. Before this, she conducted a PhD research explaining the high rates of litigation and successful litigation in the case of Dutch cartel fines on the basis of an analysis of Dutch enforcement practice, comparative research with nine other EU Member States and four other Dutch market supervisors and interviews with practitioners, judges and NCAs. For this research, Annalies was also a visiting researcher at the European University Institute under the supervision of Prof. Dr Giorgio Monti in 2017. This research was successfully defended on 25 June 2019.

Alongside her PhD, Annalies undertook many other academic activities such as attending, organising and presenting at conferences, writing the yearly chronicle on Dutch competition law judgments for the Journal of European and Economic Law (SEW), advising the board of the journal AB Rechtspraak Bestuursrecht and several teaching activities. She lectured on competition law enforcement in the Dutch and English versions of the Master's course 'Competition Law', provided training and consulted to the Fijian Competition and Consumer Commission and gave tutorials in the second year LLB course 'Europeanisation of Public Law'.

In 2015, she graduated with an LLM in Dutch Law with a specialisation in Constitutional and Administrative Law (*summa cum laude*) and the LLM Research Master (*cum laude*). After her LLB and LLM studies, she was a research and teaching assistant at the Department of Administrative Law from April 2012.

Rapporteurs

AUSTRIA

Viktoria H.S.E. Robertson is a professor of Competition Law and Digitalisation at the Vienna University of Economics and Business. She is a course director of the Competition Policy and Digital Markets course at the College of Europe and Director of The Competition Law Hub (www.complawhub.eu). Previously, she was also a professor of International Antitrust Law at the University of Graz. She holds a law diploma and a doctorate from Graz University and an MJur from Oxford University, and has clerked with the Austrian Supreme Court on competition and intellectual property matters. Among others, she has been a visiting academic with Oxford University's Centre for Competition Law and Policy (CCLP), the Max Planck Institute for Comparative and International Private Law, Stanford University and the FGV-Rio Law School. She has taught competition law at Oxford University, the European University Institute, the College of Europe, Graz University and the Vienna University of Economics and Business. She is a member of the European Law Institute and the Academic Society for Competition Law, where she acts as director for scholarship. Her current research focuses on the application of competition law in digital market environments as well as on its intersection with sustainability concerns. She is the author of *Competition Law's Innovation Factor: The Relevant Market in Dynamic Contexts in the EU and the US* (Hart Publishing 2020) and *Competition Law in Austria* (Kluwer 2021).

BELGIUM

Caroline Cauffman obtained her Master's (1998) and PhD (2004) in Law from the KULeuven (Belgium). In 1999, she obtained the Ius Commune Researcher's certificate. She specialised in EU competition law from King's College (UK, MA 2012).

Currently, she is an associate professor at Maastricht University, a visiting professor at the University of Hasselt and the China-EU School of Law and an assessor at the Belgian competition authority.

Caroline is a research leader of the Research Program General Law of Obligations and Contracts of the Ius Commune Research School, as well as the author of numerous contributions to national and international journals dealing with issues of contract law, consumer law and competition law.

She is a member of the editorial board of the Maastricht Journal of European and Comparative Law and the Tijdschrift voor Consumenten- en Handelspraktijken and a member of the advisory board of the Journal of European Consumer and Market Law.

BULGARIA

Anton Dinev is Director of Global Partnerships and assistant professor of EU and Competition Law at Northeastern University - London. Previously, he taught (European) business law as a regular or visiting lecturer at universities in France, Belgium, and the Netherlands. Additionally, he has consulted on the public policy aspects of competition enforcement for law and public affairs firms and served as a non-governmental advisor to the International Competition Network (ICN), selected by the European Commission (DG COMP). He is an established researcher with publications in leading law journals and editorial commitments for Oxford Competition Law, the European Competition Law Review (ECLR), the World Competition Law and Economics Review, and the Journal of Antitrust Enforcement (JAE).

Alexandr Svetlicinii is an associate professor of law at the University of Macau, where he also serves as Program Coordinator of the Master of International Business Law. He holds a PhD from the European University Institute and an LLM from the Central European University. Professor Svetlicinii has published extensively on competition law and market regulation topics with a special focus on Central and Eastern European jurisdictions and, more recently, on China. His works appeared in European Law Review, Common Market Law Review, World Competition Law and Economics Review, European Competition Journal, European Competition Law Review, European Law Reporter, Market and Competition Law Review, Yearbook of Antitrust and Regulatory Studies, Revue Lamy de la concurrence, Concorrenza e Mercato, Revista Română de Concurenţă, Österreichische Zeitschrift für Kartellrecht, Pravna misao: časopis za pravnu teoriju i praksu, Právník: teoretický časopis pro otázky státu a práva, etc. The recently published monographs include *Competition Law in Moldova* (Kluwer, 2018) and *Chinese State Owned Enterprises and EU Merger Control* (Routledge, 2020).

In addition to his academic work, Dr Svetlicinii served as the non-governmental advisor to the International Competition Network (working group Mergers) and acted as a consultant in a number of projects for the European Commission. Currently, Alexandr Svetlicinii heads the Southeast Europe chapter of the Academic Society for Competition Law (ASCOLA).

CROATIA

Jasminka Pecotić Kaufman is a professor of law at the University of Zagreb, where she teaches competition law and business law. She holds an LLM from the University College London and a PhD from the University of Zagreb. Her overall research interests relate to the process of transition from a collusive to a competitive paradigm in societies, in particular in European post-socialist countries. Her most recent project studies institutional capacity and cartel enforcement in Central and Eastern Europe.

Prof. Pecotić Kaufman's work appeared in the Journal of Antitrust Enforcement, the World Competition Law and Economics Review, the Review of Central and East European Law, and the Yearbook of Antitrust and Regulatory Studies. She co-edited a book on competition law in Western Balkans (Springer 2024) and co-authored a book on competition law in Croatia (Kluwer, 2nd ed., 2022). She serves on the Board of the Academic Society for Competition Law (ASCOLA) and co-chairs its Southeast Europe chapter. Prof. Pecotić Kaufman is Vice-President of the Croatian Competition Law and Policy Association and the founder of the Šoljan Competition Law and Policy Conference series. She is a Member of the Editorial Board of the Yearbook of Antitrust and Regulatory Studies and the International Advisory Board of the Institute for Consumer Antitrust Studies. She was a Non-Resident Senior Research Fellow at the Institute for Consumer Antitrust Studies, Loyola University Chicago and a Jean Monnet Fellow at the European University Institute.

CYPRUS

Marios Iacovides is an associate professor of European Law, a senior lecturer in Commercial Law at Uppsala University and a researcher of the Royal Swedish Academy of Letters. His research focuses on the goals of competition law and on EU competition law, sustainability, and degrowth.

He obtained an LLB in European Legal Studies from King's College London, an LLM in European Integration Law from Stockholm University, and an LLD in European Law from Uppsala University. Upon completion of his doctoral studies, he held the position of research fellow at the University of Oxford's Institute of European and Comparative Law and of assistant professor in EU Law at Stockholm University. He also worked as Legal Counsel at the Swedish Competition Authority, which he has represented in several competition law proceedings at the Swedish Patent and Market Court and the Patent and Market Court of Appeal. He has acted as an expert advisor on EU competition law and sustainability for the Hellenic Competition Commission, a non-governmental advisor for DG Competition in the International Competition Network, and as counsel for a Swedish boutique competition law firm.

Maria Vassiliou is a practising advocate and legal consultant in a tier-one law firm in Cyprus. Maria obtained her LLM in Commercial Law from the University of Cambridge in 2017, graduating with First Class among the top 10% of her cohort. She obtained her LLB in Law from the University of Cyprus in 2016, graduating with First Class among the top 5% of her cohort. During her undergraduate studies, she interned at a leading consulting company in Cyprus specialising in competition law, where she first gained exposure to the area of Competition Law. During her internship, she authored an article titled 'Actions for damages: Towards an Effective Enforcement of Competition Law', which was published in a local business journal. In 2018, she was also appointed as a special research assistant to Dr Thomas Papadopoulos (assistant professor of Business Law at the Department of Law of the University of Cyprus) and undertook research in the field of commercial law with a particular focus on international and EU insolvency law. In 2021, she was also appointed as a research assistant to Dr Marios Iacovides during his fellowship at the University of Oxford. She currently practices law as a qualified advocate and regularly deals with and advises clients on matters of EU and Cyprus Competition Law, advising clients on mergers and acquisitions issues arising in relation to cartels and also drafting notifications of concentrations to the Cyprus Commission for the Protection of Competition. Maria is also actively involved in high-value commercial and civil litigation regularly appearing before Courts of all jurisdictions and instances.

CZECH REPUBLIC

Michal Petr is head of the Department of International and European Law at the Faculty of Law of Palacky University Olomouc, Czech Republic, and a senior researcher there. He specialises in EU law, in particular competition law, state aid, public procurement and regulation of network industries. Before his academic career, he worked for the Czech Competition Authority, first as Head of the Legislation Department (2003–2009), then as Director of the Section of Legislation and International Relations (2009–2010) and finally as the Vice-Chairman responsible for competition law and policy (2010–2015).

Michal authored numerous publications concerning competition law, regulation of network industries and due process. He is a member of the editorial board of the Antitrust Review of Competition Law, as well as a national correspondent for the European Competition and Regulatory Law Review and a member of the advisory appellate committee of the Czech Competition Authority and the Czech National Bank.

DENMARK

Caroline Heide-Jørgensen is a professor of Competition Law at the Faculty of Law, University of Copenhagen, Denmark. She holds a PhD and a doctorate (habilitation) from the Faculty of Law at the University of Copenhagen. Extensive publications in areas of EU and national competition law. She has been a part-time professor in Competition Law at BECCLE at the University of Bergen (2014-2020). She has been a member of the Danish Competition Council for more than ten years and now serves as its deputy chair.

ESTONIA

Evelin Pärn-Lee is a junior researcher and a PhD student at Tallinn University of Technology (TalTech). She has been lecturing EU competition law and policy at TalTech and Tartu University for over ten years. Her research is related to the interface of EU competition law, intellectual property law, innovation and ICT in general, as the private and public sector endeavours to innovate and create different challenges for competition regimes. In her doctoral thesis, she studies if the EU State aid framework and implementation thereof, when fostering innovation, is adequately considering the ultimate aim of the EU's competition law and policy, which is protecting the competition in order to maintain a level playing field in the Digital Single Market. She has authored several publications in journals, but also as book chapters and books (https://www.etis.ee/CV/Evelin_P%C3%A4rn-Lee/eng?lang=ENG). Apart from academic work, she has over twenty-five years of international consultancy experience as an attorney. She has also acted as a legal expert to the European Commission and

Estonian public authorities with regard to not only innovation, research and technology projects but also artificial intelligence studies. From time to time, she also provides public lectures or trainings on topics of state aid, innovation and procurement, etc.

FINLAND

Petri Kuoppamäki is a professor of Business Law at the Aalto University School of Business (Helsinki), where he is heading the Business Law Discipline and the Master's programme. He received his LLM in 1989 and LLD from the Helsinki University in 2003. Besides working in the academia, he served from 1993 to 2001 as Secretary General of the Finnish Competition Council (today Market Court) and from 2003 to 2011 as Vice President Legal & IP at the Nokia Corporation. Before joining Aalto University, he was professor of Competition Law at Helsinki University. Petri has published many books and articles on competition law, IPR and public procurement, *inter alia*. He was a member of the Finnish Research Council (Academy of Finland, Culture and Science Board) during the years 2019–2021. He is Chairman of the Board of the Finnish Competition Law Yearbook, which he co-founded in 2001. He is a full member of the Finnish Academy of Science and Letters and also, from 2024, the Chairman of the Legal Science Group of the Academy.

FRANCE

Rafael Amaro is a professor of Private Law at Caen Normandie University. He teaches EU and French Competition Law, Human Rights, Civil Procedure and Tort Law. His research focuses mainly on the private enforcement of competition law and unfair commercial practices in B2B and B2C relationships. He is a member of the European network of legal experts, Trans Europe Experts (TEE), and the Institut Caennais d'Etudes Juridiques.

GERMANY

Rupprecht Podszun holds the chair for Civil Law, German and European Competition Law at Heinrich Heine University Düsseldorf; he leads the University's Institute for Competition Law and is a Guest Professor at Université Aix-Marseille. He is the President of ASCOLA, the Academic Society for Competition Law. In recent times, he has focused on the regulation of digital gatekeepers and on institutional issues of antitrust law. He runs the blog www.d-kart.de.

Nils Overhoff is a Candidate Notary with the Chamber of Notaries of the Rhineland. He was a researcher at the Chair for Civil Law, German and European Competition Law from 2020 to 2022 and holds a PhD from Heinrich Heine University, Düsseldorf.

GREECE

Andriani Kalintiri is a Senior Lecturer in Competition Law at King's College London. Previously, she was a Lecturer at City University and a Fellow at the London School of Economics and Political Science. She is a Fellow of the UK Higher Education Academy, and she holds a PhD from Queen Mary University of London, an LLM from Cambridge University and an LLB from the University of Athens, Greece.

Andriani's research has been published in peer-reviewed journals, including the Journal of Competition Law & Economics, the Modern Law Review, the European Law Review, the Common Market Law Review and the Yearbook of European Law. Moreover, she is the author of the monograph Evidence Standards in EU Competition Enforcement (Hart 2019).

Andriani is a member of the editorial board of the Journal of European Competition Law & Practice. She was a member of the preparatory committee for the transposition of the ECN+ Directive on the effective enforcement of the competition rules by national competition authorities in Greece, and she has also served as an expert for the Hellenic Competition Commission.

Lefkothea Nteka is a partner in Lambadarios Law Firm specialising in EU and Greek competition law since 2021. Lefkothea has served as Commissioner – Rapporteur at the Hellenic Competition Commission (HCC) since 2013 and, before that, as Director of the Legal Services Directorate, Head of Unit and case handler. She has also worked as an Intern at the Directorate General of Competition of the European Commission in Brussels.

Lefkothea was a member of the EU Council's negotiation team for the adoption of the Directive on antitrust damages actions, of the legislative committee for the transposition of the Directive on antitrust damages actions in Greece, as well as a regular delegate-representative at the OECD and the European Competition Network. She was also a member of the legislative committee for the transposition of the Directive on the effective enforcement of competition rules by national Competition Authorities (ECN +) in Greece.

She has academic publications in law journals and collective volumes and teaches European competition law as a Visitor Lecturer at Université Aix – Marseille.

She holds a Bachelor's from the Faculty of Law of the University of Athens and a Master's (DES) from the Institut d'Etudes Européennes of the Université Libre de Bruxelles in European commercial law.

HUNGARY

Csongor István Nagy is a professor of law at the University of Galway, Ireland and at the University of Szeged, Hungary, and a research professor at the HUN-REN Center for Social Sciences, Hungary. He is a recurrent visiting professor at the Central European University (Budapest/New York/Vienna) and the Sapientia University of Transylvania (Romania) and an associate member of the Center for Private International Law at the University of Aberdeen, Scotland. He is admitted to the Budapest Bar and listed at various arbitral institutions. Professor Nagy graduated from the Eötvös Loránd University of Sciences (ELTE, dr jur.) in Budapest, where he also earned a PhD. He received his LLM and SJD from the Central European University (CEU) and a DSc from the Hungarian Academy of Sciences. He had visiting appointments in The Hague (Asser Institute), Munich (three times, at the Max Planck Institute), Brno (Masarykova University), CEU Business School (Budapest), Hamburg (Max Planck Institute), Edinburgh (University of Edinburgh), London (BIICL), Riga (Riga Graduate School of Law),

Bloomington, Indiana (Indiana University), Brisbane, Australia (University of Queensland), Beijing (China-EU School of Law), Taipei, Taiwan (National Chengchi University), Florence (European University Institute), Rome (LUISS) and Ann Arbor, Michigan (University of Michigan). Professor Nagy has more than 260 publications in English, French, German, Hungarian, Romanian and (in translation) in Croatian and Spanish. His works have been widely cited, among others, by the Court of Justice of the European Union and Hungarian courts and have been relied upon in litigation before the US Supreme Court.

IRELAND

Mary Catherine Lucey is an associate professor at UCD Sutherland School of Law, Director of the UCD Centre for the Common Law in Europe, Honorary Senior Fellow at Melbourne Law School and Senior Visiting Fellow at the School of Law, University of Reading. As a Non-Governmental Adviser to the Irish Competition and Consumer Protection Commission, she is a member of ICN Working Groups on Advocacy and Agency Effectiveness.

ITALY

Michele Messina is a professor of European Union Law at the University of Messina. He is Academic Coordinator of the Bachelor's in International Relations at the Department of Political and Legal Sciences of the University of Messina. He is Module Leader of a Jean Monnet Module on EU Citizenship and the Rule of Law, co-funded by the European Commission. He has been a non-governmental advisor of the DG Competition (European Commission) at the International Competition Network (ICN). He has been a visiting professor/researcher at the Faculté de droit de l'Université Paris-Est Créteil, Europa Institute of the Leiden Law School, Columbia University in the City of New York, School of Law of King's College London, and British Institute of International and Comparative Law (BIICL). He has been Course Director and Deputy Head of Section at the Academy of European Law (ERA) in Trier, Germany. He had worked as a Bluebook Intern at the DG Competition of the European Commission in Brussels. He completed his PhD in Law from the University of Rome Sapienza. He also holds a Master of Laws (LLM) in International Business Law from the University of Manchester. He is the author of several publications on EU Law in general and EU competition law more specifically.

LATVIA

Jūlija Jerņeva is a PhD candidate at the University of Latvia and a practising attorney and partner at law firm VILGERTS. She teaches EU Competition and State Aid Law and EU Internal Market Law at the Riga Graduate School of Law, as well as teaches Public International Law at the University of Latvia. She holds a law diploma from the University of Latvia, as well as she studied at the College of Europe (Bruges) and King's College London. Jūlija is a recognised EU and Competition Law expert in Latvia and is regularly invited by the Constitutional Court of Latvia to provide expert opinions on matters related to the interpretation of EU law.

LITHUANIA

Jurgita Malinauskaite is a professor of law and the Head of Brunel Law School, Brunel University London, UK, where she teaches competition law and energy law. She is also a visiting professor at Vytautas Magnus University (Kaunas, Lithuania). She is a Senior Fellow of the UK Higher Education Academy. Prior to her academic career, Malinauskaite served as a competition lawyer at the Competition Council of Lithuania.

Her expertise is in various aspects of competition law, including harmonisation, in the Central and Eastern European (CEE) region. She is also the author of numerous journal articles as well as three books, including Merger Control in Post-Communist Countries, Routledge, 2010; and Harmonisation of EU Competition Law Enforcement, Springer, 2019 (Harmonisation of EU Competition Law Enforcement | Jurgita Malinauskaite | Springer). The latter book was based on expansive research covering eleven CEE jurisdictions.

LUXEMBOURG

Caroline Cauffman (*see* Belgium).

MALTA

Sylvann Aquilina Zahra is a consultant at Ganado Advocates, specialising mainly in EU and Maltese competition law. She advises on antitrust, merger control and State aid law and assists clients in competition investigations, litigation and merger notifications. She sits on the Board of Directors of Epic Communications Limited, one of the main communication companies in Malta. Previously, Sylvann served for a number of years in various roles at the Maltese competition authority, including as a senior case officer and Director General. She also worked as a senior legal advisor on competition and consumer policy within the Office of the Prime Minister, as a researcher at the European Commission's Directorate General for Competition (DG COMP), and as a legal officer at the former Office of the Attorney General. Sylvann is a visiting senior lecturer and examiner at the University of Malta. Her teaching areas cover competition law, State aid and human rights under EU law. She also served as a non-governmental advisor for DG COMP in the International Competition Network. She has authored and co-authored chapters and articles on competition law in different publications. Sylvann graduated as a Doctor of Laws from the University of Malta and holds a Magister Juris from the University of Oxford.

NETHERLANDS

Annalies Outhuijse (*see* co-editors).

POLAND

Maciej Bernatt (*see* co-editors).

Maciej Janik is a graduate of Law and English Studies at the University of Łódź. He also graduated from the School of German Law, organised by the University of Łódź and the School of French Law, organised by the University of Warsaw. He received an

LLM for completing the multidisciplinary European Law and Economic Analysis programme at the College of Europe in Bruges. Maciej was a Blue Book Trainee at the Directorate General for Competition of the European Commission (DG COMP) and worked with law firms in Brussels and Warsaw. As a practising advocate, he specialises in competition and copyright law. He is currently pursuing a PhD in Competition Law at the University of Łódź.

PORTUGAL

Miguel Sousa Ferro is a professor at the University of Lisbon Law School, where he lectures courses within the Economic Law Department. His main areas of specialisation are EU Law, Competition Law and Nuclear Law. He obtained his PhD and his LLB from the University of Lisbon, and an LLM in European Studies from the College of Europe. He is a practising lawyer and Managing Partner at Sousa Ferro & Associados. He has published widely with national and international publishers and periodicals, including the books *The EU Antitrust Damages Directive: Transposition in the Member States* (Oxford University Press) and *Market Definition in EU Competition Law* (Edward Elgar). He is co-director of the Portuguese Competition & Regulation Journal and a member of several associations, foundations and research institutes. He is a Judge at the European Nuclear Energy Tribunal.

ROMANIA

Adriana Almăşan is a Law professor at the Faculty of Law, University of Bucharest. She teaches Competition Law and Civil Law. She is the co-founder and the director of the 'Centre for Competition Law Studies' of the same faculty. She is the author and co-author of several books and articles on civil law, contract negotiation and competition law. She sits on the board of several law journals and acts as a national rapporteur for Oxford Competition Law. She is an attorney, currently coordinating the competition and M&A practice of 'TAMC - Attorneys at Law' in Bucharest, and is also a member of the panel of arbitrators with the Romanian Court of International Commercial Arbitration by the Chamber of Commerce and Industry of Romania.

Ştefan Bogrea is a practising lawyer in the Bucharest Bar Association (specialised in litigation, EU Law and Human Rights Law) and has defended his PhD in Human Rights Law at the Faculty of Law, University of Bucharest. He teaches EU Law at a BA Level and is the scientific secretary of the 'Centre for Competition Law Studies' at the same faculty. He has also authored and co-authored several articles on EU Law, Human Rights Law and Competition Law.

SLOVAKIA

Ondrej Blažo is a professor at Comenius University Bratislava, Faculty of Law, Institute of European Law, and Director of that institute. He is also editor-in-chief of Bratislava Law Review and holds various positions in the management of the Faculty of Law. He graduated in Law from Comenius University Bratislava and in Economics from the Faculty of National Economy at the University of Economics in Bratislava.

Previously, he was a senior state counsel at the Antimonopoly Office of the Slovak Republic as a case handler and at the legal and EU affairs department (co-authored several legislative documents on Slovak competition rules). He is the author and co-author of publications focused particularly on competition law, EU competition law and EU public procurement law, including commentary to the Slovak Act on Protection Competition (C.H. Beck, 2012). His research was supported by many national and international grants, including the following projects: Jean Monnet Centre of Excellence 'Rule of Law in the European Union' and projects supported by the Slovak Research and Development Agency (SRDA): 'Effectiveness of legal regulation of protection of economic competition in the context of its application in practice', 'Effectivization of legal regulation of public procurement and its application in the context of EU law' (the SRDA evaluated the outcome of this project as 'excellent' and, in 2023, the project was selected as a 'flagship' project in social sciences).

SLOVENIA

Ana Vlahek obtained her BA in law in 2003 from the University of Ljubljana, Faculty of Law, by defending a thesis on the Reform of EC Competition Law. She continued her education at the University of Ljubljana with postgraduate studies in civil and commercial law and wrote in 2009 her PhD on the transfer of property rights in Europe. Since 2003, she has been employed at the University of Ljubljana and currently holds positions of both associate professor for Civil and Commercial Law and associate professor of European Law. She teaches the following courses at the University of Ljubljana: EU law, Commercial Law and Procedure, Insolvency Law, Collective Actions in the EU, Judicial Remedies in the EU, etc., and mentors the ELMC and the CEEMC moot court teams. Her main research interests cover European Union law, competition law, and collective redress. In competition law, she has specialised in antitrust private enforcement and cooperation between the national courts and competition authorities. She co-authored *Competition Law in Slovenia* (Wolters Kluwer, 2016 and 2019) and *Commentary on the Slovenian Competition Act* (GV, 2008). She was involved in drafting amendments to the Slovenian Competition Act and co-authored the 2017 Slovenian Collective Actions Act. She has been active in several competition law projects, including the European Commission's projects on the Education and Training of National Judges in the Field of EU Competition Law.

SPAIN

Francisco Marcos (*see* co-editors).

SWEDEN

Lars Henriksson is a professor of Law and heads the Center for Business Law at the Stockholm School of Economics. He received his MSc in General Management at SSE in 1991 and his LLM from Stockholm University in 1998. His area of research and practice is within antitrust and competition law, contract law, EU law, company and market law and international trade law. Also, a special interest in his research is devoted to regulated markets and law-related issues of market regulations. He has chaired a governmental public enquiry on regulations and is a member of ASCOLA, the worldwide association of competition law academics. He has been appointed to the Council for Research Issues at the Swedish Competition Authority and has headed of specialisation for the LLD Programme in Law at SSE. Since 2011, he has been on the Board of the Institute of Intellectual Property Law and Market Law at the Stockholm University, Faculty of Law. In 2013, he became a non-governmental advisor to the International Competition Network (ICN) Unilateral Conduct Working Group, and he is also a member of La Ligue internationale du droit de la concurrence (LIDC). He has published numerous articles on legal matters such as competition law, copyright law, public procurement, company law and telecom and energy regulation.

UK

Barry Rodger and Or Brook (*see* editors).

Summary of Contents

Table of Contents

Acknowledgements

This book, and the underlying empirical research project, has taken a considerable period to finalise, and inevitably, there are a number of people whose support, assistance and hard work were absolutely vital in ensuring its successful completion and to whom we, the co-editors, extend our gratitude.

This project would not have been feasible without the incredible hard work of all national rapporteurs and teams in compiling case databases, coding all relevant cases on Excel spreadsheets in conformity with our lengthy coding book, and writing their national chapters following a structured template. There was more work involved than any of us envisaged at the outset of the project back in 2020, particularly for those rapporteurs in legal systems with hundreds of cases involved. We are extremely grateful to all of them for engaging with this research methodology.

Working on such an international and comparative project involving multiple partners (especially without the support of research funding) can be challenging and difficult, as well as time-consuming. It is also exceptionally rewarding and breaks new grounds in revealing how EU law enforcement relies on national legal systems, which, for a variety of historical, social and legal reasons, widely diverge.

Many thanks to Professor Andreas Stephan of the University of East Anglia (and Centre for Competition Policy, Norwich Law School), who provided really helpful feedback on the Chapters in Parts I and III of the book. We are incredibly grateful for the support received from the members of the Association of European Competition Law Judges (AECLJ) and from the European Competition Network Unit of the European Commission Directorate General for Competition and for their curiosity about the project. In particular, special thanks are due to Dr Adam Scott, Sir Peter Roth and Rainer Becker for their support throughout the project and their valuable feedback and suggestions while designing and undertaking the project, and interpreting its outcomes.

Finally, we are grateful to Kluwer Law International and Simon Bellamy for being so supportive of this research project and also for their understanding where there were delays in the delivery of the manuscript, as is often inevitable in multi-party projects.

PART I Outline and Approach

CHAPTER 1

Introduction

Barry Rodger, Or Brook & Maciej Bernatt

1 AIMS

National courts play a special role in the enforcement of EU competition law. Under the EU enforcement framework instituted by Regulation 1/2003, they constitute the main forum for the review of enforcement decisions taken by national competition authorities (NCAs).[1] This is not a simple task, as the application of the competition rules often calls for a complex economic and legal assessment.[2] At the same time, beyond the trite assertion that judicial review seeks to protect the rule of law, European competition law and legal scholarship have offered scant guidance on the functions of judicial review. The effectiveness of judicial review within the EU legal order, therefore, is often taken for granted,[3] and very little is known about its operation and impact in practice.

This project is the first to undertake a comprehensive, comparative empirical study, mapping out the judicial review of competition law public enforcement in the European Union (EU) and the United Kingdom (UK) in order to provide a greater understanding of the practical operation of the judicial review role. We undertake an empirical study of all national judgments reviewing the application of Articles 101 and 102 Treaty on the Functioning of the European Union (TFEU) and the national

1. Council Regulation (EC) No. 1/2003 of 16 December 2002 on the implementation of the rules on competition laid down in Articles 81 and 82 of the Treaty [2003] OJ L1/1 (Regulation 1/2003), Preambles 8, 21.
2. Joined cases C-215/96 and C-216/96 Bagnasco ECLI:EU:C:1999:12, 50. Also *see* Commission Notice on the co-operation between the Commission and the courts of the EU Member States in the application of Articles 81 and 82 EC OJ C 101 ('Commission Notice on Cooperation with National Courts'), para. 8.
3. Damien Geradin and Nicolas Petit, 'Judicial Review in European Union Competition Law: A Quantitative and Qualitative Assessment' in Massimo Merola and Jacques Derenne (eds), *The Role of the Court of Justice of the European Union in Competition Law Cases* (Bruylant 2012), 22.

equivalent provisions[4] by NCAs between the entry into force of Regulation 1/2003 in May 2004 and the end of April 2021. Covering 5,707 judgments, the empirical findings are used to: (i) comprehensively *map* out the judicial review practices across the EU and the UK, comparing their quantitative and qualitative aspects across the various jurisdictions, and (ii) to *assess* the operation of judicial review of the national competition law agencies.

This approach aspires to fill gaps in the existing scholarship. First, we aim to shed light on national enforcement. Thus far, the scholarship on the judicial review of EU competition law enforcement has mostly focused on appeals launched against the decisions of the European Commission ('Commission').[5]

There is limited academic literature on the judicial review of EU and national competition law enforcement at the national level. Often, legal scholars limit their studies to their own jurisdiction and national courts or in relation to a limited number of legal systems, as outlined below. As a result, although the basic institutional structures of the various national judicial systems may be transparent, little is known of their actual functioning across the EU. The lack of attention to this pillar of the national enforcement system demonstrates a clear gap in the academic competition law literature, especially since some previous studies on certain Member States have illustrated the importance of this pillar for 'controlling' the operation of the NCAs and ensuring their effectiveness.[6]

Second, and even more fundamentally, the role of national courts merits scholarly attention because of its impact on the rule of law: an EU law value expressly set out and established in Article 2 Treaty on European Union (TEU).[7] Judicial review is a key 'rule of law' safeguard. It seeks to ensure that each NCA stays within the limits prescribed by law and minimises the likelihood of abuse of power.[8] Accordingly,

4. For the definition of the national equivalent provisions *see* Chapter 2, section 3.1.
5. Martin Günster et al., 'European Antitrust Policy 1957-2004: An Analysis of Commission Decisions' (2010) 36(2) Review of Industrial Organization 97; Yannis Katsoulacos et al., 'Antitrust Enforcement in Europe in the Last 25 Years: Developments and Challenges.' (2019) 55 Review of Industrial Organization 5 DOI: 10.1007/s11151-019-09698-2; Geradin and Petit, *supra* n. 3; Olivier Guersent, 'The Fight Against Secret Horizontal Agreement in the EC Competition Policy' (2003) 30 Fordham International Antitrust 43; P. Takis Tridimas and Gabriel Gari. 'Winners and Losers in Luxembourg: A Statistical Analysis of Judicial Review Before the ECJ and the CFI (2001-2005)' (2010) 2 European Law Review 133 DOI: 10.1023/a:1010645411771; Christopher Harding and Alun Gibbs. 'Why Go to Court in Europe? An Analysis of Cartel Appeals 1995-2004' (2005) 30(3) European Law Review 349; Frank Montag, 'The Case for a Radical Reform of the Infringement Procedure under Regulation 17' (1996) 17(8) European Competition Law Review 428-443; Jan Blockx, 'The Impact of EU Antitrust Procedure on the Role of the EU Courts (1997-2016), (2018) 9(2) Journal of European Competition Law & Practice 92-103 DOI: 10.1093/jeclap/lpy004.
6. This is evident in the accounts of the 'previous studies', included in the national reports of this volume. In addition, a Pilot field study on the functioning of the national judicial systems for the application of competition law rules was commissioned by DG Justice, examining the functioning of judicial review in a limited time period from mid-October 2013 until mid-March 2014. See European Commission, 'Pilot field study on the functioning of the national judicial systems for the application of competition law rules', 7 March 2014.
7. Maciej Bernatt, 'Rule of Law Crisis, Judiciary and Competition Law' (2019) 46(4) Legal Issues of Economic Integration 345, 346-350 DOI: 10.54648/leie2019022.
8. Maciej Bernatt, *Populism and Antitrust: The Illiberal Influence of Populist Government on the Competition Law System* (CUP 2022), 106. For more on the roles played by judicial review of

Article 6 of the European Convention on Human Rights (ECHR) calls for judicial review to examine the substance of any NCA decision, as well as the procedure in the administrative proceedings leading to its adoption.[9] By doing so, an effective review system also plays another function: it promotes the accountability of NCAs.[10]

Finally, beyond the subject focus of this study, this project is also unique in its empirical methodology. Prior to modernisation, scholars provided various doctrinal-legal accounts of the (limited) role of national courts.[11] Only a few empirical studies have mapped the competencies and procedural rules governing various national courts, pointing to hurdles preventing them from playing a greater role[12] or recording the (limited) number of court judgments applying the EU competition law provisions.[13] Other empirical studies on the application of EU law by national courts beyond the field of competition law contained some interesting observations relevant to the field of competition.[14]

Whereas the 2010s witnessed dramatic growth in the empirical analysis of the operation of courts worldwide,[15] only a few empirical studies have explored judicial review of administrative agencies in Europe in general and of competition law in particular. Judicial review of national courts continued to be examined mostly by

administrative actions, *see, e.g.*, Louis Jaffe, *Judicial Control of Administrative Action* (Little, Brown and Company 1965); Paul Craig, *EU Administrative Law* (OUP 2012), 250.

9. Bernatt, *supra* n. 8, 106.
10. *Ibid.*
11. Ian Forrester, 'Complement or Overlap? Jurisdiction of National and Community Bodies in Competition Matters after SABAM', 1974 11 Common Market Law Review 171 DOI: 10.54648/cola1974012; Ian Forrester and Christopher Norall, 'The Laicization of Community Law: Self-Help and the Rule of Reason: How Competition Law Is and Could Be Applied' 21(1) Common Market Law Review 11; John Meade, 'Decentralisation in the Implementation of EEC Competition Law – A Challenge for the Lawyers' (1986) Northern Ireland Legal Quarterly 101; Richard Whish, 'The Enforcement of EC Competition Law in the Domestic Courts of Member States' (1994) 2 European Competition Law Review 60 DOI: 10.54648/eulr1994003; Ivo Van Bael, 'The Role of the National Courts' (1994) 1 European Competition Law Review 3; Bos, 'Towards a Clear Distribution of Competence Between EC and National Authorities' (1995) 7 European Competition Law Review 410-416; Claus-Dieter Ehlermann,'Implementation of EC Competition Law by National Anti-trust Authorities' (1996) 8 European Competition Law Review 88-95; Linda Hiljemark, 'Enforcement of EC Competition Law in National Courts: The Perspective of Judicial Protection' (1997) 17(1) Yearbook of European Law 83 DOI: 10.1093/yel/17.1.83.
12. August J. Braakman 'The Application of Articles 85 & 86 of the EC Treaty by National Courts in the Member States' (1997) EU Commission Publications Office, available here: https://op.europa.eu/en/publication-detail/-/publication/03d808bf-3928-4793-bcfc-72bb63da27dd. John Temple Lang, General Report on the Application of Community Competition Law on Enterprises by National Courts and National Authorities, FIDE Congress (1998).
13. J.H.J. Bourgeois, 'EC Competition Law and Member State Courts' (1993) Fordham International Law Journal 331.
14. Alec Stone Sweet and Thomas L. Brunell. 'The European Court and the National Courts: A Statistical Analysis of Preliminary References, 1961-95' (1998) 5(1) Journal of European Public Policy 66.
15. Keren Weinshall and Lee Epstein, 'Developing High-Quality Data Infrastructure for Legal Analytics: Introducing the Israeli Supreme Court Database' (2020) 17(2) Journal of Empirical Legal Studies 416-434, 416 DOI: 10.1111/jels.12250.

'traditional' legal methodologies, examining the rules[16] and jurisprudence of national courts, for example, via the lenses of coherence[17] or the impact on the rule of law.[18] Especially since the 2010s, there has been an apparent trend towards the use of more systematic empirical approaches to studying national judicial review. As will be elaborated in the national reports, some studies have examined the operation of judicial review in a single or a few Member States.

Several interesting empirical studies have examined specific issues on a comparative or multi-jurisdiction basis. *Essens*, *Gerbrandy* and *Lavrijssen* focused on national courts' standards of review in relation to competition law and other economic regulations.[19] They demonstrate that such standards may affect elements of the fining decisions that are being reviewed and how this review is performed. *Georgieva* examined the use of the Commission's soft law by national courts, focusing on Germany, France, the UK, and the Netherlands.[20]

Another clear reference point for the project is the earlier research undertaken by *Outhuijse*,[21] in which she sought to analyse and explain the high rates of (successful) litigation in Dutch anti-cartel enforcement. Her research constituted the first empirical assessment of the frequency of (successful) litigation, focusing only on cartel fines cases across ten Member States, including the Netherlands and the UK. *Brook* studied the role of non-competition interests (public policy considerations) in the enforcement of Article 101 TFEU, based on a database that also includes information on judicial review of public enforcement in five Member States (France, Netherlands, Germany, Hungary and the UK, 2004-2017).[22] *Brook* and *Eben* examined the relationship between EU and national competition and other laws, examining the practice of French and German courts.[23]

Rodger studied preliminary rulings involving competition law questions (2004-2013), providing a comprehensive account of all those rulings and in particular how they were dealt with subsequently in the legal systems of the referring Member

16. Ioannis Kokkoris and Ioannis Lianos, *The Reform of EC Competition Law: New Challenges* (Wolters Kluwer 2009); Temple Lang, 'The Duty of Cooperation of National Courts in EU Competition Law' (2014) 17 Irish Journal European Law 27.
17. Wolf Sauter, *Coherence in EU Competition Law* (OUP 2016).
18. Bernatt, *supra* n. 7.
19. Oda Essens et al., *National Courts and the Standard of Review in Competition Law and Economic Regulation* (Europa Law Publishing 2009), 173-198.
20. Zlatina Georgieva, 'The Judicial Reception of Competition Soft Law in the Netherlands and the UK' (2016) 12(1) European Competition Journal 54 DOI: 10.1080/17441056.2016.1221167; Zlatina Georgieva, 'Soft Law in EU Competition Law and Its Reception in Member States' Courts' (2017) PhD dissertation, available here:https://pure.uvt.nl/ws/portalfiles/portal/23090447/Georgieva_Soft_law_28_06_2017_emb_tot_31_1_2018.pdf.
21. Annalies Outhuijse, 'Effective Public Enforcement of Cartels: Explaining the High Percentages of Litigation and Successful Litigation in the Netherlands' (2019) available here: https://www.rug.nl/research/portal/nl/publications/effective-public-enforcement-of-cartels (e9a200be-9d1b-49b1-95d8-48cc3345e40b).html.
22. Or Brook, *Non-competition Interests in EU Antitrust Law: An Empirical Study of Article 101 TFEU* (CUP 2022).
23. Or Brook and Magali Eben, 'Article 3 of Regulation 1/2003: A Historical and Empirical Account of an Unworkable Compromise' (2024) 12(1) Journal of Antitrust Enforcement 45.

States.[24] *Mejia* analysed appeals submitted against telecoms and competition regulators in Spain and the UK (2000-2016), seeking to assess how legal traditions impact the outcomes of judicial challenges to regulators' actions.[25] *Bernatt* assessed the permissibility of deferential standards of judicial review in EU and national competition law proceedings in the light of ECHR fundamental rights standards and EU law principles, focusing on NCAs in Central Europe.[26] Bernatt also studied how judicial review in competition law operates when faced with illiberal shifts in the EU Member States (i.e., Hungary and Poland), focusing particularly on risks to national courts' independence and expertise.[27] The empirical nature of this project, therefore, gives us the opportunity to provide original and unique datasets and findings. By adopting an empirical approach, the project provides a unique and significant contribution not only with respect to EU and national competition laws but also more broadly with respect to comparative administrative law scholarship in Europe.

This chapter is structured as follows. First, section 2 outlines the growing importance of national enforcers in general and national courts in particular following the entry into force of Regulation 1/2003. This section will set the scene in terms of the national enforcement of the competition law prohibitions in order to appreciate, as discussed in the following section, the fundamental role of the national courts in this new enforcement framework. Section 3 presents the four main tasks of national courts in the enforcement system, highlighting the limited EU law guiding their operation. Section 4, in turn, discusses the parallel application of national competition rules alongside Articles 101 and 102 TFEU, the role of national courts in this regard, and why purely national competition law enforcement and the UK following Brexit were included in the study.

Section 5 outlines the legal context for the Court of Justice for the European Union (CJEU) to review European Commission competition law infringement decision-making to provide a juxtaposition for the limited legal rules for the functioning of the national courts in their parallel role. The final section of this introductory chapter outlines the structure of the book.

---

24. Barry Rodger, 'Competition Law Preliminary Rulings: A Quantitative and Qualitative Overview Post Regulation 1/2003' (2014) Global Competition Litigation Review 125-139.
25. Nuria Ruiz Palazuelos, El control jurisdiccional de la discrecionalidad de los organismos reguladores: Un análisis de casos en los ámbitos de la energía y las telecomunicaciones, Aranzadi 2018.
26. *See* among others, Maciej Bernatt, 'Transatlantic Perspective on Judicial Deference in Administrative Law', (2016) 22(2) Columbia Journal of European Law 275-325. Maciej Bernatt, 'Effectiveness of Judicial Review in the Polish Competition Law System and the Place for Judicial Deference' (2016) 9(14) Yearbook of Antitrust and Regulatory Studies 97-124 DOI: 10.7172/1689-9024.yars.2016.9.14.4.
27. Bernatt, *supra* n. 8, 106.

2 NATIONAL COURTS AND EU COMPETITION LAW ENFORCEMENT: A SHORT HISTORY

NCAs and national courts have been gaining an increasingly significant role across Europe since the early 2000s, particularly following the entry into force of Regulation 1/2003 in May 2004 and Directive 1/2019 in January 2019 (the 'ECN+ Directive').[28]

Under the old enforcement system of Regulation 17/62,[29] public enforcement of the EU prohibitions against anti-competitive agreements (governed by Article 101 TFEU) and abuse of dominance (governed by Article 102 TFEU) was mostly undertaken by the Commission and was subject to review by the General Court (GC) and European Court of Justice (ECJ). Regulation 17/62 obliged undertakings to notify the Commission about all agreements that had the potential to be considered anti-competitive prior to their implementation, and the Commission alone held the power to issue exemption decisions under Article 101(3) TFEU. In that highly centralised system, NCAs and national courts played only a limited role. Although the ECJ held that Articles 101(1) and 102 TFEU are directly applicable[30] and although around half of the NCAs were formally competent to apply Article 101(1) TFEU under their respective national laws and such actions could be reviewed by national courts,[31] the Commission's monopoly in the application of Article 101(3) TFEU had discouraged national enforcement of the EU competition law provisions.[32] The enforcement of national competition laws, moreover, was considerably limited in most of the Member States.[33]

By the 1990s, the centralised system of prior notification and exemption was being increasingly criticised as unmanageable and ineffective.[34] The Commission's 1993 Notice addressing the division of responsibilities between itself and the national courts marked a first step towards decentralisation,[35] which was reinforced in 1997 by the adoption of the Commission's guidelines on cooperation with the NCAs.[36] Yet, the Notice and the Guidelines had only limited effect in practice and were criticised for

---

28. Directive (EU) 2019/1 of the European Parliament and of the Council of 11 December 2018 to empower the competition authorities of the Member States to be more effective enforcers and to ensure the proper functioning of the internal market [2019] OJ L 11 ('ECN+ Directive').
29. Council Regulation (EEC) No. 17/1962 of 21 February 1962 First Regulation Implementing Articles 85 and 86 of the Treaty [1962] OJ 13.
30. Case 127/73 *BRT* v. *SABAM* ECLI:EU:C:1974:25, para. 15.
31. *See* the national reports in Part II in respect of both of these issues for all EU Member States and the UK.
32. Temple Lang, *supra* n. 12, 8; Wouter Wils, 'Regulation 1/2003: A Reminder of the Main Issues', in Damien Geradin (ed.) *Modernisation and Enlargement: Two Major Challenges for EC Competition Law* (Intersentia 2004), 24; Luis Ortiz Blanco, *EC Competition Procedure* (OUP 2006), 44.
33. *See* Part II of this book and Temple Lang, *supra* n. 12, 38.
34. *See, e.g.*, Wouter Wils, 'Regulation 1/2003: An Assessment after Twenty Years' (2022) 46(1)World Competition, 3-36; Wouter Wils, 'Ten Years of Regulation 1/2003: A Retrospective' (2013) 4(4) Journal of European Competition Law and Practice 293-301; Brook, *supra* n. 22, 177-179, 206-211, 308-309, 339-341, 83-87.
35. Commission Notice on Cooperation Between National Courts and the Commission in Applying Articles 85 and 86 of the EEC Treaty [1993] OJ C 39/6.
36. Commission Notice on Cooperation between National Competition Authorities and the Commission in Handling Cases Falling within the Scope of Articles 85 or 86 of the EC Treaty [1997] OJ C 313, 45-46.

failing to address many of the practical problems preventing greater national enforcement and for their lack of protection for procedural rights.[37]

The NCAs and national courts moved towards a more significant role in EU competition law enforcement towards the turn of the millennium, as the Commission's Modernisation White Paper of 1999 called for a system both requiring and facilitating the NCAs to enforce the EU competition law prohibitions in parallel to the Commission.[38] The role of NCAs, therefore, was dramatically transformed by the entry into force of Regulation 1/2003. Nowadays, the vast preponderance of Articles 101 and 102 TFEU enforcement decisions (circa 90 %!)[39] are rendered by NCAs, in addition to active enforcement of purely national cases in many Member States.

The Regulation has also significantly transformed the role of national courts. Under the Regulation, in the words of the Commission, 'national courts have become an important arm of application of the EU competition rules'.[40] It instituted a highly decentralised judicial review system, where appeals on the NCAs' decisions applying EU and/or national competition laws can only be reviewed by national courts. The EU Courts can only indirectly influence the decision-making of national courts by means of preliminary reference proceedings, and the Commission has limited powers to influence ongoing proceedings in front of NCAs and courts.[41]

This institutional choice was highly contentious. During negotiations on Regulation 1/2003, not all agreed that a decentralised judicial review system was desirable. Stakeholders warned that '[d]ivergent application of Community competition law by national courts would pose a threat to the proper functioning of the single market and the coherence of the system'.[42] The Economic and Social Committee, in particular, suggested several times that the judgments of national courts should be open to appeal to supranational courts empowered to assess both the law and the facts.[43] According to

---

37. Alan Riley, 'More Radicalism, Please: The Notice on Co-operation Between National Courts and the Commission in Applying Articles 85 and 86 of the EEC Treaty' (1993) 3 European Competition Law Review 91; Hiljemark, *supra* n. 11; Temple Lang, *supra* n. 12, 38.
38. The Commission White Paper on Modernisation of the Rules Implementing Articles 85 and 86 of the EC Treaty COM/99/0101 ('Modernisation White Paper').
39. https://competitionpolicy.ec.europa.eu/european-competition-network/statistics_en. *See also* Wils, *supra* n. 34.
40. Communication from the Commission, Ten Years of Antitrust Enforcement under Regulation 1/2003 -Achievements and Future Perspectives COM/2014/0453 final (2014) ('Regulation 1/2003's 2014 Report'), para. 22.
41. For those coordination mechanisms, *see* section 3 below. For the role of national courts, *see also* Sauter, *supra* n. 17, 172-173.
42. Explanatory Memorandum to COM(2000)582 Implementation of the rules on competition laid down in Articles 81 and 82 of the Treaty and amending Regulations (EEC) No. 1017/68, (EEC) No. 2988/74, (EEC) No. 4056/86 and (EEC) No. 3975/87 ('Regulation implementing Articles 81 and 82 of the Treaty') COM(2000)582 ('Modernisation Explanatory Memorandum'), para. 9.3.
43. Opinion of the Economic and Social Committee on the 'White Paper on modernisation of the rules implementing Articles 81 and 82 of the EC Treaty – Commission programme No 99/027' (2000/C 51/15), para. 2.3.5.11; Opinion of the Economic and Social Committee on the 'Proposal for a Council Regulation on the implementation of the rules on competition laid down in Articles 81 and 82 of the Treaty and amending Regulations (EEC) No. 1017/68, (EEC) No. 2988/74, (EEC) No. 4056/86 and (EEC) No. 3975/87 ("Regulation implementing Articles 81 and 82 of the Treaty")' (2001/C 155/14) ('Opinion of the Economic and Social Committee on Modernisation White Paper'), para. 2.13.

the Committee, 'in a decentralised system without a single appeal authority it is difficult to guarantee not only the right of defence, but also the coherent and consistent application of Community competition rules across the EU'.[44] The proposed cooperation requirements to be imposed on national courts by the draft Regulation, according to the Committee, 'are definitely not great enough to reach this objective',[45] and neither is the preliminary reference procedure.[46] Scholars, moreover, voiced concern over the ability of the national courts to perform effective judicial review, noting that most national courts had only limited experience with the provisions of competition law.[47]

The Commission, nevertheless, disagreed. The Modernisation White Paper argued that as EU competition law and policy had been clarified over the years leading to the reform, the burden of enforcement could be shared 'more equitably' with NCAs and national courts, 'which have the advantage of proximity to citizens and the problems they face'.[48]

Consequently, not only did Regulation 1/2003 vest national courts with the tremendous task of reviewing the vast majority of EU competition law enforcement, but it also contains very few provisions aiming to ensure the harmonised and consistent application of the EU competition provisions across the internal market, which will be elaborated on in the following sections.

In all other respects, the decentralised competition law enforcement system is based on the principles of procedural and institutional autonomy.[49] NCAs and national courts must rely upon the procedural enforcement powers and institutional setting prescribed by their respective domestic laws. The Commission has introduced some soft measures to facilitate some convergence within the European Competition Network (ECN),[50] which is an informal forum for discussion and cooperation between the Commission and NCAs. Notably, while the new enforcement regime resulted in voluntary harmonisation in some areas,[51] neither Regulation 1/2003 nor the ECN

44. Opinion of the Economic and Social Committee on Modernisation White Paper, para. 2.13.1.
45. *Ibid.*
46. *Ibid.*, para. 2.13.4.
47. Claus-Dieter Ehlermann and Isabela Atanasiu. 'The Modernisation of EC Antitrust Law: Consequences for the Future Role and Function of the EC Courts' (2002) 23(2) European Competition Law Review 72-80.
48. Modernisation White Paper, 5.
49. Regulation 1/2003, Article 35. At the same time Member States need to ensure that the enforcement system put in place does not undermine the effectiveness of EU law.
50. For the overview of various challenges created by the lack of procedural convergence *see* Maciej Bernatt, 'Convergence of Procedural Standards in the European Competition Proceedings' (2012) 8(3) Competition Law Review 255, 267-271.
51. Wils, *supra* n. 34. *See also* Report on the functioning of Regulation 1/2003, paras 31-33; Commission Staff Working paper, '10th Anniversary of Regulation 1/2003: Convergence and Cooperation in the ECN', ECN Brief 05/2011, accessible at http://ec.europa.eu/competition/ecn/brief/05_2011/brief_05_2011.pdf, 4-6; ECN Working Group Cooperation Issues and Due Process, Investigative Powers Report and Decision-Making Powers Report (31 October 2012), accessible at https://competition-policy.ec.europa.eu/european-competitionnetwork/documents_en.

sought to formally harmonise the domestic rules on enforcement procedures and the powers of the various NCAs.[52]

The ECN+ Directive of 2019 marked a step towards harmonisation by introducing some common rules for the institutional role of the national enforcers. Most of the Directive's provisions are directed towards NCAs, while the rules governing the operation of national courts were left largely untouched. Article 3(2) of the ECN+ Directive merely provides a general obligation, according to which: 'Member States shall ensure that the exercise of the NCA's enforcement powers is subject to appropriate safeguards in respect of the undertakings' rights of defence, including the right to be heard and *the right to an effective remedy before a tribunal.*'[53] As a consequence of the principle of national procedural autonomy, there is a landscape of different court review systems in terms of the nature and degree of specialism of national courts, their respective roles and the scope and intensity of review available.[54]

In conclusion, while Regulation 1/2003 and the ECN+ Directive harmonise *some* aspects of the *NCAs'* powers, independence, budget, institutional designs, and operation, there is a paucity of 'guidance' for appellate *courts*. EU law 'affects neither national rules on the standard of proof nor obligations of competition authorities and courts of the Member States to ascertain the relevant facts of a case, provided that such rules and obligations are compatible with general principles of Community law'.[55] Regulation 1/2003 does not demand the involvement of any specific type of institution or procedure. It does not indicate, for example, if the national courts should be constituted by a specialised tribunal, a generalist (civil, administrative, or criminal) court, or a specialised chamber of a generalist court. Similarly, it does not prescribe the number of instances of appeal, grounds of appeal, limitation periods, fees for launching appeals, which attributes the judges should have (e.g., specialised, ordinary judges, or layperson), and the number of judges sitting on any panel. The standard, scope, and

52. *See* Kris Dekeyser and Maria Jaspers, 'A New Era of ECN Cooperation, Achievements and Challenges with Special Focus on Work in the Leniency Field' (2007) 30(1) World Competition 3.
53. It has been observed that the practical added value of Article 3(2) is limited, in particular, if one takes into account that when compared with the proceedings before the European Commission the level of procedural safeguards of right of defense is lower in national procedures relied on by some NCAs, *see* Maciej Bernatt et al., 'The Right of Defense in the Decentralized System of EU Competition Law Enforcement: A Call for Harmonization from Central and Eastern Europe' (2018) 41(3) World Competition 309-334. *See also* Anna Piszcz and Michal Petr, '(Dis)Respect for Fundamental Rights in EU Competition Law Enforcement Proceedings Before National Authorities: In What Way Does Article 3 of the ECN+ Directive Prove to Be Too Open-Ended?' (2023) 54 International Review of Intellectual Property and Competition Law 1081-1104 DOI: 10.1007/s40319-023-01353-4.
54. European Commission, Pilot field study on the functioning of the national judicial systems for the application of competition law rules (2014); OECD, 'Judicial Perspectives on Competition Law. Contribution from Italy' (2017).
55. Regulation 1/2003, Preamble 5. Also *see* Modernisation Explanatory Memorandum, para. 11.3. Nonetheless, in practical terms, to some extent, cases based on the national provisions equivalent to Article 101 TFEU still hinge on the same types of evidential presumptions e.g. in relation to the establishment of a concerted practice.

intensity of judicial review also vary considerably across the EU and lead to different review processes and outcomes.[56]

3 THE ROLE OF NATIONAL COURTS: BIG TASK, LITTLE (EU) LAW

Identifying the role for and scope of judicial oversight over the decisions of administrative law enforcement by independent and highly specialised administrative authorities has been subject to debate in scholarship for many years.[57] The relationship between NCAs and the national courts is complex because, in many cases, generalist judges are called upon to review the decisions taken by highly expert regulators in matters involving legal, economic, and technical complexity.

The Treaties, EU secondary legislation and soft laws, and the EU Courts' jurisprudence generally avoid such discussions. They mostly defer to general EU law principles and do not explicitly identify the tasks of national courts. To guide the discussion and assessment of the operation of the national courts, in this study, we suggest differentiating between the four general tasks of national courts when they review the enforcement of EU and/or national competition laws. The first three tasks are common to the review of the application of both the EU and national competition rules, while the fourth is limited to competition law infringements having an effect on trade between Member States: (i) ensuring the appropriate interpretation of the *substantive norms* of the competition law provisions and their application; (ii) protecting due process and the fundamental rights of the parties involved or affected by the enforcement (*procedure*); (iii) verifying that the *fines* imposed by the NCAs are procedurally and substantively effective, proportionate and dissuasive; and (iv) in the context of the *EU internal market*, national courts must ensure that the NCAs apply the EU competition law provisions in a consistent and uniform manner, and preserve the effectiveness of EU law.

Each of those four aspects is elaborated below. The national reports in Part II and the final chapter in Part III will later demonstrate that the various national systems tend to focus on different aspects. Many of them have mainly focused on matters related to the procedure and remedies, while others have more deeply engaged with the substantive application of the rules. Those chapters will also demonstrate that the national courts have rarely engaged with matters relating to the internal market and tensions between the EU competition rules with national laws.

56. Marco Botta and Alexandr Svetlicinii, 'The Right of Fair Trial in Competition Law Proceedings: Quo Vadis the Courts of the New EU Member States?' in Paul Nihoul and Tadeusz Skoczny (eds), *Procedural Fairness in Competition Proceedings* (Edward Elgar 2015) 276-308; Christopher Bellamy, 'ECHR and Competition Law Post Menarini: An Overview of EU and National Case Law' (2012) e-competitions N47946 2012; Bo Vesterdorf, 'Judicial Review in EC Competition Law: Reflections on the Role of the Community Courts in the EC System of Competition Law Enforcement' (2005) 1 Global Competition Policy 3-27, 9 et seq.; Gerardin and Petit, *supra* n. 3.
57. This debate is aptly presented in Despoina Mantzari, *Courts, Regulators, and the Scrutiny of Economic Evidence* (OUP 2022).

3.1 Substantive

According to Regulation 1/2003, the role of national courts 'complements' the role of NCAs, and therefore, they should 'be allowed to apply Articles [101] and [102] of the Treaty in full'.[58] The national courts, therefore, have an important role in the substantive interpretation and application of the competition law provisions.

The competition law prohibitions in many jurisdictions are typically vague and open-ended.[59] They gain meaning when the surrounding political environment - from which the regulator and the law derive their authority, resources, and legitimacy - prescribes secondary legislation and rules, allocates a budget for enforcement, and the application of the rules is also influenced by the extent of the NCAs' powers.[60] A uniform substantive application of such rules is challenging in a decentralised enforcement setting, where each national socio-legal environment (described by *Fels* as the 'authorising environment') differs from other systems. In particular, the authorising environments in Member States having newly established competition policies in the 1990s (e.g., those of the 'new' Member States joining the EU since 2004, which have transitioned from state-planned to market economy) are likely to differ from those in Member States having a well-established competition policy.[61]

Court judgments reviewing the application of the competition rules are an important element in shaping the substantive meaning of the competition provisions.[62] This is true in both civil and common law jurisdictions.[63] As *Tapia* and *Montt* observe, '[t]here can be little doubt that an effective mechanism of judicial scrutiny of competition law decisions is an essential part of any competition regime. Competition authorities' powers and discretion (which may generally refer to questions of fact and law, including policy)' find their internal limit in the different levels of intervention that reviewing courts may be prepared to apply in the process of judicial scrutiny'.[64]

The EU Courts play an important role in clarifying the meaning of Articles 101 and 102 TFEU. In particular, national courts are bound by the case law of the EU Courts when applying the EU competition rules.[65] Other sources, such as the Commission's decisional practice and notices, guidelines, and other policy documents, may provide guidance but are not binding on national courts.[66] Interestingly, empirical research has

58. Regulation 1/2003, Preamble 7.
59. Ariel Ezrachi 'Sponge' (2017) 5(1) Journal of Antitrust Enforcement 49.
60. Allan Fels, 'A Model of Antitrust Regulatory Strategy' (2009) 41 Loyola University Chicago Law Journal 489, 498-499.
61. *Ibid.*, 500-501.
62. *Ibid.*
63. *See, e.g.*, Pablo Ibanez Colomo, *The Shaping of EU Competition Law* (CUP 2018).
64. Javier Tapia and Santiago Montt. 'Judicial Scrutiny and Competition Authorities: The Institutional Limits of Antitrust' in Ioannis Lianos and Daniel Sokol (eds) *The Global Limits of Competition Law* (Stanford University Press 2012), 141-157, 141.
65. Case 63/75 SA *Fonderies Roubaix Wattrelos v. Société nouvelle des Fonderies A. Roux and Société des Fonderies JOT* ECLI:EU:C:1976:15, 9-11; case C-234/89 *Delimitis v. Henninger Bräu* ECLI-:EU:C:1991:91, 46. Also *see* the Commission Notice on Cooperation with National Courts (2004), para. 8.
66. Case 66/86 *Ahmed Saeed Flugreisen and others v. Zentrale zur Bekämpfung unlauteren Wettbewerbs e.V.* ECLI:EU:C:1989:140, 27 and case C-234/89 Delimitis, 50. Also *see* the

indicated that national courts have often refrained from citing the (binding) leading cases by EU courts[67] and the (unbinding) Commission's soft law instruments,[68] although on substance, the national case law on Articles 101 and 102 TFEU tends to be consistent with that of the CJEU.

Regulation 1/2003 provides only a few provisions aimed at ensuring the substantive accuracy of the competition law provisions: First, Article 3 of the Regulation obliges the national courts (and NCAs) to apply Articles 101 and/or 102 TFEU when they apply their national competition law rules.[69] In the case of conflict, the Regulation establishes the primacy of the EU competition provisions, subject to limited exceptions.[70] Next, Articles 15-16 of Regulation 1/2003 impose on national courts some cooperation duties aimed at ensuring that the Commission and NCAs remain 'sufficiently well informed of proceedings before national courts'[71] and avoid adopting conflicting decisions on cases already dealt with by the Commission.[72] Those Articles allow national courts to request the Commission to transmit to them information in its possession or its opinion on questions concerning the application of the Community competition rules,[73] and the Commission can also participate as *amicus curiae* in national court proceedings.[74] NCAs may submit written observations to the national courts of their Member State on their own initiative and, with the permission of the court in question, may also submit oral observations.[75]

Article 16(1) of the Regulation provides that when national courts rule on matters that were already the subject of a Commission decision, they cannot take decisions running counter to the decision adopted by the Commission. They must also avoid making decisions that would conflict with a decision contemplated by the Commission in proceedings it has initiated. According to the Regulation, the national court may assess whether it is necessary to stay its proceedings. Remarkably, this duty is more limited than the one imposed on NCAs by Article 16(2) of the Regulation, according to which NCAs 'cannot take decisions' which would run counter to a decision adopted by the Commission.

Commission Notice on Cooperation with National Courts (2004), para 8. For an interesting account of conflict, *see* Kathryn Wright, 'European Commission Opinions to National Courts in Antitrust Cases: Consistent Application and the Judicial-Administrative Relationship' (2008) ESRC Centre for Competition Policy Working Paper Series, available at: https://ueaeco.github.io/working-papers/papers/ccp/CCP-08-24.pdf.

67. Saskia Lavrijssen et al., 'European and National Standards of Review: Differentiation or Convergence', in Oda Essens et al. (eds), *National Courts and the Standard of Review in Competition Law and Economic Regulation* (Europa Publishing 2009), 265-292. It should of course be noted that these findings date from early in the Regulation 1/2003 era.
68. Zlatina 2016, *supra* n. 20.
69. The meaning of the obligation to 'apply' Articles 101 and 102 TFEU is contentious. *See* Brook and Eben, *supra* n. 23, 10-12.
70. *Ibid.*, 10-11.
71. Regulation 1/2003, Preamble 21.
72. Those rules are further detailed in the Commission's Notice on Cooperation with National Courts (2004), paras 15-41.
73. Regulation 1/2003, Article 15(1).
74. *Ibid.*, Article 15(3).
75. *Ibid.*

Finally, Article 15(2) of the Regulation also obliges the Member States to forward to the Commission 'without delay after the full written judgment is notified to the parties' a copy of any written judgment by its national courts deciding on the application of Articles 101 or Article 102 TFEU. The obligation to inform the Commission of national court judgments is not fully respected in practice. As the Commission reported, it 'received very few national court judgments deciding on the application of the EU competition rules'.[76]

The above demonstrates that the cooperation obligations imposed on national courts are not only limited but are also mostly non-binding. As noted by the Economic and Social Committee in 2001, '[c]ooperation with national courts certainly raises awkward questions that are in any case difficult to regulate with binding provision', and most of those mechanisms are 'virtually optional'.[77] In fact, the original wording of Article 15, which highlighted that the Commission and NCAs may intervene in front of national courts on their 'own initiative',[78] was discarded as the European Parliament's Committee on Economic and Monetary Affairs considered that it would amount to 'an unnecessary and unwarranted intrusion in the judicial processes of national courts',[79] and following strong opposition by several Member States.[80] The only binding provision is Article 15(2), requiring the Member States to forward to the Commission a copy of any written judgment.[81] Yet, as mentioned, this notification obligation has only been partially respected in practice.

The main mechanism to ensure the correctness of the interpretation of the national courts beyond the cooperation mechanisms of the Regulation is the preliminary reference procedure of Article 267 TFEU,[82] providing for 'preliminary rulings' to be given by the Court of Justice on the application and interpretation of an issue of EU law.[83] The rulings are designed to ensure the uniform application of EU law throughout the legal systems of the various Member States. A national court may refer an issue to the Court of Justice where a ruling is necessary to enable the national court to give judgment and must do so where there is no right of further appeal. The Court of Justice

76. Regulation 1/2003s 2014 Report, para. 22 and footnote 5.
77. Opinion of the Economic and Social Committee on Modernisation White Paper, para. 2.10.2.
78. *See* Proposal for a Council Regulation on the implementation of the rules on competition laid down in Articles 81 and 82 of the Treaty and amending Regulations (EEC) No. 1017/68, (EEC) No. 2988/74, (EEC) No. 4056/86 and (EEC) No. 3975/87 (Regulation implementing Articles 81 and 82 of the Treaty) (2000/C 365 E/28), Article 15(3).
79. Committee on Economic and Monetary Affairs, Report on the proposal for a Council regulation on the implementation of the rules on competition laid down in Articles 81 and 82 of the Treaty and amending Regulations (EEC) No. 1017/68, (EEC) No. 2988/74, (EEC) No. 4056/86 and (EEC) No. 3975/87 (COM(2000) 582 n C5-0527/2000 n 2000/0243(CNS)) A5-0229/2001, 13.
80. Council of the European Union, Note from the General Secretariat of the Council to the Delegations, Proposal for a Council Regulation on the implementation of the rules on competition laid down in Articles 81 and 82 of the Treaty, 27.6.2001, 2000/0243(CNS), footnotes 33 and 37 (Austria, Ireland, Finland, France, and the Netherlands), footnotes 89-94.
81. This obligation was described as 'purely clerical', requiring 'very little additional work' from the national courts' side. *See* Modernisation Explanatory Memorandum, para. 25.
82. Ehlermann and Atanasiu, *supra* n. 47, 76.
83. Barry Rodger (ed.), *Article 234 and Competition Law: An Analysis* (Kluwer Law International 2008).

does not decide the dispute between the parties but issues an interpretative 'preliminary ruling' that provides guidance on the interpretation of the point of EU law which is at issue. The Article 267 procedure should be important for the development of EU competition law, given the role of NCAs under Regulation 1/2003. Nonetheless, as the empirical findings presented in this book will demonstrate, there has been limited use of this tool in practice in the public enforcement context.[84]

Interestingly, the ECJ has held that it is competent to provide preliminary rulings also on the interpretation of national prohibitions equivalent to Articles 101 and 102 TFEU, even when the national proceedings do not affect trade between Member States.[85]

3.2 Procedural

National courts have the important task of ensuring due process and the protection of the fundamental rights of the parties to the NCAs' (and judicial) proceedings and other affected third parties. Nevertheless, EU primary and secondary laws only provide general guidance as to the protection of such rights. This is demonstrated by the preamble of the ECN+ Directive, noting that the NCAs should exercise their powers 'subject to appropriate safeguards which at least comply with the general principles of Union law and the Charter of Fundamental Rights (CFR) of the European Union, in accordance with the case law of the Court of Justice of the European Union, in particular in the context of proceedings which could give rise to the imposition of penalties'.[86] These safeguards, according to the Directive, include the right to good administration and respect for the undertakings' rights of defence, an essential component of which is the right to be heard.[87] Accordingly, NCAs must inform the parties under investigation about the preliminary objections raised against them under Article 101 or 102 TFEU before making a finding of an infringement. Those parties should have an opportunity to make their views on those objections known effectively before such a decision is taken and have the right to access the relevant case files.

The Directive also explains that the addressees of NCAs' decisions, and in particular of those decisions finding an infringement and imposing remedies or fines, should have the right to an effective remedy before a tribunal. Therefore, the NCAs' decisions should be reasoned so as to allow addressees of such decisions to ascertain the reasons for the decision and to exercise their right to an effective remedy, and the national review proceedings should be conducted within 'a reasonable timeframe'.[88] The design of those safeguards, according to the Directive, should strike a balance

84. Rodger, *supra* n. 24, 'Competition Law Preliminary Rulings: a Quantitative and Qualitative analysis post Regulation 1/2003' [2014] GCLR 7(3), 125-139. Also *see* Part III of this book.
85. C-32/11 *Allianz Hungária Biztosító Zrt. and Others v. Gazdasági Versenyhivatal* ECLI-:EU:C:2013:160, paras 20-23; C-413/13 *FNV Kunsten Informatie en Media v. Staat der Nederlanden* ECLI:EU:C:2014:2411, paras 17-20.
86. ECN+ Directive, Preamble 14.
87. *Ibid.*
88. *Ibid.*

between respect for the fundamental rights of the undertakings and the duty to ensure that Articles 101 and 102 TFEU are effectively enforced.[89]

Yet, because the Directive and other EU law provisions do not consider matters of procedure, the procedural rules for the enforcement of EU and national competition rules by national courts are largely a matter of national law.[90] Such procedural rules, therefore, vary extensively according to the constitutional arrangements and the competencies conferred on the judicial branch,[91] which are merely limited by general EU and ECHR standards,[92] such that the basic requirements of equivalence, effectiveness and effective judicial protection are guaranteed.[93]

In recent years, the normative content of the principle of effective judicial protection as set out by Article 19 TEU and reflected in Article 47 of the EU CFR was developed by the CJEU case law, and in particular, the obligation of national courts to remain independent.[94] At the same time, the CJEU has confirmed that it is for Member States to organise their national judiciary as long as the national court structure and system safeguard effective judicial protection.[95]

---

89. *Ibid.*
90. Commission's Notice on Cooperation with National Courts (2004), para. 9. The European legislature and EU Courts have so far avoided setting guidelines for judicial review in competition law, by contrast to, for instance, telecommunications law, *see* Rolf Ortlep and Rob J.G.M. Widdershoven, 'Rechtsbescherming' in Sacha Prechal and Rob J.G.M. Widdershoven (eds), *Inleiding tot het Europees bestuursrecht* (Ars Aequi Libri 2017) 397. Also *see* Directive 2002/21/EC of the European Parliament and of the Council of 7 March 2002 on a common regulatory framework for electronic communications networks and services (Framework Directive), Article 4(2).
91. Dubravka Aksamovic, 'Judicial Review in Competition Cases in Croatia and Comparative Jurisdictions' (2017) 67 Zbornik PFZ 405, 437.
92. *See* amongst others: ECHR 23 November 2006 *Jussila v. Finland* (Application no. 73053/01); ECHR 27 September 2011 *Menarini Diagnostics v. Italy* (Application no. 43509/08); Case C-272/09 *KME Germany and Others v. Commission* EU:C:2011:810; Case C-386/10 P *Chalkor AE Epexergasias Metallon v. European Commission* EU:C:2011:815, para. 51. *See* Wouter P.J. Wils, 'The Compatibility with Fundamental Rights of the EU Antitrust Enforcement System in Which the European Commission Acts Both as Investigator and as First-Instance Decision Maker' (2014) 37 World Competition 5-25; Renato Nazzini, 'Administrative Enforcement, Judicial Review and Fundamental Rights in EU Competition Law: A Comparative Contextual-Functionalist Perspective', (2012) 49 Common Market Law Review 971-1006 DOI: 10.54648/cola2012036; Maciej Bernatt, 'Between Menarini and Delta Pekarny: Strasbourg View on Intensity of Judicial Review in Competition Law', in Csongor Nagy (ed.) *The Procedural Aspects of the Application of Competition Law: European Frameworks – Central European Perspectives* (Europa Law Publishing 2016).
93. Albert Sánchez-Graells, 'ECJ Avoids Providing Guidance on Intensity of Judicial Review of Procurement Decisions by Sticking to Strictly Formalistic Approach: The Gaping Hole Remains (C-171/15)' (How to Crack a Nut – A Blog on EU Economic Law, 15 December 2016) http://www.howtocrackanut.com/blog/2016/12/15/ecj-avoids-providing-guidance-on-intensity-of-judicial-review-of-procurement-decisions-by-sticking-to-strictly-formalistic-approach-c-17115.
94. Michał Krajewski and Michał Ziółkowski, 'Judicial Independence Decentralized: A.K.', (2020) 57 Common Market Law Review 1107 DOI: 10.54648/cola2020717.
95. Case C-619/18 *Commission v. Poland* EU:C:2019:531, para. 52 ('the organisation of justice in the Member States falls within the competence of those Member States, the fact remains that, when exercising that competence, the Member States are required to comply with their obligations deriving from EU law (...) and, in particular, from the second subparagraph of Article 19(1) TEU' (*see*, to that effect, C-64/16 *Associação Sindical dos Juízes Portugueses* EU:C:2018:117, para. 40).

It should also be noted that the preliminary reference mechanism may allow the CJEU to ensure (at least a degree of) conformity of national court review processes with those broader principles of EU law identified. This was exemplified, for instance, in its ruling in *Vebic*,[96] a case concerning the extent to which a particular NCA could participate, as a defendant or respondent, in proceedings before a national court which challenge a decision that the authority itself has taken. The Court concluded, at para 64, that 'Article 35 of the Regulation must be interpreted as precluding national rules which do not allow a national competition authority to participate, as a defendant or respondent, in judicial proceedings brought against a decision that the authority itself has taken.'[97] The Court emphasised that while in the absence of EU rules, the principle of procedural autonomy prevailed, it is imperative that fundamental rights are observed and that the effectiveness of EU competition law should not be jeopardised.

3.3 Fines-Related

Like other matters of procedure, in the absence of EU law provisions, national courts follow their domestic rules when reviewing the sanctions imposed for EU and national competition law infringements, which are only limited by the general principles of EU law.[98] Such principles were developed by the EU Courts' jurisprudence to include, inter alia, the obligation of national courts to provide remedies that are procedurally and substantively effective, proportionate and deterrent.[99] The remedies for the breach of the EU competition rules, moreover, must be as effective as those remedies for the breach of the corresponding national competition rules.[100]

The ECN+ Directive emphasises that imposing effective, proportionate and deterrent fines for the infringement of Articles 101 and 102 TFEU is necessary to ensure the effective and uniform enforcement of those provisions.[101] Yet, it provides for limited harmonisation in this regard, noting that fines should be determined in proportion to the total worldwide turnover of the undertakings and associations of undertakings concerned,[102] that NCAs should take into account the gravity of the infringement,[103] and that the maximum amount of the fine that could be imposed for each infringement in each Member State will not be lower than 10% of the total worldwide turnover of the undertaking concerned.[104]

---

96. Case C-439/08 *Vlaamse federatie van verenigingen van Brood- en Banketbakkers, Ijsbereiders en Chocoladebewerkers (Vebic) VZW* ECLI:EU:C:2010:739.
97. The Vebic pronouncement was repeated in Article 30(2) of the ECN+ Directive.
98. Also *see* Commission's Notice on Cooperation with National Courts (2004), para. 10.
99. Case 68/88 *Commission v. Greece* ECLI:EU:C:1989:339, 23-5. Also *see* Marshall N° 2, 1993 ECR I 4367; *Draehmpaehl v. Urania*, 22 April 1997 ECR I 2195: Garden Cottage Foods, 1983 2 All E.R. 770; Factortame, 1990 ECR I 2433; John Temple Lang, 'The Duties of National Courts under Community Constitutional Law' (1997), 22 European Law Review 3-18.
100. Case 68/88 *Commission v. Greece*, 2985-85: Case C-7/90 *Vandevenne et al.* ECLI-:EU:C:1991:363; Case C-382/92 *Commission v. U.K.* ECLI:EU:C:1994:233.
101. ECN+ Directive, Preamble 40.
102. *Ibid.*, Preamble 43.
103. *Ibid.*, Preamble 46.
104. *Ibid.*, Preamble 49.

Consequently, as the following chapters will demonstrate, in many Member States, the rules governing the review of fines differ from the rules governing the review of the infringement itself.

3.4 Internal Market: Consistency and Uniformity of EU Law Application

The decentralised application of the EU competition rules, as the Modernisation White Paper emphasised, should not 'stand in the way of the maintenance of conditions of competition that are consistent' throughout the internal market.[105] This is reflected by the aforementioned provisions of Article 3 of Regulation 1/2003, enacting the primacy of EU competition law over conflicting national laws, as well as the other cooperation obligations already discussed above, and the preliminary reference procedure.

In addition, the EU Courts' jurisprudence has developed the duties of national courts to ensure uniformity. Even prior to modernisation, for example, the EU Courts held that national courts must raise questions of EU competition law on their own initiative.[106] The national courts must apply the EU competition rules, even when a party with an interest in the application of those provisions has not relied on them, where domestic law allows such application by the national court. However, EU law does not require national courts to raise on their own motion an issue concerning the breach of provisions of EU law where the examination of that issue would oblige them to abandon the passive role assigned to them by going beyond the ambit of the dispute defined by the parties themselves and relying on facts and circumstances other than those on which the party with an interest in the application of those provisions bases his claim.[107] While this case law, which was later codified in the Commission's notice, was developed in relation to private enforcement actions, the Commission Notice does not appear to be limited to that context.

4 NATIONAL COMPETITION LAWS AND ENFORCEMENT (AND THE INCLUSION OF THE UK)

This book and the study behind it were designed with reference to the EU decentralised enforcement system. Accordingly, and as will be elaborated in Chapter 2, we seek to capture and assess the diverging national substantive, institutional, and procedural laws according to their common or comparative function under Regulation 1/2003.[108] Yet, it should be emphasised that the project examines judicial review in relation to the application of both EU and national competition laws. In other words, it also maps and evaluates the application of purely national cases where there was no effect on trade

105. Modernisation White Paper, 35.
106. C-312/93 Peterbroeck, *Van Campenhout & Cie SCS v. Belgian State* ECLI:EU:C:1995:437; Case 66/86 Ahmed Saeed; Case 103/88, *Fratelli Costanzo SpA v. Comune di Milano* ECLI: EU:C:1989:256.
107. Joined cases C-430/93 and C-431/93 *Van Schijndel v. Stichting Pensioenfonds voor Fysiotherapeuten* ECLI:EU:C:1995:441, 13-15 and 22; Commission's Notice on Cooperation with National Courts (2004), para. 3.
108. For this comparative functional legal approach, *see* Chapter 2, section 2.

between Member States. The inclusion of purely national cases in the database has various justifications.

First, all the Member States (and the UK) have established competition law prohibitions at the domestic level that correspond with and are equivalent to the primary EU prohibitions listed in Articles 101 and 102 TFEU. Those national prohibitions are mostly equivalent in substance and content to the EU prohibitions, except for the EU inter-state trade criterion requirement.[109] In practice, NCAs often apply the national and EU sets of rules interchangeably and, in some cases, have not even clearly distinguished between the two.[110] As mentioned, this has led the CJEU to declare that it is competent to issue preliminary rulings on the interpretation of the national equivalent prohibitions, even in purely national cases.[111] Second, the inclusion of purely national cases in the database of this study was required on pragmatic grounds to account for cases that gave no indication of whether they were based on the EU or the national provisions.[112] Third, it is clear that throughout the EU Member States (and the UK), the same framework for judicial review (in terms of the relevant court, the availability of review and the rules and procedures undertaken by the court in conducting the review) apply irrespective of whether a particular case concerns the application of the domestic and/or the EU rules. Hence, it is equally relevant to consider all appeal cases throughout the legal system. Finally, the inclusion of appeals in purely national cases provides indirect insights into the frequency of application of the EU competition law provisions. As Parts II-III of this book demonstrate, the ratio of appeals engaging with the EU prohibitions varies considerably across the Member States. While some have regularly examined the EU prohibitions, other NCAs have rarely applied them and were mostly engaged with national competition law enforcement.

It should also be noted that this project explores judicial review in the UK in addition to the EU Member States. The inclusion of the UK in the project is justified on various grounds, which will be elaborated on in the UK report. First, the UK was a part of the EU during the majority of the temporal period of this project until its formal withdrawal at the end of 2020 ('Brexit'). Therefore, the operation and effectiveness of judicial review in the EU were partly dependent on this key Member State during the project period. Second, given the relatively mature system of competition law development and enforcement in the UK and the specialist nature of its Competition Appeal Tribunal, EU judicial review can consider and reflect upon practice within that

109. Katalin Cseres, 'Multi-jurisdictional Competition Law Enforcement: The Interface Between European Competition Law and the Competition Laws of the New Member States' (2007) 3(2) European Competition Journal 465-502 DOI: 10.5235/ecj.v3n2.465; Katalin Cseres, 'Comparing Laws in the Enforcement of EU and National Competition Laws' (2010) 3 European Journal of Legal Studies 7.
110. An empirical study of five Member States demonstrated that the NCA and national courts have not distinguished between the EU and national rules even when the national differed from their EU counterpart. *See* Brook, *supra* n. 22, 177-179, 206-211, 308-309, 339-341, 356-359.
111. C-32/11 *Allianz*, paras 20-23; C-413/13 *FNV Kunsten Informatie en Media*, paras 17-20.
112. The proportion of cases where the NCAs and national courts did not indicate whether the EU or the national prohibition applies is recorded by the 'Competition prohibition(s) being appealed' graphs presented in the national reports.

jurisdiction. British judges and the British enforcement system, moreover, are still highly influential in the operation of the European Association of Competition Law Judges, even post-Brexit. Finally, in terms of substantive law, it is also important to remember that the UK Competition Act Chapter I and Chapter II prohibitions are modelled on Articles 101 and 102 TFEU, and this is likely to continue, with some potential divergences, following the UK withdrawal from the EU.[113]

5 EU COURTS' REVIEW OF THE COMMISSION'S DECISION-MAKING

An overview of the EU competition law judicial review system cannot be completed without briefly reflecting on the role of the EU Courts in the system of enforcement of Articles 101-102 TFEU in the EU.[114] Aside from the preliminary reference system mentioned above, the role of the EU Courts is limited to reviewing the Commission's enforcement of Articles 101 and 102 TFEU decisions under Article 263 TFEU. Notably, the procedural and institutional rules and the standards of review developed in the EU case law do not govern the way that national courts review NCAs' decisions. Nevertheless, they may serve the reader of this book as a known benchmark against which judicial review at the national level can be compared.

The first issue to consider is the set of grounds for review available when seeking annulment of a Commission act under Article 263 TFEU, namely lack of competence/authority; infringement of an essential procedural requirement; infringement of the Treaty or any rule of law relating to its application; or misuse of powers. These grounds are alternatives, although they overlap to a certain extent. Annulment may be sought, for instance, on the basis of failure to give a party a hearing, inadequate reasoning in a decision, a decision based on inadequate evidence, or erroneous application of the competition rules. An action for annulment is often combined with an action seeking review of a decision by the Commission to fine infringing undertakings. Article 261 TFEU provides the Court with unlimited powers to annul, vary or increase fines imposed by the Commission.

The second issue is the intensity of judicial control as exercised by the GC, which may differ from the national standards of review. This has long been one of the hottest topics in the EU competition law literature.[115] It has become clear that the GC undertakes a comprehensive (or exhaustive) review of the examination carried out by

113. *See* Barry Rodger et al., *The UK Competition Law Regime: A Twenty Year Retrospective* (OUP 2021).
114. For a description of the enforcement system of EU competition law see generally Luis Ortiz Blanco (ed.), *EU Competition Procedure* (OUP 2022); Ekaterina Rousseva (ed.), *EU Antitrust Procedure* (OUP 2020) and Maciej Bernatt and Laura Zoboli, 'Competition Law' in Miroslava Scholten (ed.) *Research Handbook on the Enforcement of EU Law* 398-414.
115. David Bailey, 'Scope of Judicial Review under Article 81 EC' (2004) 41 Common Market Law Review 1327-1360 DOI: 10.54648/cola2004046; Heike Schweitzer, 'Judicial Review in EU Competition Law' in Ioannis Lianos and Damien Geradin (eds), *Handbook on European Competition Law: Enforcement and Procedure* (Edward Elgar Publishing 2013) 491; Heike Schweitzer, 'The European Competition Law Enforcement System and the Evolution of Judicial Review', in Ehlermann and Marquis Claus-Dieter Ehlermann and Mel Marquis (eds), *European*

the Commission,[116] which concerns 'both the Commission's substantive findings of facts and its legal appraisal of these facts'.[117] However, controversies arose in relation to a lighter standard of judicial review (the manifest error of assessment standard), which applied when the GC reviewed the Commission's complex economic and technical assessment due to the declared 'margin of appreciation' of the Commission in this field.[118] The criticism against the application of that lower review standard was often based on the alleged violation of the Article 6 ECHR requirement of full judicial review of both facts and law (i.e., full jurisdiction).[119] While a comprehensive analysis of the ECtHR case law suggests that this criticism might not necessarily be strictly accurate given that the ECtHR accepts in practice a relatively light standard of judicial review exercised by national administrative courts in quasi-criminal administrative law cases as long as questions of facts are covered,[120] the GC in recent years has relied on the margin of appreciation terminology less often and may be believed to apply the same standard of review for both the Commission's factual and economic findings.[121] On the basis that these developments at the GC level may have arisen on the basis of comparative approaches (i.e., arguments that in some Member States, full judicial review is exercised by national courts),[122] a comprehensive study of the standards of

Competition Law Annual 2009: The Evaluation of Evidence and Its Judicial Review in Competition Cases (Hart Publishing 2011); Nazzini, *supra* n. 92; José Carlos Laguna de Paz, 'Understanding the Limits of Judicial Review in European Competition Law' (2014) 2 Journal of Antitrust Enforcement 203-224; Alice Setari, 'The Standard of Judicial Review in EU Competition Cases: The Possibility of Introducing a System of More Intense or Full Judicial Review by the EU Courts' (PhD Thesis University of Milan 2014) 46; Bernatt, *supra* n. 25; Andriani Kalintiri, 'What's in a Name? The Marginal Standard of Review of "Complex Economic Assessments" in EU Competition Enforcement', (2016) 53(5) Common Market Law Review, 1283-1316 DOI: 10.54648/cola2016116; José Luís da Cruz Vilaça, 'The Intensity of Judicial Review in Complex Economic Matters: Recent Competition Law Judgments of the Court of Justice of the EU' (2018) 6 Journal of Antitrust Enforcement 173-188 DOI: 10.1093/jaenfo/jny003; Fernando Castillo de la Torre and Eric Gippini Fournier, *Evidence, Proof and Judicial Review in EU Competition Law* (Edward Elgar Publishing 2017) 332-336.

116. Case 42/84 *Remia and Others v. Commission*, EU:C:1985:327, 34; Case T-168/*01 GlaxoSmithKline Services v. Commission* EU:T:2006:265, 57 (describing judicial review as comprehensive); Joined Cases T-25/95 *Cimenteries CBR and Others v. Commission*, EU:T:2000:77, 719 (describing the judicial review as exhaustive).
117. T-25/95 *Cimenteries CBR*, 719.
118. *See, e.g.*, Case T-168/01, paras 85 and 146. *See* Case T-201/04 *Microsoft v. Commission*, EU:T:2007:289, paras 88-89.
119. *See, e.g.*, AG Sharpston raised doubts in this respect in the Opinion in Case C-272/09 *KME Germany AG, KME France SAS and KME Italy SpA v. Commission*, EU:C:2011:63.
120. Bernatt, *supra* n. 115. The existence of the margin of appreciation did not mean that the Commission's complex economic assessment was not reviewed at all. The GC had to verify whether the rules on procedure and on the statement of reasons had been complied with, whether the facts has been accurately stated and whether there had been any manifest error of appraisal or misuse of powers by the Commission, *see* Joined Cases C-204, C-205, C-211, C-213, C-217 and C-219/00 *Aalborg Portland A/S and Others v. Commission*, EU:C:2004:6, 279.
121. For example, Wils, *supra* n. 34, suggested that the increased intensity of judicial review by the EU Courts may be a factor in explaining the reduction in the number of prohibitions by the Commission in recent years, given the additional resources required by the Commission to dedicate to improved reasoning and also in the work required for readopting annulled decisions.
122. *See* a review of national standards by Ian S. Forrester, 'A Bush in Need of Pruning: The Luxuriant Growth of 'Light Judicial Review' (2011) in Claus-Dieter Ehlermann and Mel

judicial review applied by the courts of the EU Member States in competition cases can also help to shed further light on the debate at the EU level.

6 THE STRUCTURE OF THIS BOOK

This book is organised into three parts. Part I includes this introduction chapter (Chapter 1) and a chapter detailing the methodology of this study (Chapter 2). Readers are encouraged to read that chapter, as it presents the systematic empirical approach forming the basis of this study, including a discussion of the common definitions, the scope and selection criteria guiding the collection of data, the coding of judgments, and the drafting of the reports included in this book.

Part II consists of the twenty-eight national reports for each of the EU's twenty-seven Member States and the UK, set out in alphabetical order. Aiming to facilitate cross-jurisdictional comparison, each of Chapters 3-30 contains a full national report by each national rapporteur(s), which follows an identical structure and makes use of the same types of graphs and figures (which are detailed in the Methodology Chapter). Accordingly, each national report is structured in six parts. Section 1 provides an introduction to the national competition law enforcement framework. Section 2 details the national appeals system set in place to review the NCA's enforcement decisions. Section 3 highlights the prior studies which have explored the operation of judicial review in that jurisdiction, focusing in particular on any existing empirical studies. Section 4 presents the empirical findings of the quantitative analysis. Section 5 takes a more qualitative analysis, putting the empirical findings in context. Finally, section 6 ends with concluding remarks.

Part III of the book seeks to provide a comparative analysis of the operation of national judicial review of competition law enforcement across the EU and the UK. It provides an analysis of: (i) the structures of the national enforcement systems, (ii) the total number of judgments rendered in each jurisdiction, the ratio of appeals, success rates and the outcome of judicial review; (iii) the types of appellants; (iv) the competition rules subject to review; (v) the grounds of review; (vi) the use of preliminary references, (vii) the appeals involving leniency and/or settlements; and (viii) the role of third parties. Based on these findings, the chapter argues that the current system of judicial review of EU and national competition law enforcement by national courts does not fully match the integration aims of Regulation 1/203. The evidence suggests that the existing EU and national rules on judicial review of the NCAs' enforcement do not ensure an effective, consistent, and uniform application of the competition rules by national courts in all Member States.

Marquis (eds) *European Competition Annual 2009: The Evaluation of Evidence and Its Judicial Review in Competition Cases* (Bloomsbury Publishing 2010), 11-14. For a study of judicial review in Poland, see Maciej Bernatt, 'Effectiveness of Judicial Review in the Polish Competition Law System and the Place for Judicial Deference', (2016) 9(14) Yearbook of Antitrust and Regulatory Studies 97 DOI: 10.7172/1689-9024.yars.2016.9.14.4. For the standard of judicial review at national level *see also* Csongor Nagy (ed.), *The Procedural Aspects of the Application of Competition Law: European Frameworks – Central European Perspectives* (Europa Law Publishing, 2016).

CHAPTER 2

Methodology and Definitions

Or Brook & Barry Rodger

This chapter presents the methodology and definitions guiding the collection of data, coding of judgments, and drafting of the reports included in this book.

1 DATABASE, REPORTS, AND DATA COLLECTION METHOD

1.1 Sources of Information

The quantitative data and qualitative analysis presented in this volume are based on an original open-access database formed for the purpose of this study by twenty-eight national teams of competition law experts (academics and practitioners, the 'Rapporteurs').[1] The database covers all publicly available judicial review judgments of final public enforcement actions in relation to Articles 101 and 102 Treaty on the Functioning of the European Union (TFEU) and the national equivalent provisions by national competition authorities (NCAs). It gathered information about judgments by national courts in the EU 27 Member States and the UK, rendered and made public between 1 May 2004 and 30 April 2021. The database is publicly available online and may be reused under the terms of a CC BY-NC licence.[2]

As elaborated below, for each jurisdiction, the study offers three categories of data: the database of judgments, the coding output (Excel spreadsheets) and national reports. In addition, Part III provides a comparative analysis report.

1. *See* the list of contributors at the opening of this volume.
2. https://creativecommons.org/licenses/by-nc/4.0/. This licence allows researchers and other reusers to distribute, adapt, and build upon the material in any medium or format for non-commercial purposes only, and only so long as attribution is given to the creator.

1.2 Database of Judgments

The online database gathers all coded judgments.[3] In some jurisdictions, not all judgments are regularly or fully published.[4] Each report, therefore, indicates whether its respective national database is expected to be comprehensive.

1.3 Excel Spreadsheets ('Coding')

For each jurisdiction, an Excel spreadsheet summarises the coding of the characteristics of all relevant judgments across thirty-one variables. The variables record information on: (i) case identification (the jurisdiction, judgment date, relevant court, judges presiding, judge rapporteur, docket number, and case name); (ii) the relevant parties in the appeal process (type of applicants and third parties); (iii) the NCA decision subject to appeal (docket/case number, the competition prohibition(s) being appealed - including whether EU or national law have been applied, the type of restriction of competition, whether it was an by-object or by-effect restriction, the type of NCA procedure, the remedies imposed including the level of fine, and whether it involved a leniency application or a settlement); and (iv) the ground of appeal (whether the appeal was deemed admissible, whether procedural or substantive grounds were raised and accepted, whether the fine was contested and reduced, whether the appeal involved questions about the tension between EU and national competition laws, and whether a preliminary reference to the European Court of Justice (ECJ) had been submitted); (v) the outcome of the appeal (in terms of success, the outcome, and the effect on the fine imposed by the NCA if applicable). In addition to those variables, the Excel contains open-text comments, recording further information about the appeals.

Notably, the coding relies on information extracted from the relevant cases. Some information related to unpublished or partially published judgments was retrieved from the NCA's decision that was subject to the appeal or from subsequent appeals on the unpublished judgment. Yet, the coding did not record exogenous information from external sources, such as background information, news items, or scholarship. Exogenous information, however, is reflected in the reports, in particular in the qualitative analysis (*see* below).

In addition to the coding of the cases, the Excel spreadsheets include information about the relevant reviewing national courts, the number of NCA's decisions that could have been subject to appeal during the relevant period, and a host of automatically generated identical figures and graphs, which summarise the findings and can be compared across jurisdictions.[5]

---

3. https://www.mappingcomplawreview.com/.
4. *See* Comparative Analysis, Chapter 31.
5. *See* section 4 below.

All Rapporteurs followed a dedicated coding book to apply systematic content analysis of legal text ('coding') to the judgments.[6] The full coding book is available on the project's website.[7] It offers detailed coding instructions, aiming to ensure uniformity between the analysis of the jurisdictions.

The coding book was drafted by the Editors, together with the Advisory Board. Before launching the study, each member of the Advisory Board coded twenty judgments in an initial 'pilot' study, aiming to test the fit and accuracy of the coding book in six representative jurisdictions. The coding book was subsequently revised, tweaked, and shared with the Rapporteurs. Next, all Rapporteurs participated in online training, followed by a second 'pilot' exercise in which twenty judgments were coded by each Rapporteur and reviewed by the Advisory Board. Small but necessary clarifications were added to the coding book and shared with all Rapporteurs. Questions arising during the coding process were answered by the Editors based on the coding book and, when necessary, were consulted among the Advisory Board. When doubts arose, we tried to follow the functional comparative approach described below to guide the answer, interpreting the coding in light of Regulation 1/2003 rather than national law (*see* section 2 below).

The raw data in the Excel spreadsheets may be used by subsequent researchers and policymakers for independent (national or comparative) research.

1.4 National and Comparative Reports

The Database of Judgments and Excel spreadsheets guided the drafting of the reports included in this volume. The twenty-eight national reports follow a similar structure. Section 1 begins with an introduction to the respective national competition law enforcement context. Section 2 details the national judicial review system, focusing on the relevant courts and procedures. Section 3 briefly outlines any prior research on judicial review of competition law in that legal system and, in particular, whether any empirical or systematic reviews had previously been undertaken. Section 4 is dedicated to quantitative analysis. It discusses the findings stemming from the coding and presents key trends and figures. The figures presented in this section were automatically generated by the formulas included in the Excel spreadsheets to allow for cross-jurisdictional comparison. Section 5 moves to a qualitative analysis of the effectiveness of judicial review, complementing the quantitative findings and reflecting on judicial practice. It comments on the level of intensity of scrutiny by the review courts and the extent to which the appeal process exhibits judicial deference to the NCA's decision-making. Section 6 in each national report provides concluding remarks.

---

6. On systematic content analysis of legal text, *see* Mark A. Hall and Ronald F. Wright, 'Systematic Content Analysis of Judicial Opinions' (2008) 96 Calif. L. Rev. 63; Or Brook, 'Politics of Coding: On Systematic Content Analysis of Legal Text', in Marija Bartl & Jessica C. Lawrence (eds), *The Politics of European Legal Research* (Edward Elgar, 2022), 109-123.
7. https://www.mappingcomplawreview.com/.

The Comparative Report in Chapter 30 takes a European-wide view, highlighting some cross-country trends and divergences. It focuses on mapping the different structures of national enforcement systems of competition law, the number of appeal instances and the types of reviewing courts, the type of NCAs' decisions subject to appeal and the standard of review. It also provides comparative empirical data on the number and ratio of appeals, their success rates, the ground of review, appeals in proceedings which involved leniency and/or settlement applications, and the involvement of third parties.

2 A FUNCTIONAL COMPARATIVE APPROACH TO STUDY MULTI-LEVEL GOVERNANCE NETWORKS

The coding and analysis of the data are based on the functional comparative approach.[8] Accordingly, it is based on the premise that different legal systems may adopt different legal measures to solve similar legal problems. The research focuses on stating the problem in purely functional terms, without being influenced by the design of each legal system and legal culture, presenting the ways the different legal systems resolve the legal problem, and comparing and evaluating such solutions from the lens of their functionality in resolving the legal problem. This approach is essential for studying multi-level governance networks such as those characterising EU competition law enforcement, in which the identical EU substantive rules are being applied by NCAs and national courts in the context of diverging national procedural rules and institutional settings.[9]

Regulation 1/2003 defines the notions of 'national competition authority' and 'national courts' in functional terms in recognition of the considerable institutional divergence across Member States. NCAs are 'the authorities designated by the Member States *including courts* that *exercise functions* regarding the preparation and the adoption of the types of decisions' foreseen in the Regulation.[10] National courts, in turn, are the institutions '*acting* (...) as review courts'.[11] The Regulation refrains from formally defining the attributes of national courts. The term 'national courts' acquires meaning only by reference to the function of a court as the institution reviewing an NCA's public enforcement actions. This choice is striking, especially as several Member States requested the adoption of a clear definition of the term during the

8. For an overview, *see* Ralf Michaels, 'The Functional Method of Comparative Law', in Mathias Reimann and Reinhard Zimmermann (eds) *The Oxford Handbook of Comparative Law* (OUP 2019).
9. Katalin Cseres, 'Comparing Laws in the Enforcement of EU and National Competition Laws' (2010) 3 *Eur. J. Legal Stud.* 7.
10. Emphasis added. Council Regulation No. 1/2003, 2003 O.J. (L 1) 1 (on the implementation of the rules on competition in Articles 81 and 82 of the Treaty) [hereinafter Regulation 1/2003], Article 35(3).
11. Regulation 1/2003, preamble 21.

negotiation procedure[12] and noted that the distinction between NCAs and courts in their judicial system is 'problematic'.[13]

EU competition law, as well as this study, therefore, are functional to the extent they do not only focus on the form of the written EU and national rules but on their effects, 'not on doctrinal structures and arguments alone but on the consequences they bring about'.[14] The operation of the different NCAs and national courts and their national procedural rules and institutional designs are deemed to be comparable even if they are doctrinally different because they are functionally equivalent, that is, because they fulfil similar roles across the European legal systems.[15]

This functional comparative approach, naturally, comes with a cost. Drawing a comparison between significantly diverging systems requires a degree of generalisation and simplification. In particular, using the same metrics and figures to interpret the national data means that those metrics and figures do not always perfectly fit national procedures, institutions, or terminology.

This was exemplified by the (apparently simple) decision regarding how to identify the relevant judgments to be included in the database. Most competition law systems in the EU adopted an 'administrative enforcement system', that is, when an administrative competition authority acts both as the investigator and the first-level decision-maker.[16] For those jurisdictions, this study examines the judicial review of the NCAs' decisions by a court. Yet, some Member States follow a 'judicial enforcement system' approach, by which Articles 101 and 102 TFEU and the national equivalent infringements decisions are taken by a court following a procedure (which varies across these States) initiated by the administrative authority (e.g., Austria, Finland, Ireland, Malta, and Sweden during all or part of the period covered by this study). In that context, the NCA, within the meaning of Regulation 1/2003, would be the court, not the administrative competition authority. Moreover, to complicate matters further, in some of those judicial enforcement systems, not all competition law decisions are taken by a court. Decisions relating to the rejection of complaints, no grounds for action

12. *See, e.g.*, Council of the European Union, Outcome of Proceedings, Proposal for a Council Regulation on the implementation of the rules on competition laid down in Articles 81 and 82 of the Treaty, 20.10.2000 12542/00, paras 13-14 (France, Finland, and Ireland); Council of the European Union, Note from the General Secretariat of the Council to the Delegations, Proposal for a Council Regulation on the implementation of the rules on competition laid down in Articles 81 and 82 of the Treaty, 27.6.2001, 2000/0243(CNS), footnotes 33 and 37 (Austria, Ireland, Finland, France, and the Netherlands); Council of the European Union, Progress Report on the Proposal for a Council Regulation on the implementation of the rules on competition laid down in Articles 81 and 82 of the Treaty, 20.12.2001, 13563/01 [hereinafter Progress Report of 20.12.2001], footnote 26 (Finland and Ireland); Council of the European Union, Progress Report on the Proposal for a Council Regulation on the implementation of the rules on competition laid down in Articles 81 and 82 of the Treaty, 21.5.2002, 8383/02, para. B(1)(e) and footnotes 31-32, 107 (the Presidency, France, Finland, and Ireland); Council of the European Union, Progress Report on the Proposal for a Council Regulation on the implementation of the rules on competition laid down in Articles 81 and 82 of the Treaty, 27.5.2002, 200/0243(CNS), footnotes 31-32 (Finland and Ireland).
13. *See, e.g.*, Progress Report of 20.12.2001, footnote 25.
14. Michaels, *supra* n. 8, 347-348.
15. *Ibid.*
16. *See* the Comparative Analysis, Chapter 31.

findings, and acceptance of commitments and/or settlements are often dealt with by the administrative authority without any need for the court's authorisation/approval or decision. That means that in certain contexts and for certain processes and decisions, the administrative authority would be considered as an NCA, while in others, it would be the court.

This bifurcation in enforcement models undoubtedly raises challenges as to how to define and code the judgments that should be considered as falling within the category/concept of 'judicial review' of competition law enforcement. As elaborated in the next section, the classification of an NCA for the purpose of this study was informed by the functional comparative approach; namely, it followed the classification offered by Regulation 1/2003 according to the function performed by the institution.

Another challenge to the comparative study of judicial review pertained to the type of NCAs' decisions that could be subject to an appeal. As elaborated in the national reports, there is considerable divergence across the Member States (and the UK) with respect to the type of NCA decisions that can be subject to review by national courts. The possibility of reviewing an NCA's decisions accepting commitments, terminating an investigation, or rejecting complaints, for example, is available only in some jurisdictions. This affects the interpretation of metrics such as the ratio of NCA's decisions subject to an appeal (*see* section 4.1 below).

These challenges should inform the reading of this volume and the interpretation of its results. Some examples of such challenges and how we believe they can be overcome will be discussed in the Comparative Report when presenting the empirical findings. We have attempted to flag such divergences in each of the national reports, which should be read alongside the coding outputs. These challenges might also explain why only limited attempts have been made prior to this project at a comparative and cross-jurisdictional study of EU competition law judicial review. At the same time, we believe that the functional comparative research design can be defended on normative grounds, not only practical ones. The functional comparative approach taken by this study is not only necessary to allow for robust comparison but is also supported by the fact that EU law relies on those considerably divergent national systems to perform a shared task – 'establish[ing] a system which ensures that competition in the common market is not distorted'.[17]

3 DEFINITIONS AND CASE SELECTION CRITERIA

The following definitions and criteria were used in the gathering and coding of data, as well as in drafting the reports included in this volume.

3.1 Articles 101 and 102 TFEU and National Equivalent Provisions

In this project, Articles 101 and 102 TFEU refer to the EU prohibitions on anti-competitive agreements and abuse of a dominant position, respectively. Unless

17. Regulation 1/2003, Preamble 1.

indicated explicitly otherwise, those references also include all national equivalent provisions. The relevant national equivalent provisions are indicated by each report and in each Excel spreadsheet. National laws on abuse of economic dependence and relative market power were not included in the study.

3.2 NCAs, National Courts, Judicial Review, and Appeal

The term NCA is used in this project to refer to the first-level decision-maker(s) on matters related to the application of Articles 101 and 102 TFEU and the national equivalent prohibitions in public enforcement settings and has the same meaning as NCA according to Regulation 1/2003. As mentioned in section 2 above, an NCA may be an administrative or a judicial body or a combination of both. The term NCA in this study does not include independent regional competition authorities but includes non-independent regional offices of the national authority.

In some jurisdictions, more than one body might be considered as an NCA. This is particularly true for national sector regulators entrusted with competition law enforcement powers.

The term national court(s) refers to the relevant institutions entrusted with reviewing the NCA's decisions on the application of Articles 101 and 102 TFEU and the national equivalent prohibitions (as defined above) across all instances of appeals. Internal review of an NCA's decisions involving, for instance, the chairperson or board of the competition authority, is not regarded as judicial review.

The terms judicial review and appeals are used interchangeably in this volume, as referring to the evaluation of the NCA decision by review courts in the meaning of Regulation 1/2003. Admittedly, this may appear to be problematic in certain jurisdictions (e.g., the UK) where, in practice, a distinction is made between 'judicial review,' which is a particular form of 'limited' review of the lawfulness of the decisions of public bodies, whereas 'appeal' signifies a full appeal 'on the merits' normally from an earlier decision by a court- yet in this context we will see that 'judicial review' of the UK NCA's enforcement decisions actually involves a full merits appeal. Nonetheless, given the divergence in the institutions acting as NCAs in EU competition law and in the rules, institutions, and approaches to the review of NCA decisions, we consider that the broader non-technical term 'judicial review' is appropriate for this study.[18]

Review of competition law decisions by constitutional courts was only included in the database where the national constitutional court examines appeals on the *NCA's* final decisions. The study does not cover constitutional complaints alleging that the *decisions of the NCA* or the *judgments of the lower courts* have violated human rights. Such judgments were not included in the database but discussed within the national reports. As the examples detailed in the Comparative Report illustrate, the latter type of complaints operate outside of the regular competition law appeals system by focusing on the protection of fundamental rights and the rule of law.

18. On the difference between the terms, also *see* Despoina Mantzari, *Courts, Regulators, and the Scrutiny of Economic Evidence* (OUP 2022), 6.

3.3 Time Frame

The database includes all judgments issued and made public between 1 May 2004 and 30 April 2021. It does not include appeals on older NCAs' decisions that were rendered prior to the modernisation of EU competition law. The starting date represents the entry into force of Regulation 1/2003, which decentralised the enforcement of competition law. While this date was adopted to ensure uniformity, it should be noted that in some Member States, the Regulation was implemented at a later date.

This timeframe was also used for those Member States which joined the EU after 2004 – namely Romania and Bulgaria (2007) and Croatia (2013) – and for those exiting the EU (the UK, 2020). Each of the relevant national reports discusses the impact of EU accession/exit, the transitional regime, and their effects on the competition law regime and judicial review.

3.4 The Material Scope of the Project

The database includes all judgments concerning judicial review of the public enforcement of Articles 101 and 102 TFEU and the national equivalent provisions by the NCAs. Namely, it *does not* include: (i) judicial review/appeals of criminal or private enforcement cases; (ii) appeals on decisions of independent regional competition authorities; (iii) internal review proceedings of the NCA; (iv) appeals on injunctions or monitoring and compliance orders adopted by NCAs.

The database only includes judicial review of *final* NCAs' decisions. This involves: (i) infringement decisions, including in cases of settlements; (ii) decisions imposing fines for an infringement, either on a company or an administrative fine on individuals; (iii) no ground for action findings; (iv) decisions to close or not to pursue a case (rejection of complaints, decisions not to investigate or stop investigation, including due to lack of evidence or prioritisation); (v) NCAs' decisions on recalculation of fines, adopted following an appeal; and (vi) decisions accepting commitments. Notably, not all of those decisions are subject to appeal in all of the jurisdictions examined by this study.

The database *does not* include judicial review of NCAs' decisions and proceedings regarding interim measures; procedural matters (e.g., decisions on dawn rights, right to be part of proceedings, on confidentiality matters, fines for lack of cooperation or non-compliance); and decisions related to monitoring previously adopted NCA decisions. Likewise, the database does not include court judgments concerning an accepted application for leave for appeal[19] and cases that were paused and referred for a preliminary ruling on the interpretation of EU law under Article 267 TFEU. The latter will only be included in the database after the ECJ has provided its ruling and the national court has consequently delivered its own judgment.

19. *Rejected* applications for leave to appeal, therefore, are included in the database.

4 FIGURES AND GRAPHS PRESENTED IN THE NATIONAL REPORTS

To facilitate comparative exploration, the figures and graphs included in each national report were automatically generated on the basis of the coding undertaken by each team of national rapporteurs. They are identified by the same title, and were generated by using identical formulas. Although the national reports vary in relation to the range of figures presented and discussed, all of the figures are available online in the Excel spreadsheets.[20] This section provides details on the figures and, where applicable, some important limitations to bear in mind when interpreting them.

4.1 Total Number of Cases and the Ratio of NCA's Decisions Subject to an Appeal

The Excel spreadsheets and the reports for each jurisdiction indicate the total number of judgments in the database and the number of NCA's decisions that were reviewed by the courts. They also provide the ratio of NCA's decisions that were subject to appeal. This ratio is calculated by dividing the number of NCA's decisions subject to first-instance appeal by the total number of NCA's decisions that could have been subject to an appeal according to the applicable national rules (on the divergence regarding the type of decisions subject to appeal, *see* section 2 above).

4.2 Number of Judgments per Instance

This figure summarises the number of judgments included in the database for each jurisdiction per year, according to the instance of appeal. For 2004, it includes judgments that were issued from 1 May onwards. For 2021, it includes judgments that were issued and made public before 30 April (*see* the time frame of this study, section 3.3 above).

In some jurisdictions, there was a considerable time lag between the rendering of a judgment and its publication. Therefore, it is possible that some published judgments were not included in the database if they were not published before April 2021. This problem is most likely to affect judgments issued towards the end of the examined period.

4.3 First/Second/Third-Instance Judgments

This set of figures indicates the number of judgments included in the database per year according to each instance (lines). It compares it with the number of NCA's decisions that were appealed in the first instance each year or the number of court judgments that were appealed in further instances (bars).

20. *See* section 1.3 above.

In some jurisdictions, all appeals on a single NCA decision have been addressed in a single judgment. In those jurisdictions, because the appeals launched by all appellants were joined, there will be a perfect overlap between the line and the bars. In other jurisdictions, multiple judgments were issued in relation to a single NCA decision. They may be separated according to each appellant or a group of appellants or even according to the different grounds of appeal raised by a single appellant.

In some jurisdictions, there was a considerable time lag between the rendering of a judgment and its publication. Therefore, it is possible that some published judgments were not included in the database if they were not published before April 2021. This problem is most likely to affect judgments issued toward the end of the examined period.

4.4 The Success of Appeals (Each NCA's Decision or Previous Instance Judgment Counts as One)

This figure summarises the success of appeals launched against either an NCA's decisions or a prior review court instance's judgment. It indicates the ratio of fully successful appeals, partially successful appeals, fully rejected appeals, and appeals that were withdrawn prior to adopting a judgment.

The data in this figure is presented from the perspective of the NCA decision or the previous instance judgment which has been appealed. For example, if three separate first-instance judgments were issued with respect to a single NCA decision, and the appeals were fully accepted in two court judgments but rejected in the third, the figure will record this case as a *single partially successful* appeal.

4.5 First/Second/Third-Instance Outcome

This set of figures indicates the ratio of possible outcomes according to each instance of appeal. When an appeal was fully or partially accepted, the range of outcomes may include, for example, a full or partial *annulment* of the NCA's decision or previous instance judgment, *replacement* of the NCA's decision or previous instance judgment by that of the reviewing court, or an order *returning* the case to the NCA or previous instance court, or a combination of outcomes.

In contrast with the previous figure, the data is presented from the perspective of each separate judgment. For example, if three separate first-instance judgments were issued with respect to a single NCA decision, the outcome of each of those three cases will be presented separately.

4.6 Competition Prohibition(s) Being Appealed

This figure indicates the ratio of the different competition law prohibitions subject to the courts' review across all instances of appeal. It differentiates between the prohibition on anti-competitive agreements and abuse of dominance and between cases in which both the EU and the national equivalent prohibitions have been applied and purely national cases in which only the national equivalent prohibitions have been applied due to the absence of an effect on trade between Member States.

The figure presents the data from the perspective of each single appeal judgment (noting that more than one judgment may be issued with respect to a single NCA decision).

4.7 Rules Being Appealed According to Years (Each Judgment Counts as One)

This figure presents similar data as the previous one. However, it pertains to the number of judgments involving particular rules being appealed (rather than a percentage) and displays the data according to years.

In some jurisdictions, there was a considerable time lag between the rendering of a judgment and its publication. Therefore, it is possible that some published judgments were not included in the database if they were not published before April 2021. This problem is most likely to affect judgments issued towards the end of the examined period.

4.8 Types of Restrictions

This figure summarises the types of restrictions of competition that were examined in the NCA's decisions subject to appeal, across all instances of appeal. For cases in which the EU and/or national prohibitions on anti-competitive agreements have been applied, the figure differentiates between horizontal and vertical restrictions. For cases in which the EU and/or national prohibitions on abuse of dominance have been applied, it differentiates between exploitative and exclusionary abuses. It also records cases involving a combination of such restrictions.

The figure presents the data from the perspective of each single appeal judgment (noting that more than one judgment may be issued with respect to a single NCA decision).

4.9 Object/Effect

This figure only examines appeals against NCA decisions where Article 101 TFEU and/or the national equivalent prohibition have been examined. It indicates the ratio of cases in which the NCA characterised or described the restriction of competition as by-object, by-effect, both by-object and by-effect, or left it unclassified. It should be stressed that this classification is based on the text of the NCA decision alone and not the coder's own assessment.

The figure presents the data from the perspective of each single appeal judgment (noting that more than one judgment may be issued with respect to a single NCA decision).

4.10 NCA's Procedure

This figure indicates the ratio of the type of NCA's procedures that were subject to judicial review, across all instances of appeal. It specifies the percentage of appeals on an NCA's finding of an infringement (distinguishing between cases where a fine was or was not imposed), of no grounds for action findings, decisions to accept formal commitments, and decisions rejecting a complaint or closing an investigation.

The figure presents the data from the perspective of each single appeal judgment (noting that more than one judgment may be issued with respect to a single NCA decision).

4.11 Grounds of Appeal (Each NCA's Decision or Previous Instance Judgment Counts as One)

This figure indicates the success of each ground of appeal launched by the parties against an NCA's decision or a previous instance judgment. For each type of ground - procedural, substantive, fines-related, or EU/national - the figure indicates whether this ground was fully accepted, partially accepted, or rejected.

The figure does not record grounds related to action taken by the court on its own motion (e.g., to raise or reduce a fine). Grounds that were raised but not discussed by the court were recorded as rejected grounds. In particular, grounds that were raised but not discussed since the court did not deal with them (e.g., when matters related to fines were not discussed since the court found there was no infringement) were marked as argued but not accepted.

The data is presented from the perspective of the NCA decision or the previous instance judgment which has been appealed. For example, if three separate first-instance judgments have been issued with respect to a single NCA decision, and the procedural grounds (e.g., limitation period) were fully accepted in two court judgments but rejected in the third, the figure will record this case as a *single partially successful procedural ground of appeal.*

Notably, some legal systems classify similar grounds of appeal differently. To ensure uniformity among the jurisdictions, the coding book included a detailed list of claims that should fall under each ground for the purpose of this study. To allow for a meaningful comparison, the grounds were classified according to the list, irrespective of their status under national law.

Procedural grounds were defined as arguments based on or related to the right to be heard, rights of the defence, due reasoning, competence, admissibility of evidence (excluding lack of sufficient evidence to support a fact), legality of obtaining evidence, limitation periods, and *ne bis in idem*. They do *not* include pleas directly related to the imposition or calculation of fines.

Substantive grounds were defined as arguments based on or related to the definition of undertakings (e.g., state action, public/mix bodies, liability of parents/subsidiaries companies); the existence of agreements/concerted practices; restrictions by-object/effect; the application of Article 101(3) TFEU, BERs, and the national equivalent prohibitions; market definition; the existence of dominance; abuse of dominance; *de minimis*; any EU or national exemptions or exceptions to the competition rules; lack of sufficient evidence to support a fact (excluding the admissibility of evidence); and burden of proof.

Fines-related grounds were defined as arguments against the amount of a penalty imposed by the NCA. They do *not* include cases in which the fine was reduced as a direct result of accepting procedural, substantive, or EU/national grounds.

EU/national grounds were defined as arguments based on or related to the tension between EU and national competition laws. For example, they include matters related to the application of the effect on trade tests, the interpretation of the obligations of Article 3 of Regulation 1/2003 and questions over the primacy of EU competition law or its uniform application.

4.12 Grounds of Appeal

This set of figures indicates the four types of grounds of appeals (procedural, substantive, fines-related and EU/national grounds) raised by one or more parties against an NCA's decision or on a previous instance's judgment per year (lines). It also specifies the number of fully and partially successful appeals (bars). Unlike the previous figure, the data is presented from the perspective of each single appeal judgment (i.e., more than one judgment may be issued with respect to a single NCA decision).

The figure does not record grounds related to action taken by the court on its own motion (e.g., to raise or reduce a fine). Grounds that were raised but not discussed by the court were recorded as rejected grounds. In particular, grounds that were raised but not discussed since the court did not deal with them (e.g., when matters related to fines were not discussed since the court found there was no infringement) were marked as argued but not accepted.

Notably, some legal systems classify similar grounds of appeal differently. To ensure uniformity among the jurisdictions, the coding book included a detailed list of claims that should fall under each ground for the purpose of this study. To allow for a meaningful comparison, the grounds were classified according to the list, irrespective of their status under national law (*see* summary in the 'Grounds of Appeal' figure above).

In some jurisdictions, there was a considerable time lag between the rendering of a judgment and its publication. Therefore, it is possible that some published judgments were not included in the database if they were not published before April 2021. This problem is most likely to affect judgments issued towards the end of the examined period.

4.13 Types of Restrictions Versus Successful Grounds of Appeal

This figure examines only the fully or partially successful grounds. It records the relationship between the type of restriction of competition (e.g., anti-competitive agreements/abuse of dominance and EU or national prohibitions) and the success of the procedural, substantive, fine, and EU/national grounds as defined above. To put this number in context, the figure also specifies the total number of judgments concerning each type of restriction.

The figure presents the data from the perspective of each single appeal judgment (noting that more than one judgment may be issued with respect to a single NCA decision).

Notably, some legal systems classify similar grounds of appeal differently. To ensure uniformity among the jurisdictions, the coding book included a detailed list of claims that should fall under each ground for the purpose of this study. To allow for a meaningful comparison, the grounds were classified according to the list, irrespective of their status under national law (*see* summary in the 'Grounds of Appeal' figure above).

The figure only includes pleas raised by the parties to the appeal. It does not include action taken by the court on its own motion (e.g., to raise or reduce a fine).

4.14 Leniency

This figure examines the relationship between leniency and the success of appeals. It indicates the percentage of appealed judgments on NCA decisions in which one or more parties have successfully applied for leniency. In addition, it specifies whether such appeals were fully successful, partially successful, rejected, or withdrawn.

The data is presented from the perspective of the NCA decision or the previous instance judgment which has been appealed. For example, if three separate first-instance judgments have been issued with respect to a single NCA decision, and the appeals were fully accepted in two court judgments, but the appeal was rejected in the third, the figure will record this case as a *single partially successful* appeal.

4.15 Settlements

This figure examines the relationship between settlements (when available in the legal system) and the success of appeals. In this context, settlements are defined as a reduction in the fine imposed for an infringement in exchange for an admission of liability and compliance with a set of requirements. It indicates the percentage of appealed judgments on NCA decisions in which one or more parties have successfully applied for settlement. In addition, it specifies whether such appeals were fully successful, partially successful, rejected, or withdrawn.

The data is presented from the perspective of the NCA decision or the previous instance judgment which has been appealed. For example, if three separate first-instance judgments have been issued with respect to a single NCA decision, and the appeals were fully accepted in two court judgments, but the appeal was rejected in the third, the figure will record this case as a *single partially successful* appeal.

Part II National Reports

CHAPTER 3
Austria Report

Viktoria H.S.E. Robertson[*]

1 INTRODUCTION TO THE COMPETITION LAW ENFORCEMENT CONTEXT IN AUSTRIA

The national Austrian competition law framework primarily consists of the Cartel Act (Kartellgesetz 2005),[1] which contains substantive and procedural provisions on antitrust and mergers, and the Competition Act (Wettbewerbsgesetz),[2] which establishes the Austrian Federal Competition Authority. In terms of further legislation, an Act on Fair Conditions of Competition (Faire-Wettbewerbsbedingungen-Gesetz) provides some stricter rules for unilateral conduct, particularly in the area of agricultural products and local supply.[3]

The Cartel Act, in its present form, entered into force on 1 January 2006 and closely mirrors EU legislation; earlier legislation will not be discussed in the following discussion as it quite significantly deviated from the European provisions. The Federal Competition Authority is a relatively young authority and was first established by the Competition Act in 2002.

* This research was made possible through a grant from the Austrian Federal Competition Authority. Many thanks to Barbara Seelos for discussions on the content of this report during her time at the Austrian Federal Competition Authority. Thank you to Felix Sturm for research assistance, and to Petar Petrov for his contribution to the coding of Austrian decisions. A big thank you to Sonja Köller-Thier, president of the 25th Senate of the Cartel Court at the Higher Regional Court Vienna, for assembling statistics on appeals from the Cartel Court's registry for the years 2006 to 2013, which are not publicly available.

1. Kartellgesetz 2005 (KartG 2005; Cartel Act 2005), Austrian Federal Law Gazette I 2005/61 as amended.
2. Gesetz über die Einrichtung einer Bundeswettbewerbsbehörde (Wettbewerbsgesetz, WettbG; Competition Act), Austrian Federal Law Gazette I 2002/62 as amended.
3. Faire-Wettbewerbsbedingungen-Gesetz (Act on Fair Conditions of Competition), Austrian Federal Law Gazette 1977/392 as amended.

The following account gives a brief overview of the substantive provisions contained in the Cartel Act, as well as the Austrian public enforcement system for these provisions.[4] In terms of substantive provisions, § 1 Cartel Act prohibits anti-competitive agreements and is almost a verbatim copy of Article 101(1) Treaty on the Functioning of the European Union (TFEU).[5] While § 1(1) Cartel Act contains the general prohibition, § 1(2) Cartel Act contains a list of examples of anti-competitive agreements that coincide with those contained in Article 101(1) TFEU. § 1(3) Cartel Act provides that anti-competitive agreements are null and void, thus containing the rule foreseen in Article 101(2) TFEU at the European level. § 1(4) Cartel Act provides that so-called recommendation cartels are also forbidden, aiming at recommended prices or other trading conditions that have the object or effect of restricting competition.

§ 2 Cartel Act contains the Austrian version of Article 101(3) TFEU, i.e., a rule on individual exemptions for anti-competitive agreements. It contains the same four criteria as Article 101(3) TFEU. To qualify for an individual exemption, an anti-competitive agreement must generate: (i) a benefit of which (ii) a fair share is passed on to consumers, (iii) not go beyond what is necessary and (iv) not eliminate all competition. Since September 2021,[6] Austrian competition law also knows a sustainability exemption, which foresees that where an anti-competitive agreement leads to a sustainability benefit, this will always be presumed to be passed on to consumers.[7]

§ 2(2) no. 1 Cartel Act contains a *de minimis* exemption that is in line with the European Commission's *De Minimis* Notice,[8] while § 2(2) no. 2 Cartel Act foresees a somewhat controversial exemption for resale price maintenance in books. § 2(2) no. 3 Cartel Act contains an exemption for cooperatives, no. 4 one for agricultural producers and their associations. § 3 Cartel Act provides that the Minister of Justice may adopt block exemption regulations that can also refer to those of the European Commission. No such regulation has been adopted yet. In practice, Austrian courts rely on the European block exemption regulations.

§ 4 Cartel Act defines the meaning of a dominant position based on qualitative and quantitative criteria. The rebuttable presumption of dominance applies from market shares of 30%, thus introducing thresholds that are lower than those usually applied in EU competition law. § 4a Cartel Act sets out what relative market power is; this provision is a stricter rule than can be found under EU competition law.

§ 5 Cartel Act contains the prohibition of abuses of a dominant position and applies both to dominant positions under § 4 Cartel Act and to relative dominance

4. For a more detailed account, *see* Viktoria H.S.E. Robertson, *Competition Law in Austria* (Kluwer 2021).
5. Treaty on the Functioning of the European Union (TFEU) [2016] OJ C202/47.
6. Kartell- und Wettbewerbsrechts-Änderungsgesetz 2021 (KaWeRÄG 2021), Austrian Federal Law Gazette I 2021/176.
7. *See* Viktoria H.S.E. Robertson, 'Sustainability: A World-First Green Exemption in Austrian Competition Law' (2022) *Journal of European Competition Law and Practice* (advance access) DOI: 10.1093/jeclap/lpab092.
8. European Commission, Notice on agreements of minor importance which do not appreciably restrict competition under Article 101(1) of the Treaty on the Functioning of the European Union (*De Minimis* Notice) [2014] OJ C291/1. The main difference is that the Austrian *de minimis* rule is contained in the law, while the European equivalent is contained in soft law.

under § 4a Cartel Act. The prohibition contains the same four examples of such behaviour as Article 102 TFEU, as well as one additional one on selling goods below cost price without any objective justification.

§ 6 Cartel Act prohibits retaliatory measures on the part of dominant undertakings that are faced with proceedings based on their (alleged) abusive market behaviour. Again, this is a provision that cannot as such be found under EU competition law.

The Austrian public enforcement system consists of a multitude of actors that need to work together in order to enforce Austrian and European competition laws. The Federal Competition Authority (Bundeswettbewerbsbehörde (BWB)), the Federal Cartel Prosecutor (Bundeskartellanwalt) and the Cartel Court (Kartellgericht (KG)) all constitute national competition authorities within the system of Regulation 1/2003.[9] The Federal Competition Authority is responsible for the public enforcement of national and European competition law. It is an independent authority installed at the Ministry for the Economy, headed by a Director General and consisting of about thirty case handlers in addition to administrative staff. While it has investigative powers in order to enforce the competition law provisions, it has no decisional powers.[10] If it wants to bring an infringement to an end or have a fine imposed on a company for anti-competitive behaviour, then it needs to make an application to the Cartel Court, which then issues a decision in the first instance.[11] The Cartel Court is installed at the Higher Regional Court Vienna. The proceedings before the Cartel Court are non-contentious and therefore rather flexible.[12]

The Federal Cartel Prosecutor is a further administrative body tasked with the public enforcement of competition law.[13] It is installed at the Ministry of Justice and is bound by the instructions it is given. It does not have investigatory or decisional powers. The Federal Cartel Prosecutor can, however, make applications to the Cartel Court. The Federal Cartel Prosecutor has one deputy. In practice, the Federal Competition Authority and the Federal Cartel Prosecutor work in unison.

While the Federal Competition Authority and the Federal Cartel Prosecutor are both national administrative competition authorities, the Cartel Court is a so-called

9. Article 35 of Council Regulation (EC) No. 1/2003 of 16 December 2002 on the implementation of the rules on competition laid down in Articles 81 and 82 of the Treaty [2003] OJ L1/1; § 83(1) Cartel Act (designating the Cartel Court as national competition authority for adopting decisions, the Federal Cartel Prosecutor as national competition authority for applications before the Cartel Court); § 3(1) Competition Act (designating the Federal Competition Authority as competent national competition authority in charge of applying the European competition rules).
10. The only exceptions to this are the Federal Competition Authority's power to impose a fine on anybody who provides wrong or misleading information to it in contravention of § 11a(2) Competition Act, and the Authority's power to order the provision of information or the submission of documents by an administrative decision based on § 11a(3) Competition Act. For more on this, *see* Viktoria H.S.E. Robertson, *Competition Law in Austria* (Kluwer 2021) paras 388 ff.
11. § 36 Cartel Act.
12. § 38 Cartel Act.
13. §§ 75 ff. Cartel Act.

national judicial competition authority, as termed by the ECN + Directive.[14] It is the first-instance decision-maker in competition law matters.

2 THE APPEAL PROCESS OF THE CARTEL COURT'S DECISIONS

As outlined above, Austria's two administrative competition authorities – the Federal Cartel Prosecutor and the Federal Competition Authority – have no decisional powers. Either of them must apply for a decision of the Cartel Court, which consists of a number of specialised senates at the Higher Regional Court Vienna. Both in private and in public competition law enforcement actions, the Cartel Court issues a decision ('Beschluss'). The decision of the Cartel Court can then be appealed before the Supreme Cartel Court (Kartellobergericht (KOG)), which is a specialised senate at the Austrian Supreme Court. No further appeal is possible.

The Federal Cartel Prosecutor and the Federal Competition Authority are designated as official parties that are party to any proceedings in competition law matters before the Cartel Court, also in the case of private enforcement actions.[15] Thanks to this position, they can also take up a case even if the private applicant withdraws their application. Should the official parties see a legal issue arise in a decision by the Cartel Court in the framework of private enforcement, they can also appeal such a decision where the private applicant or the respondent decides not to appeal.[16]

Austria's federal government works together with four major national interest groups in a so-called economic and social partnership; this is also reflected in how the expert lay judges in the Cartel Court's and Supreme Cartel Court's senates dealing with competition law issues are selected. The Cartel Court sits in panels of four judges, of which two are professional judges and two are expert lay judges.[17] The Chamber of Commerce, the Chambers of Agriculture and the Chamber of Labour nominate expert lay judges in competition law matters who have long-standing professional experience in law or business; they are then appointed by the Minister of Justice.[18]

The Supreme Cartel Court sits in panels of five judges, of which there must be three professional judges and two expert lay judges.[19] A professional judge presides. In the case of the need for a reinforced senate, the panel consists of seven professional judges and two expert lay judges.[20]

The Supreme Cartel Court reviews the Cartel Court's decisions on questions of law. Possible reasons for an appeal can relate to: (a) grounds for invalidity, such as the right to be heard not being granted; (b) inconsistency of the file, i.e., if the Cartel

14. Article 2(1) no. 1 of Directive (EU) 2019/1 of the European Parliament and of the Council of 11 December 2018 to empower the competition authorities of the Member States to be more effective enforcers and to ensure the proper functioning of the internal market (ECN + Directive) [2019] OJ L11/3 (differentiating between 'national administrative competition authorities' and 'national judicial competition authorities').
15. § 40 Cartel Act.
16. § 40 Cartel Act.
17. § 59(1) no. 1 Cartel Act.
18. §§ 66, 68 Cartel Act.
19. § 59(1) no. 2 Cartel Act.
20. § 59(1) no. 3 Cartel Act.

Court's findings were made on a basis contrary to the record; or (c) a deficiency in proceedings that was sufficient to cause an incorrect decision by the Cartel Court.[21] Since 2017, an appeal may also be lodged because the files raise significant doubt as to the correctness of the relevant facts upon which the Cartel Court based its decision. However, appeals grounded on this should be limited to exceptional cases.[22]

The fees for submitting an appeal range between EUR 17,000 and EUR 34,000. The law provides certain framework fees as court fees that vary depending on the type of case.[23] No further fees need to be paid, even in the case of an appeal.[24] The official parties (Federal Competition Authority, Federal Cartel Prosecutor) are never liable to pay these fees.

The limitation period for submitting an appeal is four weeks.[25] In the case of interlocutory injunctions, interim decisions or the presiding judge's decision on which part of the decision to publish,[26] an appeal must be brought within fourteen days. There is no leave required to bring an appeal.

3 PRIOR RESEARCH

To this author's best knowledge, no systematic studies of the judicial review of public competition law enforcement in Austria have been undertaken. This does not mean, however, that scholarship has not dealt with these issues. Austria has a journal dedicated to competition law (Österreichische Zeitschrift für Kartellrecht or Austrian Competition Journal), which is now in its 15th year and which publishes both scholarly and practitioners' contributions on competition law and policy, as well as a number of journals dedicated to business law that also publish contributions on competition law and policy. In those publications, various issues related to the public enforcement of competition law in Austria are regularly discussed, including individual cases. However, as stated above, these contributions have not, to date, included a broader analysis of the review of public competition law enforcement in Austria. The following provides a brief overview of the issues that have been covered in Austrian contributions, listed by the year in which the contribution was published: the investigation before the Austrian Federal Competition Authority and its sanctioning powers,[27] commitments offered to the competition authority,[28] competition law settlements,[29] the relationship

21. Sabine Völkl-Torggler, Iris Ingemarsson and Heinz Ludwig Majer, *Das Verfahren vor dem Kartellgericht* (3rd edn, 2023) paras 328 ff.
22. § 49(3) Cartel Act.
23. § 50 Cartel Act.
24. § 51 Cartel Act.
25. § 49(2) Cartel Act.
26. § 37(2) Cartel Act.
27. Maximilian Diem, 'Das Ermittlungsverfahren vor der Bundeswettbewerbsbehörde - Sanktionsmöglichkeiten der Bundeswettbewerbsbehörde' (2012) *Österreichische Zeitschrift für Kartellrecht* 181.
28. Heinrich Kühnert and Anastasios Xeniadis, 'Verpflichtungszusagen im kartellgerichtlichen Verfahren' (2012) *Österreichische Zeitschrift für Kartellrecht* 206.

between public and private competition law enforcement,[30] the Austrian leniency regime,[31] public relations management as an aspect of public enforcement,[32] and competition law fines.[33] Furthermore, a monograph by three judges (at the time of writing, two were professional judges at the Supreme Cartel Court, the third was the president of a senate and professional judge at the Cartel Court) outlines proceedings before the (Supreme) Cartel Court, thus addressing procedural issues.[34]

4 QUANTITATIVE ANALYSIS

The present analysis covers all decisions by the Austrian Supreme Cartel Court in the period from 1 May 2004 to 30 April 2021 that dealt with appeals of Cartel Court decisions that were taken after 1 May 2004 and that related to the public enforcement of the competition rules on anti-competitive agreements and abuse of a dominant position, be it based on Austrian or European competition rules.

4.1 Sources of Information

The data on Austrian cases was collected through a comprehensive search of the Austrian Legal Information System,[35] which contains all Supreme Cartel Court decisions that deal with appeals of Cartel Court decisions. At the Supreme Court, the 16th senate exclusively handles competition law matters. The 16th senate's President is Georg Kodek, who took on this role in March 2022. Cases from this senate can be identified by their case number, as the case number always starts with 16 Ok – indicating the 16th senate and the fact that this is a case at the Supreme Court (Oberster Gerichtshof) in competition law matters (Kartellrechtssachen). The less comprehensive Cartel Court case database was used to access decisions in the first instance.[36]

29. Anastasios Xeniadis, 'Einvernehmliche Verfahrensbeendigung in Kartellverfahren' (2012) *Österreichische Zeitschrift für Kartellrecht* 83; Clemens Appl and Martin Winner, 'Das kartellrechtliche Settlement zwischen Transparenz und Verfahrensökonomie' [2014] *Wirtschaftsrechtliche Blätter* 421; Georg Kodek, 'Absprachen im Kartellverfahren' (2014) *Österreichische Juristen-Zeitung* 69; Hanno Wollmann and Franz Urlesberger, 'Im Fokus: Settlements mit der Bundeswettbewerbsbehörde' (2015) *ecolex* 47.
30. Florian Schuhmacher, 'Das Verhältnis zwischen öffentlicher und privater Rechtsdurchsetzung im Kartellrecht' (2016) *Wirtschaftsrechtliche Blätter* 1.
31. Holger Bielesz, '(Große) Kronzeugenregelung "Reloaded"' (2017) *ecolex* 124; Corinna Potocnik-Manzouri, 'Das Offenlegungsverbot für Kronzeugenerklärungen – (K)ein Problem?' (2017) *Wirtschaftsrechtliche Blätter* 131.
32. Sarah Fürlinger and Nathalie Jeneral, 'Öffentlichkeitsarbeit als wesentliche Aufgabe des Kartellrechtsvollzuges' (2018) *Österreichische Zeitschrift für Kartellrecht* 145.
33. Cathrine Konopatsch, 'Der Kartellgeldbußentatbestand: § 29 Z 1 KartG auf dem Prüfstand der Erfordernisse des Bestimmtheitsgrundsatzes und des Sachlichkeitsgebotes' (2018) *Zeitschrift für Wirtschafts- und Finanzstrafrecht* 60.
34. Elfriede Solé, Anneliese Kodek and Sabine Völkl-Torggler, *Das Verfahren vor dem Kartellgericht* (2nd edn, 2019). This monograph is now in its third edition (2023) and co-authored by Sabine Völkl-Torggler, Iris Ingemarsson and Heinz Ludwig Majer, respectively a retired Cartel Court judge, a current Cartel Court judge and the Federal Cartel Prosecutor.
35. Republic of Austria, Legal Information System: Justiz, https://www.ris.bka.gv.at/Jus/.
36. Ediktsdatei der Republik Österreich, Entscheidungen des Kartellgerichts, https://edikte.justiz.gv.at/edikte/ek/ekedi17.nsf/suche!OpenForm&subf=e.

Information on cases was also gathered from the case law overview available in Austrian academic literature.[37] Furthermore, exchanges with case handlers at the Austrian Federal Competition Authority and judges at the Cartel Court were very helpful in this regard. Based on these multiple sources, the case coverage is likely to be comprehensive.

4.2 Total Number of Cases

In total, twenty-seven appeal cases before the Supreme Cartel Court were identified and analysed in depth for the project. They related to twenty-six decisions issued by the Cartel Court. As the Austrian Federal Competition Authority does not have any decisional powers, the Cartel Court is the judicial competition authority that issues a decision.

Since the entry into force of Regulation 1/2003, between 0 and 4 Cartel Court decisions were appealed per year (Figure 3.1). It is notable that no appeals have been brought in recent years that relate to public enforcement decisions. The overall low number of cases can possibly be attributed to the fact that the Austrian Federal Competition Authority lacks decisional powers. Any cases that are resolved before the authority applies for the imposition of a fine before the Cartel Court or for the finding of an infringement never reach the judicial system and are, therefore, never reviewed. While the Federal Competition Authority keeps a count of all files that deal with Article 101 TFEU, Article 102 TFEU or their national equivalent,[38] most of these files never lead to a case before the Cartel Court – and even less likely to lead to a case before the Supreme Cartel Court that would show up in the statistics at the basis of the present report.

Figure 3.1 Number of Judgments According to Instances

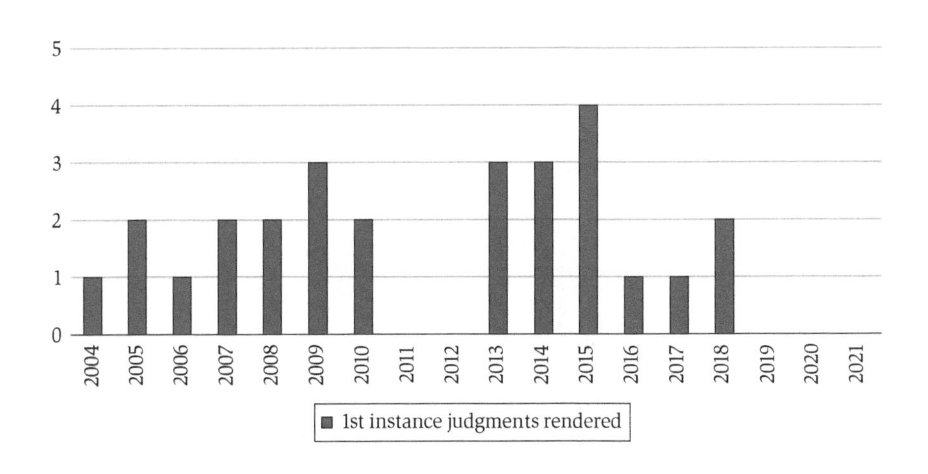

37. Johannes P. Gruber, *Österreichisches Kartellrecht* (3rd edn, Manz 2020) Entscheidungsverzeichnis.
38. *See* the annual reports available at Austrian Federal Competition Authority, 'Annual Reports', https://www.bwb.gv.at/en/factual_information/annual_reports.

Table 3.1 shows the annual number of public enforcement actions before the Cartel Court (i.e., the judicial competition authority in the Austrian system), excluding merger review, as well as appeals relating to these public enforcement actions decided by the Supreme Cartel Court. As can be observed, the Cartel Court rendered 119 public enforcement decisions regarding anti-competitive agreements and unilateral behaviour between 1 January 2006 and 30 April 2021, while the Supreme Cartel Court rendered 24 decisions relating to such public enforcement decisions in the same time period (and an additional 3 decisions between 1 May 2004 and 31 December 2005, i.e., before the entry into force of the Cartel Act 2005).[39] Overall, therefore, between 1 January 2006 and 30 April 2021, a total of 95 Cartel Court decisions remained unchallenged, amounting to 79.8% of all public enforcement decisions rendered by the Cartel Court.

Table 3.1 Number of Public Enforcement Actions Before the Cartel Court and Related Appeals Before the Supreme Cartel Court

	Number of Cartel Court (= Judicial National Competition Authority (NCA)) Decisions Relating to Public Enforcement Cases by Decision Date	*Number of Supreme Cartel Court Decisions Relating to Public Enforcement Cases by Decision Date*
2004	NA	1
2005	NA	2[40]
2006	4	1
2007	4	2
2008	1	2
2009	3	3
2010	5	2
2011	11	0
2012	6	0
2013	5	3
2014	21	3
2015	18	4
2016	7	1
2017	16	1
2018	6	2
2019	6	0
2020	4	0
2021	2	0
Total	*119*	*27*

39. No numbers are available for public enforcement cases before the Cartel Court in 2004 and 2005.
40. An additional Supreme Cartel Court decision from 2005 related to a Cartel Court decision that was issued on 28 April 2004, i.e., before the entry into force of Regulation 1/2003. For this reason, this case is not included in the table and not further discussed in this Report; *see* KOG 04.04.2005, 16 Ok 20/04, *Multiplex I*.

4.3 Success Rates and Outcomes

Overall, 70% of appeals were fully rejected, 19% were partially successful, and only 11% were fully successful (Figure 3.2). None was withdrawn. This represents a very high rate of unsuccessful appeals, perhaps indicating a lower intensity of judicial review by the Supreme Cartel Court.

Figure 3.2 Success of Appeals (Each NCA's Decision Counts as 1)

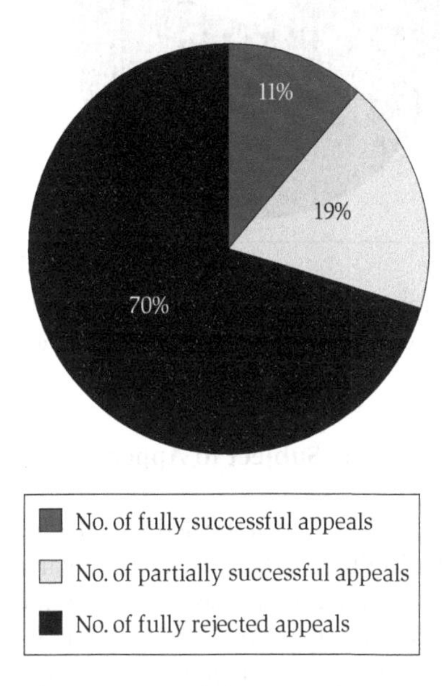

In terms of the specific outcome of the appeals, two cases each were amended only with respect to the fines or partially annulled and partially replaced (Figure 3.3). Only one case each was fully annulled, partially annulled, fully annulled and returned or resolved in a different manner. No appeals were withdrawn, and in no case was the initial decision fully replaced or partially annulled and returned. In one case, the Supreme Cartel Court annulled its own earlier dismissal of a case and went on to substantively appraise the appeals, finding that they had to be rejected.[41]

41. In an earlier case, the Supreme Cartel Court had dismissed an appeal because it believed it had been entered after the deadline; as it turned out that this was not the case, it went on to determine that appeal on the substance; KOG 01.12.2009, 16 Ok 10/09, *Pressegrosso II*.

Figure 3.3 First-Instance Outcome

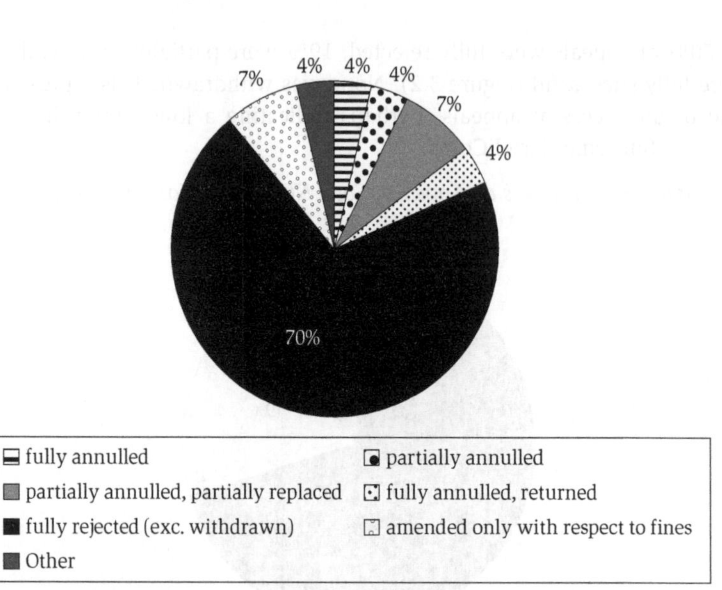

4.4 Type of NCA Decisions Subject to Appeal

An overwhelming majority of decisions appealed (nineteen cases or 70%) related to infringements of Article 101 TFEU and the Austrian equivalent, § 1 Cartel Act (Figure 3.4). Three cases only dealt with national rules on anti-competitive agreements, while two cases only dealt with national rules on abuse of dominance. Two cases dealt with national provisions on anti-competitive agreements and abuse of dominance; one case dealt with an abuse of dominance under European and national rules. It is very well possible that this data reflects the fact that public enforcement of competition law has, ever since the entry into force of the Cartel Act 2005 on 1 January 2006, focused on anti-competitive agreements and mergers while largely leaving abuse of dominance cases to private enforcement. Although this conclusion is a little speculative, this strong focus on anti-competitive agreements may have two main root causes: first of all, both sector inquiries and the Austrian leniency system have been rather successful and continue to reveal significant hardcore antitrust infringements, giving the relatively small Austrian Federal Competition Authority plenty of work in the area of anti-competitive agreements and perhaps not allowing it to deal with abuse of dominance cases in much depth. Second, Austrian business was long used to registering cartels in a cartel register rather than cartels being prohibited, meaning there was a strong cultural understanding that cartel agreements were not intrinsically bad (that, in some sectors, wrongly persists to this day). This may have contributed to a business culture that is (still) in the process of incorporating competition law rules into compliance cultures, and competition enforcement continues to be a strong impetus for doing so, meaning the authority needs to pursue hardcore restrictions as a matter of priority.

Figure 3.4 Rule Being Appealed

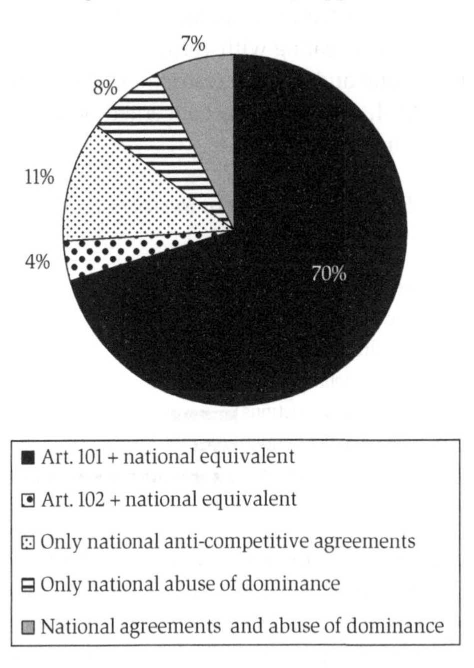

Figure 3.5 shows which rules were being appealed in which year. It shows both that the number of appeals remained relatively – and consistently – low over the years but also that anti-competitive agreements (both under EU and national law) were continuously the most prominent rules featuring in such appeals.

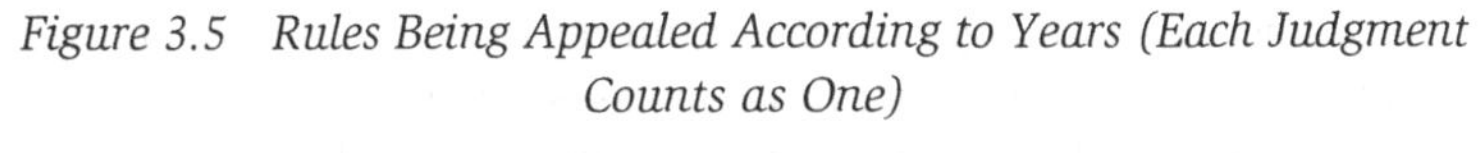

Figure 3.5 Rules Being Appealed According to Years (Each Judgment Counts as One)

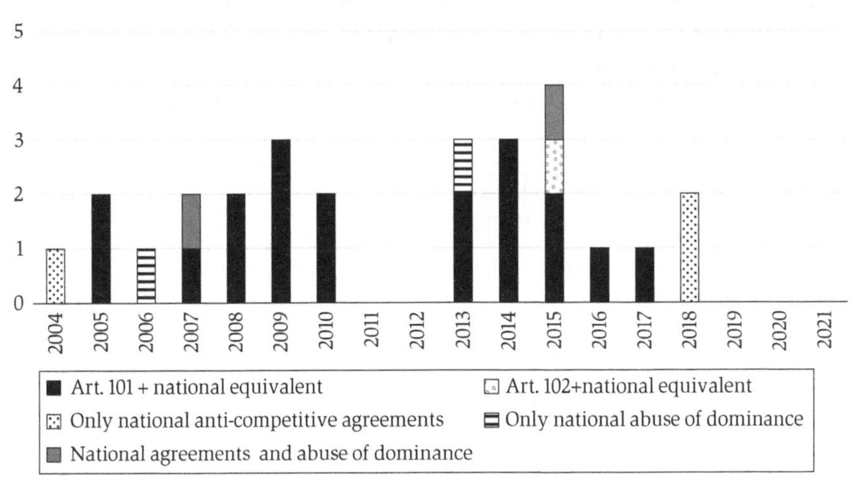

Concerning the types of restrictions being appealed, in the case of anti-competitive agreements, these were overwhelmingly horizontal restrictions (seventeen cases), with only two cases dealing with vertical restrictions alone. Three further cases dealt with both horizontal and vertical restrictions. Very few appeals of abuse of dominance cases were lodged, and only one concerned both anti-competitive agreements and abuse of dominance (Figure 3.6).

Figure 3.6 Types of Restrictions

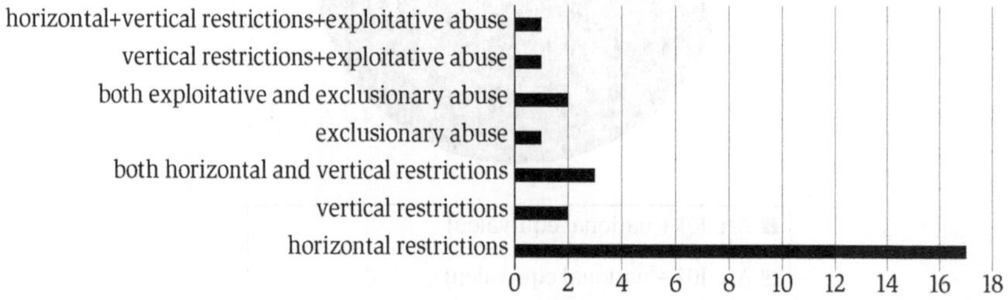

horizontal+vertical restrictions+exploitative abuse
vertical restrictions+exploitative abuse
both exploitative and exclusionary abuse
exclusionary abuse
both horizontal and vertical restrictions
vertical restrictions
horizontal restrictions
0 2 4 6 8 10 12 14 16 18

As far as anti-competitive agreements were concerned, these were all classified as restrictions by-object. As already suggested above, this could indicate that Austrian public enforcement has, in recent years, strongly focused on those types of agreements that, by their very object, restrict competition. This not only means that a more detailed effects analysis can be avoided but also signals to companies in Austria what types of competition infringements they should be particularly wary of. As such, this is likely to contribute to companies' awareness of the competition rules, which, in Austria, is still developing.

Of the Cartel Court decisions being appealed, fourteen cases related to the imposition of a fine, while in eight cases, an infringement was found and had to be terminated, but no fine was imposed. In three cases, the Cartel Court had found no ground for action, meaning that the competition authority's application for a fine or for the termination of an infringement was not granted, and the authority appealed this decision before the Supreme Cartel Court. In one case, the Cartel Court had rejected a complaint, while in another the Cartel Court's decision concerned a procedural matter (Figure 3.7).

Figure 3.7 The Competition Authority's Procedure

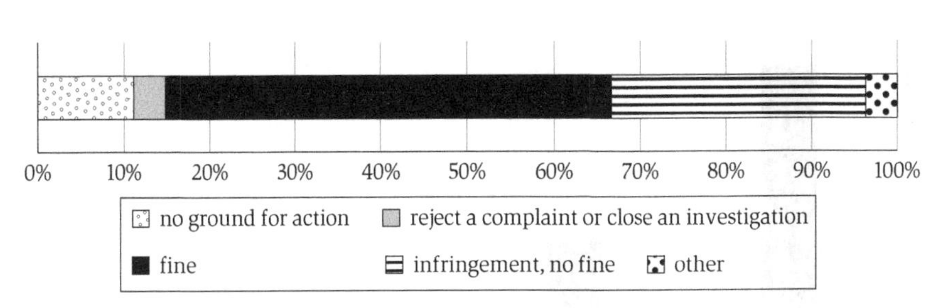

Nearly every fifth appeal before the Supreme Cartel Court related to cases in which leniency applications were successfully submitted, while 14% of appeals related to cases in which settlements had been reached with the Federal Competition Authority. These cases are further discussed below (*see* qualitative analysis). The way in which Austrian competition law handles settlements – which are not as such foreseen by the law – is by the Federal Competition Authority making an application before the Cartel Court (e.g., for the imposition of a lower fine than it would request in the case of no settlement) and the undertaking not contesting the authority's application. The functioning of settlements is based on the fact that the Cartel Act does not allow the Cartel Court to impose a fine that exceeds what the competition authority requested if the authority requested a specified amount.[42]

4.5 Grounds of Appeal

An interesting trend emerges as regards what types of appeals were successful before the Supreme Cartel Court. In particular, procedural grounds were argued in twenty cases but only accepted in three cases and partially accepted in two cases. In fifteen cases, substantive grounds were argued, and these were accepted by the Supreme Cartel Court in only one single case. Of the ten cases in which the fine was a ground of appeal, the appeal was accepted in three cases. Of the ten appeals where grounds related to the interplay between European and national law, only one appeal was accepted (Figure 3.8). Overall, this paints a picture of very few appeals of Cartel Court decisions being successful before the Supreme Cartel Court. It would be interesting to compare these numbers to success rates in appeals relating to the private enforcement of competition law before the same court.

42. On this, *see* Viktoria H.S.E. Robertson, *Competition Law in Austria* (Kluwer 2021) paras 442 ff.; Hanno Wollmann and Franz Urlesberger, 'Im Fokus: Settlements mit der Bundeswettbewerbsbehörde' (2015) *ecolex* 47; Georg E. Kodek, 'Absprachen im Kartellverfahren' (2014) 67 *Österreichische Juristen-Zeitung* 443.

Figure 3.8 Grounds of Appeal (Each NCA's Decision Counts as One)

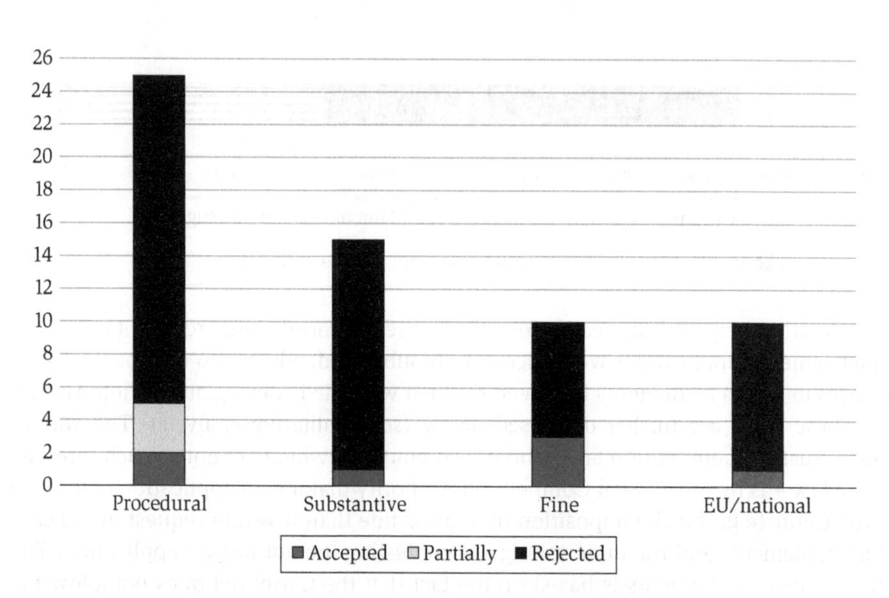

There were no cases in which the fine was reduced, but two cases in which the fine was (considerably) increased by the Supreme Cartel Court – once adding an additional EUR 2 million and thus imposing a fine of EUR 7 million, once increasing the fine by a factor of 10 to a total of EUR 30 million. This case is further considered below in section 5.3. An increase of the fine on appeal is possible when one of the official parties requests an 'adequate fine' before the Cartel Court rather than a specific amount.

Figure 3.9 shows the success of appeals in comparison to the types of restrictions at issue. It highlights that most appeals were launched in the area of anti-competitive agreements (involving both national provisions and Article 101 TFEU), and the appeals were also most often successful in that area. By comparison, no appeals on abuse of dominance or on the national provisions on anti-competitive agreements and abuse of dominance were successful. Only two appeals were launched concerning the national provisions on anti-competitive agreements as well as unilateral conduct, and one of these appeals was successful. One appeal on EU/national grounds was successful (discussed below in the quantitative analysis). As nearly all public competition enforcement cases before the Cartel Court concern anti-competitive agreements, it is not surprising that appeals also relate to this type of competition concern.

Figure 3.9 Types of Restrictions Versus Successful Grounds of Appeal

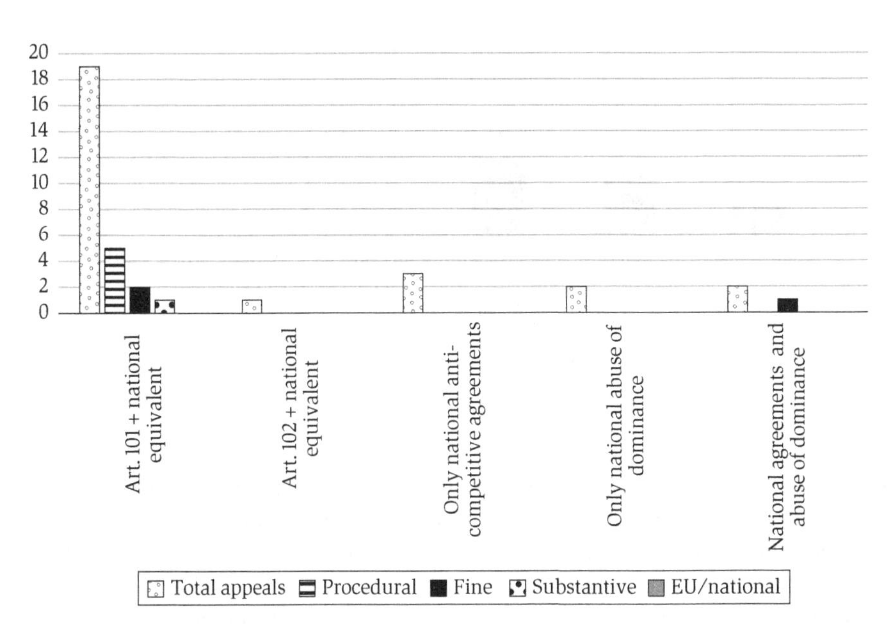

In the six cases in which leniency applications had been successfully submitted, the Federal Competition Authority appealed in three cases, while undertakings appealed in four cases.[43] Of those appeals, two were accepted, and four were rejected (Figure 3.10). However, in the four appeals that related to cases in which settlements had been concluded, two were partially successful, one was fully successful and a further one was rejected (Figure 3.11).

Figure 3.10 Leniency

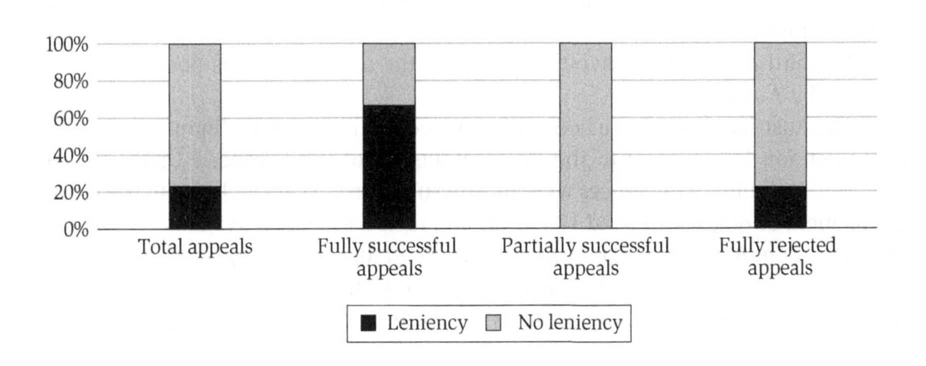

43. In one case, both the competition authority and the undertakings concerned appealed.

Figure 3.11 Settlements

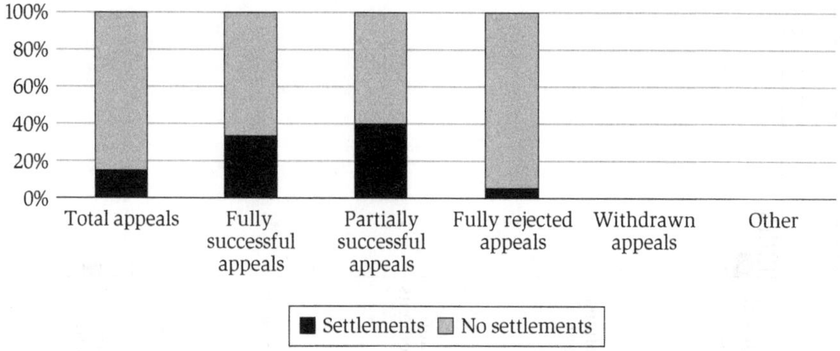

4.6 Other

In only one case was an appeal deemed fully inadmissible, while in a further case, the appeal was deemed partially inadmissible. Inadmissibility was found in a case that concerned the granting of the extension of a deadline to the Federal Competition Authority, which was appealed by the undertaking concerned.[44] The case of partial inadmissibility related to an appeal that was made after the deadline had expired.[45]

In nineteen cases, the appellants were undertakings or associations of undertakings, while in twelve cases, the appellant was the competition authority. In four of these cases, both undertakings and the competition authority simultaneously appealed a case. The relatively high percentage of appeals coming from the (administrative) competition authority may be due to the institutional set-up of competition law enforcement in Austria: as mentioned above, the Cartel Court, as the first-instance decision-maker, is a (judicial) competition authority. The (administrative) competition authority as the prime enforcer brings cases before the Cartel Court. Where it does not agree with the decision by the latter, it is inevitable that it brings the case before the next (and final) instance.

No third parties were involved in any of the appeals, as this possibility is not provided by Austrian law.

The Austrian courts have been rather active in submitting preliminary references in competition law matters to the Court of Justice of the European Union (CJEU). However, preliminary references were mostly submitted in cases relating to the private enforcement of Articles 101 and 102 TFEU and their national equivalents. Preliminary references from Austria have, for instance, arisen in the context of private enforcement or private damages claims and related to essential facilities and refusal to deal, access to file, various aspects of damages claims for competition law infringements, and most

44. KOG 22.05.2014, 16 Ok 5/14t, *Fristen*.
45. KOG 15.07.2009, 16 Ok 6/09, *Pressegrosso I*.

recently, the principle of *ne bis in idem*.[46] In the *BWB/Schenker* case, the Supreme Cartel Court made a preliminary reference to Luxembourg, and the CJEU's preliminary ruling ultimately decided the case.[47]

5 QUALITATIVE ANALYSIS

As described above, the Austrian system for judicial review of competition law decisions differs from most other jurisdictions in the European Union as the Austrian Federal Competition Authority only has investigatory rather than decisional powers. In order to bring an infringement to an end or in order to have a fine imposed for an antitrust infringement, it needs to apply to the Cartel Court. The Federal Competition Authority has around thirty case handlers, consisting of lawyers and economists, who have considerable professional expertise in competition law matters.

The Federal Cartel Prosecutor, another type of administrative competition authority in the Austrian system, has neither investigatory nor decisional powers and can only apply for the imposition of a fine or the finding of an infringement before the Cartel Court.

The Cartel Court is the decision-making instance in the Austrian antitrust enforcement system. Appeals of Cartel Court decisions come before the Supreme Cartel Court. The Cartel Court and the Supreme Cartel Court are specialised panels within the court structure, the former installed at the Higher Regional Court Vienna and the latter installed at the Supreme Court. Both professional judges and expert lay judges participate in these specialised panels. The professional judges at the Cartel Court usually exclusively deal with competition law matters and often stay with the Cartel Court for many years, allowing them to build considerable expertise in competition law matters. At the Supreme Court, judges serve both the panel on competition law matters (Supreme Cartel Court) as well as several panels dealing with other legal issues, meaning that their expertise is not exclusively focused on competition law. The expert lay judges both at the Cartel Court and at the Supreme Cartel Court are appointed on the basis of suggestions by legally acknowledged interest groups and are often professionally involved in competition law matters, for instance, at the Chamber of Commerce or at the Chamber of Labour. They are regularly involved in competition policy discussions in the Austrian context.

If one considers the high number of unsuccessful appeals that are lodged against decisions by the Cartel Court, the question may be posed whether the seemingly low

46. *See, e.g.*, the following preliminary rulings that were issued based on a reference from Austria: CJEU Case C-7/97 *Oscar Bronner v. Mediaprint*, ECLI:EU:C:1998:569; CJEU Case C-273/06 *Petschenig v. Toyota Frey Austria*, ECLI:EU:C:2007:66; CJEU Case C-138/11 *Compass-Datenbank GmbH v. Republik Österreich*, ECLI:EU:C:2012:449; CJEU Case C-536/11 *Bundeswettbewerbsbehörde v. Donau Chemie*, ECLI:EU:C:2013:366; CJEU Case C-557/12 *Kone and others v. ÖBB-Infrastruktur*, ECLI:EU:C:2014:1317; CJEU Case C-248/16 *Austria Asphalt v. Bundeskartellanwalt*, ECLI:EU:C:2017:643; CJEU Case C-435/18 *Otis v. Land Oberösterreich*, ECLI:EU:C:2019:1069; CJEU Case C-151/20 *Bundeswettbewerbsbehörde v. Nordzucker* ECLI:EU:C:2022:203.
47. CJEU Case C-681/11 *Bundeswettbewerbsbehörde v. Schenker*, ECLI:EU:C:2013:404; KOG 02.12.2013, 16 Ok 4/13, *BWB/Schenker ['Spediteurssammelladungskonferenz II']*.

intensity of review may be influenced by two factors: first of all, the fact that the first decision-maker in Austrian antitrust enforcement is a court or 'judicial' NCA rather than an administrative NCA. The second is the fact that there is only one instance available to the parties. Neither of these factors is present in the majority of national jurisdictions that were surveyed for this study.

In the quantitative assessment, a total of twenty-seven appeals before the Supreme Cartel Court could be identified that were based on a Cartel Court decision, that had their roots in an application by one of the two Austrian administrative competition authorities, and that were rendered since the entering into force of Regulation 1/2003 on 1 May 2004. Some of these are discussed below to highlight the type of review that the Supreme Cartel Court undertakes.

5.1 Appeals and Leniency

In a total of six cases, a successful leniency application had been made by one of the companies involved.[48] While leniency applications in Austria can be made in relation to horizontal as well as vertical agreements, all of these cases related to a horizontal agreement that was considered an infringement by-object and that was assessed based on Article 101 TFEU and the national equivalent.[49] This gives an indication of the type of public enforcement that has been occurring. In four of these cases, the appeal was rejected; in one case, it was accepted, and the initial decision was annulled based on a preliminary ruling by the CJEU, and in one further case, the initial decision was partially annulled.

In *Printing chemicals*,[50] an applicant argued that there had been an erroneous application of the leniency instrument as the authority had only granted it leniency status for some of the duration of the cartel; the appeal was unsuccessful. The Supreme Cartel Court held that it was not within the competence of the Cartel Court to directly assess whether the Federal Competition Authority wrongly decided on the application of the leniency instrument as set out in the Competition Act, especially as the authority has some discretion in applying it. However, the Cartel Court did – under § 30(3) Cartel Act – have the duty to consider a cartelist's contribution to the investigation of an infringement as a mitigating circumstance when fixing the amount of a fine. This allows for an indirect assessment of the application of the leniency instrument.

In one case involving leniency, the previous instance's decision was partially annulled.[51] Only one case led to the full annulment of the previous instance's decision and a return to the Cartel Court for a new decision: in *Joint liability scheme IV*, the

48. *See* KOG 25.03.2009, 16 Ok 4/09, *Industriechemikalien*; KOG 04.10.2010, 16 Ok 5/10, *Druckchemikalien*; KOG 02.12.2013, 16 Ok 4/13, *BWB/Schenker ['Spediteurssammelladungskonferenz II']*; KOG 02.12.2013, 16 Ok 6/12, *Installateure*; KOG 30.09.2015, 16 Ok 5/15v, *Rahmengebühr*; KOG 06.09.2017, 16 Ok 10/16f, *Untersuchungshandschuhe*.
49. While the Austrian leniency system also allows for leniency applications outside of horizontal agreements, in practice leniency applications usually have a horizontal background.
50. KOG 04.10.2010, 16 Ok 5/10, *Druckchemikalien*.
51. KOG 30.09.2015, 16 Ok 5/15v, *Rahmengebühr*.

Supreme Cartel Court accepted that the applicant's right to be heard had not been safeguarded and the Cartel Court's decision had to be annulled.[52]

A further case relating to a leniency application concerned its interplay with EU competition law and is discussed below at 5.2.

5.2 The Application of EU Competition Law in National Cases

The Austrian Supreme Court regularly relies on EU competition law - primary and secondary law, CJEU judgments, Commission decisions and soft law documents - in its decisions, also where it would not be bound to do so under Regulation 1/2003. Some cases are also more directly concerned with the application of EU competition law. In *Industrial chemicals*,[53] the Cartel Court had denied the Federal Competition Authority's request to establish the finding of an infringement because no fine was to be imposed on two leniency applicants. The Court held that such an isolated finding of an infringement was not covered by the powers of national competition authorities as foreseen in Regulation 1/2003. The Federal Competition Authority unsuccessfully appealed this decision. In 2013, the Austrian legislator remedied this situation and introduced a provision in the Cartel Act that now explicitly states that the finding of an infringement can also be requested where the Federal Competition Authority has granted leniency status to an undertaking.[54] This ensures that follow-on actions can be based on the finding of an infringement by the Cartel Court.

In *Federal Competition Authority/Schenker*,[55] the Cartel Court had not decided in favour of the Federal Competition Authority's application for the finding of an infringement (concerning the leniency applicant) and the imposition of a fine (on further cartelists that were not leniency applicants). Based on Article 15(3) of Regulation 1/2003, the European Commission submitted written observations to the Supreme Cartel Court, arguing that it would be an error in law to assume that undertakings were not at fault when presuming that an Austrian Cartel Court decision of 1996 relating to national law granted them cartel immunity also under EU competition law. The Commission also opined that it did not contravene EU competition law if national competition authorities found an infringement of competition law without simultaneously imposing a fine. The Supreme Cartel Court subsequently referred several questions on the interpretation of EU competition law to the Court of Justice of the European Union. In its preliminary ruling, the Court of Justice held that where an undertaking errs about the lawfulness of its behaviour based on (wrong) legal advice or based on a national competition authority's decision, it cannot escape the imposition of a fine under Article 101 TFEU. The Court of Justice also held that EU competition law - including Regulation 1/2003 - does not prevent a national competition authority from finding an infringement without imposing a fine where this applies to a successful

52. KOG 08.10.2008, 16 Ok 9/08, *Haftungsverbund IV*.
53. KOG 25.03.2009, 16 Ok 4/09, *Industriechemikalien*.
54. *See* § 28(1a) Cartel Act, as introduced by Austrian Federal Law Gazette I 2013/13.
55. KOG 02.12.2013, 16 Ok 4/13, *BWB/Schenker ['Spediteurssammelladungskonferenz II']*.

leniency applicant.[56] Already before this preliminary ruling was issued on 18 June 2013, the Austrian legislator had adopted the above-mentioned amendment to the Cartel Act explicitly allowing for the finding of an infringement without the imposition of a fine in relation to leniency applicants.

In a case involving fees for master builders,[57] the Austrian competition authorities had urged the Cartel Court to take into account Regulation 1/2003. The Supreme Cartel Court agreed that when applying Regulation 1/2003, the fee schedule for master builders at issue could not, based on Article 101(3) TFEU, be seen as exempt from the prohibition of anti-competitive agreements.

In a case involving a cartel of plumbers,[58] the Cartel Court had applied the *de minimis* rule of the Austrian Cartel Act that provided, at the time, that even hardcore cartels could come under that rule. The Federal Competition Authority and the Federal Cartel Prosecutor unsuccessfully challenged this decision before the Supreme Cartel Court.[59] The Austrian legislator remedied this by amending the Austrian *de minimis* rule, which now prevents hardcore cartels from benefitting from this exception and brings the Austrian *de minimis* rule in line with the European Commission's *De Minimis* Notice.[60]

5.3 Fines and Competition Law Appeals

In one case,[61] both the Federal Competition Authority and the undertaking concerned, major food retailer Spar, appealed the Cartel Court's decision. While the Cartel Court cannot impose a fine that goes beyond what the competition authority has requested,[62] the competition authority can simply ask for an 'adequate' fine. This enabled the Supreme Cartel Court to increase the fine originally imposed by the Cartel Court – amounting to EUR 3 million – by a factor of ten, imposing upon the food retailer a fine of EUR 30 million. This decision received widespread attention in Austria, as it means that an appeal of a Cartel Court decision can significantly affect the outcome, also to the detriment of the undertaking concerned.

In another case,[63] the Supreme Cartel Court increased a fine of originally EUR 5 million to EUR 7 million following the Federal Competition Authority's appeal. There were no cases at all in which the fine that the Cartel Court had imposed upon the competition authority's application was annulled or reduced.

56. CJEU Case C-681/11 *Bundeswettbewerbsbehörde v. Schenker*, ECLI:EU:C:2013:404.
57. KOG 20.12.2005, 16 Ok 45/05, *Honorarordnung der Baumeister*.
58. KG 13.07.2012, 27 Kt 20, 21/09-155, *Installateure*.
59. KOG 02.12.2013, 16 Ok 6/12, *Installateure*.
60. § 2(2) no. 1 Cartel Act, as amended by Federal Law Gazette I 2013/13; European Commission, Notice on agreements of minor importance which do not appreciably restrict competition under Article 101(1) of the Treaty on the Functioning of the European Union (*De Minimis* Notice) [2014] OJ C291/1.
61. KOG 08.10.2015, 16 Ok 2/15b & 16 Ok 8/15k, *Spar*.
62. § 36(2) Cartel Act.
63. KOG 12.09.2007, 16 Ok 4/07, *Bankomatvertrag III*.

In a case in relation to the elevator cartel,[64] an infringer requested to pay its fine in instalments. The Cartel Court rejected this request because the appellant had not provided proof that it was not in a position to pay the fine without severe disadvantages for its business, the Supreme Cartel Court confirmed.

In an appeal on compulsory dealing,[65] the appellant argued that the fine should be reduced; the Supreme Cartel Court did not agree and analysed the functions of a fine under competition law, also considering Commission guidance (brought up by the appellant), literature and the court's case law.

5.4 Settlements and Appeals

Three appeals concerned cases that involved settlements. In *Follow-on claims I* and *II*,[66] the Supreme Cartel Court had to rule on whether the identity of the competitors with whom the applicant had entered into an anti-competitive agreement should be named in the published decision. In both cases, the Supreme Cartel Court partially annulled the previous instance's decision on what passage should be published and replaced it with its own. In *Asphalt mixing plant III*,[67] the question revolved around the costs as decided by the Cartel Court. The undertaking's appeal was rejected.

5.5 The Competition Authority as an Official Party: Taking up Abandoned Private Cases

In *Radius clause V*,[68] the proceedings were started as a private enforcement action, but the private applicant later withdrew from the proceedings. As the Federal Competition Authority and the Federal Cartel Prosecutor are official parties to any case before the Cartel Court, the Federal Competition Authority subsequently took up the case and pursued it as its own, as a public enforcement action. This is an interesting dynamic as a settlement between private parties is not able to stop the (administrative) competition authorities from further pursuing the case – while the (judicial) competition authority can only rule on a case where there is an application before it, either by a private party or by an official party.

64. KOG 10.05.2018, 16 Ok 4/18a, *Aufzugs- und Fahrtreppenkartell X*.
65. KOG 26.06.2006, 16 Ok 3/06, *Multiplex II*. Similarly, *see* KOG 31.03.2016, 16 Ok 7/15p, *Transport von Stahlrohren*.
66. KOG 27.01.2014, 16 Ok 14/13, *Follow-on-Klagen I [vertikale Verkaufspreisvereinbarungen]*; KOG 31.01.2014, 16 Ok 15/13, *Follow-on-Klagen II*.
67. KOG 11.01.2010, 16 Ok 11/09, *Asphaltmischwerk III*. Two further appeals also concerned costs, but not in the context of a settlement: KOG 17.10.2005, 16 Ok 44/05, *Rahmengebühr*; KOG 18.05.2018, 16 Ok3/18d, *Absprachen - Trockenausbau*.
68. KOG 08.10.2015, 16 Ok 6/15s, *Radiusklausel V*.

5.6 Further Issues Raised in Appeals Before the Supreme Cartel Court

In *Liquid gas*,[69] the Supreme Cartel Court rejected the Federal Competition Authority's appeal of a Cartel Court decision that did not find an abuse of a dominant position. The same occurred in *Taxi-App*.[70]

In *Deadline extension*,[71] the Cartel Court had granted an extended deadline to the Federal Competition Authority to substantiate their application, as the electronic data upon which the authority wanted to rely was sealed. When the appellant appealed this decision, the Supreme Cartel Court found that this appeal was not admissible. This is the only case in which an appeal was found to be entirely inadmissible; in a further case, the appeal was held to be partially inadmissible.[72]

In another case,[73] the Supreme Cartel Court had previously dismissed the appeals of two appellants because they had submitted their appeals after the deadline; as this turned out to be wrong - they had submitted their appeals by fax and on time - the Court subsequently took their appeals into account.

5.7 The Supreme Cartel Court's Appellate Review in Public Enforcement Actions

The Supreme Cartel Court reviews the Cartel Court's decisions based on the appeal of an undertaking concerned or based on an appeal by a competition authority (Federal Competition Authority or Federal Cartel Prosecutor). Except for very specific circumstances, and despite the fact that it is the only appellate instance, in most cases, its review is limited to legal questions rather than extending to questions of fact,[74] a point that the Supreme Cartel Court regularly emphasises in its decisions. This may also come to bear on the intensity of the review that is performed by the Supreme Cartel Court.

The question of the degree to which the Austrian Supreme Cartel Court exercises judicial deference in competition law matters cannot be answered with any precision, not only because of the relatively small number of cases but also due to the particular set-up of public antitrust enforcement in Austria that was already discussed above. The first decisional instance is not an administrative authority but a court - which cannot become active on its own account but can only decide if an administrative competition authority makes a request. While the Federal Competition Authority uses all its expertise to make its case before the Cartel Court, it is the latter that ultimately issues the judicial decision that is open to appeal. In the past, the Supreme Cartel Court has unreservedly sided with the Cartel Court in over two-thirds of cases, perhaps indicating a high degree of (appellate) judicial deference vis-à-vis the Cartel Court.

69. KOG 01.12.2015, 16 Ok 4/15x, *Flüssiggas III*.
70. KOG 27.06.2013, 16 Ok 7/12, *Taxi-App*.
71. KOG 22.05.2014, 16 Ok 5/14t, *Fristen*.
72. KOG 15.07.2009, 16 Ok 6/09, *Pressegrosso I*.
73. KOG 01.12.2009, 16 Ok 10/09, *Pressegrosso II*.
74. § 49(3) Cartel Act.

As mentioned above, it is a peculiarity of Austrian competition law that the competition authority can request the imposition of an 'adequate fine' by the Cartel Court; in a further step, the Supreme Cartel Court can then amend this fine upon appeal. Quite to the contrary of judicial deference, this amounts to an 'administrative deference' whereby the administrative competition authority can decide not to specify the amount of an adequate fine and instead leave this to the Cartel Court and, subsequently, the Supreme Cartel Court. Indeed, the Supreme Cartel Court has held that the official parties usually only ask for the imposition of an adequate fine rather than specifying the amount.[75] However, the competition authority can also decide to ask for a specific amount of a fine, as is mentioned in § 36(1a) Cartel Act, in which case the competition authority needs to justify the specific amount it is asking for, and neither the Cartel Court nor the Supreme Cartel Court can impose a fine beyond the amount requested.[76] The criteria for calculating an adequate fine are regularly the subject of appeals, and while the Supreme Cartel Court has referred to both Commission guidance and CJEU case law in such cases, it has also acknowledged that Austrian competition law is autonomous in this respect.[77]

As the Supreme Cartel Court has repeatedly highlighted, the level of a fine is a discretionary decision[78] – but this discretion on the part of the Cartel Court is subject to review by the Supreme Cartel Court, which takes up this task without any noticeable judicial deference and assesses whether the Cartel Court has used its own discretion in line with the legal framework.

In individual cases, the Cartel Court has received legal guidance from the European Commission under Article 15(3) of Regulation 1/2003. For instance, in one case, the Commission opined on the application of EU competition law before and after the entry into force of Regulation 1/2003 and what difference the new decentralised system made for the enforcement of EU competition law.[79] In that case, the Supreme Cartel Court made a preliminary reference based on this question, and subsequently decided the case in light of the preliminary ruling issued by the CJEU.[80]

In a case on printing chemicals (already discussed above), the Cartel Court had held that it could not review the application of the leniency rules by the Federal Competition Authority, as the legal provisions in question (§ 11(3) Competition Act) exclusively addressed the latter. Upon review, the Supreme Cartel Court held that this took judicial deference too far. It found that while the Cartel Court could not directly review the Federal Competition Authority's decisions regarding the application of the leniency instrument, it was competent to decide upon the level of the adequate fine – which requires taking into account of cooperation with the authority as a mitigating factor.[81]

75. KOG 08.10.2015, 16 Ok 2/15b & 16 Ok 8/15k, *Spar*.
76. § 36 para. 1a Cartel Act.
77. *See, e.g.*, KOG 26.6.2006, 16 Ok 3/06, *Multiplex II*.
78. KOG 25.3.2009, 16 Ok 4/09, *Industriechemikalien*; KOG 31.3.2016, 16 Ok 7/15p, *Transport von Stahlrohren*.
79. KOG 2.12.2013, 16 Ok 4/13, *BWB-Schenker ('Spediteursamelladungskonferenz II')*.
80. CJEU Case C-681/11 *Bundeswettbewerbsbehörde v Schenker*, ECLI:EU:C:2013:404.
81. KOG 4.10.2010, 16 Ok 5/10, *Druckchemikalien*.

In one case, the Supreme Cartel Court found that the undertakings concerned had not engaged in abusive market conduct, and it held, therefore, that no relevant market had to be delineated and no final decision was required as to the existence of dominance.[82] As the Supreme Cartel Court is the first and final instance of appeal, it was not possible to further have this controversial finding reviewed.

The Supreme Cartel Court regularly relies on European provisions for the interpretation of Austrian competition law provisions. For instance, in a case revolving around the interpretation of the provision on the publication of Cartel Court decisions (§ 37 Cartel Act), it referred to the 'parallel provision' under European competition law, i.e., Article 30 of Regulation 1/2003.[83] In one instance, the Court also discussed different views according to the Chicago School.[84]

The Supreme Cartel Court's decisions are usually short and concise. In the sample of twenty-seven decisions analysed for this report, decisions had an average length of twenty-one pages, with the longest decision spanning seventy-one pages and the shortest covering only two pages. The median length was fifteen pages. The decisions always consist of a heading (naming the parties to the case, the case number, the type of decision, the composition of the panel and the outcome of the case), a summary of the facts as established by the Cartel Court, a summary of the arguments by the appellants, and finally a legal appraisal of these arguments by the Supreme Cartel Court. Overall, the legal appraisal carried out by the Supreme Cartel Court tends to be rather short and to the point. The Supreme Cartel Court also rarely disagrees with the Cartel Court. Of the twenty-seven decisions analysed, it fully accepted appeals in only three cases and partially accepted them in five cases; it fully rejected the appeals in nineteen cases, no matter whether the appeal was brought by the administrative competition authorities or an undertaking.

6 CONCLUDING REMARKS

The specific characteristics of the Austrian competition law system, which were outlined above, have led to a situation in which fewer appeals were available to be reviewed for the purposes of the present report. By the selection of cases that the competition authority has brought before the Cartel Court, it already becomes evident that it does not take this step lightly and prefers to focus on cases that are relatively straightforward. While the proceedings before the Cartel Court are non-contentious, the dynamics of such cases differ from cases in which the (administrative) competition authority itself decides a case – as occurs in most Member States and also at the European Union level – that can then be appealed before several judicial bodies in succession. Nevertheless, the reviewed cases allow for an insight into how competition law decisions by the decision-maker – the Cartel Court – are reviewed by the only appeal instance, i.e., the Supreme Cartel Court. With over two thirds of appeals unsuccessful before the Supreme Cartel Court, this already indicates that the appeal

82. KOG 1.12.2015, 16 Ok 4/15x, *Flüssiggas III*.
83. KOG 27.1.2014, 16 Ok 14/13, *Follow-on-Klagen I (vertikale Verkaufspreisvereinbarungen)*.
84. KOG 08.10.2015, 16 Ok 2/15b & 16 Ok 8/15k, *Spar*.

instance is only willing to overturn the lower court where there is a blatant error in the Cartel Court's decision. This points to considerable judicial deference. In addition, the intensity of review, as it became apparent in the twenty-seven decisions that were reviewed, does not appear to go beyond the minimum required, also indicating a certain judicial deference.

In substantive terms, it is remarkable that the application of EU competition law alongside national competition law has firmly established itself in Austria. While Austria does have some stricter rules for unilateral conduct as enabled by Article 3 of Regulation 1/2003 - on relative market power, retaliatory measures, and local supply - these did not once arise in an appeal in a public enforcement action. As the wording of the Austrian provisions that are equivalent to Articles 101 and 102 TFEU is modelled on the European provisions, the Austrian courts also have the habit of resorting to the CJEU's case law on these provisions in national cases. In substantive terms, it is therefore not of significant relevance whether the (Supreme) Cartel Court reviews a case under national or European competition law.[85]

In procedural terms, it is notable that, overall, very few appeals before the Supreme Cartel Court are successful. One successful appeal that particularly stood out over the years was the Federal Competition Authority's appeal of a fine imposed on an infringer that was increased by a factor of ten by the Supreme Cartel Court. This case drove the message home in Austria that competition law enforcement matters and that undertakings' appeals of Cartel Court decisions can have quite unintended effects.

85. Austria introduced a sustainability exemption in September 2021, the wording of which differs from Article 101(3) TFEU. It will be interesting to *see* whether this difference will be perceived in judicial practice. On that exemption, *see* Robertson, 'Sustainability', *supra* n. 7.

CHAPTER 4

Belgium Report

Caroline Cauffman

1 COMPETITION LAW ENFORCEMENT IN BELGIUM

1.1 Short Overview of the Belgian Competition Rules

In 1960, Belgium adopted an Act prohibiting the abuse of dominance.[1] The first Belgian legislation to also prohibit anticompetitive agreements and organise a system for merger control was introduced in 1991.[2] This Act was amended multiple times[3] until it was replaced by an Act of 2006,[4] which was, in turn, replaced by Book IV of the Code of Economic Law (CEL). However, the amendments only concerned the institutional and procedural rules. The substantive rules of antitrust corresponding to Articles 101 and 102 Treaty on the Functioning of the European Union (TFEU) have remained largely untouched since 1991. Equally, when Book IV of the CEL was replaced by a new and improved version in 2017,[5] the changes did not affect the substantive antitrust rules. Almost at the same time, however, another Act was adopted that added new

1. Act of 27 May 1960 on protection against abuse of economic dominance, *Belgian Official Journal* (*BOJ*) 22 June 1960.
2. Act of 5 August 1991 on the protection of economic competition, *BOJ* 11 October 1991.
3. Act of 22 March 1993, *BOJ* 19 April 1993; Act 26 April 1999, *BOJ* 27 April 1999. A coordinated version of the Act was realised by Royal decree of 1 July 1999, published in the *BOJ* 1 September 1999. Soon, a new amendment was adopted: Act of 15 March 2000, *BOJ* 5 May 2000.
4. Act of 10 June 2006 on the protection of economic competition, *BOJ* 29 June 2006; Act of 10 June 2006, establishing a Competition Council, *BOJ* 29 June 2006, coordinated by Royal Decree of 15 September 2006, *BOJ* 29 September 2006. The coordinated version is later referred to hereinafter referred to as: 2016 Competition Act.
5. Act of 2 May 2019 amending Book I 'Definitions', Book XV 'Law Enforcement' and replacing Book IV 'Protection of Competition' of the Economic Code, *BOJ* 24 May 2019.

rules containing a prohibition on the abuse of economic dependency[6] that has no equivalent in EU law. This prohibition falls outside the scope of the current report.

This report covers appeals of cases decided since the entry into force of Regulation 1/2003 on 1 May 2004, provided that the appellate judgment was given and made public before or on 30 April 2021. Insofar as those cases concern the Belgian equivalents of Articles 101-102 TFEU, they are subject to:

- The Act of 1991, as amended in 1993, 1999 and 2000, when they were decided by the National Competition Authority between 1 May 2004 (start of the research period) and 30 September 2006.[7]
- The Act of 2006 when they were decided between 1 October 2006 and 5 September 2013.
- The first version of Book IV of the CEL when they were decided between 6 September 2013 and 3 June 2019.[8]
- The new version of Book IV of the CEL when they were decided after 3 June 2019.

1.2 The Institutional Structure of the National Competition Authority

The 1991 Act created a Belgian competition law enforcer with a dual structure: the Competition Service (*Dienst voor de Mededinging*) was responsible for the detection and investigation of potential infringements of the competition rules. The Competition Council (*Raad voor de Mededinging*) was an administrative court, responsible for deciding cases as well as making proposals and advising on competition policy.[9] Both the Competition Service and the Competition Council were part of the Ministry of Economic Affairs.[10]

During the legislative process leading up to the 1999 reform, a suggestion was made to replace the existing institutional framework for the enforcement of competition law with an autonomous competition authority. This suggestion was rejected for financial reasons, and only a limited change was made to the institutional framework: a Corps of Reporters (*Korps Verslaggevers*) was added to the Competition Service. The

6. Act of 4 April 2019 amending the Economic Law Code with regard to abuses of economic dependence, abusive clauses and unfair market practices between enterprises, *BOJ* 24 May 2019.
7. Article 64 Act of 10 June 2006 on the protection of economic competition; Article 3 Act of 10 June 2006, establishing a Competition Council.
8. Article 28 Act of 3 April 2013 inserting Book IV 'Protection of Competition' and Book V 'Competition and Price Developments' into the Code of Economic Law and inserting the definitions specific to Book IV and Book V and the implementing provisions specific to Book IV and Book V into Book I of the Code of Economic Law, *BOJ* 26 April 2013. Article 14 Act of 3 April 2013 on the introduction of provisions regulating matters referred to in Article 77 of the Constitution in Book IV 'Protection of Competition' and Book V 'Competition and Price Developments' of the Code of Economic Law, *BOJ* 26 April 2013.
9. Article 16 Act 1991.
10. Articles 14 and 16 Act 1991.

Corps was responsible for deciding on the order of cases and for leading and organising investigations.[11]

The entry into force of Regulation 1/2003 required further reform of the Belgian competition rules. The Regulation, which decentralised the enforcement of the EU antitrust rules, was directly applicable in Belgium. However, it did not concern the application of the Belgian competition rules. This caused procedural complexities in cases where Article 101-102 TFEU were to be applied concurrently with their national equivalents. In the period leading up to the new Competition Act, which would take until 2006, the idea of creating an autonomous competition authority resurfaced but was rejected once again for financial considerations. Instead of creating an autonomous authority, the legislator emphasised the independence of the enforcer. The Council no longer formed part of the Ministry of Economic Affairs, and the Corps of Reporters, renamed as '*Auditoraat*'/'*Auditorat*' (hereinafter translated as 'Investigation and Prosecution Service' (IPS)) became part of the Council. However, the IPS was independent and decided, *inter alia*, on the priorities of the enforcement agenda and the order of dealing with cases. It carried out investigations resulting either in a decision not to pursue a case any further or in a report to the Council, which was, in any case as far as infringement cases were concerned, an administrative court.[12]

An Act of 3 April 2013 introduced a Book IV in the CEL and created a Belgian Competition Authority (BCA), an autonomous governmental service with a legal personality comprising a President, a Competition College, a Committee of Directors, a Competition Prosecutor General and an Investigation and Prosecution Service (Article IV.16, § 1 CEL). Although the BCA is a single administrative body, a functional separation exists between investigations carried out by the IPS under the supervision of the Competition Prosecutor General and decisions, taken by the Competition College.[13]

Complaints are made to the Competition Prosecutor General. The IPS has the power to decide not to pursue a complaint any further (Article IV.42, § 2 *juncto* Article IV.30, § 1, 1° CEL). The Competition Prosecutor General decides whether to open investigations and the order in which cases are to be dealt with after the advice of the Director of Economic Studies (Article IV.26, § 2, 3°CEL). The Minister of Economic Affairs may now order the opening of investigations (Article IV.41, § 1, 3° CEL), while previously, he could only request to do so (Article 44, § 1 2006 Competition Act).[14]

The Competition College decides on objections submitted by the IPS based on the file submitted by the latter. Unlike its precursor, the Competition Council, it no longer has the right to request additional investigations.

The transition from a judicial system of competition law enforcement to an administrative system in 2013 was the result of the European Court of Justice's decision

11. Article 14, §2 Act 1999 (coord.).
12. *See* Article 29 of the 2006 Competition Act; D. Vandermeersch, *De Mededingingswet*, Mechelen, Kluwer 2007, 71.
13. H. Gilliams, 'Het nieuwe Belgisch mededingingsrecht', *RDC* 2013/6, 479-481.
14. W. Devroe and H. Buelens, 'Vernieuwd mededingingsrecht in België', in *Het Wetboek van economisch recht: van nu en straks?*, Mortsel, Intersentia, 2014, 112.

in *Vebic*, according to which Article 35 of Regulation 1/2003[15] precludes national rules prohibiting a competition authority from participating, as a defendant or respondent, in judicial proceedings brought against a decision it has taken.[16] This is further elaborated on in section 2.1.3.

2 JUDICIAL REVIEW OF COMPETITION DECISIONS IN BELGIUM

2.1 First-Instance Appeal

2.1.1 General

Before the entry into force of the Acts of 3 April 2013, decisions in infringement cases were taken by the Competition Council (*Raad voor de Mededinging*), which was an administrative tribunal. These decisions could be appealed before the Brussels Court of Appeal. During this period, the concept 'appeal' could rightly be used in terms of an appeal to that Appeal Court from the first-instance judicial decision-maker. After the entry into force of the Acts of 3 April 2013, the decisions in competition cases were taken by the Competition College, part of the BCA, an administrative body. When a court reviews such administrative decisions, this is, technically speaking, not an appeal but a review procedure.[17] In the French version of the Code of Economic Law, this is reflected correctly by the use of the word '*recours*' instead of '*appel*'. The Dutch version, however, still uses the word '*beroep*', appeal.[18] Hereinafter, the words 'appeal' and 'review' will be used interchangeably.

Notwithstanding the institutional changes made to the National Competition Authority (NCA) by the 2013 revision of the competition rules, many of the rules on appeals against final decisions of the competition authority are still the same as under the first Belgian Competition Act of 1991. For instance, the competent court to hear appeals has been and still is the Court of Appeal of Brussels. Since 1991, this is the only Court hearing such appeals. Consequently, a certain degree of specialisation and uniformity in decision-making at the appellate level has always been ensured. Specialisation even increased since 2016, when within the Brussels Court of Appeal, a special section, called the Markets Court, was established and given the exclusive power to

15. Council Regulation No. 1/2003 of 16 December 2002 on the implementation of the rules on competition laid down in Articles 81 and 82 of the Treaty, *OJ* L 1, 4.1.2003, pp. 1-25.
16. Case C-439/08, *Vlaamse federatie van verenigingen van Brood- en Banketbakkers, Ijsbereiders en Chocoladebewerkers (Vebic) VZW*, EU:C:2010:739, ECR 2010 I-12471.
17. E. De Lophem, 'Aspects procéduraux des recours contre les décisions de l'autorité belge de la concurrence en matière de pratiques de restrictives de concurrence', *RDC* 2014, 237.
18. Article IV.70 CEL (version 2013); Article IV.90 CEL (version 2019). About the distinction between review and appeal, *see further* E. De Lophem, 'Aspects procéduraux des recours contre les décisions de l'autorité belge de la concurrence en matière de pratiques de restrictives de concurrence', *RDC* 2014/3, 237 et seq.

hear appeals in competition cases[19] (except for the few instances where the president of the Court of Appeal hears appeals against decisions of the IPS[20]).

Both before and after the 2013 revision, any appeal has to be launched within a period of thirty days of the notification of the decision. The appeal has no suspensory effect. However, the Court may, depending on the applicable Competition Act, suspend the obligation to pay fines or periodic penalty payments up until the day of the appellate decision. If they have already been paid, it may even order their reimbursement.[21]

Throughout the years, it has been recognised that the Court of Appeal has 'full jurisdiction'. However, the interpretation of this concept has been disputed. This will be further explained in section 2.1.3. Moreover, the various versions of the Belgian competition rules introduced changes regarding types of NCA decisions subject to appeal and the parties entitled to appeal and/or to submit observations before the Court of Appeal.

2.1.2 Type of NCA Procedures Subject to Appeal

Under the 1991 Competition Act, all final decisions in infringement cases were subject to judicial review (Article 43), including rejections of complaints. When the IPS considered that a complaint was to be rejected, it had to submit the case with its findings to the Competition Council, which could decide either to follow the opinion of the IPS to reject the complaint or to return the case to the IPS for further investigation. A decision to reject the complaint could be appealed to the Court of Appeal.[22]

The 2006 Competition Act transferred competence to make decisions to reject complaints to the IPS (Article 45, § 2). These decisions could be appealed to the Competition Council. The Council's decision was final. No further appeal was possible (Article 45, § 3).[23] Judicial review of decisions rejecting complaints was no longer available and has not been reintroduced by later revisions of the competition rules.

Book IV CEL 2013 provides in a more detailed way than the earlier Competition Acts which decisions can and cannot be appealed.[24] With respect to infringement cases, an appeal is possible against: (1) decisions of the College finding an infringement of Article 101 and/or 102 TFEU and/or their national equivalents, Article IV.1 and IV.2 CEL; (2) decisions of the College finding that there is no reason to act or that the facts

19. Act of 25 December 2016 amending the legal status of prisoners and the supervision of prisons and containing various provisions on justice, *BOJ* 30 December 2016.
20. *See* Article IV.62, § 3 and 4 CEL (version 2013); Article IV.44, IV.46, § 2 CEL (version 2019).
21. *See, e.g.*, Article 43 Act 1991, Article IV.79, § 2 CEL 2013.
22. J. Steenlant, 'De nieuwe wet tot bescherming van de economische mededinging', *TPR* 1992, 376.
23. Geert A. Zonnekeyn and Dominique Smeets, 'De hervorming van de Belgische mededingingswet: een nieuwe start of een gemiste kans?', *RDC* 2006/9, 910.
24. Decisions taken during the investigation cannot be appealed as such, only as part of an appeal against the final decision (Article IV.79, § 1, 3° CEL). An exception is made for IPS decisions to use materials obtained during searches to support the objections in the statement of objections. These decisions can be appealed as of the moment of the communication of the statement of objections (Article 79, § 1, 2 *juncto* Article 41, § 3 CEL). They fall outside the scope of this research.

do not constitute an infringement of Article IV.1 and/or IV.2 CEL; (iii) c decisions of the College finding that the concerned practice falls within a Belgian or European block exemption or finding that the effect of a Belgian or European block exemption lapses in an individual case (Article IV.79, § 1, 1° CEL). No appeal is possible against any decisions by which the College declares commitments to be binding (Article IV.49 CEL). A decision by which the College does not impose a fine or reduce a fine because of a leniency statement (Article IV.46 CEL) cannot be appealed as such. However, it could be appealed as part of an appeal against a final College decision finding an infringement.

Settlement decisions, reached between an infringer and the IPS, cannot be appealed (Article IV.57 CEL). Decisions to reject complaints by the IPS can be appealed before the President of the BCA, but they are not subject to judicial review. By contrast, when the IPS submits a proposal for a decision to the College in a case started as a result of a complaint and the College subsequently finds that there are no reasons to intervene, this decision is subject to appeal before the Court of Appeal (Article IV.47 *juncto* Article IV 79, § 1 CEL).

2.1.3 Standing

In 1991, decisions of the Competition Council could be appealed by the undertakings subject to the investigation, the complainant, or third parties who had appeared before the Council. The Minister of Economic Affairs was not given a right of appeal against any decision of the authority. The latter was justified by the fact that the appeal was to be launched against the Belgian State, represented by the Minister of Economic Affairs,[25] and the Minister could hardly be expected to launch an appeal against himself.

As a result of the 1999 amendment of the Competition Act, the right to appeal was no longer dependent on effectively having been heard by the Council, it was sufficient to have an interest and to have requested to be heard by the Council. Furthermore, the Minister of Economic Affairs was given a right to appeal without having to prove an interest. Finally, the possibility of an incidental appeal was recognised, and the Court of Appeal was given the right to involve those persons who were parties before the Competition Council in the case at any time if the main appeal or the incidental appeal might affect their interests (Article 43*bis*, § 2).

This was confirmed by Article 76, § 2 of the 2006 Competition Act, where it was specified that the Minister did not need to have been represented in the procedure before the Competition Council to be entitled to launch an appeal.

Until 2013, the NCA was not a party to the proceedings before the Court of Appeal. The 2006 Competition Act even abolished the Council's right to submit comments before the Court of Appeal. The reason for this was that the legislator found that the Council had already had the opportunity to make its position clear in the

25. Raad voor de Mededinging, Eerste activiteitenverslag 1993-1994, https://www.bma-abc.be/sites/default/files/content/download/files/1993-1994_jaarverslag_raad.pdf, p. 21.

contested decision so that there was no reason to repeat it in the course of proceedings before the Court. Moreover, if, during appeal proceedings, the Competition Council were to adopt a different position from the one it adopted in its decision, it would violate the rights of the defence as well as the principle of legal certainty.[26] The IPS did not possess such a right either. Consequently, when a party who had been found guilty of an infringement appealed the Council's decision, there was no party present to defend the general interest and the contested decision.[27] In the course of an appeal procedure against a decision imposing a fine on a baker's association for price fixing, the Brussels Court of Appeal referred a preliminary question to the Court of Justice asking, in essence, whether:

> a situation in which neither a representative of a competition authority nor a person representing the general interest with regard to competition participates in proceedings brought before a court against the decision of the competition authority[28]

is compatible with Articles 2, 15(3) and 35(1) of Regulation 1/2003.

The Court of Justice responded that Article 35 of Regulation 1/2003 precludes:

> national rules which do not allow a national competition authority to participate, as a defendant or respondent, in judicial proceedings brought against a decision that the authority itself has taken. It is for the national competition authorities to gauge the extent to which their intervention is necessary and useful having regard to the effective application of European Union competition law. However, if the national competition authority consistently fails to enter an appearance in such judicial proceedings, the effectiveness of Articles 101 TFEU and 102 TFEU is jeopardised.[29]

The Court of Justice did not specify which body or bodies of the NCA may participate in appeal proceedings against a decision taken by that NCA. In the absence of EU rules and in accordance with the principle of procedural autonomy, this is left to the Member States, provided the fundamental rights are observed and that EU competition law is fully effective.[30]

When the Belgian competition rules were revised in 2013, the Belgian legislator appointed the College as the defendant in appeal procedures against its decisions (Article IV.79, § 4 CEL). For this purpose, the authority is, in theory, represented by its

26. Proposal for an act on the protection of economic competition, *Parl. Doc. Chamber* 2005-06, n° 51 2180/001, 69.
27. *See* Y. Van Gerven, 'De Belgische mededingingsautoriteit: een evenwichtsoefening tussen doeltreffendheid en eerlijke rechtsbedeling' in W. Devroe et al. (eds), *Mijlpalen uit het Belgisch mededingingsrecht geannoteerd. Liber amicorum Jules Stuyck*, Kluwer, Mechelen, 2013, 528.
28. Case C-439/08, *Vlaamse federatie van verenigingen van Brood- en Banketbakkers, Ijsbereiders en Chocoladebewerkers* (*Vebic*) VZW, EU:C:2010:739, ECR 2010 I-12471, para 51. *See* also Brussels 30 September 2008, *Vebic*, BE:CABRL:2008:ARR.20080930.1, https://juportal.be/content/ECLI:BE:CABRL:2008:ARR.20080930.1?HiLi=eNpLtDK2qs60MrAutjK3UkoqKi0uTs1Rss60MoSIOAWFBge7+oBEjKAiMDW1AB/5EgU=R.D.C.-T.B.H., 2009/5, 473.
29. Case C-439/08, *Vlaamse federatie van verenigingen van Brood- en Banketbakkers, Ijsbereiders en Chocoladebewerkers* (*Vebic*) VZW, EU:C:2010:739, ECR 2010 I-12471, operative part.
30. Case C-439/08, *Vlaamse federatie van verenigingen van Brood- en Banketbakkers, Ijsbereiders en Chocoladebewerkers* (*Vebic*) VZW, EU:C:2010:739, ECR 2010 I-12471.

president, who may, however, delegate this to an official. In practice, the designated official is the Director for legal studies (Article IV.20, § 1, 4° CEL).[31] As under the previous Competition Act, a final decision taken by the College in an infringement case can be appealed by the undertaking or undertakings having been found to have infringed the competition rules, by interested third persons who requested to be heard in the procedure before the College and by the Minister of Economic Affairs, even when he was not represented in the procedure before the College and without having to show any interest (Article 79, § 3 *juncto* Article IV.45, § 5 and 60, § 2 CEL). The rule that interested parties not only have a right to appeal but also to intervene in an appeal procedure was also maintained.

The essence of these rules remained unchanged after the 2019 revision of Book IV CEL and later minor amendments to this Book. However, the number of the article containing the rules on appeal has changed. It is now Article IV.90 CEL.

2.1.4 Scope and Intensity of the Review by the Court of Appeal

The Belgian Competition Act of 1991 did not explicitly mention whether the Court of Appeal had full jurisdiction. However, it follows from the preparatory documents of the Act that the legislator had the intention to confer on the Court of Appeal full jurisdiction when reviewing decisions of the Competition Council.[32] This was generally understood as meaning that the Court of Appeal could review both facts and law, modify or amend the decision by the Council or even deny all its effect.[33]

After the revision of 2006, Article 75 of the Coordinated Competition Act explicitly mentions that the Court of Appeal has full jurisdiction when deciding on an appeal against a decision taken by the Competition College. The bundle of powers awarded to the Court of Appeal by this revision truly deserved to be referred to as 'full jurisdiction'. The Court of Appeal may request the IPS to carry out additional investigations (Article 44, § 1, 5° LPCE); it may take into consideration developments that took place since the contested decision of the Competition Council, and it was also awarded the power to impose fines and periodic penalties. However, while the Court of Appeal was *entitled* to carry out a full review and exercise all these powers, it considered that this did not mean that it *had* to go so far. This was recognised by the Belgian Supreme Court in its 2011 *Honda* decision (cf. *infra*, Qualitative analysis).

31. Explanatory Memorandum, *Parl. Doc. Chambre* 2012-13, 53-2591/001-53-2592/001, 10; J. Ysewyn, M. Van Schoorisse and E. Mattioli, *De Belgische Mededingingswet 2013. Een praktische en kritische analyse*, Antwerpen, Intersentia, 2013, 54.
32. Explanatory Memorandum, *Parl. Doc. Chamber*, 1989-90, nr. 1282/1, 13; Raad voor de Mededinging, Eerste activiteitenverslag 1993-1994, https://www.bma-abc.be/sites/default/files/content/download/files/1993-1994_jaarverslag_raad.pdf.
33. Brussels 29 September 1999, *BOJ* 7 October 1999; Brussels 12 February 1998, *BOJ* 12 February 1998; Brussels 29 September 2004, referred to in J. Ysewyn, T. Franchoo and T. Snels, 'Overzicht van rechtspraak van de raad voor de mededinging in 2003-2004-2005 (deel 2)', *RCB* 2006/4, 202 and S. Boullart, 'De ene volle rechtsmacht is de andere niet: over volle en minder volle rechtsmacht', *CDPK* 2007, 266. For a strongly criticised exception in the field of mergers, *see* Brussels 15 September 2005, *RCB* 2006/2, note F. Louis and F. Dierckens.

The 2013 revision distinguished between merger cases and infringement cases. While in merger cases, the Court of Appeal's power was limited to annulment, in infringement cases, the Court of Appeal decides in principle 'with full jurisdiction including the power to substitute its own decision for the challenged decision' (Article IV.79, § 2, 2° paragraph CEL). The Court of Appeal rules 'in law and in fact on the case as submitted by the parties' (Article IV.79, § 2, 1° paragraph CEL). The Court no longer has the power to request the ISP to carry out additional investigations (cf. *supra*), and the rule that the court 'may take into consideration developments that have occurred since the challenged decision of [the Competition Authority]' has been deleted (former Article 75, 2° of the 2006 Competition Act).[34]

There are, however, a few important exceptions to the Court's full jurisdiction in infringement cases. If the Court – unlike the Competition College – concludes that there has been an infringement of Articles 101 and/or 102 TFEU, the Court can only annul the decision of the Competition College and refer the case back to the College in a different composition.[35] It may not *impose* a fine itself. It is uncertain whether the Court may *increase* the fine itself when it agrees with the conclusion of the College regarding the existence of an infringement but finds (e.g., at the request of a complainant or the Minister) that the sanction imposed by the Competition College is too light.[36] Furthermore, where the Competition College has imposed orders or prohibitions on undertakings, the Court of Appeal may only confirm or annul the decision but not replace it with its own.[37]

Furthermore, it remains the case that[38] even if the court is entitled to replace the decision of the Competition College with its own decision, it is not obliged to do this, and it may limit itself to annulling the decision. In most cases of the latter type, the Markets Court explicitly refers the case back to the Competition College in order to allow it to appoint a College with a different composition to take a new decision within the limits of the annulment decision. In one case, however, the Markets Court did not explicitly refer the case back to the Competition College, which nevertheless resumed proceedings.[39] This was justified by reference to established case law: in the case of annulment of an administrative decision, the procedure before the entity whose decision was annulled starts again at the stage it was in exactly before it adopted the annulled decision.[40]

34. J. Ysewyn, M. Van Schoorisse and E. Mattioli, *De Belgische Mededingingswet 2013. Een praktische en kritische analyse*, Antwerpen, Intersentia, 2013, 139.
35. Article IV. 79, §2, 3° CEL.
36. *Contra*: H. Gilliams, '"Volle rechtsmacht" en de rol van het hof van beroep in de toepassing van het mededingingsrecht', in X., *Mijlpalen uit het Belgisch mededingingsrecht geannoteerd. Liber amicorum Jules Stuyck*, Mechelen, Kluwer, 2013, 301. Comp. with some reserve P. Wytinck, 'Boetes en sancties in perspectief' in H. Gilliams, '"Volle rechtsmacht" en de rol van het hof van beroep in de toepassing van het mededingingsrecht', in X., *Mijlpalen uit het Belgisch mededingingsrecht geannoteerd. Liber amicorum Jules Stuyck*, Mechelen, Kluwer, 2013, 472.
37. Article IV. 79, §2, 3° CEL.
38. In any case, that is how the Court of Appeal interpreted the CEL.
39. Brussels 27 June 2018, 2018/MR/1, *Global/ABC*, https://www.abc-bma.be/sites/default/files/content/download/files/20180627_cab_2018mr1_global_champions_league.pdf.
40. Competition College, Decision ABC-2018-V/M-33, 28 September 2018, Nooren, https://www.bma-abc.be/nl/beslissingen/18-vm-33-lisa-nooren-et-henk-nooren-handelsstal-sprl-fei-gcl-ttb.

The 2013 CEL contained a gap: it did not explicitly mention the consequence of the annulment of a decision of the Competition College in cases where the Court of Appeal only had the power to annul the NCA's decision. The 2019 revision intended to fill this gap. It was added in Article IV.90, §2 (5) CEL that if the Markets Court annuls such a decision, the case is referred back to the Competition College within the limits of the annulment. Yet, by limiting this provision to cases where the Markets Court only had the power of annulment, the legislator created room for discussion on the consequences of cases where the Markets Court voluntarily limited its review to the annulment of the Competition College's decision.[41]

2.1.5 Other

The 2013 revision of the competition rules introduced the rule that the Court of Appeal decides according to the procedural rules applicable 'as in summary proceedings' (Article 79, §2 (1) CEL). This implies that the parties may request their case to be decided within a short period. It does not affect the scope or the standard (intensity) of the review.

2.2 Second-Instance Appeal

During the entire period covered by the research, decisions taken by the Court of Appeal are subject to review by the Supreme Court.[42] The request for review is to be submitted within a period of three months as of the date the Court of Appeal's decision has been served (Article 1073 (1) Code of Civil Procedure). The review request has no suspensory character. The Supreme Court does not review the Court of Appeal's decision on the facts of the case (Article 147 Constitution). It only carries out a review of the legality of the decision. Moreover, it only decides on the objections put forward against the decision of the Court of Appeal by the party who launched the second (and last) instance appeal. Only objections relating to the fact that the Court of Appeal misapplied the law or disrespected any formal rules sanctioned with nullity may lead the Supreme Court to annul the Court of Appeal's decision (Article 608 Code of Civil Procedure) and to refer it back to the Court of Appeal, in a different composition, which then has to decide in line with the Supreme Court's decision. Unless the Court of Appeal does not comply with the Supreme Court's decision, its decision is final and cannot be contested before the Supreme Court again (Article 1110(4) Code of Civil Procedure).

---

41. For an NCA decision dealing with this issue outside the scope of this study, *see* Competition College, Decision ABC-2023-P/K-01, 18 January 2023 (*Caudalie*). https://www.belgiancompetition.be/en/decisions?combine=&field_decision_case_type_target_id%5B0%5D=21&field_decision_advices_target_id%5B0%5D=35&field_decision_nature_target_id=All&field_decision_pubdate_value%5Bmin%5D=&field_decision_pubdate_value%5Bmax%5D=&field_decision_infraction_target_id=All&field_decision_fine_target_id=All&field_decision_penalty_target_id=All&field_decision_commitments_target_id=All.
42. H. Swennen, 'De wijziging van de Wet tot bescherming van de economische mededinging', *RDC* 1999, 372-379.

3 PRIOR RESEARCH

There are very few publications focused on judicial review in Belgium of decisions in cases relating to Articles 101 and 102 TFEU and their national equivalents. Some research has studied judicial control of decisions by regulatory authorities, including, but not limited to, the BCA.[43] Others examined the Court that is responsible for appeals by the BCA.[44] In addition, certain judgments inspired legal scholars to discuss specific aspects of the appeal procedure, such as appeals against actions taken during the investigation phase,[45] access to file in cases before the Competition Council and the Court of Appeal,[46] the voluntary intervention of the competition authority in the appellate case,[47] and the scope of the Court of Appeal's competences.[48] Furthermore, the appellate cases are briefly reviewed in the annual reports of the competition authority and an annual scholarly overview of decisions by the competition authority and the Court of Appeal.[49] The procedure for appeal has also been discussed in various publications following the adoption of a new version of the Belgian national

43. P. Boucquey and P. De Broux, 'Les recours juridictionnels contre les décisions des autorités de regulation' in H. Dumont, P. Jadoul and S. van Drooghenbroeck (eds), *La protection juridictionnelle du citoyen face à l'administration*, Bruxelles, la Charte, 2007, pp. 209-313; D. Van Liedekerke and A. Laes, 'Les recours contre les décisions des autorités de régulation économique devant la Cour des marchés: état des lieux à la suite de l'adoption de la loi du 20 février 2017', *TRNI* 2017/2-3, 205-211.
44. P. Bondeel, 'Over twee decennia groei en ontstane bloei: bijzondere bevoegdheden in het hof van beroep te Brussel', *RDC* 2016/8, 727; M. Bosmans, 'Het Marktenhof blies zijn eerste verjaardagskaarsje uit ...', *Competitio* 2018/1, 66-79; A. Witters, 'Het vijfjarig jubileum en de werking van het Marktenhof', *RW* 2021-22/36, 1410.
45. V. Wellens and C. Schellekens, 'Bewijs verkregen tijdens huiszoekingen in Belgische mededingingszaken: leidt de voorziene beroepsprocedure tot een quasi-automatische wering van dergelijk bewijs?', *Jaarboek Marktpraktijken* 2015, 855-861; S. Raes, 'Rechtsbescherming – Beroep tegen handelingen tijdens het onderzoek' in X., *Mijlpalen uit het Belgisch mededingingsrecht geannoteerd. Liber amicorum Jules Stuyck*, Mechelen, Kluwer, 2013, 383-418. *See also*: H. Delescaille, [Les faiblesses de l'art. IV.79, § 1 CDE en matière de contrôle des perquisitions], *RCB* 2015/4, 279-280.
46. D. Vandermeersch and A. Cloots, 'De toegang tot het dossier in zaken van restrictieve mededingingspraktijken voor de Raad voor de Mededinging en het Hof van Beroep', *RCB* 2010/4, 46-60.
47. X., [La recevabilité de l'intervention volontaire de l'Autorité belge de la concurrence], *RCB* 2014/2, 136-137.
48. H. Gilliams, '"Volle rechtsmacht" en de rol van het hof van beroep in de toepassing van het mededingingsrecht', in X., *Mijlpalen uit het Belgisch mededingingsrecht geannoteerd. Liber amicorum Jules Stuyck*, Mechelen, Kluwer, 2013, 265-331; B. Gielen, 'Het Belgacom-arrest van het Hof van Cassatie. Een brug tussen de oude en de nieuwe Belgische mededingingswetgeving op het vlak van volle rechtsmacht', *RCB* 2014/3, 241-251; H. Gilliams, 'Vervolging van grensoverschrijdende kartels: bewijslast, "ne bis in idem" en rechtsmacht van het hof van beroep te Brussel', *Jaarboek Marktpraktijken* 2014, 1170-1178; S. Boullart, 'De ene volle rechtsmacht is de andere niet: over volle en minder volle rechtsmacht', *CDPK* 2007, 266.
49. The annual reports are available on https://www.bma-abc.be/nl/over-ons/publicaties. The annual doctrinal overviews, written by J. Ysewyn et al. are published in *RDC* between 1995 and 2004, in *RCB* between 2006 and 2017 and in *Competitio* as of 2018.

competition rules.[50] There has been no comprehensive study of appeals in competition law cases in Belgium to date.

4 QUANTITATIVE ANALYSIS

4.1 Source of Information

Most of the judgments of the Court of Appeal/Markets Court (first-instance appeals) are published. Exceptionally, a decision establishing the withdrawal of an appeal by some of the parties involved in a case which subsequently proceeds with the remaining parties is not published. The database was comprised based on the judgments published on the website of the Belgian NCA.[51] In addition, the legal databases *Jura* and *Strada Lex* were checked, as well as the annual reports of the competition authority and the annual doctrinal overviews of the decision-making in competition cases. All second-instance appeals have been published on the website of the NCA and on the governmental website publishing case law.[52]

4.2 Total Number of Judgments and Ratio of Appeals

The database includes thirteen judgments that were rendered and published between 1 May 2004 to 30 April 2021, from which eleven are first-instance appeals and two second-instance appeals. Those judgments pertain to ten NCA decisions.[53] When compared to the total number of NCA's decisions that are potentially subject to review, this entails that 26% of all NCA decisions were reviewed, and 5% of first-instance

50. For example, J. Stuyck, W. Devroe and P. Wytinck, *De nieuwe Belgische mededingingswet 2006*, Mechelen, Kluwer; J. Ysewyn, M. Van Schoorisse and E. Mattioli, *De Belgische Mededingingswet 2013. Een praktische en kritische analyse*, Antwerpen, Intersentia, 2013, 280 p.
51. https://www.bma-abc.be/.
52. https://juportal.be/home/welkom.
53. Competition Council, Decision 2005-I/O-40, *Professional soccer*, 29 July 2005, https://www.bma-abc.be/sites/default/files/content/download/files/2005IO40%20Liga%20Beroepsvoetbal.pdf; Competition Council, Decision 2007-I/O-27, *Ordre des Pharmaciens I*, 26 Octobre 2007, https://www.bma-abc.be/sites/default/files/content/download/files/2007IO27_Ordre_%20des_%20pharmaciens.pdf; Competition Council, Decision 2008-I/O-04, *Vebic*, 25 January 2008, https://www.bma-abc.be/sites/default/files/content/download/files/2008IO04.pdf; Competition Council, Decision 2012-P/K-20, *Presstalis*, 30 July 2012, https://www.bma-abc.be/sites/default/files/content/download/files/2012PK20_Pub.pdf; Competition Council, Decision 2013-I/O-06, *Brabomills*, 28 February 2013, https://www.bma-abc.be/sites/default/files/content/download/files/2013IO06_pub.pdf; Competition Council, Decision 2012-P/K-29, *Belgacom*, 29 November 2012, https://www.abc-bma.be/sites/default/files/content/download/files/2012PK29_Pub.pdf; Competition Council, Decision 2013-I/O-34, *Holcim*, 30 August 2013, https://www.belgiancompetition.be/sites/default/files/content/download/files/2013IO34_Pub.pdf; Competition Council, Decision 2012-P/K-32, *Bpost*, 10 December 2012, https://www.belgiancompetition.be/en/decisions/12-pk-32-bpost; Competition Council, Decision 2009-P/K-10, *Proximus*, 26 May 2009, https://www.bma-abc.be/sites/default/files/content/download/files/2009PK10.pdf; Competition college, Decision ABC-2019-I/O-14, *Ordre des Pharmaciens II*, 28 May 2019, https://www.bma-abc.be/sites/default/files/content/download/files/abc-2019-io-14_pub_0.pdf.

reviews were subject to further review. A third-instance review does not exist under Belgian law.

4.3 Judgments per Year

Figure 4.1 Number of Judgments According to Instances

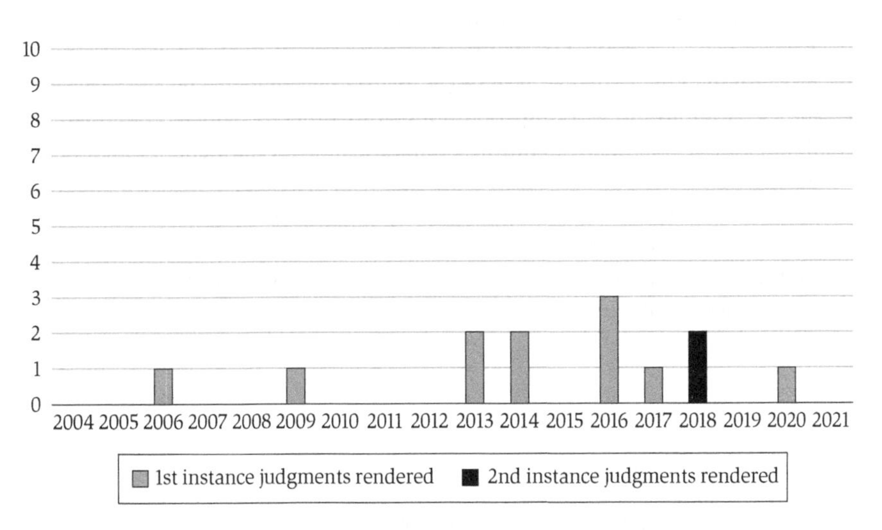

Figure 4.1 shows that the number of appeals seemed to increase until 2016 and afterwards seemed to decrease again. In 2006, 2009, 2017, and 2020, one first-instance judgment was rendered.[54] In 2013[55] and 2014,[56] two first-instance decisions were given, and in 2016, there were three first-instance decisions.[57]

54. Brussels 28 June 2006, 2005/MR/2, 2005/MR/5, *Professional soccer*, *AM* 2007/1-2, 167, note P. Valcke, *Jaarboek Handelspraktijken & Mededinging* 2006, 805, note C. Verdonck and L. Depuydt, *RCB* 2007/1, 63; Brussels 7 April 2009, 2007/MR/5, *Ordre des Pharmaciens I*, https://www.bma-abc.be/sites/default/files/content/download/files/20090407_cab_2007mr5_ordre_des_pharmaciens_ad.pdf; Brussels 8 January 2020, 2019/MR/3, *Ordre des Pharmaciens II*, https://www.abc-bma.be/sites/default/files/content/download/files/20200108_2019mr_3_op_arret_vpub.pdf, *Competitio* 2020/2, 138, *Jaarboek Marktpraktijken* 2020/1, 1382.
55. Brussels 13 February 2013, *Vebic*, 2013/MR/3, https://www.bma-abc.be/sites/default/files/content/download/files/20130213_hvbb_vebic_ea.pdf; Brussels 27 September 2013, 2012/MR/5, *Presstalis*, https://www.bma-abc.be/sites/default/files/content/download/files/20130927_cdc_2012mr5_presstalis.pdf.
56. Brussels 12 March 2014, 2013/MR/6, *Brabomills*, https://www.bma-abc.be/sites/default/files/content/download/files/20140312_cab_hvbb_brabomills_eindarrest.pdf, *Jaarboek Marktpraktijken* 2014, 1139, note H. Gilliams, *RCB* 2014/2, 108; Brussels 27 May 2014, 2013/MR/1 and 2013/MR/4, *Belgacom*, https://www.bma-abc.be/sites/default/files/content/download/files/20140527_hvbb_kpn_belgacom_eindarrest.pdf.
57. Brussels 30 June 2016, 2013/MR/11-15, *Holcim*, https://www.bma-abc.be/nl/beslissingen/2013mr11-12-13-14-et-15-cimenteries-ad, *RDC* 2017/8, 865, note J. Dewispelaere, *RCB* 2017/1, 4; Brussels 10 November 2016, 2009/MR/4-6 & 8, *Proximus*, not published, mentioned in Brussel

Two second-instance decisions were given in 2018.[58]

The increase in appeals towards 2016 might be due to the fact that since 2006, the Competition Council directed more resources to infringement cases (previously, it dealt mainly with merger cases),[59] and there was a structural revision of the national competition authority in 2013 (cf. *supra*, section 1.2). The impact on appeal cases understandably follows a few years after a change is made at the level of the competition authority since it takes some time before appellate proceedings reach the stage of a judgment. Moreover, while the 2013 restructuring aimed to increase the number of infringement decisions,[60] that number did not increase substantially. This is, to a large extent, due to the fact that the new authority struggled with a shortage of staff. The revision of the structure of the NCA in 2013 was followed by a long period of uncertainty relating to the working conditions of its officials, which, combined with other administrative and financial hurdles, hampered the recruitment of much-needed new officials.[61] The new NCA was also burdened with appeal procedures dealing with procedural issues at the investigation stage, in particular relating to searches carried out under the application of the 1999 and 2006 Competition Acts[62].

Moreover, the 2013 revision introduced a settlement procedure that was successful.[63] As mentioned above (section 2.1.2), settlement decisions are not subject

9 October 2019, 2009/MR/3, https://www.bma-abc.be/sites/default/files/content/download/files/20191009_2009mr3_proximus_arret_v_pub.pdf.

58. Cass. 22 June 2018, AR C.16.0462.F, *Holcim*, https://www.bma-abc.be/sites/default/files/content/download/files/20180622_cdc_c160462f_c160476f_cimenteries.pdf, *Competitio* 2018/3, 267, note; Cass. 22 November 2018, AR C.17.0126.F, *Bpost*, https://www.bma-abc.be/sites/default/files/content/download/files/20181122_cdc_c170126f_bpost.pdf, *Competitio* 2019/1, 21, note, *JT* 2020/6815, 401, note P. Lagasse, *JLMB* 2019/31, 1448, *RCJB* 2022/1, 37, note F. Mourlon Beernaert and B. Maes, *Rev.dr.pén.* 2019/2, 158, note F. Lugentz.
59. Conseil de la concurrence, Rapport Annuel 2007, https://www.abc-bma.be/sites/default/files/content/download/files/2007_rapport-annuel_conseil.pdf, p. 7.
60. K. Marchand et al., 'De ambitie is: beslissingen, beslissingen, beslissingen de ambitie is: beslissingen, beslissingen, beslissingen – Interview met Jacques Steenbergen – Voorzitter Belgische Mededingingsautoriteit', *Competitio* 2014/1, 4.
61. *Ibid.*
62. On these cases, *see e.g.*, J. Ysewyn and M. Van Schoorisse, 'Overzicht van de beslissingspraktijk van de Belgische Mededingingsautoriteit in 2014', *RCB* 2015/3, 165-169; J. Ysewyn and M. Van Schoorisse, 'Overzicht van de beslissingspraktijk van de Belgische Mededingingsautoriteit in 2017', *Competitio* 2018/2, 158-159; J. Ysewyn and M. Van Schoorisse, 'Overzicht van de beslissingspraktijk van de Belgische Mededingingsautoriteit in 2019', *Competitio* 2020/1, 26-27.
63. Before the 2013 revision, 'informal settlements' could be reached in the sense that the IPS could decide to terminate an investigation upon the termination of the conduct that had triggered the investigation. Such a decision could not include the imposition of penalties on the undertaking that was the subject of the investigation and any promises made by that undertaking were not binding. However, in case of non-compliance, a new investigation could be started at any moment. Furthermore, when the case was submitted to the Competition Council, the latter could use its power to accept commitments and make them binding, if desired in combination with a fine to reach some kind of 'settlement'. *See* J. Steenbergen, 'Schikkingen en de Belgische mededingingsautoriteit', *RDC* 2008/4, 16-18.

to appeal. As a result, no infringement decisions (other than settlements) were taken during the period 2015-2018 and only one per year in 2019-2020 as well as one in the first months of 2021 that are part of this research. This explains the decrease in appellate decisions after 2016.

4.4 Success Rates and Outcomes

Figure 4.2 summarises the success of appeals launched against either NCA's decisions or a prior review court instance's judgment.

Figure 4.2 Success of Appeals (Each NCA's Decision or Previous Instance Judgment Counts as One)

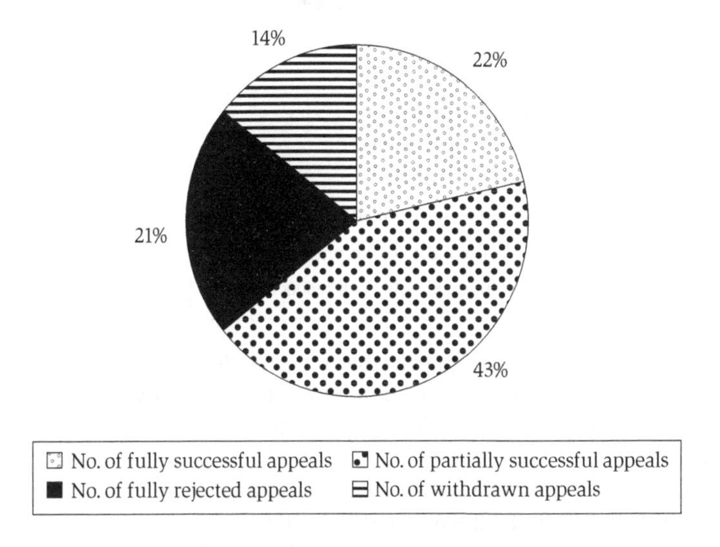

Approximately 22% of appeals were fully successful, 43% were partially successful, 21% were fully rejected and 14% were withdrawn.

Figure 4.3 indicates the ratio of possible outcomes according to each instance of appeal. In contrast with Figure 4.2, the data is presented from the perspective of each separate judgment.

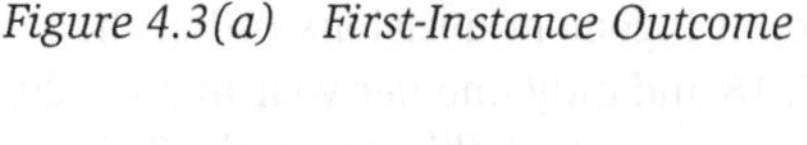
Figure 4.3(a) First-Instance Outcome

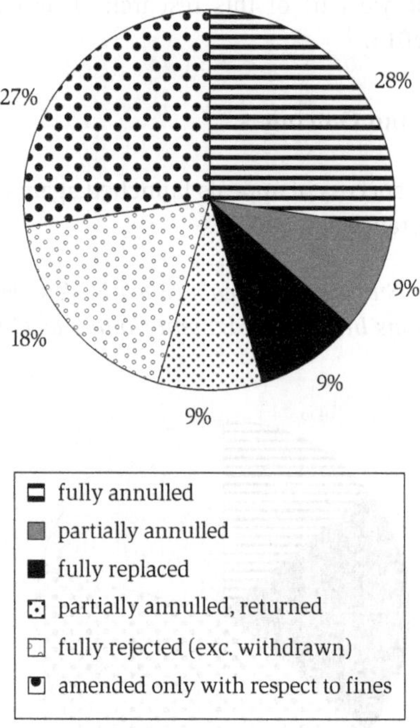

In 28 % of the first-instance appeals, the contested decision was fully annulled; in 9 % of the cases, it was partially annulled; in 9 % of the cases, it was fully replaced; in 9 % of the cases, it was partially annulled and returned. In 18 % of the cases, the appeal was fully rejected.

In 27 % of the cases, the appeal was withdrawn. The cases concerned are *Belgcacom* (2014),[64] *Proximus* (2016)[65] and *Vebic* (2017).[66]

On 1 June 2005, Belgacom introduced the Happy Time rate for callers from a fixed-line phone to another fixed-line telephone on Belgian territory for an amount of EUR 0.3 (including VAT) per call from 8 a.m. to 5 p.m., Monday to Friday. Calls outside these hours, and on Saturdays and Sundays, were free of charge. A competitor complained that with the launch of the Happy Time offer, Belgacom abused its dominant position in the retail markets for network access and fixed national telephony

64. Brussels 27 May 2014, 2013/MR/1 and 2013/MR/4, https://www.bma-abc.be/sites/default/files/content/download/files/20140527_hvbb_kpn_belgacom_eindarrest.pdf.
65. Brussels 10 November 2016, 2009/MR/4-6 & 8, *Proximus*, not published, mentioned in Brussels 9 October 2009, 2009/MR/3, belgiancompetition.be/en/decisions; Brussels 10 November 2016, 2009/MR/4-6 & 8, *Proximus*, not published, mentioned in Brussel 9 October 2019, 2009/MR/3, https://www.bma-abc.be/sites/default/files/content/download/files/20191009_2009mr3_proximus_arret_v_pub.pdf.
66. Brussels 4 October 2017, 2013/MR/7, *Vebic*, https://www.abc-bma.be/sites/default/files/content/download/files/20171004_hvbb_bma_bakkers_vlaanderen.pdf.

for residential users, as well as in the wholesale markets for call origination and for call termination, including through margin squeezing, predatory pricing and cross-subsidisation.

In 2008, the complainant submitted a letter to the NCA in which it only mentioned the problem of margin squeezing. Although this did not restrict the IPS from investigating the other alleged infringements, the IPS decided to use its discretion to focus on the alleged margin squeezing, indicating that this did not mean that no predatory pricing and/or cross-subsidisation was committed.

Belgacom was the historic telephone operator that enjoyed a legal monopoly until the liberalisation of the Belgian market in 1998. Within the framework of the liberalisation of the telecommunications market, it was possible for new entrants to offer only transportation of spoken communication while using against payment the connection services of the historic monopolist. The complainant made use of this option in its capacity as a wholesaler and bought interconnection services from Belgacom while competing with the latter on the retail market offering voice communication services from fixed phone numbers to fixed phone numbers.

The complainant argued that the difference between the Belgacom rates for the wholesale interconnection services and its rates for retail voice communication services between fixed phone numbers under the Happy Time system was too small to allow a reasonable competitor on the retail market to make profits.

The Competition Council considered that while an abuse of dominance can rarely be demonstrated merely by the mechanical application of quantitative tests, it is difficult to prove the existence of an abuse of dominance if no test leads to a negative margin.

Since neither an 'equally efficient operator' test (EEO) nor a 'reasonably efficient operator' test (REO) at the level of the Happy time tariff plan or the level of the entire retail offer of fixed voice telecommunication services led to a negative margin, the Competition Council found that there was no ground for action.[67] Both parties appealed, and about one and a half years later, they agreed to withdraw the appeals.[68]

The *Proximus* case had started as the result of a complaint by one of Proximus' competitors. Another competitor had requested to be heard by the NCA and had in fact been heard as an interested third party. The NCA imposed a massive fine on Proximus (EUR 66,300,000). After Proximus appealed, the complainant and the interested third party also appealed. The appeal was launched in 2009 and took a long time. In 2016, the complainant and the interested third party withdrew their appeal, probably because they no longer wanted to invest in the appeal proceedings.

Vebic appealed against a decision of the Competition Council in which it was fined. As mentioned above, the Court of Appeal then made a preliminary reference to the CJEU in order to find out if a national law prohibiting the NCA from participating in the appeal proceedings was compatible with EU law. After receiving a negative

67. Competition Council 29 November 2012, 2012-P/K-29, https://www.bma-abc.be/sites/default/files/content/download/files/2012PK29_Pub.pdf.
68. Brussels 27 May 2014, 2013/MR/1 and 2013/MR/4, https://www.bma-abc.be/sites/default/files/content/download/files/20140527_hvbb_kpn_belgacom_eindarrest.pdf.

answer from the CJEU, the NCA was invited to participate in the proceedings. The NCA refrained from doing so because the national law did not provide who was entitled to represent the NCA in such proceedings. The Court of Appeal annulled the contested decision. Afterwards, when the law had been amended to allow the NCA to participate in appeals against its decisions and to determine who could represent it, the NCA brought an 'objection' procedure before the Court of Appeal. This is a procedure to have a judgment by default set aside. The NCA later withdrew from the proceedings, probably because it considered that its scarce resources could be put to better use.

Figure 4.3(b) Second-Instance Outcome

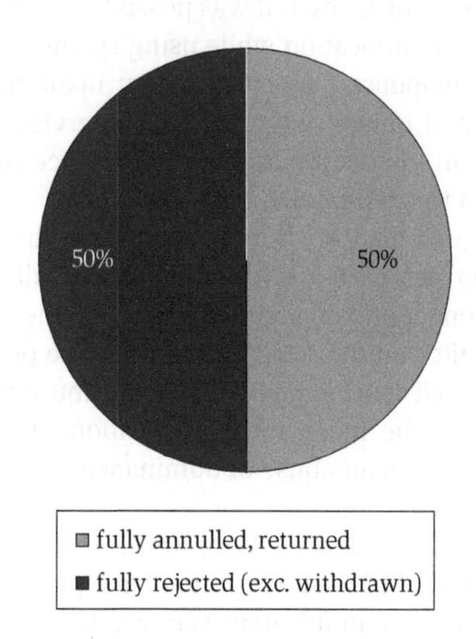

As mentioned, only two cases were examined at second instance (*Holcim* and *Bpost*).

In *Holcim*, the second-instance appeal was rejected. The Supreme Court found that the grounds put forward against the decision of the Court of Appeal were based on an incorrect reading of the decision.[69]

In *Bpost*, the second-instance appeal was successful and the case was fully annulled and returned to the Brussels Court of Appeal in a different composition. The case concerned the interpretation of the *non bis in idem* principle. Bpost had introduced a tariff system whereby the quantity discounts were calculated solely on the basis of each sender's volume of mail, with the result that intermediaries could no longer add up the volumes of their customers to obtain larger quantity discounts. By a

69. Cass. 22 June 2018, C.16.0462, *Holcim*, https://www.bma-abc.be/sites/default/files/content/download/files/20180622_cdc_c160462f_c160476f_cimenteries.pdf, *Competitio* 2018/3, 267, note.

decision of 20 July 2011, the Belgian Regulator for Postal Services and Telecommunications[70] sanctioned this system with a fine of EUR 2.3 million, mainly for breach of the principles of transparency and non-discrimination guaranteed by the Belgian transposition of Article 12, fifth indent of Directive 97/67/EC.[71] More than a year later, on 10 December 2012, the Competition Council imposed a fine of almost EUR 37.4 million for the use of the same system, which it considered to be incompatible with Article 102 TFEU and its national equivalent. The Competition Council considered the *non bis in idem* principle inapplicable because it did not sanction the same infringement as the Regulator. However, while stating that no legal rule required it to do so, it took the fine imposed by the Regulator into account when determining the amount of the fine for the infringement of the competition rules.[72] Bpost appealed and invoked the *non bis in idem* principle. By the time the Court of Appeal had to decide on the appeal, the decision of the Regulator had been annulled. Nevertheless, the Court of Appeal applied the principle *non bis in idem* and annulled the decision of the Competition Council.[73] The Competition Council lodged an appeal with the Supreme Court complaining about an erroneous application of the *non bis in idem* principle and defective reasoning. The Supreme Court annulled the decision of the Court of Appeal, referring, *inter alia*, to *Menci* and *Garlsson*,[74] the Supreme Court held that the Court of Appeal could not legally decide to apply the *non bis in idem* principle based on the mere identity of facts without examining if the two proceedings pursued complementary aims having as their object different aspects of the same infringement.[75]

4.5 Type of NCA's Decisions Subject to Appeal

Figure 4.4 indicates the ratio of the different competition law prohibitions subject to the courts' review across all instances of appeal. It differentiates between the prohibition on anticompetitive agreements and abuse of dominance and between cases in which both the EU and the national equivalent prohibitions have been applied and purely national cases in which only the national equivalent prohibitions have been applied

70. The official name is BIPT: Belgian Institute for Postal Services and Telecommunications.
71. Directive 97/67/EC of the European Parliament and of the Council of 15 December 1997 on common rules for the development of the internal market of Community postal services and the improvement of quality of service, *OJ* L 15, 21 January 1998, 14. Article 13, fifth indent of this Directive is transposed in Article 144(1)(4) and (5) of the Act of 21 March 1991 on the reform of certain public economic undertakings, *OJ* 27 March 1991, 6155, as modified by the Act of 13 December 2010, *OJ* 31 December 2010, 83267.
72. Competition Council, Decision 2012-P/K-32, 10 December 2012, https://www.belgian-competition.be/en/decisions/12-pk-32-bpost, *OJ* 22 February 2013 (fourth edition), 11727, *Jaarboek Marktpraktijken* 2012, 1181, note C. Lousberg, *RCB* 2013/2, 206.
73. Brussels 10 November 2016, 2013/MR/2, *Bpost*, https://www.bma-abc.be/sites/default/files/content/download/files/20161110_cab_2013mr2_bpost.pdf, *RDC* 2017/8, 865, note J. Dewispelaere, *RCB* 2017/ 1, 42.
74. Case C-524/15, *Menci*, EU:C:2018:197; Case C-537/16, *Garlsson Real Estate s.a.*, EU:C:2018:193.
75. Cass. 22 November 2018, AR C.17.0126.F, *Bpost*, https://www.bma-abc.be/sites/default/files /content/download/files/20181122_cdc_c170126f_bpost.pdf, *Competitio* 2019/1, 21, note, *JT* 2020/6815, 401, note P. Lagasse, *JLMB* 2019/31, 1448, *RCJB* 2022/1, 37, note F. Mourlon Beernaert and B. Maes, *Rev.dr.pén.* 2019/2, 158, note F. Lugentz.

due to the absence of an effect on trade between Member States. As the figure demonstrates, most of the appeals have examined the infringement of both EU and national prohibitions. Thirty-nine per cent of all judgments in the database concerned Article 101 TFEU and its national equivalent, 38% concerned Article 102 and its national equivalent, and only 23% the national equivalent of Article 101 TFEU alone. The reason for this might be that the competition authority focuses on the most serious cases and that in serious cases of collusion, trade between the Member States is often affected so that Article 101 TFEU is to be applied, while cases of abuse are more likely to be considered serious in purely national cases.

Figure 4.4 Rules Being Appealed

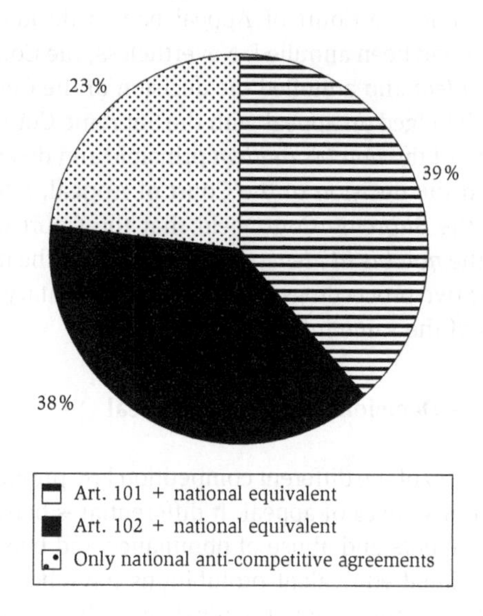

Figure 4.5 presents similar data as Figure 4.4. However, it pertains to the number of judgments involving particular rules being appealed (rather than a percentage) and displays the data according to years. The figure demonstrates that in both 2006 and 2009, one appellate decision was given. The 2006 decision concerned an alleged infringement of Article 101 TFEU and its national equivalent by the association of Belgian premier league soccer clubs, which had awarded the broadcasting rights for

premier league games to a single company (*Professional soccer*).[76] The decision taken in 2009 concerned the national equivalent of Article 101 TFEU (*Ordre des Pharmaciens I*, anticompetitive decisions by professional associations of pharmacists regarding opening and closing times as well as advertising and rebates).[77]

In 2013 and 2014, two decisions each were handed down. One of the 2013 decisions concerned the national prohibition of anticompetitive agreements (*Vebic*: an allegedly anticompetitive decision on bread prices by a professional association of bakers);[78] the other one related to Article 102 and its national equivalent (*Presstalis*: a loyalty rebate system used by a press distributor).[79]

In 2014, one decision concerned Article 101 TFEU and its national equivalent (*Brabomills*: a cartel in the flour market)[80] and another one concerned Article 102 TFEU and its national equivalent (*Belgacom*: an alleged price squeeze by a telecom operator).[81]

In 2016, three decisions were given. One decision concerned Article 101 TFEU and its national equivalent (*Holcim*: lobbying activities during a standard setting process),[82] and two decisions concerned Article 102 TFEU and its national equivalent (*Bpost*: an allegedly abusive loyalty rebate system[83] and *Proximus*: an alleged price squeeze by a mobile telecom operator[84]).

76. Brussels 28 June 2006, 2005/MR/2, 2005/MR/5, *Professional soccer, AM* 2007/1-2,167, note P. Valcke, *Jaarboek Handelspraktijken & Mededinging* 2006, 805, note C. Verdonck and L. Depuydt, *RCB* 2007/1, 63.
77. Brussels 7 April 2009, 2007/MR/5, *Ordre des Pharmaciens I*, https://www.bma-abc.be/sites/default/files/content/download/files/20090407_cab_2007mr5_ordre_des_pharmaciens_ad.pdf.
78. Brussels 13 February 2013, 2008/MR/3, *Vebic*, https://www.bma-abc.be/sites/default/files/content/download/files/20130213_hvbb_vebic_ea.pdf.
79. Brussels 27 September 2013, 2012/MR/5, *Presstalis*, https://www.bma-abc.be/sites/default/files/content/download/files/20130927_cdc_2012mr5_presstalis.pdf.
80. Brussels 12 March 2014, 2013/MR/6, *Brabomills*, https://www.bma-abc.be/sites/default/files/content/download/files/20140312_cab_hvbb_brabomills_eindarrest.pdf, *Jaarboek Marktpraktijken* 2014, 1139, note H. Gilliams, *RCB* 2014/2, 108.
81. Brussels 27 May 2014, 2013/MR/1 and 2013/MR/4, *Belgacom*, https://www.bma-abc.be/sites/default/files/content/download/files/20140527_hvbb_kpn_belgacom_eindarrest.pdf.
82. Brussels 30 June 2016, 2013/MR/11-15, *Holcim*, https://www.bma-abc.be/nl/beslissingen/2013mr11-12-13-14-et-15-cimenteries-ad, *RDC* 2017/8, 865, note J. Dewispelaere, *RCB* 2017/1, 4.
83. Brussels 10 November 2016, 2013/MR/2, *Bpost*, https://www.bma-abc.be/sites/default/files/content/download/files/20161110_cab_2013mr2_bpost.pdf, *RDC* 2017/8, 865, note J. Dewispelaere, *RCB* 2017/1, 4.
84. Brussels 10 November 2016, 2009/MR/4-6 & 8, *Proximus*, not published, mentioned in Brussel 9 October 2019, 2009/MR/3, https://www.bma-abc.be/sites/default/files/content/download/files/20191009_2009mr3_proximus_arret_v_pub.pdf.

In 2017, there was only one decision concerning the national equivalent of Article 101 TFEU, the withdrawal from the opposition by the BCA against the default judgment in *Vebic*.[85]

Two decisions given in 2018 (*Holcim*,[86] resp. *Bpost*)[87] concerned an infringement of Article 102 TFEU and its national equivalent.

In 2020, there was one case concerning Article 101 TFEU and its national equivalent (*Ordre des Pharmaciens II*: strategy of an association of pharmacists aiming at excluding pharmacists using a certain business model and/or preventing the development of that business model).[88]

Figure 4.5 Rules Being Appealed According to Years (Each Judgment Counts as One)

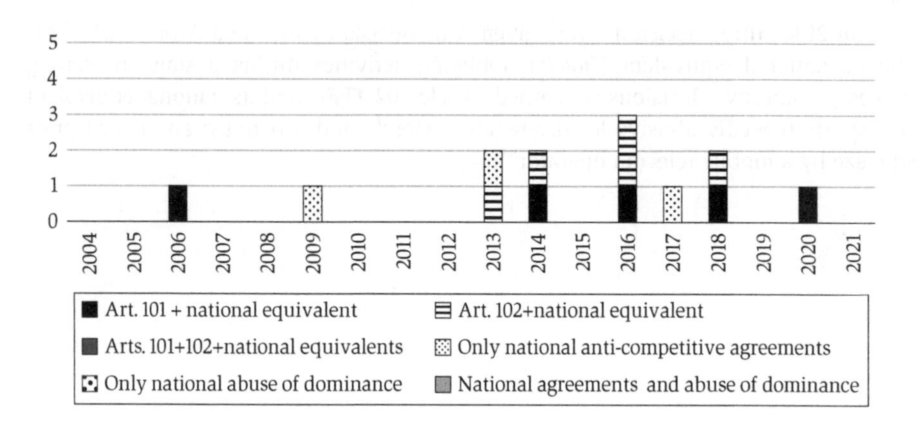

4.6. Type of Restrictions

Figure 4.6 summarises the type of restrictions of competition that were examined in the NCA's decisions subject to appeal across all instances of appeal.

85. Brussels 4 October 2017, 2013/MR/7, *Vebic*, https://www.abc-bma.be/sites/default/files/content/download/files/20171004_hvbb_bma_bakkers_vlaanderen.pdf.
86. Cass. 22 June 2018, C.16.0476.F, *Holcim*, https://www.bma-abc.be/sites/default/files/content/download/files/20180622_cdc_c160462f_c160476f_cimenteries.pdf, *Competitio* 2018/3, 267, note.
87. Cass. 22 November 2018, AR C.17.0126.F, *Bpost*, https://www.bma-abc.be/sites/default/files/content/download/files/20181122_cdc_c170126f_bpost.pdf, *Competitio* 2019/1, 21, note, *JT* 2020/6815, 401, note P. Lagasse, *JLMB* 2019/31, 1448, *RCJB* 2022/1, 37, note F. Mourlon Beernaert and B. Maes, *Rev.dr.pén.* 2019/2, 158, note F. Lugentz.
88. Brussels 8 January 2020, 2019/MR/3, *Ordre des Pharmaciens II*, https://www.abc-bma.be/sites/default/files/content/download/files/20200108_2019mr_3_op_arret_vpub.pdf, *Competitio* 2020/2, 138, *Jaarboek Marktpraktijken* 2020/1, 1382.

Figure 4.6 Types of Restrictions

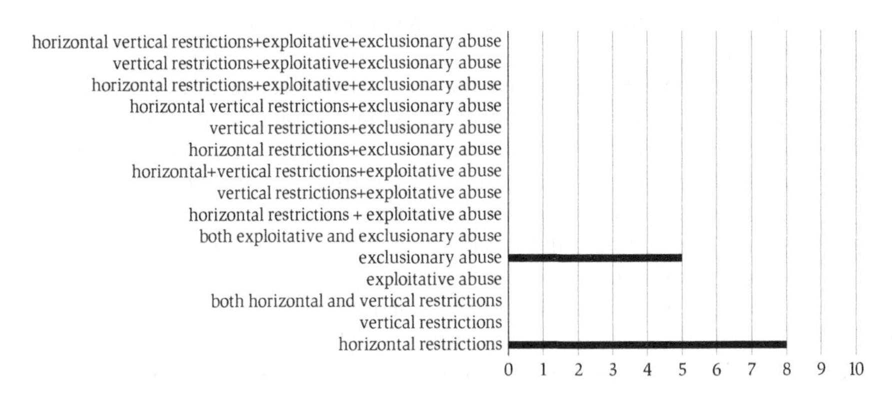

Figure 4.6 points to the relatively limited type of restriction of competition subject to the Court's review. It demonstrates that Article 101 TFEU and the national equivalent judgments, only examined horizontal restrictions, and Article 102 TFEU and the national equivalent judgments only exclusionary abuses.

Seven first-instance decisions concerned horizontal restrictions (*Professional soccer*,[89] *Ordre des Pharmacies I*,[90] *Vebic* (2x),[91] *Brabomills*,[92] *Holcim*,[93] *Ordre des Pharmaciens II*.[94]

Of the two second-instance decisions, one also concerned horizontal restrictions (*Holcim*).[95]

Four first-instance decisions (*Presstalis*,[96] *Bpost*,[97] *Proximus* (2x))[98] and one second-instance case (*Bpost*)[99] concerned exclusionary abuses.

89. Brussels 28 June 2006, 2005/MR/2, 2005/MR/5, *Professional soccer*, *AM* 2007/1-2167, note P. Valcke, *Jaarboek Handelspraktijken & Mededinging* 2006, 805, note C. Verdonck and L. Depuydt, *RCB* 2007/1, 63.
90. Brussels 7 April 2009, 2007/MR/5, *Ordre des Pharmaciens I*, https://www.bma-abc.be/sites/default/files/content/download/files/20090407_cab_2007mr5_ordre_des_pharmaciens_ad.pdf.
91. Brussels 13 February 2013, 2008/MR/3, *Vebic*, https://www.bma-abc.be/sites/default/files/content/download/files/20130213_hvbb_vebic_ea.pdf.
92. Brussels 12 March 2014, 2013/MR/6, *Brabomills*, https://www.bma-abc.be/sites/default/files/content/download/files/20140312_cab_hvbb_brabomills_eindarrest.pdf, *Jaarboek Marktpraktijken* 2014, 1139, note H. Gilliams, *RCB* 2014/2, 108.
93. Brussels 30 June 2016, 2013/MR/11-15, *Holcim*, https://www.bma-abc.be/nl/beslissingen/2013mr11-12-13-14-et-15-cimenteries-ad, *RDC* 2017/8, 865, note J. Dewispelaere, *RCB* 2017/1, 4.
94. Brussels 8 January 2020, 2019/MR/3, *Ordre des Pharmaciens II*, https://www.abc-bma.be/sites/default/files/content/download/files/20200108_2019mr_3_op_arret_vpub.pdf, *Competitio* 2020/2, 138, *Jaarboek Marktpraktijken* 2020/1, 1382.
95. Cass. 22 June 2018, C.16.0462, *Holcim*, https://www.bma-abc.be/sites/default/files/content/download/files/20180622_cdc_c160462f_c160476f_cimenteries.pdf, *Competitio* 2018/3, 267, note.
96. Brussels 27 September 2013, 2012/MR/5, *Presstalis*, https://www.bma-abc.be/sites/default/files/content/download/files/20130927_cdc_2012mr5_presstalis.pdf.

For further information on the type of restrictions, *see* the comments on Figure 4.5 above.

No review judgments in cases concerning vertical restrictions or exploitative abuses were found.

In several documents setting out the NCA's enforcement priorities, the NCA indicates that it focuses on areas where it considers its intervention to provide the greatest benefit. While it suggests an attempt to achieve a fair balance between different types of restrictions (horizontal and vertical agreements and abuse of dominance) as well as between relatively simple cases and more complex or innovative cases) it also takes into account the impact of its intervention, the resources required and the risk that its investment in a case will not lead to an infringement decision.[100] These considerations, combined with the types of infringements that led to complaints and the fact that more serious infringements are likely to lead to more serious sanctions, contribute to explaining the type of restrictions involved in appellate cases.

Figure 4.7 Object/Effect (Only for Article 101/National Equivalent Infringements)

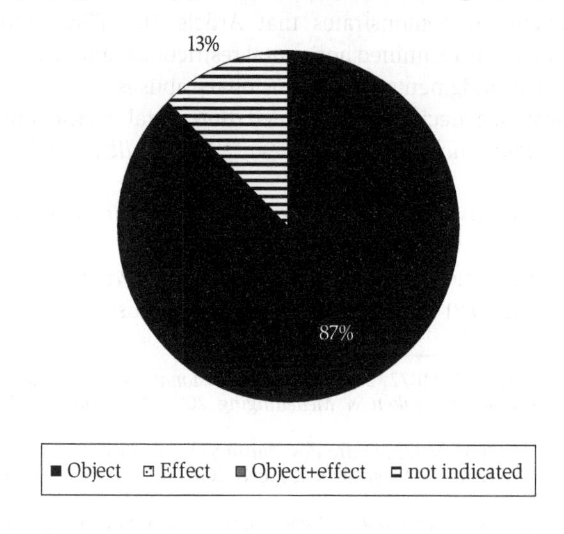

97. Brussel 10 November 2016, 2013/MR/2, *Bpost*, https://www.bma-abc.be/sites/default/files/content/download/files/20161110_cab_2013mr2_bpost.pdf, *RDC* 2017/8, 865, note J. Dewispelaere, *RCB* 2017/1, 42.
98. Brussels 10 November 2016, 2009/MR/4-6 & 8, *Proximus*, not published, mentioned in Brussel 9 October 2019, 2009/MR/3, https://www.bma-abc.be/sites/default/files/content/download/files/20191009_2009mr3_proximus_arret_v_pub.pdf; Brussels 9 October 2019, 2009/MR/3, *Proximus*, https://www.bma-abc.be/sites/default/files/content/download/files/20191009_2009mr3_proximus_arret_v_pub.pdf.
99. Cass. 22 November 2018, AR C.17.0126.F, *Bpost*, https://www.bma-abc.be/sites/default/files/content/download/files/20181122_cdc_c170126f_bpost.pdf, *Competitio* 2019/1, 21, note, *JT* 2020/ 6815, 401, note P. Lagasse, *JLMB* 2019/31, 1448, *RCJB* 2022/1, 37, note F. Mourlon Beernaert and B. Maes, *Rev.dr.pén.* 2019/2, 158, note F. Lugentz.
100. *See, e.g.*, https://www.belgiancompetition.be/en/about-us/publications/politique-de-priorites-2017; https://www.belgiancompetition.be/en/about-us/publications/priority-policy-2016; https://www.abc-bma.be/fr/propos-de-nous/publications/politique-des-priorites-2014.

The limited type of restrictions under review is also illustrated by Figure 4.7, recording whether the NCA's proceedings concerning the application of Article 101 TFEU and/or its national equivalent involved a by-object or by-effect restriction. It demonstrates that almost all cases involved hardcore (horizontal) restrictions.[101] The only case where the NCA investigated an infringement of Article 101 TFEU and its national equivalent without referring to a distinction by-object and/or by-effect was *Professional soccer*, a case where no infringement was proven.[102]

Figure 4.8 Competition Authority's Procedure

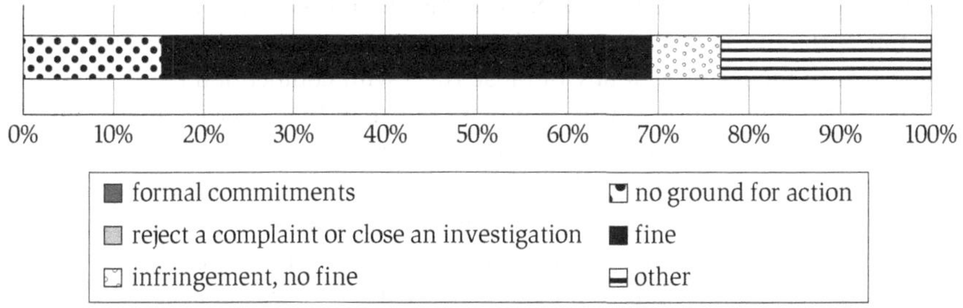

0% 10% 20% 30% 40% 50% 60% 70% 80% 90% 100%

formal commitments | no ground for action
reject a complaint or close an investigation | fine
infringement, no fine | other

Figure 4.8 presents the type of NCA's procedures subject to an appeal across all instances. Unsurprisingly, the majority of cases involved infringement decisions, where a fine was imposed. Seven first-instance appeals were brought against NCA's decisions, where a fine was imposed.[103] The first-instance appeal in *Vebic* led to an

101. Competition Council, Decision 2007-I/0-27, 26 October 2007, *Ordre des pharmaciens I*, https://www.bma-abc.be/sites/default/files/content/download/files/2007IO27_Ordre_%20 des_%20pharmaciens.pdf, *BOJ* 11 February 2008 (first edition), 9078, *Jaarboek Handelspraktijken & Mededinging* 2007, 1065, note C. Verdure, *RDC* 2008/4, 366 *RCB* 2008/1, 49; Competition College, Decision ABC-2019-I/O-14, *Ordre des Pharmaciens II*, 28 May 2019, https://www.bma-abc.be/sites/default/files/content/download/files/abc-2019-io-14_pub_0. pdf, *JLMB* 2019/32, 1522, note P. Henry, *RDC* 2019/4, 612; Competition Council, Decision 2013-I/O-06, 28 February 2013, *Brabomills*, https://www.bma-abc.be/sites/default/files/ content/download/files/2013IO06_pub.pdf, *BOJ* 2 April 2013 (first edition), 20502, *RCB* 2013/3, 300; Competition Council, Decision 2008-I/O-04, 25 January 2008, https://www.bma -abc.be/sites/default/files/content/download/files/2008IO04.pdf, *OJ* 19 February 2008 (first edition), 10525, *Jaarboek Handelspraktijken & Mededinging* 2008, 894, note F. Naert, *RDC* 2008/6, 571, *RCB* 2008/2, 26; Competition Council Decision 2013-I/O-34, 30 August 2013, https://www.belgiancompetition.be/sites/default/files/content/download/files/2013IO34_ Pub.pdf, *BOJ* 9 October 2013 (first edition), 71144, *RDC* 2013/9, 945, *RCB* 2014/1, 45.
102. Competition Council, Decision 2005-I/O-40, 29 July 2005, *Professional soccer*, https://www. bma-abc.be/sites/default/files/content/download/files/2005IO40%20Liga%20Beroepsvoetb al.pdf, *BOJ* 20 October 2005 (second edition). The NCA did not mention object or effect, but found that no infringement was proven, so in fact neither one by-object, nor one by-effect.
103. Competition Council, Decision 2008-I/O-04, 25 January 2008, *Vebic*, https://www.bma-abc. be/sites/default/files/content/download/files/2008IO04.pdf, *BOJ* 19 February 2008 (first edition), 10525, *Jaarboek Handelspraktijken & Mededinging* 2008, 894, note F. Naert, *RDC* 2008/6, 571, *RCB* 2008/2, 26; Competition Council, Decision 2012-P/K-20, 30 July 2012, *Presstalis*, https://www.bma-abc.be/sites/default/files/content/download/files/2012PK20_Pub.pdf, *BO J* 3 September 2012, 53900, *Jaarboek Marktpraktijken* 2012, 1090, *RDC* 2012/9, 946, *RCB* 2013/1, 36; Competition Council, Decision 2013-I/O-06, 28 February 2013, https://www.bma -abc.be/sites/default/files/content/download/files/2013IO06_pub.pdf, *BOJ* 2 April 2013 (first edition), 20502, *RCB* 2013/3, 300; Competition Council, Decision 2013-I/O-34, 30 August 2013,

annulment of the NCA's decision.[104] It was followed by an 'objection procedure' brought by the NCA because of its absence as a party in the proceedings. One first-instance appeal was brought against an NCA decision where an infringement was found, but no fine was imposed, only a behavioural remedy[105] (*Ordre des Pharmaciens I*). Given the long duration of the investigation (February 1998-November 2005) and the fact that very few investigatory activities had taken place for three years (between 2001 and 2004), the Competition Council had found that the reasonable time within the meaning of Article 6 ECHR had been exceeded. Therefore, it decided not to impose a fine. However, given the restrictive nature of the professional association's rules on opening and closing hours as well as on advertising and rebates, the Council considered it appropriate to impose a publication measure in order to inform its members (pharmacists) of the incompatibility of those rules with competition law.[106]

Two first-instance appeals were brought against an NCA decision that found that there were no grounds for action (*Professional soccer*,[107] *Belgacom*[108]).

Appeals against decisions of the NCA to reject a complaint were possible under the 1991 Competition Act (cf. *supra*, section 2.1.2), where it was the Council for Competition that decided on the rejection of complaints. *Professional soccer* concerned an appeal against the rejection of a complaint by a television broadcaster (Telenet)

---

https://www.belgiancompetition.be/sites/default/files/content/download/files/2013IO34_Pub.pdf, *BOJ* 9 October 2013 (first edition), 71144, *RDC* 2013/9, 945, *RCB* 2014/1, 45; Competition Council, Decision 2012-P/K-32, 10 December 2012, *Bpost*, https://www.belgiancompetition.be/en/decisions/12-pk-32-bpost, *BOJ* 22 February 2013 (fourth edition), 11727, *Jaarboek Marktpraktijken* 2012, 1181, note C. Lousberg, *RCB* 2013/2, 206; Competition Council, Decision 2009-P/K-10, *Proximus*, *BOJ* 29 June 2009, 44264, *RDC* 2009/7, 731, *RCB* 2009/3, 80, *RCB* 2010/2, 36, note K. Bourgeois & note N. Petit and E. Provost; Competition College, Décision ABC-2019-I/O-14, 28 May 2019, *Ordre des Pharmaciens II*, https://www.bma-abc.be/sites/default/files/content/download/files/abc-2019-io-14_pub_0.pdf, *JLMB* 2019/32, 1522, note P. Henry, *RDC* 2019/4, 612.

104. Brussels 13 February 2013, 2008/MR/3, *Vebic*, https://www.bma-abc.be/sites/default/files/content/download/files/20130213_hvbb_vebic_ea.pdf.
105. An obligation to publish the decision on its website; to notify the members of the Order of the content of this decision in writing, possibly by electronic means, containing at least the operative part of the decision and a link to the text of the decision or a copy of the full text; to send to the registry for the attention of the Competition Council, a copy of the communication sent to the members of the Order within one month of the notification of the decision.
106. Competition Council, Decision 2007-I/O-27, 26 October 2007, https://www.bma-abc.be/sites/default/files/content/download/files/2007IO27_Ordre_%20des_%20pharmaciens.pdf, *BOJ* 11 February 2008 (first edition), 9078, *Jaarboek Handelspraktijken & Mededinging* 2007, 1065, note C. Verdure, *RDC* 2008/4, 366 *RCB* 2008/1, 49.
107. Competition Council, Decision 2005-I/O-40, 29 July 2005, https://www.bma-abc.be/sites/default/files/content/download/files/2005IO40%20Liga%20Beroepsvoetbal, *BOJ* 20 October 2005 (second edition). The NCA did not mention object or effect, but found that no infringement was proven, so in fact neither one by-object, nor one by-effect.
108. Competition Council, Decision 2012-P/K-29, 29 November 2012, https://www.abc-bma.be/sites/default/files/content/download/files/2012PK29_Pub.pdf, *BOJ* 9 January 2013 (first edition), 776, *Jaarboek Marktpraktijken* 2012, 1124, *RCB* 2013/2, 203.

against the allocation of broadcasting rights to national soccer league matches to a competitor. More specifically, the facts were as follows. Belgian professional soccer clubs of the first division of the Belgian soccer league mandated LBV, a professional association of such soccer clubs, to jointly sell their television broadcasting rights to national soccer league matches. The broadcasting rights were granted to a certain undertaking, Belgacom Skynet, for a period of three years. Another undertaking active in TV broadcasting filed a complaint against this decision and the NCA had also started investigations *ex officio*. The cases were joined. The Council carried out an extensive analysis of similar cases brought before the Commission.[109] Based on this analysis, it held that EU competition law does not oppose the granting of broadcasting rights to a single broadcaster provided that this is the result of an open, transparent and non-discriminatory bidding procedure and the allocation of broadcasting rights is limited to a duration not exceeding three years. The Council for Competition found that these conditions had been respected. Consequently, it declared that there was no ground for action, and it rejected the complaint. The complainant and a third party appealed the decision. The Court of Appeal confirmed the Council's decision, further substantiating its legal basis: while the allocation agreement infringed Article 101(1) TFEU (then Article 81(1) EC), it satisfied the conditions of Article 101(3) TFEU and was therefore exempted. In addition to the annulment of the Council's decision, Telenet requested the Court to decide that a clause in a contract it concluded in 2003 did not infringe the competition rules, a matter that was not decided by the Council. The Court declared it lacked jurisdiction to decide on this request.[110]

Each of the two second-instance decisions concerned a case (*Bpost*[111] and *Holcim*[112]) where the NCA had imposed a fine.

109. Cf. *infra*, Qualitative analysis.
110. Brussels 28 June 2006, 2005/MR/2, 2005/MR/5, *Professional soccer*, *AM* 2007/1-2,167, note P. Valcke, *Jaarboek Handelspraktijken & Mededinging* 2006, 805, note C. Verdonck and L. Depuydt, *RCB* 2007/1, 63.
111. Competition Council, Decision 2012-P/K-32, 10 December 2012, https://www.belgian-competition.be/en/decisions/12-pk-32-bpost, *BOJ* 22 February 2013 (fourth edition), 11727, *Jaarboek Marktpraktijken* 2012, 1181, note C. Lousberg, *RCB* 2013/2, 206.
112. Competition Council, Decision 2013-I/O-34, 30 August 2013, https://www.belgiancompetition.be/sites/default/files/content/download/files/2013IO34_Pub.pdf, *BOJ* 9 October 2013 (first edition), 71144, *RDC* 2013/9, 945, *RCB* 2014/1, 45.

Figure 4.9 Grounds of Appeal (Each NCA's Decision or Previous Instance Judgment Counts as One)

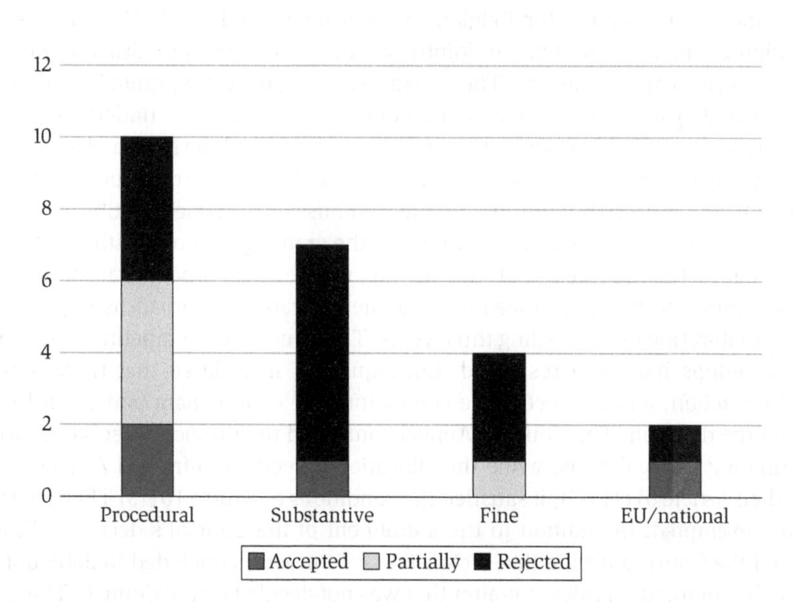

Figure 4.9 illustrates the grounds of appeal raised by the parties and their success rates across both instances. Judgments against the same NCA decision or previous instance judgment have been aggregated, and the grounds involved in them and their success or rejection have been counted as a single case.

Procedural grounds of appeal had the highest success rate. They were at least partially successful in 60% of the cases where they had been raised. They were partially accepted in the first-instance decisions in *Ordre des Pharmaciens I*,[113] *Vebic (Court of Appeal)*,[114] *Brabomills*.[115] In *Bpost*, they were accepted both in the first- and second-instance appeals.[116]

113. Brussels 7 April 2009, 2007/MR/5, *Ordre des Pharmaciens I*, https://www.bma-abc.be/sites/default/files/content/download/files/20090407_cab_2007mr5_ordre_des_pharmaciens_ad.pdf.

114. Brussels 13 February 2013, 2008/MR/3, *Vebic*, https://www.bma-abc.be/sites/default/files/content/download/files/20130213_hvbb_vebic_ea.pdf.

115. Brussels 12 March 2014, 2013/MR/6, *Brabomills*, https://www.bma-abc.be/sites/default/files/content/download/files/20140312_cab_hvbb_brabomills_eindarrest.pdf, *Jaarboek Marktpraktijken* 2014, 1139, note H. Gilliams, *RCB* 2014/2, 108.

116. Brussels 10 November 2016, 2013/MR/2, *Bpost*, https://www.bma-abc.be/sites/default/files/content/download/files/20161110_cab_2013mr2_bpost.pdf, *RDC* 2017/8, 865, note J. Dewispelaere, *RCB* 2017/1, 42; Cass. 22 November 2018, AR C.17.0126.F, *Bpost*, https://www.bma-abc.be/sites/default/files/content/download/files/20181122_cdc_c170126f_bpost.pdf, *Competitio* 2019/1, 21, note, *JT* 2020/6815, 401, note P. Lagasse, *JLMB* 2019/ 31, 1448, *RCJB* 2022/1, 37, note F. Mourlon Beernaert and B. Maes, *Rev.dr.pén.* 2019/2, 158, note F. Lugentz.

In *Vebic,* the Court of Appeal accepted the procedural ground that the investigation was initiated irregularly: it was only based on a request from the Minister of Economy, who wanted information on market behaviour, without there being any serious indications of any infringement of the 2006 Competition Act, which applied at the time of the initiation of the investigation.[117] Since this ground was sufficient to annul the Competition Council's decision, the Court did not consider it necessary to decide on the other procedural (and substantive) grounds of appeal.[118]

In *Brabomils,* the Court of Appeal accepted the procedural ground based on the infringement of the *non bis in idem* principle (*see also* further regarding the relation between this procedural ground and EU/national grounds).[119] The first and second appeal decisions in *Bpost* also concerned the *non bis in idem* principle.[120]

In *Ordre des Pharmaciens I,*[121] the Court accepted the applicant's procedural ground that the decision had been taken by a Chamber of the Competition Council that was not legally composed. Article 19 of the then-applicable 2006 Competition Act provided that the Council had to be divided into chambers composed of three judges each and that the general assembly of the Council had to yearly determine the composition of the chambers and their president. When the contested decision in *Ordre des Pharmaciens I* was taken, no such decision by the Council's General Assembly was available. According to the Court of Appeal, this justified the annulment of the decision. The Court rejected the second procedural ground invoked by the applicant, i.e. that the Council should not have decided on the case because the investigated practices of the Order had been terminated. The Court pointed out that when the IPS submits the report of an investigation to the Council, the latter has to take a reasoned decision, albeit a reasoned decision that there is no ground for action. The fact that the infringement has been terminated neither relieves the Council from its obligation to take a reasoned decision nor of finding that an infringement had occurred and to impose a remedy. In the present case, the Council found an infringement and imposed an injunction. The Court of Appeal also rejected the grounds relating to the substance and replaced the annulled decision with its own decision, imposing the same injunction for the same reasons as the Competition Council.[122]

117. Brussels 13 February 2013, 2008/MR/3, *Vebic,* https://www.bma-abc.be/sites/default/files/content/download/files/20130213_hvbb_vebic_ea.pdf.
118. *Ibid.*
119. Brussels 12 March 2014, 2013/MR/6, *Brabomills,* https://www.bma-abc.be/sites/default/files/content/download/files/20140312_cab_hvbb_brabomills_eindarrest.pdf, *Jaarboek Marktpraktijken* 2014, 1139, note H. Gilliams, *RCB* 2014/2, 108.
120. Brussels 10 November 2016, 2013/MR/2, *Bpost,* https://www.bma-abc.be/sites/default/files/content/download/files/20161110_cab_2013mr2_bpost.pdf, *RDC* 2017/8, 865, note J. Dewispelaere, *RCB* 2017/1, 42; Cass. 22 November 2018, AR C.17.0126.F, *Bpost,* https://www.bma-abc.be/sites/default/files/content/download/files/20181122_cdc_c170126f_bpost.pdf, *Competitio* 2019/1, 21, note, *JT* 2020/6815, 401, note P. Lagasse, *JLMB* 2019/31, 1448, *RCJB* 2022/1, 37, note F. Mourlon Beernaert and B. Maes, *Rev.dr.pén.* 2019/2, 158, note F. Lugentz.
121. Brussels 7 April 2009, 2007/MR/5, *Ordre des Pharmaciens I,* https://www.bma-abc.be/sites/default/files/content/download/files/20090407_cab_2007mr5_ordre_des_pharmaciens_ad.pdf.
122. *Ibid.*

Substantive grounds were raised by the parties in seven cases[123]and accepted in one.[124]

Grounds relating to the fines were at least partially successful in 25 % of the cases where they had been raised. In fact, they were only partially accepted in *Ordre des Pharmaciens II*.[125] In the same case, grounds relating to the relationship between EU law and national law were partially accepted. In fact, the two kinds of grounds were intermingled, as will be explained hereafter.

When considering the success rates of grounds of appeal, it has to be noted that the grounds of appeal are often dealt with in a specific order, starting with grounds relating to the procedure, grounds relating to the substance, and finally, grounds relating to the fine. EU/national grounds are often intermingled with other types of grounds of appeals.

The order in which the grounds of appeal are dealt with has an impact on their success rate. There are cases where the Court finds that the investigations were affected by such serious infringements of the procedural rules that it is no longer possible to decide on the substance of the case. Consequently, there is no need at that stage to analyse the grounds relating to other grounds of appeal. This occurred, for example, in the Court of Appeals 2013 decision in *Vebic*.[126] Furthermore, when the Court's task is not to decide on the substance of the case and the procedural grounds suffice to annul the case and refer it back to the lower level, it will generally not consider other grounds

123. Brussels 28 June 2006, 2005/MR/2, 2005/MR/5, *Professional soccer*, *AM* 2007/1-2, 167, note P. Valcke, *Jaarboek Handelspraktijken & Mededinging* 2006, 805, note C. Verdonck and L. Depuydt, *RCB* 2007/1, 63; Brussels 7 April 2009, 2007/MR/5, *Ordre des Pharmaciens I*, https://www.bma-abc.be/sites/default/files/content/download/files/20090407_cab_2007mr 5_ordre_des_pharmaciens_ad.pdf; Brussels 4 October 2017, 2013/MR/7, *Vebic*, https://www. abc-bma.be/sites/default/files/content/download/files/20171004_hvbb_bma_bakkers_vlaa nderen.pdf; Brussels 27 September 2013, 2012/MR/5, *Presstalis*, https://www.bma-abc.be/ sites/default/files/content/download/files/20130927_cdc_2012mr5_presstalis.pdf; Brussels 12 March 2014, 2013/MR/6, *Brabomills*, https://www.bma-abc.be/sites/default/files/content /download/files/20140312_cab_hvbb_brabomills_eindarrest.pdf, *Jaarboek Marktpraktijken* 2014, 1139, note H. Gilliams, *RCB* 2014/2, 108; Brussels 30 June 2016, 2013/MR/11-15, *Holcim*, https://www.bma-abc.be/nl/beslissingen/2013mr11-12-13-14-et-15-cimenteries-ad, *RDC* 201 7/8, 865, note J. Dewispelaere, *RCB* 2017/1, 4; Brussels 8 January 2020, 2019/MR/3, *Ordre des Pharmaciens II*, https://www.abc-bma.be/sites/default/files/content/download/files/202001 08_2019mr_3_op_arret_vpub.pdf, *Competitio* 2020/2, 138; *Jaarboek Marktpraktijken* 2020/1, 1382; Cass. 22 June 2018, C.16.0462, *Holcim*, https://www.bma-abc.be/sites/default/files/ content/download/files/20180622_cdc_c160462f_c160476f_cimenteries.pdf, *Competitio* 2018 ,/3, 267, note.
124. Brussels 10 November 2016, 2013/MR/2, *Bpost*, https://www.bma-abc.be/sites/default/files /content/download/files/20161110_cab_2013mr2_bpost.pdf, *RDC* 2017/8, 865, note J. Dewispelaere, *RCB* 2017/1, 4.
125. Brussels 8 January 2020, 2019/MR/3, *Ordre des Pharmaciens II*, https://www.abc-bma.be/ sites/default/files/content/download/files/20200108_2019mr_3_op_arret_vpub.pdf, *Competitio* 2020/2, 138, *Jaarboek Marktpraktijken* 2020/1, 1382.
126. *See also* Brussel 10 November 2016, 2013/MR/2, *Bpost*, https://www.bma-abc.be/sites/ default/files/content/download/files/20161110_cab_2013mr2_bpost.pdf, *RDC* 2017/8, 865, note J. Dewispelaere, *RCB* 2017/1, 42; Cass. 22 November 2018, AR C.17.0126.F, *Bpost*, https://www.bma-abc.be/sites/default/files/content/download/files/20181122_cdc_c17012 6f_bpost.pdf, *Competitio* 2019/1, 21, note, *JT* 2020/6815, 401, note P. Lagasse, *JLMB* 2019/31, 1448, *RCJB* 2022/1, 37, note F. Mourlon Beernaert and B. Maes, *Rev.dr.pén.* 2019/2, 158, note F. Lugentz.

of appeal. Similarly, when the Court finds that one or more of the substantive grounds are to be accepted and that there is no infringement, there is no ground to impose a fine. Consequently, there is no reason to decide on the grounds relating to the fine itself. In *Holcim*, for example, the Court of Appeal did not address the appeal ground relating to the fine because it had already annulled the decision on substantive grounds.[127]

Grounds have only been qualified as EU/national grounds when the tension between EU and national law was the main element of the ground of the appeal. This seemed to be the case in *Ordre des Pharmaciens II*,[128] where the BCA applied the EU law's approach to assessing the turnover to be taken into account for the determination of the fine to be imposed on an association of undertakings, thereby deviating from its own fining guidelines, which was contested by the appellant.

However, grounds that are mainly of a procedural, substantive or fines-related nature also contain elements that may be somewhat related to the tension between EU and national law. For example, in the *Brabomills*, the procedural ground relating to the infringement of the *non bis in idem* principle included an argument contradicting the Court of Justice's interpretation of this principle.[129] Also, in other cases concerning the application of the *non bis in idem* principle, such as the Supreme Court's decision in *Bpost*,[130] EU and European Convention on Human Rights (ECHR) case law is often discussed. In these cases, however, the procedural nature of the grounds of appeal appeared to be determinative.

Figures 4.10 (a-d), focus on the grounds argued and accepted per year and count each judgment separately, irrespective of whether there were multiple separate appeals in relation to the same NCA decision.

127. Brussels 30 June 2016, 2013/MR/11-15, *Holcim*, https://www.bma-abc.be/nl/beslissingen/2013mr11-12-13-14-et-15-cimenteries-ad, *RDC* 2017/8, 865, note J. Dewispelaere, *RCB* 2017/1, 4.
128. Brussels 8 January 2020, 2019/MR/3, *Ordre des Pharmaciens II*, https://www.abc-bma.be/sites/default/files/content/download/files/20200108_2019mr_3_op_arret_vpub.pdf, *Competitio* 2020/2, 138, *Jaarboek Marktpraktijken* 2020/1, 1382.
129. Brussels 12 March 2014, 2013/MR/6, *Brabomills*, https://www.bma-abc.be/sites/default/files/content/download/files/20140312_cab_hvbb_brabomills_eindarrest.pdf, *Jaarboek Marktpraktijken* 2014, 1139, note H. Gilliams, *RCB* 2014/2, 108.
130. Cass. 22 November 2018, AR C.17.0126.F, *Bpost*, https://www.bma-abc.be/sites/default/files/content/download/files/20181122_cdc_c170126f_bpost.pdf, *Competitio* 2019/1, 21, note, *JT* 2020/6815, 401, note P. Lagasse, *JLMB* 2019/31, 1448, *RCJB* 2022/1, 37, note F. Mourlon Beernaert and B. Maes, *Rev.dr.pén.* 2019/2, 158, note F. Lugentz.

Figure 4.10(a) Procedural Grounds

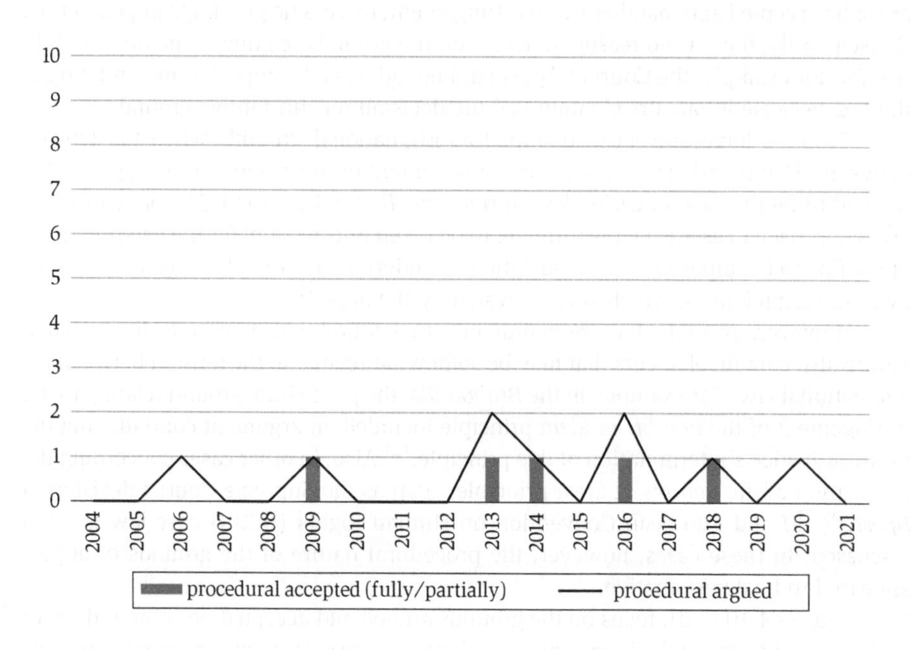

Figure 4.10(b) Substantive Grounds

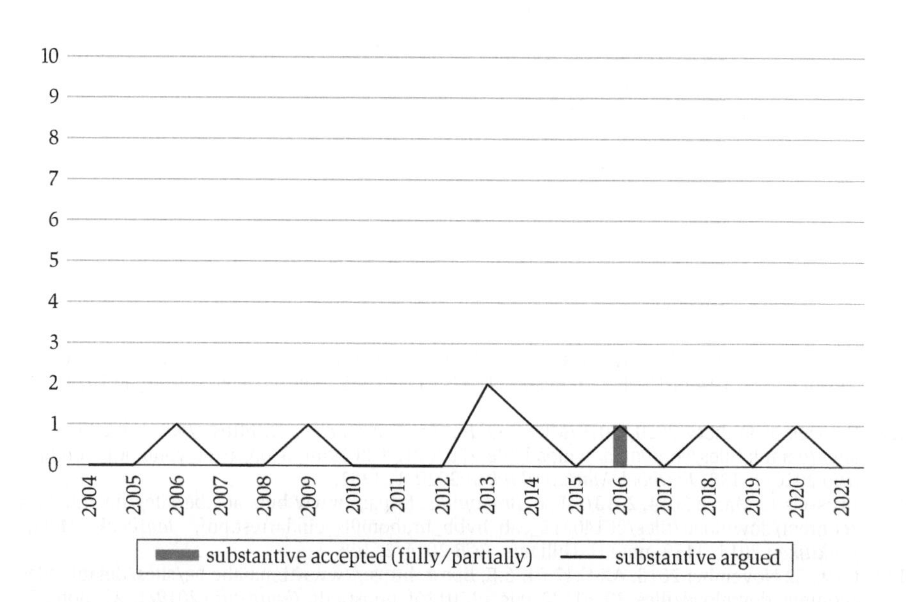

Figure 4.10(c) Fines-related Grounds

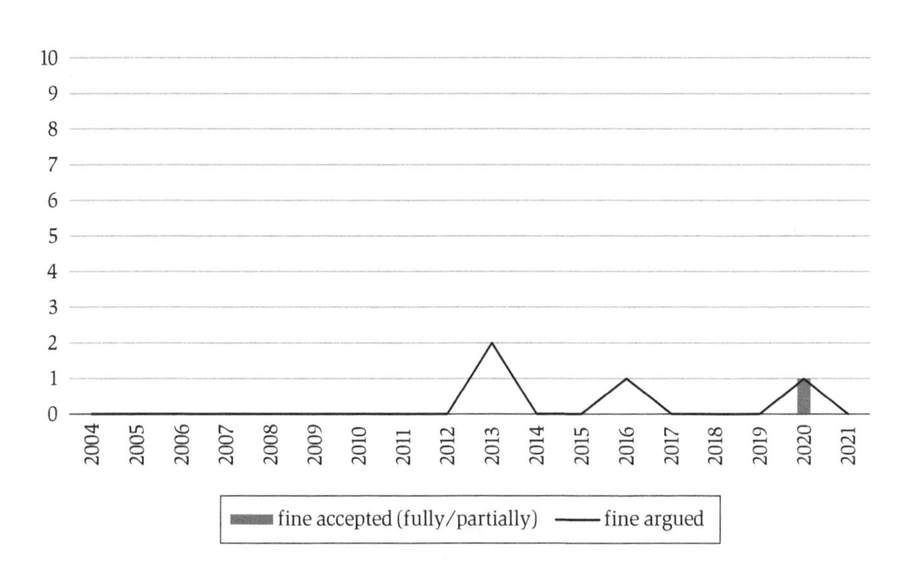

Figure 4.10(d) EU/National Grounds

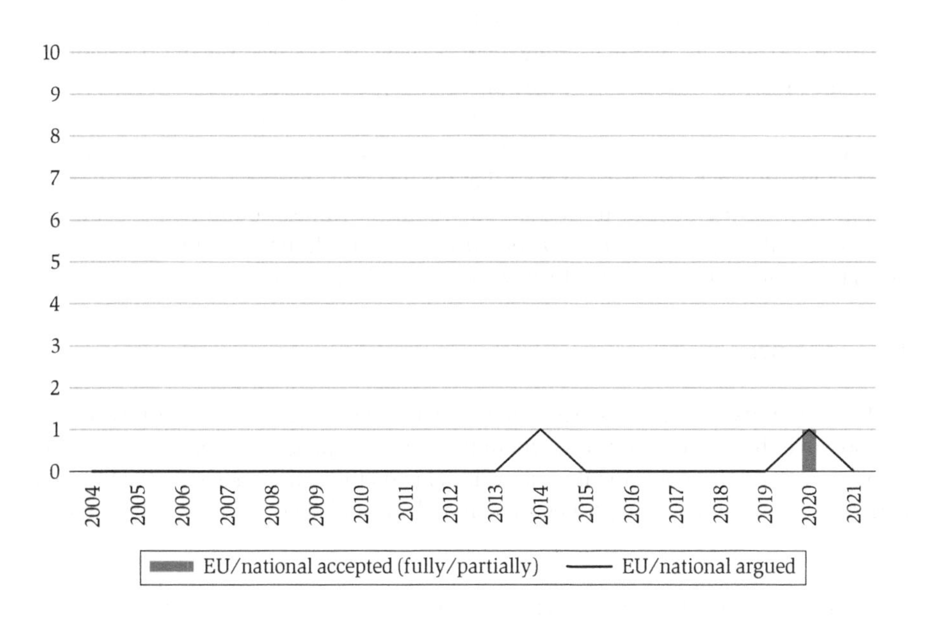

Figure 4.11 Types of Restrictions Versus Successful Grounds of Appeal

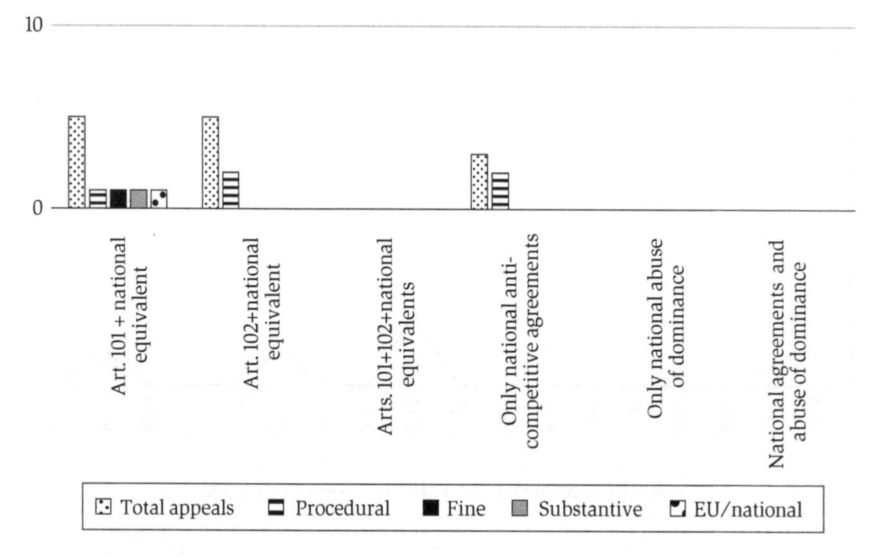

Figure 4.11 indicates the (fully or partially) successful grounds of challenge per type of restriction.

In cases relating to Article 101 and its national equivalent, procedural, substantive, fines and EU/national-related grounds were equally successful. In cases relating to Article 102 and its national equivalent, as well as in cases relating to only the national equivalent of Article 101, only procedural grounds were successful. Note that the fine may be reduced (even to zero) when substantive or procedural grounds were at least partially successful. In *Brabomills*, for example, the NCA determined the fine as a lump sum. While the NCA made clear that the fine was only intended to sanction the infringement on the Belgian territory,[131] the Court of Appeal found that it could not exclude an infringement of the *non bis in idem* principle because the fine was not calculated based on the relevant turnover on the Belgian territory.[132]

4.7 Fines

In 45% of the first-instance appeals, the fine was fully waived by the court. However, it is possible that in certain cases, where the appellate judge referred the case to the NCA or the Court of Appeal to take a new decision on the entire case or on the fine, and where this decision has not yet been taken and/or published, a fine will be imposed

131. Competition Council Decision 28 February 2013, 2013-I/O-06, www.bma-abc.be/sites/default/files/content/download/files/2013IO06_pub.pdf.
132. Brussels 12 March 2014, 2013/MR/6, *Brabomills*, https://www.bma-abc.be/sites/default/files/content/download/files/20140312_cab_hvbb_brabomills_eindarrest.pdf, *Jaarboek Marktpraktijken* 2014, 1139, note H. Gilliams, *RCB* 2014/2, 108.

eventually. In *Ordre des Pharmaciens II*, for example, the Court of Appeal returned the case to the NCA in order to determine the fine. In *Bpost*, the Supreme Court returned the case to the Court of Appeal to determine the fine.[133] It is to be noted that when a case is returned to either the NCA or the Court of Appeal, the institution hearing the case after referral needs to be composed in a different way than the one that heard the (partially) annulled decision.

4.8 Leniency

Brabomills is the only case leading to judicial review of the NCA's decision in the period under review, where a party successfully applied for leniency. The first-instance appeal in this case was partially successful. The case concerned a cartel in the flour market. In 2008, the first application for leniency was made by one of Brabomills' competitors. Two years later, a second competitor filed for leniency. Shortly after the receipt of the first leniency application, the IPS started an investigation against six undertakings active in the flour market. One of them was Brabomills. Based on the leniency applications and other evidence collected by the IPS, the Competition Council found that the six undertakings systematically exchanged information in breach of Article 101 TFEU and its Belgian equivalent. The infringement also involved the Dutch territory, but the Belgian NCA only aimed at sanctioning the infringement on the Belgian territory. Three of the undertakings involved were already fined by the Dutch NCA for the infringement on the Dutch market. Brabomills was not fined in the Netherlands. The Belgian Competition Council imposed on Brabomills a fine of EUR 100,000. Brabomills appealed the Competition Council's decision. It argued that the Competition Council based its decision on evidence that did not respect the standard of proof in competition cases, that it was unduly treated unequally compared to its co-defendants, that the decision infringed the *non bis in idem* principle and was inconsistently reasoned. As mentioned in the previous section, the appeal was successful insofar as it concerned the amount of the fine because the way in which the NCA calculated the fine did not allow the Court of Appeal to exclude an infringement of the *non bis in idem* principle.[134]

133. Cass. 22 November 2018, AR C.17.0126.F, *Bpost*, https://www.bma-abc.be/sites/default/files/content/download/files/20181122_cdc_c170126f_bpost.pdf, *Competitio* 2019/1, 21, note, *JT* 2020/6815, 401, note P. Lagasse, *JLMB* 2019/31, 1448, *RCJB* 2022/1, 37, note F. Mourlon Beernaert and B. Maes, *Rev.dr.pén.* 2019/2, 158, note F. Lugentz.
134. Brussels 12 March 2014, 2013/MR/6, *Brabomills*, https://www.bma-abc.be/sites/default/files/content/download/files/20140312_cab_hvbb_brabomills_eindarrest.pdf, *Jaarboek Marktpraktijken* 2014, 1139, note H. Gilliams, *RCB* 2014/2, 108.

Figure 4.12 Success of Appeals When Leniency Applications Were Successfully Submitted

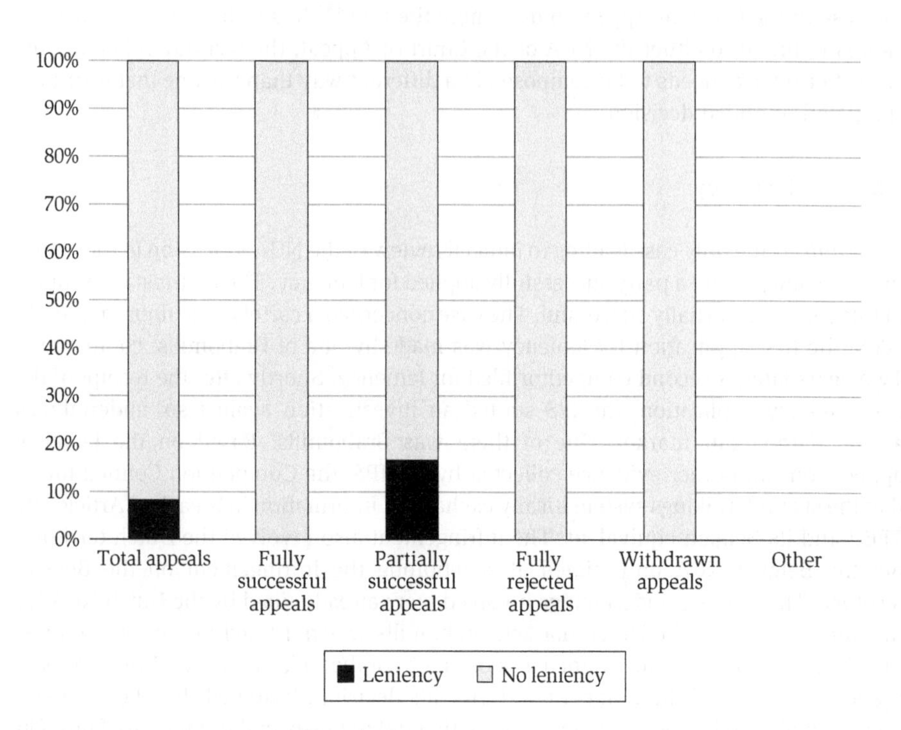

5 QUALITATIVE ANALYSIS

Although the principle that the court hearing appeals of competition decisions has full jurisdiction can be traced back to the parliamentary documents relating to the first Belgian Competition Act, the actual meaning of this principle is still unclear. In theory, one may anticipate a difference between the period before 2013, where the body responsible for making competition decisions was an administrative court, and the period after 2013 where that body became an autonomous administrative body.

Before 2013, the first-instance appeals against competition decisions were, in fact, judgments by a second-instance court hearing an appeal against a decision by a first-instance court. While this was not explicitly provided in the 1991, 1999 and 2006 Competition Acts, the appeal procedure was subject to the rules of the Code of Civil Procedure.[135] For this type of appeal, it is the rule that the court of appeal hears the facts and the law and reaches its own decision either to confirm the first-instance decision or to change it entirely or partially, albeit within the boundaries set by the appellants.

After 2013, the procedure before the Court of Appeal is, in fact, a review of an administrative decision. The traditional view regarding judicial review of administrative decisions is that the court assesses the legality of the decision, and if the law allows

135. Article 2 Code of civil procedure.

the administrative body a certain degree of discretion, the Court limits itself to a marginal review, assessing whether a reasonable administrative body could reach the contested decision.[136]

The traditional view regarding administrative review has never been fully applied in competition cases. As mentioned before, since the first Belgian Competition Act, the Court of Appeal has been awarded full jurisdiction. The subsequent statutory revisions elaborated on the powers this entailed and their limits (cf. *supra*, section 2.1.4). Nevertheless, the meaning of the concept 'full jurisdiction' in competition appeals has always been a little confused. Even the most detailed and extensive description of the powers included in the Court's full jurisdiction in the 2006 Competition Act (cf. *supra*, section 2.1.4) neither provided clarity nor caused the Court to fully exercise its powers.

Discussions about the meaning of the concept 'full jurisdiction' often touch upon one or more of the following three interrelated elements: (1) the power to review facts and/or law, (2) the standard or intensity of review: marginal control or making an own assessment, and (3) the power not only to annul a decision but to give a final decision on the substance.

There is legal scholarship which suggests that the concept of full jurisdiction should be limited to the power to give a final decision on the substance of the case, replacing the decision given by the NCA.[137]

For a long time, the Court of Appeal gave a limited interpretation to its power to substitute the NCA's decision withits own. In *Ordre des Pharmaciens* I (2009), the Court of Appeal stated, for example (unofficial translation):

> '38. [...], the court does not in principle substitute its decision for that of the [NCA]. It cannot put its own assessment of the incriminating and discharging elements in place of that of the [NCA], any more than it can submit elements of the investigation report to the parties to the case on its own initiative with a view to establishing the existence of an infringement which the [NCA] has not established.
>
> Conversely, the Court cannot decide that there is no need to find an infringement if the [NCA] has concluded that there is such an infringement (...).
>
> 39. This principle is subject to exceptions only in cases where the court may substitute a decision for the contested decision without encroaching on the exclusive competence of the [NCA].
>
> This is the case where, in the event of annulment of the contested decision, the new decision to be taken follows directly and inevitably from the relevant failings on which the contested decision was based and where these failings leave no margin of appreciation which falls within the exclusive competence of the Council as a competition authority.
>
> This is not the case where a decision is annulled solely on the basis of a formal defect, but its content is otherwise legally justified'.[138]

136. R. Tijs, *Algemeen bestuursrecht in hoofdlijnen*, Antwerp, Intersentia, 2012, 266.
137. H. Gilliams, '"Volle rechtsmacht" en de rol van het hof van beroep in de toepassing van het mededingingsrecht', in X., *Mijlpalen uit het Belgisch mededingingsrecht geannoteerd. Liber amicorum Jules Stuyck*, Mechelen, Kluwer, 2013, 294.
138. Brussels 7 April 2009, 2007/MR/5, https://www.bma-abc.be/sites/default/files/content/download/files/20090407_cab_2007mr5_ordre_des_pharmaciens_ad.pdf.

This Court gave the following justification for this view (unofficial translation):

> '36. The Court has already considered that the legislator did not designate it as a competition authority. It has deduced from this that in the exercise of its full jurisdiction (...), it cannot exercise the same powers as the [NCA].
>
> (...)
>
> 37. (....) in the exercise of its full jurisdiction, the Court examines the grounds of the contested decision in the light of all the relevant facts and rules.
>
> Its review of the facts extends to the question of whether they have been correctly established, their reliability and their overall consistency. It also covers the relevance of the facts, their correct assessment by the competition authority and the conclusions drawn from them.
>
> Within the limits of the appeal and with due regard to the public policy nature of the Competition Act, the court shall review compliance with the procedural rules and the duty to state reasons, the application of the substantive law to these facts and, where appropriate, determine whether an excess of power may have been committed'.[139]

Where the Court considers the NCA to have discretionary powers, it will therefore only examine whether the NCA could legally reach the contested decision. This implies a marginal review of the NCA's decision. This view is all the more remarkable since it was given under the 2006 Competition Act, which gave the Court of Appeal very broad powers, including the power to ask the IPS to undertake further investigations and to take into account developments that took place after the NCA gave its decision (cf. *supra*, section 2.1.4).

Nevertheless, this approach was confirmed by the Supreme Court in 2011 in relation to a case decided by the Court of Appeal outside the scope of this research (*Honda*, unofficial translation):

> 'When an unrestricted appeal is lodged against a decision of the Council concerning a restrictive competition practice which is found and a fine is imposed, the Brussels Court of Appeal is not obliged to conduct a new investigation or to decide of its own motion, to subject elements of the investigation to a debate with a view to establishing the infringement.
>
> It may (...), limit its review to the questions as to whether the procedural requirements and the requirement to state reasons have been complied with. It may also, as regards the substance of the case, limit the review to whether the facts are correctly stated, whether there is no manifest error of assessment of the facts and whether the legal qualification of the facts is correct, whereby the Court of Appeal assesses whether the evidence adduced constitutes the relevant factual framework for the assessment of the infringement and can support the conclusions drawn from it.
>
> It must assess whether the restrictive practice has been established or not on the basis of the facts established by the Court of Appeal. It must itself determine whether, on the basis of the established facts, a fine is due and, if any, the amount of the fine'.[140]

---

139. Brussels 7 April 2009, 2007/MR/5, https://www.bma-abc.be/sites/default/files/content/download/files/20090407_cab_2007mr5_ordre_des_pharmaciens_ad.pdf.
140. Cass. AR C.09.0227.N, 3 June 2011, *Honda Motor Europe (North) GmbH / Belgische Staat, Occasiemarkt bvba, Erx nv e.a.*, https://www.abc-bma.be/sites/default/files/content/

This point of view is in line with the older case law of the Court of Justice regarding the General Court's review of Commission decisions. However, in two decisions of 8 December 2011, *Chalkor* and *KME*, the Court of Justice moved to a more intensive review, in line with the case law of the ECHR on Article 6 of the ECHR.[141]

In *Honda* (2011), the Supreme Court held that the claimant had not sufficiently argued why competition investigations would be of a criminal nature.[142] Moreover, at that time, the Competition Authority was not an administrative body but an administrative court.

It should be mentioned, however, that in *Honda*, the Supreme Court had already accepted that the Court of Appeal has the power to make its own assessment as to whether a fine is to be imposed and to determine its amount.[143] This implies that a 'fuller' review was accepted with regard to the *fine* as opposed to the *existence of an infringement*.[144]

In legal scholarship, it has been argued that where an appeal is brought by the undertaking which has been held to infringe the competition rules, Article 6, § 1 ECHR requires the Court of Appeal not to limit itself to a marginal review of the legality of the NCA's decision, but to make its own assessment as to whether the infringement is proven.[145]

Support for this view is found in the Court of Appeal's decision in *Vebic* (unofficial translation):[146]

download/files/20110603_hvc_c090227n_motorfietsen.pdf, *Arr.Cass.* 2011/6-7-8, 1463, opinion C. Vandewal, *JT* 2011/6454, 758 with case note by F. Louis, *Jaarboek Marktpraktijken* 2011, 1049, with case note by H. Gilliams, *Pas.* 2011/6-8, 1583, opinion C. Vandewal, *RDC* 2012/10, 985 with case note by H. Gilliams, *RCB* 2012/1, 19 with case note by D. Gerard and B. Gielen. Note that the Supreme Court's interpretation of full jurisdiction is even more restrictive than that of the Court of Appeal in *Ordre des Pharmaciens I* where the concept 'manifestly incorrect' is not used.

141. Case C-386/10 P, *Chalkor*, EU:C:2011:815; Case C-272/09 P, *KME*, EU:C:2011:810.
142. Cass. AR C.09.0227.N 3 June 2011, *Honda*, https://www.abc-bma.be/sites/default/files/content/download/files/20110603_hvc_c090227n_motorfietsen.pdf, *Arr.Cass.* 2011/6-7-8, 1463, opinion C. Vandewal, *JT* 2011/6454, 758, opinion C. Vandewal, note F. Louis, *Jaarboek Marktpraktijken* 2011, 1049, note H. Gilliams, *Pas.* 2011/6-8, 1583, opinion C. Vandewal, *RDC* 2012/10, 985, note H. Gilliams, *RCB* 2012/1, 19, note D. Gerard and B. Gielen.
143. Cass. AR C.09.0227.N, 3 June 2011, *Honda*, para. 3. *Contra*: Brussels 2 February 2009, 2005/MR/3, *Honda*, https://www.abc-bma.be/sites/default/files/content/download/files/20090202_hvbb_2005mr3-4_occasiemarkt_hondamotoreurope_ta.pdf, para. 81 (marginal assessment regarding the fine). *See also*: Brussels 27 September 2013, 2012/MR/5, *Presstalis*, https://www.bma-abc.be/sites/default/files/content/download/files/20130927_cdc_2012mr5_presstalis.pdf, para. 16; P.-J. Van de Weyer, *De rechterlijke toetsing van bestuursrechtelijke handelingen*, Antwerp, Intersentia, 2020, 515.
144. P.-J. Van de Weyer, *ibid.*, 511 et seq.
145. H. Gilliams, '"Volle rechtsmacht" en de rol van het hof van beroep in de toepassing van het mededingingsrecht', in X., *Mijlpalen uit het Belgisch mededingingsrecht geannoteerd. Liber amicorum Jules Stuyck*, Mechelen, Kluwer, 2013, 296-297.
146. *Ibid.*, 299. Support can also be found in Cass. 20 December 2013, AR H.13.0001.F, *Jaarboek Marktpraktijken* 2013, 1302, *Pas.* 2013/12, 2688, opinion D. Vandermeersch, *RDC* 2014/3, 323, *RDC* 2014/3, 256, note E. De Lophem, *RCB* 2014/1, 41, note (a preliminary referral made to the Belgian Supreme Court by the Court of Appeal in *Belgacom*. *See and compare* P.-J. Van de Weyer, *De rechterlijke toetsing van bestuursrechtelijke handelingen*, Antwerp, Intersentia, 2020, 516.

> '29. However, following the annulment of the contested decision, the court, by virtue of its full jurisdiction, is required to examine whether, on the basis of regularly established facts that may emerge from the investigation file, there are grounds to find proved against the appellant the offence charged against her by the reasoned report'.

Moreover, in *Holcim* (2016), the Court of Appeal seemed to believe it was at least entitled to make its own assessment of the case rather than a mere analysis of the legality of the NCA's decision and to substitute its own decision for that of the NCA (within the limits set by the CEL, unofficial translation):

> 'The court may examine all the elements submitted to the debates, give its own interpretation to the writings produced by both sides, which may differ from those of the Competition Prosecutor and the Council, analyse the factual context of the case, respond to the parties' pleas in a different way than the Council by substituting its own reasons for those of the Council, annul the Decision and substitute its own, and assess the penalties in the light of the principle of proportionality. It could also order the production of documents or the hearing of witnesses.'[147]

The power to obtain additional facts, interpret the evidence submitted and substitute its own decision for the contested decision clearly goes further than a pure legality assessment. References to a marginal assessment, such as a 'manifest incorrect assessment', are also absent. Full jurisdiction appears to have become 'fuller' than before.

Still, legal scholarship was divided over the question of whether there has been a real shift in the case law since even in more recent cases, references to legality control and marginal control appear.[148] In particular, in a case decided in 2020, the Markets Court stated that its task mainly consists of controlling the legality and the regularity of the administrative decision. Even where it has the power to substitute its own decision for that of the College, the question of substitution only arises after the contested decision has been annulled. The appellant needs to prove that the contested decision is irregular or illegal (in a broad sense, including, for example, principles of good government). Only then, the Court may substitute its own decision with that of the College. The Court does not need to decide on arguments of a political nature or arguments questioning the desirability of the contested decision. According to the Court, this follows from the separation of powers between the judiciary and the executory branch of the government.[149]

The Court of Appeal/Markets Court frequently refers to EU case law in support of its views.[150] In *Brabomills*,[151] the Court of Appeal, for example, referred to *Salzgitter*

147. Brussels 10 November 2016, 2013/MR/2, *Bpost*, https://www.bma-abc.be/sites/default/files/content/download/files/20161110_cab_2013mr2_bpost.pdf, *RDC* 2017/8, 865, note J. Dewispelaere, *RCB* 2017/1, 4, para. 58.
148. *Pro:* L. Corbett and A Nys, 'De rechter en de mededinging', *RCB* 2017/3, 245-246. *Contra:* P.-J. Van de Weyer, *De rechterlijke toetsing van bestuursrechtelijke handelingen*, Antwerp, Intersentia, 2020, 516.
149. N. Neyrinck, *Manuel de droit belge de la concurrence*, Brussels, Bruylant, 2021, 565-566.
150. The same goes for the NCA.

Mannesmann[152] in relation to anonymous evidence and to Toshiba[153] in relation to the *non bis in idem* principles.[154] In *Presstalis*, the Court of Appeal included a long quote from *TeliaSonera*[155] in relation to the fact that the abuse and its effect may occur on different markets and a shorter reference to *Tomra* in relation to exclusivity rebates.[156] Even in purely national cases, EU case law is discussed. This occurred, for example, in *Ordre des Pharmaciens I*,[157] where the Court decided that the *Wouters* criteria were not satisfied. In *Ordre des Pharmaciens II*, the Markets Court referred to *Lufthansa* in support of its statement that the exceptions to the principle of full jurisdiction are to be interpreted restrictively. It did not have powers mirroring those of the General Court but held that it was entitled to carry out a review that was at least as intensive. It did not specify why the intensiveness of its review could exceed that of the General Court. In *Professional soccer*, the Court of Appeal referred in support of its decision to the Commission's decision in *UEFA Champions League*,[158] *Bundesliga*[159] and *Premier League*[160] and set aside the Commission's decision in *ARD*[161] and the CFI case *Eurovision*,[162] both invoked by the applicants as being irrelevant given the different factual circumstances. In *Holcim*, it referred to the Court of Justice's case law in, *inter alia*, *Visa* in relation to the application in competition law matters of the principle that a decision has to be given within a reasonable time.[163]

A preliminary reference to the Court of Justice was only made in *Vebic*, a case in which, somewhat surprisingly, only Belgian competition law applied (cf. *supra*, section 2.1.3 and *infra*, Concluding Remarks).

6 CONCLUDING REMARKS

Appeals have been brought before a specialised court since the 1991 Competition Act. Originally, the legislator sought to ensure that specialisation was achieved by giving

151. Brussels 12 March 2014, 2013/MR/6, *Brabomills*, https://www.bma-abc.be/sites/default/files/content/download/files/20140312_cab_hvbb_brabomills_eindarrest.pdf, *Jaarboek Marktpraktijken* 2014, 1139, note H. Gilliams, *RCB* 2014/2, 108.
152. Case C-411/04 P, *Salzgitter Mannesmann*, EU:C:2007:54, ECR 2007 I-00959.
153. Case C-17/10, *Toshiba*, EU:C:2012:72.
154. The Court of Appeal mentioned that it was aware of criticism on this CJEU decision in national legal scholarship but that it nevertheless has to decide in accordance with it.
155. Case C-52/09 P, *TeliaSonera*, EU:C:2011:83.
156. Case C-549/10 P, *Tomra*, EU:C:2012:221.
157. Brussels 7 April 2009, 2007/MR/5, *Ordre des Pharmaciens I*, https://www.bma-abc.be/sites/default/files/content/download/files/20090407_cab_2007mr5_ordre_des_pharmaciens_ad.pdf.
158. UEFA Champions League (Case COMP/C.2-37.398) Commission Decision 2003/778/EC, *OJ* L291 8 November 2003, 25.
159. *German Bundesliga* (Case COMP/C.2/37.214) Commission Decision 2005/396/EC, *OJ* L134, 27 May 2005, 46.
160. *FA Premier League* (Case COMP/38.173) Commission Decision 2006/868/EC, *OJ* C7, 12 January 2008, 18.
161. *ARD* (Case IV/31.734) Commission Decision 89/536/EEC, *OJ* L284, 3 October 1989, 36.
162. Joined cases T-185/00, T-216/00, T-299/00 and T-300/00, *Métropole Télévision SA (M6)*, EU:T:2002:242, ECR 2002 II-03805.
163. Case T-461/07, *Visa*, ECLI:EU:T:2011:181, ECR 2011 II-01729.

the Brussels' Court of Appeal exclusive jurisdiction to hear appeals of cases of the competition authority, which was, at the time, the Competition Council, an administrative court. By internal regulations of the Court of Appeal, competition appeals were centralised to allow for specialised judges to deal with those cases. In certain periods, all competition appeals were brought before the same chamber; in other periods, a linguistic distinction was made, and cases in Dutch were brought before one chamber, while cases in French were brought before another one. In 2019, a specialised Court of Appeal, the Markets Court, was created as a special section within the Brussels Court of Appeal and was given exclusive jurisdiction to hear appeals of economic regulators and of the competition authority, which, since 2013, had become an autonomous administrative authority.

An important change in the institutional organisation of the competition authority was triggered by a preliminary reference of the Court of Appeal to the Court of Justice in *Vebic*. Before *Vebic*, Belgium had a judicial system of competition enforcement, where an administrative service acted as the prosecutor and the decision on the existence of an infringement and the sanction was taken by an administrative court. As in any appeal against a judicial decision, the court that adopted the contested decision was not a party in the appeal. According to the Court of Justice in *Vebic*, the absence of the competition authority as a party in the appeal was incompatible with the efficient enforcement of competition law. Therefore, the 2013 competition law reform created the BCA as an autonomous administrative authority entitled to act as a party in the appeal against its decision. Strictly speaking, the 'appeal' is since no longer an appeal in the technical sense but rather a 'review' of an administrative decision.

Since 1991, the appellate court has had 'full jurisdiction'. The concrete meaning of this concept has been disputed ever since. Even the most detailed and extensive description of the powers included in the Court's full jurisdiction in the 2006 Competition Act neither provided clarity nor caused the Court to fully exercise its powers. Nevertheless, insofar as final decisions in infringement cases are concerned, the number of cases where the Court of Appeal limited itself to annulling an NCA decision and referring it back to the NCA has been limited.

The most important outcomes of the quantitative analysis are the following: more than half of the appeals have been at least partially accepted. Procedural grounds have the highest success rate, followed by grounds relating to the substance. Understandably, most of the appeals are launched by undertakings on which the NCA imposed a fine. Most appeals concern cases where Article 101 TFEU and its national equivalent were applied, followed by cases where Article 102 TFEU and its national equivalent were applied and finally, the national equivalent of Article 101 TFEU. Appeals in cases relating to anticompetitive agreements mainly concern cases of infringements by-object. Appeals in abuse cases exclusively concerned exclusionary abuses. Appeals appear to have become more frequent since 2013. Only the future can tell whether this trend will be confirmed.

CHAPTER 5

Bulgaria Report

Alexandr Svetlicinii & Anton Dinev[*]

1 INTRODUCTION TO THE COMPETITION LAW ENFORCEMENT CONTEXT IN BULGARIA

1.1 Historical Outline

Enforcement of competition rules in Bulgaria has been driven primarily by the process of the country's accession into the European Union during the late 1990s and early 2000s. Key prohibitions against anti-competitive conduct, such as restrictive agreements and abuse of dominance, as well as a mandatory merger control framework, essentially copied their EU counterparts. Moreover, the institutional model of administrative enforcement by a single competition authority and many procedural rules mirrored the system of enforcement set out at the EU level for the European Commission. Historically, however, Bulgarian competition law has been more concerned with unfair competition than checking anti-competitive market power.

As early as 1940, the *Law against Dishonest Competition*[1] prohibited, subject to civil and administrative liability and sanctions, a number of unfair competition practices (false or misleading advertising, unauthorised substitution, trademark infringements, offering of free gifts for sales promotion purposes, etc.). It is unclear whether, and to what extent, that statute was effectively applied during and immediately after Bulgaria's involvement in World War II, but it became *lettre morte* with the adoption of the Constitution of 1947 and was eventually repealed in 1951, along with

* In accordance with ASCOLA's Declaration of Ethics, I confirm that I have no conflicts of interest. Any and all views, errors, and omissions are solely my own. ORCID 0000-0003-1795-0240.

1. Law against Dishonest Competition (*Закон против непочтената конкуренция*), *State Gazette* No. 270, 29 November 1940.

all other legislation in force by 9 September 1944.[2] For a long period thereafter, unfair competition was only prohibited by virtue of Article 10*bis* of the 1883 Paris Convention for the Protection of Industrial Property, which Bulgaria ratified in 1965.[3] As the country moved to gradually liberalise its struggling economy in the late 1980s, *Decree No. 56 on the Economic Activity*[4] allowed nationals as well as foreigners to register firms and conduct business under State supervision, thus paving the way for the first comprehensive competition legislation.

Although it was adopted during the last days of the Constitution of 1971, the 1991 *Law on the Protection of Competition* (LPC)[5] was instrumental in ensuring a smooth democratic transition[6] before and after the adoption of the current Constitution of 1991. Most notably, it consolidated the previous prohibitions of unfair competition with modern antitrust rules on anti-competitive agreements, abuse of dominance or monopoly, acts or decisions by public authorities resulting in a legal or *de facto* monopoly, *ex ante* control of mergers and restrictive agreements. A 'monopoly position' was defined as either the exclusive right to conduct a certain economic activity or the possession of a 35% share of the national market for that economic activity. Abusing such a 'monopoly position' to restrict competition or harm the interests of consumers included exclusionary conduct and exploitative abuses, such as unfair terms and conditions, economic duress, and monopoly prices. Mergers that may lead to a 'monopoly position' were prohibited as well, subject to prior notification and approval by the competition authority. Similar approval was necessary for agreements setting uniform contractual conditions to the extent they did not affect the free negotiation of prices, restrict competition, and harm the interests of consumers.

This relatively short piece of legislation, with only twenty-five articles, was the subject of vigorous but largely ineffective enforcement by the Commission for the Protection of Competition (CPC), the first independent, specialised administrative authority in charge of competition policy in Bulgaria. Under the 1991 legislation, the CPC could open a case *ex officio* or upon complaint, but the final decision on the merits and the imposition of penalties was left to the respective district court where the competition infringement took place. Between 1991 and 1995, the CPC dealt with 910 cases, 56 (6%) *ex officio* and 854 (94%) complaints, 521 (57%) of which were investigated, resulting in 110 (12%) petitions to the competent courts.[7] Although 434 (51%) of all complaints were filed by competitors, only 157 (36%) led to an investigation. By contrast, complaints by individual consumers (91 or 10%), consumer organisations (122 or 14%), and trade unions (36 or 4%) were successful at rates of

2. Law repealing all legislation enacted prior to 9 September 1944 (*Закон за отменяване на всички закони, издадени до 9 септември 1944 г*), *State Gazette* No. 93, 20 November 1950.
3. Decree No. 633, *State Gazette* No. 75, 24 September 1965.
4. *State Gazette* No. 4, 13 January 1989.
5. *State Gazette* No. 39, 17 May 1991.
6. It is no coincidence that one of the very first complaints under the 1991 LPC concerned an alleged abuse of dominance in the newspaper distribution sector, CPC Decision No. 6, 16 December 1991, *Bulgarian Post and Telecommunications*, Case 21/1991.
7. Bernard Hoekman and Simeon Djankov, Competition Law in Post-Central Planning Bulgaria, 45 Antitrust Bulletin 1 (2000), CEPR Discussion Paper No. 1723, November 1997, pp. 1-19, available at https://repec.cepr.org/repec/cpr/ceprdp/DP1723.pdf.

80%, 67%, and 53%, respectively.[8] Importantly, 374 (72%) of the 521 investigations concerned unfair competition, followed by 104 (20%) abuse of dominance cases, and only 15 (12%) that dealt with anti-competitive agreements.[9] These figures are consistent with the competition law enforcement statistics for other Eastern European jurisdictions during the same period, in so far as the focus on unfair competition and (exploitative) abuses of dominance are concerned.[10] They also paint a picture that still holds true today: complaints are the main driver for enforcement, even though the prohibitions of anti-competitive agreements and exclusionary abuses of dominance remain relatively under-enforced.

Concerns about the overall effectiveness of its actions and the use of its resources led the CPC to propose several amendments to the 1991 LPC. However, it was the ratification of Bulgaria's European Association Agreement[11] and the European Commission's criticism of the country's slow progress towards a functioning market economy that prompted the government to table a Draft Bill introducing a new LPC, which was adopted in 1998.[12] Significantly lengthier than its predecessor, with no less than sixty articles, the 1998 LPC kept the general prohibition of unfair competition, regulated in more detail various forms of unfair competition, and copied the relevant EC provisions on anti-competitive agreements and control of concentrations.[13] As for unilateral conduct, the concept of 'monopoly position' was limited to legal monopoly, whereas the 35% market share criterion served to define a 'dominant position' to the extent that market dominance could not be established using the *United Brands* criteria.[14] Moreover, a methodology to define the relevant market was adopted based on the EC notice of 1997.[15]

Even more important were the changes to the CPC's institutional setup and procedural rules, closely following those in Regulation 17/62.[16] In addition to the mandatory notification of agreements to benefit from an individual exemption, the competition authority's enforcement powers were strengthened, including broader

8. The authors note that with 910 cases, the CPC was ahead of its counterparts in Czechia (767), Poland (535), Slovakia (512), and Hungary (275) during 1992-1995.
9. *Ibid.*, p. 11.
10. John Fingleton et al., *Competition Policy and the Transformation of Central Europe*, CEPR, London, 1996, 235 p., Roger Mastalir, Regulation of Competition in the New Free markets of Eastern Europe: A Comparative Study of Antitrust Laws in Poland, Hungary, Czech and Slovak Republics and Their Models, 19 N.C.J. Int'l L. & Com. Reg. 61 (1993).
11. Europe Agreement establishing an association between the European Communities and their Member States, of the one part, and the Republic of Bulgaria, of the other part, OJ L 358, 1994, pp. 3-222. Article 64(2) of the Agreement required Bulgaria to make its rules on competition compatible with 'the criteria arising from the application of the rules of Articles 85, 86, and 92 of the Treaty establishing the European Economic Community'. On 7 October 1997, the Association Council adopted Implementing Rules for the competition provisions of the Europe Agreement applicable to undertakings.
12. *State Gazette* No. 52, 8 May 1998.
13. Jurian Langer, The New Bulgarian Competition Act, 11(2) European Business Law Review 102-104 (2000) DOI: 10.54648/271556.
14. Case 27/76, *United Brands*, ECLI:EU:C:1978:22.
15. Commission Notice on the definition of relevant market for the purposes of Community competition law, OJ C 372, 1997, pp. 5-13.
16. Council Regulation 17/62/EEC, First Regulation implementing Articles 85 and 86 of the Treaty, OJ P013, 1962, pp. 204-211.

investigation powers, new decision-making powers to find an infringement, issue cease-and-desist orders, grant individual exemptions, and impose pecuniary penalties. In 2003, the CPC was provided new advocacy powers and the power to conduct sector inquiries. At the same time, some ambiguous provisions were challenged by opposition MPs before the Constitutional Court. A landmark decision by that court,[17] which still guides competition enforcement in Bulgaria today, clarified that, unlike the Constitution of 1971, the current Constitution of 1991 does not allow administrative authorities to exercise jurisdictional functions and act as quasi-courts or tribunals. Therefore, the CPC's power to declare anti-competitive agreements null and void, which, at any rate, arises *ex lege* or decide disputes about the very existence of such a nullity and voidness, was held to be unconstitutional. Furthermore, CPC decisions could not bind civil courts hearing private enforcement actions to the extent that such a blanket binding effect ruled out any incidental juridical review.[18] On the other hand, ordering interim measures requiring the termination of a notified agreement, but not modification of it by the parties, was allowed by the Constitutional Court.

As expected, the 1998 LPC considerably improved the effectiveness of competition law enforcement in Bulgaria. As an integrated administrative authority with powers to investigate and decide cases on the merits, adopt interim measures, impose penalties, conduct sector inquiries, and actively engage in competition advocacy, the CPC's enforcement actions increased on average to 200-300 decisions per year applying competition rules.[19] Still, most of these concerned unfair competition and exploitative abuses of dominance, and there might have been even less enforcement against anti-competitive agreements and exclusionary abuses of dominance had it not been for the notification of agreements seeking individual exemptions and the duty for the CPC to address the merits of every admissible complaint it received.

The period around when Bulgaria joined the European Union in January 2007 saw the most intensive application of the national equivalents of Articles 101 and 102 TFEU. EU membership also meant that the CPC was able to cooperate effectively within the European Competition Network (ECN). Accordingly, a new LPC was enacted in 2008[20] to align Bulgarian competition law enforcement with Regulation 1/2003 and the EC Modernisation Package of 2004.[21] Most notably, it abandoned the notification system to exempt anti-competitive agreements and provided a legal basis for leniency

17. Const. Court Decision No. 22, 24 September 1998, *Law on the Protection of Competition*, Case 18/1998, *State Gazette* No. 112, 29 September 1998.
18. This does not apply to the very fact that an infringement of competition rules has been committed by the investigated undertaking(s), in which case a non-appealed CPC decision or the review court's judgment upon appeal will be binding on civil courts in follow-on actions (cf. Article 105(4) LPC, following the implementation of Directive 2014/104).
19. The CPC is also competent to apply the Law on Pubic Procurement and the Law on Concessions. A few hundred to a little over a thousand decisions are adopted yearly under the public procurement rules as the CPC hears appeals against public tenders by central and local administrative authorities across the country.
20. State Gazette No. 102, 28 November 2008.
21. Council Regulation (EC) No 1/2003 of 16 December 2002 on the implementation of the rules on competition laid down in Articles 81 and 82 of the Treaty, OJ L 1, 2003, pp. 1-25.

and private enforcement based on the recommendations in the EC White Paper,[22] while the CPC was still bound to consider the merits of all admissible complaints. As enforcement against agreements and unilateral conduct has been on the decline ever since, the 2008 legislation was amended substantially on three occasions. First, in 2015, a new prohibition against abuse of superior bargaining power (ABSP) was introduced in Article 37a LPC (repealed), expanding the existing rules on unfair competition to vertical B2B relations to regulate, in particular, unfair trading practices (UTPs) in the food supply chain.[23] Then, in 2018[24] and 2021,[25] Directive 2014/104 (Damages Directive),[26] Directive 2019/1 (ECN+ Directive),[27] and Directive 2019/633 (UTP Directive)[28] were implemented, significantly expanding both the scope and complexity of the 1998 LPC. At the time of writing, it comprises 120 articles and a lengthy list of 59 legal definitions – almost five times more than the 1991 LPC – and prohibits anti-competitive agreements, abuse of dominance, unfair competition, UTPs, and regulates mergers, public and private enforcement of all competition rules.

1.2 Enforcement Practices and Priorities

The Bulgarian CPC's institutional setup and exclusive competence to enforce competition rules across all sectors of the economy has remained unchanged over the years. Article 3 LPC defines it as an 'independent specialised public authority' and the national competition authority (NCA) 'in charge of applying the law of [the] European Union in the competition field'. Its members – a chairperson, a deputy chairperson, and five commissioners – are appointed for a term of seven years and are accountable to the National Assembly (Parliament). The CPC operates under an integrated enforcement model, with functional separation between investigation (case handlers within the so-called specialised administration) and decision-making (by a *collège* of commissioners). The chairperson may unilaterally adopt certain decisions, essentially of a procedural nature, but the final decisions (on the merits) in individual cases are adopted by

22. European Commission, *White Paper on damages actions for breach of the EC antitrust rules*, COM(2008) 165 final.
23. *State Gazette* No. 56, 24 July 2015. *See* Anton Dinev, 'National Report: Abuse of Superior Bargaining Power under Bulgarian Law,' in Anna Piszcz and Adam Jasser (eds), *Legislation Covering Business-to-business Unfair Trading Practices in the Food Supply Chain in Central and Eastern European Countries*, Warsaw, 2019, available at https://ssrn.com/abstract=3389333.
24. *State Gazette* No. 2, 3 January 2018.
25. *State Gazette* No. 17, 26 February 2021.
26. Directive 2014/104/EU of the European Parliament and of the Council of 26 November 2014 on certain rules governing actions for damages under national law for infringements of the competition law provisions of the Member States and of the European Union, OJ L 349, 2014, pp. 1-19.
27. Directive (EU) 2019/1 of the European Parliament and of the Council of 11 December 2018 to empower the competition authorities of the Member States to be more effective enforcers and to ensure the proper functioning of the internal market, OJ L 11, 2019, pp. 3-33.
28. Directive (EU) 2019/633 of the European Parliament and of the Council of 17 April 2019 on unfair trading practices in business-to-business relationships in the agricultural and food supply chain, OJ L 111, 2019, pp. 59-72.

the *collège* of commissioners.[29] In any case, the competition authority is now required to exercise its powers in full compliance with the general principles of EU law and the Charter of Fundamental Rights. It also must cooperate closely with the European Commission and the national competition authorities (NCAs) of other Member States, exchange information on a regular basis with them and provide assistance in cross-border investigations.[30]

Unlike the European Commission or other NCAs, the CPC historically did not have the power to set an *ex ante* enforcement agenda with respect to individual cases or complaints, i.e., choosing which complaint to investigate or not. However, it has always had an institutional discretion to organise its resources and focus on specific competition issues or economic sectors, especially such that have drawn a lot of public attention (e.g., food and fuel prices). Therefore, consistent with its mission to act in the interest of the economy, the consumers, and society as a whole, the CPC could set priorities to guide, in particular, its *ex officio* investigations, sector inquiries, or decisions to accept commitments.[31] These priorities would be publicised in the annual reports to the Parliament pursuant to Article 14 LPC, which would also provide a summary of how they had been achieved during the relevant year. Examples of CPC priorities over the years include improving administrative capacity, gaining experience with conducting on-site inspections (to enable future cooperation with the European Commission), developing a 'competition culture' among economic operators, advocating for legislative amendments to allow setting and using enforcement priorities in individual cases or requiring government and public authorities to report how they have acted upon the CPC's recommendations following sector inquiries, focusing on the most harmful competition infringements such as cartels and abuse of dominance and their prevention as well as effective sanctioning, or fighting unfair competition and abuse of superior bargaining position (ASBP), etc.

Following the implementation of the ECN + Directive in 2021,[32] the CPC can now reject individual complaints based on its enforcement priorities (Article 38(4) LPC) – a welcome change for which the competition authority had advocated since at least 2014. To ensure transparency,[33] it published two sets of priorities for 2022 and 2023 concerning Articles 101 and 102 TFEU and their national equivalents, including

29. Anton Dinev, 'The Regulation of Unfair Trading Practices in Bulgaria' in Bert Keirsbilck, Evelyne Terryn, Elisa Paredis, and Tom Verdonk (eds), Unfair Trading Practices in the Agricultural and Food Supply Chain: Implementation of Directive (EU) 2019/663 (1st edn, Intersentia 2004).
30. *Ibid.*
31. For example, CPC Decision No. 131, 9 February 2010, *2010 Guidelines on accepting commitments.*
32. *See* OECD, Annual Report on Competition Policy Developments in Bulgaria 2021, DAF/COMP/AR(2022)42, 23 May 2022, https://one.oecd.org/document/DAF/COMP/AR(2022)42/en/pdf, p. 4.
33. Setting enforcement priorities for individual cases is regulated by the CPC *Rules on Prioritisation Rules on Prioritising Requests [complaints] for Commencing Proceedings under Chapter IX* [Enforcement of Articles 101 and 102 TFEU and their national equivalents] *and Chapter XII* [Enforcement of the UTP prohibitions] *of the Law on the Protection of Competition, Sate Gazette* No. 51, 18 June 2022. CPC, Decision No. 606, 10 June 2021, Rules for prioritizing requests for initiation of proceedings under Chapter Nine and Chapter Twelve of the Law on Protection of Competition.

competition law enforcement, focus on the digital economy, healthcare, financial services, energy, sustainability, food, fuels, bid rigging, no-poach agreements. A separate set of enforcement priorities concerns the application of unfair competition and UTP rules.

2 JUDICIAL REVIEW OF CPC DECISIONS

Proceedings before the CPC are administrative in nature, similar to those before the European Commission and most NCAs across Europe, and are subject to judicial review by the Administrative Court – Sofia Region (ACSR) and the Supreme Administrative Court (SAC) (Article 64(1) LPC). Unlike other national legislation, however, the LPC includes both general (Articles 38-69 LPC) and specific procedural rules depending on the substantive rules enforced – anti-competitive agreements and abuse of dominance (Articles 70-77 LPC), control of concentrations (Articles 78-90 LPC), unfair competition and UTPs (Articles 94-98 LPC), sector enquiries and competition advocacy (Articles 91-92 LPC).

Alternative enforcement decisions are available under Article 60(1) LPC, including waiving or reducing fines for leniency applicants (Articles 60(1)(4) and 101 LPC), accepting mandatory commitments by the investigated undertaking(s) (Articles 60(1)(8) and 75(1)). Interim measures under Article 56 are available whenever there is a risk of serious and irreparable harm to competition and may be decided by the CPC, either *sua sponte* or at the request of the persons whose interests have been or could be affected by the competition law infringement.

2.1 First-Instance Appeal: ACSR (Three-Member Panel of the SAC Before 1 January 2019)

The legality or lawfulness (*zakonosaobraznost/zakonosaobraznost/законосъобразност*) of CPC decisions is controlled by the ACSR. The parties to the proceedings, as well as any third party with legal interest in the case, can appeal the final CPC decision within fourteen days of its communication to the parties or publication in the competition authority's electronic register (Article 64(1) LPC). Until 1 January 2019, such first-instance appeals were heard by a three-member panel of the Supreme Administrative Court ('SAC3').

In 2018, the Administrative Procedure Code (APC)[34] was amended to ensure more effective, transparent, and speedy administrative justice by limiting the SAC's jurisdiction to its core functions under Article 125(1) of the Constitution of 1991. Relieving it from first-instance appeals against individual administrative acts by central public authorities, such as the CPC, had been put forward and supported by the government, the judiciary, and practising lawyers, who pointed out the need for optimisation as well as institutional separation when hearing administrative appeals on points of law and fact and such on points of law only.

34. *Stage Gazette* No. 77, 18 September 2018.

The ACSR is one of the twenty-eight regional administrative courts which, together with the SAC, form the system of administrative justice in Bulgaria. As an administrative court, it is a 'specialised court' within the meaning of Article 119(2) of the Constitution of 1991 since all legal disputes generally fall within the jurisdiction of the ordinary courts in civil and criminal matters.[35] At the same time, the ACSR is not specialised *ratione materiae* in the judicial review or control of legality of enforcement decisions in competition or regulatory matters, similar to the UK Competition Appeal Tribunal (CAT), and may, in principle, hear first-instance appeals against any individual administrative act within its *ratione territoriae* jurisdiction. Still, a number of statutes designate it as the competent administrative court to review the legality of acts or decisions by the authorities or regulatory bodies, such as the CPC, the Financial Supervision Commission,[36] the Communication Regulation Commission,[37] or the Council for Electronic Media.[38] Moreover, internal specialisation is possible when the general assembly of judges at a given administrative court decides to establish specialist departments (chambers) hearing certain types of cases.

First-instance appeals before the ACSR are heard by a single judge (Article 164 APC). While the appeal automatically suspends the execution of the appealed administrative act or decision (Article 166(1) APC), a preliminary execution may be granted by the court at any point of the procedure (Article 167(1) APC). Grounds of appeal at this stage include: (i) lack of competence (jurisdiction), (ii) deviation from established forms, (iii) substantial violation of procedural rules, (iv) contradiction with substantive rules, (v) inconsistency with the law's objectives (Article 146 APC). The administrative authority, as well as any party that benefits from the appealed decision, bear the burden of establishing all points of fact therein (Article 170(1) APC). At the same time, the evidence presented in the proceedings before the administrative authority is admissible and valid in the appeal as well (Article 171(1) APC). Existing witness and expert testimony may be heard again, if necessary, and new evidence collected at the request of the parties. The appeal court may appoint *ex officio* new expert witnesses (Article 171(2) APC).

Within a month of the last sitting to hear the appeal against an administrative act or decision, the first-instance court has to decide the case and issue one of four types of judgment: (i) declare the appealed act or decision null and void, (ii) annul it, partially or in its entirety, (iii) amend it, or (iv) reject the appeal (Article 172(1) and (2) APC). As long as an issue does not fall within the discretion of the administrative authority that adopted the appealed decision, an administrative court, such as the ACSR (or the SAC3 prior to 2019), may decide the case on the merits following annulment or a declaration of nullity and voidness (Article 173(1) APC). Where the nullity stems from a lack of competence (jurisdiction) or the matter is such that it cannot be decided on the merits by the first-instance appeal court, the case is remanded

35. *See, e.g.*, Const. Court Decision No. 2, 14 February 2021, *Exclusive Jurisdiction of the Administrative Courts*, Case 1/2022, *State Gazette* No. 17, 21 February 2023.
36. Article 13(3) of the Law on the Financial Supervision Commission, *State Gazette* No. 8, 28 January 2003.
37. Article 35(2) of the Law on Electronic Communications, *State Gazette* No. 41, 22 May 2007.
38. Article 38 of the Law on Radio and Television, *State Gazette* No. 138, 24 November 1998.

to the competent administrative authority together with mandatory instructions on the correct interpretation and application of the law (Article 173(2) APC).

2.2 Second-Instance Appeal: SAC (Five-Member Panel of the SAC Before 1 January 2019)

First-instance judgments by the ACSR (or the SAC3 prior to 2019) can be appealed within fourteen days, in whole or part, on points of law only (*cassation/касация*) before the SAC3 (or a five-member panel of the Supreme Administrative Court ('SAC5') prior to 2019) (Articles 208 and 211(1) APC). Such *cassation* appeals in administrative matters are lodged via the lower court and aim to enable the SAC to 'carry out supreme judicial oversight of the correct and uniform application of the laws in administrative justice', which is its core function pursuant to Article 125(1) of the Constitution of 1991.

Any person that is legally bound and adversely affected by the appealed judgment, whether or not they were a party to the proceedings before the first-instance court, as well as the Chief Public Prosecutor (or a deputy in administrative matters), may lodge an appeal on points of law, alleging that the appealed judgment is either (i) null and void, (ii) inadmissible, or (iii) incorrect, as a result of violating the substantive rules, substantial violation of the procedural rules, or because of insufficient reasons (Articles 209 and 210 APC). The SAC3 (or the SAC5 prior to 2019) may verify *ex officio* each of these grounds (Article 218(2) APC). However, its assessment of the correct application of substantive rules can only be based on the facts established by the lower court (Article 220 APC).

Since the proceedings before the ACSR are public, oral, and adversarial, appeals on points of law before the SAC may be heard in a closed-door sitting, which could reduce the overall length of the *cassation* proceedings. If the appealed judgment is null and void, and there are no grounds to dismiss the case altogether, the SAC (or the SAC5 prior to 2019) will remand it to the first-instance administrative court (Article 221(5) APC). Where a lower court judgment is inadmissible, the case is dismissed within the appealed part, remanded for further hearing, or sent to the competent court or administrative authority (Article 221(3) APC). Finally, *cassation* appeals against incorrect judgments will either be rejected or result in their full or partial annulment (Article 221(2) APC). Upon annulment, the SAC3 (or the SAC5 prior to 2019) will decide the case on its merits unless (i) the first-instance judgment has been annulled on procedural grounds, or (ii) the available written evidence is insufficient to establish certain facts, the case is then remanded to the lower court in a different composition (Article 222 APC). In any case, where the appealed judgment is being annulled for a second time by the SAC, the case will have to be decided on the merits (Article 227(1) APC).

3 PRIOR RESEARCH

To the best of the authors' knowledge, there has not been another comprehensive, empirical study of competition law enforcement in Bulgaria since Hoekman and Djankov's CEPR discussion paper in 1997.[39] However, they only studied CPC enforcement activity and decisions between 1992 and 2005. Our report, therefore, aims to provide a complete and detailed overview of all judgments upon appeal against CPC decisions applying Articles 101 and 102 TFEU and/or their national equivalents from 1 May 2004 to 30 April 2021.

4 QUANTITATIVE ANALYSIS

4.1 Source of Information

All CPC decisions are published in its electronic register within fourteen days of their adoption. The review court judgments are likewise publicly available and have been retrieved from the SAC's website[40] and Bulgaria's centralised judicial system database.[41] For the purposes of the present report, we have identified an exhaustive pool of the following types of *enforcement decisions* adopted by the CPC between May 2004 and April 2021: (i) infringement decisions, (ii) no-ground-for-action findings, (iii) commitments, and (iv) individual administrative sanctions imposed in connection to an infringement of Articles 101 and 102 TFEU and/or the national equivalent provisions. This preliminary step allowed us to track all appeals against each of the CPC decisions in the pool, guaranteeing the robustness of our dataset and empirical findings.

4.2 Total Numbers of Judgments and Ratio of Appeals

Judicial review of CPC enforcement decisions has yielded a total of 396 judgments, from which 215 were rendered by the SAC in the first instance (three-member panels) and 181 in the second instance (five-member panels). The ratio of CPC's decisions subject to appeal is 42%. The ratio of the SAC's first-instance judgments appealed is 37%. One possible reason for the high rate of appeal is the relatively low cost of legal services[42] and very low court fees to be borne by the appellants in administrative cases.

39. Hoekman and Djankov, *supra* note 7.
40. Supreme Administrative Court (cases) https://info-adc.justice.bg/courts/portal/edis.nsf/e_cases.xsp?inst=administrative.
41. Electronic Court Cases (Republic of Bulgaria), https://ecase.justice.bg/Case/Search.
42. *See* European E-Justice Portal, information about the costs of justice in Bulgaria, https://e-justice.europa.eu/37/EN/costs?BULGARIA&member=1.

Given the substantial amounts of fines imposed by the CPC,[43] an appeal challenging the competition authority's decision and subsequent appeal of the first-instance judgment thus present an attractive option for undertakings targeted by the NCA's infringement decisions. It is also an inexpensive procedural venue for the complainants dissatisfied with the CPC's decision finding no grounds for action.

4.3 Judgments per Year

Figure 5.1 summarises the number of judgments issued by the two instances of the Bulgarian courts per year.

Figure 5.1 Number of Judgments According to Instances

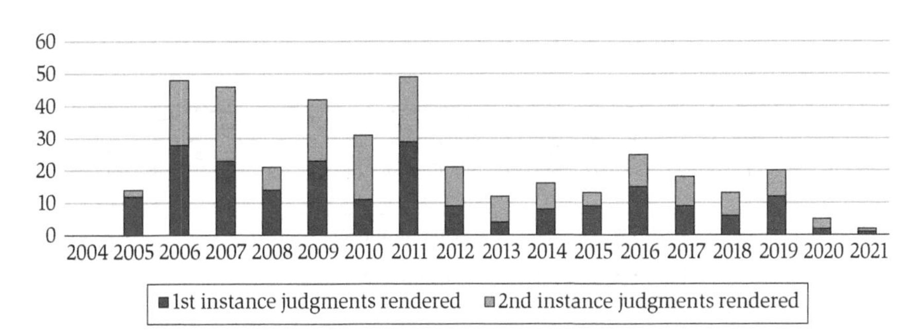

The changes in the number of judgments across the years can be explained with reference to the number of decisions issued by the CPC or the number of first-instance judgments rendered by the SAC. As Figures 5.2(a) and (b) demonstrate, in the vast majority of cases, each CPC's decision has been subject to a single first-instance judgment, and each appealed first-instance judgment has been dealt with by a single SAC's judgment.

43. *See, e.g.*, Zoya Todorova, Bulgaria: First-instance court confirms a fine of over €8 million on the distributor of Hyundai in Bulgaria for several hard-core vertical restrictions (Kluwer Competition Law Blog, 17 January 2017), https://competitionlawblog.kluwercompetitionlaw.com/2017/01/17/bulgaria-first-instance-court-confirms-a-fine-of-over-e-8-mln-on-the-distributor-of-hyundai-in-bulgaria-for-several-hard-core-vertical-restrictions/.

Figure 5.2(a) First-Instance Judgments

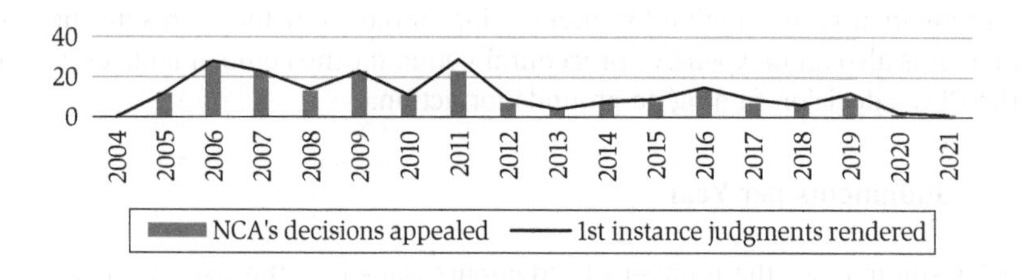

Figure 5.2(b) Second-Instance Judgments

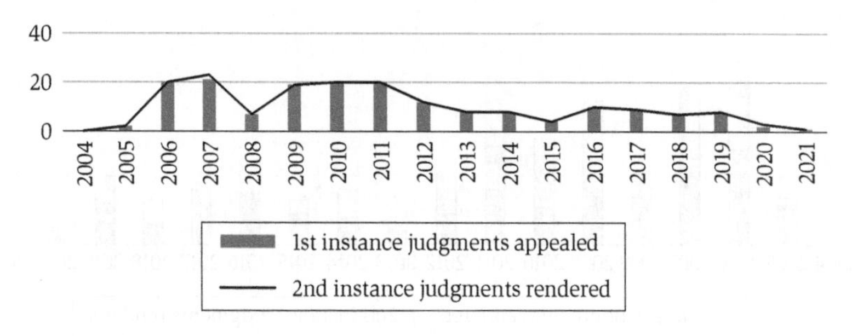

Figure 5.2(a) suggests that 2006, 2009, and 2011 were peak years in terms of the number of first-instance judgments rendered by the SAC. These trends generally follow the enforcement efforts of the CPC in terms of the number of infringement decisions issued and the number of undertakings concerned.

4.4 Success Rates and Outcomes

Figure 5.3 demonstrates the success rate of appeals and includes both appeals against the CPC decisions and appeals against the first-instance judgments rendered by SAC. The success rates shown in Figure 5.3 relate to the outcomes of all appeals, taking into account that separate appeals launched against the same CPC decision or the previous instance judgment were aggregated and counted as a single case. The category 'Number of partially successful appeals' includes cases where either certain parts of the infringement decision were overturned or set aside, as well as cases where the original penalty imposed by the CPC was reduced.

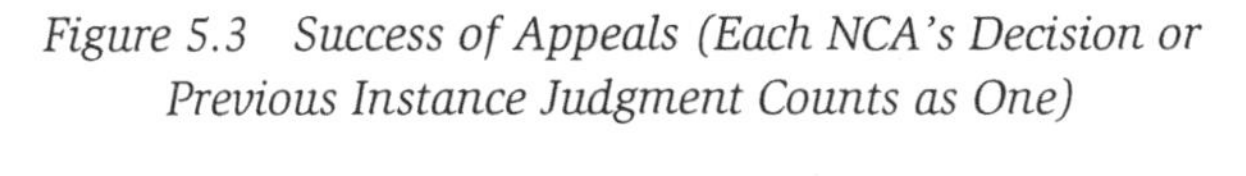

Figure 5.3 Success of Appeals (Each NCA's Decision or Previous Instance Judgment Counts as One)

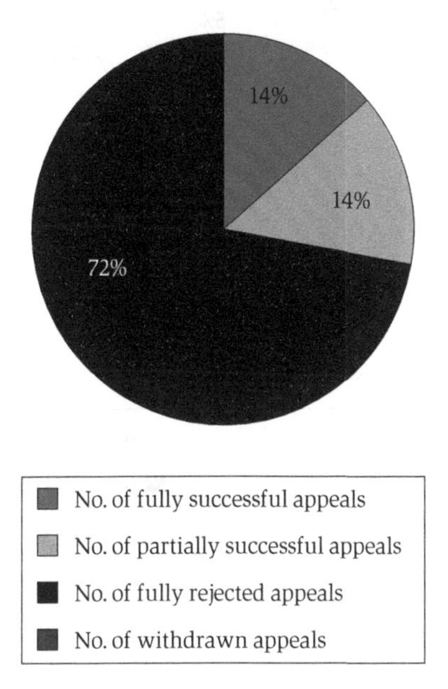

The observed rate of success is relatively low - only in 14% of the cases was an appeal fully successful, while in 14% of the cases, the appeal was partially successful. Despite the high ratio (72%) of fully rejected appeals, it does not discourage appellants from seeking to challenge decisions due to the low stakes of launching an appeal, as discussed above. The success rates are further substantiated in the following Figure 5.4(a), which identifies the specific outcomes of the appeals. Unlike Figure 5.3, it examines each appeal judgment separately.

Figure 5.4(a) First-Instance Outcome

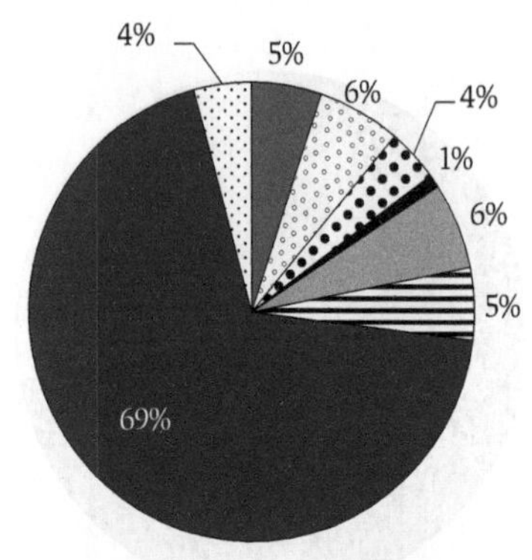

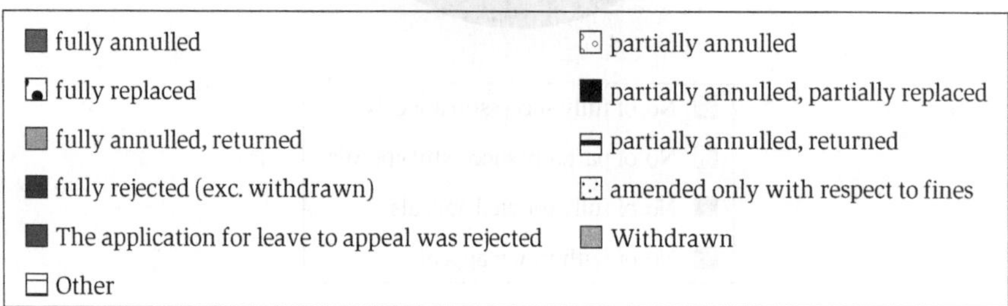

The above Figure 5.4(a) highlights that appeals were slightly more successful in the first-instance, and the outcomes of appeals that were not fully rejected were as follows: full annulment and return of the case to CPC for repeated examination (6%), partial annulment of the CPC decision (6%), full annulment (5%), partial annulment and return of the case to CPC (5%), full replacement of the CPC decision with the SAC judges deciding on the merits of the case (4%). The absence of a clear trend in the outcome of appeals when the SAC finds errors in the CPC's findings and interpretations of the law is due to case-specific circumstances. For the most part, in cases where the CPC failed to collect sufficient evidence that would allow the SAC to decide on the merits, the case is returned to the CPC for repeated investigation. In cases where the defect in the decision consists of the erroneous interpretation of the legal provisions, the SAC does not hesitate to rule on the merits of the case. For example, in 2015, SAC5 disagreed both with the CPC and the SAC3 when determining the requisite conditions for finding an abuse of dominant position in the form of imposing unfair trading conditions.[44] The court examined the standard terms and conditions of the dominant supplier of natural gas. While the CPC and the SAC3 considered that the right of the supplier to unilaterally terminate the supply contract and the obligations of the buyers

44. SAC5, Judgment 10524 of 12 October 2015 in case 9059/2015.

to provide certain additional information should be viewed as an abuse of dominance, the SAC5 emphasised that in the absence of any restriction of competition or prejudice to consumer interests, the specified contractual terms should not be viewed as abusive under the applicable competition rules.

Figure 5.4(b) Second-Instance Outcome

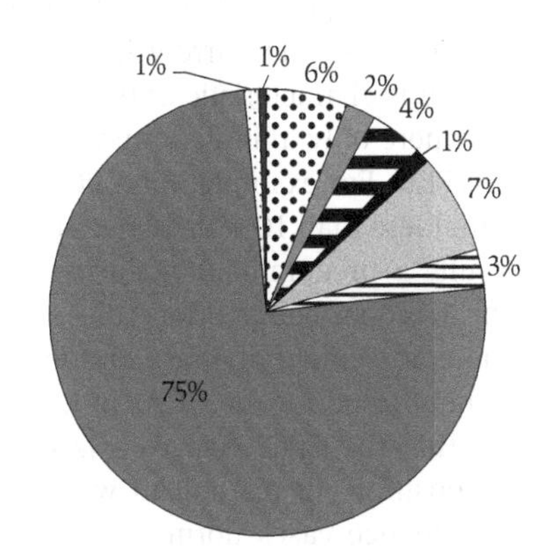

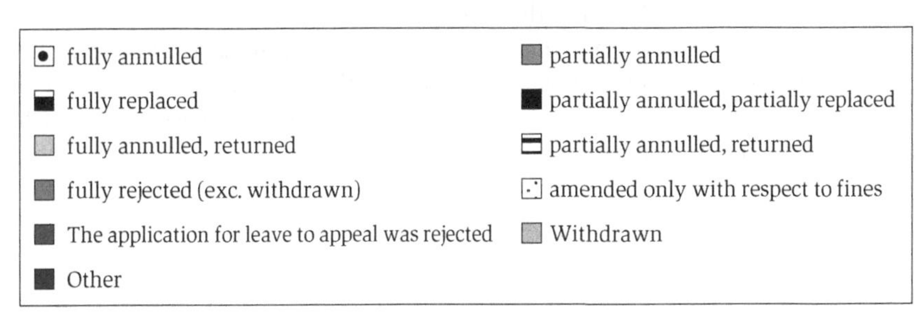

The above Figure 5.4(b) offers a similar picture in relation to the second-instance outcomes where a five-member panel of the SAC is reviewing a first-instance judgment rendered by a three-member panel of the same court.[45] The rate of rejected second-instance appeals is somewhat higher, reaching 75%. In relation to successful appeals, cases involving full annulment and return (7%) and full annulment (6%) are slightly higher than in the case of first-instance appeals. The number of cases involving partial annulments and returns is very low due to the fact that the procedural deficiencies on the part of the CPC are normally established at the first level of appeal, and if the CPC

45. *See, e.g.*, Dessislava Fessenko, The Bulgarian Supreme Administrative Court upholds the Competition Authority's decision sanctioning the telecom incumbent for exerting margin squeeze on its competitors in the markets for fixed telephone services *(Bulgarian Telecommunication Company)*, 9 January 2008, e-Competitions January 2008, Article N° 15516.

chooses to appeal, the case will be rejected by the second-instance court. The presence of the full annulment and return cases reflects the differences in interpretation of the law between the first- and second-instance courts.

4.5 Type of NCA's Decisions Subject to Appeal

The empirical findings summarised in Figure 5.5 below reflect two general trends in the enforcement practices of the CPC. *First*, the narrow interpretation of the 'effect on trade' criterion by the CPC, which is characteristic of the NCAs in the 'new' Member States,[46] leads to the situation where only a limited number of decisions concern the application of Article 101/102 TFEU. For example, the CPC's enforcement records for the period 2007-2013 suggest that less than 10% of all decisions issued applied the EU competition rules.[47] As a result, a predominant majority of judicial review cases concern the application of the national competition rules only. *Second*, the CPC is traditionally more active in the enforcement of abuse of dominance cases,[48] which is another characteristic enforcement trend for the NCAs in the 'new' Member States.[49] This is largely due to the fact that the CPC receives a large number of complaints alleging abuse of a dominant position, in relation to which it is required to react. Furthermore, the abuse of dominance cases normally do not present a significant evidentiary burden for the CPC, and the available evidence allows it to issue infringement decisions on a larger scale than in cases involving alleged anti-competitive practices, which require more substantial investigative action on the part of the competition authority. As a result, 71% of the judicial review cases concern the application of the national abuse of dominance prohibition.

46. *See* Marco Botta, Alexandr Svetlicinii, and Maciej Bernatt, 'The Assessment of the Effect on Trade by the National Competition Authorities of the "New" Member States: Another Legal Partition of the Internal Market?' 52(5) Common Market Law Review 1247-1276 (2015) DOI: 10.54648/cola2015103.
47. *Ibid.*, p. 1275.
48. *See, e.g.*, Alexandr Svetlicinii, The Bulgarian Competition Authority fines the National Health Insurance Fund for imposing maximum retail margins for medicines sold under the national health insurance scheme *(National Health Insurance Fund)*, 1 July 2010, e-Competitions July 2010, Article N° 32776.
49. *See* Alexandr Svetlicinii and Marco Botta, 'Article 102 TFEU as a Tool for Market Regulation: 'Excessive Enforcement' Against 'Excessive Prices' in the New EU Member States and Candidate Countries', 8(3) European Competition Journal 473-496 (2012) DOI: 10.5235/ecj.8.3.473.

Figure 5.5 Rule Being Appealed

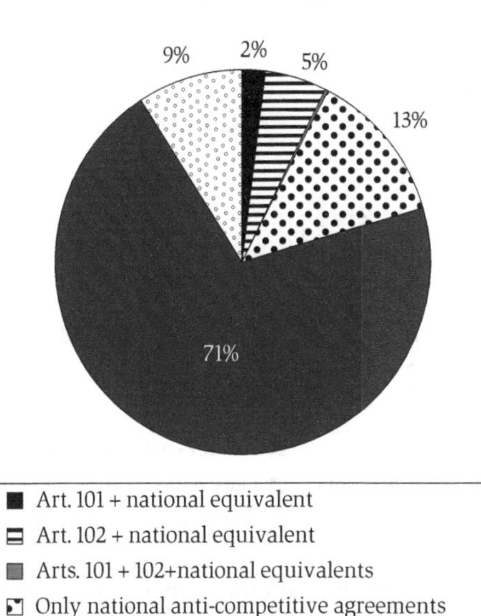

Figure 5.6 below highlights the dynamics of the judicial review cases in terms of the substantive rules applied. While the total number of cases largely follows the enforcement activity of the CPC, the prevalence of the 'domestic' abuse of dominance cases remains constant throughout the years. On the one hand, this might suggest that the CPC has never revised its narrow interpretation of the 'effect on trade' concept, which ensures the application of the EU competition rules occupies an insignificant part of its enforcement workload. On the other hand, the presence of numerous abuse of dominance cases, many of which occur in regional or local markets, is due to the CPC's obligation to follow up on complaints submitted by the customers, consumers, or trading partners of the dominant undertakings.

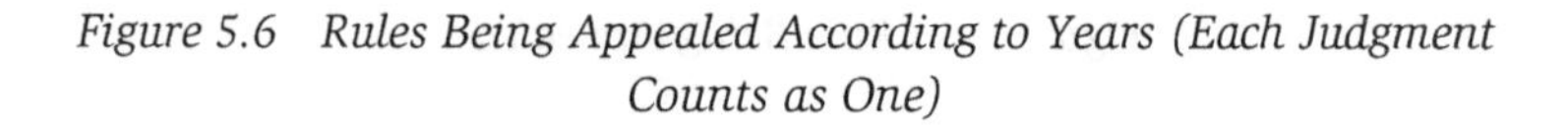

Figure 5.6 Rules Being Appealed According to Years (Each Judgment Counts as One)

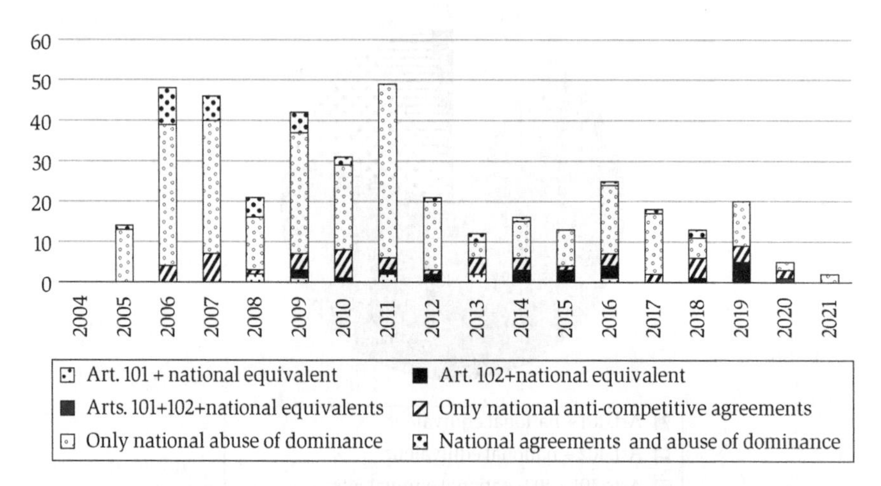

The aforementioned trends in the enforcement practice of the CPC have also conditioned the types of restrictions that feature in the judicial review cases as demonstrated in Figure 5.7. In cases concerning anti-competitive practices under Article 101 TFEU and/or its national equivalent, horizontal restrictions (42) are more frequent than vertical restrictions (10).[50] At the same time, it should be noted that one of the CPC's largest fines, subsequently confirmed by the courts, was imposed in a case concerning vertical distribution agreements in the automotive industry.[51] In abuse of dominance cases, exploitative abuses (146) are more frequent than exclusionary abuses (118). This distinction, however, is not significant because neither the CPC nor the courts operate the exclusionary-exploitative dichotomy. The abusive practices featured in the CPC's decisions frequently feature both exclusionary (in relation to competitors) and exploitative (in relation to consumers and trading partners) elements.

50. *See, e.g.*, Bulgarian Competition Authority, The Bulgarian Supreme Administrative Court confirms the sanction imposed by the Bulgarian Competition Commission on several undertakings for having implemented a vertical anti-competitive agreement in the sunflower oil market *(Zvezda and COOP – Trade and Tourism)*, 7 October 2014, e-Competitions October 2014, Article N° 69363.

51. *See* Eleonora Mateina, The Bulgarian Supreme Administrative Court inflicts a record fine for prohibited vertical agreements within a selective distribution system of cars *(Hyundai)*, 28 December 2016, e-Competitions December 2016, Art. N° 83115; Zoya Todorova, The Bulgarian Supreme Administrative Court confirms a fine of over €8 million for several hard-core vertical restrictions *(Hyundai)*, 28 December 2016, e-Competitions December 2016, Article N° 82713; Anton Dinev, 'Bulgaria: Anti-competitive Agreements – Judgment', 43(2) European Competition Law Review N22-N23 (2022).

Figure 5.7 Types of Restrictions

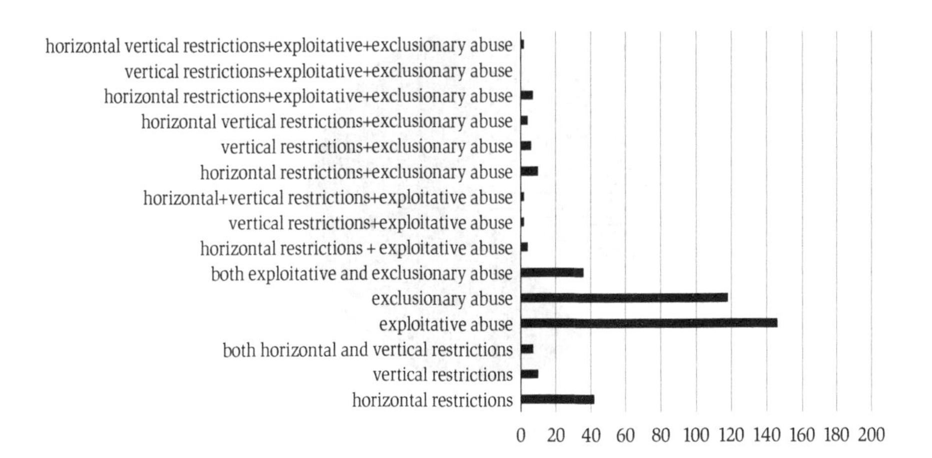

While the number of cases involving the enforcement of Article 101 TFEU and/or its national equivalent is lower than abuse of dominance cases, Figure 5.8 shows that they are dominated by cases involving the anti-competitive object (62%) of the alleged practices as opposed to its anti-competitive effect (7%) as shown in Figure 5.8. More frequent reference to the anti-competitive object stems from the CPC's decisions where the establishment of the anti-competitive object of an agreement or concerted practice relieves the CPC from the need to demonstrate the actual or potential negative effects of such agreement or practice. There is a significant number of cases (21%) where the object and/or effect of the respective infringement have not been indicated. This frequently occurs in cases where the appellants rely on purely procedural issues, such as irregularities in the CPC's investigation or sanctioning. Alternatively, the parties may dispute the CPC's application of the substantive competition rules to the alleged anti-competitive agreements and practices without disputing their object and/or effect but merely referring to the examples listed in Article 101 TFEU and/or its national equivalent.

Figure 5.8 Object/Effect (Only for Article 101/National Equivalent Infringements)

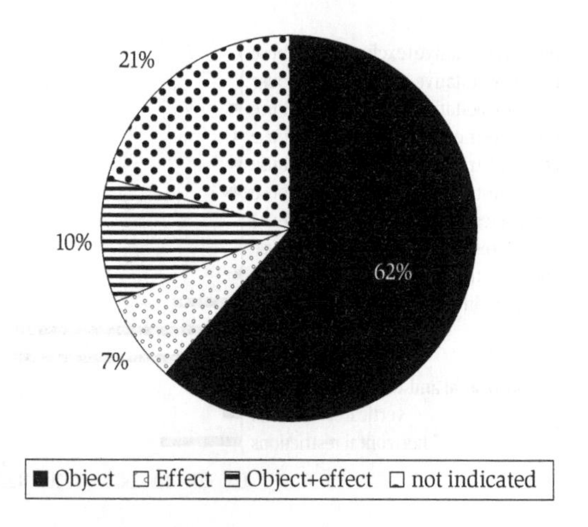

4.6 Type of NCA's Procedure

Figure 5.9 summarises the type of CPC's decisions that were subject to appeal. It indicates that approximately 50% of the judicial review cases concern appeals against the CPC's decisions whereby the competition authority imposes fines for violation of competition law. Most notable, however, is the fact that another half of the cases concern appeals against the CPC's decisions whereby the competition authority found no grounds for intervention on its part.[52] In this regard, it should be noted that unlike the national competition rules of other Member States that were substantially harmonised with the provisions of Regulation 1/2003, the Bulgarian Competition Act clearly distinguishes between EU law and national law as a basis for closing a case without finding an infringement. In line with Article 5 Regulation 1/2003, the CPC is authorised to adopt a decision concluding that there are no grounds for intervention under Article 101/102 TFEU.[53] At the same time, the Competition Act does not permit the CPC to close an investigation in the absence of sufficient evidence proving the existence of an infringement.[54] This effectively means that the case can be closed under national competition rules either with the establishment of an infringement or confirmation that no infringement was committed.[55] The equivalence between 'no-ground-for-action'

52. *See, e.g.*, Alexandr Svetlicinii, The Bulgarian Competition Authority finds no cartel on the market for banking services *(Association of Banks in Bulgaria)*, 3 June 2010, e-Competitions June 2010, Article N° 31625.
53. Competition Act, Article 8(3).
54. Competition Act, Article 41. *See also* Dessislava Fessenko, The Bulgarian Parliament adopts an act on the protection of competition, 28 November 2008, e-Competitions November 2008, Article N° 23076.
55. *See* Alexandr Svetlicinii, Maciej Bernatt, and Marco Botta, 'The 'Dark Matter' in EU Competition Law: Non-infringement Decisions in the New EU Member States Before and After Tele2 Polska', 43(3) European Law Review 424-446, p. 430 (2018).

decisions under Regulation 1/2003 and 'non-infringement' decisions under the Competition Act was confirmed by the SAC in the *BTC Cable Ducts* case, where the court reasoned that 'a decision to take no action under Articles 81 and 82 EC amounts to finding no infringement of the [national competition] law'.[56] A recent series of amendments to the Competition Act implementing the objectives of the ECN+ Directive did not change the *status quo* on the matter of 'non-infringement' decisions under national competition rules.[57]

The large number of appeals against such 'negative' decisions of the CPC is an expression of the procedural rights exercised by third parties that are not satisfied with the CPC's findings. Since the associated legal costs are relatively low, appellants normally do not hesitate to make use of their procedural rights and challenge the CPC's findings with the aim of having the court remand the case for further investigation that would address the appellants' concerns.

Figure 5.9 Competition Authority's Procedure

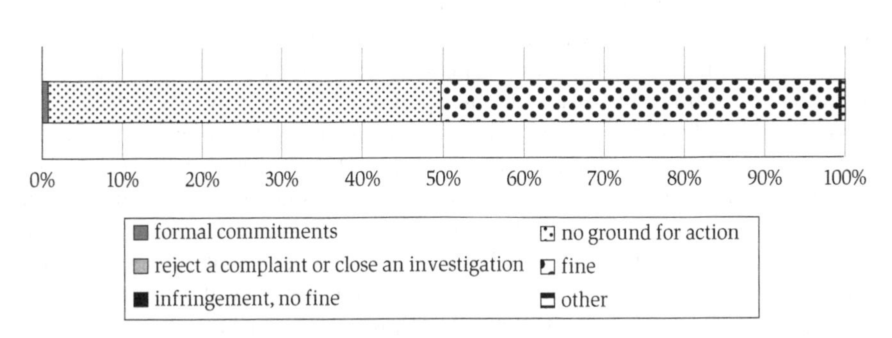

4.7 Grounds of Appeal

The empirical findings presented in Figure 5.10 reveal the grounds on which appeals were launched by the parties as well as their rate of success. This figure outlines the grounds and outcomes of all of the appeals launched against a single CPC decision or the previous instance judgments. That means that if a CPC decision was appealed by various parties in separate proceedings, the grounds invoked in all of those judgments and their success were counted as a single case. The data highlights a characteristic trend of the judicial review of administrative decisions in Bulgaria – the appellants' reliance on multiple grounds when challenging the decision of an administrative authority. Since the appellants are not required to produce evidence of procedural irregularities or

56. *See* Anton Dinev, The Bulgarian Supreme Administrative Court upholds the Competition Authority's decision finding no infringement of Article 102 TFEU in a case involving the concurrent application of competition rules and communications regulation *(BTC Cable Ducts)*, 15 February 2011, e-Competitions February 2011, Article N° 38336.

57. *See* Boyko Gerginov and Polina Westerhoven, Latest Amendments to the Bulgarian Protection of Competition Act: Three Steps Forward, One Step Back (Kluwer Competition Law Blog), 23 April 2021, and https://competitionlawblog.kluwercompetitionlaw.com/2021/04/23/latest-amendments-to-the-bulgarian-protection-of-competition-act-three-steps-forward-one-step-back/.

substantive errors in the CPC's application of the law, this task largely rests with the court conducting its own review of the CPC's investigative actions, reasoning, and sanctioning. For that reason, appeals are abound with the formalistic enumeration of the alleged 'procedural and substantive deficiencies' that are expected to be verified by the court. Due to the low evidentiary burden incumbent on the appellants, it is not surprising that the rate of rejections for both grounds of appeal is very high.

As shown in Figure 5.10, the rate of success is somewhat higher for substantive grounds (more than 50% of the CPC's decisions) of appeal due to the differences in the interpretation of the substantive competition rules and their application in specific cases between the CPC and the judicial panels of the SAC reviewing the former's decision. This effectively means that the appellants are more likely to succeed in reversing the CPC's decisions by convincing the reviewing court of the incorrect application of the substantive rules rather than the reviewing court finding procedural irregularities in the CPC's work (less than 50% of the CPC's decisions).

The number of cases where the appellants have disputed the amount of the fine (74 cases) is significantly lower than in relation to other grounds: (substantive (360 cases) and procedural (344 cases). The reason for this situation lies in the appellants' strategy of disputing the legality of the CPC's decision as a whole due to procedural irregularities or substantive errors in the application of the law. As a result, the appellants frequently do not advance specific arguments related to the imposition of the fine, as it appears redundant in cases where the CPC's decision will be quashed on procedural or substantive grounds. Any arguments disputing the amount of fine imposed by the CPC normally appear in cases where the appellants are aware of the solid evidence of infringement collected by the CPC that may result in rejection of the appeal on substantive or procedural grounds. In such cases, they attempt to bring the mitigating circumstances to the attention of SAC, which can lead to a reduction of the initial fine imposed by CPC.[58]

Another reason for the lower number of cases where the appellants challenge the fine in comparison with other grounds of appeal lies in the fact that a large number of appeals are launched in cases where the applicants are not satisfied with the CPC's decision, finding no grounds for action on its part. An insignificant number of cases where the relationship between EU law and national competition law is to be raised by the appellants reflects the general enforcement trends of the CPC, which adopts the vast majority of its decisions on the basis of national law only.

58. *See, e.g.*, Alexandr Svetlicinii, The Bulgarian Supreme Administrative Court confirms the Competition Authority's decision to fine a heating plant company for exploitative abuse of dominance *(Heating Plant Ruse)*, 18 June 2009, e-Competitions June 2009, Article N° 29126. In this case, SAC has reduced CPC's fine of BGN 300,000 to BGN 50,000 taking into account that the exploitative abuse of dominance has affected only a limited number of consumers. *See also* Alexandr Svetlicinii, The Bulgarian Supreme Administrative Court partially upholds the decision of the Bulgarian Competition Authority finding an abuse of dominance on the market for electricity distribution and accessory services (*CEZ Distribution Bulgaria*), 10 May 2010, e-Competitions May 2010, Article N° 31510. In this case, SAC has examined several abusive practices alleged by CPC. Since some of these practices were qualified as abusive while others not, the court has respectively reduced the total amount of fine from BGN 300,000 to BGN 100,000.

Figure 5.10 Grounds of Appeal (Each NCA's Decision or Previous Instance Judgment Counts as One)

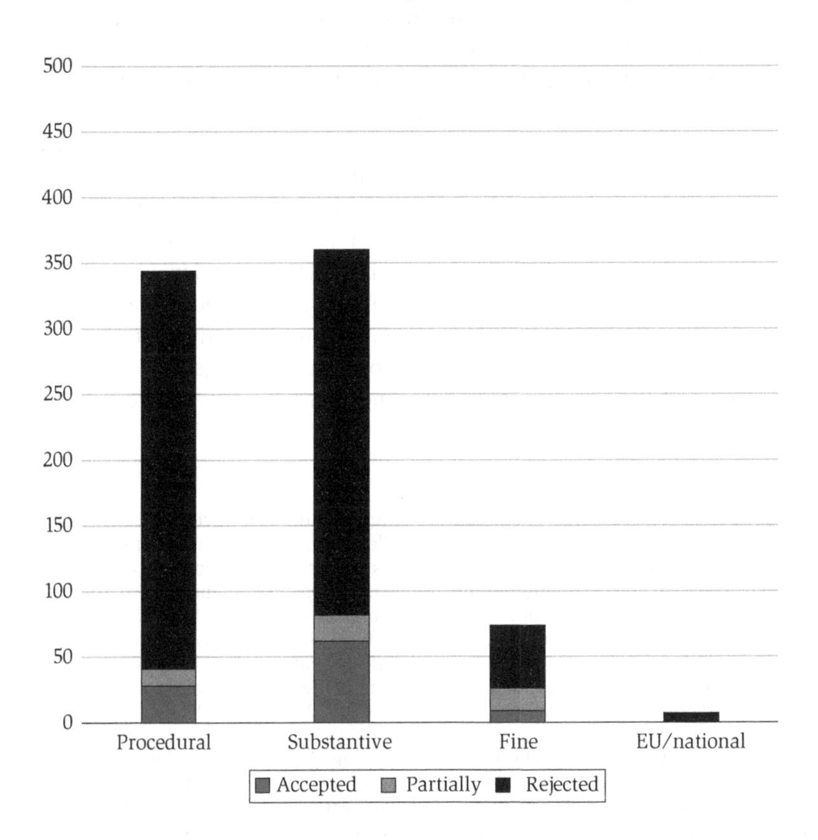

Figures 5.11(a)-(d) take a different approach and present the relationship between the grounds argued and grounds accepted throughout the years. The following trends are notable in this regard. In relation to the procedural grounds, the success rate has been consistently low throughout the years largely due to the aforementioned factors that explain the high rate of rejections of appeals. Notably, due to the low burden of proof incumbent upon the appellants as well as the low costs associated with launching an appeal, appellants frequently launch appeals that are barely supported by evidence and the majority of them are rejected by the courts, which only infrequently find any procedural deficiencies in the CPC's investigations. In relation to substantive grounds, one should note a higher rate of success in the years immediately preceding and immediately following Bulgaria's accession to the EU in 2007 (2006-2010). Without applying the EU competition rules directly, both the CPC and the SAC judges

became continuously exposed to EU competition law practice, including the Commission's enforcement practice and the case law of the CJEU. During these formative years, the interpretation of certain substantive concepts such as 'anti-competitive agreement',[59] 'undertaking',[60] 'excessive or unfair prices',[61] 'concerted practice', 'anti-competitive object and/or effect',[62] 'essential facility',[63] as well as the standard of proof applicable to the determination of these concepts, have revealed initial divergences in interpretation between the CPC and the judiciary. Continuously learning from the EU jurisprudence and setting their own precedents, the Bulgarian judiciary has increased legal certainty related to the interpretation of the key competition law concepts, which has gradually led to a further reduction of the success rate for substantive grounds of appeal. For example, in a series of judgments rejecting the appeals launched against the CPC's decisions, finding no grounds for action, the SAC panels have made a clear distinction between protecting competitors or trading parties and protecting market competition.[64] Furthermore, the SAC judges have referred to the CJEU case law and the Commission's guidelines even in cases where only national

59. *See, e.g.*, Dessislava Fessenko, The Bulgarian Supreme Administrative Court quashes an NCA decision penalising agreements thwarting parallel imports of premium branded beverages *(Diageo Brands)*, 10 August 2007, e-Competitions August 2007, Article N° 16039; Dessislava Fessenko, The Bulgarian Supreme Administrative Court dismisses liability for participation in a cartel when the undertaking is not active in the market concerned *(Vegetable Oil Cartel)*, 11 August 2010, e-Competitions August 2010, Article N° 32903; Dessislava Fessenko, The Bulgarian Supreme Administrative Court holds that the absence of a party to a hard-core arrangement from the market concerned rules out an infringement of the local equivalent of Art. 81 EC by this party *(Vegetable Oil Manufacturers and Suppliers / CPC)*, 27 March 2009, e-Competitions March 2009, Article N° 26203.
60. *See, e.g.*, Dessislava Fessenko, The Bulgarian Supreme Administrative Court endorses a fine-tuning of the notion of an 'undertaking' with respect to non-profit organisations (*Geto Productions v CPC*), 2 April 2008, e-Competitions April 2008, Article N° 17555; Alexandr Svetlicinii, The Bulgarian Competition Authority holds that the national health insurance fund is not an undertaking for competition law enforcement *(NZOK II)*, 14 August 2013, e-Competitions August 2013, Article N° 56409.
61. *See, e.g.*, Alexandr Svetlicinii, The Bulgarian Supreme Administrative Court rules on the abuse of dominant position committed by the bus terminal administration in setting the service charges paid by the bus operators *(Avtobusni prevozi)*, 12 January 2009, e-Competitions January 2009, Article N° 29685; Alexandr Svetlicinii, The Bulgarian Competition Authority applies economic value test in the assessment of the alleged exploitative abuse of dominance committed by the bus terminal administration *(Avtobusni prevozi)*, 28 July 2009, e-Competitions July 2009, Article N° 29834.
62. *See, e.g.*, Dessislava Fessenko, The Bulgarian Supreme Administrative Court endorses a minimum premium tariff for green card insurance as pro-competitive (*Vitosha*), 15 February 2006, e-Competitions February 2006, Article N° 14753.
63. *See, e.g.*, Alexandr Svetlicinii, The Bulgarian Supreme Administrative Court affirms Competition Authority's decision to prosecute the incumbent telecom operator for tying its ADSL and fixed voice services *(Bulgarian Telecom)*, 19 February 2009, e-Competitions February 2009, Article N° 29342.
64. *See, e.g.*, Alexandr Svetlicinii, The Bulgarian Supreme Administrative Court dismisses the charges of abuse of dominance launched against a domestic tobacco producer *(Iosini)*, 9 July 2009, e-Competitions July 2009, Article N° 28695; Alexandr Svetlicinii, The Bulgarian Supreme Administrative Court dismisses the charges of abuse of dominance launched against the national railway infrastructure company *(Polygraphsnab)*, 22 June 2009, e-Competitions June 2009, Article N° 29125.

competition rules were applied.[65] At the same time, the SAC has continued to exercise close scrutiny of the CPC's economic and technical assessments, for example, in cases alleging price-related abuses of dominance,[66] which at times lead to the reversal of the CPC's findings.

A similar dynamic can be observed in relation to fines. As shown in Figure 5.11(c), the success rates for this ground of appeal slightly increased during the 2006-2010 period but generally remained low as this ground of appeal is invoked relatively infrequently and is largely limited to cases where the sanctioned undertakings only dispute the calculation of fine by CPC. In terms of success rate, the fines were reduced by the court in 28% of the cases where this ground of appeal was invoked by the parties. This is consistent with the generally low rates of success of appeals against the CPC's decisions. The average fine reduction is 90%. This high percentage is due to the way these reductions were calculated for the purpose of the present study and includes those instances where the court has annulled the CPC's decision that imposed fines on the undertaking(s) concerned. For example, if a CPC decision imposed the fine of X amount and the court annulled the decision in its entirety, then the reduction of the fine was counted as 100%. Another reason for the duction in fines is connected to the methodology for the calculation of the fine, which allows consideration of various factors.[67] As a result, the SAC panels have frequently considered various mitigating circumstances that led to a significant reduction in fines.[68]

Finally, as shown in Figure 5.11(d), the role of the grounds related to the relationship between EU law and national competition rules has generally been negligible due to the low number of cases where the CPC has applied the EU competition rules.[69] For example, in one of its earlier cases, the SAC addressed the duty

65. *See, e.g.*, Anton Dinev, 'Bulgaria - Anti-competitive Practices - Judgment', 43(11) European Competition Law Review N244-N245 (2022); Anton Dinev, 'Bulgaria - Anti-competitive Practices - Judgment', 43(7) European Competition Law Review N141-N142 (2022).

66. *See, e.g.*, Eleonora Mateina, The Bulgarian Supreme Administrative Court quashes the Competition Authority's decision on an abuse of dominance case in the energy sector, due to a different economic analysis *(Energo Pro)*, 20 January 2017, e-Competitions January 2017, Article N° 84447; Alexandr Svetlicinii, The Bulgarian Competition Authority sanctions electricity supplier for an abuse of dominance in the form of temporary suspension of supply for accumulated debts *(Energo Pro)*, 8 May 2013, e-Competitions May 2013, Article N° 56412.

67. *See, e.g.*, Alexandr Svetlicinii, The Bulgarian Supreme Administrative Court upholds the decision of the Competition Authority establishing the existence of a cartel on the market for poultry meat and eggs *(Bulgarian Poultry Breeders Union)*, 15 September 2010, e-Competitions September 2010, Article N° 32777. In this case the SAC panel reviewed the CPC's differentiated sanctioning of the following groups of cartel members: (1) cartelists which were particularly active in defining the rules of the anti-competitive conduct; (2) cartelists without active involvement in the formulation of the common pricing policy; and (3) cartelists which were passive observers of the anti-competitive behaviour without expressly denouncing it.

68. *See, e.g.*, Anton Dinev, The Bulgarian Competition Authority imposes sanctions for abusive interest rates on overdue payments for water supply in Sofia *(Sofiyska voda)*, 27 May 2014, e-Competitions May 2014, Article N° 68782; Alexandr Svetlicinii, The Bulgarian Supreme Administrative Court affirms the Competition Authority's decision to prosecute a water supply operator for abuse of dominant position *(Sofiyska Voda)*, 17 June 2009, e-Competitions June 2009, Article N° 29344. The SAC reduced the original fine of BGN 250,000 to BGN 100,000 stating that previous infringements should not justify the increase in penalties.

69. *See, e.g.*, Dessislava Fessenko, The Bulgarian Supreme Administrative Court quashes an NCA decision applying Art. 3.1.g and 10 in conjunction with Art. 81 EC on grounds of separation of

of the CPC to notify its investigations and envisaged decisions applying Articles 101 and 102 TFEU (formerly 81 and 82 EC) to the European Competition Network under Regulation 1/2003.[70] The court held that although the national courts can verify compliance with this obligation by the CPC, the failure to notify an investigation or an envisaged decision does not automatically mean that the CPC has erred in application of the EU competition rules that the national courts are empowered to apply under Regulation 1/2003. The SAC also refused the appellant's claim that the CPC must pronounce the alleged infringement of Article 102 TFEU as mentioned in the complaint. The SAC panels agreed that since Article 102 TFEU was not applicable due to the absence of any effect on trade, the CPC could not be expected to address it in its decision.[71] In a rare case, the appellant challenged the CPC's conclusions on the absence of an effect on trade, which precluded application of Article 102 TFEU.[72] The SAC reviewed the CPC's assessment and concluded that in a case involving the funeral services market, which was limited geographically to a particular locality, there was no actual or potential effect on inter-state trade that would justify the application of the EU competition rules.

Figure 5.11(a) Procedural Grounds

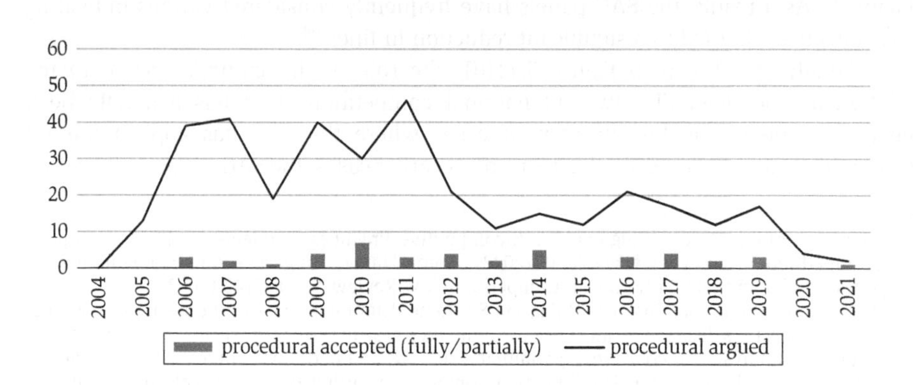

powers and national procedural autonomy *(Chamber of the design engineers)*, 11 June 2009, e-Competitions June 2009, Article N° 29703; Dessislava Fessenko, The Bulgarian Supreme Administrative Court upholds a NCA decision evoking Art. 81.1 and 3 EC for the first time *(Civil liability insurance for car drivers)*, 29 December 2008, e-Competitions December 2008, Article N° 27428; SAC3 judgment No. 15121 of 7 November 2019 in case No. 9599/2018.

70. SAC3 judgment No. 14628 of 29 December 2008 in case No. 10739/2008; SAC5 judgment No. 9407 of 13 July 2009 in case No. 5129/2009.
71. SAC3 judgment No. 310 of 9 January 2012 in case No. 14829/2010; SAC5 judgment No. 6875 of 16 May 2012 in case No. 3156/2012.
72. SAC3 judgment No. 10725 of 9 July 2019 in case No. 12053/2018.

Figure 5.11(b) Substantive Grounds

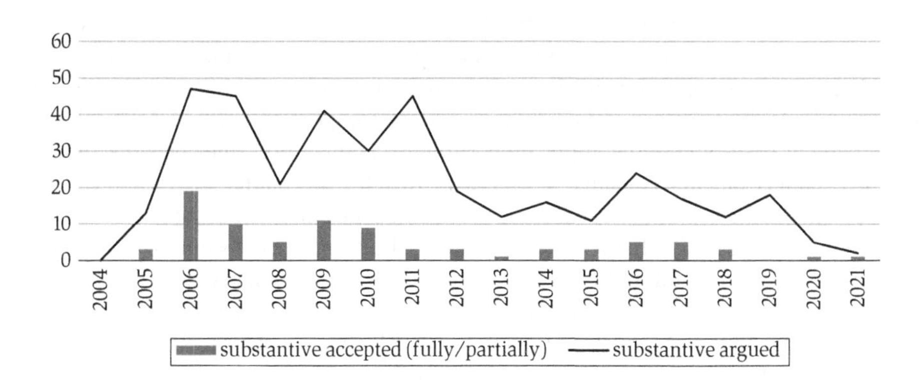

Figure 5.11(c) Fines-related Grounds

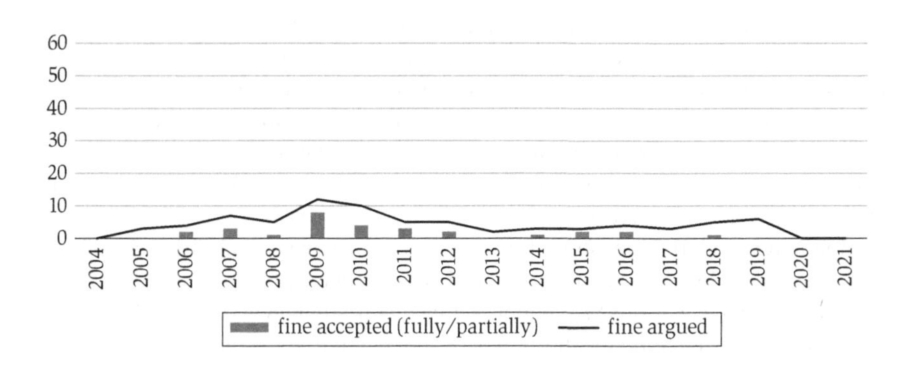

Figure 5.11(d) EU/National Grounds

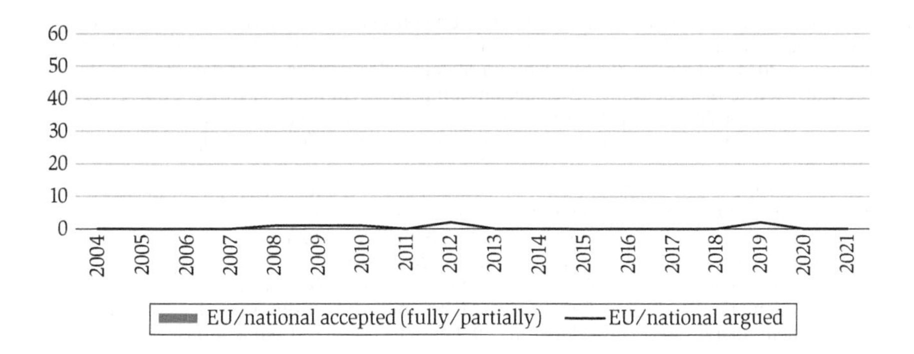

Similarly, the study has uncovered no instances where the SAC has sent a reference for a preliminary ruling to the CJEU in relation to the judicial review of a CPC's decision. The absence of such references can be partially explained by the negligible number of cases where the CPC has applied EU competition rules due to the latter's narrow interpretation of the 'effect on trade' concept, which results in the majority of decisions being issued under national competition rules.[73] At the same time, even in cases where the application of the EU competition rules was discussed, the SAC panels did not consider it necessary to refer the matter to the CJEU. For example, in the *Insurance Cartel* case, the SAC denied the parties' request to refer to the CJEU when considering whether a failure of the CPC to notify the Commission about the ongoing investigation and the envisaged draft decision under Regulation 1/2003 could serve as a ground for the subsequent annulment of the CPC's decision.[74] In 2017, the SAC3 denied another request to refer to the CJEU when considering the application of the national equivalent of Article 102 TFEU.[75] The court considered that under Regulation 1/2003, the Member States were authorised to implement stricter rules on abuse of dominance than under Article 102 TFEU, and since the CJEU only has the power to interpret the provisions of EU law, there were no grounds for making a reference for a preliminary ruling.

Figure 5.12 matches the successful grounds of appeal with the types of restrictions featured in the CPC decisions or first-instance court judgments. The empirical data displayed therein leads to the conclusion that, overall, the substantive grounds of appeal have achieved the highest ratios of success in the appeals collected for the purpose of this study. This is especially pronounced in relation to abuse of dominance cases, where an open-ended list of abusive practices included in Article 102 TFEU and its national equivalent has created room for divergent approaches as to which practices of a dominant undertaking should be considered abusive and thus contrary to competition rules. Such divergences can be observed not only between the CPC and the SAC but also between various SAC panels acting on different levels of appeal.[76] In cases of anti-competitive agreements and practices, the evidentiary standards for establishing the existence of an agreement or concerted practices have at times led to the

73. *See, e.g.*, Eleonora Mateina, The Bulgarian Competition Authority rules on parallel trade of pharmaceutical products and their limitations *(Sopharma)*, 17 December 2014, e-Competitions December 2014, Article N° 76322; Eleonora Mateina, Restrictions in Parallel Trade of Pharmaceuticals – Carte Blanche from the Bulgarian Competition Authority? (Kluwer Competition Law Blog, 22 October 2015), https://competitionlawblog.kluwercompetitionlaw.com/2015/10/22/restrictions-of-parallel-trade-in-pharmaceuticals-carte-blanche-from-the-bulgarian-competition-authority/.
74. *See* Anton Dinev, The Bulgarian Supreme Administrative Court discusses in detail the legal consequences of failure to comply with the obligation to inform the EU Commission *(Insurance Cartel)*, 13 July 2009, e-Competitions July 2009, Article N° 30028.
75. SAC3 judgment No. 6579 of 26 May 2017 in case No. 7616/2015.
76. *See, e.g.*, Dessislava Fessenko, The Bulgarian Supreme Administrative Court finds that a holder of the trademark 'Der Grüne Punkt' abused its dominant position on the collective waste management market *(Ecopack Bulgaria)*, 9 February 2007, e-Competitions February 2007, Article N° 13608.

annulment of the CPC decisions in cases where the SAC judges ruled that the requisite standard of proof was not satisfied.[77]

Figure 5.12 Types of Restrictions Versus Successful Grounds of Appeal

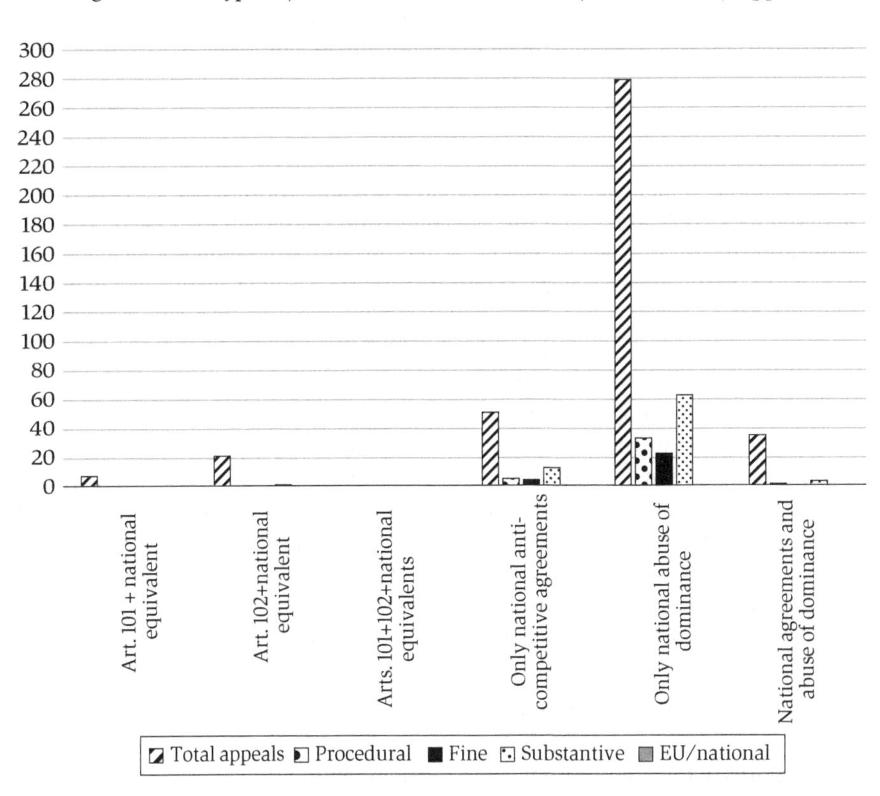

Our empirical study did not reveal any instances where the appellant has challenged a commitments decision issued by the CPC.[78] The reason lies in the

77. *See, e.g.*, Dessislava Fessenko, The Bulgarian Supreme Court dismisses mere price parallelism as a form of concerted practice in the absence of compelling evidence of such *(Travel Agencies)*, 16 September 2013, e-Competitions September 2013, Article N° 61110.

78. *See, e.g.*, Dessislava Fessenko, The Bulgarian Competition Authority considers behavioural commitments in cases of refusal to supply *(E.On Bulgaria / EVN Bulgaria)*, 11 March 2010, e-Competitions March 2010, Article N° 42070; Eleonora Mateina, The Bulgarian Competition Authority approves commitments by oil companies suspected of cartel activities *(Lukoil Bulgaria / Eco Bulgaria / Shell Bulgaria / OMV Bulgaria / NIS PETROL)*, 28 March 2017, e-Competitions March 2017, Article N° 84404; Nikolai Gouginski, The Bulgarian Competition Authority Settles an Alleged Cartel Case (Kluwer Competition Law Blog, 24 August 2012), https://competitionlawblog.kluwercompetitionlaw.com/2012/08/24/the-bulgarian-competition-authority-settles-an-alleged-cartel-case/; Eleonora Mateina, The Bulgarian Commission for Protection of Competition has Approved Commitments by Oil Companies Suspected of Cartel Activities (Kluwer Competition Law Blog, 24 July 2017), https://competitionlawblog.kluwercompetitionlaw.com/2017/07/24/bulgarian-commission-protection-competition-approved-commitments-oil-companies-suspected-cartel-activities/.

procedural stance of the SAC expressed in a 2011 case where the court refused standing to the complainant attempting to challenge a commitments decision adopted by the CPC. The court held that a commitment decision could not affect a complainant's legitimate interests, and thus, it had no cause of action. Furthermore, according to the court, the commitments procedure is an intermediate procedure rather than a ruling on substance and, therefore, cannot affect the complainant's interests.[79]

4.8 Third Parties

The most frequent appellants identified in our study are: (i) third parties (196 cases), (ii) undertakings (187 cases), and (iii) the competition authority (52 cases). The CPC normally appears as an appellant in the second-instance proceedings challenging the rulings of the first-instance courts, where they have resulted in the full or partial annulment of the CPC's decisions. Since the rejection rate of appeals is high at both first-instance and second-instance levels, the CPC acts as appellant in considerably fewer cases than the undertakings which have been the subject of enforcement action by the CPC for competition law infringements. The most numerous groups of appellants consist of complainants dissatisfied with the CPC's 'negative decisions' finding no infringements of national competition law or no grounds for action under the EU competition rules. The high rejection rate of appeals does not discourage this group of appellants due to the low costs associated with launching an appeal in comparison with private enforcement proceedings.[80] The complainants also frequently participate as third parties in cases where the CPC or sanctioned undertakings act as appellants. Our empirical study has revealed eighty-six instances of such participation.

4.9 Leniency and Settlements

For the purposes of the present study, we have not identified any instance where a CPC decision which accepted a leniency application was challenged before the court. Considering the conditions that must be satisfied for accepting a leniency application by the CPC, it is unlikely that they would be challenged either by the investigated undertakings or third parties due to a lack of legal interest and the CPC's enforcement discretion (cf. by analogy commitment decisions).

Bulgaria had no settlement programme during the period covered by this project.

79. *See* Dessislava Fessenko, The Bulgarian Supreme Administrative Court dismisses a standing to challenge commitments in an antitrust case *(Zlaten Lev Capital)*, 17 March 2011, e-Competitions March 2011, Article N° 35770.

80. *See* Eleonora Mateina, Better Later Than Never: Bulgaria Finally Implemented the Private Damages Directive in its Competition Protection Act (Kluwer Competition Law Blog, 8 January 2018), https://competitionlawblog.kluwercompetitionlaw.com/2018/01/08/better-later-never-bulgaria-finally-implemented-private-damages-directive-competition-protection-act/.

5 QUALITATIVE ANALYSIS

5.1 Scope and Intensity of Appeals

CPC decisions undergo a comprehensive judicial review of their lawfulness at two appeal instances, the ACSR (or the SAC3 before 2019) and the SAC3 (or the SAC5 before 2019). As already seen, the former hears appeals on points of law and fact, including the following grounds: (i) lack of competence (jurisdiction), (ii) deviation from established forms, (iii) substantial violation of procedural rules, (iv) contradiction with substantive rules, (v) inconsistency with the law's objectives, whereas the latter reviews first-instance judgments on points of law only, including where such judgments are either (i) null and void, (ii) inadmissible, or (iii) incorrect, as a result of violating the substantive rules, substantial violation of the procedural rules, or the provision of insufficient reasons. Since both instances of appeal control the application of the substantive competition law prohibitions, judicial review of the CPC decisions is comparatively intensive. This entails reviewing any errors of law or fact, as well as the exercise of enforcement discretion (or its control by first-instance administrative courts), including the assessment of complex economic appraisals. The substantive review is limited in principle by the parties' claims (*petitum*), and in practice, the review courts examine how the substantive competition rules were applied, depending on their *ratione temporis* applicability to the appealed enforcement decision.

5.2 Judicial Deference

Although the CPC, as any administrative authority, enjoys a significant enforcement discretion or margin of appreciation, review courts need to control it with respect to the appealed decision and assess whether it has been lawfully exercised (Article 169 APC). Therefore, judicial deference is neither automatic nor unlimited but concerns only the lawful exercise of enforcement discretion, which, as such, is subject to judicial review or control of legality. This means, in practice, that an administrative authority's margin of appreciation consists of choosing the most appropriate between two or more equally lawful (and proportionate) decisions that are also consistent with the law's purpose and objectives. And while an administrative court would defer to the actual choice, its very existence and tenor need to appear clearly in the reasons for adopting the decision under appeal.[81] Consequently, failure to provide sufficient reasons as to the lawful exercise of enforcement discretion, including due consideration of any objections or statements by the parties to the administrative proceedings or interested third parties, would constitute a substantial violation of the administrative procedure and result in the annulment of the appealed decision.[82]

The review courts have recognised and, where applicable, controlled the lawful exercise by the CPC of enforcement discretion: (i) to not commence an *ex officio*

81. *See, e.g.*, SAC5 Judgment No. 2026, 10 February 2020, Case 8875/2019.
82. SAC Interpretative Ruling No. 4, 22 April 2004, Case TR-4/2002.

investigation upon receiving a tip-off, e.g., a complaint that has not been filed in the required form,[83] (ii) to reject a complaint based on its enforcement priorities,[84] (iii) to conduct (or not) an inspection of business premises following its judicial authorisation,[85] (iv) to impose interim measures,[86] (v) to grant an individual exemption,[87] (vi) to accept (or not) and render binding the commitments offered by an investigated undertaking,[88] (vii) to set the amount of a pecuniary sanction depending on the gravity of the infringement,[89] (viii) to determine the duration of behavioural or structural remedies.[90] Additionally, in contrast to the marginal standard of review followed by the ECJ pertaining to 'complex economic assessment' and 'administrative discretion' of the European Commission, the ACSR and SAC in Bulgaria do not hesitate to engage in the review of technical and economic findings of the competition authority, and to consider various mitigating circumstances that could lead to the reduction of the imposed sanctions. Despite the relatively high intensity of the judicial review of the CPC decisions, the present study reveals a high number of rejected appeals, demonstrating that in the vast majority of the cases, the appellants are unable to identify substantive or procedural errors in the CPC's work. The low chances of success do not discourage parties from appealing due to the low costs associated with the administrative judicial review, which effectively leads to a waste of judicial resources.

5.3 Review of Fines

Although challenging the lawfulness or the amount of a fine is only subsidiary to the substantive or procedural grounds of appeal and, therefore, is rarely requested on a stand-alone basis, the review courts control how the CPC has exercised its discretion in deciding what sanctions to impose. As the SAC put it recently, since the court reviews the legality of the appealed decision in its entirety, including the reasons for imposing a pecuniary sanction, it may also rule on its amount based on the evidence that had been considered by the CPC to determine the gravity and duration of the infringement at issue.[91]

There is only one scenario where the CPC has exclusive competence to determine the sanction – where it finds no infringement under the national competition rules (or decides there are no grounds for further action under Articles 101 and 102 TFEU), but

83. ACSR Order No. 836, 5 August 2022, Case 677/2022, SAC3 Order No. 15344, 11 December 2018, Case 8996/2018.
84. SAC3 Order No. 8695, 10 October 2022, Case 8152/2022.
85. SAC3 Order No. 4472, 3 December 2014, Case 14697/2014.
86. SAC3 Judgment No. 6215, 12 May 2010, Case 16170/2009.
87. SAC5 Judgment No. 7961, 13 July 2006, Case 1493/2006.
88. SAC3 Judgment No. 7087, 11 June 2021, Case 1152/2018, SAC3 Judgment No. 15629, 13 December 2018, Case 1262/2018, SAC3 Judgment No. 9006, 2 February 2018, Case 6774/2017, SAC5 Judgment No. 2321, 16 February 2012, Case 8930/2011.
89. SAC5 Judgment No. 2478, 5 March 2008, Case 10536/2007.
90. ACSR Judgment No. 46, 12 April 2023, Case 147/2023.
91. SAC3 Judgment No. 127, 1 February 2023, Case 7166/2022. *See also*, ex multis, SAC3 Judgment No. 4071, 13 April 2020, Case 15367/2018, SAC5 Judgment No. 9190, 9 July 2020, Case 12327/2019.

that decision is later annulled on appeal, then the review court finds an infringement and, instead of the deciding the merits of the case itself, remands it for further investigation, with instructions for the CPC on how to set the amount of the sanction.[92] Even then, however, the review courts will still be able to control the legality or lawfulness of the newly imposed fine to assess its compliance with its previous instructions to the competition authority.

5.4 Coherence with Substantive EU Competition Law

It would be inappropriate to make any resolute conclusions as to the coherence of the judicial review with the substantive EU competition law, at least for the following two reasons. First, the application of EU competition rules plays an insignificant role in the enforcement practice of the CPC. Second, a limited number of cases applying EU competition rules that were reviewed by the SAC present only anecdotal evidence that cannot serve as a sufficient basis to make a conclusion on the overall coherence with the substantive EU competition law. At the same time, we have identified SAC judgments referring to and following the EU case law and European Commission guidelines in cases applying national competition rules alone.[93] While relying extensively on EU law in numerous cases, we studied, Articles 101 and 102 TFEU were applied in only 7% of the cases before the reviewing courts due to a very narrow interpretation of the 'effect on trade' condition.

5.5 Third Parties' Rights

The judicial review of CPC decisions in Bulgaria presents an impressive example of third parties' rights in competition proceedings. First, third parties are typically involved as complainants before the CPC, then they are the largest group of appellants against 'negative decisions', where the competition authority found no evidence of competition law infringements. This allows administrative courts at two levels to review the CPC's findings and remand the case for *de novo* investigation, if necessary. Most notably, almost 50% of judicial review cases concerned appeals against a decision finding no grounds for action on the CPC's part, including a non-infringement decision issued under national competition rules. Most frequently, the appellants in

92. *Ibid.*
93. SAC5 judgment of 9 July 2009 in case No. 9256; SAC5 judgment of 22 June 2009 in case No. 8248. In these cases, the SAC has referred to the interpretation of Article 82 EC by the ECJ and the Commission upholding the CPC's refusal to find an infringement of the national equivalent of Article 82 EC in cases where no anti-competitive effects or consumer harm was established. See also Alexandr Svetlicinii, The Bulgarian Supreme Administrative Court dismisses the charges of abuse of dominance launched against a domestic tobacco producer (*Iosini*), 9 July 2009, e-Competitions July 2009, Article N° 28695; Alexandr Svetlicinii, The Bulgarian Supreme Administrative Court dismisses the charges of abuse of dominance launched against the national railway infrastructure company *(Polygraphsnab)*, 22 June 2009, e-Competitions June 2009, Article N° 29125.

these cases are trading partners or competitors of the undertaking(s) under investigation which are appealing with the aim of prompting the reversal of the CPC's negative findings that would address their concerns. Many of those appeals are dismissed by the courts since the actions complained of cannot be viewed as anti-competitive agreements or abuses of dominance. Nevertheless, despite the low rate of success, third parties continuously launch such appeals since the ancillary legal costs are low, while the intervention on the part of the CPC could improve the third parties' bargaining position or competitiveness in their relationships with the undertaking(s) under investigation.

Generally, anyone can bring a legal action to ascertain the existence or non-existence of an administrative right or legal relationship, provided they have a sufficient legal interest and no other remedy is available. This follows from Article 12(2) of the Constitution of 1991, whereby citizens and legal persons whose rights, liberties, and legal interests are or might be affected by an individual administrative act or where an individual administrative act creates obligations for citizens and legal persons, have a legal interest in appealing that individual administrative act and may do so unless otherwise proved by law. At the same time, there may be limitations on the third parties' right to appeal commitment decisions under national competition law, as these are not regarded by the SAC as deciding a case on the merits, such as allowing standing to third parties.[94]

6 CONCLUDING REMARKS

Competition law enforcement in Bulgaria generally follows the EU model while accommodating the specificities of the national administrative justice system. These concern mainly the scope and intensity of judicial review, as well as third parties' right to participate in the proceedings before the CPC and the review courts. Both first- and second-instance appeals are comparatively more intensive than they are in other jurisdictions, which is consistent with the broad understanding of controlling the legality or lawfulness of individual administrative acts or decisions in Bulgarian administrative law.

Despite the lack of institutional specialisation, similar to the UK CAT, the ACSR and the SAC have developed considerable expertise in competition law cases over the years, often engaging in sophisticated discussions of economic theories and complex assessments that generally fall within the CPC's enforcement discretion. At the same time, the cases dealt with by the competition authority and, then, by the appeal courts are fairly similar, as 71% of the appeals concerned the application of the national equivalent of Article 102 TFEU, with 36% being exploitative abuse of dominance cases. Although substantive grounds of appeal are twice as likely to be accepted than procedural grounds, 69% of all first-instance appeals and 75% of second-instance cases (cassation) have been fully rejected.

94. *See* Dessislava Fessenko, The Bulgarian Supreme Administrative Court dismisses a standing to challenge commitments in an antitrust case *(Zlaten Lev Capital)*, 17 March 2011, e-Competitions March 2011, Article N° 35770.

Considered together with the high volume of cases – one of the highest in the EU, the preponderant role of third parties as complainants before the CPC and appellants in the judicial review proceedings, and the general reluctance to apply Articles 101 and 102 TFEU, these figures and other empirical findings confirm our initial observation that competition law in Bulgaria is still very much understood in terms of fairness in commercial relations. It seems that Bulgaria's accession to the EU has changed little in this traditional approach to competition enforcement despite the extensive harmonisation of substantive and procedural rules.

CHAPTER 6
Croatia Report

Jasminka Pecotić Kaufman

1 COMPETITION LAW ENFORCEMENT IN CROATIA

1.1 Historical Outline

Modern competition rules were introduced in Croatia in 1995 amidst the democratic and economic transition that ensued in the early 1990s throughout Eastern Europe.[1] The first Competition Act, adopted in 1995, predated the beginning of Croatia's EU rapprochement process.[2] It established the Croatian Competition Agency (AZTN) as an independent authority entrusted with enforcing competition rules.[3] The institutional set-up included a Director, i.e., the head of the authority, and a Competition Council, a nine-member advisory body. The legal framework at that time, somewhat lacking in precision and scope, particularly as regards procedural rules, was broadly inspired by the then valid EU competition law template, including the obligation of the parties to notify their agreements to the AZTN for clearance. Many enforcement tools, such as dawn raids or a leniency programme, were unavailable at that stage.

1. More on the early stages of competition system development in Croatia in: Jasminka Pecotić Kaufman, 'On the Development of (Not so) New Competition Systems – Findings from an Empirical Study on Croatia', 10(2) *Journal of Antitrust Enforcement* 326-364 (2022) DOI: 10.1093/jaenfo/jnab018. Some competition legislation existed already under Yugoslavia, from which Croatia declared its independence in June 1991. However, the Yugoslav 1974 Act on Fight Against Unfair Competition and Monopolistic Agreements (*Zakon o suzbijanju nelojalne utakmice i monopolističkih sporazuma, Službeni list SFRJ 24/1974, amended 72/1986 and 58/1989)* was largely unenforceable due to lacking institutional arrangements. In fact, in 1974, Yugoslavia was the first country in Eastern Europe to enact a competition statute. Tibor Varady, 'The Emergence of Competition Law in (Former) Socialist Countries', 47 *The American Journal of Comparative Law* 229 (1999) DOI: 10.2307/841040.
2. Competition Act (*Zakon o zaštiti tržišnog natjecanja*), Official Journal 48/1995, 52/1997.
3. AZTN was not operational until late 1997. Pecotić Kaufman, *supra* n. 1.

Antitrust infringements were considered misdemeanour offences, meaning that the AZTN could not impose fines. A separate proceeding had to be initiated before a local misdemeanour court, which was asked by the AZTN to decide on fines on the basis of its infringement decision. This solution proved to be ineffective. Since the late 1990s, frustration has mounted concerning the overall reluctance of the misdemeanour courts to impose fines based on AZTN infringement decisions.[4] For example, the misdemeanour courts would re-evaluate the AZTN's decision on its merits, questioning if there was indeed any infringement of the Competition Act in a particular case. In addition, the statute of limitations was allowed to expire in some cases, leaving the infringers unpunished.[5] Between 2003 and 2009, the AZTN submitted sixty requests to the local misdemeanour courts to initiate proceedings, and only ten decisions punishing undertakings and their 'responsible natural persons' with fines were adopted in this period.[6]

The beginning of the 2000s saw a process of extensive Europeanisation of the legal system taking off in the country. In 2001, the Stabilisation and Association Agreement (SAA) between the [EU] and Croatia was signed.[7] The SAA included the obligation to fully harmonise national competition law with the [EU] acquis.[8] This prompted the adoption of the new Competition Act in 2003, which changed the institutional design by introducing a collegiate decision-making Competition Council, with the Council President as head of the AZTN. Moreover, the Competition Act of 2003 introduced a more refined legal framework vis-à-vis substantive and procedural rules, alongside some basic alignment with Regulation's 1/2003 template. At this point, dawn raids were introduced. Notably, mimicking Article 70 of the SAA, the Competition Act of 2003 formally legislated the reliance on the EU competition law model, stipulating that when deciding on 'distortions of competition' that had an effect on trade between the [EU] and Croatia, the AZTN was obliged to apply 'criteria arising from the correct application of EU competition rules'.[9]

---

4. For details, *see ibid.*
5. *Ibid.*, p. 336.
6. AZTN Annual Report for 2009, p. 33. Competition Acts of 1995 and 2003 provided for an individual liability (the so-called responsible natural persons, typically company directors). As of 1 October 2010, when the Competition Act of 2009 came into force, only undertakings (be it legal or natural persons) can be sanctioned for antitrust infringements. For a call to reintroduce individual liability in order to increase the effectiveness of the competition law regime in Croatia *see* Jasminka Pecotić Kaufman, 'Sankcioniranje fizičkih osoba za povrede tržišnog natjecanja, pokajnički programi i novi čl. 65.a ZZTN-a', 72 Zbornik Pravnog fakulteta u Zagrebu 329 (2022) DOI: 10.3935/zpfz.72.12.09.
7. Stabilisation and Association Agreement between the European Communities and their Member States, of the one part, and the Republic of Croatia, of the other part, *OJ L 26, 28.1.2005, p. 3–220.* The SAA was signed on 29 October 2001 and entered into force on 1 February 2005.
8. For more details *see* Jasminka Pecotić Kaufman, Vlatka Butorac Malnar and Dubravka Akšamović, *Competition Law in Croatia* (Kluwer Law International 2019).
9. Article 35 para. 3 Competition Act of 2003. Article 70 para. 2 SAA reads: 'Any practices contrary to this Article shall be assessed on the basis of criteria arising from the application of the competition rules applicable in the Community, in particular from Articles 81, 82, 86 and 87 of the Treaty establishing the European Community and interpretative instruments adopted by the Community institutions.' In Competition Act of 2009, the relevant provision on the application of EU law criteria removed the mention of a cross-border effect, effectively extending the obligation to apply EU rules as interpretative tool also to purely domestic cases. The formulation used

The next stage in reforming national competition rules took place at the time of intensifying EU membership negotiations in the second half of the 2000s. The landmark new Competition Act was adopted in 2009 and entered into force on 1 October 2010. Its most striking feature was granting the power to the AZTN to fine the infringers directly, thus abandoning the earlier system of misdemeanour courts deciding on fines.[10] Even as the new Competition Act was being finalised in 2009, the fine collection was significantly increased. That year, 75% of all fines from 2003 to 2009 were collected.[11] However, the earlier fining system was abandoned with no regrets. As we have no precise data on the total number of fines collected under the previous system, we are not able to discern if there was a significant increase in fines after 2009.

Apart from granting the AZTN the power to impose fines directly, the Competition Act of 2009 was notable for a series of crucial updates to the legal framework, such as introducing a leniency program, the possibility of issuing a commitment decision, and the notion of legal professional privilege. Also, by introducing *ex officio* proceedings, the law changed how AZTN handled complaints. Lastly, the individual exemption system introduced in 1995 was abandoned to align the Croatian competition law regime with Regulation 1/2003.

Despite the two comprehensive reforms of the normative framework of 2003 and 2009, alignment with EU law was still a work in progress. Conditioned by the fact that Croatia was due to become an EU Member State on 1 July 2013, extensive amendments were made to the Competition Act of 2009 in order to make sure that, as of the accession date, its competition law regime was fully functional as part of the EU legal order.[12] The update ensured full compliance of national rules with Regulation 1/2003 and regulated antitrust damages actions in more detail. Moreover, the amendments changed the name of the court exercising judicial review over the AZTN's decisions (from the Administrative Court of the Republic of Croatia to the High Administrative Court of the Republic of Croatia) in line with the reform of the national administrative judiciary system which was completed on 1 January 2012 when the new Act on Administrative Disputes came into force.[13] This was a nominal change as the same court remained in charge to hear challenges against AZTN's decisions. More importantly, the amendments of 2013 introduced a change related to the notion of the suspensive effect of appeals against AZTN's decisions. Before 2013, an appeal had a suspensive effect related to both the existence of an infringement and the fine.[14] By the 2013 amendments, the suspensive effect related to the fine was retained. On the other

provided that 'criteria arising from the application of EU competition rules' will be applicable 'in particular, in case of legal lacunae or doubts related to legal interpretation' (Article 74 Competition Act of 2009). Even after Croatia's accession to the EU in 2013, this provision was kept in the Competition Act, albeit quoting Article 1 of the Accession Treaty as its legal basis, not the SAA.

10. Competition Act, Official Journal 79/2009. For more details *see* Pecotić Kaufman, Malnar and Akšamović, *supra* n. 8.
11. AZTN Annual Report for 2009, pp. 33-34.
12. Amendments to the Competition Law, Official Journal 80/2013, in force as of 1 July 2013.
13. Act on Administrative Disputes (*Zakon o upravnim sporovima*), Official Journal 20/2010, 143/2012, 152/2014, 29/2017, 110/2021.
14. Article 67 para. 4 Competition Act of 2009, Official Journal 79/2009.

hand, it was clear now that there was no suspensive effect regarding the existence of the infringement.

Finally, the 2021 amendments to the Competition Act mainly worked to ensure the transposition of the ECN+ Directive into national law.[15] In addition, a cartel settlement procedure was introduced, and the transparency of the Competition Council members' selection process was increased.

1.2 Institutional and Enforcement Framework of the AZTN

The institutional framework for enforcing competition rules in Croatia is based on the administrative model. The AZTN is a 'regulatory', 'independent legal person with public powers',[16] with investigative and decision-making powers based on national and EU competition laws. In terms of its formal legal status, it is defined as a 'public institution' (*javna ustanova*).[17] It is financed from the state budget,[18] and its revenues are considered state budget revenues.[19] For the performance of its tasks, the AZTN is responsible to the Croatian Parliament, to which it must submit a report once a year.[20] Ensuring its independence from the executive branch, the Competition Act explicitly provides that the AZTN exercises its powers 'independent of political and other external influence and without seeking and receiving instructions from the Government of the Republic of Croatia or any other public or private entity'.[21] However, in line with the wording adapted from the ECN+ Directive, this is 'without questioning the right of the Government of the Republic Croatia to, as necessary, adopt general policy rules that are not related to sector inquiries carried out by the Agency or specific proceedings within the competence of the Agency'.[22]

AZTN's proceedings are considered administrative proceedings (*upravni postupak*) in nature. Apart from specific procedural rules found in the Competition Act, which are primarily applicable, the general administrative law rules, i.e., the Act on General Administrative Procedure, are also applicable.[23] Consequently, the High Administrative Court conducts any judicial review of AZTN's decisions in the 'administrative dispute' proceedings (*upravni spor*).[24]

Although, nominally, a collegiate, five-member body – the Competition Council (*Vijeće za zaštitu tržišnog natjecanja*) – runs the AZTN,[25] it is one of its members – the President of the Competition Council – that plays a leading role. The President

15. Amendments to the Competition Law, Official Journal 41/2021.
16. Article 26 para. 1 Competition Act, Official Journal 79/2009, 80/2013, 41/2021.
17. *Ibid.*, Article 26 para. 9.
18. *Ibid.*, Article 26a para. 4.
19. *Ibid.*, Article 26a para. 7.
20. *Ibid.*, Article 26 para. 6.
21. *Ibid.*, Article 26 para. 11.
22. *Ibid.*
23. *Ibid.*, Article 35 para. 1. Act on General Administrative Procedure (*Zakon o općem upravnom postupku*), Official Journal 47/2009, 110/2021.
24. Act on Administrative Disputes.
25. Article 27 Competition Act, Official Journal 79/2009, 80/2013, 41/2021.

'represents and governs' the institution,[26] presents the annual report before the Parliament, and is responsible for its functioning. The President and other members of the Council are appointed and dismissed by the Croatian Parliament at the proposal of the Government of the Republic of Croatia for a renewable term of five years.

The internal division of work is between the Competition Council and the subordinate Expert Service. The latter conducts investigations in individual cases, proposes to the Competition Council to open proceedings, manages the proceedings, conducts the hearings, prepares draft decisions for the Competition Council, etc. The Competition Council, in turn, adopts relevant decisions in individual cases, including on any fines, orders the Expert Service to conduct market investigations, adopts the annual report, etc.

The investigative and decision-making powers of AZTN are aligned with Article 5 of Regulation 1/2003 and the relevant provisions of the ECN + Directive. The AZTN's powers are very similar to those of the European Commission. It can investigate suspected violations (*ex officio*[27] or following a complaint),[28] request information,[29] conduct interviews,[30] inspections,[31] and sector inquiries,[32] accept commitments[33] and settlements in cartel cases[34] and impose interim measures.[35] It may adopt a decision finding an infringement while imposing remedies and fines.[36] Fines, including daily fines, may be imposed for procedural and substantive law breaches or non-compliance with AZTN's decisions.[37] It may grant immunity from fines or reduce fines for leniency applicants.[38] In addition, the AZTN may issue opinions on issues relating to its mandate and on proposed or existing regulations.[39]

Infringement proceedings are opened *ex officio*.[40] In addition, the AZTN may decide to open proceedings based on a formal complaint submitted by a natural or legal person, professional or trade association, consumer association, the Government of the Republic of Croatia, state administration bodies or local and regional institutions.[41] However, it will refuse to open proceedings following a complaint if it relates to conduct which has a negligible effect on competition in the relevant market or if the complaint fails to address an enforcement priority.[42] So far, to our knowledge, there

26. *Ibid.*
27. *Ibid.*, Article 38.
28. *Ibid.*, Article 37.
29. *Ibid.*, Article 41.
30. *Ibid.*, Article 41.a.
31. *Ibid.*, Articles 42-46.
32. *Ibid.*, Article 32 para. 14.
33. *Ibid.*, Article 49.
34. *Ibid.*, Article 52.a.
35. *Ibid.*, Article 51.
36. *Ibid.*, Article 58.
37. *Ibid.*, Articles 60-64.
38. *Ibid.*, Article 65.
39. *Ibid.*, Article 25.
40. *Ibid.*, Article 38.
41. *Ibid.*, Article 37.
42. *Ibid.*, Article 38 para. 4.

have been no rejections based on prioritisation, but in several cases, the complaint was refused due to negligible effects.

AZTN is in charge of enforcing competition rules in all markets. The only exception, which lapsed on 1 July 2013, was the power of the Croatian National Bank (HNB) to apply competition rules to the banking sector. In two cases, *Société Générale - Splitska banka d.d.* and *Zagrebačka banka d.d.*, the HNB had initially started the proceedings, both related to the abuse of dominance and the same facts, but due to the transfer of the competence in 2013 the AZTN adopted the final decision.[43] The first case was ended by adopting a commitment decision. In the second case, AZTN performed a full competition law assessment and found no legal grounds to continue with the proceedings as no anti-competitive issues were found to exist, thus terminating the proceedings. The HNB unsuccessfully appealed this decision.[44]

2 REVIEW OF THE COMPETITION AUTHORITY'S DECISIONS

As explicitly provided by the Competition Act,[45] the AZTN's decision may be challenged in front of the High Administrative Court, the highest review court in administrative matters. Even though it, in principle, acts as an appellate court vis-à-vis the decisions of the first-instance administrative courts, competition cases are an exception in this regard. In other words, instead of first submitting an appeal (*žalba*) to a first-instance administrative court, which would be the common path for challenging administrative decisions, the AZTN's decisions are challenged by filing an administrative action (*upravna tužba*) with the second-instance administrative court, thus starting the administrative dispute proceedings (*upravni postupak*).[46]

The High Administrative Court judgements are not appealable. Thus, in competition matters, Croatia has a single-tier judicial review system. Exceptionally, an extraordinary legal remedy (the request for extraordinary review of the legality of a final judgement) may be used against the judgment of the High Administrative Court, which is considered a res iudicata.[47] This legal remedy is cumbersome to use since the petitioner may not directly address the Supreme Court of the Republic of Croatia with

43. Decision of the AZTN of 1 August 2013, *Société Générale - Splitska banka d.d.* UP/I-034-03/2013-01/029 (commitment decision). Decision of the AZTN of 3 June 2014, *Zagrebačka banka d.d.*, UP/I-034-03/2013-02/028 (decision to terminate the proceedings). For more details *see* Pecotić Kaufman, Malnar and Akšamović, *supra* n. 8, pp. 33-34.
44. Judgment of the High Administrative Court of the Republic of Croatia of 27 August 2015, UP/I-034-03/2013-01/028; UsII-43/14-10.
45. *Ibid.*, Article 67.
46. For the purposes of this chapter, the term appeal is used to denote the administrative action (*upravna tužba*) in the context of administrative dispute proceedings (*upravni spor*) and/or the administrative dispute proceedings themselves. Also, the term 'first-instance court' refers to the High Administrative Court of the Republic of Croatia, while the term 'second-instance court' refers to the Supreme Court of the Republic of Croatia.
47. Article 78 Act on Administrative Disputes. Another extraordinary legal remedy pursuant to Article 76 of the Act on Administrative Disputes is the reopening of administrative dispute proceedings (*obnova spora*). For a rare example see the judgment of the High Administrative Court of 17 December 2015, UsII-186/15-2 in the case *Zlatni lipanj* (the plaintiff argued he found out new facts, but was rejected by the court; this case refers to the earlier High Administrative

its request to review the legality of the final judgment. Rather, petitioners must first persuade the State Attorney's Office to ask the Supreme Court to allow this request.

A crucial difference between the courts mentioned above, as regards their jurisdiction to hear a case related to breach of the Competition Act, lies in the scope of the review they perform and in the appeal grounds the petitioners may use to address those courts. While the High Administrative Court can be seized on a wide variety of appeal grounds (including breach of procedure or violation of substantive law, incomplete determination of facts, etc.), the Supreme Court only addresses a violation of law, both procedural and substantive.

Applicants dissatisfied with the High Administrative Court judgments in competition matters may also claim violations of their fundamental constitutional rights and freedoms and launch a constitutional complaint before the Constitutional Court of the Republic of Croatia.

2.1 High Administrative Court: Administrative Dispute Proceedings

As mentioned, the High Administrative Court has jurisdiction to hear challenges to AZTN's decisions. Before 1 January 2012, the Administrative Court of the Republic of Croatia was in charge. This is effectively the same court, but its name changed due to a reform of the national administrative judiciary system that was completed in 2012.[48]

Under the current system, the High Administrative Court decides competition cases in two non-specialised chambers, each consisting of three judges. Competition cases present only a very small proportion of their overall workload, as the judges also hear cases from other administrative areas. Administrative dispute proceedings are 'urgent' in competition matters.[49]

The 2012 reform, in particular the new Act on Administrative Disputes, only had a partial bearing on the system of appeals in competition matters since the specific rules that govern the issues, such as grounds for appeal and standing, are covered by the Competition Act, and not by the general law, i.e., the Administrative Dispute Act.[50]

Court judgment UsII-10/2015 of 20 June 2015, and the AZTN's decision UP/I-034-03/14-01/021 (corrected by UP/I-034-03/14-01/021).

48. A comprehensive reform of the administrative justice system that was rolled out in 2009-2010, and completed in 2012, was aimed at modernising national administrative law, in particular at its alignment with the ECtHR standards of the right to fair trial. Upon the 1997 ratification of the ECHR, Croatia made a reservation regarding the application of the right to a fair trial in administrative dispute proceedings with regard to Article 6 para. 1 ECHR since the then valid Act on Administrative Disputes failed to adhere to the requisite ECtHR standards. One of the main deficiencies of the legal framework as it stood then was that deliberations within the administrative dispute proceedings were conducted in a closed hearing. Štefica Stažnik, 'Europski sud za ljudska prava i standardi upravnosudskog postupka' in Ivan Koprić (ed.), *Europeizacija upravnog sudovanja u Hrvatskoj* (Institut za javnu upravu 2014), pp. 123-124.

49. Article 69 Competition Act, Official Journal 79/2009, 80/2013, 41/2021.

50. For a detailed discussion see Dario Đerđa and Zoran Pičuljan, 'Nastanak i temeljni instituti novog Zakona o upravnim sporovima' in Ivan Koprić (ed.), *Europeizacija upravnog sudovanja u Hrvatskoj* (Institut za javnu upravu 2014), pp. 93, 109-110.

Most notably, mandatory oral hearings were introduced in 2012 but with 'significant exceptions' to the requirement to hold them.[51] Hearings are held in some competition cases (e.g., *Sports Betting* case), and not in others (*Hrvatska pošta* (*City Ex*)).[52]

Before 2012, under the 1977 Act on Administrative Disputes, the Administrative Court of the Republic of Croatia, a predecessor of the High Administrative Court, had a narrower role to play when it came to reviewing administrative decisions. It could only annul the contested decision and only exceptionally meritoriously decide on the dispute itself.[53] In other words, it acted as a cassation court, not a court of full jurisdiction. On the contrary, the 2012 Act on Administrative Disputes intended to turn it into a court of full jurisdiction, with the cassation function being an exception.[54] In practice, however, this was a greater challenge than expected.[55]

Administrative dispute proceedings before the High Administrative Court in competition cases are aimed at reviewing the legality of AZTN's decision rather than at rehearing the case. The High Administrative Court decides based on the facts presented in the proceedings before the AZTN, and the plaintiff may not submit new facts except if they can prove that they were not known to him/her or that he/she may not have known about them during the proceedings before the AZTN.[56] The plaintiff may introduce new evidence only if it relates to the facts already presented in the AZTN's

51. Article 7 Act on Administrative Disputes reads: 'The High Administrative Court decides on the basis of an "oral, direct and public" hearing.' However, if the appellant disputes only the application of law, the facts are not contentious, and the parties explicitly stated that they do not demand an oral hearing, no oral hearing is held (Article 36 point 4 Act on Administrative Disputes). Under the 1977 Act on Administrative Disputes, the Administrative Court could hold oral hearings, but they were not obligatory. As Đerđa and Pičuljan noted, oral hearings were theoretically possible in 'complex cases', but in practice never took place (Đerđa and Pičuljan, *supra* n. 50, p. 109). Consequently, the Constitutional Court held that the Administrative Court was not a full jurisdiction court. Decision of the Constitutional Court U-I-745/1999 of 15 November 2000, Official Journal 112/2000.
52. *Sports Betting* case: Judgment of the High Administrative Court of the Republic of Croatia of 8 July 2016, *Super Sport d.o.o. et al. v. Competition Agency*, UsII-22/16-11. An oral hearing was also conducted in the Private security companies case, judgment of the High Administrative Court of 22 April 2016, UsII-60/15-10. Cf the *City Ex* case, Judgment of the High Administrative Court of the Republic of Croatia of 22 September 2017, City Ex d.o.o., UsII-15/16-19. The position of the Supreme Court is that oral hearings must be held if the relevant facts were contentious (judgement U-zpz 1/17-5 of 12 September 2017). The Constitutional Court found no violation of the right to a fair trial in a case in which the High Administrative Court rejected the plaintiff's request to hold an oral hearing, invoking the Jussila judgment of the ECtHR (no. 73053/01, judgment of 23 November 2006). Decision of the Constitutional Court of the Republic of Croatia of 13 January 2021, Bio Save Premium, U-III-2790/2016.
53. Đerđa and Pičuljan, *supra* n. 50, p. 113.
54. The court being able to resolve the matter itself will significantly speed up the decision-making process leading to the faster achievement of the rights of the parties in administrative matters (Ljiljana Karlovčan Đurović, 'Prvostupanjski upravni spor' in Ivan Koprić (ed.), *Europeizacija upravnog sudovanja u Hrvatskoj* (Institut za javnu upravu 2014), p. 175.
55. As observed by Dario Đerđa, 'Chapter IV. Croatia' in Zbigniew Kmieciak (ed.), *Administrative Proceedings in the Habsburg Succession Countries* (Wydawnictwo Uniwersytetu Łódzkiego 2020), pp. 95-96, administrative judges generally prefer to use the cassation power rather than to decide on the merits, as they do not feel competent to adjudicate upon a specific administrative matter by themselves.
56. Article 68 paras 1, 2 and 3 Competition Act, Official Journal 79/2009, 80/2013, 41/2021.

proceedings.[57] The Competition Act narrowed the High Administrative Courts' freedom to 'evaluate the evidence and determine the facts', based on the Act on Administrative Disputes, which stipulates that the court takes into account both the facts established in the proceedings upon which the contested decision was adopted and the facts it established *itself*.[58] The presentation of evidence before the High Administrative Court is regulated by the rules of civil procedure.[59]

As regards the standard of review, the High Administrative Court decides 'within the limits of the claim but is not bound by the grounds of the claim'.[60] There are no specific rules on the intensity of judicial review in competition matters. The High Administrative Court renders its judgment according to its 'free conviction' and considers 'all legal and factual issues'.[61]

The Competition Act provides no list of reviewable AZTN acts; any substantive or procedural decision (*rješenje*) may be appealed. Procedural conclusions (*zaključak*) are non-reviewable and may be challenged only as part of an action against the reviewable AZTN decision.[62] Moreover, dawn raid warrants issued by the High Administrative Court are non-reviewable.[63]

An action against an AZTN decision must be brought within thirty days of the notification of the AZTN's decision.[64] As regards its suspensive effect, any challenge before the High Administrative Court suspends only the payment of the fine, but the execution of the AZTN decision is otherwise not halted.[65] Furthermore, challenging an AZTN's procedural decision by advancing arguments related to a procedural irregularity while the proceedings are still ongoing does not stop the proceedings pending before the AZTN.[66]

As regards the issue of standing, an AZTN infringement decision, adopted either on the basis of national law or Articles 101 or 102 TFEU, may be challenged by 'a party to the proceedings in the framework of which such a decision was adopted'.[67] An AZTN decision terminating the proceedings (*obustava*) may be challenged before the High Administrative Court both by the parties and the complainant, including 'a person to which the AZTN granted the same procedural rights as to the complainant'.[68] Furthermore, the High Administrative Court will *ex officio* invite an 'interested person' to submit its reply to the action filed with the court, although there is no duty for this

57. Article 68 para. 2 Competition Act.
58. Article 33 paras 1 and 2 Act on Administrative Disputes. *See* Dubravka Akšamović, 'Sudska kontrola u sporovima zbog povrede propisa o tržišnom natjecanju u hrvatskom i poredbenom pravu', 67 Zbornik Pravnog fakulteta u Zagrebu 405 (2017).
59. Article 33 para. 5 Act on Administrative Disputes.
60. *Ibid.*, Article 31.
61. *Ibid.*, Article 55 para. 3.
62. Article 67 para. 3 Competition Act, Official Journal 79/2009, 80/2013, 41/2021.
63. *Ibid.*, Article 67 para. 6.
64. *Ibid.*, Article 67 para. 1.
65. *Ibid.*, Article 67 para. 4. However, the plaintiff may ask the High Administrative Court for interim measures, Article 47 Act on Administrative Disputes.
66. Article 67 para. 2 Competition Act, Official Journal 79/2009, 80/2013, 41/2021.
67. *Ibid.*, Article 67 para. 5.
68. *Ibid.*

person to participate in the administrative dispute proceedings.[69] In the administrative dispute proceedings, the defendant will always be the AZTN since its decision is being contested.

As regards the appeal grounds, the Competition Act lists as follows: (a) a contravention of the substantive competition rules, (b) a material breach of procedural rules, (c) erroneous or incomplete determination of facts, and (d) an erroneous decision on fine or other matters decided upon by the AZTN.[70]

As regards the possible appeal outcomes, the High Administrative Court may, on the one hand, reject the action as 'unfounded'[71] or it may reject it due to procedural reasons.[72] On the other hand, it may accept the appeal (in its entirety or partially) and annul the AZTN's decision, or it may accept the appeal (in its entirety or partially), annul the AZTN decision and return it to the AZTN.[73] As of 2012, the High Administrative Court may accept the appeal, annul the AZTN's decision and replace it with its own judgment, except if the 'nature of the matter' prevents it from doing so or if the defendant's administrative act contains a discretionary decision.[74]

2.2 Supreme Court: Extraordinary Review of Legality

As already mentioned, judgments of the High Administrative Court cannot be further appealed. Exceptionally, the Supreme Court of the Republic of Croatia may be seized based on an extraordinary legal remedy, i.e., the request for an extraordinary review of the legality of a final judgment (*zahtjev za izvanredno preispitivanje zakonitosti pravomoćne odluke*). The applicant is not allowed to address the Supreme Court directly. It must first ask the State Attorney's Office of the Republic of Croatia (DORH) if it is willing to submit this remedy to the Supreme Court. Depending on the discretion of the DORH, and provided the Supreme Court accepts this request, the latter - if it finds the request founded - may set aside the High Administrative Court judgment and remand the case for a new trial (*ukinuti presudu i vratiti predmet na ponovno rješavanje*) or it may reverse the judgment (*preinačiti presudu*).[75]

The Supreme Court can only be seized for a violation of procedural or substantive law. In this context, it would typically concern a violation of the Competition Act. This legal remedy is not available for erroneous or incomplete determination of facts; also, this remedy is not appropriate if the petitioner submits new facts.[76]

69. Article 19 para. 3 Act on Administrative Disputes.
70. Article 67 para. 1 Competition Act, Official Journal 79/2009, 80/2013, 41/2021.
71. Article 57 Act on Administrative Disputes.
72. *Ibid.*, Article 30.
73. *Ibid.*, Article 58 para. 1.
74. *Ibid.*
75. *Ibid.*, Article 78. The Supreme Court decides in a chamber of five judges, in a closed session, and examines the disputed decision only within the limits of the request (*ibid.*, Article 78).
76. Meri Dominis Herman, 'Izvanredni pravni lijekovi u upravnom sporu', 42 Zbornik Pravnog fakulteta Sveučilišta u Rijeci 537, p. 553, (2021).

In general, this legal remedy is used relatively rarely, with twenty to forty requests submitted yearly and some ten cases adjudicated every year.[77] It was used only once in a competition case (the *Croatian Association of Orthodontists* case).[78]

2.3 Constitutional Court: Constitutional Complaint

An additional avenue for parties which were unsuccessful in the administrative dispute proceedings is to challenge the High Administrative Court's judgement before the Constitutional Court of the Republic of Croatia by means of a constitutional complaint (*ustavna tužba*).[79] A constitutional complaint is based on a claim that the parties' human rights or fundamental freedoms guaranteed by the Constitution[80] have been violated through an 'individual' act of a state authority, which decided on their rights and obligations.[81] The legal bases most often invoked before the Constitutional Court in competition cases were the right to a fair trial[82] and the right to equality before the law.[83]

77. Alan Uzelac, 'Pravni lijekovi u upravnom sporu: kreću li se upravno i parnično sudovanje u suprotnim smjerovima?' in Ante Galić (ed.), *Novosti u upravnom pravu i upravnosudskoj praksi* (Organizator 2019), p. 81 and references cited *supra* nn. 19 and 20. Looking at the 2013-2017 period, Uzelac noted that the Supreme Court accepted eighteen requests only, out of which in eleven cases the administrative court judgment was reversed (*preinačena*), and in seven cases set aside (*ukinuta*).
78. The AZTN successfully petitioned the State Attorney's Office to file the request for extraordinary review of legality concerning a High Administrative Court judgment which annulled the AZTN's infringement decision (AZTN Decision of 12 June 2014; judgment of the High Administrative Court of the Republic of Croatia of 5 March 2015, UsII-70/14-6). Eventually, in 2021, the Supreme Court reversed the High Administrative Court judgement, thereby confirming the 2014 AZTN's decision. Judgment of the Supreme Court of the Republic of Croatia of 2 March 2021, U-zpz 16/2015-4.
79. In case the constitutional complaint is accepted the contested decision or judgment will be revoked. In such a case, if a new decision or judgment must be adopted by the relevant administrative or judicial body, the Constitutional Court shall return the judgment/decision to the body which adopted it (i.e., to the High Administrative Court or the AZTN). *See, e.g.*, Sokol Marić decision. In such a case, the relevant body is obliged to respect the legal position of the Constitutional Court expressed in its decision. Articles 73, 76, 77 Constitutional Court of the Republic of Croatia, Official Journal 49/2002-consolidated text.
80. Constitution of the Republic of Croatia, Official Journal 56/90, 135/97, 113/00, 28/01, 76/10, 5/14.
81. Article 62 para. 1 Constitutional Act on the Constitutional Court of the Republic of Croatia, Official Journal 49/2002-consolidated text. A constitutional complaint is allowed solely if administrative dispute proceedings have been exhausted as a remedy, i.e., if the AZTN's decision has been appealed before the High Administrative Court., Article 62 para. 3.
82. Article 29 para. 1 Constitution. The cases include Zlatni lipanj, U-III-4930/2015; Sokol Marić, U-III-2791/2016; Presečki U-III-1678/2014; Presečki U-III-952/2017; Klemm sigurnost U-III-2826/2016; Bilić-Erić U-III-2820/2016; V Grupa U-III-6196/2016; I.-I.n U-III-2397/2012; Hyundai U-III-2934/2011; E.H/N.M.G. U-III-4257/2012; Zlatni lipanj U-III-3189/2015; Presečki U-III-1711/2014; Auctus U-III-2225/2015.
83. Article 14 para. 2 Constitution. The cases include Zlatni lipanj, U-III-4930/2015; Tisak U-III-4082/2010; Presečki U-III-1678/2014; Presečki U-III-952/2017; Klemm sigurnost U-III-2826/2016; Bilić-Erić U-III-2820/2016; V Grupa U-III-6196/2016; I.-I.n U-III-2397/2012; Hyundai U-III-2934/2011; E.H/N.M.G. U-III-4257/2012; Zlatni lipanj U-III-3189/2015; Presečki U-III-1711/2014; Auctus U-III-2225/2015, bio Save Premium, Sretan Jukić, Selec.

Considering the specific narrow nature of this remedy, focusing solely on asserting the parties' fundamental rights vis-à-vis the state, it has been considered that Constitutional Court decisions in competition matters do not fall within the project's scope. Therefore, such cases do not constitute part of the data on appeals discussed in this chapter. On the other hand, it did not escape our attention that the involvement of the Constitutional Court definitively impacts the outcome of the case. For this reason, as illustrated below (section 5.2.), this chapter also includes a discussion on its role in competition matters.

3 PRIOR RESEARCH

The literature review we conducted for this research project did not produce any examples of a comprehensive and quantitative survey of competition law enforcement in Croatia. However, there are examples of more limited studies, such as a survey by Akšamović examining the High Administrative Court case law between 2015 and 2020 to analyse the arguments used by the plaintiffs in administrative dispute proceedings initiated against the AZTN's infringement decisions. She found a higher success rate in cartel/anti-competitive agreements appeals (35%) compared to the average success rate of 17%.[84] Another systematic study by *Petrović* critically examined the Croatian Constitutional Court case law in competition cases.[85]

We have also identified several studies focusing on specific aspects of judicial review concerning competition matters. The topics covered include the appropriate level of judicial scrutiny and whether a one-tier administrative justice system in competition matters meets the requisite legal standards (with Akšamović, and Popović & Maričić taking opposing views),[86] the suspensive effect and interim measures in the administrative dispute proceedings in Croatia,[87] excessive judicial formalism in the post-accession case law of the High Administrative Court and the Constitutional Court,[88] the standard of proof in judicial review of cartel cases,[89] and the use of the fair

84. Dubravka Akšamović, 'Judicial Review in Competition Cases in Croatia: Winning and Losing Arguments before the High Administrative Court of the Republic of Croatia', 13 Yearbook of Antitrust and Regulatory Studies 7 (2020) DOI: 10.7172/1689-9024.yars.2020.13.22.1.
85. Siniša Petrović, 'Tržišno natjecanje u praksi Ustavnog Suda Republike Hrvatske – Osvrt na recentne odluke Ustavnog suda (U-III-952 / 2017 /" Presečki "/ i U-III-2791/2016, U-III6196/2016, U-III-2826/2016, U-III-2820/2016 /"Zaštitari"/)', (2018), https://hdpptn.hr/wp-content/uploads/2018/06/usud-tr%C5%BE-natj.pdf.
86. Akšamović, *supra* n. 58. Nikola Popović and Domagoj Maričić, 'Postupci pred nezavisnim eegulacijskim tijelima i novi Zakon o upravnim sporovima' in Ivan Koprić (ed.), *Europeizacija upravnog sudovanja u Hrvatskoj* (Institut za javnu upravu 2014).
87. Dubravka Akšamović, 'Privremene mjere i odgodni učinak uužbe u sporovima za zaštitu tržišnog natjecanja u hrvatskom pravu i europskom pravu', 72 Zbornik Pravnog Fakulteta u Zagrebu 119 (2022) DOI: 10.3935/zpfz.72.12.03.
88. Jasminka Pecotić Kaufman, 'Judicial Interpretation and Competition Law Enforcement: Authoritarian Legal Culture, Semantic Dissonance and Skewed Agencification in Post-Socialist Croatia', 48 Review of Central and East European Law 275 (2023) DOI: 10.1163/15730352-bja10084.
89. Alexandr Svetlicinii, 'The Judicial Review of the Standard of Proof in Cartel Cases: Raising the Bar for the Croatian Competition Authority Case Comment to the Judgment of the Constitutional

trial legal basis in competition cases as a trigger for the involvement of the Constitutional Court as another review instance.[90]

There is also a general book in English covering all aspects of competition law in Croatia, which includes a chapter on judicial review of the AZTN's decisions.[91]

Overall, the consulted sources have been beneficial in gaining insight into the main strands of discussion related to judicial review in competition matters in Croatia, though not engaging in the type of comprehensive quantitative and qualitative analysis that we undertake here.

4 QUANTITATIVE ANALYSIS

This section examines the empirical findings from applying a systematic analysis of all judicial reviews of competition law enforcement in Croatia issued and made public between May 2004 and April 2021. During this period, in 2013, Croatia acceded to the EU. However, already since the early 2000s, on the basis of international agreements signed with the EU, EU competition law was applied in Croatia as an interpretative tool alongside national law. Thus, the dataset explored includes the pre-accession and post-accession case law of the Croatian courts in competition matters. The dataset includes the case law of the following courts: first, the High Administrative Court of the Republic of Croatia, the first and final instance for judicial review of the AZTN's decisions to be reached using an 'ordinary' legal remedy (*redovni pravni lijek*), i.e., an administrative action (*upravna tužba*); second, the Supreme Court of the Republic of Croatia, which can be seized using an 'extraordinary' legal remedy (*izvanredni pravni lijek*), i.e., the request for extraordinary review of the legality of a final judgment. Constitutional complaints do not fall within the dataset, as explained in section 2 of this chapter.

4.1 Source of Information

To our knowledge, all appeal rulings concerning competition law matters have been published in Croatia so far. This is mainly thanks to the efforts of the AZTN, which by law makes appeal court decisions available on its website in a timely manner.[92] Thus, the AZTN's open online database was used for this project to collect the judgments. This database contains all AZTN's decisions in full text from late 2002 until the present,

Court of the Republic of Croatia No. u-Iii-2791/2016 of 1 February 2018 (Sokol Marić D.)', 11 Yearbook of Antitrust and Regulatory Studies 311 (2018) DOI: 10.7172/1689-9024.yars.2018.11.18.13.

90. Lovorka Kušan and Siniša Petrović, 'Ustavna jamstva i gospodarski ustroj Republike Hrvatske (o poduzetničkoj i tržišnoj slobodi i pravu vlasništva)', 7 Zagrebačka pravna revija 255, p. 274 (2018).
91. Pecotić Kaufman, Malnar and Akšamović, *supra* n. 8.
92. www.aztn.hr/odluke. From 1998 until 2010, the judgments of the High Administrative Court (previously, the Administrative Court) were also by law published in the Official Gazette. However, there may be a significant time lag between the adoption of the appeal judgment and its publication in the Official Gazette. For a minor number of appeal judgments, we were able to find them in the AZTN's database but not in the Official Gazette.

as well as the judgments of the High Administrative Court (previously the Administrative Court) and the Supreme Court related to the AZTN's decisions.[93] Hence, the database of this study is expected to be comprehensive.

4.2 Total Number of Judgments, Judgments per Year and Ratio of Appeals

The database includes a total of 104 rulings, which fell within the scope of this research project (the period between May 2004 and April 2021). Out of this number, 103 were adopted at the first instance and one at the second-instance level.

The first-instance judgments include sixteen adopted by the Administrative Court of the Republic of Croatia (until 31 December 2011), eighty-six by the High Administrative Court of the Republic of Croatia (as of 1 January 2012), and one judgment adopted in 2013 by the Administrative Court in Zagreb.[94] Only one second-instance judgment was adopted by the Supreme Court of the Republic of Croatia.

The proportion of AZTN's decisions being appealed is relatively low. Only some 22% of AZTN's decisions from May 2004 to April 2021 were appealed. In other words, slightly more than a fifth of AZTN's decisions were challenged before the High Administrative Court (previously, the Administrative Court). We can think of several explanations for such a low appeal ratio. First, over the years, the AZTN adopted infringement decisions and imposed fines in a limited number of cases; also, in a considerable number of cases, it adopted a non-infringement decision, meaning that the undertakings had no incentives to appeal them.[95] Second, for a prolonged period (from 1995 until late 2010), the AZTN had no power to directly fine undertakings; thus, the incentive for the parties to appeal an AZTN's declaratory infringement decision was arguably not entirely functional, in particular, due to the fact that fines were most often not imposed in individual cases by the misdemeanour courts.

Figure 6.1 summarises the number of judgments issued per year. It points to notable trends in the average number of decisions issued annually.

First, there is a striking difference in the number of appeals before and after 2012. In almost eight years (1 May 2004-31 December 2011), the Administrative Court adopted sixteen judgments, while in almost ten years thereafter (1 January 2013-30 April 2021), the High Administrative Court adopted sixty-six judgments. In other words, the Administrative Court issued an average of two judgments annually, while the High Administrative Court had an average of 6.6. This means that, on average, the High Administrative Court heard more than three times more appeals than its predecessor. Thus, appeals against AZTN's decisions increased considerably after 2012, which coincided with the new Competition Act of 2009 (in force as of late 2010), based on which the AZTN started imposing fines directly for antitrust infringements.

Second, 2016 appears to be a tilting point in the operation of the High Administrative Court. In the first period (2012-2016), sixty-eight appeal judgments were

93. www.aztn.hr/odluke/odluke-sudova.
94. A gap case due to changes in the administrative justice system: UsI-17/12-9 Akton (VIPnet).
95. For details concerning the number of cases, *see* Pecotić Kaufman, *supra* n. 1.

adopted, with a peak in 2015 (twenty-seven judgments in a single year). In the second period, eighteen appeal judgments were adopted, almost four times less. This pronounced difference seems to indicate that the golden years of AZTN's antitrust enforcement were in the period of most intensive negotiations for EU membership, the time when there was considerable pressure from the European Commission for the AZTN to demonstrate a credible enforcement record or immediately thereafter (seventeen appeal judgments in 2012, ten in 2014, twenty-seven in 2015, thirteen in 2016).[96] Thus, the significant decrease in the number of AZTN decisions in 2017 seems to be related directly to the decrease in the number of appeals as of 2017.

Third, the appeals were largely driven by a large number of decisions rejecting initiatives to start proceedings (i.e., complaints) produced by the AZTN in the period leading up to the conclusion of Croatia's membership negotiations.[97]

Figure 6.1 Number of Judgments According to Instances

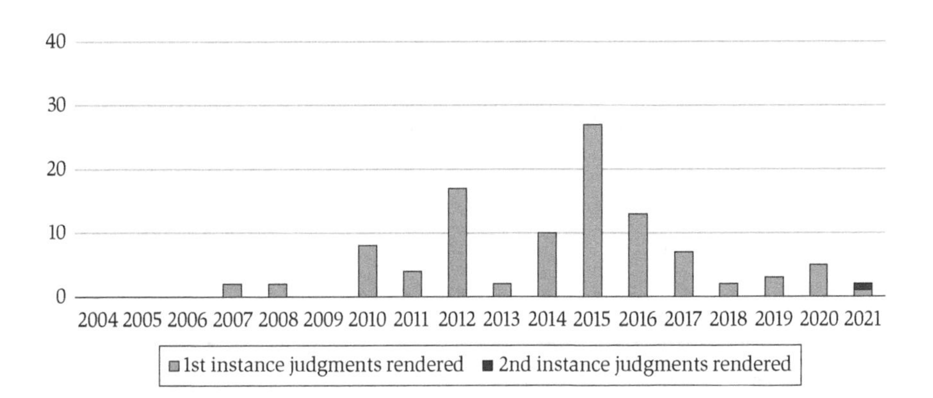

Figures 6.2(a) and (b) compare the number of judgments in the database per year according to each instance (lines) with the number of AZTN's appealed decisions (bars). They reveal that in most instances, each appealed AZTN decision was subject to a single judgment.

96. Indeed, there is a notable difference between the total number of the AZTN's substantive decisions (decisions rejecting a complaint, infringement or non-infringement decisions, and commitment decisions) in the period between 2010 and 2016, and 2017-2020. We take 2016 as a cut off year, as in that year the total number of substantive decisions peaked (43 decisions), while it more than halved in 2017, remaining around that level until 2020. In the first period (2010-2016), the AZTN adopted a total of 222 decisions (31.7 decisions per year), while in the second period 2017-2020, it adopted a total of 81 decision (20.25 decisions per year). This is an astonishing 44% drop in the enforcement activity measured in the number of decisions. Calculated using data from *ibid.*, pp. 351-352.

97. As regards AZTN's decisions rejecting complaints, in the period 2010-2020, 21 decisions were adopted each year. The peak was in 2016 (34 decisions), with a pronounced decrease in 2017 (15 decisions). There is a striking difference in the yearly number of decisions rejecting a complaint

Figure 6.2(a) First-Instance Judgments

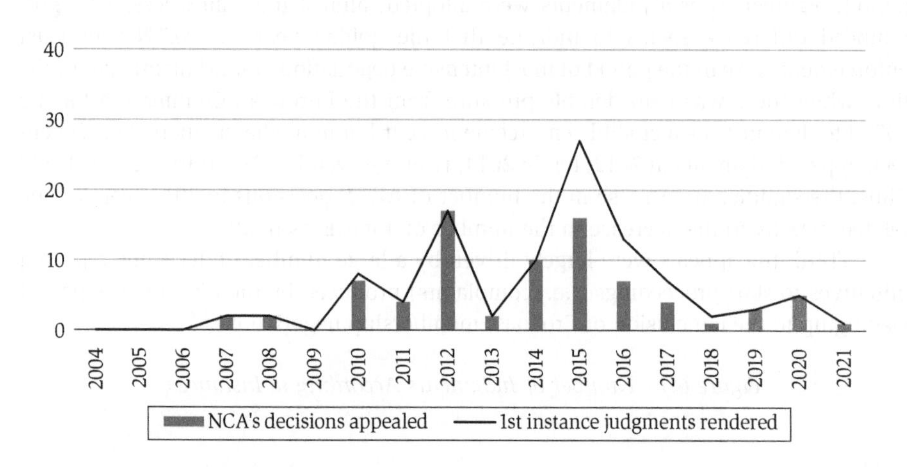

Figure 6.2(b) Second-Instance Judgments

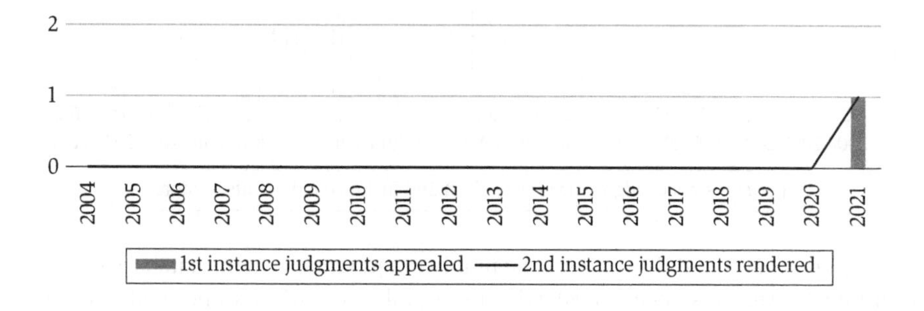

4.3 Success Rates and Outcomes

The overall success of appeals against AZTN decisions is low. As shown in Figure 6.3, which presented the data from the perspective of the NCA decision or the Previous Instance Judgment which has been appealed, 84% of the appeals have been fully

and other categories of substantive decisions (infringement/non-infringement/commitment decisions), former being four to six times higher when compared to the latter. In the 2010-2016 period, there were 173 decisions rejecting complaints and 49 other substantive decisions (more than two times less), and in 2017-2020, there were 62 decisions rejecting a complaint and 19 other substantive decisions (more than three times less). Calculated using data from ibid., pp. 351-352.

rejected (sixty-nine appeals), while 11 % were fully successful (nine appeals), and 5 % partially successful (four appeals). In other words, in most cases, the appeal court has followed the position of the AZTN.

Figure 6.3 Success of Appeals (Each NCA's Decision or Previous Instance Judgment Counts as One)

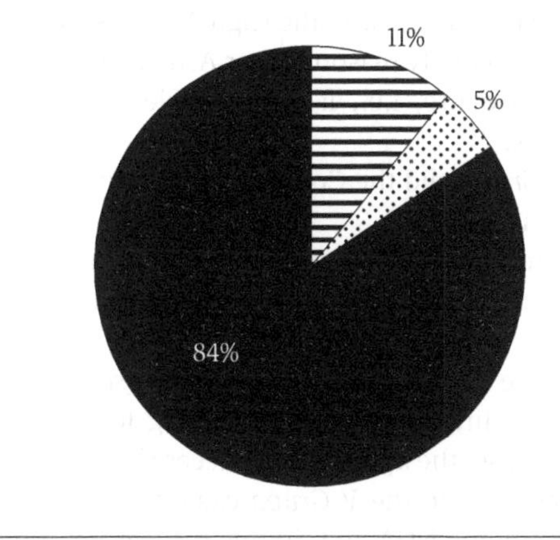

No. of fully successful appeals	No. of partially successful appeals
No. of fully rejected appeals	No. of withdrawn appeals

Figures 6.4(a) and (b) move to examine the ratio of possible outcomes according to each instance of appeal. In contrast with the previous figure, the data is presented from the perspective of each separate judgment.

Figure 6.4(a) demonstrates that when the High Administrative Court (previously, the Administrative Court) finds the AZTN's decision to be 'unlawful', it might either fully annul the AZTN's decision[98] (five judgments) or fully annul and return it to the AZTN (six judgments).[99]

Examples of fully annulled AZTN's decisions include the judgment of the High Administrative Court in the *Sports Betting* case, where it held that the AZTN made an erroneous determination of facts,[100] as well as the *Croatian Association of Composers* case,[101] and the *Croatian Association of Orthodontists* case,[102] where it held that the AZTN erroneously applied the law.

98. Article 58 para. 1 Act on Administrative Disputes.
99. *Ibid.*
100. UsII-22/16-11.
101. In this case, the court held that the law was applied retroactively, with the AZTN imposing a fine based on the Competition Act 2009, while the infringement was committed at the time when Competition Act 2003 was in force. Under Competition Act 2003 the AZTN had no power to impose fines directly. UsII-6/2014-7.
102. UsII-70/14-6.

Examples of fully annulled and returned AZTN's decisions include the *Neven Perica* (*BAT*) case,[103] the *H1* case,[104] and the *Bilogora* case,[105] where the High Administrative Court found a significant violation of procedural law.[106] In the *Presečki* case, the AZTN decision was annulled and returned based on the Constitutional Court decision, which set aside the High Administrative Court judgment and returned for reassessment.[107] In the *Marinas* case, the High Administrative Court held that the facts were not sufficiently determined, preventing it from assessing whether substantive law was correctly applied.[108] In the ABIES case, the High Administrative Court held that the AZTN's decision was not sufficiently reasoned, per Article 98 paragraph 5 of the Act on General Administrative Procedure, i.e., it was not clear what was the reason for terminating the proceedings.[109]

Only in one case, *V Grupa*, did the Court partially annul the AZTN decision and return it for further examination.[110]

Although the High Administrative Court can replace the AZTN decision with its judgment,[111] there has been no such case. This instead occurred at 'second instance', when the Supreme Court, in the *Croatian Association of Orthodontists* case, fully replaced the judgment of the High Administrative Court (*see* Figure 6.4(b)).[112]

Two judgments at the first-instance level belong to the category 'Other' outcomes. In the *Zlatni lipanj* case, the applicant unsuccessfully requested a retrial due to new facts and new evidence.[113] In the *V Grupa* case, the High Administrative Court annulled the fine imposed by the NCA and, in this respect, returned it to the NCA for retrial, and as regards the rest of the NCA's decision, it rejected the appeal.[114]

---

103. UsII-69/17-5 Neven Perica (BAT).
104. UsII-65/2014-9 H1 Telekom (HT).
105. UsII-98/13-13 Bilogora.
106. Article 67 para. 1 point 2 Competition Act.
107. UsII-171/18-2 Presečki Grupa (Međimurska županija).
108. UsII-39/15-10 Marine.
109. UsII-109/15-6 ABIES (Hrvatske šume).
110. UsII-45/15-12.
111. Pursuant to the Act on Administrative Disputes, which came in force in 2012.
112. In *Croatian Orthodontists Association*, the AZTN used extraordinary remedy to challenge the High Administrative Court judgment which annulled the AZTN's infringement decision. Eventually, in 2021, the Supreme Court reversed the HAC judgment in this case ordering that the challenge to the AZTN's decision before the HAC was rejected, thereby confirming the 2014 AZTN decision.
113. UsII-186/15-2 Zlatni lipanj. The retrial refers to the previous the HIG judgment UsII-10/2015 of 20 June 2015 and NCA decision UP/I-034-03/14-01/021 (corrected by UP/I-034-03/14-01/021) and return to NCA for retrial (*obnova sudskog postupka*).
114. UsII-45/15-12 V Grupa (Zaštitari).

Figure 6.4(a) First-Instance Outcome

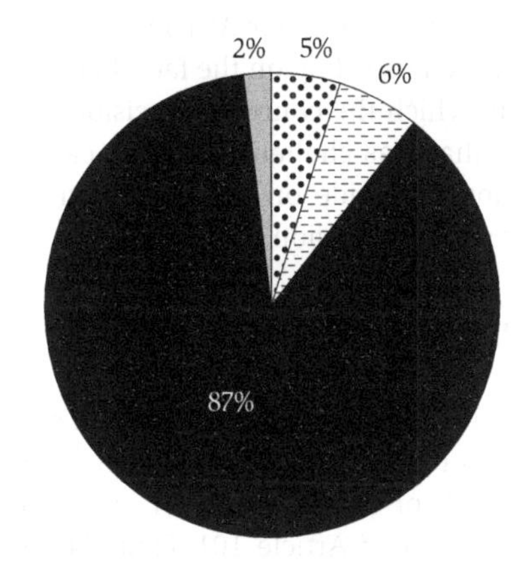

Figure 6.4(b) Second-Instance Outcome

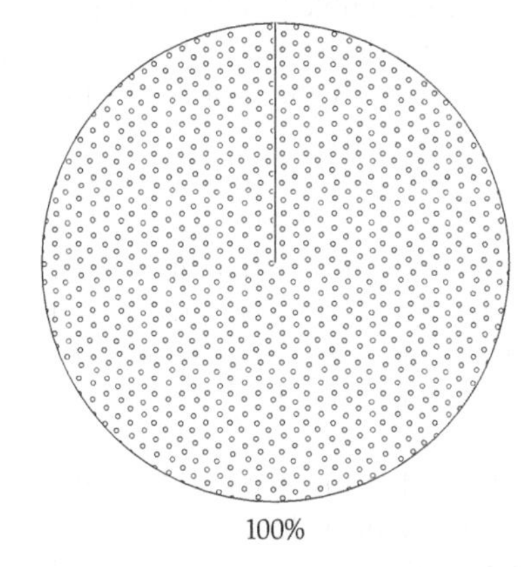

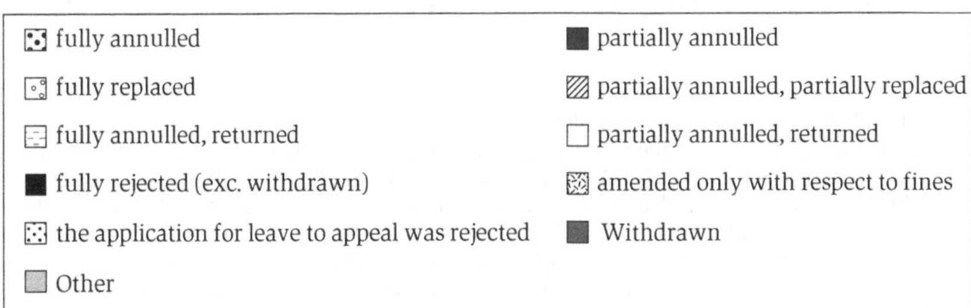

The issue of admissibility rarely arises. In addition to the *Croatian Association of Orthodontists* case, we have no information on any requests to the DORH to petition the Supreme Court that were rejected or any possible rejections by the Supreme Court in the event the DORH was willing to submit such a remedy. To the best of our knowledge, such cases have not occurred.

In only one case, *HNB*, the appeal was deemed fully inadmissible, as the High Administrative Court held that the applicant (the Croatian National Bank, HNB) had no standing.[115] The appeal was dismissed under Article 30(1)(2) of the Act on Administrative Disputes. The court based its ruling on the fact that HNB was not a party in the administrative proceeding in which the contested decision was adopted. Namely, the AZTN adopted the decision that was challenged in this case, not the HNB, since the latter institution's jurisdiction to decide on competition matters regarding financial institutions ceased as of Croatia's accession to the EU.

4.4 Type of NCA's Decisions Subject to Appeal

Figure 6.5 shows that the AZTN decisions subject to appeal concerned either the abuse of a dominant position subject to the national equivalent of Article 102 TFEU (50% of all decisions subject to appeal, or 52 decisions) or an anti-competitive agreement, subject to the national equivalent of Article 101 TFEU (40% of all decisions, or 42 decisions). The rest concern decisions relying on both national rules equivalent to Articles 101 and 102 TFEU in the same case (7%, or 7 decisions). A very small minority of decisions relate to cases where a double legal basis has been invoked, both national and EU competition rules (3%, or 3 decisions related to both Article 102 TFEU and its national equivalent being relied upon, with no cases in which Article 101 TFEU and its national equivalent would be relied upon).

As the figure demonstrates, judicial review of AZTN decisions was mainly confined to national competition law. As very few AZTN decisions have Articles 101 and/or 102 TFEU as their legal basis, the fact that this is mirrored in the appeals process is not a surprise. However, one would have expected that after Croatia's EU accession in 2013, the AZTN would issue more decisions based on a double legal basis (both national law and Articles 101 and 102 TFEU), and it is surprising that this did not happen.[116]

As regards the three cases that involved an appeal against an AZTN decision adopted under Article 102 TFEU, alongside its national equivalent, the first was the *Hrvatska pošta* (*City Ex*) case,[117] the second was the *HT* (*H1*) case,[118] while the third

115. UsII-43/14-10 Hrvatska narodna banka.

116. For explanations for this apparently broader phenomenon, at least as regarding Central and Eastern Europe, see Marco Botta, Maciej Bernatt and Alexandr Svetlicinii, 'The Assessment of the Effect on Trade by the National Competition Authorities of the "New" Member States: Another Legal Partition of the Internal Market?', 52 Common Market Law Review 1247 (2015).

117. *HP-Hrvatska pošta (City Ex)*, AZTN decision based on the national equivalent of Article 102 TFEU, and Article 102 TFEU for the period after 1 July 2013); found no infringement of the national equivalent of Article 102, but terminated proceedings (*obustava postupka*) in relation to Article 102, AZTN decision of 26 November 2015, UP/I 034-03/13-01/010. Judgment of the High Administrative Court of the Republic of Croatia of 22 September 2017, City Ex d.o.o., UsII-15/16-19.

118. Case *HT (H1)*: AZTN decision of 8 May 2014 terminating proceedings against HT, annulled and returned UsII-65/2014-9 due to a lack of reasons for termination of proceedings; new AZTN decision, of 17 December 2014, again annulled UsII-8/15-10 with the appeal court holding that the AZTN must adopt a substantive decision, not a termination decision; new AZTN decision,

was the Bio Save Premium case.[119] In the first two cases, the AZTN adopted a non-infringement decision concerning the national rule on the abuse of a dominant position while terminating proceedings concerning Article 102 (based on Article 5 Regulation 1/2003 and Tele2 Polska judgment).[120] In the *Bio Save Premium* case, the initiative to start proceedings based on Articles 102 and 106 TFEU and the national equivalent of Article 102 was rejected by the AZTN. Although this decision was appealed, the appeal invoked only national law appeal grounds.

In three additional cases that were not appealed, the AZTN adopted a non-infringement decision alongside a termination decision concerning Article 102 TFEU.[121] Moreover, we are only aware of one case before the AZTN that was started based on Article 101 TFEU and its national equivalent.[122] Here, the AZTN decided to terminate the case (*obustava*) as regards Article 101 due to its negligible effect on trade between Member States, and concerning the national equivalent of Article 101, it adopted a commitment decision.

As already mentioned, half of all the AZTN's appealed decisions relate to the abuse of a dominant position. This is disproportionate to the amount of abuse of dominance decisions adopted by the AZTN overall. In the 2004-2020 period, the AZTN adopted ten infringement decisions for an abuse of dominance, while in the same period, the total number of infringement decisions related to anti-competitive agreements was 32.[123] Notably, in the 2012-2020 period, there were no AZTN infringement decisions related to the abuse of dominance. Regarding non-infringement decisions, between 2004 and 2023, there were sixteen such decisions for an abuse of dominance (including one with a double legal basis in 2020) and eight for anti-competitive agreements.[124] It seems that many of the potential infringement decisions were supplanted by commitment decisions (the AZTN was able to adopt them as of 2011). In the 2011-2020 period, a total of twenty-seven commitment decisions were adopted by the AZTN for anti-competitive agreements and the abuse of dominance.[125] In addition, a probable explanation for the disproportionately higher number of abuse of

of 14 November 2018, non-infringement under Article 13 Competition Act and termination under Article 102, invoking Tele2 Polska judgment.

119. *Bio Save Premium* case: AZTN decision UP/I 034-03/15-01/015 of 28 September 2015, High Administrative court judgment, Usll-191/15-12 of 22 April 2016, and Constitutional Court judgment, U-III-2790/2016 of 13 January 2021.
120. An NCA does not have the power under Article 5 of Regulation 1/2003 to reach a decision stating that there has been no breach of Article 102 (Tele2 Polska C-375/09 (2011) ECR I-3055, EU:C:2011:270, paras 27-30), (David Bailey and Laura Elizabeth John (eds), *Bellamy & Child European Union Law of Competition* (8th edn, Oxford University Press 2018). P. 1323).
121. UP/I 034-03/17-01/010, AZTN protiv Hrvatski Telekom d.d. (termination of proceedings both in relation to Article 102 TFEU and its national equivalent); UP/I 034-03/14-01/028, AZTN protiv Grand Auto d.o.o. (no infringement in relation to the national equivalent of Article 102 and termination in relation to Article 102 TFEU); UP/I 034-03/2012-01/023, AZTN protiv Hrvatski Telekom d.d. (no infringement in relation to the national equivalent of Article 102 and termination in relation to Article 102 TFEU).
122. UP/I 034-03/2014-01/026, AZTN protiv Drezga d.o.o. (commitment decision; the proceedings were terminated in relation to Article 101 TFEU).
123. Pecotić Kaufman, *supra* n. 1, Table 2, p. 352.
124. *Ibid.*
125. *Ibid.*

dominance decisions being appealed overall is that a clear majority of AZTN decisions reject a complaint related to an abuse of dominance situation.[126]

Figure 6.5 Rule Being Appealed

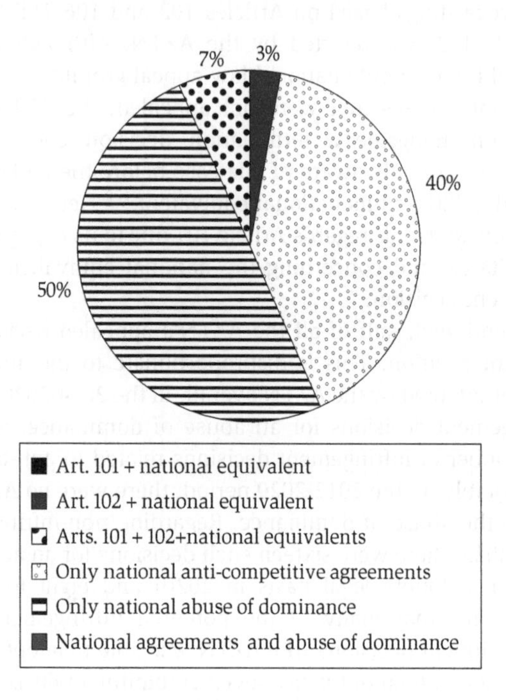

Figure 6.6 presents the rules being appealed according to years. It shows that the peak year of 2015 mostly involved challenges to AZTN decisions related to the abuse of dominance. However, caution is needed when interpreting this result. Some two-thirds of the appeal decisions adopted in 2015 on account of an abuse of dominance concern the one and same case (*Zlatni lipanj*). This is a prime example of a situation in which the applicant stubbornly but unsuccessfully (ab)used all and any procedural weapons to contest the AZTN decision, which consistently rejected its complaints.

126. *Ibid.*, Table 1, p. 351.

Figure 6.6 Rules Being Appealed According to Years (Each Judgment Counts as One)

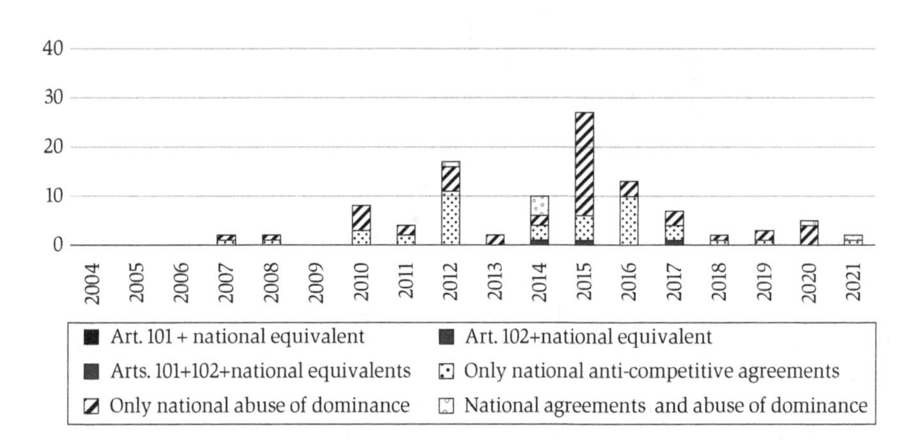

As regards the types of competition restrictions addressed by the AZTN's decisions that were appealed (Figure 6.7), a clear majority of the Article 102 TFEU-type restrictions relate to exclusionary abuse (forty-nine appeal judgments), while the rest relate to exploitative (five judgments) and both exclusionary and exploitative (one judgment). To our knowledge, those types of abuses are also more generally subject to AZTN's decisions. However, it is worth noting that, in general, no clear indication is given either by the AZTN or an appeal court on the more precise categorisation of the relevant restriction, at least concerning the abuse of a dominant position.

As regards Article 101 TFEU-type restrictions, 50% more appeal judgments relate to horizontal restraints (twenty-eight judgments) than to vertical restraints (fourteen judgments). This finding matches the general AZTN's enforcement focus on hardcore horizontal restrictions.

Finally, only a very small number of appeal judgments related to Article 101 and 102-type restrictions (seven judgments).

Figure 6.7 Types of Restrictions

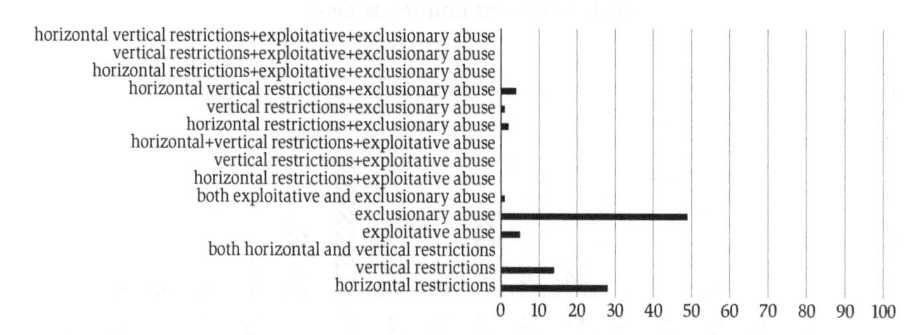

Figure 6.8 illustrates that an overwhelming majority of appeal judgments concerning anti-competitive agreements involved by-object restrictions (80% or thirty-nine judgments), with no judgments relating to by-effect restrictions. In 18% of judgments (a total of nine), the type of restriction was not indicated. The focus on by-object restrictions is consistent with the enforcement focus of the AZTN on hardcore infringements, both horizontal and vertical.

A closer look at those judgments demonstrates that the courts seemingly struggle with the concept of horizontal hardcore restraints, particularly in the context of collusive conduct between competitors.[127]

Figure 6.8 Object/Effect (Only for Article 101/Nationa Equivalent Infringements)

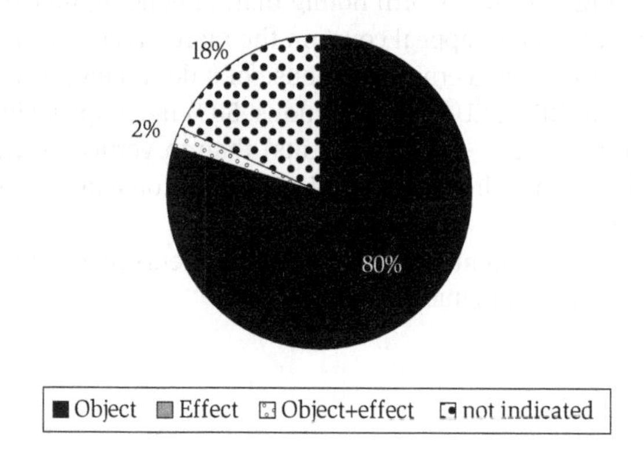

Most appealed AZTN's decisions – thirty-seven judgments – concern the rejection of a complaint (Figure 6.9). This is consistent with the finding that such decisions were adopted in great numbers by the AZTN, especially between 2011 and 2016.[128]

127. The legacy of an authoritarian legal culture, excessive judicial formalism, disassociation between the legal norm and its socio-economic context and a lack of 'constitutionalisation effects' in competition cases were, inter alia, offered as explanations contextualising the occurrence of several controversial rulings. For an extensive discussion, *see* Pecotić Kaufman, *supra* n. 88.

128. See Pecotić Kaufman, *supra* n. 1, Table 1, p. 351.

Many appeal judgments relate to AZTN's infringement decisions without a fine (twenty-six judgments), while only nineteen judgments concerned an infringement decision imposing a fine. Since AZTN had no power to sanction competition law violations directly until late 2010, these findings do not come as a surprise.

Seven relate to an AZTN's decision, which found that there were no grounds for action.

Figure 6.9 Competition Authority's Procedure

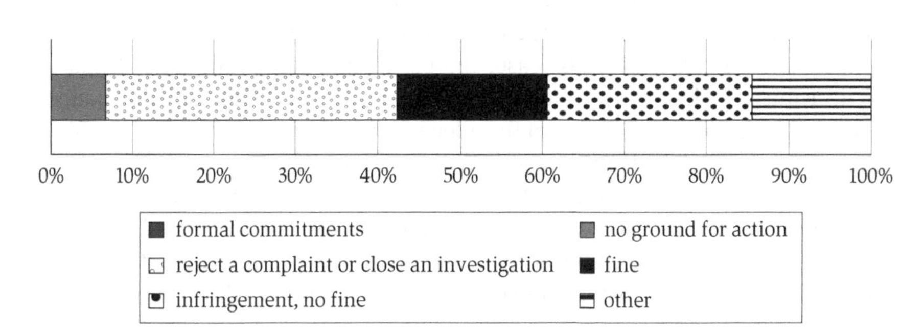

Finally, our findings reveal that none of the appeals related to proceedings in which leniency and settlement applications were successfully submitted. These findings are unsurprising: the cartel settlement procedure was unavailable before 2021,[129] while the leniency programme was available in late 2010 but had no significant effects.[130]

4.5 Grounds of Appeal

Figure 6.10 indicates the success of each ground of appeal launched by the parties to the procedure against an NCA's decision or on a previous instance judgment. The data is presented from the perspective of the NCA decision or the previous instance judgment, which has been appealed. For example, if three separate first-instance judgments have been issued concerning a single NCA decision and procedural grounds were fully accepted in two court judgments but rejected in the third, the figure will record this case as a single partially successful procedural ground of appeal.

Our findings indicate a similar number of procedural and substantive grounds of appeal used by the applicants overall. In most cases, they were rejected (fifty-seven rejected appeals relied on procedural grounds, sixty-eight on substantive grounds). A limited number of appeals were successful: five on procedural grounds, four on substantive grounds, and two on fine grounds. One appeal was partially successful on substantive grounds as well as on procedural grounds.

129. Introduced by amendments to the Competition Act in 2021, Article 52.a, Official Journal 41/21.
130. A leniency programme was introduced by the Competition Act 2009 that entered into force on 1 October 2010, Official Journal 79/09.

Remarkably, almost no appeals related to fines (nine overall, from which six were rejected; one partially accepted, and two fully accepted). This finding is consistent with a relatively small number of appealed decisions relating to infringements with a fine imposed, as discussed above.

Given that none of the cases under appeal was considered to have an effect on trade between Member States, EU/national arguments were discussed relatively frequently (eight unsuccessful appeal judgments had an EU/national aspect, and in two judgments, the claim was fully accepted). In these cases, the applicant raised issues related to the tension between EU and national competition law. Such arguments were, in particular, raised in the pre-accession period.

In the 2007 *Tisak/Distri-Press* case, the parties unsuccessfully argued that the AZTN decision relied on an 'undefined [EC] practice' but also that the national competition law in force at the time of the alleged infringement only foresaw as illegal agreements those which had anti-competitive effect in practice, and that the agreement in question was no longer in force.[131] The defendant (i.e., AZTN) invoked [CJEU] case law to claim that Article [101] was still applicable to a formally rescinded agreement which still produced negative effects on competition.[132] The appeal court confirmed that the AZTN was correct to apply the criteria arising from the [EU] competition law based on Article 70 SAA.

Arguments based on the inapplicability of EU law before Croatia's accession to the EU were entertained by the appellants in several appeals. For instance, in the 2011 *Hyundai Auto Zagreb* case, the applicant, *inter alia*, argued that the AZTN decision was illegal since, concerning some allegedly anti-competitive clauses of the relevant distribution contracts, it entirely relied on 'interpretative instruments for the application of Croatian rules' even before the country was an [EU] member state.[133] The appeal court dismissed this claim, holding that the AZTN appropriately applied the criteria arising from the [EU] acquis. Based on the SAA, the appeal court held that the entire acquis communautaire was 'an important interpretative instrument for the application of Croatian laws in case of legal lacunae or interpretational doubts'.[134]

Similarly, in the 2012 Autoškole Rijeka Matulji case, the applicants unsuccessfully attempted to contest the AZTN's decision, arguing that applying EU rules before accession was not lawful.[135] One of the applicants argued that the agreement did not affect trade between Croatia and [EU]. However, the appeal court based its ruling

131. Us-533/2006-7 Tisak/Distri-Press.
132. The following case law was mentioned: *SCA Holding v. Commission*, *Petrofina v. Commission*, *Acerinox v. Commission*; the AZTN also referenced Van Bael & Bellis, *Competition Law of the European Community*, Kluwer Law International, pp. 43-44.
133. Us-6075/2010-9 Hyndai Auto Zagreb.
134. *Ibid.*
135. Us-10674/2009-4 Autoškole Rijeka i Matulji.

entirely on national law, not tackling any of the EU law-related arguments raised by the applicants.[136]

Another appeal in which it was unsuccessfully argued that [EU] law and [CJEU] practice were not applicable and that the AZTN's decision had to be annulled due to the application of rules which 'did not belong to the positive law of the Republic of Croatia', was the *Stanouprava et al.* case.[137] Here, the applicants' also attempted to show that the non-existence of concrete effects on the market was relevant to the agreement's legality. The appeal court rejected this argument, confirming AZTN's reliance on the Commission's Guidelines on the application of Article [101] paragraph 3 [TFEU].

In the 2015 *TDR/Adris Grupa* case, the applicants unsuccessfully argued that the AZTN 'unconstitutionally' applied the EU acquis directly since it was not a valid 'source of law'.[138] The AZTN argued that it was correct to apply the acquis as an auxiliary interpretation tool, based on Article 35 paragraph 5 Competition Act and the Constitutional Court's interpretation in previous rulings.[139] The appeal court confirmed the AZTN's stance.

The argument that no EU rules should be relied upon by the AZTN continued to be used after Croatia's EU accession. In the *Private Security Companies* case, the appeal court rejected the applicant's argument that only national rules should have been applied in the concrete case. The court explicitly relied on Article 74 paragraph 1 Competition Act, which provided that criteria arising from the application of EU competition rules are applicable in case of legal lacunae or any doubt concerning the interpretation of the rules laid in the Competition Act in line with Article 1 of Croatia's Accession Agreement.[140]

In the *Marinas* case, one of the applicants, the Croatian Chamber of Commerce, relied on Article 101 TFEU and its interpretation by the CJEU to dispute the association's liability for an alleged breach of competition rules.[141] In this richly argued case, the applicants claimed that the AZTN incorrectly applied EU competition law, relying, *inter alia*, on CJEU case law and the Commission's Horizontal Cooperation Guidelines. One of the applicants argued that criteria based on EU law had no primacy over the national legal standards. The appeal court referred to the standards established by the CJEU related to the illegal exchange of information between competitors. However, it found that an infringement of the national competition law was not sufficiently established, thus annulling and returning the AZTN's decision.

136. In the *Kutjevo* case too, the applicant argued that EU rules were not applicable before Croatia's accession to the EU. The appeal court had not tackled this issue in its reasoning. UsII-85/14-5 Kutjevo.
137. Us-1700/2010-6 Stanouprava et al.
138. Us-9222/11-4 TDR/Adris grupa.
139. The following rulings were invoked U-III-1410/2007, and U-III-4082/2010.
140. UsII-60/15-10 Securitas Hrvatska. Cf. *supra* n. 9.
141. UsII-39/15-10 Marine.

The tension between EU law and national law was particularly relevant in the HT (H1) case, where a misaligned provision of national law prompted the appeal court to twice annul and return an AZTN's decision.[142]

The national courts submitted no preliminary references in competition cases. There is no indication in the judgments that the parties proposed submitting any preliminary references.

Figure 6.10 Grounds of Appeal (Each NCA's Decision or Previous Instance Judgment Counts as One)

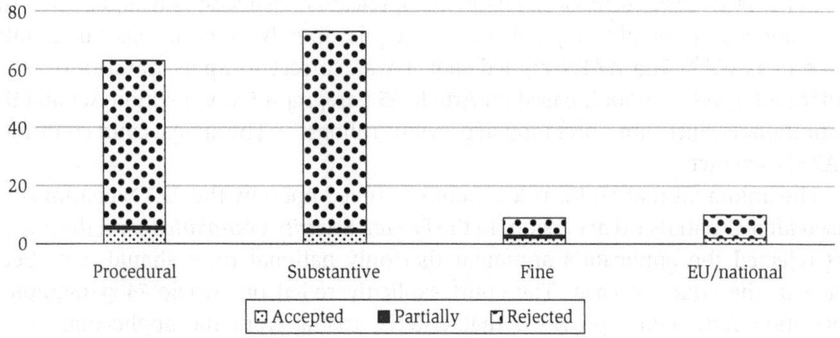

80
60
40
20
0
Procedural Substantive Fine EU/national
Accepted ■ Partially Rejected

The fine was reduced in 7% of cases at the administrative dispute level.[143] The fine was also annulled in all cases where the AZTN's decision was annulled. There are no cases where the fines were only reduced.

The findings related to the issue of which grounds of appeal were most successful in what types of restrictions (Figure 6.11) reveal that almost all of the fully or partially successful substantive grounds were in anti-competitive agreements cases and not in abuse cases. Successful abuse cases are related primarily to matters of procedure. Accordingly, substantive grounds were successful in five anti-competitive agreement cases,[144] while procedural grounds were successful in three abuse of dominance cases.

142. UsII-65/2014-9, and UsII-8/15-10.

143. At the constitutional complaint level, the fine was reduced in 33% of cases. Thus, the Constitutional Court was more willing to reduce fines compared to the High Administrative Court.

144. U-zpz 16/2015-4 Hrvatsko društvo ortodonata, UsII-39/15-10 Marine, UsII-171/18-2 Presečki Grupa (Međimurska županija), UsII-70/14-6 Hrvatsko društvo ortodonata, UsII-22/16-11 Sportske kladionice.

Figure 6.11 Types of Restrictions Versus Successful Grounds of Appeal

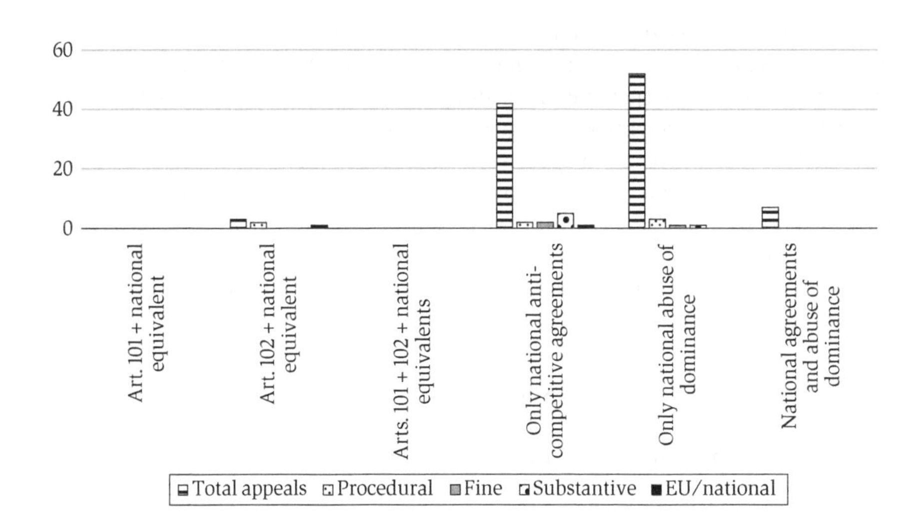

4.6 Third Parties' Participation

The challenges to AZTN's decisions were submitted by two types of appellants: the undertakings concerned and third parties. It might be expected that the largest group to submit an appeal would be the undertakings against which the decision was adopted. However, in Croatia, primarily due to the large number of AZTN's decisions rejecting a complaint (especially in the 2011-2016 period), the largest number of appeals have been submitted by a third party, i.e., an undertaking or an individual person, which submitted an initiative to the AZTN to start proceedings (complainants). A total of sixty appeal judgments relate to such a situation, while forty-four judgments concern an appeal submitted by the undertakings concerned.

Pursuant to the Act on Administrative Disputes, the High Administrative Court has to send the 'appeal', i.e., the administrative action (*upravna tužba*), to the respondent and any 'interested persons'.[145] The interested third parties have procedural rights and are considered a party in the 'appeal' procedure, i.e., the administrative dispute proceedings.[146] Quite surprisingly, in many instances, the third parties – as interested persons in the administrative dispute proceedings – would disregard the invitation to submit their response. Remaining passive, they effectively ceded their involvement to the defendant, i.e., the AZTN. In only eleven cases out of sixty were the complainants actively involved in the proceedings challenging the AZTN's decision.

In one case, a company harmed by the abusive conduct by the appellants but which was not the complainant in the AZTN proceedings joined the administrative

145. Article 32 Act on Administrative Disputes.
146. Articles 16 and 20 Act on Administrative Disputes.

dispute proceedings i.e., submitted a reply to the administrative action submitted by the appellants.[147]

Consumer organisations are rarely involved in competition cases. Some exceptions, where NGOs acted as complainants, include the *Stambeni inžinjering et al.* case,[148] in which the infringement proceedings in front of the AZTN related to a cartel agreement between residential management companies in Pula. In this case, the complaint was submitted by a local consumer NGO (*Potrošač-Društvo za zaštitu potrošača Istre*). In a similar case concerning a different locality (the town of Split), the *Stanouprava et al.* case,[149] the infringement proceedings in front of the AZTN were again based on the complaint submitted by a local consumer NGO (*Dalmatinski potrošač*). However, in neither case did the consumer organisation join the appeal procedure as a third party.

5 QUALITATIVE ANALYSIS

5.1 Scope and Intensity of Judicial Review

As it currently stands, the Competition Act prevents the High Administrative Court from establishing facts on its own, significantly narrowing the scope and intensity of judicial review.[150] Even though appeals in competition matters benefit from an increased level of legal protection due to stricter rules on oral hearings imposed as of 2012, there have been no competition cases where the High Administrative Court acted as a full jurisdiction court.[151] Engaging in merits review seems to be a broader issue. At the administrative judiciary level, there seems to be a prevailing opinion that 'the role of the court in the administrative dispute proceedings is, as a rule, exhausted in assessing the legality of the contested decision, and not in the immediate solving of the administrative relationship'.[152] Indeed, administrative law scholars have noted that when an administrative body decides based on their 'discretion', as is the case in the competition matters, the administrative court cannot decide on the merits because it would go beyond the scope of judicial authority and step into the competences of the administration.[153]

147. *Adris grupa/TDR* case Us-5855/2006-9. BAT (British American Tobacco), the company harmed by the plaintiffs' abusive conduct, joined the appeal procedure.
148. Us-2248/2010-6.
149. Us-1700/2010-6.
150. Akšamović, *supra* n. 84, pp. 12-13, 16.
151. The law grants it discretion to avoid deciding on the merits. For example, in the *Marinas* case, the High Administrative Court annulled the AZTN's decision and returned the case to AZTN, invoking the exception related to 'the nature of the administrative case' from the obligation to decide in the case at hand pursuant to Article 58 para. 1 Act on Administrative Dispute, while ordering the AZTN to comply with the legal position elaborated in its judgment. The AZTN's decision was annulled because the High Administrative Court held that the contested decision was founded on facts that had not been sufficiently established; thus, the court held it was unable to examine whether substantive law has been applied correctly. UsII-39/15-10 Marine.
152. Bosiljka Britvić Vetma and Boris Ljubanović, 'Ovlasti upravnog suca u sporu pune jurisdikcije', 50 Zbornik Pravnog fakulteta Sveučilišta u Splitu 429. p. 433 (2013).
153. Đerđa and Pičuljan, *supra* n. 50, p. 116. However, they note that in practice, it will be very

However, some authors see no difficulties with the High Administrative Court acting as a cassation court. Noting that only a small number of EU Member States, i.e., those with a long market economy tradition, have judiciary specialised in competition matters, Popović and Maričić argue that there is no need for the High Administrative Court to conduct a *de novo* review, as this would demand a 'significant level of judicial specialisation' alongside with increased costs related to expert opinions.[154] Also, since the AZTN's decisions are based on extensive economic analysis, and since in light of Article 6 of the ECHR, AZTN should be regarded as a specialised administrative court of the first instance, the appropriate level of judicial scrutiny by the High Administrative Court may well be limited to examining material and procedural legality, which does not necessarily have to include a reassessment of all relevant facts.[155]

This discussion should probably take into account the fact that within the EU Croatia stands out with its quite limited appeal options. Reforming the Competition Act to provide the appellants with the possibility to challenge the AZTN's decision before the first-instance administrative court(s) seems an obvious solution, as the appeal to the first-instance administrative courts (*žalba*) allows new facts to be submitted. Such a reform would allow a more thorough examination of the appellants' arguments by a younger generation of judges with more exposure to EU law, albeit protracting the process of reaching a *res judicata*.

5.2 The Role of the Constitutional Court

The Constitutional Court decisions in competition matters were sporadic and sparse throughout the relevant period but included some notable cases.[156] The cases in which a constitutional complaint was submitted concerned equally anti-competitive

difficult to assess when the nature of the matter prevents the court from solving the administrative matter by itself; if the court interprets this provision too extensively, it will exceed its authority, if it is interpreted too strictly, it will fail to fulfil the task entrusted by the law.

154. Popović and Maričić, *supra* n. 86, pp. 220-221.
155. *Ibid.*, pp. 203-204. However, they warned that particular care must be taken to respect the procedural rights of the parties, guaranteed by Article 6 ECHR, in the proceedings before the AZTN.
156. In the 2004-2021 period, the Constitutional Court adopted altogether eighteen rulings related to AZTN's decisions; some relate to a single AZTN's decision (four rulings concerning the *Private Security Companies* case: 2018 rulings in *Sokol Marić, V grupa, Klemm, Bilić Erić* cases; three concerning the *Presečki* case (2016 Presečki infringement decision, Presečki complaint rejection, 2018 Presečki infringement decision second time); four concerning the *Zlatni lipanj* case (2016 complaint related to an abuse of dominance rejected two times, 2020 complaint related to an anti-competitive agreement rejected). Thus, the eighteen Constitutional Court rulings concern ten AZTN's cases (*Tisak, Selec et al., EHP/NCL, I.-I.n, Hyundai, Zlatni lipanj, Presečki, Auctus, Private Security Companies*, and *Bio Save Premium*).

agreements and the abuse of dominance.[157] Most Constitutional Court rulings were related to an AZTN's infringement decision.[158]

It was argued that because of very limited appeal options, both in terms of the number of instances and in terms of the scope of the review, recourse to the Croatian Constitutional Court has been (ab)used in competition cases in order to create an additional (*de facto*) appeal level.[159]

The constitutional complaint itself was intended only as an exceptional remedy, and the Constitutional Court has no direct jurisdiction vis-à-vis administrative bodies' decisions and administrative courts' judgments. However, by deciding on the protection of fundamental and constitutional guarantees, the Constitutional Court becomes actively involved in adjudicating administrative matters. Since its introduction in 1990, the constitutional complaint has grown into a remedy almost routinely filed in all types of proceedings, regardless of the actual existence of violations of constitutional rights in the earlier proceedings.[160] Competition cases are no exception in this regard. The distortion of its original role was criticised for effectively turning the Constitutional Court, 'completely unnecessarily and contrary to the Constitution', into a regular court of the highest instance controlling the correct application of law by other courts.[161]

5.3 Overall Enforcement Trends and Sanctions

There seem to be two distinct competition law enforcement periods in Croatia. The first one ended in 2016, with a peak in both the number of the AZTN's substantive decisions and decisions rejecting an initiative to start proceedings[162] and in the number of appeal judgments. The second one, starting in 2017, features an overall drop in the AZTN's enforcement activity, alongside the number of appeal judgments showing a downward

157. If we count cases and not each individual decision, five AZTN cases concerned national equivalent of Article 101, while five concerned national equivalent of Article 102 and one concerned both national equivalent of Article 102, and Article 102 and Article 106 TFEU.
158. Ten concerned an infringement decision adopted by the AZTN (seven if we count on the basis of cases), one concerned a non-infringement decision, and seven concerned an AZTN's decision rejecting a complaint (four if we count on the basis of cases).
159. Akšamović, *supra* n. 84.
160. The review of constitutional complaints equals about 85% of cases within the jurisdiction of the Constitutional Court. The total number of constitutional complaints that are endorsed is approximately 4%, while about 50% will be rejected for various procedural reasons, and roughly 46% for substantial reasons. During constitutional complaint proceedings, the Court will also look into any erroneous application of substantive law, provided the application constitutes a violation of constitutional rights. If the decision of the competition authority was rescinded and sent for retrial, the competition authority is bound by the legal reasoning of the Constitutional Court. See Mario Jelušić and Duška Šarin, 'Vladavina prava i uloga Ustavnog suda Republike Hrvatske u izvršavanju upravnih i upravnosudskih odluka', 52(1) *Zbornik radova Pravnog fakulteta u Splitu* 175-201, at 184-186, 188 (2015).
161. Kušan and Petrović, *supra* n. 90, p. 274. Kušan and Petrović criticise invoking the right to a fair trial legal basis in competition cases as a trigger for the involvement of the Constitutional Court.
162. As substantive decisions we count infringement decisions, no infringement decisions, commitment decisions. Decisions rejecting initiatives provide a substantive analysis of the reasons for rejection.

trend.[163] As visible from Figure 6.1, the number of appeal judgments peaked in 2015, continuing somewhat in 2016, with a significant downward trend from 2016 onwards.

Concerning fines, the dynamics are somewhat different. Prior to late 2010, the fines were imposed by the misdemeanour courts based on the AZTN's infringement decision.[164] After the AZTN obtained the power to impose fines, the fines initially remained symbolic.[165] However, several years after Croatia's EU accession, a stricter fining policy by the AZTN encountered challenges at the appeals level. In a series of more prominent, mostly cartel cases, the courts (High Administrative Court, but also Constitutional Court) annulled its decisions. Although Constitutional Court rulings are outside this project's scope, their effect on fines imposed by AZTN was in fact significant.[166] In the *Presečki* saga, the judgment of the High Administrative Court confirming the AZTN decision to impose a fine of HRK 1,009,000.00 on a cartel between bus operators was twice annulled by the Constitutional Court.[167] Most notably, in the 2015 *Private Security Companies* case, the Constitutional Court annulled the highest-ever total fine imposed by the AZTN (HRK 5,035,000), which the High Administrative Court earlier confirmed.[168]

The High Administrative Court invalidated sanctions imposed by AZTN in several notable horizontal price-fixing cases. In the 2015 *Sports Betting* case, the total fine of HRK 9,374,000.00 was annulled by the High Administrative Court.[169] In the 2015 *Marinas* case, the total fine of HRK 2,363,000.00 was annulled by the High

163. We observe a one-third drop in the number of AZTN's substantive decisions between the first and the second period (in the 2011-2016 period, on average seven substantive decisions, while on average 4.75 substantive decisions in the 2017-2020 period). In addition, the overall number of the AZTN's decisions rejecting initiatives was relatively consistent in the first period (on average, twenty-eight decisions per year), dropping substantially in the second period (on average, 15.5 decisions in the 2017-2020). For data concerning the AZTN's enforcement between 2011 and 2020 *see* Pecotić Kaufman, *supra* n. 1, p. 353, Table 3.

164. For this period, we have no reliable data in terms of actual fines imposed/collected. In addition, no information on any appeals to the misdemeanour court decisions imposing fines is available.

165. Symbolic fines were imposed in the following cases: the *Osijek Bakeries cartel* case (CCA Decision of 26 July 2012, the first ever fine directly pronounced by the competition authority); the *Croatian Orthodontist Association* case (CCA Decision of 12 June 2014, annulled: judgment of the High Administrative Court of the Republic of Croatia of 5 March 2015, *Hrvatsko društvo ortodonata v. CCA*, UsII-70/14-6); the *Carlsberg/KTC* case (CCA Decision of 23 October 2014); the *Kutjevo/KTC* case (CCA Decision of 30 July 2014); and the *Dukat/Konzum* case (CCA Decision of 30 July 2014). Pecotić Kaufman, *supra* n. 1, p. 358. Malinauskaite compared Estonia, where a stricter fining policy was applied from the beginning, and Croatia which opted for a 'soft start with symbolic fines being imposed'. Jurgita Malinauskaite, 'Public EU Competition Law Enforcement in Small "Newer" Member States: Addressing the Challenges', 12 Competition Law Review 19, 52 (2016).

166. In any case, in the 2010-2018 period, most of the fines eventually collected relate to gun jumping in merger cases.

167. UsII-65/2013-6 & UsII-60/16-2. After the first annulment, the AZTN again adopted an infringement decision, imposing a slightly reduced total fine of HRK 991,040.

168. UsII-61/15-9 Arsenal Ivezić (Zaštitari) HRK 171,000.00, UsII-54/15-9 Klemm Sigurnost (Zaštitari) HRK 657,000.00, UsII-53/15-9 AKD-Zaštita (Zaštitari) HRK 905,000.00, UsII-93/15-10 Bilić-Erić (Zaštitari) HRK 942,000.00, UsII-60/15-10 Securitas Hrvatska (Zaštitari) HRK 1,027,000.00, UsII-40/15-10 Sokol Marić (Zaštitari) HRK 1,333,000.00.

169. Judgment of the High Administrative Court of the Republic of Croatia of 8 July 2016, *Super Sport d.o.o. et al. V. CCA*, UsII-22/16-11.

Administrative Court.[170] In the *2015 Orthodontists* case, the fine of HRK 150.000,00 was annulled by the High Administrative Court;[171] however, this ruling was later reversed by the Supreme Court.[172] In one case, the annulment of the fine by the High Administrative Court was due to retroactive application of the law.[173]

In very few cases, the High Administrative Court confirmed sanctions imposed by the AZTN. This occurred in a series of RPM cases: *Kutjevo* (a fine of HRK 130,000.00),[174] *Carlsberg Croatia* (a fine of HRK 500,000.00),[175] and *Narodni trgovački lanac/Kraš* (a fine of HRK 2,582,600.00).[176] In a rare case, the High Administrative Court accepted the plaintiffs' arguments related to the financial difficulties it was enduring and annulled the part of the AZTN's decision related to the fine.[177]

Arguably, rulings by the High Administrative Court and the Constitutional Court annulling the AZTN's decisions imposing fines undermined the effectiveness of cartel enforcement by the AZTN in the long run.[178] From 2015 until the present, the AZTN's cartel enforcement efforts were almost non-existent, arguably indicating a low level of institutional resilience. The rulings were also criticised for establishing a disproportionately high standard of proof for illegal cartel conduct that did not comply with the standards established by the CJEU.[179]

Finally, in the vast majority of cases, as analysed for this project, the position of the appeal court is one of deference. However, in the post-accession period, a less deferential attitude by the High Administrative Court is observed, mainly due to the above-mentioned more prominent price-fixing cases, in which the AZTN, reversing its previously relaxed fining policy, imposed considerable sanctions, only to be repudiated at the appeal stage.[180]

170. Judgment of the High Administrative Court of the Republic of Croatia of 17 March 2016, *Ilirija d.d. et al. v. AZTN*, UsII-39/15-10; eventually the AZTN decided to suspend proceedings in this case (AZTN's decision of 13 December 2016.
171. UsII-70/14-6 judgment of the High Administrative Court.
172. Judgment of the Supreme Court of the Republic of Croatia of 2 March 2021, U-zpz 16/2015-4.
173. In the *KMAG* case, the infringement related to conduct that occurred prior to the Competition Act 2009, i.e., before the AZTN obtained the power to impose fines. UsII-60/2013-8.
174. UsII-85/14-5.
175. UsII-103/14-5.
176. UsII-4/15-5.
177. *V Grupa* case (one of the Private Security Companies cases). The Court returned the decision for retrial on this aspect and asked the AZTN to consider a reduction of the fine or imposition of a symbolic fine. UsII-45/15-12. The AZTN reduced the fine to HRK 145,000 (from HRK 289,000). The decision of the AZTN of 28 July 2016, UP/I 034-03/14-01/002. However, the Constitutional Court annulled subsequently both the judgment of the High Administrative Court and the AZTN's decision, so no fine was eventually collected. U-III-6196/2016.
178. The High Administrative Court and the Constitutional Court's role in reversing sanctions was not significant in quantitative terms. However, the few rulings annulling AZTN's infringement decisions had a lasting effect as the AZTN's decisions were its first attempt to use direct fining powers in a more prominent fashion. Moreover, it was argued that the excessively stringent legal standard of proof for cartel agreements, established by the Croatian courts following accession, indicated an incomplete semantic alignment with the EU competition law. For details *see* Pecotić Kaufman, *supra* n. 88.
179. Svetlicinii, *supra* n. 89.
180. The same is true for the Constitutional Court, acting in competition cases on the basis of a constitutional complaint.

5.4 The Application of EU Competition Law

The reliance on the EU competition law as an (indirect) source of law was observable in AZTN's decisional practice even before Croatia acceded to the EU in 2013, i.e., ever since 1 March 2002, when the Interim Agreement on trade and trade-related matters between the [EU] and Croatia took effect, mandating EU rules to be applied as interpretative tools in cases with a cross-border effect on trade.[181] However, references to EU legal sources in AZTN's decisions, which were made in purely domestic type of situations, typically without any assessment on the issue of the cross-border effect performed by the AZTN, was not left unchallenged as the parties argued that reliance on a foreign body of law, prior to Croatia's EU membership, was unconstitutional.[182]

In 2008, in the *PZ Auto* case, the Constitutional Court notably held that it was both the right and the obligation of the AZTN and of the appeal court to take the relevant EU law into account when applying national competition rules, as the EU 'criteria, standards and interpretative instruments' were 'not applied as the primary source of law, but only as auxiliary instruments of interpretation'.[183] Furthermore, the Constitutional Court held that the Competition Act had to be applied 'within the meaning and the spirit' of the EU rules with which national rules were harmonised.[184] As noted subsequently, this 'judgment paved the way for the full alignment of Croatian substantive competition rules with EU competition rules and enabled the Competition Agency to continue considering EU competition law as a point of reference even in the assessment of purely domestic cases, with beneficial results on the convergence of competition law enforcement and the quality of decisions'.[185]

The EU-friendly stance, established firmly in the pre-accession era, saw some backsliding after the accession to the EU. Notably, the Constitutional Court's 2018 rulings in the *Private Security Companies* case, annulling the AZTN's decision to impose its highest-ever total fine for cartel infringement, were criticised as departing from the well-established EU competition law standards. For example, Svetlicinii observed that they disregarded several substantive presumptions developed by the EU Commission and EU courts when applying competition rules in relation to anti-competitive agreements, effectively deviating 'from [Constitutional Court's] previous practice of accepting EU competition law standards as auxiliary sources of law for interpretation purposes even prior to Croatia's formal accession to the EU'.[186] Svetlicinii noted that this approach placed 'a heavier burden of proof on the Croatian NCA in

181. Interim Agreement on trade and trade-related matters between the European Community, of the one part, and the Republic of Croatia, of the other part (OJ L 330, 14.12.2001, p. 3-210).
182. Pecotić Kaufman, Malnar and Akšamović, *supra* n. 8, para. 31.
183. Vlatka Butorac Malnar and Jasminka Pecotić Kaufman, 'The Interaction Between EU Regulatory Implants and the Existing Croatian Legal Order in Competition Law' in Mitja Kovač and Ann-Sophie Vandenberghe (eds), *Economic Evidence in EU Competition Law* (Intersentia 2016).
184. Decision of the Constitutional Court of Croatia of 13 February 2008, U-III-1410/2007.
185. Pecotić Kaufman, Malnar and Akšamović, *supra* n. 8, para. 32.
186. Svetlicinii, *supra* n. 89, p. 318.

cartel cases when compared to its own preceding practice or the enforcement practices of the EU Commission or other European NCAs'.[187]

In addition, the departure from the well-established principles of EU competition law has been noted in the *Croatian Association of Orthodontists* case. (In)famously, the High Administrative Court held that for an anti-competitive agreement to be sanctioned, it 'must be enforceable in practice, meaning that the AZTN should have proved that there was price fixing or that there was an intention to fix prices'.[188]

However, in most cases where judicial review of the AZTN decisions has been sought, the court rulings seem to be based on well-settled principles established by the CJEU. Overall, relevant legal issues are usually neither complex nor novel. The courts frequently confirm the AZTN's decisions based on relatively straightforward legal arguments.[189] A notable exception is the *H1 Telekom/HT* case, in which the question of interpretation of Regulation 1/2003 was at the forefront of the proceedings.[190] The key issue was whether the AZTN could adopt a negative infringement decision. The AZTN claimed this would be contrary to Article 5 of Regulation 1/2003 and suspended its proceedings. On the contrary, the High Administrative Court held that the AZTN must adopt a substantive decision and not a decision suspending the proceedings.

Most of the AZTN's decisions that have been reviewed by the High Administrative Court (previously the Administrative Court) relate only to the application of the national prohibitions. This is unsurprising since very few AZTN's decisions have Articles 101 and/or 102 TFEU as their legal basis.[191] Only in two cases were appeals related to AZTN's decisions, which had been adopted based on Article 102 TFEU, alongside its national equivalent.[192] In both cases, the AZTN adopted a non-infringement decision concerning the national rule while terminating proceedings concerning Article 102 (under Article 5 of Regulation 1/2003 and Tele2 Polska judgment). Thus, the appeals referred only to the national equivalent of Article 102.[193]

187. *Ibid.*
188. Judgment of the High Administrative Court of the Republic of Croatia of 5 March 2015, UsII-70/14-6. Annulled by the judgment of the Supreme Court of the Republic of Croatia of 2 March 2021, U-zpz 16/2015-4.
189. For example, *see POS sistemi*, where the High Administrative Court rejected the appeal against the AZTN decision which rejected the request to start proceedings against undertakings that were a single economic entity. Erste card club et al. UsII-474/18-13.
190. UsII-65/2014-9, and UsII-8/15-10. As the corollary of this case, a corrigendum of the Croatian translation of the Regulation 1/2003 was made in 2016 on the initiative of the AZTN. However, practitioners involved in this case correctly argued that the national court was obliged to disrespect the misaligned national rule and directly apply Regulation 1/2003. *See* Veršić Marušić, Mucalo, Kolak, Wrong translation of Regulation 1/2003 and inappropriate provisions of the Croatian Competition Act cause problems in practice, Antitrust News - Newsletter of the International Bar Association Legal Practice Division, vol. 29, no. 3, December 2016, pp. 21-23.
191. This is similar to other CEE jurisdictions, *see* Botta, Bernatt and Svetlicinii, *supra* n. 116. According to the ECN statistics, between 1 May 2004 and 31 December 2021 the AZTN, acting under Article 101 or 102 TFEU, informed the Commission, pursuant to Article 11 para. 3 Regulation 1/2003, on commencing formal investigation in 9 cases, and pursuant to Article 11 para. 4 Regulation 1/2003, of 4 envisaged decisions. https://competition-policy.ec.europa.eu/european-competition-network/statistics_en.
192. HP-Hrvatska pošta (City Ex) case, and HT (H1) case.
193. In the *Bio Save Premium* case, the initiative to start proceedings on the basis of Articles 102 and 106 TFEU and the national equivalent of Article 102 was rejected by the AZTN. AZTN decision

It is notable that the AZTN's decisions rarely analyse the effect on cross-border trade.[194] This does not imply that all the cases dealt with by the AZTN are related to purely domestic situations. It just means that an analysis of whether there is an effect on trade between Croatia and the EU was, for some reason, not entertained. An explanation for this may lie in the fact that the tradition has developed in the AZTN since 2001 (based on Article 70 SAA) that the EU rules were being applied indiscriminately to all cases, whether purely domestic or not.

Consequently, judgments of the High Administrative Court fail to discuss the effect on trade criteria. Even in the two rulings mentioned above *(HP-Hrvatska pošta (City Ex)* and *HT (H1))*, the effect on trade was not discussed. In this regard, Svetlicinii observes that, unlike other NCAs, the AZTN does not consider that the application of EU competition rules 'would support its reliance on ECJ case law and strengthen its decision against a possible judicial challenge'.[195] However, EU competition law is used by the AZTN as an indirect source of law, even in purely domestic cases. Based on the Constitutional Court ruling in *PZ Auto*, the High Administrative Court (previously the Administrative Court) accepted that the EU rules are applicable as interpretative tools based on Article 35/3 Competition Act and Article 70 SAA.[196] This approach was also featured in more recent case law. When the applicant, in *Securitas Hrvatska (Zaštitari)*, argued that the EU rules should not be applicable since the legal basis for the NCA decision was the national rules, the High Administrative Court routinely rejected this argument.[197]

It seems that the absence of the analysis of the effect on trade criterion, as well as the application of Articles 101 and 102 TFEU by the AZTN, can be explained by the continued use of the pre-accession rule ordering the use of EU competition law standards as an interpretative tool even after the accession. Arguably, this practice effectively prevents the AZTN from fully complying with Regulation 1/2003 that the NCAs must apply Articles 101 and/or 102 TFEU in cases where there exists an effect on cross-border trade between the Member States. Indeed, this has adverse consequences

---

UP/I 034-03/15-01/015 of 28 September 2015. On appeal, the High Administrative Court failed to engage with the issue of a violation of Article 102, simply confirming the position of the AZTN concerning Article 106 TFEU. High Administrative court judgment, Usll-191/15-12 of 22 April 2016. The constitutional appeal was rejected; the Constitutional Court made no reference to Article 102 or 106 TFEU. Constitutional Court judgment, U-III-2790/2016 of 13 January 2021.

194. A rare example is the *Drezga* case, UP/I 034-03/2014-01/026, AZTN protiv Drezga d.o.o. (the proceedings were terminated in relation to Article 101 TFEU due to negligible effect on trade between Member States; in relation to the national equivalent of Article 101 the AZTN adopted a commitment decision). In some cases, the national rule was applied for the whole duration of an alleged infringement, while Article 101 or 102 were applied for the conduct related to the period after 1 July 2013. For example, in the *Hrvatska pošta* case, Article 102 was applied (alongside its national equivalent), holding that the allegedly abusive rebates could affect trade between Member States, 'by preventing new competitors from entering the postal service market services' on the territory of Croatia after its EU accession. AZTN decision of 26 November 2015, UP/I 034-03/13-01/010. *See* also *HT (H1)* case. AZTN decision, UP/I 034-03/2013-01/007 14 November 2018.
195. Svetlicinii, *supra* n. 89, p. 320.
196. For example, Us-533/2006-7 Tisak/Distri-Press, Us-12765/2007-5 Distri-Press (Media-Ideja), Us-6075/2010-9 Hyundai Auto Zagreb.
197. UsII-60/15-10.

for the use of the preliminary reference procedure. Thus, it is not surprising that there have been no preliminary rulings by the CJEU so far based on references from the Croatian courts in competition matters.

References to relevant case law (European or national) in court judgments in competition matters are rare.[198] This is true both for the High Administrative Court and the Constitutional Court.[199] A rare exception is a reference to relevant CJEU judgments by the Supreme Court in the *Croatian Association of Orthodontists case*, to be considered as a notable push in the opposite direction by the highest court in the country.[200] Indeed, *Ivančan & Petrić* find that the Croatian Supreme Court has 'repeatedly held that the interpretive obligation mandates all national courts to interpret domestic law in accordance with EU law', while the Croatian Constitutional court 'still has not openly adopted a position on the interpretive obligation following accession'.[201]

As a related issue, it is difficult to appreciate to what extent the applicants, i.e., their legal representatives, rely on EU competition law in their legal arguments. Based on anecdotal evidence, such arguments are being invoked on a regular basis. However, this is visible only in a limited number of rulings, and the courts seem not overly receptive to addressing those arguments in the explanatory part of the judgment.[202] For example, in *Marine*,[203] the applicants referred to many CJEU judgments to support their arguments; however, the court did not address them in its judgment. In *Totalna televizija (A1)*,[204] the AZTN, the applicant, and the interested party invoked the case law of the CJEU. However, the appeal court did not rely on any specific CJEU judgment to base its decision. In *V Grupa (Zaštitari)*,[205] the judgment noted that the plaintiff complained that the defendant, i.e., the AZTN, did not react to its arguments based on

198. Also, references to literature or case law in Croatian courts' rulings are rare, and this is also true as regards competition cases.
199. An exception is the *Sports Betting* case, where the *Woodpulp II* judgment was mentioned by the High Administrative Court. On the contrary, the AZTN's decisions regularly reference CJEU judgments and European Commission decisions. Curiously, the AZTN's decisions rarely invoke Article 101 or 102 TFEU; instead, secondary legislation, even soft law, such as European Commission guidelines, are regularly relied on to substantiate the AZTN's arguments. Regularly, the High Administrative Court (earlier the Administrative Court), copying the arguments offered by the AZTN as the defendant, invokes secondary EU legislation. On the difference in legal cultures between the courts and the AZTN *see* Pecotić Kaufman, *supra* n. 88.
200. Holding that in case of a restriction of competition by-object concrete effects of the agreement were irrelevant the Supreme Court made a reference to the judgment of the Court of Justice in case C-49/92 P *Commission v. Anic Partecipazioni SpA*, 8 July 1999, ECLI:EU:C:1999:356. *See* Judgment of the Supreme Court of the Republic of Croatia of 2 March 2021, U-zpz 16/2015-4 (the Orthodontists case).
201. Antonija Ivančan and Davor Petrić, 'Are Croatian Courts Prepared for the Interpretive Obligation?', 44 Review of Central and East European Law 493, 524-525 (2019) DOI: 10.1163/15730352-04404003.
202. For observations on appellate courts ignoring references to EU law in lawyers' appellate briefs or the competition authority briefs *see* Zdenek Kuhn, 'The Authoritarian Legal Culture at Work: The Passivity of Parties and the Interpretational Statements of Supreme Courts', 2 Croatian Yearbook of European Law and Policy 19, p. 19 (2006) DOI: 10.3935/cyelp.02.2006.12.
203. UsII-39/15-10.
204. UsII-43/20-7.
205. UsII-45/15-12.

CJEU judgments and AG opinions in the administrative proceedings. However, there have been instances indicating that the value of CJEU case law as a source of law for national courts has not been recognised by national practitioners, with a lack of appreciation for the fact that EU law permeates the national competition law and that the CJEU judgments are a source of law for the NCA when it applies Articles 101 and/or 102 TFEU.[206]

Furthermore, appeal judgments seem to fail to provide a clear insight into the grounds invoked by the plaintiff when they rely on the case law of the CJEU. For example, in *HP-Hrvatska pošta (City Ex)*, in the judgment, we read that the interested party in the appeal proceedings (i.e., HP) mentioned 'all the judgments of the Court of Justice of the EU invoked by the plaintiff'. However, in the part of the judgment where plaintiffs' arguments were summarised, no CJEU judgments were mentioned. It seems that Croatian courts are largely not appreciative of the CJEU case law when deciding on competition cases. The difficulties which the national judges are faced with mostly relate, we believe, to the specific role of case law in EU law, unlike in Croatian law where case law has no precedential value.

It has been argued that the judicial style of the Croatian courts - which omits references to CJEU landmark cases, academic literature, or even their own previous case law - discourages practitioners and the competition authority from submitting quality briefs and harms the overall quality of judicial adjudication.[207] Moreover, ignoring CJEU case law post-accession indicates the difficulty for the national courts in assuming their role as European courts, participating in the decentralised application of EU competition rules.[208]

5.5 Excessive Formalism in Judicial Interpretation

Excessive legal formalism is an overarching issue that needs to be considered when discussing judicial review in competition cases in Croatia.[209] As the Constitutional Court itself noted in 2011, 'legal ("textual") positivism still prevails in the Republic of Croatia'; it is 'characterized by a narrow and partial interpretation of individual legal norms without their necessary contextualization, without finding their social purpose

206. *See, e.g.*, HP-Hrvatska pošta (City ex) case.
207. Pecotić Kaufman, *supra* n. 88.
208. *Ibid.*
209. Many scholars have warned of excessive formalism in judicial interpretation as a widespread feature of legal cultures in ex-socialist jurisdictions. Among others, Siniša Rodin, 'Discourse and Authority in European and Post-Communist Legal Culture', 1 Croatian Yearbook of European Law and Policy 1 (2004) DOI: 10.3935/cyelp.01.2005.01. Tamara Ćapeta, 'Courts, Legal Culture and EU Enlargement', 1 Croatian Yearbook of European Law and Policy 1 (2005) DOI: 10.3935/cyelp.01.2005.02. Zdenek Kuhn, 'European Law in the Empires of Mechanical Jurisprudence: The Judicial Application of European Law in Central European Candidate Countries', 1 Croatian Yearbook of European Law and Policy 55 (2008) DOI: 10.3935/cyelp.0 1.2005.03. Alan Uzelac, 'Survival of the Third Legal Tradition?', Supreme Court Law Review 377 (2010). For a detailed discussion, *see* Pecotić Kaufman, *supra* n. 88.

based on the principle of proportionality and without looking at the whole constitutional values on which the Croatian constitutional state is based'.[210]

We observe textual formalism as a feature of judicial adjudication in judgments related to competition matters made by the High Administrative Court and the Constitutional Court.[211] Although the latter court's decisions are not within the project's scope, they play an important role vis-à-vis the function and interpretation of the appeal court, and our analysis cannot omit the Constitutional Court's impact on the validity of AZTN's decisions.

Excessive formalism as a feature of judicial interpretation can be observed in the *Marinas* case. Here, the High Administrative Court returned the matter for reconsideration by the AZTN following a decision which had found a prohibited restrictive agreement and concerted practice between major Croatian marinas operators, in which the chairman of the trade association discussed prices at the meeting between competitors. This was duly recorded in the meeting minutes, which were relied upon by the AZTN as proof of prohibited collusion on prices. In a very formalistic fashion, the High Administrative Court held that to find collusion, the competition authority must prove that all parties to the agreement signed the meeting minutes.[212] Faced with the unrealistic prospect of obtaining such proof from the applicants, the AZTN eventually decided to suspend the case.[213]

In the *Private Security Companies* case, the Constitutional Court disapproved of the AZTN's decision, which was previously confirmed by the High Administrative Court, which found an illegal price-fixing cartel agreement between private security companies.[214] Finding a breach of the constitutional right to a fair trial, as claimed by the applicants, the Constitutional Court undertook a formalistic analysis of what constitutes a price, effectively overturning the AZTN's decision. The controversial legal test introduced by the Constitutional Court to establish the existence of illegal price fixing unduly raised the standard for finding cartel agreements in breach of competition rules, departing from the CJEU standards.[215]

210. Memo of the Constitutional Court of the Republic of Croatia, U-VII-529/2011 of 12 November 2011 (Official Gazette, No. 133/11).
211. In a study focused on this issue, the post-accession case law of the High Administrative Court and the Constitutional court was described as 'illustrative of excessive judicial formalism' and featuring 'a disassociation between the legal norm and its socio-economic context in judicial interpretation'. It was argued that an excessively stringent standard of proof for cartel agreements, established by Croatian courts post-accession, indicated incomplete semantic alignment with EU competition rules. Pecotić Kaufman, *supra* n. 88.
212. The *Marinas* case (AZTN Decision of 17 March 2015, *Adriatic Croatia International Club d.d. et al.*; annulled: judgment of the High Administrative Court of the Republic of Croatia of 17 March 2016, *Ilirija d.d. et al. v. AZTN*, UsII-39/15-10.
213. AZTN Decision of 13 December 2016, *Adriatic Croatia International Club d.d. et al.* (decision to suspend the proceedings).
214. Decision of the AZTN of 17 March 2015, *Sokol Marić d.o.o., et al.*, UP/I-034-03/2014-01/002, confirmed: Judgment of the High Administrative Court of the Republic of Croatia of 22 April 2016, *Sokol Marić d.o.o. v. Competition Agency*, UsII-40/15-10 (and other cases), annulled: Judgment of the Constitutional Court of the Republic of Croatia of 1 February 2018, *Sokol Marić d.o.o.*, U-III-2791/2016 (and other cases).
215. For critical overview of the Croatian Constitutional Court judgments in competition cases *see* Petrović, *supra* n. 85. Also *see* Svetlicinii, *supra* n. 89 and Pecotić Kaufman, *supra* n. 88.

Finally, in the *Croatian Association of Orthodontists* case, the High Administrative Court annulled the AZTN's infringement decision.[216] The key question in this case was whether a pricelist made publicly available on the association's website for three years, recommending prices to its members, was illegal under the Competition Act. The High Administrative Court held that the association was not liable under national competition rules since its mother association, the Croatian Dental Association, had, by law, the power to adopt such a price list. Moreover, it held that to be deemed illegal, a price-fixing agreement 'must be enforceable in practice, meaning that the AZTN should have proved that there was price fixing or that there was an intention to fix prices'.[217] Finding that the High Administrative Court's ruling was incompatible with the CJEU standards, some eight years after the AZTN issued its infringement decision, the Supreme Court eventually annulled this judgment.[218]

Judicial rulings, such as those discussed above, seem to show a lack of understanding of the broader economic context of competition rules. The capacity of the courts to consider policy goals in competition cases would ensure they were well-placed to adopt a judgment on the soundness of the competition authority's decision. In any case, the rulings presented above contradict the ethos established within the AZTN ever since its inception: the use of the EU competition law template as a source of interpretative strength and a source of non-formalistic legal interpretation.[219]

5.6 Miscellaneous

As can be seen from the judgments collected in this project, procedural grounds are invoked almost mechanically by the appellants. This is visible in all appeals before the High Administrative Court (previously Administrative Court). An example of a case where procedural grounds were invoked only superficially in the appeal, but no real arguments were discussed in the judgment was MUZIKA I TO (HDS).[220]

Uneasiness with a more expansive interpretative role can be observed in the judicial drafting style, with a relatively small portion of a judgment devoted to explaining the courts' position and elaborating its own reasoning. Generally, the part of the judgment in which the court explains its stance is usually quite limited, with the reviewing court rarely venturing into discussing substantive notions and providing its reasoned opinion and approach.[221] In judgments by the High Administrative Court, in cases where the competition authority's decision has been confirmed, the court mostly

216. AZTN Decision of 12 June 2014; judgment of the High Administrative Court of the Republic of Croatia of 5 March 2015 (*Croatian Orthodontist Association v. AZTN*), UsII-70/14-6.
217. More details on this case *see* in Pecotić Kaufman, Malnar and Akšamović, *supra* n. 8, p. 215.
218. Judgment of the Supreme Court of the Republic of Croatia of 2 March 2021, U-zpz 16/2015-4 (the Orthodontists case).
219. On the difference in legal cultures between the courts and the AZTN, in particular in terms of legal interpretation *see* Pecotić Kaufman, *supra* n. 88.
220. UsII-519/18-12.
221. For example, in the Bio Save case, the crucial AZTN argument was that the Ministry of Health could not be considered as an undertaking. Although the appeal was rejected, in the part of the judgment where it explained the reasons for such a decision the High Administrative Court avoided engagement with this argument. UsII-191/15-12.

relies on the findings and approach of the competition authority. As a rule, the court repeats the arguments of the AZTN and accepts them without developing an original interpretation narrative. When the court annuls the competition authority's decision, the reasoning is often not very well-developed.[222] This might be due to the large workload and limited time for adjudication in individual cases but also to legal culture features that downplay judges' role as independent and impartial servers of justice.[223]

Finally, the outstanding concern is the ease of access to the courts' case law. This issue is more pronounced when it comes to private enforcement of competition law. Concerning public enforcement, as noted in section 4 of this chapter, the judgments of the High Administrative Court (and previously Administrative Court) in competition matters are, by law, published on the AZTN's website. However, the Supreme Court rulings are notoriously difficult to access digitally.

As mentioned, access to private enforcement rulings is cumbersome.[224] Although by law, the courts must inform the AZTN of any such cases,[225] this has not been implemented in practice.

It has been noted that, in Croatia, 'the right of access to judgments is understood as a judge's privilege'.[226] Similar problems regarding access to case law exist throughout the CEE region.[227] Difficulties in accessing the case law of the courts have detrimental consequences on the ability of scholars to assess the judiciary's work critically. Non-publication of judicial decisions prevents the development of a discourse between the judiciary and the academic community.[228]

6 CONCLUDING REMARKS

This chapter has examined the judicial review process in the context of competition cases in Croatia. This jurisdiction is an outlier in the EU context with its one-tier appeal system. Both the appeal rate (22%) and the rate of appeal success (15%) are low compared to other EU jurisdictions. In particular, the number of appeals against fines is very low. Roughly the same number of appeals relate to abuses of a dominant

---

222. For example, *see* the judgment of the High Administrative Court of the Republic of Croatia of 5 March 2015 (*Croatian Orthodontist Association v. AZTN*), UsII-70/14-6.
223. Pecotić Kaufman, *supra* n. 88. Transparency and legibility would be enhanced with the High Administrative Court numbering the paragraphs in its judgments.
224. It is not clear if all decisions of the first-instance commercial courts and the High Commercial Court, the second-instance court in antitrust damages cases, are publicly accessible as rulings are published selectively without clear criteria (only the 'most important' judgments), and in any case it is very cumbersome to find concrete rulings, https://sudskapraksa.csp.vsrh.hr/.
225. Article 69.a para. 4 Competition Act.
226. Open letter by Professor Zlata Đurđević, https://www.jutarnji.hr/vijesti/hrvatska/zlata-durdevic-mjesecima-me-diskreditiraju-mocnici-iz-politickih-i-sudackih-redova-jer-sam-im-pri jetnja-15083412 (25.06.2021). She noted that the county courts (*županijski sudovi*) published 2%-6% of their decisions, while the number of the Supreme Court decisions that were published was rapidly declining and in 2018 it was less than 50%.
227. *See* Frank Emmert, 'Editorial: The Independence of Judges: A Concept Often Misunderstood in Central and Eastern Europe', 3 European Journal of Law Reform 405, p. 408 (2002).
228. Capeta, *supra* n. 209. On the importance of academic literature for the interpretation of the Company Act, *see* Jakša Barbić, 'Utjecaj njemačkog prava na stvaranje hrvatskog prava društava' 44 Zbornik Pravnog fakulteta u Splitu 339, p. 362 (2007).

position (50%) and to anti-competitive agreements (40%), all based on national rules. It is extremely rare for the AZTN to use a double legal basis (Articles 101 and/or 102 TFEU and their national equivalents) in its decisions, and no rulings relate to Articles 101 and/or 102 TFEU.

In the pre-accession period, the appeal court had an important function of confirming the application of EU competition law standards, heavily relied upon by the AZTN, as lawful. While in that period, the appellants' arguments often focused on arguing against applying EU law as a foreign body of law, in the post-accession period, their efforts transitioned to arguing that EU competition law standards were incorrectly applied.

Overall, the golden age of competition enforcement in this jurisdiction was around 2016, which saw a peak in AZTN's decisions and appeal rulings. In the years before the accession, and around that time, the appeal court had plenty of time to practice adjudicating in competition cases. Nowadays, the challenge seems to be incorporating EU competition law standards in the judicial interpretive matrix amid a low influx of new cases.

CHAPTER 7

Cyprus Report

Marios Iacovides & Maria Vassiliou[*]

1 INTRODUCTION TO THE COMPETITION LAW ENFORCEMENT CONTEXT IN CYPRUS

1.1 Competition Law in Cyprus

In Cyprus, the primary piece of legislation governing competition law is currently the Protection of Competition Law of 2022 (Law 13(I)/2022) (the '2022 Competition Law'). The 2022 Competition Law was enacted in February of 2022[1] in order to transpose Directive 2019/1 (the 'ECN+ Directive'),[2] and it repealed the previous legal framework, i.e., the Protection of Competition Laws of 2008 and 2014.[3] The 2022 Competition Law mainly focuses on reinforcing the powers of the Cyprus Commission for the Protection of Competition (CPC), which is the national competition authority entrusted with competition enforcement and with providing it with the essential resources to carry out its mandate effectively.[4] The CPC was established in 1990 with the enactment of the Protection of Competition Law of 1989 (Law 207/1989) and is considered to be an independent administrative authority whose status differs from that of other

* The authors would like to thank P Agisilaou for valuable feedback during the drafting of this Report. All errors and omissions remain the authors. All links in the footnotes last visited 15 September 2022.
1. Published in Annex I(I) of the Official Gazette of the Republic, Issue 4875 on 23.2.2022.
2. Directive (EU) 2019/1 of the European Parliament and of the Council of 11 December 2018 to empower the competition authorities of the Member States to be more effective enforcers and to ensure the proper functioning of the internal market [2019] OJ L 11/3 (14 January 2020).
3. The Protection of Competition Law of 2008, L.13(I)/2008 and the Protection of Competition Law of 2014, L.41(I)/2014.
4. P Agisilaou and S Hettinger, 'Cyprus Enacts New Competition Law', Mondaq (9 March 2022).

governmental authorities.[5] Throughout its existence, the CPC has been the subject of scrutiny and criticism, mostly in relation to delays in issuing decisions as well as due to the various judicial annulments of the appointments of its members over the years, resulting in even more delay as all of its decisions had to be re-examined.[6]

Cyprus' accession to the European Union (EU) in 2004 signalled the implementation of the *acquis communautaire* in the field of competition and the adoption of competition policy rules focusing on the smooth and free function of the market.[7] Therefore, a few years later, Law 207/1989 was abolished with the enactment of the Protection of Competition Law of 2008 (Law 13(I)/2008) seeking to implement EU Regulation 1/2003.[8] With the enactment of the Protection of Competition Law of 2008, the powers of the CPC were broadened to incorporate the application of competition rules as provided for in (what were then) Articles 81 and 82 of the Treaty establishing the European Community, and it was designated as the competent National Competition Authority (NCA) in the Republic of Cyprus responsible for applying EU Regulation 1/2003. In that regard, and subject to the provisions of EU Regulation 1/2003, the CPC was entrusted with, among others, the following competences: (a) to investigate and decide regarding infringements of sections 3 and/or 6, either on its own initiative or upon a complaint; (b) to decide whether the illegal collusions of subsection (1) of section 3 fulfil the conditions of section 4(1) and can thus be considered permissible and valid; (c) to investigate and decide regarding infringements of Articles 101 TFEU and/or 102 TFEU, either on a complaint or on its own initiative or as otherwise determined by EU Regulation 1/2003; (d) to decide whether the collusions falling within the provisions of paragraph 1 of Article 101 TFEU may be allowed and considered valid, as defined in paragraph 3 of Article 101 TFEU; and (e) to impose administrative fines and administrative sanctions, as defined in the provisions of this Law and/or the regulations made thereunder; (f) to decide upon the taking of interim measures.

The Protection of Competition Law of 2008 was later amended once again by Law 41(I)/2014, the objective of which was the 'further convergence of the national legislation with European law' and also to 'ensure a higher level of competition in the market by strengthening and expanding the powers of the Commission'.[9] One of the most important powers granted to the CPC pursuant to Law 41(I)/2014 was the power to make sector inquiries as well as the power to decide on undertaking commitments. Lastly, the CPC was now empowered to set, by a decision, the criteria for examination of cases in priority for infringements of sections 3 and/or 6 and/or Articles 101 TFEU and/or 102 TFEU and to examine cases based on these priority criteria.[10] It should be

5. Case 1023/2012 *Pagkyprios Organismos Ageladotrofon (POA) Public Ltd v. CPC* (30 November 2012).
6. *See further*, section 5 below.
7. Cyprus Commission for the Protection of Competition, Annual Report 2004.
8. Council Regulation (EC) No. 1/2003 of 16 December 2002 on the implementation of the rules on competition laid down in Articles 81 and 82 of the Treaty [2003] OJ L 1/1.
9. Cyprus Commission for the Protection of Competition, Annual Report 2014.
10. Law 41(I)/2014, section 23(2)(p).

noted that the CPC's aforementioned decision-making powers and other competences remain unchanged by the 2022 Competition Law.

In other words, the 2022 Competition Law does not actually alter substantive competition law in Cyprus, which – as in all Member States and in accordance with Regulation 1/2003 – must be applied consistently (and, sometimes, in parallel) with EU competition rules when it comes to agreements and abuse of dominance. Thus, section 3 of the Law which has remained mostly unchanged since it was first introduced, is the national equivalent to and essentially mirrors Article 101(1) of the Treaty on the Functioning of the European Union (TFEU) and provides that all agreements between undertakings, all decisions by associations of undertakings and any concerted practices which have as their object or effect the prevention, restriction or distortion of competition within the Republic, shall be prohibited, and in particular those which (a) directly or indirectly fix purchase or selling prices or any other trading conditions; (b) limit or control production, markets, technical development or investments; (c) share markets, geographically or otherwise, or sources of supply; (d) apply dissimilar conditions to equivalent transactions thereby placing certain undertakings at a competitive disadvantage; (e) make the conclusion of contracts subject to acceptance by other parties of supplementary obligations which, by their nature or according to commercial usage, have no connection with the subject of such contracts. Furthermore, section 3(2) of the Law provides that agreements, decisions and concerted practices mentioned in section 3(1) shall be void *ab initio*. Section 4(1) of the Law is the exception from section 3 and essentially corresponds to Article 101(3) TFEU. Moreover, according to section 5 of the Law, the Council of Ministers of the Cypriot government, following a prior reasoned opinion of the CPC, may issue a decree exempting specific categories of practices from the application of section 3 of the Law (the so-called Block Exemptions). Such block exemption decrees have in the past been issued in relation to, among others, research and development agreements,[11] agricultural products,[12] air transport,[13] and insurance.[14]

Section 6(1) of the 2022 Competition Law has also remained largely unchanged by the recent amendments of the Law and corresponds to Article 102 TFEU. Section 6(1) provides that any abuse by one or more undertakings of a dominant position within the internal market or in a substantial part of it in respect of a product shall be prohibited. Especially so if this practice results or may result in: (a) direct or indirect fixing of unfair purchase or selling prices or any other unfair, under the circumstances, trading conditions; (b) limiting production, distribution or technical development to

11. P.I. 98/2002 – Block Exemption (Agreements, Decisions and Concerted Practices in relation to Research and Development Agreements) Order of 2002.
12. P.I. 7/98 – Block Exemption (Agreements, Decisions and Concerted Practices in relation to the Production or Trade in Agricultural Products) Order of 1998.
13. P.I. 207/2000 – Block Exemptions (Agreements Between Air Transport Undertakings concerning Consultations on Passenger Tariffs on Schedule Air Services and Slot Allocation at Airports) Order of 2000.
14. P.I. 341/97 – Block Exemptions (Agreements, Decisions and Concerted Practices in the Insurance Sector) Order of 1997.

the prejudice of consumers; (c) applying dissimilar conditions to equivalent transactions, thereby placing certain undertakings at a competitive disadvantage; (d) making the conclusion of contracts subject to acceptance by the other parties of supplementary obligations which, by their nature or according to commercial usage, have no connection with the subject of such contracts.

Section 6(2) of the Law introduces a national prohibition on abuse of economic dependence. This provision does not have any equivalent in EU law. It concerns the abuse by one or more undertakings of the economic relations of dependency between one or more such undertakings and an undertaking which is a customer, supplier, producer, representative, distributor, or trading partner thereof, even regarding as a specific kind of product or service, and which does not have an equivalent alternative solution (i.e., the dependent undertaking does not have the possibility to find alternative suppliers, trading partners, etc.). The abuse of such economic dependence is prohibited.

1.2 The Cypriot Commission for the Protection of Competition

According to section 26 of the 2022 Competition Law, the CPC is the independent authority vested with the exclusive jurisdiction for competition law enforcement.[15] The Commission has exclusive competence, among others: (i) to investigate restrictive agreements and concerted practices by undertakings, having as their object or effect the elimination, restriction or distortion of competition; (ii) to investigate any probable abuse of dominant position possessed by one or more undertakings; (iii) to decide on interim measures, (iv) to impose terms and behavioural and/or structural remedies as necessary to bring the infringement to an end; and (v) to conduct investigations in a specific sector of the economy or in specific types of agreements pursuant to section 31. Furthermore, in accordance with section 29 of the 2022 Competition Law, the Commission, designated as the National Competition Authority, is empowered to apply Articles 101 and 102 TFEU in accordance with Regulation 1/2003.[16]

According to section 47 of the 2022 Competition Law, for every infringement of sections 3 and/or 6 of the Law and of Articles 101 and/or 102 TFEU, the Commission has the power to:

(a) impose an administrative fine, according to the gravity and duration of the infringement, not exceeding 10% of the combined annual revenue of the undertaking or not exceeding 10% of the revenue of every undertaking member of the association of undertakings in the year within which the infringement took place or in the year which immediately preceded the infringement;

15. The CPC has been the independent authority vested with the power of competition law enforcement since 1990, pursuant to the provisions of Law 207(I)/1989, which was later abolished by the Law 13(I)/2008 and later amended by Law 41(I)/2014. All the foregoing were repealed by the 2022 Competition Law.
16. Reg. 1/2003 (*supra* n. 8).

(b) require that the undertakings or association of undertaking bring the infringement to an end within a prescribed timeframe and avoid repetition in the future;
(c) where the Commission intends to adopt a decision requiring that the infringement is brought to an end and the undertakings concerned offer commitments, the CPC may, by decision, make those commitments binding on the undertakings;
(d) in case the undertakings or associations of undertakings concerned do not comply with the Commission's decision issued pursuant to paragraphs (b) and (c) above, the Commission may impose an administrative fine of up to 5% of the average daily turnover in the year within which the infringement took place or in the year which immediately preceded the infringement for each day during which the infringement continues;
(e) impose an administrative fine of up to 1% of the turnover of the undertaking or association of undertakings in the preceding financial year in case an undertaking intentionally or negligently provides false, incomplete, inaccurate or misleading information, refuses to accept a summons from the Commission pursuant to the provisions of section 36 of the Law or provides incomplete and/or altered records, books, accounts or other documents relating to the business activity in the context of an inspection under the provisions of section 38;
(f) impose an administrative fine not exceeding EUR 25,000 on natural persons who intentionally or negligently provide false, incomplete, inaccurate or misleading information during an investigation;
(g) impose an administrative fine not exceeding EUR 5,000 on natural persons who fail to provide information to the Commission within the time prescribed for doing so or fail to comply with a summons issued by the Commission to provide a statement.

Before imposing an administrative fine for an infringement of competition law, the CPC allows any interested party to submit representations[17] and grants them the right of access to the case file.[18] Administrative fines are imposed by means of a reasoned decision following due investigative process and considering both the severity and the duration of the infringement.

One of the most interesting changes that the 2022 Competition Law introduces is the enhancement of the protection of confidential information and personal data. The Law aims to achieve this by expressly requiring the duties and powers of the CPC to be

17. This is in accordance with the General Provisions of Administrative Law 158(I)/1999, and section 43 thereof, which safeguards the right to be heard.
18. Section 42 of the 2022 Competition Law; Joined cases T-236/01, T-239/01, T-244/01 to T-246/01, T-251/01 and T-252/01 *Tokai Carbon Co. Ltd and Others v. Commission* EU:T:2004:118.

in accordance with the provisions of the General Data Protection Regulation (GDPR).[19] Specifically, although it is the responsibility of the relevant parties in each transaction to identify the information, documents and any other material they consider to contain confidential information,[20] the CPC retains the discretion to declare additional information and/or documents as business secrets or confidential information for specific undertakings. Furthermore, the Law expressly prohibits any natural or legal persons who have lodged a complaint, as well as third persons, from accessing any internal documents, ensuring that any information which relates to personal data will be dealt with in accordance with the GDPR. Lastly, it is also provided that in issuing its decisions, the CPC shall ensure that such decisions are published without disclosing personal data of natural persons, except in cases where it considers that such publication is strictly necessary and proportionate.

The Law also introduces significant changes in relation to the members of the CPC, requiring them to be persons of high professional and moral standing, capable of performing their duties and contributing to achieving the objectives of the Law.[21] The Law highlights the importance of impartiality and independence of the CPC, as it is expressly stated that the President and members of the CPC must not have any economic or other benefit which may affect their judgement in the exercise of their powers.[22] Furthermore, it is clearly provided that the President and members of the CPC, while performing their duties and exercising their powers under the Law, shall, among others, not seek or receive instructions from a governmental or any other public or private body and act independently of any political or external interference.[23] This is a welcome and much-anticipated change insofar as, in the past, decisions of the CPC have been annulled on the ground that its composition was unlawful due to the participation of person(s) with conflicting interests in that particular composition, thus seriously impeding its effectiveness, causing severe delays in the investigation of cases, and curtailing its efforts to enforce competition law.[24]

Furthermore, to ensure the proper functioning of the CPC and effective enforcement of competition law, the CPC has been vested by section 45(1) of the Law with the power to continue, at its own discretion, investigating a complaint which has been withdrawn, if it has already reached a preliminary conclusion as to the infringement of the law. This, too, is a welcome change since a significant number of complaints are withdrawn every year and not necessarily because they lack merit. Additionally, the CPC is now empowered to summon persons in order to obtain statements and

---

19. Regulation (EU) 2016/679 of the European Parliament and of the Council of 27 April 2016 on the protection of natural persons with regard to the processing of personal data and on the free movement of such data, and repealing Directive 95/46/EC (General Data Protection Regulation) [2016] L 119/1.
20. Section 18(7) of the 2022 Competition Law.
21. Section 9(2)(a) of the 2022 Competition Law.
22. Section 10 of the 2022 Competition Law.
23. Section 10(2) of the 2022 Competition Law.
24. A. Antoniou, *Competition Law in Cyprus: 30 Years of the CPC*, Oxford Competition Law (Oxford University Press, 2021), available at https://oxcat.ouplaw.com/page/cypriot. *See also*, further, section 5 in this Report.

information in connection with investigations carried out by it.[25] The Law also introduced a deadline regarding the payment of an administrative fine imposed by the CPC with the provision that such fines shall be subject to annual interest if not paid within the prescribed time frame.[26] Furthermore, the CPC has the power, in the event the undertaking fails to pay the administrative fine imposed by the CPC, to take legal action in civil courts and collect the amount due as a debt owed to the Republic.[27]

Lastly, the cooperation and mutual assistance between the CPC and other national competition authorities has been further enhanced, as the CPC is now able to share documents and conduct investigations related to the cross-border implementation of Articles 101 and 102 TFEU.[28]

1.3 Leniency Programme and Other Relevant Provisions

Beyond the main 2022 Competition Law, in 2011, the Immunity from and Reduction of Administrative Fines in Cases of Restrictive Collusions Infringing Section 3 of the Law or/and Article 101 of the TFEU (Leniency Programme) Regulations were adopted (the 'Leniency Programme') via the issuance of Regulatory Administrative Act No. 463/2011 by decision of the Cypriot Council of Ministers. The Leniency Programme codifies the procedure, conditions and criteria for granting an exemption or reduction of the administrative fine imposed by the CPC to an undertaking or association of undertakings wishing to cooperate with the CPC and, to a large extent, mirrors the EU Commission's leniency programme.[29] Briefly, if an undertaking participating in a secret cartel comes forward and voluntarily provides information to the CPC which leads to the finding of an infringement and to the imposition of fines on the other undertakings in the cartel, the CPC will consider granting such undertaking immunity from or reduction of any fine that would otherwise have been imposed on it. For the avoidance of doubt, we note that there are no procedural guidelines or regulations for reaching settlements other than in the context of the Leniency Programme.[30]

Finally, the Cypriot competition legal framework is complemented by three other pieces of legislation, namely: (i) the Control of Concentrations Between Undertakings Law, Number 83(I)/2014, which deals with concentrations of undertakings and implements Council Regulation (EC) No. 139/2004 of 20 January 2004 on the control of concentrations between undertakings (the 'EC Merger Regulation'), (ii) the Actions for Damages for Infringements of Competition Law of 2017 (113(I)/2017) which transposes Directive 2014/104/EU, and (iii) the Interchange Fees for Card-Based Payment Transactions Law of 2018 which implements Regulation (EU) 2015/751 of the European Parliament and of the Council of 29 April 2015, on 'interchange fees for card-based payment transactions'. However, these are outside the scope of this study.

25. Section 37 of the 2022 Competition Law.
26. Section 51 of the 2022 Competition Law.
27. Section 52 of the 2022 Competition Law.
28. Part IX of the 2022 Competition Law, sections 53-58.
29. N. Constantinides, The Cartels and Leniency Review: Cyprus, Law Reviews Ed. 10, 01/02/2022.
30. Anti-cartel enforcement template, Cartels Working Group, Cyprus 29/04/2020.

2 THE APPEAL/REVIEW PROCESS OF THE CYPRIOT COMPETITION AUTHORITY'S DECISIONS

2.1 Judicial Review of Administrative Acts in Cyprus

The Constitution of the Republic of Cyprus, enacted in 1960, introduces judicial review of administrative acts as a separate jurisdiction, distinguishable from all other judicial processes.[31] In particular, pursuant to Article 146 of the Constitution, acts, decisions, and omissions of regulatory authorities emanating from the exercise of powers in the public domain are amenable to judicial review. The CPC is one of such regulatory authorities, whose decisions may be challenged through administrative recourse.[32] Any person with a legitimate interest in a decision of the CPC, whether a party to the decision or not, may file an appeal against this decision by initiating an administrative recourse before the competent court (today, the Administrative Court) under the provisions of Article 146 of the Constitution. Such recourse must be filed within seventy-five days of notification of the decision.

Originally, according to the Cyprus Constitution, exclusive jurisdiction for judicial review of administrative acts was vested in the Supreme Constitutional Court.[33] The Supreme Constitutional Court decided cases in the first and final instance.[34] In other words, its decisions were final and conclusive. The Supreme Constitutional Court was, however, short-lived. The withdrawal of the Turkish-Cypriot community from participation in governmental functions in 1964 led to the paralysis of the judiciary insofar as the Constitution originally prescribed, among others, that the Supreme Constitutional Court would consist of one Greek-Cypriot Justice, one Turkish-Cypriot Justice and one 'neutral' Justice who would also preside (Article 133). Once the Turkish-Cypriot Justice participating in the Supreme Constitutional Court's composition withdrew, the Court's operation was effectively halted.

As a result, the Administration of Justice (Miscellaneous Provisions) Law of 1964 was enacted to safeguard the functionality of the judiciary.[35] According to the Administration of Justice Law, judicial review of administrative acts was to be exercised by a single Justice of the Supreme Court, which is a different body than the Supreme Constitutional Court as originally provided for by the Constitution. Furthermore, such decisions were subject to appeal before a panel consisting of at least three Supreme Court Justices, a provision which was amended in 1991 in order for the appellate jurisdiction to be exercised by five Justices of the Supreme Court. Hence, until

31. M Nicolatos, L Parparinos and M Hadjiprodromou, Administrative Justice in Europe, Supreme Court of Cyprus, June 2018.
32. *The Judicial review of Regulatory Authorities, Answers to questionnaire*: Cyprus (Paris, 6 December 2021).
33. Article 146 of the Constitution.
34. E Nicolaou and P Michaelides, *Cyprus Administrative Law: Fundamental Principles – Judicial Review* (Nomiki Vivliothiki, 2019) 127.
35. The constitutionality of this legislation was confirmed in the seminal judgment *Republic v. Mustafa Ibrahim* [1964] 1 C.L.R. 195 invoking the law of necessity. The Court referred to the Latin maxim *salus populi suprema lex esto* and *necessitas non habet legem* to conclude that no state is to be destroyed by its own Constitution.

2015, the Supreme Court (sitting as a single Justice panel) carried on first-instance administrative review of decisions of the CPC and the Supreme Court (sitting as a panel of three and subsequently five Justices) heard appeals. Therefore, administrative recourses were heard by the Supreme Court (both on first and final instance), which reportedly accounted for more than half of its time.[36] Interestingly, although judicial review in Cyprus was traditionally and still remains to this day heavily influenced by the continental legal traditions of Greece and France,[37] the Supreme Court and now the Administrative Court appear to follow the common law doctrine of stare decisis - a creature of the common law - in recourses under Article 146 of the Constitution.[38] In fact, the Supreme Court has repeatedly held that the stare decisis principle also applies in administrative law cases on the basis of the principles of judicial hierarchy, legal certainty and predictability.[39]

A significant milestone in administrative justice took place in 2015 when a general restructuring and reformation of administrative justice was effected through the eighth constitutional amendment as well as the enactment of a new piece of legislation pursuant to which two new first-instance Administrative Courts were formed through the enactment of the Establishment and Operation of the Administrative Court Law of 2015 (Law No. 130(I)/2015) (the 'Administrative Court Law') and through the enactment of the Establishment and Operation of the Administrative Court of International Protection Law of 2018 (Law 73(I)/2018).[40]

The primary aim of establishing the Administrative Court was to lighten the caseload of the Supreme Court and to reduce the delay in the hearing of cases.[41] Furthermore, the Cypriot legislator aimed to stabilise the system and expedite the procedure to stave off the threat of public law cases overwhelming it.[42]

This specialist Administrative Court, established pursuant to the Administrative Court Law, has exclusive jurisdiction to adjudicate on first instance every administrative recourse under Article 146 of the Constitution in relation to decisions, acts and omissions of administrative and executive authorities, including the CPC.[43] The Supreme Court, which was previously entrusted with exercising judicial review on both first instance and appellate review, now enjoys exclusive jurisdiction to adjudicate appeals from decisions of the Administrative Court.

36. NE Hatzimihail, 'On Law, Legal Elites and the Legal Profession in a (Biggish) Small State: Cyprus' in P Butler and C Morris (eds), Small States in a Legal World (Springer, 2017) 228.
37. NE Hatzimihael, 'Cyprus as a Mixed Legal System' (2013) 6:1 *Journal of Civil Law Studies* 37, 66-67.
38. P Polyviou, *Cyprus: A Study in the Theory Structure and Method of the Legal System of the Republic of Cyprus* (2015) 262.
39. Cases *Demetriades v. The Republic*, (1977) 3 C.L.R. 213 and *Elefetheriou-Kanga v. The Republic*, (1989) 3 C.L.R. 262.
40. C Paraskeva, *Cyprus Administrative Law: General Part* (Nomiki Vivliothiki, 2017) 42.
41. Functional Review of the Courts System of Cyprus, 2017-2018 Final Report.
42. N Mouttotos, 'Reform of Civil Procedure in Cyprus: Delivering Justice in a More Efficient and Timely Way' (2020) 49 *Common Law World Review* 99 DOI: 10.1177/1473779520924441.
43. P Polyviou, *Administration and Justice: The Commission for the Protection of Competition and the Securities and Exchange Commission in Cyprus Law* (Chryssafinis & Polyviou Publications, 2017) 35.

Under section 13 of the Administrative Court Law and section 11 of the Administration of Justice Law of 1964, in exercising its jurisdiction as an Appellate Administrative Court, the Supreme Court sits in formations of three Justices. Furthermore, judgments of the Administrative Court can be appealed to the Supreme Court on points of law only and within forty-two days from the decision of the Administrative Court. The Supreme Court does not need to give leave to appeal for the appeals to proceed. Appeals raising issues of utmost importance are heard by the Full Bench of the Supreme Court.

The Supreme Court, acting under Article 163 of the Constitution and section 17 of the Administration of Justice Law 33/64, has issued Procedural Regulation 6/2015, which is applicable to administrative recourses filed after 1 January 2016. These Regulations deal with various procedural matters such as the form of the recourse and opposition, matters of service of the recourse to all interested parties, as well as timeframes for filing the same. For example, it is stated that the applicant shall file a written address within thirty days from the filing of the opposition of the respondent and the latter shall file a written address within thirty days from service of the applicant's written address. The interested party (if any) shall have the right to file its own written address within twenty-one days, whereas if such interested party appearing in the proceedings omits to file a written address, it shall be presumed that such party adopts the positions and written address of the respondent. Thereinafter, the applicant shall have the right to file a written address in reply within ten days. In practice, the above-mentioned timeframes are never followed, and the Administrative Court grants applicants and respondents six weeks each to file their written address and another four weeks to file the written address in reply. The content of the written address is also governed by the Procedural Regulations, section 8 thereof, stating that it shall present in summary each party's 'skeleton argument' and shall only deal with the legal issues which the applicant brings forward for annulment of the administrative decision and which the respondent argues in support of such decision. Evidently, therefore, the hearing of the administrative recourse is primarily conducted on the basis of the parties' written positions as advanced through their respective written addresses. In the end, the case is fixed for oral clarifications, at which stage the parties have the option to orally address the Court for a short time as the Court may deem necessary, and the Court has the opportunity to ask any questions it wishes or request to hear argument from both sides on a specific legal point.[44]

2.2 The Powers of the Administrative Court: Scope of Judicial Review

The Administrative Court has jurisdiction to review an administrative decision, act, or omission on both points of law and fact. Pursuant to Article 146(4) of the Constitution (as amended), the Administrative Court may, by its decision:

44. E Nicolaou & G Tsaousis, *Manual on Cyprus Administrative Procedure* (Nomiki Vivliothiki, 2021) 111.

(a) uphold, in whole or in part, such decision or act or omission; or
(b) declare the decision or act, in whole or in part, null and void and of no effect whatsoever; or
(c) declare the omission to be wholly or partly void; or
(d) modify the decision or act in whole or in part, provided that it relates to a *tax matter* or is a decision relating to *international protection* under the law of the European Union.

As is apparent from points (a) to (c) above, the Administrative Court exercises marginal review of administrative decisions, acts or omissions. In other words, the Court's powers are limited to testing the legality of administrative decisions rather than their correctness, thus not exercising 'full jurisdiction'.[45] This also means that in most cases, the Administrative Court is not empowered to amend or replace the impugned administrative act with its own (such as, for example, reducing the fine imposed by CPC). The law expressly provides for only two exceptions to the above rule, in the case of international protection (asylum)[46] and tax cases, whereby the Court has jurisdiction to review both the legality and the correctness of the decision and to substitute the decision of the administrative authority with its own.[47] After the recent amendment of the Constitution in July 2022, Article 146 also provides for another two exceptions, namely for administrative decisions relating to EU law or any other matter, as prescribed by the law. These two new exceptions are vaguely formulated, but the idea is that Parliament will be able to legislate specific instances and decisions which will be open to full judicial review. As this is a recent amendment to the Constitution, all the cases we have reviewed for the purposes of this research project involve a marginal type of administrative review, as described above and further discussed in section 5.1.

When reviewing the legality of a decision, the Court examines whether the public organ has exercised its discretionary powers within lawful limits, whether the decision was reasoned and not a product of legal or factual error, but its jurisdiction does not extend to issues of technical nature,[48] issues pertaining to the substance of the decision[49] or issues that require specialised knowledge.[50] The Court does not substitute the administrative organ and, in fact, will only intervene if, after taking into account all the facts of the case, it concludes that the findings of the administrative organ are the result of an error of fact or law or are in excess of its discretionary powers.

45. Polyviou (*supra* n. 43) 48.
46. In 2018, the Law on the Establishment and Functioning of the Administrative Court of International Protection of 2018 (Law 73 (I)/2018) was enacted pursuant to which another specialist Court was established dealing solely with international protection (asylum) cases.
47. Article 11(4) of the Administrative Court Law *juncto* Article 146(4) of the Constitution.
48. For example, the Supreme Court in the Case 612/2009 *Akis Ioannou v. CPC* dated 23.9.2010 stated that 'market analysis is also a technical matter and this court's power to review the decision is limited'.
49. Case *Varnavas Nicolaides v. Republic* (1989) 3C CLR 1961.
50. Cases *Republic v. C. Kassinos Constructions* (1990) 3 (E) C.L.R. 3835; *Lambrou v. Republic* (2009) 3 C.L.R. 79; *Georghiou v. SALA* (2002) 3 C.L.R. 475; and *Eva Ttousouna v. Republic* (2013) 3 C.L.R. 151.

The Constitution does not provide for a definition of administrative authorities or organs whose decisions are subject to judicial review. The term is understood to include public legal entities, local governmental authorities, and statutory bodies performing public functions. The CPC is considered to be an administrative organ whose decisions can be challenged by recourse to the Administrative Court.[51]

There exists a right to appeal the decision of the Administrative Court for every party who participated in the first-instance proceedings, provided that they retain their legitimate interest.[52] This also includes the right of the winning party to appeal if, for example, not all the grounds put forward for annulment were successful, and therefore, there are still negative consequences stemming from the decision.[53] This jurisdiction is termed 'revisional'. The nature of the Supreme Court's appellate revisional jurisdiction differs from that of civil appeals.[54] The subject matter of the appeal, just like the proceedings before the first-instance Court, is legality of the administrative act or decision,[55] such as a decision issued by the CPC imposing a fine. The Supreme Court conducts a full review of the case on points of law, referring to the issues raised by the appellant on appeal, or to the extent not decided by the first-instance court, or to the issues raised on cross-appeal.[56]

The Supreme Court, in exercising its Appellate Revisional Jurisdiction, primarily deals with the legal argumentation which the parties have already advanced before the first-instance Court,[57] unless the latter, in exercising judicial review, has annulled a decision on a ground not raised by the applicant, in which case the appellant can also invoke this ground as a ground for appeal before the Supreme Court.[58] However, it is understood that administrative proceedings are of an inquisitorial nature, as opposed to the purely adversarial nature of civil proceedings.[59] The Supreme Court may also examine *ex proprio motu*, that is on its own initiative, some irregularities such as competence and lawful composition or establishment and legal grounds such as breach of *res judicata*. The scope of review, however, does not differ much from that of the first-instance court. Documents and other evidence relevant to the issues in dispute are admissible at all stages of the proceedings, both at first instance in the review of the legality of the administrative decision or act and on appeal. Lastly, an appeal against the Administrative Court's decision must be served on all parties, including an

51. Section 20(5) of the 2022 Competition Law expressly provides that the CPC's decisions are subject to judicial review.
52. E Nicolaou and G Tsaousis, *Manual on Cyprus Administrative Procedure* (Nomiki Vivliothiki, 2021) 205.
53. Case *Kantounas Constantis v. Republic of Cyprus* (2010) 3 CLR 344.
54. Case *Republic (Council of Ministers) v. Christakis Vassiliades* (1967) 3 C.L.R. 82.
55. Cases *Costas Pikis v. Republic (Minister of Interior and Another)* (1968) 3 C.L.R. 303, 305, 306; *George Constantinides v. Republic (Minister of Finance)* (1969) 3 C.L.R. 523; *Miltiades Papadopoulos v. Republic (Council of Ministers)* (1970) 3 C.L.R. 169; *Republic (Minister of Finance) v. Sawas Pericleous* (1972) 3 C.L.R. 63.
56. Case *University of Cyprus v. Constantinou et al.* (1994) 3 CLR 145.
57. Case *Tsangaridou et al. v. Republic et al.* (No.1) (1995) 3 CLR 31.
58. Nicolaou and Tsaousis (*supra* n. 52) 202.
59. Case *Republic of Cyprus v. C. Kassinos Construction Ltd* (1990) 3 CLR 3835.

interested party who appeared in the first-instance proceedings; otherwise, the proceedings could be annulled pursuant to the Supreme Court's inherent jurisdiction to restore justice.[60]

3 PRIOR RESEARCH

The literature review we conducted for the purposes of this research project did not produce any examples of a comprehensive and quantitative survey of the enforcement of competition law in Cyprus or the CPC's track record in the Cypriot courts following the adoption of Regulation 1/2003. However, there are examples of more limited studies that we have consulted. One such example is a 2011 book by Agisilaou et al., containing summaries of the Supreme Court's decisions on competition law matters issued between 1989 and 2009, as well as summaries and commentary on all published decisions of the CPC for the same period.[61] Another example is a book by Polyviou updated most recently in 2017.[62] As one would expect, there are also general books in English covering all aspects of competition law in Cyprus, including on judicial review of the CPC's decisions, for instance, Chapter III.3 in the recently published Emilianides and Antoniou, Competition Law in Cyprus.[63] Overall, the consulted sources have been very useful in gaining an overview of the topic, though mostly descriptive and not engaging in the type of quantitative or comprehensive qualitative analysis that we undertake here.

Beyond judicial review, when it comes to the CPC's enforcement of competition rules in Cyprus, there were recurrent updates in the European Competition Journal, but these have stopped as of 2007.[64] There are papers on increased enforcement against abuses of dominance,[65] on the implementation of the ECN+ Directive,[66] and on the enforcement of antitrust rules vis-à-vis groups of companies.[67]

60. Case *Republic of Cyprus v. Zena Poulli* (2001) 3 CLR 1060.
61. P Agisilaou, D Kalli and KK Kleanthous, *Competition Policy in Cyprus 1989-2009 Introductory Concepts, Historical Background, Legislation, Decisions of the Competition Protection Commission, Decisions of the Supreme Court* (Nomiki Vivliothiki, 2011).
62. Polyviou, *supra* n. 43.
63. A Emilianides and A Antoniou, *Competition Law in Cyprus* (Wolters Kluwer, 2021).
64. M Eliades and G Mountis, 'Cyprus Current Developments in Member States' (2006) 2 *European Competition Journal* 190; M Eliades and G Mountis, 'Cyprus Current Developments in Member States' (2006) 2 *European Competition Journal* 402; M Eliades and G Mountis, 'Cyprus Current Developments In Member States' (2007) 3 *European Competition Journal* 226.
65. A Antoniou, 'Abuse of Dominance Enforcement on the Rise Reports: Cyprus' (2020) 4 *European Competition and Regulatory Law Review* (CoRe) 23 DOI: 10.21552/core/2020/1/6.
66. E Poulladou, 'Implementation of the ECN+ Directive in Cyprus: Draft Bill Setting the Foundations for a New Era of Competition Law Enforcement? Reports: Implementation of the ECN+ Directive' (2021) 5 *European Competition and Regulatory Law Review* (CoRe) 230 DOI: 10.21552/core/2021/3/10.
67. T Papadopoulos, 'National Report on Cyprus' in Rafael Mariano Manóvil (ed.), *Groups of Companies: A Comparative Law Overview* (Springer International Publishing, 2020).

4 QUANTITATIVE ANALYSIS

4.1 Source of Information

The database used to collect the court cases covered by this research is http://www.cylaw.org/index.html. CyLaw is the online service of the Cyprus Institute of Legal Information (KINOP/CyLII), which offers free access to Cypriot and international sources of law. The database includes all Supreme Court case law, consolidated and numbered legislation, civil procedure rules and other pieces of secondary legislation. After 2008, the database also includes first-instance decisions in civil and criminal cases, although not all decisions are publishable. After the establishment of a specialist Administrative Court in 2016, it also includes all the case law of the Administrative Court. The judgments are available electronically in Greek. The judgments which were used for the purposes of the present research project are also available on the website of the Cyprus Commission for the Protection of Competition, in Greek as well.[68] To the best of our knowledge, our database includes all available decisions that were within the scope of the research project.

4.2 Total Number of Cases

In total, we coded twenty-nine judgments that fell within the scope of this research project in the database. These court cases involved the review of twenty-six of the CPC's decisions. On the basis of the CPC's annual reports, which indicate the total number of decisions adopted per year, we estimate the ratio of CPC's decisions subject to appeal to be 18%. Only 1% of judgments at first instance (a single case) had been further reviewed at second instance.

4.3 Total Number of Cases per Year

In total, for the period covered in our research, there were twenty-eight judgments delivered at first instance on appeals from the CPC's decisions and one judgment on appeal from the first-instance court, bringing the total number of catalogued judgments to twenty-nine (*see* Figure 7.1). In the same period, there were twenty-six appeals from decisions of the CPC (*see* Figure 7.2(a)). The only appeal judgment covered by the scope of this research was rendered in 2011. In section 5.2, we discuss the possible reasons for the scarcity of appeals from the judgments at first instance.

The small number of appeals and judgments does not allow for drawing safe conclusions as to historical trends. There seems to be a stable output of a couple of judgments at first instance per year, whereas the increasing trend observed in years 2015-2019 seems to have been broken in years 2020 and 2021.

68. Available at http://www.competition.gov.cy/competition/competition.nsf/page19_gr/page19_gr?OpenDocument.

Figure 7.1 Number of Judgments According to Instances

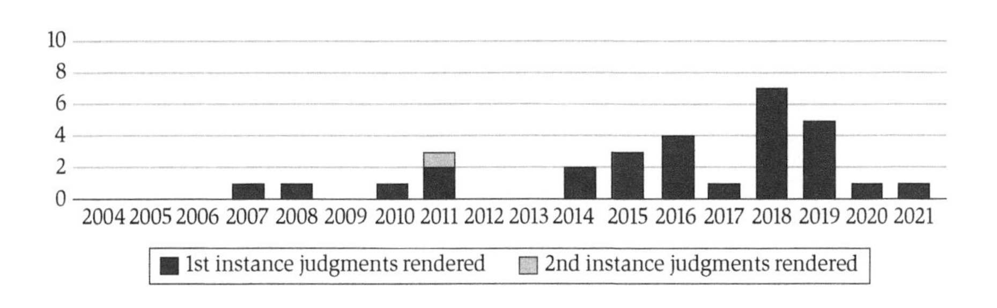

Figure 7.2(a) First-Instance Judgments

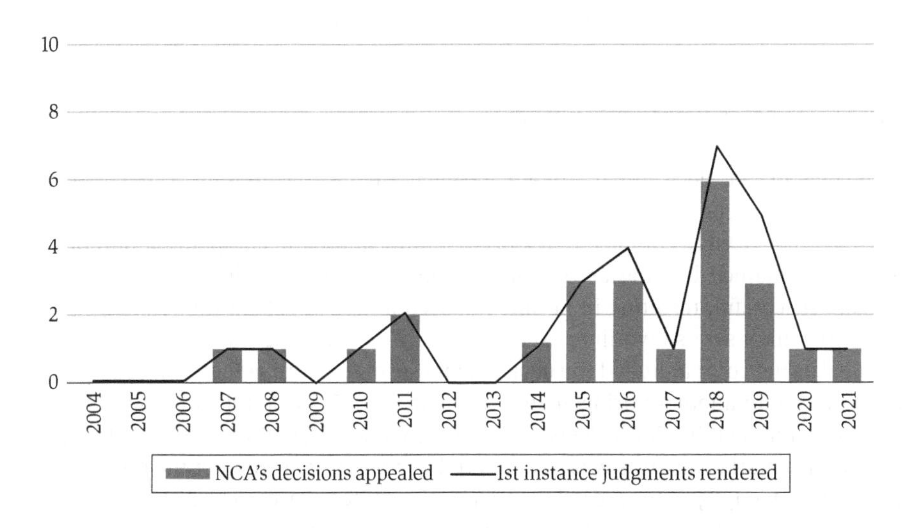

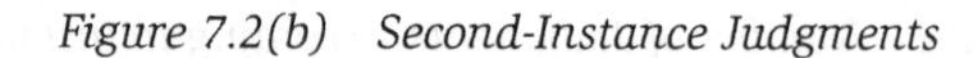

Figure 7.2(b) Second-Instance Judgments

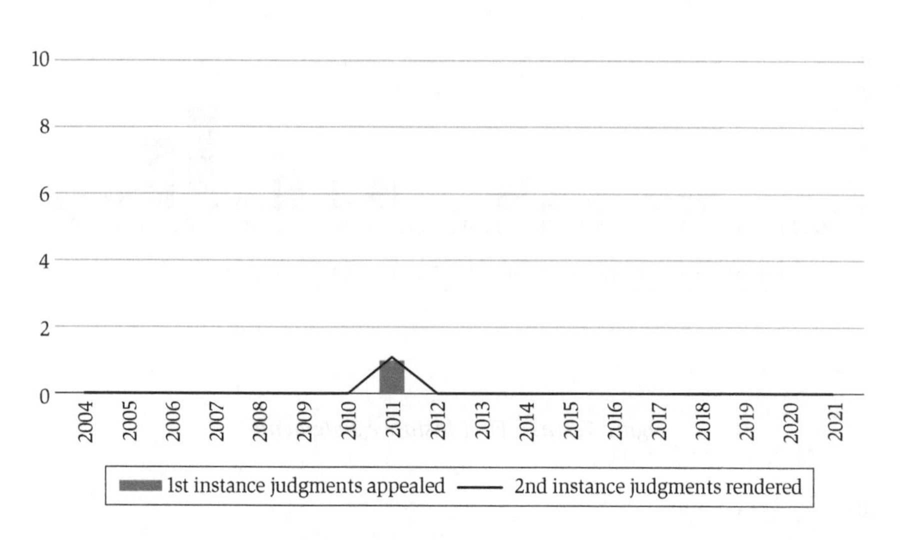

4.4 Success Rates and Outcomes

Of the overall CPC decisions that were appealed, only 8% were fully accepted across both first and second-instance appeals. Almost two-thirds of the appeals from CPC decisions (64%) were completely unsuccessful, meaning the competition authority's decisions remained binding as originally adopted, whereas a significant 28% were partially successful, resulting in no fine imposed on the appellant undertakings since the court cannot set its own fine, except in one case where the fine was only partially annulled as the court annulled the decision for one of the infringements in the case but maintained it for another infringement (*see* Figure 7.3). For example, in Case 741/2013 the Court annulled the CPC's decision on the ground of lack of reasoning as to why a comparative market analysis was not undertaken to ascertain whether the undertaking involved had engaged in excessive pricing. In Joined Cases 843/2017, 844/2017, 845/2017, 963/2017 and 971/2017, the Court annulled the CPC's decision since the lawfulness of the composition of the CPC had been affected by the participation of a person who lacked impartiality. The Court decided that being a debtor of the Bank of Cyprus, 'the existence of a special relationship and the creation of the special interest of hostility on the part of the member concerned had been established' and annulled the decisions on this ground. In Case 2003/2012, the Court held that the CPC had acted unlawfully in extending the investigation, and thus, the imposition of the administrative fine beyond a certain date was also unlawful.

Figure 7.3 Success of Appeals (Each NCA's Decision or Previous Instance Judgment Counts as One)

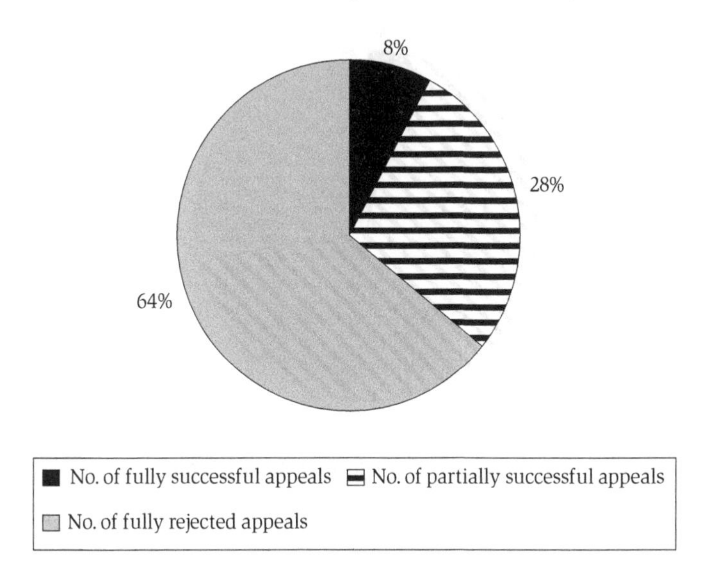

As most appeals only involved one instance (*see* Figure 7.1), the outcomes per instance reflect the general outcomes from Figure 7.3. Discounting the single second-instance appeal, 68% of appeals were unsuccessful, whereas 29% were partially successful, and 3% resulted in a partial annulment of the CPC's decision (*see* Figure 7.4(a)). The one and only appeal on second instance was successful and led to a full annulment of the CPC's decision (*see* Figure 7.4(b)). The case related to the unlawfulness of the appointment of the CPC's president. We discuss this case further in section 5.1 below. Note here that according to national law, a partially successful appeal (e.g., successful on only one of many grounds of appeal) may still result in a full annulment of the NCA's decision; hence, in our data, there are partially successful appeals corresponding to fully annulled decisions.

Figure 7.4(a) First-Instance Outcome

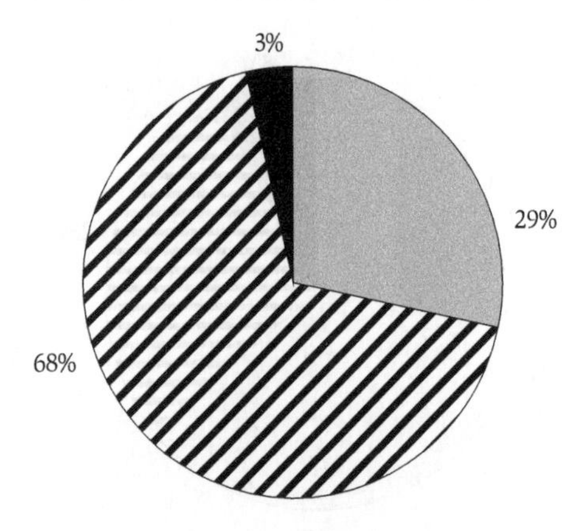

Figure 7.4(b) Second-Instance Outcome

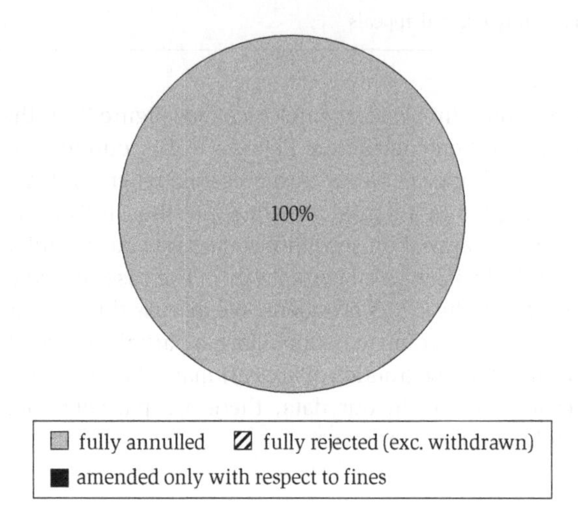

4.5 Type of NCA's Decisions Subject to Appeal

4.5.1 The Rules Being Appealed

In two-thirds of the judgments we included in the database, the appeal related to a CPC decision based on the national provision against abuse of dominance. In section 5.4 below, we discuss the possible reasons for the predominance of cases relating to the national provision against abuse of dominance. Only 17% of the CPC decisions were based on the national provision against anti-competitive agreements, and 3% related to decisions adopted on the basis of both national provisions against anti-competitive agreements and abuse of dominance, bringing the total percentage of appeals involving only the national rules up to 86%. Generally, this seems to be in line with a very low application of EU competition law in Cyprus in comparison to national competition law, as seen in statistics from the European Competition Network.[69] Nevertheless, it should be noted that Member States with small populations that joined the EU at the same time as Cyprus, such as Malta and Estonia, display a similarly low number of cases where EU competition law was applied. One out of ten decisions that were appealed involved violations of both Articles 101 and 102 TFEU and their national equivalents, whereas 3% involved only Article 101 TFEU and its national equivalent (*see* Figure 7.5).

Figure 7.5 Rule Being Appealed

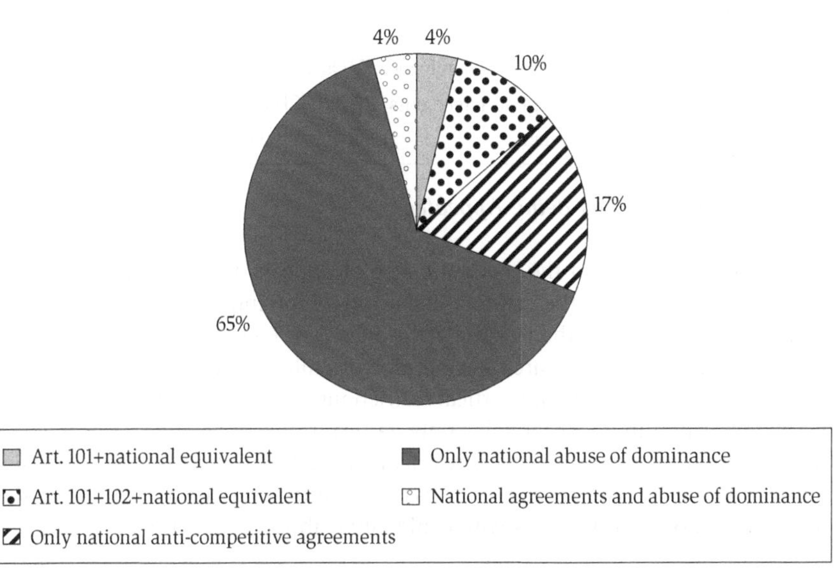

Breaking this down to the rules involved in the decisions being appealed per year does not reveal any significant trends. Given their general predominance, cases that have to do with the national provision on abuse of dominance come up steadily throughout the years covered by this research project. All other types appear only sporadically, as expected, given their relative rarity (*see* Figure 7.6).

69. https://competition-policy.ec.europa.eu/european-competition-network/statistics_en.

Figure 7.6 Rule Being Appealed According to Years (Each Judgment Counts as One)

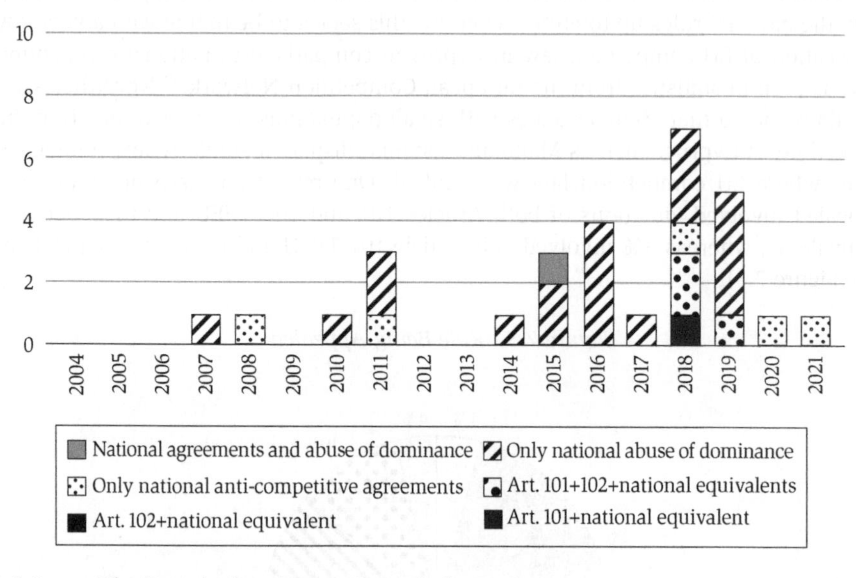

4.5.2 *The Restrictions Being Appealed*

As one would expect, given the predominance of appeals against CPC decisions on abuse of dominance and the general focus on enforcing antitrust rules against exclusionary abuses rather than exploitative ones (*see* Figure 7.5), most judgments (fourteen) covered by this research have to do with alleged exclusionary abuse. Two cases involve both horizontal and vertical restrictions, one case involves only horizontal restrictions, and three cases involve only vertical restrictions. Two cases involve a mix of horizontal restrictions, vertical restrictions, exploitative abuse, and exclusionary abuse, and there is one of each of the cases on vertical restrictions with exclusionary abuse and vertical restrictions with exploitative abuse (*see* Figure 7.7).

Figure 7.7 Types of Restrictions

4.5.3 *By-Object or By-Effect Restrictions in Agreements*

Zooming in on the judgments that involved decisions adopted on the basis of alleged violations of Article 101 TFEU and its national equivalent, we observe that there were no cases that involved purely an alleged effects-based violation. Half the cases (five out of ten) classified the agreements as anti-competitive by-object and effect, three cases out of ten involved a by-object restriction, and in two cases out of ten, there was no classification whatsoever (*see* Figure 7.8).

The lack of classification in some cases may seem rather surprising, given the fact that it ought to have been crucial in terms of burden of proof and the type of evidence that has to be put forward by the competition authority and economic analysis that it has to undertake to prove its case. However, both cases concern appeals against rejections of complaints about alleged anti-competitive vertical restrictions. Case 5550/2013 *Bacenco v. CPC* was an appeal against a rejection of a complaint which concerned alleged violations of the national rule against anti-competitive agreements.[70] The alleged restrictions were vertical in nature. Case 919/2013 *Koutroupi v. CPC* also concerned a vertical relationship in the form of a franchise agreement and claims made, *inter alia*, under the national provision against anti-competitive agreements.[71] The court found that the applicant had not put forward any arguments as to the alleged violation of the national provision against anti-competitive agreements.

Figure 7.8 Object/Effect (Only for Article 101/National Equivalent Infringements)

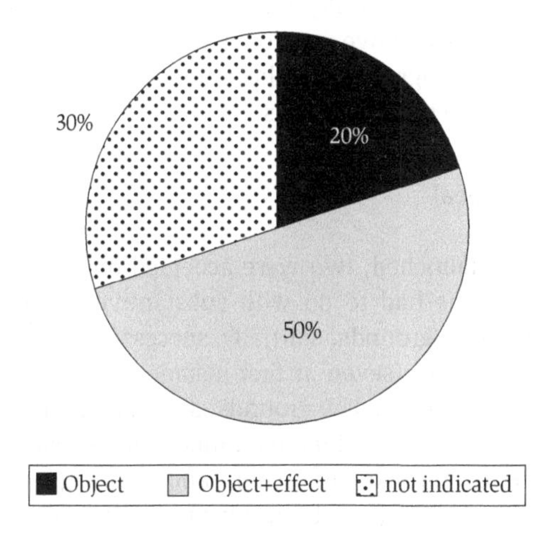

70. Case 5550/2013 *Bacenco v. CPC* CY:DD:2018:540.
71. Case 919/2013 *Koutroupi v. CPC* CY:DD:2018:276.

4.5.4 Type of NCA's Procedure

The large majority of CPC decisions that were appealed were decisions finding an infringement and imposing a fine (twenty-two decisions). Six decisions were rejections of complaints or decisions for the closing of an investigation, and one case involved the finding of an infringement but with no fine imposed.

Figure 7.9 Competition Authority's Procedure

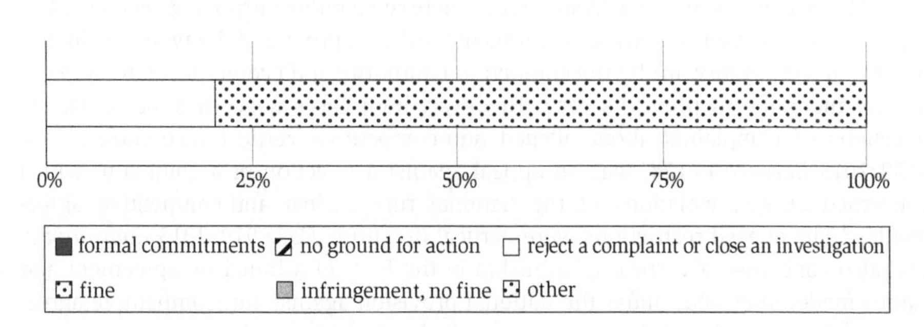

4.5.5 Leniency and Settlement Applications

We found no instances of appeals relating to proceedings in which leniency and settlement applications were successfully submitted despite the Leniency Programme being available since 2012 (*see* above, section 1). Unfortunately, we were unable to verify whether the Leniency Programme has been utilised, thus making it impossible to gauge the reasons behind the lack of appeals.

4.6 Grounds of Appeal

Of the successful appeals launched, two were accepted on procedural grounds, one related to the fine, and none had to do with substantive law issues in the CCA's decision or any EU/national grounds. Partially successful appeals related to eight instances of procedural matters (seven at first-instance and one on second-instance appeal), one instance of substantive law grounds, and one on the fine. Of the rejected appeals, fourteen related to procedural matters, nine regarded substantive law issues, six had to do with the fine, and two with EU or national law grounds. Note that each appeal may relate to several issues (e.g., both substantive and procedural issues); thus, the total number of grounds for appeal here does not reflect the number of appeals (*see* Figure 7.10).

Figure 7.10 Grounds of Appeal (Each NCA's Decision or Previous Instance Judgment Counts as One)

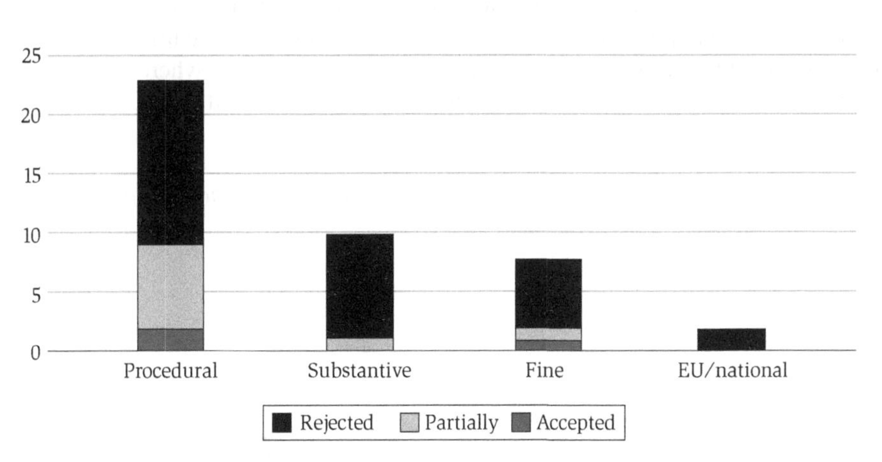

The small number of appeals does not allow us to draw any safe conclusions as to trends in the numbers per year of appeals launched and accepted under each ground just presented above. The only exception is, perhaps, for appeals on procedural grounds, where we see an increase in the number of appeals both launched and accepted up until 2019 and a drop again for the years 2020 and 2021 (*see* Figure 7.11). These make up the majority of appeals; thus, naturally, they follow the same trends as the total number of cases, as demonstrated by a comparison of Figure 7.11 with Figures 7.1 and 7.2a.

Figure 7.11 Procedural Grounds

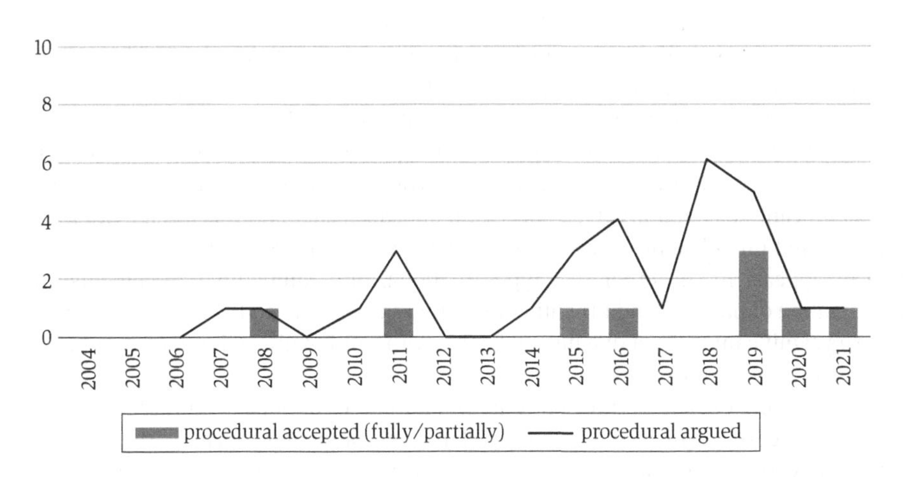

In 31% of the total appeals in which the fine was contested, the fine was reduced. In fact, in all these cases, the fine was not only reduced but cancelled completely. This is explained by the type of review procedure. As noted above, the jurisdiction of the court at appellate review does not allow for it to set its own fine. Instead, the decision of the CPC can be vitiated completely (meaning no fine is imposed), or the case must return to the CPC for the imposition of a new fine. The cases which were returned to the CPC are the ones which were 'partially successful', whereas the ones where the decision was vitiated in its entirety are the ones which were fully annulled (*see* above, section 4.4).

Figure 7.12 Types of Restrictions Versus Successful Grounds of Appeal

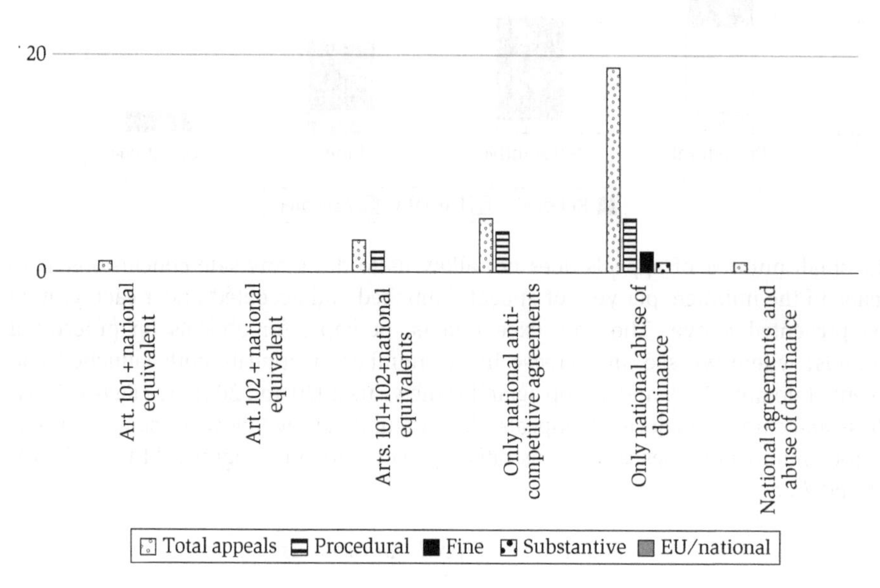

Appeals were successful in three types of restrictions that were alleged by the CPC in its contested decision, namely cases only relating to the national provision against abuse of dominance, cases where the alleged violation was based on an application of the national provision against anti-competitive agreements, and cases that involved a combination of the two national provisions and the two EU ones. The ratio of successful appeals regarding the first type (i.e., national abuse of dominance) is a significant 40% and involved successful appeals based on procedural matters, on the fine, and on substantive law issues as well as one successful appeal The success rate of appeals in the other two types (national anti-competitive agreements and combination of national and EU anti-competitive agreements and abuse of dominance) appears significant too, yet one must take this with caution given the small numbers of appeals in these categories.

A possible explanation for both the small number of appeals in these cases and the good success rate may be that the appellants only launched appeals in the few cases where they knew they had a strong case against the CPC's decisions. Moreover, as discussed further *infra*, the success of appeals in the majority of cases is, in fact, unrelated to substantive law issues and, therefore, also unrelated to the type of restriction that the CPC had found in the appealed decision.[72] We discuss the procedural issues that have arisen in these cases further below in section 5.1.

4.7 Other

4.7.1 Admissibility Matters and Preliminary Rulings

Admissibility issues may be raised on appeal by means of a preliminary objection. That is, prior to raising the substantial or procedural grounds of objection, a party may argue that the case is inadmissible because the applicant lacks locus standi and that there is no legitimate interest to challenge the decision of the CPC. In none of the cases we reviewed was admissibility in this sense an issue. However, there were instances of certain arguments of the parties being challenged as inadmissible for procedural reasons, such as when a ground of appeal had been raised too late. Moreover, there were no requests for preliminary rulings from the Court of Justice made in any of the cases we catalogued.

4.7.2 Appellant Types

Most appeals, as one would expect, are brought by the undertakings against which the CPC decision is directed. Beyond these, we found two appeals launched by individuals whose complaints had been rejected by the CPC and one by a group of individuals against a CPC decision, finding the appellants had breached competition law. The first individual was an importer of goods and equipment relating to eye laser surgeries through companies he owned, who launched a complaint against another company, owned by seventeen ophthalmologists, for allegedly defamatory comments as to the suitability of his equipment and eye surgery methods.[73] The second individual was an owner of a private employment agency who had launched a complaint against the Ministry of Labour and Social Security for its own programme of matching unemployed persons to possible jobs.[74] Finally, the group of individuals that appealed a decision against them appealed as private individuals, as members of the Board of Directors of the Limassol Licenced Porters Association (LLPA), and as licensed porters against a decision of the CPC that had found the LLPA had engaged in anti-competitive behaviour.[75] All three appeals were rejected.

4.7.3 Third-Party Participation

When it comes to third-party participation, we found two instances in which undertakings that had been part of the CPC's decision joined proceedings brought by other

72. *See further, infra* section 5.1.
73. Case 612/2009 *Akis Ioannou v. CPC.*
74. Case 1782/2012 *Georgios Stylianou v. CPC* CY:AD:2014:D448.
75. Case 259/2013 *Andreas Charilaou et al. v. CPC* CY:AD:2015:D818.

parties as interested parties. We also found 15 instances where complainants before the CPC joined the proceedings in support of the CPC, where the undertaking against which they had launched a complaint appealed the CPC decision that had found a violation of the competition rules.

5 QUALITATIVE ANALYSIS

5.1 Intensity and Depth of Judicial Review

The single most important aspect of the judicial review of CPC decisions in Cyprus is the relative lack of substantive review. As the CPC is an administrative authority whose decisions are subject to an administrative type of review, the national courts do not engage in the kind of in-depth discussions of the substantive competition law issues that competition lawyers are used to seeing from the General Court or Court of Justice or even from specialised courts in other Member States. Thus, court decisions on judicial review of the CPC's decisions cannot 'substitute the judgment of the administration', and courts cannot 'intervene unless the administration during the exercise of its judgment has exceeded the outer limits of its discretion'.[76] That does not mean that the courts' jurisdiction is limited to only a *formal* review of legality. As the administrative court itself has remarked, the courts must fully guarantee a fair trial and ensure:

> the provision of effective judicial protection by examining the grounds for annulment, [which are] error of law and appreciation of facts, lack of proper investigation, breach of principles of natural justice, review of the reasoning, whether the reasoning exists, is adequate and lawful (as not being mistaken as to the law and facts in the case), whether it goes beyond the outer limits of administrative discretion, whether it complies with the principle of proportionality and other principles governing the procedure before the CPC, and other grounds laid down in the relevant case law.[77]

Thus, although review of the fines does not exist and review on substance is limited, judicial review on matters of procedure and based on administrative law procedures is rather intense, even if limited in scope. That narrow scope, coupled with the CPC's role as investigator, prosecutor, and *de facto* first-instance adjudicator, has been criticised as potentially violating the right to fair trial as safeguarded by Article 6(1) of the European Convention on Human Rights (ECHR) and the case law of the EU courts.[78] No case has yet reached the Strasbourg court and, as noted above, no reference for a preliminary ruling has ever been requested from the courts in Luxembourg either. On the other hand, *Bernatt* considers that judicial deference to administrative authorities may be permissible so long as due process guarantees are provided in the administrative proceedings, there is a division of prosecutorial and investigative

76. Case 256/2003 *Cyprus Telecommunications Authority v. CPC and Republic* CY:DD:2016:424, 15 (authors' translation).
77. Case 741/2013 *Cyprus Telecommunications Authority v. CPC* CY:DD:2019:334, 9 (authors' translation).
78. Polyviou (*supra* n. 43) 123 et seq.

functions from decision-making ones at the competition authority, and the authority possesses an established expertise proven in the justification of its decisions.[79] We note that at least the first two criteria are satisfied with regard to the CPC. We comment on the third criterion further in this subsection.

From the cases covered by the scope of this research project, the *only* successful appeal on substantive grounds is case 741/2013 *Cyprus Telecommunications Authority v. CPC*, where the court examined the appellant's arguments regarding the relevant market, the finding of dominance, and the abuse, and found that the CPC had not substantiated its findings of excessive pricing, since it had not explained its choice of methodology and why it had not conducted price comparison analysis.[80]

All other successful or partially successful appeals were won, or partially won, by the applicants either on procedural grounds or because of matters relating to irregularities as to the CPC's composition and impartiality.

When it comes to procedural matters, there are two successful appeals. The first case concerned the legality of a dawn raid and led to a full annulment of the CPC's decision.[81] The second case had to do with the limitation period for the imposition of a fine having been exceeded by the CPC for one of three findings of predatory pricing, leading to a partial annulment of its decision.[82]

The remaining cases where appellants were successful, which in fact are the *majority* of successful appeals, were won on irregularities as to the composition of the CPC, on findings that members of the CPC were possibly compromised but had not recused themselves, and on a lack of impartiality (at least as subjectively experienced) on the part of the CPC.[83] The track record of the CPC in this regard is rather embarrassing and has negatively impacted its reputation for a large part of its thirty-year existence. Polyviou is, therefore, right in describing the CPC's history as one of *'constant adventures and upheavals'*.[84] One of the CPC's chairs has been prosecuted for forgery of minutes of meetings of the CPC, two other chairs resigned for other reasons, and three members of the CPC, including one of its chairs, have had their appointments judicially annulled on distinct occasions over the span of just a decade.[85]

Two judicial annulments of the appointments had to do with members' concurrent engagements at the time of serving at the CPC, as mayor in a municipal council in one case[86] and a member of the central committee of a major political party in another

79. M Bernatt, Transatlantic Perspective on Judicial Deference in Administrative Law (2016) 22(2) *Columbia Journal of European Law* 275, 325.
80. Case 741/2013 *Cyprus Telecommunications Authority v. CPC* CY:DD:2019:334, 26-27.
81. Case 1646/2017 *ExxonMobil Cyprus Ltd v. CPC* CY:DD:2021:187.
82. Case 256/2003 *Cyprus Telecommunications Authority v. CPC and Republic* CY:DD:2016:424, 20.
83. Case 2003/2012 *Cyprus Telecommunications Authority v. CPC* CY:DD:2016:261; Case 804/2017 *Bank of Cyprus v. CPC* CY:DD:2018:287; Joined Cases 843/2017, 844/2017, 845/2017, 963/2017 and 971/2017 *Emporiki Bank et al. v. CPC* CY:DD:2019:263; and Case 1462/2017 *SEMIEK v. CPC*.
84. Polyviou (*supra* n. 43), 53.
85. Antoniou, 30 Years of the CPC (*supra* n. 24).
86. Supreme Court decision in *Cyprus Telecommunications Authority v. Republic* [2007] 3 CLR 560.

case, although the Supreme Court overturned the latter judgment on the ground that such a position did not constitute 'holding of political office'.[87]

The removal of the CPC's chair by the Supreme Court, moreover, had to do with a total lack of apparent criteria for the appointment of the chairperson as well as a total lack of any investigation and justification in the relevant decision of the Cypriot Council of Ministers to appoint the chairperson.[88] As a result of the above, the CPC had no other choice but to revoke all the decisions issued while the said persons were participating in its composition.[89]

It is worth mentioning here that the appointments for the five-member CPC have hitherto been made by the Cypriot Council of Ministers on a recommendation of the (then) Minister of Commerce, Industry, and Tourism and may have been mostly politically motivated rather than been made based on objective and meritocratic criteria and the persons' credentials. This begs the question as to whether the judicial deference to CPC decisions we see in the reviewed judgments is indeed permissible. Recall that the third of *Bernatt's* conditions for permissibility of judicial deference is that the administrative authority must possess proven expertise. According to *Bernatt*, the criterion entails that appointment of the people who are the final decision-makers in the authority should be contingent on adequate education and experience.[90] Seen in this light, the appointment of members to the CPC (and even its chairperson) without any clear criteria relating to the candidates' credentials would render the judicial deference shown by Cypriot courts to the CPC's decisions with regard to the substantive application of competition law impermissible, for instance by ECHR standards. That said, as noted above, on account of the transposition of the ECN+ Directive into Cypriot law, the 2022 Competition Law seeks to address some of these issues.[91] Thus, we can expect fewer appeals in the future to have to do with the CPC's composition, though issues about recusals and impartiality may remain.

A case where a member of the CPC should have recused himself from the case but did not concerned a bitter dispute between that member in his private capacity as a debtor of one of the banks that were being investigated for their participation in anti-competitive agreements and collusions. The relevant member had engaged in certain email discussions (the said emails having been sent from his work email address at the CPC) with representatives of the bank, asking for a restructuring of his

87. The Supreme Court eventually overturned this first-instance judgment on appeal in the Supreme Court decision, *CPC v. Cyprus Telecommunications Authority*, Apps 2/16 and 7/16, 3 March 2017.
88. Supreme Court decision, *Exxon Mobil Ltd and others v. CPC* [2011] 3 CLR 449.
89. In other words, the effect of a finding that an organ's composition was unlawful is serious because if the Court decides the formation of an organ such as the CPC is problematic, then all the CPC's decisions taken up to that point are vitiated and will need to be re-examined and a new decision issued.
90. M Bernatt, *Populism and Antitrust: The Illiberal Influence of Populist Government on the Competition Law System* (Cambridge University Press, 2022) 230.
91. *See* above, section 1.

loan while arguing that the profit margins were illegal and mentioning his capacity as a member of the CPC.[92]

Overall, our conclusion is that there are qualitative differences across the intensity of review with relation to procedure, substance, and fines, with the procedural review being rigorous, the review of substance almost lacking, and the review of fines not undertaken at all due to the Administrative Court's limited permissible scope of review.

5.2 Lack of Appeals at Second Instance

Another striking feature of judicial review of CPC decisions in Cyprus is the apparent scarcity of appeals in second instance. In reality, there are a few more appeals than the single one we reported, but they were outside the scope of this research project as they had to do exclusively with legal matters beyond competition law, such as the lawfulness of the composition and formation of the CPC. In our opinion, the scarcity of appeals on matters relating to the interpretation of the substantive competition law provisions may have three possible explanations. It may depend: (i) on the relative scarcity of appeals in first-instance dealing with substance rather than procedural or administrative matters, (ii) on losing parties not bringing appeals, suggesting the existence of a legal culture of compliance with court rulings and trust that the court on first instance arrived at a result that would seem difficult to reverse on second-instance appeal, and (iii) on delays in hearing appeals at second instance, due to a backlog in the Supreme Court.

5.3 Predominance of Enforcement of National Abuse of Dominance Provision

We note that the CPC's enforcement of the national equivalent to Article 102 TFEU against abuse of dominance seems to be rather prominent, contrary to what is common on the EU level and at other Member States, where Article 101 TFEU and its national equivalents are enforced more. Although we cannot speculate on why this is the case, we note that this trend has been observed by other commentators with experience of competition law enforcement in Cyprus.[93] One possible reason is that the majority of complaints made to the CPC concern an alleged abuse of dominance, whereas *ex officio* investigations conducted by the CPC mostly (if not entirely) concern the existence of anti-competitive agreements between undertakings.[94]

92. Case 804/2017 *Bank of Cyprus v. CPC* CY:DD:2018:287 and Joined Cases 843/2017, 844/2017, 845/2017, 963/2017 and 971/2017 *Emporiki Bank et al. v. CPC* CY:DD:2019:263.
93. Antoniou (*supra* n. 65).
94. Cyprus Commission for the Protection of Competition, Annual Report 2010.

5.4 Use of EU Law and Case Law

From the types of rules that the appeals relate to, one can deduce that competition law enforcement by the CPC relates mostly to the national provisions rather than the EU ones, presupposing, of course, that the appeals are a representative part of the CPC's enforcement. We can only assume that the CPC does not consider the effect on trade criterion to be satisfied in the cases it pursues, most likely because of the appreciability aspect of the criterion not being satisfied. This is not remarkable: the Cypriot economy is small relative to the EU and other Member States, and its companies are predominantly small and local.

Regardless, in the court rulings we examined, we found references to case law from the General Court and the Court of Justice, where it was relevant. The cases to which Cypriot courts relied upon relate both to competition law procedure, for instance, how dawn raids are to be conducted,[95] and to substantive law issues, for instance, what is an undertaking[96] or how exploitative excessive prices are to be shown.[97] That said, we did not observe any in-depth engagement with the cited rulings; they are simply used to verify whether the CPC has correctly conducted its investigation and is not mistaken as to the law. The sense that EU law is relied upon but without any in-depth engagement is supported by the fact that there were no requests for preliminary rulings in the cases we reviewed for the purposes of this research project and that rulings from the EU courts are often cited as a legal source alongside academic opinion and even competition law textbooks as if they carry the same weight.

6 CONCLUDING REMARKS

This is the first time a comprehensive empirical study of the application of EU competition law in Cyprus on the basis of Regulation 1/2003 has been undertaken. Our research revealed certain peculiarities of competition law enforcement in Cyprus, such as the emphasis on enforcement against unilateral conduct, the predominance of cases dealing with matters other than substantive competition law, such as matters of procedure, composition, independence, and impartiality, and the apparent scarcity of appeals on second instance. Overall, in our view, it does not seem that public competition law enforcement in Cyprus has been particularly strong despite a system of judicial review that gives significant deference to the decisions of the NCA and only engages in marginal administrative review.

This gap in public enforcement has not been countenanced by any significant private enforcement. This may, however, be about to change as a Cypriot District Court recently issued the first-ever court judgment in the area of private enforcement of competition law in an action for damages based on an infringement of competition pursuant to law 113(I)/2017. In February 2022, the District Court of Larnaca awarded damages in the sum of EUR 257,716.11 plus statutory interest to an undertaking as

95. *See, e.g.*, Case 1646/2017 *ExxonMobil Cyprus Ltd v. CPC* CY:DD:2021:187.
96. Case 259/2013 *Andreas Charilaou et al. v. CPC* CY:AD:2015:D818, 8.
97. Case 741/2013 *Cyprus Telecommunications Authority v. CPC* CY:DD:2019:334, 23-24.

compensation for losses incurred due to the abuse of dominant position in which the Cyprus Grain Commission had engaged (in particular, predatory pricing).[98] On that note, the recently enacted 2022 Competition Law introduced a significant change to provide that a final decision of the CPC finding an infringement of the provisions of Articles 3 and/or 6 of the Law and Articles 101 and/or 102 TFEU constitutes an irrebuttable presumption and may be used by any person who has suffered loss caused by the infringement in order to bring a claim for an action for damages.[99] This may signify a new era for actions for damages as the prospective claimant will now be able to rely on the CPC's decision and will presumably require no further evidence to prove a claim.

Furthermore, in light of the very recent amendment of the Competition Law, it is also expected that the Leniency Programme will follow suit. Accordingly, the CPC has issued draft leniency regulations entitled the Leniency Programme Immunity from and Reduction of Administrative Fines in cases of Restrictive Collusions Infringing Section 3 of the Law or/and Article 101 of the TFEU (Leniency Programme) Regulations of 2021, which would bring the Cyprus Leniency Programme into conformity with the ECN+ Directive. At the time of writing this chapter, the Regulations had not yet been adopted by the Cypriot Parliament.

Overall, it remains to be seen whether reforms introduced by the 2022 Competition Law, on the basis of the ECN+ Directive[100] and the expected review of Regulation 1/2003,[101] will have an impact on EU competition law enforcement in Cyprus, though the latest developments are certainly in the right direction. We can only hope that on account of these changes, judicial review will shift from matters of procedure and administrative law more towards the substance of competition law, albeit with judicial deference shown towards the CPC as an expert administrative authority.

While authoring this chapter, on 12 July 2022, the Cyprus Constitution was amended pursuant to the provisions of Law 103(I)/2022. In what has been termed as the 'biggest reform in justice' in the history of the Republic of Cyprus, Article 146 of the Constitution was amended, among others. Article 146(4)(d) of the Constitution, as amended, stipulates that the Administrative Court shall, subject to provision of the law, exercise full judicial review. In other words, it is expected that the Administrative Court will in the future be able to amend in part or in full the relevant administrative decision under question in cases where secondary legislation specifically allowing this has been passed. Thus, the House of Representatives is now empowered to pass new secondary legislation providing for the types of administrative decisions that may be subject to full judicial review, leaving the door open for decisions of the CPC to be subject to full judicial review in the future.

98. Case *AGS Agrotrading Ltd* v. *Cyprus Grain Commission*, Action No. 2431/2013, 9/2/2022.
99. Section 63 of the 2022 Competition Law.
100. ECN+ Directive (*supra* n. 2).
101. Reg. 1/2003 (*supra* n. 8).

CHAPTER 8

Czech Republic Report

Michal Petr

1 INTRODUCTION TO COMPETITION LAW ENFORCEMENT IN THE CZECH REPUBLIC

1.1 Historical Outline of Czech Competition Law

From an economic point of view, the era of communism was unique in the former Czechoslovakia. The entire economy was fully state-controlled and subject to central planning, without any form of private entrepreneurship, which was to some extent allowed or tolerated in other countries of Central Europe. Therefore, the liberalisation of the economy in the nineties had to begin with massive 'privatisation' of hitherto state-controlled enterprises (e.g., shops, restaurants, hotels etc.) and companies.

To accompany this process, Czech competition law was first introduced in 1991.[1] It was inspired by EU competition law, regulating anti-competitive agreements, abuses of dominance and control of concentrations; in addition, it contained a specific provision prohibiting public authorities from distorting competition, which was justified by the fact that the entire economy had hitherto been subject to central planning of the Government. A specific ministry was responsible for the enforcement of competition law; competition policy being part of the process of 'privatisation', for which the Government was responsible. This changed in 1996 when the Office for the Protection of Competition (in Czech 'UOHS') was established as an independent public authority[2] responsible for competition policy and enforcement.

1. Act No. 63/1991 Coll., on the protection of competition.
2. Act No. 273/1996 Coll., on the competences of the Office for the Protection of Competition.

Czech competition law was fully rewritten in 2001 when the new Competition Act entered into force.[3] The new act was adopted in the course of preparations for the accession of the Czech Republic to the EU. Section 3 of the Competition Act prohibited anti-competitive agreements, and section 11 abuse of dominant position; merger control was also introduced. Conversely, the distortion of competition by public authorities was no longer prohibited by the law; it was, however, re-introduced in 2012.[4]

Even though it was claimed that the Competition Act would be fully compatible with EU law, it was not. For example, undertakings were not defined as economic entities but as legal ones (i.e., individual companies), and the law did not distinguish between by-object and by-effect agreements. It took more than a dozen subsequent amendments adopted in the course of the following years to reach full alignment with EU law.[5] For the purposes of this study, however, section 3 of the Competition Act may be considered fully in line with Article 101 TFEU and section 11 of the Competition Act fully in line with Article 102 TFEU. In accordance with the principles of effectiveness and equivalence, Czech courts insist that Czech competition law needs to be interpreted in the same way as EU competition law.[6]

1.2 Enforcement Framework

Since 1996, the Office for the Protection of Competition (UOHS) has been responsible for the enforcement of competition law. In addition to competition law, it was made responsible for the supervision of public procurement procedures.[7] Later, it gained powers in state aid control[8] and regulation of significant market power of grocery stores.[9]

The authority is headed by the Chairman, selected by the Government, and appointed by the President for six years. The authority is divided into different sections, entrusted with different competences. The Competition Section, responsible for competition policy and enforcement, oversees investigation and decision-making. The section is headed by a Vice-Chairman, appointed by the Chairman for an indefinite period.

The decisions of the Vice-Chairman (known as 'first-instance decisions' in Czech law) may be appealed to the Chairman of UOHS by the parties to the proceedings. The

3. Act No. 143/2001 Coll., on the protection of competition, as amended (hereinafter referred to as 'Competition Act'). English version of the Competition Act is available at: https://www.uohs.cz/en/legislation.html.
4. Act No. 360/2012 Coll., amending the Competition Act.
5. The compatibility of Czech and EU competition law is discussed in detail in Petr, M. *Vztah českého a unijního soutěžního práva [The Relationship between Czech and EU Competition Law]*. Praha: C. H. Beck, 2018.
6. Judgment of the Supreme Administrative Court of 25 February 2009, Ref. No. 1 Afs 78/2008.
7. Currently, public procurement is regulated by Act No. 134/2016 Coll., on public procurement.
8. Czech legislation implementing EU state aid rules is contained in Act No. 215/2004 Coll., on certain relationships in the area of state aid.
9. Act No. 395/2009 Coll., on significant market power in the sale of food and agricultural products and on abuse thereof.

Chairman has full jurisdiction and may, in principle, confirm the decision, annul, and return it for further investigation or amend it himself/herself. Only the decision of the Chairman (known as 'second-instance decision') may be reviewed by the courts; conversely, if the 'first-instance decision', i.e., the decision of the Vice-Chairman, is not appealed to the Chairman, it is not subject to court review. For the purpose of this study, however, only the decisions of the Chairman would be regarded as final national competition authority (NCA) decisions, as only they are subject to judicial review by courts.[10]

The initiation of antitrust proceedings is left to the discretion of the Competition Authority. Only those undertakings suspected of illegal conduct are parties to the proceedings, and complainants or affected parties cannot be included in the proceedings.[11]

Most investigations end with a declaration of an infringement. Such decisions are typically accompanied by a fine amounting to up to 10% of the annual turnover of the undertakings concerned.[12] In the case of bid-rigging, a prohibition from taking part in public procurement for up to three years may also be imposed.[13]

The UOHS may declare that there was no infringement. Yet, such decisions amount to less than 20% of all the cases.[14] The UOHS may also impose commitments on the undertakings investigated, i.e., instead of finding an infringement, it closes the investigation on condition that the undertakings concerned fulfil some remedies that dispel the authority's concerns ('commitments').[15] The number of such decisions is limited and adopted in practice only in cases of abuse of dominance. Both the decision to close an investigation and the decision to accept commitments can be appealed only by the parties to the proceedings, i.e., the undertakings under investigation; no decision closing an investigation without finding an infringement or imposing commitments has ever been subject to court review.

A significant proportion of infringement decisions (circa 50%) are 'settled', meaning that the UOHS decreases the fine by 20% if the undertakings concerned do not contest its findings.[16] As the parties to settlement proceedings do not have any incentive to challenge the findings of the competition authority, settlement decisions are almost never appealed. Out of the considerable number of settlement decisions issued since 2012, when the settlement procedure was introduced, there has only been a single appeal to the court; it concerned only the fine, not the merits of the case, and was dismissed by the court.[17]

10. For the methodology, and case selection criteria, see the Methodology chapter of this book.
11. Section 21 of the Competition Act.
12. Section 22a(2) of the Competition Act.
13. Section 22a(4) of the Competition Act.
14. Petr, M., Zorková, E. *Kvantitativní analýza rozhodování soutěžního úřadu [Quantitative Analysis of Decisions of the Czech Competition Authority]*. ANTITRUST, 2018, č. 3, p. 77.
15. Section 7(2) and 11(3) of the Competition Act.
16. Section 22ba(2) of the Competition Act.
17. Judgment of the regional Court in Brno of 14 December 2020, Ref. No. 29 Af 54/2019.

1.3 Enforcement Practices and Priorities

The UOHS is obliged to investigate every suspicion of an infringement of competition law, and it is not allowed to set priorities. As of 2012, the UOHS may decide not to open an investigation if the effects of the potential infringement were limited.[18] This provision is not perceived as 'prioritisation', an enforcement policy available to other NCAs, as the UOHS cannot decide to concentrate on a specific sector or type of practice; the only criterion is that the effects of the practice are close to negligible. In any event, the UOHS has not yet reported any use of this provision.

Investigations by the UOHS have been heavily focused on anti-competitive agreements, accounting for more than 90% of all decisions, all of which were by-object infringements.[19] Most of the cases concerned horizontal cartels, in particular bid-rigging, which clearly constitutes a 'flagship' of the UOHS's enforcement record.

2 COURTS OF APPEAL

Under Czech terminology, the term 'appeal', whether administrative or judicial, is restricted to the description of a review of a decision that is not yet final and legally enforceable by a higher-instance authority. In Czech terminology, such an appeal is an 'ordinary remedy'. Conversely, if a decision becomes final, it cannot be appealed (ordinary remedies are no longer available; there is no higher instance to perform the review). Judicial review by courts is labelled as 'extraordinary remedies'.

Similarly, the Czech terminology concerning judicial review of administrative decisions does not refer to the different courts performing the review as 'instances'. Instead, it is possible to file an 'action' to the Regional Court against the decision of the Chairman of the UOHS, a 'cassation complaint' against the judgment of the Regional Court to the Supreme Administrative Court and a 'constitutional complaint' against all the preceding decisions (decisions of UOHS, judgments of the Regional Court and the Supreme Administrative Court) to the Constitutional Court.

Thus, there are three levels of judicial review of decisions of administrative authorities by three judicial institutions in the Czech Republic. The specific terminology used in Czech, though different from terminology used in other jurisdictions, does not influence the analysis performed by this study. For the sake of coherence, I will therefore further refer to court review as 'appeals' and to the different courts as 'instances', i.e., to the Regional Court in Brno as the court of first instance and to the Supreme Administrative Court as the court of second instance.

All final decisions of all the administrative authorities in the Czech Republic are reviewed by administrative courts. These courts are not specialised in competition law and they decide disputes on any matter of administrative law. A judgment is delivered by a panel of three judges.

18. Section 21(2) of the Competition Act.
19. Petr, M., Zorková, E. *Kvantitativní analýza rozhodování soutěžního úřadu [Quantitative Analysis of Decisions of the Czech Competition Authority]*. Antitrust, 2018, č. 3, s. 77.

2.1 First-Instance Appeal: Regional Court in Brno

All decisions of the UOHS's Chairman are reviewed by the Regional Court in Brno, where the competition authority is located. Only parties to the proceedings before the UOHS may file an appeal, i.e., only the undertakings that have allegedly breached the law. In practice, most decisions of the UOHS Chairman are challenged before the Regional Court.[20]

The court may either confirm the UOHS's decision and dismiss the appeal or annul the decision (or its part) and return the case to UOHS. If the fine imposed by the UOHS is disproportionately high, the court may itself decrease it. Any judgment of the Regional Court is final and may be enforced, even if a cassation complaint is filed.

2.2 Second-Instance Appeal: Supreme Administrative Court

Judgments of the Regional Court may further be appealed to the Supreme Administrative Court. This court is competent to hear all appeals against judgments of all the Regional Courts in the Czech Republic and it is also not specialised in competition law. A panel of three judges delivers its judgments. Only parties to the proceedings before the Regional Court may file an appeal, i.e., the parties to the proceedings before UOHS (the undertakings that have allegedly breached the law) and the UOHS itself.

The Supreme Administrative Court has full jurisdiction and may review both matters of fact and law. The court may either confirm the Regional Court's judgment and dismiss the appeal or annul the judgment (fully or partially) and return the case to the Regional Court.

2.3 Third-Instance Appeal: Constitutional Court

It is possible to file a constitutional complaint to the Constitutional Court against any judgment of the Supreme Administrative Court. Only the private entities that were parties to the proceedings before the Supreme Administrative Court may file such a complaint; however, the UOHS does not have such a right.

The Constitutional Court only reviews whether claimants' rights guaranteed by the Constitution were infringed. It may dismiss the claim as inadmissible or review the decisions under appeal (on matters of constitutional law only) and either dismiss the complaint or accept it and annul the judgment under appeal.

None of the constitutional complaints against any judgments discussed in this study were found admissible by the Constitutional Court.[21]

---

20. Petr, M., Zorková, E. *Kvantitativní analýza rozhodování soutěžního úřadu [Quantitative Analysis of Decisions of the Czech Competition Authority]*. Antitrust, 2018, č. 3, s. 77.
21. In fact, there has been only a single admissible case so far, where it was originally found inadmissible, but after the intervention of the European Court of Human Rights, the Constitutional Court returned to it and allowed the review. This case however precedes the time period covered by this study.

3 PRIOR RESEARCH

Research concerning competition law is rather limited in the Czech Republic. Specifically in relation to judicial review, existing research so far only covers analyses of specific judgments. The author is aware of only a single article concerning the quantitative analysis of the judicial review of UOHS's decisions.[22]

4 QUANTITATIVE ANALYSIS

This section examines the findings resulting from a systematic analysis of all judgments reviewing administrative competition law enforcement in the Czech Republic between May 2004 and the end of April 2021.

4.1 Source of Information

In the Czech Republic, only the judgments of 'top' courts are systematically published. Thus, both the Supreme Administrative Court[23] and the Constitutional Court[24] have databases containing their judgments published online. These databases are not interconnected. Conversely, not all judgments of Regional Courts are published by the courts themselves, although some of them are contained in the database of the Supreme Administrative Court.

Nevertheless, the UOHS publishes all judgments reviewing its final decisions on Articles 101 and 102 Treaty on the Functioning of the European Union (TFEU) or their Czech national equivalents (in Czech terminology, decisions 'on the merits') on its website. The judgments are listed (and their full text is downloadable), primarily in chronological order, even though they are frequently (though not always) 'grouped', i.e., judgments of the Regional Court in Brno, the Supreme Administrative Court and the Constitutional Court concerning the same decision of the UOHS are typically listed next to each other.[25]

The database compiled for this study was based on the information published on the UOHS's website and cross-checked with the database of the Supreme Administrative Court. The author thus believes that it includes all relevant judgments. For the purposes of this study, we only included judgments concerning final decisions of the UOHS issued after 1 May 2004.[26]

22. Petr, M., Zorková, E. *Přezkum rozhodnutí ÚOHS ve správním soudnictví [Court Review of the Decisions of the Czech Competition Authority]*. Antitrust, 2018, č. 4, s. 102.
23. The search engine of the Supreme Administrative Court is available at: https://vyhledavac.nssoud.cz/Home/Index?formular=4.
24. The search engine of the Constitutional Court is available at: https://nalus.usoud.cz/Search/Search.aspx.
25. The judgments are available at: https://www.uohs.cz/cs/hospodarska-soutez/soudni-prezkum-rozhodnuti.html.
26. On condition the decision of the Vice-Chairman was also issued after this date.

The study also considers the decisions of the UOHS issued during the same period that are published on its website.[27] With respect to these decisions, two remarks need to be made.

First, the statistics on the number of decisions which the UOHS publishes in its annual reports, are not suitable for this study. They reflect the absolute number of decisions issued in a given year but do not take into account the links between the decision of the Chairman and the Vice-Chairman; the absolute number of reported decisions is thus higher than the number of cases the UOHS had actually closed.[28] Therefore, the author undertook a 'manual' search through the database, searching for decisions concerning the same 'case' (i.e., a single investigation) and identified only those final decisions.[29]

Second, the total number of final decisions issued by the UOHS, identified in the way described in the previous paragraph, does not correspond with the number of decisions subject to judicial review. Only if the decision of the Vice-Chairman is appealed to the Chairman and the Chairman issues a decision confirming it, making it the final decision of the UOHS, may this decision be appealed to court. As a significant proportion of all the cases end with a decision of the Vice-Chairman (in particular, settlement decisions), they cannot be appealed to the court, which accounts for the relatively low ratio of appeals overall (see below).

4.2 Total Number of Judgments and the Ratio of Appeal

The dataset includes 99 judgments, of which 55 were issued by the first-instance Regional Court in Brno, 37 by the Supreme Administrative Court, and 7 by the Constitutional Court. In this period, the UOHS issued a total of 149 final decisions on the application of Articles 101 and 102 TFEU and the national equivalents; out of these, only 61 were the decisions of the Chairman and thus subject to court review. As mentioned, if the decision of the Vice-Chairman is not challenged, it becomes final and cannot be reviewed by courts. This is the case with most of the decisions of the UOHS. Of all the 149 UOHS decisions included in this study, 88 were final decisions of the Vice-Chairman; most of them were settlement decisions.

The appeal rate of more than 66% is relatively high. Materially, the appeal rate is, in fact, even higher, as most of the decisions of the Chairman that were not appealed were those in which the Chairman upheld the appeal, annulled the decision of the

27. The search engine is available at: https://www.uohs.cz/cs/hospodarska-soutez/sbirky-rozhodnuti.html.
28. For example, if a decision of the Vice-Chairman is appealed and the Chairman confirms it, the official statistics would show two decisions, even though only one (the decision of the Chairman) may be reviewed by court; if the Chairman annuls the decision and refers the proceedings back, which is often the case, there would be another decision of the Vice-Chairman and if appealed, another decision of the Chairman, i.e., four decisions in total, even though only one (the final decision of the Chairman) may be subject to court review.
29. This means the decisions of the Vice-Chairman, if they were not appealed to the Chairman; if there was an appeal to the Chairman, only the final decisions of the Chairman were calculated.

Vice-Chairman and returned the case back to him; the parties to the proceedings have no incentive to challenge such a decision before the court.

4.3 Judgments per Year

Figure 8.1 summarises the number of judgments issued by the various instances of the Czech courts per year.

Figure 8.1 Number of Judgments According to Instances

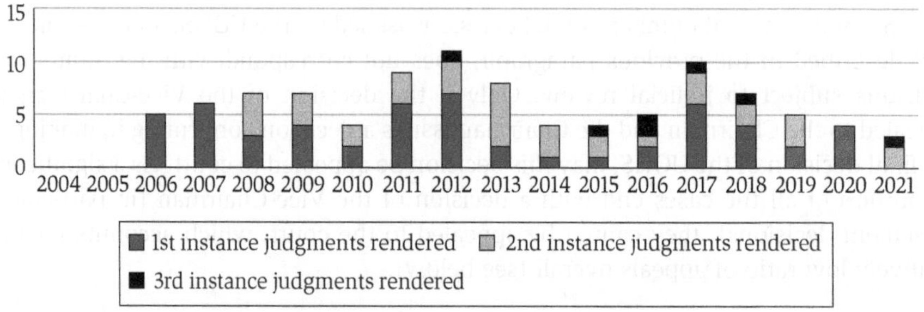

15
10
5
0
2004 2005 2006 2007 2008 2009 2010 2011 2012 2013 2014 2015 2016 2017 2018 2019 2020 2021

1st instance judgments rendered
2nd instance judgments rendered
3rd instance judgments rendered

The number of first-instance judgments does not fully correlate with the number of UOHS's decisions appealed; in some years, there are more first-instance judgments than the number of UOHS decisions. This may be explained by the fact that the number of first-instance judgments is also influenced by the number of second-instance ones, as the Supreme Administrative Court may annul the judgment of the Regional Court and refer the case back to it for another judgment.

It is also interesting to note the decrease in the number of first-instance judgments in the years 2013–2015; this reflects the fact that the number of final decisions of the UOHS decreased significantly in 2012 and 2013, and even though the number of decisions recovered in 2014, no decision was subject to court review. The court was thus deciding on 'old' cases, returned to it by the Supreme Administrative Court.

Conversely, the number of second-instance judgments fully correlates with the number of first-instance judgments rendered, as no cases were returned to it by the Constitutional Court.

It is interesting to note that the number of constitutional complaints has increased during the second half of the period covered by this study, despite the fact that none of them was found admissible. This might have been caused by the fact that after the European Court of Human Rights found in 2014 that a dawn raid carried out by the UOHS infringed the European Convention on Human Rights,[30] the Constitutional Court

30. ECtHR judgment of 2 October 2014, *DELTA PEKÁRNY v. Czech Republic*, application number 97/11.

annulled a decision based on evidence from that dawn raid in 2016.[31] It is the only competition case in which the Constitutional Court found the constitutional claim admissible and the only intervention of the Constitutional Court concerning a case decided by UOHS so far.

4.4 Success Rates and Outcomes

Figure 8.2 summarises the success of appeals against NCA's decisions or a previous instance's judgment across all instances. The figure demonstrates that the courts tend not to interfere with the UOHS's discretion, with two-thirds of the appeals being fully rejected. The quality of the NCA's decision-making is probably increased by the internal review of the Chairman, who must deal with all claims by the parties to the proceedings.

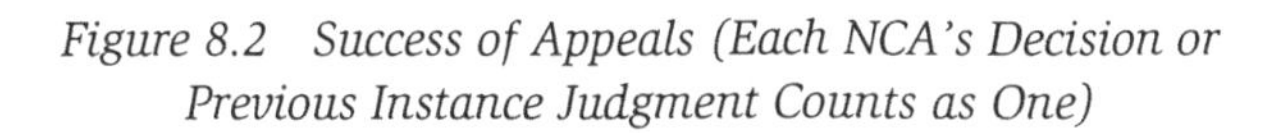

Figure 8.2 Success of Appeals (Each NCA's Decision or Previous Instance Judgment Counts as One)

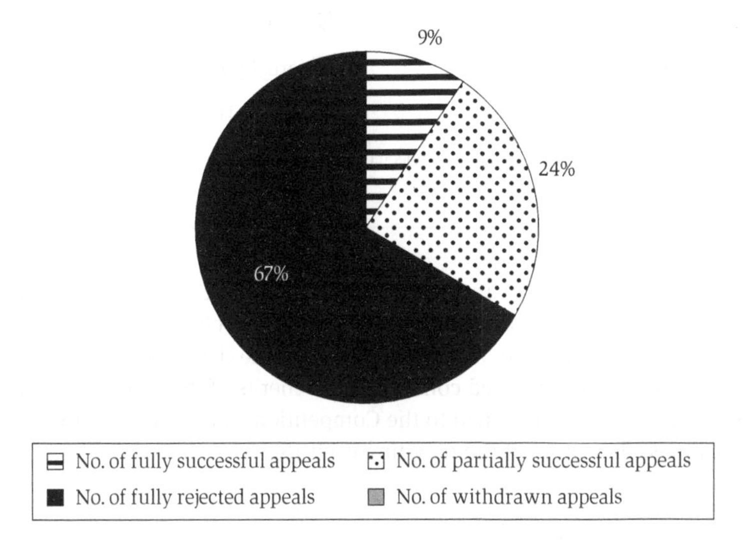

The success rate, however, varies significantly at different instances of appeal, as is evident from Figure 8.4. Notably, in contrast with Figure 8.3, Figure 8.4 presents the data from the perspective of each single judgment.

31. Ruling of the Constitutional Court of 9 February 2016, Ref. No. IV. ÚS 4397/12; originally, the Constitutional Court dismissed this constitutional complaint as inadmissible, and it only returned to it after the judgment of the ECtHR.

Figure 8.3(a) First-Instance Outcome

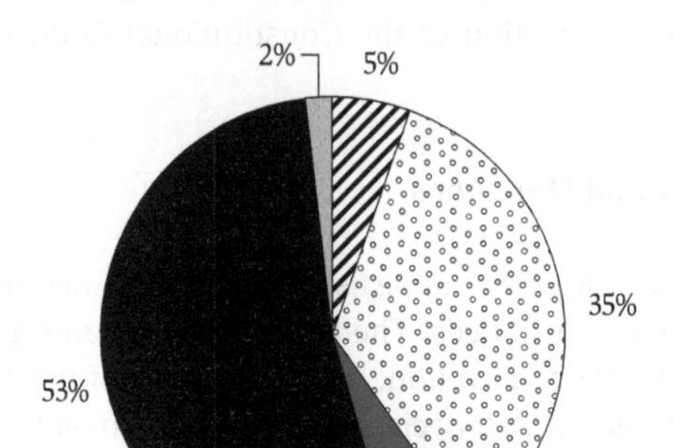

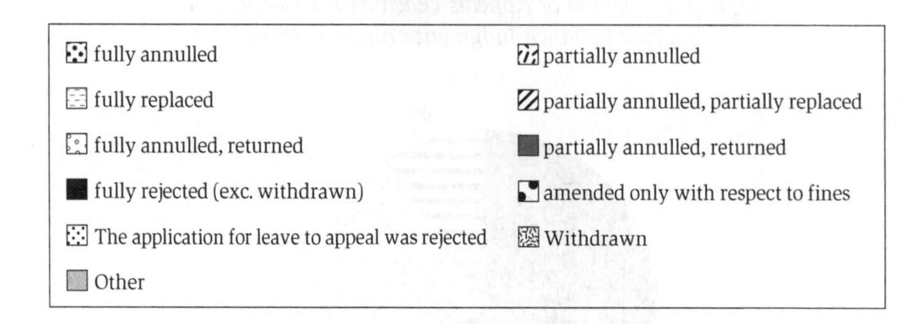

It is clear from Figure 8.3(a) that before the Regional Court, the UOHS has been fully successful in a slight majority of cases (53%); conversely, more than a third of the UOHS's decisions were fully annulled and returned to the UOHS (35%). In some cases, the UOHS's decision was endorsed concerning the merits of the case, but the fine was annulled, and the case was returned to the Competition Authority to set the fine anew (5%); sometimes, the court set the new fine itself (5%).[32]

32. The 'other' type of outcome stands for a specific case when the appeal proceedings were stopped by the court as the complainant did not pay the court fees. Judgment of the Regional Court in Brno of 27 March 2006, Ref. No. 62Ca2/2006-85.

Figure 8.3(b) Second-Instance Outcome

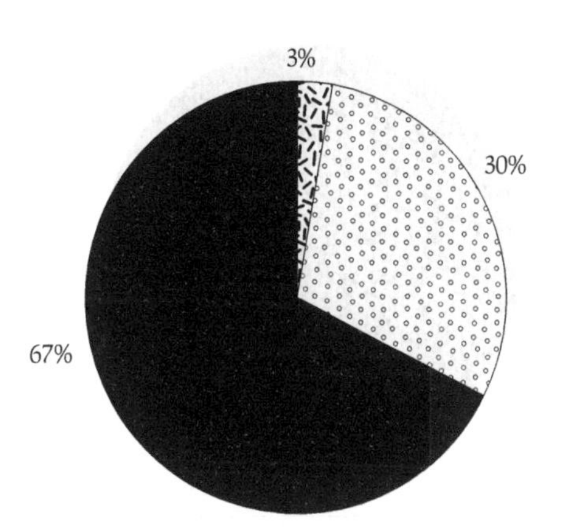

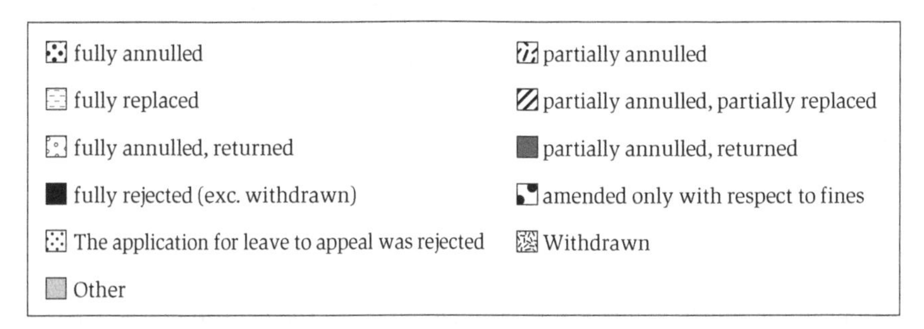

Whereas an appeal against the final decisions of UOHS may only be brought by the parties to the proceedings – the undertakings that allegedly infringed competition law, an appeal against a judgment of the Regional Court may be brought by both those parties and by the UOHS. Figure 8.3(b) shows that these appeals are largely unsuccessful, with two-thirds of them being rejected in full. In 30% of cases, the Supreme Administrative Court annulled the Regional Court's judgment and returned the case to it, frequently on appeals by the UOHS, which explains its overall high success rate. The 'partially annulled' decision stands for a single case when the Supreme Administrative Court found that the investigation was time-barred with respect to one of the undertakings concerned and annulled part of the decision in which it was found responsible for a cartel.[33]

33. Judgment of the Supreme Administrative Court of 29 January 2015, Ref. No. 8Afs25/2012-351.

Figure 8.3(c) Third-Instance Outcome

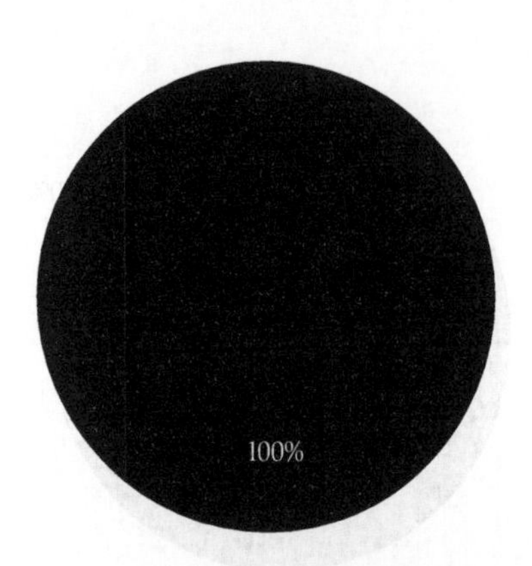

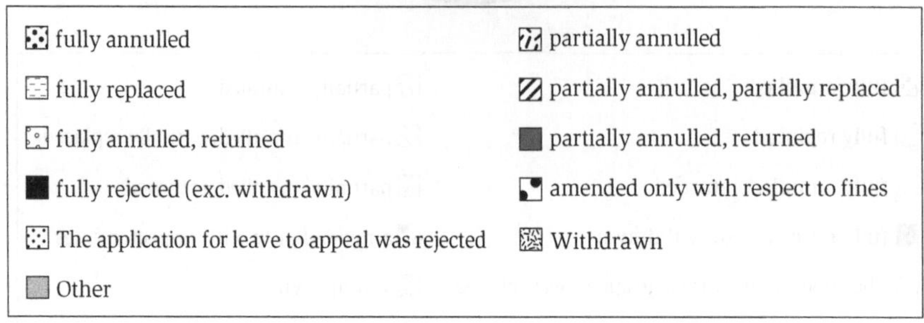

Concerning finally Figure 8.3(c), as mentioned, all the constitutional claims by the undertakings concerned were rejected as inadmissible by the Constitutional Court.

4.5 Type of Competition Authority's Decisions Subject to Appeal

The type of UOHS's decisions subject to appeal corresponds with the type of decisions issued by the NCA. As Figure 8.4 shows, three-quarters of the judgments (75%) were only concerned with Czech law, whereas only 25% were concerned with both EU law and its Czech equivalent. The Czech Republic is one of a group of countries where the effect-on-trade criterion is interpreted very narrowly, resulting in a relatively low number of cases in which EU competition law is applied.[34]

34. Botta, M., Svetlicinii, A., Bernatt, M. *The Assessment of the Effect on Trade by the National Competition Authorities of the 'New' Member States: Another Legal Partition of the Internal Market?* Common Market Law Review, 2015, No. 5, p. 1247.

Figure 8.4 Rules Being Appealed

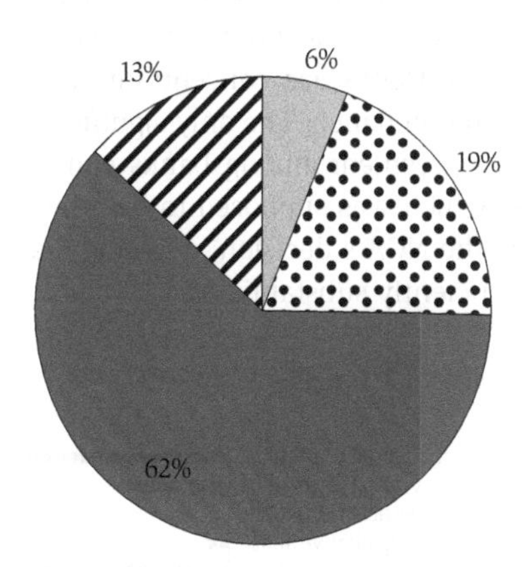

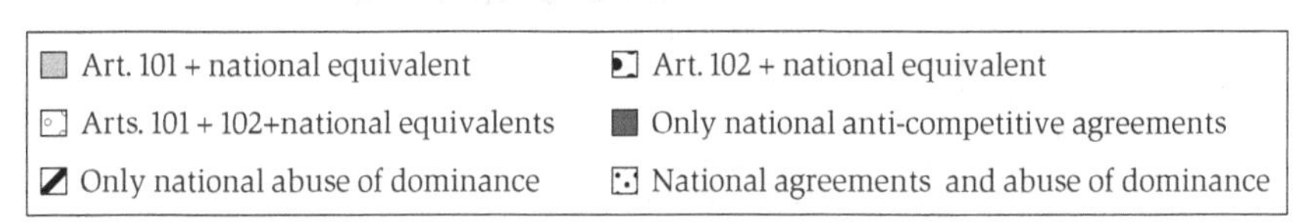

Figure 8.5 Rules Being Appealed According to Years (Each Judgment Counts as One)

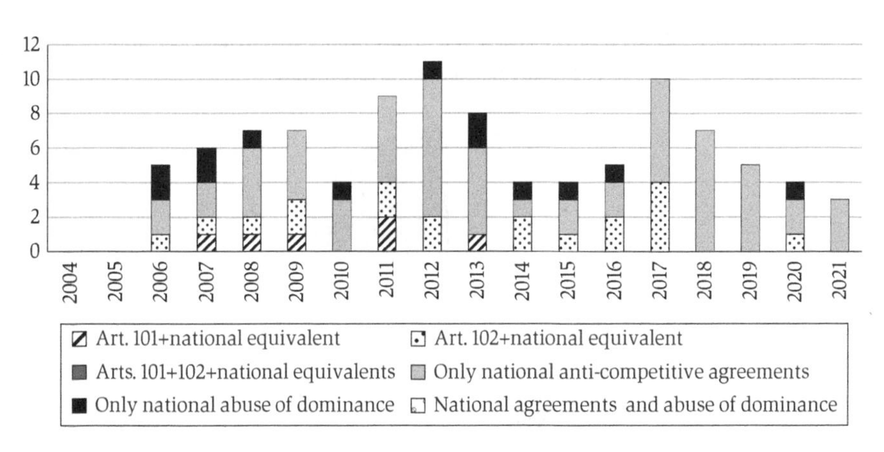

Figure 8.6 shows that the vast majority of all the cases concerned horizontal agreements (fifty-four judgments in total, standing for 55% of all the judgments and 81% of all judgments on restrictive agreements); in the case of abuse of dominance, the cases reviewed were predominantly exclusionary ones (twenty-eight out of thirty-one judgments).

Concerning anti-competitive agreements, it is unclear from the data what percentage of the cases concerned by-object and by-effect agreements; Figure 8.7 shows that it was not indicated in 82% of the cases. That is because, until 2009, the Czech Competition Act did not distinguish between by-object and by-effect restrictions. Judged by the practice itself, however, most of the cases could have been classified as by-object infringements, as the UOHS has concentrated particularly on bid-rigging, price-fixing and resale price maintenance. The only significant exception was the case of an information exchange agreement among banks concerning a specific form of making deposits and loans, which was supposed to be a by-effect infringement. The courts nonetheless annulled the NCA's decision, deeming that the detrimental effects on competition were not sufficiently substantiated.[35]

Figure 8.6 Types of Restrictions

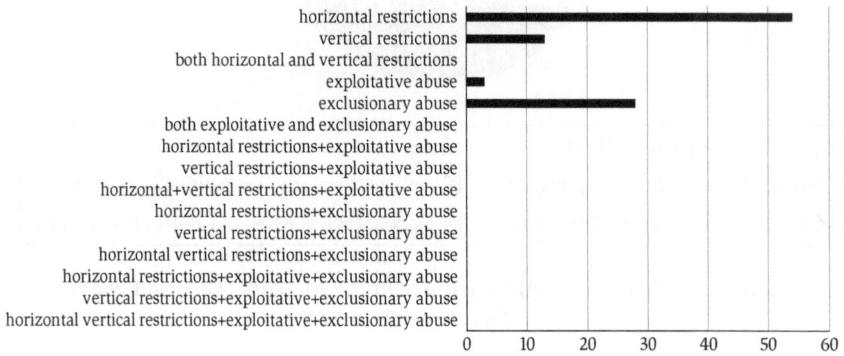

horizontal restrictions
vertical restrictions
both horizontal and vertical restrictions
exploitative abuse
exclusionary abuse
both exploitative and exclusionary abuse
horizontal restrictions+exploitative abuse
vertical restrictions+exploitative abuse
horizontal+vertical restrictions+exploitative abuse
horizontal restrictions+exclusionary abuse
vertical restrictions+exclusionary abuse
horizontal vertical restrictions+exclusionary abuse
horizontal restrictions+exploitative+exclusionary abuse
vertical restrictions+exploitative+exclusionary abuse
horizontal vertical restrictions+exploitative+exclusionary abuse
0 10 20 30 40 50 60

Figure 8.7 Object/Effect (Only for Cases Involving Article 101 and the National Equivalent Prohibition)

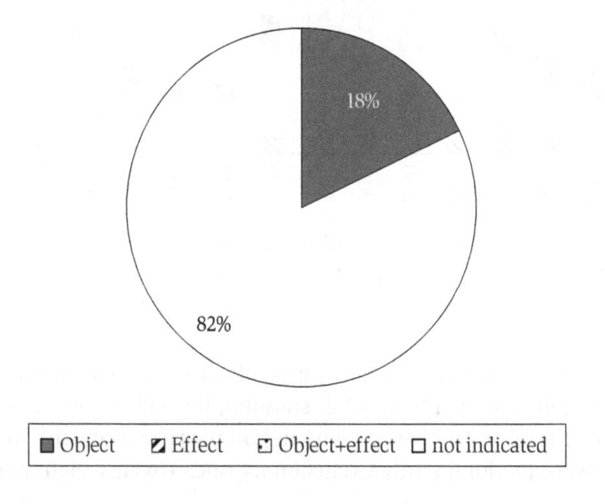

35. Judgment of the Regional Court in Brno of 8 January 2008, Ref. No. 62 Ca 15/2007-519.

Almost all the UOHS decisions reviewed by courts are decisions in which it found an infringement and imposed a fine. Because only those decisions that were appealed to the UOHS Chairman may be reviewed by courts, decisions 'in favour' of the participants are never appealed, including any closure of proceedings without finding an infringement, commitments, settlements, etc.[36]

For this reason, settlement decisions were generally not appealed to the courts; there has been only one exception, when one of the parties to the proceedings that had settled later appealed the fine, first to the UOHS Chairman and then to the Regional Court in Brno, which rejected the appeal.[37]

Leniency applications are still rather rare in the Czech Republic. Naturally, in those cases, the leniency recipient does not file an appeal; the other parties to the proceedings, however, do, and thus, these decisions are subject to court review. So far, two leniency cases have been reviewed by courts (in six separate judgments). Both cases were quite specific and required some explanation.

The first one was the UOHS decision on the global GIS cartel. The merits of the case, based on the leniency application, were never discussed; the Regional Court in Brno first annulled the UOHS's judgment because, according to its interpretation, the *ne bis in idem* principle was breached, as the European Commission had earlier ruled on the same case.[38] This judgment was annulled by the Supreme Administrative Court, according to which the *ne bis in idem* principle was not breached.[39] When the case returned to the Regional Court, it annulled it again, because, when imposing the fine, the UOHS did not sufficiently consider the fact that the undertakings involved were composed of several companies.[40] After this was confirmed by the Supreme Administrative Court,[41] the UOHS stopped the proceedings as any further investigation was time-barred.

The second case was the UOHS decision on the global CRT cartel, based again almost entirely on a successful leniency application. The Regional Court in Brno largely confirmed the UOHS's findings and only decreased the fine by 15% with respect to one of the undertakings concerned.[42] This was later confirmed by the Supreme Administrative Court, which, however, annulled a part of the decision with respect to one of the undertakings for being time-barred.[43]

Occasionally, the UOHS's proceedings were divided into separate infringement and fine decisions. This happens when the Chairman of the UOHS on appeal rejects the claims concerning the merits of the case but annuls the fine and returns the case back to the Vice-Chairman, where a new decision – only on fines – is issued;[44] similarly, the court may annul only the decision on fine and return it back to the UOHS, while

---

36. With a single exception of a settlement decision, *see* below.
37. Judgment of the Regional Court in Brno of 14 December 2020, Ref. No. 29Af54/2019-82.
38. Judgment of the Regional Court in Brno of 25 June 2008, Ref. No. 62 Ca 22/2007-489.
39. Judgment of the Supreme Administrative Court of 10 April 2009, Ref. No. 2 Afs 93/2008-920.
40. Judgment of the Regional Court in Brno of 14 June 2012, Ref. No. 62 Ca 22/2007-2067.
41. Judgment of the Supreme Administrative Court of 13 August 2008, Ref. No. 2 Afs 93/2008-716.
42. Judgment of the Regional Court in Brno of 23 February 2012, Ref. No. 62 Af 75/2010-318.
43. Judgment of the Supreme Administrative Court of 29 January 2015, Ref. No. 8 Afs 25/2012-351.
44. There would be two separate decisions, both being subject to separate court review; the courts review them independently, not merging the review proceedings. The first decision would find

confirming the merits of the case. These decisions, imposing a fine but not finding an infringement (as the infringement is found in another decision), stand for the 'other' category in Figure 8.8.[45]

Figure 8.8 Competition Authority's Procedure

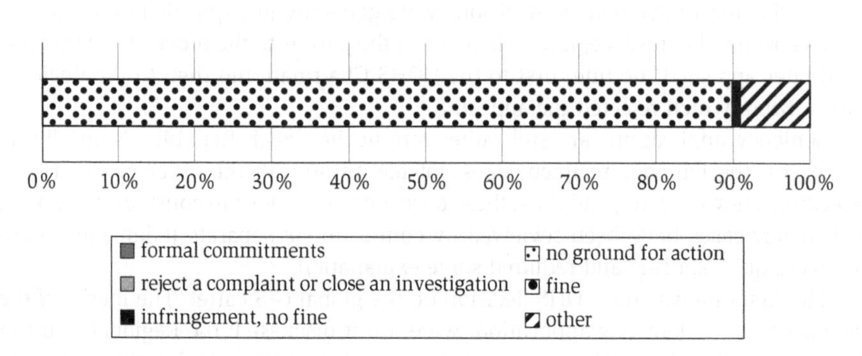

4.6 Grounds of Appeal

Figure 8.9 indicates the success of each ground of appeal launched by one or more parties to the appeal against a UOHS decision or on a previous instance court judgment issued on its review. The empirical data demonstrates that the undertakings have often raised various grounds of appeal, even though they are largely unsuccessful. This was especially the case with procedural grounds, which are raised most frequently. Such grounds were discussed in almost seventy judgments, i.e., in 70% of the appeals. Their success rate was nevertheless rather low (only 18% of the judgments accepted – fully or partially – on procedural grounds).

The same is true for substantive grounds and appeal grounds concerning the fine. Both of these grounds were discussed in approximately sixty judgments, i.e., they were raised in 60% of appeals. Even though they are frequently raised, they are rarely successful (17% of cases). Also, the success is often only partial. Frequently, a single UOHS decision condemns more than one infringement. On appeal, a court may annul the decision in its entirety. But it is also common for a court to annul only one of more infringement findings by the UOHS. The court may also confirm that there was an infringement but decide that only part of it was sufficiently substantiated by the UOHS, typically that it lasted only for a shorter period of time.

---

an infringement and prohibit the conduct for the future, the other would refer to the infringement, established by the first decision, and impose a fine (or other sanction).

45. This list covers also the judgment of the Regional Court in Brno of 6 June 2006, Ref. No. 31 Ca 152/2005, the final 'clearance' case, i.e., a decision issued in proceedings initiated by the undertaking concerned in which the UOHS assessed whether the undertakings' conduct is in line with competition law. This type of procedure was abandoned in 2004, but the proceedings already initiated were left to be finished.

Concerning specifically fine reductions, this was the outcome in 4% of the cases, with an average ratio of reduction of 48%; although this ratio looks rather dramatic, it is caused by the fact that in one case, the Regional Court in Brno reduced the fine to a symbolic level of CZK 1,000 (EUR 40), and when the Supreme Administrative Court ruled that conditions for a symbolic fine were not met, the Regional Court reduced it to CZK 7,000 (EUR 280).[46]

By comparison, the grounds of appeal concerning the relation between Czech and EU competition law were raised less frequently in 16% of the cases. Intriguingly, such judgments often pertained to purely national cases where the EU prohibitions were not applied. The appellants typically claimed that the UOHS failed to interpret Czech law in line with EU law, yet such a claim was almost never successful. The only instance in which this ground of appeal was successful concerned a trio of cases in which the Regional Court in Brno found that the UOHS breached the *ne bis in idem principle*, either by applying Czech law in parallel with EU law in the same proceedings[47] or by deciding on the effects of a global cartel in the Czech Republic;[48] the Supreme Administrative Court, however, annulled all these judgments on appeal and confirmed that the UOHS did not breach this principle. Interestingly, the number of appeals concerning the relationship between Czech and EU law dropped almost to zero in the last five years.

During the seventeen years studied, there was only a single preliminary reference to the Court of Justice. The reference did not concern any specific aspect of the case but rather a general issue concerning parallel proceedings – whether the same cartel may be investigated in parallel by the Commission and by the NCA.[49]

Figure 8.9 Grounds of Appeal (Each NCA's Decision or Previous Instance Judgment Counts as One)

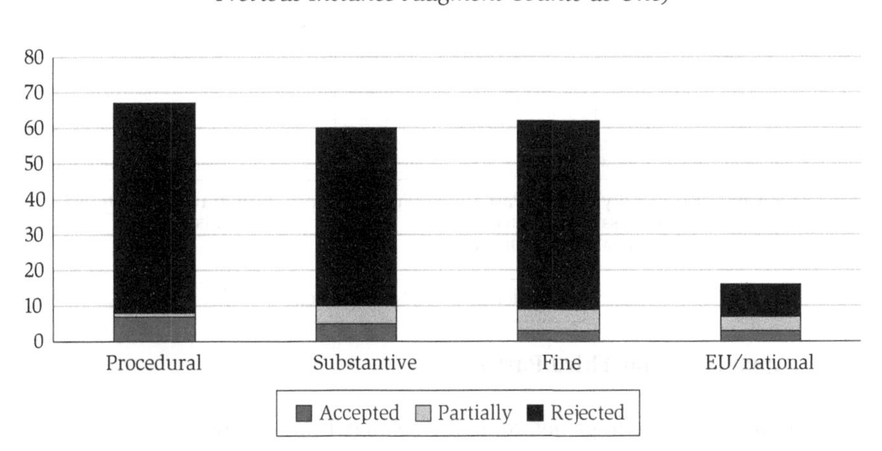

46. Judgment of the Regional Court in Brno of 16 August 2020, Ref. No. 62 Af 58/2012-227; judgment of the Regional Court in Brno of 12 march 2013, Ref. No. 62 Ad 58/2012-273.
47. Judgment of the Regional Court in Brno of 1 November 2007, Ref. No. 62 Ca 4/2007-115; judgment of the Regional Court in Brno of 22 October 2007, Ref. No. 62 Ca 8/2007-171.
48. Judgment of the Regional Court in Brno of 25 June 2008, Ref. No. 62 Ca 22/2007-489.
49. Judgment of 14 June 2012, Ref. No. 62Ca22/2007-2067. The Court of Justice decided by judgment of 14 February 2012 C-17/10 *Toshiba Corporation et al.*

As has already been discussed above, the number of leniency applications is low in the Czech Republic; so are the appeals against such decisions, as is evident from Figure 8.10. However, those appeals have been more successful than the average data seem to suggest, but this was due not to leniency as such but to peculiarities of Czech law concerning the concept of an undertaking as an economic unit and the relevant limitation period (see above). Moreover, settlement decisions have never been challenged since the settlement programme was introduced (Figure 8.11).[50]

Figure 8.10 Leniency

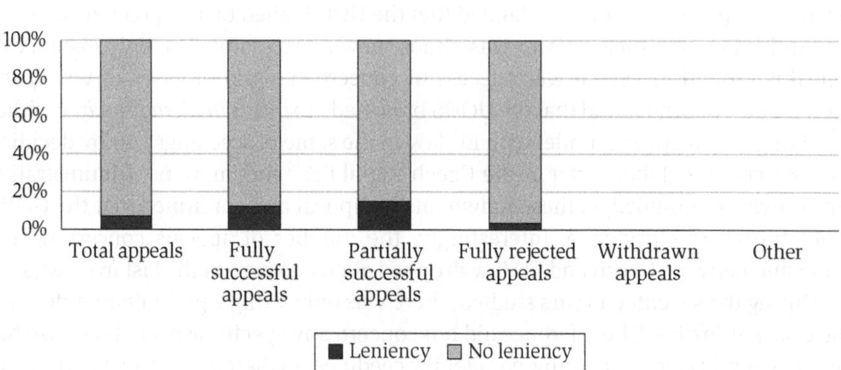

Figure 8.11 Settlements

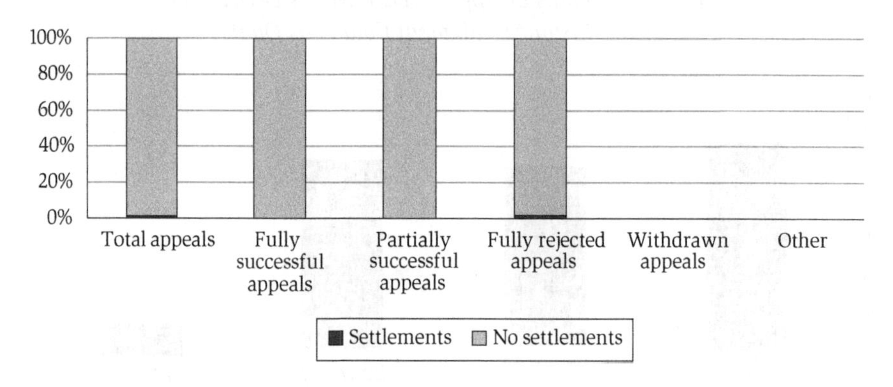

4.7 Appellants and Third Parties

Only parties to the proceedings before the UOHS may bring an appeal to the court. In addition to that, the UOHS may further appeal a judgment of the Regional Court in Brno if it was (partially or fully) unsuccessful. If the UOHS was unsuccessful before the Supreme Administrative Court, it cannot appeal to the Constitutional Court. A vast majority of all the appeals (84%) were launched by undertakings. Interestingly, the

50. With a single exception concerning only the fine, as discussed above.

share of appeals brought by the undertakings and the UOHS to the Supreme Administrative Court (the only court to which the UOHS can appeal) is very similar, with 58% being brought by undertakings and 42% by the UOHS.

According to Czech law, third parties cannot be involved in judicial review.

5 QUALITATIVE ANALYSIS

This section will make a few comments explaining the quantitative analysis, concentrating on the outcome of the statistics, the relationship between administrative and judicial review and the review of fines.

5.1 The Intensity of Court Review

Before discussing the intensity of court review, It ought to be mentioned that there is absolutely no specialisation of judges in matters of antitrust; they have to decide appeals on antitrust cases infrequently, amidst the vast majority of cases stemming from other areas of administrative law, from electoral matters to the issues of social security, as the judges of administrative courts review all decisions of all the administrative authorities in the Czech Republic. This leads to the inevitable situation that judges cannot specialise in particular areas of substantive law, but they are experienced in relation to procedure and fines.

Conversely, substantive claims are less frequent, and their full success is infrequent. Partial success is nonetheless relatively more common. The intensity of judicial review concerning substantive questions is, however, very high, as the courts do not leave the UOHS any margin of appreciation in complex economic assessments. For example, the definition of relevant markets is subject to in-depth court review; it is not uncommon for the Regional Court in Brno to declare that a relevant market was not assessed properly,[51] even though ultimately, the UOHS won all these cases on the relevant market issue before the Supreme Administrative Court. Similarly, in the only by-effect infringement case the UOHS has dealt with, the courts annulled the decision, claiming that the anti-competitive effects were not sufficiently substantiated.[52] The same also happened on several occasions with respect to by-object infringements and in abuse of dominance cases,[53] where the courts found that the evidence gathered by the UOHS was not sufficient.[54] The intensity of judicial review has, however, never been raised, questioned, or critiqued in the academic literature in the Czech Republic.

51. For example, judgment of the Regional Court in Brno of 9 November 2012, Reg. No. 62Af27/2011-409. This judgment was annulled by the Supreme Administrative Court and in its subsequent judgment of 25 September 2014, Ref. No. 62Af27/2011-554, the Regional Court in Brno approved the relevant market as defined by the UOHS.
52. Judgment of the Regional Court in Brno of 8 January 2008, Ref. No. 62Ca15/2007-519.
53. For example, judgment of the Regional Court in Brno of 19 January 2012, Ref. No. 62Af56/2011-647.
54. For example, judgment of the Regional Court in Brno of 23 February 2018, Ref. No. 29Af7/2016-107.

Conversely, the judicial review of fines is relatively constrained. The courts appear to have afforded the UOHS a significant margin of appreciation, limiting themselves only to the issue of whether the fine was imposed in accordance with the principles set by law; the Supreme Administrative Court has held that 'administrative discretion of public authorities while setting a fine is in principle not subject to judicial review'.[55] Still, the courts are entitled to decrease the fine if they find it *manifestly disproportionate*, though they may not increase it. Accordingly, the extent of judicial review of fines set by the UOHS is limited; the courts decreased the fine in only 4% of all cases. The nature and level of court review of fines have never been discussed in the academic literature to date.

5.2 Coherence with EU Law

The number of claims concerning the relationship between Czech and EU law is relatively low and seems to be decreasing over time. This can probably be explained by the very high level of harmonisation of Czech and EU competition law since 2009 when the Competition Act was significantly amended.[56]

Even in cases decided based only on Czech law, the EU jurisprudence is fully taken into account. The UOHS, as well as the courts involved in the review of its decisions, extensively discuss the relevant case law of the Court of Justice. In fact, references to the decisions of EU institutions are more frequent than references to Czech case law.

As Czech competition law was from the very beginning based on the EU prohibitions, and given that both the UOHS and the courts referred to EU law even before the accession of the Czech Republic to the EU, there has never been any significant discrepancy between these two legal systems. It is also telling that since the accession of the Czech Republic to the EU, only a single preliminary reference has been sent to the CJEU, concerning not the material competition law and its interpretation but the question of *ne bis in idem* and the parallel competences of UOHS and the European Commission.[57]

6 CONCLUDING REMARKS

The UOHS decisions are subject to full judicial review in relation to substantive and procedural issues on two levels, both subjecting those decisions to very intensive review without any signs of judicial deference; conversely, the review of fines is rather relaxed. Despite this intense level of review of the merits of the case, the UOHS remains relatively successful, even though a significant minority of decisions have been annulled on procedural and, more importantly, substantive grounds. The review of UOHS decisions by the Constitutional Court remains only theoretical.

55. Judgment of the Supreme Administrative Court of 3 April 2012, Ref. No. 1 Afs 1/2012-36.
56. Act No. 155/2009 Coll., amending the Act on the Protection of Competition.
57. Judgment of the Court of Justice of 14 February 2012 C-17/10 *Toshiba Corporation et al.*

Despite this intensive review, judges are not specialised beyond the very broad realm of 'administrative law'. In this regard, it could be argued that the lack of specialisation of judges at both the Regional Court in Brno and the Supreme Administrative Court contributes to the number of decisions annulled, in the sense that judges are more restrictive in interpreting the competition law than current trends might demand. Indeed, the UOHS has itself informally suggested this rationale, although it has never been raised officially. The UOHS has also called for more competition-specific education of judges.

It might be added that after the current model of judicial review of administrative decisions was introduced in 2002, judicial review of competition matters was for eight years concentrated in specialised panels of judges, one before the Regional Court in Brno and one before the Supreme Administrative Court. This changed around 2010 when the courts decided that judges should be more 'generalist' rather than specialists in a particular area of law. Still, as is apparent from the data, the number of judges involved in making decisions on antitrust appeals remains relatively low, allowing, to some extent, for *de facto* specialisation.

Nonetheless, the reputation of the Czech judiciary in matters of competition law is rather low. Judges are not engaged in any public debate, nor do they publish antitrust articles or monographs,[58] and generally, they do not frequently participate in antitrust events, such as conferences or workshops. This, however, is a problem not only of the courts, but of the discourse on competition law in the Czech Republic in general. The number of people specialising in competition law is limited, both among private lawyers and university professors and, indeed, also the judges.

58. With a notable exception of a single Regional Court judge, who published numerous, highly relevant articles on Czech competition law and co-authored one of the leading commentaries to the Competition Act.

CHAPTER 9
Denmark Report

Caroline Heide-Jørgensen

1 INTRODUCTION TO THE COMPETITION LAW ENFORCEMENT CONTEXT IN DENMARK

1.1 Historical Outline

Competition law was in force in Denmark long before it entered the EEC in 1973. Denmark's first real competition law was the Law on Monopolies from 1955,[1] but legislation governing competition has been in place since 1929. Originally, rules in this area were based on the principle of control of anti-competitive agreements and market dominance rather than prohibitions, as known from US antitrust and European Economic Community (EEC) competition legislation. Denmark's entry to the EEC did not alter the domestic competition law for many years, but gradually, during the late 1980s and early 1990s, the debate about whether national competition law should be reformed to mirror EEC rules also made its way to Denmark. In 1993, the Parliament decided that the Danish competition law should be brought into line with EEC competition law and a governmental committee was composed and asked to do a report on the matter.[2] The Competition Law Act was passed in 1997.[3] At that time, merger control was not introduced, and the level of fines did not mirror the EEC standards. Therefore, conformity with the EEC rules was in no way complete, but, nonetheless, the law marked an important step in the direction of harmonisation. The basic rules on anti-competitive agreements and abuse of dominance mirrored the EEC

1. Law No. 102 of 31 March 1955.
2. Folketingstidende 1992/1993, tillæg A 7941, *see also* in general about the development in the legislation C. Heide-Jørgensen, *Lærebog i Konkurrence- og Markedsføringsret*, 5th ed., 2022, p. 171, Kirsten Levinsen, *Konkurrenceloven*, 3rd ed., 2009, pp. 64ff. The result of the committee's work came in 1995 in *Betænkning 1297/1995, Konkurencelovgivningen i Danmark.*
3. Law No. 384 of 10 June 1997, which entered into force on 1 January 1998.

rules,[4] and the principle of EU conformity in interpretation of the rules was introduced.[5] The principle of EU conformity in interpretation has been further developed since and has had a great impact on the interpretation of national rules both in terms of the administrative practice of the competition authorities and in the Danish courts' case law.

Since the first EEC-style competition Law legislation of 1997, the Danish Competition Act has been amended several times.[6] Many of the amendments have been small changes and adjustments, but there have also been several major changes. Merger control was introduced in 2000,[7] and in 2005, the entry into force of Regulation 1/2003 required further changes;[8] leniency was introduced in 2007;[9] in 2012, cartels were more severely sanctioned than before, and the possibility of a prison sanction for individuals was introduced,[10] and in 2021 the necessary amendments to implement the ECN + Directive were passed.[11]

A general trend has been increasingly EU-compliant rules, especially in the years after Council Regulation 1/2003, and the growing use of the EU competition law rules by the Danish authorities either alone or in combination with the corresponding national rules. Today, Danish competition law is modelled carefully on the EU role model of Articles 101 and 102 Treaty on the Functioning of the European Union (TFEU). The wording of the Danish provisions is almost verbally identical to those of the EU equivalents. As for its coherence with substantive EU competition law, this study seems to confirm at least the attempt to ensure a coherent interpretation. As in many other EU jurisdictions, EU law plays a predominant role in the enforcement of competition law in Denmark.

1.2 Enforcement Framework

Competition law enforcement in Denmark is based on an administrative model.

Public enforcement of competition law is in the hands of the Danish Competition and Consumer Authority (DCCA) and the Competition Council (CC). The DCCA investigates, and the CC takes final decisions on infringements and – since the implementation of the ECN + Directive – also on sanctions in the form of civil fines[12] in bigger and/or principled cases, which are those involving matters regarding the correct interpretation of the law. The DCCA also takes decisions in minor cases,

4. Anti-competitive agreements are regulated in section 6 of the act, and abuse of dominant position in section 11. The numbering – and the content – is, with few national additions, the same today.
5. Section 4 of the law.
6. A complete overview of the changes (in Danish) can be seen in C. Heide-Jørgensen, *Lærebog i Konkurrence- og Markedsføringsret*, 5th ed. 2022, Ch. IV, and Kirsten Levinsen, *Konkurrenceloven*, 3rd ed., 2009, pp. 61 ff.
7. Law No. 416/2000.
8. Law No. 1461/2004.
9. Law No. 572/2007.
10. Law No. 1385/2012. No one has yet been in prison for infringement of the cartel prohibition.
11. Law No. 207/2021.
12. The final decision about the size of the fines lies with the courts, see section 24a in the Danish Competition Act.

whereas only the major and/or principled ones are brought before the CC. In 2016, the composition of the CC was greatly modified, and the CC now consists of seven members.[13] Together, the DCCA and the CC form one united and independent competition authority. The CC is an independent tribunal composed of seven members appointed by the Minister for Industry, Business, and Financial Affairs. The entire CC is appointed for four years. Members represent different backgrounds; four must have insight into competition matters or other appropriate backgrounds; two members must have experience in business management, and one member must have specialised knowledge of consumer affairs. They can be reappointed for additional mandates. They carry out the tasks assigned to them pursuant to the Competition Act independently of political or other external influence and do not seek nor take any instructions from the Government or any public or private entity. The members may only take on other employment to the extent that it is compatible with the performance of the duties attached to their position.[14] CC decisions are subject to appeal to the Competition Appeal Tribunal (CAT).

Most cases are initiated by formal complaints, typically against an alleged anti-competitive agreement or abuse of dominance. Cases can also begin following informal whistleblowing, e.g., from traders or others who experience conduct that they believe to be harmful or illegal, or by the DCCA's own investigations into markets on a more general level or via results stemming from dawn raids. In recent years, the leniency programme has also begun to play a role in uncovering secret cartels.

The DCCA has a high level of discretion to manage investigations. It decides which cases to investigate. However, differently from other jurisdictions, the Danish DCCA does not have written Prioritisation Principles. Section 15 of the Danish Competition Act instead gives the DCCA (and not the CC) full competence to decide what cases to investigate. It also allows the DCCA to give up an investigation at any time without this being subject to complaint to higher instances on grounds of priorities or because the DCCA finds no basis for action.[15] Apart from situations where the investigation is closed before it reaches a decision,[16] the DCCA and the CC have various options in dealing with a case. The CC has powers to accept binding commitments, although this remedy has not been used very frequently.[17] Settlements, as known from the EU Commission's settlement procedure, do not exist under Danish competition law. Penalty issues may be issued to undertakings that confirm that they have broken the law. Penalty notices are a general instrument and not regulated in the Competition Act. Instead, they are governed by criminal and procedural law and are based on case law. In penalty notice cases, the amount of the fine is not subject to negotiation, but an

13. Section 14 in the Competition Act.
14. Sections 14 and 14a in the Competition Act. The four members with academic background are university professors in law and economics (two in law and two in economics). The chair of the CC is for the time being a professor of economics and the deputy chair is professor or law. The author of this report is – for the time being – the deputy chair of the CC.
15. Except cases referred from the EU Commission or other national competition authorities. This had not yet happened in practice.
16. Which can occur at any stage of the process according to section 15 in the Competition Act.
17. According to section 16a in the Competition Act.

offer is made by the public prosecutor/the authority and if the undertaking is willing to accept it, the infringement case process will not be undertaken.

The CC (and the DCCA in smaller cases) also has the power to adopt a formal decision, declaring that the rules have been infringed and ordering the parties in breach to cease the infringing conduct. For the period covered by this study, the key sanction in public enforcement was the power to stop the infringement by a formal decision, whereas the imposition of fines was a matter for ordinary courts. This system of competences changed with the implementation of the ECN + , and now the CC impose civil fines on companies[18], whereas fines on individuals (and possible imprisonment) are initiated by the public prosecutor and imposed by the courts.

The level of fines imposed in practice has increased over the years but has not yet reached the level of the fines imposed by the Commission. According to section 23, b, (5) of the Competition Act, the fine may not exceed 10% of the annual turnover worldwide. It also follows from section 23, b, that when calculating a fine, the seriousness and duration of the infringement are of importance. The law also states mitigating and aggravating criteria in setting the amount of the fine.[19] The present formulation of section 23, b, (5) stems from the implementation of the ECN + Directive, Article 13 on civil fines. After the implementation of the ECN + Directive, all fines on undertakings are therefore considered civil, and the principles for imposing fines apply to all competition law infringement cases. The preparatory works also note that the final calculation of a fine will depend on the specific assessment by the courts. The fines on individuals are still considered criminal.

The leniency program is modelled very closely on the ECN Model Leniency Programme. Leniency was introduced in Denmark as late as 2007 (section 23d of the Danish Competition Act). It is only in recent years that the DCCA has received leniency applications.

1.3 Enforcement Practices and Priorities

There is no legislation on how the DCCA should prioritise, and the DCCA has no written principles on how to prioritise the cases. The DCCA publishes statistics about

18. The final decision about the size of the fine is for the courts, see section 24a in the Competition Act.
19. Section 23, b, 2, states, that it should be considered as an aggravating circumstance that the undertaking etc. for example (i) after a previous decision finding that the undertaking, etc., has infringed this Act or Article 101 or 102 TFEU, proceeds with the same infringement or commits a similar infringement, (ii) has played a leading role or has encouraged the infringement or (iii) has subjected another undertaking to retaliatory measures in order to compel it to respect an anti-competitive agreement or conduct in contravention of section 6 or 11 of this Act or Article 101 or 102 TFEU. According to section 23, b, 3, it is considered a mitigating circumstance, that the undertaking: (i) has played only a passive role in connection with the infringement, (ii) has not complied with an illegal agreement, a decision or a concerted practice pursuant to section 6 of this Act or Article 101 TFEU, (iii) through an internal policy of compliance with the competition rules has constantly made an active effort to ensure that all employees of the undertaking comply with this Act, or (iv) has contributed to the detection of the case outside the scope for leniency in section 23d or 23e being met.

the number of cases over the years.[20] It follows that the CC issues approximately ten decisions a year. Moreover, infringements of the prohibition on anti-competitive agreements tend to dominate, while findings of an infringement of the prohibition on abuse of dominance are rare, with approximately only one to two cases per year and none in some years. As also seen in other jurisdictions,[21] most anti-competitive agreement cases are about 'by-object' infringements. Likewise, there have been many cases over the years related to vertical restrictions, mostly on resale price maintenance. Those cases were often referred directly to the public prosecutor or, in recent years, settled by penalty notices.[22] Whether it can be concluded that the dominance of cases on anti-competitive agreements is the result of a deliberate prioritisation by the Competition authorities or not is hard to say, but in Denmark - as in many other jurisdictions - it holds true that a number of factors make those cases simpler than those involving abuse of dominance. This goes for by-object cases, while by-effect cases (which are very rare in Denmark) demonstrate similar difficulties in establishing proof of the infringement as with abuse of dominance cases. The more economic approach to competition law over the last two decades has probably intensified this trend.

2 REVIEW OF THE COMPETITION AUTHORITY'S DECISIONS

Denmark has a well-developed and rather complex system of appeal tribunals/appeal courts in competition law cases.

Any decision by the CC/DCCA can be appealed to first the CAT and from there to the ordinary courts. The Danish legal system does not operate with specialised courts, as seen in other jurisdictions. There is only one type of court that handles all cases - civil, criminal or administrative - the matter of the case may differ, but the judge(s) remain the same. In competition cases, there are as many as four possible appeal instances. The multiple appeal instances mean that it can take several years for competition law cases to be final, an issue that has been criticised by the OECD in its 2015 in-depth review of Competition Law and Policy in Denmark.[23]The first instance of appeal is the CAT, a 'hyper-specialised' appeal body.

A decision by the CAT may be appealed further to the ordinary courts, with the Maritime and Commercial Court first in line. The judgments from the Maritime and Commercial Court can be appealed to one of the two Danish High Courts or the Supreme Court, depending on whether the case in question is a principled one. When a case is appealed directly from the Maritime and Commercial Court to the Supreme Court, it is for the Supreme Court to decide if the appeal should be accepted by the Supreme Court or instead referred to the High Court. If the case ends up in the High

20. www.en.kfst.dk/competition/about-competition-matters/.
21. *See, e.g.*, the UK report, Chapter 30.
22. Because of the settled case law from the Danish courts on the level of fines for infringement of the ban on resale price maintenance.
23. Competition Law and Policy in Denmark. A Peer Review, OECD in-depth review on Danish Competition Law and Policy, 2015, see the executive summary, p. 7, oecd-peer-review.pdf (kfst.dk). Please, be aware that there have been some changes in the Danish system because of the implementation of the ECN+ Directive.

Court, it can only be appealed further on to the Supreme Court if permission is granted, as further explained below. The system for appeal is, therefore, rather complex. The CAT is composed of a tribunal, but it operates on administrative law principles. This has consequences for the scope and intensity of the review, as further explained below. At the outset, the CAT has a full review of cases appealed to it, although in practice, reluctance towards overruling the discretionary decision-making of the CC can perhaps be observed.

If a matter is appealed from the CAT to the ordinary courts, the legal point of view changes in the sense that it is now the principles for review of administrative decisions that govern the review of cases appealed. In this context, one should bear in mind that Denmark does not have courts of cassation, as known in many other jurisdictions. In Denmark, the paradigm for review of the competition authority's decisions has been that they are subject to full review when appealed to higher instances. This is a general rule from administrative law, also applicable in principle to competition law cases.[24] Over the years some modifications have developed in practice. At least two aspects must be emphasised in this context.

First, according to the Danish Administration of Justice Act, section 196, it is possible to ask for the use of expert statements from experts appointed by the court. Traditionally, this was not permitted in cases involving appeal of decisions from the Danish competition authorities, but over the last ten years, a new trend has evolved, and it is now settled law that experts' statements on the facts and the economics of a case are allowed. The Supreme Court has confirmed this development, and therefore, such statements are used on a regular basis.[25]

Second, there was a trend towards a more intense review of the circumstances of the appealed case, perhaps partly because of the more frequent use of expert reports. The Danish Supreme Court had the chance to consider the matter in a couple of judgments, and in the leading case from 2020 in *Eurostar*,[26] the Supreme Court ruled that there should be a full review of all facts in a case but that the overruling of judgments which are essentially based on an assessment of the competitive situation presupposes a secure basis for the appeal court to assume that the previous instance had erred in their assessment of the case,[27] This reflects a Danish tradition of restraint in the review of decisions/judgments based on the previous instance's discretion, at least when the previous instance is considered to have special expertise within the field in question. The full effect of this ruling remains to be seen, but one may expect courts in future to be even more reluctant to overturn decisions from the CC and the CAT when appealed.

24. Also founded in the Danish Constitution section 63 that allows for court review of administrative acts.
25. Supreme Court order issued 13 October 2011 in the case of *Dong Energy v. the Competition Council.*
26. UfR (Weekly Law Report) 2020. 524 H, Eurostar on a road marking consortium.
27. *See* about this development C. Heide-Jørgensen, *Lærebog i Konkurrence- og Markedsføringsret,* 5th ed., 2022, p. 237; J. Pinborg and Kr. H. Straton-Andersen, *Konkurrenceloven med kommentarer,* 5th ed., 2022, pp. 1395, 1426 ff.

2.1 First-Instance Appeal: The CAT

Decisions of the CC can be appealed to the CAT, which is composed of five members with different competences. The president of the CAT must be a Supreme Court judge, and of the four other members, two must be legal experts and two economic experts. The President and the other members of the CAT are appointed by the Minister for Industry, Business and Financial Affairs, and they must all be independent of any business or commercial interests.[28] Before the implementation of the ECN + Directive, the CAT's competence as an appeal tribunal covered all decisions issued by the CC. The CAT had competence to decide on all issues regarding the substance of the case as well as all formal matters such as access to documents, party status and other formal questions.[29] A decision from the CAT was, therefore, a prerequisite for any further appeals through the Danish courts. This has changed as of 2021 with the implementation of the ECN + Directive. The CAT is now optional as an appeal tribunal for the substance of the matter, and the parties of a case can, therefore, choose to bring a decision from the CC directly before the courts for the merits of the case.[30] Formal questions must still be brought before the CAT before taking the case to the courts. It remains to be seen what practical consequences this alteration of the appeal instances will have.[31]

The scope of the CAT's right of review has not been determined in the Competition Act nor preparatory works. Therefore, it is generally assumed that the general principles from Danish administrative law on review apply.[32] This means that the CAT has full review powers in relation to any case appealed to them. The CAT may confirm, set aside, or vary the CC's decision, send the matter to the CC or adopt any other decision the CC could have made.[33] In principle, there is, therefore, a full review of both the facts of a case as well as of the application of the law and in relation to any discretion exercised by the CC/DCCA. In practice, a tendency towards caution in overruling the discretion of the CC can perhaps be observed.[34] This aligns with the Danish tradition of caution in overruling decisions made by independent expert boards

28. Competition Act, section 21.
29. But not penalties/fines as they were part of the criminal system. The competence for the CAT is seen in the Danish Competition Act No. 155 of 1 March 2018, section 18, which is now replaced with the Competition Act No. 360 of 4 March 2021. Hereinafter, the Competition Council can issue civil fines on companies as part of the case, whilst fines on individuals are still a matter for the criminal system. If a case give rise to the question of fining an individual person (e.g., a leading employee), it is referred to the public prosecutor that has the competence to decide whether or not to press charges. If the public prosecutor decides to prosecute it is for the court to decide if and in the affirmative how much the person should be fined.
30. Section 20 of the Danish 2021 Competition Act.
31. Since the alteration no cases has been brought before the CAT as for the substance matter of the case, and no decisions from the Competition Council has yet been brought directly for the courts.
32. Pinborg and Kr. H. Straton-Andersen, *Konkurrenceloven med kommentarer,* 5th ed., 2022, p. 1403.
33. The CAT is regulated in Executive Order No. 496 of 17 March 20221 on the CAT.
34. *See, e.g.,* J. Pinborg and Kr. H. Straton-Andersen, *Konkurrenceloven med kommentarer,* 4th ed., 2022, p. 1426.

as well as Supreme Court case law on the court's right to review.[35] Hearings before the CAT are oral and court-like.

The Danish Competition Act, section 19 indicates exhaustively which decisions can be appealed to the CAT. It includes all decisions on the substance of a case but as just mentioned, the CAT is now optional as for the matter of substance, whilst formal decisions must still be appealed to the CAT. It is a condition that there is a 'decision' as defined in Danish administrative law before an appeal can be issued. This means that informal guidance and 'decisions' on closing a matter according to section 15(1) in the Danish Competition Law are not subject to appeal.[36] The main party or parties against whom the CC has made decisions can appeal, as can also 'qualifying third parties' with a sufficient individual, interest in the issue.[37]

In relation to penalties, the CAT has not, before the implementation of the ECN+ Directive, had as one of its tasks to decide on this as this power was reserved to the ordinary courts. After implementation of the ECN+ Directive as of 4 March 2021, the review of civil fines on companies (not individuals) is still a matter for the courts, according to section 24a in the Danish Competition Act.

2.2 Second-Instance Appeal: Maritime and Commercial Court

Decisions of the CAT and decisions of the CC on the substance of the case can be appealed to the Maritime and Commercial Court in Copenhagen, covering all of Denmark.[38] The Maritime and Commercial Court has the power to carry out a full review of the appealed case. In principle, this goes for both law and facts. The Maritime and Commercial Court can therefore confirm, set aside/repeal, or vary the CC's/CAT's decision. Over the years, there have been several examples of judgments from the Maritime and Commercial Court setting aside the appealed decision from the CAT (or CC). Due to the 2020 Supreme Court judgment in the *Eurostar* case, restraint in this respect must be expected in the future. The Supreme Court has clarified the role of the courts in competition law cases as follows: 'The examination in cases like this covers full review of the facts in the case and the legal application, whilst it requires a secure basis to disregard the competitive discretion.'[39] The paradigm on full review of both

35. *See, supra* n. 23, UfR (Weekly Law Report) 2020. 524 H, Eurostar.
36. *Ibid.*, p. 1386.
37. There is quite a few cases on who can appeal. The condition on 'individual' interest means, that consumers/consumer organisations do not have the right to appeal, *see* J. Pinborg and Kr. H. Straton-Andersen, *Konkurrenceloven med kommentarer,* 5th ed., 2022, p. 1395.
38. Retsplejeloven (The administration of justice act), section 225(2)(5). Cases can in principle also be brought to the district court, according to section 224 in the Retsplejeloven. It does not happen in practice, probably because the Maritime and Commercial court is a specialised body (contrary to the district courts).
39. The Supreme Court's judgment in UfR (weekly law report) 2020.524 H in *Eurostar* on a road marking consortium (translation by the Danish rapporteur). *See also* judgment of 24 May 2014 by Western High Court, and in the same direction the Supreme Court's judgment in UfR 2014.2663 H. *See also* J. Pinborg and Kr. H. Straton-Andersen, *Konkurrenceloven med kommentarer,* 5th ed., 2022, p. 1426.

fact and law therefore has some very important restrictions in practice, and in recent years, judgments setting aside decisions from the CAT/or CC have been rare.

2.3 Third- and Fourth-Instance Appeals: High Courts or Supreme Court

Further appeal as the third appeal is available to either the High Courts or the Supreme Court of Denmark. The case can be appealed directly to the Supreme Court when it concerns principled matters and has general importance. It is for the Supreme Court to decide in these cases whether an appeal should be accepted or should instead be referred to one of the two High Courts.[40] If the case is not accepted by the Supreme Court, the High Court should instead decide on the matter. There have been very few cases from the High Courts within the scope of this project. When a case is decided by the High Courts, a further appeal to the Supreme Court, as the fourth appeal, is only available with special permission.[41] There have been some cases before the Supreme Court within the scope of this project.

2.4 2015 OECD Review of Competition Law and Policy in Denmark

In 2015, the OECD performed a peer Review of Competition Law and Policy in Denmark.[42] The study is interesting for many reasons, one of them being the careful explanation of the complex dual enforcement system in Denmark during the period covered by this study. The system can be illustrated by the following figure from the OECD study.[43]

Figure 9.1 Competition Law Institutions Prior to the ECN+ Directive

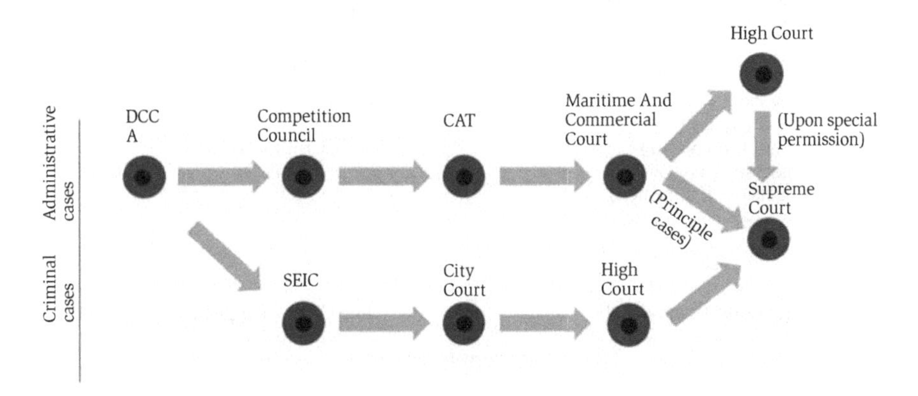

40. Section 368(4) and (5) in the Danish administration of justice act.
41. According to section 368(2) in the Administration of Justice Act. The permission is given by a special appeal board, the so-called Process Grant Board.
42. Competition Law and Policy in Denmark. A Peer Review, https://web-archive.oecd.org/2015-10-07/374692-COMP_A%20Peer%20Review_Denmark__web_2015.pdf. The OECD was rather critical towards the institutional setup in competition law cases.
43. The figure can be found in section 4.10 of the OECD study.

As can be seen, the enforcement of the Competition Act in the period covered by this study involved a dual authority of the DCCA/CC and the State Prosecutor for Serious and International Economic Crimes (SEIC)/the courts.

As explained above, investigations of infringements of the Competition Act may be terminated by administrative determinations by the CC, but imposition of fines was not within the CC's powers or part of the infringement case before the CC. Instead, imposition of fines followed the 'the below row' in the figure. Infringements of the Competition Act may be punished with fines on undertakings or natural persons, typically leading employees, but such cases were considered criminal by nature. Therefore, investigation and prosecution of these cases were undertaken by the SEIC and the fines were imposed by the district Courts with possible appeal to higher instances. Typically, the infringement cases had to find their final solution before the criminal part of the case could be initiated, meaning that it would easily take several years for a case to make its way through both the administrative and criminal path illustrated in the figure.

The implementation of the ECN+ Directive has meant some simplification and especially the introduction of civil fines as part of the infringement case before the CC has meant changes. However, the enforcement system in Denmark remains complex. As of today, it can be illustrated in Figure 9.2[44]

Figure 9.2 Competition Law Institutions Following the ECN+ Directive

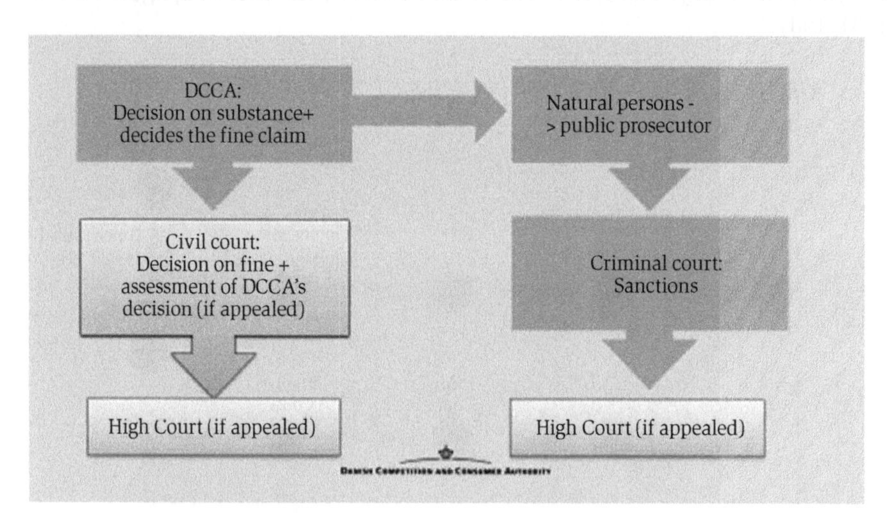

3 PRIOR RESEARCH

Denmark is a small jurisdiction and the legal writing in Danish on competition law is limited. The focus in the competition law literature has – at least up until now – been

44. Reproduced with permission from the DCCA.

on the substantive competition law rules. There has been limited, sporadic discussion of judicial review of competition law enforcement in Denmark. There have been no scholarly studies regarding appeals in the competition law context in Denmark.[45] The above-mentioned OECD in-depth review from 2015 is the only study available.

4 QUANTITATIVE ANALYSIS

This section moves to examine the findings resulting from a systematic analysis of judicial review of competition law enforcement, with respect to judgments and decisions rendered and made public between May 2004 to April 2021.

4.1 Source of Information

All judgments and decisions of the relevant courts in Denmark are published. Hence, it is anticipated that the decisions in the database will provide comprehensive coverage of all relevant appeals during the relevant period. The judgments were identified primarily via the Competition and Consumer Authority's website and were cross-cheeked with the database of the Maritime and Commercial Court as well as the Weekly Law Report.[46]

Note that the CAT's rulings in Denmark are not considered judgments according to Danish law and therefore are referred to as 'decisions'.

4.2 Total Numbers of Judgments and Ratio of Appeals

A total of forty-eight judgments and decisions were rendered during the relevant period, of which thirty-four by the CAT in the first instance, seven from the Maritime and Commercial Court, 4 from the High Courts and three from the Supreme Court. Of the NCA's relevant decisions, 24% were appealed in front of the CAT, 5% in front of the Maritime and Commercial Court, 3% in front of the High Courts, and 2% in front of the Supreme Court.

4.3 Judgments per Year

Figure 9.3 summarises the number of judgments issued by the various instances of the Danish courts per year.

---

45. For references regarding competition law in Denmark, *see* the following (all in Danish): Christian Bergqvist, *Konkurrenceretten,* 2019, Caroline Heide-Jørgensen, *Lærebog i Konkurrence- og Markedsføringsret,* 5th ed., 2022, Palle Bo Madsen, *Markedsret del 1,* 8th ed., 2021, and J. Pinborg and Kr. H. Straton-Andersen, *Konkurrenceloven med kommentarer,* 5th ed., 2022.
46. In Danish. Ugeskrift for Retsvæsen, abbreviated UfR, can be accessed here Ugeskrift for Retsvæsen – Karnov Group. Decisions and judgments published on the DCCA web can be found here Afgørelser (kfst.dk) (both in Danish).

Figure 9.3 Number of Judgments According to Instances

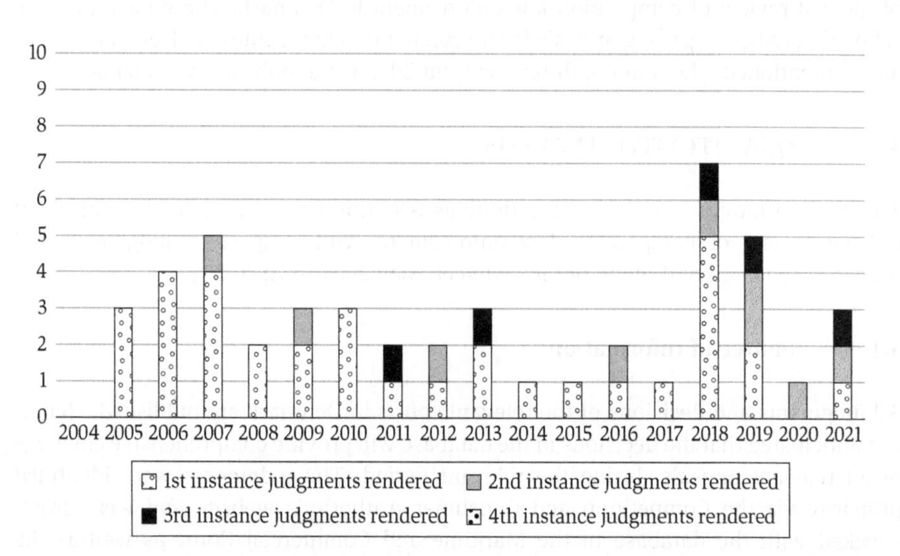

The findings in Figures 9.3 and Figures 9.4(a)-4(c) indicate that it was not until recently that competition law cases reached the ordinary courts. From 2005 to 2018, decisions from the Danish CAT predominated. Subsequent appeals to the Danish courts were rare, at least in the first years of the period explored. In this early period, it was more likely for a case to end with a decision by the Danish CAT than to reach the ordinary courts. It was only from 2019 until 2021 that a pattern of more court cases can be seen. In connection with the implementation of the ECN+ Directive, the CAT's status and function in regard to appeals has changed, as explained above under section 2, and the parties in a case can now choose to take a CC decision directly to the Maritime and Commercial Court as for the substance of a case. The CAT is therefore now only optional and not mandatory, apart from formal questions. Therefore, further changes may be expected onwards.

Figure 9.4(a) First-Instance Judgments (CAT Decisions) According to Years

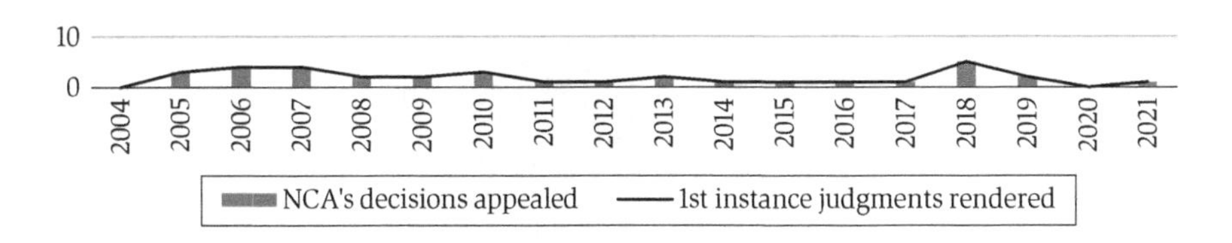

Figure 9.4(b) Second-Instance Judgments (MCC) According to Years

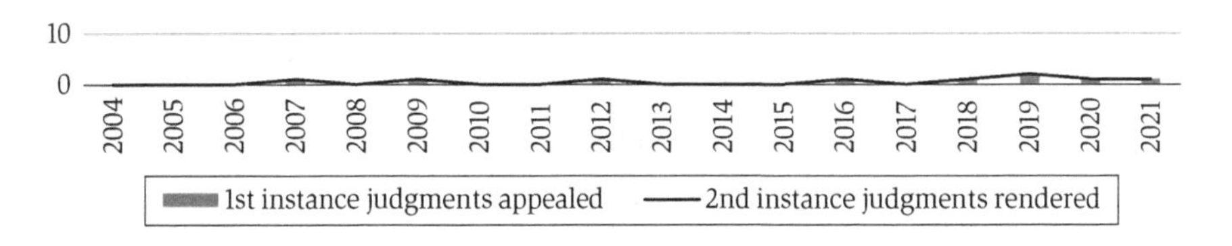

Figure 9.4(c) Third-Instance Judgments (MCC) According to Years

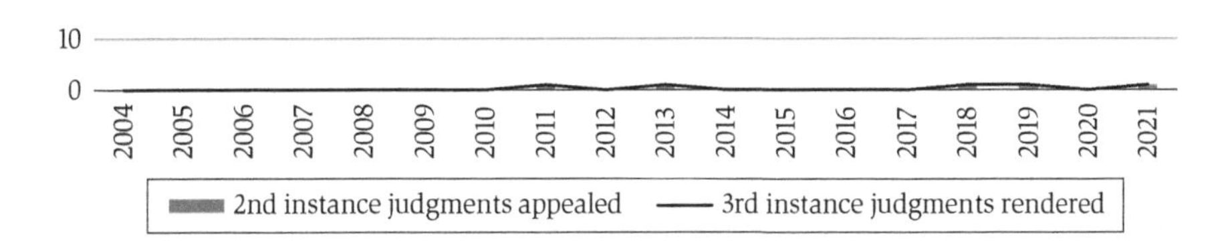

4.4 Success Rates and Outcomes

Figure 9.5 shows that in 65% of the cases, the appeal was fully rejected, and in the remaining 35% of the cases, appeals against the competition authority's decisions or previous instance judgment were either partially or fully successful. The partially successful category includes cases where either substantive aspects of the infringement decision were overturned or set aside and cases where the original penalty was reduced in some way.

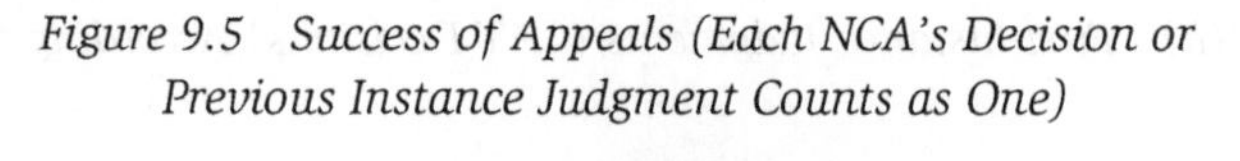

Figure 9.5 Success of Appeals (Each NCA's Decision or Previous Instance Judgment Counts as One)

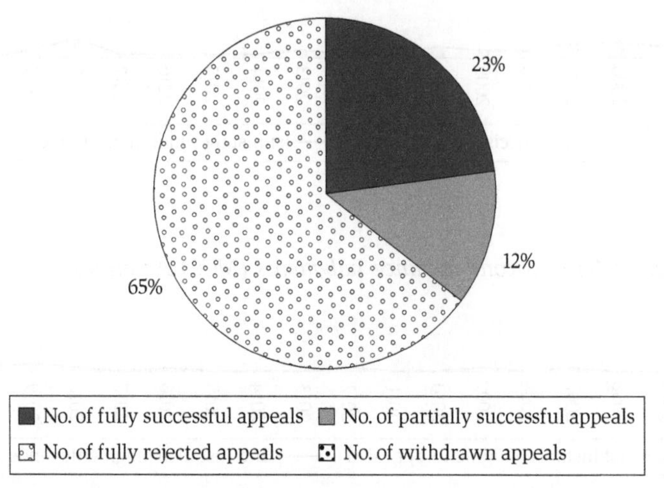

The success rates are further elaborated by Figure 9.6(a)-(c), which identifies the outcome of the appeals. Figure 9.6(a)-(c) sheds further light on these numbers by showing the outcome of each judgment in the first, second, and third instances separately.

Figure 9.6(a) First-Instance Outcome

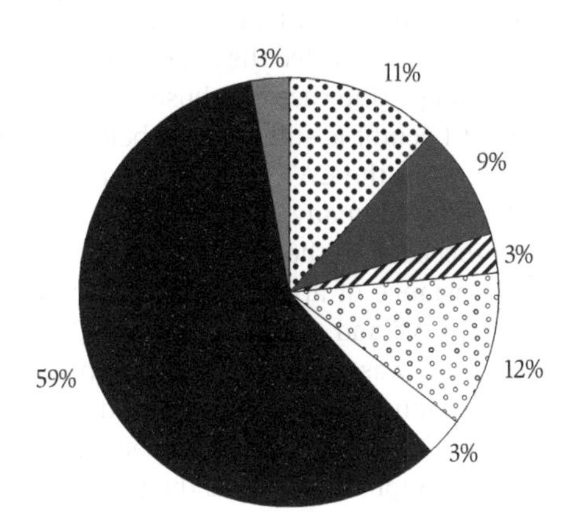

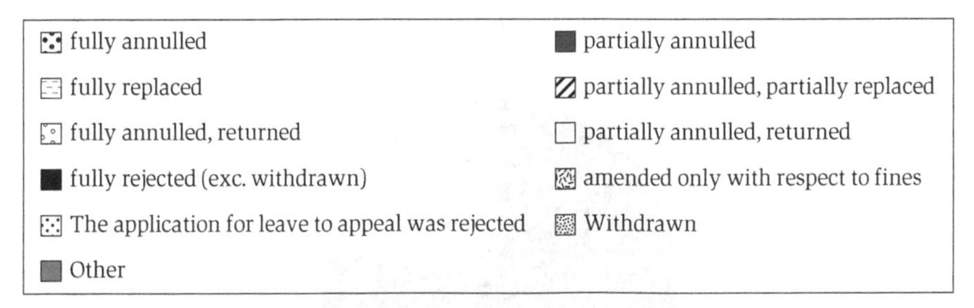

Figure 9.6(a) shows that in 59% of the cases, the CAT, being the first-instance appeal, rejected the appeal. In the rest of the cases, i.e., 41%, the decision was either partially or fully annulled or had another outcome. A total annulment is rare and only arose in 11% of the cases, while in 12 of the cases where the CAT annulled the CC's decision, the CAT at the same time returned the case to the CC. In 9% of the cases, the CAT only partially annulled the CC's decision, and in 3% of the cases, the CAT partially annulled and returned the case. The rest of the cases, i.e., 6%, either had a different outcome or the application for leave to appeal was rejected. No cases at all ended with the CAT replacing the CC's decision with its own. The possibility of doing so therefore seems more theoretical than practical, at least at this stage of the competition process. It also seems fair to suggest that the CAT is reluctant to overturn the CC's decisions when appealed. This aligns with the Supreme Court jurisprudence on the need for a secure basis for setting aside any discretionary assessments by the competition authorities. In this context, it should also be borne in mind that in the period covered by this study, fines were not part of the infringement cases but were instead imposed by the courts according to the dual enforcement system explained above in section 2. This also explains why there are no cases in Denmark, unlike in other jurisdictions where the judicial outcome has been an amendment only with respect to the fine.

Figure 9.6(b) summarises the outcome of the nine cases in front of the Court of Appeal: the Maritime and Commercial Court. Seven were unsuccessful in the sense that the Maritime and Commercial Court rejected the appeal. In all these cases, the CAT had affirmed the CC's earlier findings. One case on abuse of dominance in the market for repairs of railway equipment (Deutz) is still pending before the Eastern High Court - the third instance of appeal. Both the CAT and the Maritime and Commercial Court confirmed CC's decision that the company (Deutz) had abused its dominant position. Of the seven cases, three proceeded to the third instance of appeal. Only three cases were resolved in the third instance of appeal, and in all cases, the applicants were unsuccessful both before the CAT and the Maritime and Commercial Court; accordingly, the original CC's decision was confirmed by all appeal instances. Only in two cases did the Court of Appeal annul the decision from the CAT. Both cases - one on abuse of dominance and one of anti-competitive agreements in the form of an illegal consortium - proceeded to the Supreme Court as the third instance of appeal.

Figure 9.6(b) Second-Instance Outcome: The Maritime and Commercial Court

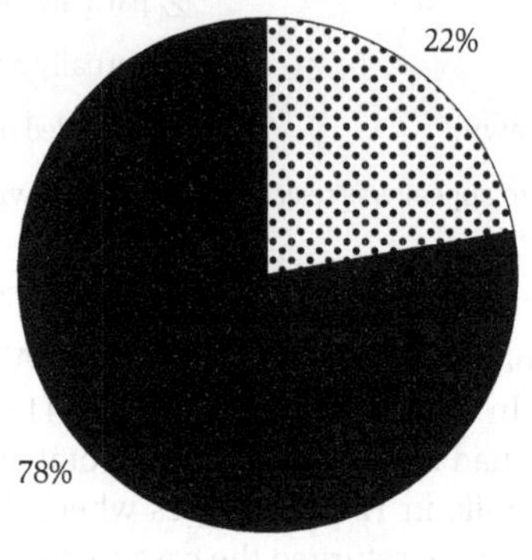

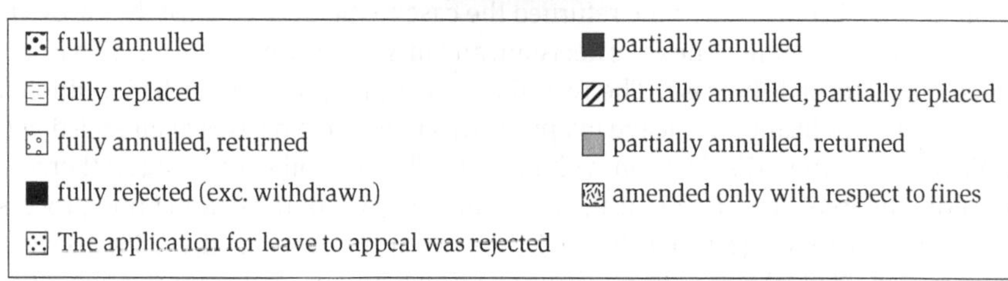

As already explained, Denmark has a complicated appeal system. After an appeal to the Maritime and Commercial Court, the case can be further appealed to either the Supreme Court or the High Court, depending on the subject matter. In the period examined in this study, there have been five third-instance appeal judgments, two by the High Courts and three by the Danish Supreme Court. The number of third-instance rulings appears to have increased in recent years. As seen in Figure 9.6(c), in 4 out of the total of five cases, the third instance annulled the previous instance judgment. Prima facie, one might, therefore, get the impression that there were very different outcomes across the different instances. Upon closer inspection, the picture becomes more nuanced. Three judgments involved the same l outcome as reached by the CC and the CAT, while only two judgments resulted in a different outcome after appeal.

In only one case, the Eastern High Court rejected the appeal by the applicant. This was a case about anti-competitive agreements in the business of repair services for natural gas boilers.[47] The case had the same outcome in all instances from the CC to the third instance of appeal, namely that there had been an infringement of the prohibition against anti-competitive agreements. The other High Court case was a case on the abuse of dominance for excessive pricing in the Danish wholesale market for electricity.[48] In particular, the case concerned the test for excessive pricing. The High Court annulled the decision and, thereby, the test used by the competition authorities. The case had very special circumstances, but it represented a rejection of the approach adopted by the competition authorities.

Three Supreme Court cases have been rendered in the period covered by this study, two about abuse of dominance and one about anti-competitive agreements. The first Supreme Court case was about loyalty rebates in the Danish television broadcaster TV2, and here, the Supreme Court, like the CC – but unlike the CAT – found that the broadcaster had abused its dominant position in the years 2001-2005.[49] The second Supreme Court case was the ruling in Post Danmark, where the Supreme Court had to follow the ruling by the Court of Justice of the European Union (CJEU) in the case.[50] As anticipated, the Supreme Court used the test provided by the CJEU in its ruling and thereby rejected the CC's approach in the case. This resulted in the Supreme Court ruling that Post Danmark had not abused its dominant position in the years covered by the case. The final Supreme Court case concerned an anti-competitive agreement about a consortium in the road marking industry, and the core of the dispute concerned the conditions for establishing a legal consortium.[51] The case is one of the most debated in the competition law context in Denmark in recent years, concerning when participants in a consortium should be considered to be competitors. The Maritime and Commercial Courts ruled in favour of the applicants at the second instance, while the Supreme Court annulled this decision and ruled on the same basis as the CC and the CAT at the first-instance appeal.

47. Judgment of 13 March 2021 in *HNM Naturgas* by the Eastern High Court.
48. Judgment of 24 May 2018 from the Western High Court.
49. Judgment of 18 March 2011 from the Supreme Court.
50. CJEU's judgment of 27 March 2012 in case C-209/10, ECLI:EU:C:2012.172.
51. Judgment of 21 November in *Eurostar* from the Supreme Court.

Figure 9.6(c) Third-Instance Outcome

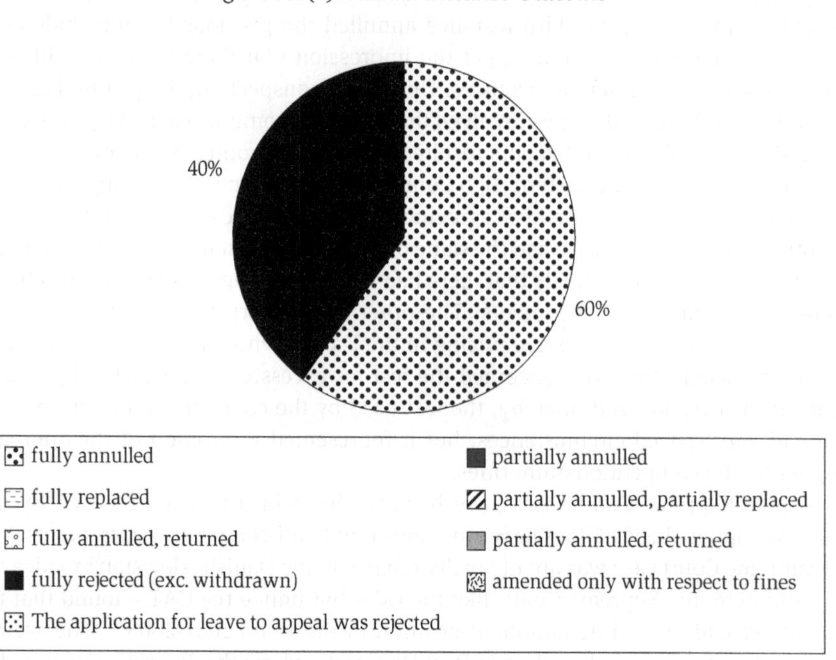

4.5 Type of Competition Authority's Decisions Subject to Appeal

The empirical findings illustrate that only limited types of competition law rules are being subject to review on appeal. Figures 9.7 and 9.8 show what competition law rules were appealed. Figure 9.7 illustrates what kind of competition law rules in the challenged decisions were appealed, and Figure 9.8 shows the rules being appealed over the years. The two figures allow for some interesting observations. First, as can be seen from Figure 9.7, 65% of the cases involve some kind of enforcement of both EU rules and national equivalents on anti-competitive agreements (23%), abuse or dominance (36%) or both in the same case (6%). Second, it is quite interesting to observe that the number of cases on abuse of dominance is quite large compared to other jurisdictions where the cases on anti-competitive agreements seem to be predominant. This is perhaps because some very large cases on abuse of dominance found their way through the - complicated - Danish system during the study period. However, the number of cases on abuse of dominance is not necessarily a general trend in Danish competition law, but rather some few remarkable cases, and in total numbers, there are more cases on anti-competitive agreements than cases on abuse of dominance. Third, the number of cases on anti-competitive agreements increased in the second half of the period, as shown in Figure 9.8. Perhaps one can also observe a trend towards more cases involving enforcement of both the national rule and the EU equivalent over the years, which is perhaps not surprising given the time for Council Regulation 1/2003 to make an impact on domestic enforcement.

Figure 9.7 Rule Being Appealed

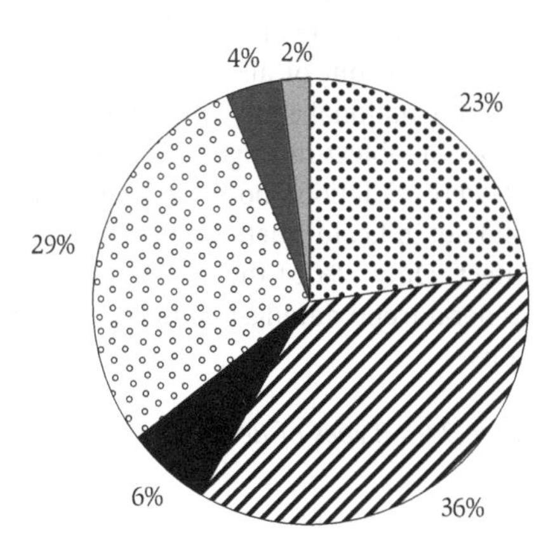

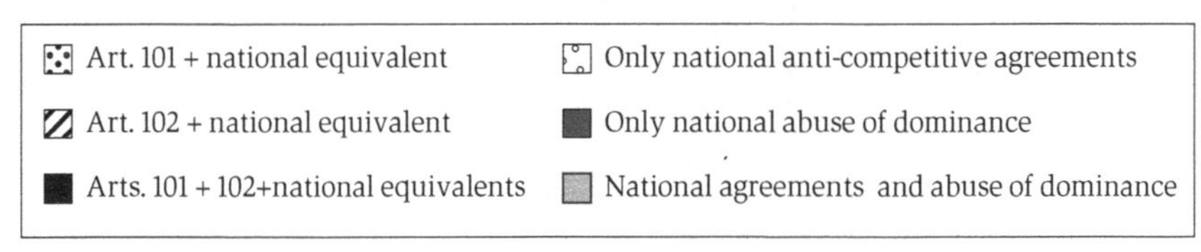

Figure 9.8 Rules Being Appealed According to Years (Each Judgment Counts as One)

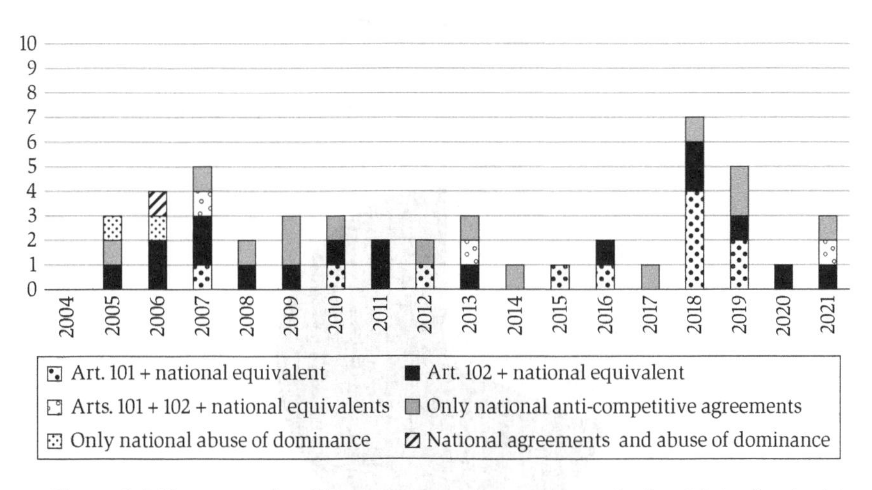

Figure 9.9 illustrates the different types of restrictions dealt with in the decisions that were appealed. The majority (twenty-two judgments) concerned horizontal restrictions, mostly some form of cartel, while only a small number (two judgments) concerned vertical restrictions. Only one judgment involved both horizontal and vertical restrictions. The rest of the cases concerned different kinds of abuse of dominance. A great majority of these judgments concerned exclusionary abuse

(thirteen judgments), six judgments were about exploitative abuse, and the rest of the cases (four judgments) concerned cases where both Articles 101 and 102 and/or the national equivalent provisions were the issue in some form.

Figure 9.10 below illustrates that out of all the judgments that challenged the decisions on Article 101 TFEU or the national equivalent, the great majority, namely as many as 69%, were classified as by-object infringements. As can be observed, 17% concerned infringements that were violations both by-object and by-effect and 7% (primarily in the early cases) did not indicate whether the infringement in question was a violation by-object or by-effect. Only 7% of the cases were classified as by-effect cases, probably mirroring a general trend amongst competition authorities across the EU to prefer by-object violations.

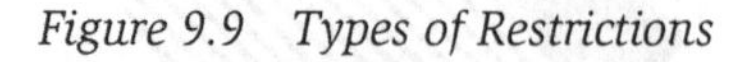

Figure 9.9 Types of Restrictions

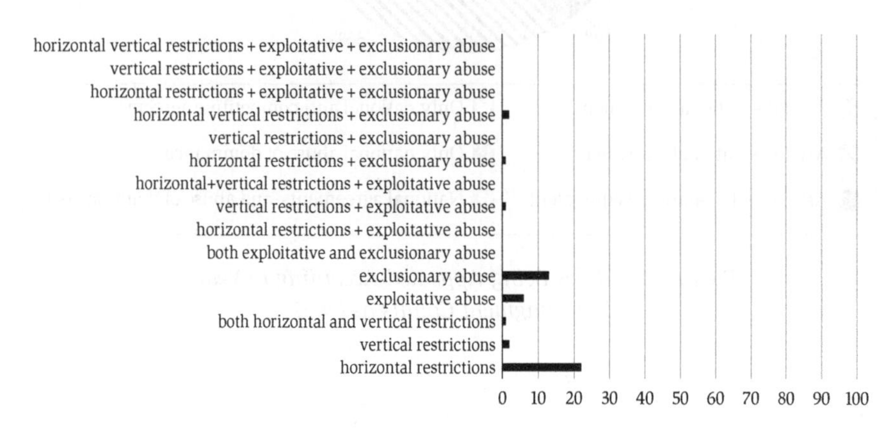

Figure 9.10 Object/Effect (Only for Article 101/National Equivalent Infringements

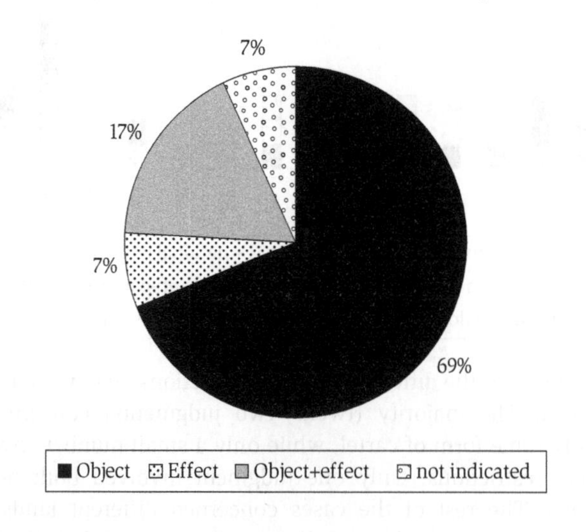

4.6 Types of Competition Authority Procedures

Figure 9.11 summarises the type of competition authority actions that were subject to appeal. Eight-five per cent of cases involved the mere findings of infringements with no imposition of fines. This reflects the pre-ECN+ enforcement system in Denmark as described in section 1, where all questions on fines were a matter for the courts and not the DCCA/CC, and it also explains why there are no cases in the study period involving the imposition of fines. The figure also shows that less than 10% of the cases involved a rejected complaint or closed investigation. This reflects particularities in the Danish enforcement system, notably a very wide discretion for the DCCA to decide on whether or not to close an investigation at any stage of the proceedings without this being subject to appeal.[52] The number also includes the rare cases where a complaint was initiated by a third party, and that complaint was rejected by the CAT. This category covers only three older cases from the CAT dating back to 2006 and 2008. Commitments are not subject to appeal in Denmark,[53] and the figures reflect this.

Figure 9.11 Competition Authority's Procedure

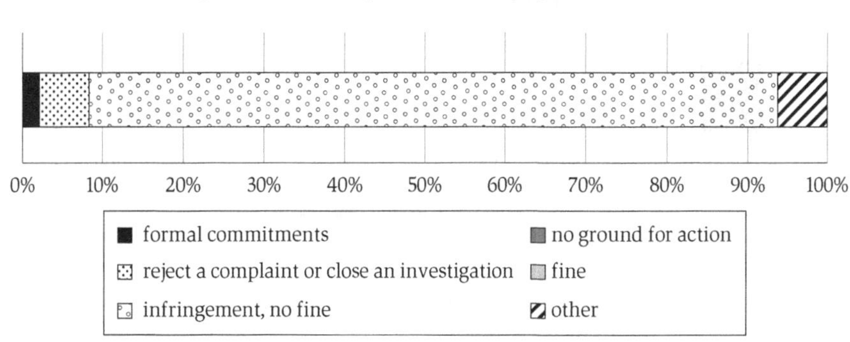

4.7 Grounds of Appeal

Figure 9.12 shows the grounds of appeal raised by the parties and the rate of success across appeal instances. Most of the cases involve more than one ground. It shows that procedural grounds were normally rejected, whilst substantive grounds were accepted more often. Due to the special pre-ECN+ dual enforcement system in Denmark, there are no appeal cases involving appeals in relation to fines. Danish competition law rules have been consistent with the EU competition law rules for many years, at least in their wording. Questions on the tension between the applicability of national law and/or EU law are not visible in the case judgments. Substantive arguments about the right interpretation of the relevant prohibitions have been put forward in cases by the appellants, but the national rules are reflections of the EU role model, and there is consensus on the interpretation and application of those national rules in accordance with EU law. Figures 9.13(a)-(b) show the grounds argued and accepted per year and

52. Section 15.1.2 in the Danish Competition Act.
53. *See* section 19.1 in the Danish Competition Act in connection with section 16a on commitments.

count each judgment separately, and Figure 9.14 shows the successful grounds of challenge per type of restriction.

Figure 9.12 Grounds of Appeal (Each NCA's Decision or Previous Instance Judgment Counts as One)

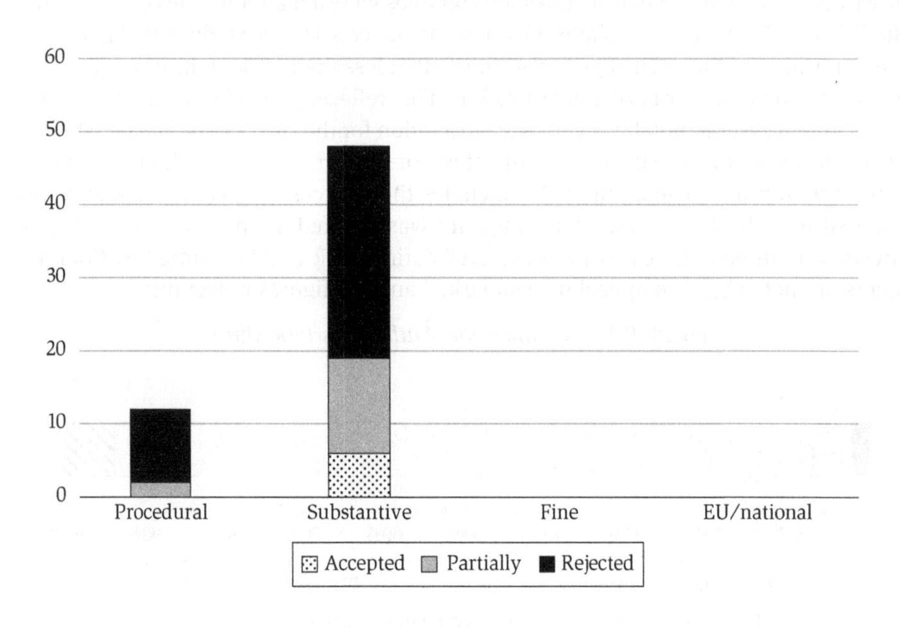

Figure 9.13(a) Procedural Grounds

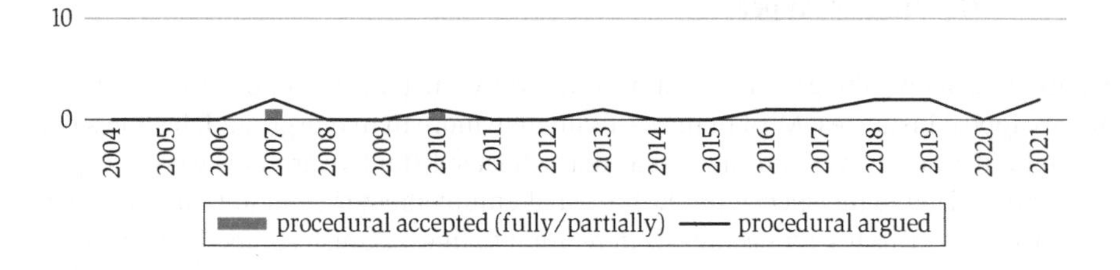

Figure 9.13(b) Substantive Grounds

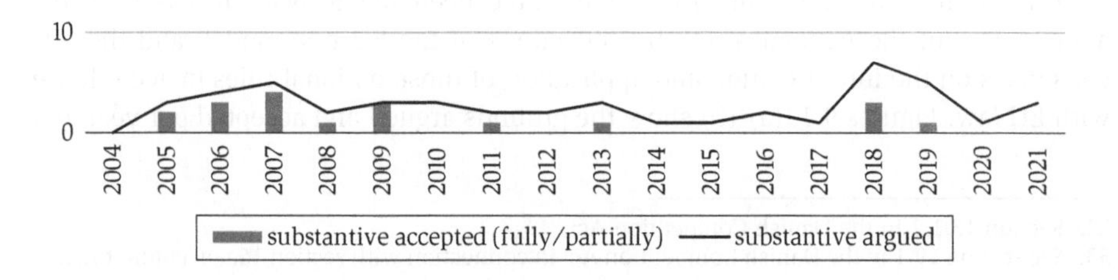

Figure 9.14 Types of Restrictions Versus Successful Grounds of Appeal

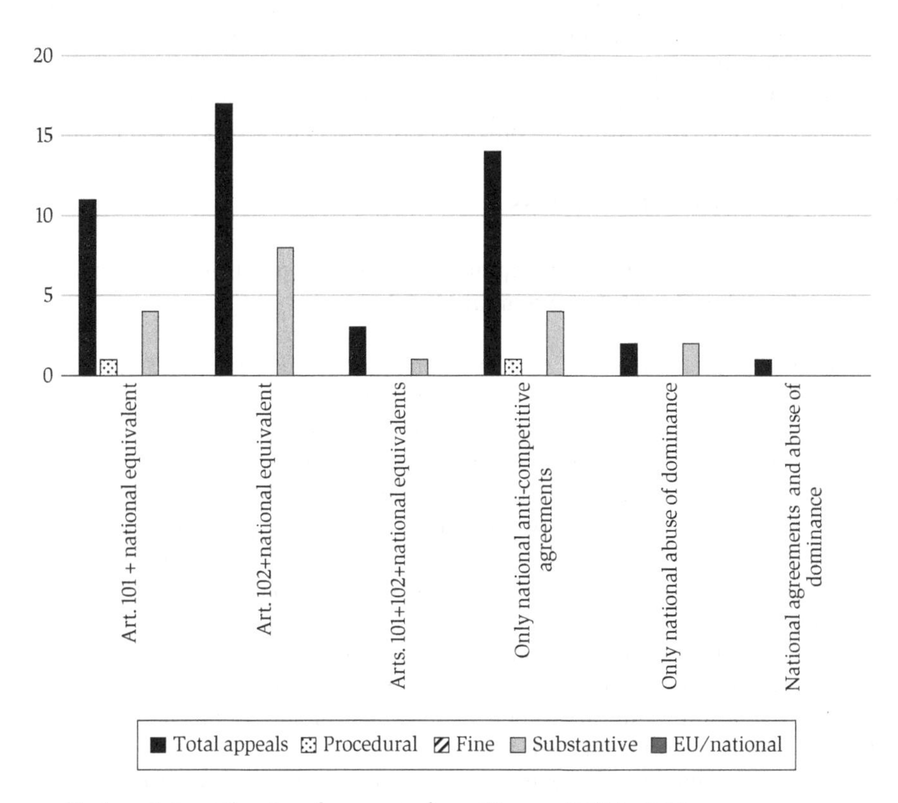

Various interesting trends emerge from Figures 9.12 to 9.14.

First, substantive grounds of appeal were the appeal grounds most frequently raised by the parties and more likely to succeed. Their success, however, was not equally distributed across the years. Such grounds were by and large accepted by the courts between 2004 and 2009, but after then appeals where substantive grounds were accepted have been rare. Successful substantive grounds of appeal concern arguments that the CC had erred in its interpretation of the law. In particular, abuse of dominance cases have given rise to substantive appeals. Second, it is noteworthy that procedural grounds have not been raised in any appeals since 2011. There have been legal challenges based on procedural grounds involving such issues as access to documents, status as a party in a case, etc., but such administrative law matters do not constitute final competition law decisions for the purposes of this study. Other procedural grounds like lack of competence, illegally obtained evidence, *ne bis in idem* or other possible procedural grounds have not been raised.

Third, the pre-ECN + enforcement system in Denmark means that appeals for the purposes of this study have not involved the imposition of fines, as explained in section 1.

Finally, it flows from Figure 9.14 that both the cases on anti-competitive agreements and abuse of dominance have led to questions about the right interpretation of the law. It is a very common argument by appellants that the competition authorities and the appeal courts have erred in their interpretation of the law. Sometimes, the argument succeeds, like in Post Danmark, but the figures show that the interpretation put forward by the CC prevails most frequently across appeal instances.

5 QUALITATIVE ANALYSIS

5.1 The Structure and Development of Danish Competition Law and the Complex Danish Enforcement Model

Although the Danish Competition Act has adopted rules based on the EU Treaty and its substantive structure is generally aligned with the EU system, there are – as explained above – several differences between the Danish enforcement system and those followed by the EU Commission and in other Member States.

First, and foremost, there are some institutional particularities of importance in the enforcement of competition law rules in Denmark in the period covered by this study. As explained above, the enforcement of the Danish Competition Act lies primarily with the DCCA and the CC in bigger or principled cases. The CC took (administrative) decisions in infringement cases as for the substance matter of the case deciding on whether there had been an infringement of the competition law rules. The CC did not have the competence to issue fines. It was for the public prosecutor to raise proceedings concerning the imposition of fines and/or imprisonment and for the district city courts to decide on these issues.[54]

The present study covers the review process of the infringement decisions issued by the CC. As explained above in section 2, there are no less than four possible instances of appeal. The judicial review of competition law cases was, therefore, in the words of the OECD, 'complex'.[55] This complexity could easily be criticised from several perspectives. The review process simply took too long and left the parties uncertain about their final legal position for too long, meaning that it could be discussed if the enforcement framework provided for a full and effective enforcement of the Danish Competition Act simply because of the institutional setup.[56]

5.2 Other Enforcement Particularities

Apart from this very complex enforcement system, it is also a special feature of the Danish enforcement system that many formal questions, like access to documents, the right to be heard and who has the competence to complain about a decision, are dealt with in special cases, isolated from the question of the competition law infringement in

54. Figure 3, p. 101 in the OECD study.
55. The OECD study, p. 99.
56. See the recommendation by the OECD in the study at p. 139 and in the executive summary at p. 9.

question. Such questions are considered administrative law issues and are, therefore, almost always separated from the infringement decision.

5.3 The Scope and Intensity of Review

The CAT, as the first instance of appeal, is composed of a 'hyper-specialised' appeal tribunal and is, in many ways, a hybrid between a court and an administrative body. In many ways, its workstyle and the principles upon which it operates are court-like, with oral proceedings and decisions following the national traditions for drafting a court verdict. During the period of this study, all decisions from the CC could be appealed to the CAT and should be appealed to the CAT before appealing onwards to the ordinary courts. As for the scope, all material and formal questions could be appealed to the CAT with two very important modifications. First, as just mentioned and further explained above in section 2, imposition of fines was not part of the infringement cases handled by the CC and therefore also not part of the appeal process. Second, commitment decisions are not subject to appeal.[57] As for the intensity of the review process carried out by the CAT, its nature as a hybrid plays a role. The CAT operates on administrative law principles regarding the intensity of the review. Those principles are not regulated in law but are unwritten principles developed in administrative law. The outset is that the CAT has the right to full review of any case appealed to it as for both facts and law. However, in practice, there is a Danish tradition of being cautious in overruling decisions made by independent expert boards like the CC. This tradition is reflected in the figures above in the quantitative analysis. As seen in Figures 9.5 and 9.6, the number of fully rejected appeals is rather high. The CAT seems to be reluctant to overthrow the CC's decision when appealed.

When appeals move on from the CAT to the ordinary courts there are no limitations in respect of what can be appealed. All issues decided by the CAT can be appealed to the ordinary courts. As for the intensity of the review, the same reluctance, as seen in the CAT's review process, is also present in these subsequent appeal instances. Again, the outset here is the principle of full review. Courts may carry out a full review of both law and facts, and the courts can, therefore, confirm, set aside/repeal or vary the former instance's decisions. The figures seem to tell another story. As seen in Figures 9.6(b) and 9.6(c), most of the appeals are fully rejected. Only 22% of the appeal cases have been successful in the second instance, and in the third instance, only 24%.

The figures and the low rate of success in appeal shown may be understood in light of the case law of the Danish Supreme Court. The Supreme Court has explicitly stated in the *Eurostar* case that the principles for review should be a full review of the facts and legal application but that it should require a secure basis to disregard the

57. Section 16a in the Competition Act on commitment decisions and section 19 on appeals. The preparatory works, Lovforslag L 63 Forslag til ændring af konkurrenceloven, fremsat 27.10.2004, explain the absence of any possibility for review based on the fact that the undertakings involved have negotiated the commitments themselves and that the possibility of an appeal therefore would remove the resource-saving effects of the commitment.

discretionary competition assessments.[58] From time to time, appeals are successful, especially when previous instances have erred in the interpretation of the law. An example of this is seen, e.g., in the ruling from 2013 in the Supreme Court in Post Danmark, where the ruling from the CJEU in case C-209/10 meant a different outcome in the Supreme Court than at lower levels. The Post *Danmark* case is of course very special and reflects somehow the 'battle' for the right interpretation of EU Competition law as the CJEU, with its ruling, in many ways, embraced the more economic approach in interpretation. Perhaps it is fairer to categorise this as a development in interpretation rather than an 'error' by previous instances, and it illustrates the sometimes very dynamic nature of competition law.

5.4 Interpretation: Questions of Coherence with EU Competition Law

From time to time, parties apply for preliminary rulings in pending cases, but during the period covered by this study, it was only in the *Post Danmark* case that the court decided to refer a question to the CJEU.

Nonetheless, such questions on the right interpretations of the EU competition law are present in most of the cases. Since the entry into force of Regulation 1/2003, most cases involve the application of both EU competition law and the national equivalent. As seen in Figure 9.7, approximately two-thirds of the cases involve some kind of enforcement of both national rules and the EU equivalent.

There is no doubt that the Danish appeal instances, as well as the CC, try to ensure the coherence of Danish competition law with EU competition law. All instances consistently draw on EU competition law, even in cases that only involve the application of national competition law. Occasionally, parties argue that the different (appeal) instances have erred in their interpretation of the law, and sometimes, these arguments are accepted, as the *Post Danmark* case illustrates. However, the overall trend is that the different competition law instances in Denmark cite both Danish and EU competition law when deciding the cases, and this underlines the significance of EU doctrine in Danish competition law.

6 CONCLUDING REMARKS

The Danish enforcement system is complex. The many instances of appeal and the dual enforcement of competition law in the period covered by this study made the review process lengthy and complicated. The complexity can be seen as an obstacle to an effective review of competition law cases, as also stressed by the OECD in its in-depth review of Danish Competition Law and Policy in 2015.[59] This study seems to confirm this.

Despite the principle of the right to full review for the appeal instances, the outcome of the review process seems to draw another picture of the reviewing courts'

58. *See* above in section 2, and the judgment i UfR 2014.2663H (Weekly Law Report), Eurostar.
59. For example, in the executive summary, p. 138 and in the recommendation p. 139.

reluctance to overrule decisions from previous instances. The reluctance is now also directly articulated by the Danish Supreme Court in its ruling from 2020 in *Eurostar*.[60] The principle of full review of both fact and law therefore has some very important limitations in practice, and in recent years, decisions from the CAT or CC are only rarely set aside.

The Danish cases mostly involve a parallel application of both EU rules and the national equivalent, and all instances in the enforcement system draw on EU law when deciding cases, even those cases that only involve national provisions. EU competition law, therefore, plays a predominant role in Danish Competition law, and the appeal instances all seem to undertake the task of ensuring real coherence with EU law when deciding cases.

60. The Supreme Court's judgment in UfR (weekly law report) 2020.524 H in *Eurostar* on a road marking consortium (translation by the Danish rapporteur). See also judgment of 24 May 20014 by Western High Court, and in the same direction the Supreme Court's judgment in UfR 2014.2663 H. See also J. Pinborg and Kr. H. Straton-Andersen, *Konkurrenceloven med kommentarer*, 5th ed., 2022, p. 1426.

CHAPTER 10
Estonia Report

Evelin Pärn-Lee

1 INTRODUCTION TO THE COMPETITION LAW ENFORCEMENT CONTEXT IN ESTONIA

1.1 Estonian Competition Law

Estonia has had competition law rules since 1993. The current set of national competition rules is one of the strictest in Europe, as competition law violations are regulated by criminal law alone. Enforcement takes the form of either criminal offences or misdemeanours rather than administrative enforcement. The investigative and sanctioning body depends on the type of infringement. Parties to an unlawful restrictive agreement (cartels) face criminal fines as well as jail time. The prosecutor, rather than the (administrative) Competition Authority, is responsible for enforcing these criminal offences. All other competition law violations, including abuse of a dominant position and violations of merger review procedures, are treated as misdemeanours that may be subject to misdemeanour fines and are handled by the Competition Authority.

Paragraph 31 of the Constitution of the Republic of Estonia[1] guarantees the right to engage in business, i.e., the freedom to conduct a business, including the freedom of competition. From the latter follows the obligation to ensure an appropriate legal environment for the functioning of the free market in Estonia. Estonian national competition law is harmonised with European Union competition law. The national provisions equivalent to Articles 101 and 102 of the Treaty of Functioning of the European Union (TFEU) are set out respectively in Chapters 2 and 4 of the Estonian

1. In Estonian: Eesti Vabariigi Põhiseadus, passed on 28.6.1992. Entry into force on 3.7.1992. English version available here: https://www.riigiteataja.ee/en/eli/530122020003/consolide.

Competition Act (CA).[2] Accordingly, paragraph 4 of the CA mirrors Article 101(1) TFEU, stating the prohibition on agreements, concerted practices, and decisions by associations of undertakings that restrict competition.[3] The regulation on the nullity of agreements restricting competition is set forth in paragraph 8 of the CA.[4] Paragraphs 5, 6, and 7, respectively, provide *de minimis*[5] provisions and exemptions.[6] Paragraph 16 of the CA is the national equivalent of Article 102 TFEU, prohibiting any direct or indirect abuse by an undertaking or several undertakings of a dominant position in the

2. In Estonian: Konkurentsiseadus, passed on 5.6.2001. Entry into force on 1.10.2001. English version available here: https://www.riigiteataja.ee/en/eli/505012022002/consolide.
3. The provision reads as follows:

   (1) The following are prohibited: agreements between undertakings, concerted practices, and decisions by associations of undertakings (hereinafter *agreements, practices and decisions*) which have as their object or effect the restriction of competition, including those which:
   1) directly or indirectly fix prices or any other trading conditions, including prices of goods, tariffs, fees, mark-ups, discounts, rebates, basic fees, premiums, additional fees, interest rates, rent or lease payments applicable to third parties ;
   2) limit production, service, goods markets, technical development or investment;
   3) share goods markets or sources of supply, including restriction of access by a third party to a goods market or any attempt to exclude the person from the market;
   4) exchange information which restricts competition;
   5) agree on the application of dissimilar conditions to equivalent agreements, thereby placing other trading parties at a competitive disadvantage;
   6) make the entry into agreements subject to acceptance by third parties of supplementary obligations which have no connection with the subject of such agreements.

   (2) The prohibition provided for in subsection 1 of this section shall apply to agreements and practices, and decisions of agricultural producers, their associations and federations of such associations, which concern the production or sale of agricultural products or the use of joint facilities, only to the extent determined on the basis provided for in Article 42 of the TFEU.

4. According to this *any agreement or decision or a part thereof which has as its object or effect the consequences specified in § 4 of CA is void unless it is permitted on the basis of §§ 5–7 of CA.*
5. According to the CA the ban provided on agreements restricting competition does not apply to agreements, practices and decisions of minor importance. Whereas agreements, practices or decisions are considered to be of minor importance if the combined market share of the undertakings which enter into the agreement, engage in concerted practices or adopt the relevant decision does not exceed: (i) 10% for each party of in the case of a vertical agreement, practice or decision; (ii) 10% in total for all parties of a horizontal agreement, practice or decision; (iii) 10% in the case of an agreement, practice or decision which includes concurrently the characteristics of both vertical and horizontal agreements, practices or decisions.
6. The exemptions provisions also mirror to a considerable extent Article 101(3) of TFEU stating in para. 6 of CA that the ban on restrictions of competition shall not be imposed concerning an agreement, activity or decision which: (i) contributes to improving the production or distribution of goods or to promoting technical or economic progress or to protecting the environment, while allowing consumers a fair share of the resulting benefit; (ii) does not impose on the undertakings which enter into the agreement, engage in concerted practices or adopt the decision any restrictions which are not indispensable to the attainment of the objectives specified in CA; and (iii) does not afford the undertakings which enter into the agreement, engage in concerted practices or adopt the decision the possibility of eliminating competition in respect of a substantial part of the goods market. Block exemptions are granted by regulations of the Government of the Republic, and they also mirror the EU relevant block exemptions.

goods market.[7] Just like Article 102 TFEU, paragraph 16 of the CA sets out only a sample list of possible abuses.

Under that provision, a dominant position is held by an undertaking whose position enables it to operate on that product market to an appreciable extent independently of competitors, suppliers, and buyers. A dominant position is presumed when an undertaking or several undertakings active on the same product market account for at least 40% of its turnover. The possession of a dominant position is not prohibited; however, the abuse of such a position is prohibited.

1.2 The Enforcement Framework

In terms of procedural law, as mentioned, Estonia has a multiplicity of procedures. The current system allows and obliges the Competition Authority to ensure compliance with Articles 101 and 102 TFEU and Chapters 2 and 4 of CA through four different procedures as set out in Figure 10.1.

Figure 10.1 Rules Applicable to Competition Law Procedures

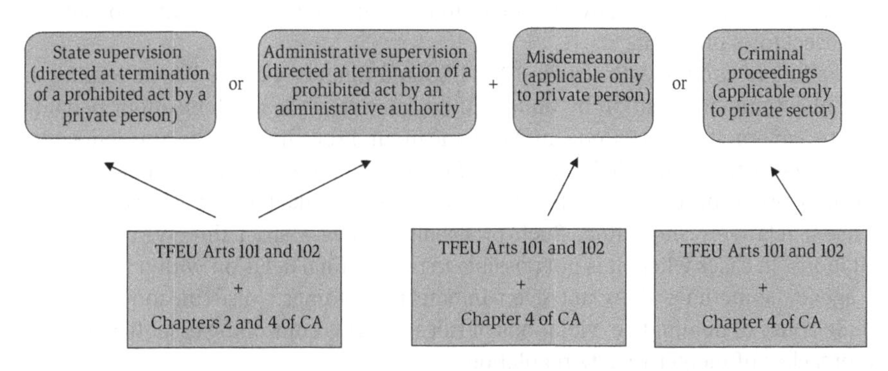

The choice of procedure depends on various factors, such as the nature of the prohibited act, the statute of limitations, and whether the offender is a private legal entity or an individual. The enforcement of Article 101 TFEU and Chapter 2 of the CA,

7. The provision reads as follows: Any direct or indirect abuse by an undertaking or several undertakings of the dominant position in the goods market is prohibited, including:

(1) directly or indirectly establishing or applying unfair purchase or selling prices or other unfair trading conditions;
(2) limit production, service, goods markets, technical development or investment;
(3) offering or applying dissimilar conditions to equivalent agreements with other trading parties, thereby placing some of them at a competitive disadvantage;
(4) making the entry into agreements subject to acceptance by the other parties of supplementary obligations which have no connection with the subject of such agreements;
(5) forcing an undertaking to concentrate, enter into an agreement which restricts competition, engage in concerted practices or adopt a decision together with the undertaking or another undertaking;
(6) unjustified refusal to sell or buy goods.

which address agreements, concerted practices, and decisions of associations of undertakings, is governed by Section 400 of the Estonian Penal Code,[8] which establishes corresponding criminal offences. The Estonian Code of Criminal Procedure, moreover, provides procedural rules in this context.[9]

The enforcement of Articles 101 and Chapter 2 of the CA can take the form of state supervision or criminal proceedings, which can be conducted simultaneously. State supervision investigations are conducted by the Competition Authority, which also adopts the final decision. In criminal proceedings, by comparison, the Competition Authority is only the investigative body under the supervision of the prosecutor's office. For example, while the interrogation of suspects is performed by the Competition Authority, the decision of whether to press charges and file the matter before a criminal court is taken by the prosecutor. Occasionally, the prosecutor has chosen not to press charges despite the Competition Authority's opinion that the case is strong. After concluding its investigation, the prosecutor brings the case to the court,[10] which takes the final decision as to the existence of an infringement and sanctions. Participation in an anti-competitive arrangement is punishable by either a financial penalty of 5%-10% of the company's turnover or up to one year's imprisonment in the case of infringements by a natural person (although such punishment has not yet been used in practice). The court has the power to determine the amount of the fine after considering the prosecutor's proposal.

Failure to comply with Article 102 TFEU and Chapter 4 of the CA, governing the abuse of a dominant position by undertakings, may result in misdemeanour penalties that are governed by the Code of Misdemeanour Procedure.[11] The misdemeanour procedure is a somewhat 'light' version of the criminal procedure. It is conducted by the Competition Authority, which is also authorised to make the final decision and can impose a relatively small fine. Such proceedings have a strict three-year statute of limitations. In cases where it is not possible to reach a final decision within three years, the agency sometimes does not even initiate proceedings. Misdemeanour offences include abuse of dominance, violations of rules on firms controlling essential facilities, and breaches of merger review regulations.

In both misdemeanour and criminal proceedings, the presumption of innocence applies, which places the burden of proof on the state. According to Article 22 (3) of the Estonian Constitution, the defendants are also not compelled to testify if they will incriminate themselves. This constitutional privilege against self-incrimination is widely used and seems to be the main reason why Directive (EU) 2019/1 of the European Parliament and the Council (the ECN+ Directive[12] has not yet been

---

8. In Estonian: Karistusseadustik, passed on 6.6.2001. Entered into force on 1.9.2022. English version available here: https://www.riigiteataja.ee/en/eli/510052022003/consolide.
9. In Estonian: Kriminaalmenetluse seadustik, passed on 12.2.2003. Entered into force on 1.7.2004. English version available here: https://www.riigiteataja.ee/en/eli/527122021006/consolide.
10. Estonian Competition Act, para. 9.
11. In Estonian: Väärteomenetluse seadustik. Passed on 22.5.2002. Entered into force on 1.9.2002. Available in English: https://www.riigiteataja.ee/en/eli/528042022001/consolide.
12. Directive (EU) 2019/1 of the European Parliament and of the Council of 11 December 2018 to empower the competition authorities of the Member States to be more effective enforcers and to ensure the proper functioning of the internal market, OJ L 11, 14.1.2019.

transposed into Estonian legislation). Business circles lobbied strongly against transposing Article 8 of the ECN+ Directive, claiming that enabling the Competition Authority to request information in criminal or misdemeanour cases would infringe the constitutional right to remain silent.

Finally, enforcement of Articles 101 and 102 TFEU and the national equivalent may take the form of an administrative procedure. This procedure, however, is limited as it only allows the Competition Authority to bring an infringement to an end without imposing sanctions. The only sanction that can be imposed in an administrative procedure is aimed at forcing the infringer to bring the violation to an end. The Competition Authority has used the administrative procedure quite often.

As elaborated below, only judicial review of the administrative procedure is covered by the scope of this study. During the relevant period, there were no appeal cases involving judicial review of administrative enforcement of Articles 101 and 102 TFEU or the national equivalents.

The current enforcement system is complex and can be confusing. Some argue that this complexity is the reason behind the relatively lower number of public enforcement actions in Estonia compared to neighbouring countries like Latvia and Lithuania, which share similar market structures and players.

1.3 The Proposed Reform: A Shift to Administrative Enforcement

Recently, there has been discussion in Estonia about whether the current enforcement framework is suitable for fulfilling the objectives outlined in Protocol 27 TFEU[13] and section 31(1) of the Constitution of the Republic of Estonia,[14] which guarantees the right to engage in entrepreneurship and freedom of competition. It is believed that the state's obligation to ensure a legal environment for a functioning free market through competition supervision and enforcement can and should be reformed.

This was further emphasised by the obligation to transpose the ECN+ Directive into Estonian law. In fact, Estonia is one of the last member states where the so-called ECN+ Directive has still to be transposed, and in July 2023, the European Commission announced that it had decided to refer Estonia to the European Court of Justice for its failure to fully transpose the ECN+ Directive into national legislation.

In response to these challenges, a major reform is currently underway, which will introduce a new special administrative procedure that combines all necessary measures for effective enforcement, including behavioural, structural, and punitive measures such as fines for the first time. As a result, not only will the Competition Authority be transformed, but the national administrative court proceedings and enforcement proceedings will also undergo changes.

A draft bill prepared by the Ministry of Justice for transposing the ECN+ Directive seeks to introduce a new sector-specific special administrative procedure –

13. *Providing that the internal market as set out in Article 3 of the Treaty on European Union includes a system ensuring that competition is not distorted.*
14. In Estonian: Eesti Vabariigi põhiseadus, passed on 28.6.1992. Entry into force on 3.7.1992. English version available here: https://www.riigiteataja.ee/en/eli/530122020003/consolide.

the competition supervision procedure, which, if accepted, will replace the previous procedures for ensuring compliance with the competition rules. It will abolish the criminal, misdemeanour, and state supervision proceedings in favour of a purely administrative procedure, granting the Competition Authority both law enforcement and punitive powers. Criminal proceedings may be preserved for infringements by natural persons, at least according to the latest drafts.

The reform will impact not only the activities of the Estonian Competition Authority but also the administrative court, the police, and the prosecutor's office. It is anticipated that the reform will indirectly benefit consumers by improving the competitive landscape through enhanced competition supervision in Estonia. However, it should be noted that Estonia is significantly delayed in enacting the ECN + Directive, as the deadline for transposition was 4 February 2021. As the bill has not yet been presented to parliament, it is too early to predict how the final version will look, but according to the latest versions, the enforcement framework should be transformed in future as follows (*see* Figure 10.1).

Figure 10.2 The Proposed Rules Applicable to Competition Law Procedures after Transposing ECN + Directive

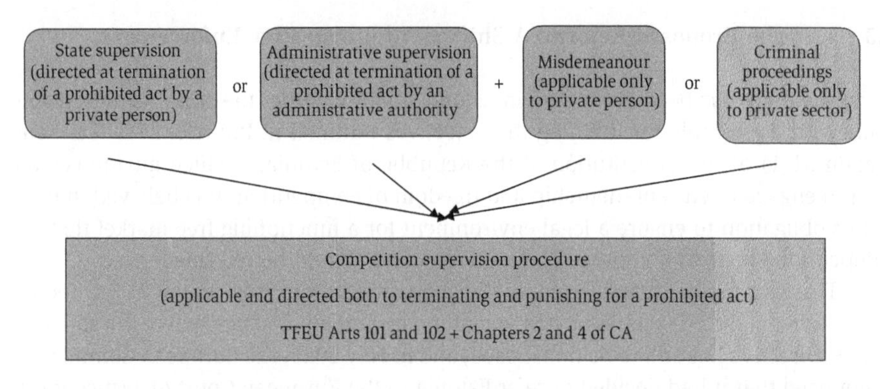

One of the objectives of this amendment is to achieve harmonisation between the application of national competition law and EU competition law. The current enforcement framework may lead to an unequal and legally ambiguous situation, where the rights and obligations of individuals subject to proceedings would vary based on the location of the investigation, even though the infringement itself may be the same (with the difference lying only in the (non-) existence of cross-border effects). The Estonian Supreme Court has previously emphasised the importance of interpreting competition law in line with EU competition law, considering the domestic rules as based predominantly on EU principles.[15] This approach ensures consistency, even in cases where there is no impact on trade between Member States. By avoiding the existence of two different sets of competition rules within the same country, the planned competition supervision procedure aims to prevent any potential conflicts and

15. Estonian Supreme Court case 3-16-1267, p. 20.

inconsistencies.[16] The Ministry of Justice has emphasised that the enforcement of Articles 101 and 102 TFEU, as well as Chapters 2 and 4 of the Estonian CA, should be carried out using the same (administrative) procedure to avoid legal fragmentation and promote a cohesive approach to competition law enforcement in Estonia.

In addition to public enforcement, both Estonian and European competition laws can be applied in civil courts to resolve disputes between private parties, such as claims for damages. Additionally, the Competition Authority can directly intervene against acts by local authorities that impede competition under specific authorisation under the CA. In such cases, the Competition Authority does not issue a formal decision but provides recommendations to advise the local government on improving the competitive situation. Such cases typically relate to public procurement, where public sector bodies restrict competition by their actions. Although there is no regular follow-up to check compliance, it appears that the addressees of any recommendations regularly follow the Competition Authority's advice. This procedure is not used frequently.

1.4 The Estonian Competition Authority

The Estonian Competition Authority (In Estonian "Konkurentsiamet"[17]) turned thirty in 2023. Generally, there are typically two kinds of competition authorities in Europe, some dealing exclusively with competition supervision, whereas some others operate also as a regulatory body. The Estonian Competition Authority undertakes both functions.

Since the adoption of the first competition law in 1993, the Competition Authority has consistently played the most important role in enforcing competition law. It is an independent agency whose decisions are made by the Director General and are subject to judicial review. As mentioned, it serves as the investigatory and decision-making body for misdemeanour proceedings (and for the proposed administrative enforcement proceedings, should it become operational in the future). In criminal cases, the Competition Authority's role is limited to investigation, while all pre-trial proceedings are overseen by the State Prosecutor, who also technically leads the Competition Authority's activities during this stage of a criminal case. In addition, the Authority also has the power to conduct market studies, propose new measures to the government to promote competition and make other recommendations to rectify competition law problems.

The Competition Authority has the power to open administrative proceedings on its own initiative. In most cases, however, proceedings began with a complaint. It possesses extensive investigatory powers as set out in Chapter 8 of CA. For example, it can request information from natural and legal persons, as well as state agencies, local governments, and their officials. The Authority can request documents, copies, and other written materials, and it may conduct inspections to obtain such documents. Inspections can be unannounced and conducted without the consent of the target,

16. *See* for that purposes also Estonian Supreme Court cases 3-3-1-66-02, p. 15 and 3-1-1-12-11, p. 12.
17. www.konkurentsiamet.ee.

provided they occur in relation to the use of an office or plant. Consent from the target would be required at other times. Although there are no statutory limits on the duration of an investigation, the Competition Authority has implemented self-imposed deadlines, aiming to resolve cases within a year or less. If a party believes that its rights were violated during the administrative procedure, it can file a challenge with the authority.

The decision on the challenge by the authority can be appealed to the administrative court. Administrative procedures can lead to recommendations, decisions, or precepts (administrative orders).

2 REVIEW OF THE COMPETITION AUTHORITY'S DECISIONS

The route for appeal or review of the authority's decisions depends on the procedural framework under which any enforcement action is taken. Decisions made in administrative procedures can be appealed to the administrative court. Appeals from administrative court decisions go to a circuit court and subsequently to the Supreme Court.

Decisions made in misdemeanour procedures can be appealed to a county court, offering different avenues for competition cases to reach the Supreme Court. Appeals from the county court go directly to the Supreme Court, where the Court's Criminal Chamber handles any such appeal.

The courts review the legality of the Competition Authority's decisions without conducting a *de novo* review of the case or gathering new evidence. The courts may issue a decision to annul the Competition Authority's decision in part or in full or reduce a misdemeanour fine if the appeal is upheld.

In Estonia, no specialised courts have been appointed to handle competition law appeals.

3 PRIOR RESEARCH

We are not aware of any research specifically addressing the topic of judicial review of competition law enforcement in Estonia. However, in 2020, the University of Tartu conducted a study commissioned by the Ministry of Finance, aiming to examine the conformity of Estonian penal law with the concepts of intent and negligence in EU competition law.[18] The study sought to determine whether the administrative sanctions provided for in European Union law could be applied under Estonian law. The findings of the study indicated that the Estonian penal law aligns with the concepts of intent and negligence in EU competition law.

18. Soo, A., Lott, A., Kangur, A. (2020) Euroopa Liidu õiguses sätestatud halduskaristuste kohaldamine Eesti õiguses. Aruanne. Tartu: Tartu Ülikool. The report in Estonian available here: file:///C:/Users/Evelin/Downloads/Euroopa%20Liidu%20%C3%B5iguses%20s%C3%A4testatud%20halduskaristuste%20kohaldamine%20Eesti%20%C3%B5iguses.pdf.

4 QUANTITATIVE ANALYSIS

As mentioned, during the relevant period of this project, the competition authority did not have the power to impose sanctions in administrative law procedures regarding the infringements of Articles 101 and 102 TFEU and the equivalent national prohibitions. While in some proceedings it issues an order demanding an infringement to be brought to an end, such decisions were not subject to any appeal during the period of the project. This means that there are no appeals within the selection criteria of this study (see Chapter 2). This is likely to change if the proposed reform to the enforcement system takes place.

In general, all Estonian court decisions are publicly accessible and can be accessed, for example, via the Estonian Supreme Court website[19] or through the online judicial information portal ('sept') provided by the Estonian State Chancellor's Office.[20]

5 QUALITATIVE ANALYSIS

To ensure the effective and consistent enforcement of Articles 101 and 102 TFEU, it is expected that national administrative competition authorities should have the authority to impose fines that are effective, proportionate, and dissuasive for violations of these articles. Enforcement proceedings should allow for the direct imposition of fines that meet these criteria, either through administrative procedures or through other types of non-criminal judicial proceedings. This chapter has demonstrated that the Estonian competition authority does not yet hold such powers. It argued that the criminal and misdemeanour routes do not sufficiently ensure the protection of competition in Estonia, given the high burden of proof and the protection awarded to defendants against self-incrimination.

The limited powers of the Competition Authority to conduct administrative proceedings, in turn, means that national courts have not played a role in ensuring effective competition law. Although the Competition Authority made some use of its administrative powers, on the basis that it did not impose sanctions, undertakings have not contested its decisions before the courts.

6 CONCLUDING REMARKS

Administrative competition law enforcement has played a limited role in Estonia. By transposing the fines outlined in the ECN+ Directive as administrative fines, the Estonian legal system could cohere more fully with European Union law while maintaining its unique characteristics.

19. Online search engine available here https://www.riigikohus.ee/et/lahendid/marksonastik.
20. Online search engine available here https://www.riigiteataja.ee/kohtulahendid/koik_menetlused.html.

While the impact and effectiveness of this new competition supervision procedure remain uncertain, it is evident that after twenty years of criminal enforcement[21] of competition law violations, this experiment is coming to an end, and Estonian public enforcement of competition law is entering a new era. This new era is also likely to provide a greater role for national courts in the competition law enforcement environment.

21. In the Penal Code which entered into force on 6.6.2021 violations of competition law were declared to be criminal in nature, A chapter with appropriate regulations was added to the draft law during the parliamentary procedure, and unfortunately the justification for that development is not publicly available. It can only be assumed that the view was that if cartels, abuse of dominant position, etc., were criminalised, this would act as a deterrent. It would be interesting to see if the standard of the subject's rights in national criminal proceedings was viewed as significantly higher than the one set by the European courts, ultimately leading to double standards as well as inefficiency in the Estonian supervisory process.

Chapter 11
Finland Report

Petri Kuoppamäki

1 INTRODUCTION TO THE COMPETITION LAW ENFORCEMENT CONTEXT IN FINLAND

1.1 History

Finland has had competition legislation since 1958[1] based on the so-called lenient abuse principle.[2] The abuse principle entailed the absence of any outright prohibitions in the competition legislation, with the exception of bid-rigging, that had been prohibited by law since 1958. Accordingly, the competition authority could intervene only if restrictions of competition were shown to have negative effects on the market.[3]

A major shift in the competition law framework took place in 1992 when Finland adopted competition rules similar to the European Communities (EC) competition law.

1. For a treatise on Finnish competition law in English language *see* Hiltunen, Sari - Kuoppamaki, Petri - Nieminen, Jussi - Kärkelä, Susanna: Competition Law in Finland, Kluwer 2017; for literature in Finnish, *see, e.g.*, Kuoppamäki, Petri: Markkinavoiman sääntely EY:n ja Suomen kilpailuoikeudessa 2003; Kuoppamäki, Petri: Uusi kilpailuoikeus 2018; Aine, Antti: Kilpailu ja sopimus 2011.
2. The Act on Control of Economic Competition Restrictions was adopted in (47/1957) and came into force in 1958. There were many changes since then. For instance, in 1988, an extensive price regulation system was abolished, a new act, i.e., the Act on Competition Restrictions (709/1988) was adopted, and the Finnish Competition Authority (FCA) was established. For details of the historical development *see* Hiltunen, Sari - Kuoppamäki, Petri - Nieminen, Jussi - Kärkelä, Susanna: Competition Law in Finland, Kluwer 2017, Chapter 4, Historical Background of Antitrust Law, Kluwer 2017. *See also* Kilpailulainsäädännön uudistaminen - yrityskauppojen valvonta ja toimivaltakysymykset, Kauppa- ja teollisuusministeriön työryhmä- ja toimikuntaraportteja 3/1997, p. 13.
3. *See, e.g.*, Kuoppamäki, Markkinavoiman sääntely EY:n ja Suomen kilpailuoikeudessa 2003 p. 76.

The new rules prohibited restrictive trade practices and abuse of a dominant position.[4] Finland had the aim of joining the EC, which ultimately happened in 1995. Alignment of the domestic competition rules with those of the EC was seen as an important part of that integration process. The new prohibitions were in wording very similar to Articles 81 and 82 EC (now Articles 101 and 102 Treaty on the Functioning of the European Union (TFEU)). The preparatory works of the Act on Competition Restrictions of 1992 stated that the material provisions were to be interpreted in a consistent way with the EC antitrust rules. Subsequently, EU case law was routinely relied on as underpinning the interpretation of the domestic prohibitions and no significant conflicts arose between EU and national competition law.[5] In practice, since Finnish competition law is fully harmonised with the EU competition law prohibitions, the interpretation of the national provisions generally follows that given in the EU context.[6]

1.2 Key Provisions

The key Finnish competition law rules are now set out in the Competition Act of 2011.[7] Section 3 of the Act provides that '[w]hen a restraint on competition may affect trade between the EU Member States, the provisions of Articles 101 and 102 of the Treaty on the Functioning of the European Union shall also apply'. This clarifies that the Finnish Competition Act and Articles 101 and 102 TFEU may be applied simultaneously, where trade between EU Member States may be affected. In practice, Articles 101 and 102 TFEU have been applied alongside the national law in many important cases. Furthermore, the Finnish Consumer and Consumer Authority (FCCA), the Market Court, and the Supreme Administrative Court (SAC) often refer to precedents of the EU General Court and the Court of Justice of the European Union (CJEU) when analysing and interpreting national law. This ensures consistency with the EU competition rules, in particular where no differences in law exist.

Section 5 of the Competition Act is a blueprint of Article 101(1) TFEU, with the obvious difference that no effect on trade between EU Member States is required. All agreements between undertakings, decisions by associations of undertakings, and concerted practices by undertakings which have as their object or effect the significant prevention, restriction or distortion of competition shall be prohibited. An exemption to section 5 prohibition is laid down in section 6 of the Competition Act. Similarly to Article 101(3), it allows an exception, based on efficiency benefits, from the prohibition of restrictive agreements on the same grounds as Article 101 TFEU. Section 7 of the Competition Act provides that 'any abuse by one or more undertakings or association of undertakings of a dominant position shall be prohibited'. This wording is identical

4. Act on Competition Restrictions (480/1992), Government proposal (162/1991). For literature, *see, e.g.*, Kuoppamäki, Petri: Markkinavoiman sääntely EY:n ja Suomen kilpailuoikeudessa 2003 pp. 66-77.
5. *See* Kuoppamäki, Petri: Markkinavoiman sääntely EY:n ja Suomen kilpailuoikeudessa 2003 p. 1367.
6. *See Ibid.*, p. 1348; Kuoppamäki, Petri: Uusi kilpailuoikeus (2018) p. 29.
7. The Competition Act (948/2011), Government proposal (88/2010).

to Article 102 TFEU, with the exception that no effect on trade between Member States is required.

1.3 Competition Law Enforcement in a Judicial System: The Competition and Consumer Authority (FCCA) and Market Court

Most European competition authorities are based on an *administrative system,* by which the competition authority is the investigator as well as the decision-maker at first instance. Other enforcement systems are based on a *judicial system* (also known as the judicial model),[8] in which the competition authority is competent to investigate cases, but the final decision is taken by a court.

While these typologies are rather generic in nature, Finland appears to be closer to the judicial system model. The Finnish system is based on the premise that the undertakings' rights of defence are better protected if a single authority in a particular case does not investigate, prosecute and impose fines. One example of this approach is the classification of fines under Finnish competition law. The division of powers between the FCCA and the Market Court takes into account the 'quasi-criminal' nature[9] of EU competition law sanctions by creating a decision-making structure whereby the competition law fines are imposed by a court instead of an administrative authority. Accordingly, the FCCA has the authority to supervise compliance with the competition law rules and to enforce the competition law in Finland. Furthermore, it deals with competition law infringements as the decision-making body. It can issue prohibition decisions in restrictive practices and abuse of dominant cases, but the imposition of fines is reserved for the Market Court.

The FCCA investigates competition restraints both on its own initiative and on the basis of complaints. It holds powers necessary for carrying out investigations. The FCCA is entitled to pursue dawn raids and/or to request the undertakings to provide it with all information and documentation necessary for its investigation.

The FCCA has the right to prioritise matters and use its resources for cases the FCCA deems most important from a competition law enforcement point of view. In accordance with section 31 of the Competition Act, if the FCCA finds that a business undertaking or an association of business undertakings restrains competition, it shall initiate the necessary proceedings to eliminate the competition restriction or the harmful effects thereof. However, the FCCA may decide not to take action if, regardless of the competition restriction, competition in the market can be deemed to be effective as a whole. Similarly, it may also decide not to investigate a matter if it deems that it is of minor importance (*de minimis*) or, more generally, not important for the functioning of the Finnish economy. The FCCA will also not pursue the matter further if its investigation deems that there is no competition law violation in a matter.

8. *See, e.g.*, OECD: Directorate for Financial and Enterprise Affairs Competition Committee. Working Party No. 3 on Co-operation and Enforcement. The standard of review by courts in competition cases – Background Note by the Secretariat, 4 June 2019. https://one.oecd.org/document/DAF/COMP/WP3(2019)1/en/pdf.
9. *See, e.g., Société Stenuit v. France* (1992) 14 EHRR 509.

Upon the conclusion of an investigation, the FCCA normally issues a formal infringement decision.[10] The infringement decisions are the most important cases under the Finnish system, often dealing with serious infringements like cartels or abuse of dominant position. Since 2004, the FCCA has been empowered to order a competition restriction to be terminated. The FCCA may also impose on the company an obligation to supply its products. Prior to that, an order to bring an infringement to an end had also required a Market Court decision.[11]The proceedings may end with a settlement or a commitment decision if the parties commit to change their behaviour in a manner that terminates the restrictive practice or abusive behaviour. In commitment decisions, the FCCA normally sets a 'notice of conditional fine' to ensure compliance going forward.[12] In other words, the addressee of the decision (violating company) has to change its illegal behaviour (for instance, refusal to supply or discriminatory pricing) within the timeframe prescribed in the decision of the competition authority, or else the fine will be imposed. In some cases, the FCCA has terminated an investigation after the company under investigation altered its behaviour.

As mentioned, although the FCCA has no power to impose fines itself, it may propose that the Market Court impose a competition infringement fine on the company.[13] In such cases, the FCCA conducts a full investigation, normally lasting several years and issues a detailed decision on the existence of a competition law violation a well as a detailed motivation for the fines proposed. The Market Court is not bound by the FCCA's proposal. There is a full review of the case as the companies concerned typically try to avoid fines from being imposed or at least seek their reduction from the levels proposed by the FCCA, whether for substantive, procedural or evidentiary reasons. In practice, fines imposed by the Market Court have normally been lower than the original proposals made by the competition authority.

When fines are proposed by the FCCA, the Market Court acts as the first decision-maker (a *public enforcer* in the meaning of Article 35 subparagraph 4 of Regulation 1/2003[14]). In cases where the FCCA makes a full final decision, for instance,

10. A file may be closed before the investigation leads to the stage where a formal decision is given, if it becomes evident that there is no reason to suspect a violation.
11. Annual Report on Competition Policy Developments in Finland, March 2004-March 2005.
12. A conditional fine is not a sanction for past infringement but a forward-looking administrative tool to ensure that the companies concerned fulfil the commitments they have given to the FCCA.
13. Section 12 of the Competition Act.
14. *See* Regulation 1/2003, preamble 21: 'Consistency in the application of the competition rules also requires that arrangements be established for cooperation between the courts of the Member States and the Commission. This is relevant for all courts of the Member States that apply Articles 81 and 82 of the Treaty, whether applying these rules in lawsuits between private parties, acting as public enforcers or as review courts. In particular, national courts should be able to ask the Commission for information or for its opinion on points concerning the application of Community competition law. The Commission and the competition authorities of the Member States should also be able to submit written or oral observations to courts called upon to apply Article 81 or Article 82 of the Treaty. These observations should be submitted within the framework of national procedural rules and practices including those safeguarding the rights of the parties. Steps should therefore be taken to ensure that the Commission and the competition authorities of the Member States are kept sufficiently well informed of proceedings before national courts.' Emphasis added.

to reject a complaint, the Market Court acts as the first appellate court (as will be elaborated in the following section).

For the purpose of this study, only the judgments in which the Market Court acted as an appeal court were included in the database.[15] Market Court judgments concerning the imposition of fines following the FCCA's recommendations were regarded as a first-instance decision by the national competition authority (NCA) and were not included in the empirical analysis.

Under the EU competition law system, special courts dealing with competition law cases are courts in the sense that they do not need to send their decision applying Article 101 or 102 TFEU to the European Commission for review in advance. This is quite understandable, as courts need to be independent in any legal system based on the rule of law.

It should be borne in mind that under the old classification of the DG Competition, special courts dealing with competition law matters by making first-level decisions are regarded as 'NCAs', whereas general courts are regarded as 'courts'. However, this does not mean that national administrative authorities and special courts dealing with competition law matters would be treated alike. In fact, quite important differences exist.

First, when NCAs plan to apply Article 101 or 102 TFEU directly, they are under a duty to consult the European Commission in advance; this obligation does not apply to special courts. The independence of the judiciary would be harmed if courts were under an obligation to consult an administrative authority in advance. This is spelt out in Article 35(4) of Regulation 1/2003, the so-called Finnish clause that reads as follows: '4. Notwithstanding paragraph 3, in the Member States where, for the adoption of certain types of decisions foreseen in Article 5, an authority brings an action before a judicial authority that is separate and different from the prosecuting authority and provided that the terms of this paragraph are complied with, the effects of Article 11(6) shall be limited to the authority prosecuting the case which shall withdraw its claim before the judicial authority when the Commission opens proceedings and this withdrawal shall bring the national proceedings effectively to an end.'

Second, in cases where there is a need for guidance on the interpretation of EU law, special courts, such as the Finnish Market Court, and general courts may refer the case to the European Court of Justice under Article 234 TFEU.

The referral procedure is used in cases where the interpretation or validity of an EU law is in question, where a decision is necessary for a national court to give judgment, or where there is no judicial remedy under national law.[16] By comparison, administrative authorities such as the Finnish FCCA cannot refer a case for a preliminary ruling.

15. According to the methodology and definitions of this project, see Chapter 2 in this book.
16. *See, e.g.*, Recommendations to national courts and tribunals in relation to the initiation of preliminary ruling proceedings OJ C 380, 8.11.2019, pp. 1-9.

2 THE APPEAL PROCESS IN COMPETITION LAW MATTERS

2.1 Market Court

Final decisions of the FCCA can be appealed to the Market Court,[17] that is the final decision by the authority concerning the application of the competition rules. Preparatory steps are not appealable. Interim decisions cannot be appealed separately but the FCCA has to bring the case to the Market Court within a year from the imposition of the interim decision. The Market Court is a specialised court that hears market law cases, competition cases and public procurement cases as well as cases regarding energy market regulation. The Market Court Act (1527/2001) entered into force on 1 March 2002. As far as competition cases are concerned, the Market Court has replaced the Competition Council, which was previously the tribunal empowered to hear appeals in relation to the FCCA's decisions. In competition matters, the Market Court's tasks include the imposition of infringement fines and prohibiting mergers, both following a proposal by the FCCA.

The Market Court is led by the Chief Judge. In addition, there are judges, technical experts, legal secretaries and administrative staff. There are also part-time expert members who participate in the consideration, *inter alia*, of competition cases.[18] Competition law cases are normally heard in a panel of three judges. In addition, a part-time competition expert is added to the panel in the most significant cases. The Market Court annually decides on hundreds of public procurement cases and only a handful of competition law cases (normally 1-3 cases annually).[19]

2.2 Supreme Administrative Court

The Market Court's decisions may be appealed to the SAC as a second-instance appeal (or first-instance appeal in the case of fining decisions taken by the Market Court), which is the highest court dealing with competition law cases in Finland. However, even if decisions by the SAC can be regarded as precedents, they do not have formally binding authority. Nevertheless, precedents do have a strong *de facto* influence on the interpretation of the rules in practice.

3 PRIOR RESEARCH

There has been very limited research on court procedures in antitrust matters in Finland in general and no prior comprehensive research on enforcement and appeals in competition law cases.

---

17. *See* on market Court, e.g., Kuoppamäki, Petri: Uusi kilpailuoikeus (2018) p. 82.
18. The Market Court, presentation, http://www.markkinaoikeus.fi/fi/index/markkinaoikeus/markkinaoikeudenesittely.html.
19. In addition to competition law, the Market Court is the special court for various other matters as well like public procurement, consumer protection law, energy and telecom regulation as well as certain patent cases. In practice, most cases deal with public procurement law.

Kuoppamäki has investigated, *inter alia*, the application of economics in courts dealing with competition law matters.[20] He also stressed that in Finland, complainants enjoy weaker procedural rights compared to the EU system and proposed law reform in this regard.[21] This critique follows from case law of the Market Court and the SAC, interpreting the concept of 'directly affected' extremely narrowly. As a result, most complainants do not have standing in cases where the FCCA investigated the matter but found no violation of competition law.

Havu[22] and Aine[23] researched the application of damages and nullity rules in private enforcement. Almost all research at doctoral level or above has concentrated on substantive matters. There are articles written by practising lawyers which tend to provide case commentary on enforcement in particular cases.

4 QUANTITATIVE ANALYSIS

4.1 Source of Information

In Finland, all court judgments and FCCA's decisions are published. Therefore, the database guiding this study is expected to be comprehensive. The judgments were collected by the Market Court and the SAC via a request for information and were directly sent to the researchers by the courts.[24]

The relevant case law consists of the judgments on appeal in relation to the NCA's decisions rendered between May 2004 to April 2021 on the application of Articles 101 and 102 TFEU and the national equivalent prohibitions.

While more recent decisions are easily accessible, this does not apply to decisions that are more than ten to fifteen years old. The gathering of the judgments was achieved through the court archives to ensure a comprehensive list and to have ease of access via an already combined list, to focus on the workbook analysis.

4.2 Number of Judgments

The database includes a total of thirty-six judgments. Of these, thirty-one judgments are first-instance appeals, of which sixteen were heard in front of the Market Court and fifteen in front of the SAC. A further five judgments were appeals to the SAC in its role as a second-instance appeal (on the classification of first and second instance for the purpose of this project, *see* section 2.1 above).

The appeals can be divided generally into two categories. The first category consists of 'big cases', where the FCCA initiated proceedings and the companies

20. Kuoppamäki, Petri: Markkinavoiman sääntely EY:n ja Suomen kilpailuoikeudessa (2003).
21. Kuoppamäki, Petri: Uusi kilpailuoikeus (2018) pp. 77–80.
22. Havu, Katri: Oikeus kilpailuoikeudelliseen vahingonkorvaukseen (2013).
23. Aine, Antti: Kilpailunrajoitusvahinko (2015).
24. The collection process was the following. The principal author of this report Professor Petri Kuoppamäki contacted the presidents of the Market Court and the SAC. The cases were collected by the administrative personnel of the courts. In both courts, a judge was appointed to oversee that the material is complete.

concerned were represented by the competition bar; these are usually hard-fought cases between antitrust professionals. The second category consists of 'small' or 'laymen' cases. In such cases, complainants contest the FCCA decisions to reject a complaint (for instance, because of *de minimis*, no appreciable effect, or no infringement was found). Under Finnish administrative law, the parties are not under an obligation to be represented by a lawyer in such cases, and many choose not to in practice. Hence, the term 'laymen cases' reflects the appellants' general knowledge of the judicial process and the chances of the appeal being successful a priori due to the generally low level of preparation and substantive argument in the original case before the appeal. These figures suggest that only relatively few FCCA's and Market Court's infringement decisions have been appealed. Approximately 18% of such decisions were appealed in the first instance and only 3% in the second instance.

This relatively low rate of appeals can be explained by the Finnish system that reduces the number of appeals. In some cases, as was already identified in section 2.1, the SAC is the first and last possible instance of appeal. In theory, FCCA decisions rejecting a complaint are subject to appeals. Yet, the FCCA has a great margin of appreciation on which cases it decides to investigate or to bring forward, and the Market and Supreme Court have been relatively unwilling to challenge that.[25] The autonomy of the FCCA in this regard acts as a threshold to the appeals. This is supported by the data in section 4.3 that shows that complaints aimed at limiting the FCCA's margin of appreciation as to what cases it brings forward have not, to a great extent, been a success story.

Figure 11.1 Number of Judgments According to Instances

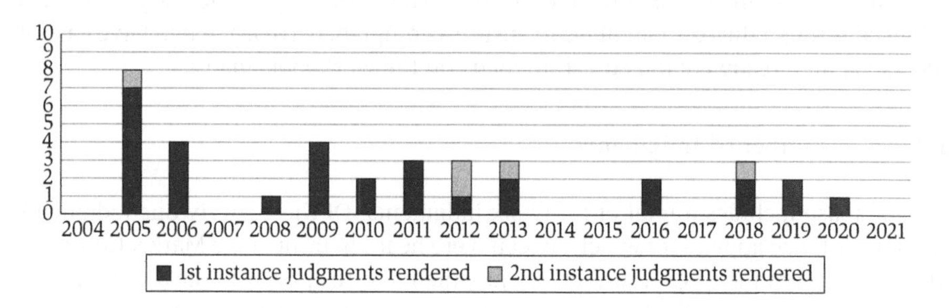

Figure 11.1 summarises the number of judgments included in the database per year, according to the instance of appeal. Only the years 2005, 2006 and 2009 are notable in terms of a relatively high number of appeal judgments, especially in 2005, when there were eight judgments. There is not any clear reason for the higher number

25. *See* Kuoppamäki, Uusi kilpailuoikeus (2018) pp. 74, 77-80.

of appeals in these years. It should also be noted that there are also certain years with no appeal judgments at all.

4.3 Success Rates and Outcomes

As can be seen from Figure 11.2 and Figure 11.3, the majority of the appeals within the scope of the project were unsuccessful: No appeals were fully successful. Approximately 55% of appeals at the first instance and 60% of appeals in the second instance were fully unsuccessful. Partially successful appeals constituted 39% of all judgments (fourteen appeals), from which only two cases were partially successful in the second instance.

A significant number of rejected appeals at the first instance were linked to matters of inadmissibility. In fact, a third of the appeals (eleven of thirty-one) were deemed fully inadmissible, and one appeal was deemed partially inadmissible. This was based on the broad margin of appreciation given to the FCCA as regards which matters it decides to investigate. In a significant number of cases, the appellants tried to challenge the findings of the FCCA not to investigate or to bring the case further, but these appeals were largely unsuccessful.

The low number of successful appeals, especially the first instance before the SAC, demonstrates the difficulty of successfully appealing the Market Court rulings. This is linked to the FCCA's margin of appreciation and expertise, as discussed in section 4.2, signalling that the chances of success in appeal were limited or that the undertakings' claims were weak when the FCCA decided that there were no grounds for action.

The empirical findings suggest that the SAC rarely adopts a fundamentally different approach from the Market Court, as there were only partially successful appeals at first instance in the SAC. These successful appeals, furthermore, only concerned the amount of fines. In one case, the SAC confirmed the decision of the Market Court where a fine had been refused because the limitation period for the fine had lapsed before the FCCA brought the case to the Market Court.

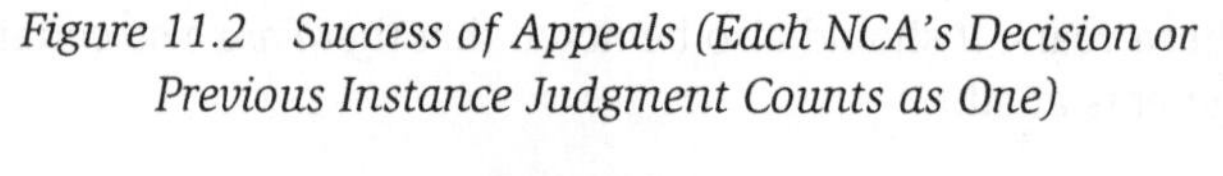

Figure 11.2 Success of Appeals (Each NCA's Decision or Previous Instance Judgment Counts as One)

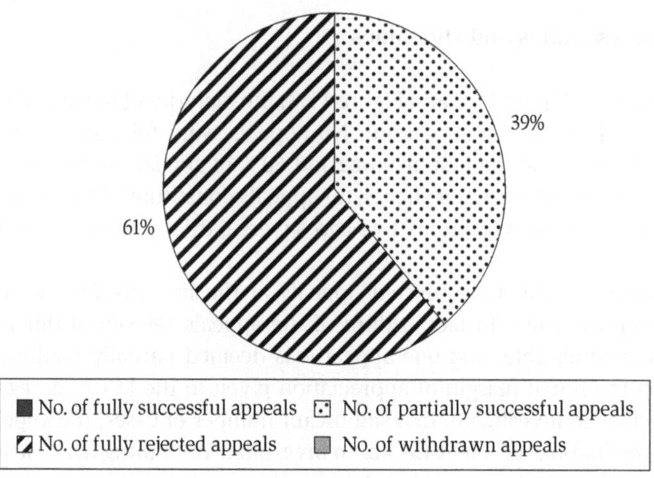

Figure 11.3(a) and Figure 11.3(b) indicate the outcomes of the appeals according to each instance. In contrast with Figure 11.2, they present the data from the perspective of each single judgment. The figures illustrate that once the court partially or fully accepted the appeal, the common remedy involved partial annulment of the FCCA's or Market Court's decision, sometimes while returning the case to the previous instance.

Figure 11.3(a) First-Instance Outcome

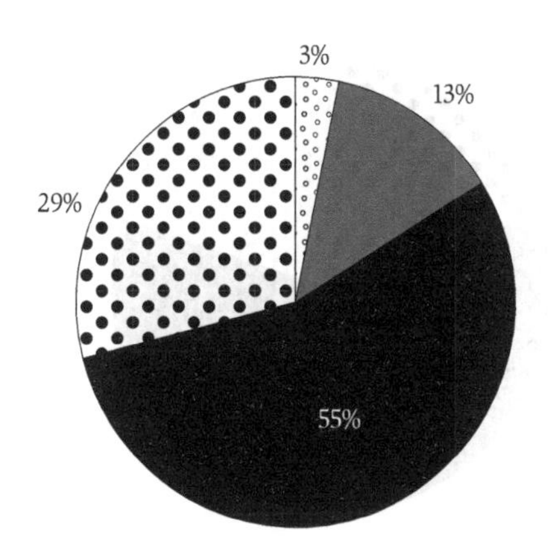

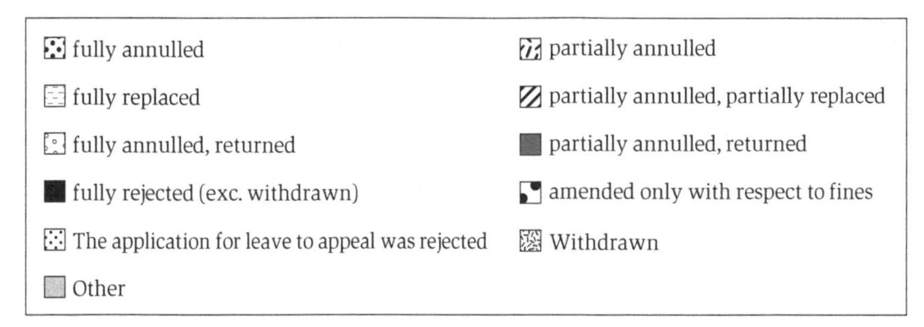

It can be seen that 29% of the first-instance appeals were amended only with respect to the fines, and 13% were partially annulled and returned to the Market Court or FCCA. Only a single case (3%) was fully annulled and returned. In that decision, the FCCA terminated an investigation of abuse of dominance and the appellant, *Blue1*, a Finnish flying operator, appealed to the Market Court. The Market Court decided in *MAO 39/2010* that the party accused of market dominance, *Ilmailuvirasto*, a Finnish Airport Governing Organisation, apparently had discriminatory and opaque pricing, and the Finnish NCA did not present reasonable justifications to dismiss the case. Therefore, the case was returned to the FCCA, and the FCCA was forced to pay half of the appellant's court costs.[26]

26. https://www.markkinaoikeus.fi/fi/index/paatokset/kilpailu-javalvonta-asiat/1377502876399.html.

Figure 11.3(b) Second-Instance Outcome

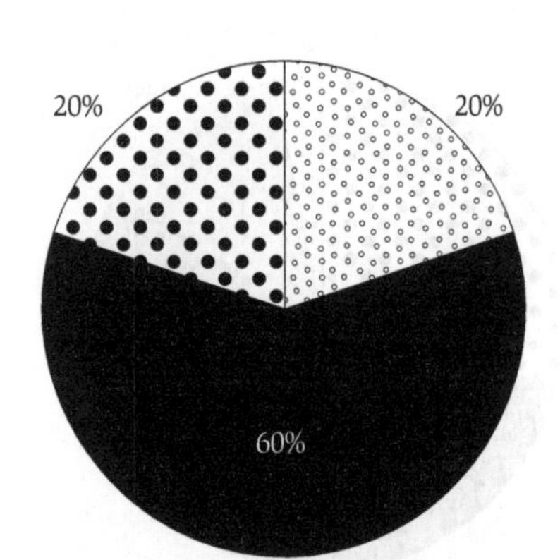

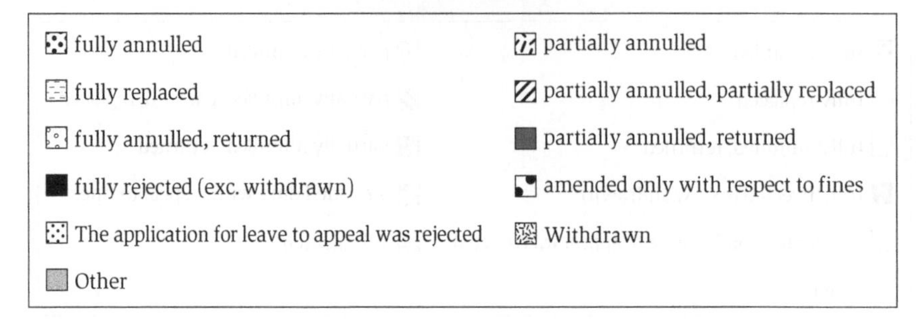

The two partial successful appeals at the second instance resulted in partial annulment of the fine in one case and in a return of the case to the FCCA in the other. In the latter, the judgment of the SAC in *KHO 100/2012* annulled both the FCCA decision and the Market Court judgment *MAO 373/2010*. The SAC stated that the FCCA had not thoroughly investigated whether the accused party, *Suomen Yrittäjät* (Finnish Entrepreneurs), accrued significant income from an informational web portal and how it affected the organisation's income. Therefore, the case should have been investigated more rigorously and the case was returned to the FCCA level.

One particularly interesting example was the *Asfalttikartelli* judgment, *KHO 2839/2009*, where the SAC imposed an increase of over 60 million in the original fines sentenced in the Market Court. Both the undertakings and the FCCA appealed the original Market Court case. To date, in Finland, this judgment contains the highest fines ever imposed, and the significant increase in both percentage and absolute terms from the Market Court judgment is notable. The court was satisfied by the testimony of the witnesses and other evidence to enable it to sanction harsher penalties.

4.4 Type of Competition Authority's Decisions Subject to Appeal

Most appeals in Finland concerned the abuse of dominance provision. Figure 11.4 reveals that 79% of the NCA's decisions subject to appeal involved abuse of dominance, from which 50% involved only the national provision on abuse of dominance, and 29% together with the national prohibition on anti-competitive agreements and/or the EU equivalents. This is probably accounted for by the fact that many product markets in Finland are heavily concentrated. In most of these cases, smaller competitors had filed a complaint, and the FCCA saw no reason to intervene, leading to an appeal to the Market Court by the complainant.

Figure 11.4 Rule Being Appealed

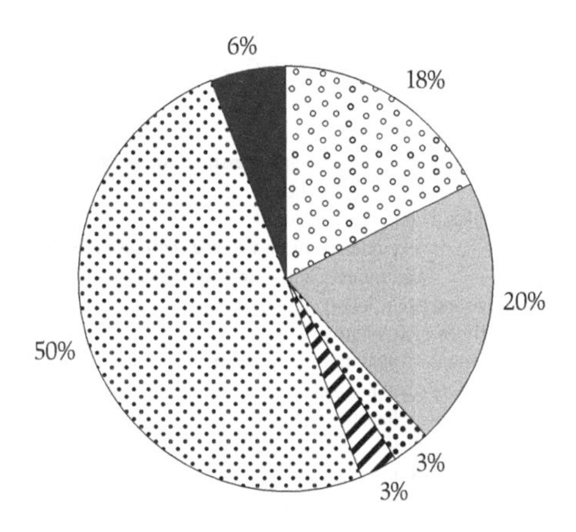

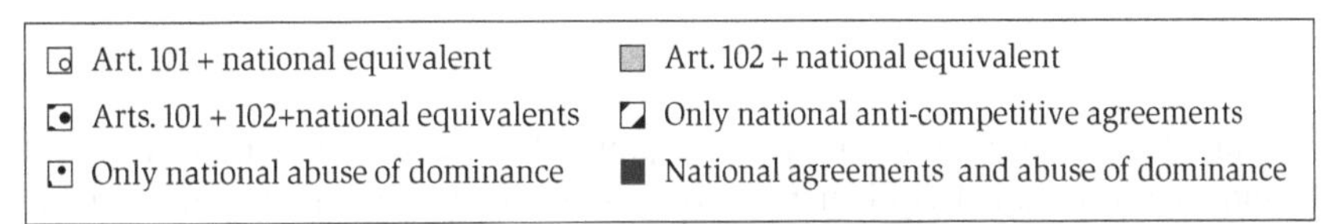

Figure 11.4 also demonstrates that most appeals (59%) focused on the national prohibitions. Only seven appeals concerned Article 102 TFEU and six on Article 101 TFEU. One appeal involved the application of both Article 101 and Article 102 TFEU. In this case, *Lännen Puhelin,* the appellant was the FCCA when the Market Court had ruled that there was no breach of competition law. Originally the FCCA had suspected that the telecommunications company *Lännen Puhelin* had abused its local monopoly position in the ADSL[27] communications and had also used excessive pricing. The SAC, in their ruling *KHO 1057/2011*, decided in favour of the *Lännen Puhelin* and rejected the fine proposal made by the FCCA to the court. The appeal supported the appellant's

27. Asymmetric Digital Subscriber Line.

arguments in relation to the definition of markets and the pricing of services related to costs.

Figure 11.5 further demonstrates that the most common NCA decisions subject to appeal involved exploitative abuse under Article 102 TFEU and/or the national equivalent. Altogether, 58% of the NCA's decisions subject to appeal involved exploitative abuse (from which, 8% together with exclusionary abuse, and 3% with vertical restrictions). This was particularly noticeable in the second instance, in which 80% of the cases involved exploitative abuse (from which, 20% together with exclusionary abuse).

The reason for the predominance of appeals involving exploitative abuses of dominance might be that markets in Finland are more likely to be heavily concentrated at a local level because of the small size of the country, arguably increasing the likelihood of some form of exploitative abuse or at least suspicion of it.

Figure 11.5 Types of Restrictions

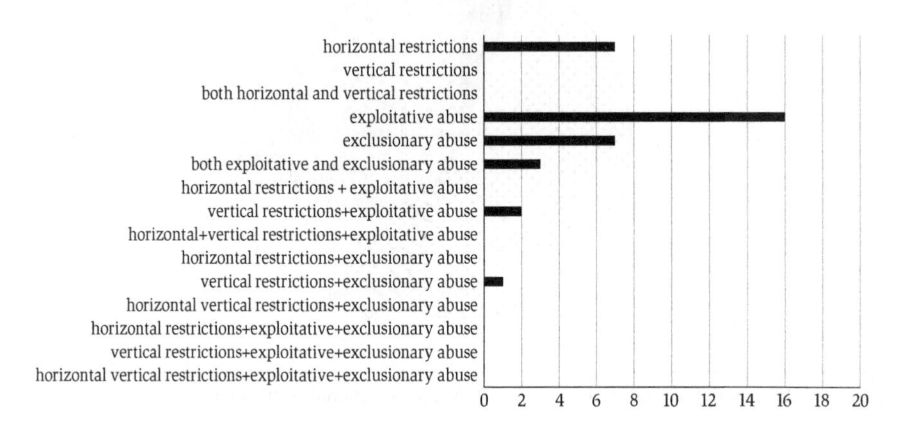

Figure 11.6 focuses only on appeals against NCA decisions where Article 101 TFEU and/or the national equivalent were examined. It demonstrates the extent to which the restrictions were classified as by-object or by-effect. Out of the ten NCA decisions subject to appeal, five were labelled as by-object restrictions, one as a by-object and by-effect, and 1 as a by-effect restriction. In three of the NCA decisions appealed, the infringements were not classified at all.[28]

28. The reason for this is that these three appeals were so generic and poorly written that even the type of the claimed competition restriction remained unclear.

Figure 11.6 Object/Effect (Only for Article 101/National Equivalent Infringements)

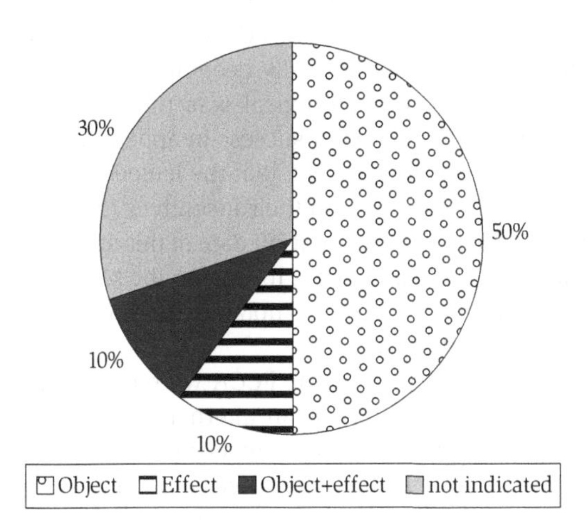

Figure 11.7 demonstrates that the most common type of NCA's decision subject to an appeal was a no ground for action decision, amounting to 61 % of decisions subject to appeal (from which, eighteen in first instance, and four in second instance). As noted, the FCCA no grounds for action decisions can be appealed to the Market Court and, thereafter possibly to the SAC. The high number of appeals launched against such decisions mirrors the wide margin of appreciation of the FCCA, which was discussed above in sections 1.3 and 4.2, respectively.

The second largest category of decisions subject to an appeal concerned judgments by the Market Court where fines were ordered, amounting to 30 % (from which, ten were first-instance judgments and only one was a second-instance judgment).

This distribution between appeals launched against fines and no grounds for action decisions epitomises the competition law enforcement in Finland. The courts are either deciding hard-fought professional cases with severe fines or appeals on the basis of FCCA no grounds for action outcomes.

Figure 11.7 Competition Authority's Procedure

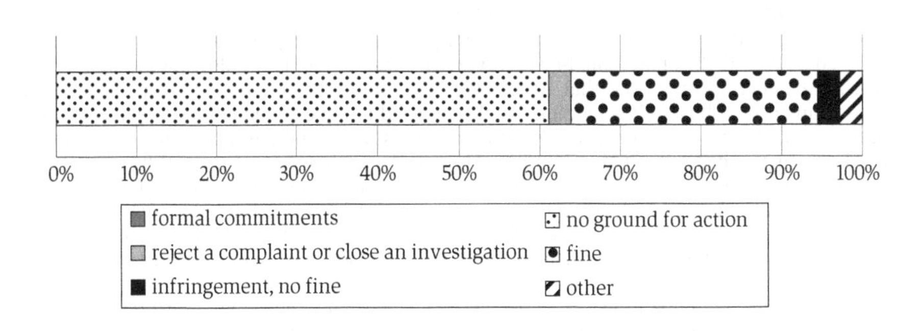

Interestingly, only 3 % of the decisions subject to an appeal involved a leniency application, and none involved a settlement. This is remarkable as the Market Court accepted leniency applications granted by the FCCA in its role as a first-level decision-maker, but those decisions have not normally been appealed to the SAC. The single case where leniency was subject to an appeal was fully rejected.[29] This seems to suggest that parties view the likelihood of success in appeals as low where there has been a leniency application or, alternatively, that the leniency reductions obtained by the other undertakings may have lessened their incentives to appeal.

In one recent case adopted after the cut-off date of this study, the appeal was fully accepted because the FCCA brought the case too late to the Market Court for fines, and the limitation period had lapsed. This case is notable because, on appeal, the case was referred to the European Court of Justice.[30]

Commitment decisions adopted by the FCCA were not subject to appeal.[31] The FCCA has used commitment decisions as an alternative to infringement decisions. While infringement decisions may have a stronger preventive effect as fines can be imposed by the Market Court, commitment decisions enable the FCCA to avoid protracted litigation and use these resources elsewhere. The companies under investigation quite often offer commitments as a resolution of the pending competition case. Also, the complainant may propose commitments in the administrative process. If the FCCA thinks that a commitment decision could be a suitable resolution, it will send a draft for comments to the parties of the case. From the suspected company's point of view, a commitment decision avoids other sanctions than the commitment decision that has been negotiated and agreed upon between the parties. While cartel cases are brought to the Market Court for fines, during the past twelve years, all remedies in the investigated abuse cases have been reached through commitment decisions. It seems obvious that the more widespread use of commitment decisions has limited the number of appeals in Finland.

4.5 Grounds of Appeal

Figure 11.8 indicates the success of each ground of appeal launched by one or more parties to the appeal against an NCA decision or on a previous instance court judgment

29. *KHO 1429/2012, Autojen varaosamarkkinoiden kartelli.*
30. The Supreme Administrative Court had made a preliminary ruling request to the CJEU on 10 June 2019. The CJEU opined on 14 January 2021 (Case C-450/19), following the opinion of Advocate General Pitruzzella, that Article 101 TFEU must be interpreted such that alleged anti-competitive collusion in a bidding cartel is deemed to have ended on the date of signature of the contract concluded between the infringing undertaking and the contracting authority on the basis of the concerted bid submitted. The CJEU concluded that, to qualify as such an infringement-ending contract, the contract must specifically set out the essential characteristics of the project in question, including the contract price. The CJEU did not see any relevance in one of the FCCA's main arguments, namely that the completion of the project concerned and the payment schedule for the work delivered took place much later than the conclusion of the contract.
31. While remedies decisions in merger cases are not appealable under the Finnish law, FCCA's commitment decisions on restrictive practices and abuse of dominant position can be appealed to the Market Court.

issued on its review. The figure includes seventy-one different grounds of appeal, meaning that many judgments involved more than one ground of appeal, combining, for instance, procedural and substantive grounds of appeal.

Figure 11.8 Grounds of Appeal (Each NCA's Decision or Previous Instance Judgment Counts as One)

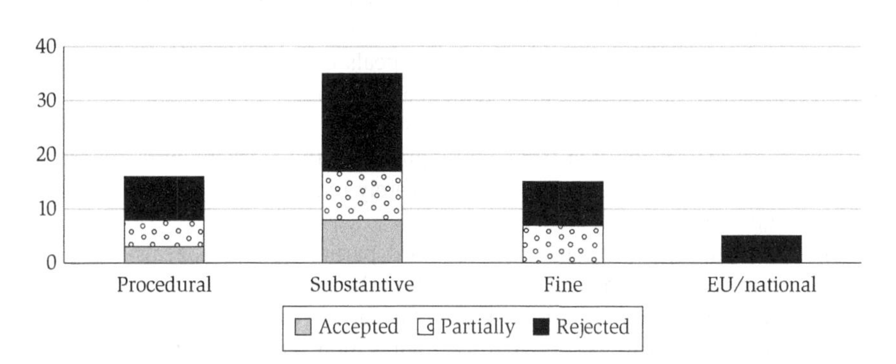

Only eleven judgments involved fully accepted one of the grounds of appeal. The most frequently rejected grounds of appeal were substantive grounds in eighteen cases.

The data suggests that the SAC rarely changes the application of the substantive competition rules by the Market Court. However, in relation to the level of fines, the success rate of appeals is slightly higher. There are cases where the FCCA has succeeded in an appeal to increase the fine set by the Market Court, whereas in some appeals, the fines have been reduced. In one of the partially successful appeals at second instance, the reduction amounted to a minor reduction of 10% of the overall fine, from EUR 100,000 to EUR 90,000. In the second partially successful appeal, the outcome was that the case was returned to the FCCA. Not a single appeal was deemed fully successful. There were only five appeals involving the issue of the potential tension between EU/national law, and those grounds were unsuccessful in each of those appeals. This seems to indicate that the tension is raised by laymen appeals as a 'shot in the dark', but due to the harmonisation of Finnish competition law with EU competition law, these tend not to succeed at all.

In total, eight appeals on substantive grounds were fully accepted, and these were the most numerous, as only in three judgments procedural claims were fully accepted. Procedural, substantive and fine reduction-based arguments were partially accepted in five, nine, and seven cases, respectively.

Only 11% of the appeals resulted in a reduction in the fines. The average fine reduction was a sizeable 49%. It should be noted that the first-instance reduction was, on average, 63%, and the second-instance reduction was only 10%. Some of the cases, at first instance, were appeals before the SAC.

4.6 Appellant and Third-Parties' Participation

The special nature of the Finnish system is demonstrated by the types of appellants. Naturally, most of the appeals were launched by the undertakings in question (46%). Yet, approximately 30% of the appeals were launched by complainants, mostly in relation to FCCA decisions to terminate an investigation. The appellants in these appeals are usually smaller competitors operating in the more remote areas of Finland, such as *Lasmak Oy,* which appeared three times in the database and is a small to minuscule company in the media sector. Its appeals can be thought of as trying to survive competition via law instead of actual competition.

Remarkably, 23% of all appeals were launched by the FCCA. In these cases, the FCCA appealed against the first-instance judgment of the Market Court, where the court either found no grounds for action or severely reduced the fines the FCCA had originally suggested.[32]

Governmental organisations acted as third parties in four appeals. These included, for example, the Finnish National Aviation Organisation, the national telecommunications regulator and the National Post Office, and in these instances, the appeals were raised in their capacity as a regulatory organisation. There were twenty-six third parties otherwise listed in the appeals. Most of these are the original alleged infringers, and the appellant was the competitor (complainant) who instigated the investigation; therefore, the alleged infringer appears in the judgment as a third party.

5 QUALITATIVE ANALYSIS

5.1 Low Number of Appeals

As discussed above, there has been a relatively low number of competition appeals between May 2004 and April 2021. This is clear when compared with the number of appeals raised between 1993 and 2003, a period that could be called the formative era of the Finnish competition law.[33] While in the 1990s and 2000s, many abuse of dominance cases were brought forward by the FCCA, the number of such cases has decreased in recent years. In fact, the FCCA brought its last abuse of dominant position case to the Market Court back in 2012.

The data on appeals reflects the FCCA's prioritisation of cartels. The data reflects the extent to which the approaches of the competition authority and the courts, and between the courts themselves, namely the Market Court and SAC, may differ. A number of appeals were successful on the substance, but indeed, many of these coincide with prior success at the Market Court. There have been cases where the FCCA's decision has been quashed partly for lack of sufficient evidence, for instance.

32. That is, Asphalt Cartel, Bus Cartel, Household appliance Cartel.
33. No separate analysis was conducted but the principal rapporteur served as Secretary General of the Finnish Competition Council during the years 1993-2002 and was actually writing most of the decisions on that era.

The second reason for the low number of appeals is the apparent preference given by FCCA to commitment decisions over infringement decisions with sanctions. A commitment decision avoids a lengthy and costly court proceeding, the outcome of which is not known in advance. As was outlined above, commitment decisions have never been subject to appeal in Finland.

Overall, given the relatively limited number of appeal cases it is difficult to discern any clear and distinct trends, but the quantitative data helps us to identify the following key points.

5.2 Standard of Review

Appeal to the Market Court involves a review of the facts and application of the law. The same applies to the SAC. In practice, the actual level of review depends on the particular case.

As regards appeal cases in the sample, the success rate of the applicants was relatively low, but this also has to do with the nature of the case (*de minimis*, etc.).

The SAC has occasionally taken a stricter view on the level of fines than the Market Court. The most prominent example is the asphalt case mentioned above where the SAC imposed a record fine in 2009. Although administrative court proceedings are mostly written proceedings in Finland, the case shows that even the highest instance court will organise oral hearings as necessary and appropriate. The case is also interesting for evidentiary standards in Finland.

The case involved a national asphalt cartel, that had operated in Finland during 1994–2002, involving all of the biggest actors in the field. Originally, in 2004, the FCCA had proposed to the Market Court that the companies in question should have a fine imposed totalling EUR 97 million.[34] Yet, in 2007, the Market Court imposed a fine totalling only EUR 19.4 million.[35] The Market Court considered that the cartel was partly national (work done for the Finnish state) and partly areal/local (work done for municipalities). The Market Court considered the evidence piece by piece and area by area. It deemed some of the proof submitted by the FCCA to be inadmissible (e.g., issues heard from third parties) and rejected some of the FCCA's claims.

The Market Court's decision was appealed to the SAC by the Finnish competition authority and six asphalt companies. The SAC held an oral hearing in the case, which is atypical in competition cases in Finland at the highest court level. The reason for the hearing was that the Court wanted a direct impression of the credibility of certain witnesses.

The authority's appeal to increase the infringement fine was approved in large part by the SAC, while the appeals by the asphalt companies were dismissed. The SAC stated that the asphalt companies in question had breached Finnish competition law and Article 81 EC (now Article 101 of the TFEU) by bid-rigging and market sharing and that the cartel was nationwide (i.e., covered the whole of Finland) and that it was a

34. FCA's proposal to the Market Court, 31 March 2004, register number 1198/61/2001.
35. Market Court's decision, 19 December 2007, MAO:441/07, register number 94/04/KR.

long-lasting and severe breach of the law. The companies which participated in the cartel were subjected to fines totalling EUR 82.55 million.[36]

The SAC referred to the case law of the European Commission, the EU Courts and the European Court of Human Rights. It also emphasised that in accordance with the Administrative Judicial Procedure Act, the guiding principle is 'free (i.e., comprehensive) consideration of all the evidence'. The SAC pointed out that the evidence should be considered as a whole, not piece by piece or area by area and that also indirect evidence (e.g., issues heard from third parties) could be taken into account. The SAC also held that in cartel cases, there is typically no extensive evidence available that would cover all aspects of the illegal activity and that the burden of proof in competition cases is lower than in criminal cases. The Court also considered the witnesses called by the competition authority to be more credible than those called by the asphalt companies.[37]

Generally, the Finnish legal system shows only limited judicial deference to administrative discretion. Instead, more value is generally accorded to effective judicial protection and other related factors, such as adequate access to a court, guarantees of procedural fairness, the sufficiently broad scope of judicial review, effective remedies and a relatively active role for the administrative courts. In Finland, procedural law tends to attribute an active role to the courts. The courts exercise judicial power and play a central role in offering legal protection to individuals affected by administrative decision-making. Hence, judicial review constrains the exercise of executive power because of its emphasis on adherence to the law and legal principles. On the other hand, for instance investigation of the appropriateness and expediency of an administrative decision falls outside the jurisdiction of the administrative courts. A further limit to judicial power is based on constitutional principles, more precisely on the separation of powers doctrine. According to that doctrine, the actual adoption of an administrative decision belongs exclusively to the sphere of executive power.[38]

There is no stare decisis in Finland, and courts do not normally refer to their earlier decisions. Lower courts are formally not bound by the decisions of the highest instances, but these decisions may have a practical precedential value and are followed without there being a legal obligation to do so. However, decisions of the CJEU can be regarded as binding and are normally also treated as such by the Finnish judiciary.

It can be said that in competition law matters in Finland, the level of judicial review is intense. Yet, even if the formal ability to review administrative acts is broad, there may be considerable case-by-case differences in the depth and intensity of the review and the active role of the courts in relation to the FCCA. The decisions of both the Market Court and the SAC are very detailed in the bigger cases but less detailed in cases where there is an appeal against the decision by the FCCA. It seems that the SAC

36. Supreme Administrative Court's decision, 29 September 2009, KHO:2009:83, register numbers 188/3/08, 189/3/08, 190/3/08, 191/3/08, 196/3/08, 197/3/08 and 199/3/08, file copy 2389.
37. In accordance with section 51 of the Administrative Judicial Procedure Act, the Court 'shall review all evidence available and determine on which grounds the resolution can be based'.
38. *See, e.g.*, Mäenpää, Olli (2019): Deference to the Administration in Judicial Review in Finland, p. 1. https://helda.helsinki.fi/bitstream/handle/10138/321846/M_enp_Deference_to_Administration_Finland.pdf.

only seldom deviates from the substantive antitrust-specific evaluation of the Market Court, which may have to do with the fact of the latter being a specialist court. However, the SAC has been willing to change (increase) the level of fines imposed. If the SAC has considered that the evidentiary situation has been unclear it has organised a full hearing with witnesses being re-heard (for instance, the Asphalt case).

The Market Court and the SAC have the power to uphold or annul a contested decision. The powers of the Finnish courts are limited in the sense that a court may not substitute itself for the administrative authority which made the contested decision. After annulling an administrative decision, the courts usually refer the case back to the administrative authority in question while usually also indicating what amendments or improvements should be made. Moreover, in addition to affirming or annulling the decision subject to review, the court may also amend it. If the competition law matter has not been properly investigated, the court sends it back to the FCCA. If the Market Court finds, for instance, that a cartel has had a shorter duration than the FCCA has claimed, it is likely to lower the fines. The SAC may still find that the competition restriction was nevertheless more severe, and it may set the fines higher.

The applicable standard of judicial review is a full and unrestricted review of the FCCA's decisions on questions of facts and law. The court decisions often contain long analyses of the case law of the EU courts, not only to ensure the similarity of the standards in Finland and the EU but also to fill the gaps in the preparatory works of the national law. There have been a few references to the CJEU in competition law matters, albeit none within the scope of this project, but in any event, the courts tend to use EU law as a material source even in cases where the claim does not involve the direct application of Article 101 or 102 TFEU.

6 CONCLUDING REMARKS

Finland has had competition law rules similar to Articles 101 and 102 TFEU in place for thirty years now. The most interesting, foundational procedural struggles took place during the first decade and are not covered in this study that starts from 1 May 2004. The system is now relatively mature, and the key principles of competition law, following the example of EU precedents, are well-established. No significant conflicts with EU law have occurred, which can be explained by the fact that the key legislation introduced in 1992 and early court precedents sought to harmonise with EU rules.

There has been a relatively low number of competition appeals between 2004 and 2021. This is clear when compared with the number of appeals raised between 1993 and 2002, a period that could be called the formative era of the Finnish competition law. The data on appeals reflects the FCCA's prioritisation of cartels that are routinely brought to market court due to their severity. As to other types of competition restrictions, the FCCA has given preference to commitment decisions over infringement decisions with sanctions. A commitment decision avoids a lengthy and costly court proceeding, the outcome of which is not known in advance, but given there is no scope for appeal in relation to commitments, it has clearly limited the scope for judicial consideration of the competition rules in appeal cases.

With regard to cases that the FCCA files at the Market Court in order to have fines imposed, the Market Court is not bound by the FCCA's proposal. There is a full review of the case as the companies concerned typically try to avoid fines from being imposed or at least seek their reduction from the levels proposed by the FCCA, whether for substantive, procedural or evidentiary reasons. In practice, fines imposed by the Market Court have normally been lower than the original proposals made by the competition authority. The level of the fines has also been one of the key topics in the appeals made to the SAC.

It can be said that in competition law matters in Finland, the level of judicial review is intense. Nonetheless, even if the formal ability to review administrative acts is broad, there may be considerable case-by-case differences in the depth and intensity of the review and the active role of the courts in relation to the FCCA. The decisions of both the Market Court and the SAC are very detailed in the bigger cases - where the Market Court is not, in fact, acting as an appeal court - but less detailed in cases where there is an appeal against the decision by the FCCA. It appears that the SAC only seldom deviates from the substantive antitrust-specific evaluation of the Market Court, which may have to do with the fact of the latter being a specialist court. However, the SAC has been willing to change (increase) the level of fines imposed, as evidenced in various cases.

CHAPTER 12
France Report

Rafael Amaro

1 COMPETITION LAW ENFORCEMENT IN FRANCE

1.1 Historical Outline

In France, the origins of what would later be called 'competition law' can be traced back at least to the French Revolution. Two founding texts from 1791 - during its first liberal phase - are most often cited. The best known is the *Loi Le Chapelier* of 14 June 1791, which prohibits professional guilds, many of which dated back to the Middle Ages.[1] Today, we would say that this was the first piece of legislation designed to combat regulatory barriers to market entry.[2] The second text is the *Loi d'Allarde* (better known by the misnomer *Décret d'Allarde*) of 2 and 17 March 1791. Article 7 of this act sets out the principle of freedom of trade and industry, which has become one of the general principles of French law. Then, under Napoleon the 1st, Article 419 of the 1810 Penal Code prohibited behaviour that today would be considered anti-competitive agreements: 'coalitions' to manipulate prices 'above or below what free and natural competition would have determined'. This article, which was rarely applied, remained in force for 176 years.

Despite these founding texts, which laid down the legal foundations for the regulation of competition in French law, free competition was not a reality in France until the 20th century. This situation can be explained by the strong state interventionism during the 18th and the beginning of the 19th century, dating back to the 'Absolute

1. Usual legislative instrument issued by the Parliament. It may be translated by 'act' but the French word would be used to avoid confusions with other legislative instruments, especially those issued by the Government.
2. For the record, the French Revolution went so far as to abolish bar associations and the very title of barrister (*avocat*) to promote free access to the judicial system.

Monarchy': the *colbertism.*[3] Then, as we move into the 19th century, it is instead private barriers to free competition that replaced public barriers and explained the state of the French economy. The rapid development of industrial capitalism throughout this century worried French economic circles. They then organised themselves to avoid the destabilising effects of competition. This led to the development of the so-called *ententes industrielles* (industrial agreements), which today would be seen as the purest form of hardcore cartels.

In other words, an embryonic competition law did not result in the French economy obeying the current standards of the market economy. It can also be explained – and this explanation is linked to the previous ones – by the absence of public bodies in charge of enforcing competition law.

It was the beginning of the European integration process that led to the first French law provisions close to our modern competition law: a *Décret* No. 53-704 of 9 August 1953.[4] On this occasion, the first French competition authority was created (*la Commission technique des ententes*) with an advisory role limited to cartels. Subsequent reforms gradually expanded the role of the French competition authority while changing its name and composition:

- 1963: *Loi* No. 63-628 of 2 July 1963 extended the competence of the authority to abuses of dominant position.
- 1977: following the economic troubles resulting from the first oil crisis of 1973, a more significant liberalisation of the French economy was undertaken. *Loi* No. 77-806 of 19 July 1977 created the Competition Commission (*la **Commission de la concurrence***) with broader powers than the previous commission. It was responsible for giving opinions to the Government on mergers, with the Minister of the Economy remaining the decision-maker.
- 1986: an important *ordonnance*[5] – *Ordonnance* No. 86-1243 of 1 December 1986 – replaced this Commission by the Competition Council (*le **Conseil de la concurrence***), now empowered to fine anti-competitive practices. This *ordonnance* also introduced the possibility for companies to refer cases to the *Conseil*.
- 1992: *Loi* No. 92-1282 of 11 December 1992 empowers the *Conseil de la concurrence* to apply former Articles 85 to 87 of the Treaty of Rome.
- 2001: *Loi* No. 2001-420 '*Nouvelles régulations économiques*' of 15 May 2001 introduces important procedural changes, including settlement and leniency programs.
- 2008/2009: *Loi* No. 2008-776 '*Modernisation de l'économie*' of 4 August 2008 transforms the Council into the current Competition Authority (*l'Autorité de la*

3. Named after Louis XIV's main minister.
4. Usual instrument issued by the Government in its own field of legislative activity. In the French hierarchy of norms, *ordonnances* and *lois* prevail over *décrets*. *See* the following footnote.
5. An *ordonnance* is a legislative instrument issued by the Government to rule on matters which are usually reserved to the *loi* and the two chambers of the French Parliament: the *Assemblée nationale* – the lower house, and the *Sénat* – the upper house. *Ordonnances* have been very common for half a century because of the strong political legitimacy of the executive branch and the corresponding weakness of the legislative branch.

concurrence) and transfers to it all its powers, adding merger control, as of March 2, 2009. This transfer brings the French authority closer to its EU counterparts. The new *Autorité* also has the power to issue opinions on its own initiative on any competition subject, as well as to issue recommendations aimed at improving the functioning of markets to the minister responsible for the sector.
- 2015: *Loi* No. 2015-990 '*Loi Croissance*' of 6 August 2015 gives the *Autorité* new powers to regulate certain legal professions. Every two years, the *Autorité* must make proposals to the Government on changes to regulated fees and on the establishment of professionals.
- 2020/2021: *Loi* No. 2020-1508 *DADDUE* of 3 December 2020 authorises the transposition of the ECN+ Directive by an *ordonnance*, which was undertaken by the *Ordonnance* No. 2021-649 of 26 May 2021. This reform gave the *Autorité* the power to set its own priorities and to reject complaints for lack of priorities,[6] which it was previously prohibited from doing. It therefore now has identical powers to those of the European Commission.[7]

For the purposes of this study, we will note that between 2004 and 2021, the French competition authority was renamed. As this timeline indicates, the *Conseil de la concurrence* has been replaced by the *Autorité de la concurrence* as of 2 March 2009. The decisions dealt with in this study are therefore those of the *Conseil* between 2004 and February 2009 and those of the *Autorité* between March 2009 and 2021.[8]

1.2 Enforcement Framework

Since its inception in March 2009, the *Autorité de la concurrence* is an independent administrative authority with extensive powers, as in most other Member States. It investigates and makes final decisions on infringements and remedies. It also exercises its powers concurrently with a variety of utility regulators for audiovisual and digital communication, telecommunications and post, rails, and energy. The *Autorité* has a high level of discretion to manage investigations. It decides which cases to investigate and has considerable powers to investigate potential infringements of the domestic and EU prohibitions once a formal investigation has been opened. The *Autorité* has various options in dealing with a case. It can close the investigation on the grounds of administrative priorities or issue a no grounds for action decision. It has the power to accept binding commitments and frequently uses it. Most importantly, the *Autorité* can make a formal decision declaring that the rules have been infringed and order the parties in breach to cease the infringing conduct, as well as impose penalties of up to 10% of the turnover of an undertaking.

6. Article L. 462-8, al. 2 Commercial Code.
7. It used this new power for the first time in October 2022: Aut. Conc., 20 October 2022, No. 22-D-19 (2022).
8. Article R. 464-10 Commercial Code.

The *Autorité*'s enforcement activities are governed by Book IV of the French Commercial Code. Title V of this Book deals with its investigation powers,[9] and Title VI with its organisation (Chapter 1),[10] attributions (Chapter 2),[11] the procedural framework of the trials conducted by its services (Chapter 3)[12] and its decisions (Chapter 4).[13]

1.3 Major Trends in the Activity of the French Competition Authority

Without attempting to be exhaustive, three trends can be highlighted.

1.3.1 One of the Most Active National Competition Authorities in Europe

First trend: the *Autorité* appears to be among the most active national competition authorities, judging by the number of decisions it issues each year. For example, in 2021, the last year for which statistics were published at the time of writing, the *Autorité* issued 321 decisions and opinions, including a record number of merger decisions (272 decisions), the remaining decisions being issued in antitrust cases. The amount of penalties imposed in 2021 was EUR 873.7 million including EUR 720 million for Google.[14] Over ten years, the average annual amount is EUR 719.7 million.

1.3.2 Changes in the Type of Cases Handled by the French Competition Authority

Second trend: the evolution of enforcement in France includes a change in the type of cases dealt with by the French competition authority, which is partly reflected in the reviewing Courts' activity. To my knowledge, there are no empirical studies on this subject. However, the former *Conseil* and then the *Autorité*'s annual reports since 2004 provide a better understanding of these trends and some explanations for them. Two interesting features of this evolution can be underlined here.

First, over time, the French competition authority progressively focused on the most harmful conduct, even if this development has not yet led to the complete

9. Articles L. 450-1 et seq. Commercial Code.
10. Articles L. 461-1 et seq. Commercial Code.
11. Articles L. 462-1 et seq. Commercial Code.
12. Articles L. 463-1 et seq. Commercial Code.
13. Articles L. 464-1 et seq. Commercial Code.
14. Aut. Conc., Decision No. 21-D-11 (2021): Google was sentenced to EUR 220 million fine for favouring its own services in the online advertising sector. The case was settled and Google proposed commitments to end the trial. Aut. Conc., Decision No. 21-D-17 (2021): Google was sentenced to a EUR 500 million fine in a case where it was suspected to breach the IP rights of major French media groups and did not comply with several injunctions imposed by a previous decision. As the previous one, the case was settled by a commitments decision by another decision: Aut. Conc., Decision No. 22-D-13 (2022).

disappearance of low-stakes cases.[15] This evolution was experienced mostly in anti-competitive agreement enforcement. Bid-rigging cases, which accounted for up to a third of the former *Conseil*'s decisions in the 1990s, have been replaced by nationwide cartels between producers or suppliers. In the same period, vertical agreement litigation has decreased significantly.

It is not easy to explain this feature, but it seems to be the result of a combination of procedural reforms and spontaneous changes in stakeholders' behaviour. Among the procedural reforms, at least four devices have helped the authority to refocus its activity on the most serious cartels. It should also be noted that all these procedural developments date from the same period (between 2008 and 2011) and roughly coincide with the very first years of the *Autorité's* activity:

- Since 2008, the *Rapporteur general* has been empowered to conduct investigations on his own initiative without any prior procedure having been initiated.[16] This helped to uncover several harmful cartels.
- Since 2008, the Minister of the Economy has had a special competence to deal with local cartels and abuses (*'micro-pratiques anticoncurrentielles'*) through negotiated procedures[17] which relieved the *Autorité* of cases of minor importance.
- Progress in leniency procedures helped to detect hardcore cartels.
- The *Autorité* has made more systematic use of its power to open *ex officio* cases and directed toward serious infringements,[18] as shown by the figures taken from its annual report: eight in 2009, three in 2013, but twenty-one in 2018 and twenty-two in 2019.[19]

Regarding the decrease in the number of vertical agreement cases, three evolutions may have played a role:

- The new 2010 block exemption regulations have dried up cases.
- Vertical agreement cases are now brought more frequently to courts in stand-alone actions.
- A particularly active complainant - the astonishing Mr Chapelle, a home electronics equipment retailer - who was able to bring several cases a year before the former *Conseil* retired.

15. *See* on this trend: Laurence Idot, Réflexions sur l'évolution de la preuve des pratiques anticoncurrentielles devant les autorités de concurrence, novembre 2017, Concurrences N° 4-2017, Article N° 84879, pp. 45-59.
16. Article L. 450, I. Commercial Code.
17. Articles L. 464-9 et seq. Commercial Code.
18. Article L. 462-5, III. Commercial Code. As recalled at section 1.3, it is important to note that the *Autorité* has only had the power to set its own priorities, like the Commission, since the transposition of the ECN + Directive. It is therefore since this transposition that it can reject a complaint for lack of priority.
19. This is a significant change compared to the 2010s: *see* Ali Massadeh, *Empirical Assessment of Public Enforcement of Competition Law: Criteria and Three Case Studies (EU, UK and France)*. Doctoral thesis, University of East Anglia (2015), https://ueaeprints.uea.ac.uk/id/eprint/67068/1/A_Massadeh_4130626_final_thesis_Jan_15.pdf, p. 186.

Second feature: the evolution of the enforcement structure has also been accompanied by a notable development of abuse of dominant position enforcement. This development first concerned network industries involving former State-owned companies. In the telecommunications sector, Orange's practices (former France Telecom) gave rise to a significant number of cases,[20] but the energy and transport sector was also at the heart of certain widely commented trials against EDF[21] or GDF (now Engie).[22] Abuse of dominant position enforcement has also diversified. In recent years, the rapid development of the digital economy has led the *Autorité*, like some of its European counterparts, to initiate proceedings against the GAFA. For instance, Google has been recently prosecuted before the *Autorité* in several high-profile cases.[23]

1.3.3 *Decrease in the Number of Cases Handled by the French Competition Authority*

Third trend: the number of decisions handed down in antitrust cases by the French competition authority has fallen. For example, in 2005, the former *Conseil* issued seventy-nine decisions on the merits in antitrust cases, whereas, in 2017, the *Autorité* issued only twenty-seven decisions.

This can be partly explained by the refocusing of the enforcement activity on high-stakes cases, but not exclusively. The main explanation seems to me to be a reduction in the overall number of referrals since 2008. More specifically, two types of referrals have fallen significantly, as the tables below show: referrals from the Minister for the Economy and referrals from undertakings. For instance, the number of cases referred to the former *Conseil* and then to the *Autorité* by the Minister fell from sixteen in 2006 to six in 2008 and zero in 2011, 2012, 2013 and 2018. Although referrals by the Minister for the Economy are still possible, they are now unusual. This trend was depicted in an annual report as the consequence of the creation of the *Autorité*, a more powerful authority than the former *Conseil*, and that has been empowered with some of the Minister's responsibilities.[24] As a result, the Minister seems to have partially disengaged from the enforcement of competition law. Regarding the decline in the number of cases referred by undertakings, we note that it fell from thirty-nine in 2009 (the peak) to eighteen in 2013 and then around twenty since 2016 (thirty-six in 2015).

20. For instance: Cons. Conc., Decision No. 01-D-46 (2001); Cons. Conc., Decision No. 05-D-59 (2005); Cons. Conc., Decision No. 07-D-33 (2007); Aut. Conc., Decision No. 09-D-36 (2009); Aut. Conc., Decision No. 15-D-20 (2015). In the last decision the *Autorité* fined Orange EUR 350 million for having abusively hindered the development of competition in the business market. In the previous decisions, the same kind of practices was also found unlawful.
21. Aut. Conc., Decision No. 22-D-06 (2022); Aut. Conc., Decision No. 13-D-20 (2013).
22. Aut. Conc., Decision No. 17-D-06 (2017); Aut. Conc., Decision No. 14-MC-02 (2014).
23. Aut. Conc., Decision No. 22-D-13 (2022), *relative à des pratiques mises en œuvre par Google dans le secteur de la presse*; Aut. Conc., Decision No. 21-D-17 (2021) *relative au respect des injonctions prononcées à l'encontre de Google dans la décision n° 20-MC-01 du 9 avril 2020*; Aut. Conc., Decision No. 21-D-11 (2021), *relative à des pratiques mises en œuvre dans le secteur de la publicité sur Internet;* Aut. Conc., Decision No. 19-D-26 (2019) *relative à des pratiques mises en œuvre dans le secteur de la publicité en ligne liée aux recherches;* Aut. Conc., Decision No. 19-MC-01 (2019) *relative à une demande de mesures conservatoires de la société Amadeus.*
24. Aut. Conc., *Rapport annuel 2008*, p. 49.

I have no explanation for this other than a change in mentality and perhaps the development of stand-alone private enforcement.

1.4 French Competition Law Cases Outside the Scope of This Study

In order to have an overview of the application of competition law in France, it would be necessary to include certain provisions of domestic competition law that sanction behaviour other than those prohibited by Articles 101 and 102 of the TFEU- albeit they fall outside the specific scope of this study. One may consider, in particular, the abuse of economic dependence (*'abus de dépendance économique'*) prohibited by Article L. 420-2, paragraph 2 of the Commercial Code.[25] The prohibition of this 'other' abuse was included in the French Commercial Code to address the unresolved problem of unbalanced contractual relations in the food supply chain. As none of the powerful French groups operating the main networks of supermarkets (e.g. Carrefour, Leclerc, Auchan, Intermarchés) is in a dominant position, it was proven impossible to combat their contractual abuses under Article 102 of the TFEU or its French counterpart. The notion of economic dependence was created to address this market power that operates as a sort of relative dominance.[26] This prohibition also falls within the competence of the French competition authority and is subject to the same reviewing proceedings before the Paris Court of Appeal and the Court of Cassation. For example, in 2020, Apple was fined a record amount of more than EUR 1 billion for an abuse of economic dependence.[27]

This type of case is still quite rare, and as noted, most of the French competition authority's enforcement has been focused in the past fifteen years on cartels and abuses of dominant position.[28]

---

25. This article provides that: 'The abuse of the state of economic dependence of a client or supplier by an undertaking or group of undertakings is also prohibited, if it is likely to affect the functioning or structure of competition. This abuse may include a refusal to sell, tie-in sales or discriminatory practices mentioned (...).'
26. Economic dependence is established according to the usual criteria used to define a dominant position (market shares, notoriety etc.) except that the point of reference is not the market but the economic relationship. For example, an undertaking which achieves 100% of its turnover with another powerful contractor may be in a situation of economic dependence on its contractor even if the latter does not dominate the market.
27. Aut. Conc., Decision No. 20-D-04 (2020) – the *Autorité* fined Apple EUR 1.1 billion, as well as two wholesalers: Tech Data and Ingram Micro EUR 76.1 million and EUR 62.9 million, respectively. However, the amount of these fines was significantly reduced by the Paris Court of Appeal.
28. There are also three other 'typically French' anti-competitive practices that follow the provisions on anti-competitive agreements and abuses of dominant position: abusive low prices (Article L. 420-5), the prohibition of exclusive import rights in overseas markets (Article L. 420-2-1) and the prohibition of certain commercial practices in passenger transport. These prohibitions are more rarely enforced and give a good idea of the clumsiness of the French legislator. The latter has thus inserted in the Commercial Code these three anti-competitive practices which also fall within the competence of the French competition authority without any in-depth reflection on their articulation with the prohibitions of cartels and abuses of dominant position.

2 JUDICIAL REVIEW OF COMPETITION DECISIONS IN FRANCE

2.1 A Dualist Court System

Review procedures against the *Autorité*'s decisions are subject to a rather complex regime:

- Merger decisions are reviewed by the *Conseil d'Etat*, the supreme court of the administrative order.[29]
- Antitrust decisions, on the other hand, are reviewed by an ordinary court - the Paris Court of Appeal - and then the Commercial Chamber of the Court of Cassation, the supreme court of the ordinary order. This is a derogation from a fundamental principle of French law which reserves to the administrative order the annulment or reversal of decisions taken by executive bodies in the exercise of the prerogatives of public power. This exception was validated by the *Conseil constitutionnel*, the French Constitutional Court[30] and the *Conseil d'Etat*, which has adopted an extensive conception of it.[31] Within the Paris Court of Appeal, a specialised chamber, the *chambre de la régulation économique et financière*, most known by its number: chamber 7 of division 5 (noted chamber 5-7), is systematically designated to rule on appeals against the *Autorité*'s decisions. This chamber is composed of four professional judges (in January 2023) who have expertise in competition law. In general, these judges go back and forth between the *Autorité* and the Paris Court of Appeal. Some of them also reach the Commercial Chamber of the Court of Cassation, where they hear appeals against decisions of the Paris Court of Appeal. Recently (end of 2020), two economic advisers were added to the four professional judges of chamber 5-7.

The decisions covered by this study are therefore the judgments of this chamber of the Paris Court of Appeal and those of the Commercial Chamber of the Court of Cassation.

That said, the procedures before these two chambers and their respective powers require a number of clarifications.

29. Article R. 311-1 Administrative Justice Code: 'The *Conseil d'État* is competent to hear appeals in the first and last instance (...) '4o (...) against decisions taken by the bodies of the following authorities in the exercise of their supervisory or regulatory functions: (...) the *Autorité de la concurrence* (...).' The Conseil itself added in a landmark judgment that: 'In the absence of an express legislative provision derogating from this principle, it is up to this court to hear the legality of acts taken for the application of Article L. 430-9 of the French Commercial Code, which appears in Title III of Book IV, relating to economic concentration.' (CE, 7 November 2005, No. 271982).
30. Cons. const., dec. No. 86224 DC, 23 January 1987, *Rec. Cons. const.*, p. 8.
31. CE, 6th and 2nd ss-sect, 21 October, 1998, No. 174803, *Union des coopératives agricoles – Union laitière normande, RJDA* 1999, No. 98 concerning an appeal against a decision of the *Conseil de la concurrence* refusing to withdraw its decision imposing a sanction.

2.2 The *Recours en Réformation et en Annulation*: The Review Procedure in the Paris Court of Appeal

2.2.1 Scope and Intensity of Judicial Review Exercised by the Paris Court of Appeal

In the French legal system, there is a distinction between the notions of *réformation* that may be translated by 'appeal' and *annulation* that may be translated by 'judicial review'. *Réformation* refers to the merits of the case, allowing the court to substitute the decision of the primary decision-maker. *Annulation*, by comparison, is linked to the validity of the decision rather than its merits. For example, if a court's composition is not regular, its decision can be annulled even though it would not have been reformed on the merits.

An *appel* is a common review procedure - *voie de recours* - that allows the *appellant* to seek the *réformation* and/or the *annulation* of the previous judgment in one of the thirty-seven French courts of appeal. This *appel* is ruled by the general rule of the Code of Civil Procedure.[32]

That said, the review procedure in the Paris Court of Appeal against the *Autorité*'s decisions is not exactly an *appel*. It is a *sui generis* review procedure, called *recours en réformation et en annulation*, ruled by the special provisions of the Commercial Code.[33] Only in the absence of clear rules in the Commercial Code on certain points of law are the general rules of the Code of Civil Procedure on *appel* applicable.

The scope and intensity of judicial review exercised by the Paris Court of Appeal are not governed by any statutory provisions. The procedural provisions of the Commercial Code only regulate procedural delays and procedural acts and specify the modalities of participation in the proceedings of each stakeholder.[34]

However, the case law provides several solutions that bring the appeal before the Paris Court of Appeal into line with European standards. Generally, the judicial review exercised by the Paris Court of Appeal bears similarities to the scrutiny carried out by the General Court in the EU. Therefore, the scope of the appeal depends on the nature of the decision, and the Court may either accept the appeal fully or partially and may annul fully or partially, modify the challenged decision, or it may reject the appeal.

But three further observations can be made.

First, the Court has full jurisdiction on questions of fact and questions of law for usual infringement decisions,[35] whereas its role is more limited to decisions accepting commitments,[36] according to the *Alrosa* ruling,[37] settlements decisions[38] and leniency

32. Articles 542 et seq. and 899 et seq. Code of Civil Procedure.
33. Article L. 464-8 paras. 1 and 2 Commercial Code.
34. Article R. 464-11 - R. 464-24 Commercial Code.
35. Cass. com., 10 May 2006, No. 05-14.501 and No. 05-15.187, *Bull. civ.* 2006, IV, No. 115.
36. The Court of Appeal's review is limited to the *Autorité's* manifest error of assessment as to whether the facts complained of by the plaintiffs - generally the appellants - are or are not competition concerns: Paris Court of Appeal, 19 December 2013, No. 2012/19484.
37. CJEU, Case C-441/07, *Alrosa*, paras 59-69, 94 and 115.
38. The Court admitted appeals against these decisions: Paris Court of Appeal, 13 June 2019, No. 18/20229, *Alcyon c/ Ministre chargé de l'Économie.*

decisions. For the latter, the Court is only empowered to verify the legality of the leniency agreement considering the statutory rules.[39]

Second, the legality of the *Autorité's* decision will be assessed to the extent that this has been challenged and within the limits of the submitted grounds for reformation or annulment. Thus, the Court is not empowered to review the contested decision in its entirety on its own motion.

However, and this is the third point, when the Court annuls, and not only reforms, all or part of the *Autorité*'s decision, its role needs to be clarified. The Court is then not allowed to refer the case back to the *Autorité* and must decide on each of the points raised in the statement of objections and on which the *Autorité*'s previous ruling has been annulled.[40] Nevertheless, there is an important limitation to this rule. If the *Autorité*'s decision is annulled because of insufficient investigation, the Paris Court of Appeal has to refer the case back to the *Autorité* to further investigate the case,[41] as it is not empowered to undertake its own investigation.

2.2.2 *Period to Lodge an Appeal with the Paris Court of Appeal*

Article L. 464-8 of the Commercial Code provides that the Autorité's decisions are notified to the Minister of the Economy and to the parties involved. They then have one month to lodge an appeal with the Paris Court of Appeal.

2.2.3 *Defendants' and Complainants' Participation*

The appeal is open to the parties involved, i.e., those whose complaint has been declared inadmissible or rejected or those who have been subject to an injunction or a fine.[42] The notion of party involved is interpreted strictly. For instance, undertakings that only answered to requests for information from investigative services are not considered as parties. Consequently, they don't have standing to lodge an appeal.[43]

If they have not appealed, the undertakings that took part in the proceedings before the *Autorité* also have the right to intervene in the proceedings before the Paris Court of Appeal. As provided for in Article R. 464-17 paragraph 1 of the Commercial Code: 'Where the appeal may affect the rights or obligations of other persons who were

39. Article L. 464-2, IV Commercial Code; Paris Court of Appeal, 19 January 2010; *Contrats, conc. consom.* 2010, comm. 79, obs. G. Decocq; Cass. com., 14 April, 2015, No. 12-15.971.
40. Cass. com., 31 January 2006, No. 04-20.360; Cass. com., 27 September 2005, No. 04-16.677, Bull. civ. 2005, IV, No. 181, p. 195.
41. Cass. com., 26 February 2008, No. 07-14.126, *Bull. civ.* 2008, IV, No. 44; *RLDA* 2008, No. 1580, obs. C. Anadon; *RLC* 2008, No. 1110, obs. B. C., *BRDA* 2008, No. 6, No. 29, *D.* 2008, p. 844, obs. E. Chevrier.
42. Article L. 464-8 Commercial Code.
43. Paris Court of Appeal, 11 March 2003, *Chronopost et al. v. Ufex et al., BOCCRF* 11 July 2003.

parties before the Competition Authority, such persons may intervene in the proceedings before the Court of Appeal.'[44]

It should also be noted that at any time during the proceedings, the Paris Court of Appeal, through its President, may also call into question *ex officio* the parties who have not appealed and have not intervened in the proceedings.

2.2.4 Minister of the Economy's Participation

An appeal is also open to the Minister of the Economy[45] who will then be considered as a party. Moreover, even if he/she does not lodge an appeal, the Minister may intervene in the procedure.[46] In this case, he/she is not a party and will not be able to make an application to the Court of Appeal (e.g., confirmation of a fine or rejection of a complaint) but will be able to develop arguments in writing and orally at the hearing.

2.2.5 The Autorité*'s Participation*

The participation of the Autorité itself has given rise to developments in case law and legislation.

Prior to the *Vebic* judgment of the Court of Justice,[47] former Article R. 464-11 of the French Commercial Code provided that in an appeal proceeding before the Paris Court of Appeal against its decisions, the former *Conseil* shall not be a party to the proceedings. The Conseil only had the right, through its President, to appeal to the Court of Cassation. This procedural framework was contrary to the interpretation of the Court of Justice, which requires national competition authorities to participate in the reviewing proceedings.

In a judgment of 17 January 2012,[48] the Court of Cassation admitted, as required by Article R. 464-11 of the Commercial Code, the admissibility of the appeal lodged by the President of the *Autorité* in the Court of Cassation, but it added, based on the same text, that the *Autorité* also had the status of party before the Paris Court of Appeal. Subsequently, a *Décret* introduced new provisions aiming to bring French statutory provisions into line with the Court of Justice's requirements.[49] A new Article R. 464-11 of the Commercial Code now provides that 'the Competition Authority shall be a party to the proceedings in accordance with the procedures laid down in this chapter'.[50]

---

44. Unofficial translation of the French provisions: '*Lorsque le recours risque d'affecter les droits ou les charges d'autres personnes qui étaient parties en cause devant l'Autorité de la concurrence, ces personnes peuvent intervenir à l'instance devant la cour d'appel.*'
45. Article L. 464-8 Commercial Code.
46. Article L. 490-8 Commercial Code.
47. CJEU, Case C-4397, *Vebic* (2010).
48. Cass. com., 17 January 2012, No. 11-13.067.
49. *Décret* No. 2012-840, 29 June 2012 *relatif aux recours exercés devant la cour d'appel de Paris contre les décisions de l'Autorité de la concurrence: JORF* 1 July 2012, p. 10838.
50. Unofficial translation of the French provisions: '*L'Autorité de la concurrence est partie à l'instance selon les modalités prévues au présent chapitre.*'

2.2.6 *Third Parties' Rights*

The French review system provides some rights for third parties, allowing interested parties to participate in the proceedings before the Paris Court of Appeal in accordance with the general rules on appeals.[51] For instance, in a recent decision, the Paris Court of Appeal admitted the intervention of an undertaking in an appeal procedure initiated by Google following an infringement decision.[52] This undertaking considered that it had been the victim of Google's abuse of a dominant position and was therefore able to join the appeal to defend its views.

2.3 The *Pourvoi en Cassation*: The Review Procedure in the Court of Cassation

The *pourvoi en cassation* – or 'appeal in cassation' according to an official translation of the Code of Civil Procedure that used to be published on légifrance.gouv.fr – can be brought in one of the six chambers of the Court of Cassation against a previous decision of a Court of Appeal or even a court of first instance for cases that are not appealable (claims below EUR 5,000). For competition litigation, the Commercial Chamber (noted Cass. com.) has jurisdiction.

The *pourvoi* 'tend(s) to ask the Court of Cassation to quash the non-conformity of the judgement to the rules of law'.[53] In other words, the Court shall not rule on the merits but only on the points of law.[54]

For example, the Court of Cassation can verify that the Paris Court of Appeal and before it, the *Autorité*, have applied properly the rules for calculating a fine (e.g., the 10% threshold has been respected), but it cannot substitute its own fine to the one imposed by the Court or the *Autorité*. It can also verify that all the conditions for qualifying an abuse or a cartel have been applied (e.g., the relevant market has been defined or the notion of anti-competitive object has been correctly applied), but it will not examine the evidence to rule on the responsibility of the defendant companies.

3 PRIOR RESEARCH

To my knowledge, no academic study comparable to the present project has been undertaken in relation to judicial review of the competition authority's decisions in France. This may be because the former *Conseil* and the *Autorité* have been publishing

51. Article 554 of the Code of Civil Procedure.
52. Paris Court of Appeal, 7 January 2021, No. 20/03811, *Amadeus*.
53. Article 604 Code of Civil Procedure.
54. The Court of Cassation itself defines its role as follows: 'it does not constitute a third level of jurisdiction above the lower courts and the courts of appeal. It is mostly called upon not to decide on the merits of the case, but to say whether the rules of law have been correctly applied, based on the facts sovereignly assessed in the decisions. (...). It acts in fact as the judge of the judges' rulings: its role is to say whether they have applied the law correctly in the light of the facts, determined by them alone, of the case submitted to them and the questions put to them'. https://www.courdecassation.fr/en/about-court.

very comprehensive statistics on their activities in their annual report since 2004. It could also be explained by the fact that this type of research is unusual in French legal studies.[55] Only four studies have adopted a methodology comparable to the one proposed here, with a more limited scope. Not surprisingly, three of them were not carried out by French scholars: those of Annalies Outhuijse,[56] Ali Massadeh[57] and Or Brook.[58] The last one was conducted by a French professor based in Belgium, assisted by a lawyer in a Brussels law firm: Nicolas Petit & Louise Rabeux.[59]

Annalies Outhuijse's paper is the closest to the present study.[60] She studied Court review of cartel cases in 10 EU Member States, including France from 1 January 2009 to 31 July 2017. She focused on fines review and showed that out of 56 cases, the appeal rate was 61% (34 of 56 cases), and the success rate was 50% (17 of 34 cases).[61]

Ali Massadeh's findings are also interesting. Although he mainly focused on the enforcement activity of the French competition authority between 2004 and 2012, he devoted a short but enlightening section to the review of the Paris Court of Appeal.[62] He found that out of 138 infringement decisions, 78 were appealed and reached the following outcome: 37 were upheld (26%), 12 were largely upheld (8.7%), 11 were partly upheld (7.9%), 4 were annulled (2.9%) and the remaining 14 cases were pending. He also highlighted that 'when the fine is high, the likelihood of appealing the FCA's decision is higher. Whereas, when the fine is comparatively low the possibility of appealing a decision is much lower'.[63]

Or Brook has coded all of the enforcement of Article 101 TFEU and the national equivalent provisions by the French NCA and courts from the entry into force of Regulation 1/2003 to 2017. Her research points to some general enforcement patterns of those provisions yet focuses on the consideration of public policy within the enforcement.

---

55. If not despised: Alain Bernard, 'Law and Economics, une science idiote?', *Recueil Dalloz*, No. 40, 2008, p. 2806.
56. Annalies Outhuijse, 'Effective Public Enforcement of Cartels: Rates of Challenged and Annulled Cartel Fines in Ten European Member States' (2019) 42(2) World Competition, pp. 171-204, https://kluwerlawonline.com/journalarticle/World+Competition/42.2/WOCO2019013 DOI: 10.54648/woco2019013.
57. Ali Massadeh, *Empirical Assessment of Public Enforcement of Competition Law: Criteria and Three Case Studies (EU, UK and France)*. Doctoral thesis, University of East Anglia, (2015); https://ueaeprints.uea.ac.uk/id/eprint/67068/1/A_Massadeh_4130626_final_thesis_Jan_15.pdf.
58. Or Brook, Non-competition Interests in EU Antitrust Law. In Non-competition Interests in EU Antitrust Law: An Empirical Study of Article 101 TFEU (Global Competition Law and Economics Policy, p. I). Cambridge: Cambridge University Press (2022).
59. Nicolas Petit and Louise Rabeux, Judicial Review in French Competition Law and Economic Regulation – A Post-Commission v. Tetra Laval Assessment (26 October 2008). Available at SSRN: https://ssrn.com/abstract=1290143 or http://dx.doi.org/10.2139/ssrn.1290143.
60. Or Brook focused on non-competition interest in the enforcement of Article 101 TFEU and Nicolas Petit and Louise Rabeux only seeked, thank to qualitative analysis, to assess the standard of judicial review in France between 2005 and 2008 (*ibid.*, pp. 16-18).
61. Annalies Outhuijse, *supra*, p. 178.
62. Ali Massadeh, *supra*, pp. 204-212.
63. *Ibid.*, p. 211.

Mention should also be made of a report commissioned by the Ministry of the Economy in 2010 on the fines imposed by the former *Conseil*.[64] This report did not carry out a statistical analysis as undertaken in this study, but based on a qualitative study of several emblematic cases, it came to a rather worrying conclusion about the fining policy of the French authority and the Court of Appeal.[65]

4 QUANTITATIVE ANALYSIS

This section moves to examine the findings resulting from applying systematic content analysis of a review of competition law enforcement by French courts between May 2004 and April 2021.

4.1 Source of Information

It is only since 2016 that there has been an obligation to publish online all courts and administrative authorities' decisions.[66] Previously, French constitutional rules, Article 6, § 1 of the ECHR and various domestic rules[67] only required that such decisions be 'public' in the legal sense of the word, meaning that they had to be accessible to anyone who requested them but not necessarily published online.

As regards the *Autorité*'s decisions, since 2009, a special rule in the Commercial Code already required online publication.[68] But the *Autorité*'s services had anticipated this legal duty by publishing all decisions on the *Autorité*'s website on their own initiative. As for the decisions of the Paris Court of Appeal and the Court of Cassation – the two main courts of the ordinary order – they are generally available on public and private databases, even if their online accessibility has only been mandatory since 2016.

Therefore, the database used for this study is presumed to be comprehensive. The judgments in the database were identified as primary via the *Autorité*'s website and were cross-checked using four databases: a public one[69] and three private ones.[70]

64. Folz-Schaub-Raysseguier, *Rapport sur l'appréciation de la sanction en matière de pratiques anticoncurrentielles*, September 2010, vie-publique.fr/rapport/31343-lappreciation-de-la-sanction-en-matiere-de-pratiques-anticoncurrentiell.
65. It deplored: 'a lack of consistency in the assessment of fines for anti-competitive practices between the *Autorité* and the Court of Appeal, which leaves companies in a state of legal uncertainty. This divergence of approach highlights the need to define a more precise method for assessing fines'. (p. 18).
66. *Loi* No. 2016-1321 of 7 October 2016 *pour une République numérique* (Articles 20 and 21). This *Loi* was specified for court decisions by two subsequent instruments: *Loi* No. 2019-222 of 23 March 2019 *de programmation de 2018-2022 et de réforme pour la justice* (Article 33) and *Décret* No. 2020-797 of 29 June 2020 *relatif à la mise à la disposition du public des décisions des juridictions judiciaires et administratives*.
67. Article 11-2 *Loi* n° 72-626 du 5 juillet 1972 instituant un juge de l'exécution et relative à la réforme de la procédure civile ; CE, 4 october 1974, No. 88930, *David*, publié au recueil Lebon (N° Lexbase: A3098B7U), p. 464.
68. Article D. 464-8-1 Commercial Code.
69. légifrance.gouv.fr.
70. concurrences.com, dalloz.fr and lexis360.fr.

As noted, since 2004, the former *Conseil* and the *Autorité* have also published very informative annual reports. These reports provide detailed statistics and I have often referred to them to check that the broad level of the figures provided in this report were comparable. However, it should be noted that the *Conseil* and the *Autorité*'s figures essentially reflect their volumes of activity. They are not intended to support a qualitative analysis such as that provided in this study. For example, when the *Autorité* publishes figures on the number of appeals, it does not distinguish between appeals against infringement decisions and appeals against rejection decisions. This type of distinction is relevant to this study, which is why some of the results discussed here complement those of the annual reports of the former *Conseil* and the *Autorité*.

4.2 Total Number of Judgments and Ratio of Appeals

A total of 297 relevant judgments were rendered during the temporal scope of the study: 199 by the Paris Court of Appeal in first instance and 98 by the Court of Cassation in second instance.

This number of judgments pertains to 164 different former *Conseil* and *Autorité*'s decisions that were appealed in the first instance and judgments of the Paris Court of Appeal that were appealed in the second instance. Compiling the figures published each year since 2004 by the former *Conseil* and by the *Autorité* in their annual report, 635 decisions could have been appealed.[71] This means that the appeal rate for the French competition authority's decisions is 26%. Fifteen per cent of the Paris Court of Appeal judgments have been subsequently appealed to the Court of Cassation.

Figure 12.1 Judgments per Year According to Instances

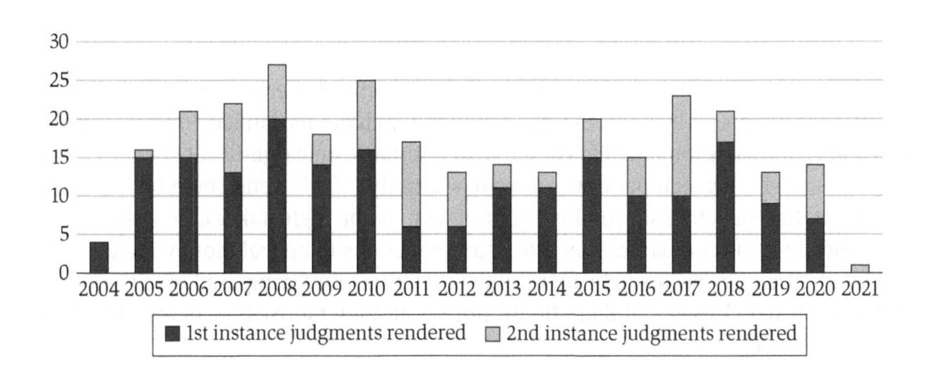

71. This number was calculated on the basis of the figures provided by the *Conseil* and the *Autorité* in their annual reports. It does not take into account decisions on interim measures or decisions declaring that the complainant has withdrawn. However, it does include infringements decisions, commitments decisions, decisions to reject a complaint or to dismiss a case following an investigation as these decisions may be appealed. These decisions are those noted 'D' by the NCA in its reports.

Figure 12.2(a) First-Instance Judgments

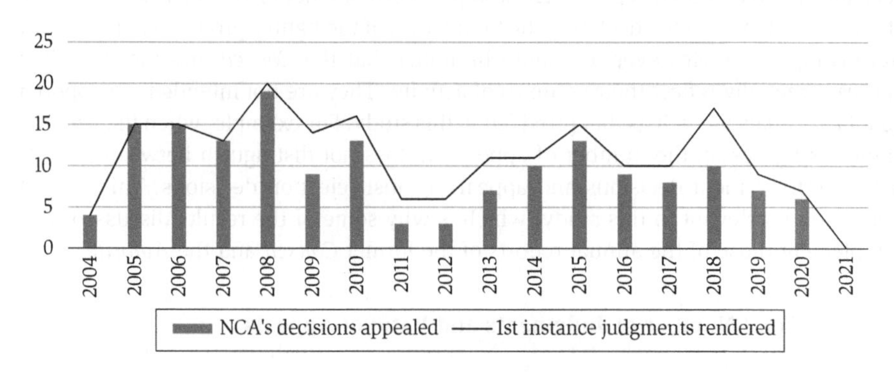

Figure 12.2(b) Second-Instance Judgments

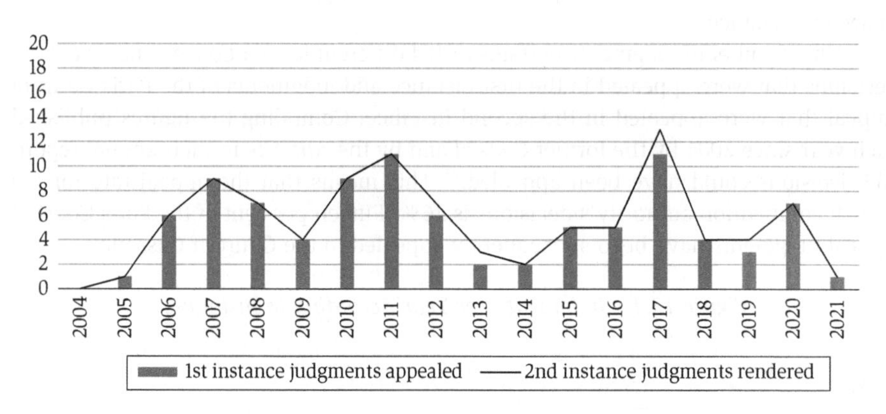

Figure 12.1 summarises the number of judgments issued per year according to the instance of appeal. It shows that the number of judgments handed down by the two reviewing courts has remained fairly stable over time despite significant changes in the volume of the French competition authority's activity.[72] This trend could be explained by the fact that the refocusing of the *Autorité's* activity on high-stakes cases (*see* section 1.3) logically leads companies that risk heavy sanctions to appeal more willingly. The appeal rate therefore seems to be increasing in relative terms compared with the period when the former *Conseil* and then the *Autorité* dealt with more cases, many of them of minor importance.

For instance, the appeal rate on NCA decisions was high in 2013 (43%), in 2014 (64%) and in 2019 (44%) and significantly lower in 2004 (28%), in 2009 (29%) or 2010 (20%).

72. This decrease is particularly noticeable from 2011 onwards. The *Autorité* itself explains it in its annual report by a decrease in the number of referrals by economic operators: 30 referrals in 2011, 57 in 2007, 47 in 2004. *See* Aut. Conc., *Rapport annuel 2011*, p. 13.

These figures seem to me to be consistent with those of Annalies Outhuijse (2019) for cartel cases, which show an overall appeal rate of 61% over the period 2009-2017.[73] As cartel cases generally result in high penalties, the appeal rate is logically higher than the average rate of all infringements combined.

Figure 12.2 indicates the number of judgments issued per year according to each instance (lines), in comparison to the number of the French competition authority's decisions (Figure 12.2(a)) and the Paris Court of Appeal's judgments (Figure 12.2(b)) that were appealed. The figure reveals that appeals of some of the competition authority's decisions were examined in several different proceedings in front of the Paris Court of Appeals. However, the judgments of the Paris Court of Appeal have almost always been the subject of a single cassation procedure and, therefore, of a single review judgment.

4.3 Success Rates and Outcomes

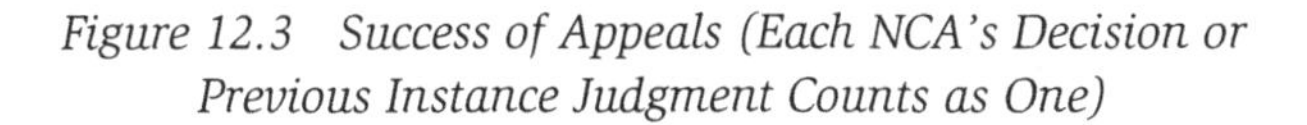

Figure 12.3 Success of Appeals (Each NCA's Decision or Previous Instance Judgment Counts as One)

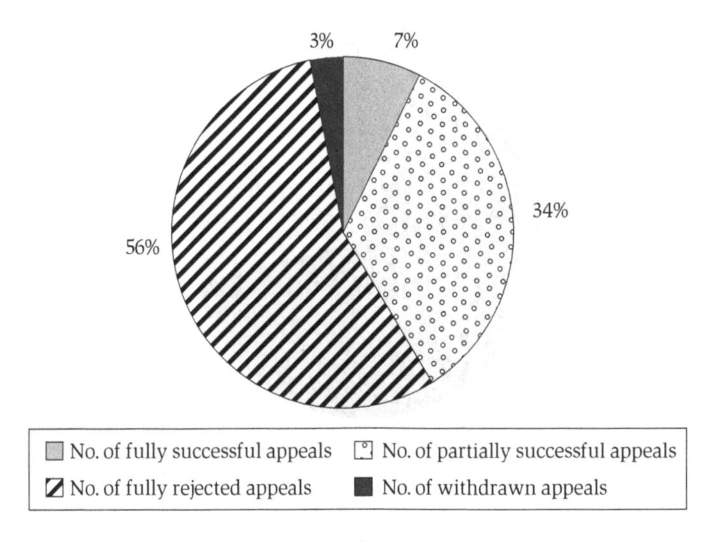

Figure 12.3 presents the success of appeals launched against either NCA's decisions or a prior review court instance's judgment. It indicates the ratio of fully successful appeals, partially successful appeals, fully rejected appeals, and appeals that were withdrawn prior to adopting a judgment. It shows that 56% of the appeals were fully rejected. Forty-one per cent were either partially (34%) or fully (7%) successful. The partially successful category includes cases where either substantive aspects of the infringement decision were overturned or set aside (or there was a success in some appeals but no other separate appeals in relation to the same infringement decision) and cases where the original penalty was reduced in some way (see discussion below).

73. Annalies Outhuijse, *supra*.

Figure 12.4(a) First-Instance Outcome

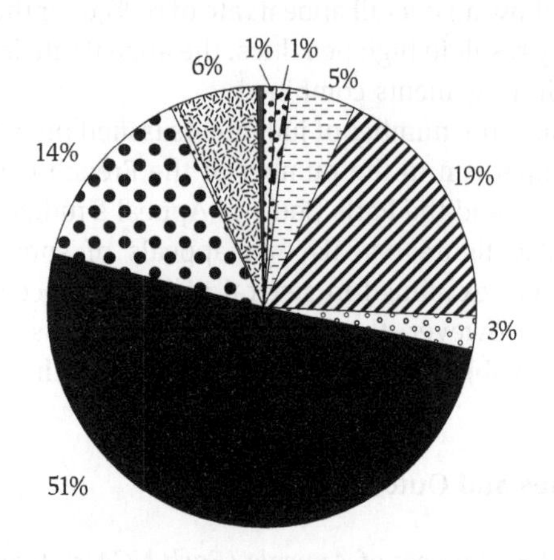

Figure 12.4(b) Second-Instance Outcome

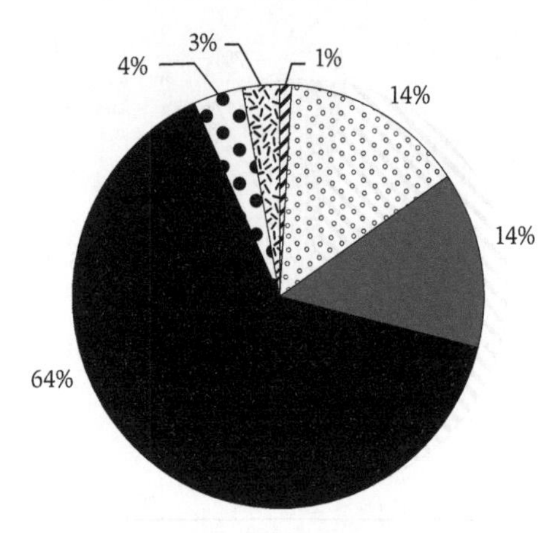

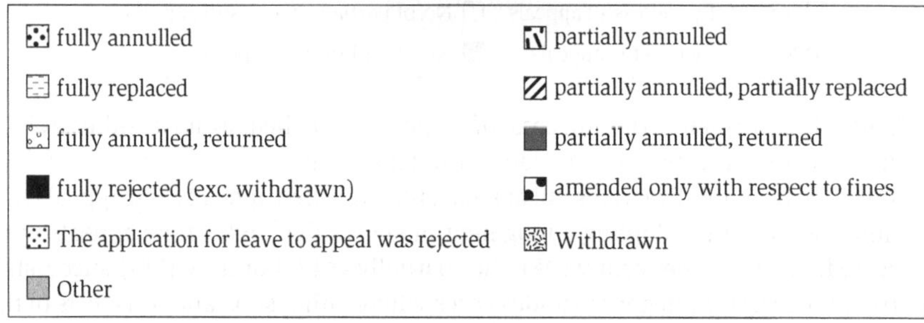

Figure 12.4 indicates the ratio of outcomes of appeals according to each instance. In contrast with Figure 12.3, the data is presented from the perspective of each separate judgment and differs between the appeal's instances. The figure demonstrates that

second-instance appeals were fully rejected more often than first-instance appeals (64% and 51%, respectively).

Figure 12.4(a) shows that in 57% of its judgments, the Paris Court of Appeal did not modify the decisions of the French competition authority, either because the appeal was totally rejected (51%) or withdrawn (6%). Consequently, this means that in 43% of its judgments, the Paris Court of Appeal fully or partially annulled and/or changed the *Autorité's* decision, including 14% of judgments that amended the decision only with respect to the fines.

Only 9% of the Paris Court of Appeal's judgments fully annulled and/or replaced the competition authority's decision. In other words, the court at least partially confirmed 91% of the *Autorité's* decisions. A qualitative analysis also tends to show that, with rare exceptions, partial reversals are, in most cases, on relatively minor points. The following are examples of this point: the material participation of one undertaking was not established, but the unlawful conduct remains established for all others;[74] the facts were time-barred;[75] part of the conduct was not unlawful;[76] the wording of the publication at the expense of the infringing public entity was not accurate;[77] the duration of the infringement was reduced,[78] EU law was not applicable, only French law,[79] etc.

These figures are consistent with those published by the *Autorité* in its annual reports, as the tables below tend to show.

Figure 12.4(b) summarises the outcome of the cases decided by the Court of Cassation. The figure shows that when the Court of Cassation accepted all or some of the arguments of the applicants, it mostly returned the case back to the Paris Court of Appeal, for re-examination of the case.

It is important to note that due to the peculiarities of the role of the Court of Cassation discussed above, the outcome of its judgments does not always coincide precisely with the classification of outcomes in this project (*see* section 1.2). This is the case, for

74. Paris Court of Appeal, 9 November 2004, No. 04/08123, *See Camille Bayol et al.* against Aut. Conc. Decision No. 04-D-08 (2004); Paris Court of Appeal, 07 March 2007, No. 2005/12604, *Ineo et al.* against Aut. Conc., Decision No. 05-D-19 (2005); Paris Court of Appeal, 04 April 2006; No. 2005/14057, *Établissement Horticoles Georges Truffaut et al.* against Aut. Conc. Decision No. 05-D-32 (2005); Paris Court of Appeal, 25 April 2006, No. 2005/13773, *SADE – Compagnie Générale de Travaux d'Hydraulique* against Aut. Conc. Decision No. 05-D-26 (2005); Paris Court of Appeal, 19 June 2007, No. 2006/00628, *Philips France et al.* against Aut. Conc. Decision No. 05-D-66 (2005); Paris Court of Appeal, 03 July 2008, No. 2007/10671, *Eiffage Construction et al.* against Aut. Conc. Decision No. 07-D-15 (2007); Paris Court of Appeal, 26 October 2017, No. 2017/01658, *Groupe Caisse des dépôts et consignations et SCET* against Aut. Conc. Decision No. 16-D-28 (2016).
75. Paris Court of Appeal, 23 May 2006, No. 2005/20727, *DBS et al.* against Aut. Conc. Decision No. 05-D-51 (2005); Paris Court of Appeal, 04 July 2006, No. 2005/24344, *Unidoc*, against Aut. Conc. Decision No. 05-D-67 (2005).
76. Paris Court of Appeal, 26 September 2006, No. 2005/23649, *Le syndicat des eaux d'Île de France et al.* against Aut. Conc. Decision No. 05-D-58 (2005).
77. Paris Court of Appeal, 12 December 2006, No. 2006/01743, *Ministre de l'Economie (Monnaie de Paris)* against Aut. Conc. Decision No. 05-D-75 (2005).
78. Paris Court of Appeal, 06 May 2008, No. 07/06172, *Lafarge Ciments et al.* against Aut. Conc. Decision No.07-D-08 (2008).
79. Paris Court of Appeal, 15 September 2016, No. 2015/06968, *TDF et al.* against Aut. Conc. Decision No. 15-D-01 (2001).

example, in relation to the fine. When the Court of Cassation overturns an appeal judgment on the merits, it does not rule that the fine should be zero. It simply invites the Paris Court of Appeal to re-examine the case. If the infringement is not established after this second trial before the Court of Appeal, the amount of the fine may be zero. But it would be incorrect to consider that this amount has been established by the Court of Cassation. For this reason, for all decisions that lead to a partial or total reversal of the appeal judgment on the merits, the code referring to recalculation has been indicated as a result, even though the reversal may lead to the recalculation being zero.

Figure 12.4(b) shows that in 31% of its judgments, the Court of Cassation partially (14%) or fully (14%) accepted the appeals or amended it only with respect to the fine (2%).[80]

This rate is identical to the average rate of *cassation* of the commercial chamber of the Court of Cassation for all types of business litigation combined (around 31%[81]), and it is lower than the average rate of successful appeals in the Paris Court of Appeal. However, the qualitative analysis carried out below (*see* section 5.2) shows that overturning decisions tend to arise on important points at first instance, whereas overturning decisions issued by the Paris Court of Appeal seem to concern minor points.

4.4 Type of Competition Authority's Decisions Subject to Appeal

Figure 12.5 Rules Being Appealed

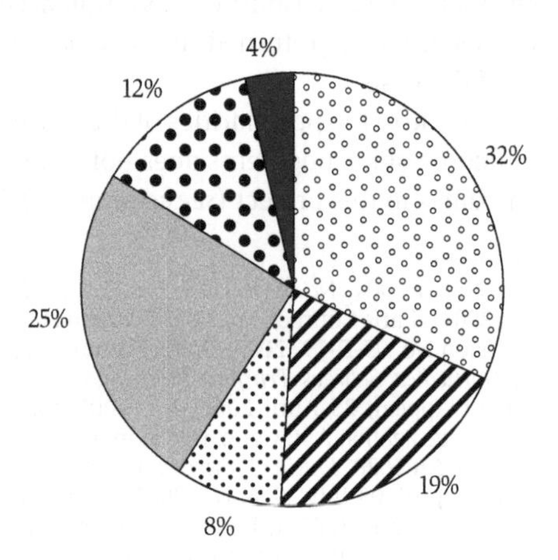

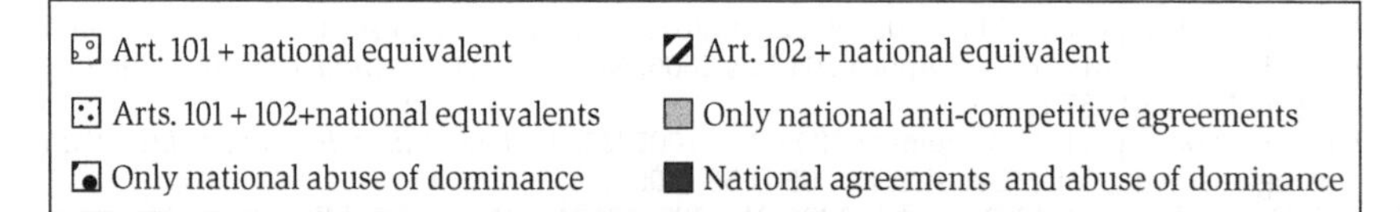

80. The remaining 1% being a decision that corrected a material error.
81. Cour of Cassation, *Rapport annuel 2020*, p. 263, Figure 5 d), published in the Court's website.

Figure 12.5 indicates the ratio of the different competition law prohibitions subject to the courts' review across all instances of appeal. It differentiates between the prohibition on anti-competitive agreements and abuse of dominance and between cases in which both the EU and the national equivalent prohibitions have been applied and purely national cases in which only the national equivalent prohibitions have been applied due to the absence of an effect on trade between Member States.

In terms of subject matter, it reveals that French courts have reviewed a relatively balanced mix of agreements cases (57%) and abuses cases (31%), the remaining judgments involving abuse plus agreements cases (12%).

This is in line with the diverse range of cases handled by the French competition authority. More specifically, on the basis of Article 101 TFEU or its French equivalent (Article L. 420-1 of the Commercial Code), the former *Conseil*, the *Autorité* and the Paris Court of Appeal dealt with a variety of disputes involving both horizontal and vertical agreements.

Figure 12.5 also demonstrates that appeal judgments in France have not predominately focused on the enforcement of national law alone: 59% of the appeals involved the enforcement of both the EU and national competition law prohibitions.

Figure 12.6 shows, however, that this trend has changed over time. In the decade 2010-2020, the number of cases involving only French law has decreased. The trend is more pronounced for abuse cases than for agreement cases: eight out of nine of the abuse cases involved only French law in 2005, ten out of eleven in 2006 but zero out of six in 2016, two out of eight in 2017 and zero out of ten in 2018. This may be explained by the fact that abuses tend to be committed by undertakings operating at the national level and whose practices will more likely affect trade between Member States. It may also be the result of the application of Regulation 1/2003. A few years were needed before the French NCA fully enforced EU law.

Figure 12.6 Rules Being Appealed According to Years (Each Judgment Counts as One)

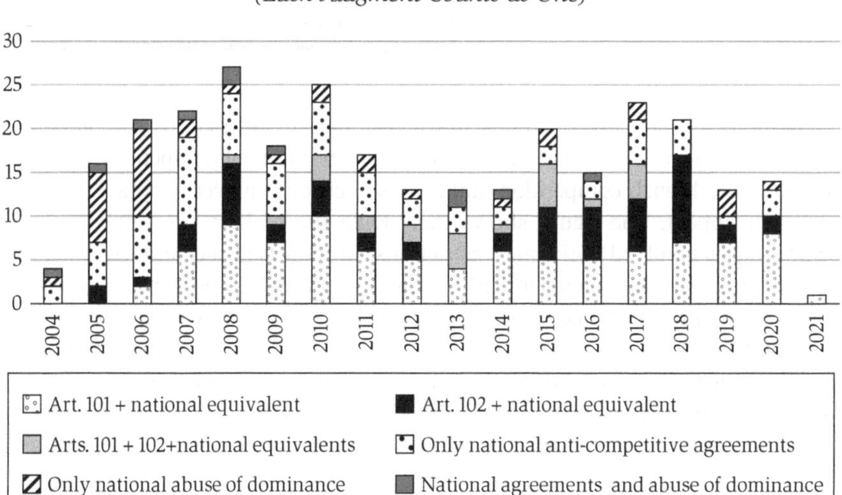

Figure 12.6 also demonstrates that the distribution between abuse and agreement cases can vary quite significantly from year to year. For instance, regarding judgments that involved the enforcement of the abuse prohibition(s), the following figures appear:

- 68% of the judgments in 2005 (11 out of 16);
- 40% of the judgments in 2008 (11 out of 27);
- 47% of the judgments in 2018 (10 out of 21);
- 21% of the judgments in 2020 (3 out of 14).

This unpredictable trend is difficult to explain other than by the random evolution of the number of complaints, leniency applications, or self-referrals by the *Autorité* (*see* section 1.3).

We can, though, detect a slight but noticeable trend in the later years of the study: the number of abuse cases decreased slowly: 38% in 2019 and 21% in 2020. This could be explained by the fact that many abuse cases were settled by the *Autorité,* and that settlement decisions in abuse cases, unlike those in cartel cases (*see* section 4.6), are very rarely appealed.

Figure 12.7 Types of Restrictions

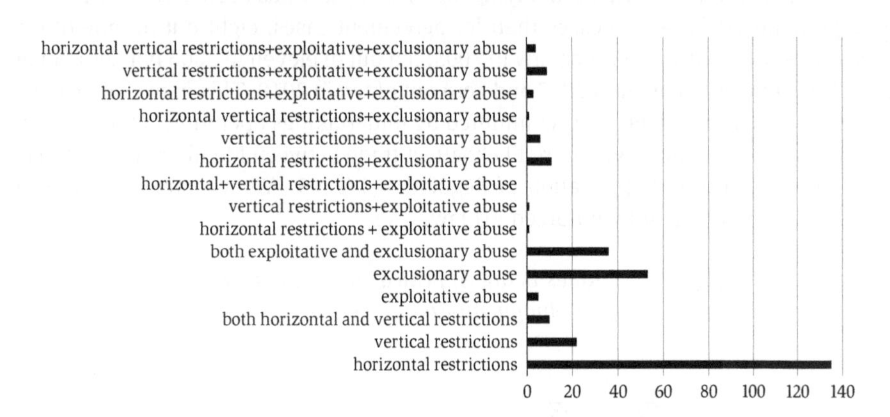

Figure 12.7 again demonstrates the wide range of restrictions of competition subject to an appeal. It summarises the types of restrictions of competition that were examined in the French competition authority's decisions subject to appeal across all instances of appeal. The figure shows that while the majority of anti-competitive agreement cases involved horizontal restrictions, the courts also examined appeals on vertical and mixed restrictions. Similarly, abuse cases involved both exclusionary and exploitative practices and mixed cases. It should be noted, however, that conclusions on this point must be formulated carefully in relation to abuse cases. Some decisions, in particular those from the early period, did not identify with precision the nature of the abusive restriction. It is therefore necessary to undertake the complicated task of interpretation of the former *Conseil* or the *Autorité*'s decision to determine the nature

of the abuse. In some cases, it is difficult to precisely reach clear-cut conclusions as the abuse potentially caused various restraining effects.[82]

Figure 12.8 Object/Effect (Only for Cases Involving Article 101/National Equivalent Infringements)

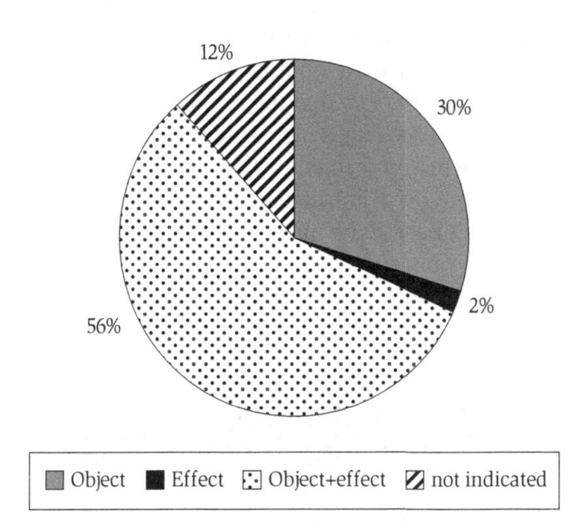

Figure 12.8 focuses on appeals against the French competition authority's decisions involving anti-competitive agreements. It indicates the ratio of cases in which the competition authority characterised or described the restriction of competition as by-object, by-effect, both by-object and by-effect or left it unclassified. It should be stressed that this classification is based on the text of the NCA's decision alone and not the coder's own assessment. It is worth adding that French law distinguished between by-object and by-effect infringements also in abuse of dominance cases.[83] Yet, according to the definitions of this study (see methodology chapter), Figure 12.8 only refers to the classification of cases involving Article 101 TFEU and Article L. 420-1.

The figure reveals that in most instances, the former *Conseil* and the *Autorité* either classified the restriction as both by-object and by-effect restriction (56%) or left

82. For example, Aut. Conc., 04-D-32 (2004): The Decaux group, which operates in the street furniture market for the public sector, has implemented a number of practices aimed at delaying the change of service provider in the city of Rennes, discouraging local authorities from considering awarding the contract to a service provider other than Decaux when contracts come up for renewal, and dissuading its competitors from responding to invitations to tender issued by these authorities. These practices therefore appear to have an exploitative effect on public bodies and an exclusionary effect on competitors, even if in this case the effects have not been precisely measured.
83. Article L. 420-2 para. 1 of the Commercial Code prohibits abuse of a dominant position, specifying that such conduct is prohibited under the 'same conditions' as agreements prohibited under the preceding article (L. 420-1), which states that agreements are prohibited if they have the object or effect of restricting competition.

it unclassified (12 %). The remaining 30 % involved by-object restrictions, and only 2 % of the judgments pertained to by-effect infringements.

These findings can be explained by two factors. First, the former *Conseil* and the *Autorité* tended, at least until the mid-2010s, to deal superficially with the classification of anti-competitive conduct as a by-object or by-effect restriction. Not infrequently, after a detailed description of the suspected conduct and a reference to their previous decision-making practice or to European case law, they concluded with a standard formula that the practice 'may have the object or the effect' of harming competition. This trend is itself explained by the fact that the progress of the effects-based doctrine is recent and coincides with the *Autorité*'s increasing expertise in competition economics.[84] Second, the refocusing of enforcement activity on cartels has led the *Autorité* to maintain this habit, as this type of infringement generally has an anti-competitive object and effect that doesn't need to be measured in detail.

Figure 12.9 The Competition Authority's Procedure

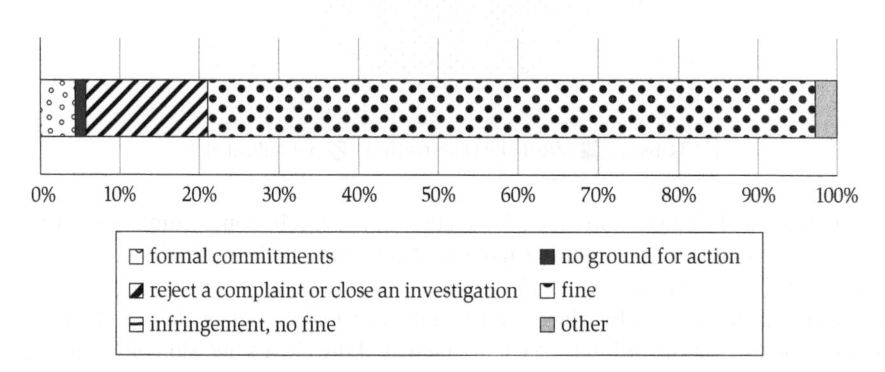

Figure 12.9 indicates the ratio of the type of NCA's procedures that were subject to judicial review, across all instances of appeal. It shows that 76 % (224 cases) of those decisions involved findings of infringements, together with the imposition of fines; 4 % (13 cases) were commitments decisions; 1 % (4 cases) of the decisions were no grounds for action, and 13 % (45 cases) were decisions to reject a complaint or to close an investigation. The remaining 8 decisions are unusual cases.[85]

84. *See* Guy Canivet, 'Regard sur 25 ans de construction du droit de la concurrence...', p. 28, *in 25 ans*, 2012, published by the *Autorité* on its website: https://www.autoritedelaconcurrence.fr/sites/default/files/2019-05/livre_25ans.pdf 'One of the main (developments of the recent years) is the progression of economic reasoning and its better integration into legal reasoning, whether in private or public law. There is now a competition law doctrine built by the Autorité de la concurrence through its decisions based on rigorous economic analysis and a clearly defined competition policy.'

85. For example, Paris Court of Appeal, 3 December 2015, *Société Concurrence,* No. 2015/13861, against Aut. conc. Decision No. 15-D-11. The NCA's decision found the complaint partially inadmissible, rejected it for lack of evidence and also decided to continue the investigation for only one of the objections (vertical agreement). However, it refers to all the texts of European law (Articles 101 and 102) and their equivalent in national law. The complainant's appeal was rejected in its entirety.

4.5 Grounds of Appeal

Figure 12.10 Grounds of Appeal (Each NCA's Decision or Previous Instance Judgment Counts as One)

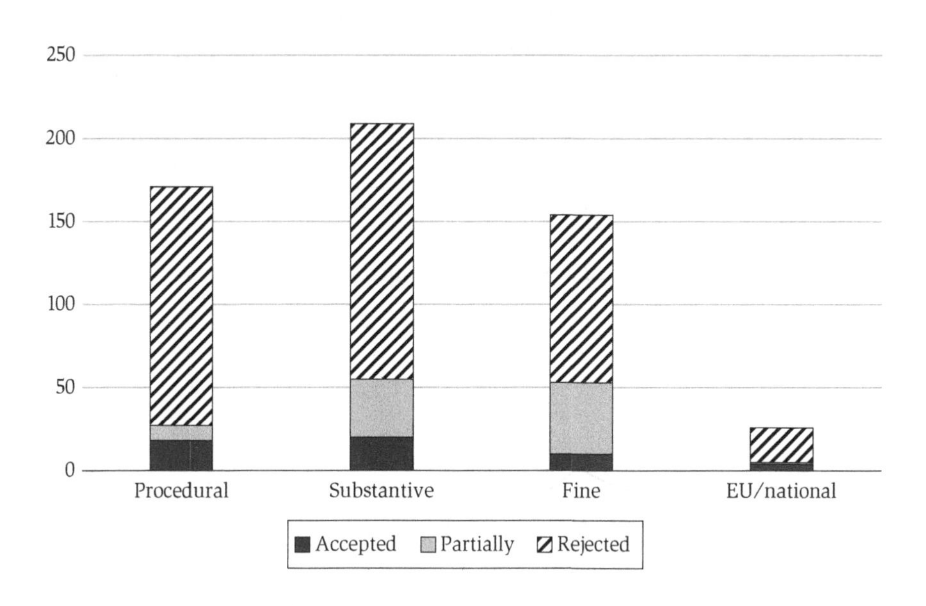

Figure 12.11(a) Procedural Grounds

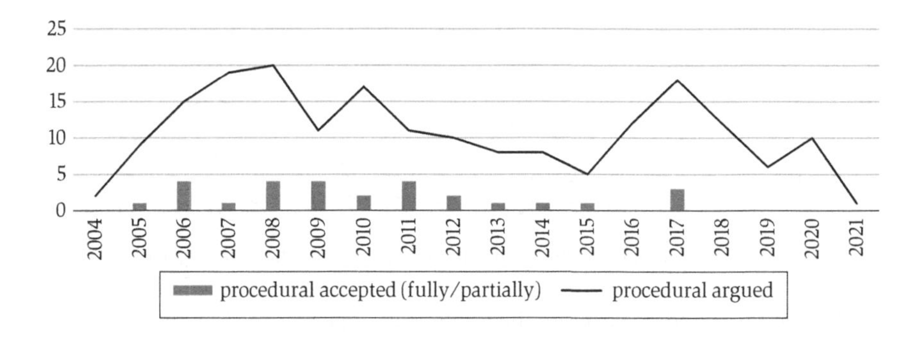

Figure 12.11(b) Substantive Grounds

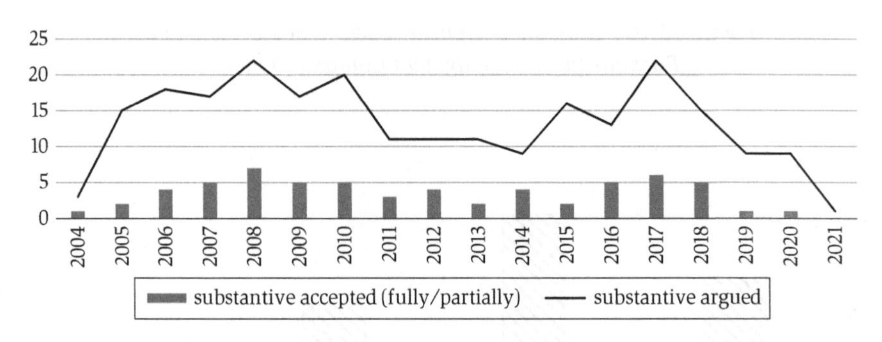

Figure 12.11(c) Fines-Related Grounds

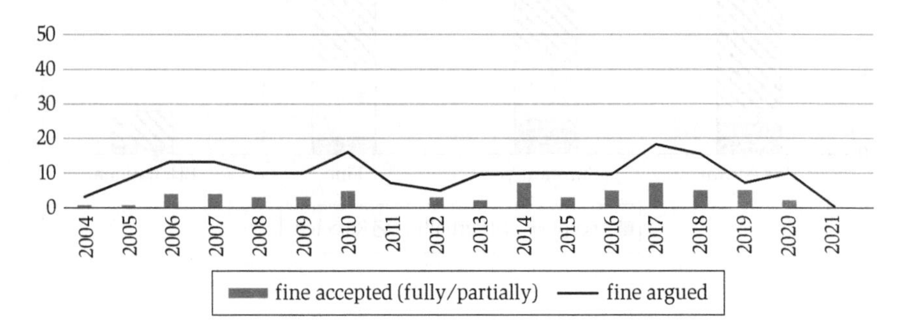

Figure 12.11(d) EU/National Grounds

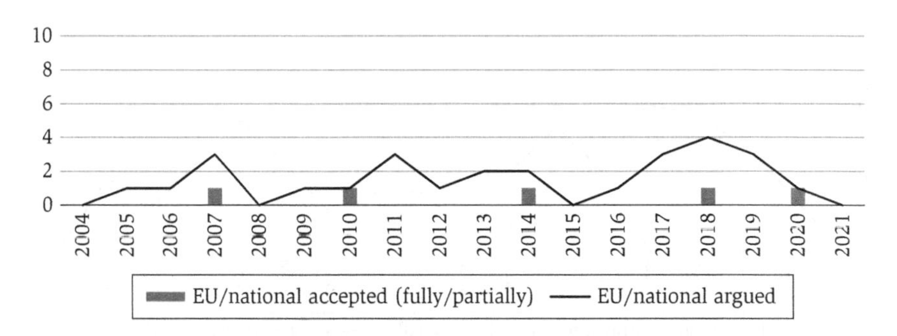

The empirical findings explore the grounds of appeals raised by the parties and their success rates. To this effect, Figure 12.10 indicates the success of each ground of appeal across all instances. For each type of ground – procedural, substantive, fine, or EU/national – the figure indicates whether this ground was fully accepted, partially accepted, or rejected. The success rates relate to the outcomes of all appeals, taking into account that separate appeals were aggregated where launched against a single decision of the NCA or a previous instance judgment. That means that when a single decision was appealed by various parties in separate proceedings, the outcome of all those judgments will be counted as a single case for the purposes of this figure. In practice, more than one appeal ground has often been invoked in the same case.

Figure 12.10 shows the following success rates (full and partial success):

- The success rate for procedural grounds: 15%, 27 out of 171 cases.
- The success rate for substantive grounds: 26%, 55 out of 209.
- The success rate for fine grounds: 32%, 53 out of 164 cases.
- The success rate for EU/national grounds: 19%, 5 out of 26 cases.

Figure 12.11 takes a different approach, focusing on the appeal grounds argued and accepted according to years. Unlike Figure 12.10, the data is presented from the perspective of each single appeal judgment (i.e., more than one judgment may be issued with respect to a single NCA decision). Some interesting trends emerge.

First, parties have most often raised substantive grounds (and next procedural grounds), although they are not often accepted (Figure 12.10). From 2010, there appears to be a decline in the tendency to raise procedural grounds (Figure 12.11(a)).

Second, the (full/partial) success rate indicated by Figure 12.10 is twice as high for grounds of appeal pertaining to fines imposed (32%) as in relation to procedural grounds (15%). The success rate for substantive grounds is higher than for procedural grounds, at 26%, as is the success rate for grounds based on tensions between French and EU law (19%).

Third, Figure 12.11 confirms that these trends were stable over time. This can probably be explained by a simple factor: in general, appeals mobilise arguments relating to the first three grounds measured by Figures 12.11(a) to (c). The curves therefore simply follow the curve of the number of appeals.

Fourth, Figure 12.11(d) measures the tensions between EU and French law. Although less easy to assess,[86] it appears that this ground is raised less frequently than the other three and that its chances of success are low. This can be explained by the fact that, since Regulation 1/2003, the former *Conseil*, the *Autorité*, and the Paris Court of Appeal have aligned French law with EU law in many (if not all) matters.

Fifth, it should be added that for grounds of appeal pertaining to fines imposed, the 32% rate displayed in Figure 12.10 is the one that measures the chances of success before the Paris Court of Appeal (36%) and the Court of Cassation (24%). It may be added that before the Paris Court of Appeal, the recalculation resulted in an average fine reduction of 41%, which is quite significant. However, as has already been pointed out, it is not possible to indicate this rate for the Court of Cassation insofar as it cannot rule on the amount of the fine but can only overturn the decision of the Court of Appeal on the grounds that the calculation criteria have not been respected.

86. To be detected, this type of ground must be accurately reported by the Court of Appeal or the Court of Cassation in the presentation of the parties' arguments, which is not always the case. It is then necessary to read these arguments in detail and sometimes interpret what the parties meant when their arguments lack clarity.

Figure 12.12 Types of Restrictions Versus Successful Grounds of Appeal

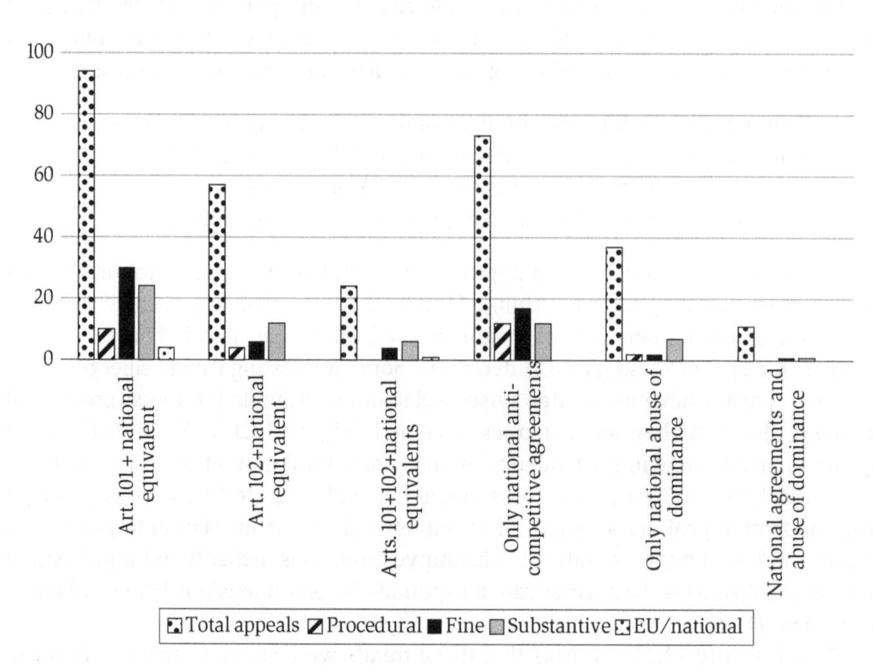

Next, Figure 12.12 records the relationship between the type of restriction of competition (e.g., anti-competitive agreements/abuse of dominance and EU or national prohibitions; *see* Figure 12.7) and the success of the procedural, substantive, fine, and EU/national grounds as defined above. To put this number in context, the figure also specifies the total number of judgments concerning each type of restriction.

It shows three interesting findings:

- fine and procedural grounds were mostly successful in agreement cases;
- successful abuse of dominant position cases mostly involved substantive grounds;
- EU/national grounds were only accepted in agreement cases.

The first two trends can be explained by the nature of the infringements involved. In horizontal agreement cases, particularly those that have given rise to leniency applications, substantive arguments are unlikely to succeed. The unlawfulness of the practice is beyond doubt. However, the calculation of the fine can often give rise to complex debates that explain certain differences in assessment between the NCA and the Paris Court of Appeal.

Where abuse is concerned, the unlawfulness of suspected behaviour is often less clear-cut and relies heavily on economic analyses debated during the trial. This may explain why substantive arguments are more likely to convince the Paris Court of Appeal.

4.6 Leniency and Settlements

Figure 12.13 Leniency

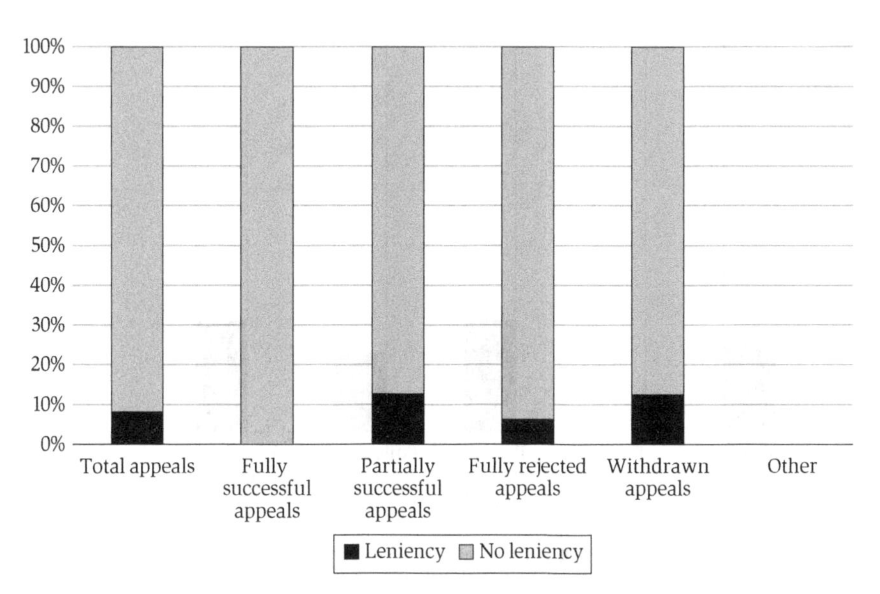

Figure 12.13 examines the relationship between leniency and the success of appeals. It indicates the percentage of appealed judgments on the French competition authority's decisions in which one or more parties have successfully applied for leniency. In addition, it specifies whether such appeals were fully successful, partially successful, rejected, or withdrawn. As expected, the number of such appeals is limited compared to the total number of appeals: 8% of the total, twenty-one cases. As also expected, there were no cases where the appeal resulted in full success for the appellants. If the partial success rate of these appeals is not negligible - eleven out of twenty-one - in almost all these cases, with three exceptions, the partial success is simply a reduction in the fine.[87] In the three judgments where this is not the case, the

87. Paris Court of Appeal, 29 September 2009, No. 2008/12495, *Etablissements A. Mathé et al.*, against Aut. conc. Decision No. 08-D-12; Paris Court of Appeal, 19 January 2010, No. 2009/00334, *AMD Sud-Ouest et al.*, against Aut. conc. Decision No. 08-D-32; Paris Court of Appeal, 14 April 2016, No. 2015/18055, *Graham & Brown France et al. against*, Aut. conc. Decision No. 14-D-20; Paris Court of Appeal, 20 December 2018, No. 17/21459, *Graham & Brown France et al. against*, Aut. conc. Decision No. 14-D-20; Paris Court of Appeal, 27 October 2016, No. 2015/01673, *Beiersdorf et al.* and Paris Court of Appeal, 18 June 2020, No. 19/08826, *L'Oréal* both against Aut. conc. Decision No. 14-D-19; Paris Court of Appeal, 04 July 2019, No. 16/23609, *Goodmills Deutschland* against Aut. conc. Decision No. 12-D-09.

partial reversal of the *Autorité*'s decision is explained either by an infringement of the rights of the defence,[88] a lack of reasoning in the calculation of one undertaking's fine and a lack of evidence of another one's participation in the cartel,[89] and by the fact that the restriction was only by-effect and not by-object.[90]

Figure 12.14 Settlements

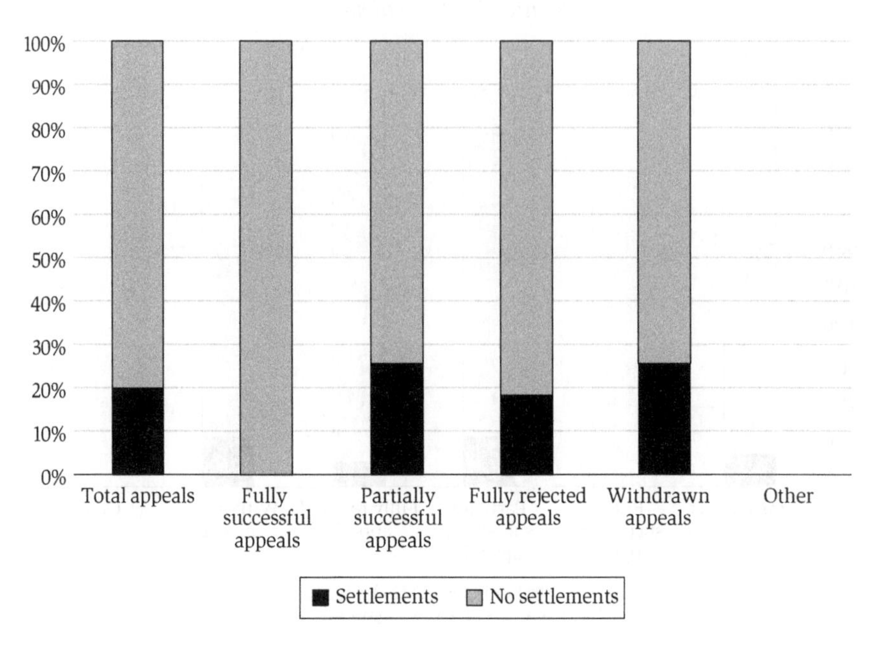

Figure 12.14 examines the relationship between settlements and the success of appeals. It shows comparable results for similar reasons. The only difference is that the number of settled cases that were appealed is higher: 20% (fifty-one cases).

At first glance, this rate may seem high, but it is well explained by the nature of the cases in which one party has successfully applied for a settlement. Out of these fifty-one cases, forty-five involved a horizontal agreement (thirty-eight involved only a horizontal agreement and seven a horizontal agreement and another practice), three cases involved only an abuse of dominant position and three cases involved only a vertical agreement. The appeals are therefore lodged by defendants who did not benefit from the settlement or, having benefited from it, contested the method used to

88. Paris Court of Appeal, 23 May 2017, No. 2015/08224, *Laïta et al.*, against Aut. conc. Decision No. 15-D-03.
89. Paris Court of Appeal, 19 July 2018, No. 16/01270, *Chronopost et al.*, against Aut. conc. Decision No. 15-D-19.
90. Paris Court of Appeal, 20 November 2014, No. 2012/06826, *Grands Moulins de Paris et al.* against Aut. conc. Decision No. 12-D-09.

calculate the fine. The success rate is logically limited (twelve cases out of fifty-one) and essentially leads to limited reductions in fines.[91]

5 QUALITATIVE ANALYSIS

5.1 Scope and Intensity of Appeals in the Paris Court of Appeal

The key point already made (*see* section 1) is that the intensity of review of the *Autorité's* (and its predecessor, the *Conseil*) decisions by the Paris Court of Appeal is considerable. The Court has the competence to review any error of law, fact, or discretion; to review decisions finding a prohibition, non-prohibition, and the rejection of complaints; and it has the power to replace the *Autorité*'s decisions. The Court of Cassation, on the other hand, has more limited powers, in line with French tradition: it does not review the entire case but only deals with errors of law.

As highlighted in Figures 12.4(a) to (c), the rate of reversal of the French competition authority's decisions is quite low. We can recall here the figures that we consider most important from this study: 26% of the Paris Court of Appeal's judgments fully or partially changed the competition authority's decision. This includes 14% of judgments that amended the decision only with respect to the fines. In these cases, however, the level of fine reduction is significant. As Figure 12.10 shows, companies that contest the amount of the fine can expect a reduction of 41% when they win their case.

But most importantly, only 9% of the Paris Court of Appeal's judgments fully annulled and/or replaced the competition authority's decision. In other words, in 91% of the appeals, the court at least partially confirmed the competition authority's decisions. As noted above, and stressed again here, a qualitative analysis tends to show that usually partial reversal is only on relatively minor points.

It is not easy to explain this finding, especially over such a long period when a variety of factors may come into play. It can be the result of the undeniable expertise of the former *Conseil* and *Autorité*'s investigating services and adjudicating formation (the 'Collège'). The *Autorité*'s lawyers and economists display a wide range of experience and solid training. For this reason, it may be difficult to prove them wrong. But there could be another explanation mentioned in an official Senate report: the lack

91. Paris Court of Appeal, 25 September 2014, No. 2015/18055, *Graham & Brown France et al.*, against Aut. conc. Decision No. 13-D-03; Paris Court of Appeal, 21 January 2016, No. 2014/22811, *Ineo réseaux Sud Ouest*, against Aut. conc. Decision No. 11-D-13; Paris Court of Appeal, 14 April 2016, No. 2013/05595, *Groupe Bigard et al.*, against Aut. conc. Decision No. 14-D-20; Paris Court of Appeal, 4 July 2019, No. 16/23609, *Goodmills Deutschland*, against Aut. conc. Decision No. 12-D-09; Paris Court of Appeal, 27 October 2016, No. 2015/01673, *Beiersdorf et al.*, against Aut. conc. Decision No. 14-D-19; Paris Court of Appeal, 19 July 2018, No. 16/01270, *Chronopost et al.*, against Aut. conc. Decision No. 15-D-19; Paris Court of Appeal, 6 July 2017, No. 2016/22365, *Smith & Smith Characters et al.*, against Aut. conc. Decision No. 16-D-20; Paris Court of Appeal, 15 March 2018, No. 16/14231, *Sermetal et al.*, against Aut. conc. Decision No. 16-D-09.

of resources at the Paris Court of Appeal, which does not really allow it to challenge the authority's assessments.[92]

Regarding the different types of infringement, two features should be recalled.

First, a particularity in relation to abuse of dominant position enforcement has been noted: it gives rise to a more limited number of appeals on the merits to the Paris Court of Appeal because of the prominence of negotiated procedures, such as settlements and commitments. And when appeals are lodged, they very rarely seek to challenge the decision in its entirety but generally contest it on anecdotal points, such as the criteria for calculating the penalty, the duration of the practice or the imputation of the practice to certain legal entities that make up the undertakings involved in the infringement.

Second, a more nuanced assessment applies to major cartels. Almost all the cases dealt with by the *Autorité* over the last decade have been the result of leniency proceedings, and when this is not the case, the companies have settled.[93] But despite the importance of negotiated procedures, appeals are almost systematic, even if they are on minor points. This trend was explained above (*see* section 4.4). This enlightens an observation already made when commenting on Figure 12.2: the number of appeals increases in relative terms as the number of cases decreases over the past decade.

5.2 Scope and Intensity of Appeals in the Court of Cassation

Concerning the review process in the Court of Cassation, we highlighted (*see* section 4.3) that the overall success rate was 31%, including 2% of reviewing on fine, only 14% for partial success and 14% for total success. While this rate is slightly lower than the rate of success before the Paris Court of Appeal (41%), a qualitative analysis tends to show that decisions are rarely overturned on minor points. Albeit there are some decisions related to errors in fine calculation[94] or errors of law with limited consequences for the outcome of a case,[95] there have been a significant number of decisions

92. It said: '*Les décisions de l'Autorité de la concurrence sont soumises à un contrôle juridictionnel, mais celui-ci est de fait handicapé par le manque de moyens de la cour d'appel de Paris*'; Free translation: 'The decisions of the Autorité de la concurrence are subject to judicial review, but this is hampered by the lack of resources at the Paris Court of Appeal.' P. Bonnecarrère *Proposition de résolution sur l'harmonisation de l'application des règles européennes de concurrence par les autorités nationales: Mieux appliquer le droit européen de la concurrence au niveau national: pour une convergence maîtrisée, Rapport d'information n° 396* (2015-2016), déposé le 11 février 2016.
93. One important case could be mentioned her: the Cartel in the Floor Coverings Sector: Aut. Conc., Decision No. 17-D-20 (2017). In this case, the *Autorité* imposed a EUR 302 million fine on the three leading manufacturers of PVC and linoleum floor covering, for a price fixing agreement and a collusive exchange of information.
94. Cass. com., 27 March 2019, No. 16-26.472 et al., *L'Oréal et al.*; Cass. com., 12 December 2018, No. 14-19.589, *Président de l'Autorité de la concurrence*; Cass. com., 8 November 2017, No. 16-17.226; 16-17.330; *Graham & Brown France et al.;* Cass. com., 27 September 2017 No. 15-20.087; 15-20.291, *Président de l'Autorité de la concurrence et EDF*; Cass. com., 21 October 2015, No. 13-16.602; 13-16.696; 13-14.905, *Ineo et al.*; Cass. com., 18 February 2014, No. 12-27.643; 12-27.697; 12-27.689; 12-27.700; 12-28.026, *Pradeau et Morin et al.*
95. Cass. com., 11 June 2013, No. 12-13.961, *Guerlain et al.*; Cass. com., 29 June 2007, No. 07-10.303; 07-10.354; 07-10.397; *Bouygues Télécom et al.* This judgment partially quashed the

on important points, especially in the 2000s and the beginning of the 2010s. Decisions were taken on the following issues: limitation,[96] fair trial,[97] anti-competitive object,[98] anti-competitive effect in exclusionary abuse cases[99] and effect on trade between Member States.[100]

One explanation for this trend may lie in the fact that on most of these issues, the case law and even the Commercial Code, over the past twenty years, lacked precision. It is therefore not entirely surprising that the Court of Cassation has had to establish its case law. Most of the decisions of the Court of Cassation, which quashed the Paris Court of Appeal's judgments, also relate to the economic aspects, especially those rulings rendered before 2015. They therefore reflect the progress in the use of economic analysis and the increasing requirement that the Court of Cassation has set for the Paris Court of Appeal in assessing the anti-competitive effects of suspicious conduct.

That said, there can be no doubt that the Court of Cassation is not particularly sympathetic towards the Paris Court of Appeal and that it fully exercises its control within the limits of the French *cassation* technique's scope.[101] In most cases where it quashed the Paris Court of Appeal's decisions, it ruled in favour of the appealing undertakings. More rarely, it also ruled in favour of the Minister of the Economy or the President of the *Autorité* when the competition authority's decision was partially overturned by the Court of Appeal. This was the case, for example, regarding the application of the rules on aggravating circumstances,[102] the requirement for an effect

judgment of the Court of Appeal on the grounds that it had erred in law by accepting that an exchange of information relating to commercial and non-public information was in itself a sign anti-competitive without investigating whether this exchange actually had such an impact on competition. As a result, the fine was slightly reduced, and the appeal judgment was largely upheld; Cass. com., 7 July 2009, No. 08-15.609, *Lafarge Ciments*: this judgment also partially quashed the Paris Court of Appeal judgement for an error of law in the qualification of a collective dominant position but upheld most of this judgment that fined two undertakings for a horizontal agreement.

96. Cass. com., 15 May 2012, No. 11-18.507, *Ministre de l'Economie*; Cass. com., 6 November 2007, No. 06-16.194, *SADE – Compagnie Générale de Travaux d'Hydraulique.*
97. Cass. com., 14 April 2015, No. 12-15.971, *Président de l'Autorité de la concurrence et UFC-Que choisir;* Cass. com., 15 November 2011, No. 10-20.527; 10-20.851; 10-20.881, *Véolia et al.*; Cass. com, 2 November 2011 No. 10-21.103, *Colas Rail et al.;* Cass. com., 23 November 2010, No. 09-72.031, *L'Oréal*; Cass. com., 02 February 2010, No., 08-70.449, *Ministre de l'Economie*; Cass. com., 02 February 2010, No., 08-70.450, *Ministre de l'Economie;* Cass. com., 13 October 2009, No. 08-17.269, *Colas Ile-de-France Normandie et al.*
98. Cass. com., 29 January 2020, No. 18-10.967; 18-11.001, *Banque postale et al.*
99. Cass. com., 10 May 2006, No. 05-14.5013 and Cass. com., 9 March 2009, No. 08-14.435 and 08-14.464, *SFR et France Télécom* (same case); Cass. com., 17 June 2008, No. 05-17.566, *RDPEV, VIIV (Vedettes vendéennes)*: the Court of Cassation censured the Paris Court of Appeal on its analysis of the incremental cost test that grounded the finding that an undertaking implemented a predatory strategy.
100. Cass. com., 31 January 2012, No. 10-25.772; 10-25.775; 10-25.882, *France Télécom, Préisdent de l'Autorité de la concurrence et al;* Cass. com., 1 March 2011, No. 09-72.655; 09-72.657; 09-72.705; 09-72.830; 09-72.894, *Total Réunion et al.*
101. The particularities of the *cassation* technique suggest that one should be wary of jumping to conclusions here too. As stated in section 1, the Court of Cassation only reviews errors of law. The economic assessment of cases therefore remains outside the scope of its review.
102. Cass. com., 27 September 2017, No. 15-20.087; 15-20.291, *Président de l'Autorité de la concurrence et EDF.*

on trade between Member States[103] or the *ratione temporis* application of new rules governing limitation.[104]

5.3 Public Enforcement and the Right to a Fair Trial

Another important issue that has not yet been addressed is the question of the compliance of competition enforcement in France with fair trial principles.

Review procedures in the Paris Court of Appeal and the Court of Cassation are judicial proceedings. As such, they must comply in every respect with the principles of a fair trial. It is therefore very rare that the compliance of these proceedings with Article 6 ECHR is questioned.

In contrast, debates about compliance with the *Autorité*'s procedures are much more frequent. While the separation of the investigative function from the adjudicative function provides guarantees that do not exist, for example, before the European Commission,[105] it is the investigations that have most often given rise to appeals by infringing undertakings alleging possible violations of the rights of a fair trial. These discussions seem to have become less common recently, but in the earlier phase of this study, there were important decisions on the subject by the Paris Court of Appeal and the Court of Cassation.

For instance, in the Philips France case, both courts declared the illegality of the clandestine recording of a telephone conversation and ruled that it was impossible for the French authority to use it as evidence.[106] They also decided that the same panel of judges cannot assess both the lawfulness of court orders authorising the search of premises and seizure of documents and the legitimacy of the French competition authority's decision without infringing the right to a fair trial.[107] In agreement with the Court of Appeal and based on Article 6 paragraph 1 of the ECHR, the Court of Cassation also extended the applicability of the reasonable time principle and the right of defence to the administrative phase prior to the statement of objections.[108] More recently, albeit in exceptional circumstances, the Paris Court of Appeal also ruled that the inclusion by the *Autorité* in its investigation file and in its report, without concealment, of documents containing unfounded personal accusations against the lawyer of a company, was contrary to the rights of the defence and consequently annulled the *Autorité*'s decision.[109]

---

103. Cass. com., 31 January 2012, No. 10-25.772; 10-25.775; 10-25.882, *France Télécom, Préisdent de l'Autorité de la concurrence et al.*
104. Cass. com., 15 May 2012, No. 11-18.507, *Ministre de l'Economie.*
105. *See* on this old topic: M. Merola & D. Waelbroeck (eds), Towards an Optimal Enforcement of Competition Rules in Europe. Bruxelles, Bruylant, 2010, p. 206. – W. Wils, The Combination of the Investigative and Prosecutorial Function and the Adjudicative Function. *World Competition: Law and Economic Review*, vol. 27, 2004, p. 202.
106. Paris Court of Appeal, 16 February 2012, No. 2011/00951, *Philips France et al.*, against Cons. conc. Decision No. 05-D-66 and Cass. ass. plén., 7 January 2011, No. 09-14316 and 09-14667.
107. Cass. com, 2 November 2011 No. 10-21.103, *Colas Rail et al.*
108. Cass. com., 23 November 2010, No. 09-72.031, *L'Oréal* – but it censured the application of this principle by the Court of Appeal, deeming its assessment too severe.
109. Paris Court of Appeal, 2 February 2017, No. 13/13058, *GEA Group, Brenntag S.A. et al.*

5.4 Coherence with Substantive EU Competition Law

Subject to the reservations mentioned above concerning the difficulty of identifying with precision the arguments highlighting the divergences between French and EU competition law, it seems that these arguments are relatively rare before the review courts and that their success rate is very low. This outcome can be explained by the competition law expertise of the members of the *Autorité* and the Paris Court of Appeal and by the convergence that Regulation 1/2003 has accelerated.

There are only three cases in which the Paris Court of Appeal or the Court of Cassation referred a question to the Court of Justice for a preliminary ruling. This was the case in the well-known cases in France: the '*Pierre Fabre*' case,[110] the '*Expedia*' case[111] and the '*endives*' case.[112] There have also been cases where the Cour de cassation has refused to refer to the Court of Justice on the basis of the *CILFIT* jurisprudence[113] when it was certain that French law was compatible with EU law. This was the case in the *Brenntag* case concerning certain investigative powers.[114]

There are, however, cases in which it has been considered that EU law has not been correctly applied. For instance, in one case where the former *Conseil* had imposed heavy fines for a market-sharing cartel on three undertakings that shared the oligopolistic market of public transport.[115] The Paris Court of Appeal upheld this decision in a subsequent ruling[116] before the Court of Cassation overturned this confirmatory ruling.[117] The Court of Cassation quashed the Court of Appeal for misapplying the Court of Justice's *Anic*[118] and *Aalborg Portland*[119] case law. The wording of the Court of Justice is even adopted almost word for word. More specifically, the Court of Cassation held that the Court of Appeal had not established that one of the undertakings '*was aware of the unlawful conduct of the other participants, or could reasonably foresee such conduct, and was prepared to accept the risk*'. In other cases, the Court of Cassation found that the Court of Appeal had not correctly applied Article 3 of Regulation 1/2003 and Articles 101 and 102 of TFEU in raising the standard of proof required to establish the effect on trade between Member States.[120]

---

110. CJEU, Case C-439/09, *Pierre Fabre*, question referred to the Court of Justice by the Court of Appeal: Paris Court of Appeal, 29 October 2009, No. 2008/23812, *Pierre Fabre Dermo-cosmétiques* against Cons. Conc., Decision No. 08-D-25 (2008).
111. CJEU, Case C-226/1, *Expedia;* question referred to the Court of Justice by the Court of Cassation: Cass. com., 10 May 2011, No. 10-14.881.
112. CJEU, Case C-671/15, *APVE*, 14 November 2017; question referred to the Court of Justice by the Court of Cassation: Cass. Com., 8 December 2015, No. 14-19.589 against Aut. Conc., Decision No. 12-D-08 (2012).
113. CJEC, Case C-283/81, 6 October 1982, point 16.
114. Cass. Com., 26 April 2017, Nos. 15-25701 et 15-25699.
115. Aut. Conc., Decision No. 05-D-38 (2005).
116. Paris Court of Appeal, 7 February 2006, No. 2005/15051, *TRANSDEV*.
117. Cass. com, 9 October 2007 No. 06-12.446; 06-12.596.
118. CJEU, 8 July 1999, Case C-49/92.
119. CJEU, 7 January 2004, Case C-204/00.
120. Cass. com., 31 January 2012, No. 10-25.772; 10-25.775; 10-25.882, *France Télécom, Préisdent de l'Autorité de la concurrence et al.*

These rulings of the Court of Cassation show its determination to ensure that the *Autorité* and the Paris Court of Appeal rigorously apply EU Law. Nonetheless, it is important not to over-extrapolate their scope, as this type of decision is, as has been stated, rare.

6 CONCLUDING REMARKS

Looking at the figures as a whole, it would appear that the rate of reversals of decisions taken by the French competition authority is fairly low, although not anecdotal. For the record, of the 635 decisions handed down during the period covered by the study, only 164 were appealed (26%). Of these 164 decisions, only 8 were completely overturned by the Paris Court of Appeal (5%), and 71 were partially overturned (43%). Of the 635 decisions handed down, these 8 decisions represent 1% and the 71 decisions nearly 11%.

These figures allow us to draw the conclusion that has already been hinted at by practitioners in the field but which is commonplace without (until now!) being backed up by data: over the period covered by the study, the Paris Court of Appeal has tended to follow the French competition authority if we disregard the calculation of fines.[121] For the Court of Cassation. a more nuanced conclusion should be drawn. As noted above (*see* section 4.2), the Court's overturning decisions frequently related to important points of law. Yet the rate of success remains low: 31%. Of the 199 Court of Appeal's decisions, only 11 were completely quashed (5%) and 23 were (11%) partially quashed.

From the qualitative analysis carried out in section 4, it could also be concluded that the Court of Appeal and the Court of Cassation are undoubtedly willing to exercise a degree of control over the French authority, but it does not seem that this can be interpreted as a desire to promote a certain competition policy. As other national reports have highlighted, the Court of Appeal and the Court of Cassation understand their role as a supervisory body in individual cases aimed at ensuring that the rules of law are applied fairly.

The only discernible 'agenda' for the two reviewing courts may be the aspiration to ensure the rigorous application of EU law, and for the Cour de cassation alone, it may be added that some of its decisions have clearly reflected its desire to promote a more effects-based approach.

121. It should be noted, however, that in the last year (outside the scope of this study) there has been an increase in the number of Court decisions overturning the *Autorité*'s, some of which relate to high-profile cases.

CHAPTER 13
Germany Report

Rupprecht Podszun & Nils Overhoff

1 INTRODUCTION TO COMPETITION LAW ENFORCEMENT IN GERMANY

Germany introduced a modern competition law as early as 1958 with the Gesetz gegen Wettbewerbsbeschränkungen (GWB), the Act against Restraints of Competition.[1] In Germany, the Act is often called the 'basic norm' or the 'constitution of the market economy'. This wording displays the high regard competition law enjoys in Germany but also mirrors a long-standing tradition of legal thinking – that competition law forms part of a strong commitment to a certain economic order. In a country divided for decades with a market economy in the West and a socialist planned economy in the East, the competition mechanism became a main principle of state belief in the free part of Germany. Strong public enforcement by an institution trusted by the German population paved the way for a healthy competition culture.

Competition law in Germany now rests on two pillars: public enforcement through competition authorities and private enforcement by ordinary law courts. Public enforcement is dominant. Damages cases by private claimants are usually brought as follow-on actions, but there is also a considerable number of stand-alone competition law cases.[2] In this contribution, we focus on public enforcement but wish to make it clear that private parties and courts play an integral role of growing importance in the competition law environment in Germany.

1. An English translation of the German provisions provided by the Federal Ministry of Justice can be found at http://www.gesetze-im-internet.de/englisch_gwb/.
2. For examples, *see* the list in Zöttl/Schlepper, EuZW 2012, 573.

1.1 Substantive Framework

The GWB serves to create a market-based, competitive economic system for all market participants. Participants are expected to use their individual economic freedoms in an unrestrained manner. Germany has never subscribed to an isolated consumer welfare approach in the same way as other jurisdictions. In a 2021 ruling, the highest German competition law court explicitly stated the aims of competition law as 'ensuring competition on the merits and openness of market access'.[3]

The GWB is designed to achieve these goals in three ways: by prohibiting restrictive agreements (sections 1 ff. GWB), by prohibiting unilateral actions by dominant companies and companies with superior market power (sections 18 ff. GWB), and by controlling mergers (sections 35 ff. GWB). Merger control is not subject to the scope of this project and will therefore not be mentioned hereafter.

The national provisions on the prohibition of restrictive agreements mostly resemble the provisions in Article 101 TFEU. The provisions deviate in some respects where only national law is applicable. For example, section 3 GWB introduces an exception for cartels of small- or medium-sized undertakings. This exemption allows for the cooperation of small- and medium-sized enterprises if it serves to improve their competitiveness and competition is not significantly impeded. Obviously, the exemption is only granted if trade between Member States is not affected in an appreciable way.

In the field of unilateral actions, the German provisions are stricter than Article 102 TFEU. The German legislator used the leeway granted by Article 3(2) of Regulation 1/2003. Section 20 GWB deals in a rather encompassing way with practices by undertakings with relative or superior market power. Section 21(1) GWB prohibits boycotts. Section 19a GWB, a new provision introduced in 2021, targets undertakings with paramount significance for competition across markets, i.e., digital gatekeepers.[4] Further rules on market definition and market power in section 18 GWB and the examples in section 19 GWB for abusive practices supplement this field. The database does not include cases that exclusively rely on such specific national antitrust rules.

There are specific rules within the GWB for the press sector, water supplies, energy and the agricultural sector. These rules amend the general German competition law rules, providing exceptions or stricter rules for these sectors.

1.2 Competition Agencies

The Bundeskartellamt, statutorily established in section 48 GWB, is the main German competition authority. It is the National Competition Agency in the meaning of Article 35 Regulation 1/2003, applying European competition law in Germany (section 50 GWB).

3. Bundesgerichtshof, 6 July 2021, Case KZR 11/18, at para. 24 – *wilhelm.tel*.
4. There is no case of section 19a GWB included in this investigation.

The enforcement practice of the Bundeskartellamt varies each year in terms of the number of decisions and type of restrictions examined (Article 101/102 TFEU and/or national equivalents). This also depends on the number and complexity of pending or new merger control cases. The Bundeskartellamt had around 400 members of staff in 2022, some of whom are working in related fields to antitrust enforcement (in particular, public procurement law, market transparency units, and the competition register[5]).

In each of the sixteen German Länder, the federal states, there is one regional competition authority dealing with cases that are only relevant in the geographical territory of that Land. These authorities are of minor importance in practice regarding the number and the importance of cases and often coordinate with the Bundeskartellamt if they investigate cases. This is due to the limited geographical scope of the cases investigated by the regional competition authorities: According to section 48 GWB, the Bundeskartellamt is solely competent for competition law cases if the effect of the undertaking's conduct extends beyond the territory of a single German Land.

1.3 Administrative and Fining Procedures

The competition framework is enforced in administrative proceedings, either with or without fines. The fines are not criminal in nature but administrative ('Ordnungswidrigkeiten'). One notable exception is the criminal sanction for bid rigging in cases with a formalised tender procedure (section 298 of the German Criminal Code).[6] The nature of the proceedings needs to be determined beforehand and cannot be changed during proceedings. This is due to differing procedural requirements - stricter ones in fining procedures as opposed to more lenient ones in purely administrative proceedings.

In administrative antitrust proceedings, the Bundeskartellamt can open and close investigations at will. It enjoys an enormous leeway to set priorities. If it wishes to pursue a case, it does not have statutory time limits.[7] In administrative cases, the Bundeskartellamt has powers similar to those available to the Commission under Regulation 1/2003: It may declare the behaviour to be unlawful and to be stopped, it can order the undertakings to take certain measures, it may accept binding commitments, it can declare that there are no grounds for action, and it can take interim measures. The most common decision seems to be a cease-and-desist order, combined with some specifications on how to stop the infringement.

5. The Competition Register for Public Procurement provides public contracting authorities, sector contracting entities and concession grantors with information about their sector. Further information on the competition register can be found at https://www.bundeskartellamt.de/EN/Tasks/Competitionregister/competitionregister_node.html.
6. The cases dealing with section 298 of the German Criminal Code (Strafgesetzbuch) were not included in the database. While these cases deal with infringements of free competition, they are dealt with under German law in an institutional and procedural setting that is completely different from the cases that are dealt with under Articles 101 and 102 TFEU or according to the respective national provisions. Decisions based on section 298 seem to be rare or are not published.
7. In merger cases, there are time limits that need to be observed.

Fine proceedings end with the setting of a fine (or closing the case). A fine is often levied not only against the undertakings but also against its directors and managers. Differing from EU law, in other words, natural persons are not exempt from personal fines. The fines are determined by the Bundeskartellamt. For natural persons, the fines may not exceed EUR 1 million, and for undertakings, they may not exceed 10% of the undertaking's total turnover in the previous year. The amount of the fine depends on a number of factors, including the gravity and length of infringement, damages caused and profits made with the infringement, behaviour during proceedings, and the turnover of the undertaking. When determining the amount of fine, lenience may apply. The requirements for leniency are set in sections 81h–81n GWB ('Bonusregelung'). The provisions go back to the Bundeskartellamt's leniency program and play a key role in uncovering secret cartels.

1.4 Decision-Making in the Bundeskartellamt

The Bundeskartellamt operates independently from the Federal Government and determines the subject and outcome of its investigations autonomously (section 51 paragraph 1 GWB). The Ministry of Economics and Climate Protection is the supervisory body in organisational terms for the Bundeskartellamt, and it is this Ministry in government responsible for reforms of the GWB. The Bundeskartellamt enjoys independence in substance: Each of the 13 Decision Divisions decides in chambers of three persons, similar to judges (cf. sections 51 paragraph 3, 52 GWB) without interventions from either the President of the Bundeskartellamt or the Ministry. This is a remarkably different system from the one practised at the European Commission.

There are no formalised prioritisation principles. The Bundeskartellamt as a whole and the decision divisions specifically have great power to choose their own focus and set an internal agenda.[8] The Bundeskartellamt has no official agenda and is not required by law to investigate specific industries or practices. It reports every two years to Parliament (section 53 GWB).

The internal structure shifts a lot of decision-making power to individuals. The decisions are made in the thirteen so-called decision divisions ('Beschlussabteilungen'). In 2022, nine of these divisions were responsible for a specific industry or sector, three were exclusively responsible for investigating hardcore cartels, and one was responsible for competition cases closely linked to consumer protection. The divisions decide independently and without instruction from any superior officer. They do not need to consult with a legal team or other units at the Agency. Each deciding committee is composed of one chairperson (the leader of the respective decision division) and two committee members. All have the same voting rights. The decision is made using the majority principle. As is typical for courts in Germany, it is clear from the outset, thanks to an allocation of cases plan, who sits on what case. Because of this internal structure and the high degree of freedom, the Bundeskartellamt seems to be pretty immune from political influence. The internal structure is more similar to the internal organisation of

8. Brook/Cseres, Priority setting in EU and national competition law enforcement, pp. 29 et seq.

courts than to the internal structure of typical hierarchically organised executive agencies.

2 THE JUDICIAL APPEAL PROCESS OF THE COMPETITION AUTHORITY'S DECISIONS

Two courts are involved in the judicial review process of decisions issued by the Bundeskartellamt.[9] Judicial review is first undertaken by the Oberlandesgericht Düsseldorf (Higher Regional Court of Düsseldorf, OLG Düsseldorf), and in second instance, by the Bundesgerichtshof (the Federal Supreme Court, BGH).

2.1 OLG Düsseldorf

The OLG Düsseldorf is the first-instance court for appeals against decisions of the Bundeskartellamt. It is competent to assess questions of fact and of law. Interestingly, it is a civil and criminal law court and does not form part of the administrative branch of the judiciary (Verwaltungsgerichtsbarkeit). Also, it is not the locally competent review court for the city of Bonn, where the Bundeskartellamt is located. Instead, this is a special attribution of competencies to the OLG Düsseldorf. It is a historic peculiarity that the administrative cases of the Bundeskartellamt are heard here.[10]

The competence for competition-law-related cases is concentrated in specialised cartel senates, with approximately fifteen judges dealing with competition law. This means that the judges reviewing the Bundeskartellamt's decisions do so relatively frequently. Outside of competition law, the OLG Düsseldorf usually deals with cases on appeal from the Regional Courts. According to the 2022 allocation of business plan,[11] the first Cartel Senate is exclusively competent for appeals against purely administrative decisions. The 2nd, the 4th and the 6th Cartel Senate deal with fining cases.[12] The senates also review cases of private enforcement. Most of the cases in the scope of this study, accordingly, are dealt with by the first Cartel Senate of the Düsseldorf Court.

Each Senate decides with three professional judges. They do not necessarily have a specific competition law expertise when starting their assignment since they come from the general judiciary and may have dealt with matters of general civil law before. However, they usually stay with the cartel senates for a long time, i.e., until the age of retirement, unless they wish to change themselves or are appointed to a more senior position. This length of appointments leads to the judges being, on average, highly competent and experienced in evaluating and applying competition law.

9. The jurisdiction of the courts is determined in the GWB according to sections 73, 83 and 91 for the OLG Düsseldorf and sections 77, 84 and 94 for the Bundesgerichtshof. Jurisdiction is exclusive.
10. Dicks, in: Loewenheim/Meessen/Riesenkampff/Kersting/Meyer-Lindemann, Competition Law, 4th ed., section 92 GWB.
11. Available at https://www.olg-duesseldorf.nrw.de/aufgaben/geschaeftsverteilung/gvp_rechtsprechung/gvp_recht_2022/index.php.
12. The 3rd and the 5th Cartel Senate mainly deal with matters of energy law coming from the networks regulator.

2.2 Bundesgerichtshof

The Bundesgerichtshof is the Federal Supreme Court of Germany in civil and criminal law matters, located at Karlsruhe. The Bundesgerichtshof has a specialised senate for competition law, the Cartel Senate ('Kartellsenat'), with around eight professional judges. The Senate sits with five judges in cases. All judges are also members of other senates dealing with different matters, except for the presiding judge. Until 2019, the Cartel Senate was traditionally presided over by the President of the Bundesgerichtshof and was only called on an *ad hoc* basis. This changed in 2019 when the Cartel Senate was established as a permanent body because the higher caseload (with a higher number of damages cases and appeals against fines) meant that it was necessary to establish the Senate as a regular one. The Cartel Senate also deals with private enforcement cases and energy law. It is only competent for legal review and takes the facts as stated by the lower courts (with the exception of cases of section 19a GWB, *see* below).

In our study, all cases determined by the Bundesgerichtshof originated from the OLG Düsseldorf. Theoretically, the Bundesgerichtshof can also review cases that came from regional competition authorities of the Länder with first-instance review undertaken by the relevant Oberlandesgericht in that respective Land.

If the Bundesgerichtshof holds that the OLG Düsseldorf has misapplied one or more legal provisions, there are two ways to resolve this: If all necessary facts have been determined by the OLG Düsseldorf, the Bundesgerichtshof can make a final judgement. Otherwise, the case is returned to the OLG. A decision by the Bundesgerichtshof on substantive or procedural law is binding for the OLG Düsseldorf.

These proceedings may take time: If a case is sent back to the OLG Düsseldorf it may take years before conclusion. There may even be a referral back and forth (if necessary, even with a preliminary reference to the European Court of Justice, which is, however, extremely rare). In all of these cases, the Bundesgerichtshof does not review the decision made by the Bundeskartellamt but the decision made by the first-instance court, the OLG Düsseldorf.[13]

2.3 The 2021 Reform: Limiting the Scope of Judicial Review

In 2021, the German Parliament introduced a notable exception to the usual procedural path of Bundeskartellamt decisions being reviewed by the OLG Düsseldorf and the Bundesgerichtshof. Accordingly, decisions made on the provisions within section 19a GWB (the new digital gatekeeper regulation provision in Germany) are directly reviewed by the Bundesgerichtshof. The OLG Düsseldorf is circumvented, meaning that the Bundesgerichtshof rules on facts and legal matters as the first and final instance of judicial review in such matters.

There have been no section 19a-proceedings in the scope of this study (for the late introduction of the rule), but the step is nonetheless significant since it raises the

13. This is with the notable exception of section 19a cases as explained below.

question of the necessary level of judicial review. In the official reasoning accompanying the statute, the lawmakers refer to the speed of changes in digital markets. They imply that the judiciary does not keep up with this speed:

> The exception to the concept of the Federal Court of Justice as the appellate court of last resort takes into account the special interest in a quick and conclusive clarification of the legal issues associated with such proceedings. The speed of the changes brought about by digitalisation is one of the special challenges the state is facing in dealing with the digital economy. (...) these companies [the digital gatekeepers] can completely reshape markets in a very short time. Intervention by the authorities against competitive strategies not based on competition on the merits of such companies can therefore only achieve the effectiveness necessary to protect competition if the corresponding orders by the antitrust authorities can also be implemented in practice. In recent years, the perception has increasingly prevailed that the special features of digital markets require particularly swift intervention compared to other economic sectors in order to have an effective impact.[14]

We see this reduction in the availability of judicial review by one stage as a significant development for the political discussion of judicial review. Even if proceedings take too long - is it the right way to cut down judicial protection for the parties?

2.4 Different Treatment of Cases

The German judicial review system works differently depending on whether a fine or an administrative decision is at stake.

2.4.1 Cases with Fines

Decisions by the Bundeskartellamt that levy a fine against an undertaking and/or a natural person[15] are treated according to the special law on administrative offences, the Ordnungswidrigkeitengesetz, which is similar in nature to the provisions for criminal cases. Unlike EU law, under German competition law, it is possible to fine individuals, e.g., the managers of undertakings.[16] The fine against an undertaking is - from a legal viewpoint - always derived from the responsibility of an individual. The cases against undertakings and the responsible managers are usually dealt with in a single proceeding.

If a party objects to the decision by the Bundeskartellamt, the case goes to the OLG Düsseldorf as a first-instance court. At the OLG Düsseldorf, the Bundeskartellamt is a party to the proceedings together with the public prosecutor (cf. section 82a GWB). Up to 2021, the public prosecutor was leading the appeals cases, while the Bundeskartellamt only had an assisting role.

14. Deutscher Bundestag, Drucksache 19/25868, p. 120 f. (translated by the authors).
15. Hereafter, any statements on the procedure governing the judicial review of fines levelled against an undertaking are also applicable to fines levelled against natural persons.
16. In these proceedings, the provisions of the Ordnungswidrigkeitengesetz are modified by sections 82a-86 GWB.

The OLG Düsseldorf does not review the decision of the Bundeskartellamt in the sense of examining and controlling whether the Bundeskartellamt acted in conformity with the law. Instead, the court issues its own independent decision that replaces the original decision. The court starts the case anew (with very limited exceptions). It takes evidence again, hears the witnesses anew, and looks at the facts as presented by the prosecutor and the Bundeskartellamt on the one hand and the defendants on the other hand. It adopts its own decision, determining the fine independent from the fine set before. Obviously, the case rests on the assumptions and evidence gathered by the Bundeskartellamt since this is what the prosecutor presents to court. Yet, the prosecutor (particularly in the time before 2021) takes the case as its own case and may also deviate from the Bundeskartellamt findings. Technically and practically, this is not a review of what the Bundeskartellamt has done. This also means that the fine may be higher than before, even on appeal by the defendants.

In the second instance, it is the Cartel Senate of the Bundesgerichtshof that is competent for all competition law matters. The decisions taken by the OLG Düsseldorf are subject to legal review. The Bundesgerichtshof does not review the case as decided by the competition agency but as decided by the preceding court. This is a pure review of points of law. The decision by the OLG Düsseldorf can be confirmed or replaced with a decision of the Bundesgerichtshof. If the Bundesgerichtshof considers it necessary to go back to the factual stage, it usually returns the case to the OLG Düsseldorf. In fining cases and sometimes in administrative cases, a new senate has to review it. This guarantees a fresh pair of eyes, at least in fining cases.

The applicable law in fining cases varies from case to case. Since the fine is a sanction close to a criminal sanction, it is not possible to apply laws retroactively. In general, the law in force at the time of the offence is applicable. However, if at any point in time from then to the last judgment, a more lenient legal provision entered into force, the offence is judged against this more lenient provision. This means that it is possible for the court to apply different legal standards for different legal questions relevant to the same case. Furthermore, the court may apply a different version of the Competition Act than the Bundeskartellamt. In a considerable number of fining decisions with this study the OLG Düsseldorf or the Bundesgerichtshof has applied provisions pre-dating 1 May 2004 even though the judgment was given years later (after the detection of the cartel and the proceedings at the Bundeskartellamt).

2.4.2 Infringement Cases/No-Fining Cases

In all other cases, the applicable legal regime and treatment of cases is a specific competition law regime that differs in some respects from normal administrative or civil procedures. The GWB provides for some amendments to usual procedures, which is also rooted in the fact that the proceedings do not go to administrative courts.[17]

17. The provisions governing the rules of procedure for these proceedings are laid down in sections 63-80 GWB.

If the competition authority orders cease and desist of a certain practice, an appeal does not have a suspensive effect (cf. section 66 GWB).[18] In such cases, undertakings may want to seek immediate redress by asking a court to grant an order for suspensive effect. In parallel, the undertaking will challenge the order in the main proceedings. Even if an undertaking appeals an infringement decision of the Bundeskartellamt, enforcement may still continue while the court proceedings are ongoing unless the Bundeskartellamt and the applicant strike a deal, e.g., a non-enforcement agreement. The two proceedings are distinct, but they are both aimed at assessing the original decision of the NCA against the provisions of competition law.

The suspensive effect can be imposed in a court order by the first-instance court, the OLG Düsseldorf. During these proceedings, the decision by the Bundeskartellamt is subject to full legal review with one caveat: The court usually does not take any evidence but decides on the basis of the files forwarded to it by the Bundeskartellamt and the writs provided by the undertaking. In general, the court will impose a suspensive effect if it finds the original decision was unlawful or if enforcement would result in undue hardship for the undertaking. If a suspensive effect is mandated, the prohibition order is suspended for the duration of the court proceedings and can only be enforced after the proceedings are concluded. The OLG Düsseldorf's decision mandating suspensive effect is subject to judicial review by the Bundesgerichtshof. During this second-instance judicial review, the Bundesgerichtshof only reviews the decision by the OLG Düsseldorf in terms of legal plausibility. In terms of the judicial review system, the decisions made in these proceedings can be seen as equally important as decisions made in the full appeal proceedings.

The main proceedings against Bundeskartellamt decisions start at the OLG Düsseldorf. In such appeals, questions of facts and law can be brought to the attention of the court. The original decision is subject to full legal review. Depending on the outcome, the original decision is annulled, or the appeal is rejected or partly upheld/rejected. The decision of the OLG Düsseldorf is subject to further review by the Bundesgerichtshof. Here, the ruling of the OLG Düsseldorf is reviewed on points of law. If the OLG Düsseldorf made a relevant procedural mistake or misapplied substantive law, the decision is overturned. If the facts determined by the OLG Düsseldorf are sufficient, the Bundesgerichtshof will make a final ruling in the case. Otherwise, the case will be referred back to the OLG Düsseldorf.

Not all cases have automatic access to review by the Bundesgerichtshof. The OLG Düsseldorf must admit the case for further review according to section 77 GWB or the parties have to claim a very significant violation of procedural laws. If there is no admission of the case and if there is no such procedural violation, the parties may still plea for admission to the Bundesgerichtshof (section 78 GWB). The decision is then taken by the Bundesgerichtshof whether it hears the case.

Not all cases decided by the Bundeskartellamt are subject to judicial review. If the proceedings are closed with commitments entered into by the undertaking specifying which conduct they will refrain from in the future, there is hardly ever judicial review.

18. Up to 12 July 2005, an application against an order by the Bundeskartellamt did have a suspensive effect.

While the undertakings concerned usually do not waive their legal right to litigate, they have no incentive to challenge the decisions. The same is true for settlements or other ways to close the proceedings.

Third parties have standing to trigger a review only if their interests are substantially affected by the decision and when they have been admitted to the proceedings upon their application by the competition authority (section 63 GWB).

If the OLG Düsseldorf fully or partly overturned the Bundeskartellamt's original decision, the agency may challenge this court decision and seek judicial review of the Bundesgerichtshof.

3 PRIOR RESEARCH

Up to this point, no comprehensive research on questions of judicial review of decisions issued by the Bundeskartellamt has been conducted. In general, empirical work on German case law is relatively rare. Only recently, some authors presented empirical findings, particularly on damages claims.[19] We suspect that empirical work is not as deeply embedded in German legal and philosophical tradition as may be the case in other countries.

Podszun conducted an empirical analysis of the second instance's, i.e., the Bundesgerichtshof's, judicial review of antitrust cases[20] in the period from 2000 to 2019.[21] His key findings were:

- The number of cases on judicial review decreased, in particular in proportion to the rising number of cases dealt with by the agency. So, while the Bundeskartellamt had more cases, these were less frequently subject to judicial review.
- Many subject matters of competition law were never or very rarely subject to judicial review. Hence, the influence of the judiciary and the control of the Bundeskartellamt in these fields have been weak. For instance, third-party rights and procedural issues hardly ever played a role in the Bundesgerichtshof rulings.

That study also provided data on the length of proceedings, the quota of success for the parties and the involvement of individual judges, but not on questions of the relationship with European law.

19. *See*, for instance, Loy, Kartellschadensersatzverfahren am Justizstandort Deutschland, 2022; Rengier, WuW 2018, 613; Klumpe/Thiede, NZKart 2018, 136; Isikay, WuW 2020, 650; Marx, Konsensuales Kartellverfahrensrecht, 2016; more generally Risse, NJW 2020, 2382.
20. The study also included merger control cases, but excluded private enforcement.
21. *See* Podszun, Die Überprüfung kartellbehördlicher Entscheidungen durch den BGH - Eine empirische Analyse des Zeitraums 2000-2019, WuW 2021, 216-222; Podszun, Die Stellung des BGH im Kartellrecht - ein empirischer Ansatz, GRUR 2021, 316-321.

There has been no comparable research to date regarding the Bundeskartellamt's decisions or the first-instance level at the OLG Düsseldorf. To our knowledge, there is no further research involving empirical study or coding of decisions nor research focussing on questions primarily associated with judicial review.

4 QUANTITATIVE ANALYSIS

This project maps the judicial review of competition law cases, focusing on restrictive business practices or unilateral conduct in Germany. Any cases dealing with private enforcement or merger control were excluded from this analysis. All actions were brought by German competition authorities, and they cover the period from May 2004 to the end of April 2021.

4.1 Source of Information

The data was collected from the official databases of the OLG Düsseldorf[22] and the Bundesgerichtshof.[23] Additionally, the commercial databases provided by Beck-Online[24] and Juris[25] were used to find additional decisions not published in the official databases. Eighteen decisions issued by the OLG Düsseldorf were not published on the database of the OLG Düsseldorf but could be found on Beck-Online or Juris. To our knowledge, there is no decision published elsewhere that is not included in one of these sources.

It is important to note that in Germany, not all judicial decisions are published or included in official databases. National law does not require administrative authorities or courts to publish their decisions and judgments, and there is no public register indicating which cases have been decided. Publication decisions primarily lie in the hands of the judges: If they believe a case is worth publishing they may do so, but this often takes a long period of time.

In light of the above, the database is inherently partial. We take an educated guess, having checked numbers with the Bundeskartellamt, that roughly 60% of decisions involving judicial review of Bundeskartellamt decisions are published. Regarding decisions by the Bundesgerichtshof we estimate that all decisions on administrative cases and most fining decisions (79%) are published. We estimate that 54% of all fining decisions of the OLG Düsseldorf are published, and 50% of administrative decisions.

22. www.justiz.nrw/BS/nrwe2/index.php.
23. juris.bundesgerichtshof.de/cgi-bin/rechtsprechung/list.py?Gericht = bgh&Art = en&Datum = Aktuell&Sort = 12288.
24. www.beck-online.de.
25. www.juris.de.

We asked judges and members of the competition authority regarding which cases were and were not being published. But even the answer to this question was hardly verifiable. It seems that the issue is a black box also for those directly involved in the process. Even when published, court judgments are anonymised to a significant degree. This leads to a loss of information (e.g., regarding names of parties, names of judges, sum in dispute, preceding decisions, relevant legal norms, timeline of the case). The published reasoning often consists of an abbreviated justification, which does not always include all information about every document presented by the parties. It is often unclear from the decision about what aspects of a previous decision parties complained about. The decisions usually do not deal with matters that are not relevant to the final outcome of the decision or matters that are not litigious but may be informative for understanding the case and its review. This means that it can be very difficult to understand many issues from the decision alone.

The same is true with respect to fines. The original fine imposed by the Bundeskartellamt is hardly ever mentioned in the court decision and is not always traceable in other documents. Since the OLG Düsseldorf reconsiders the whole case, it seldom refers to the specific amount of the fine in its reasoning. The same is true for review by the Bundesgerichtshof. It is not a given that the fine as set by the OLG Düsseldorf is published or mentioned in the Bundesgerichtshof case. The lack of available information renders the understanding and coding of the cases difficult and to trace the development of the case given that it is not mandatory to give the case number of the preceding case in publications.

4.2 Total Number of Cases

As stated above, we estimate that only 60% of the relevant court judgments are published and that the judgments by the Bundesgerichtshof are more often published. This may also mean that the history of some cases cannot be completely recorded since one judgment may not be published.

Including all available judgments, the database contains sixty-five judgments pertaining to thirty-one decisions by the Bundeskartellamt. The ratio of decisions subject to appeal is approximately 20% in the first instance. Of the judgments made by the first-instance courts, 22% are appealed. In total, there are thirty-one first-instance judgments and thirty-four second-instance judgments coded in the database. Any proceedings concerning the suspensive effect of an appeal were coded as if they were appeal proceedings.[26] The fact that these were proceedings concerning the suspensive effect was documented.

The number of judgments rendered - per year - is summarised in Figure 13.1.

Figure 13.1 Number of Judgments According to Instances

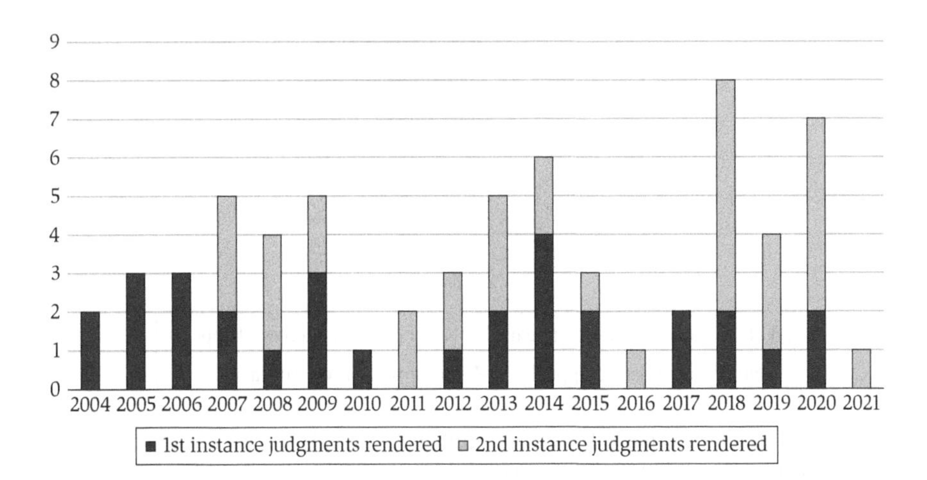

On average, the OLG Düsseldorf issued 1.72 and the Bundesgerichtshof issued 1.83 published judgments per year. Over time, a decline in the number of judgments issued and published by the first-instance court can be observed. For example, in 2011, 2016 and 2021, the first-instance court did not render a single judgment that fell into the scope of this study. The second-instance judgments, by comparison, are equally spread over the whole time period. Only during the first three years (2004-2006) were there no second-instance judgments that were included in the database. This is due to the scope of the study, where only decisions made after the enactment of Regulation 1/2003 came into view.

4.3 Success Rates and Outcomes

Figure 13.2 summarises the success of appeals launched against the NCA's decisions or the first-instance court's judgment. It indicates the ratio of fully successful appeals, partially successful, and fully rejected appeals.

26. As explained above, parties usually formally first seek to reverse the rule that the appeal does not have suspensive effect. In substance, this is an appeal of the decision.

Figure 13.2 Success of Appeals (Each NCA's Decision or Previous Instance Judgment Counts as One)

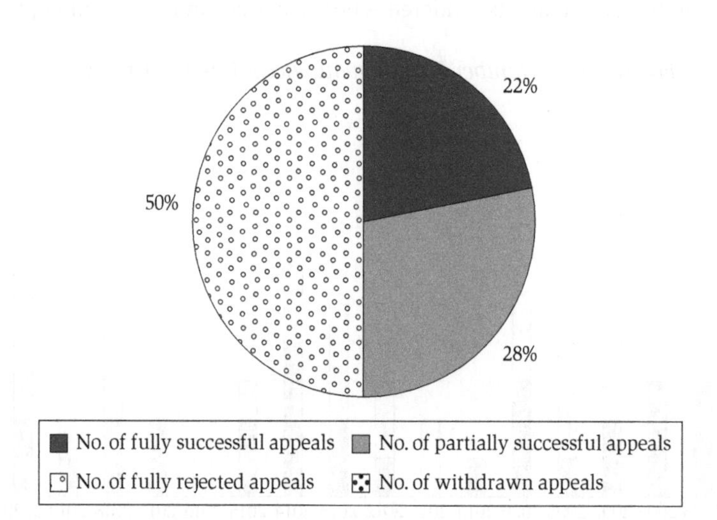

Figure 13.2 shows that 50% of the published appeals were fully rejected, 28% partially successful, and 22% fully successful.

The relatively high level of fully or partially successful appeals is even more striking when examining only first-instance appeals. To this end, Figures 13.3(a) and (b) indicate the ratio of possible outcomes according to each instance of appeal. Figure 13.3(a) demonstrates that from all recorded first-instance judgments, only 26% were fully rejected, leaving the NCA's decision unchanged. By comparison, 14% of appeals were fully successful, 16% of the NCA's decisions were fully or partially annulled, 36% were amended only with respect to the fines, and 19% of the NCA's decisions were fully replaced by the court. In other words, the data shows that in most cases the amount of the fine or a part of the original decision was successfully appealed against.

The rejected cases also include appeals deemed to be inadmissible by the courts. The appeal was found to be fully inadmissible in five cases (8%)[27] and partially inadmissible in two cases (3%). If the formal requirements of proceedings are observed (e.g., time period, providing grounds of appeal, appealing to the correct court, power of attorney), the appeal is admissible. In the cases where the courts held the appeal to be inadmissible parties did not have formal standing (third party), did not show up for tactical reasons or did not succeed in claiming a substantive violation of their rights. Any other legal questions regarding the case are covered insofar as the court determined that the appeal was admissible.

27. Five cases out of sixty-five cases investigated is 7.69%, rounded up to 8% here.

Figure 13.3(a) First-Instance Outcome

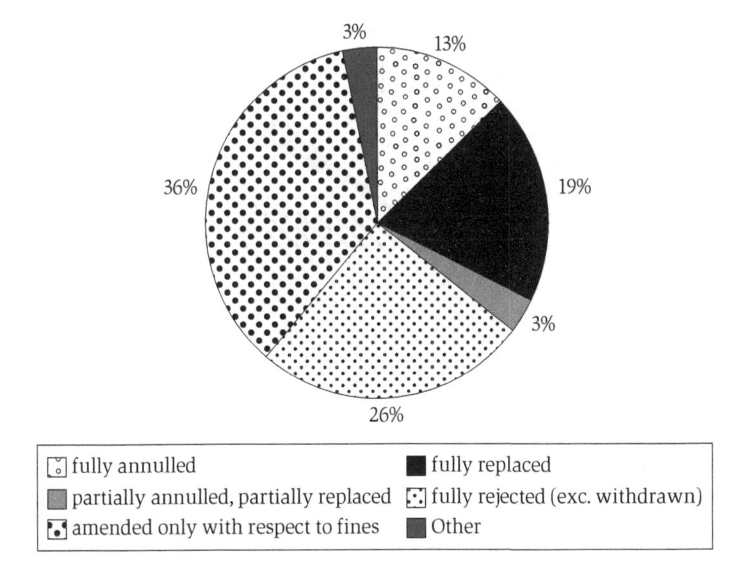

It is important to note that any amendment made with respect to the fines may not necessarily be beneficial to the undertaking launching the appeal. In several prominent rulings, the OLG Düsseldorf raised the fine considerably upon appeal of the parties.[28] For instance, in the 'Coffee Cartel' case, the Bundeskartellamt imposed a fine of EUR 5.25 million against retailer Rossmann in 2015. When Rossman objected, the OLG Düsseldorf levied a fine of EUR 30 million in 2018. This ruling was set aside by the Bundesgerichtshof for procedural reasons in 2019. After another back and forth between OLG Düsseldorf and Bundesgerichtshof, the OLG Düsseldorf dealt with the case anew and set the fine for Rossmann at EUR 20 million in 2022.[29]

Second-instance appeals were less successful. As Figure 13.3(b) shows, 44% of the appeals were fully rejected. The BGH partially annulled 18% of the OLG Düsseldorf's judgments and returned them to the first-instance court, 18% were fully annulled and returned to the first-instance court, and only in 6% of all cases was the first-instance decision fully annulled.

28. This is not always reflected in the code sheet since the amount of fines is redacted from the decisions.
29. The final ruling is available https://www.justiz.nrw.de/nrwe/olgs/duesseldorf/j2022/1_Kart_1_22_OWi_Urteil_20221111.html.

Figure 13.3(b) Second-Instance Outcome

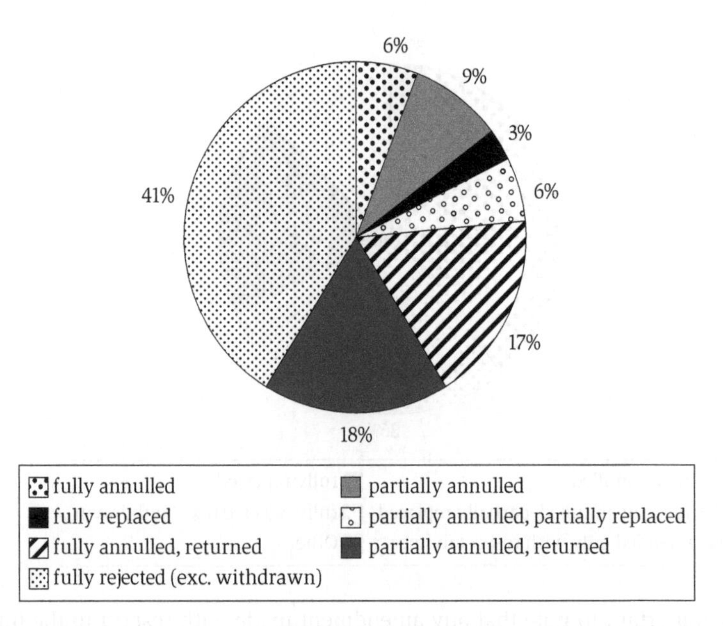

Assessing the success rate is difficult without a detailed analysis of the decision. It makes a difference whether a decision is upheld in all major points but annulled in a minor point or vice versa. This is not reflected by the formal question that formed the basis for this issue.

4.4 Type of NCA's Decisions Subject to Appeal

Figure 13.4 shows that a vast majority (77%) of appeals concerned the prohibitions against restrictive agreements. Purely national cases, reviewing the application of section 1 GWB alone (the German equivalent to Article 101 TFEU) were the subject of a little more than half (51%) of all appeals, and 26% of appeals concerned both Article 101 TFEU and section 1 GWB. The focus on anti-competitive agreements may result from the fact that in Germany, fines are usually imposed in cartel cases alone, that cartel cases often have several participants (who sometimes appeal in separate procedures), and that for a while, there was no 'deal-making' or settlement in such cases so that judicial redress was the only way to challenge the fine.

The provisions on abuse of dominance were reviewed in 17% of the appeals. A small number of appeals (6%) examined all provisions. The different rules being appealed are evenly distributed across all years. There are no discernible patterns.

Figure 13.4 Rule Being Appealed

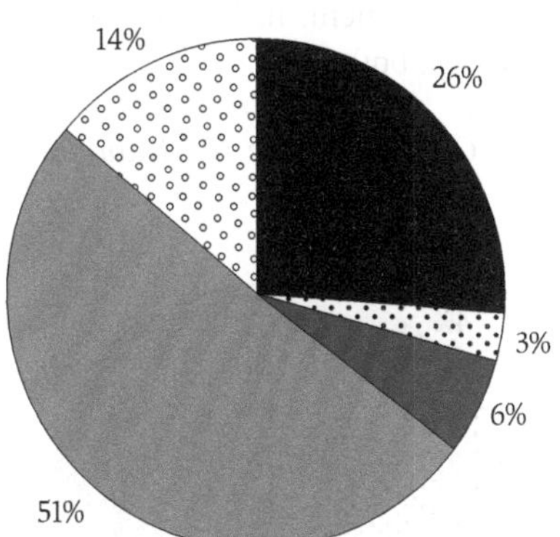

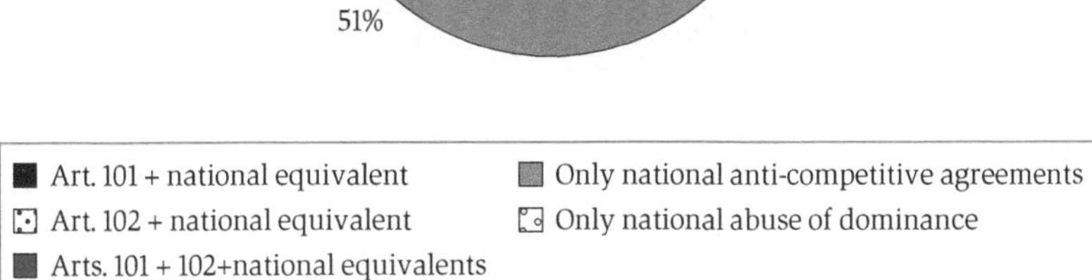

Figure 13.5 examines the type of restrictions subject to appeal. In line with the above findings pointing to the frequency of appeals concerning anti-competitive agreements, it demonstrates that a clear majority (74%) of all appeals concerned horizontal restrictions, 11% of appeals concerned vertical restrictions (5%) or vertical restrictions as well as exclusionary abuse (5%). An additional 11% of all restrictions covered were concerned with exclusionary abuse. Finally, 3% of all restrictions were concerned with exploitative abuse, and 2% of all cases were concerned with exploitative and exclusionary abuse.

Figure 13.5 Types of Restrictions

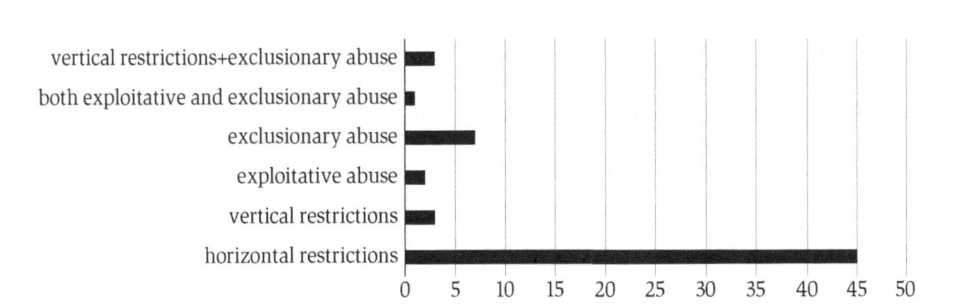

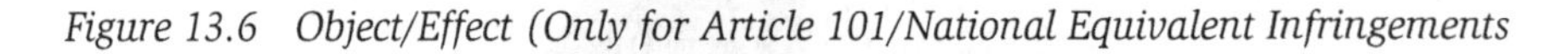

Similarly, Figure 13.6 shows that a majority (72%) of all cases on Article 101 TFEU and section 1 GWB concern agreements where the restriction of competition was found to be the object of the agreement. In 15% of cases, a restriction by-effect was involved, and in 4% of all cases, both.

Figure 13.6 Object/Effect (Only for Article 101/National Equivalent Infringements

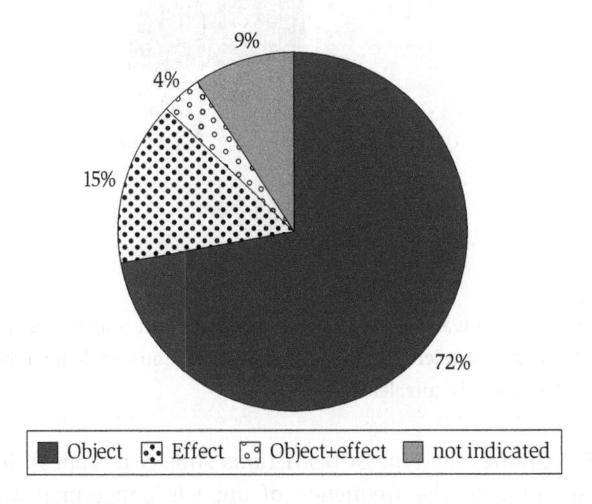

The above findings point to relatively narrow areas of law subject to appeals in Germany, namely mostly horizontal restrictions in purely national cases. This raises the question of whether this matches the focus of the Bundeskartellamt's enforcement more generally or is a phenomenon uniquely associated with appeals. While full data on the practice of the Bundeskartellamt is missing, we have figures for the year 2017 that give some indication of the Bundeskartellamt's practices: in 2017, the Bundeskartellamt gave the following statistics on new cases:[30]

- fifteen cases: restrictive agreements, only national law, two of these hardcore cartels, no vertical case;
- twenty-four cases: restrictive agreements, national law and EU law, nine of these hardcore cartels, one of these vertical case;
- eight cases: abusive practices, only national law;
- four cases: abusive practices, national and EU law;
- one other case.

30. Bundeskartellamt, Tätigkeitsbericht 2017/2018, 2018, BT-Drucksache 19/10900, p. 135.

This is a snapshot for the year 2017 only. According to our impression of other years where we have not verified the data but got an overview, it seems that this is representative of general practice: the vast majority of cases deal with horizontal restrictive business practices. For restrictive business practices, it is quite common to apply European law in parallel today. This is less so for the smaller overall number of abuse cases.

Finally, Figure 13.7 summarises the types of Bundeskartellamt decisions subject to an appeal. It shows that with one exception, all cases involved findings of infringements. Sixty-six per cent of the published appeals related to Bundeskartellamt's decisions, making a finding of an infringement and levelling a fine, and 38% of the cases involved findings of an infringement with no fine.

In the case of *Flüssiggas*,[31] the Bundeskartellamt's proceedings were terminated after some form of settlement. The undertaking accepted the determination by the Bundeskartellamt that its actions were unlawful and only challenged the amount of fine. This meant that the determination that competition law was infringed became binding, and only the amount of fine was still subject to appeal. The OLG Düsseldorf levied a fine of EUR 6,000,000 against the undertaking.[32]

Figure 13.7 Competition Authority's Procedure

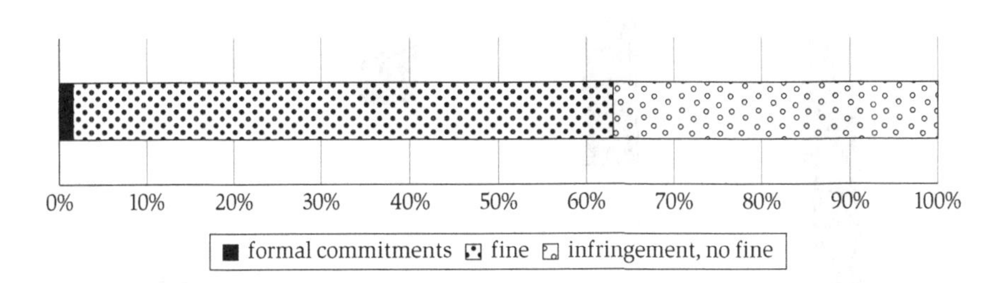

31. Translated 'Liquid Gas', 13.05.2014, docket no. V-4 Kart 8/10 (OWi).
32. The original fine levelled by the Bundeskartellamt was not mentioned in the reasoning of the OLG Düsseldorf.

4.5 Grounds of Appeal

Figure 13.8 summarises the grounds of appeals raised in first- and second-instance appeals and their success.

Figure 13.8 Grounds of Appeal (Each NCA's Decision or Previous Instance Judgment Counts as One)

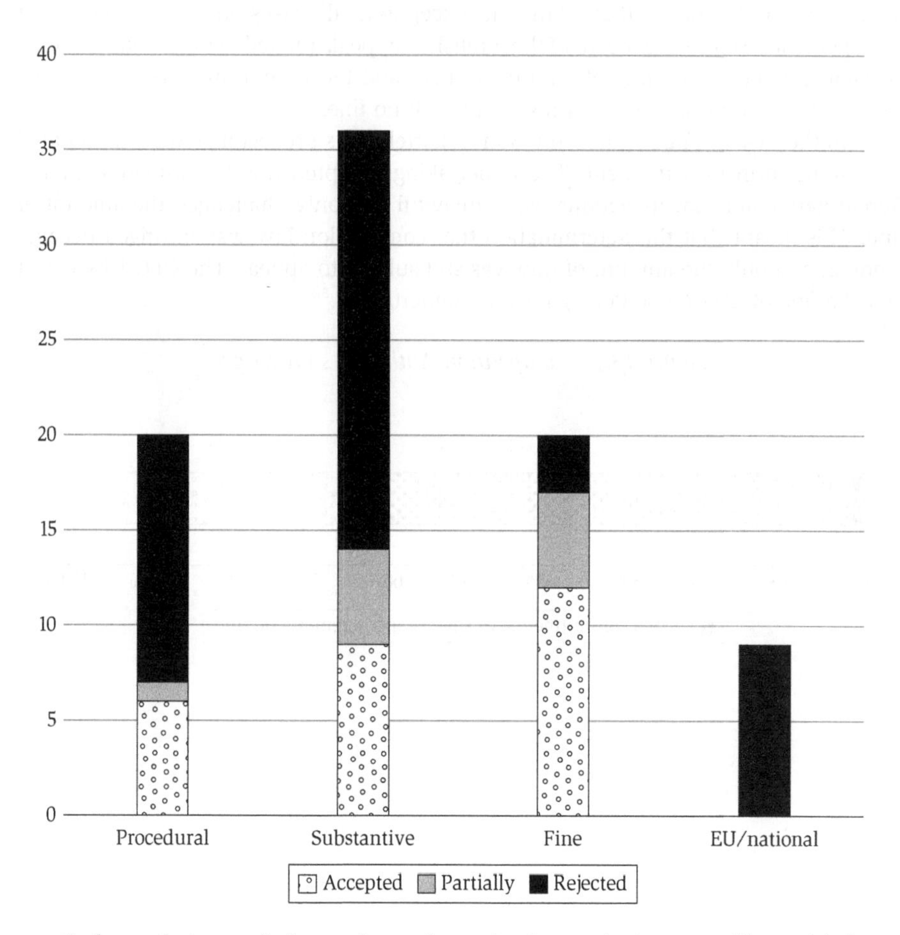

It shows that appeals focused on substantive law and – in proceedings with fines – the amount of fines levelled.[33] Our impression is that procedural aspects of competition law are not scrutinised with intensity by courts. We assume that there are several reasons that could explain this.

33. Procedural grounds are less frequently invoked, and judging from the cases, it often looks as if procedural grounds were raised rather additionally, with less vigour (this is a qualitative statement that cannot be read from the numbers).

First, the Bundeskartellamt has established procedures in place that have been tried and tested before. If one of the procedures was substantially flawed, this could have been corrected over time. While matters of substance may differ from case to case, procedures usually remain the same. There is a higher chance that, at least regarding the general set-up of the procedures, these are in conformity with the law.[34]

Second, it may play a role that judges on the competition benches institutionally act in a civil law setting. They are mostly (but not exclusively) recruited from prior positions where they dealt with other civil law cases. (As noted, the cartel senates at OLG Düsseldorf and BGH are embedded in the civil law strand of the judiciary). It is a characteristic of civil law that administrative procedures do not play a role. Therefore, the mindset and training of these judges have not been trained in public or criminal law, where much more scrutiny is put on procedures.

Third, in proceedings involving fines, the OLG Düsseldorf redetermines all facts of the case and takes its own decision. In such cases, there is little room for analysing procedures at the Bundeskartellamt.

Finally, for the undertakings, the legally binding determination that the actions were unlawful is the most effective point of attack. An appeal against procedural aspects potentially just delays enforcement and leads to repeat proceedings (if at all) where the same practices are examined. Sometimes, the review of procedures does not even lead to a revision or a different outcome at all. This lowers the incentive for undertakings to emphasise this point, and consequently, judges are focussing less on procedure.

The tension between EU and national competition laws has been examined in only a few cases, and in all of those cases, this ground was unsuccessful.

In several cases, the undertakings do not appeal the substantive assessment but only the level of fines. The fine is determined on the basis of a lot of factors (object/effect, length of illegal behaviour, breadth of infringement, damage caused, cooperation during proceedings, leniency, etc.). These factors are open to different assessments; there is no schematic right or wrong in this. The OLG Düsseldorf[35] often comes to a different outcome than the Bundeskartellamt, not necessarily because of huge differences in substance but because of different perceptions when weighing the different factors. This, incidentally, also means that EU law does not play a role in such cases since fines are calculated according to national law only.

The findings show that different grounds of appeals are - mostly - evenly distributed across all years. Yet, procedural grounds were only successful between 2018 and 2020.

34. This does not mean, of course, that in each case procedures are followed correctly by staff.
35. The OLG Düsseldorf is the only court that determines the amount of the fine. If the Bundesgerichtshof finds that the determination of fine made by the OLG Düsseldorf was done incorrectly, it annuls the decision and refers the case back to the OLG Düsseldorf. The OLG Düsseldorf is bound by the decision of the Bundesgerichtshof and redetermines the fine taking into account the legal reasoning of the Bundesgerichtshof why the previous determination of fine was incorrect.

4.6 Undertakings and Individuals as Appellants

The Bundeskartellamt's decision was appealed by undertakings in 75 % of all cases and by individuals in 23 % of all cases. These individuals are usually the directors or employees in influential (managing) positions within the undertaking. Proceedings against undertakings are usually accompanied by proceedings against the directors/managers responsible. It is impossible to state from the data how many mixed cases there were where appeals by individuals and by companies were taken together in one. The rulings of the OLG Düsseldorf were appealed by the Bundeskartellamt in 27 %, by undertakings in 53 % and by individuals in 18 % of all cases.

Most appeals, in the first instance, are made by undertakings. In the second instance, undertakings account for 73 % of all appeals not made by the Bundeskartellamt. In fining cases, undertakings and natural persons often appeal the same decision in the same appeal proceedings. It was not always possible to determine whether this was the case, who and how many applicants were party to the proceedings and how they fared.

4.7 Third Parties

Third parties rarely challenge decisions at all, be it for commercial reasons or on the basis that the impact of the case is limited. This means that the interests of third parties are only seldom heard in a meaningful way. This is all the more true for the involvement of associations that represent collective interests, e.g., consumer associations. It is uncommon in German courts to have such parties involved in competition cases or to give their point of view a considerable meaning. There is no tradition of amicus briefs in German courts (but for the Bundeskartellamt in private enforcement cases).

Within the scope of the study, two cases were a third-party appeal. In these cases, the third parties were advantaged by a decision made by the Bundeskartellamt. In both cases, the Bundeskartellamt found that a specific practice of a business partner of this third party was unlawful. This decision would have led to better contract conditions for both third parties. Therefore, in each case, the third party appealed against the OLG Düsseldorf's decision, annulling the Bundeskartellamt's decision. Both appeals were unsuccessful.

In one case, the case *Bau und Hobby*,[36] the appellant was a hardware store franchisee. The Bundeskartellamt determined that the franchisor infringed competition law because the prices set for franchise products were too high. The franchisor successfully appealed against this decision. The Bundeskartellamt's decision was annulled by the OLG Düsseldorf. The franchisee appealed against this decision and argued that the original decision by the Bundeskartellamt determining an infringement of competition law was correct. The appeal was unsuccessful. In the other case,[37] a

36. Decision made by the Bundesgerichtshof on 11.11.2008, docket no. KVR 17/08.
37. Decision made by the OLG Düsseldorf on 17.09.2014, docket no. VI Kart 1/13 (V).

broadband network provider challenged the decision by the Bundeskartellamt to declare commitments made by another undertaking legally binding. The appellant argued that this commitment effectively bound the network provider and that this was unlawful because of a lack of legal basis. The appeal was unsuccessful.

4.8 Role of EU Law

European law is relevant in fewer cases than we expected.

We have not found a single case with a preliminary reference to the European Court of Justice.[38] In their rulings, the courts do not refer to case law from the European Court of Justice. It needs to be pointed out that there is no strict pattern of citing case law in decisions - each ruling (or each rapporteur?) is different regarding the quantity of cited sources. It is still remarkable that there is no citation of European jurisprudence, be it in cases involving Articles. 101, 102 TFEU or national law (where the wisdom of the European courts could still be used by analogy).

Tensions between national law and EU law were only relevant in two cases. The Bundesgerichtshof decided one of these cases in 2007 and one in 2008. Both cases dealt with Article 4(3) TEU (ex Article 10 EC, *effet utile*) and the consequences that need to be observed when applying national competition law. In the first case, Article 102 TFEU (ex 86 EC) was also relevant to the decision. Other than that, European law and its relationship with national law were not relevant. In Article 102 TFEU cases, the German law is stricter and thus easier to apply than the European law.

5 QUALITATIVE ANALYSIS

5.1 Independence of the Bundeskartellamt and Judicial Review

As stated before, each division within the Bundeskartellamt operates independently from the Ministry of Economics and Climate and the President of the Bundeskartellamt. This aspect of true independence of the divisions and the principle of majority decisions by three individuals within the divisions needs some emphasis, particularly with respect to judicial review: The Bundeskartellamt is not a hierarchical organisation with one decision-making body at its top. Instead, there are very many people individually involved in different decisions. There is no formal coordination of decisions. For an agency, this opens up pluralist and diverse paths to exercising power. The internal division of tasks and the non-hierarchical mechanism of coming to a decision amounts to a form of internal control mechanism that puts individual decisions very much into perspective: The impact of each decision is limited, not only because it only deals with this or that case, but because of the freedom of other decision divisions to differ from the path taken by one of them.

38. The well-known Facebook case where the OLG Düsseldorf sent questions to the European Court of Justice is not in the scope of this study.

The system has in-built mechanisms of 'peer review'. There is no person or committee that can drive its agenda forward. Power is divided into many. We suggest taking this institutional design into consideration when discussing the level of judicial review. It might be suggested that judicial review becomes ever more important, the more power is concentrated in a few hands. On the one hand, in a setting like the German one, it could be seen as less likely that a state agency abuses its powers to any significant extent. On the other hand, individual decisions are more likely to reflect the idiosyncratic nature of the decision-making context. We do not advocate that there should be no judicial review of Bundeskartellamt decisions, but at least the danger of a politically driven agency, directed by one person at its helm, is limited.

If judicial review of administrative decisions is primarily seen as an instrument to control the power of state actors, it can be pointed out that power in the Bundeskartellamt is distributed to many people. This decentralisation is the first level of internal control. Judicial review is more centred on individual cases, not so much on shaping the application of competition law in general and limiting the power of the Bundeskartellamt.

5.2 Specialisation of Courts

Germany decided to set up specialised competition law benches at two courts to review decisions by the Bundeskartellamt, namely at the Cartel Senates at the OLG Düsseldorf and at the Bundesgerichtshof. At both courts, judges do not necessarily come from the field of competition law when starting in their positions but are part of the general judiciary. Judges on both courts need to pass a rigorous selection process. These judicial appointment processes are usually long. Therefore, the judges of each senate are, on average, highly experienced in applying competition law. They generally have a high reputation and are seen as highly professional judges. In our analysis, we had the impression that all rulings were in conformity with a high standard of judicial care and professionalism. No outsiders other than professional judges are involved (i.e., lay judges).

The judges are part of the branch of the judiciary that deals with private law or criminal law cases ('ordentliche Gerichtsbarkeit'). This is a peculiar feature since the cases to be investigated are administrative in nature and would - normally - go to the branch of the German judiciary that deals with administrative law. It is often said that the mindset is different in the two branches and that previous experiences matter a lot for the approach taken by judges towards a case. According to this perception, administrative law judges are more concerned with procedural issues than others. Judges with a history in criminal law allegedly tend to be particularly attentive to facts and proof. Civil law judges are assumed to be more likely to focus on the substance of the case and try to reconcile the interests of the parties.

While we are not able to show such differing approaches in detail within the scope of this project, we share the general assumption that the prior experiences of judges and their legal mindsets may play an important role in judicial review. The approach to cases and the style of rulings, in our perception, resembles the usual reasoning and style of civil law cases much more than classic administrative cases.

This civil law background could theoretically be corrected by the influence of two other courts, the German Constitutional Court (Bundesverfassungsgericht) or the European Court of Justice. Yet, these courts are practically not involved in competition law cases in Germany. As seen before (section 4.h), there are hardly any preliminary references to the European Court of Justice. The Bundesverfassungsgericht is hardly ever hearing competition law cases.

5.3 Intensity of Legal Review

It is difficult to comment on the intensity of legal review with the findings made here. As seen from Figure 13.3(a), there is a significant number of cases, but this number seems to be declining when taking into account that more and more decisions are taken by the Bundeskartellamt. The outcome of appeals (Figure 13.3(b)) shows that the judiciary is willing to exert control of the Bundeskartellamt, even if the limited number of total cases does not allow for an encompassing control of all aspects of competition law. Judicial review, even at the level of the Bundesgerichtshof, does not seem to be oriented towards 'educating' the Bundeskartellamt. There is no discernible 'agenda' for competition policy. The courts understand their role as instances of control in individual cases, trying to do justice to the parties of the particular case.

The courts do not assess cases comprehensively but focus on the specific points that are (deemed) important for the specific case. This is particularly true for the Bundesgerichtshof, where cases are not scrutinised in full but only with a view to the litigious aspects.

Regarding the legal standard, it is often difficult to discern the exact standards in a positive way since judicial review does not give the right solution but only determines where there has been an error by the authority in enforcing the law.

In the period of the study, economic evidence in the sense of modern economic tests (as advocated by proponents of the *more economic approach*) has not played a role in German courts. The courts refrain from references to a consumer welfare standard and have usually not engaged in discussing economic theories or models. Cases have mostly been resolved by purely legal reasoning.

For proceedings involving fines, the level of control appears to be relatively high, but the system does not allow for 'judicial review' in the sense of an examination of the activities taken by the agency. As stated above, the OLG Düsseldorf does not review the agency's decision or proceedings. Instead, the proceedings start anew as judicial court proceedings, where the court examines the whole case in terms of facts and law. This includes hearing witnesses (including competitors), involving expert witnesses, and carefully examining any facts or legal arguments presented by the undertakings' legal representation. The level of factual scrutiny required of the OLG Düsseldorf is high and is the main reason for the length of court proceedings. If the court finds that the undertaking or individual did infringe competition law, it takes its own decision with a completely new reasoning and determines an appropriate fine. This means that the proceedings do not lead to a review of the original fine.

This system comes with different effects: On the one hand, appellants get a completely new assessment of the case. This goes beyond simple review and reduces biases that may exist when the court heavily relies on the findings of the prosecuting agency. On the other hand, this also means that the outcome of the appeal can be less favourable than the outcome at the agency stage. Fines can be set at a higher level. Parties have no certainty what happens upon appeal. This may be a disincentive to parties considering an appeal.

For all parties, this system raises the costs of proceedings in terms of fees and time. This is shown by the liquid gas cartel case (*Flüssiggaskartell*): after completion of the Bundeskartellamt investigation in 2007, the undertakings involved got a fine of EUR 180 million. Upon appeal to the OLG Düsseldorf, the court took 130 days of hearings to assess the case anew and ended the proceedings in 2013 with a fine of EUR 244 million. This ruling went to review by the Bundesgerichtshof and was overturned in 2019. The Bundesgerichtshof returned the case to another senate at the OLG Düsseldorf that had to deal with the matter again. This time, it took 6 court days and ended with a fine of approximately EUR 40 million in 2020.

5.4 The Courts Dealing with EU Law

European law plays a big part in the development of German competition law. In turn, German competition law - along with the competition law of the other member states - contributes ideas to the development of European competition law. In light of this interplay of European and German competition law, it was surprising that the reasoning of many court decisions solely refers to the German antitrust provisions. As far as European law is concerned (mostly in more recent cases), it is often seen as parallel to German law (as in cases of cartels). The lack of preliminary references and the omission of citations of European law during the period we studied is a stunning result of this study.

In abuse cases, this is understandable since German law is stricter than EU law, so it makes sense to focus on German law.

Still, we consider it a weakness of the German case law that it does not offer more references to European law. This would be fruitful for the exchange with courts in other countries, and it may also increase the impact of German decisions in the EU. Harmonisation would be further eased with more consideration of national and EU law on all levels. It is our impression that in very recent times the attitude changed.

We speculate that this 'blindness' to European law is rooted in the historical development of German competition law. Its rich history dating back to the 1950s may have given competition lawyers in Germany a more national perspective than in Member States where competition law was introduced only later or under the auspices of the European Commission. If you have a national tradition and national precedents, it may be harder to turn to the EU than if not. This may be reinforced by the system of state examinations in law that place little emphasis on EU law or specialisations like competition law. When Regulation 1/2003 was introduced many German competition policy experts (lawyers and economists) had very strong reservations towards the changes introduced. The same is true for the more economic approach that was met in Germany with criticism. Both developments may have contributed to a rather cautious integration with European law in the period studied here.

6 CONCLUDING REMARKS

Germany has a robust competition law enforcement and judicial review system in place that, generally speaking, is well-respected by stakeholders. It is said that all institutions fulfil high legal standards when applying competition law. Yet, determining in detail whether confidence in the system is justified is difficult with the empirical framework of this study. We still believe that it is fair to state that Germany has a robust and effective judicial review system that ensures that the enforcement practice of the Bundeskartellamt adheres to EU and national competition law. The judiciary seems well-equipped for the coming years to ensure effective and lawful competition law enforcement. Nonetheless, we conclude by pointing at five findings that merit further attention.

Before doing so, the limits of this research should be pointed out:

First, the important topic of judicial review has not as yet been addressed intensely with an empirical or theoretical methodology. Perhaps the long-standing traditions of the German competition law framework, in action ever since 1958, have obscured the view for questioning the institutional setting. This mapping exercise provides a starting point for further endeavours.

Second, we are unable to answer many questions comprehensively. This is partly due to a lamentable lack of transparency. Our ignorance is also partly due to the complexity of the issue and the necessity to have implicit knowledge about a legal system. Judges know very well what they do, but it is still very complicated to trace the different steps and find an explanation for each of them in their published verdicts.

The third aspect does not come as a surprise but still needs to be borne in mind: Rules, procedure, and practice of enforcement and judicial review are heavily entrenched in the national legal system, are very complex and have not yet been harmonised within the EU. Whether this can be changed over time or not will be one of the tough questions of updating the institutional framework for the judiciary.

Now, we turn to the five substantive conclusions.

6.1 Incentives for Seeking Judicial Review

If cases are not brought to court, the matter is not reviewed, the competition agency is not controlled, and the field of competition law is not developed further through judges. In the long run, conformity with the law may falter.

As we have set out in our prior research and as is visible from the above results presented in section 4.2, the level of judicial review of competition law enforcement seems to be on the decline. This may have different reasons. At the stage of the agency, more cases are completed with settlements and commitment decisions or in cartel cases with leniency applications where the parties have little room to question facts. Another reason may be the uncertainty and risk associated with the jurisprudence (e.g., regarding the raising of fines by the Düsseldorf court).

We suggest that it is a considerable disincentive for seeking judicial redress when the parties need to fear that the outcome of their appeal is worse than before (as happened in one of the cases). This tendency increased after the period we investigated. If undertakings see litigation as a matter of business (and not a matter of principle) they will undertake a cost-benefit analysis before going to court. Germany needs to pay attention to the incentives for potential applicants. If they risk too much when going to court, judicial review will decline further.

This raises the question of the influence of the judiciary. There are - for such a long period of study - relatively few competition law cases make it to the OLG Düsseldorf and the Bundesgerichtshof (*see* section 4.2)). The Bundeskartellamt therefore takes the prime role in shaping competition policy.

6.2 Ignorance of Procedures and Third Parties

Judicial scrutiny of some aspects of competition law enforcement is particularly scarce. There are areas in German competition law that have hardly been inspected by the courts in the past two decades. This relates particularly to questions of procedure and third-party rights. Both aspects rarely play a role. One may assume that procedural aspects are not in the spotlight of civil law judges and do not feature prominently in applications by parties. In fining cases, the peculiar system often makes it superfluous to check procedures in any detail. For third parties, the incentives to litigate are lower than for parties that are directly affected.

6.3 Length and Complexity of Proceedings

It makes a fundamental difference whether a case goes on appeal or not. If a case is not appealed, the parties and the Bundeskartellamt save many resources and a lot of time that would otherwise be spent on court proceedings that they are not able to steer themselves. This is especially relevant for fining cases where judicial review does not only mean to review of the decision itself but includes a full new gathering of facts by the OLG Düsseldorf. The length and complexity of proceedings are further increased if a case is sent back from the Bundesgerichtshof to the OLG Düsseldorf. This back and forth can consume a considerable amount of time and resources. The whole matter is made more complex since it is often a certain complex of cases, e.g., stemming from the same cartel, that go to courts and take different routes or outcomes. This may happen when there are decisions on procedural issues, interim relief, appeals by different parties independently from another etc. In total, the incentive to seek judicial review is low if a case is costly and lengthy and drags on for years. We advocate a substantial reform of the judicial system to deal with cases more swiftly.

6.4 Available Data

In Germany, not all decisions are published.[39] Even if the decisions are published with reasoning, the rights of the individuals and undertakings involved are protected by anonymising the content of decisions. Decisions are often published at a late point of time with heavy redactions. This study makes it plain again (as experienced by others before) that Germany needs a much better publication culture for the judiciary and better access to public data.[40] Digital means should enable courts to give a good overview of what they are working on and of their work products.

This is not an end in itself for academia (even though the value of academic work for the law should not be underestimated). Empirical research or even the simple possibility of reading cases in a meaningful way means guidance for the competition law community. It also makes it possible to control the judiciary, which is otherwise beyond control. Especially in competition law, where there are many general clauses and open-ended provisions, publication would help with self-assessment and the development of the law. We are strongly in favour of a system where all cases are published with as many unredacted files as possible.

6.5 European Perspective

Finally, it came as a surprise to us that the German judiciary rarely relies on European law to solve cases. It neither makes use of asking the Court of Justice through the preliminary ruling process nor does it cite EU material in a meaningful way. This indicates that there is still considerable potential for a growing European culture within the judiciary. This requires more information and better access to information from other Member States. This study of the review of German competition law enforcement decisions during the project timeframe serves as a first building block for this endeavour.

39. It needs to be noted that rulings may be requested from courts by interested parties, including the public. Yet, decisions are not made available by default. For requesting a decision, you first need to be aware of the case – which is not always the case. It often takes time before the decision is made available and even if it is made public it is not always meaningful for external readers, e.g., due to redactions, the lack of a reasoning or references to statements by the parties on file.
40. Cf. Klumpe, NZKart 2023, 16.

CHAPTER 14

Greece Report

*Andriani Kalintiri & Lefkothea Nteka**

1 COMPETITION LAW ENFORCEMENT IN GREECE

1.1 Legal Framework

Laws on the control of monopolies and the protection of free competition have been in place in Greece since 1977. Notwithstanding the multiple reforms of the enforcement regime over the years, the Greek competition provisions on anti-competitive agreements and abuses of dominance have always mirrored Articles 101 and 102 of the Treaty on the Functioning of the European Union (TFEU).

The first Greek Competition Law was Law 703/1977.[1] Its substantive and procedural provisions followed the model of the EU (then EC) competition rules, i.e., Articles 85 and 86 EC Treaty and Regulation 17/1962.[2] Article 1(1) prohibited all agreements between undertakings, decisions by associations of undertakings and concerted practices which had as their object or effect the prevention, restriction or distortion of competition; Article 1(2) provided that anti-competitive collusive arrangements were void; and Article 1(3) identified the conditions for an exemption from the prohibition of Article 1(1).[3] Article 2 of Law 703/1977 banned abuses of a dominant position in the Greek market or in a substantial part thereof. For some time, Law

* We are indebted to the Hellenic Competition Commission and its former President, Professor Ioannis Lianos, for their kind assistance with the collection of data.

1. Law 703/1977 on the -Control of Monopolies and Oligopolies and the Protection of Free Competition was enacted by the Greek Parliament on 19 September 1977 and published in the Government Gazette on 26 September 1977. The Law entered into force on 26 March 1978.
2. [1962] OJ 13/204.
3. Under Law 703/1977 the Hellenic Competition Commission (HCC) had the exclusive competence to apply Article 1(3) thereof.

703/1977 also banned abuses of economic dependence, but in 2009, this prohibition was abolished[4] and transferred to Law 146/1914 on Unfair Competition Practices.[5]

Law 703/1977 also provided for a notification system for agreements, concerted practices and decisions by associations of undertakings falling within the ambit of Article 1 of Law 703/1977, which was similar to the notification regime of Regulation 17/1962, but this was also abolished in 2005 by Law 3373/2005.[6] The latter Law adopted the 'legal exemption' regime as introduced in Regulation 1/2003[7] but with a 'twist'. While it abolished the negative exemption system, it retained an *ex lege* self-standing obligation to notify all likely restrictive agreements. The obligation served the sole purpose of 'mapping the market', thus setting up a monitoring mechanism for agreements falling under the scope of Article 1(1) of Law 703/1977 that would presumably allow the Hellenic Competition Commission (HCC) to intervene and initiate an investigation if necessary.[8]

In 2011,[9] Law 703/1977 was replaced by Law 3959/2011,[10] which is the Competition Law currently in force in Greece. With the exception of certain small revisions,[11] Articles 1 and 2 of Law 3959/2011 replicate Articles 1 and 2 of Law

4. With Article 2 of Law 3784/2009. The prohibition on abuse of economic dependence was initially introduced by Law 2000/1991 (which amended Law 703/1977). Following Law 2296/1995, it took the form of a standalone Article 2A in Law 703/1977. It was then abolished by Article 1(1) of Law 2837/2000 and came into force again by Article 1 of Law 3373/2005. On the history and enforcement of the Greek provision on abuse of economic dependence see, among others, Assimakis Komninos, 'The New Amendment of the Greek Competition Act: Harmonization with or Departure from the EU Model?' (2006) European Competition Law Review 293; Michalis-Theodoros Marinos, 'Comments to Article 18a of Law 146/1914' [2011] Chronika Idiotikou Dikaiou 532 (in Greek); Ilias Soufleros, 'Abuse of economic dependence' [2010] Dikaio Epixiriseon and Etairion 408 (in Greek); Ilias Soufleros, 'Athens Administrative Court decision 2498/2010' [2013] Dikaio Epixiriseon and Etairion 49 (note) (in Greek); Dimitrios Tzouganatos, 'The Aim of Upgrading the Competition Commission' [2005] Dikaio Epixiriseon kai Etairion 1028 (in Greek); Emmanuela Truli, 'Relative Dominance and the Protection of the Weaker Party: Enforcing the Economic Dependence Provisions and the Example of Greece' (2017) 9 Journal of European Competition Law and Practice 579 DOI: 10.1093/jeclap/lpx022; Georgios Mpampetas, 'Economic Dependence and its Abuse' (Sakkoulas 2008) (in Greek).
5. Both Law 703/1977 (now abolished) and Law 3959/2011, the Competition Law currently in force in Greece, also set up a system of *ex ante* merger control, similar to that established by the EU Merger Regulation. *See* Articles 5-10 of Law 3959/2011. Given the subject of this report, the Greek merger control rules will not be discussed any further.
6. Law 3373/2005 amending and partially replacing Law 703/1977 was published in the Government Gazette on 2 August 2005 and entered into force on the same day, with the exception of specific provisions.
7. [2003] OJ L1/25.
8. *See* in this respect HCC 492/2010 *Ixthyokalliergeies*. Under the regime of Law 3375/2005, five fish farming companies notified to the HCC a memorandum of cooperation, pursuant to which they jointly agreed to limit/control the sales and fix the selling prices of sea bream, for a limited period of six months due to overproduction. Following the notification the HCC initiated an *ex officio* investigation and fined the companies in question.
9. Previous amendments (which did not affect the letter of Articles 1 and 2 of Law 3959/2011) were introduced with Law 3784/2009. The most important amendment was the introduction of Commissioners-Rapporteurs (*see* below under Institutional Framework).
10. Law 3959/2011 on the Protection of Free Competition replacing Law 703/1977 was published in the Government Gazette on 20 April 2011 and entered into force on the same day.
11. Article 1(3) of Law 703/1977 identified three conditions for granting an individual exemption from the prohibition of Article 1(1) which largely mirrored but did not fully match the four

703/1977 and Articles 101 and 102 TFEU. Law 3959/2011 introduced a number of institutional and procedural arrangements aimed at increasing the effectiveness of the HCC and strengthening its independence while further promoting harmonisation with EU competition law and practice, such as a system for the prioritisation of cases, the abolition of the notification requirement for 'mapping' purposes introduced in 2005,[12] and the streamlining of the overall time frame and corresponding deadlines for antitrust cases.[13] Law 3959/2011 was most recently amended by Law 4886/2022.[14] The main goal of the latest amendments was to implement the ECN+ Directive (Directive 2019/1)[15] and render the Greek competition rules fit for the digital age. While Articles 1 and 2 remained intact, a new Article 1A was introduced, which outlaws invitations to collude and unilateral future price disclosures.[16]

---

conditions of Articles 101(3) TFEU (the requirement for consumers to receive a fair share of the resulting benefits was rather implied). Article 1(3) of Law 3959/2011 lists four conditions for individual exemptions which mirror the four conditions of Article 101(3) TFEU. Importantly, a fourth paragraph has been introduced to Article 1(1) which provides for the application by analogy of EU block exemption regulations in the Greek legal order.

12. While it had been argued that this notification requirement was not inconsistent with the level-playing-field rule established by Article 3(2) of Regulation 1/2003, as it was meant to pursue different policy objectives, it was criticised as resulting in disproportionate administrative costs for the HCC, while further increasing costs for undertakings (*see* Dimitrios Loukas and Lefkothea Nteka, 'The Memorandum of Understanding on specific economic and competition policy conditionality for granting financial assistance: Greek point of view' [2011] e-Competitions N° 37517).
13. For detailed references to the changes brought by Law 3959/2011 to the Greek competition regime, *see*, among others, Dimitrios Loukas and Lefkothea Nteka, 'The Memorandum of Understanding on specific economic and competition policy conditionality for granting financial assistance: Greek point of view' [2011] e-Competitions N° 37517; Ilias Soufleros, 'The new law 3959/2011 on the protection of free competition – Critical review of its main provisions' [2012] Nomiko Vima 1108 (in Greek); Ioannis Dryllerakis, 'The new Greek competition law regime – Law 3959/2011' (Nomiki Vivliothiki 2011) 5-45 (in Greek); Emmanuela Truli, 'New Greek Law on the Protection of Free Competition: Key Changes and First Impressions' [2013] ECLR 280. *See also* below under Institutional Framework and Enforcement Framework.
14. Law 4886/2022 on the modernisation of the Greek competition regime and the transposition of Directive 2019/1 was published in the Government Gazette on 24 January 2022 and entered into force on the same day, with the exception of specific provisions. The full text of Law 3959/2011, as amended by Law 4886/2022, is available (in English) at https://www.epant.gr/en/legislation/protection-of-free-competition.html.
15. Directive (EU) 2019/1 of the European Parliament and of the Council of 11 December 2018 to empower the competition authorities of the Member States to be more effective enforcers and to ensure the proper functioning of the internal market [2019] OJ L11/3.
16. Ioannis Lianos and Florian Wagner-von Papp, 'Tackling Invitations to Collude and Unilateral Disclosure: The Moving Frontiers of Competition Law?' (2022) 13(4) Journal of European Competition Law & Practice 249. Article 2A on abuse of market power in ecosystems, included in the proposal on the amendment of Law 3959/2011 as posted for public consultation, was not included in the draft bill as tabled in the Greek Parliament. See, among others, Konstantinos Stylianou, 'The Modernization of Competition Law and the Lost Opportunity of Article 2A on Economic Ecosystems' (2022) Synigoros 56 (in Greek) DOI: 10.1093/jeclap/lpac017; Michael Jacobides and Ioannis Lianos, 'Ecosystems and Competition Law in Theory and Practice' (2021) 30(5) Industrial and Corporate Change 1199 DOI: 10.1093/icc/dtab061.

Table 14.1 Competition Laws in Greece

Period	*Competition Laws in Greece*
1977-2011	*Law 703/1977*, as had been amended by Laws 1934/1991, 2000/1991, 2296/1995, 2837/2000, 3373/2005 and 3784/2009
2011-current	*Law 3959/2011*, as has been amended by Laws 4013/2011, 4072/2012, 4364/2016, 4389/2016, 4623/2019, 4635/2019, 4714/2020, 4753/2020, 4782/2021, 4795/2021, 4796/2021, 4886/2022, 4914/2022

1.2 Institutional Framework

Competition enforcement in Greece is modelled upon administrative justice systems. The HCC[17] is the main institution responsible for enforcing Articles 1 and 2 of Law 3959/2011 and Articles 101 and 102 TFEU.[18] In Greece, there are also sector-specific regulators (SSRs) for telecommunications, post, rails, energy and ports.[19] However, the division of competences between the HCC and the SSRs does not follow a uniform framework. Interestingly, the respective public consultations and parliamentary discussions do not reveal why different solutions were adopted across regulated industries and which factors weighed in in each specific choice.

In the telecommunications and post sectors, the exclusive competence for the application of the Greek and EU competition rules lies with the Hellenic Telecommunications and Post Commission (EETT),[20] which may consult with the HCC where it deems necessary.[21] By contrast, the Rail Regulator (RAS)[22] has parallel competence to

17. https://www.epant.gr/en/.
18. Article 14(1) of Law 3959/2011.
19. *See* Article 24 of Law 3959/2011 and Article 113(2)(z) of Law 4727/2020 on cooperation mechanisms between the HCC and SSRs (assistance, memoranda of understanding and information sharing). In this context, the HCC has signed memoranda of understanding with RAE (https://www.epant.gr/en/enimerosi/press-releases/item/1099-press-release-memorandum-of-understanding-between-hcc-and-rae.html) and RAL (https://www.epant.gr/enimerosi/deltia-typou/item/1378-deltio-typou-mnimonio-synergasias-epitropis-antagonismoy-rythmistikis-arxis-limenon.html).
20. https://www.eett.gr/opencms/opencms/EETT_EN/index.html. To the best of our knowledge, EETT's legislative framework has not been amended thus far in transposition of the ECN+ Directive.
21. Article 113(2)(st) of Law 4727/2020 and Article 14 of Law 4070/2012 for the electronic communications sector and Article 5(1)(ka) and 5(2)(a) of Law 4053/2012 for the postal services sector. Article 113(2)(st) of Law 4727/2020 replaced the almost identical provision of Article 12(st) of Law 4070/2012 which had in turn replaced the equivalent provision of Article 12(st) of Law 3431/2006. The competence to apply competition law in the telecommunications sector was initially entrusted to EETT by virtue of Article 3(14)(id) and (15) of Law 2867/2000. The competence to apply competition law in the postal services sector was entrusted to EETT by virtue of Article 7 of Law 2668/1998 which was then abolished by Law 4053/2012. Article 14(1) of Law 3959/2011 on the competences of the HCC, as amended in 2022 by Law 4886/2022, expressly mentions the above provisions regarding EETT's powers ('Without prejudice to the competences of […]').
22. https://ras-el.gr/.

enforce the competition rules in the rails sector, alongside the HCC.[23] It adopted its first decision enforcing Article 2 of Law 3959/2011 and Article 102 TFEU in 2020.[24] On the other hand, the Energy Regulator (RAE)[25] lacks competence to enforce the competition rules, although in the past RAE and the HCC have worked closely to ensure the proper application of competition law in the energy sector.[26] The latter model seems to have been favoured also in the port sector and the Regulatory Authority for Ports (RAL), established in 2016.[27]

Overall, significant institutional shifts have occurred over the years. From 1977 to 1995, the HCC lacked independence and was part of a Ministry. From 1995 onwards, however, the HCC was recognised as an independent agency and acquired administrative[28] and eventually financial autonomy,[29] separate legal personality, and standing to appear before courts in its own name.[30] Still, for a very long time, the HCC was supervised by a Minister (the Minister). The scope of this supervision was not clearly defined in law, although in practice, it was construed narrowly.[31] Over time, several provisions introduced in the competition regime further prescribed the Minister's

23. Articles 28(1) and 32(4) of Law 3891/2010. Article 56(2) and (8) of Law 4408/2016 on the competences of RAS as a regulator refer to the HCC's competence to enforce competition law in the rail transport services markets ('Without prejudice to the powers of the HCC under law 3959/2011 to protect competition in the rail transport services' markets [...]'). According to the Rail Regulator's (RAS) annual report for 2020-2021 (available at https://ras-el.gr/wp-content/uploads/2022/07/ekthesi-pepragmenwn-ras-2020-2021.pdf, pp 148-149), since November 2020 RAS is a member of the European Competition Network (ECN) as a sectoral competition authority in the railway services sector in Greece. According to the annual report a letter was sent in this respect to the European Commission by the Greek government, presumably the designation letter provided under Article 35 of Regulation 1/2003.To the best of our knowledge, RAS's legislative framework has not been amended thus far in transposition of the ECN+ Directive.
24. RAS Decision 14006/2020. RAS accepted the commitments offered by the incumbent dominant rail transport services' operator, following a complaint by a competitor. In 2021 RAS initiated proceedings to investigate compliance with the imposed commitments. *See* https://ras-el.gr/2020/10/14/%ce%b4%ce%b5%ce%bb%cf%84%ce%af%ce%bf-%cf%84%cf%8d%cf%80%ce%bf%cf%85-%ce%b4%ce%b5%cf%83%ce%bc%ce%b5%cf%8d%cf%83%ce%b5%ce%b9%cf%82-%cf%84%ce%b7%cf%82-%ce%b5%cf%84%ce%b1%ce%b9%cf%81%ce%af%ce%b1%cf%82/ and https://ras-el.gr/2021/05/11/%ce%ad%ce%bd%ce%b1%cf%81%ce%be%ce%b7-%cf%80%ce%b1%cf%81%ce%b1%ce%ba%ce%bf%ce%bb%ce%bf%cf%8d%ce%b8%ce%b7%cf%83%ce%b7%cf%82-%ce%bf%cf%81%ce%b8%ce%ae%cf%82-%ce%ba%ce%b1%ce%b9-%ce%b1%cf%80%ce%bf%cf%84-2/. *See also* RAS' annual report for 2020-2021 pp. 58-59.
25. https://www.rae.gr/?lang=en.
26. *See* HCC 551/2012, as amended by HCC 589/2014, 596/2014, 618/2015, 631/2016 and 651/2017 regarding commitments imposed on the Greek incumbent dominant gas supplier in the context of an abuse of dominance investigation, with a view to speeding up the liberalisation of the Greek gas supply market.
27. http://www.raports.gr/en. *See* Article 112(1)(d) and Article 113(1)(st) of Law 4389/2016 on measures and 'regulatory measures' respectively. According to Article 113(1)(st) of Law 4389/2016 RAL's powers should not impinge on the HCC's competence under Law 3959/2011.
28. Article 4(1) of Law 2296/1995.
29. Article 1(7) and (8) of Law 2837/2000.
30. Article 10(9) of Law 3373/2005.
31. It comprised mainly of (a) addressing means of parliamentary control regarding the activities of the Authority and (b) approval of the HCC's budget, to be annexed to the budget of the Ministry.

supervisory role, thus limiting any room for unwarranted intervention.[32] The most recent amendments to Law 3959/2011 in 2022 eliminated this supervision.[33]

The HCC consists of two separate bodies: the Directorate General for Competition (Directorate General), which is the body responsible for investigations, and the Board, which is the decision-making body of the Authority. While the dualist structure of the HCC has been preserved since its establishment, changes in the institutional design of the Board, in particular the introduction of Commissioners-Rapporteurs, signified a softening of the strict separation between the HCC's investigatory and decision-making functions. In addition to their duties as regular members of the HCC Board, Commissioners-Rapporteurs are entrusted with overseeing the final stages of the investigation process and are responsible for formulating a proposal to the HCC's Board on the merits of the cases assigned to them.[34] The trend towards a monist system has been reinforced in recent years: the President of the HCC serves as both the senior administrative officer and the senior officer exercising disciplinary authority over HCC personnel.[35]

Proceedings before the HCC bear similarities to judicial proceedings, such as the submission of written pleadings before the HCC Board (written memorandum in response to the Report – Proposal, rebuttal of other parties' memoranda, post-hearing memorandum) and a fully fledged oral hearing before the Board, quite similar to ordinary court proceedings, where parties enjoy the right to be legally represented and can examine and cross-examine witnesses and experts.

1.3 Enforcement Framework

For the first time, Law 3959/2011 introduced provisions regarding the prioritisation of cases. The HCC is entrusted to set strategic goals and prioritise cases based on the

32. *See*, *e.g.*, 14(2)(r) of Law 3959/2011 regarding the modalities and content of any information request addressed by the Minister to the HCC. Such requests should be filed in writing and the HCC is to provide information of a general nature, not including information on ongoing investigations or leniency programme applications.
33. Article 9 of Law 4886/2022, implementing the ECN+ Directive. The Greek text of the law mentions that the Minister oversees ('παρακολουθ') administratively and financially the HCC. Interestingly, the English translation of the law as published in the HCC's website still uses the term 'supervise'.
34. Article 15(7) of Law 3959/2011 provides that Commissioners-Rapporteurs do not vote in the cases assigned to them. *See* in this respect DEA 869/2013, para 15; DEA 2741/2012, para. 7; DEA 2742/2012, para. 7; DEA 3529/2013, para. 2; DEA 3657/2013, para. 5, finding that the participation of the Commissioner-Rapporteur with a vote in the deliberations of the HCC Board in the cases assigned to them, as initially provided, did not infringe the principle of impartiality and the right to a fair trial.
35. *See*, among others, Articles 19(1)(m), 21(9) and 21B(10) of Law 3959/2011. Under the previous regime, the dual role of the HCC President as a senior administrative officer and as Chair of the decision-making body of the Authority had been found not to contravene the principle of impartiality, in view of the nature of the oversight he/she exercised over the Directorate General for Competition (DEA 1616/2009, para 15; DEA 1617/2009, para. 13; DEA 2221/2009, para. 10; DEA 1833/2010, para. 10; DEA 2803/2009, para. 8; DEA 559/2010, para. 8; STE 2007/2013, paras 4, 6, 9 and 10).

public interest.[36] Public interest considerations in individual cases are assessed in light of the estimated impact of the practices under investigation on the functioning of effective competition, and especially on consumers, along with other factors, such as available resources and the number of pending cases.[37] In this respect, the most innovative feature of Law 3959/2011 was the introduction of a 'point system' for the investigation of cases by the HCC,[38] which exemplifies and quantifies the prioritisation criteria.[39] It functions as an internal management tool to rank and investigate cases,[40] as well as to revise the ranking of pending cases and decide on their treatment depending on the results of the investigation. The HCC may not examine complaints that get a low ranking under the point system.[41]

The investigative and decision-making powers of the HCC are aligned with Article 5 of Regulation 1/2003 and the ECN+ Directive. The HCC has powers similar to those of the European Commission. Among others, it can investigate suspected violations, whether *ex officio* or following a complaint;[42] it may request information[43] and conduct interviews[44] and inspections;[45] it may conduct sector inquiries;[46] it may accept commitments[47] and impose interim measures;[48] it may adopt a decision finding an infringement;[49] it may impose fines for procedural and substantive law breaches, or

36. Article 14(2)(jd)(aa).
37. HCC 525/2011. According to the decision priority is given to *ex officio* investigations or complaints pertaining to: (a) hardcore restrictions (price-fixing, market sharing and sales or production restrictions) of national scope, especially in cases of horizontal agreements (cartels), taking particularly into account the market position of the undertakings involved, the structure of the relevant market and the estimated number of the affected consumers; (b) products and services of key importance to the Greek consumer, where the anti-competitive practice under examination may have a significant impact on the increase of prices and/or the quality of the products/services supplied (especially as compared to other EU Member States); and (c) anti-competitive practices with likely cumulative effect. Other factors considered in the assessment are the resources available to the Authority, the possibility of establishing proof of an infringement, the necessity of providing guidance on novel issues, as well as the assessment of whether the HCC is the best-placed body to act (particularly comparing to the competence of national courts). *See also* HCC decision of 15 February 2007 on criteria for investigating cases, in file with the authors.
38. Article 14(2)(o).
39. HCC 696/2019, replacing HCC 539/2012 and 616/2015.
40. Article 14(2)(o) expressly stipulates that the point system is intended solely for internal use and that the ranking of each individual case is not made public nor notified to the complainant. The provision attempts to immunise the system from litigation, i.e., discovery and/or judicial challenges by interested parties.
41. Article 14(2)(o) and HCC 696/2019. At the time of writing, the issue of the competent court to review HCC decisions rejecting complaints for low priority and the appropriate legal remedy (review on the merits of the case or review on points of law) has not yet been resolved by national courts.
42. Articles 14(2)(a), 25(1) and 36. Law 4886/2021 abolished the privilege of the Minister to request the initiation of proceedings by the HCC, with the exception of regulatory sector inquiries (Article 11) and opinions on (draft) legislation (Article 23).
43. Article 38(1).
44. Article 38(2A).
45. Article 39.
46. Article 40.
47. Article 25C.
48. Article 25D.
49. Article 14(2)(a) and Article 25(1)(h) on infringements committed in the past.

for non-compliance with its decisions;[50] it may impose remedies in case of an infringement of competition law;[51] and, instead of imposing a fine, it may address recommendations to undertakings which have committed an infringement.[52] The HCC may also conduct regulatory interventions in a sector of the economy, whether *ex officio* or following a request by the Minister, and it may impose remedies to rectify the potential absence of conditions of effective competition.[53] In addition, the HCC may issue opinions on issues relating to its mandate, as well as on proposed or existing regulations.[54] Law 4886/2022 entrusted the HCC with a new set of information-gathering powers for which there is no equivalent in EU legislation.[55] These powers are not to be used in the context of specific investigations, though, but only for the mapping of competitive conditions in specific sectors of the economy or markets.

In enforcing the competition rules within the scope of their competence, the SSRs do not enjoy as wide powers as the HCC.[56]

2 JUDICIAL REVIEW OF COMPETITION DECISIONS IN GREECE

2.1 Review Courts

In Greece, there are three types of courts: administrative courts, civil courts and criminal courts.[57] HCC decisions adopted pursuant to Articles 1 and 2 of Law 3959/2011 and Articles 101 and 102 TFEU are administrative acts and may be challenged by means of an appeal (*Προσφυγή*) before the Athens Administrative Court of Appeal (Dioikitiko Efeteio Athinon (DEA)), which acts as the first instance court. For an appeal to be admissible, the applicant must pay a fee of EUR 750 to initiate proceedings;[58] the application must be submitted within sixty days of the applicant

50. Articles 25, 25B and 38-39.
51. Article 25(1)(c).
52. Article 25(1)(a). The HCC has rarely opted to exercise its power to impose recommendations on an undertaking having committed an infringement of competition law, instead of a fine. *See, e.g.*, HCC 517/2011.
53. Article 11 of Law 3959/2011. This tool resembles the UK's market investigation regime.
54. Article 23.
55. Pursuant to Article 38(1A) of Law 3959/2011, the HCC may request the submission of information of a particular type, such as access to electronic data held on a private or public network. Pursuant to Article 38(2B), the HCC may invite to an interview any representative of the undertaking or representatives of other legal persons, as well as any natural person. Under both provisions the natural and legal persons to whom the investigative measure is addressed are under no obligation to provide the requested information.
56. EETT is empowered to apply Articles 38 and 39 of Law 3959/2011 on requests for information and inspections of premises (Article 14 of Law 4070/2012) and may impose fines and sanctions, as provided by Law 3959/2011 (Article 113(2)(kh) Law 4727/2020). As to RAS, while Article 32(4) of Law 3891/2010 expressly provides that, in case of an infringement of the competition provisions in the market of rail services, RAS may impose the sanctions provided for in Law 3959/2011, there is no specific provision on powers of investigation.
57. For an overview in English, *see* https://e-justice.europa.eu/content_judicial_systems_in_member_states-16-el-en.do?member=1.
58. Article 45(2). In the case of actions for annulment against fining decisions of the HCC, for the action to be deemed admissible, under Article 14(5) of Law 703/1977, applicants had to pay a fee amounting to 20% of the imposed fine, up to a maximum of EUR 100,000.

being notified of the decision in question;[59] and the applicant must meet the standing requirements of Article 30(3) of Law 3959/2011. Pursuant to this, a competition decision may be challenged by its addressees, the complainant, the Minister on behalf of the Government, and any third party with a sufficient legal interest. The appeal does not suspend the effect of the challenged decision, but applicants may submit an application for interim measures pending such an action.[60]

DEA judgments may be challenged on points of law by means of an appeal (*αναίρεση*) before the Council of State (Symvoulio tis Epikrateias (STE)), which is the highest administrative court in Greece and acts as the second and last instance court.[61] Appeals against the judgments of the DEA must be submitted within 60 days of their publication.[62] Appellants must also pay a fee of EUR 750 to initiate proceedings before the STE, although the Government and the HCC are exempted from this obligation.[63] Only the parties to the first-instance proceedings may bring an appeal, as well as the General Prosecutor of the State for the ordinary administrative courts, even if he/she did not participate in the trial before the DEA.[64] Co-infringers and any third party with a legitimate interest may file a third-party intervention.[65] In appeals brought before the STE, the HCC may submit observations on questions concerning the application of the competition rules as an *amicus curiae*, including in cases where the HCC was party to the proceedings before the DEA but opted not to challenge its judgement.[66] Since 2011, for appeals to the STE to be admissible, two further conditions must be satisfied: the value of the dispute in question must exceed EUR 40,000, and there must be no STE case law on the points of law raised in the appeal, or the DEA judgment must contradict existing case law.[67]

The DEA and the STE are generalist courts. Law 3959/2011 envisions the creation of specialised competition law chambers within the DEA. Article 33 provides that such chambers may be set up by means of a Presidential Decree,[68] following a joint proposal by the Minister of Justice and the Minister. However, no such order has been issued

59. Article 30(1). Under Article 14(1) of the now abolished Law 703/1977 this deadline was twenty days.
60. Article 30(2).
61. For the institution of appeal in the Greek legal framework *see* among others Ioannis Gravaris (ed.), *The institution of appeal (on points of law) before the Hellenic Council of State* (Nomiki Vivliothiki 2022) (in Greek).
62. Article 32. For procedural issues relating to the institution of appeal before STE *see*, among others, Maria Gkana, 'Procedural Issues of the Appeal' in Ioannis Gravaris (ed.), *The Institution of Appeal (on Points of Law) Before the Hellenic Council of State* (Nomiki Vivliothiki 2022) pp. 469ff (in Greek).
63. Article 45(2).
64. Article 32(2). The General Prosecutor of the State for the ordinary administrative courts may also file an action for annulment of judgements of the DEA in the interest of the law (Article 34).
65. Article 32(6).
66. STE 166/2018 interpreting Article 14(2)(i).
67. Article 53(3) and (4) of Presidential Decree 18/1989 as amended by Article 12(1) of Law 3900/2010. *See*, among others, Panagiotis Chalioulias, 'Specific Issues in the Interpretation of Articles 37 of Law 3772/2009 and 2, 12 of Law 3900/2010' in Ioannis Gravaris (ed.), *The Institution of Appeal (on Points of Law) Before the Hellenic Council of State* (Nomiki Vivliothiki 2022) pp. 548ff. (in Greek).
68. This is essentially an executive order by the President of the Hellenic Republic.

until now, presumably in view of the low number of cases per year and, most importantly, the generalist character of both courts and judges in Greece. In practice, competition cases are normally assigned to specific chambers within the DEA, while at second instance, they are typically heard by the 6th STE Chamber in a five-member panel. These practical arrangements allow a certain degree of specialisation, evidenced also in the identity of the judges presiding over appeals or serving as rapporteurs.

2.2 Judicial Review

The scope and intensity of judicial review exercised by Greek administrative courts are clarified in the Code of Administrative Procedure (Kodikas Dioikitikis Dikonomias (KDD)). Article 79(1) KDD provides that, in an appeal (*προσφυγή*), the court reviews the legality of the challenged act to the extent that this has been challenged and within the limits of the submitted grounds for annulment. In appeal proceedings, the court may examine *ex officio* questions of lack of competence of the administration, errors in the legal basis of the adopted act, violations of precedent,[69] questions of lack of jurisdiction[70] and non-fulfilment of procedural requirements.[71] Article 79(2) KDD further states that the court may accept the appeal fully or partially and annul fully or partially or modify the challenged act, or it may reject the appeal. Pursuant to Article 79(3) KDD, the court may refer the case back to the administration where the act has been issued by an incompetent or unlawfully composed body, where the act was adopted in violation of an essential procedural requirement, or where the administration has not exercised its margin of discretion.

The judicial review exercised by the DEA bears similarities to the scrutiny carried out by the General Court in the EU. The applicable standard of judicial review for infringement decisions is a full and unrestricted review of the HCC's decisions on questions of facts, law and facts and law (*πλήρης έλεγχος ουσίας*): the DEA may hear pleas on questions of procedure, substance and fines.[72] The review comprises a *stricto sensu* review of legality with respect to competence and procedural requirements for the adoption of the challenged HCC decision, a full and unrestricted review of the facts and grounds of the case, as well as of the sanctions imposed, and the power of DEA to substitute its opinion for that of the HCC and modify the challenged decision.[73] In view of the *inter partes* nature of the proceedings, the full and unrestricted review which the DEA is obliged to carry out is limited by the claims of the parties to the proceedings. Thus, the DEA is not required to review the contested decision in its entirety, nor is it

69. The proceedings before the DEA are *inter partes* and, with the exception of pleas which the Courts is required to raise of its own motion, it is for the applicant to raise pleas in law against and to adduce evidence in support of those pleas.
70. Article 12(1) KDD.
71. Article 35 KDD.
72. *See* section 5 below.
73. Georgios Dellis and Konstantina Scandali, 'The HCC: Structure, Process, Judicial Review' in Dimitris Tzouganatos (ed.), *Free Competition Law* (Volume 2, 2nd ed., 2020) pp. 160ff. (in Greek).

competent to undertake of its own motion a new and comprehensive investigation of the case, substituting the functions of the HCC.[74]

With respect to fines, the DEA has unlimited jurisdiction to reform them as it deems appropriate in cases where the HCC has already exercised its discretion and has imposed a fine, and the parties contest the relevant chapter of the HCC decision.[75] The judicial control exercised by the DEA has been deemed to comply with the requirements of the right to a fair trial as enshrined in Article 6 of the European Convention of Human Rights (ECHR) following *Menarini*, although the DEA has not explicitly acknowledged the criminal nature of antitrust fines.[76] In relation to decisions accepting commitments, the DEA will scrutinise whether the authority exceeded the outer limits of its discretion.[77] This standard is very similar to the marginal review of the European Commission's commitment decisions by the EU Courts.[78]

An appeal before the STE lies on points of law only. The applicable standard of judicial scrutiny before the STE is again full review,[79] and the STE may set a DEA judgment aside where this is vitiated by a legal error.

3 PRIOR RESEARCH

To the best of our knowledge, there has been no comprehensive investigation of the judicial review of competition decisions in Greece. The most relevant study is probably OECD's Peer Review of Competition Law and Policy in Greece, which was published in October 2018[80] and provides an overview of judicial review in Greece along the lines outlined above, along with some empirical data on the number and outcome of first and second-instance judgments on HCC decisions published during 2012-2017, as compiled by the HCC. The data shows that most HCC decisions had been upheld. Furthermore, the EU Justice Scoreboard shows that review proceedings of HCC decisions have improved in 2018-2020,[81] but as with the OECD Peer Review there is no further information on the number of challenged decisions, success rates and the grounds for appeal.

74. STE 166/2018, paras 11 and 12.
75. STE 1933/2013, para. 10.
76. STE 2007/2013, para. 4; STE 2365/2013, para. 6; STE 2390/2012, para. 7; DEA 869/2013, para. 15.
77. DEA 2265/2010, para. 9; DEA 869/2013, para. 24; DEA 1552/2012, para. 8; DEA 1554/2012, para. 8.
78. Case C-441/07 *Commission v. Alrosa*, EU:C:2010:377, paras 59-69, 94 and 115.
79. *See* STE 166/2018, para. 12, which refers to 'power of review of increased density'.
80. https://www.oecd.org/daf/competition/GREECE-OECD-Reviews-of-Competition-Law-and-Policy-2018.pdf.
81. https://ec.europa.eu/info/policies/justice-and-fundamental-rights/upholding-rule-law/eu-justice-scoreboard_en.

4 QUANTITATIVE ANALYSIS

4.1 Source of Information

The judgments of Greek administrative courts, including the DEA and the STE, are not consistently published online in a manner accessible to the public. The websites of the DEA and of the STE contain a database of judgments issued by them,[82] but in practice, these are not reliably searchable due to the ineffectiveness of the available filtering criteria.[83] Private databases of Greek case law suffer from similar shortcomings or returned results which were not comprehensive.[84] As required under Law 3959/2011,[85] the HCC has published on its website the texts of seventy-four relevant judgments, but there are many more that were not available at the time of writing. While the HCC kindly shared with us a record of relevant judgments, some may still be missing from the dataset used for this report. Furthermore, the text of competition decisions issued by EETT is not comprehensively available online, neither on EETT's website[86] nor through the existing databases. Although we formally requested this information from EETT, at the time of writing, we have not received a response.[87] Since we are not aware of any other source where this information may be available, the dataset used for this report does not include any judicial review cases against EETT's competition decisions in the telecommunications and post sectors. Finally, some data were retrieved from the Annual Reports published by the HCC,[88] in particular, the total number of enforcement actions by the HCC, including and excluding rejections of complaints. However, this information may not be entirely accurate either since the HCC's decisions are not reported in the same manner in all the Annual Reports (in particular, rejections of complaints and decisions to close an investigation).[89] To verify the above data, we also retrieved information about the HCC's enforcement action from its website, as the HCC publishes the full text of most of its decisions, as required by Article 27(1) of Law 3959/2011.[90] Still, this information is incomplete since

82. https://www.adjustice.gr/webcenter/portal/defeteioath/services/search-caselaws?_adf.ctrl-state=59rukqskm_68&_afrLoop=16390923963291026#!,
83. For example, it is not possible to locate all judgments on Law 3959/2011 or Law 703/1977 or on HCC decisions. Moreover, the full text of the judgments may not be available – only a summary.
84. We tried ISOKRATIS (accessible at https://www.dsanet.gr/), NOMOS (accessible at https://lawdb.intrasoftnet.com/nomos/nomos_frame.html) and Qualex (accessible at https://www.qualex.gr/el-GR/periexomeno/nomologia). ISOKRATIS is accessible to all qualified lawyers in Greece through their bar membership, while NOMOS and Qualex require a separate subscription.
85. Articles 30(7) and 32(7). There was no similar provision in Law 703/1977.
86. https://www.eett.gr/opencms/opencms/EETT/EETT/EETT_Decs/competiondecs.html.
87. 31 July 2022.
88. Article 29 of Law 3959/2011 and formerly, Article 13C of Law 703/1977.
89. https://www.epant.gr/enimerosi/dimosieyseis/ektheseis-pepragmenon.html.
90. Article 13A of Law 703/1977 also imposed a similar obligation on the HCC to publish its decisions in the Official Governmental Gazette, but it did not require it to also publish them online.

rejections of complaints are not always published online.[91] As a result of the above difficulties, the estimated total number of the HCC's enforcement actions from May 2004 to April 2021 has most likely been underrepresented.

4.2 Total Number of Judgments and Ratio of Appeals

Notwithstanding the challenges in locating the relevant judgments, we were able to identify and record 257 first and second-instance judgments against HCC competition decisions rendered during the relevant period. The DEA rendered 170 judgments in the first instance, while 87 judgments were rendered by the STE in the second instance. From the estimated 266 decisions taken by the HCC in the relevant period (excluding summary rejections of complaints and dismissals of complaints on low prioritisation grounds),[92] 69 were challenged before the DEA. Thus, the ratio of HCC decisions subject to appeal at first instance is 26%. From those decisions, 27% of the DEA judgments have been subsequently appealed to the STE.

4.3 Judgments per Year

Figure 14.1 summarises the number of judgments issued per year by the two instances of Greek courts, i.e., the DEA and the STE. With the exception of 2014, where the DEA and the STE issued almost double the number of judgments compared to any other year in the relevant time frame, overall, the total number of judgments rendered over the years has not changed significantly. The data for 2020 and 2021 should not be taken at face value to imply a decline in judicial review since judgments rendered this year may not have become available yet and thus may not have been recorded. Moreover, during these two years, most of the decisions issued by the HCC relating to antitrust enforcement were adopted in the context of settlement proceedings, and consequently, they were not challenged before the DEA.

Figures 14.2(a) and 14.2(b) provide further insights in that they indicate the number of judgments per year and per instance and the number of HCC decisions that were appealed each year. Figure 14.2(a) suggests that appeals against the same HCC decision are examined in multiple proceedings at first instance rather than being joined together and addressed in a single judgment. The observed peak in 2010 can be explained by the judicial review of two cartel decisions – the milk cartel in 2007[93] and the car insurance cartel in 2009[94] – which had been addressed against twelve and four undertakings, respectively, and which led to more than one-third of the first-instance judgments issued that year.[95] By contrast, Figure 14.2(b) suggests that at second and

91. Rejection of complaints on low priority grounds (Article 14(2)(ie)), and summary rejections of complaints that clearly fall outside the scope of the HCC's competence or are manifestly unfounded (Article 37).
92. Calculated based on information on the HCC's website and the Annual Reports.
93. HCC Decision 373/2007.
94. HCC Decision 460/2009.
95. Nine judgments out of the twenty-five issued in 2010.

last instance, there is a significantly lower degree of multiplication of proceedings.[96] Nevertheless, although appeals by multiple parties against the same HCC decision are generally dealt with in separate judgments, in practice, they are usually heard by the same judges whose judgments are often published on the same day. This, in turn, reduces the risk of conflicting and inconsistent rulings, and thus, the multiplication of proceedings with respect to the same HCC decision does not seem to have an impact on the effectiveness of judicial review.

Figure 14.1 Number of Judgments According to Instances

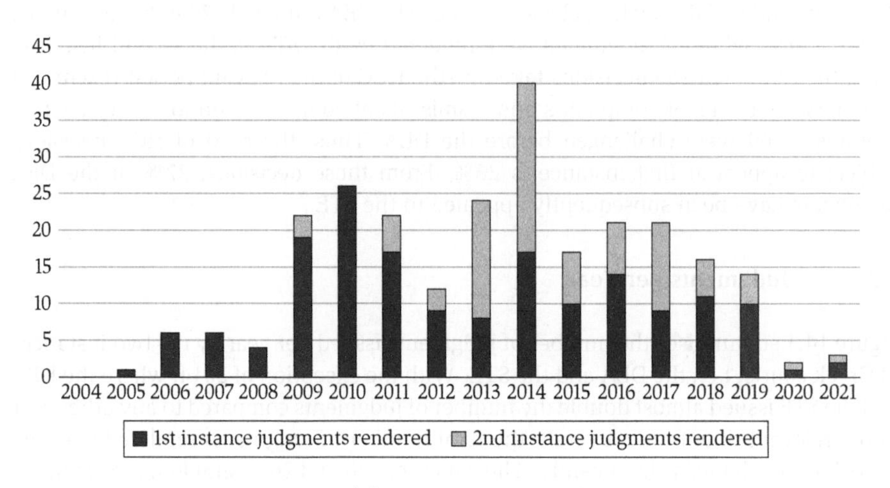

Figure 14.2(a) First-Instance Judgments

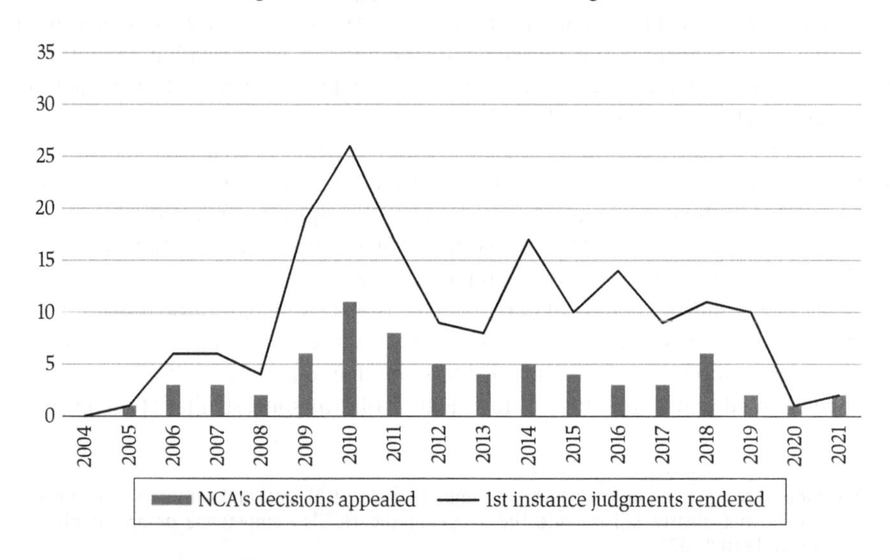

96. This finding should not be taken at face value though since some of the parties may not have appealed the DEA judgment or some of the STE judgments may not have been published yet.

Figure 14.2(b) Second-Instance Judgments

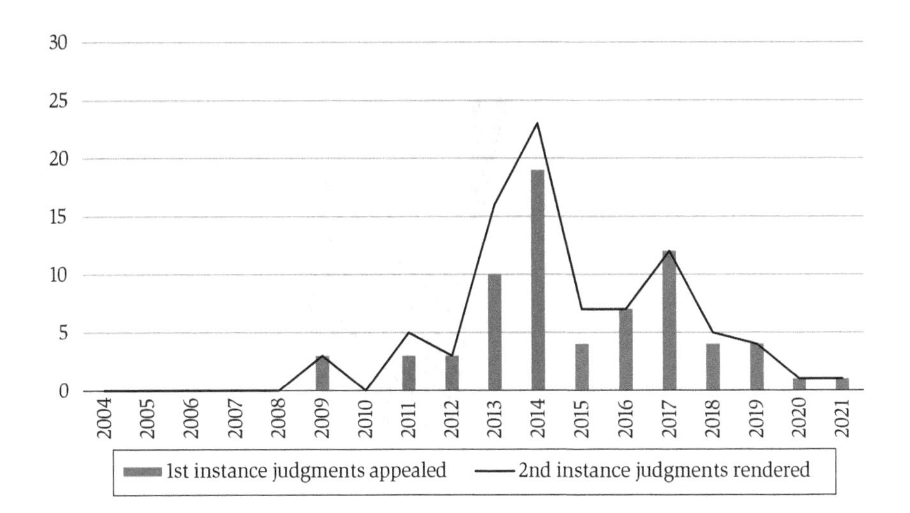

4.4 Success Rates and Outcomes

Figure 14.3 presents the success rates of judicial review across all instances. For this purpose, multiple judgments against the same HCC decision or Previous Instance Judgment have been aggregated and counted as a single case. Figure 14.3 indicates that in 48% of the reviewed HCC decisions, the appeals were fully rejected. At the same time, the success rate is not negligible: in 49% of the HCC decisions that were challenged, the appeals were fully (16%) or partially successful (33%). Figure 14.4 sheds further light on these numbers by showing the outcome in each judgment at first and second instance, separately. At first instance (Figure 14.4a), 36% of the actions for annulment were fully rejected, while in 19% of them, the HCC decision was fully annulled (and 4% returned to the HCC for reconsideration). In 36% of the judgments concerned, the DEA amended the HCC decision solely with respect to fines while leaving the substantive assessment intact. At second instance (Figure 14.4b), 68% of the appeals were fully rejected, while 17% were fully or partially accepted and returned to the DEA for reconsideration. Importantly, most STE judgments annul DEA judgments that had, in turn, annulled HCC decisions.[97]

97. *See* below under Grounds of Appeal.

Figure 14.3 Success of Appeals (Each NCA's Decision or Previous Instance Judgment Counts as One)

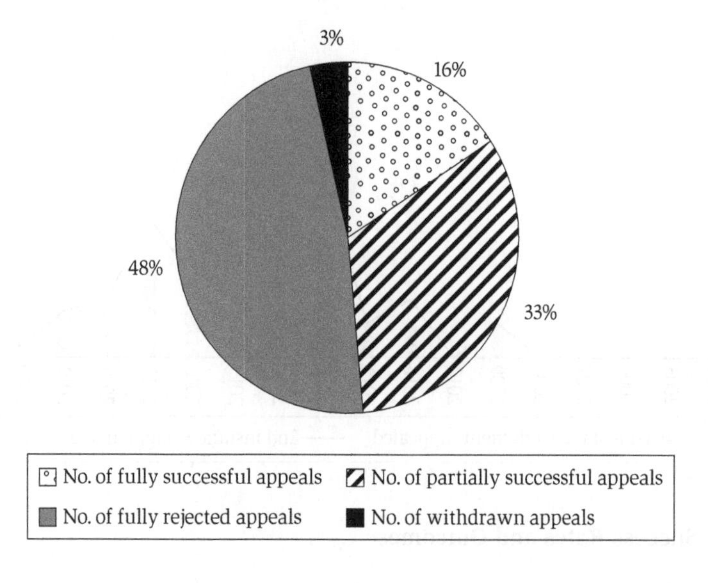

Figure 14.4(a) First-Instance Outcome

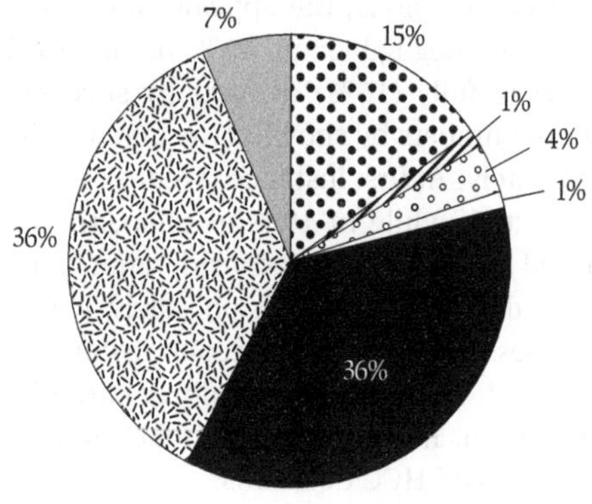

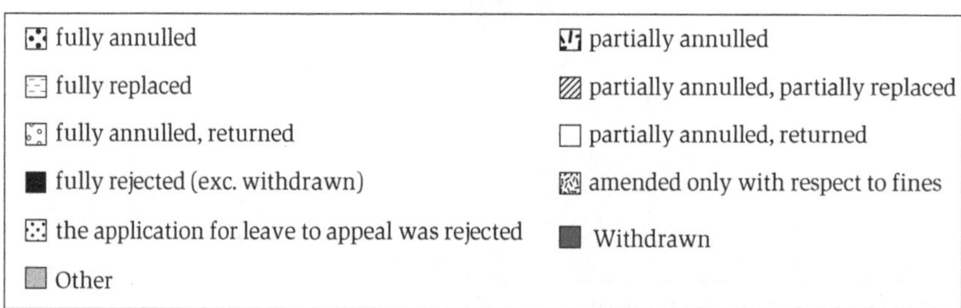

Figure 14.4(b) Second-Instance Outcome

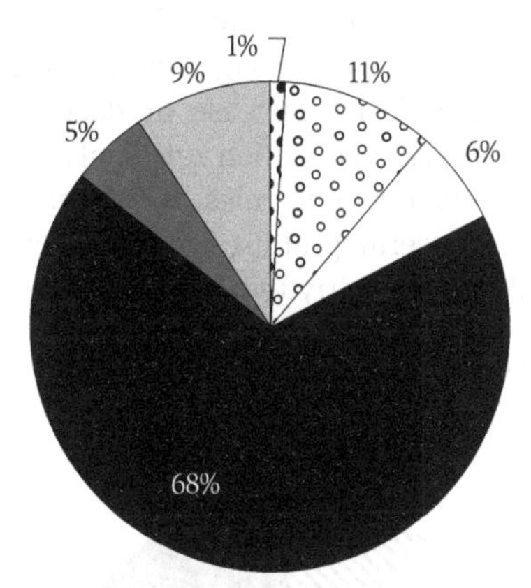

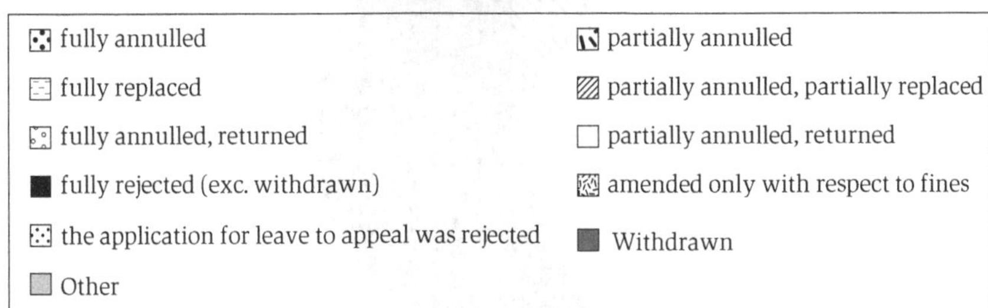

4.5 Type of Competition Authority's Decisions Subject to Appeal

Figure 14.5 indicates the type of competition law prohibitions that were enforced by the HCC in the challenged decisions, while Figure 14.6 illustrates the type of rule that the relevant judgments published over the years pertained to (each judgment counting as one). The combined reading of the two figures allows for certain interesting observations. First, the majority of HCC decisions involved the parallel application of the EU and the national rules on anti-competitive agreements and abuses of dominance. Sixty-eight per cent of the cases concerned Articles 101 and/or Article 102 TFEU, alongside their national equivalents (57% for anti-competitive agreements, 3% for abuses of dominance and 8% for both), while a smaller 32% of the cases involved the application of the national competition rules only (23% for anti-competitive agreements and 9% for abuses of dominance). Second, the overwhelming majority of HCC decisions, i.e., 80%, concerned anti-competitive agreements and only 12% pertained to abuses of dominance, while 8% concerned both. Interestingly, in relation to anti-competitive agreements, the HCC has more often relied on Article 101 TFEU and the national equivalent in parallel (57%) rather than on the national rule on anti-competitive agreements only (23%). By contrast, the majority of abuse of dominance cases were decided based on the national rule alone (9%) rather than in combination with Article 102 TFEU (3%). This is largely because the conduct investigated was of local character and was not expanded to the entire Greek territory,[98] although in a few cases, the choice to rely on the national rule only might imply a perceived discordance between national and EU law.[99] Thirdly, although variations may be observed per year, overall, there has been no significant increase or decrease in the ratio between judgments concerning the national competition rules only and judgments concerning both the national and the EU competition rules. By contrast, Figure 14.6 suggests a small decline in judgments concerning abuses of dominance since 2016 (nineteen judgments during 2015-2022 versus thirty-two judgments during 2008-2015).

Figure 14.5 Rule Being Appealed

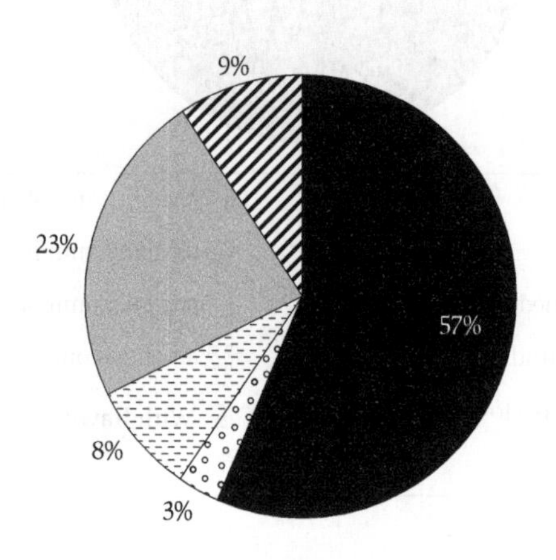

98. HCC 317/2006, HCC 426/2008, HCC 438/2009, HCC 486/2010, HCC 516/2011.
99. *See* HCC 318/2006 on GlaxoSmithKline's refusal to supply wholesalers with the requested quantities of certain drugs following the CJEU's judgment in Joined cases C-468/06 to C-478/06 *Sot. Lélos*, EU:C:2008:504. In view of the latter, the HCC refrained from applying Article 102 TFEU on the ground that the existence of a common market assumes that prices are determined by supply and demand. According to the HCC, where competition is distorted due to the presence of national price regulation, as in the pharmaceutical sector, such distortions cannot be properly dealt with under Article 102 TFEU, but only through the adoption of appropriate measures by competent EU authorities. This HCC decision was overturned by the DEA (*see* n. 116).

Figure 14.6 Rule Being Appealed According to Years (Each Judgment Counts as One)

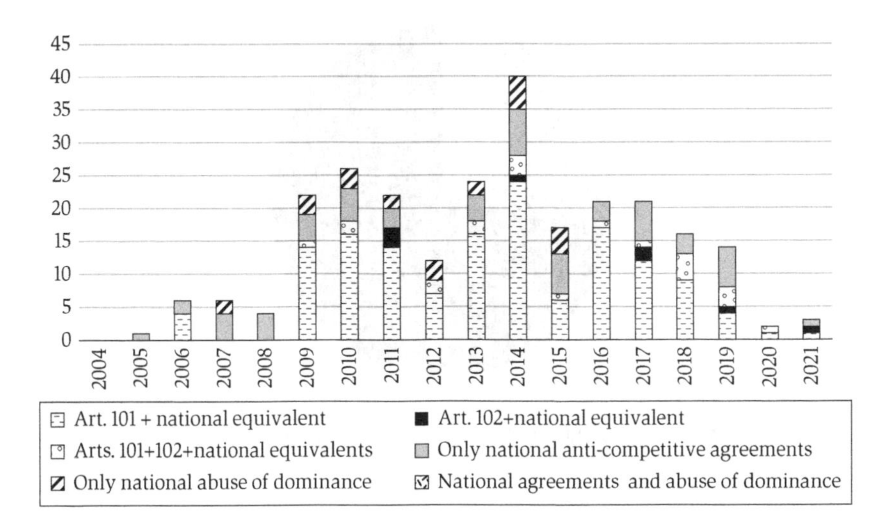

Considering now the type of restrictions that the relevant judgments concerned, Figure 14.7 clearly shows that the great majority, i.e., 124 judgments, concerned horizontal restrictions - mostly, cartels. A significant number, i.e., seventy-nine judgments, concerned vertical restrictions, while twenty-eight judgments concerned exclusionary abuses and another twenty-six judgments concerned more than one type of restriction in different combinations. Out of the judgments challenging HCC decisions that pertained to anti-competitive agreements, 72% were classified as by-object violations, 17% were prohibited as both by-object and by-effect violations, and only 5% concerned by-effect restrictions of competition.

Figure 14.7 Types of Restrictions

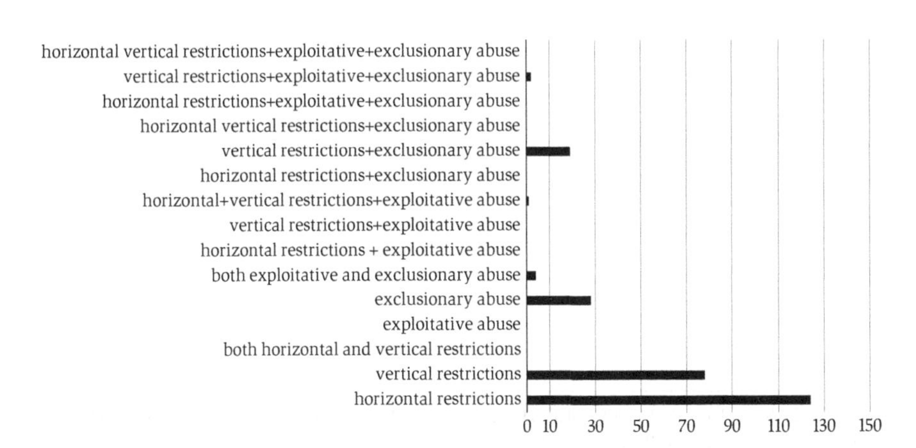

Figure 14.8 Object/Effect (Only for Article 101/National Equivalent Infringements)

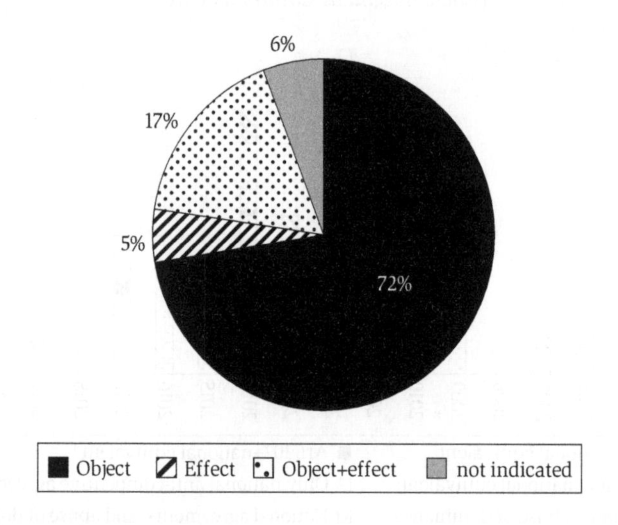

4.6 Type of NCA's Procedure

Figure 14.9 summarises the type of HCC decisions that were challenged based on the procedure followed. Unsurprisingly, more than 80% of the relevant judgments concerned infringement decisions where a fine was imposed. It is worth noting that in six HCC decisions that were subsequently appealed before the Greek courts, the HCC had adopted an infringement decision without imposing a fine (more than 5% of the relevant judgments).[100] By contrast, commitments were the relevant procedure only in one judgment.[101]

100. HCC 292/2005; HCC 317/2006; HCC 317/2006; HCC 438/2009; HCC 517/2011; HCC 604/2015.
101. DEA 2415/2018, pertaining to HCC 612/2015.

Figure 14.9 Competition Authority's Procedure

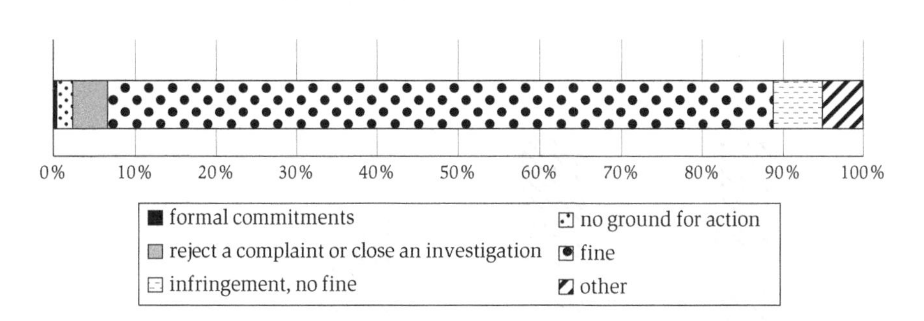

HCC decisions granting leniency have not been challenged so far.[102] Only one appeal has been examined by the DEA against an HCC decision issued in the context of settlement proceedings in the relevant time frame. The appeal was filed by a co-infringer, a non-party to the settlement proceedings and was dismissed as inadmissible.[103]

4.7 Grounds of Appeal

Figure 14.10 illustrates the grounds of appeal raised by the parties and their rate of success across both instances. Judgments against the same NCA decision or previous instance judgment have been aggregated, and the grounds involved in them and their success or rejection have been counted as a single case. Most cases involve more than one ground. Figure 14.11 focuses on the grounds argued and accepted per year and counts each judgment separately, irrespective of whether there were multiple separate appeals in relation to the same HCC decision. Figure 14.12 shows the successful grounds of challenge per type of restriction.

102. HCC 642/2017; HCC 703/2020.
103. DEA 538/2021.

Figure 14.10 Grounds of Appeal (Each NCA Decision or Previous Instance Judgment Counts as One)

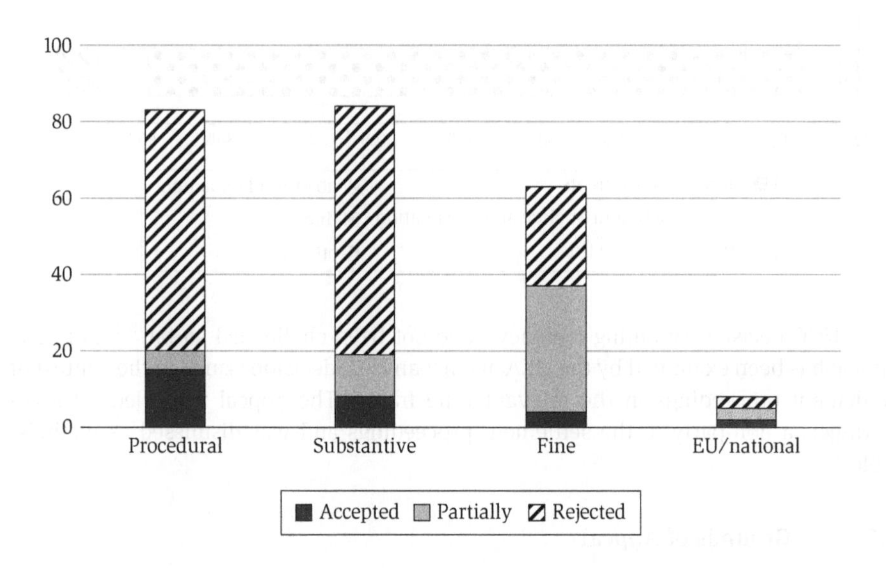

Figure 14.11(a) Procedural Grounds

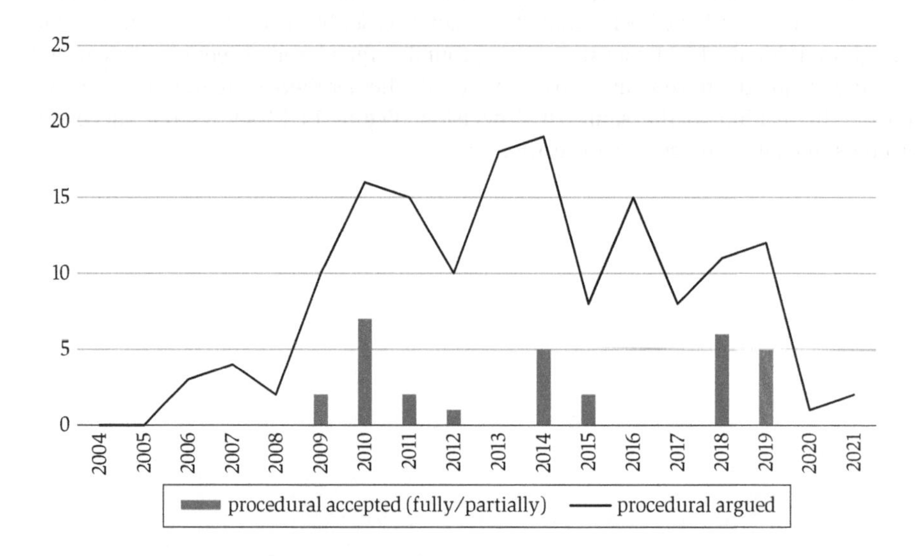

Figure 14.11(b) Substantive Grounds

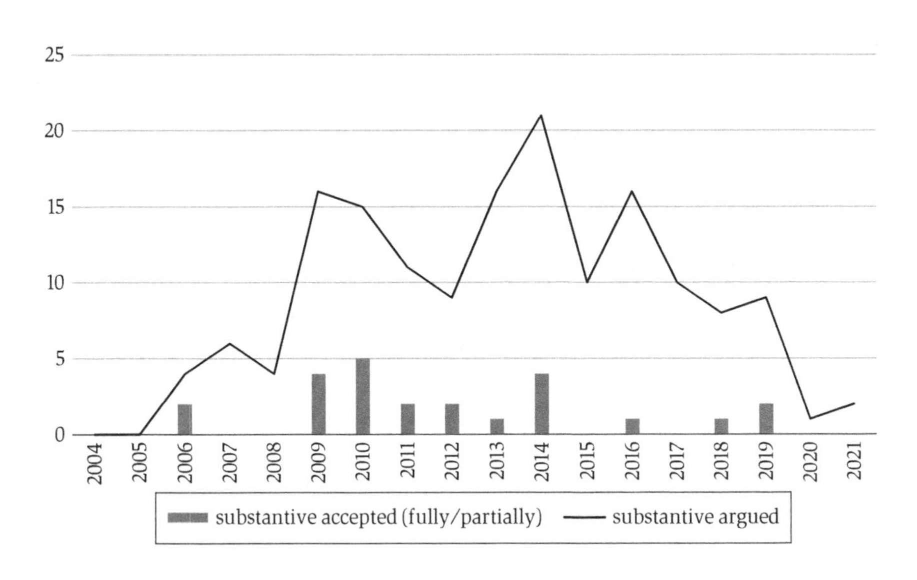

Figure 14.11(c) Fines-related Grounds

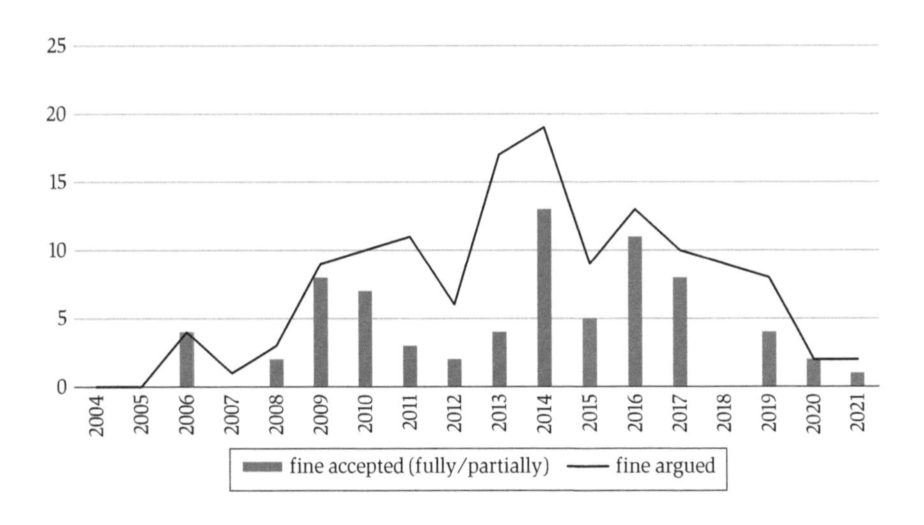

Figure 14.11(d) EU/National Grounds

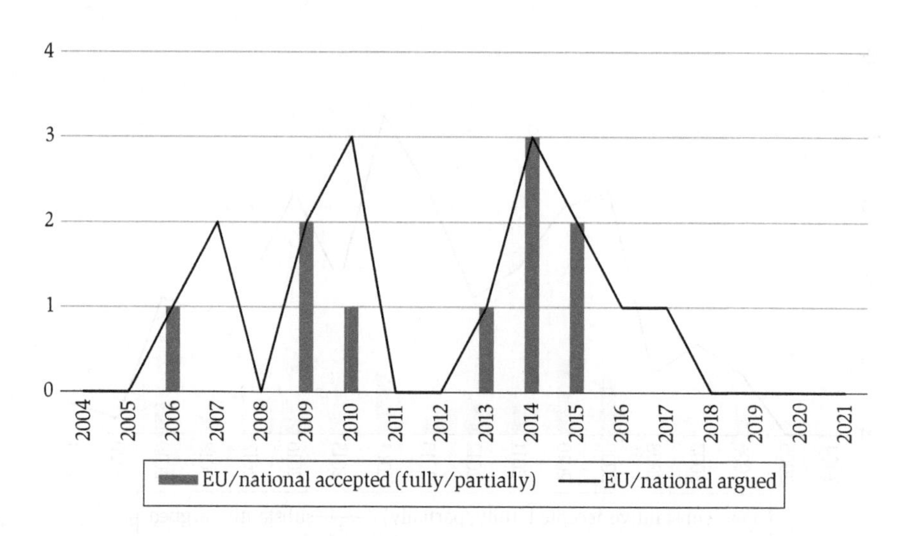

Figure 14.12 Types of Restrictions Versus Successful Grounds of Appeal

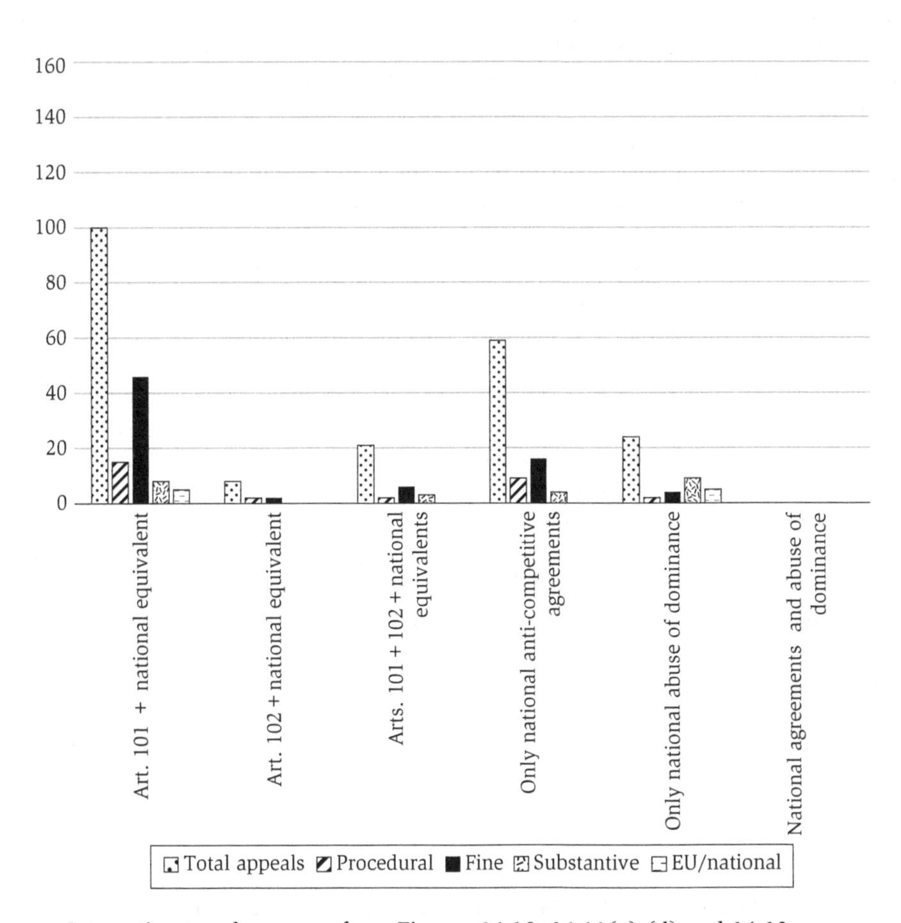

Interesting trends emerge from Figures 14.10, 14.11(a)-(d) and 14.12.

First, procedural and substantive grounds were the most frequently raised by the parties, almost in equal measure. Such grounds have been fully or partially accepted in about 23% of the challenged HCC decisions, respectively (Figure 14.10). The distribution of successful grounds per judgment over the years varies somewhat and is more evenly spread out in the case of substantive grounds. Indeed, most procedural grounds were partially or fully accepted in a number of judgments published in 2010, 2014, 2018 and 2019.[104] Taking a closer look at DEA judgments that fully annulled an HCC decision, in about two-thirds of them, the successful ground was procedural,[105] while in the remaining almost one-third, the successful ground was substantive.[106] Successful procedural grounds in appeals included three types of arguments: that the HCC had

104. Seven, four, six and five judgments, respectively.
105. Nineteen out of thirty-two full annulments of an HCC decision.
106. Nine out of thirty-two full annulments of an HCC decision.

not been lawfully composed at the time of the decision,[107] that the decision had been adopted after the limitation period,[108] and that the applicant's right to a fair trial had been violated.[109] Successful substantive grounds in appeals included arguments that the HCC had erred in its interpretation of the law or had failed to discharge its burden of proof.

More specifically, in *Lavicosmetica* (overturned by STE), the DEA concluded that the requirement for a pharmacist to be present at the points of sale in a selective distribution system was not a restriction of competition, contrary to the HCC decision.[110] In *Hyundai*, the DEA found that the HCC had failed to demonstrate that the agreement between the parties was not a genuine agency agreement escaping the application of the competition rules.[111] In *OLP* and *Mediterranean Shipping*, the DEA concluded that, in light of the evidence and the circumstances of the case, the agreement in question did not restrict competition by-object or by-effect.[112] In *DEH/HRON*, the DEA found that the HCC had not adequately demonstrated that the conditions for granting an exemption were satisfied.[113] In *Fiat* the DEA held that the HCC had failed to establish the existence of an RPM agreement.[114] In *EPA Thessalonikis* and *EPA Thessalias* (overturned by STE), the DEA took the view that the addresses of the HCC decision were not an 'undertaking' in the meaning of the competition rules since they had acted in the exercise of public authority.[115] In the *Glaxo* judgments, the DEA concluded that the HCC had erred in law in finding that GlaxoSmithKline's conduct did not amount to an abuse of dominance under Article 102 TFEU, following the preliminary ruling of the Court of Justice.[116] In *Colgate Palmolive*, the DEA held that the HCC had failed to prove that the parent company had exercised decisive influence over the conduct of its subsidiary.[117] Last but not least, in *Limeniki*, the DEA concluded that the HCC had not adequately established the applicant's participation in the infringement in question.[118]

107. DEA 1495/2011 *Shell* and DEA1494/2011 *BP* regarding HCC 421/2008; DEA 2930/2010 *IRON* regarding HCC 442/2009; DEA 2132/2010 *Groupama*, DEA 2133/2010 *Ethniki*, DEA 2134/2010 *Agrotiki Asfalistiki* and DEA 2135/2010 *Interamerican* regarding HCC 460/2009; DEA 4761/2014 *DESFA* regarding HCC 555/2012.
108. DEA 3040/2014 *Veropoulos*, DEA 2017/2010 *Atlantic*, DEA 3039/2014 *Masoutis* and DEA 3045/2014 *Makro* regarding HCC 441/2009; DEA 3597/2018 *Securities* regarding HCC 609/2015; DEA 2245/2018 *Notos*; DEA 2246/2018 *Sarantis*; DEA 2247/2018 *Parfums Christian Dior*; DEA 2248/2018 *Estee Lauder* regarding HCC 646/2017.
109. DEA 1717/2019 *Merkourakis* regarding HCC 24/29-12-2017 (decision not adopted within a reasonable time); DEA 1364/2010 *Hillside Press* regarding HCC 455/2009 (violation of the right to be heard).
110. DEA 1817/2005 *Lavicosmetica* (set aside on appeal: STE 1408/2015 *Lavicosmetica*.
111. DEA 1935/2006 *Hyundai*.
112. DEA 3132/2010 *OLP* and DEA 3134/2010 *Mediterranean Shipping*.
113. DEA 2617/2010 *DEH/HRON* (set aside on appeal: STE 166/2018 *DEH/HRON*).
114. DEA 458/2011 *Fiat*.
115. DEA 2741/2012 *EPA Thessalonikis* and DEA 2742/2012 *EPA Thessalias*.
116. DEA 821/2014; DEA 5484/2014; DEA 1983/2010; DEA 2019/2009; DEA 2100/2009 (*see also supra* n. 99).
117. DEA 1626/2019 *Colgate Palmolive*.
118. DEA 840/2019 *Limeniki*.

Procedural grounds were more successful than substantive grounds also in appeals before the STE. Procedural grounds succeeded in eight STE judgments. In *Lavicosmetica*, the STE held that the DEA failed to satisfy its duty to state reasons when concluding that the requirement for a pharmacist to be present at the points of sale in a selective distribution system was not a restriction of competition.[119] A failure to state reasons was also why the STE set DEA's judgments aside in *Dimovasilis*[120] and in *Nestle*.[121] In *Lava*[122] and in *Veropoulos*,[123] the STE concluded that the DEA had erred in its application of the rules on limitation periods (in *Lava*, the DEA mistakenly held that administrative action had not been time-barred, while in *Veropoulos* the DEA erroneously found the HCC decision to be time-barred). Last but not least, in *Coral/BP-Shell*,[124] *BP*[125] and *DESFA*,[126] the STE did not agree with the DEA that the HCC had not been lawfully composed at the time of the decision. Substantive grounds succeeded before the STE in three cases. In *EPA Thessalias and EPA Thessalonikis*, the STE held that the DEA had erred in law by holding that the addressee of the HCC was not an undertaking for the purposes of competition law.[127] More recently, in *DEH/HRON*, the STE concluded that the DEA failed to examine properly whether the HCC had correctly classified the agreement as a restriction of competition when denying negative clearance before considering whether the conditions for granting an exemption were satisfied.[128]

In any event, while procedural and substantive grounds were most frequently raised by the parties, the grounds with the higher rate of success were those pertaining to fines. In about 60% of the HCC decisions where the fine was challenged, the ground was partially or fully upheld (Figure 14.10). Looking at the judgments, the fine was reduced in 47% of them across instances. In particular, the fine was reduced in 53% of the DEA's judgments and in 37% of the STE's judgments.[129] The average fine reduction was 68%. This suggests that sanctioned undertakings may have a strong incentive to challenge a fine before the Greek courts since the chances of success are considerable and the expected fine reduction significant.

In contrast, grounds challenging the application of the EU competition rules, alongside their national equivalents, were less common, albeit relatively successful when raised. Such grounds were invoked in about 7% of the judgments and were accepted in approximately 4% of them.[130] In *Supermarkets*, the DEA found that there was an infringement of the national competition rules but not of Article 101 TFEU since

119. STE 1408/2015 *Lavicosmetica*.
120. STE 764/2014 *Dimovasilis*.
121. STE 2390/2012 *Nestle*.
122. STE 1976/2015 *Laval*.
123. STE 582/2019 *Veropoulos*.
124. STE 1769/2019 *Coral/BP-Shell*.
125. STE 1770/2019 *BP*.
126. STE 2700/2019 *DESFA*.
127. STE 2075/2014 *EPA Thessalias*; STE 2076/2014 *EPA Thessalonikis*.
128. STE 166/2018 *DEH/HRON*.
129. The Greek courts have never increased the fine. Article 79(6) KDD provides that, subject to limited exceptions, the court may not worsen the applicant's position. Whether the applicant's position would be worsened is to be determined based on the overall outcome of the appeal.
130. Eleven out of seventeen judgments.

the HCC had not explained in its decision why the agreement had an effect on trade between Member States, nor had it produced any evidence to this effect.[131] Similarly, in *Masoutis* and in *Sklavenitis*, the STE held that the DEA had not provided adequate reasons for the conclusion that the agreement had an effect on trade between Member States and returned the cases to the DEA for reconsideration,[132] which eventually found that the effect of the agreement on inter-state trade had not been adequately established by the HCC.[133] The opposite issue arose in the *Glaxo* judgments, where the complainants in the HCC proceedings successfully challenged the HCC's decision that GlaxoSmithKline's conduct did not amount to an infringement of Article 102 TFEU.[134]

Last but not least, the grounds that were most successful varied depending on the type of restriction. In judgments pertaining to anti-competitive agreements, whether based on national law only or national law and EU law in conjunction, fine-related grounds were the most upheld, followed by procedural grounds. By contrast, in abuse of dominance cases based on national law, substantive grounds were the most successful. This divergence in the type of successful grounds, depending on the type of behaviour in question, is unsurprising. The overwhelming majority of anti-competitive agreements pursued by the HCC in the relevant time frame were cartels and RPM arrangements, whose qualification as by-object restrictions is well-established. Thus, it is only normal that undertakings would concentrate their efforts on having the fine reduced or on challenging aspects of the procedure before the HCC. By contrast, abuse of dominance cases may raise more difficult substantive questions, as the *Glaxo* judgments exemplify.[135] Having said this, one must be cautious against overly broad generalisations, considering the significant gap between enforcement against anti-competitive agreements and enforcement against abuses of dominance since the latter category comprises much fewer cases.

4.8 Other

A few additional findings are worth highlighting regarding the admissibility of appeals, references for a preliminary ruling submitted by the Greek courts, and appellant types and third parties' participation in judicial proceedings.

First, about 17% of all the recorded appeals were fully dismissed as inadmissible, while another 15% were deemed only partially admissible.[136] The two most common reasons for an appeal to be fully dismissed as inadmissible were that (a) the applicant

131. DEA 163/2006 *Supermarkets*.
132. STE 1324/2013 *Sklavenitis*; STE 1677/2014 *Masoutis*.
133. DEA 2874/2015 *Masoutis*; DEA 114/2015 *Sklavenitis*.
134. DEA 821/2014; DEA 5484/2014; DEA 1983/2010; DEA 2019/2009; DEA 2100/2009.
135. Also note *EPA Thessalias* (DEA 2742/2012 and STE 2075/2014) and *EPA Thessalonikis* (DEA 2741/2012 and STE 2076/2014).
136. Forty-four judgments before the DEA: sixteen judgments were dismissed as fully inadmissible and twenty-eight as partially inadmissible. Thirty-eight judgments before the STE: twenty-seven judgments were dismissed as fully inadmissible and eleven as partially inadmissible.

lacked legal interest,[137] or (b) the representing lawyer had not been properly authorised to act on their behalf.[138] Three cases are noteworthy. In *Stathis Kokkinis – Texnologia 2020*, the appeal was dismissed as inadmissible since the applicant had been investigated by the HCC as a suspected participant but had not participated in settlement discussions, and thus, the challenged settlement decision had not been addressed against it.[139] In *Dikigoroi*, the reason for the inadmissibility was that the relevant fees had not been paid.[140] Last but not least, in *NEOSET*, the complainant asked the DEA to amend the decision of the HCC dismissing part of its complaint and to find the existence of further violations, but the action was dismissed as inadmissible on the basis that the DEA lacked jurisdiction to do so.[141] In the case of partially admissible appeals, the most common reason was that the action had been brought against both the HCC and the Greek Government, as represented by the Minister. Since the HCC acquired a separate legal personality and could represent itself in court autonomously, these appeals were partially dismissed as inadmissible with respect to the Greek Government.[142] Turning now to admissibility questions before the STE, the most common reasons for an appeal to be dismissed on this basis were: (a) again that the representing lawyer had not been properly authorised to act on behalf of the appellant,[143] and (b) that the appeal did not satisfy the admissibility criteria introduced in 2011, namely that the value of the dispute in question must exceed EUR 40,000; and that there must be no STE case law on the points of law raised in the appeal or the DEA judgment must contradict existing case law.[144] In *Procter & Gamble*, the appellant argued that the obligation to pay a fee as a condition for the admissibility of the appeal contravened the right to a fair trial, but the STE dismissed this claim.[145]

Second, DEA and STE have never filed a reference for a preliminary ruling under Article 267 TFEU. It is worth noting though that Greek civil courts have done so once – in *Glaxo*. Wholesalers of medicinal products complained to the HCC that GlaxoSmithKline was abusing its dominance by refusing to meet their orders to prevent parallel exports to other Member States.[146] The HCC concluded that aspects of GlaxoSmithKline's conduct violated the national prohibition on abuse of dominance but did not constitute an infringement of Article 102 TFEU.[147] The complainants challenged the HCC's decision before the DEA, while in parallel, they filed actions for restitution and/or damages before Greek civil courts, which decided to submit a reference for a

137. For example, DEA 3034/2006 *Procter & Gamble*; DEA 106/2010 *Ntourakis*; DEA 107/2010 *Mouzakis*.
138. For example, DEA 1779/2011 *Blue Container Line*; DEA 322/2015 *IRON*.
139. DEA 538/2021 *Stathis Kokkinis – Texnologia 2020*.
140. DEA 2459/2011.
141. DEA 2464/2019.
142. For example, DEA 263/2011 *Apollo*, para. 6.
143. For example, STE 601/2014 *SESME*; STE 1882/2014 *RENPA*; STE 3811/2011 *Procter & Gamble*.
144. For example, STE 2121/2013 *Carrefour*, para. 7; STE 3161/2014 *AB*; STE 1014/2014 *Sarlis*.
145. STE 3811/2011 *Procter & Gamble*, para. 4.
146. Following the complaint, the HCC submitted a reference for a preliminary ruling seeking guidance on the meaning of Article 102 TFEU, but the Court of Justice dismissed the reference as inadmissible on the ground that the HCC was not a court or tribunal (Case C-53/03 *Syfait and Others*, EU:C:2005:333).
147. HCC 318/2006. *See also supra* n. 99.

preliminary ruling to the Court of Justice, asking whether GlaxoSmithKline's conduct amounted to a violation of Article 102 TFEU.[148] The Court of Justice answered the question in the affirmative, where the dominant company refuses to meet 'ordinary orders'.[149] With this ruling in mind, the DEA annulled the HCC decision to the extent that it found no violation of Article 102 TFEU and returned the case back to the HCC, which eventually found that aspects of Glaxo's conduct had infringed both Article 2 of Law 703/1977 and Article 102 TFEU.[150] Both Glaxo and the complainants whose main activity was parallel exports filed appeals against the HCC decision, which were rejected by the DEA.[151] Appeals against the DEA judgment are currently pending before the STE.

Thirdly, about 73% of all actions for annulments and appeals were brought by the undertakings that were the addressees of the HCC decision.[152] Naturally, this percentage is higher when one considers first-instance proceedings only, 82% of which were initiated by addressees of the HCC decisions.[153] The HCC has appealed about 30% of DEA judgments, a relatively high number.[154] The remaining actions and appeals were initiated by third parties, mostly complainants. Turning now to third parties' participation in judicial proceedings, a third party – whether a complainant, the government or others – intervened in about 20% of cases across instances. Unsurprisingly, complainants were the most common category of intervener (about 50% of all recorded interventions).[155] The remaining interventions were often made by the undertakings against which an unsuccessful complaint had been filed.[156] The government – through public authorities – intervened only in a limited number of proceedings, all of which concerned actions for annulment against the HCC decision finding a cartel in poultry farming.[157]

5 QUALITATIVE ANALYSIS

5.1 Scope and Intensity of Judicial Review

As explained, the scope and intensity of the judicial review exercised by administrative courts are mandated by Article 79(1)-(3) KDD. DEA judgments do not typically elaborate on the matter – contrary, for instance, to the practice of the EU Courts. Interestingly, the Greek courts do not seem to afford the HCC any margin of appreciation with respect to complex economic assessments in the establishment of an infringement – at least not explicitly – and fully scrutinise all questions of law and of

148. Joined Cases C-468/06 to C-478/06 *Sot. Lélos kai Sia*, EU:C:2008:504, paras 28-29.
149. *Ibid.*, para. 77.
150. HCC 608/2015.
151. DEA 1040/2021 *Glaxo.*
152. One hundred eighty-seven out of two hundred fifty-seven judgments.
153. One hundred and forty out of one hundred and seventy judgments.
154. Twenty-seven out of eighty-seven STE judgments.
155. Twenty-five out of fifty-seven judgments involving third parties.
156. For example, DEA 2415/2018 *Distribution of tobacco products*.
157. HCC 563/2013; DEA 1075/2016; DEA 1076/2016; DEA 1082/2016; STE 1105/2018; STE 1106/2018; STE 1115/2018.

fact. Thus, the intensity of the Greek courts' scrutiny of HCC infringement decisions appears to be considerable. Based on the text of the recorded judgments, there seems to be little to no deference to the findings of the HCC regarding the existence of a violation, as the epistemically superior expert institution,[158] even in relation to findings which traditionally involve complex economic evaluations, such as findings of a dominant position or harm to competition.[159] To some extent, this might be due to the type of cases that have reached DEA and STE. As explained earlier, more than 80% were concerned with anti-competitive agreements and out of those, 73% were concerned with by-object violations. Such cases generally raise questions of fact - for instance, about the parties' participation in the infringement and its duration - or questions about the calculation of the fine and thus do not entail the type of complex economic assessments that may trigger the application of marginal review in EU jurisprudence.

In any event, it is worth noting that on several occasions, the STE did not hesitate to rectify errors made by the first-instance court in annulling HCC decisions. The following examples illustrate this vividly. In *Supermarkets*, the DEA annulled the HCC decision with respect to one of its addressees, TROFINO, on the basis that the latter's short presence in one of the anti-competitive meetings was not sufficient to prove its participation in the illegal arrangement in question.[160] The STE, however, recalled the *Aalborg Portland* presumption according to which one's attendance at a meeting whose object is anti-competitive suffices to prove that their will concurs with that of the other attendees and thus to establish its participation in the agreement in question.[161] On this

158. It may be worth noting that in DEA 1067/2014 *AEPI*, para. 8 (not included in the dataset since the relevant HCC decision was issued before 2004), the DEA commissioned an expert on the appropriate cost method for assessing excessive pricing, a matter which required specialist economic knowledge that the court lacked. To the best of our knowledge, this is the only case where the DEA has made use of its ability to order the production of expert economic evidence to assist it in its judicial review function.

159. For example, DEA 1040/2015 *Glaxo*, para. 19 (upholding the HCC's finding of a dominant position); DEA 2395/2011 *Efstathiadis*, paras 14-20 (upholding the HCC's finding of a collective dominant position and that the parties' rebate policy amounted to an abuse); DEA 869/2013 *Tasty*, para. 38 (examining the results of the econometric tests conducted by the party and upholding the HCC's definition of the relevant market); DEA 2458/2017 *Procter & Gamble*, para. 26 (upholding the HCC's finding of a dominant position). In STE 166/2018 *DEH/HRON*, para. 12 the STE explains that the power of review exercised by the STE is 'of increased density' while it affirms as a matter of principle that the full and unrestricted review of the HCC's decisions on questions of facts, law and facts and law (*πλήρης έλεγχος ουσίας*) exercised by the DEA is restricted to the extent that certain aspects of the HCC's decisions relate to the margin of discretion enjoyed by the HCC when exercising its competence to shape and enforce competition policy, without providing further concrete clarifications to this effect. In STE 1410/2022 *Procter & Gamble*, para. 9 (not included in the dataset since the relevant HCC decision was issued after April 2021), the STE further elaborates on the above principle stating that the dismissal by the HCC of the findings of an as-efficient-competitor test conducted by an undertaking under investigation or the HCC's assessment as to the degree of competitive pressure exercised by the said undertaking's competitors relate to complex economic assessments and are subject to 'marginal' review by the DEA.

160. DEA 163/2006, para. 21.

161. STE 1933/2013 *Atlantik*, para. 7. *See also* Joined Cases C-204/00 P, C-205/00 P, C-211/00 P, C-213/00 P, C-217/00 P and C-219/00 P *Aalborg Portland and Others v. Commission*, ECLI:EU:C:2004:6, para. 81.

basis, it clarified that the mere fact that the undertaking was present at the meeting only briefly is irrelevant, and the burden of proof remains with it to reverse the *Aalborg Portland* presumption.[162] Another example is *Lavicosmetica*, discussed earlier, where the STE held that the DEA failed to satisfy its duty to state reasons when concluding that the requirement for a pharmacist to be present at the points of sale in a selective distribution system did not go beyond what was necessary and thus was not a restriction of competition.[163] Last but not least, as explained earlier, in *EPA Thessalias* and *EPA Thessalonikis*, the STE took issue with the first-instance court's conclusion that the entities in question were not 'undertakings' on the ground that they had acted in the exercise of public authority and referred both cases back to DEA for reconsideration.[164]

Considering now the scope and intensity of the judicial review of commitment decisions, this differs significantly from infringement decisions insofar as the HCC enjoys a margin of discretion in this regard. Accordingly, as long as the HCC's decision to accept or reject commitments is adequately reasoned, so as to allow for its judicial review, the DEA may only annul it where the HCC has exceeded the outer limits of its discretion. *Colgate* is illustrative in this regard. In this case, the HCC decided to reject the undertaking's in question offer of commitments and to continue the investigation.[165] The undertaking, however, challenged this decision as illegal. Hearing the matter, the DEA recalled the HCC's margin of discretion to accept commitments or not and the limited judicial scrutiny to which such decisions are subject and noted that the applicant did not claim that the HCC had exceeded the outer limits of this discretion. In any event, the DEA stressed that the HCC's decision to reject the commitments was adequately justified: the proposed commitments not only concerned obligations of the undertaking that were already mandated by law but also pertained to past behaviour, in which case commitments do not constitute an effective measure.[166]

5.2 Review of Fines

Grounds pertaining to the fine have been the most successful, as Figures 14.10 and 14.11(c) demonstrate. In more than one-third of the recorded first-instance judgments, the DEA amended the fine imposed by the HCC. Despite the fact, however, that the

162. STE 1933/2013, para. 8. Three STE judges (Gravaris, Tsimekas and Lazaraki) disagreed though on the ground that participants in the relevant meeting discussed a variety of matters, beyond those that were deemed to amount to by-object restrictions of competition, and that given the limited presence of TROFINO in the meeting, it must be given the benefit of the doubt.
163. STE 1408/2015, para. 8.
164. STE 2075/2014, paras 5-8; STE 2076/2014, paras 5-8.
165. HCC 453/2009.
166. DEA 1552/2012, para. 8; DEA 1554/2012, para. 8. It is worth noting that the President of the DEA disagreed, citing the judgment of the General Court in *Alrosa*, and took the view that the HCC's margin of discretion in relation to commitments does not relieve the HCC from its obligation to comply with the principle of proportionality. In accordance with this principle, in her dissenting opinion, the HCC should have accepted the offered commitments, which were adequate and suitable, given the limited duration of the violation and the fact that its impact on the Greek market had not been proved.

Greek courts have not shied away from scrutinising the penalties imposed by the HCC, they have not been particularly vocal on the scope of their judicial review function in relation to fines.

The most comprehensive statement on this may be found in *Veropoulos*,[167] a judgment published in 2017. Drawing on EU case law, the STE noted that antitrust fines constitute an important aspect of competition policy and that, subject to the principle of proportionality, the European Commission, as well as NCAs, enjoy a margin of discretion in this regard to ensure the effectiveness of competition law and the deterrent effect of sanctions.[168] The STE further emphasised that neither the HCC nor the Greek courts may decline to impose a penalty in case of an antitrust violation and clarified that, to be deterrent, fines must be sufficiently higher than the profits that the undertaking could expect from the commission of the violation, without becoming though too burdensome.[169] Considering the principle of proportionality, the STE stressed that this is safeguarded through the 15% cap provided by Law 703/1977 (10% under Law 3959/2011) and the obligation to take into account all the circumstances of the case when setting the fine.

Turning to the applicable scope and intensity of judicial control, the STE noted that the reviewing court may not substitute its own assessment for that of the HCC but may scrutinise all errors in its decision, whether pertaining to the finding of a violation or the setting of the fine. In particular, the court may amend the fine in case of a legal error, such as a violation of the principle of proportionality or the principle of the deterrent effect of sanctions, or in case of factual errors - for instance, in relation to the duration and the scope of the infringement or the existence of any mitigating or aggravating circumstances. In the presence of such an error, the reviewing court has full jurisdiction to modify the fine as appropriate. The STE further clarified that where the fine does not exceed the maximum cap and was calculated based on the criteria provided for in the law, the review of its proportionality entails verifying the legality, comprehensiveness and factual accuracy of the determination of the fine, although the court must not go as far as exercising competition policy itself. Last but not least, the STE noted that the global turnover is lawfully used as a proxy for an undertaking's commercial power and the potential extent of the harm caused by the infringement and that the principles of proportionality and equal treatment may require setting a different fine for each perpetrator.

Notwithstanding this detailed presentation of the scope and intensity of judicial review of antitrust fines, the DEA has been occasionally terse in its reasoning when annulling or decreasing penalties imposed by the HCC. *Supermarkets* offers an extreme example. The HCC had found a cartel among six supermarkets and had imposed on them varying fines, which represented approximately 0.08% of their turnovers (with the exception of one of them, TROFINO, for which the fine had been calculated based

167. STE 1695/2017, para. 19.
168. Also note STE 1933/2013 *Atlantik*, paras 9-10, and in particular para. 10, where the STE justified this margin of discretion based on the HCC's expertise and its competence not only to prosecute antitrust violations but also to exercise general competition policy.
169. The STE framed this in terms of the 'costs of doing business'.

on 0.03% of its turnover).[170] Examining the addressees' actions for annulment, the DEA concluded that the HCC had failed to establish the participation of TROFINO in the infringement and set the fine for each of the remaining five supermarkets at EUR 120,000.[171] However, the DEA provided no explanation as to how it arrived at this calculation and why this approach was compatible with the principle of equal treatment but rather cited vague reasons for its judgment: that the intended objective of the infringement had not materialised, its duration was short and its seriousness limited, since the chosen means could not have led to the desired outcome, and the initiative for the violation belonged to the five supermarkets eventually sanctioned in the judgment.[172] Fortunately, this was rectified on appeal.[173] In addition to finding that the DEA had erred in law in concluding that TROFINO's participation in the violation had not been established, the STE chastised the DEA for failing to state reasons for its calculation of the fines and referred the case back to the first-instance court for reconsideration.[174]

Overall, the picture is somewhat mixed. In some judgments where the fine was reduced, the DEA's reasoning has been laconic. *Ixthyokalliergeies* offers a telling illustration. Although in principle the HCC may decide not to impose a fine for an antitrust infringement only exceptionally, in this case, the DEA annulled the penalty in question and concluded that the appropriate sanction was merely a recommendation not to repeat the violation.[175] However, the DEA hardly explained why and vaguely cited reasons pertaining to the type and seriousness of the breach, its short duration, the particular circumstances of the case and the fact that the applicant had collaborated with the HCC during the investigation.[176] In other judgments, though, the reasoning of the DEA when lowering the fines imposed by the HCC has been more detailed. For instance, in *SERGAL*, the DEA justified the nearly 67% fine reduction based on the severe financial difficulties faced by the applicant.[177] Likewise, in *Ergasis*, the 97% decrease in the sanction was due to errors in the HCC's calculation of the relevant sales and the end date of the violation, taking into account the type and seriousness of the violation, its impact on the market, its duration and the financial struggles of the undertaking.[178]

In any event, the Greek courts have had the opportunity to examine two interesting questions regarding fines. The first question arose in *Supermarkets* and was whether the HCC may find an infringement in one decision and impose fines for this infringement in a separate decision. Acting in full composition in *Veropoulos, Metro* and *Sklavenitis*, the STE addressed this preliminary issue and agreed with the DEA that, as long as the relevant procedures had been properly followed and the undertakings'

170. HCC 277/2005 and HCC 284/2005.
171. DEA 163/2006, para. 24.
172. *Ibid.*
173. STE 1933/2013 *Supermarkets*, para. 13.
174. *Ibid.*
175. DEA 548/2010 *Ixthyokalliergeies*, para. 19.
176. *Ibid.*
177. DEA 906/2010 *SERGAL*, para. 15.
178. DEA 5002/2019 *Ergasis*, para. 10.

rights of the defence had been respected, the HCC could lawfully adopt two separate decisions: one establishing the existence of a violation and another one imposing penalties for this violation.[179] The second question arose in *Nestle* and was whether the HCC could impose a single fine for breaches of the rules on anti-competitive agreements and on abuses of dominance committed by the same undertaking in the same case. Considering the matter at first instance, the DEA deemed this illegal. As the DEA explained, the national rules on anti-competitive agreements and abuses of dominance constitute standalone prohibitions, which cannot be absorbed by one another, and thus, a separate fine must be set for their violation. Since the HCC had imposed a single fine and had not exercised its discretion in setting a separate sanction for each violation, the DEA lacked jurisdiction to determine the penalties itself and referred the case back to the HCC.[180]

Last but not least, an interesting question arose in *Atlantik*, where the STE reviewed the DEA's annulment of the HCC decision sanctioning Atlantic for its participation in the milk cartel. Citing EU jurisprudence on the imposition of penalties in vertical agreements, the DEA noted that where the infringement has been initiated by a powerful supplier and forced on the commercially weaker distributors, it is not appropriate to impose a fine on the latter.[181] The HCC had established that this was not the issue regarding several involved supermarkets, but it did not consider the specific position of Atlantic and did not demonstrate that it was not commercially weaker than the suppliers in question.[182] On this ground, the DEA annulled the fine imposed on the latter.[183] However, the HCC successfully appealed the judgment before the STE, which emphasised that whether the participants in an anti-competitive arrangement are in a similar position is irrelevant for the establishment of an infringement or for the imposition of a fine.[184] Rather, the size and economic strength of an undertaking and its role in the commission of the infringement are considered in the evaluation of the seriousness of the infringement when setting the individual fine, and only exceptionally may the HCC not impose a penalty for an antitrust violation in the context of the margin of discretion it enjoys with respect to fines.[185] The STE also noted that the weaker party may always challenge the validity of the agreement and seek damages.[186] On these grounds, the STE set the first-instance judgment aside and returned the case to the DEA for reconsideration.[187]

---

179. STE 1297/2011 *Veropoulos*, paras 6-7; STE 1298/2011 *Metro*, paras 7-8; STE 1299/2011 *Sklavenitis*, paras 7-8. Also note DEA 527/2016 *Germanos*, para. 46, where the DEA *ex officio* annulled the fine imposed by the HCC (without examining the arguments put forward by the applicant) on the ground that the HCC should have imposed three fines, instead of one - one for each separate infringement found (RPM, restriction of cross-supplies between distributors, and non-compete obligation).
180. DEA 2265/2010 *Nestle*, paras 41-44.
181. DEA 604/2009 *Atlantic*, paras 12-13.
182. *Ibid.*
183. *Ibid.*
184. STE 2872/2020 *Atlantik*, paras 9-10.
185. *Ibid.*
186. *Ibid.*
187. *Ibid.*

5.3 Coherence with Substantive EU Competition Law

As noted above, DEA and STE have never submitted a reference for a preliminary ruling under Article 267 TFEU, while Greek civil courts have done so only once in *Glaxo*. However, the dearth of preliminary ruling references must be put into context. To some extent, it can be explained by the type of restrictions that have been challenged before the DEA and the STE. As Figures 14.5 and 14.8 illustrated, 88% of the challenged HCC decisions involved anti-competitive agreements (80% exclusively and 8% in combination with the rules on abuse of dominance), and 73% of these cases concerned by-object restrictions, whose legal qualification is well-established and does not normally raise questions of interpretation. This percentage rises to 90% when one considers only the cases involving the application of Article 101 TFEU and the national equivalent on their own and in conjunction with the EU and national rules on abuses of dominance.[188]

A closer look at the recorded DEA and STE judgments further confirms the general coherence of Greek competition law with EU competition law in the relevant time frame. Both courts have consistently drawn on EU case law, even in cases involving the application of the national competition rules only. For example, in *EPA Thessalias* and *EPA Thessalonikis,* which was decided under the national rule on abuse of dominance and where the notion of undertaking was at stake, the DEA and the STE heavily cited relevant EU jurisprudence.[189] Likewise, in *Samiakes Ploes*, the DEA referenced EU case law on rebates when interpreting the notion of abuse under Article 2 of the Greek Competition Law.[190] Similarly, in *ELPE,* the STE relied on the EU Courts' definition of the notion of concerted practice in its application of the national rule on anti-competitive agreements.[191] The fact that DEA and STE do not often cite relevant Greek case law only reinforces the significance of EU doctrine in Greek competition law.[192] In this regard, it is noteworthy that the Greek courts have cited EU judgments not only on matters of substantive interpretation but also on matters of procedure. For instance, in *Mixaniki Perivallontos* and in *Karkanias Texnologia Perivallontos* (which concerned the application of national law), the DEA relied on EU jurisprudence to clarify the HCC's obligation to make decisions within a reasonable time in view of the principles of legality and legal certainty and undertakings' rights of defence.[193]

---

188. One hundred and fifty out of the one hundred and sixty-six relevant judgments in the dataset involved by-object violations (118 judgments) or both by-object and by-effect violations (32 judgments).
189. DEA 2742/2012, para 10; DEA 2742/2012, para 10; STE 2075/2014, para 5. STE 2076/2014, para 5.
190. DEA 1333/2011, para. 7.
191. STE 3859/2014, para. 5.
192. STE judgments are more often cited in subsequent cases in relation to substantive issues (e.g., STE 1036/2016 *Art Gas Stations*, para. 6; DEA 4049/2018 *Ergonet*, para. 3) but not nearly as frequently as EU judgments.
193. DEA 5005/2019, para. 5; DEA 4559/2019, para. 4.

5.4 Third Parties' Rights

The Greek review system provides some rights for third parties: they may bring an appeal against an HCC decision, or they may intervene in competition proceedings, assuming they have sufficient legal interest.

Two cases are worth noting in particular. The first is *Distribution of tobacco products*, where an association of tobacco product wholesalers complained that a supplier's decision to switch to an exclusive distribution model for the distribution of their products violated the competition rules. Following its investigation, the HCC decided to dismiss the complaint and accept the commitments offered by the suppliers in question.[194] The complainant challenged this decision before the DEA, alleging that the HCC erred in law in accepting the offered commitments rather than imposing structural remedies which would restore the previous distribution system in place and that the commitments in question did not eliminate the concerns, insofar as the wholesale distribution market had been closed off. However, the DEA dismissed both claims, noting that structural remedies may only be imposed in case of an infringement, which had not been established on the facts, and that, while the new distribution system had reduced intra-brand competition at the wholesale level, this was a business choice with which the HCC could not interfere, absent a competition violation.[195]

The second case worth highlighting is *Merkourakis*.[196] Pursuant to Article 37 of Law 3959/2011, the Directorate General may propose that complaints that are manifestly unfounded be dismissed through an act by the HCC President within nine months from their submission. The HCC dismissed the applicant's complaint as manifestly unfounded, but the applicant complained that the HCC had failed to adopt a decision within the applicable deadline and, in any event, within a reasonable time. Hearing the matter, the DEA noted that, while the HCC enjoys a margin of discretion in the way it handles complaints and may prioritise certain investigations, this discretion must be exercised consistently and transparently, taking into account appropriate prioritisation criteria, pertaining, among others, to the seriousness, complexity and urgency of the complaints.[197] Moreover, the DEA stressed that, while administrative deadlines are indicative, the HCC President must adopt an act on the matter within nine months, either dismissing the complaint or ordering further investigative measures or explaining the priority and overall progress of the case if a different decision is not possible at the time.[198] In any event, administrative proceedings must be concluded within a reasonable time, which is for the DEA to determine.[199] On the facts, the DEA concluded that the HCC failed to comply with its obligation to decide within a reasonable time insofar as it dismissed the complaint as manifestly unfounded five years after its

194. HCC 612/2015.
195. DEA 2415/2018 *Distribution of tobacco products*, para. 27. The court also noted that complainants had initiated civil litigation, seeking among others, interim measures, but nearly all actions and requests had been dismissed.
196. DEA 1717/2019.
197. *Ibid.*, paras 2-3.
198. *Ibid.*
199. *Ibid.*

submission and did not adopt a decision within nine months as provided for by Article 37 Law 3959/2011.[200] The HCC decision was thus annulled.

6 CONCLUDING REMARKS

As the above analysis exemplifies, the number of appeals against HCC decisions post-Regulation 1/2003 is relatively high and overall, appellants have frequently been successful, at least partially. What is more striking, though, is the low number of cases where the DEA reviewed and annulled or amended HCC decisions in substance. In practice, the judicial review exercised by the DEA mostly centres on procedural issues as well as sanctions, where the DEA enjoys unlimited jurisdiction and the DEA shows no to little deference to HCC's assessments. This may explain the rather high number of appeals filed against HCC decisions. While the DEA's focus on process has contributed substantially to the streamlining of the proceedings before the HCC and the development of a robust procedural framework, the lack of any substantial reasoning with regard to fine reductions has not allowed for the design of a more coherent fining policy that will better serve deterrence and compliance and will persuade undertakings of its fairness. On the other hand, the STE has been pivotal to the development of competition policy and enforcement in Greece by thoroughly scrutinising DEA judgments on both procedural and substantive issues.

200. *Ibid.*, para. 6.

Chapter 15
Hungary Report

Csongor István Nagy

1 COMPETITION LAW ENFORCEMENT CONTEXT IN HUNGARY

Hungarian competition law has a relatively long history. Its origins date back way before the Second World War. The country's first act on unfair competition was adopted in 1923,[1] while the first antitrust legislation was Act XX of 1931 on Agreements Regulating Economic Competition.[2] The latter did not prohibit restrictive agreements in general but only those that were contrary to the public interest. The law established a duty of notification. Restrictive agreements were required to be registered with the competent ministry.

After the communist party took power in Hungary after the Second World War, Hungary was converted into a state-planned economy, making antitrust law unnecessary. However, in 1968, an economic reform was introduced (entitled the 'new economic mechanism'), which gave some room for the free market and enabled the creation of small- and medium-sized enterprises (SMEs). This process resulted in a dual economy. The 'state' sector embraced the country's big public enterprises and was managed according to the rules of state planning, while the private sector was made up of SMEs, which could operate in a relatively autonomous manner. The

1. Act V of 1923 on unfair competition (in Hungarian: '*1923. évi V. törvénycikk a tisztességtelen versenyről*').
2. In Hungarian: '*1931. évi XX. törvénycikk a gazdasági versenyt szabályozó megállapodásokról*'. *See* Norbert Varga, A kartellfelügyelet bevezetése Magyarországon: Az 1931:XX. tc. kodifikációja és gyakorlata (2020); Norbert Varga, The European Roots of Hungarian Regulation of the Cartels Special Attention to the Foundation of Cartel Supervisory Public Authorities, 11(2) Journal on European History of Law 111 (2020); Norbert Varga, The Antecedents of the Regulation of the Economic Competition Agreement in the First Part of the 20th Century in Hungary, 14(1) Krakowskie Studia z Historii Panstwa i Prawa 17 (2021); Norbert Varga, Introduction to the Hungarian Cartel Regulation in the Interwar Period, 15(2) Krakowskie Studia z Historii Panstwa i Prawa 215 (2022).

gradual extension of the free market made economic regulation necessary, including company law and antitrust law. As part of this process, Hungary enacted a competition law in 1984, when the country was still a planned economy.

After the socialist regime collapsed in 1989, a new competition act was adopted in 1990 (Act LXXXVI of 1990 on the Prohibition of Unfair Market Conduct), which established the Hungarian Competition Office ('HCO', in Hungarian: '*Gazdasági Versenyhivatal*'). This act essentially followed the mainstream legislation practice, addressing restrictive agreements, abuses of dominance and mergers. Perhaps the most important shortcoming of the act was that, with the exception of resale price fixing, it did not prohibit vertical restrictive agreements.[3]

In 1996, the Hungarian parliament adopted a new competition act (Act LVII of 1996, hereinafter referred to as the 'Hungarian Competition Act' (HCA)), which entered into force on 1 January 1997. This act replaced the act of 1990 and is still effective, albeit it has been amended several times.

The HCA was modelled after the EU competition law. Substantive rules and their interpretation are highly influenced by EU competition law and policy, albeit there are a few points where Hungarian competition law diverges from EU law. In procedural law, the differences are more significant.

The HCA regulates most fields of competition law in the wider sense. In addition to antitrust, it contains rules on unfair competition law and on the prohibition of unfair manipulation of business decisions (unfair commercial practices in a business-to-business context). Under Hungarian law, competition law, in its widest sense, also covers the law of unfair commercial practices against consumers, which is regulated in a separate act (Act XLVII of 2008 on the Prohibition of Unfair Commercial Practices).[4] This act implements the UCP Directive (Directive 2005/29/EC concerning unfair business-to-consumer commercial practices in the internal market) and provides that matters substantially affecting competition come under the HCO's competence. Initially, the HCA contained a separate chapter on the unfair manipulation of consumer decisions (the prohibition of misleading consumers), which had a broadly similar regulatory aim as the UCP regime. With the implementation of the UCP Directive, this chapter was amended to address the unfair manipulation of business decisions (misleading communication in a business-to-business context), leaving the prohibition of unfair commercial practices in a business-to-consumer context to the UCP Act. However, as noted, this field is supervised primarily by the HCO.

Hungarian substantive antitrust law has three fields: the rules on restrictive agreements, abuses of dominance and merger control (concentrations). Sections 11-20 HCA deal with restrictive agreements and are the equivalent of Article 101 TFEU. They equally apply to horizontal and vertical agreements. Section 11 contains a general prohibition on restrictive agreements, in line with Article 101(1) TFEU, and distinguishes between agreements anti-competitive by-object and by-effect. Section 17 HCA contains the rules on individual exemption, which converge with the requirements

3. Section 14 of Act LXXXVI of 1990 on the prohibition of unfair market conduct.
4. In Hungarian: '*2008. évi XLVII. törvény a fogyasztókkal szembeni tisztességtelen kereskedelmi gyakorlat tilalmáról*'.

embedded in Article 101(3) TFEU. Section 16 HCA empowers the government to adopt block exemption regulations; these regulations, as a rule of thumb, are in line with EU block exemption regulations.[5] Section 21 HCA prohibits any abuse of a dominant position. It contains a general prohibition and an illustrative list of prohibited practices, while section 22 HCA defines economic dominance essentially in accordance with EU competition law. Sections 23-32 HCA contain the rules of merger control: concentrations above a certain turnover have to be notified to the HCO for clearance.

The rules of competition law enforcement are partly included in the HCA, and partly in the 'Administrative Procedure Act' ('APA', Act CL of 2016),[6] whose rules apply only in case the HCA expressly provides so. The rules on the judicial review of HCO decisions are included in the HCA, the APA and the 'Code on Administrative Court Procedure' (Act I of 2017).[7] This also implies that the judicial review of HCO decisions takes place under the general rules applicable to the judicial review of administrative decisions.

The administrative authority responsible for enforcing competition law (both Hungarian and EU) is the HCO, which is an autonomous central administrative body. The HCO's head, deputy heads and members of the Competition Council (CC), which is the HCO's internal decision-making body, have fixed tenure for six years[8] and cannot be removed before the end of this term, with the exception of certain cases of grave breaches of duty.[9] The leaders' fixed tenure and the protection against dismissal are meant to guarantee the HCO's independence and are constitutionally protected.[10]

The HCO has an idiosyncratic twofold structure, which features a split administrative competition procedure involving an investigative and a *quasi*-judicial branch. The competition investigation is carried out by case handlers, who are part of the hierarchy controlled by the head of the HCO. Case handlers work in different bureaux, which are responsible for the HCO's investigative and analyst functions. Case handlers are responsible for discovering the facts, collecting evidence and, at the end of the investigation, submitting the file together with the 'case handler's report' to the CC. After the investigative phase, the case handlers submit the file accompanied by a report to the CC, which is the HCO's adjudicatory body and responsible for making any final decision on the merits. The status of the CC is somewhat controversial: while it is part of the HCO from an institutional and budgetary perspective, it is an independent, *quasi*-judicial body whose members have independence in making their decisions and act as quasi-judges.[11]

The HCO's president is appointed by the president of the republic (head of state) upon the proposal of the prime minister.[12] The president of the HCO nominates the two

5. Csongor István Nagy, Versenyjogi kézikönyv 267 (2021).
6. In Hungarian: '*2016. évi CL. törvény az általános közigazgatási rendtartásról*'.
7. In Hungarian: '*2017. évi I. törvény a közigazgatási perrendtartásról*'.
8. Sections 35(2), 37(3) and 38(1) HCA.
9. Section 38(1) and (5) HCA.
10. *See* decision of the Constitutional Court in Case *183/2010*. For a case-note on the Constitutional Court's decision *see* Levente Szabó, *Az Alkotmánybíróság határozata a szervezetátalakítás szabadságáról*, 2(special issue) Jogesetek Magyarázata 26 (2011).
11. Section 37(1) HCA.
12. Section 35(2) HCA.

vice presidents (one of them serves as the chair of the CC) to the prime minister, who - in case he agrees with the proposal - submits the nominations to the head of state. The vice presidents of the HCO are appointed by the head of state, who charges one of them with the responsibility of heading the CC.[13] The president and the vice presidents of the HCO are appointed for six years and can be reappointed.[14]

The members of the CC are appointed and dismissed by the head of state upon the proposal of the president of the HCO. They are appointed for a term of six years.[15]

2 JUDICIAL REVIEW OF COMPETITION DECISIONS IN HUNGARY

2.1 Review Courts

The HCO's administrative decisions can be challenged before the Budapest-Capital Regional Court (*'Fővárosi Törvényszék'*), whose judgment can be appealed to the Supreme Court by means of an extraordinary appeal limited to questions of law. The general deadline for challenging an administrative decision on the merits by the HCO before the courts is thirty days.[16] Before 2020, HCO decisions were reviewed in a three-tier system, where the first-instance court was the Budapest-Capital Administrative and Labour Court (*'Közigazgatási és Munkaügyi Bíróság'*)[17] and the Budapest-Capital Regional Court acted as second-instance court with a full-review power. The Supreme Court heard extraordinary appeals concerning questions of law. Until 2013, the first-instance court was the Budapest-Capital Regional Court, and the High Court of Appeal of Budapest acted as second-instance court with a full-review power. The Supreme Court heard extraordinary appeals concerning questions of law.

2.2 Judicial Review

Standing as to judicial review of decisions on the merits is limited to the defendants in the administrative procedure and to those third parties whose right or legal interest is directly affected by the matter.[18] Courts interpret standing as to third parties rather narrowly, and, in practice, third-party challenges are extremely rare.[19] The complainant in the administrative procedure has no privileged status to challenge the decision on the merits; that is, it can appeal the decision on the merits only if his right or legal interest is directly affected. If, however, the HCO refuses to open a competition procedure or terminates it, the complainant is entitled to appeal this decision without the need to prove legal interest.[20]

13. Section 35(2) HCA.
14. Section 35(2) HCA.
15. Section 37(3) HCA.
16. Section 134(4) of the Code on Administrative Court Procedure.
17. *See* Rita Csőke, A közigazgatási és munkaügyi bíróság megszervezése a Budapest Környéki Törvényszéken, 11(2) Themis 61 (2013).
18. Csongor István Nagy, Versenyjogi kézikönyv 562-566 (2021).
19. *Ibid.*
20. Section 43/H(9)-(10) HCA.

The basis of review in Hungarian administrative and procedural law, including competition matters, is 'illegality'.[21] Nonetheless, in competition cases, the Supreme Court developed a full-review standard. In *Railway Constructors*,[22] the Supreme Court held that the HCO's decision must not be examined under the provision on discretionary acts, enabling a margin of appreciation, but in undertaking any judicial review, the HCO's decision has to be fully reviewed. In the court procedure, the plaintiff is not expected to demonstrate that the HCO assessed the evidence in a blatantly unreasonable manner or the legal assessment was obviously unreasonable. It suffices if they demonstrate that there is a more reasonable assessment of the evidence and there is a more reasonable legal assessment. The Supreme Court deduced the above approach from Article 6 of the European Convention of Human Rights as interpreted in the judgment of the European Court of Human Rights in *Menarini*.[23] The principle of full review was confirmed by the Supreme Court in Case Kfv.III.37.690/2013/29, Case Kfv.II.37.110/2017/13 and in Case Kf.38050/2018/8.

The appeal practice features three important characteristics.

First, notwithstanding the declaration of the principle of full review, the judicial procedure cannot ignore the fact that the court does not try the case directly but reviews an existing administrative decision and the underlying administrative procedure. Courts have been reluctant to use their powers to carry out a full review as to substance and, as a matter of practice, have still afforded considerable deference to the HCO. Although under the law, they are not prevented from second-guessing HCO decisions, in practice, they may lack the institutional capacity to carry this out. This implies that courts have been less interventionist with respect to substantive issues, including questions of proof, and proved to be increasingly active in relation to procedural issues. Still, the courts' willingness to engage with substantive issues increased considerably. Although still deferential, the review practice features a significant intensification as compared to the judicial practice of two decades ago. This has shifted the development of the law from the HCO to the courts. Of course, the HCO still plays a crucial role in the development of competition law. Courts review HCO decisions, and the HCO has a distinguished professional reputation. The radical change in the judicial practice can mainly be attributed to the fact that in the 2000s, the judicial practice featured a minimalist approach. This manifested itself not only in the high success rate of the HCO but also in the language of court judgments, which rarely provided guidance as to substantive issues of interpretation and limited themselves to a 'technical' review of any administrative decision.

It has to be noted that, under Hungarian law, a number of issues that are treated in this study as substantive grounds,[24] qualify as procedural grounds under the Hungarian system and courts have had the tendency to use a 'procedural' justification even if perceiving substantive errors. The lack of or insufficient proof of the facts by the HCO, as well as the decision's weak evidentiary basis, amount to a breach of the rules

---

21. Section 37(1)(f) Code of Administrative Court Procedure.
22. Case Kfv.III.37.690/2013/29.
23. Judgment rendered in Case 43509/08 *Menarini Diagnostics S.R.L. v. Italy* on 27 September 2011.
24. *See* the 'methodology' chapter in this collection.

on evidence and on establishing the facts of the case. In these matters, the court may quash the HCO decision for breach of the rules on evidence and failure to establish the facts and may even order the HCO to retry the case, although the real issue may be that the evidence collected by the HCO does not prove the violation to the requisite standard. Furthermore, judgments establishing that the rules on reasoning were breached may hide substantive concerns on the side of the court. Courts have a tendency to quash the decision for insufficient or contradictory reasoning instead of establishing that the HCO's substantive analysis was flawed.

Second, under Hungarian law, violations of the rules of procedure may lead to the annulment of an administrative decision only if it had a substantial impact on the substance of the case. This requirement implies that, in addition to demonstrating the violation of the rules of procedure, the plaintiff is also expected to prove that the HCO may have decided differently if the rules of procedure had been respected. In certain cases, this requirement may make the rules of procedure a *lex imperfecta*. Nonetheless, the Supreme Court has developed certain categories of procedural violations where the negative impact on the substantive outcome is presumed. Although the Supreme Court has never conceptualised it, judicial practice suggests that there are certain procedural violations that are in themselves sufficient reasons to annul the HCO decision. For instance, if the HCO's final decision substantially departs from its preliminary position, which is the rough equivalent of a statement of objections, the decision has to be annulled. The plaintiff is not required to prove that if the preliminary position had defined the 'indictment' properly, he could have argued effectively to avoid the HCO's condemnation or to reduce the fine.[25] A similar approach was followed by the Supreme Court as to the time limit of the procedure. For decades, the HCO's violation of the rules on the terms of the competition procedure had been treated as *lex imperfecta*. The HCO regularly exceeded the statutorily fixed deadline, but the courts consistently rejected all objections to this violation on the basis that it had no substantial impact on the substantive outcome of the case, and the HCO would have adopted no different decision, even if it had respected the deadline.[26] Nonetheless, in Case Kf.II.37.959/2018/14, the Supreme Court suddenly changed its approach and held that with the expiry of the deadline, the HCO loses the power to impose a fine. The plaintiff is not required to prove that the ignorance of the deadline had a substantive impact on the case.[27]

Third, legal counsel have developed an omnibus appeal practice. Appellants usually base their appeal on a wide variety of legal grounds that embrace all the potentially relevant substantive and procedural grounds and which also extend to the

25. Csongor István Nagy, Versenyjogi kézikönyv 526-528 (2021).
26. *See, e.g.*, the judgment of the BCA in Case 2. Kf.27.280/2008/7, also published as ÍH 2009.98, and in Case 2.Kf.27.463/2009/5 and the judgment of the HSC in Case Kfv.37827/2015/19, Case Kfv.III.37.441/2016, also published as EH 2017.06.K16, and in Case Kfv.38108/2016/26.
27. For a critical analysis of this case law, *see* András Tóth, Észszerűen az észszerű idő követelményéről versenyügyekben, 30(1)-(2) Gazdaság és Jog 3-11 (2022).

amount of the fine. This implies that appeals list a wide set of legal grounds, even weak ones, and appeals are rarely limited to specific main issues. This practice may be explained on the basis of various reasons, including issues of professional liability, the unpredictability of court decisions and the strict rules of procedure that prevent the plaintiff from raising new legal grounds during the court procedure.

HCO decisions are reviewed by general (administrative) courts. Hungary has a unitary court system and has no separate courts to deal with administrative matters. Nonetheless, separate chambers are set up for administrative (and civil, criminal, etc.) matters.[28] Their judgments could be appealed to the regional court. Although the administrative chambers and the setting-up of administrative and labour courts secure a level of specialisation in administrative law, courts reviewing HCO decisions have no specific specialisation in antitrust matters, and this has mainly affected the quality of first-instance judgments. In reality, antitrust matters usually account for a small part of the cases a judge has to deal with, and this makes specialisation, especially for lower-level courts, very difficult.

There is a special mechanism in Hungarian law that is meant to ensure the consistency of judicial practice; this is the 'procedure for the consistency of the case law' (in Hungarian: '*jogegységi eljárás*'), at the end of which a 'decision for the consistency of the case law' (in Hungarian: '*jogegységi határozat*') is rendered. The Supreme Court is obliged to ensure the consistency of the case law, and 'decisions for the consistency of the case law' are binding on the courts. It is very important to note that these decisions are not judgments in the sense that they do not adjudicate on a particular matter but simply decide questions of legal interpretation. No such procedure has ever been raised in the field of competition law. This can be traced back to the fact that EU law questions, such as the interpretation of Articles 101 and 102 TFEU, cannot be settled in the frame of this procedure, while the interpretation of Hungarian competition rules, which could be the subject of a 'procedure for the consistency of the case-law', are for the most part determined by EU law. If a question of interpretation of EU law emerges, the court is expected to refer to the Court of Justice of the European Union (CJEU). As far as the national equivalents of Articles 101 and 102 TFEU are concerned, the Supreme Court established that these have to be interpreted in the same way.[29] This implies that a preliminary reference is a more effective way to handle questions of interpretation related to the national equivalents of Articles 101 and 102 TFEU than a 'decision for the consistency of the case law'. Although this does not rule out a procedure concerning merger control law and procedural issues, courts have never made use of this possibility in this regard.

28. The only exception is the administrative and labour courts, which were set up as first-instance courts hearing administrative and labour matters.
29. *See* Case Kfv.IV.37.077/2010/11; Case Kfv.III.37.072/2013/15; Case Kfv.III.37.441/2016/7., also published as EH 2017.06.K16.

3 PRIOR RESEARCH

Hungarian legal scholarship on judicial review in antitrust matters has been extensive but has focused on the legal (or legalistic) aspects of the subject.[30] No empirical analysis has been carried out and no statistics are available as to the operation of judicial review in competition matters. This chapter is the first attempt to provide such an analysis and a quantitative and qualitative overview of judicial review in competition cases in Hungary.

4 QUANTITATIVE ANALYSIS

4.1 Source of Information

In Hungary, court judgments are published after having been anonymised. They are freely available on the courts' website (www.birosag.hu). Court orders are not published and are publicly accessible only if they are selected by one of the court reporters (collections) and published by them. Courts adopt decisions in the form of an order, for instance, when the HCO's decision not to open a competition procedure or to terminate a competition procedure is challenged by the complainant, when a procedural fine is challenged and when there is a dispute as to whether or not a document is covered by legal privilege. Given that the research focused on court judgments (the review of HCO decisions on the merits), the survey is expected to be comprehensive. Nonetheless, given that all court judgments are anonymised, it is not possible to search for court cases on the basis of the case number of the administrative procedure and to formally link anonymised court judgments to the HCO decision reviewed. This linking can be accomplished only manually if the administrative case can be identified on the basis of the description in the judgment. This may give rise to occasional errors or omissions.

As an alternative source of case law, the HCO also runs a publicly available database on court judgments revising HCO decisions. Although aiming to provide comprehensive data and link court judgments to the HCO decisions they reviewed, it usually contains only the final and conclusive judgments. Lower court judgments are not available here. Though not comprehensive, the HCO's database contains an extensive collection of court orders, which are otherwise not publicly available, given that the courts' official website publishes only court judgments.

30. *See, e.g.*, András Tóth, A magyar versenyügyek 2010-2020 közötti bírósági felülvizsgálatának tapasztalatai, 17(4) IUSTUM AEQUUM SALUTARE 139 (2021); András Tóth, A Versenytanács kartelljog-fejlesztő gyakorlata, 69(5) Magyar Jog 305 (2022); András Tóth, Kortárs magyar versenyjog (Ludovika Egyetemi Kiadó, 2022); Csongor István Nagy, Versenyjogi kézikönyv 559-577 (2021).

There are also different court reporters (collections) who publish judicial decisions concerning matters of principle. One of these is 'Judicial Decisions' (in Hungarian: '*Bírósági Határozatok*'). Cases reported here receive the collections' special numbering, which starts with 'BH'.

The cases for the present study were collected by means of the above public databases. First, the potentially relevant HCO decisions were identified, and then the corresponding judgments were collected using the courts' website (www.birosag.hu). Second, I linked the relevant judgments and reproduced the procedural history. Third, the dataset was supplemented with cases on an *ad hoc* basis, based on the scholarship, the court reporters and the database of the HCO. The purpose of this step was to correct eventual errors in the collection process and to identify court orders which are not published by the courts' website. Some of these orders are, however, selected by a court reporter or are reported in the scholarship. Furthermore, the HCO also runs a database of court cases, which contains several unpublished court orders.

4.2 Total Numbers of Judgments and Ratio of Appeals

The coding identified one hundred judgments of the courts at different instances, fitting the selection criteria of the database. During the relevant period of study, the HCO adopted 414 decisions applying Articles 102 and 102 TFEU and their Hungarian equivalents. This figure embraces both decisions on the merits and orders declining to open an investigation. The latter are formal administrative decisions subject to appeal to the court. These orders may refuse to open an investigation either for legal reasons (lack of infringement), factual reasons (lack of evidence) or administrative reasons (the investigation is not justified by the public interest). Technically, under Hungarian law, these are procedural orders, but in reality, they are substantive decisions. Unfortunately, these orders are not published, and there is no publicly available data concerning appeals against them; hence, the ratio of appeals cannot be established. However, decisions on the merits and appeals against them are published. Forty-two decisions on the merits were challenged before the court of first instance. A comparison of the number of appeals to the decisions on the merits shows that in antitrust matters, about 50%-60% of the HCO decisions on the merits are appealed to the court.[31] First-instance judgments are regularly, almost routinely, appealed. Thirty-eight out of the forty-three first-instance judgments were appealed to the second-instance court, producing an 88% ratio of appeals. Appeals against the second-instance court feature a lower ratio: nineteen out of the thirty-eight judgments were appealed, producing a

31. *See* https://www.gvh.hu/pfile/file?path=/kozerdeku_adatok/tevekenysegre-mukodesre-vonatkozo-adatok/gvh-eljarasok/GVH_eljarasok_230208.xlsx1&inline=true.

50% ratio of appeals. It has to be noted, however, that in five of the judgments, the matter was tried in a two-tier procedure where the HSC acted as the second-instance court whose judgment could not be appealed. If taking this into account, nineteen out of the thirty-three appealable second-instance judgments were actually appealed, producing a ratio of appeals of 58%.

These figures suggest that if the parties appeal the HCO decision, they tend to make use of all the legal remedies available. Although the ratio of appeals against second-instance judgments is lower than that of first-instance judgments, it also has to be taken into account that generally, only an extraordinary appeal is available against second-instance judgments, which is limited to points of law, and this may also contribute to the somewhat lower level of ratio of appeals in this regard.

4.3 Judgments per Year

Figure 15.1 presents the total number of judgments rendered by year across all three instances of appeal.

Figure 15.1 Number of Judgments According to Instances

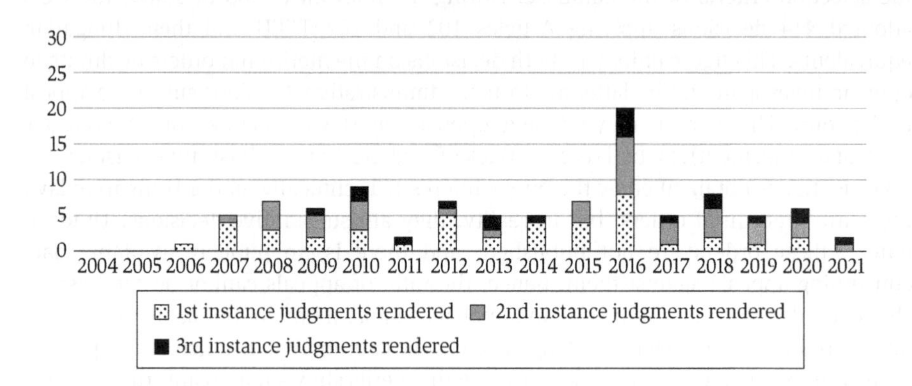

4.4 Success Rates and Outcomes

Figure 15.2 summarises the success rate of appeals across all three instances. The data is presented from the perspective of the appealed NCA's decision or previous instance judgment which has been appealed. The figure reveals that in 70% of the cases, the appeal was fully rejected, 21% of the appeals were partially successful, and only 8% were fully successful. The low success rate suggests that courts are highly deferential to the HCO's decisions.

Figure 15.2 Success of Appeals (Each NCA's Decision or Previous Instance Judgment Counts as One)

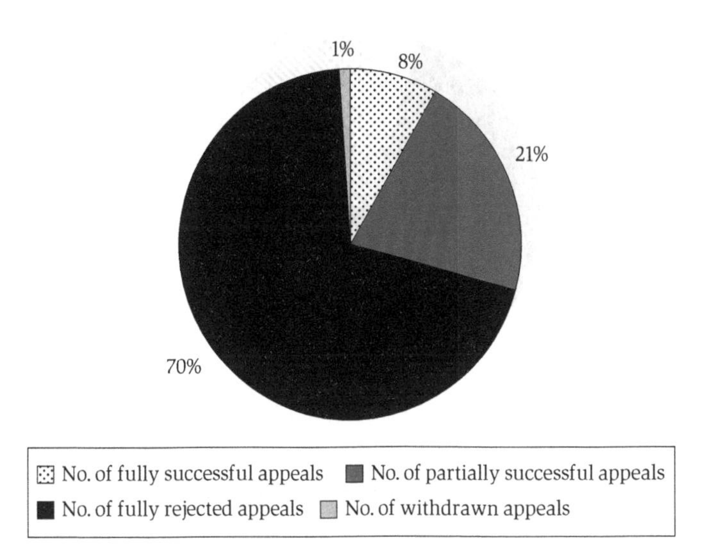

Figure 15.3 indicates the ratio of possible outcomes according to each instance of appeal. In contrast with Figure 15.2, the data is presented from the perspective of each separate judgment. For example, if three separate first-instance judgments were issued with respect to a single NCA decision, the outcome of each of those three cases would be presented separately. The figure demonstrates that the ratio of rejected appeals remains stable across instances of appeal, but higher-level courts are more willing to intervene in antitrust matters and to annul HCO decisions or replace them with their own decision: 74% of the appeals were fully rejected by the first instance; 71% by the second instance; and 62% by the third.

Figure 15.3(a) First-Instance Outcome

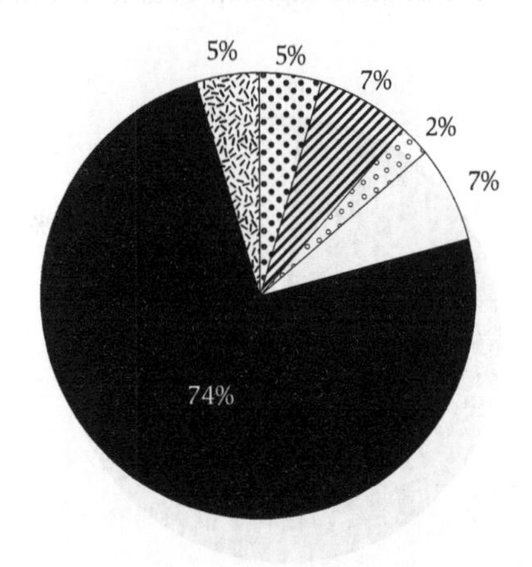

Figure 15.3(b) Second-Instance Outcome

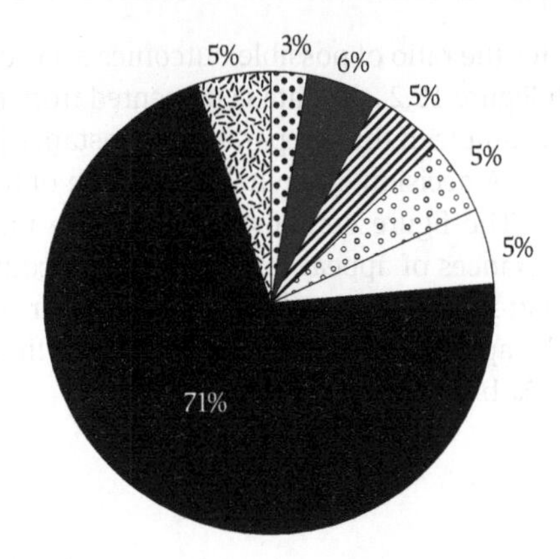

fully annulled	partially annulled
fully replaced	partially annulled, partially replaced
fully annulled, returned	partially annulled, returned
fully rejected (exc. withdrawn)	amended only with respect to fines
the application for leave to appeal was rejected	Withdrawn
Other	

Figure 15.3(c) Third-Instance Outcome

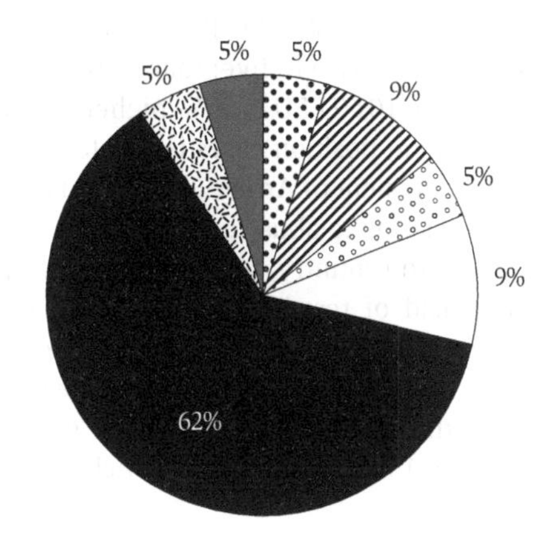

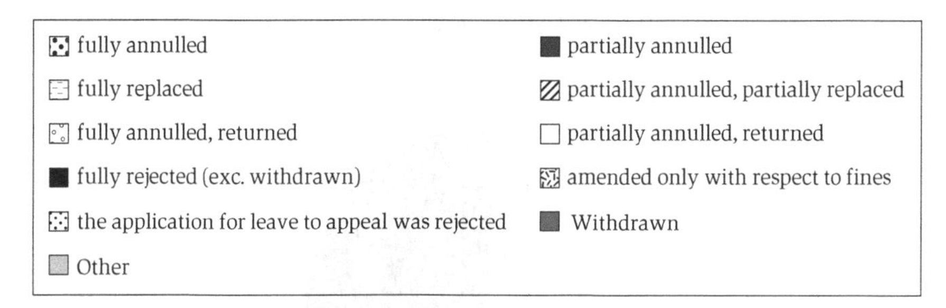

The tendency that higher-level courts are more willing to intervene is also salient when it comes to the adjudication of the fine. On average, courts have reduced the fine in 31% of the judgments rendered, from which first-instance courts reduced the fine in only 19% of the cases, second-instance courts in 37% of the cases, and third-instance courts in 47% of the cases.

A possible explanation for this trend is that higher lever courts may consider themselves to have a higher professional authority and capacity to decide the merits of the case and, hence, may engage in a closer review and afford less deference to the HCO. It has to be noted, however, that the rejection rate is still significant, and the HCO prevailed in about two-thirds of the cases.

4.5 Type of Competition Authority's Decisions Subject to Appeal

Figure 15.4 indicates the ratio of the different competition law prohibitions subject to the courts' review across all instances of appeal. The figure presents the data from the perspective of each single appeal judgment (noting that more than one judgment may be issued with respect to a single NCA decision). The composition of the antitrust cases in terms of the rules applied shows two important and salient features.

First, almost half of the cases (43%) involved the application of EU law. This implies that the jurisdictional requirement of the effect on inter-state trade criterion is conceived widely by the HCO. Interestingly, the ratio between EU and Hungarian anti-competitive agreement cases is two to five; that is, the number of cases based on the national equivalent of Article 101 TFEU is 50% higher, while the ratio between EU and Hungarian abuse of dominant position cases is five to two, that is, the number of cases based on the national equivalent of Article 102 TFEU is 50% higher. This may be explained by the fact that, in relation to abuse of dominance, the HCO focuses on cases covering the whole territory of the country, which have a high probability of having a cross-border impact in the field of restrictive agreements, especially in relation to cartels, local and national level cases are equally an enforcement priority.

Second, the overwhelming majority of the cases dealt with restrictive agreements. In essence, 87% of the judgments were based on Article 101 TFEU or its national equivalent and only 15% of them on Article 102 TFEU or its national equivalent.

Figure 15.4 Rules Being Appealed

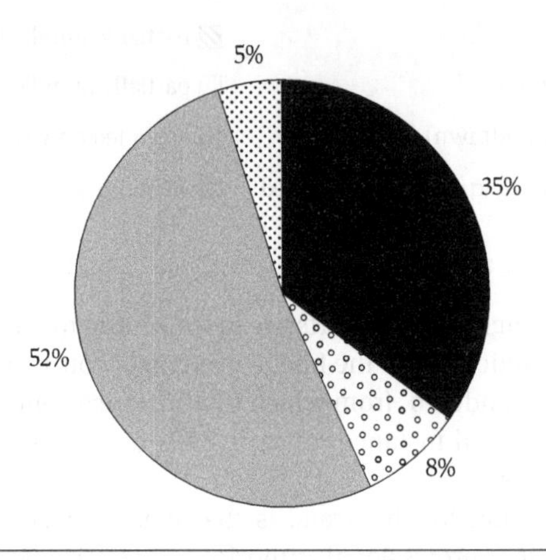

The per-year presentation of the data reveals no particular trends. It is clear, however, that the number of cases where EU competition law was applied has been increasing.

Figure 15.5 Rules Being Appealed According to Years (Each Judgment Counts as One)

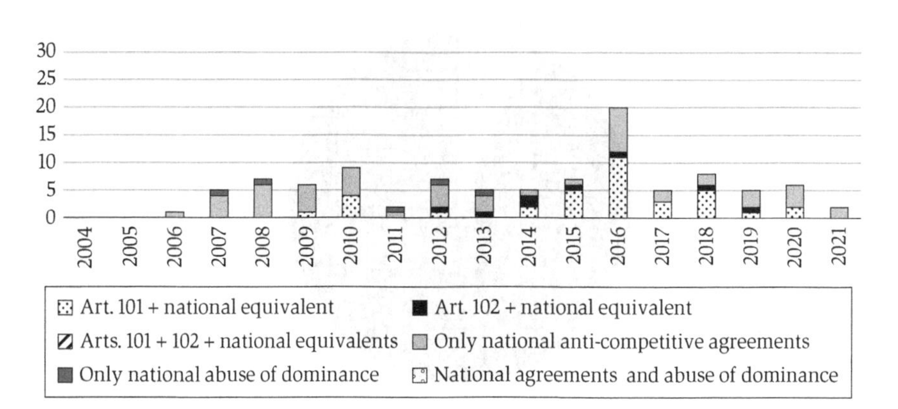

As noted above, the overwhelming majority of the antitrust cases dealt with Article 101 TFEU or its national equivalent. Figure 15.6 shows that these cases were made up predominantly of cartel cases.

Figure 15.6 Types of Restrictions

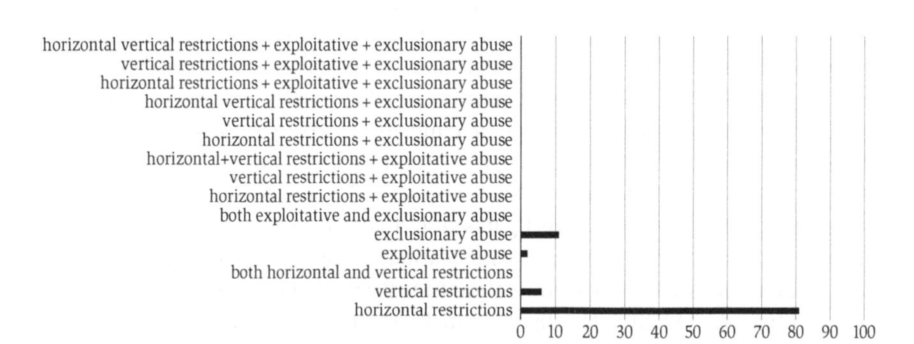

Figure 15.7 focuses only on appeals against the HCO's decisions where Article 101 TFEU and/or the national equivalent prohibition have been examined. It indicates the ratio of cases in which the HCO described the restriction of competition as by-object, by-effect, both by-object and by-effect, or left it unclassified. The figure demonstrates that the overriding majority of cases, 93%, involved by-object restrictions, while only 6% of the cases dealt with anti-competitive conduct by-effect (both dominant position and restrictive agreements) and 1% of cases with both object and effect restrictions. This shows that the HCO predominantly focuses on violations that call for no effects analysis, and, in reality, the enforcement of the antitrust rules in the field of restrictive agreements consists essentially of investigations of by-object restrictions. A joint reading of Figures 15.6 and 15.7 indicates that the focus of the HCO's enforcement efforts is on horizontal hardcore restrictions.

Figure 15.7 Object/Effect (Only for Article 101/National Equivalent Infringements)

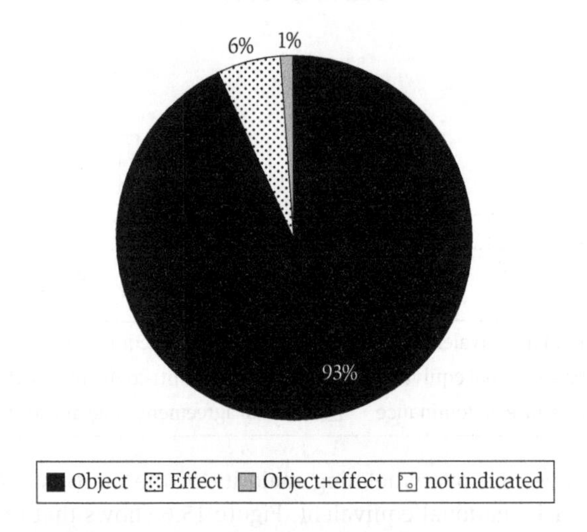

4.6 Type of Competition Authority's Procedure

Figure 15.8 indicates the ratio of the type of HCO's procedures that were subject to judicial review, across all instances of appeal. The figure presents the data from the perspective of each single appeal judgment (noting that more than one judgment may be issued with respect to a single NCA decision). The figure reveals that 99% of the judgments pertained to infringement decisions in which the HCO imposed a fine.

In antitrust matters, the imposition of a fine, in case of an infringement, is usually inevitable. Although the HCO has the right to establish any violation without imposing a fine, the composition of the cases taken up by the HCO makes this rare. In relation to abuse of dominance, the HCO investigates only major cases where the abuse had a significant impact on competition in the market,[32] and this also implies that the imposition of a fine is warranted. In relation to restrictive agreements, the focus is on anti-competitive agreements by-object, which are the most serious violations of antitrust law and, hence, call for a fine. It also has to be noted that the study identified HCO decisions that were challenged before the court, and the number of cases where the violation was established but no fine was imposed may be slightly higher, as the parties may be less inclined to challenge these decisions. The reason may be the limited exposure to actions for damages, which implies that, in the absence of an administrative fine, the party may have no financial interest in attacking the decision. Private enforcement cases are rare,[33] and they were especially rare in the first part of the period of inquiry; hence, the HCO's establishment of a violation alone without a fine triggered limited practical consequences.

32. Csongor István Nagy, Versenyjogi kézikönyv 285-325 (2021) (Substantial impact on competition in the market is a precondition of intervention in virtually all abuse of dominant position cases).
33. *Ibid.*

The study identified only a single case where a commitment decision was challenged before the courts. This does not mean that commitment decisions are rare. Quite the contrary, the HCO has relied extensively on this arrangement in particular in abuse of dominance cases and at times, it uses it as a surrogate of private enforcement by accepting commitments to provide restitution to injured parties.[34] Nonetheless, commitment decisions are very rarely challenged before the courts, the sole identified exception being Case Vj-22/2008 Országos Takarékpénztár (OTP).

Figure 15.8, however, should be interpreted with caution. Decisions rejecting a complaint or closing an investigation, including findings of no ground of action, are not published in a systematic way by the HCO, and if they are challenged before the courts, the judicial decision is not published either. This implies that these categories of cases are missing from Figure 15.8 for lack of data and not for lack of cases. According to the general rule, orders are not published but only decisions on the merits. The rejection of a complaint, as well as the closing of the investigations occurs in the form of an order, as it does not concern the merits of the case. The finding that there is no ground of action is usually also made in the form of an order. The only exception is no-infringement decisions, where the HCO closes the procedure because the investigated conduct is lawful. It has to be noted that pursuant to the ruling of the CJEU in *Tele2Polska*, the HCO has no power to adopt no-infringement decisions,[35] so it has to reject a complaint or close the investigation on procedural grounds, such as lack of evidence.

Figure 15.8 Competition Authority's Procedure

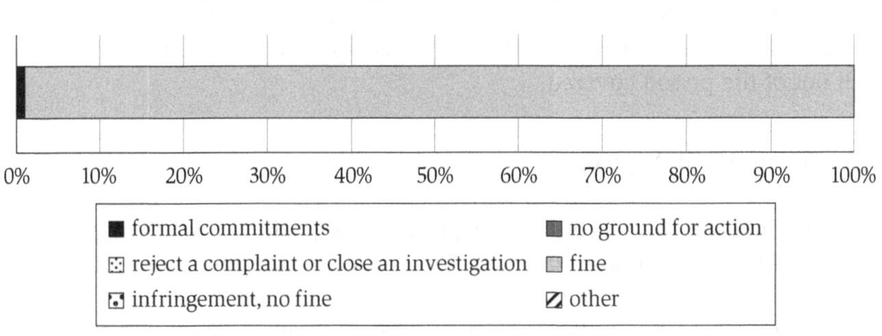

Figure 15.9 examines the relationship between leniency and the success of appeals. It indicates the percentage of appealed judgments on HCO decisions in which one or more parties have successfully applied for leniency.

34. Csongor István Nagy, Commitments as Surrogates of Civil Redress in Competition Law: The Hungarian Perspective, 33(11) European Competition Law Review 531-536 (2012).
35. Case C-375/09 Tele2 Polska, ECLI:EU:C:2011:270, paras 27-28 and 32. The ruling was applied by the HCO for instance in Case Vj-2/2010/740.

Figure 15.9 Leniency

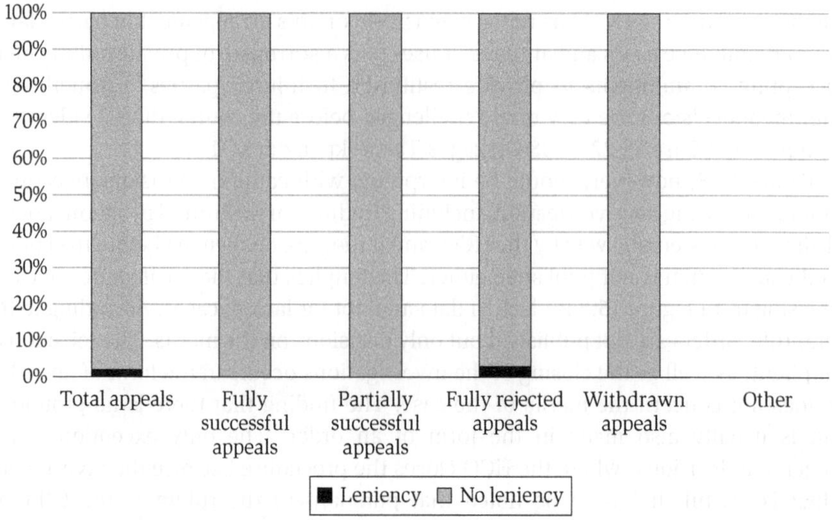

	Leniency	No leniency
Total appeals		
Fully successful appeals		
Partially successful appeals		
Fully rejected appeals		
Withdrawn appeals		
Other		

The settlement procedure was introduced in Hungary in 2013.[36] Since then, these procedural means have been regularly used, and HCO decisions involving a settlement with some of the parties have already been challenged, for instance, in Case *MENTO*.[37] In the judicial review of this HCO decision,[38] the HSC held that the settlement declaration of one of the defendants could be used as evidence against those defendants of the case who entered no settlement. This case was not included in the study, as it fell out of the period covered.

4.7 Grounds of Appeal

Figure 15.10 indicates the success of each ground of appeal. For each type of ground – procedural, substantive, fines-related, or EU/national – the figure indicates whether this ground was fully accepted, partially accepted, or rejected. It has to be noted that the overwhelming majority of the cases involve more than one ground of appeal. As a matter of practice, the parties raise a number of potentially relevant grounds of appeal. Appeals limited to one or a few grounds of appeal are rare. Out of the one hundred judgments, substantive grounds were raised in ninety-four, grounds related to the fine in eighty-six, while procedural grounds were raised in fifty cases, demonstrating the much greater likelihood of substantive as opposed to procedural grounds being raised.

36. Act CCI of 2013.
37. Case Vj-77/2016.
38. Case Kfv.VII.38.167/2021/15.

Figure 15.10 Grounds of Appeal (Each NCA's Decision or Previous Instance Judgment Counts as One)

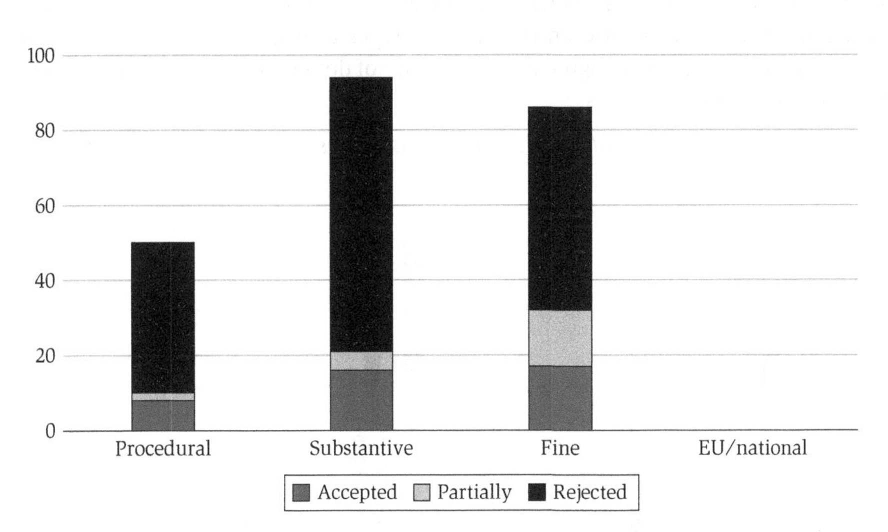

Upon assessment of the success rates as to the individual grounds of appeal, it is salient that appeals specifically against the fine have a substantially higher chance of success than procedural and substantive arguments (in 31% of the cases, the fine was fully or partially annulled). In cases where the fine was reduced, the average reduction was 80%. In interpreting this figure, it has to be noted that it also includes cases where the whole fine was quashed and remanded to the HCO for recalculation. This could occur because, as a substantive issue, the court found that the investigation had to be repeated. It is standard practice that if the HCO's decision on a violation is based on insufficient evidence, the court does not simply quash the decision but simultaneously remands it to the HCO. Thereafter, the HCO may rectify the deficiency and find an infringement in a new decision or terminate the repeated procedure if no further evidence can be collected. In other cases, the court accepted the legal basis for the fine and found only the HCO's calculation of the fine inconsistent or illegal, but instead of setting the fine, it remanded the case and required the HCO to recalculate it. These cases figure as a reduction of 100%, although in the repeated administrative procedure a recalculated (and very likely lower) fine was imposed. The court has never increased the fine imposed by the HCO, and it is uncertain if they are legally authorised to do so. The role of the court is confined by the plaintiff's statement of claim. The court cannot rule outside the *petitum,* and the only *petitum* in the case is the request of the plaintiff or the plaintiffs, which, in turn, targets the reduction of the fine. The HCO submits no statement of claim and cannot have any *petitum*. It follows from this that the court has no power to increase the fine, as that would be *ultra petita.*[39]

39. Csongor István Nagy, Versenyjogi kézikönyv 393-395 (2021).

This discussion implies that courts are comparatively more inclined to reduce or even quash the fine than to overrule the substance of the decision or to establish substantial procedural errors affecting the substance of the case. In this regard, there is no significant difference between the different types of restrictions, so the foregoing equally applies to restrictive agreement and abuse of dominance cases as well as to EU and Hungarian antitrust cases.

Figure 15.11 Types of Restrictions Versus Successful Grounds of Appeal

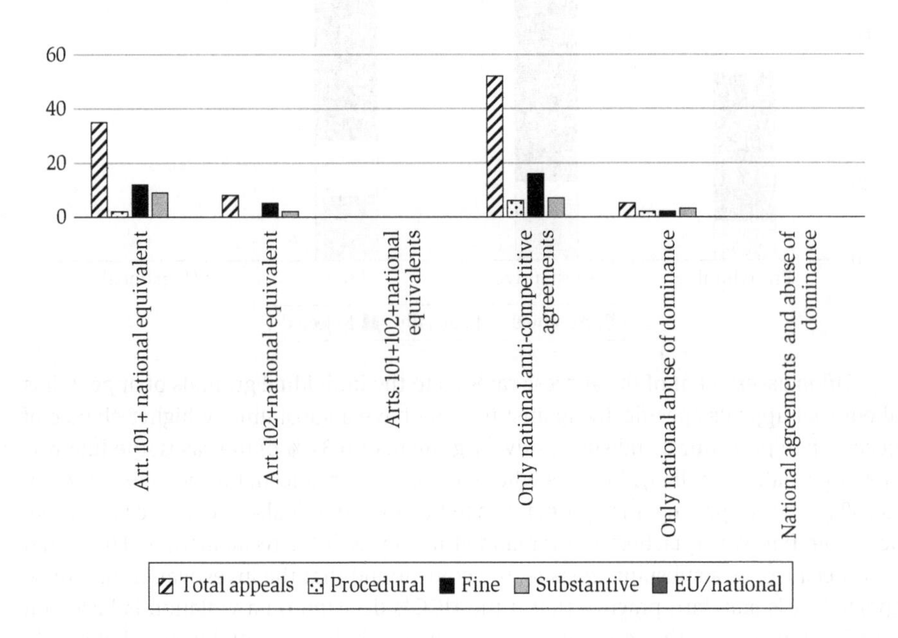

4.8 Other

Admissibility is not an issue in judicial practice. The survey identified no case where the appeal was deemed fully or partially inadmissible. The parties need no leave to appeal an HCO decision or a court judgment. Appeals result in a full review, except for extraordinary appeals to the HSC, which are limited to points of law.

Hungarian courts have been active in referring competition cases to the CJEU[40] and some of these resulted in important CJEU rulings. Two judicial review cases reached the CJEU. The principal procedure of *Allianz*[41] was the HCO's decision in Case Vj-51/2005. In this case the CJEU redefined the concept of anti-competitive object and, in essence, accepted the line of interpretation advocated for by the HCO. *Budapest*

40. Márton Varju, Ernő Várnay, After the Judgment: The Implementation of Preliminary Rulings in the Hungarian Judicial System 2004–2019 and Beyond, 59(6) Common Market Law Review 1743-1770 (2022) DOI: 10.54648/cola2022117.
41. C-32/11, Allianz Hungária Biztosító, ECLI:EU:C:2013:160.

Bank[42] emerged from the HCO's investigation of Hungarian banks' multilateral interchange fee in Case Vj-18/2008. In this case, the CJEU provided an interpretation of the doctrine set up in *Allianz* in the context of banks' multilateral interchange fees. Case C-102/15 *Gazdasági Versenyhivatal v. Siemens*[43] emerged from a civil action brought by the HCO for the payment of interest after the competition fine.

In antitrust matters, appeal practice is dominated almost exclusively by the defendants. Third parties play no practical role in the judicial review of HCO decisions. The survey identified a single case where the appellant was a third party. Although, as a matter of law, they have standing to challenge an HCO decision if that concerns them directly, courts have interpreted this rule very narrowly in antitrust cases.[44] As noted above, the complainant has a special status in this regard: if the competition procedure is terminated, the complainant is entitled to challenge that decision before the court.

5 QUALITATIVE ANALYSIS

5.1 Scope and Intensity of Judicial Review

The practice of judicial review in antitrust matters features two important tendencies.

First, courts have become increasingly active in these matters, primarily as a result of two developments. In the 1990s, courts were reluctant to intervene in antitrust cases and afforded considerable deference to the HCO. Nonetheless, in the last two decades, courts' review has been increasingly close, while the deference afforded to the HCO has decreased (though still significant). This manifests itself in the success rate of appeals. Furthermore, courts are increasingly willing to engage in substantive analysis, and this manifests itself also in the length and depth of appeal court judgments. Until the 2000s, court judgments were very laconic with little substantive analysis. This is in stark contrast with current judicial practice, where courts are less reluctant to engage with substantive issues and do engage with questions of interpretation and are important actors of legal development. This does not mean that the HCO's role has decreased in absolute terms. Quite the contrary, courts can deal only with cases investigated by the HCO and their role is to review and assess the HCO decision. However, the courts became more active in the development of antitrust law, and instead of deferring to the HCO as a matter of routine, they became increasingly willing to engage with substantive analysis.

Second, the review standard governing antitrust appeal cases also changed significantly, and Hungarian courts replaced the initially quite deferential approach with the principle of full review. In the wake of the ECtHR's judgment in *Menarini*[45] and the CJEU's rulings in Case C-272/09 *KME Germany*, Case C-386/10 *Chalkor* and Case C-389/10 *KME Germany*,[46] Hungarian judicial practice, starting with the judgment

42. C-228/18, Budapest Bank, ECLI:EU:C:2020:265.
43. ECLI:EU:C:2016:607.
44. Csongor István Nagy, Versenyjogi kézikönyv 562-566 (2021).
45. Judgment rendered in Case 43509/08 *Menarini Diagnostics S.R.L. v. Italy* on 27 September 2011.
46. ECLI:EU:C:2011:810; ECLI:EU:C:2011:815; ECLI:EU:C:2011:816.

in *Railway Constructors*,[47] embraced the notion that any HCO decision can be reviewed fully both in terms of facts and legal issues. Although courts do not retry the case but review an existing administrative decision and the underlying competition procedure, they have full power of review and can replace the HCO's assessment with their own. This also implies that any HCO decision should be affirmed only if it is based on the most reasonable interpretation and application of the law and assessment of the evidence. Under the earlier deferential approach, an HCO decision could still survive judicial scrutiny if it was based on a reasonable interpretation and factual assessment, even if the HCO's interpretation and assessment were not the most reasonable. In other words, if there were more than one reasonable assessment of the evidence, the HCO could choose any of these without its decision being quashed. Under the full review standard, however, the HCO is obliged to choose the most reasonable option for interpretation and assessment. A reasonable interpretation and assessment must be quashed if it is not the most reasonable of the available options. This approach has had a substantial impact on the judicial review of HCO decisions and has also led to a more pro-active approach and increased the rate of success of appeals.

Nonetheless, the new review standard ushered by *Railway Constructors* should not be overestimated. Although courts certainly have the power, they may lack the capacity to fully review HCO decisions. Although deference is no longer required by law, it continues to be afforded as a matter of practice. Given that the judicial review of antitrust decisions is carried out by general, non-specialised courts, there is a clear asymmetry between the professional resources and capacities of the HCO and the reviewing courts. This is exacerbated by the fact that the appeal procedure centres around an existing administrative decision. The quantitative analysis also corroborated the general perception that lower instance courts are more reluctant to intervene in antitrust cases than higher instance courts, and this implies that appellants need to overcome additional hurdles in terms of time and cost to ensure a more 'professional' and less deferential review of any HCO decision. Appellants have a much greater chance of success before higher instance appeal courts, whereas first-instance courts tend to be particularly reticent both in terms of engaging with the arguments set out in an appeal and in taking responsibility for annulling any prior decision. This is clearly demonstrated by the fact that first-instance courts reduced the fine in only 19% of the cases, while third-instance courts reduced fines in 47% of cases.

The relevance of procedural grounds of appeal increased during the period of study, but the approach of the courts still evidences a particularly lenient treatment of procedural errors, turning various procedural rules into *lex imperfecta*. The reason for this is that according to the traditional rules of judicial review, only those procedural violations that had a substantial impact on the substantive outcome of the case are relevant, and the respective burden of proof rests on the appellant. This implies that even the most outrageous and deliberate violation of the procedural rules is overlooked if the appellant cannot prove that without the procedural violation, the HCO would have decided otherwise. On the one hand, this approach is in line with the general rules and

47. Case Kfv.III.37.690/2013/29.

principles of judicial review of administrative decisions. On the other hand, however, it is difficult to reconcile it with the quasi-criminal nature of antitrust procedures and sanctions, which calls for a more rigorous approach to compliance with procedural rules.

5.2 Review of Penalties

The most successful grounds of appeals against HCO decisions are in relation to fines. This is somewhat contradictory, as under the applicable review standards the HCO should have a narrower playing field as to legal and factual assessment than as to the determination of the fine. Still, courts have been more willing to intervene in relation to the fine, either by reducing or quashing it or remanding it to the HCO for re-setting.

5.3 Coherence with Substantive EU Competition Law

Substantive Hungarian competition law is completely harmonised with EU competition law. Hungarian courts have referred altogether two judicial review cases to the CJEU.

In *Allianz,*[48] the HSC applied Hungarian competition law (the case was based on facts arising before Hungary's accession to the EU) but referred the case to the CJEU because EU and Hungarian substantive competition rules require consistent interpretation.[49] The CJEU found the case admissible, considering that 'the concepts referred to in Paragraph 11(1) of the (...) [HCA] must in fact be interpreted in the same way as the equivalent concepts in Article 101(1) TFEU and that it is bound in that regard by the interpretation of those concepts provided by the Court'.[50] Accordingly, the CJEU held that section 11(1)-(2) HCA, as the national equivalent of Article 101 TFEU, effectively reproduces Article 101(1) TFEU. 'It is clearly apparent, moreover, from the preamble to and the explanatory memorandum for the (...) [HCA] that the Hungarian legislature sought to harmonise domestic competition law with that of the European Union.'[51] Although the statement related specifically to the rules on restrictive agreements, it may be extrapolated to all the substantive rules of antitrust law, including abuse of dominance, provided that such rules do not contain an express deviation from the EU rules. This approach was subsequently confirmed in practice.[52]

The congruence between the two systems is reinforced by the Hungarian block exemption regulations, which are essentially in line with their EU competition law counterparts, and the fact the Commission's various competition law guidelines and notices are regularly applied in practice. Hungarian courts have made two references to the CJEU in public enforcement cases.[53]

48. C-32/11. Allianz Hungária Biztosító, ECLI:EU:C:2013:160.
49. Case Kfv.IV.37.077/2010/11.
50. Paragraph 22.
51. Paragraph 21.
52. Case Kfv.III.37.072/2013/15; Case Kfv.III.37.441/2016/7, also published as EH 2017.06.K16.
53. In *Allianz,* C-32/11, ECLI:EU:C:2013:160, and *Budapest Bank,* C-228/18, ECLI:EU:C:2020:265.

5.4 Third Parties' Rights

Appeals by third parties have been of limited practical significance in Hungarian competition law practice. The standing of third parties is interpreted narrowly. In the field of antitrust law, third-party appeals against decisions on the merits are virtually non-existent, although in principle this possibility is provided for in law. Appeals against an HCO decision not to open an investigation or to close an investigation are relatively common. These are, however, adjudicated in the form of a court order, which is not automatically published. It has to be noted that the HCO has a clear statutory authorisation to set enforcement priorities and refuse to investigate cases if the competition procedure is not warranted by the public interest.[54]

6 CONCLUDING REMARKS

Modern Hungarian competition law is more than thirty years old. Its current trajectory started with the adoption of Act LXXXVI of 1990 on the Prohibition of Unfair Market Conduct and culminated in the currently effective Competition Act (Act LVII of 1996 on the Prohibition of Unfair Market Conduct and Restriction of Competition). It should of course be noted that there was a history of competition law regulation, including the Act CC of 1931 on Agreements Regulating Economic Competition, which was one of the first pieces of legislation on cartels in Europe. During the period starting in 1990, Hungarian competition law gained an outstanding role in economic regulation and evolved into a regional success story.

In the period between 1990 and the mid-2000s, competition law and policy were focused on and developed by the decisional practice of the HCO. Judicial practice was restrained and highly deferential to the competition authority and this found clear reflection in the HCO's success rate before the appeal courts. In this period, the sole driver of competition law was the HCO, which had the appropriate expertise, human resources and recognition arising from its professional reputation and independence. This situation has changed radically in the mid-2000s and the beginning of the 2010s. The courts developed as the main actors of competition law. Although the HCO retained its prominent role, courts have accumulated significant knowledge and experience and developed from a technical review forum to a central actor of competition policy. They no longer limit their role to following and approving (or quashing) HCO decisions, but they actively and confidently shape the law. To date, the courts have worked out several fundamental competition law principles and have been active in referring cases to the CJEU. This brought with itself a more vigorous judicial review practice and a closer scrutiny in competition matters, which are reflected in the success rate of appeals.

54. Section 67(2) HCA.

Chapter 16
Ireland Report

Mary Catherine Lucey

1 INTRODUCTION TO THE COMPETITION LAW ENFORCEMENT CONTEXT IN IRELAND

The competition law enforcement regime in Ireland is a distinctive one which does not mirror the EU model, even though Irish substantive provisions closely reflect Articles 101 and 102 Treaty on the Functioning of the European Union (TFEU).[1] The Irish regime has been described as being 'out of step' with the administrative models found in many other Member States of the EU.[2] This section explains the development of the judicial and rather prosecutorial model under which EU and national competition law is enforced in Ireland.[3]

1. Imelda Maher, *Competition Law: Alignment and Reform* (Round Hall Sweet & Maxwell, 1999); Alan McCarthy and Vincent J.G. Power, *Irish Competition Law: The Competition Act 2002* (Tottel Bloomsbury Professional 2003); Nathy Dunleavy, *Competition Law: A Practitioner's Guide* (Bloomsbury Professional 2010); Philip Andrews, Paul Gorecki and David McFadden, *Modern Irish Competition Law* (Wolters Kluwer 2015); Vincent J.G. Power, 'Reflection on Irish Competition Law 1991-2005' (2004-2005) 5 Hibernian LJ 195. Imelda Maher, 'The Irish Courts and EC Competition Law' (1993) 15 DULJ 118; Imelda Maher. 'Ireland' in (Behrens (ed.)) *EEC Competition Law in National Courts vol II* (Nomos Baden-Baden 1994); Imelda Maher, 'The Implementation of EC Competition Law in Ireland: The Transition to a New Statutory Regime' (1995) Irish Jurist 21; Barry Doherty, 'EC Competition Law Before Irish Courts: The First 25 Years' (1999) 20 ECLR 78.
2. OECD Annual report of Competition Policy Developments in Ireland 2003 para. 9 available at http://www.oecd.org/ireland/34720597.pdf; Competition Authority Annual Report 2003 Foreword p. 5; Mary Catherine Lucey, 'Ireland: "Out of Step": Coping with Its Constitutional Concerns about Civil Fines' (2017) 2 Concurrences.
3. *See* further Mary Catherine Lucey, 'Public Enforcement of EU Competition Law in Ireland; Appraising Divergence' (2016) 12(1) Comp L. Rev 9.

The Competition Act 1991 introduced substantive prohibitions which closely mirrored the EC Treaty competition law substantive provisions. However, the institutional architecture for their enforcement, as set out by the 1991 and subsequent enactments, has created a distinctive enforcement regime. The 1991 Act did not provide for public enforcement by an administrative agency but only for private enforcement.[4] Public enforcement was introduced by the Competition (Amendment) Act 1996. Notably, it did not grant the administrative competition agency either competence to make determinations of substantive infringements of competition law or to impose fines. Instead, during the period covered by this study, the Competition Authority (CA) (and later the Competition and Consumer Protection Commission (CCPC))[5] enjoyed power only to investigate (either on its own initiative or following a complaint) suspected infringement of domestic and/or EU competition law and the right to initiate an action before a court seeking either a declaration that particular conduct violated competition law and/or an injunction. The explanation for this particular design derives from certain interpretations of Bunreacht na hÉireann (the Constitution), whose Article 34.1 stipulates that justice must be administered by *courts*.[6]

The *High Court* adjudicates alleged infringements of EU and/or national competition law in civil actions initiated by the administrative competition agency (or by private litigants). The civil public enforcement model entails the agency (CA/CCPC) deciding to commence a legal action seeking an Order from the High Court against undertaking(s). Such Orders may be subsequently challenged by either the agency or the undertaking(s) before superior courts, as detailed in section 2.

The balance of probabilities before the High Court is the usual civil standard of proof in civil actions. This standard applies to competition law actions.[7] Indeed, the Supreme Court has expressly stated that the CA/CCPC 'carries the normal civil burden of proof'.[8]

In 2005, procedural rules were introduced (and amended in 2006) for 'Competition Proceedings' in the High Court.[9] One of their innovations was the creation of a so-called 'Competition List' which is a listing of competition proceedings for hearing before the High Court- a court sometimes described as the 'Competition Court'. Typically, a single High Court judge hears the 'Competition List'. Order 63B of the Rules of the Superior Court provides that 'competition proceedings, and any motions or other

4. It has been suggested that this can be explained by a wish to avoid drawing on State funds for enforcement Vincent J.G. Power, 'Irish Innovations to Facilitate Competition Litigation: Ireland's Competition (Amendment) Act 2012' (2012) 4 GCLR 168, 170.
5. ComReg is another administrative agency which was granted competence to enforce competition legislation in relation to the communications sector.
6. Mary Catherine Lucey, 'The New Irish Competition and Consumer Protection Commission: Is This "Powerful Watchdog with Real Teeth" Powerful Enough under EU Law?' (2015) 6(3) Journal of European Competition Law and Practice, 185 DOI: 10.1093/jeclap/lpu103.
7. *Masterfoods Ltd t/a Mars Ireland v. H. B. Ice Cream Ltd* [1993] ILRM 145, Keane J.
8. *Competition Authority v. O Regan & Others* [2007] IESC 22, para. 103.
9. SI No 130 of 2005 Rules of the Superior Courts (Competition Proceedings) 2005 introduced Order 63 B and replaced by SI No. 461/2006 Rules of the Superior Courts (Competition Proceedings) 2006. https://www.courts.ie/superior-court-rules.

applications in the competition proceedings, shall be heard in the Competition List by the Judge'.

Order 63B also allows the Court to appoint an economist to offer expert advice to the Court and further states that where 'the expert provides advice or any other information to the Court, the Court shall, where it considers it appropriate in the interests of justice, inform the parties of such advice or information and afford each of them an opportunity to make submissions in respect of it'.[10]

That Ireland did not adopt an administrative model created some challenges in the aftermath of Article 35 of Regulation 1/2003, which obliges Member States to designate *national competition authorities* (NCAs) to carry out the range of activities listed in Article 5 of the same regulation. Satisfying this EU requirement without risking domestic constitutional uncertainty required an unusual approach to be adopted in Ireland in relation to its designated NCA. The creative solution contained in *European Communities (Implementation of the Rules on Competition Laid Down in Arts 81 and 82 of the Treaty) Regulations 2004* entailed designating Irish courts as well as the Competition Authority as being 'NCAs' in Ireland.[11] These Regulations were amended by *European Communities (Implementation of the Rules on Competition Laid Down in Arts 81 and 82 of the Treaty) (Amendment) Regulations 2007*, which additionally designated the Commission for Communications Regulation ('ComReg') as the designated NCA in respect of electronic communications and networks.[12]

The roles performed within the atypical constellation of NCAs in Ireland were succinctly captured recently by the Court of Appeal,[13] statement that '[W]here the CCPC would otherwise exercise the powers specified in Article 5 if it were a competition authority of another member state and could make a decision of the kind specified in Article 5 without recourse to court, the CCPC must instead apply to the High Court for such orders or reliefs. In those circumstances, where the CCPC issues proceedings seeking orders pursuant to Article 5 of Regulation 1/2003, the High Court is acting as a competition authority.'[14]

Splitting the NCA roles and responsibilities among different domestic administrative and judicial institutions creates a more intricate public enforcement landscape in Ireland than found in most other Member States. This is especially the case in relation to the precise responsibilities of NCAs under Article 11 of Regulation 1/2003. Article 11(4) provides that:

> [N]o later than 30 days before the adoption of a decision requiring that an infringement be brought to an end, accepting commitments or withdrawing the benefit of a block exemption regulation, the competition authorities of the Member States shall inform the Commission. To that effect, they shall provide the Commission with a summary of the case, the envisaged decision, or, in the absence thereof, any other document indicating the proposed course of action. This information may also be made available to the competition authorities of the other

10. Rule 63B, 23(4).
11. SI No. 195 of 2004.
12. SI No. 525 of 2007.
13. *Goode Concrete v. CRH plc* [2020] IECA.
14. *Ibid.*, para. 12.

Member States. At the request of the Commission, the acting competition authority shall make available to the Commission other documents it holds which are necessary for the assessment of the case.

The High Court has recognised that 'Ireland occupies a somewhat unusual position, even within the enlarged community, in designating under Article 35 its national courts as competition authorities responsible for the application of Articles 81 and 82 of the Treaty (S.I. 195/2004). Most of the functions under Chapter IV of R. 1/2003 are assigned in Ireland to the Competition Authority, so that the court's function and obligation under Article 11(4) of R. 1/2003 to notify a proposed or "envisaged" Decision made under Article 5 to the Commission may be seen as an exception to the various other obligations contained in Chapter IV which, by virtue of S.I. 195, all fall on the Irish Competition Authority.'[15]

The earliest instance of an Irish NCA operating under Article 11(4) procedure occurred on 30 July 2004. On that date, the High Court, acting in its capacity as an NCA, provided its envisaged decision in the *ILCU* case to the European Commission. Interestingly, the Commission gave the Irish Court an undertaking to maintain confidentiality around the content and outcome vis-à-vis any Member State competition authority including the plaintiff (i.e., the Competition Authority). For completeness, it should be noted that it has been observed by the High Court that the Article 11(3) obligation on an NCA 'shall, when acting under Article 81 or Article 82 of the Treaty, inform the Commission in writing before or without delay after commencing the first formal investigative measure', is an obligation which falls on the Irish administrative agency [CA/CCPC] and not the national court.[16]

2 THE APPEAL/REVIEW PROCESS OF THE COMPETITION AUTHORITY'S DECISIONS

Bunreacht na hÉireann (Irish Constitution) governs the system of courts in Ireland.[17] It provides for: (i) Courts of First Instance (including a High Court and courts of local and limited jurisdiction); (ii) a Court of Appeal (following a Constitutional referendum in Oct 2013); and (iii) a Court of Final Appeal (namely the Supreme Court). The term 'Superior Courts' is used to refer collectively to the High Court, the Court of Appeal and the Supreme Court. Courts of First Instance are those courts where a case may be started and include the High Court.

Judges are appointed by the President of Ireland and are designated to a particular court. The threshold of minimum experience for eligibility for an appointment to a Superior Court for a practising solicitor/barrister is set at twelve years.

To convey thoroughly the process in which an Irish court considers a 'prior determination' of an infringement took place, it is essential to present two separate

15. *Competition Authority v. O Regan & Others* [2004] IEHC 33 p. 63.
16. *Ibid.*
17. Relevant legislation includes the Courts (Establishment and Constitution) Act 1961; Courts (Supplemental Provisions) Act; Court of Appeal Act 2014. For all legislation and the text of the Constitution see www.irishstatutebook.ie and www.courts.ie, for procedural court rules.

areas of law. These are, firstly, the operation *of judicial review of administrative activities* and, secondly, the *appeals* mechanism. It is the latter mechanism which is relevant to this project because it is the process which may arise following a determination by the High Court (acting as NCA) that a competition law infringement either occurred or did not occur. Nonetheless, for the sake of providing a fuller picture and a keener contrast with other Member States, a brief overview will be provided of the system of 'judicial review' before we focus on the appeals system.

2.1 Judicial Review

Judicial review in Ireland is largely founded on the doctrine of ultra vires. The core idea of this doctrine is that a public body should not act beyond or outside the limits of the powers granted to it by the Oireachtas (Parliament). When engaging in judicial review, the court does not focus on the merits of the case but, instead, on 'the lawfulness of the decision under review'.[18]

Bunreacht ns hÉireann (Irish Constitution) in Article 15.2.1 vests legislative power in only the Oireachtas (Parliament). Thus, as Hogan et al. observe, 'to permit a public body to transgress the limits of its statutory authority would (arguably) be to give it law-making power, which would be anathema to Ireland's constitutional structure'.[19]

The High Court enjoys inherent power to supervise the legality of the activities of inferior courts, tribunals, and other types of public bodies. The High Court, the Court of Appeal, and the Supreme Court as Superior Courts of record are not amenable to judicial review.[20] However, the Supreme Court has inherent jurisdiction to set aside its own judgment in exceptional circumstances.[21]

While not strictly relevant to the remit of this project (whose focus is on reviewing determinations of infringements), it may be of interest to note that a small number of judicial review actions involving the application of competition legislation have resulted in judgments from a court. Judicial review proceedings have been taken against the administrative competition agency (CA/CCPC). One strand of judicial review case law has involved challenging the (comparatively) limited competences of the administrative agency, for example, in relation to a CCPC inspection of the undertaking's premises.[22] Another, more interesting, strand of judicial review judgments involving competition law arguments in legal actions are those taken against government ministers where improper exercise of statutory powers is alleged. For example, the High Court found that a Minister (when adopting fees) had acted *ultra vires* and the Court made a conditional finding of an abuse of a dominant position as

18. David Gwynn Morgan, Gerard Hogan and Paul Daly, *Administrative Law in Ireland* (Thomson Reuters Ireland Ltd, 5th ed., 2019) 10-03.
19. *Ibid.*, 10-02.
20. *People (DPP) v. Quilligan* (no.2) [1989] I.R 46, 57.
21. *Re Greendale Developments (no 3)* [2000] 2I.R. 514.
22. *CRH Plc, Irish Cement Limited and Seamus Lynch v. The Competition and Consumer Protection Commission*, 65/2016 (WLIE 1), Supreme Court, 29 May 2017, unreported, [2017] IESC 34/1, Ms Justice Laffoy, 29 May 2017.

prohibited by Irish competition law.[23] Later, the High Court awarded compensatory damages for the *ultra vires* aspect but not for an infringement of the competition legislation.[24] These cases show a rather imaginative recourse to the doctrine of judicial review in circumstances where competition law issues have been argued, albeit they fall outside the scope of this project.

2.2 Appeals

The focus of this project is on the review *of determinations that an infringement of competition law has or has not occurred.* As detailed above, a determination of a civil infringement of national or EU competition law cannot be delivered by an Irish administrative competition agency. Instead, only the High Court has the competence to find an infringement (or not) of competition law. For clarity, it is important to emphasise that, for this project, in Ireland, the pertinent NCA determination is a judgment from the High Court in proceedings initiated by the CA/CCPC, and the subsequent 'reviewing' stage is an *appeal* to a Superior Court.

As noted above, a new appeal court was established during the period covered by this project. The Court of Appeal, established on 28 October 2014 by the Court of Appeal Act 2014,[25] is solely concerned with appeals, including appeals from judgments of the High Court.[26] Composed of a President and up to nine judges, the Court of Appeal may sit in divisions of three judges.

Before the establishment of the Court of Appeal, only the Supreme Court heard appeals from the High Court at first and last instance. Since 2014, the Supreme Court's appellate jurisdiction has included two instances of appeals: the Court of Appeal and the High Court. The Supreme Court will grant leave to appeal from a decision of the Court of Appeal only if it is satisfied that the decision sought to be appealed involves either a matter of general public importance or the interests of justice.[27]

Direct appeals from the High Court to the Supreme Court are possible only in exceptional circumstances, and in such cases (of a direct appeal from the High Court to the Supreme Court), it is not possible to appeal to the Court of Appeal. The effect of the criterion of exceptional circumstances is to set a threshold which limits appeals to those instances where the matter is either of general public importance or otherwise in the interests of justice.[28]

---

23. *Island Ferries Teoranta v. Minister for Communications, Marine and Natural Resources, Ireland and Ors* [2011] IEHC 388.
24. *Island Ferries Teoranta v. Minister for Communications, Marine and Natural Resources, Ireland and Ors* [2012] IEHC 256.
25. The legislation followed a constitutional referendum in October 2013.
26. *See* Rules of the Superior Courts (Court of Appeal Act 2014) SI 485/2014 for more information on its operation. It can also hear appeals from the following courts which are not relevant to this project.
27. Article 34.5.3 Bunreacht na hÉireann *Shay Sweeney v. VHI* [2021] IESCDET 36, para. 2 O'Donnell J., McKechnie J., Dunne J.
28. Article 34.5.3 Bunreacht na hÉireann.

Judgments of the High Court may be appealed only on a point of law.[29] Witnesses are not called before the appellate court. The Court usually considers a transcript of the evidence heard by the High Court and, on that basis, reaches a view as to whether the findings of fact of the trial judge are founded in the evidence admitted.[30] Generally, the appellate court will not interfere with the findings of fact once there is a foundation in the evidence given.[31]

Appeals from decisions of the High Court in civil cases must be brought within twenty-eight days of the perfection (signing by the court registrar) of the order to be appealed. It is possible to lodge a notice of appeal outside the twenty-eight-day limit if the respondent (the party on the other side) provides a letter consenting to the late filing by the other party. If the party does not consent, it is possible to apply to the Court of Appeal by way of notice of motion for an extension of time. Changes to the procedures for Supreme Court appeals came into effect on 10 January 2019.[32] In general, the notice of application for leave and an attested copy of the order of the court below must be lodged not later than twenty-one days from the perfecting of the order in respect of which leave to appeal is sought.[33]

There has been very little civil public competition law enforcement in Ireland. In fact, between April 2004 and May 2021, only two cases initiated by the CA/CCPC yielded a High Court judgment on a possible substantive infringement. As elaborated below, both infringement decisions were subsequently appealed to a higher court, which issued a judgment.

3 PRIOR RESEARCH

It appears that there has been no empirical research to date on the judicial review of public enforcement of competition law in Ireland. Nonetheless there has been some academic analysis of the CA/CCPC's competences[34] and of its priorities.[35] Competition litigation before the Irish courts has also been appraised.[36]

29. Raymond Byrne, J. Paul McCutcheon, Laura Cahillane and Emma Roche-Cagney, *Byrne and McCutcheon on the Irish Legal System* (Bloomsbury Professional, 7th ed., 2020), [7.23].
30. *Ibid.*, [7.05]. Order 86A rule 4 Rules of the Superior Court allows the Court of Appeal full discretionary power to receive further evidence on questions of fact.
31. *Ibid.*
32. Rules of the Superior Courts (Supreme Court) 2018 (SI 583 of 2018).
33. Order 58 Rule 16 Rule of Superior Court.
34. Mary Catherine Lucey, 'The New Irish Competition and Consumer Protection Commission: Is This "Powerful Watchdog with Real Teeth" Powerful Enough under EU Law?' (2015) 6(3) Journal of European Competition Law and Practice, 185 DOI: 10.1093/jeclap/lpu103; Philip Andrews, Paul Gorecki and David McFadden, *Modern Irish Competition Law* (Wolters Kluwer 2015).
35. Vincent J.G Power, 'An Analytical Review of the Choices/Priorities Made by Ireland's Competition Authority/Competition and Consumer Protection Commission 1991-2016' (2018) 13(1) Comp LRev 83.
36. Philip Andrews, Paul Gorecki and David McFadden, *Modern Irish Competition Law* (Wolters Kluwer 2015); Vincent J.G. Power, 'Irish Innovations to Facilitate Competition Litigation: Ireland's Competition (Amendment) Act 2012' (2012) 4 GCLR 168; Paul K. Gorecki, 'The Courts and Competition Law: The Irish Experience' (2021) 14(2) Comp L. Rev 109, 112.

4 QUANTITATIVE ANALYSIS

4.1 Source of Information

The database is expected to be comprehensive. The chosen sources of information are two free (non-subscription) websites. The website www.courts.ie lists and offers access to copies of judgments from Irish courts. The second source is www.ccpc.ie, which is the website of the CCPC and contains a section dedicated to public civil enforcement which includes reference to judgments in cases initiated by the CA/CCCPC.

4.2 Total Number of Cases

As mentioned, there are only two judgments in the database, which pertain to two NCA decisions. This gives a ratio of 100% appeal. Both judgments are first-instance appeals given by the Supreme Court against the judgments of the High Court (acting as NCA) in cases initiated by the Competition Authority. The first NCA decision is the 2004 High Court judgment in *Competition Authority v. O Regan & Others* (more commonly known as *ILCU*)[37] whose appeal judgment was delivered by the Supreme Court in 2007.[38] The second NCA decision is the 2006 High Court judgment in *Competition Authority v. Beef Industry Development Society and Barry Bros (Carrigmore) Meats Ltd* (often known as *BIDS*),[39] whose judgment on appeal was delivered by the Supreme Court in 2009.[40]

4.3 Success Rates and Outcomes

As Figures 16.1 and 16.2 demonstrate, in the period of this study, as mentioned, that there were two appeals. The appeal in *ILCU* was fully successful. The Supreme Court unanimously overturned the High Court judgment finding of an infringement.[41] In the second appeal (*BIDS*), the Supreme Court remitted the case back to the High Court to determine whether the agreement complied with Article 101(3) TFEU.[42]

37. [2004] IEHC 330.
38. *Competition Authority v. O Regan & Others* [2007] IESC 22.
39. [2006] IEHC 294.
40. [2009] IESC 72.
41. *Competition Authority v. O Regan & Others* [2007] IESC 22.
42. [2009] IESC 72.

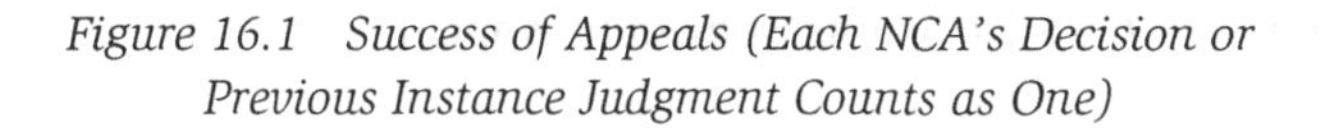

Figure 16.1 Success of Appeals (Each NCA's Decision or Previous Instance Judgment Counts as One)

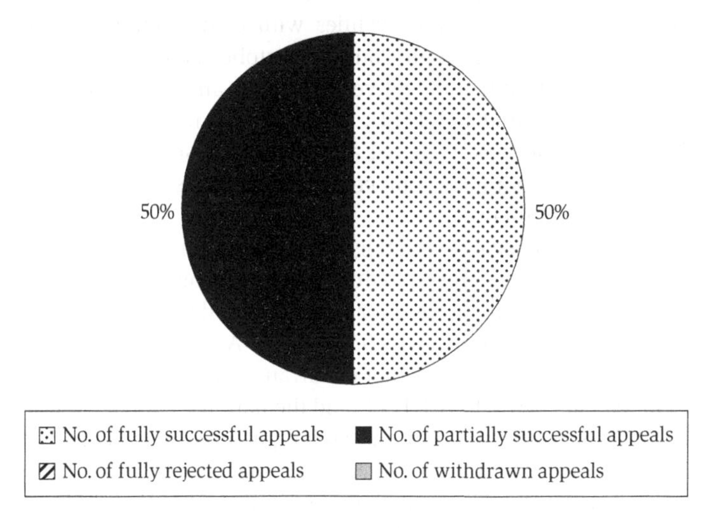

Figure 16.2 First-Instance Outcome

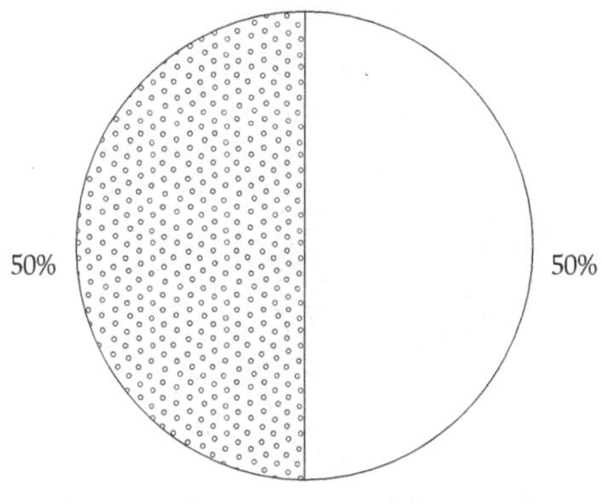

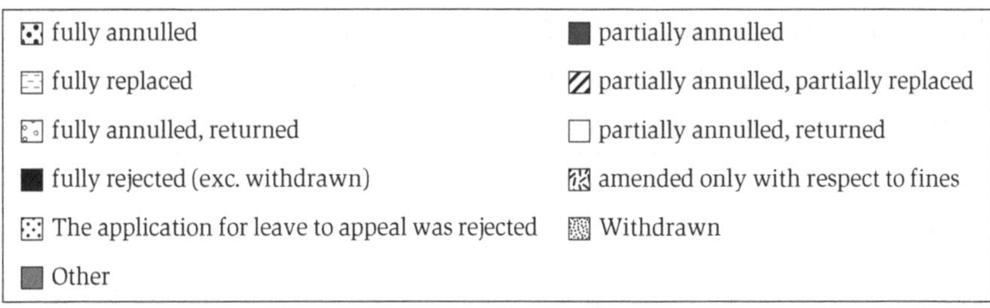

4.4 Type of NCA's Decisions Subject to Appeal

As Figure 16.3 summarises, in *ILCU*, the CA sought High Court orders to require an association of credit unions to share facilities with credit unions which were not members of the association. The High Court, in October 2004, found an abuse of a dominant position and an anti-competitive agreement and made orders to provide access.[43] Both Articles 101 and 102 TFEU, as well as the national equivalents, were applied, and the restriction was classified as horizontal restriction and exclusionary abuse. The High Court did not have competence in a civil case to impose a fine for an infringement of competition law.

In 2003, the CA began legal proceedings in the High Court against BIDS. The High Court decided that the arrangements (to reduce capacity throughout the industry) were not anti-competitive in either their object or effect.[44] This determination was appealed by the CA to the Supreme Court, which made an Article 267 TFEU preliminary reference in 2007. The CJEU reply was that the arrangements constituted a 'by-object' horizontal infringement of Article 101 TFEU and the national equivalent prohibition.[45] In November 2009, the Supreme Court, in two judgments (Judge Fennelly J. issued a separate judgment), decided to send the case back to the High Court to determine whether the Article 101 (3) TFEU exception criteria were satisfied.[46] However, BIDS withdrew its claim in 2011 before the High Court reached a determination.

Neither of the two appeals involved either leniency or settlements.

Figure 16.3 Rule Being Appealed

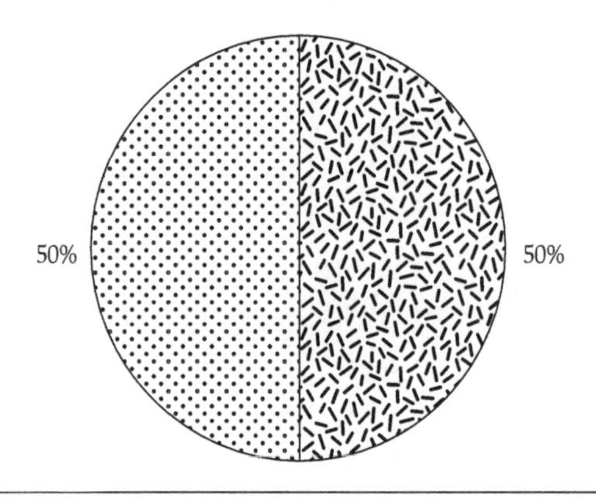

43. [2004] IEHC 330.
44. [2006] IEHC 294.
45. Case C-209/07 *Competition Authority v. Beef Industry Development Society Ltd and Barry Brothers (Carrigmore) Meats Ltd*, ECR 2008 I-08637.
46. [2009] IESC 72.

Figure 16.4 shows that in *ILCU*, the restriction was classified as 'by-effect' while in *BIDS*, the appeal court did not make an express specific finding of anti-competitive object nor effect on account of how the parties framed the issue to be determined by the appellate court but returned the case to the High Court to assess whether the arrangement satisfied the criteria of Article 101(3) TFEU. This is discussed later in section 5.

Figure 16.4 Object/Effect (Only for Article 101/National Equivalent Infringements)

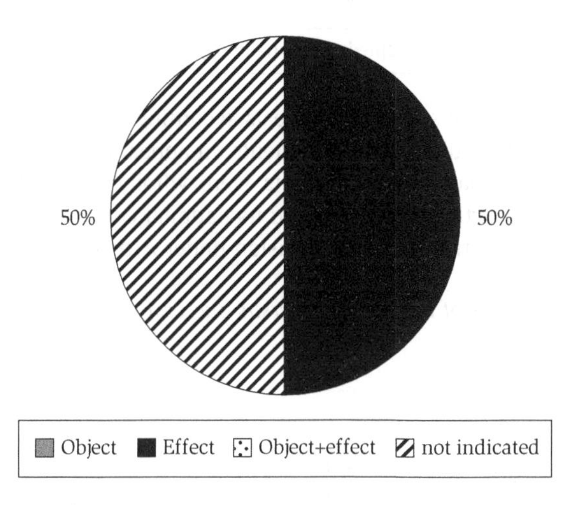

Figure 16.5 Competition Authority's Procedure

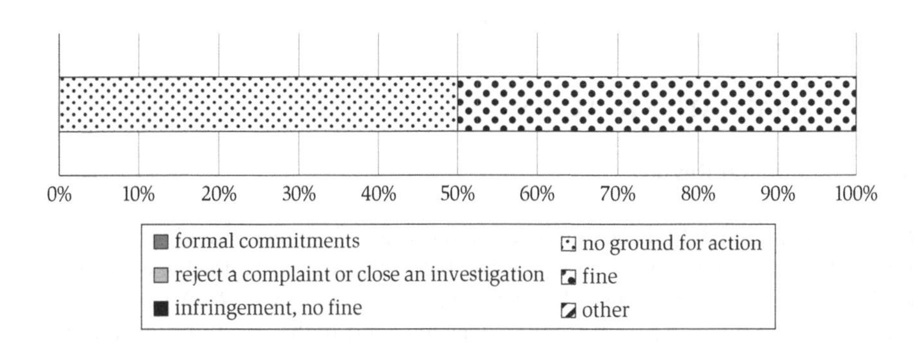

4.5 Grounds of Appeal

As Figure 16.6 indicates, both of the appeals were made only on substantive grounds.

Figure 16.6 Grounds of Appeal (Each NCA's Decision or Previous Instance Judgment Counts as One)

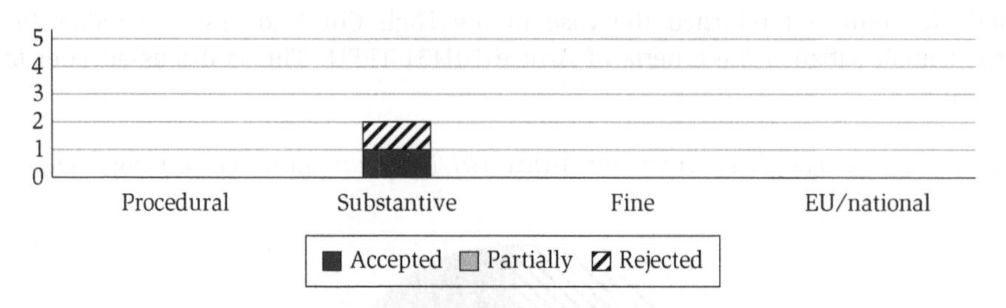

Figure 16.7 reports the successful appeals according to the type of restriction of competition. In *ILCU*, the substantive arguments on appeal in relation to Articles 101 and 102 TFEU and the national equivalents were wholly successful. In *BIDS*, the Supreme Court applied Article 101 TFEU and its national equivalent and remitted the case back to the High Court to reach its decision under Article 101(3) TFEU.

Figure 16.7 Types of Restrictions Versus Successful Grounds of Appeal

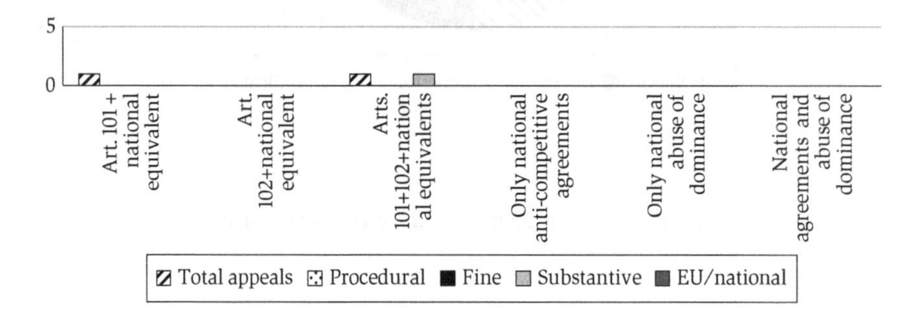

5 QUALITATIVE ANALYSIS

5.1 Judicial Review

Bernatt's definition of 'judicial deference' in the sense of courts restraining themselves from substituting their own assessment for that of the NCA is somewhat awkward to apply in the Irish system. This is because, in Ireland, the relevant NCA is, in fact, the High Court and the matter reaches the reviewing court (either the Court of Appeal or the Supreme Court) by way of appeal (rather than by means of judicial review of administrative action). In addition, while fines are within the range of effective judicial review under *Bernatt's* approach, no fine can be imposed by an Irish NCA in the context of civil enforcement.

The Supreme Court, at an early stage, displayed an acute awareness of the peculiarity of its role within the Irish enforcement regime model, which is atypical compared to the EU model. In *ILCU*, it noted the existence of:

> two fundamentally different ways of incorporating competition principles into law. The first model assigns investigation and decision-making power to an independent expert administrative body designated as a competition authority. Under that model, primary decisions are made by the authority. Consequently, the role of the court is normally limited to judicial review. This is the model of the European Union .... The second model entails assigning to the courts the task of making substantive decisions. It is true that under the direct effect of Articles [101] and [102]...The present case arises from the special role assigned by section 14 of the Competition Act 2002 to the Authority. The Authority has not made any decision other than to institute proceedings. It identifies market conduct and invites the Court to condemn it. There is no *prima facie* legal presumption in favour of the Authority's view. The Authority carries the normal civil burden of proof.[47]

In the same case, it noted that this 'appeal is the first occasion on which this Court has been faced with the need to assess the economic effect of market behaviour and to decide substantive issues of the law relating to competition'.[48]

This project considers judgments (all from the Supreme Court), which are appeals from the two cases (*ILCU* and *BIDS*) in which the High Court delivered judgments in cases initiated by the CA alleging substantive infringements of competition law. In *BIDS*, Kearns P. delivered a judgment on behalf of the Supreme Court and, additionally, Judge Fennelly delivered a separate judgment. While Fennelly J. agreed with the decision of Kearns P. to remit the case to the High Court, Fennelly J. believed the High Court should consider the matter *de novo*. In so doing, thus, the individual judgment of Fennelly J. indicates an interesting difference in attitude to the remit of the review.

In both *ILCU* and *BIDS*, the judgments of the Supreme Court set out precise and detailed information about the High Court hearings. These accounts include considerable detail about the evidence adduced before the High Court judge and the particular arguments presented by each of the parties to the High Court. This information is presented before the appellate court offers its appraisal of the High Court judgment and indicates that a careful and meticulous methodology is adopted by the appellate court.

Indeed, the level of detail (often involving direct quotation) from the contested High Court judgments reproduced in the judgments of the Supreme Court is notable. To illustrate the depth of attention paid to High Court judgments by the appellate court, some detailed illustration from the ILCU appeal is next set out.[49]

In *ILCU*, the Supreme Court expressly noted that the parties, under the direction of the High Court judge, had agreed on a list of the issues to be decided by the High

47. *Competition Authority v. O Regan & Others* [2007] IESC 22 per Fennelly J., para. 103.
48. *Ibid.*, para. 100.
49. *Ibid.*, paras 89-99.

Court. The Supreme Court found it striking that, notwithstanding the lengthiness of the list of agreed issues, the list did not cover the one which succeeded before the High Court and, most importantly, which was the subject of the appeal to the Supreme Court. The particular issue was whether there 'was a distinct market for the provision of stabilisation services (SPS) for credit unions, whether ILCU enjoyed a dominant position in such a market, whether ILCU had abused such a market, whether by tying the provision of SPS to the provisions of credit union representation services or otherwise'.[50]

When conducting its appraisal, the Supreme Court approached the High Court judgment under three principal headings and framed each heading in the shape of a question. The Supreme Court took the view that the second and third questions only arose if the first question was answered in the affirmative. Thus, the answer to the first question became pivotal in the reviewing process.

The first question was '[w]hether credit union representation services and SPS should be considered as distinct products and in different relevant product markets'.[51] The Supreme Court outlined the rival contentions that had been put before the High Court[52] before noting the High Court's finding that SPS constituted a product distinct from representation services.[53] The Supreme Court noted that the High Court had decided that the tying arrangements infringed the national equivalent of Article 101 by reason of anti-competitive effect.[54] It observed that the appeal really was more concerned with the abuse of dominant position prohibition.

The Supreme Court in *ILCU* also noted various contributors to the High Court hearing. The level of detail contained in the appellate (Supreme Court) judgment attests to the careful consideration given to the matter under appeal. There is reference by name not only to the barristers who represent each side but also to the individual expert witnesses[55] and academic authors whose work was considered.[56] Moreover, the Supreme Court noted that the High Court, with the consent of the parties, appointed its own economic assessor.[57] This appointment likely indicates the need felt by the High Court to have access to a tailored degree of economic expertise. Access to such an expert enhances the level of expertise associated with the decision-making of the High Court acting as NCA.

On the issue of deference to the administrative competition agency, it is clear the Supreme Court does not consider itself to be beholden to the position adopted by the

50. *Ibid*, para. 54.
51. *Ibid.*, para. 60. The second question was '[W]hether ILCU enjoys a dominant position in the market for either of these services (especially SPS) assuming them to be in separate markets.' The third question is 'whether ILCU has abused its alleged dominant position in the market for SPS, principally by tying its provision to the provision of a separate product, namely credit union representation services but alternatively by abusive refusal to supply'. *Ibid.*
52. *Competition Authority v. O Regan & Others* [2007] IESC 22 per Fennelly J., paras 63-67.
53. *Ibid.*, para. 68.
54. *Ibid.*, paras 78-80.
55. *Ibid.*, paras 109-110, 129, 131-132.
56. *Ibid.*, paras 113-118.
57. *Ibid.*, para. 58. Such an appointment is permitted by Order 36, Rule 41 of the Rules of the Supreme Court.

competition agency. The Court does not shy from subjecting the agency's arguments to close scrutiny. In *ILCU*, having found a particular analysis of a substantive matter to be 'clear and compelling', the Supreme Court expressly rejected the criticism of that analysis, which was advanced by the CA. Indeed, the Supreme Court went so far as to comment that 'the unfavourable view held by the Authority does not appear to be shared by the leading English writer on competition law ...'.[58] While the Supreme Court accepted that the text does not 'enjoy the status of a judicial decision' but continued by observing that its 'emphasis on the role of consumer demand is, nonetheless, entirely consistent with the long-established case law of the Court of Justice'.[59] After reviewing the evidence (including expert witnesses for each party), the Supreme Court in *ILCU* reached 'the clear conclusion that the Authority has not established that SPS constitutes a distinct product, still less that it is in a separate product market'.[60] It immediately followed this conclusion with the stinging (and certainly far from deferential) observation that:

> [I]t is not altogether surprising that the Authority has failed to provide a convincing analysis of ILCU's activities as being anti-competitive. The history shows that it has changed its position in relation to ILCU on several occasions. It was permitted finally to change its stance from that advanced in the statement of claim only because Mr Collins decided not to object, believing that this radical change of position demonstrated the lack of credibility in the Authority's case. It certainly seems to me to undermine confidence in the Authority's consistency.[61]

The Supreme Court concluded that if the SPS and representation services are not distinct products in distinct product markets, the CA's case for tying abuse fails, and it also found that the CA's case under the Irish equivalent of Article 101 TFEU also failed.[62] The Supreme Court had set aside the order of the High Court in its entirety and substituted its order to dismiss the claim of the CA.[63] This is an example of the High Court judgment on the existence of a substantive infringement being overturned on appeal. That unanimous conclusion was reached by the Supreme Court after a very careful dissection of the High Court judgment and close consideration of the parties' arguments on appeal.

Some detail from the second case (*BIDS*) is next offered to convey further the attitude to and level of scrutiny afforded by the appellate court in its two judgments dealing with the High Court determination. The first judgment was delivered by Kearns P. (President) on behalf of the Court, and the second was by Fennelly J.

The Kearns P. judgment noted the parties' agreement that the only issue requiring determination from the Supreme Court (following the reply under the preliminary reference procedure) was whether the arrangements could benefit from the exemption under Article 101(3) TFEU. Although their consensus effectively disposed of the Article 101(1) TFEU matter, Kearns P., nonetheless, made some more general observations

58. *Competition Authority v. O Regan & Others* [2007] IESC 22 per Fennelly J., para. 119.
59. *Ibid.*, para. 120.
60. *Ibid.*, para. 134.
61. *Ibid.*, para. 135.
62. *Ibid.*, paras 143-144.
63. *Ibid.*, para. 145.

that offer insights into the High Court's determination (which was not supported by the ECJ) that Article 101(1) TFEU had *not* been infringed. The Supreme Court judgment remarked that, as was found by the High Court judge, the industry-wide restructuring arrangement 'was as far removed as one could imagine from objectionable cartel practises. The scheme was not hatched in a smoke filled room'.[64]

Kearns P. further remarked on how both sides to the appeal 'refrained from disputing the key elements in the economic analysis conducted by the learned trial judge. However, both sides strongly contend that the learned trial judge drew incorrect inferences from his analysis'.[65] The question for the Supreme Court, according to Kearns P., was 'having regard to the ruling delivered by the European Court of Justice in relation to the anti-competitive object of the BIDS arrangement under Article [101](1), whether it can itself, acting in effect as a court of first instance, conduct the economic analysis required under Article [101](3)'. This quotation is important as it draws attention to the parameters of the role of the Supreme Court in these particular circumstances.

For Kearns P., it was clear that both parties considered that the High Court analysis 'while detailed and comprehensive, was not one specifically undertaken in the context of the different requirements and different onus of proof arising under Article [101] (3)'.[66] Kearns P. decided that 'the proper course in these circumstances is to refer the matter back to the High Court so that the appropriate analysis under Article 101(3) TFEU can be carried out as soon as may be possible by the judge who saw and heard the various witnesses. He is thus the arbitrator best qualified to assess the credibility and weight of their evidence'. Then, Kearns P. proceeded 'to express a view on some general legal points which were canvassed in this appeal in the hope that it may be of assistance to the learned trial judge'. Kearns P. concluded the judgment by stressing that the High Court judge had no obligation to conduct the full analysis under Article 101(3) TFEU 'at the time of writing his judgment in light of the findings he was making under Article [101](1)'.[67]

As noted above, a separate judgment was delivered by Fennelly J., although he too was of the view that the case should be returned to the High Court. The tenor of the Fennelly J. judgment seems to emphasise the importance of the High Court considering particular substantive aspects of Article 101(3) TFEU (indispensability), which had not been addressed previously. Fennelly J. took the view that this was 'understandable in view of the conditional character of the learned judge's findings on this issue. However, clearly, these issues will now need to be addressed'.[68] Thus, it seems to this

64. *Competition Authority v. Beef Industry Development Society and Barry Bros (Carrigmore) Meats Ltd*, [2009] IESC 72.
65. 'BIDS contends that the learned trial judge was in error in holding that the efficiency gains to consumers had to be demonstrated "with precision". The [Competition Authority], on the other hand contend that it is well established under the Commission's guidelines that precise and measurable efficiencies must be demonstrated.'
66. *Competition Authority v. Beef Industry Development Society and Barry Bros (Carrigmore) Meats Ltd*, [2009] IESC 72.
67. *Ibid.*
68. *Competition Authority v. Beef Industry Development Society and Barry Bros (Carrigmore) Meats Ltd*, [2009] IESC 72, para. 7.

author that there was not complete consensus among the members of the Supreme Court in respect of the type of exercise to be undertaken by the High Court. In the event, the High Court did not get the opportunity to deliver any judgment because BIDS withdrew the case.

5.2 EU Aspect

The Supreme Court's judgments in both cases engage to a considerable degree with EU competition law,[69] even when considering violations of Irish competition law. In *ILCU*, the Supreme Court expressly remarked it was not entirely bereft of sources of guidance and noted the 'rich body' of EU case law[70] and cited from monographs on EU and Irish competition law.[71]

The EU aspect of the Supreme Court judgment in *ILCU* is interesting because the *orders* made by the High Court referred only to the Irish competition law equivalents of Articles 101 and 102 TFEU. However, the Supreme Court judgment details of the High Court hearing in June and July 2004 reveal a complete embrace of EU competition law not only for the substantive interpretation but also in terms of procedures introduced by Regulation 1/2003. Indeed, the Supreme Court judgment records that the High Court judge noted that the parties 'had been able to agree that the same economic analysis is required and the same legal principles apply' under EU and Irish competition law.[72]

Furthermore, the Supreme Court noted that the High Court judge had considered in some detail as to whether this case fell to be decided under Irish or EU competition law. It stated that the High Court judge, after concluding that the impugned practice probably had the potential to affect interstate trade, decided that the case should be assessed by reference to EU competition law.[73]

The notable consequence of this conclusion (on the applicability of EU competition law) was to bring into play processes (at that time very recently) introduced by Regulation 1/2003. The Supreme Court paid close attention to how the High Court discharged its responsibility on the key point of the newly introduced procedure of Article 11 of Regulation 1/2003. The Supreme Court remarked that the High Court, in advance of adopting its judgment, had provided a copy to the European Commission in line with the obligation in Article 11(4) of Regulation 1/2003 of an NCA to notify the Commission of an intended decision which envisages requiring an infringement be

69. For example, *Competition Authority v. O Regan & Others* [2007] IESC 22 per Fennelly J. para. 113 Microsoft Decision on 24.3.2004 Case COMP C-3/37.792 and noted that the decision from the then CFI was still pending; paras 120-123.
70. *Competition Authority v. O Regan & Others* [2007] IESC 22 per Fennelly J., para. 104.
71. *Ibid.*, paras 117-118.
72. *Ibid.*, para. 59.
73. *Ibid.* CA initially asked the High Court to make orders based on infringement of *Irish* competition law (ss 4 and 5). During the hearing which was conducted in June 2004 and, in particular, following evidence relating to Northern Ireland it was agreed that there was a possibility of interstate trade effect (p. 62). The High Court took the clear view that, on account of the possibility of interstate trade effect that 'this is a case where Articles 81 and 82 of the Treaty do apply and it will accordingly adopt the procedural measures demanded in those circumstance by R.1/2003'. (p. 63).

ended. The Commission gave the Irish court an undertaking to maintain confidentiality around the content and outcome vis-à-vis any Member State competition authority including the plaintiff (notably the Irish Competition Authority). The Supreme Court stated that the Commission had notified the High Court (on 8 October 2004) that it had no observations to make.[74]

In *BIDS* too, there is a strong presence of EU law. As noted earlier, this case involved a preliminary reference to the ECJ. Both judgments in *BIDS* from the Supreme Court pay close attention to the ruling made by the ECJ (Third Chamber) following the preliminary reference procedure being invoked by the Supreme Court. Kearns P.'s judgment directly cites from the ECJ response that 'an agreement with features such as those ... has as its object the prevention, restriction or distortion of competition within the meaning of Article [101] (1)'. Fennelly J. delivered a separate judgment in *BIDS*. In Fennelly's view, the High Court should consider the matter:

> de novo, having regard, in particular, to the terms of the judgment of the Court of Justice. It is true that the latter court was responding only to the very precise question which had been referred to it by this Court by way of reference for preliminary ruling. Nonetheless, it pronounced its judgment on the very important question of the very object of the BIDS arrangement, which it found to conflict patently with the concept inherent in the Treaty regarding competition. Clearly the learned trial judge will have to have regard to the terms of the judgment in Case C-209/07.

Then, Fennelly J. cited directly paragraphs 33 to 39 of the ECJ judgment.[75] He continued by saying that it is 'for the High Court to consider the matter in light of these remarks as well as the relevant observations of the Advocate General'.[76] These remarks indicate the strength of regard that Fennelly J. felt was owed to EU sources, including the non-binding Opinion of the Advocate General.

6 CONCLUDING REMARKS

Within the period of this study, only two civil cases were initiated by the CA/CCPC, which yielded a judgment from the High Court delivering a determination on a substantive aspect of competition law in Ireland (comprising national and/or EU competition law). Both such High Court determinations were challenged before the Supreme Court, as the Court of Appeal had yet to be established.

The low level of competition law enforcement in Ireland is likely to be, at least partially, due to the peculiar design of the domestic public enforcement, where, in respect of infringement determinations, it is the High Court (rather than an administrative agency) which acts as the NCA and, consequently, any subsequent review of the determination must take the form of an appeal to either the Supreme Court or, since 2014, the Court of Appeal.

74. *Competition Authority v. O Regan & Others* [2007] IESC 22 per Fennelly J., para. 82.
75. *Competition Authority v. Beef Industry Development Society and Barry Bros (Carrigmore) Meats Ltd*, [2009] IESC 72 *per* Fennelly J., para. 3.
76. *Ibid.*, para. 4.

For an investigation of a suspected infringement to finally reach the stage of an NCA determination (i.e., a High Court judgment) in Ireland entails the CA/CCPC committing itself to pursuing resource-intensive, expensive and highly visible litigation before the High Court. It has been suggested that the CA/CCPC reaching some sort of settlement with the investigated parties is preferred by the agency to pursue litigation before the court.[77] It is true that the CA/CCPC has commenced a number of court actions which did not reach the stage of final judgment because of some sort of resolution with the undertakings.[78] One member of the Competition Authority (in the period between 2000 and 2008) has recently suggested that the lack of cases 'reflects a number of factors including a hostile political environment following the financial crisis of 2008 (e.g. the lack of appointments to the CCPC which led to emergency legislation to prevent the agency becoming inquorate...)'.[79]

Another factor which may throw further light on the reason for such low level of litigation before the High Court is the high level of cost. Conducting an oral hearing can be an important aspect of due process before an NCA. That said, in Ireland, because the NCA is the High Court, the oral aspect usually entails parties being represented by qualified lawyers, and moreover, expert economic evidence is admitted only according to particular rules of evidence and is subject to cross-examination. This all contributes to the length of the proceedings before the High Courts and, potentially, the appellate courts. Indeed, the duration of the proceedings before the courts in the cases considered in this study is noteworthy; for example, in *ILCU*, the High Court hearing was conducted over eleven days. Thus, the oral aspect of proceedings within the peculiarly designed Irish system creates a level of expense which may not be inevitably incurred in administrative proceedings conducted before NCAs in other Member States.

Significant change to the public enforcement landscape is effected by the Competition (Amendment) Act 2022. It was signed into law on 29 June 2022. This Act intends to transpose Directive 2019/1 ('ECN+').[80] It, among other things, introduces an administrative penalty mechanism for enforcing competition law. Its legislative purpose is stated as including providing for 'a system of non-criminal enforcement of certain provisions of competition law, including the appointment and empowerment of independent adjudication officers, and the issuing of prohibition notices in response to certain suspected infringements of competition law; to provide for a system of enforcement and non-criminal penalties in relation to certain breaches of competition law, including by the imposition of non-criminal structural and behavioural remedies and certain non-criminal financial sanctions, and to provide for processes by which

77. Philip Andrews, Paul Gorecki and David McFadden, *Modern Irish Competition Law* (Wolters Kluwer 2015).
78. *See* www.ccpc.ie for details of instances which were resolved by means of undertakings or commitments.
79. Paul K. Gorecki, 'The Courts and Competition Law: The Irish Experience' (2021) 14(2) Comp L. Rev. 109, 112.
80. https://www.irishstatutebook.ie/eli/2022/act/12/enacted/en/html; https://data.oireachtas.ie/ie/oireachtas/act/2022/12/eng/enacted/a1222.pdf, *see* Laura McGovern and Jessica Egan, 'Competition Law Enforcement: A New Era' (2023 January/February) Law Society Gazette, 56.

such non-criminal sanctions may be appealed, remitted or confirmed by the High Court'.

The newly introduced legislative provisions are quite intricate. Their essential gist is that an independent 'Adjudication Officer', after reviewing a 'full investigation report' of CCPC (and/or ComReg) and possibly an oral hearing, may find an infringement of competition law on the balance of probabilities and, then, may impose administrative, financial sanctions which take effect only after being confirmed by the High Court. The ceiling on the permitted level of the sanction is either EUR 10 million or 10% of turnover.

There is no doubt that this legislation radically amends the public enforcement architecture. Compared to the administrative models in other Member States the new mechanism, with its involvement of the High Court, appears rather complicated. The complexity is presumably a response to the requirement of Article 34.1 of the Irish Constitution that the administration of justice be undertaken by courts. This report has highlighted the influence of the Irish Constitution on designing a distinctive model of public enforcement of national and EU competition law, which has evolved at several junctures from 1991 to the present, often in light of EU developments such as Regulation 1/2003 and Directive 2019/1. The extent to which this new mechanism will increase the *incidence* of public enforcement remains to be seen.

Chapter 17
Italy Report

Michele Messina

1 INTRODUCTION TO THE COMPETITION LAW ENFORCEMENT CONTEXT IN ITALY

1.1 Historical Outline

The Italian Republic and its legislators have been rather late in introducing national antitrust rules in the Italian Legal System, as compared to some other Western and industrialised countries.[1] Law 10 October 1990, n. 287 ('The Italian Antitrust Law'),[2] in fact, was adopted more than thirty years after the entry into force of the EEC Treaty.[3] Before the entry into force of the 1990 legislation, the Italian Legal Order regulated unfair competition only in its Civil Code.

The reasons for such delay have to be found in the model of economic development implemented in Italy between the 1920s and late 1980s.[4] A model characterised by a massive public intervention in the economy in a context of structural weakness in the national production system, fuelled by a strong distrust towards a mercantilist framework in which market forces are left free to operate.

1. Reference here is made, in particular, to the United States, which adopted its Sherman Act in 1890, and to Germany and France, which adopted their national antitrust rules at the end of 1940s. On the contrary, the same cannot be affirmed, for example, for The Netherlands, which introduced their national competition law rules in 1988.
2. Legge 10 ottobre 1990, n. 287, *Norme per la tutela della concorrenza e del mercato*, in *Gazzetta Ufficiale della Repubblica italiana* of 13 October 1990, n. 240.
3. The so-called Treaty of Rome, establishing the then European Economic Community (EEC), was signed in 1957.
4. *See, ex multis*, P. Fattori, M. Todino, *La disciplina della concorrenza in Italia*, Third edition, 2019, Bologna: Il Mulino, pp. 13-14.

At the end of the 1980s,[5] the political and cultural framework in Italy started to change, influenced by the rather sensible development of the European integration process and the increasing achievements of the liberalisation process in the then EC Common Market. In Italy, the idea that the crisis of public undertakings, and of public industry as a whole, was a direct consequence of the intervention of the State in the economy, which characterised the Italian economic system for so many years, increasingly developed. Such a context brought a re-thinking of the role of the State in the economy,[6] giving increasing importance to the market and its forces in driving economic operators' conducts, thus promoting a privatisation process of public undertakings and the liberalisation of sectors of the economy previously not opened to competition.

It was in this specific context that the debate on the introduction of antitrust rules in Italy was revamped, bringing to the final adoption of Law 287/90,[7] whose late adoption allowed it to enrol in the wake of modern antitrust rules.[8] The Italian Antitrust Law characterises itself as promoting a rather maximum harmonisation, though not total, of the national rules to the EU relevant ones with regard to substantive as much as procedural aspects.

As far as substantive aspects are concerned, the prohibitions and the exceptions provided in Articles 2, 3 and 4 of the Italian Antitrust Law, with regard to anticompetitive agreements and abuses of dominant positions, reflect faithfully the corresponding EU provisions in Articles 101 and 102 of the Treaty on the Functioning of the European Union (TFEU). At the same time, also procedural aspects are highly inspired by the EU model, opting, at national level, for an administrative enforcement system, with the concentration of investigative and decisional powers to a single administrative authority, independent from other public or private powers, the Autorità Garante della Concorrenza e del Mercato (AGCM).[9] Proceedings carried out by the AGCM are quite similar to those carried out by the European Commission, pursuant to Articles 101 and 102 TFEU, in particular, with regard to the protection of the rights of defence of the parties involved.

The harmonisation of Italian antitrust rules to the EU corresponding ones is further explained and affirmed, more generally, by Article 1, paragraph 4, of the Italian Antitrust Law, which, quite evidently according to the EU general principle of sincere cooperation, enshrined in Article 4, paragraph 3, of the Treaty on the European Union

5. It is interesting to note that, at the end of the 1980s, Italy and Turkey were the only two members of the OECD not having a national antitrust legislation in force. *See*, F. Ghezzi, G. Olivieri, *Diritto antitrust*, 2nd ed., 2019, Turin: Giappichelli, p. 17.
6. On that process, *see*, S. Cassese, *La nuova Costitutizione economica*, 2012, Rome-Bari: Laterza.
7. For a comment on that Law, in general, *see*, *ex multis*, F. Ghezzi, G. Olivieri, *Diritto antitrust*, 2nd ed., 2019, Turin: Giappichelli; and P. Fattori, M. Todino, *La disciplina della concorrenza in Italia*, 3rd ed., 2019, Bologna: Il Mulino.
8. For that purpose, it has been affirmed that antitrust rules also constitutes an instrument of democracy, aiming at the protection of the general interest and preventing the affirmation of market power in its worst forms. *See* G. Amato, *Antitrust and the Bounds of Power*, 1997, Oxford: Hart Publishing; and G. Amato, *Il potere e l'antitrust*, 1998, Bologna: Il Mulino.
9. The AGCM is a collegiate body made up of the President and two other Members appointed for a seven-year mandate by the presidents of the two branches of the Italian Parliament. A Secretary-General oversees and coordinates the activities of the offices.

(TEU), provides that substantial rules therein must be interpreted in the light of the EU Competition Law principles.

The choice of a national antitrust law system strongly anchored to the EU one, nevertheless, proved to be decisive in allowing the AGCM to fill in the temporal gap accumulated by the delay in adopting national antitrust rules, thus making it possible to immediately inherit the wealth of principles developed by EU practice and jurisprudence; while also contributing to a smoother national transition towards the Modernisation of EU Competition Law rules entered into force in 2004 – just fourteen years after the adoption of the Italian Antitrust Law in 1990 – which has almost entirely shifted the centre of gravity of AGCM's enforcement activity from national to EU rules.[10]

Law 287/90, more than thirty years after its adoption, is still in force, though it went through several amendments, whose most important ones are indeed related, to a greater extent, to the necessity to transpose into the Italian legal system, the EU Directive on empowering the National Competition Authorities of EU Member States of more effective actions (the so-called ECN+ Directive),[11] and, to a much lesser extent, to the transposition of the EU Directive on private enforcement of EU antitrust rules.[12]

The 1990 legislation, alongside substantial aspects of the Italian antitrust regime, also provides some procedural rules, which are further completed by the D.P.R. 217/98, on preliminary procedures falling within the competence of the AGCM,[13] adopted to implement Article 10, paragraph 5, of Law 287/90, which provides specific procedural rules and guarantees for the parties involved in proceedings before the AGCM. Such procedural rules, despite their specificity due to the peculiarity of antitrust proceedings, remain nevertheless highly inspired by Law 241/90 on administrative procedure in general.[14]

10. Reference here is made to Council Regulation (EC) No. 1/2003 of 16 December 2002 *on the implementation of the rules on competition laid down in Articles [101] and [102] of the [TFEU]*, in Official Journal of the EU, L 1 of 4 January 2003, p. 1, and, in particular, to Article 3 therein on the parallel application of national and EU competition law rules. On the influence of the Modernisation of EU Competition Law rules to the Italian system of antitrust enforcement, *see, inter alia*, G.L. Tosato, L. Bellodi, *Il nuovo diritto europeo della concorrenza. Aspetti procedurali*, 2004, Milan: Giuffrè.
11. Directive (EU) 2019/1 of the European Parliament and of the Council of 11 December 2018 *to empower the competition authorities of the Member States to be more effective enforcers and to ensure the proper functioning of the internal market*, in Official Journal of the EU, L 11 of 14 January 2019, p. 3. The ECN+ Directive has been transposed into the Italian Legal Order by the Legislative Decree of 8 November 2021, n. 185, which amended Law 287/90 in several parts.
12. Directive 2014/104/EU of the European Parliament and of the Council of 26 November 2014 *on certain rules governing actions for damages under national law for infringements of the competition law provisions of the Member States and of the European Union*, in Official Journal of the EU, L 349 of 5 December 2014, p. 1. The EU Directive on private actions has been transposed into the Italian Legal Order by the Legislative Decree of 19 January 2017, n. 3, which, for our purposes, amended Article 1 of Law 287/90, by affirming, also in the Italian Antitrust Law, the principle of the parallel application of EU and National rules on the prohibition of anti-competitive agreements and of abuses of dominant positions.
13. Decreto del Presidente della Repubblica 30 aprile 1998, n. 217, *Regolamento in materia di procedure istruttorie di competenza dell'Autorità garante della concorrenza e del mercato*, in *Gazzetta Ufficiale della Repubblica Italiana* of 9 July 1998, n. 158.
14. Legge 7 agosto 1990, n. 241, *Nuove norme in materia di procedimento amministrativo e di diritto di accesso ai documenti amministrativi*, in *Gazzetta Ufficiale della Repubblica Italiana* of 18

1.2 Enforcement Framework

Law 287/90 provided that antitrust enforcement powers were entrusted to the AGCM, which was initially competent to apply Articles 2-4 of the Italian Antitrust Law only, and, successively, also Articles 101 and 102 TFEU, on a full and decentralised basis after the entry into force of Regulation 1/2003.

The AGCM belongs to the category of the Italian independent Administrative Authorities, consisting of a series of bodies entrusted with the pursuance of public interests, characterised by the exercise of technical or administrative discretionary powers and a very high level of impartiality vis-à-vis the Executive Power.[15] The AGCM, making no exception to the characteristics above, has experienced a constant increase in its competences, ranging from the protection of competition to consumer protection and to a series of specific sectorial competences. AGCM's competences, in fact, have further developed with regard to the application of antitrust rules to regulated markets, usually submitted to the control of sector-specific Authorities, which, as explained below, in some cases, exercise an advisory function, by reason of their specialisation, towards the National competition authority.

The AGCM is called to guarantee a primary constitutional interest, competition and expression of that freedom of economic initiative provided in Article 41 of the Italian Constitution, which is, at the same time, the basis for the undisputed independence of the AGCM itself, by reason of the interest protected.[16] The AGCM is called to guarantee the protection of competition in the market in a position of total independence from any political or administrative influence,[17] although the lack of any such links does not mean lack of any control, as the AGCM's conduct is subject to a judicial control by the Administrative Judge.[18]

The possible enforcement models available to the Italian legislator for the mandate to be entrusted to the AGCM ahead of the adoption of Law 287/90 were of two different types. The first one conferred the enforcement of antitrust law, including the imposition of criminal sanctions, to a Court (so-called US model), whereas the second one conferred the enforcement of antitrust law rules to an independent authority, whose decisions are subject to judicial control by a Court (the so-called European model); let alone the possibility of direct actions before civil judges for the protection of subjective rights of natural or legal persons, which might have been impaired by an antitrust law violation. The option taken by the Italian legislator in 1990 was the second

August 1990, n. 192. This quite extensive piece of legislation contains the general rules on administrative procedure in Italy.

15. *See*, F. Squillante, 'La procedura nell'ordinamento italiano', in G.L. Tosato, L. Bellodi, *Il nuovo diritto europeo della concorrenza. Aspetti procedurali*, 2004, Milan: Giuffrè, p. 505.
16. *See*, P. Fattori, M. Todino, *La disciplina della concorrenza in Italia*, 3rd ed., 2019, Bologna: Il Mulino, p. 341.
17. Directive ECN+ contributed to a further increase of the independence of National Competition Authorities. For that purpose, in 2021, the Italian legislator, in transposing the Directive above, amended Article 10 of Law 287/90, by giving particular importance to the independence of the members and the personnel of the AGCM.
18. Let alone the obligation of the AGCM to present its annual report on its institutional activity to the Parliament and the Government, pursuant to Article 23 of Law 287/90.

one, conferring to the AGCM the task of implementing the provisions on the protection of competition and the market.[19]

Alongside the enforcement of Italian Antitrust Law rules, in most of the cases in parallel with EU competition law ones, the AGCM exercises several other powers, which, however, go beyond the scope of the present contribution.[20]

The Italian legislator also opted for a complete subordination of regulated industries to the activity of the AGCM for the enforcement of Italian competition law rules in those sectors, thus guaranteeing a direct application, by a single authority, of competition law rules in all economic sectors, even those under the control and the regulation of a sector-specific authority.[21]

Turning to the AGCM's competition law enforcement powers, preliminarily, it should be noted that the Authority does not have exclusive competence for the application of competition law, as Article 33, paragraph 2, of Law 287/90 expressly provides civil judges with a specific competence to decide on actions for nullity and for damages, interim measures and violations of Articles 101 and 102 TFEU producing effects in the Italian market; thus creating, in the Italian legal order, a system of private enforcement of antitrust law rules entrusted to civil judges, alongside a system of public enforcement entrusted to the AGCM, under the judicial control of administrative judges.

---

19. *See*, F. Ghezzi, G. Olivieri, *Diritto antitrust*, 2nd ed., 2019, Turin: Giappichelli, p. 295.
20. These competences concern, for example, Advocacy, whereby the AGCM, pursuant to Articles 21 and 22 of Law 287/90, may inform the Government, Parliament, Regions and Local Authorities of possible restrictions on competition deriving from existing or potential legislative or administrative measures, as provided in Article 21-*bis* of the Italian Antitrust Law, introduced by Law 214/2011, whereby the AGCM has acquired *locus standi* before administrative Courts against those administrative acts, adopted by any other body of the Italian Public Administration, for an alleged distortion of competition. The AGCM may also carry out fact-finding inquiries, pursuant to Article 12, para. 2, Law 287/90, similar to sector inquiries carried out by the European Commission, according to Article 17 of Regulation 1/2003. On the broader consumer protection side, the AGCM has also been granted powers to pursue misleading advertising, unfair commercial practices and unfair contractual terms. Since 2004, the AGCM has also a specific power in the quite sensible area of conflict of interests, preventing those holding public positions to pursue private interests, which might be in conflict with each other. The AGCM, pursuant to Law 62/2012, has also the power to confer a legality rating to undertakings operating in Italy, consisting in an instrument whereby the Authority may promote ethical behaviours undertaken by the companies involved.
21. All that prompted the necessity to coordinate the activity of the AGCM with that of sector-specific control authorities. In particular, as for the insurance sector, the AGCM exercises a general competence in antitrust law matters, with an advisory role to the sector-specific authority (IVASS, previously ISVAP), consisting in a request for a mandatory but not binding opinion. The same pattern applies to the communications sector since 1997, with a general antitrust competence to the AGCM and an advisory role for the sector-specific authority (AGCOM). Before the adoption of Law 249/97 establishing the AGCOM, in fact, the competence to apply competition law rules in the communications sector was exercised by the sector-specific regulator. In the energy sectors (electricity and gas), instead, the AGCM has an exclusive role with no explicit coordination provided with sector-specific regulators, except in the cases where the AGCM, on a voluntary basis, requests a technical opinion to the energy authority on issues of a regulatory nature. That technical opinion, however, does not seem to have neither a mandatory nor a binding nature. As for the banking sector, the initial competence of the Bank of Italy, also in the application of competition law rules, has been replaced, in 2005, by that of the AGCM, in accordance with the principle of functional specialisation.

With regard to the public enforcement of competition law rules in Italy, the AGCM, as a specific body of the Italian Public Administration, although independent, must comply with the general rules governing the activity of the Public Administration – ranging from those of a constitutional nature (Articles 97 ff. of the Italian Constitution) to those regulating the administrative procedure (the above-mentioned Law 241/90) and those on sanctions (Law 689/81) – as not expressly derogated by the Italian Antitrust Law. This means that the decisions adopted by the AGCM must comply with the general principle of proportionality and must be adequately motivated. It also means that any conduct or practice of the AGCM must be based on a rule of law or provided in an administrative act. All this, nevertheless, did not prevent the AGCM, more recently, from adopting more atypical acts, like communications, following the experience initiated by the European Commission. Examples of that trend are quite evident in the area of interim measures, assessment of commitments, leniency programme competition law sanctions, and compliance.[22]

The AGCM can act on its own initiative (*ex officio*) or following a complaint coming from competitors of the undertaking concerned, consumers, or other bodies of the Public Administration.[23] The AGCM has discretion on bringing forward or not a complaint and, therefore, on which cases to investigate, not having a legal obligation to do so.[24] The procedure consists of three different phases: pre-investigation, formal investigation and conclusion of the case. The AGCM has considerable powers to investigate potential infringements of national antitrust rules, in parallel with the EU law ones, once a formal investigation has been opened.[25] The AGCM has various options in dealing with a case. On the basis of a largely discretionary assessment, it can close the investigation on the grounds of administrative priorities or issue a no grounds for action decision. In that case, the complainant is allowed to act before the Regional Administrative Tribunal for Latium (TAR Latium) against the decision of the Authority.[26] The AGCM, pursuant to Article 14-*bis* of Law 287/90, may adopt interim measures *ex officio* in those cases where the competition law violation is *prima facie* founded (*fumus boni iuris*) and there is serious and irreparable damage for the competition (*periculum in mora*).[27] The AGCM can also accept binding commitments with a procedure similar to the one provided at the EU level by Article 9 of Regulation 1/2003.[28] More recently, the Italian legislator introduced Article 14-*quater* to Law 287/90 providing for a so-called settlement procedure, which, nevertheless, does not

22. *See*, F. Ghezzi, G. Olivieri, *Diritto antitrust*, 2nd ed., 2019, Turin: Giappichelli, p. 301.
23. Article 12 of Law 287/90, whose para. 2 provides the AGCM with the possibility to carry out sector inquiries, not dissimilar from those provided in Article 17 of Regulation 1/2003.
24. Although the AGCM has not a legal obligation to bring forward a complaint, thus having a high discretion on that. The decision rejecting a complaint must nevertheless be motivated.
25. Article 14 of Law 287/90, which, following the transposition of Directive 2019/1 (ECN+), provides the AGCM with even more powers as compared to the past.
26. The decision of no grounds for action of the AGCM, nevertheless, does not prevent the same Authority to pursue the same case if the factual or legal circumstances have changed.
27. The possibility for the AGCM to adopt interim measures has been introduced in the Italian competition law system in 2006, in order to adapt Law 287/90 to the Regulation 1/2003. A further reform of interim measures has occurred with the transposition of the ECN+ Directive.
28. *See* Article 14-*ter* of Law 287/90, introduced by Law 248/2006.

apply to cartel cases only, as in the EU system, but in general to infringements of Article 101 or 102 TFEU and/or Article 2 or 3 of Law 287/90.[29] Furthermore, and most importantly for our purposes, the AGCM can also adopt formal decisions declaring that the rules have been infringed, ordering the parties involved to bring the infringing conduct to an end, as well as imposing penalties.[30] As far as sanctions are concerned, the most important power is to impose fines under Article 15, paragraph 1-*bis* of Law 287/90, which, having regard to the gravity and the duration of the infringement at stake, may not exceed 10% of the turnover of an undertaking in the preceding business year.[31] The AGCM may also impose periodic penalty payments – which may not exceed 5% of the average daily turnover in the preceding business year – applied per day in order to compel the undertaking involved to comply with either the infringement decision, the interim measures decision or the commitments one.[32]

Law 287/90 now provides the AGCM with the power to adopt a leniency programme very similar to the EU Law one in order to uncover secret cartels.[33] Its success in the Italian legal system, nevertheless, is not as high as it is at the EU level, with very limited use by small- and medium-sized enterprises. This may be due to the late adoption of a leniency programme in Italy, together with a general distrust of undertakings going for leniency in industrial sectors characterised by strong corporate interests and cooperation relationships. Moreover, it is not excluded that further distrust might come from the transposition of the Directive on the private enforcement of EU competition law rules, which exposes leniency applicants to additional risks before national civil judges.

2 REVIEW OF THE COMPETITION AUTHORITY'S DECISIONS

Decisions adopted by the AGCM in the application of Italian competition law rules may be subject to the judicial control of the Administrative Judge, namely the TAR Latium, in the first instance, and the Council of State (CoS), on appeal.[34] The rulings of the TAR Latium and the CoS can also be challenged by revocation.[35] The limitation period for submitting an appeal in both instances is two months. Fees for submitting an appeal amount to EUR 500 or above depending on the value of the case, whereas costs are, in

29. Article 14-*quater* of Law 287/90 has been introduced by the Law 118/2022. On 22 May 2023, the AGCM published a communication to define the procedural application of Article 14-*quater* above.
30. *See*, Article 15 of Law 287/90.
31. The quantification of sanctions imposed by the AGCM will be made in accordance with the 2014 guidelines adopted by the Authority itself.
32. *See*, Article 15, para. 2-*bis*, of Law 287/90.
33. *See*, Articles 15-*bis*, 15-*ter*, 15-*quater*, 15-*quinquies*, 15-*sexies*, 15-*septies*, of Law 287/90, which are providing the AGCM of the power to adopt a Leniency programme. Such a programme was first implemented in Italy in 2007 through a Notice on the non-imposition or reduction of fines. The Italian Leniency Notice is essentially modelled on the 2006 ECN Model Leniency Programme.
34. *See*, Article 33, para. 1, of Law 287/90, which also provides that judicial protection before the administrative judge is regulated by the Code of Administrative Process, adopted in 2010.
35. *See*, Articles 395 and 396 of the Code of Civil Procedure and Articles 106 and 107 of the Code of Administrative Process.

principle, charged to the losing party, with the exception of the compensation of costs when duly motivated by the administrative judge.[36]

2.1 First-Instance Appeal: The Tribunale Amministrativo Regionale per il Lazio (TAR Latium)

Among the different Regional Administrative Tribunals in Italy, the TAR Latium, sitting in Rome, although not a specialised Court in the area of competition law, has a mandatory functional competence with regard to the decisions adopted by the AGCM and other independent administrative authorities. This specific competence entrusted to the TAR Latium - and for the AGCM's decisions entirely to its First Section - is justified by the necessity to ensure a certain coherence and uniformity in the interpretation of the relevant rules.

A Chamber/section composed of a president and two other members, including the Judge-rapporteur, hears appeals in front of the TAR Latium. The president and the other members are career judges with a legal background.

With regard to *locus standi* before the Administrative Judge, a decision adopted by the AGCM can be challenged before the TAR Latium by the addressees of that decision (typically parties to the proceedings before the Authority), but also by third parties (competitors, consumers or suppliers/distributors), complaining for the failure to act or the finding of non-infringement by the AGCM.[37]

The types of appealable decisions are those finding an infringement, ordering its termination, and/or imposing a fine (pecuniary administrative sanction), pursuant to Article 15, paragraph 1, of Law 287/90, together with those ordering interim measures, according to Article 14-*bis*, of Law 287/90. Also, decisions containing periodic penalty payments and those imposing fines for not supplying or supplying incorrect, incomplete or misleading information or documents can be appealed. Appeals may also be made where the AGCM has adopted a decision accepting commitments offered by undertakings under investigation. In particular, third parties *lato sensu* - meaning not necessarily parties involved in the proceedings - which consider themselves injured by such decisions may bring these appeals. Whereas the undertaking offering commitments may appeal the decision accepting them only if the AGCM has made additions to the initial offer.[38] The decision to reject commitments may be appealed by the proposing undertaking but only jointly with the final decision once this has been adopted.

The scope of the first-instance administrative judge's review covers both questions of facts and law, whereas the intensity of the administrative judge's review of the decisions adopted by the AGCM is the result of a jurisprudential development, which

36. *See*, Article 26 of the Code of Administrative Process.
37. *Locus standi* before the administrative judge against decisions adopted by the AGCM used to be much stricter in the past, allowing access to addressees only. It was in the 2000s that the Italian administrative judge departed from the stricter approach, by declaring admissible an application made by a competitor. See, *Sagit/Contratti di distribuzione e vendita gelati* [2004] TAR Latium, n. 1715; and, *Nokia Italia/Marconi Mobile/OTE* [2004] CoS, n. 3865.
38. *Mastercard (intercharge Fee)* [2010] TAR Latium, n. 33474.

has seen the administrative judge initially adopting a quite timid approach towards in-depth scrutiny of the AGCM's decisions, in particular with regard to the Authority's discretionary activity. Such a 'limited-review' approach, therefore, did not allow the administrative judge to encroach upon the AGCM's competence on technical assessments, including its economic analysis.[39]

Nevertheless, the distinction between a 'limited review' and an 'in-depth review' has been soon, if not abandoned, at least discontinued by the Italian administrative judge, which increasingly showed a higher sensibility towards the principle of effective judicial protection, hardly ensured by the adoption of a 'limited review' approach. The CoS, in particular, affirmed that the administrative judge has the power to exercise an in-depth, full and effective review, similar to that exercised by the EU judge, bringing the same administrative judge to exercise a full review of even technical aspects of the AGCM's decision, like the definition of the relevant market.[40]

In relation to sanctions, the TAR Latium's competence goes well beyond the judicial control of its legitimacy. In fact, Article 134, paragraph 1, let. c), of the Code of Administrative Process, provides that the administrative judge exercises a competence extended to the merits with regard to controversies concerning pecuniary sanctions decided by the Independent administrative authorities to which the AGCM belongs, as seen above. Before the adoption of the Code of Administrative Process in 2010, the Italian legal order lacked an *ad hoc* rule on the competence on the merits of the administrative judge with regard to competition law pecuniary sanctions; unlike, therefore, the EU legal order, which, since its founding treaties, expressly provided the Court of Justice of the EU with a specific competence on the merits ('unlimited jurisdiction') in the area of pecuniary sanctions.[41] Nevertheless, before the 2010 reform, the CoS, in the 2002 *Car insurance* case, had already affirmed that the competence on the merits with regard to the quantification of the pecuniary sanction could find its implicit legal basis in Article 23 of Law 689/81, which allows the judge to reform the amount of the sanction.[42] Moreover, it was on that same occasion that the CoS elaborated the now discontinued above-mentioned distinction between a 'limited review' on the finding of an infringement implying a technical assessment and an 'in-depth review' extended to the merits on the amount of the pecuniary sanction. Before 2010, therefore, the competence on the merits of the administrative judge with regard to pecuniary sanctions in the Italian competition law system was the result of jurisprudential development.

39. *See*, *RC Auto (Car insurance)* [2002] CoS, n. 2199.
40. *See*, *Pellegrini/Consip* [2004] CoS, n. 926; *Jet fuel* [2008] CoS, n. 597; *Tariffe Traghetti Sardegna* [2015] CoS, n. 4123.
41. *See*, jointly, Article 103, para. 2, let. a), TFEU, Article 261 TFEU, and Article 31 of Regulation 1/2003, which provides that: 'The Court of Justice shall have unlimited jurisdiction to review decisions whereby the Commission has fixed a fine or periodic penalty payment. It may cancel, reduce or increase the fine or periodic penalty payment imposed.'
42. *See*, *RC Auto (Car insurance)* [2002] CoS, n. 2199.

2.2 Second-Instance Appeal: CoS

Decisions of the TAR Latium can be appealed on a point of law to the CoS. In undertaking its task, the CoS has not expressed any particular deference to the TAR Latium. As a consequence, it is not unusual for the CoS to set aside TAR Latium's judgments, both with regard to the finding of an infringement and the quantification of a sanction. In a good number of cases, the CoS seems to show, instead, higher deference towards the more specialised AGCM adopting the administrative decision, in particular, with reference to appeals lodged by the AGCM against a first-instance judgment, which annulled an administrative decision.

Appeals before the CoS against first-instance judgments are heard by a Chamber/Section (Sixth Section for competition law matters) of five judges, constituted by a president and four other judges, including the Judge-rapporteur.

3 PRIOR RESEARCH

Various studies carried out by Administrative Law Academics and Lawyers examined the review of competition law enforcement in Italy.

Prior research was more concerned with the dichotomy between a 'limited review' and an 'in-depth review' by the administrative judge towards the AGCM's decisions and how it has been overcome by the development of the relevant case law of the CoS. In particular, *Goisis*, in a 2015 paper, focusing specifically on the notion of 'full jurisdiction' elaborated by the European Court of Human Rights (ECtHR) and on how the Italian Administrative Justice system complied with it, observed that the latter was still far from achieving that objective,[43] although the ECtHR a few years before, in the famous *Menarini* case, considered itself satisfied, for the purposes of full jurisdiction, by the fact that the TAR Latium exercised a control of the legitimacy of the AGCM's decisions on questions of facts and law. The CoS probably made a step too far in its landmark decision in the *Roche/Novartis case*, in which it delivered a judgment still considerably influenced by the jurisprudence of the ECtHR,[44] but most importantly by the recent Italian legislation transposing the so-called EU antitrust damages Directive, which, by providing the binding nature of AGCM's decisions on Civil Law Judges with regard to the finding of the infringement for the purposes of antitrust damages cases, could no longer tolerate too much deference from the Administrative Judge towards national competition authority's (NCA) decisions.[45]

Greco, in particular, already in 2016, assessing the impact of the EU antitrust damages Directive into the Italian Administrative Law system, affirmed that competition law proceedings before the TAR Latium and the CoS must be qualified as

43. *See*, F. Goisis, *La full jurisdiction nel contesto della giustizia amministrativa: concetto, funzione e nodi irrisolti*, in *Diritto processuale amministrativo*, 2, 2015, pp. 546 ff.
44. It is worth recalling that one of the most important judgments of the ECtHR on a competition law enforcement system concerned Italy, in the 2011 landmark decision in *Menarini* case.
45. *See*, in this sense, F. Cintioli, *Giusto processo, sindacato sulle decisioni antitrust e accertamento dei fatti (dopo l'effetto vincolante dell'art. 7, d. lg. 19 gennaio 2017, n. 3)*, in *Diritto processuale amministrativo*, 4, 2018, p. 1207.

judgments between private parties, as it happens with stand-alone actions before Civil Law Judges, and must therefore be based on a full exercise of the powers of the administrative courts.[46]

4 QUANTITATIVE ANALYSIS

This section moves to examine the findings resulting from a systematic analysis of a review of competition law enforcement between May 2004 and April 2021.

4.1 Source of Information

All judgments of the relevant courts in Italy are published. For the purposes of this research, they were identified via the Italian Administrative Justice's portal at www.giustizia-amministrativa.it.

4.2 Total Number of Judgments and Ratio of Appeals

A total number of 462 judgments were rendered during the period object of the analysis, from which 283 by the TAR Latium in the first instance and 179 in the second instance by the CoS. Of the 405 appealable actions taken by the Italian Competition Authority (AGCM) in the relevant period, 119 were appealed. Therefore, the *ratio* of competition authority's decisions subject to appeal is 29%.

This number of judgments is definitely high. This hyperactivity of the AGCM and the Italian administrative judge might be explained by the necessity to develop a competition law tradition in Italy, considering the quite recent adoption of a national competition law enforcement system in 1990, which has been further enhanced and rooted by the necessity to apply in parallel EU and Italian competition law rules, following the entry into force of Regulation 1/2003. A parallel application which ensured coherent and uniform enforcement of both sets of rules, favoured by the high number of AGCM's decisions whose almost half have been appealed before the TAR Latium.

The necessity to develop and consolidate a competition law tradition in Italy seems to be further confirmed by an even higher percentage (43%) of the TAR Latium judgments being subsequently appealed to the CoS.

---

46. *See*, G. Greco, *L'accertamento delle violazioni del diritto della concorrenza e il sindacato del giudice amministrativo*, in *Rivista italiana di diritto pubblico comunitario*, 2016, pp. 999 ff., 1017, where the author considers that the full review of greater reliability affirmed in *Roche/Novartis* should not differ much from the power exercised by the Civil Judge in stand-alone cases with regard to the qualification of the conduct of the undertakings involved.

4.3 Judgments per Year

Figure 17.1 summarises the number of judgments issued by the two instances of the Italian courts per year.

Figure 17.1 Number of Judgments According to Instances

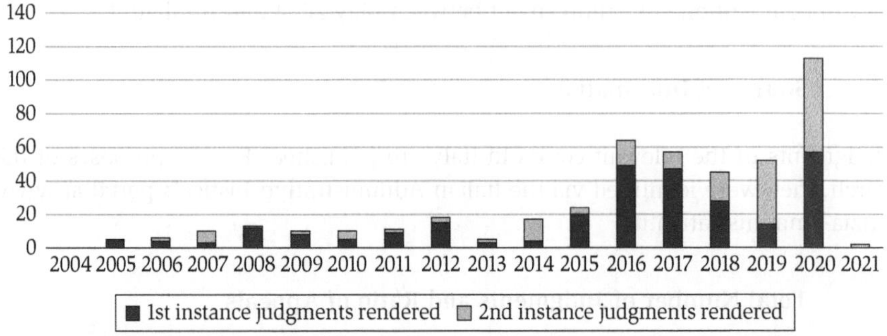

The findings indicate that the changes in the number of judgments across the years can be explained with reference to the number of competition authority's or previous instance's decisions issued.

Next, Figure 17.2(a) highlights the number of TAR Latium's judgments issued every year in comparison to the number of the competition authority's decisions the court reviewed. It demonstrates that in some instances, a single NCA decision has been subject to multiple first-instance appeals, especially from 2014 onwards. Similarly, Figure 17.2(b) examines the number of second-instance judgments in comparison to the number of the TAR Latium's decisions they examine.

Figure 17.2(a) First-Instance Judgments

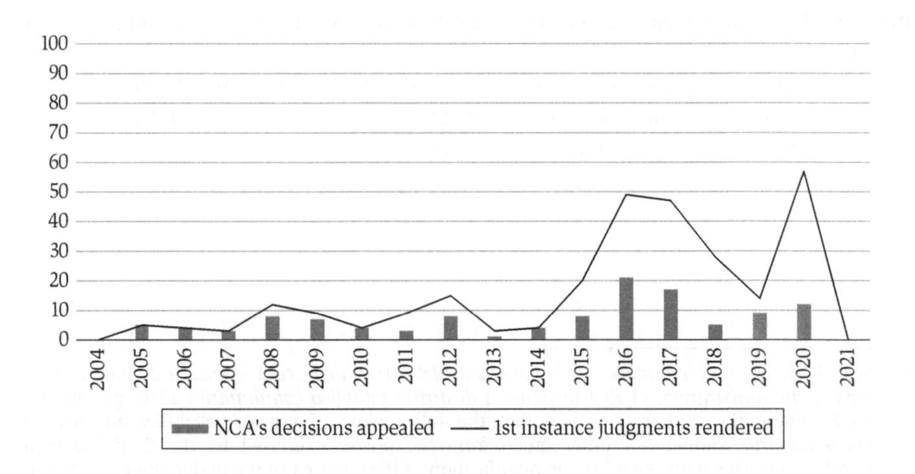

Figure 17.2(b) Second-Instance Judgments

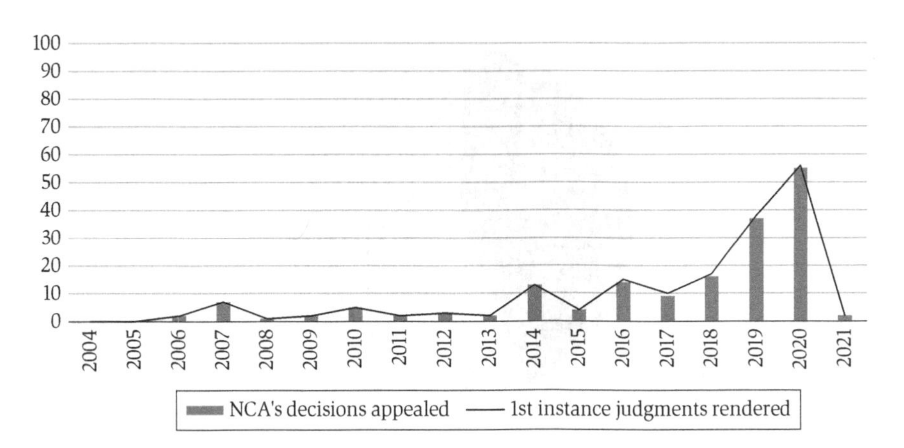

Accordingly, the figures point out that 2020 was the peak year in terms of the number of judgments delivered by TAR Latium, followed by 2016 and 2017. This was the result of some cases decided by the AGCM in 2019 concerning price-fixing in the helicopter services market, bid-rigging in the market for the nationwide supply of facility management services, and the market for the management of hazardous medical waste in the Campania Region. Probably the most numerous judgments delivered by the TAR Latium in 2020, nevertheless, concerned a late 2018 AGCM's decision on the car financing cartel involving several car makers' banks and financial services companies. The slightly lower peak in 2016 was mainly the result of the AGCM's finding of a concerted practice among twenty-one companies operating in the post-production television programmes market.

Figure 17.2(b) points out that 2020 was the peak year for the second-instance judgments delivered. This was the result of several appeal cases brought before the CoS in 2019 (cement cartel and bid-rigging practices in the auditing services market for co-funded EU programmes), in 2018 (bid-rigging practices in the market for home oxygen therapy services in the Campania Region), and in 2017 (a concerted practice in the banking sector).

4.4 Success Rates and Outcomes

Figure 17.3 presents the success of the appeals across all instances. The success rate shown in Figure 17.3 relates to the outcomes of all appeals, taking into account that separate appeals were aggregated where launched against a single decision of the competition authority or a previous instance judgment. That means that if a single decision was appealed by various parties in separate proceedings, the outcome of all those judgments will be counted as a single case for the purposes of this figure.

Figure 17.3 Success of Appeals (Each NCA's Decision or Previous Instance Judgment Counts as one)

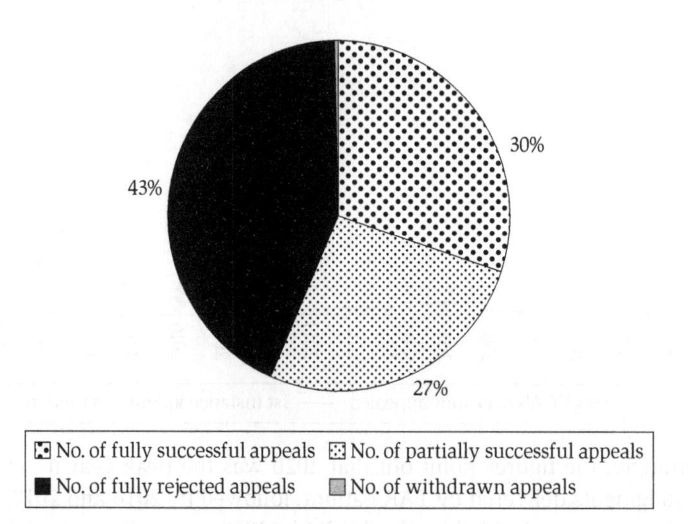

Figure 17.3 indicates a rather high success rate of appeals. Appeals in relation to 57% of the competition authority's decisions or previous instance judgments were either partially or fully successful. The partially successful category includes cases where either substantive aspects of the infringement decision were overturned or set aside (or there was a success in some appeals but not in other separate appeals in relation to the same infringement decision) and cases where the original penalty was reduced in some way (see discussion below).

The success rates are further elaborated upon by Figure 17.4, which identifies the outcome of the appeals, by examining each judgment separately and differing between the appeal's instances.

Figure 17.4(a) First-Instance Outcome

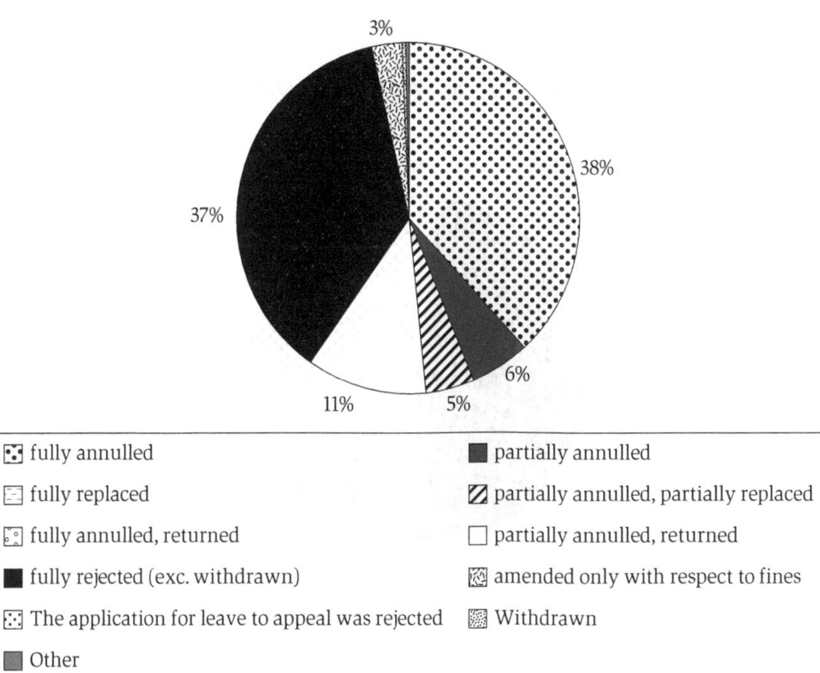

Figure 17.4(a) shows that in more than a fifth of its judgments (22%), the TAR Latium partially changed the AGCM's decision. In particular, in 11% of cases, the TAR Latium partially annulled the AGCM's decision and returned the case to the AGCM, mainly for the re-determination of the fine. In 5% of cases, the TAR Latium, while partially annulling the decision, decided to partially replace itself with the amount of the fine by exercising its unlimited jurisdiction with regard to sanctions. Similarly, the TAR Latium, in the 3% of cases, decided to amend the Authority's decision only with respect to fines.

The TAR Latium, in its judgments, fully annulled more than one-third (38%) of the AGCM's decisions, thus showing that the TAR did not shy away from properly scrutinising the AGCM's decisions. All this is nevertheless somehow counterbalanced by the 37% of TAR Latium's judgments fully rejecting the appeals lodged by the undertakings involved.

Figure 17.4(b) summarises the outcome of the cases in front of the CoS. Half of the judgments (49%) rendered by the second-instance judge have fully rejected the appeal, thus upholding the first-instance judgment of the TAR Latium. At the same time, a considerable 28% of the CoS's judgments fully annulled the TAR Latium's first-instance ruling, whereas in the 20% of cases, the CoS partially annulled the previous-instance judgment, within which, in 6% of cases, it decided to partially replace itself the amount of the fine, and, in 7% of cases, it returned the decision to the previous instance judge or to the AGCM for the recalculation of the fine only, according to its findings. Finally, in the 2 % of cases, the CoS decided to amend the TAR Latium's judgment only with respect to the amount of the fine, and in the 1 % of cases, it decided to fully replace the fine.

Figure 17.4(b) Second-Instance Outcome

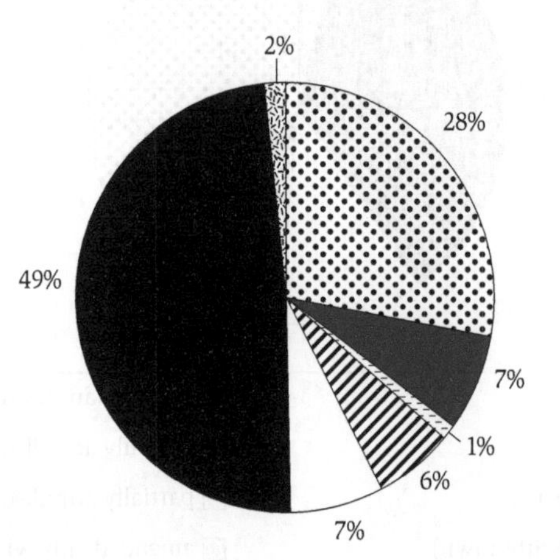

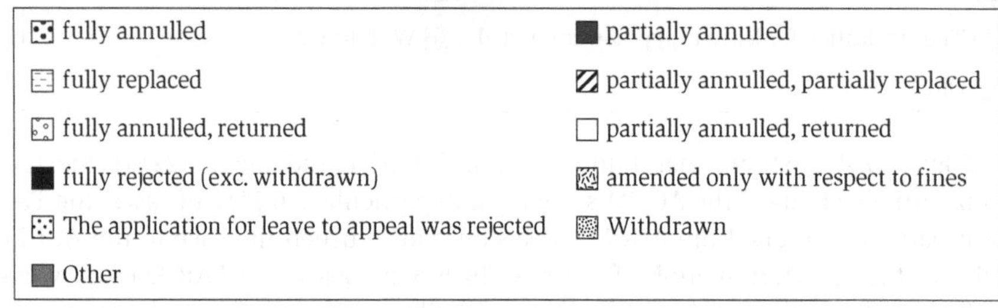

4.5 Type of Competition Authority's Decisions Subject to Appeal

The empirical findings point out a full synergy between the enforcement of national and EU competition law rules in parallel by the AGCM, pursuant to Article 3 of EU Regulation 1/2003. In fact, in the vast majority of cases, the AGCM, when enforcing national rules on anti-competitive agreements and on abuse of a dominant position, decided to apply also the EU equivalent rules. All this has been justified by the fact that cases investigated by the AGCM have quite often affected trade between EU Member States.

Figure 17.5 Rules Being Appealed

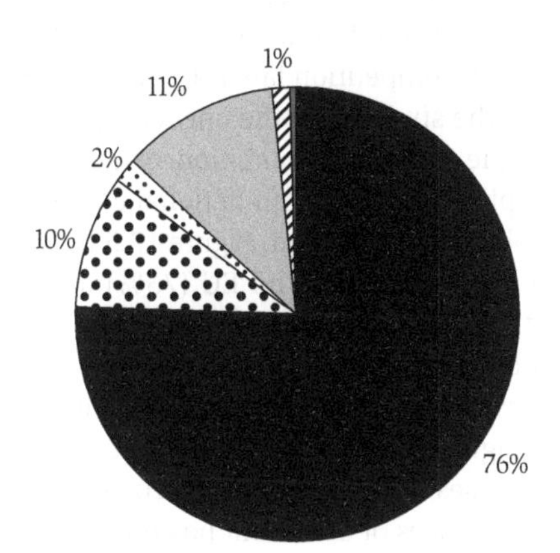

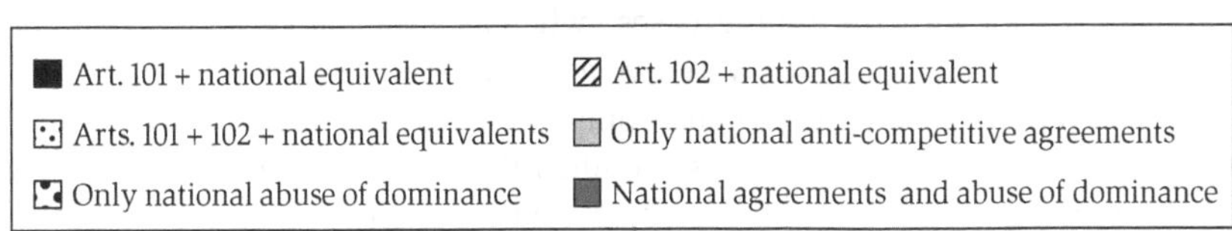

Figure 17.6 Rules Being Appealed According to Years (Each Judgment Counts as One)

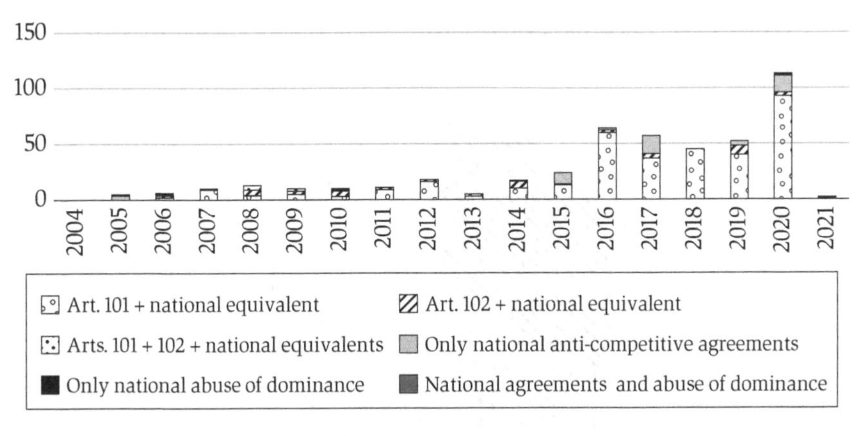

Figure 17.5 demonstrates that appeal judgments in Italy have almost exclusively focused on the parallel enforcement of the EU and national competition law rules. In fact, 88% of appeals concerned either the parallel enforcement of Article 101 TFEU and Article 2 of Law 287/90 (76%) or a combination of Article 102 TFEU and Article 3 of Law 287/90 (10%) or to a less extent, a combination of both Articles 101 and 102 TFEU and Articles 2 and 3 of Law 287/90 (2%). This means that only a small 12% of appeals concerned exclusively the enforcement of national competition law rules, with the

almost totality of cases concerning the prohibition of national anti-competitive agreements (11%) and only 1% concerning the prohibition of national abuse of dominance.

Figure 17.6 shows that the trend concerning the highly predominant parallel enforcement of EU and national competition law rules has been constant in almost the totality of the years object of the study, with the only exception of 2005, the only year where the enforcement of the national prohibition of anti-competitive agreements prevailed on the parallel application of EU and national corresponding rules.[47]

With regard to the prohibitions involved, Figure 17.5 further illustrates that 87% of appeal judgments pertained to national and EU (76%) and to the national (11%) prohibitions of anti-competitive agreements, whereas Figure 17.6 shows that this trend is noticeable across the whole period of the study.

As for the types of restrictions pursued, the vast majority by far (85%) concerned anti-competitive horizontal agreements with 390 cases, followed by very few vertical restrictions (five cases) and cases concerning both horizontal and vertical restrictions (seven cases). With regard to abuses of dominant positions, exclusionary abuses were predominant (79%) with thirty-nine cases, whereas exploitative abuses and both exclusionary and exploitative ones were five and six cases, respectively.

In relation to the prohibition of anti-competitive agreements, Figure 17.7 further points out that 68% of those decisions classified the restrictions as by-object by the AGCM (from which 11% were both by-object and by-effect). It is interesting to note that in 32% of cases concerning the infringement of Article 101 TFEU and the national equivalent, the AGCM did not indicate whether the infringement pursued was by-object or by-effect. From a more in-depth analysis, it follows that these cases were most likely by-effect infringements.

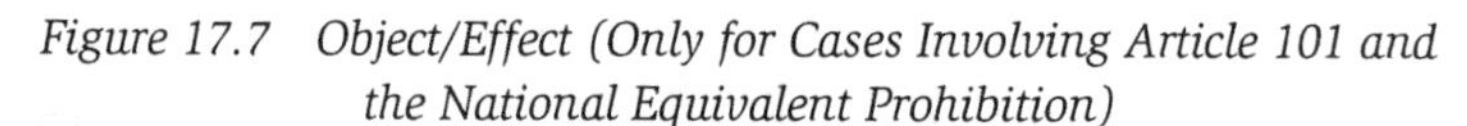

Figure 17.7 Object/Effect (Only for Cases Involving Article 101 and the National Equivalent Prohibition)

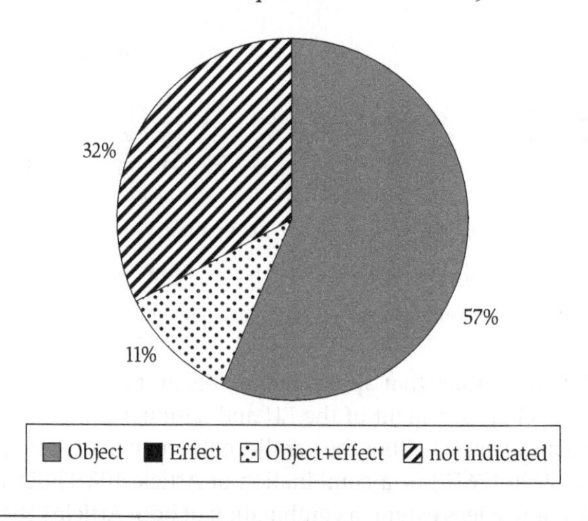

47. To be precise, also in 2021, with one appeal each, parallel enforcement appeals did not prevail on appeals concerning the enforcement of national rules only. This is maybe due, nevertheless, to the fact that the study covered only the first four months of 2021. In fact, with an extended deadline of two month, or less, parallel enforcement appeals would have prevailed also in 2021.

Only 3 % of the appealed AGCM's decisions involved cases where one or more of the parties successfully submitted a leniency application.

4.6 Type of Competition Authority's Procedure

Figure 17.8 summarises the type of competition authority's actions that were subject to appeal. Eighty-five per cent of those decisions involved findings of infringements, together with the imposition of fines. In less than 2 % of cases, decisions concluded with no grounds for action. Figure 17.8 also shows that formal commitments were subject to appeal in Italy in twenty-five cases, meaning that about 30 % of commitment decisions adopted by the AGCM have been appealed before TAR Latium.[48] This is regardless of the fact that appeals in relation to commitments involve a different standard of review as compared to that applicable to infringement decisions, most importantly with regard to the application of the principle of proportionality, which does not seem to apply with its full stringency when commitments decisions are at stake, as emerged from the jurisprudence of the Court of Justice of the EU,[49] from which the Italian administrative judge does not seem to depart.

Figure 17.8 The Competition Authority's Procedure

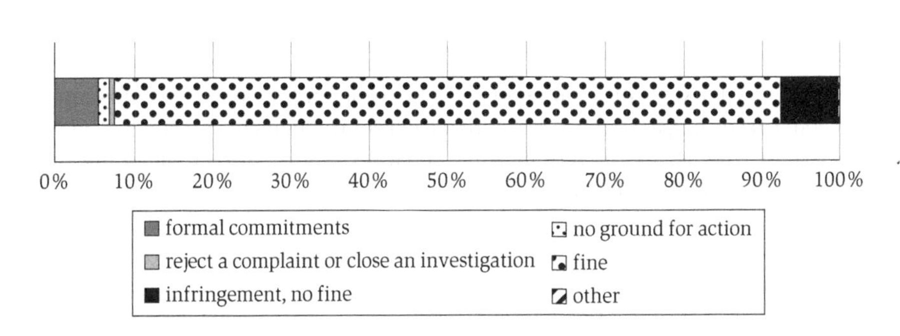

4.7 Grounds of Appeal

The empirical findings reveal the grounds on which appeals were raised by the parties and their success rates. To this effect, Figure 17.9 sets out the grounds of appeals across all instances. The success rates relate to the outcomes of all appeals, taking into account that separate appeals were aggregated where launched against a single decision of the competition authority or a previous instance judgment. That means that if a single decision was appealed by various parties in separate proceedings, the

48. In fact, according to the Annual reports published by the AGCM, between 2006 and 2021, the Authority adopted a decision accepting commitments, pursuant to Article 14-*ter* of Law 287/90, in eighty cases, with more than 60% of them concerning an alleged abuse of a dominant position.
49. Reference here is made to *Alrosa v. Commission* [2010] CJEU, C-441/07 P.

outcome of all those judgments will be counted as a single case for the purposes of this figure. More than one appeal ground has often been invoked in the same case.

Figure 17.9 Grounds of Appeal (Each NCA's Decision or Previous Instance Judgment Counts as One)

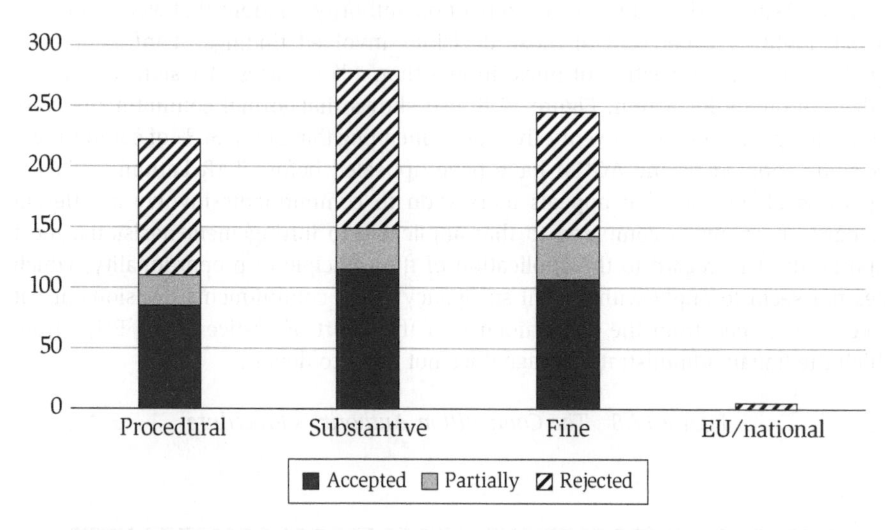

Figure 17.10 takes a different approach, focusing on the appeal grounds argued and accepted according to years and counting each court judgment as a single decision, irrespective of whether there were multiple separate appeals in relation to the same competition authority's decision.

Figure 17.10(a) Procedural Grounds

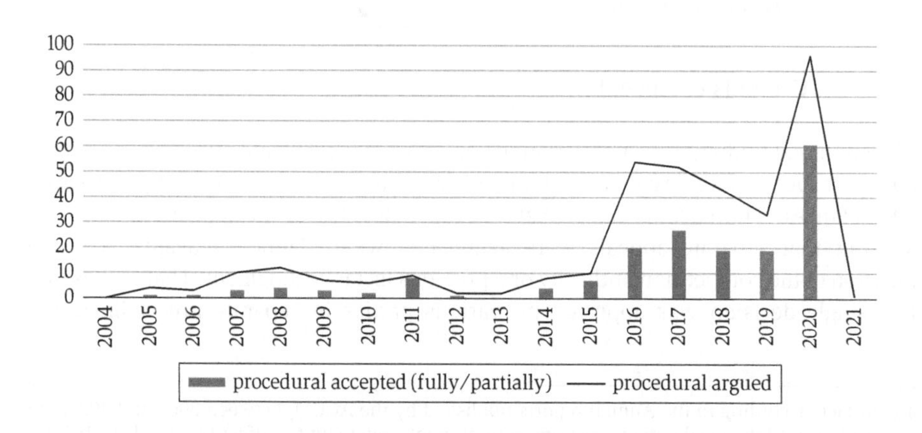

Figure 17.10(b) Substantive Grounds

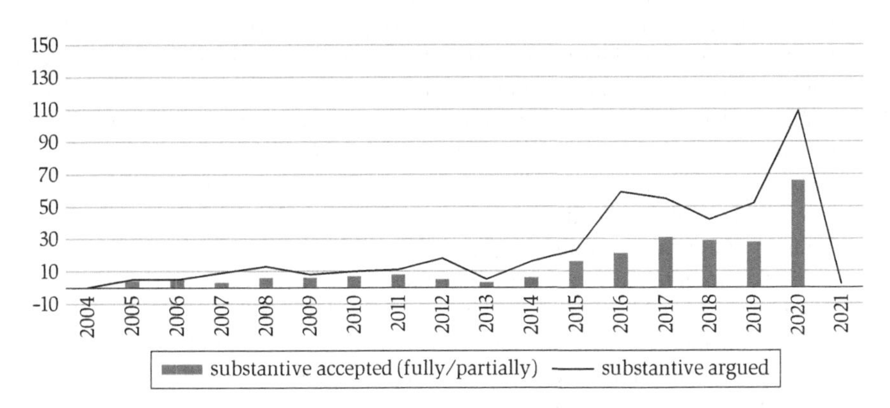

Figure 17.10(c) Fines-related Grounds

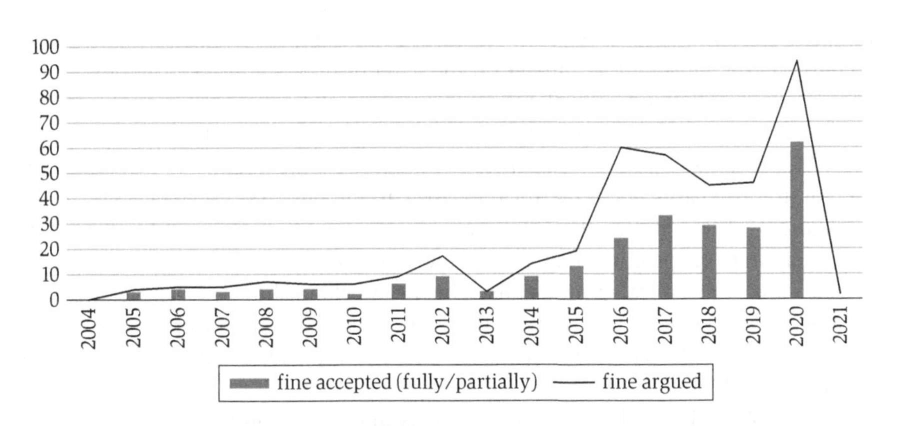

Figure 17.10(d) EU/National Grounds

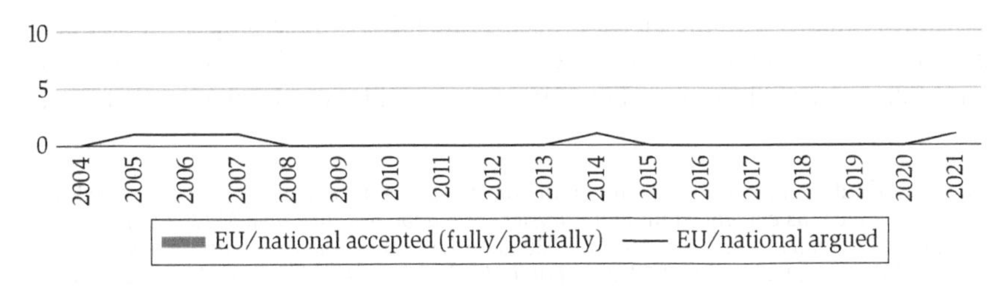

Various interesting trends emerge from Figures 17.10 and 17.11. Substantive grounds of appeal were most frequently raised by the parties, with a success rate of around 52 %, including fully accepted and partially accepted ones.[50] The success rate of substantive grounds of appeal was rather equally distributed across the years, with the highest number, in absolute terms, of substantive grounds accepted in 2020. This is quite understandable, considering that 2020 was the year with the highest number of judgments rendered by the Italian administrative courts, as already shown in Figures 17.1, 17.2(a) and 17.2(b). Most of these cases concerned various cartels in different markets, like those on helicopter services, the supply of facility management services, the management of hazardous medical waste, car financing, cement, home oxygen therapy services, vending machine operators, and the banking sector.

Grounds of appeal pertaining to fines imposed have also been rather frequent, with an overall acceptance rate for their reduction of 58%. The year in which the highest number of appeals arguing fines has been lodged was still, and not surprisingly, 2020, with a considerable 66% of fine reduction requests being either accepted or partially accepted by the Italian administrative judge.[51] It is worthwhile noting that the grounds of appeal regarding fines shown in Figures 17.10 and 17.11(c) only indicate cases where the fining calculation process was challenged in itself. Fines instead have been reduced also because the court accepted the substantive ground of appeal. Empirical findings reveal, therefore, that the appeal rulings by the Italian administrative courts had a considerable impact on the level of fines imposed. A review of the change of fines following appeal judgments during the time period analysed and regardless of the grounds of appeal indicates that fines were reduced in more than 44% of the TAR Latium's judgments and in 15% of the CoS's judgments. The average fine reduction in those cases was 92% for the TAR Latium and 76% for the CoS.

Figure 17.10(a) shows that also procedural grounds were raised quite often, though quantitatively positioned at a lower level as compared to the other two grounds analysed above. Procedural grounds raised by the appellants have been either accepted or partially accepted in almost half of the cases (48% to be precise), with a higher success rate before the TAR Latium (55%) and a lower one, but still not negligible, before the CoS (46%).

Figure 17.11 shows the success of appeals in comparison to the type of restrictions being appealed. In that regard, Article 101 TFEU and its Italian equivalent in Article 2 of Law 287/90 contain the most appealed type of restrictions before the Italian administrative judge, with the highest success rate (52%) concerning the full or partial reduction of the fine imposed by the AGCM or the TAR Latium, followed by substantive grounds fully or partially accepted in 50% of cases, and procedural ground successful

50. The lack of sufficient evidence is among the most successful substantial grounds raised by the parties involved, as evidenced in: *Fiat Chrysler Automobiles Italy v. AGCM* [2020] TAR Latium, n. 12542; *Herambiente S.p.A. v. AGCM* [2020] TAR Latium, n. 13888; *Firema Trasporti S.p.A. v. AGCM* [2016] TAR Latium, n. 3077; and, *Eon Italia S.p.A. v. AGCM* [2013] TAR Latium, n. 4478.

51. The wrong determination of the duration of the infringement is among the most successful grounds raised with regard to fine reductions, as evidenced, *inter alia*, in *Moby S.p.A. v. AGCM* [2019] TAR Latium, n. 7175; together with the wrong determination of the turnover used for the calculation of the fine, as evidenced in *Sellmat S.r.l. v. AGCM* [2018] TAR Latium, n. 7658. Another successful ground raised for the purposes of a fine reduction was that concerning the determination of a very serious instead of a serious infringement of competition law rules, as evidenced in *Romor S.r.l. v. AGCM (concrete market)* [2017] TAR Latium, n. 11886.

in the 41% of cases. A slightly different trend characterises the success of appeals concerning the application of national rules on anti-competitive agreements only, with a prevalent success of substantive grounds in 57% of cases, as compared to fine reduction (55%) and procedural grounds (38%). The success of substantive grounds of appeal has been sensibly higher (63%) with regard to the application of Article 102 TFEU in parallel with its national equivalent provided in Article 3 of Law 287/90.

Figure 17.11 Types of Restrictions Versus Successful Grounds of Appeal

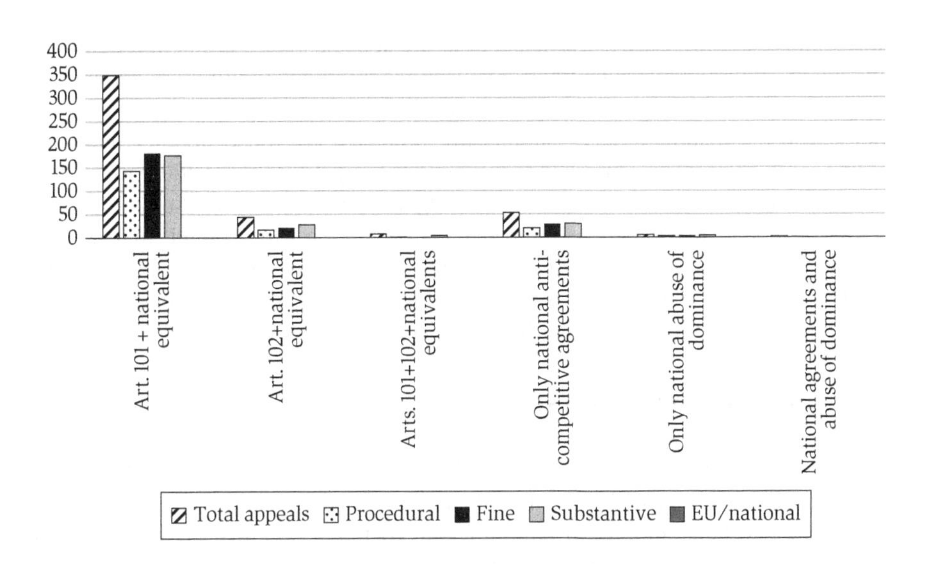

4.8 Admissibility, Preliminary References and Appellant Types

The empirical analysis shows that the appeals declared either partially or fully inadmissible were only twelve, with two-thirds of them declared by the TAR Latium and the remaining third by the CoS.[52]

There have been only three preliminary references to the EU Court of Justice, all of them referred by the CoS, in accordance, therefore, to Article 267, paragraph 3, TFEU, which provides an obligation to refer to the EU Judge only for national last instance courts, like the CoS in the Italian legal system of administrative justice, and not for other instances judges, who they only have a mere faculty in that sense, pursuant to Article 267, paragraph 2, TFEU.

52. The inadmissibility of appeals was declared for several reasons. More specifically, in some cases, the inadmissibility was due to the failure to comply with the prescribed deadline for the appeal, like in *BM S.r.l. v. AGCM* [2017] TAR Latium, n. 3263. In other circumstances, the appeals have been declared inadmissible for a *bis in idem* situation in *IMS at al. v. AGCM* [2009] CoS, n. 1009; whereas, the appeal was declared inadmissible for the lack of *locus standi* in *IACT v. AGCM* [2006] TAR Latium, n. 10013. Furthermore, it is interesting to note that in two cases the Council of State declared inadmissible an application for revocation, in *AGCM v. Sapio S.r.l.* [2008] CoS, n. 6279; and, in *Buzzi Unicem S.p.A. v. AGCM* [2020] CoS, n. 5684.

With regard to the different types of appellants, while it goes without saying that, in the first instance, almost the totality was constituted by undertakings, except in three cases where appellants were third parties, it is interesting to note that the number of second-instance appeals brought before the CoS by the undertakings involved and by the AGCM is almost equivalent, with ninety and eighty-eight appeals lodged, respectively.

4.9 Third Parties' Participation

A limited range of third parties participated in the appeals before the Italian administrative judge. In particular, consumer organisations intervened both *ad opponendum* and *ad adiuvandum* in eighteen appeals lodged by undertakings operating in those markets whose consumers were supposedly protected by those organisations. In forty-five cases, third parties intervened were either competitors of the addressee of the AGCM's decision, like in the TAR Latium's judgments in *ENI v. AGCM* of 2007[53] and *FCA Italy .v AGCM* of 2020,[54] or interested parties like a City Council in the TAR Latium's judgment in *Trambus v. AGCM* of 2008,[55] or, still, victims of the addressee of the AGCM's decision like in the case of some local public transport operators in the TAR Latium's judgment in the *Unipolsai and Generali v. AGCM* of 2015.[56]

5 QUALITATIVE ANALYSIS

The nature of judicial scrutiny of the AGCM's enforcement of Italian competition law rules is not different, in principle, from that exercised by the administrative judge with regard to the decisions adopted by the other independent administrative authorities operating in the Italian legal system. Nevertheless, the nature of the judicial scrutiny of the AGCM's decisions when enforcing competition law rules, shaped by the high number of cases scrutinised in this specific area of law, inevitably constituted an invaluable example to be followed by the administrative judge in reviewing decisions adopted by the other independent administrative authorities in the Italian legal order.

This section builds on the quantitative analysis described in the previous section to highlight the key rulings of the TAR Latium and, most importantly, the CoS to demonstrate how the courts have undertaken their appellate function. This will include the analysis of the scope and intensity of appeals developed by the competent courts, with regard in particular to their compliance with Article 6 European Convention on Human Rights (ECHR) as interpreted by the European Court of Human Rights, *inter alia*, in the seminal case *Menarini v. Italy*, and to their compatibility with EU law and jurisprudence. The analysis in this section will also include the review of penalties and

53. *See*, *ENI S.p.A. v. AGCM* [2007] TAR Latium, n. 2798.
54. *See*, *Fiat Chrysler Automobiles Italy v. AGCM* [2020] TAR Latium, n. 12542.
55. *See*, *Trambus v. AGCM* [2008] TAR Latium, n. 120.
56. *See*, *Unipolsai Assicurazioni v. AGCM* [2015] TAR Latium, n. 14282; and *Generali Italia v. AGCM* [2015] TAR Latium, n. 14281, where the local public transport operators intervened as alleged victims of the two applicants in the car insurance sector.

how this has evolved in the Italian system, and third parties' rights, in particular with regard to their *locus standi*.

5.1 Scope and Intensity of Appeals

The review of the Italian administrative judge, as affirmed by the CoS in the 2014 *TNT Post Italia v. Poste Italiane* case, involves not only a full assessment of the facts underlying the decision of the Authority but also a full and penetrating review extended to technical aspects aimed at verifying without any limitation whether the power attributed to the Authority has been correctly exercised or not.[57] At the same time, nevertheless, the administrative judge cannot, in any case, substitute its own assessment to that of the Authority by proposing an alternative view, like substituting its own identification of the relevant market to that of the AGCM or qualifying differently the breach of the competition law rules ascertained by the Authority.

According to that line of jurisprudence, the review of the administrative judge involves the direct evaluation of the facts underlying the contested decision, also extending to technical aspects; although, when those technical aspects concern assessments presenting an objective margin of questionability, the review exercised, in addition to checking the reasonableness, logic and consistency of the motivation of the contested decision, is limited to verifying that that same decision has not exceeded the margins of the above-mentioned questionability, as the judge cannot substitute his own appreciation for that of the Authority where this has remained within the aforementioned margins, as affirmed by the Joined Chamber of the Italian Court of Cassation in the 2014 *ACEA-SUEZ Environment* case.[58]

The intensity of the review exercised by the Italian administrative judge, with regard to the decisions adopted by the AGCM, has been influenced, on one side, by the jurisprudence of the European Court of Human Rights (ECtHR), which requires a full review by the Administrative Judge, in order to avoid a possible breach of the right to a fair trial, provided in Article 6 ECHR, and, on the other side, by a review model shaped on that exercised by the EU Judge. In that sense, in a 2019 judgment delivered in the *Roche/Novartis* case, the CoS, questioning itself on the intensity of its review and taking into account the jurisprudence of the ECtHR, has emphasised the evolution of its own jurisprudence, which has reached technical reliability, but non-substitutive, review, based on full knowledge of the facts and on an intrinsic control of the AGCM's assessment, though limited, with regard to questionable technical problems, to verify

57. *See, TNT Post Italia/Poste Italiane* [2014] CoS, n. 2302, pp. 11 ff.
58. *See, ACEA-SUEZ Environment/Publiacqua* [2014] Court of Cassation (Civil Division), Joined Chambers, n. 101. According to some commentators, the Italian legislator has been largely inspired by the judgment above when drafting Article 7, para. 1, second sentence, of the Legislative Decree n. 3/2017, which transposed, into the Italian legal order, Article 9, para. 1, of EU Directive 2014/104. *See*, P. Fattori, M. Todino, *La disciplina della concorrenza in Italia*, 3rd ed., 2019, Bologna: Il Mulino, pp. 438-439, where they pointed out that later on the Council of State made use of both the 2014 judgment of the Court of Cassation and the provision in Article 7 above to delimit the judicial control of the administrative judge in those circumstances. On that specific aspect, *see, Manutencoop Facility Management S.p.A. v. AGCM* [2017] CoS, n. 928, p. 37.

whether the answer provided by the Authority in the decision does or does not fall within the narrow range of plausible, reasonable and proportionate answers that can be given to that problem in the light of technology, the relevant sciences and all the facts.[59]

The CoS, on that same occasion, has even gone further by considering somehow inadequate that non-substitutive review model, in light of the then latest national legislative developments necessary to transpose the EU Directive on the so-called antitrust damages actions, which expressly provides that 'an infringement of competition law found by a final decision of a national competition authority or by a review court is deemed to be irrefutably established for the purposes of an action for damages brought before their national courts'.[60] According to the CoS, the consequence of the adoption of that new piece of national legislation was that the non-substitutive reliability review model developed so far might have needed to be replaced by a full review of greater reliability,[61] meaning that it is up to the administrative judge to compare the reliability of the AGCM's assessment with that proposed by the applicants. In so doing, the administrative judge would be able to consider the assessment of the AGCM, although intrinsically reliable, as not deserving to be confirmed if less reliable than that offered by the applicant undertaking.

The CoS Judgment in the *Roche/Novartis* case has therefore tried to produce a further departure from the already established 'in-depth review' model consisting of a non-substitutive technical reliability review, shaped on the basis of the EU relevant case law[62] and duly taking into consideration the jurisprudence of the ECtHR, which, in the *Menarini* case, produced invaluable scrutiny of the Italian judicial control system of the decisions adopted by the AGCM,[63] based on a non-substitutive technical reliability review.

This stark departure towards a more 'in-depth review' produced by the CoS in *Roche/Novartis*, nevertheless, has not been followed by the same court in some rulings delivered just two weeks later in the *Vending machine operators* case,[64] in which the CoS turned back to a technical reliability but non-substitutive review model. That same line of jurisprudence was confirmed later on by the Sixth Section of the CoS in the 2020 *Yellow Taxi Multiservice case*, where it affirmed that 'with regard to the intensity of the

59. *See*, *Roche – Novartis/Farmaci Avastin e Lucentis* [2019] CoS n. 4990, para. 1.4, p. 28. On a similar footing, *see*, F. Cintioli, *Giusto processo, sindacato sulle decisioni antitrust e accertamento dei fatti (dopo l'effetto vincolante dell'art. 7, d. lg. 19 gennaio 2017, n. 3)*, in *Diritto processuale amministrativo*, 4, 2018, p. 1207.
60. *See*, Article 9, para. 1, of EU Directive 2014/104; and, P. Fattori, M. Todino, *La disciplina della concorrenza in Italia*, 3rd ed., 2019, Bologna: Il Mulino, p. 439.
61. *See*, *Roche – Novartis/Farmaci Avastin e Lucentis* [2019] CoS n. 4990, para. 1.6, p. 34.
62. *See*, in particular, *Groupement des cartes bancaires v. European Commission* [2014] CJEU, C-67/13 P, para. 46, where the EU Judge affirmed that 'Although the General Court must not substitute its own economic assessment for that of the Commission, [...], it is apparent from now well-settled case-law that not only must the EU judicature establish, [...], whether the evidence relied on is factually accurate, reliable and consistent but also whether that evidence contains all the relevant information which must be taken into account in order to assess a complex situation and whether it is capable of substantiating the conclusions drawn from it.'
63. *See*, *Menarini Diagnostics v. Italy* [2011] ECtHR appl. n. 43509/08.
64. *See*, *Vending Machine Operators* [2019] CoS, nn. 5558-5564, and nn. 6022-6030.

judicial review of the decisions on sanctions issued by the antitrust authority, this Section believes that it is appropriate to give continuity to the jurisprudential approach which, while affirming the need for a technical reliability review model, implying direct access to the facts of the case and a check on the legal qualification of the elements of an economic nature necessary to integrate the infringement at stake, does not allow the judge to substitute his own assessment to that of the administration'.[65] Furthermore, still in 2020, in the cartel case concerning the *Concrete market in the Veneto Region*, the CoS affirmed that 'the technical discretion exercised by the AGCM cannot be considered subject to a substitutive review model, the judge having to limit himself to verifying whether the answer provided by the authority in the contextualisation of the undetermined legal parameters and in their comparison with the ascertained facts falls within the narrow range or not of plausible, reasonable and proportionate answers that can be given in the light of technology, relevant sciences and all the elements of fact'.[66]

It can be concluded, therefore, that the non-substitutive technical reliability review model is now the prevailing, if not the only, one in the Italian system of judicial control of AGCM's decisions; considering, instead, the substitutive greater reliability review model proposed by the CoS in the *Roche/Novartis* case, as a sort of one of a kind experience, and in any case maybe excessive in order to comply with the recent national legislation transposing the EU Directive 2014/104. The technical reliability model has been confirmed ever since by the last instance administrative judge in Italy, thus bringing the national case law on the scope and intensity of review in line with the relevant EU jurisprudence,[67] from which the Italian administrative judge did never show the intention to depart, and that of the ECtHR. In fact, the TAR Latium and the CoS tried to operate a balancing exercise between an effective enforcement of national and EU competition law rules, on one side, also via the respect of the principle of separation of powers between the administration and the judiciary, and the necessity to ensure effectiveness to the right to an effective judicial protection of the parties involved, on the other.

With regard to the three broad grounds of appeal (review on procedure, on substance and on fines), there was not a huge, though still sensible, difference between them in terms of their success rate before the administrative judge. As we have seen above, in Figures 17.10 and 17.11, appellants have seen their claims either partially or fully accepted in quite a high number of cases, regardless of the ground raised. The grounds of appeal, which somehow starkly prevailed, were those relating to fines reduction, with an acceptance rate of 58%, followed by appeals on substantive grounds, with an acceptance rate of 52%, and, finally, appeals on procedural grounds with an acceptance rate of 48%. This means that it is possible to identify in fines

---

65. *See*, *AGCM v. Yellow Taxi Multiservice* [2020] CoS, n. 3501, para. 4.3, p. 17.
66. *See*, *Ilsa Pacifici Remo S.p.A. v. AGCM (Concrete market in the Veneto Region)* [2020] CoS, n. 1943, p. 4.
67. *See* the reference to the EU Court of Justice's ruling in case C-67/13 P, mentioned above, and to *Chalkor v. Commission* [2011] CJEU, C-386/10 P, para. 62, and *Otis and others* [2012] CJEU, C-199/11, para. 61, where the EU judge affirmed that 'the General Court cannot use the margin of assessment which the Commission enjoys by virtue of the role assigned to it in relation to competition policy [...], as a basis for dispensing with an in-depth review of the law and of the facts'.

reduction claims the specific ground of appeal where the administrative judge, on average, has ensured a more effective judicial protection to parties involved as compared to a non-negligible protection ensured by the same judge through the other two grounds of appeal. According to data collected, nevertheless, appeals on substantive grounds concerning the parallel application of Article 102 TFEU and Article 3 of Law 287/90 have been successful in the higher 63 % of cases. This is most probably due to the higher difficulties experienced by both the AGCM and the national judge in interpreting the rules on the abuse of a dominant position, as compared to those on anti-competitive agreements. Difficulties which have not been entirely solved by the same EU legal order.

The vast majority of appeals involved a parallel application of EU and national rules on competition law. As a consequence, the Italian administrative judge had to engage quite often with the interpretation of EU law contained in the rulings of the EU judge, from which he never tried nevertheless to depart when applying both national and, *a fortiori*, EU competition law rules. The satisfaction of the Italian administrative courts with the existing interpretation of EU law rules delivered by the EU judge is clearly shown by the very few cases, only three, in which the national judge opted for a preliminary reference, pursuant to Article 267 TFEU. The three preliminary references concerned, in particular, the interpretation of Article 101, paragraph 1, TFEU, and its application to decisions of associations of undertakings in the 2015 *Consiglio Nazionale dei Geologi (National Committee of Geologists)* case;[68] the interpretation of the 2006 ECN Model Leniency Programme and its applicability in the 2016 *DHL (International Logistics)* case;[69] and, finally, the interpretation of Article 101, paragraph 1, TFEU, and the definition of the relevant market for some pharmaceuticals products in a circumstance where the relevant market seemed to be defined by the competent national medicines authority in the exercise of its regulatory powers, in the 2019 *Roche/Novartis* case.[70] The latter seems to be by far the most interesting of the three preliminary references presented by the Italian administrative courts within the time period of the research. In fact, the EU Court of Justice, on that occasion, had to decide whether the definition of the relevant market adopted by the sector-specific regulatory agency with regard to some pharmaceutical products could have been derogated by the alternative definition adopted by the AGCM for the purposes of the application of competition law rules.

5.2 Review of Penalties

In relation to penalties, as seen above, the TAR Latium's competence goes well beyond the judicial control of their legitimacy; in fact, Article 134, paragraph 1, lett. c), of the Code of Administrative Process, provides that the administrative judge exercises a competence extended to the merits with regard to controversies concerning pecuniary sanctions decided by the Independent Administrative Authorities, to which the AGCM

68. *See, AGCM v. Consiglio Nazionale dei Geologi* [2015] CoS, n. 238.
69. *See, DHL et al. v. AGCM* [2016] CoS, n. 4374.
70. *See, Roche – Novartis/Farmaci Avastin e Lucentis* [2019] CoS n. 4990.

belongs, as seen above. This competence extended to the merits, constituting a perfect synonym of the 'unlimited jurisdiction' exercised by the Court of Justice of the EU, pursuant to Article 261 TFEU, means that the TAR Latium and the CoS may amend the pecuniary sanction decided by the AGCM, whenever they consider the conduct of the Authority as being illegal or inappropriate.[71] The intervention of the Italian administrative judge with regard to the fines determined by the AGCM has always been quite frequent and particularly intrusive, scrutinising both subjective and objective aspects concerning the quantification of the fine, otherwise left to the determination of the AGCM through a rigid application of the Guidance on the quantification of administrative pecuniary sanctions, adopted by the Authority itself. Not infrequently, in more than one-third of cases, the TAR Latium and the CoS, in the exercise of their competence on the merits, have reduced the fines originally decided by the AGCM, whereas, in more than half of cases where the fine was contested, the competent judge decided not to change it. Though depending on the circumstances of the case, the administrative judge often limited himself to indicate the criteria which the AGCM needed to take into account in quantifying the re-determination of the sanction annulled when the Authority was called to a new quantification in accordance with the indications provided by the administrative judge.[72] More rarely, the same administrative judge determined himself, directly through the judgment of annulment, a new *quantum* for the due sanction.[73] It is interesting to note, furthermore, that when the administrative judge decided to reduce the fine imposed by the AGCM, it considerably curtailed its original amount by an average of almost 90%. As already seen in Figure 17.9 above, the reduction of fines by the administrative judge was almost equally based and distributed between procedural and substantive grounds of appeal. The lack of due reasoning from the AGCM's side was quite often the procedural ground determining a fine reduction, like in the 2020 *Waste management* case,[74] whereas the determination of the relevant market or the lack of sufficient evidence to support the case was among the most frequent substantive grounds determining a fine reduction, like in the *Car financing cartel case*,[75] where the TAR Latium, finding 'illogic and incomplete' the AGCM's investigation with regard to the determination of the relevant market and the suitability of the conducts at stake to produce distorting effects in that market, did not only reduce the fine but it completely cancelled it. Furthermore, in the 2018 *KPMG S.p.A. v. AGCM* case,[76] the TAR Latium ordered to the administrative authority a

71. The competence on the merits of the Italian administrative judge with regard to the quantification of competition law sanctions was formally provided in a specific piece of legislation with the adoption of the Code of Administrative Process in 2010. Nevertheless, its introduction, at jurisprudential level, dated back to a 1994 Judgment of the Italian Court of Cassation in the case *AGCM v. ENI*, whereas, as far as the administrative judge is concerned, the Council of State, already in 2002, in the *Car insurance case*, affirmed that competence.
72. *See*, *Moby/Cin* [2019] TAR Latium, n. 7175, p. 33, where the first-instance judge, in giving indications to the AGCM on the determination of the new amount of the fine, recalled its competence on the merits with regard to pecuniary sanctions, pursuant to Article 134, para. 1, let. c), of the Code of Administrative Process.
73. *See*, *Logistica Internazionale* [2012] TAR Latium, n. 3025.
74. *See*, *Herambiente S.p.A. v. AGCM* [2020] TAR Latium, n. 13888.
75. *See*, *inter alia*, *Ford Motor Company v. AGCM* [2020] TAR Latium, n. 12530, para. 2.6.
76. *See*, *KPMG S.p.A. v. AGCM* [2018] TAR Latium, n. 10996.

reduction of the original fine because, while acknowledging the existence of a restriction by-object, pursuant to Article 101 TFEU, at the same time, it found unsatisfactory the AGCM's analysis of the effects of the anti-competitive practice at stake. In other cases, as evidenced above in the quantitative part of this research, the Italian administrative judge decided to amend the decision only with respect to the fine imposed, like in the 2012 *Geodis Wilson Italia v. AGCM*, concerning the cartel on the International shipment of goods by road, where the TAR Latium reduced the fine, pursuant to its competence on the merits, because of the limited participation of the appellant to the cartel at stake;[77] in the 2014 judgment of the CoS in the *Auditel v. AGCM* case, concerning the abuse of a dominant position by the appellant in the market for the daily publication of the audience data;[78] and, in the 2016 *Manutencoop Facility Management v. AGCM* case, concerning the cartel on Cleaning services for the Public Administration, where the TAR Latium decided to amend the decision only with respect to the fine imposed, sending back the case to the AGCM for the recalculation in light of its guidance.[79]

5.3 Coherence with Substantive EU Competition Law

From the entry into force of Regulation 1/2003 and until the end of the period object of the present research, the Italian administrative judge sought a preliminary ruling from the EU Court of Justice only in three cases, all of them submitted by the last instance court, that is, the CoS.[80] This means indeed that the Italian administrative judge did consider submitting questions to the EU judge only as a last resort, when strictly necessary and where it could not ultimately solve the case in light of the existing EU case law in the field. For that purpose, the Italian administrative courts, in their judgments, made a recurrent application of the EU case law in order to determine both procedural and substantive aspects of their cases, like when they are called to assess the definition of the relevant market or the determination of an infringement by-object or by-effect. The respect for the EU case law has never been put into question by the Italian administrative judge, thus ensuring a maximum level of coherence and uniformity between the enforcement of national and EU competition law rules.

5.4 Third Parties' Rights

Initially, the Italian administrative judge, in the enforcement of competition law rules, seemed to allow only an objective protection of free market but not the protection of individual instances of the economic operators involved. As a consequence, the different positions at stake were, on one side, that of the administrative authority

77. *See*, *Geodis Wilson Italia S.p.A. (International shipment of goods by road)* [2012] TAR Latium, n. 3038, para. 18. Similarly, *Saima Avandero S.p.A. v. AGCM* [2012] TAR Latium, n. 3041; and, still concerning the same cartel, *Villanova S.p.A. v. AGCM* [2014] CoS, n. 3170, para. 9.
78. *See*, *Auditel v. AGCM* [2014] CoS, n. 3849, para. 2.2.
79. *See*, *Manutencoop Facility Management v. AGCM* [2016] TAR Latium, n. 10309.
80. The three requests for preliminary rulings lodged by the Council of State have been concentrated between 2012 and 2016.

exercising its enforcement powers and, on the other, that of the undertakings addressees of the contested decision. Between those two positions, therefore, there was no room for the protection of another private interest of a third party, like a consumer or a competitor.

This approach was later abandoned for a new line of jurisprudence allowing the appeal also against no-ground-for-action decisions adopted by the AGCM[81] or decisions whereby the same authority concluded for the rejection of a complaint.[82] An AGCM's decision may thus be appealed not only by the undertaking to which a decision is addressed but also by a competitor of the undertaking involved or a consumer opposing a no-ground-for-action decision or claiming a more severe action from the AGCM.[83]

6 CONCLUDING REMARKS

The Italian legislator adopted its national competition law system in 1990 only, more than thirty years after the entry into force of the European Communities' founding treaties. Law 287/90 established a system highly, if not totally, inspired by what today is the EU system of competition law enforcement, which had the chance to develop since the late 1950s. Well-established EU principles concerning procedural and substantial grounds, together with those related to the determination of the amount of the fine, like the principle of proportionality, the principle of equal treatment and that of sincere cooperation, were of key importance for the AGCM and the administrative courts in order to ensure coherence in the enforcement of national competition law rules, in parallel, after the entry into force of Regulation 1/2003, with EU ones.

Law 287/90 empowered the AGCM with the competence to ensure the administrative enforcement of the Italian competition law rules. Decisions adopted by the AGCM in this area of law may be subject to the judicial control of the TAR Latium on questions of facts and law, in the first instance, and of the CoS on questions of law only, on appeal.

In relation to this research, there appear to be a considerable number of appeal cases. This is indeed partly due to the high number (254) of appealable administrative decisions adopted by the AGCM in the seventeen years period object of the research, on one side, and partly due to the high percentage (47%) of those decisions being actually appealed by the undertakings involved, on the other.

As mentioned above, this hyperactivity of the AGCM and the Italian administrative judge might be explained by the necessity to develop a competition law tradition

81. *See*, *Acquedotto pugliese* [2010] TAR Latium, n. 1027.
82. *See*, *Operating systems and Internet browsers* [2006] TAR Latium, n. 10013.
83. Alongside the two mentioned above, there was also a third case, within the time interval object of the present research, concerning third parties' right to appeal an AGCM's decision. *See*, *Sales of cosmetic products* [2014] CoS, n. 5278. The Italian administrative judge, nevertheless, had already affirmed third parties' right to appeal an AGCM's decision before the starting date of the present research. *See*, in particular, *Chianti extra-virgin olive oil* [2006] CdS, n. 660, where a consortium for the protection of the origin of that specific product had lodged a complaint before the AGCM, which, in July 2003, rejected it as manifestly unfounded.

in Italy, which has been further enhanced and rooted by the necessity to apply in parallel EU and Italian competition law rules, following the entry into force of Regulation 1/2003. A parallel application which ensured coherent and uniform enforcement of both sets of rules, favoured not only by the high number of AGCM's decisions appealed before the TAR Latium but also by an even higher percentage (69%) of TAR Latium's judgments being appealed before the CoS.

The quantitative data collected in this research helps us to identify some important key points. First of all, appellants have frequently been successful, with the most successful outcome being a fine reduction, followed by substantive grounds and procedural grounds. Secondly, appellants were not only the undertakings addressees of the administrative decisions, or, though limited to second-instance appeals, the AGCM, but also third parties, although in very few cases. Thirdly, the intensity and scope of the judicial review exercised by the administrative courts have been highly debated both in the case law and by commentators. What has emerged is that the Italian administrative judge now exercises an 'in-depth review' of the decisions adopted by the AGCM, consisting of a thorough check of facts, in particular their legal qualification and law. The application of such judicial control model, moreover, would not be precluded by the technical assessments of the administrative authority either. This model has been considered in line with the relevant jurisprudence of the Court of Justice of the EU and as fully compliant with the rulings of the European Court of Human Rights, in particular in its *Menarini* case, where the Strasbourg Court went through the assessment of the compatibility with Article 6 ECHR of exactly the Italian system of competition law enforcement, with a specific focus on its judicial control mechanism and its respect for the right to a fair trial. Such compliance has been further reinforced by the fact that the Italian administrative judge also exercises competence on the merits with regard to pecuniary sanctions. In fact, that 'unlimited jurisdiction', to use the expression in Article 261 TFEU, being exercised on the only 'quasi-criminal' aspect of a competition law decision, namely the imposition of a pecuniary sanction, contributes further to a full compliance of that national system with the guarantees provided in Article 6 ECHR. Most probably, the ECtHR, in *Menarini*, could not have done otherwise, considering the quite evident similarities, to say the least, between the Italian legal system of competition law enforcement and judicial control and the EU corresponding one.

This research has demonstrated the high prolificacy of the AGCM and the competent administrative courts in producing a sensible amount of administrative infringement decisions followed by judgments in relation to the competition law prohibitions in Italy. It also demonstrated how the competition law enforcement system in Italy is somehow dynamic and mature despite its quite recent tradition. Maturity is probably due to the fact that such system is fully and inevitably founded and forged by the EU legal order.

CHAPTER 18

Latvia Report

Jūlija Jerņeva

1 INTRODUCTION TO THE COMPETITION LAW ENFORCEMENT CONTEXT IN LATVIA

1.1 Historical Outline

The first competition law regulation in Latvia, the Law on Competition and Restriction of Monopoly, was adopted just over three months after 21 August 1991, the day when Latvia regained its independence. On 1 February 1992, the law entered into force, and on 12 November 1992, a Monopoly Supervision Committee (the Committee) was established to oversee compliance with the law.

At a time when the free market economy and the underlying concept of private property were in the process of being understood and developed, the Committee first acted as an economic ombudsman, working on the broadest range of issues that inevitably arise when principles of cooperation between citizens, businesses and the state are still being established.

Initially, the Committee lacked the power to impose sanctions and lacked the requisite independence to always adopt and enforce its decisions, but there was at least evidence of a determination to seek a solution - explaining, persuading, and cooperating. One of the Committee's original goals was to explain the new role of the state (and state-owned monopolies). However, initially, the authority continued to apply the methods typical to a planned economy. It was only gradually that the state and businesses understood the necessity for and the benefits of deregulation and economic freedoms.

Despite a certain lack of experience and knowledge, the first infringements of competition law were detected in these early years between 1992 and 1999. During this period, the first cartels were detected, the first cases of abuse of a dominant position were also detected, and privatisation processes were monitored to ensure that they did not result in excessive concentration of market power.[1]

On 27 October 1995, Latvia applied for membership in the EU. It is in this context, as well as taking into account the plans to accede to the Organisation for Economic Co-operation and Development (OECD) and the World Trade Organization (WTO), that antitrust law became one of the government's priorities. On 10 February 1999, Latvia became the 134th member of the WTO, and on 1 July 2016, Latvia became a member of the OECD. Latvia finally joined the EU on 1 May 2004 following a referendum held on 20 September 2003, in which most voters supported accession.

Already on 18 June 1997, in light of Latvia's application to join the EU, a new Competition Law was adopted with a view to ensuring consistency with the EU competition rules, in anticipation of the signing of the 1995 Europe Agreement.[2] In 1998, the Competition Committee was reorganised to become the Competition Council.

During the early years following the introduction of the Competition Law of 1997, the Competition Council remained passive and focused on the task of informing undertakings about those rules. Most cases decided during those years concerned the application of rules on unfair advertisement and general unfair competition practices.

A more active role of the authority can be observed from the beginning of the 2000s. The current Competition Law was adopted on 4 October 2001.[3] The law gave substantially broader investigative powers and allowed the Competition Council to conduct more effective enforcement. Its substantive provisions followed the model of the EU (then EC) competition rules. Article 11 of the Latvian Competition Act is a provision virtually identical to Article 101 TFEU, and it contains a prohibition of agreements and concerted practices which have as their object or effect the prevention, restriction, or distortion of competition. Article 13 contains a prohibition on the abuse of a dominant position and is modelled upon Article 102 TFEU.

Harmonious interpretation of the Latvian competition law rules, in line with EU law, has been recognised in the practice of the Competition Council and in the case law of the Latvian courts. The case law of the courts and decisional practice of the authority, especially during the last fifteen years, is characterised by consistent reference to the case law of the CJEU and decisional practice, regulations and guidelines of the European Commission.[4] Consequently, when applying the substantive competition rules, the courts and the authority take into account the observations of the CJEU in relation to the relevant Articles of TFEU.

Although EU law prior to 1 May 2004 is not directly applicable in Latvia, judgments of the CJEU interpreting relevant provisions prior to that date are, in fact,

1. Twenty years of competition monitoring in Latvia – important tasks and events, Competition Council, available here: https://www.kp.gov.lv/files/documents/vesture.pdf.
2. The Europe Agreement established an association between the (then) European Communities, its Member States, and the Republic of Latvia. It was signed on 12 June 1995.
3. 4 October 2001 Competition Law, *Latvijas Vestnesis* (151) 23 October 2001.
4. 16.6.2017 judgment of the SCA, *FMS Software* case, court case ID SKA-61/2017 (A43010414), para. 7; 29.122015 judgment of the SCA, *Maxima* case, court case ID SKA-8/2015 (A43011212), para. 7; 7.1.2016 judgment of the SCA, *Palink* case, court case ID SKA-3/2016 (A43012612), para. 7; 8.10.2008 judgment of the SCA, *Eggs cartel* case, court case ID SKA-344/2008 (A42206105), para. 12.

applicable to the interpretation of Latvian legal acts, including the provisions of the Competition Law. Reference to the EU competition law concepts and the case law of the EU Court is admissible through the use of the historical and teleological interpretation methods and is explained by the fact that Latvian competition rules were adopted to ensure the transposition of EU competition rules.

To a great extent, the Latvian competition rules mirror those of the EU competition rules (including also the merger control rules, which fall outside the scope of this project). It must nonetheless be emphasised that the case law of the CJEU and the decisional practice of the European Commission are not automatically applicable in all national competition cases.[5] Thus, deviation is possible where the Latvian authority considers that the national rules are aimed at protecting interests other than those defined in the EU competition rules.

1.2 Enforcement Framework

The Competition Council is the only competent institution empowered to investigate violations of competition law and is responsible for the implementation of competition policy in Latvia. The Competition Council is an institution of direct administration that is subordinate to the Ministry of Economics. To date, the Competition Council has not managed to persuade the legislator that its independence from the Ministry of Economics or other executive branches of the state must be guaranteed.

The Competition Council is bifurcated into a decision-making arm, known as the Council, and an executive arm, the Executive Directorate. The former, composed of five members, including the Chairperson, renders decisions and decides on the signing of administrative agreements (i.e., settlements; *see* comments to Figure 18.12 below). Appointed by the Cabinet of Ministers for five-year terms, their decisions are made by a simple majority, and the sessions of the Council are not public.

The Executive Directorate, led by a single official, conducts investigations authorised by the Council. It oversees markets and represents the authority in legal proceedings, among other duties.

A case investigation commences upon the Council's resolution to initiate an investigation. The investigation of the case is conducted by the Executive Directorate, subject to regular reporting to the Council. The final text of the decision is approved by the Council, taking into account any objections raised by the addressees of the decision.

The determination of the amount of any fine is also a matter for the sole discretion of the institution.[6] Nonetheless, as discussed below in section 2, a court may, without interfering with the competence of the Competition Council, assess whether the

5. 22.1.2013 judgment of the SCA, *Rimi Sigulda* case, court case ID SKA-37/2013 (A43004011), para. 8.
6. Supreme Court, Compendium of Case Law in Competition Matters (case law findings and current case law: 2007-2018), 2018, point 9.1.

authority correctly disposed of its discretionary powers when deciding on the imposition and the amount of a fine.[7]

1.3 Enforcement Practices and Priorities

As evidenced by the empirical data presented in this report (*see* section 4 below), the main attention of the Competition Council lies with cartel cases. This may be explained by two factors: the expected impact on consumer welfare from such arrangements; and the relative ease/difficulty in establishing infringements under the two prohibitions.

Over the last decade, the Competition Council has primarily focused its efforts on raising competition law awareness. It has proven easiest to do so through bid-rigging cases. The authority regularly organises training for the entities involved in organising public procurement procedures. As a result, a substantial percentage of the cases in recent years have been spotted by public buyers. Similarly, the authority has developed efficient cooperation with prosecutors, specifically, the Corruption Prevention and Combatting Bureau (KNAB). Many investigations into potentially corruptive practices result in relevant evidence being submitted by KNAB to the Competition Council. While this strategy results in a high number of cases, many of the bid-rigging cartels identified are of a small scale for which only relatively small fines could be imposed.

During the project period, from the appealed decisions of the Competition Council, there were sixteen pure vertical restrictions cases,[8] and in several cases, both vertical and horizontal restrictions were identified.[9] The overall trend in terms of the total percentage of decisions adopted also shows that horizontal cases are a clear priority for the Competition Council.

The statistics in relation to abuse cases appear to demonstrate a sharp decline in the effort by the Latvian authority to take on abusive conduct, which may be due to the difficulties in pursuing an abuse case and finding an infringement.

7. Supreme Court, Compendium of Case Law in Competition Matters (case law findings and current case law: 2007-2018), 2018, point 9.1; 28.12.2015 judgment of the SCA, *Empower, RIO et al* case, court case ID SKA-1286/2015 (A43014713), para. 17; 28.12.2015 decision of the SCA action sitting, *Vidzemes Energoceltnieks, Telms, Spriegums* case, court case ID SKA-1357/2015 (A43012514), para. 15.
8. *Rīgas satiksme and Rīgas mikroautobusu satiksme* 27.2.2017 decision No. E02-5; *Kempmayer Media* 7.6.2004 decision No. E02-45; *Akvaparks and GDG Holdings* 6.8.2008 decision No. 85; *Apgads Zvaigzne ABC* 9.1.2008 decision No E02-3; *FMS Software, RPG et al.* 9.12.2013 decision No. E02-61; *Hanzas maiznīcas* 29.3.2006 decision No. E02-25; *KIA Auto* 7.8.2014 decision No. E02-40; *Lielvards* 28.5.2008 decision No. E02-60; *Maxima* 27.1.2012 decision No. E02-7; *MOBI-LUX* 14.5.2009 decision No. E02-12; *Optimums* 8.6.2023 decision No. E02-45; *Palink* 23.3.2012 decision No. E02-18; *Pet Pro Service* 28.9.2012 decision No. E02-78; *Rimi and Marno* J 8.4.2011 decision No. E02-5; *Rīgas satiksme and Rīgas mikroautobusu satiksme* 27.2.2017 decision No. E02-5; and *Samsung, RD Elektroniks et al.* 30.10.2009 decision No. E02-40.
9. *See also Knauf, Depo, TNK, Kesko, Kruza* 31.8.2017 decision No. E02-17 *Terra Serviss and Preiss Agro* 4.11.2011 decision No. E02-70 for cases, involving both vertical and horizontal agreements.

2 THE APPEAL/REVIEW PROCESS OF THE COMPETITION AUTHORITY'S DECISIONS

In Latvia, adjudication of competition cases occurs through both civil and administrative judicial pathways. Administrative courts are vested with the authority to review decisions made by the Competition Council. Concurrently, civil courts have the mandate to ascertain violations of both national and EU competition law and to determine claims for damages resulting from such infringements, although this second aspect of the role of the Latvian courts in competition law disputes is not within the scope of this project.

Before 15 April 2008, Latvia had a three-tier system, with the Administrative District Court (ADC) serving as the first instance for appeals against decisions of the Competition Council. The judgments of the ADC were appealable before the Administrative Regional Court (ARC), and the Supreme Court (SCA) ruled on cassation appeals. Post 15 April 2008, a two-tier appeal system was established.

Currently, the ARC acts as the first instance for appeals against the Competition Council's decisions. Administrative courts are entitled to review the legality of the contested administrative act, including a review of whether the administration has properly used its discretion. They are empowered to annul such an act, declare it illegal in cases where no alternative remedy is available, or uphold a claim demanding the making of a positive administrative act.

It should be noted that the principle of impartial investigation laid down in the Law on Administrative Procedure, mandates an active role for the court in uncovering case facts. According to section 103(2) of the Administrative Procedure Law, the ARC must independently and objectively ascertain the facts and legally assess them. The responsibility of the ARC is to determine if the evidence presented by the parties suffices to uncover the objective truth. Nevertheless, the court's obligation under this principle is not absolute or boundless. In line with the objective investigation principle, the ARC must ensure that the evidence collected is comprehensive and reliable, providing a full understanding necessary for a thorough examination of all facets of the contested administrative act or practice, as specified in the relevant legal provision. Should the authority fail to adequately justify the appealed decision, the ARC is still required to investigate unmentioned but relevant circumstances.

Judgments of the ARC can then be appealed before the SCA, to which a cassation appeal on points of law and procedure can be submitted. The SCA does not decide on the facts of the case.

Neither the ARC nor the SCA are specialised courts. The ARC is competent to adjudicate all administrative cases, of which competition cases only represent a fraction. The SCA, as the highest court in Latvia, hears competition cases in its Administrative Department. Judges typically specialise in a limited range of case types and therefore can develop a degree of competition law expertise over time (although competition cases may also be decided by judges who do not have experience in competition law). This frequently occurs when a case returns to the same court multiple times, requiring a new panel of judges. Typically, the procedure before the ARC takes place in oral format. Conversely, the SCA is not required to conduct oral hearings, even if requested by the parties, and in a majority of cases, no oral hearings take place in competition cases.

As detailed below, not all decisions of the Competition Council are subject to appeal. Furthermore, certain interim decisions may be appealed, and complaints against the conduct of Competition Council officials can only be lodged in conjunction with an appeal of the final decision that establishes a violation of competition laws.

On 15 June 2016, amendments to the Competition Law entered into force, which significantly expanded the discretion of the Competition Council in deciding whether to initiate a case. It is now provided that the Competition Council can initiate cases only on its own initiative. Until June 2016, the Competition Law provided a right to submit a complaint, and refusals to initiate an investigation could be challenged before the administrative court. While the information provided by the complainant may still serve as a basis to initiate proceedings, the Competition Council has full discretion on whether or not to initiate the case. Consequently, refusals to initiate the case can no longer be appealed. Moreover, the Supreme Court has clarified that an individual does not have a subjective right to request the Competition Council to initiate a case regarding the continued fulfilment of legal obligations specified in a decision, addressed to a third party.[10]

Moreover, any interim decisions by the authority, for instance, the decision to extend an investigation, are excluded from judicial appeal. These exclusions underscore the discretionary powers vested in the Competition Council and reflect a balance between administrative efficiency and judicial oversight.

In addition, the review mechanisms for conduct by the officials of the Competition Council are narrowly defined in Latvian Competition Law. Per Article 9^1 of Competition Law, complaints regarding most conduct are to be addressed to the Chairman of the Competition Council and his/her decision is typically not subject to appeal in court apart from when the behaviour in question constitutes so-called actual conduct. Under Article 89 of the Administrative Procedure Law, only actions that signify a conclusive resolution qualify as 'actual conduct.'[11] The jurisprudential interpretation of 'actual conduct' was notably addressed in the *Moller* case. The case hinged on whether the Competition Council's actions during a dawn raid constituted 'actual conduct.' The Administrative Regional Court, affirmed by the Supreme Court, concluded that such investigative measures do not amount to 'actual conduct' as they are not final settlements but rather part of an ongoing enquiry and are therefore, not subject to separate appeal.[12] Instead, the possible procedural violations are to be reviewed in the context of the final decision, if and when it is appealed.

In exceptional cases, conduct by the Competition Council may be subject to judicial review even if it does not conform to the standard definition of 'actual conduct'.[13] This is the case when the actions in question significantly affect a person's

10. Appeal against the *Latvijas Gaze* 1.10.2013 decision No. E02-48, 2.9.2015 judgment of the ARC, court case ID A43017613; *see also* 17.12.2012 judgment of the SCA, court case ID SKA-369/2012.
11. 7.4.2014 judgment of the SCA, court case ID SKA-510/2014 (7-002-14/16), para. 6.
12. 31.1.2014 judgment of the ARC, court case ID A-7-0002-14/16.
13. 31 January 2014 judgment of the ARC, court case ID A-7-0002-14/16, para. 6.

substantial rights or interests or when they impose a considerable burden on the exercise of such rights or interests.[14] It should be stressed that the database developed under this project only includes judicial review of *final* NCA's decisions and does not include review of purely procedural cases.

3 PRIOR RESEARCH

To date, the systematic examination of competition law enforcement in Latvia has not been addressed in any academic studies. Moreover, there has not been, to date, a dedicated monograph that comprehensively addresses Latvian Competition Law. While the leading legal journal, *Jurista Vārds*, sporadically touches upon issues related to the interpretation and application of the competition rules in Latvia, these discussions do not constitute a thorough scholarly focus on the subject. This gap presents a significant opportunity for academic enquiry and scholarly discourse to contribute to the understanding and development of competition law within the Latvian context.

4 QUANTITATIVE ANALYSIS

4.1 Source of Information

The judgments of the administrative courts are published in a public database, accessible online.[15] The database does not, however, contain all relevant judgments, and there is no reliable search tool that would allow the identification of all relevant judgments. The decisions of the Competition Council are always published on the authority's website, and the database includes information on the status of the decision. Where the decision is appealed, a relevant note is included. However, the identification of the appeal judgments in relation to a decision in question is not always possible. The authority does not publish all the judgments in its database. Instead, only the final decision ruling is made available. Therefore, while the litigation is ongoing, the court case ID number is only known to the parties and is not published. In some cases, it was possible to find the information through the search engine of the court judgments database, but the search engine is not reliable, and it does not show the relevant results in many cases.

Once the final ruling in the case is available, the Competition Council includes it in its database. When the text of the final ruling is available, the court case ID number is normally indicated. It is possible to see a summary of the proceedings using that case ID number.[16] The summary shows how many rulings were issued within the proceedings in question. The case ID numbers are not, however, helpful in all cases. Some rulings only include the so-called archive number of the case, which cannot be used to retrieve the summary of the proceedings. Furthermore, the Supreme Court uses, in

14. 7 April 2014 judgment of the SCA, court case ID SKA-510/2014 (7-002-14/16), para. 7.
15. https://manas.tiesas.lv/eTiesasMvc/nolemumi.
16. https://manas.tiesas.lv/eTiesasMvc/e-pakalpojumi/tiesvedibas-gaita.

addition to the main case ID number, its own numbering system, which is also not helpful in finding other rulings in the same case. Thus, a search through keywords was used for the purposes of the present project. Unfortunately, and as mentioned above, such a search does not provide reliable results. Thus, some of the judgments in the database are missing. Where possible, the database includes such data on the missing judgments that can be extracted from the other rulings on the same decision. Namely, the judgments generally include a statement of facts, which consists not only of a summary of the arguments of the parties but also a summary of the judgments already issued in the same case. The summaries may be detailed but it is only in some cases that coherent information on the missing judgments is available.

If the case is heard in open court, the court decision (consisting of an introductory part, a descriptive part, a reasoned part and an operative part) becomes public information from the date of its pronouncement. Before judgments are published in the public database, the texts are checked, and sensitive data is removed. Article 108[2] of the Administrative Procedure Law provides that those parts of the judgment which contain information that has the status of restricted access information are not published or are published with the relevant information replaced by an indication of why the relevant part of the ruling is not generally accessible. Data on legal persons is generally not anonymised because it is not protected by the right to privacy. However, in certain cases, anonymisation also affects certain types of data of legal persons where there is a legitimate aim to protect commercial interests. In the context of competition cases, the excluded information mostly contains commercial secrets of the parties, but some of the judgments in the database were anonymised to the extent that all data, allowing for the identification of the applicant, and even the decision of the Competition Council itself, were removed.

If the case is heard in closed proceedings, then only the operative part of the judgment is published (i.e., the outcome is published, not including the statement of facts and argumentation). Closed proceedings are, however, extremely rare in competition cases.

4.2 Total Numbers of Cases and Ratio of Appeals

Notwithstanding the challenges in identifying the relevant judgments during the project period, a total of 193 judgments were successfully identified and incorporated into the database.

Prior to 15 April 2008, the judicial system had three tiers, with the ADC serving as the court of first instance. Appeals from ADC judgments were heard by the ARC, while the SCA was responsible for cassation appeals. In this period, the ADC issued sixteen first-instance judgments, twelve of which were appealed to the ARC. The SCA initiated cassation appeal procedures in eight cases and subsequently issued judgments. Of these, the initial SCA judgment was overturned in five cases, leading to a retrial at the ARC. Moreover, in four cases, the proceedings resulted in a second initiation of cassation appeals.

Since 2008, the ARC has functioned as the court of first instance, with its judgments only subject to cassation appeals adjudicated by the SCA. The database includes eighty-five cases where the ARC delivered first-instance judgments (in ten other cases the ARC examined an appeal returned to it from the second-instance appeal). Within this group, sixty-two cassation appeals were initiated before the SCA during the project period, leading to corresponding SCA judgments. When the SCA annuls a judgment from the ARC, the case is remanded back to the ARC. This occurred in seven instances. Additionally, in three cases, the litigation triggered a second round of cassation appeals. Notably, the *Liepājas SEZ* case encompassed a record of three ARC judgments and two subsequent retrials before the SCA.[17] In four cases, the litigation continued after the end of the project period.

Out of an estimated total of 323 decisions made by the Competition Council during the relevant period, excluding summary rejections and dismissals of complaints due to low prioritisation that cannot be subject to appeal, 101 were contested before the administrative courts. Consequently, the proportion of decisions appealed at first-instance level stands at 30%. First-instance courts' judgments subsequently appealed to the second instance stand at 21%.

4.3 Total Number of Cases per Year

Figure 18.1 summarises the number of judgments included in the database per year, according to the instance of appeal.

Figure 18.1 Number of Judgments According to Instances

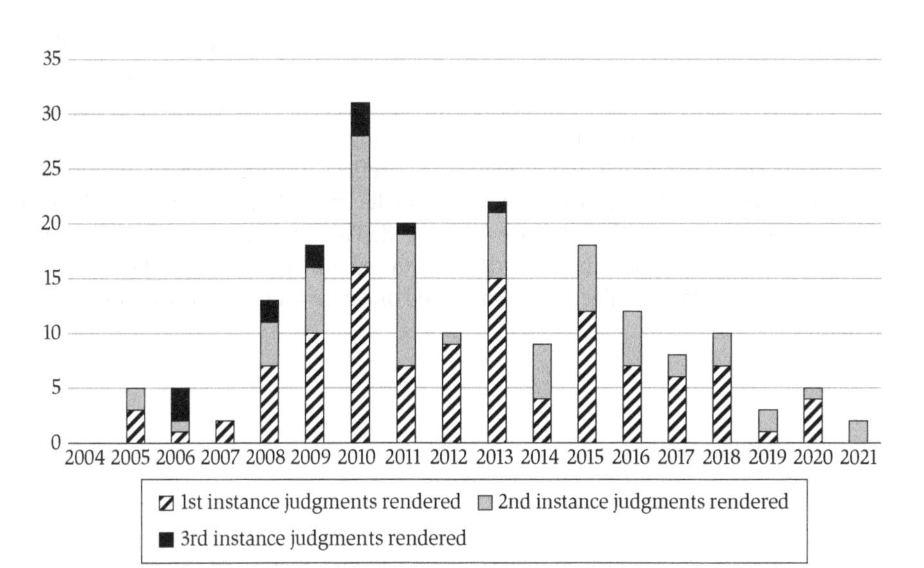

17. Court case number A42569106.

The findings indicate that the changes in the number of judgments across the years can be explained by the number of Competition Council or previous instance decisions issued. The Competition Council rendered an average of 24.75 decisions per year in the 2004-2015 period, the average number falling dramatically to an average of 4.3 in the 2016-2021 period. This explains the comparatively lower number of judgments rendered by the administrative courts in the period since 2018.

Fifty-two out of the eighty-five appeals against the Competition Council's decisions have been examined in a single first-instance judgment. Hence, in most of the cases, appeals by different parties against the same decision are joined into one court case.

Notable exceptions are the *Moller*[18] and *Būvenergoserviss, SZMA et al* cases.[19] The *Moller* litigation commenced following submissions from three entities. Subsequently, the proceedings were split into two distinct cases. As a result, the claims made by the parent companies, which contested the application of the parental liability doctrine (case ID A43009415), were separated from the primary case on substance (case ID A43007317). The Competition Council's *Būvenergoserviss, SZMA et al* decision established the existence of a prohibited agreement between twenty-six undertakings. Most of the undertakings challenged the decision, leading to the initiation of seven distinct cases in the administrative court.[20] These cases were never joined.

Also, in subsequent practice, the Administrative Regional Court typically consolidated proceedings involving appeals against the same Competition Council's decision.

4.4 Success Rates and Outcomes

Figure 18.2 summarises the success of appeals launched against either the Competition Council's decisions or a prior review court instance's judgment. It indicates the ratio of fully successful appeals, partially successful appeals, fully rejected appeals, and appeals that were withdrawn prior to adopting a judgment.

The success rates illustrated in Figure 18.2 reflect the outcomes of all appeals, considering that multiple appeals against a single decision of the Competition Council and or previous instance judgments are aggregated. This aggregation approach means that if different parties appeal the same decision in separate proceedings, the outcomes of all these judgments are collectively considered one case for the analysis presented in this figure.

18. Appeal against the *Buvenergoserviss, SZMA et al.* 17.06.2013 decision No. E02-68.
19. Appeal against the *Moller* 15.12.2014 decision No. E02-31.
20. Court cases' IDs: A43015813, A43015713, A43015313, A43014713, A43012514, A43015213, and A43016313.

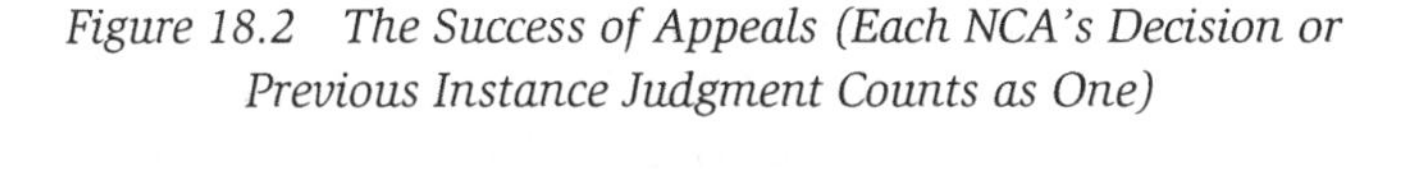

Figure 18.2 The Success of Appeals (Each NCA's Decision or Previous Instance Judgment Counts as One)

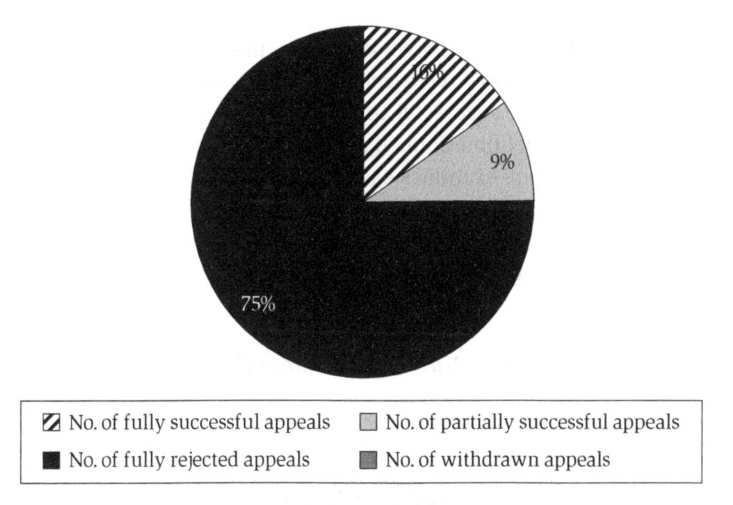

The above figure does not reveal the ultimate resolution of the case (i.e., the final success of the applicant's appeal against the Competition Council's decision). Rather, it specifically reflects the success of appeals against the most recent decision or judgment. For example, if the first-instance court initially rules in favour of the applicants, and the Competition Council's subsequent appeal against this ruling is successful, Figure 18.3 will represent this outcome accordingly. Nonetheless, the percentage of fully rejected appeals is strikingly high.

The analysis undertaken for the purposes of this project covers 101 decisions contested before administrative courts. The Competition Council's database may provide additional insights, revealing that out of the decisions rendered and appealed within the reference period, the courts annulled only three decisions: the *Rīgas brīvostas pārvalde,*[21] the *Latvenergo*[22] and the *Palink.*[23] This represents a 2.97% success rate for the applicants.

The above figure, therefore, highlights that the successful appeals were brought by the Competition Council against the first-instance courts' judgments made in favour of the undertakings in question.

For the sake of completeness, it should be noted that at least one more case should have been added to the list of successful appeals against decisions by the Competition Council. While the litigation in the *Maxima* case[24] ended formally by settlement between the Competition Council and the Maxima company, the settlement was a means for the authority to terminate the proceedings as it was destined to lose.

21. Appeal against the *Rīgas brīvostas parvalde* 5.1.2011 decision No. 1, court case ID A43004311.
22. Appeal against the *Latvenergo* 7.9.2006 decision No. E02-98, court case ID A42526106.
23. Appeal against the *Palink* 23.3.2012 decision No. E02-18, court case ID A43012612.
24. Appeal against the *Maxima* 27.1.2012 decision, court case ID A43011212.

In the preliminary ruling issued by the CJEU in the case C-345/14, *SIA 'Maxima Latvija' v. Konkurences padome*, it was explained that the authority had erred, classifying the agreements of Maxima as by-object agreements. The ARC was expected to rule in favour of Maxima in that case.

Figure 18.2 reveals that the overwhelming majority of appeals against the first-instance court's judgments were rejected. A closer look at the data further demonstrates that most of the successful appeals were rendered by the second-instance courts, accepting the Competition Council's position. This is illustrated in Figure 18.3. Unlike Figure 18.2, this figure examines each judgment separately and differs between the appeal instances.

Figure 18.2(a) first indicates the ratio of the outcomes at first instance, and it shows the success of the applicant's appeal against the Competition Council's decisions.

Figure 18.2(a) First-Instance Outcome

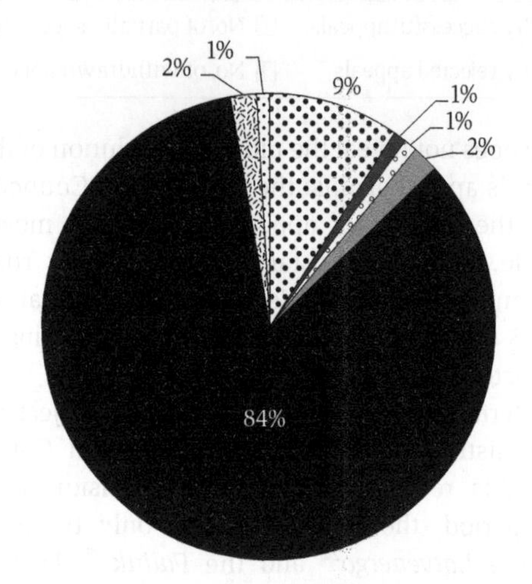

It illustrates that 84% of the first-instance courts' judgments have fully rejected the appeal over the competition authority's decision. Only in ten cases (11.9%), did the first-instance court rule entirely in favour of the applicants. Additionally, there was one instance where the judgment was partially favourable to the applicants. Of the judgments issued, one fully annulled and two partially annulled the Competition Council's decision, requesting the authority to amend the respective decisions. In two other cases, the judgments modified the Competition Council's decisions, specifically concerning the fines imposed. Figure 18.2(a) also includes first-instance courts' judgments, which re-examine matters that were returned to the court by the second-instance judgment.

Next, Figure 18.2(b) summarises the outcome of the cases at the court of second instance.

Figure 18.2(b) Second-Instance Outcome

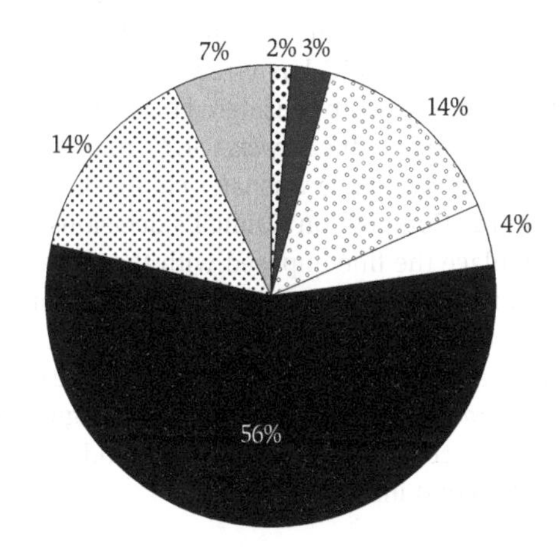

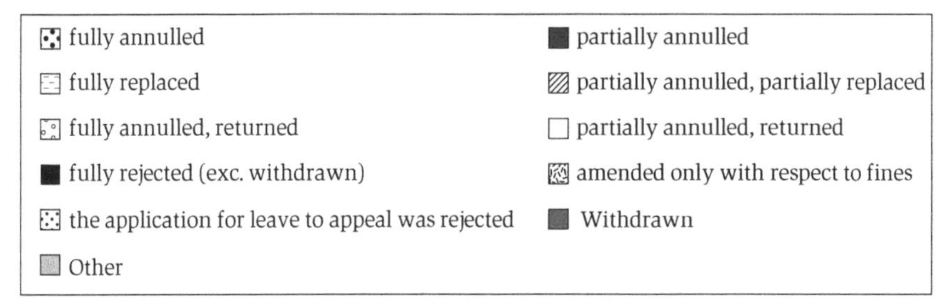

Figure 18.2(b) centres on the success rates of appeals in administrative court proceedings at second instance, irrespective of the appellant's identity, whether it be the concerned undertaking, a third party, or the Competition Council. For the sake of clarity, it should be noted that all participants in the administrative court proceedings are entitled to challenge the decision of the first-instance court (in full or in part).

The study indicates that 56% of the appeals against the judgments of the previous instance failed. In 14% of the cases, the SCA declined to initiate cassation proceedings, resulting in the judgments of the lower-instance court becoming final. In 7% of the cases, the SCA fully or partially accepted the appeal and returned the case to the previous instance court, but the proceedings were closed or settled by the parties, and no judgment was necessary by the ARC (these cases are classified as 'Other' outcomes in Figure 18.3(b)).[25]

Additionally, in 10% of the cases, the SCA fully or partially overturned the judgment of the ARC. While the ARC acted as a court of second instance (until the reform of 2018), it fully or partially overturned the judgments of ADR in 35% of the instances. In most cases, the previous instance judgments are fully or partially overturned by the SCA when the ARC has erred on the points of law or procedure. Initially, the administrative courts were considered to be competent to amend fines. For instance, the fines were amended in the *Liepājas SEZ*[26] and *EL Plūsma and ENERGOREMONTS*[27] cases. However, this practice was later changed.[28] The courts still have the power to partially annul the Competition Council's decisions on fines, but there is no longer competence to replace the fine imposed with the court's judgment.

Figure 18.2(c) summarises the outcome before the third instance. Given the national enforcement system, it should be recalled that a three-tier system functioned until 15 April 2008. Thus, applications filed after that date are only subject to a two-tier appeal system. Thus Figure 18.2(b) covers both those judgments by the ARC, which were issued by the court as a court of a second instance and also judgments by the SCA, which is now a court of second instance.

25. Appeal against the *EL Plusma and ENERGOREMONTS* 25.10.2006 decision No. E02-127, court case ID A42568206; appeal against the *Alpha Ekspress* 22.10.2009 decision No. A43006209, court case ID A43006209; appeal against the *Rīgas brīvostas parvalde* 05.01.2011 decision No. 1, court case ID A43004311; appeal against the *AGA* 7.9.2006 decision No. E02-97, court case ID A42537406; appeal against the *Maxima* 27.1.2012 decision No. E02-7, court case ID A43011212.
26. Appeal against the *Liepajas SEZ* 11.10.2006 decision, court case ID A42569106.
27. Appeal against the *EL Plusma and ENERGOREMONTS* 25.10.2006 decision, court case ID A42568206.
28. 22 December 2017 judgment of the Constitutional Court in case No. 2017-08-01.

Figure 18.2(c) Third-Instance Outcome

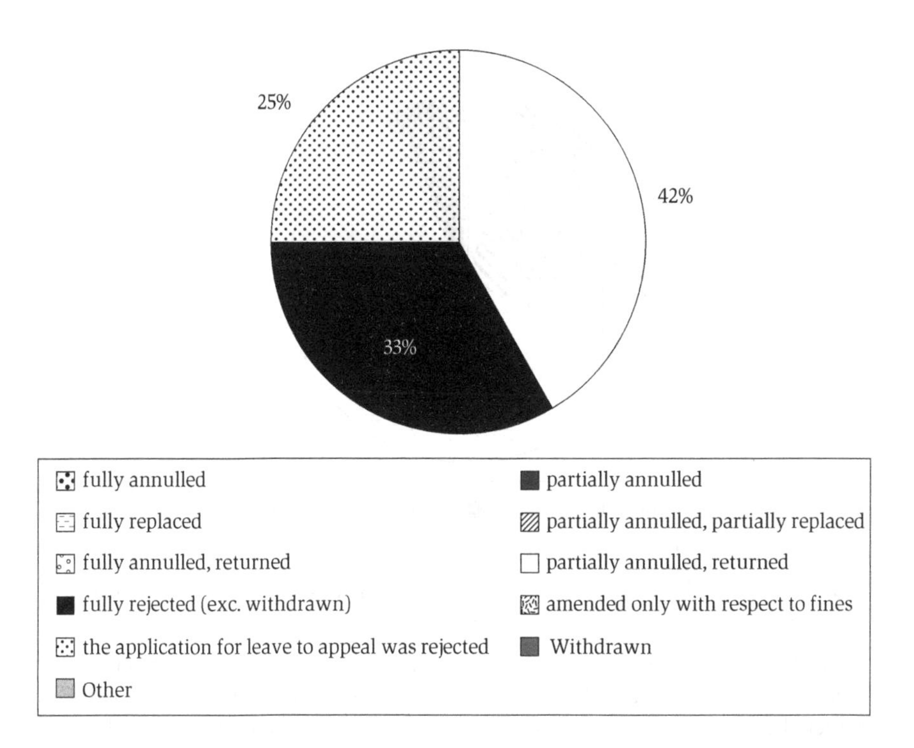

4.5 Type of NCA's Decisions Subject to Appeal

Figure 18.3 indicates the ratio of the different competition law prohibitions subject to the courts' review across all instances of appeal.

Figure 18.3 Rules Being Appealed

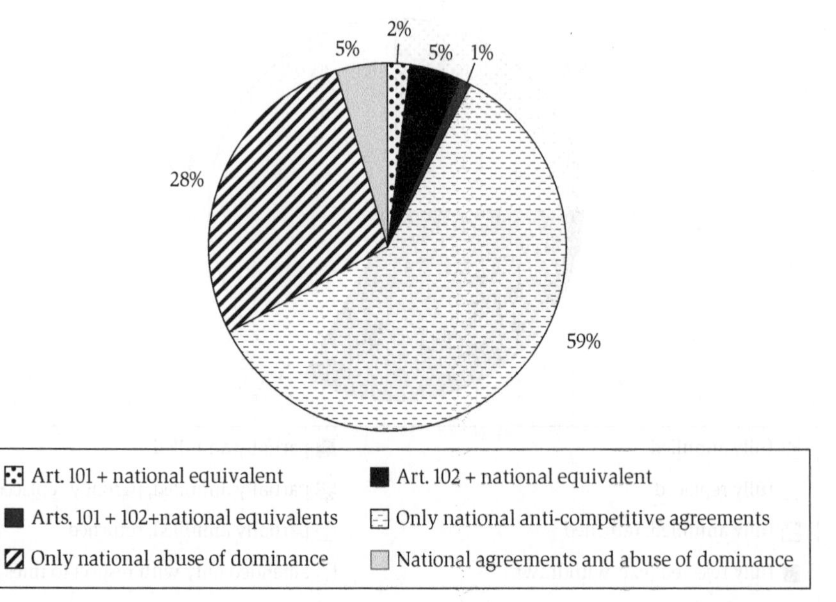

Most of the judgments dealt with cartel cases. In most cases, 59% (115 of 193 judgments), the only applicable rule was the national equivalent of Article 101 TFEU, as depicted in Figure 18.4. Both Article 101 TFEU and its national equivalent were considered in four judgments. Cases concerning solely the national equivalents of Article 102 TFEU constituted approximately 28% of the cases, and both Article 102 TFEU and its national equivalent were applied in nine judgments Mixed cases involving both Articles 101 and 102 TFEU, along with their national equivalents, accounted for about 4.6% of the cases (nine judgments).

Historically, the Competition Council's approach was more diverse, with investigations into abuse of a dominant position and both vertical and horizontal restriction cases occurring in roughly equal measures. In recent years, however, there has been a significant shift towards a focus on the investigation of anticompetitive agreements, which now constitute an absolute majority of cases. Notably, during the 2016-2021 period, the Competition Council identified an abuse of a dominant position in merely five decisions.

Figure 18.4 visually reinforces the aforementioned point, highlighting that anticompetitive agreements accounted for 100% of the judicial review judgments in 2020 and 2021. This pattern began to emerge as early as 2014, as depicted below.

Figure 18.4 Rules Being Appealed According to Years (Each Judgment Counts as One)

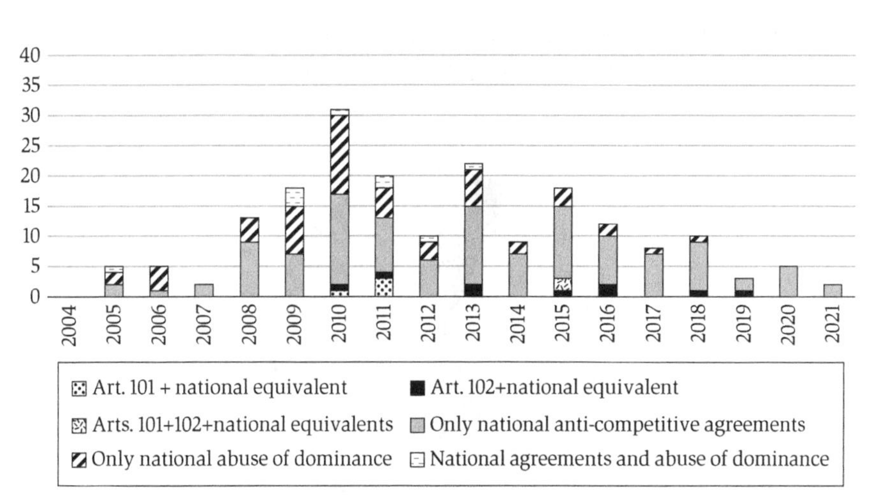

Analysis of the judgments across all instances of appeal, as depicted in Figure 18.5 below, clearly shows that the most frequently reviewed type of rule is horizontal restrictions (in eighty-five judgments), primarily cartels. Vertical restrictions were the focus of thirty judgments, while exclusionary and exploitative abuses were addressed in twenty-one and thirty-nine judgments, respectively. Additionally, another eighteen judgments involved multiple types of restrictions in various combinations.

Figure 18.5 Types of Restrictions

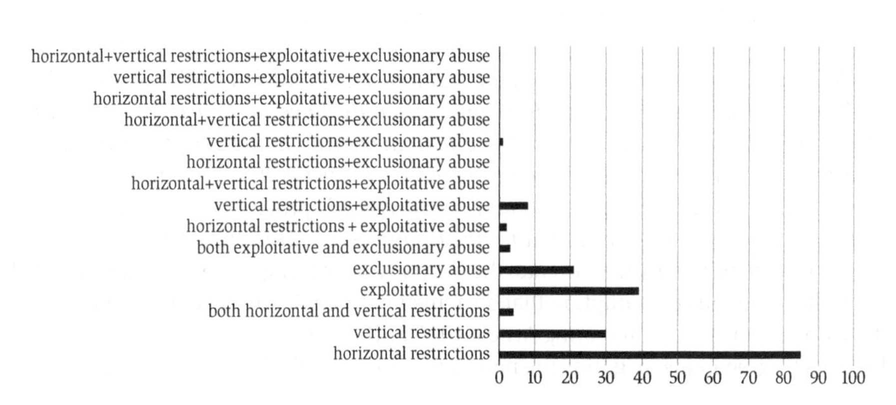

As previously mentioned, in recent years there has been a significant shift by the Competition Council towards primarily focusing on anticompetitive agreements. The vast majority of these cases deal with bid-rigging cartels.

Figure 18.6 below shows that of all appeals against decisions by the Competition Council related to anti-competitive agreements, 93% of those judgments dealt with violations 'by-object'. Only four cases were by-effect violations and four where both by-object and by-effect restrictions were established by the Competition Council.

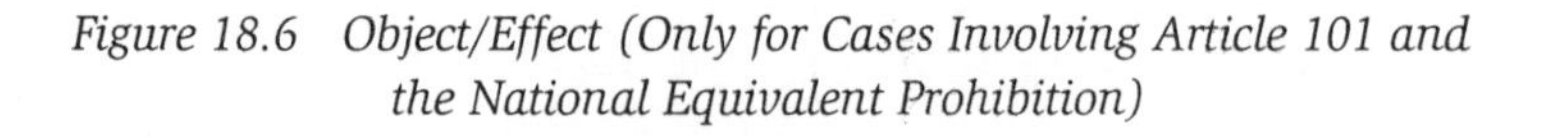

Figure 18.6 Object/Effect (Only for Cases Involving Article 101 and the National Equivalent Prohibition)

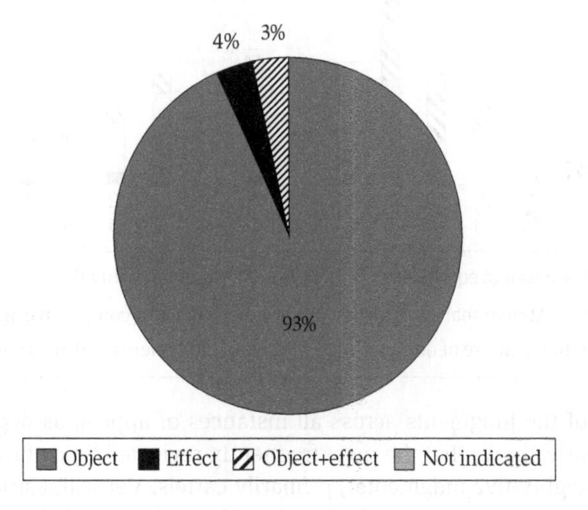

The striking statistics shown in Figure 18.6, are explained by the erroneous approach that dominated Latvian competition law for more than five years.

Similarly to Article 101 TFEU, the Latvian national equivalent - Article 11 of the Competition Law - distinguishes between agreements, restricting competition by-object or by-effect. However, until 2014, the authority and the courts followed the concept formulated by the Supreme Court in its 2009 judgment.[29] In that case, the Supreme Court stated that: '*Agreements concerning the activities listed in Points 1-7 of Article 11(1) [of the Competition Law] are prohibited and null and void since their object is always objectively anti-competitive and generally have the effect of preventing, restricting or distorting competition. The aim of the parties to the agreement referred to in Article 11(1) of the Competition Law to prevent, restrict or distort competition, or the corresponding effect on competition, must be specifically proven by the enforcer only if the factual case does not correspond to [the examples listed] in the norm.*'[30]

Consequently, for several years, the courts and the Competition Council operated under the erroneous presumption that all agreements, explicitly set out in Article 11(1) of the Competition Law (mirroring Article 101 TFEU), should invariably be classified as 'by-object' agreements, negating the necessity to prove their effects. This approach was

29. Appeal against the *STATS, ALTI A et al.* 14.9.2005 decision No E02-31, court case ID A42426505.
30. 29.6.2009 judgment of SCA, *Stats, Alti A et al* case, court case ID A42426505, para. 20.

officially abandoned in 2014.[31] Despite the change in approach, the Competition Council continues to favour a 'by-object' qualification, even in less evident cases.

Next, Figure 18.7 illustrates the ratio of decision types subject to judicial review across all appeal instances. An absolute majority, comprising 154 cases, concerned the imposition of a fine.

Figure 18.7 The Competition Authority's Procedure

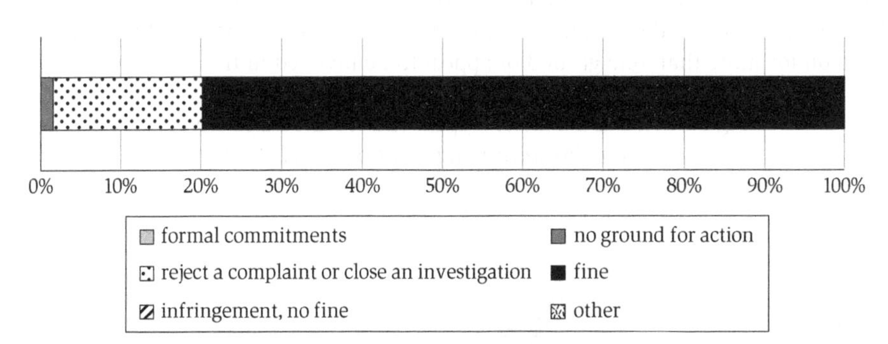

As can be seen from Figure 18.7, in thirty-six of the cases subject to an appeal, the complaint had either been rejected, the investigation had been closed, or the authority had found no grounds for action. Prior to June 2016, under the Competition Law, third parties had the right to submit a complaint, and decisions not to initiate an investigation could be appealed in the administrative court. However, following the amendments to the Competition Law on 15 June 2016, the Competition Council gained exclusive competence to decide on whether to initiate cases. Consequently, decisions not to initiate or to close an investigation are no longer subject to appeal.[32] Although facts provided by the complainant may still prompt the Council to initiate proceedings, it now has full and exclusive discretion in this matter.[33] Moreover, the Supreme Court has clarified that individuals cannot compel the Competition Council to initiate proceedings based on third-party legal obligations, such as failure to comply with a decision of the Competition Council.[34]

31. 3 February 2014 judgment of the SCA, *Rimi and Marno J* case, court case ID SKA-3/2014 (A43009211), para. 9; 28 December 2015 judgment of the SCA, *Empower, RIO et al* case, court case ID SKA-1286/2015 (A43014713), para. 13.
32. Supreme Court, Compendium of Case Law in Competition Matters (case law findings and current case law: 2007-2018), 2018, point 8.1.
33. 10 July 2018 judgment of the SCA, *Sentor Farm Aptiekas* case, court case ID SKA-370/2018 (A43007816), para. 7; Supreme Court, Compendium of Case Law in Competition Matters (case law findings and current case law: 2007-2018), 2018, point 8.1.
34. 17 December 2012 judgment of the SCA, *Rīgas brīvosta* case, court case ID SKA-368/2012 (A43006910).

4.6 Grounds of Appeal

The empirical findings map the grounds on which appeals were raised by the parties and their success rates. To this effect, Figure 18.8 presents these appeal grounds across all instances. The success rates relate to the outcomes of all appeals, considering that separate appeals may have been aggregated and launched against a single decision of the competition authority or a previous court's judgment. That means that if a single decision was appealed by various parties in separate proceedings, the outcome of all those judgments would be counted as a single case for the purposes of this figure. It is common for more than one ground of appeal to be invoked in the same case.

Figure 18.8 Grounds of Appeal (Each NCA's Decision or Previous Instance Judgment Counts as One)

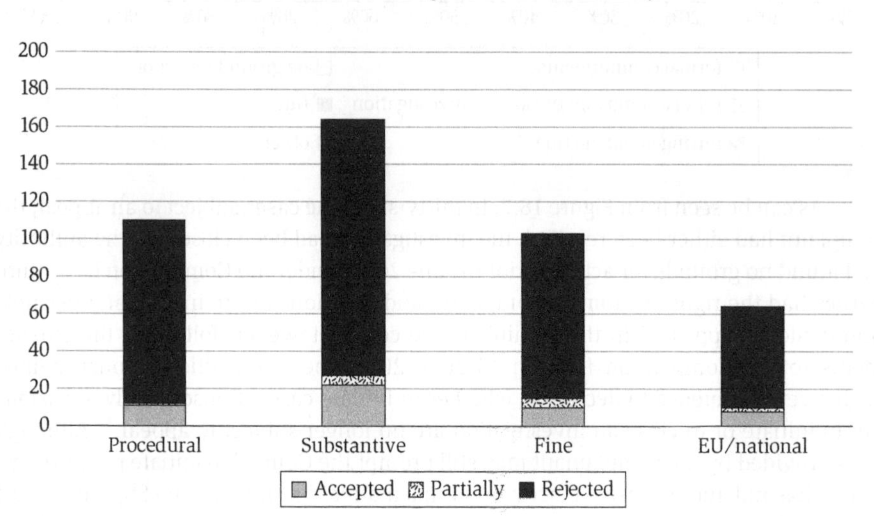

Figures 18.9(a)-(d) take a different approach, focusing on the appeal grounds argued and accepted according to years, and counting each court judgment individually, irrespective of whether there were multiple separate appeals in relation to the same competition authority's decision. Note that Figure 18.9 does not reveal the final result of the case but shows individual results per separate judgments.

It should be noted that the reference to the appeal ground of fines in Figure 18.8 and Figure 18.9(c) only indicates cases where the fining calculation process was challenged in itself. They do not reveal those cases where the fine was reduced because the court accepted another ground of appeal.

Figure 18.9(a) Procedural Grounds

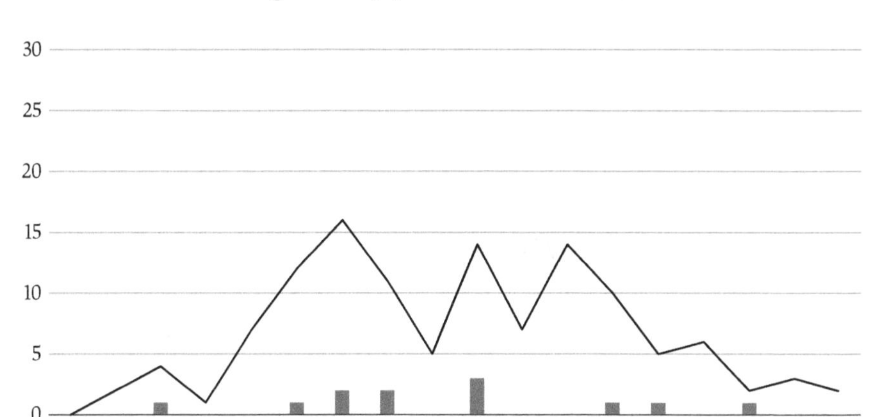

Procedural grounds were raised by the parties in approximately 62% of the cases (121 judgments, each judgment viewed as a separate case) but fully or partially accepted in less than 10% of the cases (in 12 judgments), though no decision of the Competition Council was annulled solely on procedural grounds.

Figure 18.9(b) Substantive Grounds

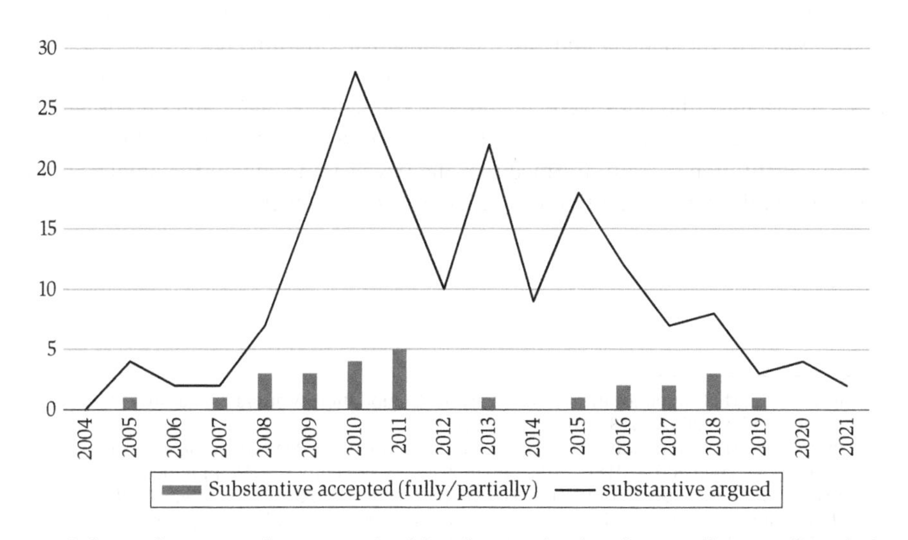

Substantive grounds were raised by the parties in almost all cases (174 judgments, each judgment viewed as a separate case) but were fully or partially accepted in approximately 15.5% of the cases (in 27 judgments).

Figure 18.9(c) Fines-related Grounds

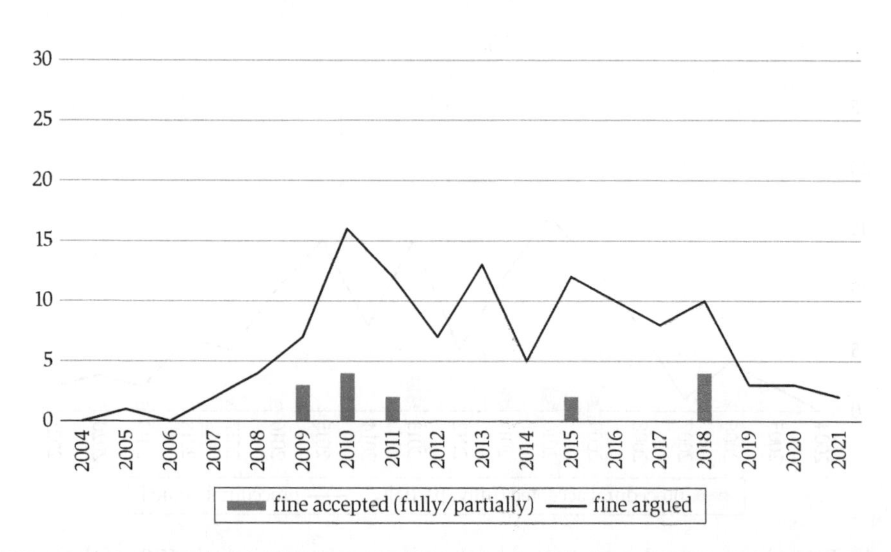

Arguments related to the imposition or the correctness of the calculation of the fines were raised by the parties in almost 60% – 115 cases (each judgment viewed as a separate case) – but were fully or partially accepted in approximately 12.9% of the cases (in fifteen judgments).

Generally, the determination of the amount of the fine is a matter of the sole discretion of the Competition Council.[35] The court may, without interfering with the competence of the institution, assess whether there were procedural irregularities in the imposition of the penalty and whether it was disproportionate.[36]

Initially, the administrative courts were considered to be competent to amend fines. For instance, the fines were amended in the *Liepājas SEZ*[37] and *EL Plūsma and ENERGOREMONTS*[38] cases. However, this practice was later changed. In 2017, the Latvian Constitutional Court affirmed that the power to decide on the amount of the fines falls within the Competition Council's exclusive competence.[39]

35. Supreme Court, Compendium of Case Law in Competition Matters (case law findings and current case law: 2007-2018), 2018, point 9.1.
36. Supreme Court, Compendium of Case Law in Competition Matters (case law findings and current case law: 2007-2018), 2018, point 9.1; 28 December 2015 judgment of the SCA, *Empower, RIO et al* case, court case ID SKA-1286/2015 (A43014713), para. 17; 28 December 2015 decision of the SCA action sitting, *Vidzemes Energoceltnieks, Telms, Spriegums* case, court case ID SKA-1357/2015 (A43012514), para. 15.
37. Appeal against the *Liepajas SEZ* 11.10.2006 decision, court case ID A42569106.
38. Appeal against the *EL Plusma and ENERGOREMONTS* 25.10.2006 decision, court case ID A42568206.
39. 22 December 2017 judgment of the Constitutional Court in case No. 2017-08-01.

Figure 18.9(d) EU/National Grounds

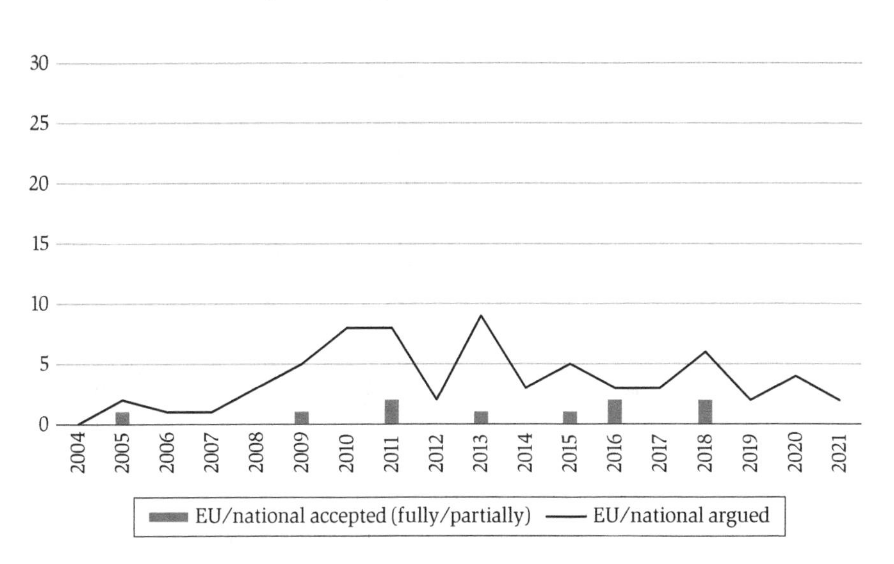

EU law-related arguments were raised in approximately 35% of the cases (sixty-seven, each judgment viewed as a separate case), but only fully or partially accepted in about 15% of the cases (ten judgments). Section 5 below includes some additional considerations on the peculiarities of the process of alignment of Latvian competition law with the EU law.

Next, Figure 18.10 examines the success of appeals in comparison with the types of restrictions at issue. It highlights that most appeals were launched in the area of anti-competitive agreements (involving, mostly, the national equivalent of Article 101 TFEU), and appeals were thus also most often successful in that area.

Figure 18.10 Types of Restrictions Versus Successful Grounds of Appeal

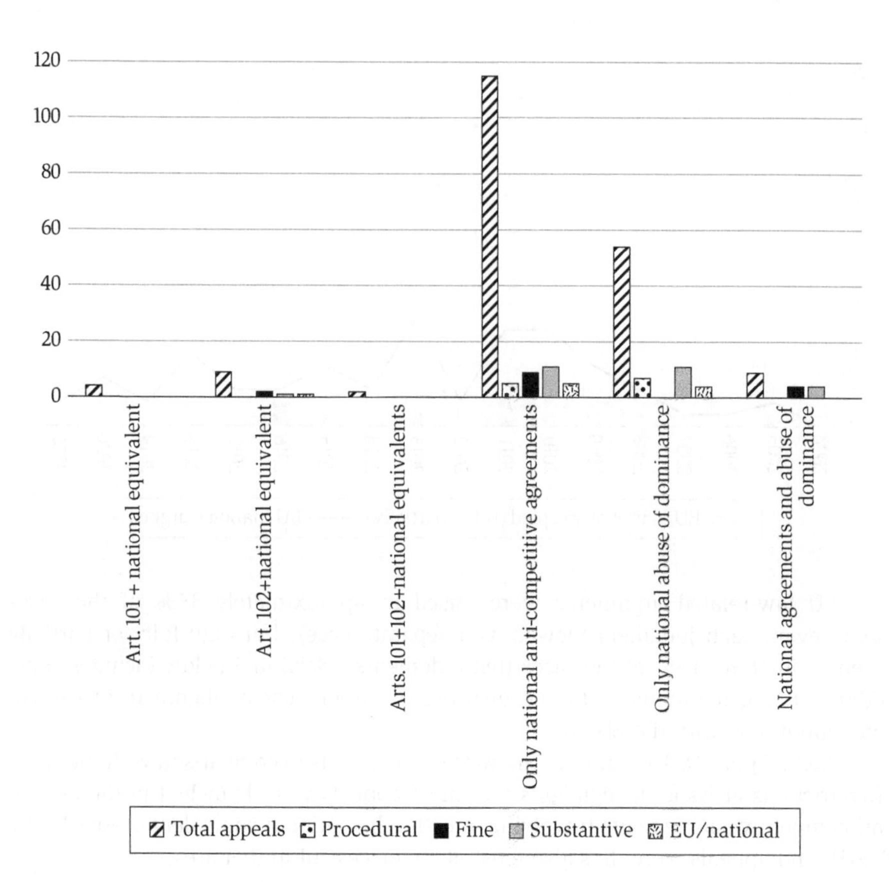

Figures 18.8, 18.9(a)-(d), and 18.10 reveal noteworthy trends. First, procedural, substantive, and fine-related grounds were those most commonly raised by the parties, with their frequencies being almost equal. The (full or partial) success rates for these grounds are also similar – 10%, 15.5%, and 12.9%, respectively. Second, the success rate of substantive grounds of appeal varied over the years. These grounds were more frequently accepted by courts between 2008-2011, with an average of three successful appeals, and less so between 2015-2019, with an average of 1.8 successful appeals. Notably, there were six years within the project period when substantive grounds did not succeed in a single case.

Next, Figure 18.11 indicates that several cases involving leniency applications were subsequently appealed by the undertakings. Yet, while the first-instance court had accepted some of their claims, subsequent court decisions reinstated the Competition Council's decisions with no changes (such cases are classified as partially successful by the figure). Hence, all related decisions by the Competition Council remain in force, as these appeals proved unsuccessful.

Figure 18.11 Leniency

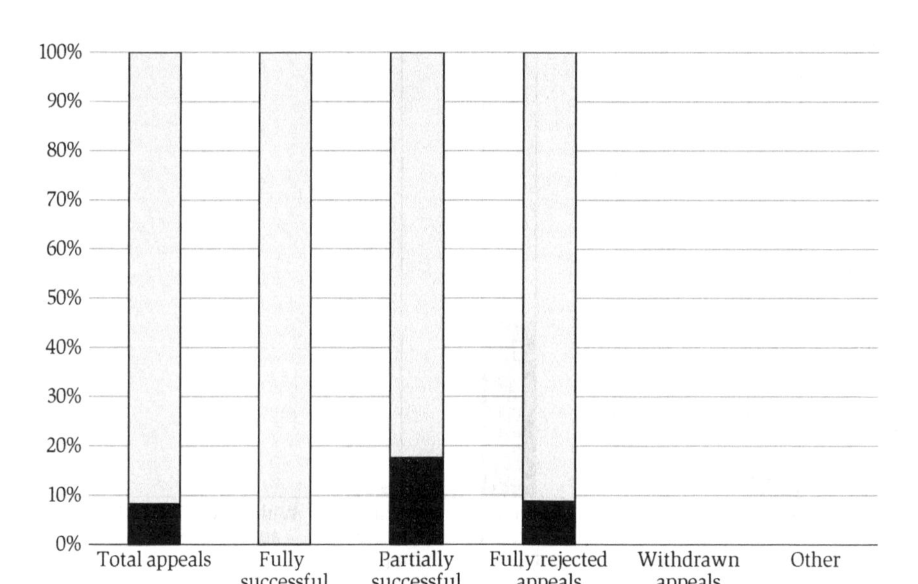

Figure 18.12 below shows the statistics in relation to the settlements between the undertakings and the Competition Council.

Figure 18.12 Settlements

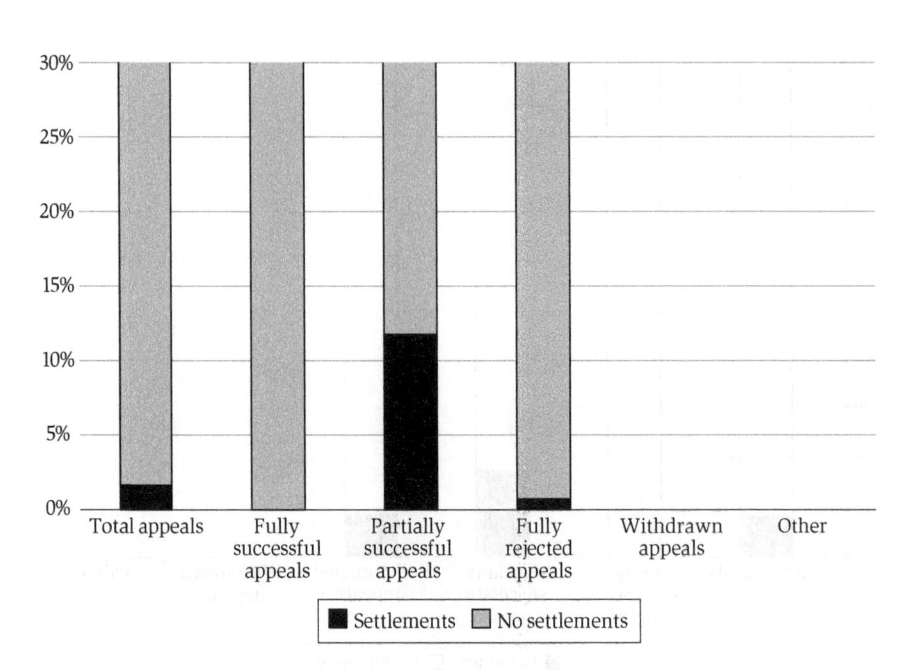

Figure 18.12 reveals that in 2% of all decisions appealed, the undertakings entered into a settlement agreement with the Competition Council during the investigation of the case.

Generally, there are two types of settlements in Latvia.

The first type, which is the focus of the present project, and which is depicted in the above Figure 18.12, allows undertakings to admit guilt before the final decision by the authority is adopted. This early settlement often does not involve leniency. Typically, it includes the undertaking's admission of guilt, commitment to pay the fine, and agreement not to appeal against the final decision. In exchange, they receive a 10% fine reduction[40] (unless under a leniency program, in which case the reduction can be more substantial).

The second type occurs after an appeal is filed and before the decision is finally enforced. Of the cases reviewed for this project, the second type represents a majority. Most settlements of this kind are reached during court proceedings to resolve the legal dispute. Their terms are generally similar to the first type. A key practical difference arises in cartel cases. Under Latvian law, cartel participants face a three-year ban from public procurement following the decision's enforcement. However, this ban can sometimes be lifted if the undertaking agrees to settle before the decision is adopted

40. The 10% reduction is explicitly mentioned in the template settlement agreement, published by the Competition Council within its 2019 Guidelines for settlement in competition cases (available here: https://www.kp.gov.lv/sites/kp/files/kp_old/local/documents/Vadlinijas_izligums_konkurences_tiesibas.pdf).

and commits to implementing a competition compliance program. These types of settlement cases fall outside the scope of the present project.

4.7 Other

A few additional findings are worth highlighting regarding requests for preliminary rulings and third parties' right to participate in judicial proceedings. Only three judgments included in the database were rendered after a preliminary ruling was issued.[41] Nevertheless, preliminary references played an important role in the development of competition in Latvia. In the initial years after Latvia joined the EU in 2004, the primary concern of the courts was to transpose EU competition law accurately and to solidify its proper interpretation. During the first years since Latvia joined the EU, the Latvian courts[42] were frequently addressed with issues that fell within the realms of the *'acte claire'* or *'acte éclairé'* doctrines. The number of clear cases gradually diminished, however. To date, there were six preliminary ruling requests, submitted by the Latvian courts within the scope of the study: *KIA Auto,*[43] *Visma Enterprise,*[44] *Riga Airport,*[45] *AKKA/LAA,*[46] *VM Remonts,*[47] and *Maxima*[48] cases.

In relation to the rights of third parties, the research reveals that a third party – whether a complainant, the government or others – intervened in thirty-seven judgments across all appeal instances. The most common category of intervener was the undertakings concerned (about 57% of all recorded interventions). This category mostly covers cases that historically were admissible but are no longer subject to appeal when the complainant appealed against the refusal to initiate the case (*see* comment to Figure 18.7 above). The government – through public authorities – only intervened in one case.[49]

41. Appeal against the *Partikas kompanija, DIV un Ko* and *Ausma grupa* 21.10.2011 decision No. E02-65, court case ID A43014511; appeal against the *Maxima* 27.1.2012 decision No. E02-7, court case ID A43011212; appeal against the *AKKA LAA* 2.4.2013 decision No. E02-14, court case ID A43012613 Maxima 2015 and A43012613 *AKKA LAA* 2018.
42. Both the ARC and the SCA possess the prerogative to pose preliminary questions to the CJEU under Article 267 TFEU, a mechanism that facilitates uniform interpretation of EU law. While awaiting a CJEU preliminary ruling, the relevant proceedings are typically stayed. Furthermore, at any stage, the courts may seek constitutional review should there be doubts regarding the conformity of a legal provision with higher-ranking legal norms, including the Constitution or international law, although again, it should be stressed that these latter types of cases fall outside the scope of this project.
43. *Tallinna Kaubamaja Grupp un KIA Auto* case C-606/23.
44. *'Visma Enterprise' SIA pret Konkurences padomi* case C-306/20.
45. *Starptautiska lidosta Riga VAS pret Konkurences padomi* case C-159/16.
46. *Autortiesību un komunicešanas konsultaciju aģentura/Latvijas Autoru apvienība pret Konkurences padomi* case C-177/16.
47. *SIA 'VM Remonts' (agrak SIA 'DIV un KO') u.c. pret Konkurences padomi* case C-542/14.
48. *SIA 'Maxima Latvija' pret Konkurences padomi* case C-345/14.
49. Appeal against the *Rīgas satiksme and Rīgas mikroautobusu satiksme* 27.2.2017 decision, court case ID A43007717.

5 QUALITATIVE ANALYSIS

This section builds on the previous quantitative analysis to highlight key elements to review the level of intensity of judicial review undertaken by the Latvian courts, their diverging views on competition law and the consequences involved for the effectiveness of judicial review and the extent to which they demonstrate a degree of judicial deference.

5.1 Scope and Intensity of Judicial Review

An adequate scope and intensity of judicial review are crucial in competition cases, given the well-known severity of the sanctions imposed.

In alignment with the principle of separation of powers, executive institutions possess the authority to initiate and issue administrative acts. Courts are empowered to adjudicate upon the legality of these acts. When an administrative body exercises its discretion, courts generally refrain from prescribing a specific course of action to avoid overstepping into the realm of administrative functions.

The courts have jurisdiction to rule on the legality of an administrative act. Thus, a court must examine whether there have been errors in the exercise of that discretion - exceeding it, failing to exercise it, incorrect use of their discretion or failure to comply with procedural requirements.

As administrative proceedings are designed for expedient decision-making and are capable of considering a broader array of information, they are more suited to efficiency assessments than court proceedings. The courts' domain, distinct from that of public authorities, is not to evaluate expediency but to protect individuals from executive overreach and uphold the separation of powers. Thus, administrative procedures must balance the protection of individual rights with respect for the distinct and independent roles of executive and judiciary branches.

Overall, the Latvian legal system provides for considerable scrutiny of the decisions of the Competition Council - both on questions of law and of fact. In practice the application of the principle of impartial investigation is key. The main objective of the principle is that administrative courts seek to establish the objective truth and courts are also entitled (even obliged, *see* section 2 above) to independently check the sufficiency of the evidence and arguments supporting or refuting the reasoning behind decisions of the Competition Council.

The SCA long stands by its established case law, according to which, '*when reviewing such a decision, the court must comply with the provisions of Section 250(2) of the Administrative Procedure Law that when assessing the legality of an administrative act, the judgment shall take into account only the reasoning included by the institution in the administrative act*'.[50]

50. 29.12.2015 SCA judgment in case No. A43011212 (SKA-8/2015) on the appeal against the *Maxima* 27.1.2012 decision No. E02-7, para. 22 of the judgment.

At the same time, the *Moller* case[51] illustrates that this rule is not interpreted and applied strictly. The case also highlights the intricacies of the sometimes tense dialogue between the courts. The applicants argued that the authority had failed to prove that the restrictions on intra-brand competition should be qualified as restrictions by-effect, not by-object. The ARC annulled the decision of the Competition Council, agreeing with the applicants. Then, the SCA quashed the ARC judgment, emphasising that '*the court should not impose [on the authority] disproportionate requirements for the justification of an administrative act*'.[52]

Therefore, the approach of the administrative courts is, rather, explained by the focus on identifying if there are any deficiencies pertaining to the decision under appeal. If the deficiencies are established, the courts proceed to determine if these significantly impact the case's outcome, thereby constituting a grave error, which, if corrected, could have led to the adoption of a different decision on the substance.[53] The Latvian rule is hardly unique, but the statistics, as presented in this study, speak for themselves.

5.2 Substantive and Procedural Grounds

Turning to success in relation to the separate grounds of appeal (procedural, substantive, fine-related), the empirical data shows that, on average, between 10% to 15.5% of grounds of appeal were successful. The success rate for substantive grounds of appeal was the highest, but there were six years within the project period when substantive grounds did not succeed in a single case. The reluctance of the courts to accept substantive grounds may be explained by the fact that statistically most ARC judgments, siding with the applicants, even in part, are quashed by the SCA.

The SCA is anything but reluctant to rectify errors it sees in judgments by the ARC. The most striking example could be the *AGA* case.[54] The ARC sided with the applicants twice, heavily criticising the Competition Council's decision on excessive and discriminatory pricing. Both times the SCA fully annulled the judgments by the ARC.

As *Bernatt* correctly formulates, judicial deference should be understood as a directive of judicial behaviour under which the courts restrain themselves from substituting their own assessment for those of the competition authority where it is based on the authority's expertise (economic assessments).[55]

51. Appeal against the *Moller* 15.12.2014 decision, court case ID A43007317.
52. 23.9.2021 judgment of the SCA, *Moller* case, court case ID A43007317, para. 26.
53. Judgment of the SCA in cases SKA-73, SKA-88/04, SKA24/04, referred to in the Compendium of the case law 'The Principle of Impartial Investigation – Interpretation and Application', prepared by the SCA, dated 2005 (available here: https://www.at.gov.lv/files/uploads/files/6_Judikatura/Tiesu_prakses_apkopojumi/2016/1-Obj_izm_princips_visparinajums-2005.doc).
54. Appeal against the *AGA* 07.09.2006 decision, court case ID A42537406.
55. M. Bernatt, *Effectiveness of Judicial Review in the Polish Competition Law System and the Place for Judicial Deference,* Yearbook of Antitrust and Regulatory Studies, 9(14), 2016, s. 97-124, https://ssrn.com/abstract=2896823.

Latvian cases do not show, however, a stable tendency for the level of scrutiny exercised by the courts. It is therefore too early to conclude if the current high rate of success for the Competition Council, in defending its cases, is due to the requisite expertise in assessments or due to deficiencies in the proper evaluation of the said expertise by the courts.

Judicial deference is also evaluated with reference to the appropriateness of the fining policy. The grounds pertaining to fine determination have proven to be moderately (compared with the general Latvian data) successful. However, recalculations of fines have not, to date, been made pursuant to final judgments by the Latvian administrative courts. It is therefore impossible to estimate the precise impact of the judgments, which included criticism of the authority's fine-setting methods. Nonetheless, over the years, the reasoning of the authority has evolved and it seems to take into account the case law of the courts on the topic.

Furthermore, *Bernatt* suggests that the courts are to give an appropriate assessment regarding whether the decision was reached after properly conducted administrative proceedings.[56] Procedural grounds were raised by the parties in approximately 62% of the cases (121 judgments, each judgment viewed as a separate case) but fully or partially accepted in less than 10% of the cases (in 12 judgments), though no decision of the Competition Council was annulled solely on procedural grounds.

In a number of cases, seemingly material breaches of procedural law were not accepted as sufficient for the annulment of the administrative acts. A pivotal case was the *Būvfirma L.B.K. and KaimS* case.[57] Article 27 of the Latvian Competition Law prescribes that the Competition Council must adopt a final decision within a maximum period of two years following the formal opening of the case. In *Būvfirma L.B.K. and KaimS* case, the authority exceeded the said maximum period by a couple of months. Nonetheless, the SCA ruled that the authority's decision could still stand, as it was not deemed to be material.

5.3 Alignment with EU Law

Formally, Latvian competition law and practice are aligned with EU competition law and both the authority and the courts regularly emphasise that interpretation of the national equivalents of Articles 101 and 102 TFEU cannot be undertaken if the relevant case law of the CJEU is not duly taken into account.

At the same time and as evidenced by the discussion following Figure 18.6 above, between 2009 and 2014 it was an accepted practice to qualify all anti-competitive agreements, explicitly listed in the national equivalent to Article 101 TFEU, as by-object cases. This is only one example, albeit illustrative, of the structural failure of Latvian competition law to properly align with EU law as a matter of rule.

One of the cases stands out in relation to the Article 267 preliminary ruling procedure. In fact, there were three identical decisions adopted by the Competition

56. *Ibid.*
57. Appeal against *the Buvfirma L.B.K. and KaimS* 21.10.2011 decision, court case ID A43014911, SCA 27.8.2013 decision in the same case, para. 6.

Council in 2012: *Rimi and Marno J*,[58] *Maxima*[59] and *Palink*.[60] In all three cases, the Competition Council assessed the existence of a prohibited agreement, which manifested itself as the obligation of the owners of shopping centres to seek consent from anchor tenants (supermarket chains) prior to leasing the premises in the same shopping centre to a competitor of the anchor tenant. The Competition Council decided that while no actual impediment to competition took place in these cases, the very aim of the restrictive practice was to create an impediment to actual or potential competition. Therefore, the authority did not analyse the existence of the effects of these vertical agreements on competition and confined its analysis to the object of the agreements. All three undertakings appealed against the relevant decisions.

First, the litigation initiated in 2012 by Rimi developed. Even though the correctness of the applicability of the by-object doctrine was argued by the applicant, and the applicant asked the courts to make a preliminary request, both motions were denied. The SCA rejected the need to refer the case to the CJEU, because '*the decision of the Competition Council is not based upon [Article 101 TFEU] and thus the direct applicability thereof is irrelevant in the case*'.[61] The *Rimi and Marno J* decision entered into force in early March 2014.

Second, the *Maxima* case progressed. Similar arguments were made by the applicant. The court of first instance rejected the appeal by Maxima but, this time, in July 2014, the SCA judges accepted that the interpretation of CJEU was crucial for determining the case. In November 2015, the preliminary ruling by the CJEU rejected the notion that vertical agreements of this type should be classified as by-object agreements.[62]

The CJEU accentuated not only the importance of a thorough analysis of all circumstances of the case but also the economic or legal nature of a restriction, contained in a contract.[63] Following the interpretation provided by the CJEU, the SCA concluded that in those circumstances it was not sufficient for the authority to give a very general description of the market, emphasising that the mere existence of the restrictions to sign lease agreements in specific shopping centres was not sufficient to prove a foreclosure effect. Consequently, the SCA reversed the judgment of the first-instance court and ordered a retrial. At this point, the Competition Council settled the case with Maxima.

Third, the *Palink* decision followed the steps of the *Maxima* case and the Competition Council's decision was finally reversed in July 2016.[64]

The *Rimi and Marno J*, *Maxima* and *Palink* cases demonstrate a more general inconsistency in the Latvian judiciary's application of competition law to comparable

58. *Rimi and Marno J* 08.04.2011 decision No E02-20, court case ID A43009211.
59. *Maxima* 27.1.2012 decision No. E02-7, court case ID A43011212.
60. *Palink* 23.3.2012 decision No. E02-18, court case ID A43012612.
61. 3.2.2014 judgment of the SCA, *Rimi and Marno J* case, court case ID A43009211, para. 16.
62. CJEU 26.11.2015 judgment in Case C-345/14, *SIA 'Maxima Latvija' pret Konkurences padomi*, para. 31.
63. 26 November 2015 CJEU judgment in case no. C-345/14, *SIA 'Maxima Latvija v. Konkurences padome'*, ECLI:EU:C:2015:784, para. 31.
64. 29.7.2016 judgment of the ARC, *Palink* case, court case ID A43012612.

scenarios. For instance, while in the *Rimi and Marno J*, the SCA concurred with the court of the first instance that The Court had correctly taken into account that '*the market power of the applicant and Maxima, the significant level of market concentration [...] allows the co-applicants [...] to further strengthen their market power and to exploit the advantages of market power*'. Meanwhile, in the *Maxima* case, only three months later, the SCA changed its approach dramatically and urged the ARC and the Competition Council against the use of a presumption that high concentration or certain market shares prove the existence of market power and, most importantly, the SCA declined to accept the argument that existence of market power and use thereof may be a valid ground for classifying the agreement as by-object.[65]

Although judicial perceptions evolve and the comprehension of competition law principles intensifies over time, the markedly contrasting judgments in these cases, issued within a short span of months, are noteworthy.

5.4 Third Parties' Rights

The law provides that third parties may indeed intervene in competition cases, assuming they have sufficient legal interest. The case law of the Latvian courts reveals that the granting of the status of a third party has become gradually more complex. Thus, a third party can join the proceedings even if it is not the addressee of the appealed decision, but only if the party's rights or legal interests may be limited as a result of the relevant administrative act or may be affected by a court judgment in a case.[66]

According to the current case law of the Latvian courts, purely economic, financial, abstract or social interests (including defence of the general interest) of a person, which are not based on a specific provision of the law, granting subjective rights, are not accepted as an appropriate basis for a person to acquire the status of a third party.[67] Further, a creditor's interest in ensuring that the addressee of the Competition Council's decision is able to meet its financial obligations is purely economic and insufficient to allow participation in the process of reviewing the legality of the Competition Council decision.[68] The SCA also decided that undertakings do not have a subjective right to request the application (maintenance) of a penalty imposed on another undertaking - the addressee of the decision of the Competition Council.[69]

---

65. 29.12.2015 judgment of the SCA, *Maxima* case, court case ID A43011212, paras 19 and 20.
66. Supreme Court, Compendium of Case Law in Competition Matters (case law findings and current case law: 2007-2018), 2018, point 10.1; 29 November 2010 decision of the SCA, *Samsung* case, court case ID SKA-1020 (A43006009), para. 7; 12 February 2015 decision of the SCA, *Procter & Gamble* case, court case ID SKA-540/2015 (A43018013), para. 7; 2 July 2014 decision of the SCA, court case ID SKA-659/2014, para. 4; 4 June 2014 decision of the SCA, court case ID SKA-358/2014, para. 13.
67. 29 November 2010 decision of the SCA, *Samsung* case, court case ID SKA-1020 (A43006009), paras 8 and 10; Supreme Court, Compendium of Case Law in Competition Matters (case law findings and current case law: 2007-2018), 2018, point 10.1.
68. Supreme Court, Compendium of Case Law in Competition Matters (case law findings and current case law: 2007-2018), 2018, point 10.1.
69. 16 November 2016 decision of the SCA, *Rezeknes autoosta* case, court case ID SKA-1551/2016

The existence of a subjective right to participate in the proceedings related to a merger clearance decision has, however, been accepted when the decision is appealed against by a competitor and the addressee of the merger clearance was then invited to participate in the status of a third party. In another case, the SCA refused to accept that the chairman of the board of a commercial company was entitled to be admitted to the case as a third party.[70]

While most of these examples seem correct, the result of the narrow interpretation adopted is that for admission as a third party, the interested party, in most cases, must prove that its interests stem beyond 'purely economic, financial' interests. In competition matters, however, most third parties do have purely economic and financial interests to pursue.

The courts justify their stringent stance on third-party involvement by citing the potential for increased duration and complexity in the proceedings.[71] Although minimising complex and protracted procedures is vital, third-party participation often enhances understanding of the case specifics and can reduce the need for multiple proceedings across various courts. One key advantage of third-party involvement is the provision of market-specific knowledge, assisting courts in navigating intricate technical and economic aspects of a case. This is particularly beneficial given the infrequency of administrative courts initiating expert consultations and their ongoing development of economic expertise. Moreover, third-party contributions can bring diverse perspectives, ensuring a more holistic and equitable judicial process. Their participation may also promote transparency and public trust in judicial outcomes, as it demonstrates the court's commitment to considering all relevant viewpoints. Additionally, third parties can provide critical counter-arguments to the positions of the principal parties, leading to a more robust and thorough adjudication process. In light of these considerations, the advantages of active third-party participation may significantly outweigh the accompanying complexities.

6 CONCLUDING REMARKS

The judicial review of public enforcement of competition law in Latvia was addressed in this chapter. Overall, the Latvian courts are competent to review all the substantive and procedural elements of decisions by the Competition Council. The courts are also competent to review (but not to substitute with their own assessment) those elements of any decision related to the setting of a fine. The courts are not limited to facts, evidence and the assessment presented by the Competition Council in its decisions, but when additional assessments are made they should strictly serve to ascertain that even regardless of any new considerations, the authority's decision remains. The Latvian

(A43010516), para. 6; Supreme Court, Compendium of Case Law in Competition Matters (case law findings and current case law: 2007-2018), 2018, point 10.1.

70. 27 January 2016 decision of the SCA, *Daugavpils energoceltnieks* case, court case ID SKA-SKA-700/2016 (A43015813), para. 5; Supreme Court, Compendium of Case Law in Competition Matters (case law findings and current case law: 2007-2018), 2018, point 10.1.
71. 29 November 2010 decision of the SCA, *Samsung* case, court case ID SKA-1020 (A43006009), para. 6.

legal framework's approach to reviewing Competition Council decisions underscores a delicate balance between ensuring rigorous judicial scrutiny and respecting the autonomous roles of the judiciary and executive branches. While the courts' role is pivotal in safeguarding against executive overreach, particularly in the context of competition law with its potential for severe sanctions, the rules on intervention are generally well-designed and calibrated to avoid encroaching upon the discretion of administrative bodies. The intensity of review undertaken by the Latvian courts can, therefore, in general, be described as comprehensive.

The low annulment rate of Competition Council decisions, as evidenced by the specific cases cited, reflects a tendency towards strong judicial restraint in overturning administrative decisions. This restraint is further manifested in the nuanced approach of the courts to different types of appeal grounds, with a slightly higher, but highly fluctuating over the years, success rate for substantive appeals. The dynamic interplay between the ARC Council and the SCA, for instance, in cases like *AGA* and *Moller*, illustrates the robustness of judicial review in Latvia.

CHAPTER 19
Lithuania Report

Jurgita Malinauskaite

1 INTRODUCTION TO THE COMPETITION LAW ENFORCEMENT CONTEXT IN LITHUANIA

After regaining independence in 1991, Lithuania started major transformations to return to its European roots, and joining the EU was seen as the best option to achieve this. These transformations involved dealing with outmoded technology; setting up capital markets; creating banking, financial and monetary systems; overcoming embedded political systems; re-drafting their laws to allow for new forms of economic organisations; and even changing deep-rooted socialist mentality.[1]

In preparation for the membership of the EU, Lithuania had to implement modern EU-compliant competition laws and establish attendant institutions as part of the harmonisation of their legal framework with the *acquis communautaire* - an essential pre-condition for admittance. Considering that competition itself was non-existent while Lithuania was part of the Soviet Union, competition law presented a new and challenging branch of law. Among other things, the Lithuanian public administration system also had to change.

In common with other candidate countries at that time, Lithuania had a high degree of flexibility in designing their national competition authorities. However, strong emphasis was placed on the requirement that competition authorities are independent of government and enjoy a sufficient level of resources and expertise to deal with competition issues. The aim was to ensure that their decisions were viewed as legitimate by the business community and that corruption was abandoned.[2]

1. J. Malinauskaite, *Merger Control in Post-communist countries*, Routledge, 2010, Chapter 4.
2. *Ibid.*

Lithuania enacted its first Law on Competition in 1992.[3] The first institutions dealing with competition issues were highly influenced by the government. Under the 1992 Competition law, the Competition Council initially existed within the Agency of Prices and Competition under the Ministry of Economy and was formed on the basis of the former State Price Committee. In 1995, the Agency was reorganised into two state administrative bodies: (i) the State Competition and Consumer Protection Office, a governmental agency, which had the status of a permanent executive institution, and (ii) the Competition Council, which acted as a collegial decision-making body applying sanctions for violations of competition (while all the preparatory and investigatory work was carried out by the Competition Office). Both institutions were governmental agencies lacking formal independence from the government. The 1999 Law on Competition re-organised these two organs into a single Competition Council (*Konkurencijos Taryba* – KT), which is an independent body (in terms of decision-making) responsible for the enforcement of competition law. KT has separation of investigation and decision-making: while investigations are conducted by different Divisions, decisions (final and procedural) are taken by the KT Board. Lithuania applies the bifurcated judicial model only with regard to the sanctions imposed on individuals.[4] After examination of the case, the KT adopts a resolution which specifies the circumstances of the violation of the Law on Competition, evidence of the fault of the offender, explanations of the offender, the applicant and other persons submitted to the KT, and their evaluation, reasons for the ruling and legal basis.

The main objectives of competition policy are summarised in the Law on Competition and in the Constitution, which is a supreme law in the Republic.[5] According to Article 46 of the Constitution, 'the law shall prohibit the monopolisation of production and the market, and shall protect freedom of fair competition. The State shall defend the interests of the consumer'. The Law on Competition, however, keeps it simple stating that its purpose is 'to protect freedom of fair competition in the Republic of Lithuania'.[6]

In terms of the anti-competitive provisions, Article 5 of the Law on Competition mirrors Article 101 TFEU (save a 'cross-border trade' element), whereas the national equivalent of Article 102 TFEU is Article 7 (previously, Article 9) of the Law on

3. The Law on Competition, 15 September 1992, No. I-2878.
4. The Law on Competition of Lithuania has an exception with regard to CEOs where only the Vilnius Regional Administrative Court can impose sanctions (i.e., disqualification or a financial penalty) on these individuals. See Article 41(1) of the Law on Competition 23 March 1999 No VIII-1099, (*No. XIII-193, 2017-01-12, announced TAR 2017-01-18, i. k. 2017-01075, as amended*).
5. Article 7 of the Constitution provides that 'Any law or other act, which is contrary to the Constitution, shall be invalid'. 1992, No. 33-1014 (1992-11-30). The current Constitution of the Republic of Lithuania was adopted by way of a referendum on 25 October 1992, following the re-establishment of the independence of Lithuania after fifty years of Soviet occupation. For further discussion, *see* Irmantas Jarukaitis and Gintaras Švedas, 'The Constitutional Experience of Lithuania in the Context of European and Global Governance Challenges', in A. Albi and S. Bardutzky (eds), *National Constitutions in European and Global Governance: Democracy, Rights, the Rule of Law*, 2019, Asser Press, Springer, https://doi.org/10.1007/978-94-6265-273-6_21.
6. Article 1(1) of the Law on Competition, 23 March 1999 No. VIII-1099, (*No. XIII-193, 2017-01-12, announced TAR 2017-01-18, i. k. 2017-01075, as amended*).

Competition.[7] In line with Article 5 of Regulation 1/2003, KT may take the following decisions: (i) require an infringement be brought to an end; (ii) order interim measures; (iii) accept commitments; (iv) impose fines, periodic penalty payments or any other penalty provided by the Law on Competition.

In light of the transposition of the ECN + Directive which intended to empower the competition authorities of Member States to be more effective enforcers and ensure the proper functioning of the internal market, the Law on Competition was amended[8] to incorporate additional safeguards ensuring the KT independence, specifically, that the KT acts independently when enforcing antitrust rules and works in a fully impartial manner, without taking instructions from politicians or other entities, including state institutions and public or private entities. Furthermore, Article 17(4) of the Law on Competition has been amended by adding an explicit provision that the KT would have sufficient qualified staff, and adequate financial, technical and technological resources to carry out its functions and tasks. It will be interesting to see how this provision will be implemented in practice, as currently, the KT has issues in obtaining and retaining qualified personnel. The best university graduates prefer better-paid jobs in the private sector than lower-paid jobs in public bodies.[9]

As part of the amendments, a new provision was incorporated where staff responsible for the adoption of the decisions in KT (i.e., the Chairperson and Council Members, as well as the administrative staff), after leaving state civil service will have a duty to abstain for seven years (an average length of court processes in Lithuania) from representing the other party in matters related to infringements or merger control procedures that they participated in the adoption of the decisions.

Furthermore, the amended Law clarifies the rules on immunity from fines or their reduction where undertakings involved in cartels can be exempted from fines or offered a reduced fine if they cooperate with KT and provide substantial evidence. KT will also be able to impose stricter fines on undertakings for continuous or repeated infringements committed not only in the territory of Lithuania but also in other EU Member States. The amended Law also now explicitly states that the maximum amount of fines will be calculated based on the undertaking's total worldwide turnover in the preceding business year. To improve deterrence there are also new rules for undertakings forming a single economic unit and on liability succession ensuring that undertakings could not escape fines through re-structuring.

Finally, the amended Law also incorporated new provisions for cross-border cooperation with other EU authorities, for instance, requests for information about the documents related to the application of Articles 101 and/or 102 TFEU as well as requests on the recovery of fines imposed on KT or accrued interest in other Member States.

7. The Law on Competition, 23 March 1999 No. VIII-1099, (*No. XIII-193, 2017-01-12, announced TAR 2017-01-18, i. k. 2017-01075, as amended*).
8. On 1 November 2020 amendments to the Law on Competition of Lithuania transposing the ECN + Directive entered into force.
9. J. Malinauskaite, *Harmonisation of EU Competition Law Enforcement*, Springer, 2019; J Malinauskaite, 'Public EU Competition Law Enforcement in Small "Newer" Member States: Addressing the Challenges', *Competition Law Review*, 2016, 12(1). pp. 19-52.

2 THE APPEAL PROCESS OF THE COMPETITION COUNCIL'S DECISIONS IN LITHUANIA

2.1 Overview of the Court System

Lithuania does not have a specialised court for competition law-related infringements. The court system consists of courts of general jurisdiction and courts of special jurisdiction with administrative courts falling under the latter category. The introduction of administrative justice into the Lithuanian legal system occurred in preparation for joining the EU.[10] The intention of this new mechanism was to increase the protection of individual rights by means of the control of the legality of the actions of the administration and to enhance administrative accountability.[11] Two cornerstone acts of this reform were the Law on Public Administration and the Law on Administrative Proceedings, which were adopted in 1999 followed by the establishment of administrative courts the same year.

Specifically, Administrative courts, comprise the Supreme Administrative Court and two regional administrative courts (Vilnius Regional Administrative Court and Regional Administrative Court of Regions which contains four chambers – Kaunas, Klaipėda, Šiauliai and Panevėžys, *see* Figure 19.1). The Regional Administrative Courts hear cases wherein at least one of the parties to the proceedings is the State, a municipality or a State or municipal institution, an agency, a service, or a public servant. Following further reforms in 2001, administrative courts are now fully separated from the system of courts of general jurisdiction. This also led to the establishment of the Supreme Administrative Court, which is the appellate instance for cases heard by the regional administrative courts as courts of the first instance. The order, according to which cases in the disputes arising from the administrative legal relationship are solved, is provided in the Law on Administrative Proceedings.[12] Article 3(1) of the Law on Administrative Proceedings notes that administrative courts settle disputes arising in the domain of public administration. Mostly, administrative courts deal with cases in the following sectors: competition, data protection, financial industry, electronic communications, energy market, waste management, food industry and alcoholic beverages.

Pursuant to a general rule, administrative courts carry out a full review of administrative acts and decisions. This means that the judicial review of administrative acts and decisions is based on both, the legality of the decision and also on factual questions and circumstances.

10. A. Andrijauskaite, 'Administrative Procedure and Judicial Review in Lithuania' Chapter 12. In Giacinto della Cananea and Mauro Bussani (eds), Judicial Review of Administration in Europe (OUP, 2021) DOI: 10.1093/oso/9780198867609.003.0012.
11. B. Pranevičiene and E. Bilevičiute, Administrative Justice System in Lithuania: Genesis, Development and Tendencies, *Visuomenes Saugumas Ir Viešoji Tvarka/Public Security and Public Order* 2020 (25).
12. Law on Administrative Proceedings of the Republic of Lithuania, 14 January 1999, No. VIII-1029 as amended.

In the context of competition law, two courts require special attention – Vilnius Regional Administrative Court and Supreme Administrative Court. There are no specific competition law divisions or chambers in these courts devoted to solving competition law cases. Yet, the judges specialise in different fields, for instance, competition, data protection, etc. and engage in continuous professional development.[13]

Figure 19.1 The Supreme Administrative Court

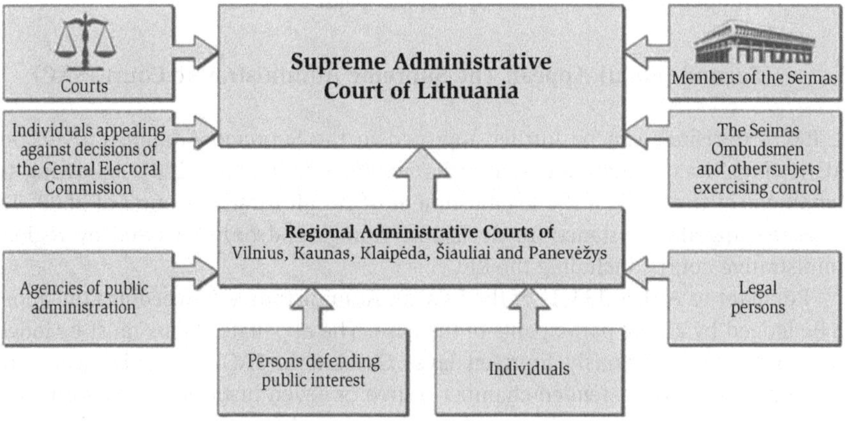

Source: Supreme Administrative Court of Lithuania, Annual Report of 2014.

2.2 First-Instance Appeal: Vilnius Regional Administrative Court (REC)

The KT decisions (resolutions) can be appealed to the Vilnius Regional Administrative Court (REC) in writing within one month (previously, twenty days) after receipt of the resolution of the Competition Council, or after the date of publication of the resolution, depending on which one is first.[14]

The filing of an appeal regarding a resolution of the KT, by which a fine is imposed on an undertaking, does not suspend the enforcement of the KT's decision unless either the KT or the court decides otherwise. The Vilnius Regional Administrative Court (REC) has exclusive jurisdiction to hear these appeals. The KT's decisions may be appealed on both procedural and substantive grounds. Upon hearing the appeal against the KT resolution, the REC shall adopt one of the following decisions:

13. Association of the Councils of State and Supreme Administrative Jurisdictions of the European Union, 'The Judicial review of Regulatory Authorities'. Answers to questionnaire: Lithuania (The Supreme Administrative Court of Lithuania). Paris, 6 December 2021. Available at: Lithuania.pdf (aca-europe.eu) (accessed 21 December 2022).
14. Article 33(2) of the Law on Competition.

(1) to uphold the resolution and reject the appeal;
(2) to revoke the resolution or its individual sections and refer the case back to the KT for a supplementary investigation;
(3) to revoke the resolution or its individual sections;
(4) to amend the resolution on concentration, application of sanctions or interim measures.[15]

According to Article 98(1) of the Law on Administrative Proceedings, the judgments of the REC (or judgments of the other administrative courts of first instance) become final after the term for their appeal has passed.

2.3 Second (Final) Appeal: The Supreme Administrative Court (SAC)

The REC's decisions can be further appealed to the Supreme Administrative Court (SAC), which was formed and started its activities in January 2001, following the amendment of the Law on the Establishment of Administrative Courts of 2000. The SAC is the appellate instance for decisions, rulings and orders passed by regional administrative courts, including the REC.

Pursuant to Article 134(1) of the Law on Administrative Proceedings the appeal can be lodged by all the participants of the case. The appellate claims must be lodged within thirty days (previously, fourteen days). Cases at the SAC are heard by a chamber of three justices.[16] An extended chamber of five or seven justices may be formed for hearing complex cases or such a case may be referred to the plenary session of the court. The SAC reviews the contested rulings in full. The SAC decisions are final and definitive (they cannot be reviewed in the cassation instance). In case unlawful conduct attributable to the public authorities is established, the SAC has the power to revoke administrative acts or to set an injunction to do or not to do something. Lithuanian law recognises the state's liability for the damages caused by public institutions (and their officials). The duty to remedy the damage is also a constitutional principle.[17] The SAC is also responsible for the formation of the uniform practice of administrative courts in applying laws.[18]

Specifically, pursuant to Article 144(1) of the Law on Administrative Proceedings, the SAC may issue one of the following decisions:

(1) leave the decision of the court of first instance (or the REC in this case) unchanged and reject the appellate claim;
(2) annul the REC decision and issue a new judgment;
(3) change the REC decision;

15. Article 34 of the Law on Competition.
16. Supreme Administrative Court, Annual Report of 2017. Available at: uju5t7qv w2geekc96bmtqccpnswc6867 (lvat.lt) (accessed 15 September 2022).
17. Association of the Councils of State and Supreme Administrative, 'The Judicial review of Regulatory Authorities', December 2021. Available at: Lithuania.pdf (aca-europe.eu) (accessed 15 September 2022).
18. *Ibid.*

(4) annul - in whole or in part - the REC decision and send the case back to the REC;
(5) annul the REC decision and close the case or leave the claim unsolved if there are circumstances listed in Articles 103 and 105 of the Law on Administrative Proceedings.[19]

3 PRIOR RESEARCH

There is no comprehensive research conducted in the field of judicial review of the NCA's decisions in Lithuania. Previous studies have focused on more general aspects, such as the development of competition law in Lithuania.[20] Those studies to some extent have also included a description of the judicial review of administrative decisions. There has been empirical research undertaken by Grigaraviciene,[21] with the emphasis being placed solely on restrictive agreements in the context of public procurement; *inter alia*, this study also covered judicial review of the KT's decisions in this context.

4 QUANTITATIVE ANALYSIS

This section examines the findings resulting from applying a systematic analysis of the review of competition law enforcement during the period May 2004 to April 2021. It embraces judicial review of final decisions (resolutions) of KT issued after Lithuania joined the EU.

4.1 Source of Information

As far as the information on the courts' decisions in Lithuania is concerned, there are several options. First, the courts publish annual as well as monthly reports of their cases.[22] Second, there is a publicly available database 'eTeismai' (based on the LITEKO system) where non-confidential decisions of all the courts are available.[23] However, this database is not comprehensive. Any search by some keywords or other defined

19. For instance, Article 103 of the Law on Administrative Proceedings specifies eleven scenarios when the court can decide to terminate the claim, including when the case does not fall under administrative courts competence. Article 105 of the Law on Administrative Proceedings defines further six circumstances when a claim can be dismissed. Law on Administrative Proceedings (consolidated version from 16 November 2022 to 31 December 2022), No VIII-1029.
20. *See*, for instance, J. Gumbis et al., *Competition Law in Lithuania* (Kluwer, 2014); J Gumbis et al., *Competition Law in Lithuania* 3rd ed. (Kluwer, 2019) J. Gumbis et al., Lithuania. In F Denozza and A Toffoletto (eds) IEL Competition Law (Kluwer, 2019).
21. R. Grigaraviciene 'Problems of Qualifying the Agreements Restricting the Competition during the Public Procurement in Lithuanian Law: Theory and Practice', Master's thesis, Vilnius 2017 (in Lithuanian).
22. Naujausia teismo praktika | Lietuvos vyriausiasis administracinis teismas (lvat.lt).
23. Pagrindinis - eTeismai.

criteria is completely unworkable and unreliable. It has also been noted that this database does not include all the administrative court decisions.[24] Third, there is a sophisticated database INFOLEX.PRAKTIKA with all Lithuanian laws, by-laws and all the courts' decisions. This database is largely used by practitioners and public bodies. However, its subscription is very expensive. Therefore, there is limited accessibility to this database and the general public cannot easily retrieve the courts' decisions.

In terms of this project, the KT database was used to find the relevant cases. This was conducted manually by reviewing all KT's decisions/resolutions using a year-by-year mode, then identifying the decisions that were appealed and finally, selecting only the decisions related to Articles 101 and 102 TFEU and/or domestic equivalents, therefore, excluding any decisions related to unfair competition, concentration etc. The period searched was all judgments issued and made public from 1 May 2004 to April 2021 relating to NCA decisions rendered in this timeframe. Specifically, the appeals were searched from the KT's decisions decided after Lithuania joined the EU, which was 1 May 2004. It included not only infringement decisions but also settlements, commitments, as well as decisions not to launch an investigation or discontinue an investigation. Most certainly, decisions related to fines were also incorporated, as this is the most common ground for appeal.

In terms of limitations, some first-instance decisions were not available on the KT platform. Therefore, the input on the first-instance decisions was taken from the second-instance decisions (as the SAC reviews the previous court's decision). Yet, this meant that some aspects, such as the judges' names or the REC case numbers were not identified.

4.2 Total Number of Cases

The database includes 103 judgments (both first instance and second instance). The data reveals that the NCA's decisions are appealed on a regular basis. Specifically, 81 % of the NCA's decisions were appealed to the REC, and 83 % of the REC's judgments have been appealed to the SAC. In other words, the majority of cases are appealed in both instances, with fifty-five judgments decided by REC and forty-eight decided by SAC. On average, there are approximately five appeal decisions per year across both instances. In 2011, there were the highest number of recorded cases – fifteen under both instances of appeal, followed by 2012, which recorded twelve cases and 2016 – eight cases (Figure 19.2). It is difficult to explain this peak. However, there are a few facts that may explain the decline in the number of cases from 2013. First, the new chairman of the KT Keserauskas was appointed in April 2011 followed by some further changes in the Board and its directions. Second, the KT launched its prioritisation policy in 2012, enabling it to set its own priorities and concentrate its limited resources in specific areas identified as being of greatest importance.[25]

24. J. Batura, *The implementation of the doctrine 'stare decisis' in administrative rulings in Lithuania: theoretical and practical aspects*, Master's thesis, Vilnius, 2010 (in Lithuanian).
25. Resolution No. 1S-89 'Concerning Priority of the Activities of the Lithuanian Competition.'

Figure 19.2 Number of Judgments According to Instances

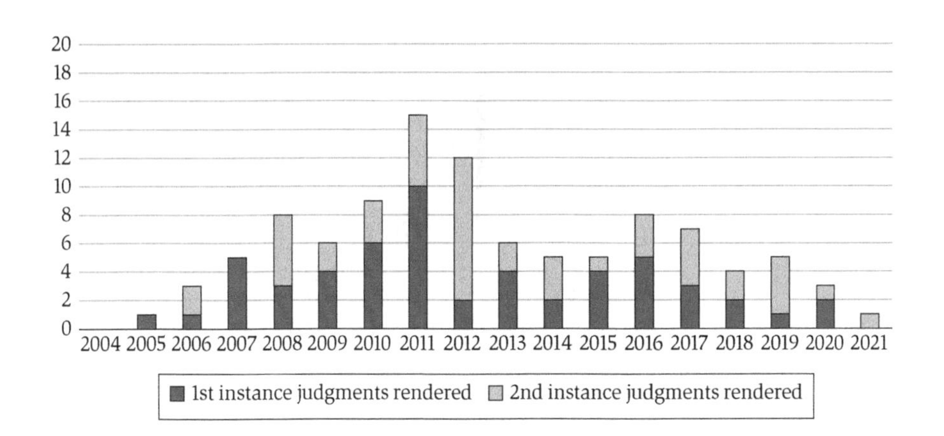

4.3 Success Rates and Outcomes

Figure 19.3 demonstrates the success rate of appeals launched against NCA's decisions or on a previous instance's judgment. The success rates shown in Figure 19.3 relate to the outcomes of all appeals, meaning that separate appeals launched against a single NCA decision or previous court judgment were aggregated. Therefore, for the purpose of this study, if an NCA decision was appealed by various parties in separate proceedings, the outcome of all those judgments was counted as a single case.

Overall, Figure 19.3 indicates that the success rate of appeal is relatively low – 51 % of the appeals on the NCA's or REC decisions were fully rejected. It seems that the courts in general confirm the KT's decisions. This is in line with general administrative courts' practice in Lithuania, as only rarely do administrative courts amend and modify the appealed decision themselves.[26] Appeals in relation to approximately 48% of the NCA decisions were either partially or fully successful. The partially successful category – 33 % predominantly includes cases in relation to the reduction of fines. One must note that there is an overlap between substantive grounds and fines, as in most cases, the courts would uphold an infringement decision but would reduce a fine imposed by the KT. In most cases, the fines imposed by the KT were reduced by the courts either in the first or second instance. This is a possible explanation for the high number of appeals.

26. Association of the Councils of State and Supreme Administrative Jurisdictions of the European Union, 'The Judicial review of Regulatory Authorities'. Answers to questionnaire: Lithuania (The Supreme Administrative Court of Lithuania). Paris, 6 December 2021. Available at: Lithuania.pdf (aca-europe.eu) (accessed 21 December 2022).

Figure 19.3 Success of Appeals (Each NCA's Decision or Previous Instance Court Counts as One)

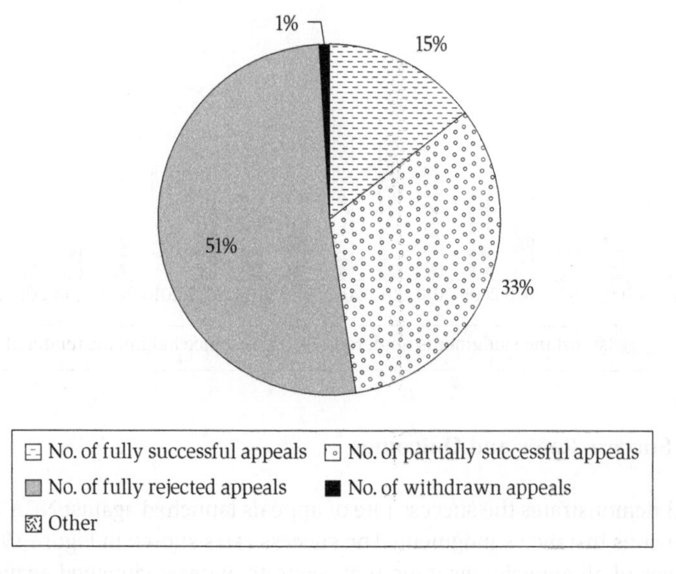

Figure 19.3 shows in more detail the first-instance outcome. Similar to Figure 19.3 above, approximately 58% of all appealable cases were fully rejected by the REC and 44% by the SAC. In most cases, the changes were made in relation to fines (i.e., the fines were reduced). There has not been a single case where the court (in either instance) would increase the fine.

Figure 19.4(a) First-Instance Outcome

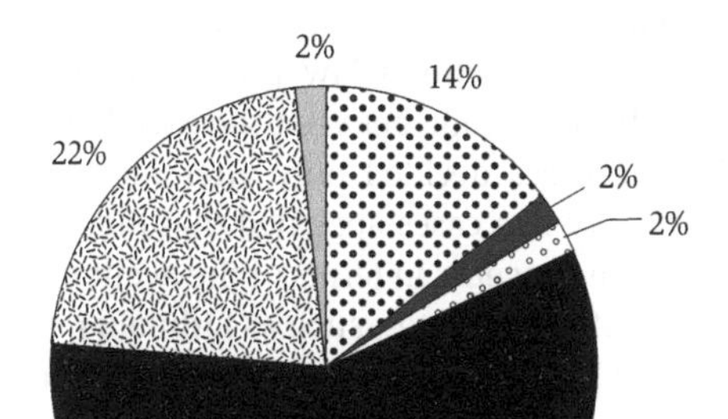

Figure 19.4(b) Second-Instance Outcome

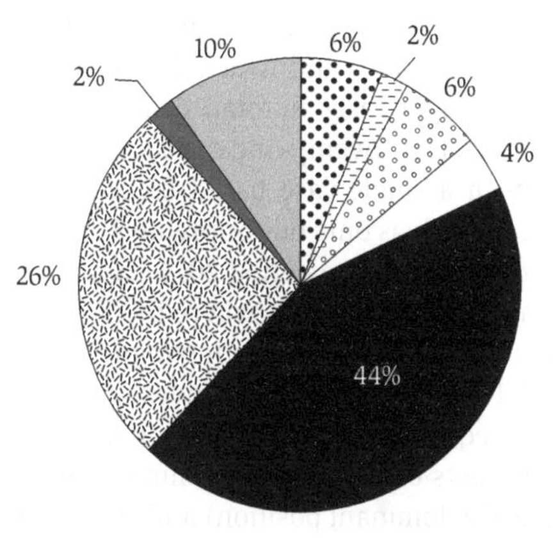

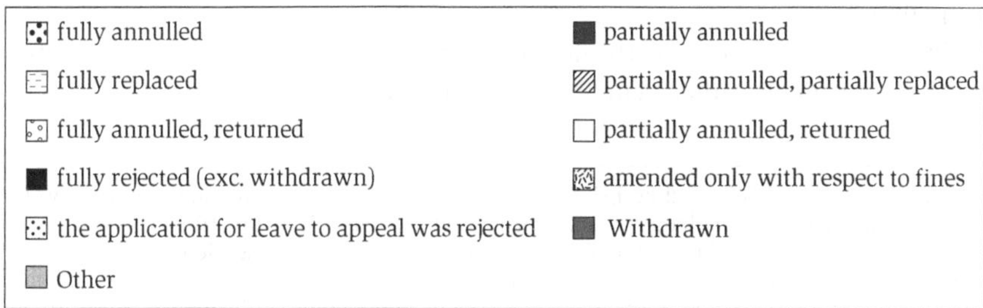

4.4 Types of NCA's Decisions Subject to Appeal

This report has also investigated the cases decided by the KT based on the different antitrust provisions over seventeen years. Figure 19.5 indicates that competition cases have predominantly focused on the national rules (i.e., 79 out of 103 cases were decided on the Law on Competition). The rest of the proceedings involved a combination of both the EU and domestic provisions. It must be noted that Lithuania had an obligation to enforce the EU competition law provisions under Regulation 1/2003 (provided the element of effect on trade between the Member States was met), as the statistical data includes the cases decided only after May 2004. In the 2004–2021 period, there were only twenty-five cases appealed that involved an EU law element. These empirical findings raise concerns in terms of the accurate application of EU law. One may argue that smaller Member States, such as Lithuania, are more exposed to the obligation of enforcement of EU competition provisions, as there are many businesses where economies of scale exceed the demand of a small country. Furthermore, prioritisation policies drive the NCAs to focus on severe anti-competitive cases instead of following all meritless complaints. Therefore, provided the element of 'effect on trade between Member States' is properly applied, this aspect should be easily met in small Member States due to their integrated national markets and the EU competition law provisions should be applied instead (or simultaneously) of national law. Logically, the application of national law should be diminishing.[27]

Furthermore, there is a clear domination of the national equivalent of Article 101 TFEU, as 54% of appeals were related to national anti-competitive agreements (in total 73% – based on both Article 101 TFEU and Article 5, and solely on Article 5). While there were some (i.e., twenty-eight cases in total) dealing with abuse of a dominant position based on both national law (twenty-one cases) and EU law (seven cases) over the years, there has not been a single case based on Article 102 TFEU or national equivalent since 2016 (e.g., there was only one Supreme Administration court decision in 2016 related to this article). During the period 2016–2021, there have been thirteen cases related to abuse of a dominant position where the KT has refused to initiate an investigation or terminated the investigation (with two of them subject to the commitments). For instance, the KT[28] in 2018 closed the investigation into the compliance of *Swedbank* actions with the requirements of the Law on Competition upon *Swedbank* submitting written commitments essential for the elimination of the alleged competition law breach (i.e., abuse of a dominant position) and creating preconditions to avoid it in the future.[29]

Overall, Figure 19.5 clearly demonstrates that the KT places its priority on restrictive agreements rather than abuse of a dominant position.

27. J. Malinauskaite, (2016) 'Public EU competition law enforcement in small "newer" Member States: addressing the challenges'. *Competition Law Review*, 12(1). pp. 19-52.
28. Under Article 28(3)2 of the Law on Competition No. VIII-1099 as amended.
29. During the investigation the KT examined whether *Swedbank* abused its dominant position by including certain provisions into *Bank Link* service agreements with undertakings providing online payment collection services to e-shops. Such provisions were seen as restricting the aforementioned undertakings' ability to offer new online payment collection services – payment initiation services – to *Swedbank* customers. To assess the suitability and appropriateness of these commitments, the KT published them on its website for public consultations and sent them to the interested parties. After considering the comments and proposals received during the public consultations, *Swedbank* amended the proposed commitments. KT (2018) Newsletter.

Figure 19.5 Rule Being Appealed

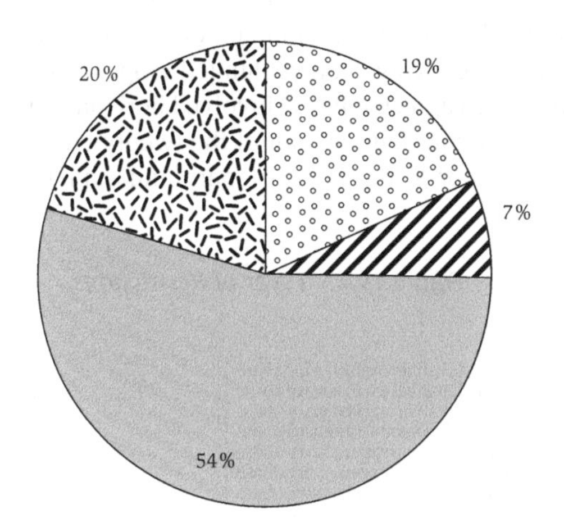

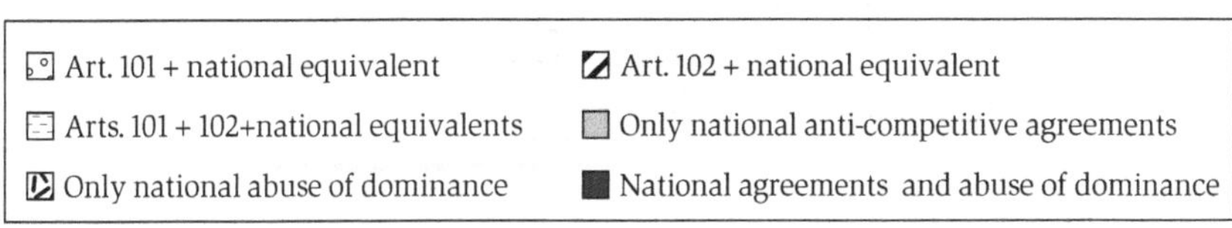

Figure 19.6 further identifies the trend when examining the type of prohibitions according to years. There is a clear focus on restrictive agreements, especially based on national law. Only in 2006, 2009 and 2014, there were a slightly higher number of cases decided on the national provision of abuse of a dominant position.

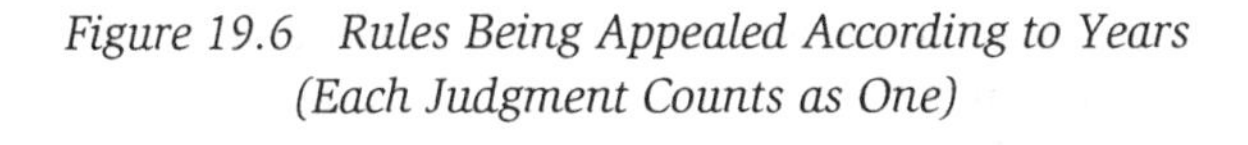
Figure 19.6 Rules Being Appealed According to Years (Each Judgment Counts as One)

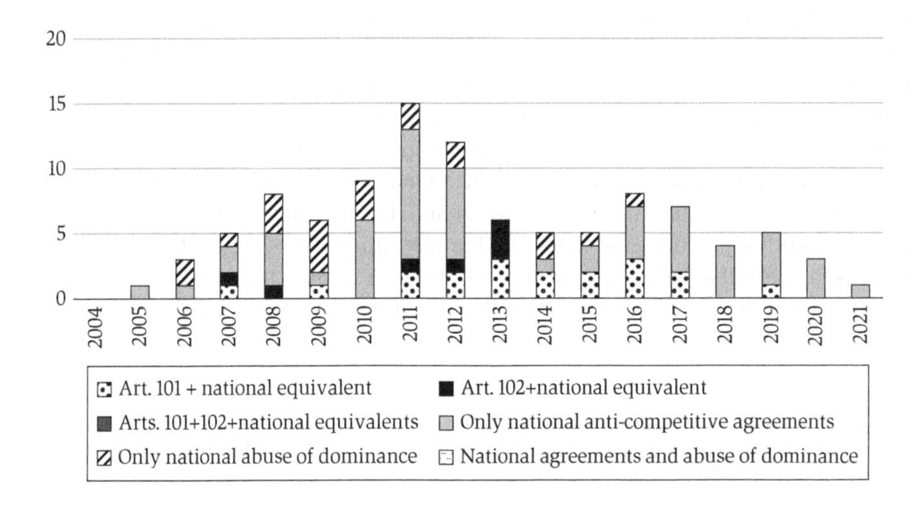

The report has also explored the specific restrictions being appealed, such as horizontal, vertical restrictions; exploitative, and exclusionary abuse. Figure 19.7 indicates that even in relation to the prohibition of anti-competitive agreements under national law, appeals have involved only a limited range of issues. 73% (75 cases out of 103) related to restricted agreements, 62 involved horizontal agreements. In terms of abuse of a dominant position, fourteen out of the twenty-eight NCA decisions related to exclusionary practices or to both exclusionary and exploitative practices (twelve cases).

Figure 19.7 Types of Restrictions

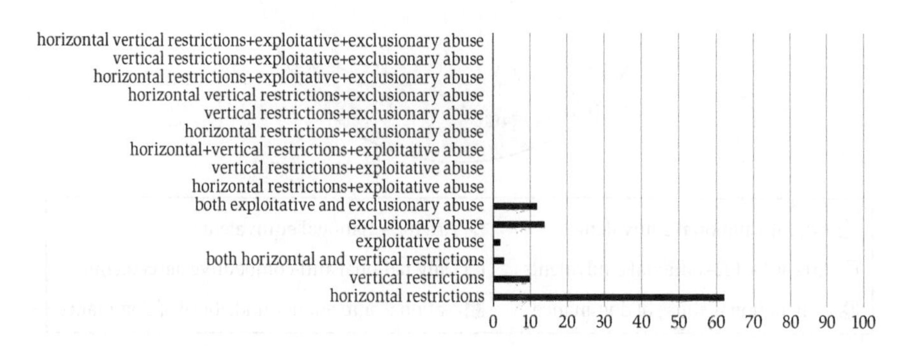

Limitations continue in relation to the 'by-object' and 'by-effect' boxes. Figure 19.8 points out that 95% of those decisions are classified as restrictions as by-object (with only one case decided by the KT based on 'by-effect' and one decided on both 'by-effect' and 'by-object'). The KT's narrow approach (with its exclusive priority given to the hard-core restrictions) has been challenged in the literature, especially in the context of highly debatable fields, such as the submission of joint bids in public procurement cases, in which the EU clarification is lacking and the NCAs approaches differ. For instance, Paukštė in her article[30] noted that both the KT and the courts unjustifiably found the restriction 'by-object' in the *UAB Irdaiva and AB Panevezio statybos trestas v. Competition Council* case (known as the *PST/Irdaiva* case), as it eliminated any potential efficiency or other legitimate interests of the consortium members in their joint tender. One must also note that the majority of undertakings in Lithuania are under the SME (small and medium enterprise) category.

A predominant focus on hard-core cartels may also raise concerns in terms of the effectiveness of competition law enforcement. This can suggest that other types of anti-competitive practices are ignored. One may question whether this approach is employed due to the limited resources of KT or the KT decides to go for the 'easy' cases, as restrictions 'by-effect' or proving an abuse requires 'more in-depth investigations'.

30. R. Paukšte, Report: Lithuania. Competition Law Enforcement in Public Procurement Markets: Joint Bidding, CoRe 2|2022.

Figure 19.8 Object/Effect (Only for Article 101/National Equivalent Infringements)

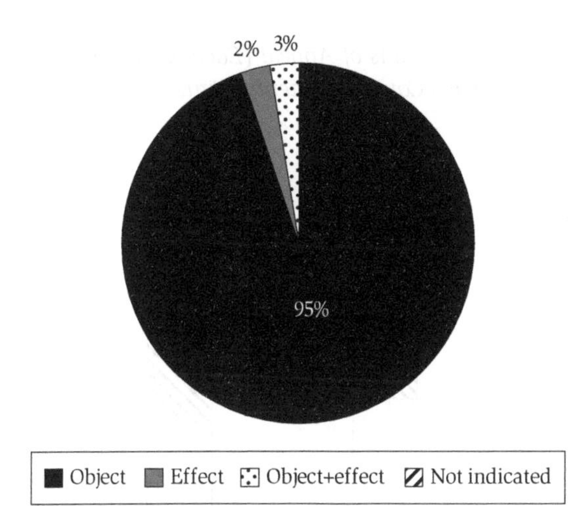

Figure 19.9 summarises the type of KT's decisions that were subject to appeal. The majority of those decisions (81%) involved findings of infringements with the imposition of fines. In 11% of those decisions refer to the rejection of a complaint or closure of an investigation.

Figure 19.9 Competition Authority's Procedure

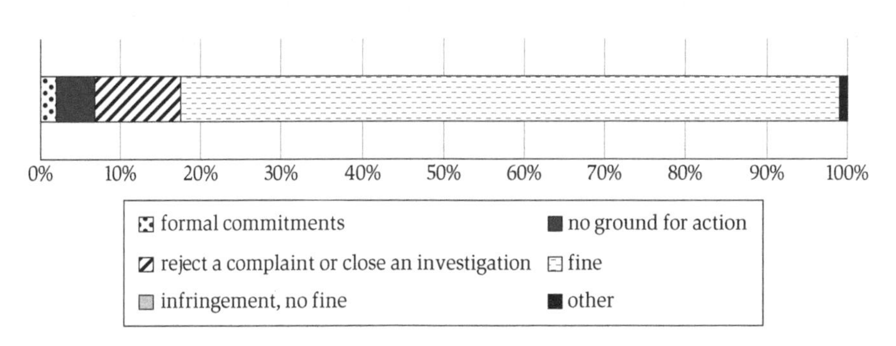

Figure 19.9 also demonstrates that commitments were seldom subject to appeal, yet, the commitments remedy is not very often utilised by the KT.

4.5 Grounds of Appeal

Further empirical data focus on the grounds on which appeals were raised by the parties and their rate of success. The success rates relate to the outcomes of all appeals, taking into account that separate appeals were aggregated where they were launched against a single KT decision or previous court's judgment. Specifically, the highest success rate is in relation to substantive grounds and fines, whereas procedural grounds were largely unsuccessful.

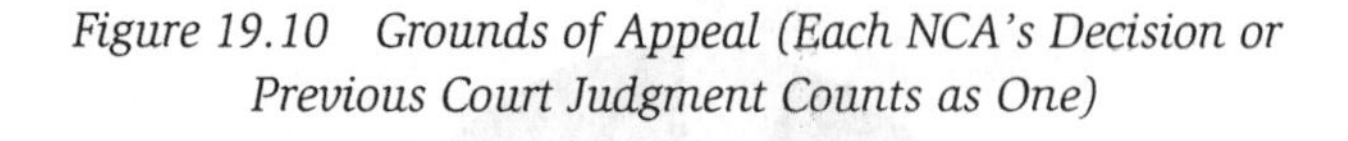

Figure 19.10 Grounds of Appeal (Each NCA's Decision or Previous Court Judgment Counts as One)

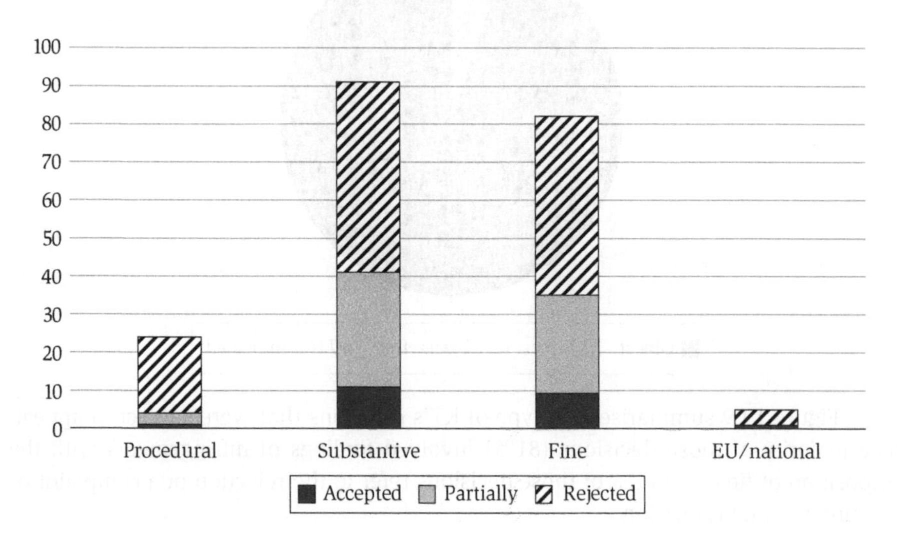

Figure 19.11 takes a different approach, it places emphasis on the appeal grounds argued and accepted over years, and counts each court judgment as a single decision, irrespective of whether there were multiple separate appeals in relation to the same KT's decision.

Figure 19.11 Types of Restrictions Versus Successful Grounds of Appeal

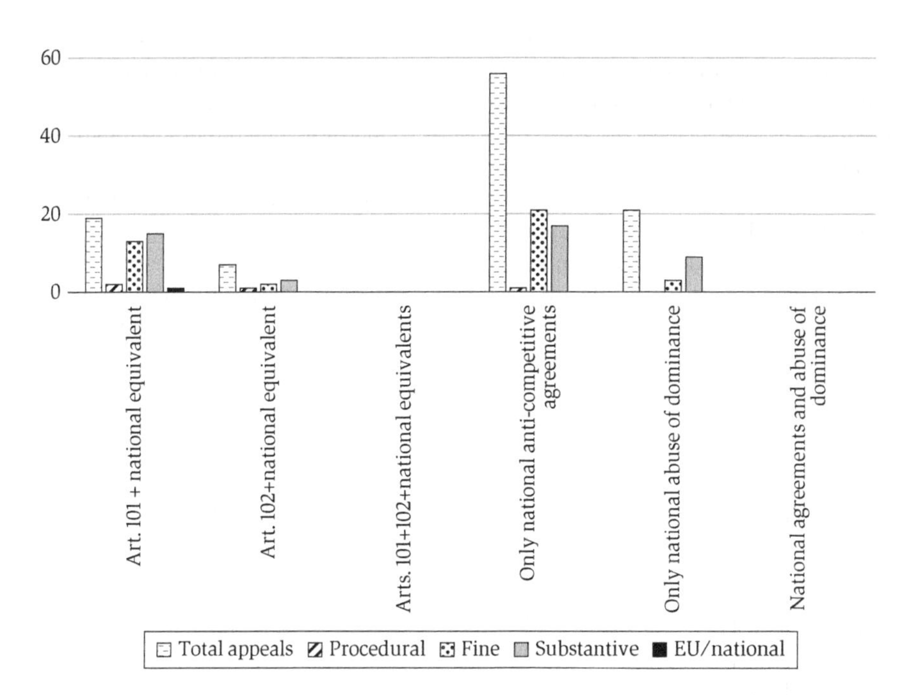

The most common substantive ground of appeal was pertaining to infringement decisions and then, fines imposed. As discussed above, the fine was reduced in approximately 42% of the cases (i.e., 36% of the cases decided by the REC and 48% by the SAC). On average, the fine was reduced by a significant 59% (62% by the REC and 55% by the SAC). The most notable appeal cases with a significant fine reduction are the *Eturas* case[31] where the fine was significantly reduced by both courts, the REC and SAC, from LTL 5,433,000 down to LTL 727,255.[32] In 'AB SEB BANKO', 'SWEDBANK', AB, AB DNB BANKO, UAB 'FIRST DATA LIETUVA', UAB 'G4S LIETUVA' the fine was reduced from LTL 57,119,800 to LTL 27,566,820 by the REC with a further reduction by the SAC to LTL 9,437,800.[33]

Finally, Figure 19.11 indicates the success of appeals in comparison to the type of restrictions being appealed. Given that most cases were in relation to the national equivalent of Article 101 TFEU, the parties were most successful in their appeal proceedings in this type of restriction, especially in relation to the fine.

31. The case is also known as Eturas. I. 121-135/2013 (first instance); and A-97-858/2016.
32. Lithuania joined the Euro on 1 January 2015.
33. I. 134-186/2013; A502-253/2014.

4.6 Leniency and Settlements

The first leniency programme was launched in Lithuania in 2008.[34] However, KT noted ineffective usage of its first leniency programme. One may speculate that this was mainly due to wide discretion being placed on the KT when imposing sanctions and potential mistrust placed on state authorities, which did not provide enough legal certainty for undertakings.[35] This study identified only five NCA's infringement decisions involving leniency that went through different stages of appeal (five REC's judgments and five SAC's judgments). In all the cases the leniency applicant was successful with full immunity granted, save one case where there was no infringement found in relation to the leniency applicant.[36] All these cases involved numerous undertakings, therefore, the table below demonstrates all leniency and 'no leniency' cases and their overall success.

Figure 19.12 Leniency

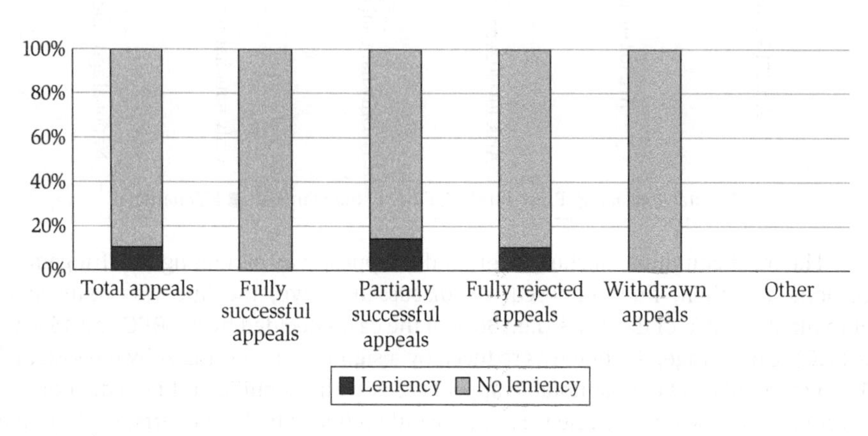

Settlement practice in Lithuania is gaining momentum, but settlements are still relatively rare. The KT regularly notes in its annual reports that it is actively engaging in advocacy activities to promote both its leniency and settlement programmes.[37]

4.7 Other Aspects: Preliminary References

Generally speaking, Jarukaitis and Švedas observed that applicants in Lithuania are still rather reluctant to rely on EU law;[38] therefore, courts do not have enough opportunities to utilise the preliminary reference procedure.

---

34. Rules on immunity from fines and reduction of fines for the parties to prohibited agreements, Council Resolution No. 1S-27. 28 February 2008, Vilnius.
35. J Malinauskaite, *Harmonisation of EU competition law enforcement*, Springer, 2019, p.203.
36. KT decision No. 2S-2; on appeal, I-2092-580/2011.
37. OECD, Annual Report on Competition Policy Developments in Lithuania, 2021. Available at: pdf (oecd.org) (accessed 3 January 2023).
38. I Jarukaitis and G Švedas, 'The Constitutional Experience of Lithuania in the Context of

However, in terms of administrative courts, once this opportunity comes, the SAC does not shy away from referring preliminary questions to the CJEU in the field of activities of regulatory authorities (including competition authority) comprising around one-fourth of all preliminary references (though the number of administrative cases related to the activities of regulatory authorities is not high).[39] While there have not been many preliminary questions submitted by the SAC in the competition field, they are significant in their importance surging debates at the European level. The SAC noted that the preliminary ruling procedure gives not only impetus for the development of the Lithuanian case law but also raises legal issues relevant to Europe. In the *Eturas* case,[40] the SAC sent the following questions to the CJEU: (1) whether based on the actions performed by the platform administrator can be presumed that the platform users were aware of the anti-competitive measure or ought to be aware of it, and thus, by failing to oppose the application of such a discount restriction, tacitly engaged in a concerted practice?; (2) provided the answer to the first question is negative, what factors should be considered to establish whether the users of the platform were engaged in concerted practices within the meaning of Article 101(1) TFEU?[41] The *Eturas* case marks a historical moment as one of the first cases demonstrating how online platforms can facilitate unlawful cooperation amongst platform users, therefore, distorting markets in the digital space. This case has also influenced the judgments of other national courts, including the recent case decided by the Federal Supreme Court of Switzerland.[42]

Most recently, in February 2021 the SAC sent another request for a preliminary ruling to the CJEU in the highly debatable Notaries case.[43] In this case, the KT found that the Lithuanian Chamber of Notaries and eight members of its Presidium concluded an anti-competitive agreement by setting the amount of notary fees and agreeing upon the calculation procedure, thereby restricting the ability of the notaries to apply lower notary fees and offer more favourable fees to consumers. As a result, the KT imposed a fine of EUR 88,400 on the Chamber of Notaries and other fines ranging from EUR 100 to EUR 20,800 on eight members of the Presidium for the infringements of Article 5 of the Law on Competition and Article 101(1) TFEU.[44] In addition, the KT sent a

European and Global Governance Challenges', in A. Albi and S. Bardutzky (eds), *National Constitutions in European and Global Governance: Democracy, Rights, the Rule of Law*, 2019, Springer, https://doi.org/10.1007/978-94-6265-273-6_21.

39. Association of the Councils of State and Supreme Administrative, 'The Judicial review of Regulatory Authorities', December 2021. Available at: Lithuania.pdf (aca-europe.eu) (accessed 15 September 2022).
40. In this case, the KT (in its decision No. 2S-9) found that the applicants – information system's E-TURAS sole rights holder and administrator as well as travel agencies which have used this system – engaged in concerted practices and therefore, infringed Article 5 of the Law on Competition and Article 101(1) TFEU. The SAC No A-97-858/2016.
41. Case C-74/14 *Eturas*, ECLI:EU:C:2016:42.
42. Judgment 2C_149/2018 of 4 February 2021. For further discussion, *see* Damiano Canapa, Non-binding 'recommended price' as concerted practices – The Federal Supreme Court of Switzerland rules on recommended prices that are communicated electronically to retailers, *Journal of European Competition Law & Practice*, 2022; lpac024, DOI: 10.1093/jeclap/lpac024.
43. Case No. eA-25-629/2021.
44. KT decision, No. 2S-2(2018).

recommendation to the Government to initiate amendments to the Law on Notaries and eliminate the obligation on the Ministry of Justice to negotiate notary fees with the Chamber of Notaries (which is a self-government institution that unites all notaries).[45] The REC repealed the KT's decision. The case is now pending in the SAC,[46] which suspended the proceedings, as the question was referred to the CJEU whether notaries should be considered undertakings and therefore, whether competition law should apply to them.

5 QUALITATIVE ANALYSIS

The Constitution and the Law on Courts regulate that the administration of justice courts are independent of other government institutions, officials, political parties, organisations and other persons. The SAC has further stressed that the principle of good administration is enshrined in the main national acts[47] and the Charter of Fundamental Rights of the EU.[48] As noted in section 2.1, unlike the court system of general jurisdiction, administrative cases do not have the cassation instance. Nevertheless, administrative courts (i.e., the REC and the SAC) aim for effective judicial review of public authorities' (including, competition authority) decisions. In addition, the SAC is also responsible for the formation of the uniform practice of administrative courts in applying laws similar to the Supreme Court (under the general jurisdiction system). Therefore, arguably, there is no need for the cassation instance.[49] However, a recent case (which fell beyond the scope of this study) may raise some concerns in relation to the effectiveness of judicial review of the REC and SAC, notably, in terms of accessibility to justice. In 2018, the KT opened an investigation against five undertakings engaged in the production and retailing of construction materials and household goods suspecting that several major producers and retailers, including the applicant, UAB Kesko Senukai, had agreed to fix the prices of certain goods sold in their stores, thereby potentially, breaching Article 5 of the Law on Competition as well as Article 101 TFEU.[50] Upon obtaining the authorisation from REC, the KT carried out dawn raids in the businesses under investigation, including UAB Kesko Senukai. Even though KT terminated this investigation, UAB Kesko Senukai, nevertheless, lodged a complaint

45. On 21 November 2018, the amendments to the Law on the Notary Office and the Law on Bailiffs entered into force, where the Minister of Justice shall set the amount of fees for the services of notaries and bailiffs upon the approval by the Minister of Finance only.
46. Case No. eA-25-629/2021.
47. For instance, Law on Public Administration or Law on Administrative Proceedings. 14 January 1999 No. VIII - 1029, Vilnius.
48. Case law of the Supreme Administrative Court of Lithuania applying the provisions of the Law on Public Administration of the Republic of Lithuania. Approved by the justices of the Supreme Administrative Court of Lithuania on 1 June 2016, pp. 464 -465. For further discussion, *see* I Deviatnikovaite, Constitutional Principles in Public Administrator's Decision-Making under the Case Law of the Supreme Administrative Court of Lithuania, *Bratislava Law Review*, 1/2018.
49. D Joksas, E Katisevskaja, Why administrative procedure does (not) need the cassation instance?, 2021, Vilnius University Press (in Lithuanian). Available at: https://doi.org/10.15388/TMP.2021.11.
50. Del ukio subjektų, užsiimančių statybos, remonto ir buities prekių gamybos ir pardavimo veikla, No. 1S-40 (2020), 24 March 2020.

with KT itself and then with the domestic courts about the manner in which the inspection was carried out, including that the large amount of information was seized and copied in 'an indiscriminate manner, without even attempting to assess whether certain documents were related to the investigation in question' during the inspection. The KT and the courts refused to examine the claim, with the SAC arguing that the KT's decision 'had constituted a procedural document of an interim nature that had not given rise to any material legal consequences for the applicant company'.[51] The European Court of Human Rights reached a decision in April 2023 finding a violation of Article 8 of the ECHR, as the absence of an *ex post facto* judicial review of the manner in which the KT's officials carried out the inspection of the applicant's business premise meant that there were no adequate and effective safeguards against abuse and arbitrariness and consequently, the interference with its right to respect for its home and correspondence could not be considered proportionate to the aim pursued or necessary in a democratic society, as required by Article 8 of the Convention.[52]

Furthermore, it should be noted that judicial deference embraces the principle that judges recognise the decision-making authority of other actors.[53] As Allan stated, even though courts must respect the sphere of decision-making autonomy enjoyed by a public body, a general doctrine of deference is unlikely to provide a useful means of defining the limits of the court's jurisdiction. Therefore, the appropriate degree of judicial deference is dependent on all the circumstances, such as the correct balance between constitutional rights and the general public interest (defined in the context in which a specific legal issue arises).[54] In the competition law context, Bernett specifies four conditions to define the permissibility of judicial deference, where the first three conditions are related to the proceedings before the NCA,[55] whereas the final condition explains the character of judicial review itself.[56] This latter condition should ensure that effective judicial review is offered by the court reviewing the NCA's decision. In Lithuania, the judicial review of administrative acts/decisions is based on both the legality of the decision and also on factual questions and circumstances. In addition, the administrative courts can also review how certain discretion attributed to regulators (including the KT) is exercised. The Law on Public Administration[57] sets out a principle of separation of functions. For instance, in terms of judicial review of any

---

51. Case of *UAB Kesko Senukai Lithuania v. Lithuania*. Application no. 19162/19, at para. 45. Available at: *UAB KESKO SENUKAI LITHUANIA v. LITHUANIA* (coe.int).
52. Ibid., at paras 126-127.
53. E Shirlow, *Judging at the Interface: Deference to State Decision-Making Authority in International Adjudication* (2021), 16.
54. TRS Allan, Deference, Defiance, and Doctrine: Defining the Limits of Judicial Review, *The University of Toronto Law Journal*, Vol. 60, No. 1, The Role of the Courts in Constitutional Law (Winter, 2010), pp. 41-59.
55. M Bernatt, *Transatlantic Perspective on Judicial Deference in Administrative Law,* Columbia Journal of European Law, 22(2), 2016, pp. 275-325. Available at: http://ssrn.com/abstract=2648232; at pp. 324-325.
56. M Bernatt, *Effectiveness of Judicial Review in the Polish Competition Law System and the Place for Judicial Deference,* Yearbook of Antitrust and Regulatory Studies 9(14), 2016, ss 97-124. Available at: https://ssrn.com/abstract=2896823; at p. 100 and pp. 106-107.
57. Law on Administrative Proceedings of the Republic of Lithuania, 14 January 1999, No. VIII-1029 as amended.

technical or economic assessments, the courts should not replace such assessments carried out by the regulatory authority with its own assessment due to the principle of separation of powers.[58] In this context, judicial review is limited to an assessment as to whether the regulator has exceeded its discretion or has made a manifest error or has misused its powers as well as whether the regulatory authority has followed procedural rules and has duly assessed all relevant factual circumstances.[59] For instance, in the *UAB 'Vilniaus Energija'* case,[60] the SAC stated that it could only to a limited extent review the legality and soundness of the economic analysis conducted by the KT. Nevertheless, it was able to evaluate whether the KT had complied with the procedure, based its findings on sound arguments, had not made a mistake in its assessment or had not misused its powers. In this case, the KT's infringement decision of Article 7 (now Article 9) of the Law on Competition where *UAB 'Vilniaus Energija'* was annulled by both the REC[61] and subsequently by the SAC.[62] The SAC noted that the KT failed to assess all the circumstances which were relevant to the establishment of abuse of a dominant position.[63]

Generally speaking, the effectiveness of the judicial review system in the competition law context is gradually improving in Lithuania. The administrative courts' rulings (especially by the SAC) are supported by findings and reasoning from earlier national cases (including constitutional cases). EU courts' jurisprudence is also observed, especially in complex cases with EU law elements (i.e., Articles 101 and 102 TFEU). This can be demonstrated by the SAC's role in utilising the preliminary ruling procedure to ensure the uniform application of EU competition law, leading to, for instance, changing the KT's decision, as in the *Eturas* case. As discussed above, the SAC in *Eturas*,[64] following the preliminary reference proceeding, concluded that it could not be established that all travel agencies participated in the concerted practice. Therefore, the KT's decision was partly annulled in relation to a number of the undertakings previously found to have infringed both Article 5 of the Law on Competition and Article 101 TFEU.

Furthermore, the concept of judicial deference is upheld in the context of the KT's infringement decisions. It is worth noting that the KT in its annual reports regularly indicates that administrative courts uphold approximately 90% of its decisions and

58. Association of the Councils of State and Supreme Administrative Jurisdictions of the European Union, 'The Judicial review of Regulatory Authorities'. Answers to questionnaire: Lithuania (The Supreme Administrative Court of Lithuania). Paris, 6 December 2021. Available at: Lithuania.pdf (aca-europe.eu) (accessed 21 December 2022).
59. Confirmed in the administrative Case No. A-502-72/2009.
60. Decision of the KT on the compliance of actions of *UAB 'Vilniaus Energija'* with the requirements of Article 9(1) (now Article 7) of the Law on Competition, 13 September 2007, No. 2S-18.
61. Initially, the REC upheld the KT's decision. However, the SAC sent the case back for additional investigation. The KT did not change its original infringement decision after further investigation. On appeal, both courts were in agreement to annual the KT's decision. Judgment of REC, 24 October 2011, Case No. I-3681-562/2011.
62. Judgment of SAC, 13 August 2012, Case No. A858-1516/2012.
63. OECD (2019), The standard of review by courts in competition cases. Contribution from Lithuania. Available at: pdf (oecd.org) (accessed 30 December 2022).
64. Judgment of the SAC, 2 May 2016, Case No. A-97- 858/2016, para. 474.

requests.[65] This is in line with the general trend whereby the SAC upholds, approximately 70% of its decisions[66] without any changes made.[67] For instance, the SAC upheld the KT's infringement decision of Article 5 in 2018[68] whereby the largest cinema chain Forum Cinemas encouraged its competitors, namely, *Multikino Lietuva* and *Cinamon Operations*, to refrain from applying discounts to blockbuster movies during the first two weeks of their screenings. Furthermore, competing cinema operations in the two largest cities (Vilnius and Kaunas) restricted discounts and fixed prices for certain movies in support of a Forum Cinemas initiative. However, 'judicial deference' appears to be more limited in relation to fines imposed by the KT. For instance, while the SAC upheld KT's resolution in the Driving Schools cartel[69] in 2021, where the KT established that twenty-six driving schools and the Association agreed to increase the prices of driving lessons in three cities of Lithuania, it, nonetheless, reduced the fines imposed on two undertakings (*Jonas Jasučis* enterprise and *Jurbarko saugaus eismo centras*) by 50% and 10% respectively due to their financial situation. The empirical research of this study indicates that the courts are willing to reduce the fines imposed by the KT on undertakings. A similar conclusion was reached by another study, which focused predominantly on public procurement cases involving cartels (based on both - the domestic provision Article 5; and the EU provision - Article 101 TFEU), where the author noted that the SAC either upheld the REC's decision to reduce the KT's imposed fine(s) or reduced the fine(s) itself in over 60% of all the analysed cases.[70] This may be due to the fact that KT seems to impose fines closer to a higher end rather than a lower end of the annual worldwide turnover 10% range.[71] Potentially, this can be rectified by the most recent development. Indeed, the KT launched a more detailed resolution of the methodology for setting fines (effective from 1 May 2023) providing more clarity on the application of the competition law provisions related to setting sanctions.[72] The KT expects that this new resolution will decrease the number of disputes concerning the

65. *See*, for instance, KT Annual Reports of 2015; 2018; 2019.
66. The SAC hears around 3,000 administrative cases per year. Association of the Councils of State and Supreme Administrative Jurisdictions of the European Union, 'The Judicial review of Regulatory Authorities'. Answers to questionnaire: Lithuania (The Supreme Administrative Court of Lithuania). Paris, 6 December 2021. Available at: Lithuania.pdf (aca-europe.eu) (accessed 21 December 2022).
67. D Joksas, E Katisevskaja, Why administrative procedure does (not) need the cassation instance?, 2021, Vilnius University Press (in Lithuanian). Available at: https://doi.org/10.15388/TMP.2021.11.
68. Case No. eA-143-624/2018.
69. A-109-556/2021.
70. R Grigaraviciene 'Problems of Qualifying the Agreements Restricting the Competition During the Public Procurement in Lithuanian Law: Theory and Practice', the Master's thesis, Vilnius 2017 (in Lithuanian).
71. Likewise, under Article 23 of Regulation 1/2003, undertakings in Lithuania can be fined a maximum of 10% of the total annual worldwide turnover.
72. Nutarimas del baudų, skiriamų už Lietuvos Respublikos Konkurencijos įstatymo pažeidimus, dydžio nustatymo tvarkos aprašo patvirtinimo, No. 64. *No. 1102, 2022-11-09, announced TAR 2022-11-10, i. k. 2022-22722.*

calculation of fines imposed by the KT, simultaneously, saving the resources of businesses, the KT, and courts.[73]

Pursuant to Article 104(1) of the Law on Administrative Proceedings, the court which analyses the case under the appeal procedure reviews the soundness and the legitimacy of the judgment of the court of first instance without overstepping the boundaries of the appellant's case. In the competition law appeals context, one must note disagreements between the administrative courts and indication of the lack of experience and knowledge of handling competition cases, for instance, with the REC's initial persistence of the need to prove a 'fault' element. For instance, in the *Advertising and Media cartel* case, the KT found that the Lithuanian association of the communication agencies and several undertakings providing advertising and media planning services violated Article 5(1) of the Law on Competition 'by-object', as they agreed to set a fixed fee to be paid by the competition organisers to these undertakings for their participation in the competitions on the purchase of advertising services. This decision was annulled by the REC,[74] which, among other things, noted that the KT unjustifiably failed to analyse the effects the agreement might have had on competition. Upon further appeal, the SAC annulled the REC's decision and explained two types of restrictions 'by-object' and 'by-effect' under Article 5 of the Law on Competition.[75] Therefore, it decided that the KT was correct in its findings that once the fixing of prices was found, it was to be considered a restriction 'by-object' without it being necessary to analyse the effects of such an agreement on competition. In the most recent Lithuanian Basketball League case once again the REC challenged the KT's 'by-object' findings. The KT found that Lithuanian Basketball League and ten basketball clubs entered into an anti-competitive agreement when they decided to stop paying basketball players salaries or other financial remuneration for the rest of the season after the termination of the basketball championship 2019-2020 due to the COVID-19 pandemic, therefore, infringing both Article 5(1) of the Law on Competition as well as Article 101 TFEU. The fines imposed ranged from EUR 1,070 to EUR 16,510. Šarūnas Keserauskas, Chairman of the KT, noted that competitors could not use the COVID-19 pandemic to justify cartels, which sought to collectively mitigate the consequences of the crisis at the expense of employed persons or consumers. However, the REC ruled that the KT failed to prove that a restrictive agreement had been reached and had not fully assessed the relevant context – that is the unprecedented circumstances during the COVID-19 pandemic as well as the specific features of this sport sector.

73. KT Newsletter 'Procedure for setting fines for Competition Law infringements has been improved', 9 November 2022. Available at: *Procedure for Setting Fines for Competition Law Infringements Has Been Improved* | Competition Council of the Republic of Lithuania (kt.gov.lt) (accessed 15 July 2023).
74. Vilnius Regional Administrative Court, 21 January 2010, Case No. I-515-602/2010.
75. Supreme Administrative Court of Lithuania, 28 March 2011, Case No. A525- 2577/2011.

6 CONCLUDING REMARKS

Administrative justice in the Lithuanian legal system was introduced at the dawn of the preparation for joining the EU and the standard of judicial review has been evolving ever since. In the competition law context, the report discussed two administrative courts involved in this review process: the REC and the SAC (which review the REC's judgments and check their soundness and legitimacy without overstepping the boundaries of the claim). Given that administrative cases do not have the cassation instance, the SAC is also responsible for ensuring the uniform practice of administrative courts in applying laws.

Specifically, this study has revealed that the KT's resolutions (decisions) are regularly appealed to the Administrative Courts. During the 2004–2021 period, 103 cases were identified dealing with Articles 101 and 102 TFEU (and/or national equivalents). The success rate of appeal is relatively low. The administrative courts mostly confirmed the KT's decisions. The SAC noted that even though there are not many competition cases, disputes in this area, as a rule of thumb, tend to be large in scope and feature a wide range of problematic issues and unusual factual circumstances.[76] This explains the SAC's willingness to utilise the preliminary ruling procedure to ensure the uniform application of EU competition law. However, surprisingly, only 25 out of 104 rulings contained an EU law element.

The partially successful category in terms of appeals predominantly includes cases in relation to the reduction of fines. It seems that the administrative courts quite often reduce the fines imposed by the KT. One may argue that this is because the majority of businesses belong to the SME category, therefore, they are unable to 'afford' high fines, as the courts in several cases noted the relatively poor financial situation of undertakings in their justification for the fine reduction. To enhance transparency and legal certainty, the KT has recently amended its guidelines of the methodology for setting fines.

In terms of the specific provisions, there is a clear focus of the KT on restrictive agreements 'by-object', as the majority of the analysed cases fall under this category (Article 5 of the Law on Competition). This may raise concerns in terms of the effectiveness of competition law enforcement, as other types of anti-competitive practices should not be ignored. One must also note whether the KT should embrace 'by-effect' investigations, especially, in some borderline cases, such as the submission of joint bids in public procurement cases,[77] as these aspects are not settled at the EU level.

Given that competition cases are complex, featuring a wide range of problematic issues and unusual factual circumstances, it is yet to be seen whether the administrative courts will take a more intrusive recourse and how judicial review will develop in the future in Lithuania.

76. Annual report of Supreme Administrative Court 2017.
77. For instance, the *PST/Irdaiva* case.

CHAPTER 20
Luxembourg Report

Caroline Cauffman

1 INTRODUCTION TO THE COMPETITION LAW ENFORCEMENT CONTEXT IN LUXEMBOURG

1.1 Historical Outline

Luxembourg does not have a long-standing competition culture. Its first general act on anticompetitive practices dates back to 1970 and conferred the power of enforcement on the Minister of Economic Affairs. However, hardly any enforcement action was taken. In 1993, the Minister of Economic Affairs was designated as the authority to assist the European Commission in investigations on infringements of Articles 101 and 102 TFEU.[1]

Up until 2004, Luxembourg maintained a Price Office (*Office des prix*). This Office was created in 1944 in order to allow the public authorities to counteract potential price surges resulting from speculation in scarce goods. It was intended to be of limited duration, but it remained in place and was used to control inflation. The multitude of regulations governing price levels in the most diverse sectors were only abolished slowly and Luxembourg was repeatedly encouraged by the European Commission to abandon its system of price regulation and to introduce modern competition rules.[2]

1. Loi du 2 septembre 1993 créant les conditions requises pour l'application: 1. de la loi modifiée du 17 juin 1970 concernant les pratiques commerciales restrictives, 2. du règlement No 17 du conseil de la communauté européenne du 6 février 1962, prise en exécution des articles 85 et 86 du traité de Rome, 3. du règlement (CEE) No 4064/89 du 21 décembre 1989 relatif au contrôle des opérations de concentration entre entreprise, *Mémorial A*, n° 76, 20 septembre 1993.
2. For further details, *see* Projet de loi relative à la concurrence, Exposé des motifs, Chambre des députés, Session ordinaire 2003-2004, n° 5229, 13 novembre 2003, pp. 26 et seq.

Only after Regulation 1/2003 made the enforcement of EU competition law a joint responsibility of the Commission and the national competition authorities, Luxembourg adopted its 2004 Competition Act,[3] based on the idea that prices are determined by competition (Article 2), introducing for the first time national equivalents of Articles 101 and 102 TFEU (Articles 3-5) and creating a dualistic enforcement structure comprising a Competition Inspection (*Inspection de la concurrence*) and a Competition Council (*Conseil de la concurrence*) as well as procedural rules for the enforcement of both Articles 101-102 TFEU and their national equivalents (Articles 6 et seq.).

As further explained below, the dualistic enforcement structure was replaced by a monistic structure through the 2011 Competition Act,[4] which also modified the rules on the appeal of NCA decisions. Further modifications of the Luxembourg competition rules served, *inter alia*, to implement the Antitrust Damages Directive.[5] This chapter focuses on the period between May 2004 and April 2021. Since then, the legislative framework has undergone further changes. The most important changes concern the transposition of the ECN+ Directive[6] and the modification of the name of the Competition Council into Competition Authority (*Autorité de concurrence*).[7] These changes will not be further elaborated on.

1.2 Enforcement Framework

The 2004 Competition Act introduced a dualistic system for the enforcement of competition law, meaning that the investigatory and decisional tasks related to the enforcement of competition law were assigned to different bodies, both newly introduced by the 2004 Act.

The Competition Inspection (*Inspection de la Concurrence*) was a department within the Ministry of Economic Affairs that was tasked with the investigatory part of

3. Loi du 26 mai 2004 relative à la concurrence, *Mémorial A*, n° 76, 26 mai 2004.
4. Loi du 23 octobre 2011 relative à la concurrence, *Mémorial A*, n° 218, 28 octobre 2011.
5. Loi du 5 décembre 2016 relative à certaines règles régissant les actions en dommages et intérêts pour les violations du droit de la concurrence et modifiant la loi modifiée du 23 octobre 2011 relative à la concurrence, *Mémorial A*, n° 245, 7 décembre 2016, p. 4534.
6. Directive (EU) 2019/1 of the European Parliament and of the Council of 11 December 2018 to empower the competition authorities of the Member States to be more effective enforcers and to ensure the proper functioning of the internal market, *OJ* L 11, 14 January 2019, p. 3.
7. Loi du 30 novembre 2022 relative à la concurrence et portant: 1° organisation de l'Autorité nationale de concurrence; 2° modification de la loi modifiée du 10 août 1991 sur la profession d'avocat; 3° modification de la loi modifiée du 21 juin 1999 portant règlement de procédure devant les juridictions administratives; 4° modification de la loi modifiée du 10 février 2015 relative à l'organisation du marché de produits pétroliers; 5° modification de la loi modifiée du 25 mars 2015 fixant le régime des traitements et les conditions et modalités d'avancement des fonctionnaires de l'État; 6° modification de la loi modifiée du 23 juillet 2016 relative à la profession de l'audit; 7° modification de la loi du 5 mars 2021 relative à certaines modalités de mise en œuvre du règlement (UE) n° 2019/1150 du Parlement européen et du Conseil du 20 juin 2019 promouvant l'équité et la transparence pour les entreprises utilisatrices de services d'intermédiation en ligne; 8° modification de la loi du 1er juin 2021 sur les relations entre entreprises au sein de la chaîne d'approvisionnement agricole et alimentaire, *Mémorial* A, n° 588, 30 novembre 2022, consolidated version available on http://data.legilux.public.lu/eli/etat/leg/loi/2022/11/30/a588; Loi du 17 mars 2023 portant modification de la loi du 30 novembre 2022 relative à la concurrence, Mémorial A, n° 145, 17 mars 2023.

the enforcement of competition law. It was responsible for receiving and investigating complaints and for starting an investigation on its own initiative in relation to potential infringements of Articles 101 and 102 TFEU and its national equivalents. In case a decision by the Competition Council (*Conseil de la concurrence*) was appealed, the Inspection could lodge written arguments in judicial and administrative proceedings. With judicial approval, it could also make oral observations and produce official reports.[8]

The Competition Council was an independent administrative body competent for the decision-making in relation to competition law enforcement. It was the competent national authority for Luxembourg within the meaning of Regulation 1/2003.[9]

The attribution of the investigatory and decisional tasks to different bodies was introduced following the Advice of the Council of the State that expressed concerns about the compatibility of the accumulation of both tasks within one authority with Article 6 ECHR.[10]

The 2011 Competition Act replaced the dualistic structure with a unified structure. The Competition Inspection was abolished and its tasks were transferred to the Competition Council. The change was motivated by the fact that the coexistence of two administrative authorities active within the same field without any organic or hierarchical link between them and without a mechanism for resolving divergent views, led to a waste of resources. The drafters of the proposal for the 2011 Competition Law carried out extensive research on Article 6 ECHR and concluded that this article did not oppose the accumulation of investigatory and decisional tasks within a single authority.[11] Furthermore, they supported their view by the fact that, at the time twenty-one Member States of the EU had conferred both tasks to a single administrative competition authority and that even a number of Luxembourg administrative authorities active outside the field of competition combined both tasks.[12] In addition, the dualistic structure was expensive and confused the public as illustrated by the fact that letters meant for the Inspection were often addressed to the Council and vice versa.

8. Article 29 of the 2004 Competition Act; Guy Harles and Philippe-Emmanuel Partsch, 'Chapter 18: Luxembourg', in Marjorie Holmes and Lesley Davey (eds), *A Practical Guide to National Competition Rules across Europe* (Second Edition), *International Competition Law Series*, Volume 13 (Kluwer Law International 2007) p. 562.
9. Council Regulation (EC) No. 1/2003 of 16 December 2002 on the implementation of the rules on competition laid down in Articles 81 and 82 of the Treaty, *OJ* L 1, 4 January 2003, pp. 1-25. It was also the competent authority to withdraw the benefit of the application of vertical block exemption regulations where vertical agreements to which the exemption applied had effects incompatible with the conditions laid down in Article 101(3) TFEU in Luxembourg or in a part thereof, which had all the characteristics of a distinct geographic market (Article 6 of the 2004 Competition Act).
10. Projet de loi relative à la concurrence, Exposé des motifs, Chambre des députés, Session ordinaire 2003-2004, n° 5229/5, p. 3; Projet n° 5816 portant réforme de la loi du 17 mai 2004 relative à la concurrence, Chambre des députés, Session ordinaire 2007-2008, Annex 1, p. 32.
11. Projet n° 5816 portant réforme de la loi du 17 mai 2004 relative à la concurrence, Chambre des députés, Session ordinaire 2007-2008, p. 3-4 and Annex 1.
12. *Ibid.*

1.3 Enforcement Practices and Priorities

The Luxembourg NCA does not publish its enforcement priorities explicitly on a regular basis. However, for 2014, the Council announced its priority to carry out sectoral investigations likely to uncover vertical restrictions affecting the competitiveness of certain Luxembourg companies that are unable to obtain supplies freely on the international market.[13] Similarly, *ex post* its enforcement priorities for other years can be derived from the sectoral investigations carried out. In 2019, for example, it published a report on sectoral investigations it carried out in the food distribution sector.[14]

Furthermore, during the 2020 COVID-19 crisis, the Council not only published a joint statement adopted within the ECN[15] but also published an additional document clarifying the prioritisation of the Council's action in this time of crisis as well as how it intended to interpret the criteria for exemption from anti-competitive practices in that specific situation and the extent to which it would take steps to prevent harm to consumers from any behaviour that seeks to exploit the crisis in an opportunistic manner.[16]

2 REVIEW OF THE COMPETITION AUTHORITY'S DECISIONS

During the entire research period (May 2004 to April 2021), first-instance appeals on NCA's enforcement decisions have been heard by the Administrative Tribunal (*Tribunal Administratif*) and second-instance appeals by the Administrative Court (*Cour Administrative*).[17] Administrative Courts (*juridictions administratives*) hear cases relating to administrative decisions[18] while judicial courts (*juridictions judiciaires*)[19] hear all other cases. In this sense, the Administrative Tribunal and Court are specialised. The Administrative Tribunal has four chambers. There is no formal system of specialisation or attribution of specific matters to specific chambers. Nevertheless, in the interests of the proper administration of justice, certain matters are grouped

13. https://concurrence.public.lu/fr/actualites/2014/Rencontre-Conseil-avec-Federation-Artisans.html.
14. Conseil de la Concurrence, *Rapport d'enquête sectorielle dans le secteur de la grande distribution*, https://concurrence.public.lu/content/dam/concurrence/fr/avis-enquetes/enquetes/2019/Rapport-enquete-2019-1-18.pdf.
15. https://concurrence.public.lu/fr/actualites/2020/declaration-commune-REC-covid-19.html.
16. Conseil de la Concurrence, *Document d'orientation à destination des entreprises. Impact du Covid-19 sur les actions du Conseil de la concurrence*, https://concurrence.public.lu/content/dam/concurrence/fr/actualites/2020/2020-03-31-Document-d-orientation-entreprises-Covid-19.pdf.
17. In this chapter, the concepts 'appeal' and 'review' are used interchangeably. Strictly speaking, the correct term would be 'review' (*recours*), since, in any case in first instance, an administrative decision is contested and the concept 'appeal' (*appel*) refers to the contestation of a judicial decision.
18. Articles 2(1) and 7(1) de la loi du 7 novembre 1996 portant organisation des juridictions administratives, *Mémorial A* 79, 19 novembre 1996, as amended, for the applicable version, *see* http://data.legilux.public.lu/eli/etat/leg/loi/1996/11/07/n1.
19. Further divided in civil, criminal, commercial, social and labour branches.

together and assigned to specific chambers, in order to allow, as far as possible, a certain specialisation of the various chambers and to take account of the affinities of the various judges. For this reason, all competition law cases have lately been assigned to the First Chamber of the Administrative Tribunal.[20] The Administrative Court of Luxembourg does not have a formal division of matters between its different chambers. The Administrative Court only has one chamber that deals with all types of cases within the jurisdiction of the administrative branch of the court system.[21]

No court fees are due to file an appeal. However, the unsuccessful party is ordered to pay court costs. Court costs are also due in case an appeal is withdrawn.[22] Each party must, regardless of the outcome of the case, bear its own lawyer's fees. In certain cases and upon request, the administrative judge may award a procedural indemnity. A party in need may claim legal aid, in which case the State bears all the costs, including the lawyer's fees.[23]

2.1 First-Instance Appeal

Under the 2004 Competition Act, a distinction was made between appeals against decisions of the Council regarding fines and appeals against other decisions of the Council. A *recours en réformation* could be launched against decisions imposing a fine, meaning that the Administrative Tribunal could replace the appealed decision. This appeal had to be launched within a period of two months (Article 26 (2)) as of the day the decision has been notified to the appellant or the day as of which the appellant could take notice of it.[24]

A *recours en annulation* could be brought against other types of decisions taken by the Council. In such a case, the Administrative Tribunal could only confirm or annul the appealed decision. If it annulled the decision, it had to refer the case back to the Council (Article 26 (1)). This appeal could be launched within a period of three months as of the day the decision has been notified to the appellant or the day as of which the appellant could take notice of it. This was not explicitly mentioned in Article 26 of the 2004 Competition Act but followed the general rules on administrative procedures.[25] Practically, this meant that a decision finding an infringement could be appealed in order to obtain the nullity of the decision (*recours en annulation*) within a period of

20. All first-instance appeals falling within the scope of the research have been decided by the first chamber of the Tribunal. The registrar's office confirmed the intentionality of the attribution to the first chamber and the reasons for this.
21. https://justice.public.lu/fr/organisation-justice/juridictions-administratives.html.
22. Article 25(2) Loi du 21 juin 1999 portant règlement de procédure devant les juridictions administratives, *Mémorial A*, 26 juillet 1999 as modified. For the applicable, coordinated version, *see* http://data.legilux.public.lu/eli/etat/leg/loi/1999/06/21/n2 (hereafter: Texte coordonné de la loi modifiée du 21 juin 1999 portant règlement de procédure devant les juridictions administratives).
23. Article 2(1) de la loi modifiée du 7 novembre 1996 portant organisation des juridictions administratives.
24. Article 13(1) Texte coordonné de la loi modifiée du 21 juin 1999 portant règlement de procédure devant les juridictions administratives.
25. *Ibid.*

three months while a decision imposing a fine could only be appealed within a period of two months. Consequently, when the infringement and the fine were determined in the same decision, the time for launching an appeal against the fine was shorter than that for launching an appeal against the infringement. This could lead to a situation where the appellate decision on the fine became final before the decision on the infringement, and the undertaking subject to the decision had to pay a (possibly decreased) fine to learn afterwards that the decision determining the infringement was annulled. The 2011 Competition Act no longer makes this distinction. The NCA's decisions on the infringements and fines, orders to do or not to do something (injunctions), periodic penalty payments, leniency, and commitments, are now all subject to a full review (*recours en réformation*) (Article 28) within a period of forty days.[26] By contrast, decisions taken by a single member of the NCA, the *Président* in the case of interim measures and confidentiality and the *Conseiller-rapporteur* in the case of inspections, are subject to a *recours en annulation*.[27]

Recours en annulation is the standard type of review under Luxembourg administrative law. It is available against all administrative decisions for which no specific rules on appeal procedures exist. *Recours en annulation* only allows the appellate judge to carry out a marginal review of the decision subject to the appeal.[28] The appellate judge will only verify whether the decision does not exceed the boundaries of 'legality' (lack, excess or misuse of power, violation of the law and violation of forms designed to protect private interests).[29]

However, case law and legal scholarship point out that the Court's task is not limited to a pure assessment of the correct application of the applicable legal rules. It also has a duty to verify that the facts on which the contested decision is based, have been established beyond doubt.[30] Furthermore, the Court has to check whether the contested decision is duly motivated.[31] Although the Court must assess the legality of the contested decision at the time the latter was given,[32] the NCA has the right to provide the Court with additional reasons supporting the contested decision.[33] The Court may even *ex officio* establish the existence of legal reasons following from the law

26. Article 38 Texte coordonné de la loi modifiée du 21 juin 1999 portant règlement de procédure devant les juridictions administratives.
27. Articles 12, 14(2), 16(5), 26(4) of the 2011 Competition Act; Projet de loi portant réforme de la loi du 17 mai 2004 relative à la concurrence, n° 5816, Chambre des députés, Session ordinaire 2007-2008, p. 29.
28. *See* Article 5 Texte coordonné de la loi modifiée du 21 juin 1999 portant règlement de procédure devant les juridictions administratives.
29. Marc Feyereisen and Jérôme Guillot, *Procédure Administrative Contentieuse*, Windhof, Larcier, 2018, n° 88 et seq.
30. *Ibid.*, n° 108 referring to Cour Adm. 22 octobre 1998, n° 10746C and Cour Adm. 9 juin 2005, n° 19242C.
31. *Ibid.*, n° 109.
32. *Ibid.*, n° 107 referring to Cour Adm. 16 juin 1998, n° 10649C and Cour Adm. Case 2 décembre 2004, no 18456C.
33. *Ibid.*, n° 111 referring to Cour Adm. 8 janvier 2002, n° 13891C and 8 mai 2003, n° 15632C.

or from elements of the case file that justify the contested decision.[34] It may even replace false reasons with good ones provided that they correspond with the purpose of the contested decision.[35]

The Court's review is limited to deciding on the grounds invoked by the appellant. It may not carry out *ex officio* a review of elements which were not contested by the appellant.[36]

The appeal *en annulation* does not allow the judge to review the appropriateness of the administrative decision or to replace it with its own assessment, even if other decisions seem more appropriate or if other decisions are more favourable to the applicant.[37] If the court gives judgment for the appellant, it is not entitled to take a decision replacing the contested decision. It may only annul the contested decision in whole or in part and return the case back to the NCA, or in case the NCA was held not to be the competent authority, to the competent authority.[38] The authority to which the case is referred will have to take the court's decision into account when deciding on the case.

Recours en réformation is the exception. It is only available when it is explicitly provided for by law. In *EPT (Entreprise des Postes et Télécommunications)*, the Administrative Tribunal describes the *recours en réformation* as 'the legal attribution to the administrative judge of the special competence to rule again, in place of the administration, on all the aspects of a challenged administrative decision. The judgment replaces the contested decision in that it confirms or reforms it. This formal attribution of competence by the legislator calls on the judge of the reversal not only to control the legality of the decision that the administration took on the basis of a situation of law and fact such as it presented itself to it at the time when it was called upon to rule but also to verify if its assessment is consistent with that of the administration and, in the negative, to substitute its own decision for that of the administration, independently of the legality of the decision referred to'.[39] Normally, the Court hearing a case in a *recours en réformation* procedure, will give a final decision on the merits. However, it is recognised that the Court could also set out the principles according to which the case is to be decided and leave it to the authority that gave the contested decision to elaborate the technical details and or calculations taking into

34. *Ibid.*, n° 112 referring to Cour Adm. 5 février 1998, n° 10207C.
35. *Ibid.*, n° 112 referring to Trib. Adm. du 10 janvier 1997, n° 9755 and Cour Adm. 17 février 2005, n° 18899C.
36. *Ibid.*, n° 113 referring to Cour Adm. 15 février 2000, n° 11420C.
37. Marc Feyereisen, *La justice administrative en Europe*, https://www.aca-europe.eu/seminars/2005_Trier/Luxembourg_fr.pdf.
38. Marc Feyereisen and Jérôme Guillot, *Procédure Administrative Contentieuse*, Windhof, Larcier, 2018, n° 112 referring to Cour Adm. 5 février 1998, n° 10207C.
39. Trib. Admin. 21 novembre 2016, n° 35847a, *Entreprise des Postes et Télécommunications*, https://ja.public.lu/35001-40000/35847a.pdf referring to Cour Adm. 23 novembre 2010, n° 26851C, *Pas. Adm.* 2016, V° *Recours en réformation*, n° 11 (unofficial translation); Cour Adm. 6 mai 2008, n° 23341C.

account the criteria set by the review Court.[40] Furthermore, when the case is not yet ready for a decision on the merits, the review court may return the case to the authority.[41] When the contested decision has been taken by an incompetent authority, the Court will annul the decision and refer it to the competent authority.[42] When the contested decision is affected by a defect that cannot be repaired, for example, because the duration of the procedure is incompatible with the reasonable time principle, the Court may limit itself to merely annul the decision, even in the case of a *recours en réformation.*[43]

While the Court hearing a *recours en annulation* has to assess whether the decision was legal at the moment it was given by the authority, the Court hearing a *recours en réformation* has to assess the legality at the moment it has to give its decision.[44] As in cases of the *recours en annulation*, the power of the court deciding *en réformation* is limited to ruling upon the arguments (or grounds) put forward by the applicant against the contested decision.[45] It is not entitled to carry out an examination of the contested decision exceeding those limits on its own motion.[46] A further similarity with cases of *recours en annulation*, is also that the Court may add to an incomplete decision legal reasons following from the law or from the case file.[47] It would also be too blunt to conclude that the appeal *en réformation* deals with facts and law and the appeal *en annulation* only with the law. In both cases, law and facts can be reviewed, albeit within certain limits.[48]

2.2 Second-Instance Appeal

The second appeal is heard by the Administrative Court of Appeal. If the first appeal was a *recours en annulation*, the second appeal is too. Likewise, if the first appeal was an appeal *en réformation*, the second appeal is too.[49]

40. Marc Feyereisen and Jérôme Guillot, *Procédure Administrative Contentieuse*, Windhof, Larcier, 2018, n°121 referring to Cour Adm. 13 mars 2001, n° 12596C.
41. *Ibid.*, n°122, referring to Cour adm. 28 février 2002, n° 13884C.
42. *Ibid.*, n° 125 referring to Cour Adm. 28 mai 2002, n° 14586C.
43. *Ibid.*, n° 126 referring to Cour Adm. 11 mars 2003, n° 15767C; Trib. Adm. 6 janvier 1999, n° 10599.
44. *Ibid.*, n° 123 referring to Cour Adm. 19 février 1998, n° 10259C.
45. Trib. adm. 21 novembre 2016, n° 35847a, *Entreprise des Postes et Télécommunications*, https://ja.public.lu/35001-40000/35847a.pdf.
46. *Ibid.*
47. Marc Feyereisen and Jérôme Guillot, *Procédure Administrative Contentieuse*, Windhof, Larcier, 2018, n° 123 referring to Cour Adm. 5 février 1998, n° 10207C.
48. In this sense, X, 'Le droit administratif dans l'Union européenne. Les procédures applicables à l'édiction des décisions administratives individuelles. Cologne, 2 – 4 décembre 2018. Réponses au questionnaire: Luxembourg', https://aca-europe.eu/seminars/2018_Cologne/Luxembourg.pdf, p. 19. *See also*, regarding the review of facts in the course of a *recours en annulation*: Marc Feyereisen and Jérôme Guillot, *Procédure Administrative Contentieuse*, Windhof, Larcier, 2018, n° 106-108.
49. Marc Feyereisen, *La justice administrative en Europe*, https://www.aca-europe.eu/seminars/2005_Trier/Luxembourg_fr.pdf.

3 PRIOR RESEARCH

Not much academic research is available on Luxembourg competition law. In addition to a manual on Luxembourg competition law, there are a few academic articles on the Luxembourg system of competition law as such,[50] or on specific issues,[51] but not on judicial appeal/review of NCA decisions.

4 QUANTITATIVE ANALYSIS

This section moves to examine the findings resulting from applying a systematic analysis to all appellate judgments on the enforcement of Articles 101 and 102 TFEU and the national equivalent provisions that were issued and made public between 1 May 2004 and 31 April 2021.

4.1 Source of Information

The numbers of the decisions of the Competition Council and the appeals before the Administrative Courts are based on the annual reports of the Competition Council. The cases were identified on the basis of two summarising overviews: The annual report of 2017 gives an overview of all the decisions of the Council since the entry into force of the 2011 Competition Act and indicates whether or not they have been appealed. The annual report of 2011 provides a similar overview of all decisions and appeals since the entry into force of the 2004 Competition Act. Individual annual reports were used for identifying the cases decided after 2017. The full text of all the concerned decisions on appeal is available at https://justice.public.lu/fr/jurisprudence/juridictions-administratives.html. The database is expected to be comprehensive, as there is no reason to believe that cases would have been left out.[52]

4.2 Total Number of Decisions and Ratio of Appeals

During the period under investigation, the Competition Council gave forty-seven final decisions. This number includes twenty-five decisions rejecting complaints, which can

50. Philippe-Emmanuel Partsch and Elie Raimond, 'State of competition law in Luxembourg further to the 2011 reform', *Concurrences* N° 4-2013, Art. N° 57661, www.concurrences.com.
51. Lena Hornkohl, 'Implementation of the ECN+ Directive – Luxembourg: A New Competition Law And Institutional Framework', *European Competition and Regulatory Law Review* 2021/3, pp. 280-286, DOI: 10.21552/core/2021/3/21; Bruno Lasserre, Louis Vogel, Alexander Italianer and Marc Jaeger, 'Échange d'informations confidentielles dans le cadre de l'application privée du droit de la concurrence (10 ans d'application du règlement 1/2003 et de la loi luxembourgeoise relative à la concurrence, Luxembourg-Kirchberg, 6 juin 2014)', *Concurrences* N° 4-2014, Art. N° 69496, pp. 54-74.
52. At least, for the period under review.

also be appealed. Only three of the Council's decisions have been appealed. Two decisions[53] were appealed at one level only, that of the Administrative Tribunal.[54] One of these decisions concerned the rejection of a complaint.[55] Only one decision of the Council[56] was appealed on two levels: that of the Administrative Tribunal[57] and that of the Administrative Court.[58]

The ratio of the appeals on at least one level compared to the decisions taken (including rejections of complaints) during the period under investigation is 3/47 or 6%. Leaving aside the rejections of complaints it is 2/22 or 9%. The number of second-instance appeals is 1/47 or 2%. Appeals can thus be considered rather exceptional in the Luxembourg system of public enforcement of competition law.

4.3 Judgments per Year

The first decision of the Council that was appealed since the start of the period under investigation in 2004, was given in 2015,[59] a second one in 2016[60] and the last one in 2021.[61] The decision of the Administrative Tribunal on the appeal followed each time within the same calendar year. The Tribunal's decision from 2016 in *Entreprise des Postes et Telecommunications* (*EPT*)[62] was appealed at second instance before the Administrative Court. The second-instance decision followed in 2017.[63]

Figure 20.1 summarises the number of judgments issued by the various instances of the Luxembourg courts per year.

53. Case 2013-FO-03, *RFA*, https://concurrence.public.lu/content/dam/concurrence/fr/decisions/ententes/2013/decision-2013-fo-03/Entscheidung-n_2013-FO-03---oeffentliche-Version.pdf and Case 2019-R-01, https://concurrence.public.lu/content/dam/concurrence/fr/decisions/classements/Decision-2019-R-01-Version-unique.pdf.
54. Trib. Adm. 30 mars 2015, n° 33903a, *RFA*, https://ja.public.lu/30001-35000/33903a.pdf and Trib. Adm. 25 janvier 2021, n° 43114, *Fédération des Artisans*, https://ja.public.lu/40001-45000/43114.pdf.
55. Case 2019-R-01, *Fédération des Artisans*, https://concurrence.public.lu/content/dam/concurrence/fr/decisions/classements/Decision-2019-R-01-Version-unique.pdf, on appeal Trib. Adm. 25 janvier 2021, n° 43114, *Fédération des Artisans*, https://ja.public.lu/40001-45000/43114.pdf.
56. Case 2014-FO-07, *Entreprise des Postes et Télécommunications*, https://concurrence.public.lu/content/dam/concurrence/fr/decisions/abus-de-position-dominante/2014/decision-2014-fo-07/Decision-n_2014-FO-07---version-non-confidentielle.pdf.
57. *See* judgment cited in n. 45.
58. Cour Adm. 1 juin 2017, *Entreprise des Postes et Télécommunications*, n° 38930C, https://ja.public.lu/35001-40000/38930C.pdf.
59. Trib. Adm. 30 mars 2015, n° 33903a, *RFA*, https://ja.public.lu/30001-35000/33903a.pdf.
60. *See* judgment cited in n. 45.
61. Trib. Adm. 25 janvier 2021, n° 43114, https://ja.public.lu/40001-45000/43114.pdf.
62. *See* judgment cited in n. 45.
63. *See* judgment cited in n. 58.

Figure 20.1 Number of Judgments According to Instances

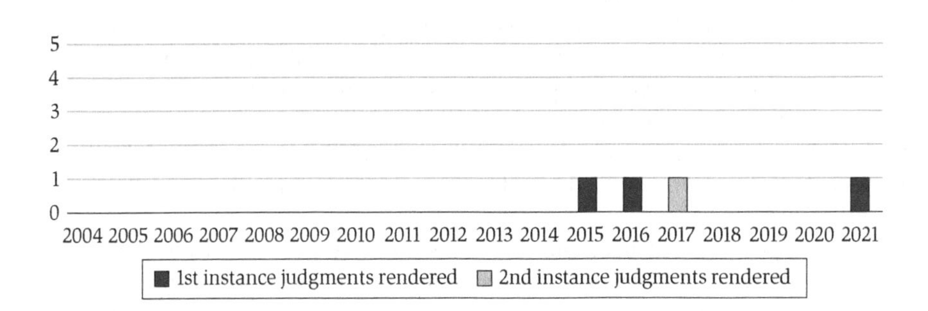

4.3.1 First Instance

As mentioned above, first-instance judgments were handed down only in 2015,[64] 2016[65] and 2021.[66]

One NCA decision that was appealed, concerned the rejection of a complaint; two NCA decisions concerned the imposition of a fine.

The case where a complaint was rejected, was a somewhat peculiar one: the complainant argued that a merger constituted an infringement of Article 102 TFEU and its national equivalent.[67] To understand this case it is important to know that Luxembourg did not have any national rules on merger control at the time the complaint was filed. In fact, at the time of writing, the preparation of a merger control law is still ongoing. When the thresholds for notification under the EU Merger Regulation are met, the merger must of course be notified to the European Commission. When those thresholds are not met, the Competition Council may only take action against anticompetitive mergers via Articles 101 and 102 TFEU and their national equivalents.

The complainant argued that the merger entailed serious risks that the merged entity would resort to abusive behaviour resulting in restrictions of competition such as driving competitors out of the market by cross-using databases, tying services offered by various companies forming part of the merged entity, by using advertising or communication strategies, etc. Moreover, the merger as such would negatively affect the structure of competition and constitute an abuse of dominance in itself thereby infringing Article 102 TFEU and its national equivalent.

64. *See* judgment cited in n. 59
65. See judgment cited in n. 45.
66. *See* judgment cited in n. 60.
67. *Ibid.*

The Council rejected the complaint on the grounds that Article 102 TFEU and its national equivalent do not allow it to rule on a purely potential abuse of a dominant position. Only concrete elements constituting a possible abuse on the part of an undertaking in a dominant position on a given market could justify the opening of a case file. Such elements were not presented by the complainant.

The complainant appealed arguing in essence that the Council had insufficiently motivated its decision, that it had wrongfully concluded that no abuse of dominance was established and wrongfully decided not to carry out an investigation following the complaint.

The appeal was unsuccessful. While recognising the duty of the Competition Council to motivate its decisions,[68] the Court did not find an infringement of this duty. The contested decision of the Competition Council was sufficiently motivated by the summary indication of the factual and legal elements on which it was based. Moreover, the Court notes that a failure to state reasons does not *ipso facto* lead to the annulment of the decision. The sanction of the obligation to state reasons for an administrative decision consists in the suspension of the time limits for appeal, the decision remaining a priori valid and the administration being able to produce or complete the reasons afterwards and even for the first time in the litigation phase.

Regarding the substance, the Court held that the conditions for the application of Article 102 (or Article 101) TFEU may not be stretched in such a way as to introduce a preventative merger control which was not foreseen by the legislator.

The Court further noted that while the principle of the opportunity of prosecution was not formally enshrined in the law, it nevertheless derives implicitly, but necessarily from the spirit of the provisions of the law of 23 October 2011. Therefore, the Competition Council had the power to reject a complaint on the sole basis of the observation that the elements submitted to it were manifestly insufficient to be likely to constitute an infringement of Article 101/102 TFEU or their national equivalents, subject to the obligation of the Competition Council to give reasons for its decision.

In the case concerned, the only concrete fact of which the Competition Council was seized, was the undisputed takeover of company D by company B. Beyond this fact, the reproaches of the plaintiff boiled down to simple hypotheses and fears of only potential, unproven violations of Article 102 TFEU and its national counterpart. The appellant's premise that the acquisition of company D would constitute *per se* an abuse of position dominant regardless of any concrete fact and regardless of any foreclosure effect or foreclosure capability was erroneous. The Court concluded that the Competition Council had not committed a manifest error of assessment and it rejected the appeal.

Fines were imposed in the judgment on the matter of *RFA*[69] and *EPT*. *RFA* will be discussed in section 4.6. *EPT* is the only case that gave rise to a second-instance

68. Based on Article 6 Règlement grand-ducal du 8 juin 1979 relatif à la procédure à suivre par les administrations relevant de l'Etat et des communes, *Mémorial A*, n° 54, 6 juillet 1979.
69. *See* judgment cited in n. 59.

appeal.[70] That case will be discussed in the next section, dealing with second-instance judgments.

4.3.2 Second Instance

As mentioned, only one second-instance decision is available, the Administrative Court's decision in *EPT*, handed down in 2017.[71] The facts of the case were as follows. In April 2006, three competing companies submitted a complaint against EPT following which the former Competition Inspectorate, opened an investigation. An interim decision was taken by the former Competition Council, but this was annulled on appeal. The newly formed Competition Council took over the case in May 2013. In the course of its investigation, the inspector in charge of the case identified nine complaints made (in)directly by the complainants, of which he included four in the SO which determined the scope of the proceedings before the Competition Council. In its decision of 13 November 2014, the Council finally retained only one as constituting an infringement of Article 102 TFEU or its national equivalent. The infringement that was retained related to coupling discounts, i.e., price reductions granted by EPT to customers of its multi-product offer 'INTEGRAL'. Within this offer, Post Telecom granted significant advantages to people who are customers for telephone, broadband internet and mobile phone services at the same time.

The Competition Council reached its decision after defining the relevant markets as on the one hand, the retail markets for fixed telephony,[72] and on the other hand, the broadband Internet markets.[73] The Council concluded that there was no need to define a separate market for bundled offers for the relevant period from 2006 to 2007. Next, based on a test carried out via the method *'par composante'*, the Council held that companies competing with EPT in the market of mobile phone telecommunication were not in a position to offer, without making losses, to their customers or potential customers the same discounts as EPT offered (via 'INTEGRAL') to people who are already EPT customers for fixed telephony and broadband Internet. As such, companies competing with EPT in the mobile phone market risked being crowded out or prevented from entering the market. The Council held that this amounted to an abuse by EPT of its dominant position in the fixed-line and Internet markets, foreclosing competition in the mobile markets for this part of the customer base. The Council recognised that over time, EPT's competitors also introduced multi-product offers such as 'INTEGRAL'. Therefore, the period of infringement selected by the Council was limited to that between late 2005 to early 2008,[74] when multi-product offers were still clearly in competition with individual services. When deciding on the fine, the Council applied a reduction by 50% in view of various circumstances such as the fact that the

70. *See* judgment cited in n. 58.
71. *Ibid.*
72. Subdivided into the markets for access to the public telephone network and those for fixed telephony services.
73. Subdivided into the retail market for broadband Internet access and the wholesale market for broadband Internet access, and finally the retail market for mobile network services.
74. According to the operative part. Elsewhere the decision mentions 2006 and 2007.

regulator approved the reference offer for the resale of the subscription, the pro-competitive effects in terms of benefits for the consumer of the discounts, the cooperation of EPT and the length of the procedure. The amount of the fine was ultimately determined at EUR 2,520,000.[75]

On 12 February 2015, EPT applied for a review of the Competition Council's decision. By judgment of 21 November 2016, the Administrative Tribunal declared EPT's application for review admissible in form, while declaring the State's incidental request for review *in peius* (increasing the fine) inadmissible. On the merits, the Tribunal declared EPT's application for review to be justified. It annulled the contested decision of the Competition Council and discharged EPT from the fine imposed on it. The Tribunal reached this conclusion based on four sets of grievances. 1) there had been a blatant failure to comply with the reasonable time limit, 2) a violation of the EPT's right to access the file, 3) an irregularity in the request for information sent to the EPT, and 4) the application of a methodology that was at variance with the European Commission's notice on the matter, which the Competition Council had stated it wished to follow. The Tribunal declared the examination of the other pleas presented by EPT to be superfluous. It motivated the discharge from the fine stating that any other decision to reduce the fine would have run up against the principle of reasonable time, in addition to the defect of the irregular investigation of the case, the extrinsic irregularities retained and the erroneous methodology applied, in an even more accentuated manner. The imposition of a lower fine by the Tribunal more than eight years after the allegedly anti-competitive activity had ceased would be largely inconsistent with the aim pursued by competition law in general and by the sanctions imposed in this area in particular. Moreover, if the Tribunal had decided, following the annulment of the defended decision, to send the case back for further investigation by the Competition Council, the additional time required would only add to the failure to comply with the reasonable time limit.[76]

On 2 January 2017, the State of the Grand Duchy of Luxembourg, declaring that it was acting through its body, the Competition Council, submitted a request for review of the Tribunal's decision. The Court rejected the State's pleas. It agreed with the first judges' opinion that the action of the competition authorities must be swift. It must reflect the economic reality of the challenged behaviour and set an example so that other actors do not adopt the same behaviour. This is even more important for economic activities, such as those in the contested decision, whose regulatory framework, and the ways in which they are carried out, are evolving, changing and fluctuating, particularly in view of technological developments. The Court confirmed the Tribunal's approach which, although not having exhausted all the pleas, retained

75. Case 2014-FO-07, https://concurrence.public.lu/content/dam/concurrence/fr/decisions/abus-de-position-dominante/2014/decision-2014-fo-07/Decision-n_2014-FO-07---version-non-confidentielle.pdf.
76. *See* judgment cited in n. 45.

four of them, considered them together and concluded that they required the annulment of the Council's decision, together with the decision not to refer the case back to the competent authority.[77]

4.4 Success Rates and Outcomes

Figure 20.2 Success of Appeals (Each NCA's Decision or Previous Instance Judgment Counts as One)

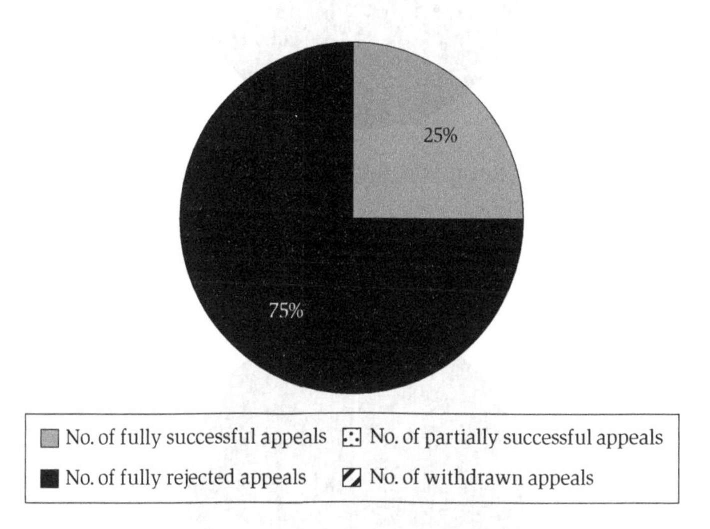

Out of the three decisions of the Council that were appealed in first instance, only one appeal was successful: the Council's decision imposing a massive fine of EUR 2,520,000 on EPT (cf *supra*, 4.3(b)) was annulled by the Administrative Tribunal.[78] The Council launched a second-instance appeal before the Administrative Court which, however, confirmed the first-instance decision.[79] Counting each appellate decision in either first or second instance as one, it can be concluded that 25% of the appeals were successful.

At first instance, a third of the appeals were fully annulled.

77. *See* judgment cited in n. 58.
78. *See* judgment cited in n. 45.
79. *See* judgment cited in n. 58.

Figure 20.3(a) First-Instance Outcome

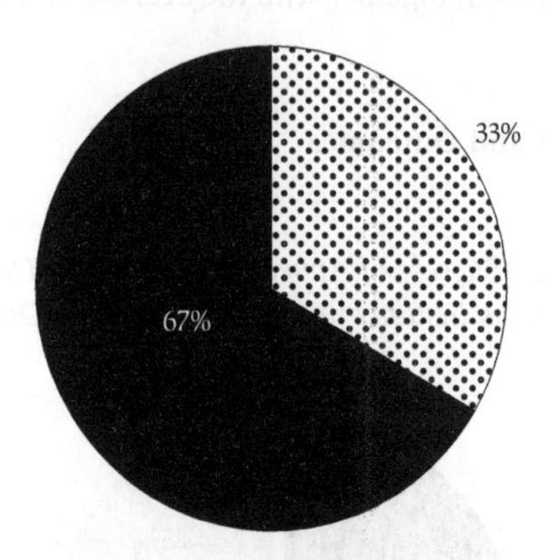

The second-instance appeal was fully rejected, meaning that the first-instance decision was fully confirmed.

Figure 20.3(b) Second-Instance Outcome

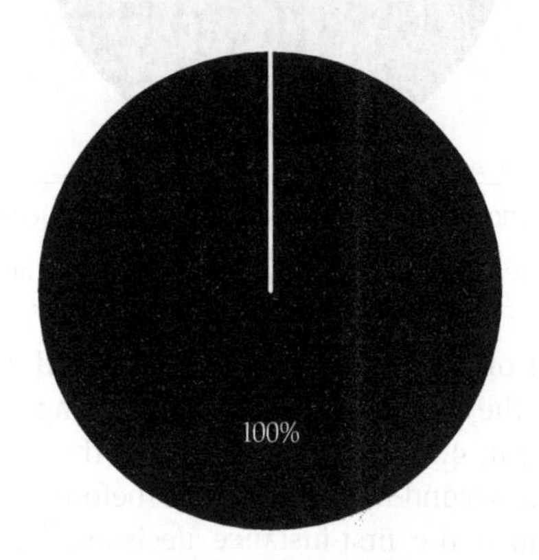

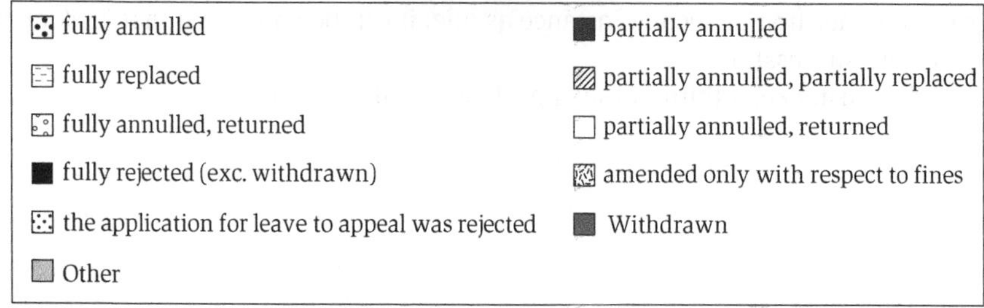

4.5 Types of NCA's Decisions Subject to Appeal

During the period under review, 75% of the appeals concerned an alleged infringement of Article 102 TFEU and its national equivalent, while 25% concerned an infringement of Article 101 TFEU and its national equivalent. Given the fact that only four appellate decisions have been given, that means that three out of the four cases concern Article 102 TFEU and its national equivalent. Moreover, two appellate decisions relating to Article 102 TFEU and its national equivalent concern the same case, *EPT*, in which a first-instance and a second-instance judgment was given. The relative importance of the type of infringement for the number of appeals in first and/or in second instance must therefore not be overestimated. Before the Council, the number of cases concerning Article 101 TFEU and/or its national equivalent (twenty-three) is also almost equal to that of cases concerning Article 102 TFEU and/or its national equivalent (twenty-four).

It is noteworthy that all decisions subject to appeal involve the combination of national and EU competition law provisions.

Figure 20.4 Rules Being Appealed

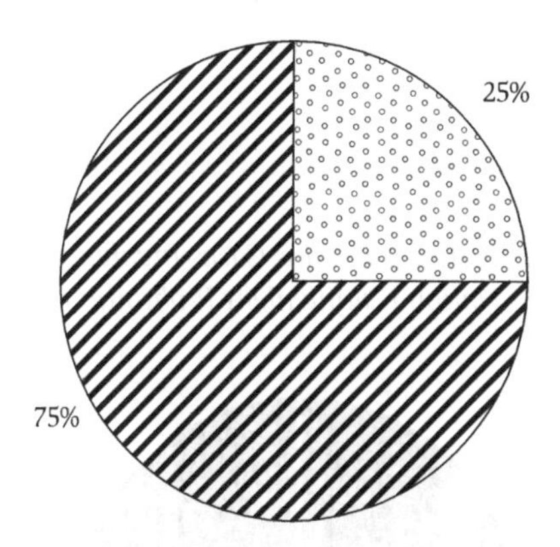

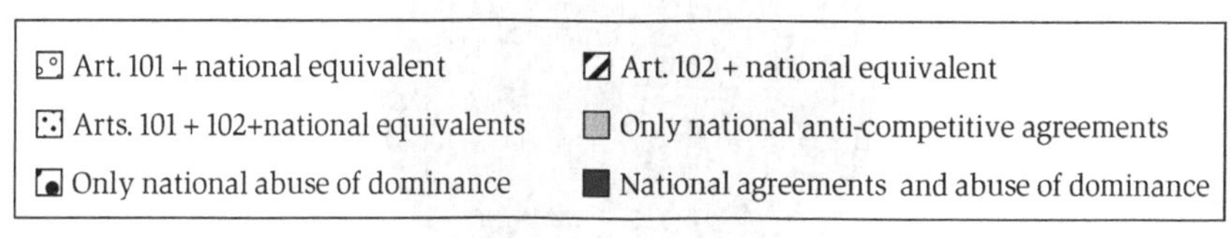

The appeal relating to the infringement of Article 101 TFEU and its national equivalent was decided in 2015.[80] The appeals relating to alleged infringements of Article 102 TFEU and its national equivalent were decided in 2016,[81] 2017[82] and 2021.[83]

All appeals in cases of an alleged infringement of Article 102 TFEU and its national equivalent concerned exclusionary abuse (75% of the appeals). The appeal relating to an infringement of Article 101 TFEU and its national equivalent concerned a cartel (25% of the appeals).

80. *See* judgment cited in n. 59.
81. *See* judgment cited in n. 45.
82. *See* judgment cited in n. 58.
83. Trib. Adm. 25 janvier 2021, n° 43114, *Fédération des Artisans*, https://ja.public.lu/40001-450 00/43114.pdf.

Figure 20.5 Types of Restrictions

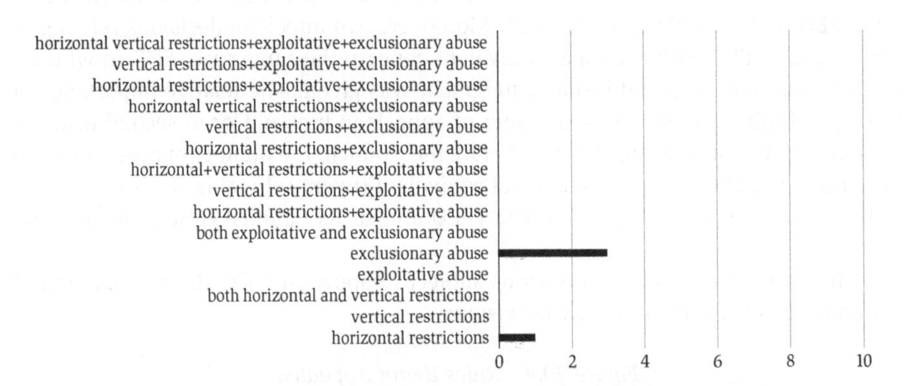

As mentioned before, the appeal relating to an infringement of Article 101 TFEU and its national equivalent, *RFA*,[84] concerned a cartel, and therefore an infringement by-object.

Figure 20.6 Object/Effect (Only for Cases Involving Article 101 and the National Equivalent Prohibition)

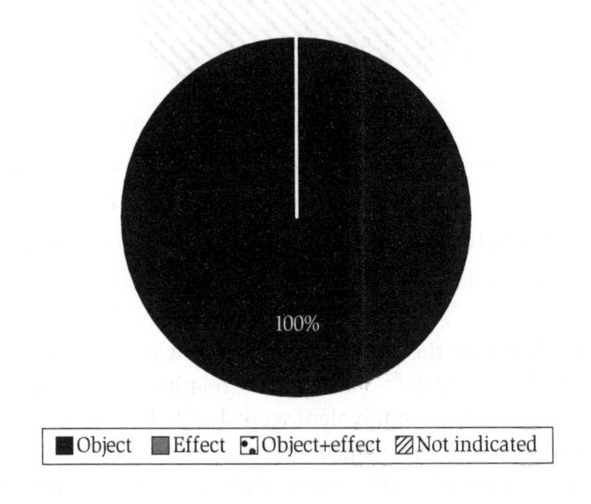

84. *See* judgment cited in n. 59.

Figure 20.7 The Competition Authority's Procedure

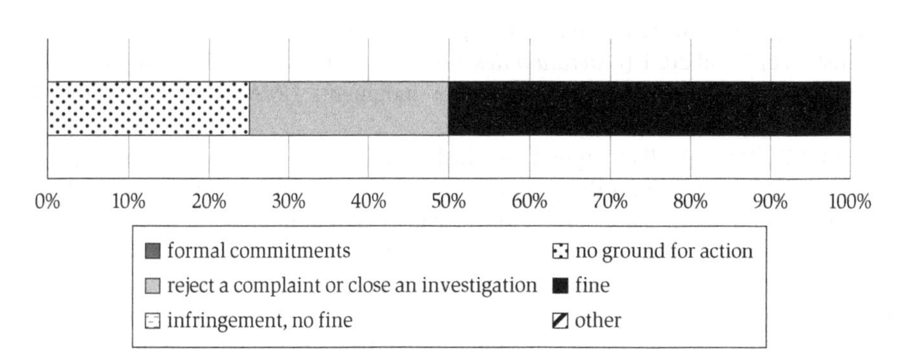

In two cases, *RFA*[85] and EPT,[86] the Council imposed a fine. In one case, *Fédération des Artisans*, it rejected a complaint.[87]

4.6 Grounds of Appeal

Figure 20.8 Grounds of Appeal (Each NCA's Decision or Previous Instance Judgment Counts as One)

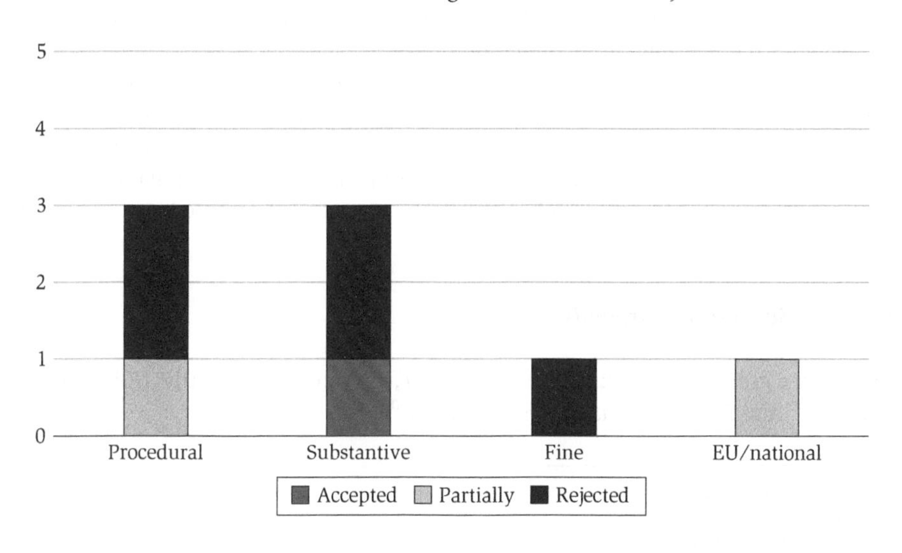

85. Case 2013-FO-03, https://concurrence.public.lu/content/dam/concurrence/fr/decisions/ententes/2013/decision-2013-fo-03/Entscheidung-n_2013-FO-03---oeffentliche-Version.pdf.
86. Case 2014-FO-07, https://concurrence.public.lu/content/dam/concurrence/fr/decisions/abus-de-position-dominante/2014/decision-2014-fo-07/Decision-n_2014-FO-07---version-non-confidentielle.pdf.
87. Case 2019-R-01, https://concurrence.public.lu/content/dam/concurrence/fr/decisions/classements/Decision-2019-R-01-Version-unique.pdf.

4.6.1 *Procedural Grounds*

Procedural grounds were argued in the appeals decided in 2015 (*RFA*),[88] 2016 (*EPT*, first instance)[89] and 2021 (*Fédération des Artisans*).[90] In the 2016 *EPT* judgment, they were partially accepted,[91] in the two other judgments (*RFA*[92] and *Fédération des Artisans*[93]) they were not accepted.

In *RFA*,[94] the appellant argued that the Luxembourg NCA's decision infringed the *ne bis in idem* principle on the ground that the latter by taking into account RFA's market share on the German market for the calculation of the fine for its infringement of the competition rules on the Luxembourg market. The Tribunal rejected this argument because the said principle does not oppose different competition authorities imposing sanctions on the same infringer, for the same set of facts when the protected interest is different. The territorial application of the (national) competition rules would therefore exclude the application of the *ne bis in idem* principle.[95]

In *Fédération des Artisans* the appellant argued that the NCA had insufficiently motivated its decision to reject its complaint. The Tribunal rejected the argument. It held that the decision was sufficiently motivated by the summary indication of the factual and legal elements on which it was based. Moreover, the Tribunal noted that in any case, a failure to state reasons does not *ipso facto* lead to the annulment of the decision. The sanction of the obligation to state reasons for an administrative decision consists in the suspension of the time limits for appeal, the decision remaining *a priori* valid and the administration being able to produce or complete the reasons afterwards and even for the first time in the litigation phase.[96]

In *EPT*, three of the four grounds on which the Tribunal based its annulment of the NCA's decision were procedural: a blatant disrespect of the reasonable time limit, a violation of EPT's right of access to the file (but not to the extent claimed by EPT) and an irregularity in the request for information sent to the EPT (irregularities in the requests for information sent to other undertakings were not accepted as a ground of appeal).[97]

4.6.2 *Substantive Grounds*

Substantive grounds were argued in 2016 (*EPT*, first instance),[98] 2017 (*EPT*, second instance)[99] and 2021 (*Fédération des Artisans*).[100]

88. *See* judgment cited in n. 59.
89. *See* judgment cited in n. 45.
90. *See* judgment cited in n. 83.
91. *See* judgment cited in n. 45.
92. *See* judgment cited in n. 59.
93. *See* judgment cited in n. 83.
94. *See* judgment cited in n. 59.
95. The Tribunal refers for this statement to Case COMP/E-1/36.604 *Citric Acid.*
96. *See* judgment cited in n. 83.
97. *See* judgment cited in n. 45.
98. *Ibid.*
99. *See* judgment cited in n. 58.

Only in the *EPT* judgment given by the Administrative Tribunal in 2016, they were accepted. More specifically, the Administrative Tribunal accepted the appellant's argument that while the NCA had stated to apply the Commission's Guidelines on its enforcement priorities in relation to Article 102 TFEU, it had not applied them correctly when assessing the rebate system applied by EPT. Without discussing all of the arguments the appellants put forward against the NCA's application of Article 102 TFEU, the Tribunal concluded that the way in which the NCA had applied the Article was wrong and did not find any support in the case law of the CJEU or the Commission's guidelines.[101]

In *Fédération des Artisans*, the appellant complained that a takeover led to a distortion of competition, and to abuses of dominance due to the cross-use of databases, coupled sales, advertising or communication strategies, the creation of barriers to market entry and a limitation of financial risks in the context of public contracts. The NCA rejected the complaint. The complainant appealed, arguing that the NCA was obliged to carry out an *ex post* merger control, and in particular, an investigation in order to detect the potential abuses mentioned above. The appellant added that for an infringement of Article 102 TFEU and its national counterpart to be upheld, it is sufficient to point to a potential abuse of a dominant position in order to demonstrate the serious risks that the transaction would pose to competition. The Tribunal rejected the argument. It pointed out that Luxembourg did not have specific legislation on merger control and that the thresholds for the application of the EU Merger Regulation were not met. Only when the conditions of Article 101 and/or 102 TFEU or their national counterparts are fulfilled, competition law sanctions can be imposed on undertakings involved in anti-competitive behaviour. The conditions for the application of these articles could not be stretched in such a way as to introduce a preventative merger control which was not foreseen by the legislator. Given the principle of the opportunity of prosecution, the Competition Council had the power to reject a complaint on the sole basis that the elements submitted to it were manifestly insufficient to constitute an infringement of Articles 101 and 102 TFEU and their national equivalents[102]

4.6.3 Fines-Related Grounds

Only in one appeal case, the *RFA* decision given by the Administrative Tribunal in 2015, arguments aiming at a reduction of the fine were put forward by the appellant and discussed by the Administrative Tribunal.[103] The case concerned four undertakings involved in bid-rigging. The undertakings had agreed that only one of them would

100. *See* judgment cited in n. 83.
101. *See* judgment cited in n. 45.
102. *See* judgment cited in n. 83.
103. The arguments put forward against the Competition Council's rejection of the appellant's application for a reduction of the fine under the national leniency programme is discussed further on in this chapter.

bid for public contracts for railway switches in Luxembourg; in return, that undertaking would refrain from bidding for similar contracts in Germany. Two undertakings applied for immunity under the national leniency programme in Luxembourg. More than a year later, a third undertaking applied for leniency in the form of a reduction of fines under the same programme. The immunity applications were successful. The application for a reduction of fines was not. By the decision of 23 October 2013, the Competition Council fined two undertakings, the unsuccessful leniency applicant and a competitor. The former launched an appeal against the Decision of the NCA and requested the fine to be reduced or to annul the decision. The appellant specified it was not contesting the infringement, only the fine. The appellant criticised the decision on various grounds relating essentially to the calculation of the fine imposed on it.

The appellant argued that by referring to the Commission Guidelines on the method of setting fines, the Competition Council had undertaken to apply these Guidelines to all aspects of the case. By deviating from the Guidelines on certain points, e.g., when determining the market, it had rendered its decision illegal. The Court rejected this argument. Even when the Council would have undertaken to comply with the Commission's Guidelines, it was still entitled to deviate from them where this was justified by the particular circumstances of the case or in the general interest. The Tribunal pointed out that this is recognised in point 37 of the Guidelines themselves.

The Tribunal also rejected the appellant's argument that the principle of *ne bis in idem* prohibited the Council to take into account the appellant's market shares on the German market for private switches because it had already been sanctioned for violations of competition law in this market by the German competition authority. According to the Tribunal, the principle *ne bis in idem* does not *a priori* preclude different authorities from different States from dealing with different offences arising from the same event.

The appellant furthermore argued[104] that the application of a gravity coefficient of 17% infringed the principle of non-discrimination on the grounds of nationality, the principle of equality before the law and the principle of legitimate expectations, because the Council had applied lower coefficients in three other cases. The Court rejected these arguments because it did not consider the earlier cases similar. Moreover, it found that a certain gravity and unpredictability in the amount of competition fines was required for the fines to have a dissuasive character. In view of the seriousness of the infringements, the Court considered a 17% coefficient appropriate, even moderate.

The appellant finally complained that the Competition Council rejected the mitigating circumstances invoked[105] without any motivation thereby infringing national procedural law. The Tribunal rejected this argument as well, *inter alia*, because the requirements for mitigating circumstances set by the Commission's Guidelines on the method of setting fines were not met.

104. *See* judgment cited in n. 59.
105. Except for the absence of dilatory measures, which was honoured by a 10% reduction of the fine.

4.6.4 *EU/National Grounds*

In *EPT*, the tension between EU and national law manifested itself on the one hand in the appellant's argument that the NCA did not correctly apply the Commission's Guidelines on its enforcement priorities in relation to Article 102 TFEU, although it had stated to comply with them and on the other hand in its argument that the duration of the national proceedings was incompatible with the principle of the reasonable time, recognised as a general principle of Union law and also referred to in the ECHR.[106]

4.7 Leniency and Settlements

Of the three NCA decisions appealed, only the *RFA* case involved a leniency application. The unsuccessful applicant for a reduction of the fine under the national leniency programme contested the Competition Council's decision to reject its leniency application.

It argued that it provided the Competition Council with relevant written evidence on the existence and scope of the alleged cartel and that it also fulfilled the other conditions of Article 21 of the Act of 23 October 2011, namely that it ended its participation in the alleged cartel without delay after filing its application and that it provided the Competition Council with genuine, full and permanent cooperation from the time it filed its application until the final decision. It therefore requested the Tribunal to reduce the fine by at least 50%.

The Tribunal rejected these arguments. First, it noted that the company submitted its leniency application after the immunity application by two of its co-conspirators. Under the applicable rules, it could therefore not obtain a reduction exceeding 50%.

Second, when the appellant submitted its leniency application, more than a year had passed since the Council had received the immunity application from two other cartel members and more than nine months after it had appointed a staff member for the investigation. This relatively late timing disqualified the appellant in any case from claiming a reduction at the top of the 30%-50% scale of the reduction that can be granted to the first successful applicant for a reduction: irrespective of the quality of the cooperation, the maximum reduction cannot be granted if the application is late.

Third, a reduction is granted only if the applicant provides evidence with 'significant added value' to the evidence already in the possession of the competition authority. The evidence provided must enhance the ability of the competition authority to establish the existence of the alleged cartel, by its nature or by its level of precision. That was not the case.[107]

106. *See* judgment cited in n. 45.
107. *See* judgment cited in n. 59.

Figure 20.9 Leniency

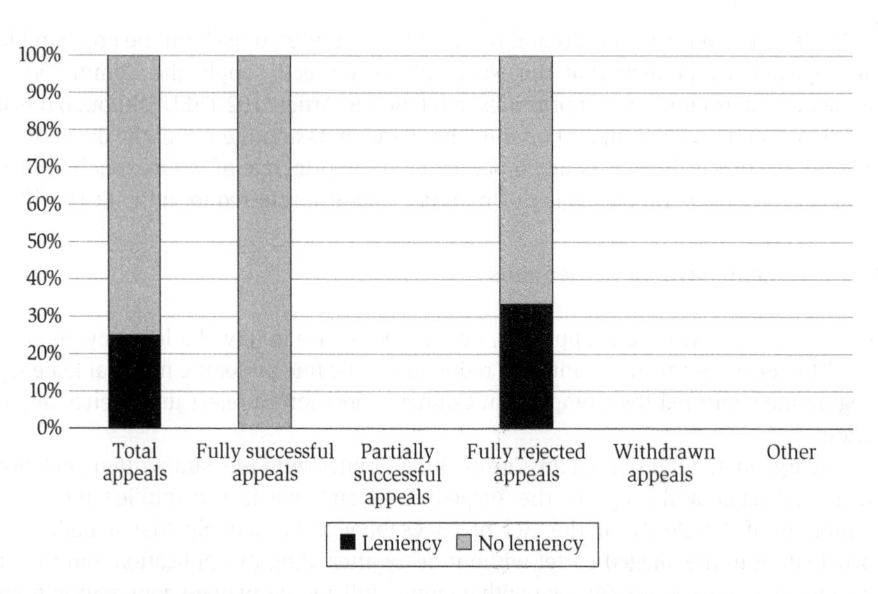

Luxembourg does not have a settlements programme, only commitment decisions. While the latter can be appealed, no appeals of such decisions are reported.

5 QUALITATIVE ANALYSIS

The limited number of infringement cases and appeals is due to a combination of two elements: the small size of the Member State and the absence of a long-standing competition culture. The first NCA decision in the period under review (starting on 1 May 2004) was given in 2007. The first review was launched and the first review decision was given in 2015. This shows that it takes time to develop a competition culture.

Luxembourg is one of the Member States that provides for judicial review of complaints that are rejected without an in-depth investigation of the case. The system of review that existed under the 2014 Competition Act, in which only final decisions imposing a fine were subject to a *recours en réformation* and other final distinctions were only subject to a *recours en annulation* led to practical difficulties. Since the entry into force of the 2011 Competition Act, this distinction is no longer made: all final decisions given by the Competition Council are subject to a *recours en réformation*.

What is remarkable is that 75 % of the appeals concern alleged infringements of Article 102 TFEU and its national equivalent. The only cartel case that was decided on during the period under review was triggered by a leniency application. No grounds of appeal were accepted in the case where the Council had found an infringement of Article 101 TFEU and its national equivalent. The appeal was fully rejected.

Where the appeal concerned an alleged infringement of Article 102 TFEU and its national equivalent, procedural and substantive grounds were successful. In two-thirds of the decisions, the appeal was unsuccessful. Two of those decisions were first-instance decisions. One decision was a second-instance decision, in which the Administrative Court rejected the appeal, launched by the State/Competition Council against the first-instance decision by the Administrative Tribunal, which had annulled the Competition Council's decision.

Overall, 75% of the appeals were rejected. Nevertheless, the courts did not shy away from overhauling a massive fine imposed by the Competition Council after proceedings whose duration exceeded a reasonable time mainly as a result of the long period of inactivity of the NCA as established by the 2004 Competition Act.

While Luxemburg does not have a long-standing experience with competition law, no preliminary references to the Court of Justice in order to obtain guidance on the interpretation of the rules of EU competition law were made. The Commission did not intervene in any of the cases as an *amicus curiae* either.

As mentioned in section 2, Luxembourg distinguishes between the *recours en annulation* and the *recours en réformation*. All the decisions analysed above are decisions against the final decisions of the Competition authority given after the entry into force of the 2011 Competition Act. In all these cases, the appeal provided for by the law was an *appeal en réformation*. The appeal in *RFA*[108] and the second-degree appeal in *EPT*[109] were correctly labelled as such by the applicants. However, in *Fédération des Artisans*, the appellants labelled their action as a *recours en réformation*, alternatively *en annulation*. The Tribunal declared the *recours en réformation* admissible and decided there was therefore no reason anymore to decide on the *recours en annulation*. Things were a bit more complicated in the first-instance appeal in *EPT*. Here, the applicant requested primarily the annulment of the decision and subsidiary its reformation. The Tribunal held that, if in a matter in which the law has instituted a *recours en réformation*, as was the case here, the applicant seeks only or principally the annulment of the contested decision, the appeal is admissible insofar as the applicant confines himself to invoking grounds of legality, provided that he observes the procedural rules and time limits for the *recours en annulation*[110] and provided the annulment sought is usefully underpinned by a ground of annulment.[111] Given that these requirements were fulfilled, the Tribunal declared the appeal admissible as an appeal *en annulation* and decided according to the rules relating to these procedures.[112] The second-degree appeal brought by the State was labelled and decided as an appeal *en réformation*.

Irrespective of whether the appeal is *en annulation* or *en réformation*, the scope of the review is determined by the arguments the appellant brings forward against the

108. *See* judgment cited in n. 59.
109. *See* judgment cited in n. 58.
110. The Tribunal refers for this to Trib. adm. 3 mars 1997, n° 9693, *Pas. adm.* 2016, V° *Recours en réformation*, n° 2 with further references.
111. Here the Tribunal refers to Trib. adm. 13 juin 2005, n° 19368, *Pas. adm.* 2016, V° *Recours en réformation*, n° 6.
112. *See* judgment cited in n. 45.

contested decision. The intensity of the review differs. When deciding on an appeal *en annulation* the review court will only assess the legality of the contested decision. It has to uphold the decision insofar as the latter is in line with the law, given the law and the facts submitted to the NCA at the time when it was called upon to rule, even if the review court itself would reach a different result.

By contrast, when deciding on an appeal *en réformation*, the review court is not limited to controlling the legality of the contested decision. The review court will also verify whether that decision corresponds to its own assessment, which is to be made taking into account new elements submitted to it during the review procedure. If that is not the case; the review court will substitute its own decision for the contested decision.

6 CONCLUDING REMARKS

Luxembourg does not have a long-standing tradition in competition law enforcement. Under Luxembourg's first general act on anticompetitive practices dating back to 1970, hardly any enforcement action was taken. Also, it took Luxembourg until 2004 to introduce national equivalents of Articles 101 and 102 TFEU. The enforcement system established in 2004, was dualistic, based on a strict division between the responsibility for investigations of competition law infringements (Competition Inspection) on the one hand and decision-making on the existence of infringements and imposing sanctions (Competition Council) on the other hand.

In 2011, the dualistic enforcement structure was replaced by a monistic structure and the rules on the appeal of NCA decisions were reformed. A first-instance appeal before the Administrative Tribunal and a second-instance appeal before the Administrative Court remained available. However, changes were made to the nature of the appeal. Under the 2004 Competition Act, a distinction was made between appeals against decisions of the Council regarding fines and appeals against other decisions of the Council. Against decisions imposing a fine, a *recours en réformation* could be launched, meaning that the Administrative Tribunal could replace the appealed decision with its own decision. Against other types of decisions taken by the Council, a *recours en annulation* could be brought. In such a case, the Administrative Tribunal could only confirm or annul the appealed decision and refer it back to the Competition Council. Both the reform of the enforcement structure and the reform of the appeal system served to render competition enforcement more effective. Given the evolution in the number of decisions by the Competition Council and requests for review, this seems to have worked. Only nine decisions were taken by the Competition Council as established by the 2004 Competition Act; thirty-eight by the Competition Council as established by the 2011 Competition Act. All appeals were decided after 2014.

Nevertheless, the number of enforcement decisions and requests remains low. This is not only the result of the absence of a long-standing competition culture but also of the limited size of the country.

What is remarkable is that 75% of the appeals concern alleged infringements of Article 102 TFEU and its national equivalent. The only cartel case that was decided on during the period under review was triggered by a leniency application.

No grounds of appeal were accepted in the case where the Council had found an infringement of Article 101 TFEU and its national equivalent. The appeal was fully rejected.

Where the appeal concerned an alleged infringement of Article 102 TFEU and its national equivalent, procedural and substantive grounds were successful. In two-thirds of the decisions, the appeal was unsuccessful. Two of those decisions were first-instance decisions. One decision was a second-instance decision, where the Administrative Court rejected the appeal, launched by the State/Competition Council against the first-instance decision by the Administrative Tribunal, which had annulled the Competition Council's decision.

Chapter 21
Malta Report

*Sylvann Aquilina Zahra**

1 INTRODUCTION TO THE COMPETITION LAW ENFORCEMENT CONTEXT IN MALTA

1.1 Historical Outline

In Malta, the Competition Act (CA)[1] came into force on 1 February 1995.[2] The substantive provisions are contained in Articles 5 and 9 CA which are respectively modelled on Articles 101 and 102 of the Treaty on the Functioning of the European Union (TFEU), henceforth referred to as the national and EU competition rules. The changes to the national competition rules since the CA's enactment have generally aimed to align them further with the EU competition rules. Less plain sailing have been the changes to the procedural rules and institutional framework for the enforcement of competition law which, as shall be discussed, have been amended significantly a number of times over the years.

Uniform interpretation of EU and national competition law has been secured through specific provisions of the CA.[3] As evidenced by Malta's competition enforcement and judicial practice, there is consistent reference to the decisional practice and guidance of the European Commission (Commission) and the case law of the Court of

* The content of this report is intended for general information and should not be considered to constitute legal advice. The views expressed are entirely personal and should not be attributed to the firm or any entity.

1. Chapter 379 of the laws of Malta.
2. Legal Notice 13 of 1995.
3. *See* CA as originally enacted, Schedule, rule 14 (renumbered as rule 13 by the amendments in 2004); Malta Competition and Consumer Affairs Authority Act (MCCAA Act) as originally enacted, Second Schedule, rule 9; CA, Articles 12A(7) and 13B(7).

Justice of the European Union (CJEU) in the interpretation of the substantive provisions. EU procedural rules relating to competition proceedings have also sometimes been relied upon with respect to national enforcement.[4]

The CA applies to all sectors of the economy. Initially, public undertakings were excluded unless the relevant Minister declared by an order that a public undertaking was subject to it. This was subsequently reversed so that public undertakings became subject to the CA unless exempted.[5] In 2004, the provision enabling exemption was replaced by a provision modelled on Article 106(2) TFEU[6] and the last exemption order for certain public undertakings was repealed.[7]

The power to investigate alleged breaches under the CA is vested with the competition authority, currently the Office for Competition (OC),[8] and formerly the Office for Fair Competition (OFC). Sector regulators do not have shared competence to apply *ex post* the competition rules under the CA although they generally have the duty to ensure *ex ante* that competition on the relevant market is maintained in terms of their own regulatory regime.

Originally, the CA allocated the investigatory role to the OFC and the decision-making role to the then Commission for Fair Trading (CFT). In an attempt to hasten the procedure for less serious cases, this strict division of functions was partially relaxed in 2001, when the OFC was granted the power to take decisions concerning non-serious infringements and issue cease and desist orders, subject to review by the CFT. In parallel, the CFT continued to decide cases alleging serious infringements.[9] Further, whereas originally, the OFC had to refer a complaint which it considered inadmissible to the CFT for its determination on admissibility, in 2001, the OFC was given the power to reject complaints on the ground of inadmissibility subject to review by the CFT. Thus, in some cases, the CFT acted as a competition authority adopting a decision following the OFC's investigation, whereas in others it acted as a reviewing tribunal scrutinising decisions by the OFC. In this respect, as at 2001, Malta's institutional structure, insofar as investigations and decisions on substance were concerned (fines aside), involved a combination of the elements of both the judicial and administrative

4. *See* Application No. 1/2011, *Onorevoli Joe Mizzi v. L-Ufficcju għall-Kompetizzjoni* (*Mizzi*), partial judgments of 21 March 2012, 27 February 2013 and 28 January 2016, discussed below.
5. Act No. XXVIII of 2000, which came into force on 1 October 2001 (LN 240 of 2001).
6. Act No. IV of 2003, Part VI, which came into force on 1 May 2004 (LN 332 of 2004).
7. LN 144 of 2002 repealed by LN 331 of 2004. The application of this exemption arose in Complaint No 1/2009 *Hompesch Service Station Limited v. Korporazzjoni Enemalta et,* 29 March 2010 (*Hompesch* CFT decision); Application No. 938/2010 *Korporazzjoni Enemalta v. Direttur tal-Ufficcju tal-Kompetizzjoni Gusta et,* 9 October 2014 (*Hompesch* FHCC judgment), confirmed on appeal on 28 February 2020 (*Hompesch* Court of Appeal judgment) all subsequent to the OFC's decision addressed to *Hompesch Service Station Ltd et, 17 March 2009.*
8. CA, Article 3; MCCAA Act, Article 14(1)(a) and (c).
9. *Supra* n. 5. The determination of a serious infringement was based on the gravity and duration of the infringement. In practice, there were some cases involving the typical serious infringements, such as cartels, where a decision finding an infringement was adopted by the OFC. *See*, for instance, CCD/97/07 *Decision relating to proceedings pursuant to Articles 5 & 9 of the Competition Act, 1994, in respect of conduct by the Burdnara Bulk Cargo Group and Central Cement Ltd,* 6 January 2010.

models. These models are discussed in Chapter 31. The CFT's dual role continued through part of the project period.

Initially, criminal offences for infringements of the substantive provisions arose where the CFT found that the investigated conduct was in breach of the CA and, following publication of its decision, a person engaged in any act pursuant to that conduct.[10] This meant that criminal proceedings had to be instituted separately before the Court of Magistrates and this only when the unlawful behaviour was pursued notwithstanding the CFT's decision. Upon conviction, the Court of Magistrates could impose fines.[11] While still allowing for the possibility to launch criminal proceedings, in 2001, in an attempt to make the CA more effective, alternatives to criminal proceedings became applicable. These were, first, compromise penalties consisting of a low fine within a specified range to be imposed by the OFC where a person breached the OFC's cease and desist order,[12] and, second, the possibility to extinguish criminal liability by virtue of an agreement in writing between the offender and the OFC, stipulating the payment of a sum determined by the OFC, in agreement with the CFT, consisting of a percentage of the penalty applicable for the offence.[13]

In 2004,[14] in light of Malta's accession to the European Union,[15] the CA was amended to enable the concurrent application of Articles 101 and 102 TFEU with Articles 5 and 9 CA in cases involving an effect on trade between Malta and any one or more Member States,[16] in line with *Council Regulation (EC) No 1/2003* (Regulation 1/2003).[17] The 2004 amendments repealed the provisions providing for individual exemption and negative clearance, thereby adopting a system of self-assessment akin to Regulation 1/2003. The 2004 amendments did not alter the division of functions between the OFC and the CFT. However, the determination of any breaches of Articles 101 and 102 TFEU was allocated to the CFT, irrespective of the seriousness of the breach. The power of the OFC and the CFT to issue compliance orders setting behavioural or structural remedies was introduced. Another amendment was that an infringement of the competition rules immediately amounted to an offence without the need for subsequent conduct following an infringement decision.[18] Yet, it was still necessary to file separate criminal proceedings for the imposition of fines.

In 2011, the Malta Competition and Consumer Affairs Authority Act (MCCAA Act)[19] established the Malta Competition and Consumer Affairs Authority (MCCAA), a public authority, consisting of a Board of Governors (Board) and four functionally

10. Original CA, Articles 16(1), 17. In 2001, this was extended to OFC decisions and cease and desist orders (*supra* n. 5).
11. Original CA, Article 21(1).
12. CA as amended by Act No. XXVIII of 2000 (*supra* n. 5), Article 26A.
13. *Ibid.*, Article 26B.
14. Act No. III of 2004, Part XXIV, which entered into force on 1 May 2004.
15. Malta became an EU Member State on 1 May 2004.
16. Articles 5(5) and (6), and 9(4).
17. [2003] OJ L1/1.
18. *See* Complaint No. 5/2006, *Ilment ta' Cassar Fuels Limited v. Korporazzjoni Enemalta (Cassar Fuels)*, 30 April 2007, p. 11.
19. Chapter 510 of the laws of Malta. The MCCAA Act entered into force on 23 May 2011 (LN 190 of 2011).

independent entities, each fulfilling distinct responsibilities under separate laws, with one of these entities being the OC[20] which replaced the OFC.[21] Provisions were included in the MCCAA Act to ensure the independence and autonomy of the OC, including from the Board and the other entities.[22] Indeed, one of the main political considerations motivating the reform was to guarantee the OC's independence and autonomy from the government and to make such independence more visible to the public (in comparison to the OFC which was a Government department).

Simultaneously, in 2011, significant amendments were made to the CA aiming to make enforcement more effective. Administrative fines for breaches of the competition rules were established replacing the previous criminal penalties, compromise penalties and penalties extinguishing criminal liability. Further, the settlement and commitments procedures were introduced, alongside sectoral inquiries, the possibility to ask for guidance letters on novel points[23] and an ad hoc action for antitrust damages. Notably, the 2011 amendments overturned the previous institutional structure by introducing the administrative model and providing procedural provisions more aligned with the EU procedural provisions under Regulation 1/2003 and Regulation 773/2004.[24] Thus, in addition to its power to investigate, these amendments empowered the OC, with respect to new cases, to decide all competition infringements and impose administrative fines.[25] Its decisions were subject to appeal on points of law and fact before the Competition and Consumer Appeals Tribunal (CCAT), also established by the 2011 amendments, and the CCAT's decisions were then subject to appeal on points of law before the Court of Appeal. The greatest benefit of this institutional reform was that competition proceedings could come to a swifter conclusion as the OC, following its investigation and after notifying the parties with a statement of objections and giving the parties the opportunity to be heard, could proceed with a decision together with the appropriate remedies without having to prove its case *ab initio* before

20. In terms of Article 3 CA and Article 7 MCCAA Act, the powers vested in the OC are exercised by the Director General heading the OC.
21. The other three entities are the Office for Consumer Affairs, the Technical Regulations Division and the Standards and Metrology Institute.
22. MCCAA Act, Articles 3(3)(a)(second proviso), 7(3), 11(1)(d), 12(4); CA, Article 3. These provisions continued to be strengthened by the reform in 2021 implementing *Directive (EU) 2019/1* (ECN+ Directive), [2019] OJ L11/3, which contains provisions aimed at strengthening the independence of competition authorities - *see* MCCAA Act, Articles 13(4), 13A and 58 (proviso). *See also* Case COMP-MCCAA 4/2017, *OC Decision relating to a proceeding under article 15(1) of the Competition Act*, 18 September 2017, paras 206-214.
23. This possibility, which does not seem to have ever been used, was removed by the reform in 2019.
24. Commission Regulation (EC) No. 773/2004 of 7 April 2004 relating to the conduct of proceedings by the Commission pursuant to Articles 81 and 82 of the EC Treaty [2004] OJ L123/18.
25. New cases included infringements occurring before the coming into force of the 2011 amendments in respect of which no investigation had ever been initiated. In these cases, the undertaking concerned, in the application of punitive measures only, was given the option of choosing those applicable before the 2011 amendments rather than those created by the 2011 amendments. The law as it stood prior to the 2011 amendments continued to apply to pending investigations, pending CFT proceedings and decisions which were not yet final at the time when the 2011 amendments came into force. Thus, for pending investigations, the OC absorbed the more limited powers and responsibilities of its predecessor as they existed prior to the 2011 amendments. *See* MCCAA Act, as originally enacted, Article 70(1)(a), (2) and (4).

a separate tribunal. Further, the CA's deterrent effect was enhanced since administrative fines could be imposed simultaneously with the OC's decision.

The administrative model was however short-lived as it soon came under attack in *Federation of Estate Agents v. Direttur Generali (Kompetizzjoni) et* (*FEA*).[26] This case sparked the need for further reform culminating in the 2019 amendments,[27] which introduced the judicial model discussed in the next subsection. The 2019 amendments were further reinforced by another reform in 2021.[28] Yet, the principal thrust of the 2021 reform was to transpose the ECN+ Directive[29] into Maltese law, aiming at 'strengthening and enhancing the efficiency of Malta's competition law enforcement system and further align Malta's competition rules to the European Union's competition law.'[30]

Between the 2011 and 2021 reforms, there were also important developments relating to private enforcement. In 2012, the *Collective Proceedings Act* was enacted, providing for 'opt-in' class actions for competition infringements.[31] In 2017, the EU Damages Directive[32] was transposed into Maltese law.[33]

At the time of writing, no further reform of a substantive or procedural nature or to the institutional set-up has been announced.

1.2 Enforcement Framework

Since 2019, as mentioned, the public enforcement of competition law in Malta has pursued the judicial model whereby the OC carries out investigations[34] and, where it considers that a breach of the competition rules may have occurred, initiates judicial

26. Constitutional Application No. 87/2013, decided by the First Hall of the Civil Court (FHCC) in its constitutional jurisdiction on 21 April 2015 and, on appeal, by the Constitutional Court on 3 May 2016.
27. Act No. XVI of 2019, which entered into force on 29 July 2019 (LN 179 of 2019).
28. The reform in 2021 consisted of the following three instruments: (i) Competition Act and the Malta Competition and Consumer Affairs Authority (Amendment) Act, 2021, Act XLV of 2021, which entered into force on 31 August 2021 (LN 339 of 2021); (ii) Immunity from Penalties and Reduction of Penalties in Cartel Investigations Regulations (Leniency Regulations), LN 264 of 2021; (iii) Mutual Assistance between National Competition Authorities Regulations, LN 265 of 2021. The latter Regulations and the Leniency Regulations entered into force on 18 June 2021.
29. *Supra* n. 22.
30. Government response to the Consultation on the National implementation of the ECN+ Directive (2019/1) into Maltese Competition law and other proposed amendments to the Competition Act, 10 November 2020, p. 4, https://mccaa.org.mt/media/5629/141220_final-report-consultation-ecnplus-directive.pdf. For the main changes introduced by the 2021 reform, *see* Aquilina Zahra S, Implementation of the ECN+ Directive in Malta: The Journey Towards Effective Enforcement – Where Does Malta Stand? European Competition and Regulatory Law Review (CoRe), Volume 5, Issue 3 (2021), p. 287, available at CoRe - European Competition and Regulatory Law Review: Implementation of the ECN+ Directive Malta: The Journey Towards Effective Enforcement - Where Does Malta Stand? (lexxion.eu).
31. Chapter 520 of the laws of Malta, retitled Collective Proceedings (Competition) Act.
32. Directive 2014/104/EU of the European Parliament and of the Council of 26 November 2014 on certain rules governing actions for damages under national law for infringements of the competition law provisions of the Member States and of the European Union [2014] OJ L 349/1.
33. CA, Article 27A; Competition Law Infringements (Actions for Damages) Regulations, Schedule to the CA.
34. CA, Article 12.

proceedings before the Civil Court (Commercial Section) (CC(CS)).[35] Accordingly, in delivering the decisions explained in this subsection, the CC(CS) acts as a competition authority.[36]

Together with the court application initiating proceedings, the OC may include a report with its findings and propose the amount of the penalty that should be imposed. To date, there are no fining guidelines, but in proposing any fine, the OC is likely to be guided by the Commission's Fining Guidelines.[37]

Under the current framework, the OC still retains some limited decision-making powers, in that it may reject or decide not to act on a complaint[38] and, following the 2021 reform, may adopt commitment decisions.[39] The OC may also conduct sector inquiries and publish the results thereon.[40] The OC has discretion in deciding which cases to prioritise.[41] It has always enjoyed considerable powers of investigation, and those powers were further strengthened by the 2021 amendments.

Leniency was introduced in Malta only following the implementation of the ECN+ Directive. Leniency applies to both secret cartels[42] and other partially or wholly concealed infringements of Article 101 TFEU and Article 5 CA.[43] The leniency applicant, as a result of its cooperation with the OC to uncover an infringement, benefits from leniency by virtue of the OC, when filing judicial proceedings, either refraining from requesting the CC(CS) to impose a penalty or asking the CC(CS) to apply a reduction to the penalty which it would otherwise have requested the CC(CS) to impose.[44]

As mentioned, the CC(CS) determines whether there has been an infringement following proceedings filed by the OC.[45] In its judgment finding an infringement, the CC(CS) may impose penalties, taking into account the gravity and duration of the infringement and any aggravating or mitigating circumstances, while ensuring that the penalties imposed are effective, proportionate and dissuasive. The penalty for an infringement of the EU and/or national competition rules must not exceed 10% of the total worldwide turnover of an undertaking in the business year preceding the

35. CA, Article 12A. This model started to apply immediately to all investigations that were commenced following the 2011 reform and which were still pending before the OC when the 2019 reform was adopted (MCCAA Act, first proviso of Article 70(2)).
36. MCCAA Act, Article 14(1)(c) designates the CC(CS) together with the OC as the national competition authority for the purposes of Article 35(1) of Regulation 1/2003.
37. Guidelines on the method of setting fines imposed pursuant to Article 23(2)(a) of Regulation No 1/2003 [2006] OJ C 210/2.
38. CA, Articles 14(2) and 14B. It may, for instance, reject a complaint on the ground that the complaint is not an enforcement priority (MCCAA Act, proviso to Article 15(1)).
39. CA, Article 17. Prior to the 2019 amendments, the power to take commitment decisions vested in the OC and between the 2019 and 2021 amendments it vested exclusively in the CC(CS). Currently, both the OC and the CC(CS) may adopt commitment decisions.
40. CA, Article 11A.
41. MCCAA Act, Article 15(1). According to the MCCAA 2021 annual report, the OC started working on negative priorities guidelines, but these appear to be still in progress.
42. Leniency Regulations, Regulation 3(3).
43. CA, Article 16.
44. Leniency Regulations, Regulations 2 (definition of leniency), 3(2), 5(1) and 9(1).
45. CA, Article 13.

judgment imposing the penalty.[46] The CC(CS) may also issue cease and desist orders and compliance orders imposing behavioural or structural remedies.[47]

The investigation before the OC or the proceedings before the CC(CS) may be terminated by a judgment of the CC(CS) applying the settlement procedure, following a joint request by the OC and the undertaking concerned to this effect.[48] The settling undertaking is rewarded by virtue of the OC reducing the penalty which it would otherwise have recommended to the CC(CS) to impose by a figure between 10% and 35%.[49]

The CC(CS) may also take commitments decisions in cases pending before it.[50] It may also deliver judgments finding no breach of the national competition rules and judgments declaring no grounds for action where it finds no breach of the EU competition rules.[51]

Compliance with the general principles of EU law and the Charter of Fundamental Rights of the European Union (European Charter) must be ensured by the OC in the exercise of its powers and by the CC(CS) in proceedings before it.[52]

1.3 Enforcement Practices and Priorities

The OC and the OFC before it have continuously been plagued by lack of resources, with few officers handling cases. In practice, the transposition of the ECN+ Directive does not seem to have solved this problem.[53] While, admittedly, a competition authority's work cannot be measured solely by the number of decisions invoking the competition rules,[54] lack of sufficient resources obviously has an impact on the number of investigations initiated and cases concluded.

Although there have been some own-initiative investigations, most investigations were initiated following a complaint. Within this context, while there were a number of decisions rejecting complaints or finding no infringement, the OFC and the OC also tried to focus on cases raising serious allegations, so that cases of both anticompetitive conduct, like cartels, and abuse of dominance have featured over the

46. CA, Article 21.
47. CA, Article 13A.
48. CA, Article 12B. Prior to the 2019 amendments, the settlement procedure was limited to cartel cases and the decision was adopted by the OC.
49. CA, Article 12B(9).
50. CA, Article 12C.
51. CA, Article 13(2).
52. CA, Article 13B(8).
53. Article 13(3) MCCAA Act, introduced in 2021, requires the OC to have 'a sufficient number of qualified staff and sufficient financial, technical and technological resources' necessary for the effective performance of its functions.
54. For instance, following the strengthening of non-enforcement tools in 2011, the OC started to resort to advocacy and sectoral inquiries. Indeed, non-enforcement tools are strategically significant for a competition authority with scarce resources for a wider and quicker outreach. Merger control also takes up some of the OC's resources. Advocacy, sectoral inquiries and merger control all fall outside the project's scope.

years.[55] The nature and number of decisions taken by the CFT and the CCAT (where these acted as competition authorities[56]) have been dictated by the cases brought before them by the OFC or the OC following an investigation. Similarly, the number and nature of cases decided by the CC(CS) under the judicial model will depend on the number and type of investigations undertaken by the OC.

Since their introduction in 2011, the settlements procedure was never applied, while the commitments procedure was used once.[57] Leniency, which, as noted, was introduced more recently, has never been granted and it remains to be seen how effective the leniency programme will be in Malta, especially if a robust public enforcement stance is not adopted.[58]

While cease and desist and compliance orders were often imposed, no fines for infringement of the EU and national competition rules under the CA have ever been imposed.[59] Prior to 2011, no criminal proceedings were ever instituted. Following the 2011 amendments, *FEA* was the first case where the OC in its statement of objections in 2013 raised the possibility of imposing administrative fines but this possibility was frustrated by the outcome of the constitutional proceedings. Since the adoption of the judicial model up to the time of writing, the OC has not filed proceedings for breach of the competition rules before the CC(CS). Hence, the CC(CS)'s approach to penalties is yet to be seen.

2 REVIEW OF THE COMPETITION AUTHORITIES' DECISIONS

This section explains the possibilities for judicial scrutiny of the decisions of the OC and OFC, and the CFT and the CCAT, where the latter two acted as competition authorities over the project's timeframe. For simplicity, such decisions, where necessary, shall collectively be termed national competition authority (NCA) decisions. This section describes the competent tribunals and courts before which NCA decisions and subsequent review proceedings or appeals could be challenged. It also illustrates how the possibilities for judicial control varied according to the institutional structure in force.

55. Albeit not a complete picture since not all decisions were challenged, a picture of the public enforcement trends in Malta for the project's period emerges from section 4 of this chapter, while for an earlier period regard may be had to *Judgements of the Malta Commission for Fair Trading 1996-2005* (Silvio Meli, Guttenberg Press, 2006). A few examples of some early infringement decisions of the CFT acting as a competition authority are Case 3/2000 *The Director, Ministry of Public Works and Construction Re Road Groups Limited following the call for tenders for the hot asphalt surfacing of roads*, 11 June 2001, involving anticompetitive conduct; Case 2/2000 *Complaint submitted by Portanier Brothers Limited re Discount Schemes adopted by the General Soft Drinks Company Limited on the sale of soft-drinks and mineral water*, 11 June 2001, involving abuse of dominance; Complaint No 3/2003, *Ilment minn W.J. Parnis England Limited v. Sea Malta Company Limited et*, 10 October 2005, involving both cartel behaviour and abuse of dominance.
56. *See* section 2.
57. Case COMP-MCCAA 27/2014 *Decision to accept binding commitments offered by St Edward's College and In Design (Malta) Limited*, 29 May 2018.
58. Aquilina Zahra (*supra* n. 30).
59. Only two very minor fines have ever been imposed, both for procedural issues falling outside the scope of the project (Reply to Parliamentary Question 27947, 12th Legislature).

In Malta, there is a distinction between 'appeal' and 'judicial review'. In an appeal, the court has full jurisdiction to examine all questions of fact and law relating to the dispute before it.[60] Thus, the court must assess the evidence and determine whether the decision is correct on the merits, and unless it confirms the earlier decision, is able to quash or modify the decision being challenged, thereby substituting the prior decision with its own judgment. In the case of judicial review, the court is concerned with the validity of a decision and, unless it considers it lawful, may declare the decision concerned invalid and without effect and annul the decision, but may not replace that decision with its own. In judicial review, the court engages in a limited review to establish that the rules of natural justice have been complied with and the decision is not contrary to law.

Where no provision is made in the law for a right of appeal, judicial review may be sought both against the decisions of administrative authorities and statutory tribunals. English administrative law serves as an important source of judicial review in Malta.[61]

The project covers both judicial review and appeal. In this chapter, unless otherwise specified as in section 4, the two terms are used according to their meaning explained above, so as to distinguish between the instances where an appeal or judicial review is or was possible under the law over the project timeframe. The project also covers constitutional review where decisions of a competition authority may be challenged before a constitutional court. Except where mentioned by their specific name, the relevant tribunals and courts entrusted with judicial review, appeals and constitutional proceedings shall for ease of reference be referred to as 'reviewing tribunal/s' and 'reviewing court/s' respectively, or collectively as 'reviewing tribunals and courts'.

2.1 The Commission for Fair Trading (CFT)

The CFT was a specialised competition tribunal composed of a magistrate,[62] who presided it, and two lay members (an economist and a certified public accountant) appointed by the President of Malta (President) acting on the advice of the Prime Minister. The lay members were appointed for a period of three years and could be reappointed.

60. The law may limit the appeal to points of law only.
61. In Application No. 592/2009 *L-Awtorità dwar it-Trasport ta' Malta v. L-Avukat Generali et*, 12 May 2011 (*Garden of Eden Garage*, FHCC's first judgment) the FHCC, referring to the seminal cases, *Lowell et noe v. Caruana noe*, 14 August 1972; *Sciberras v. Housing Secretary et*, 21 July 1973; *Il-Prim Ministru et v. Sister Luigi Dunkin noe*, 26 June 1980, agreed with the defendants' submission that Maltese administrative law is based on English administrative law, so that reference could be made to it where a lacuna exists under Maltese law (pp. 18, 20). On appeal, the Court of Appeal confirmed this principle but clarified that this applied only to substantive law and not to prescription, peremptory time-limits or procedural rules where recourse had to be made to Maltese law (27 March 2015, pp. 20-22).
62. In terms of the Constitution, the judiciary in Malta is composed of judges sitting in the superior courts and magistrates sitting in the inferior courts. The law may also provide for a judge or magistrate to sit on a statutory tribunal.

The CFT had the power to determine competition infringements following a non-binding report submitted to it by the OFC on the results of the investigation and after hearing the parties. These decisions have not been considered to be judicial review or appeal judgments for the purpose of this study, because the CFT was acting as the competition authority in such cases.[63] As mentioned, the CFT also acted as a reviewing tribunal where the OFC itself adopted a decision. In the latter case, CFT decisions falling within the scope of the project have been coded and are considered 'first-instance' decisions in line with the project's methodology and assessed in sections 4 and 5 of this chapter.

Decisions taken by the CFT following a reference to it by the civil court hearing a case involving the application of the competition rules were also not included in this study as the CFT in such cases was not acting as a reviewing tribunal.[64] Nor were they included as NCA decisions as the CFT's involvement in such cases arose in the context of private proceedings.

The Rules of Procedure regulating the proceedings before the CFT[65] required the CFT to determine any matter before it with fairness and impartiality and to motivate its decisions.[66] Procedures before the CFT were commenced by a request in writing by the OFC, or by an undertaking or complainant through the OFC where the said undertaking or complainant decided to challenge the OFC's decision.[67] The CFT had the powers vested in the Civil Court and could summon witnesses and appoint experts.[68] The CFT's sittings were held *in camera.*[69] The OFC had the right to be present in all sittings,[70] while the relevant undertaking and any complainant had the right to make submissions on the matter before the CFT and to present evidence.[71] Undertakings able to show that their operations were directly affected by the proceedings before the CFT and persons adversely affected by the alleged breach, including consumers or a registered consumers association, could intervene before the CFT at any stage of the proceedings.[72] Following the 2004 amendments, the Commission had a right to make submissions and present evidence before the CFT in cases involving the application of the EU competition rules.[73]

63. See Chapter 2, section 3.2.
64. CA (prior to the 2011 amendments), Article 27.
65. Found at the time in the Schedule to the CA.
66. Rules 1 and 4.
67. Rule 7(a). Although, the request was made through the OFC, for coding purposes, the appellant was considered to be the undertaking concerned or the complainant making the request, since it, rather than the OFC, triggered the proceedings before the CFT.
68. Rule 11.
69. Rule 8. The CFT strongly criticised this holding it disregarded transparency and limited the beneficial outreach of its proceedings to the public. *See* Case No. 5/2007 *Investigazzjoni ex officio mill-Ufficcu tal-Kompetizzjoni Gusta fir-rigward ta' Federated Mills plc ai termini ta' l-Artiklu 13A ta' l-Att dwar il-Kompetizzjoni* (*Federated Mills*), 28 April 2008, pp. 7-8.
70. Rule 8, proviso (a).
71. Rule 8, proviso (b).
72. Rule 7(b).
73. Rule 8, proviso (c).

2.2 The Competition and Consumer Appeals Tribunal (CCAT)

The CCAT was a specialised tribunal created by the 2011 amendments to hear both competition and consumer cases. The CCAT was composed of a judge, who presided it, and two other members selected by the judge from a panel of six ordinary members.[74] The panel consisted of two economists, one certified public accountant and three other persons with recognised competence and knowledge in competition law matters, consumer protection, industry and commerce, all with at least ten years of relevant experience.[75] The ordinary members were appointed by the President acting on the advice of the Prime Minister for a period of three years and could be reappointed. The CCAT was independent in the performance of its functions and the ordinary members had to act on their own independent judgment, free from the direction or control of any person.[76] Cases had to be decided by unanimity or majority decision which majority had to include the judge.[77]

In competition cases, the CCAT's main purpose under the administrative model was to hear appeals from infringement decisions, cease and desist or compliance orders and administrative fines adopted or imposed by the OC.[78] The CCAT could confirm fully or partially or quash the OC's decisions and confirm, revoke or vary administrative fines.[79] OC decisions rejecting a complaint or finding no infringement could also be appealed before the CCAT.[80]

Once the 2011 amendments abolished the CFT, the CCAT assumed the cases pending before the CFT at the time.[81] In such cases, the law as existing prior to the 2011 amendments applied, so that the CCAT acted either as a reviewing tribunal[82] or as a competition authority depending in which capacity the CFT had been acting in the particular case. The CCAT also heard cases as a competition authority where the OC, acting in the capacity of its predecessor, submitted a report on its investigation to the CCAT for its decision. Given the scope of the project, decisions taken by the CCAT acting as a competition authority were not coded.[83] Further, as explained vis-à-vis the CFT, decisions of the CCAT on cases that had been referred to the CFT by the civil court have also been excluded. Conversely, decisions adopted by the CCAT in its capacity as a reviewing tribunal are coded and considered 'first-instance' decisions in line with the project's methodology.

74. MCCAA Act (as originally enacted) Article 32(1).
75. *Ibid.*, Article 32(2).
76. *Ibid.*, Article 32(8).
77. *Ibid.*, Article 36(2).
78. CA, following the 2011 amendments, Article 13A(1); MCCAA Act, as originally enacted, Article 36(1).
79. CA, following the 2011 amendments, Article 13A(4).
80. *Ibid.*, Article 14(5).
81. MCCAA Act (as originally enacted), Article 70(1)(b) and (3)(a).
82. As in, for instance, Application No. 1/2011 *Liquigas Malta Limited v. Ufficcju għall-Kompetizzjoni* (*Liquigas* CCAT decision) 14 April 2015.
83. *Supra* n. 63.

Many of the Rules of Procedure regulating the proceedings before the CFT were adopted for the CCAT.[84] However, unlike the case before the CFT, a party wishing to challenge the OC's decision could proceed directly before the CCAT rather than through the OC, and the proceedings were held in public, although it was possible to request to be heard *in camera* where the evidence or submissions were confidential.[85] The OC was a party in appeals against its decisions under the administrative model. Interested parties could intervene on the basis of ordinary civil procedural rules. Complainants could participate in the proceedings.

The role of the OC in cases which it took over from the OFC[86] in proceedings before the CCAT, where the latter assumed the CFT's role, was clarified by the CCAT in *Mizzi*.[87] The CCAT, relying on the Rules of Procedure before the 2011 amendments,[88] held that the OC had a more limited role in the proceedings before the CCAT than the undertaking concerned, the complainant or an interested third party intervening in the proceedings.[89] It explained that the OC should be included as a defendant, given that the case concerned the review of its decision. In this respect, the OC had to assume an active role in explaining and substantiating its conclusions on the basis of the evidence collected during its investigation. The CCAT clarified that the OC's role was however not adversarial in nature but more akin to that of a watchdog ensuring that its decision is construed properly. Therefore, while the OC could make submissions and defend its position, the OC could not bring new evidence on its own motion, unless requested to do so by the CCAT. The CCAT justified its reasoning by holding that '[o]therwise it would not make sense for the [CCAT] to review what was decided by the [OC] if the [OC] is not bound by the [evidence] gathered by it and which led it to its decision or report.'[90]

2.3 The Civil Court

The Civil Court is a superior court vested with judicial authority in civil matters.[91] It consists of different sections and hears all cases of a civil and commercial nature and cases which are expressly assigned to it by law.[92] One judge sits in any one case. The role of the Civil Court is discussed in this chapter only insofar as competition cases are concerned.

84. MCCAA Act (as originally enacted), Second Schedule.
85. Rule 5.
86. *See supra* n. 25.
87. *Supra* n. 4, 21 March 2012.
88. Rule 8, proviso (a) in comparison to rules 8, provisos (b) and (c) and 7(b). *See* MCCAA Act, Article 70(1)(b).
89. At pp. 9-10.
90. At p. 10 (author's translation).
91. Code of Organisation and Civil Procedure (COCP), Chapter 12 of the Laws of Malta, Articles 2 and 3(a).
92. COCP, Article 32(2).

2.3.1 *The First Hall of the Civil Court (FHCC)*

The FHCC has general jurisdiction in civil matters which have not been assigned to other sections. On the basis of its general and residual jurisdiction, the Maltese courts were able to ground the FHCC's inherent jurisdiction to review the decisions of administrative tribunals where the applicable law does not provide for the right of appeal, holding:

> It is a principle of law, however, that the inherent jurisdiction of the courts of 'judicial review' can never be removed by any law, because it cannot be accepted that the legislator could ever permit that a decision is taken in breach of the principles of natural justice or against the law.[93]

On the basis of this jurisprudence, the FHCC played an important part in the institutional structure as originally created by the CA as judicial review proceedings against the CFT's decisions (and the CCAT's decisions where it absorbed the CFT's previous role), both where the CFT (or CCAT) acted as a reviewing tribunal[94] or as a competition authority could be filed before it, given that the CA at the time did not provide for a right of appeal from the CFT's decision.

Over the project timeframe, only FHCC decisions reviewing the CFT decisions where the latter had acted as a reviewing tribunal were found. Under Maltese procedural law, the FHCC is a first-instance court. However, since the project looks at the number of appeal or review proceedings following a competition authority's decision, the FHCC decisions found are considered 'second-instance' decisions for the purposes of the project.

The FHCC also exercises constitutional jurisdiction. This is discussed in section 2.3.3.

93. Civil Appeal No. 65/2008 *Paul Washimba v. Bord tal-Appelli dwar ir-Rifugjati et,* Court of Appeal, 28 September 2012, p. 13 (author's translation). *See also* Writ of Summons No 2770/1996 *Simonds Farsons Cisk Ltd v. Agent Direttur ta' L-Ufficcju tal-Kompetizzjoni Gusta et,* 27 October 2004, pp. 8-9; Application 379/2010, *Central Cigarette Company Limited vs Direttur tal-Ufficcju tal-Kompetizzjoni Gusta,* 26 March 2024, p. 6 (*Austria Tabak* FHCC judgement); Application No. 592/2009, *L-Awtorità dwar it-Trasport ta' Malta v. L-Avukat Generali et,* 5 October 2016, p. 6 (*Garden of Eden Garage,* FHCC's second judgment). In Application No. 210/2009 *S&D Yachts Limited v. Direttur ta' L-Ufficcju tal-Kompetizzjoni Gusta et,* 20 April 2010 (*S&D Yachts* FHCC judgment), the FHCC clarified that Article 469A of the COCP, an ad hoc provision providing for the judicial review of administrative decisions by administrative authorities, did not apply to the decisions of the CFT, it being a tribunal, p. 8.

94. *See, Hompesch, supra* n. 7; *S&D Yachts* FHCC judgment, *supra* n. 93; *Garden of Eden Garage* FHCC judgments, *supra* n. 61, 93. However, the *Liquigas* CCAT decision, *supra* n. 82, and Application No. 2/2010 *A.A.J.E. Abela Brothers Partnership et v. L-Ufficcju għall-Kompetizzjoni,* 27 October 2014 (partial judgment) and 21 February 2017 (*Burdnara Bulk Cargo Group*), where the CCAT had absorbed the cases from the CFT as a reviewing tribunal, were appealed directly before the Court of Appeal. The appeal from the *Liquigas* CCAT decision was delivered on 8 October 2020. The appeal from the *Burdnara Bulk Cargo Group* CCAT decision, decided on 22 June 2023, is not coded as it falls outside the project's temporal scope.

2.3.2 *The Civil Court (Commercial Section)*

The CC(CS) is a section of the Civil Court, which hears cases arising under competition, company, insolvency and bankruptcy, and consumer law.[95] Apart from its role as an NCA under the judicial model, the CC(CS) also acts as a reviewing court in certain circumstances.

The CC(CS) took over those proceedings pending before the CCAT when the latter was abolished by the 2019 amendments. In this absorbed role, the CC(CS) could act as a review court or as a competition authority depending in which capacity the CCAT had been acting on the case before.[96] Within the project's scope, only one CC(CS) case was found.[97] In this case, the CC(CS) absorbed the CCAT's previous role hearing an appeal against the OC's decision. It is considered 'first instance' for the purposes of the project.

Following the 2019 reform, in the limited circumstances, where the OC may take a decision, such decisions may be challenged before the CC(CS). Thus, where the OC rejects or decides not to act on a complaint, the complainant may file proceedings before the CC(CS) and, if the CC(CS) considers the complaint justified, it will order the OC to initiate the investigation or issue any other order the CC(CS) considers appropriate.[98] No such CC(CS) judgments were found over the project period. Further, a commitment decision adopted by the OC following the 2021 reform may be contested before the CC(CS), which may confirm in whole or in part, or modify or quash the OC's decision.[99] No such decisions have yet been taken by the OC and, since this power came into force in August 2021, they would fall outside the project scope.

In proceedings before the CC(CS), whether it is acting as a competition authority following infringement proceedings instituted by the OC under the judicial model, or as a court scrutinising the OC's decision to reject a complaint or adopt commitments, the OC is a full party to the suit before the CC(CS) enjoying the same rights which pertain to its counterparty.[100] Third parties with sufficient interest are able to intervene.[101] The Commission has a right to make submissions before the CC(CS) in cases involving the application of the EU competition rules.[102]

2.3.3 *The FHCC (Constitutional Jurisdiction)*

Constitutional proceedings may be instituted before the FHCC in its constitutional jurisdiction where the parties believe that there has been a breach of their fundamental rights as protected by the Constitution of Malta (Constitution) or the European

95. Civil Courts (Establishment of Sections) Order (SL 12.19), Articles 3 and 5A.
96. MCCAA Act, Article 70(4)(a) and (6).
97. Application No. 1/2016, *Falzon Group Holdings Limited et v. Direttur Generali (Kompetizzjoni)*, withdrawn on 12 February 2020.
98. CA, Article 14(3).
99. CA, Article 17(4) and (5).
100. MCCAA Act, Article 14(1)(a); CA, provisos to Articles 14(4) and 17(6).
101. COCP, Article 960.
102. CA, Article 13B(4).

Convention Act.[103] The FHCC (constitutional jurisdiction) may make orders, issue writs and give directions as it may consider appropriate for the purpose of ensuring the protection of fundamental rights.[104] Customarily, constitutional judgments make extensive reference to the judgments of the European Court of Human Rights.

Over the project period, there was only *Falzon Group Holdings Limited et v. Direttur Generali (Kompetizzjoni) et (Falzon),*[105] where constitutional proceedings were filed against the OC's decision. The FHCC's judgment is considered 'first instance'.

2.4 The Court of Appeal

The Court of Appeal, consisting of three judges, one of whom may be the Chief Justice, hears and determines all appeals from judgments of, *inter alia*, the FHCC, in its general jurisdiction, and the CC(CS).[106]

For those cases determined under the CA as it stood before the 2011 amendments, an appeal could be filed from the FHCC decision reviewing the CFT decision (or the CCAT decision where the latter absorbed the CFT's role). The judicial system in Malta does not offer the possibility of a third-instance appeal. In fact, for the purposes of Maltese law, the Court of Appeal is a second-instance court, examining the FHCC's (first-instance) decision. However, for the purposes of this project, which looks at the number of challenges following a competition authority's decision, where a decision of the OFC was challenged before the CFT, and judicial review of the CFT's decision was sought before the FHCC, and subsequently the FHCC's judgment was appealed, the proceedings before the Court of Appeal actually constituted a third round of review following the OFC's decision. These decisions have therefore been considered 'third instance' for the purposes of the project.[107] However, where the appeal from the CCAT's decision was filed immediately before the Court of Appeal, the latter's decision was considered 'second instance'.[108]

Following the 2011 amendments, where the administrative model was applied, the Court of Appeal could hear appeals from the CCAT's decisions on points of law. The CCAT's appeal decisions on OC's rejection of complaints decisions were however deemed to be final, meaning that no appeal could be filed, although judicial review

103. Constitution, Article 46(1); European Convention Act (ECA), Chapter 319 of the laws of Malta, Article 4(1). The ECA incorporates the Convention for the Protection of Human Rights and Fundamental Freedoms (ECHR) into Maltese law. In Application No. 95/2018 *Cecil Herbert Jones v. Avukat Generali*, 15 February 2019, the FHCC (constitutional jurisdiction) considered that the provisions of the European Charter may also be invoked before it together with the Constitution and ECHR provisions.

104. Constitution, Article 46(2); ECA, Article 4(2).

105. Application No. 94/2016, partial judgments delivered by the FHCC on 8 November 2018, and, on appeal, by the Constitutional Court on 12 July 2019. The case was later withdrawn.

106. COCP, Articles 34, 41; CA, Article 13B.

107. *See* Court of Appeal's judgments in *Hompesch*, *supra* n. 7, and *Garden of Eden Garage*, *supra* n. 61.

108. *Liquigas* Court of Appeal judgment, *supra* n. 94.

before the FHCC remained always an option in terms of Maltese jurisprudence. During the project timeline, none of these remedies were exercised.

Following the 2019 amendments, under the judicial model, the Court of Appeal hears appeals on points of law and fact from judgments of the CC(CS), so that it can confirm, set aside or vary the CC(CS)'s decision, including on penalties.[109] The appeal may be filed by the OC or any party to the proceedings before the CC(CS). Interested third parties may also intervene at the appeal stage.[110] In an attempt to avoid delay, the Court of Appeal must appoint the case for hearing within six months from the date of service of the appeal application.[111] There was no such appeal before the Court of Appeal over the project timeframe, since no judgment has been adopted by the CC(CS) acting as an NCA under the judicial model so far.

Further, following the 2019 amendments, in those limited cases where the OC is able to take a decision,[112] and that decision is challenged before the CC(CS), an appeal on points of law and fact from the CC(CS)'s judgment may be filed before the Court of Appeal.[113] In such cases, there is, therefore, an additional layer of appeal, in comparison with infringement decisions taken by the CC(CS). There was no such CC(CS) judgment over the project timeframe. Consequently, nor was there any Court of Appeal judgment in this respect. In all appeal cases, the OC is a full party with the same rights as the counterparty.

2.5 The Constitutional Court

Appeals from judgments of the FHCC (constitutional jurisdiction) are heard by the Constitutional Court.[114] The Constitutional Court is composed of three judges who may sit in the Court of Appeal.[115] Within the project's scope, there was only the appeal from the FHCC's judgment in *Falzon*.[116] The Constitutional Court's judgment is considered 'second instance'.

3 PRIOR RESEARCH

The author is not aware of any empirical study specifically dedicated to mapping judicial scrutiny of NCA decisions in Malta from both a qualitative and a quantitative aspect over the project timeframe. Several works have been produced analysing various aspects and cases under Maltese competition law, but these do not focus

109. CA, Article 13B(1). However, where the settlement procedure is adopted, the settling undertaking is required to waive its right to appeal or challenge the settlement procedure, the investigation concerned and the CC(CS)'s judgement on the merits and the fine (CA, Article 12B(7)(f)).
110. COCP, Article 960.
111. CA, Article 13B(1), proviso.
112. Rejection of complaints and commitment decisions.
113. CA, Article 14(4) and Article 17(6).
114. Constitution, Articles 46(4) and 95(2)(c); ECA, Articles 3(4) and 4(4).
115. Constitution, Article 95(2).
116. *Supra* n. 105.

specifically and exclusively on the mechanisms and intensity of judicial control of NCA decisions. One comprehensive study of the CFT's decisions, both where the CFT acted as a competition authority and a reviewing tribunal, over the period 1996–2010, was conducted by Azzopardi.[117] The main purpose of Azzopardi's work was to examine the various substantive competition law issues arising in these decisions and some procedural matters. This work was not intended as an empirical study mapping judicial control. Nevertheless, among the various matters discussed, Azzopardi briefly addressed, from a qualitative perspective, the extent of judicial control exercised by the CFT and judicial review of the CFT's decisions.

4 QUANTITATIVE ANALYSIS

This section presents the results of the quantitative mapping of the judicial scrutiny of public enforcement action in Malta between 1 May 2004 and 30 April 2021.

4.1 Source of Information

The CFT judgments from May 2004 to 2009 are currently available in the law courts library and are not accessible online. CFT judgments rendered between 2010 and May 2011 do not appear to be presently available or published anywhere. However, two CFT judgments over the latter period were found in two court files, but it is not definite that these were the only two judgments delivered over this period. The relevant CCAT judgments are available through the ecourts' website[118] and should all be included in the database.

The judgments of the relevant courts are also available through the ecourts' website. Since these courts do not deliver only competition law-related judgments and since the ecourts' website provides judgments delivered by the courts in Malta without distinction as to the area of law concerned, keywords were used in the search tool to identify any possible judgment within the scope of the project. While a thorough attempt was made to trace all relevant judgments, it cannot be guaranteed that through this methodology the database is absolutely comprehensive.

4.2 Total Number of Cases

A total of thirty-one judgments[119] within the material and temporal scope of the project were delivered, of which twenty-two were at first instance, six at second instance, and three at third instance.[120] These judgments refer to appeals, judicial review, and constitutional proceedings. All types of proceedings have therefore been combined in

117. Azzopardi Annalies, *A Critical Analysis of the Leading Decisions of the Commission for Fair Trading*, University of Malta, 2010.
118. https://ecourts.gov.mt/onlineservices/.
119. 'Judgments' covers not only decisions rendered but also withdrawn cases according to the project's methodology, see Chapter 2.
120. *See* section 2 describing the instance of the judgments.

calculating the number of judgments. In this section, in order to ensure consistency with other national reports, the word 'appeal' covers not only appeal as described in section 2 but also judicial review and constitutional proceedings.

Within the project's scope, thirty-three national competition authority (NCA) decisions that could be challenged were traced. Out of those decisions traced, twenty-one NCA decisions were appealed. The ratio of NCA's decisions subject to appeal is therefore 64%. However, this figure is not reliable, because the OFC did not publish its decisions, the reporting of the OC's decisions in the MCCAA's annual reports and website does not appear exhaustive, the CFT's judgments over 2010 and 2011 are not available and the appeal of one NCA decision was still pending at the end of the project period thus falling outside the project's scope, although it was taken into account when calculating the NCA's decisions.

4.3 Total Number of Cases per Year

Figure 21.1 summarises the number of judgments delivered by the reviewing tribunals and courts in Malta per year according to the instance of appeal.

Figure 21.1 Number of Judgments According to Instances

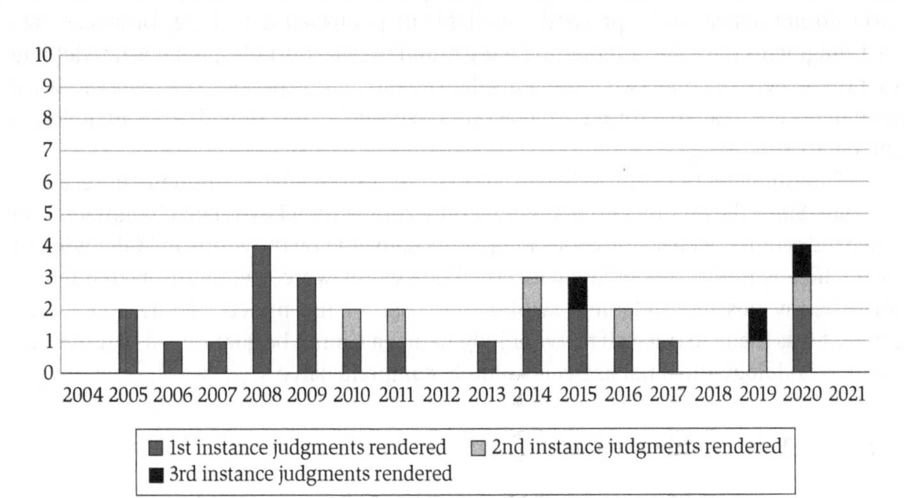

None of the NCA decisions and consequent appeals were subject to multiple appeals by different appellants, meaning no cases were joined together or decided separately. Hence, the appeal on each NCA's decision has been subject to a single first-instance judgment, and consecutive appeals have similarly been subject to a single judgment,[121] except for one NCA decision appealed before courts with different

121. Partial judgments in any one case are considered leading to one judgment.

jurisdictions at the same instance by the same parties[122] and another one involving two appeal judgments at both second and third instances following remittance.[123]

4.4 Success Rates and Outcomes

Figure 21.2 summarises the success of appeals launched against the NCA's decisions or the prior instance judgments. It indicates the ratio of fully successful appeals, partially successful appeals, fully rejected appeals, and appeals that were withdrawn prior to adopting a judgment. The two withdrawn cases at first instance relating to the *Falzon* OC decision were calculated as one in Figure 21.2.[124]

Figure 21.2 Success of Appeals (Each NCA's Decision or Previous Instance Judgment Counts as One)

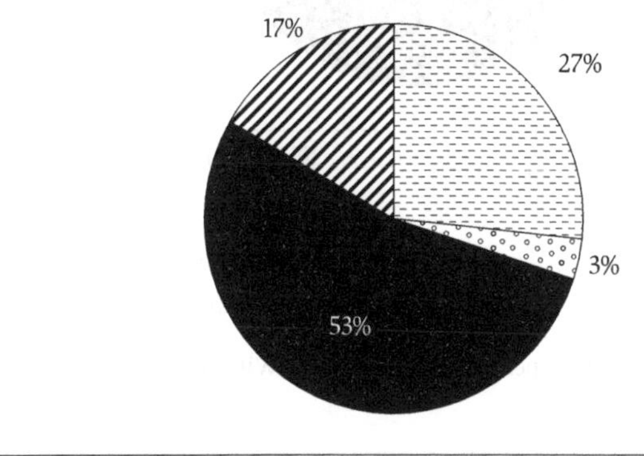

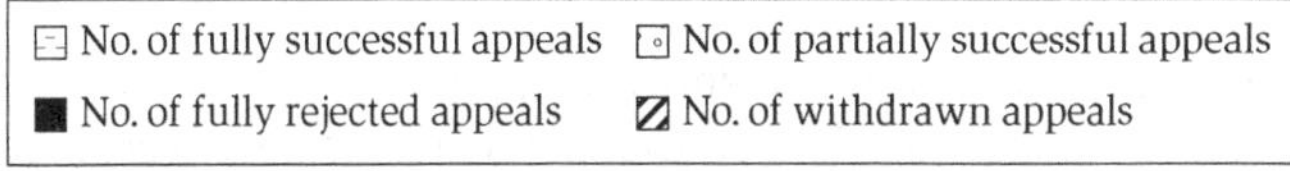

Figures 21.3(a)-(c) indicate the proportion of possible outcomes according to each instance of appeal.

Figure 21.3(a) shows that approximately 45% of the appeals at first instance were fully rejected. The 5% in the 'other' category also involved an appeal that in substance was rejected.[125] Since these appeals were filed either by the undertakings concerned or by the complainants whose complaints were rejected, 50% of these appeals confirmed the NCA's decisions. 23% of the first-instance appeals were withdrawn. This leaves

122. The *Falzon* OC decision (Case COMP-MCCAA 3/2015 *Decision of the Office for Competition of 04.10.16 relating to a proceeding under Article 5 of the Competition Act)* was challenged at first instance before the FHCC in its constitutional jurisdiction, *supra* n. 105, and before the CC(CS), *supra* n. 97.

123. *Garden of Eden Garage, supra* n. 61, 93. The *Garden of Eden Garage* FHCC's second judgment was also appealed, but the appeal was withdrawn on 11 January 2019.

124. *Supra* n. 122.

125. *Hompesch* CFT decision, *supra* n. 7, where the CFT confirmed the OFC's decision insofar as it found a breach by the undertaking and association concerned, but, unlike the OFC, also found a breach by the Government and the public authority involved.

only around 27% of cases where the relative NCA decisions were fully or partially annulled or fully replaced.

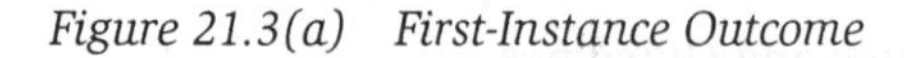

Figure 21.3(a) First-Instance Outcome

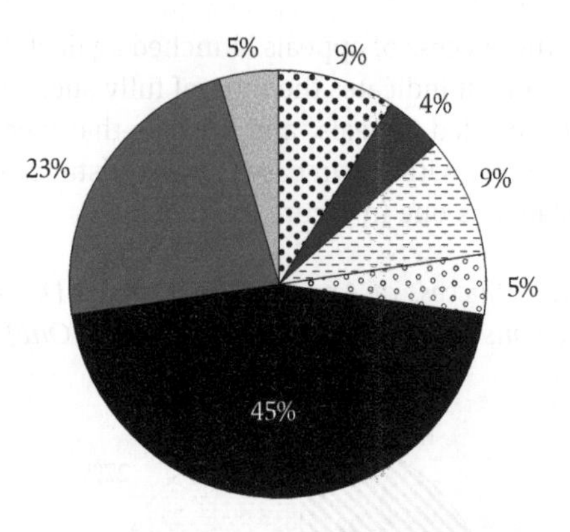

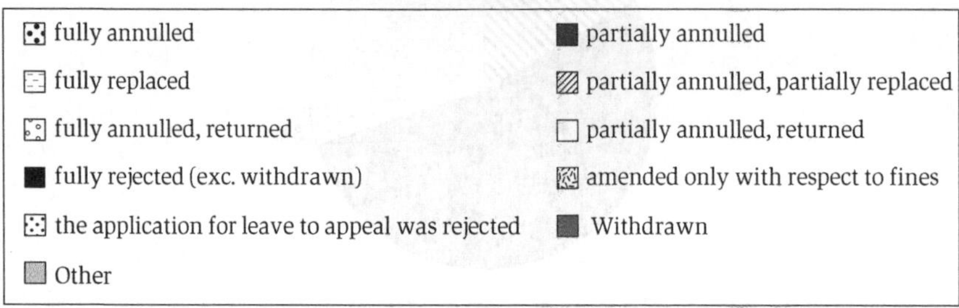

Figure 21.3(b) shows that the majority of appeals at second instance confirmed the previous instance judgments. Two appeals at second instance were filed by the OC, one was rejected,[126] while the other was accepted with the first-instance decision being replaced.[127]

126. *Liquigas* Court of Appeal judgment, *supra* n. 94.
127. Constitutional Court's partial judgment in *Falzon*, *supra* n. 105.

Figure 21.3(b) Second-Instance Outcome

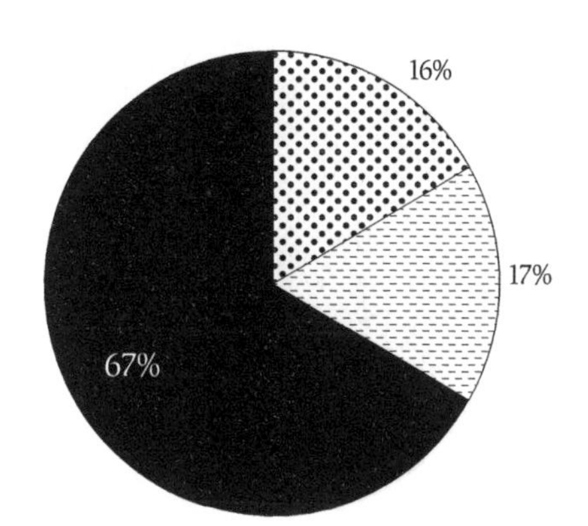

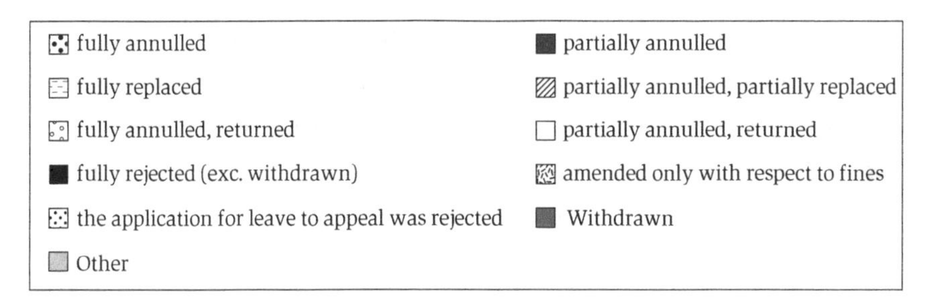

Figure 21.3(c) depicts the three judgments at third instance. Two of these concerned the *Garden of Eden Garage* case where, in one, the Court of Appeal disagreed with the FHCC's first judgment that the action was time-barred,[128] thus upholding the appeal and remitting the case back, and, in the other, the appeal filed by the complainant against the FHCC's second judgment[129] was withdrawn. In the third judgment, the appeal filed by the undertaking concerned was rejected.[130]

128. *Supra* n. 61.
129. *Supra* n. 123.
130. *Hompesch* Court of Appeal judgment, *supra* n. 7.

Figure 21.3(c) Third-Instance Outcome

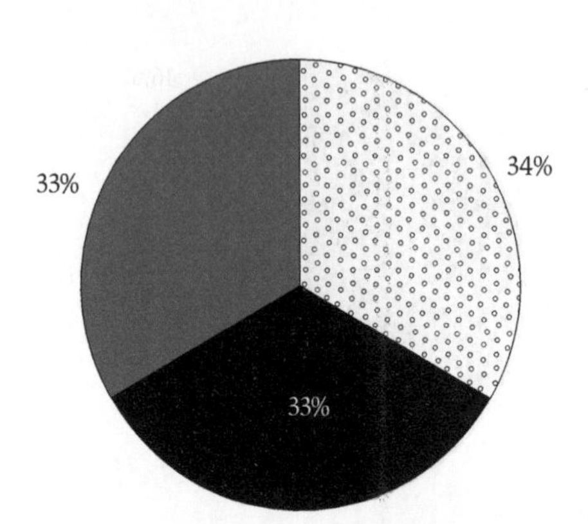

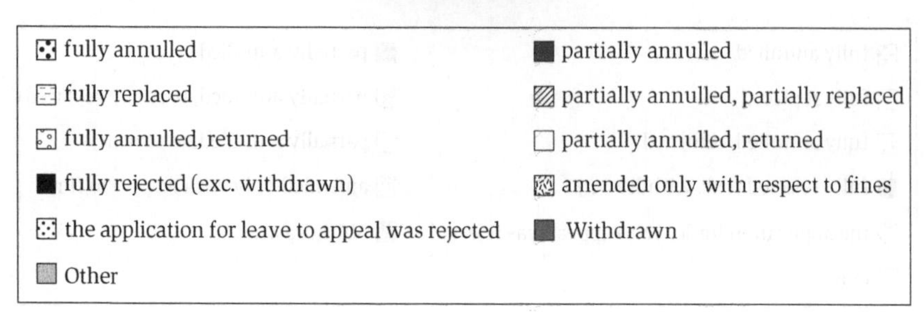

4.5 Type of NCA's Decisions Subject to Appeal

Figure 21.4 indicates the extent to which each national and EU competition rule was subject to appeal across all instances. It presents the data from the perspective of each appeal judgment, so that more than one judgment may be presented for a single NCA decision.[131] Clearly, most judgments have focused on the enforcement of the national prohibitions. This mirrors the NCA's work involving primarily enforcement of the national prohibitions. The national prohibition on abuse of dominance was the principal focus of appeal proceedings. This can be explained by the five judgments concerning the *Garden of Eden Garage* case, all involving Article 9 CA.[132]

131. The percentages in Figure 21.4 have been calculated on the basis of thirty judgments since in one withdrawn case it was not possible to identify the type of infringement alleged.
132. *Supra* nn. 61, 93, 123, *infra* n. 145.

Figure 21.4 Rule Being Appealed

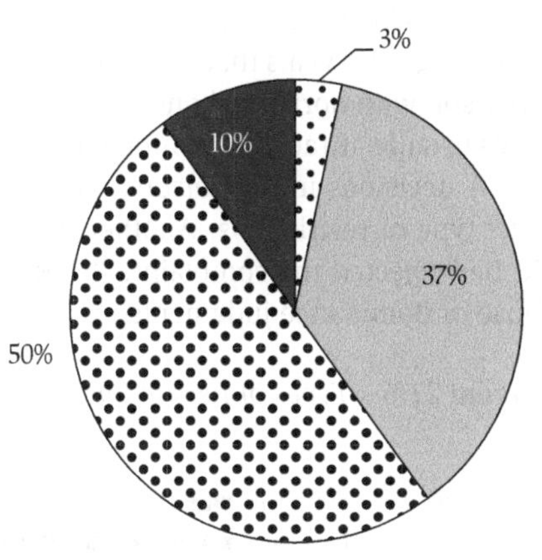

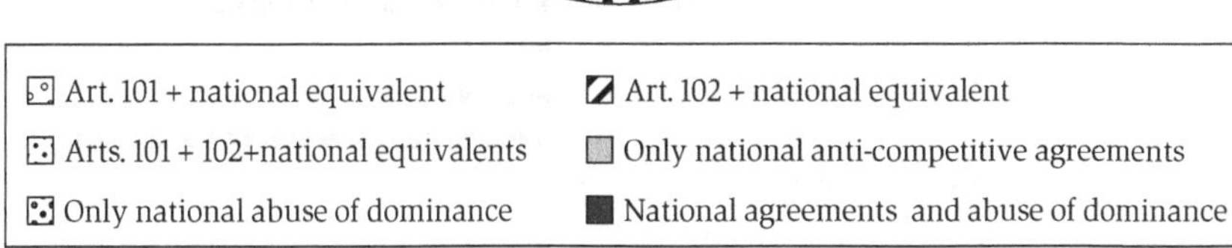

Figure 21.5 displays the number of judgments in relation to the competition rules applied over the project period. With the exception of certain years, judgments concerning both types of national competition rules were delivered across the reference period. The judgments related both to appeals from decisions where the NCA rejected a complaint and where the NCA found an infringement.

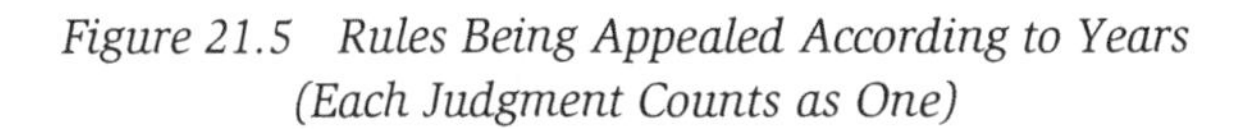

Figure 21.5 Rules Being Appealed According to Years (Each Judgment Counts as One)

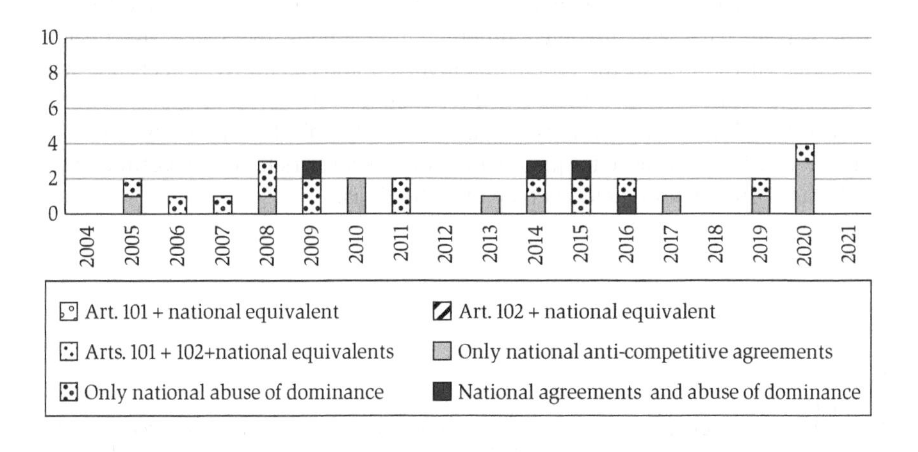

Figure 21.6 summarises the types of restrictions of competition that were examined in the NCA's decisions subject to appeal across all instances. Figure 21.6 does not reflect six judgments in which the type of restriction examined in the NCA decision was not indicated. The figure reveals that vertical restrictions were examined by more judgments in comparison with horizontal ones. While this may seem unusual given that horizontal practices usually attract more enforcement action, in practice, six judgments concerned the NCA decisions in the *Falzon*[133] and the *Hompesch*[134] cases which involved the by-object type of restrictions. Another two judgments concerned *S&D Yachts* where the OFC had rejected the complaint.[135] Less surprising, the figure reveals that most of the abuse of dominance judgments involved exclusionary abuse.

Figure 21.6 Types of Restrictions

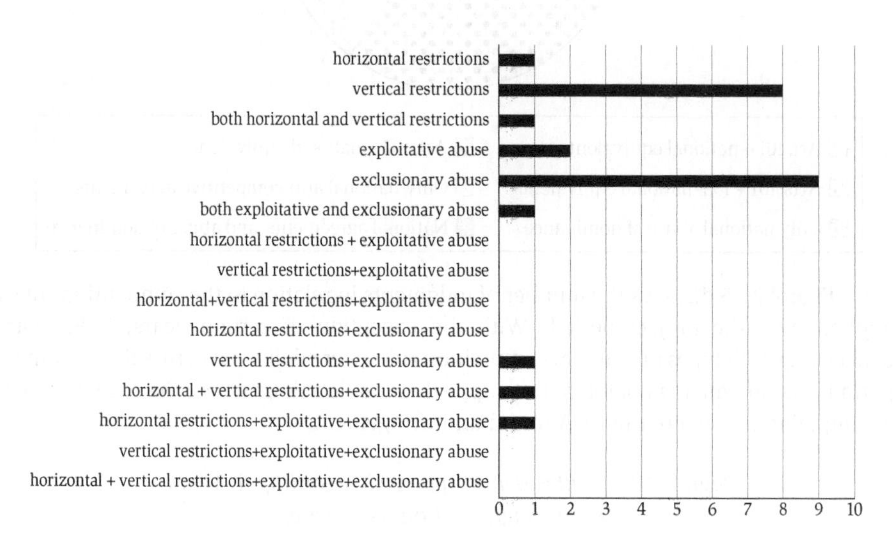

Figure 21.7 examines judgments against NCA decisions where Article 101 TFEU and/or Article 5 CA was involved differentiating among by-object, by-effect and unclassified cases. 40% of the judgments involved appeals on NCA decisions which had not specifically classified the alleged restriction as by-object and/or by-effect, as the NCA found no infringements of the rules. By-object restrictions have been examined considerably more frequently than by-effect restrictions, suggesting that the NCA focused on the more heinous type of restrictions.

133. *Supra* nn. 97, 105, 122.
134. *Supra* n. 7.
135. *S&D Yachts* FHCC judgment, *supra* n. 93; Complaint No. 2/2007, *Rikors tad-Direttur ta' l-Ufficcju tal-Kompetizzjoni Gusta fuq ilment mis-socjetà S&D Yachts Limited v. Il-Gvern ta' Malta et* (*S&D Yachts* CFT decision), 6 October 2008.

Figure 21.7 Object/Effect (Only for Article 101/National Equivalent Infringements)

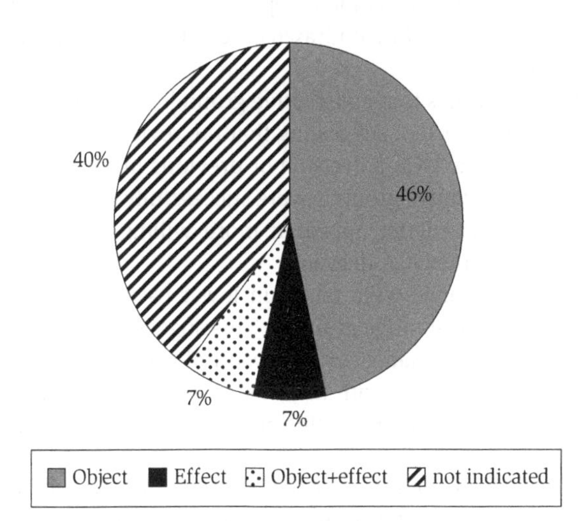

Figure 21.8 indicates the type of NCA's procedures that were subject to appeal across all instances of appeal. It shows that while the majority of judgments concerned the rejection of complaints, only 45% concerned infringement decisions. This trend may change should the OC engage in more rigorous prioritisation of cases, thereby focusing its resources on cases involving a more likely finding of an infringement. Further, as noted earlier, no fines for breaches of the national and EU competition rules have been imposed as at the date of writing. This trend is likely to change following the 2019 amendments, so that, going forward, infringement decisions are likely to include fines.

Figure 21.8 Competition Authority's Procedure

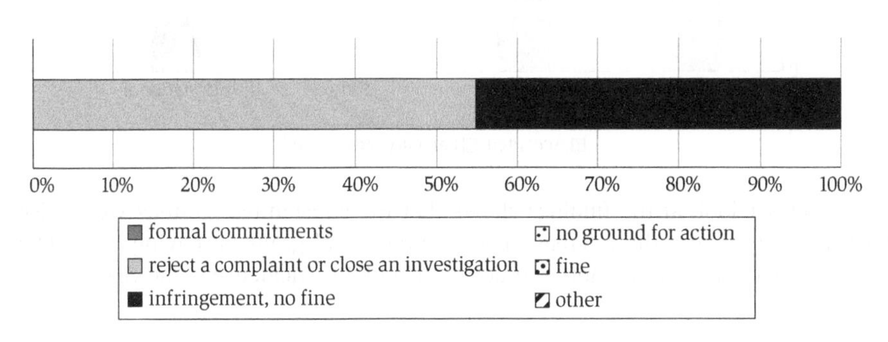

4.6 Grounds of Appeal

Figure 21.9 indicates the type of grounds raised by the appellants in all instances and their success rates. The grounds were classified as procedural or substantive in line with the definitions of this project elaborated in Chapter 2, which aim to ensure uniform classification across all national reports. Different types of grounds were sometimes invoked in one case. In withdrawn cases, the types of grounds raised could not always be determined.

Figure 21.9 demonstrates that substantive grounds were raised more frequently. In most cases, they were rejected, suggesting that the reviewing tribunal or court was more inclined to confirm the NCA's decision or previous instance judgment. The few judgments where the substantive grounds were successfully raised were mostly before the CFT, indicating that the latter appeared more willing than the CCAT and the reviewing courts to revise the NCA decision.

While procedural grounds were raised in fewer cases, they were accepted the same number of times as substantive grounds. This suggests that the reviewing courts and tribunals scrutinised compliance with procedural rules more intensely.

Finally, very few cases dealt with the tension between EU and national competition law, and in all, apart from one,[136] this ground was unsuccessful.

Figure 21.9 Grounds of Appeal (Each NCA's Decision or Previous Instance Judgment Counts as One)

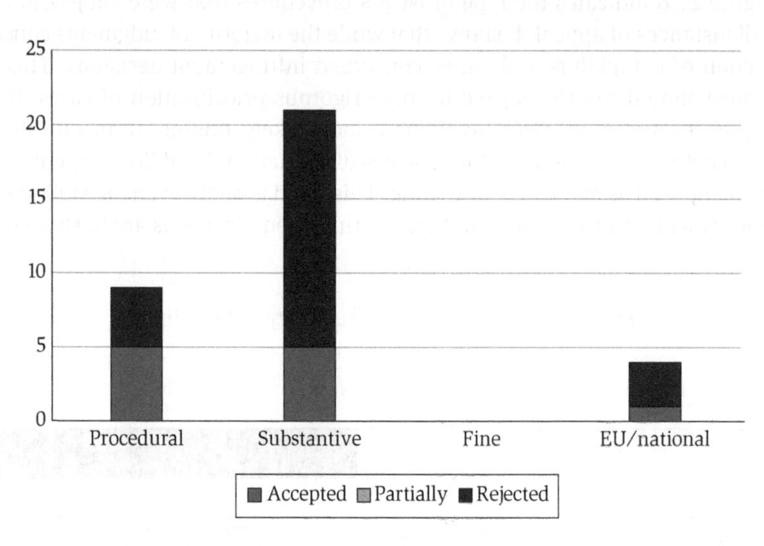

A closer look at the findings shows that the substantive grounds were raised mostly evenly across the reference period. Procedural grounds, having been relied upon less frequently, were more sporadic with a higher incidence in the years 2015 to 2020.

136. Complaint No. 1/2004, *Bargain Holidays Limited et v. Awtorità tat-Turizmu ta' Malta* (*Bargain Holidays*), 17 October 2005.

4.7 Appellants and Third-Party Participation

At first instance, naturally, the appellants were generally the undertakings concerned in appeals against infringement decisions, or the complainants in appeals against decisions rejecting complaints. Only in one appeal concerning an infringement decision, did the complainant raise grounds of appeal together with the undertaking concerned.[137] The OFC never appealed when its decision was overturned, indicating reluctance on its part to challenge any CFT decisions. The OC, however, appealed the two judgments delivered against it, i.e., the *Liquigas* CCAT decision[138] and the FHCC partial judgment in the *Falzon* constitutional case.[139]

Where the NCA decisions arose from a complaint, the respondents to the judicial proceedings at first instance, apart from the OFC or OC, were usually the undertakings concerned where complaints had been rejected, or complainants in infringement cases. In appeals concerning infringement decisions before the reviewing courts, complainant participation was less frequent. In a few cases, the State Advocate (then Attorney General), representing the Government, participated as respondent or appellant. No involvement by other third parties was recorded.

5 QUALITATIVE ANALYSIS

The scope and intensity of judicial control have varied depending very often on whether appeal, judicial review or constitutional review was exercised, the level of expertise of the reviewing tribunal or court and the nature of the pleas raised. This section provides a qualitative assessment of the judicial scrutiny exercised over the project period complementing the quantitative assessment undertaken in the previous section.

5.1 Substantive and Procedural Grounds

5.1.1 Substantive Grounds: CFT and CCAT

The CFT's approach, as a specialist competition law tribunal, was marked by its eagerness to interpret the law in a way as to allow it a full examination of the merits of the case with the possibility of reaching a new decision rather than merely exercising judicial review to either declare lawful or annul the challenged decision. Prior to the 2011 amendments, the English version of the CA provided that the OFC's decisions could be submitted for 'review' before the CFT.[140] As in some other laws,[141] in the

137. *Hompesch* CFT decision, n. 7.
138. *Supra* nn. 82, 94.
139. *Supra* n. 105.
140. Then Article 13A and Article 14(1)(b).
141. *See*, for instance, translation of 'review' in the term 'judicial review' in COCP, Article 469B, and marginal note to Article 469A.

Maltese version of the CA, 'review' was translated as 'stħarriġ'.[142] Neither version provided explicitly for an appeal to the CFT. Yet, the CFT repeatedly noted that there was a discrepancy in meaning between the two terms, holding that 'stħarriġ' meant a profound, complete and detailed examination of the merits of the case so that the case would be examined *ex novo* and decided upon afresh, while 'review' meant a limited, critical examination of the administrative decision to see if that decision was taken according to law.[143] The CFT motivated its choice on the basis of the aim and purpose of the law, holding that otherwise '*the benefit of the re-examination of the case by an expert and independent body would be stultified with serious repercussions for the consumer*',[144] and on multiple occasions pleaded for legislative alignment of the two versions in the interest of legal certainty.[145] The FHCC's second judgment in *Garden of Eden Garage* supports the CFT's interpretation as in that case the FHCC expected the CFT to examine carefully the facts and the law and then apply the law to those facts.[146]

In practice, the CFT heard and assessed the evidence, examined the merits of the case and generally reached a decision on substance based on its own appraisal of the facts and law, confirming,[147] varying,[148] revoking[149] or replacing with its own[150] the OFC's decision. In cases where the CFT did not agree with the OFC's decision that a complaint was inadmissible, the law required the CFT to send the case back to the OFC

142. In Malta, laws are enacted in English and Maltese. According to the Constitution, Article 74, the Maltese version prevails in case of conflict between the two versions.
143. *Bargain Holidays, supra* n. 136, p. 8; *Federated Mills, supra* n. 69, p. 7; *S&D Yachts* CFT decision, *supra* n. 135, pp. 14-15. In *Hompesch*, the CFT rejected the plea that the CFT could not take a decision on the merits, *supra* n. 7, p. 13.
144. *Hompesch* CFT decision, *supra* n. 7, p. 13 (author's translation). Although in *Bargain Holidays, supra* n. 136, the CFT justified its choice on the basis that *ex lege* the Maltese version prevails (p. 8).
145. *Hompesch* CFT decision, *supra* n. 7, p. 12; *Federated Mills, supra* n. 69, p. 7; *S&D Yachts* CFT decision, *supra* n. 135, p. 14; *Cassar Fuels, supra* n. 18, pp. 7-8; Complaint No. 6/2006 *Rikors tad-Direttur tal-Ufficcju tal-Kompetizzjoni Gusta fuq ilment minn Marianna Spiteri et v. l-Awtorità Dwar it-Trasport ta' Malta*, 15 October 2008, (*Garden of Eden Garage* CFT decision), pp. 15-16; Complaint No. 3/2007, *Rikors tad-Direttur ta' l-Ufficcju tal-Kompetizzjoni Gusta wara ilment mill-Federation of Associations of Travel and Tourism Agents (FATTA) v. Air Malta p.l.c. (FATTA)*, 19 October 2009, p. 6; Complaint No. 4/2005 *Rikors tad-Direttur tal-Ufficcju tal-Kompetizzjoni Gusta fuq ilment minn Austria Tabak (Malta) Limited illum Interbrands Limited v. Central Cigarette Company Limited et (Austria Tabak), 19 October 2009*, p. 15; Interim Measure 5/2005, *Talba mressqa mis-socjetà Medical Laboratory Services Limited operatrici ta' St James Hospitals et (Medical Laboratory Services)*, 9 October 2006, p. 4 (although the reference number carries 'Interim Measure', the decision concerns the merits of the case).
146. *Supra* n. 93, pp. 11-15.
147. *See*, for instance, Request No. 2/2004, *Talba għall-istħarrig tal-Kummissjoni għall-Kummerc Gust sottomessa mid-Direttur ta' l-Ufficcju tal-Kompetizzjoni Gusta fuq talba ta' Retail Marketing Limited et (Retail Marketing)*, 10 October 2005; *FATTA, supra* n. 145; *Austria Tabak, supra* n. 145; Interim Measure No. 5/2009 *Golden Shepherd Group Limited v. Korporazzjoni Enemalta (Golden Shepherd)*, 31 January 2011 (although the reference number carries 'Interim Measure' the decision concerns the merits of the case).
148. *See*, for instance, *Cassar Fuels, supra* n. 18.
149. *See*, for instance, *Federated Mills, supra* n. 69.
150. *See*, for instance, *Medical Laboratory Services, supra* n. 145; *Garden of Eden Garage* CFT decision, *supra* n. 145.

to resume its investigation.[151] While not all cases were sufficiently complex to merit a profound assessment, the level of depth in the CFT's legal assessment was not consistent throughout, with the CFT in some cases providing an explanation of the law supported by EU case law and guidance to sustain its conclusions,[152] while in others coming to a swift conclusion on the facts before it without sufficient legal analysis.[153] In relation to any required economic analysis, its decisions often deferred to the OFC's conclusions.[154]

The CFT, through its decisions, insisted and encouraged the OFC to reach high standards in its analysis. Thus, while it often confirmed the OFC's conclusions, and while, the OFC's decisions, with some exceptions, tended to be detailed and motivated, the CFT did not hesitate in rebuking the OFC where it was dissatisfied with the OFC's analysis or lack of it, holding "it should be agreed that the [OFC's] decision must be one that at least satisfies the rigour of logic, rationality and reasonableness, where after showing that [it] examined carefully all the circumstances brought before [it], determines and decides on the basis of legality, reinforced by the relative doctrine and jurisprudence".[155] Nor was it reluctant to criticise where in its opinion the OFC failed to act with the required objectivity in order to protect government interest, calling upon those responsible to detach the OFC as much as possible from the government to guarantee its independence.[156]

From a substantive point of view, the CFT showed considerable enthusiasm to apply the competition rules to deal with matters that could harm competition on the market, not only vis-à-vis anticompetitive behaviour by undertakings[157] but also with respect to legislative[158] and executive action. Its eagerness sometimes led it to go beyond the parameters of the competition rules as interpreted by the CJEU.[159] This can notably be seen in its interpretation of the CA's application to public authorities when exercising public functions (rather than economic activities). One such case is *Garden*

151. *See Bargain Holidays, supra* n. 136, p. 14. Although the CFT does not appear to have always followed this procedure rigorously, passing on to deliver judgment on the merits immediately, as in *Garden of Eden Garage* CFT decision, n 145.
152. *See*, for instance, *Austria Tabak, supra* n. 145. The CFT's decision was deemed lawful in judicial review proceedings in the *Austria Tabak* FHCC judgement, *supra* n. 93. The latter judgment is not coded as it falls outside the temporal scope of the project.
153. *See*, for instance, *Garden of Eden Garage* CFT decision, *supra* n. 145 and *Garden of Eden Garage* FHCC's second judgment, *supra* n. 93.
154. *See*, for instance, *Austria Tabak, supra* n. 145, p. 22. But *see Federated Mills, supra* n. 69, where the CFT, upholding the workings of the undertaking concerned, disagreed with the OFC.
155. *Garden of Eden Garage* CFT decision, *supra* n. 145, p. 13 (author's translation). *See also S&D Yachts* CFT decision, *supra* n. 135, p. 13.
156. *Federated Mills, supra* n. 69, p. 10.
157. *See*, for instance, *Retail Marketing, supra* n. 147; *Austria Tabak, supra* n. 145; *Cassar Fuels, supra* n. 18; *Hompesch* CFT decision, *supra* n. 7.
158. *See*, for instance, *Bargain Holidays, supra* n. 136.
159. *See*, for instance, *Medical Laboratory Services Limited, supra* n. 145, p. 10, where the CFT declared legal provisions as themselves amounting to an abuse of dominance in breach of the CA instead of advocating through recommendations to amend that law. In contrast, in *Golden Shepherd, supra* n. 147, the CFT declined jurisdiction as the matter complained of arose from legal provisions which the undertaking concerned was obliged to implement and which provisions could be scrutinised from a State aid perspective rather than under the CA, while noting that the said provisions could still defeat the CA's objectives.

of Eden Garage, where the CFT overturned the OFC's decision that the complaint against the Malta Transport Authority (MTA) was inadmissible as it was a public authority exercising public functions.[160] Instead, the CFT found the MTA in breach of Article 9 CA for failing to issue the required licences permitting Garden of Eden Garage to operate a number of open-top buses, thereby excluding it from the market to the advantage of its competitors which were allowed to operate. While condemning the MTA, the CFT considered that insofar as there is a real possibility that decisions of public entities are "preventing, restricting or distorting competition in Malta and, as a consequence, falsifying the market under scrutiny, the [CFT] has the duty to analyse the situation and offer a remedy in the interest of justice."[161] Clearly, the intention of the CFT was to restore conditions of competition on the market and to act as an effective shield where public authorities in the exercise of their public powers were distorting competition. However, in doing so, the CFT wrongly assumed jurisdiction under the competition rules with respect to the exercise of public power. The FHCC did not entertain such an approach, and in judicial review proceedings, the FHCC found that the CFT had acted ultra vires and made an error of law.[162] On its part, the CCAT adopted a more realistic interpretation of the CA's scope and in a similar context, it agreed with the OC's interpretation, that the public authority in question was not acting as an undertaking for the CA's purposes.[163]

In those cases where the CCAT succeeded the CFT and was bound by the provisions existing prior to the 2011 amendments, the CCAT, subject to the condition that the OC could not submit new evidence on its own motion before it, heard the evidence and generally undertook a detailed examination of the facts of the case and the legal points involved. Like the CFT, it adopted the approach of re-examining the case. Thus, for instance, in *Imnara Limited v. Ufficcju ghall-Kompetizzjoni*, the CCAT explained that it would examine from scratch the conduct complained of, and proceeded to assess the facts of the case and whether the CA could apply to the said conduct, before confirming the OFC's decision.[164] Again, in *U Communications Limited v. l-Ufficcju ghall-Kompetizzjoni*, the CCAT in its decision often referred to the case before it as 'an appeal' and to the complainant challenging the OFC's decision as 'appellant', and, before confirming the OFC's decision, undertook a complete assessment of the facts before applying the relevant legal principle to the facts.[165] The *Burdnara Bulk Cargo Group* case offers an excellent example where the CCAT dealt

160. *Supra* n. 145.
161. *Ibid.*, p. 14 (author's translation). *See also S&D Yachts Limited* CFT decision, *supra* n. 135, pp. 13-14; *Hompesch* CFT decision, *supra* n. 7, pp. 13-15. For an opposite approach *see* an earlier case outside the project's scope, Complaint No. 2/2003 *Application submitted by the Director of the Office for Fair Competition following his decision dated the 21st April 2003 on the complaint of Carmel Mifsud v. Malta Transport Authority*, 5 July 2004, where the CFT, confirming the OFC's decision, decided that MTA is not an undertaking under the CA and instead opted for advocacy by providing recommendations to the authorities concerned, rendering its decision still meaningful.
162. *Garden of Eden Garage* FHCC's second judgment, *supra* n. 93, pp. 13-15.
163. Application No. 1/2015 *Malta Bargains Limited (UK) v. Awtorita tat-Turizmu ta' Malta et* (*Malta Bargains*), 19 May 2015.
164. Application No. 3/2010, 20 March 2013.
165. Application No. 4/2010, 22 October 2014.

with the case as an appeal.[166] In this case, the CCAT examined at length whether there was an effect on trade, whether certain EU sectoral block exemption regulations (BERs)[167] could be applied in the national context and whether the anti-competitive conduct satisfied the conditions for exemption in Article 5(3) CA, reaching its own conclusion on all three, without these having been previously examined or examined in detail by the OFC in its decision. The same approach can be seen in *Miqna Systems Limited et v. Uffiċċju għall-Kompetizzjoni*, except that the CCAT quickly embraced the OFC's conclusions on market definition and the undertaking's market position on the tying market, deferring to the OFC's economic assessment, after noting that there was no disagreement between the parties in this respect.[168]

Where the CCAT heard appeals under the administrative model, the CCAT, true to its role, also exercised a full assessment in practice. Thus, in *Malta Bargains,* the CCAT examined thoroughly the facts and the notion of undertaking in terms of CJEU case law before it confirmed the OC's decision.[169]

In its very first pronouncement following its creation, the CCAT too, after outlining the OC's functions, laid strict standards for the OC to follow in its investigations and decisions:

> [I]n its public administrative and quasi-judicial functions of finding an infringement, the [OC] must build every investigation on respect and observance of the rule of law and on natural justice principles so as to ensure that it has the necessary, adequate, credible and true information to arrive to its conclusion, which conclusion must be fair and just.[170]

5.1.2 Substantive Grounds: FHCC and the Court of Appeal

The FHCC established clearly and carefully the parameters of its power to review the CFT's decisions on substantive grounds in its second judgment in *Garden of Eden Garage,*[171] holding from the outset that the case involved judicial review proceedings. The FHCC, after observing that under the CA at the time there was no right of appeal from the CFT's decision, referred to existing case law in terms of which, where no right of appeal exists, the courts have a general jurisdiction to review the decisions of administrative tribunals and, where it is alleged that a tribunal did not adhere to the law, the courts must examine the allegation and provide a remedy where necessary.[172] According to the case law, the courts can exercise marginal review to ensure that the administrative tribunal did not act ultra vires and adhered to the principles of natural

166. *Supra* n. 94.
167. *Council Regulation (EC) No 169/2009 of 26 February 2009 applying rules of competition to transport by rail, road and inland waterway*, OJ [2009] L 61/1; *Regulation (EEC) No 1017/68 of the Council of 19 July 1968 applying rules of competition to transport by rail, road and inland waterway*, OJ [1968] L 175/1.
168. Application No. 3/2008, 29 January 2014.
169. *Supra* n. 163.
170. *Mizzi, supra* n. 4, 21 March 2012, p. 8 (author's translation).
171. *Supra* n. 93.
172. *Ibid.*, p. 6.

justice and that its decision is not contrary to law.[173] The FHCC considered that MTA's action fell squarely within these limits since it was based on the allegation that the CFT acted ultra vires when it erroneously applied the CA to the facts of the case.[174]

The FHCC further clarified that its competence in judicial review proceedings was not to decide whether the CFT in the evaluation of the evidence before it arrived at the right decision, or reassess the evidence, or substitute the decision of the CFT on the merits by determining itself whether the public authority acted as an undertaking.[175] Rather, according to the FHCC, it could only exercise a limited review, so that its competence was to scrutinise whether the CFT had examined in the first place if MTA was acting as an undertaking by carrying out an economic activity vis-à-vis the conduct complained of, which point determined the application of Article 9 CA to MTA and established the CFT's own jurisdiction to deal with the case.[176] Upon finding that the CFT had not carried out this exercise, and after the FHCC analysed the meaning of 'undertaking' to establish its significance for the application of the competition rules, the FHCC declared the CFT's decision null and void.

The *Hompesch* CFT decision was also challenged before the FHCC.[177] In this case, the FHCC noted that the action was not based on an appraisal of the facts, but on the thesis that the CFT's decision was invalid due to an error of law, and, when the FHCC's decision was appealed, the Court of Appeal immediately stated that the case before the FHCC concerned judicial review proceedings.[178] Both the FHCC and the Court of Appeal, after considering at length the legal issues raised by the applicant and whether the CFT and the OFC (and, upon subsequent appeal, the FHCC itself) had adequately addressed these issues in their decisions, rejected the appeal.

In *Liquigas*, the Court of Appeal manifested its reluctance to accede to the respondent's plea that the appeal should be rejected.[179] Liquigas, relying on when the OFC's decision had been delivered, argued, in line with the transitory provision,[180] that no right of appeal existed under the CA preceding the 2011 amendments. The Court of Appeal, relying on another part of the transitory provision,[181] however, considered that, since the CCAT's decision was delivered following the 2011 amendments which provided for an appeal from the CCAT's decision, the appeal was admissible. The approach of the Court of Appeal indicates that, faced with a choice, it would do its utmost to save the appeal proceedings.

173. *Ibid.*, pp. 6-7.
174. *Ibid.*, p. 7.
175. *Ibid.*, pp. 10 and 13.
176. *Ibid.*, pp. 13-15.
177. *Supra* n. 7.
178. *Ibid.*
179. *Supra* n. 94.
180. MCCAA Act, Article 70(1)(c).
181. MCCAA Act, Article 70(2)(b).

5.1.3 *Procedural Grounds*

Where procedural grounds were raised, one can observe intense review by the reviewing tribunals and courts. This can probably be attributed to the fact that procedural grounds are usually less peculiar to competition law than substantive grounds, and all the reviewing tribunals and courts have been presided by members of the judiciary with many years of experience in dealing with procedural issues.[182] In particular, the reviewing tribunals and courts emerge as staunch defenders of the fair hearing rule, especially when raised by the undertakings investigated.

In *Cassar Fuels*,[183] the CFT did not hesitate to annul part of the OFT's compliance order in respect of conduct that was not raised in the complaint or addressed in the investigation, holding that the undertaking concerned was not given the opportunity to defend itself with respect to that conduct before the OFC in breach of natural justice, while stressing that the latter must always be observed in the exercise of public functions.

In *Liquigas*, both the CCAT and the Court of Appeal made it very clear that they would fiercely defend the principles of natural justice, no matter how urgent and pressing the issue before the OFC may have been from a public interest perspective. The issue arose between the plaintiff company, Liquigas, the dominant supplier of gas cylinders, and its distributors a couple of days before Christmas. It was alleged that Liquigas was refusing to supply gas cylinders unless the distributors honoured their contractual obligation to sell and distribute solely Liquigas' cylinders. In retaliation, the distributors had ceased to supply cylinders on the market. The OFC, concerned that the dispute would lead to no supplies over the Christmas period, found the contractual obligation in breach of Article 9 CA and delivered a decision within two days ordering Liquigas to resume supplies of gas cylinders. In its decision, the CCAT explained that the OFC was obliged to adhere to the principles of natural justice, including giving Liquigas sufficient opportunity to understand the complaint made against it and to adequately submit its position.[184] The CCAT underlined that this obligation in administrative decisions resulted not only from national jurisprudence and legislation but also from EU jurisprudence.[185] The CCAT further considered that Liquigas' procedural safeguards providing for access to the OFC's file and the right to be informed in writing of the objections against it and to be given a reasonable timeframe within which to reply as provided in Regulation 1/2003 and Regulation 773/2004 had not been followed. The CCAT thus annulled the OFC's decision. On appeal, the OC argued that the EU procedural provisions relating to competition proceedings before the Commission did not necessarily apply vis-à-vis the OFC's proceedings. The Court of Appeal,

182. *See*, for instance, *Garden of Eden Garage* FHCC's first judgment and subsequent appeal involving prescription and time-limits based on general law and not on competition law, where the Court of Appeal annulled the FHCC judgment (*supra* n. 61).
183. *Supra* n. 18, pp. 8-9.
184. *Supra* n. 82, pp. 7 et seq.
185. Referring to Case 17/74, ECLI:EU:C:1974:106, *Transocean Marine Paint Association v. Commission*, 23 October 1974, para. 15; Joined cases 100 to 103/80, ECLI:EU:C:1983:158, *SA Musique Diffusion Française and others v. Commission*, 7 June 1983, para. 36.

upholding the CCAT's decision, held that Liquigas' rights to know the allegations against it and to prepare its defence applied irrespective of whether the EU procedural provisions were applicable.[186]

The *Liquigas* case may be contrasted with the *Mizzi* case, where the complainant alleged a breach of the fair hearing rule by the OFC for failing to give it the opportunity to make submissions to sustain its complaint and reply to the defence of the undertakings under investigation.[187] The CCAT rejected the complainant's plea, after noting that the CA, unlike in proceedings before the CCAT, did not give the complainant the right to make such submissions during an investigation before the OFC, and upon drawing on the EU approach that competition proceedings by the Commission do not constitute adversarial proceedings between the complainant and the companies being investigated, so that the procedural rights of complainants are not as extensive as those of the companies concerned.[188] The CCAT also rejected the complainant's allegation of a breach of the fair hearing rule based on the duration of the administrative procedure, holding, after taking into account all the investigatory steps undertaken by the OFC, that the decision was delivered within a reasonable time.

In *Mizzi*, the CCAT also clarified, again on the basis of EU sources,[189] the complainant's situation regarding access to the OFC's file, holding that the complainant was only entitled to see those documents on which the OFC had relied in arriving at its conclusions.[190]

5.2 Review of Fines

Although there were no fining decisions to be challenged, there have been two significant constitutional challenges relating to fines under the CA.

In the *FEA* case,[191] the OC had investigated the FEA for an alleged breach of Article 101 TFEU and Article 5 CA under the administrative model. After being served with the OC's statement of objections, the FEA filed constitutional proceedings before the FHCC, in its constitutional jurisdiction, alleging that the powers of the OC to determine competition law breaches and impose fines following its own investigation, and the CCAT's power to hear appeals from the OC's decisions violated Article 39(1) of the Constitution and Article 6(1) ECHR. The FHCC found for FEA, and the OC and the Advocate General appealed before the Constitutional Court.

The Constitutional Court rejected the appellants' argument that the proceedings should not have been filed before the OC reached a decision on the merits, holding,

186. *Supra* n. 94, pp. 9-10.
187. *Supra* n. 4, 28 January 2016.
188. Commission Notice on the handling of complaints by the Commission under Articles 81 and 82 of the EC Treaty, OJ [2004] C 101/05, para. 59.
189. Regulation 773/2004, Article 8; Commission Notice on the rules for access to the Commission file in cases pursuant to Articles 81 and 82 of the EC Treaty, Articles 53, 54 and 57 of the EEA Agreement and Council Regulation (EC) No. 139/2004, OJ [2005] C 325/07, paras 30-32; Commission Notice on the handling of complaints, *supra* n. 188, para. 69.
190. *Supra* n. 4, 27 February 2013, pp. 3-8.
191. *Supra* n. 26.

inter alia, that the proceedings were challenging the very process stipulated in the law, particularly the fact that the authority carrying out the investigation also decided on the breach, which process was already affecting the FEA, independently of the potential outcome of the OC's decision.[192] Since the OC had not yet reached a decision and since the project only covers appeals from NCA decisions, the *FEA* judgments are not included in the database. However, the case merits discussion as it sheds important light on the Constitutional Court's scrutiny and impact on the public enforcement of competition law.

Article 6(1) ECHR provides:

> In the determination of his civil rights and obligations or of any criminal charge against him, everyone is entitled to a fair and public hearing within a reasonable time by an independent and impartial tribunal established by law.

Article 39 Constitution, unlike Article 6 ECHR, distinguishes between criminal and civil cases. Thus, Article 39(1) provides:

> Whenever any person is charged with a criminal offence he shall, unless the charge is withdrawn, be afforded a fair hearing within a reasonable time by an independent and impartial court established by law.

In contrast, under Article 39(2), cases concerning civil rights and obligations may be heard by 'any court or other adjudicating authority prescribed by law'.

The Constitutional Court, referring to *A. Menarini Diagnostics S.R.L. v. Italie*,[193] considered that the guarantees in Article 39(1) applied to competition proceedings as these are criminal in nature since the CA protects the general interest of society and serves as a deterrent, the fine is severe, intended as a penalty and not as compensation for damages, and, prior to the 2011 amendments, breaches of Article 5 CA were considered criminal offences.[194]

The Constitutional Court, agreeing with the FHCC, explained that the word 'court' in Article 39(1), in terms of the Constitution and the COCP,[195] covered only the superior and inferior courts in Malta and did not cover tribunals or other adjudicating authorities, even if impartial, independent and established by law.[196] On this basis, the Constitutional Court considered that the CCAT could not be classified as a court and did not satisfy the requirement of Article 39(1), discarding the appellants' arguments that regard had to be paid to the functional reality of the CCAT by looking at its structure and characteristics more than at its name or classification.

The Constitutional Court agreed with FEA that the right of appeal on points of law before the Court of Appeal could not serve to shield the proceedings initiated by the OC

192. Paragraph 9 of the judgment.
193. Application no. 43509/08, (ECtHR, 27 September 2011), paras 40-44.
194. Paragraph 28, confirming the FHCC's judgment on the nature of the proceedings, which had relied on ECtHR judgments including *Engel and Others v. The Netherlands* Application nos 5100/71, 5101/71, 5102/71, 5354/72, 5370/72 (8 June 1976); *Jussila v. Finland* Application no. 73053/01 (23 November 2006); *Bendenoun v. France* Application no. 12547/86 (24 February 1994).
195. *Supra* n. 91.
196. Paragraphs 20, 32 to 35.

from Article 39(1), since the Constitution requires the hearing and the determination of a criminal charge to be carried out by a court. It, however, went on to note that, in any case, even if one had to consider that part of the process took place before a court, the appeal before the Court of Appeal was still a limited appeal.[197] This left some doubt as to whether a full appeal before a court would have remedied the situation, but the Constitutional Court clarified its position in a subsequent case, *Rosette Thake noe et v. Kummissjoni Elettorali et* (*Thake*), holding unequivocally that the right to be heard by a court under Article 39(1) was triggered as soon as a person was accused of an offence and that a subsequent full appeal before a court could not serve to neutralise this right or to save the administrative proceedings.[198] This steered the legislator's choice in favour of the judicial model rather than leaving intact the administrative model subject only to an amendment requiring a full appeal before the Court of Appeal.[199]

In *FEA*, the Constitutional Court, relying on *Janosevic v. Sweden*,[200] found no breach of Article 6 ECHR since there was a full right of appeal before the CCAT[201] and the law provided sufficient guarantees to ensure that the CCAT satisfied the conditions of an independent and impartial tribunal for the purposes of Article 6 ECHR.[202] However, it found that the relevant CA provisions, insofar as they enabled the OC to issue infringement decisions and impose fines or other remedies, and insofar as they enabled the CCAT to hear appeals from OC decisions, were in breach of Article 39 Constitution and therefore invalid and without effect vis-à-vis the FEA, and that the proceedings commenced under those provisions breached the FEA's right to a fair hearing under Article 39 insofar as they could lead to an infringement decision.[203]

The effect of the *FEA* decision was to frustrate the OC proceedings on the basis of the national constitutional provision. Whether this is correct from a supremacy of EU law point of view, considering that the application of Article 101 TFEU was at stake, is a matter of useful and important discussion but outside the scope of the project. At this stage, it suffices to highlight the rigour and enthusiasm with which the Constitutional Court was willing to uphold the fair hearing principle as guaranteed by the Constitution, which is stricter than the ECHR, at the cost of preventing competition law enforcement. The protection of fundamental rights is imperative in a legal system upholding the rule of law. Nonetheless, one consequence was that the CA's deterrent effect through the imposition of fines was effectively paralysed until the 2019 amendments.

197. Paragraph 36.
198. Application No. 25/17, 8 October 2018, para. 67. This case, which falls outside the realm of competition law, concerned the Electoral Commission's powers to investigate, decide breaches and impose penalties under the law relating to political parties.
199. *See Objects and Reasons* of Bill 80 of 2019 leading to the 2019 amendments, p. C2674, https://parlament.mt/media/99642/bill-80-competition-act-and-consumer-affairs-act-and-other-laws-amendment-bill.pdf; MCCAA Annual Report, 2018, p. 10.
200. Application no. 34619/1997 (ECtHR, 23 July 2002).
201. Paragraphs 43-48.
202. Paragraphs 51-54.
203. Paragraph 56(ii). The Constitutional Court thus overturned the FHCC's decision finding a breach of Article 6(1) ECHR and confirmed it where it found a breach of Article 39(1) Constitution.

In an attempt to avoid bringing public enforcement to a complete halt until the law was amended following *FEA*, the OC's approach was to continue to investigate cases and decide thereon, declaring expressly however that it would desist from imposing fines. This approach, seen in the *Falzon* OC decision,[204] was in line with the CCAT's own approach. Following *FEA*, the CCAT refused to abstain from taking cognisance of the cases pending before it where the OC declared that it would not impose a fine if an infringement was found. According to the CCAT, in such cases, the principal obstacle leading to the Constitutional Court's conclusion in *FEA* had been removed.[205]

This approach was tested in the *Falzon* constitutional case, where the Constitutional Court reversed the earlier partial judgment of the FHCC.[206] Falzon challenged the OC infringement decision claiming that the *FEA* ruling nonetheless applied. The Constitutional Court clarified that the question was not whether the OC unilaterally had discretion to alter the nature of the proceedings merely by deciding not to impose the fine, as Falzon argued, but rather whether the OC's declaration that no fine was going to be imposed was sufficient for the proceedings to cease to be criminal in nature for the purposes of Article 6 ECHR and Article 39 Constitution.[207] The Constitutional Court, highlighting the need to pay attention to the principle of proportionality, held that, if the only factor rendering the law unconstitutional was the imposition of fines by the OC, it would be a sufficient remedy to remove this power rather than invalidate all the relative CA provisions.[208] It further explained that the Constitutional Court in *FEA* had considered the factors leading to the conclusion that the proceedings are criminal in nature cumulatively.[209] Thus, not every factor was necessarily sufficient by itself to determine the criminal nature of the proceedings, and each factor carried a different weight.[210] The Constitutional Court considered that the most important factor, which could, even by itself, make the proceedings criminal in nature, was the severity of the fine, to which the other factor relating to deterrence is tied.[211] Conversely, proceedings intended to safeguard the public interest may not necessarily be of a criminal nature.[212] The Constitutional Court, thus, concluded that, since no fine was imposed, the proceedings before the OC in *Falzon* were not of a criminal nature so the safeguards concerning criminal proceedings in Article 6 ECHR and Article 39(1) Constitution did not apply,[213] thereby confirming the CCAT's and OC's approach.

In *Falzon*, the Constitutional Court, by adopting a moderate, proportionate stance, restored some balance, enabling the OC to continue to enforce competition law and find infringements without however imposing fines. Moving forward, the judicial

204. *Supra* n. 122, para. 170.
205. *Ibid.*, para. 164.
206. *Supra* n. 105.
207. Paragraph 14.
208. Paragraph 15.
209. Identified above, *FEA*, para. 28.
210. Paragraph 21.
211. *Ibid.*
212. *Ibid.*
213. Paragraphs 24-25.

model has put these issues to rest by conferring infringement decisions and fines onto the CC(CS).

5.3 Time Factor

The effectiveness of judicial remedies depends on their timely delivery. Cases appear to have been best managed in terms of time before the CFT. The length of proceedings increased significantly for cases going to the FHCC and the Court of Appeal. For instance, in *Hompesch*, almost 11 years lapsed between the OFC decision in 2009 to the Court of Appeal decision in 2020.[214] The *Garden of Eden Garage* case is also marked by the number of years of litigation spanning from the OFC's decision in 2006 to when the case was ultimately withdrawn before the Court of Appeal in 2019. In *Liquigas* almost 10 years spanned from the OFC's decision in 2010 to the Court of Appeal decision in 2020.

5.4 Reflections on Effectiveness and Judicial Deference

The CFT and the CCAT, showed a clear preference for a full review when defining their parameters, reassessing the case on the merits. The FHCC, faithful to the limitations of judicial review, was prepared to exercise only marginal review, while the Court of Appeal exercised full review vis-à-vis the arguments raised by the parties. The cases indicate that the reviewing tribunals and courts exercised intense judicial scrutiny on procedural aspects, particularly with respect to fair hearing and natural justice principles. Appellants were less likely to succeed if they contested the OFC's or OC's legal and economic assessment. Few NCA decisions were overturned on substance, indicating either that the OFC or OC had undertaken a comprehensive assessment under the CA or that the reviewing courts and tribunals, while insisting on an intense review, were less willing to depart from the OFC's or OC's conclusions or previous instance judgment. Further, one cannot fail to note the Constitutional Court's impact on the public enforcement of competition law instigating a fresh overhaul of the institutional structure.

Going forward, under the judicial model, as noted, apart from the limited cases where the OC may take a decision, the CC(CS) will be acting as a competition authority and its decisions may be appealed before the Court of Appeal. The Court of Appeal should therefore be exercising full and unrestricted review. In practice, vis-à-vis procedural issues, in line with the pattern observed, one would expect the Court of Appeal to be very vigilant, exercising an in-depth appraisal, although certain procedural issues, particularly those relating to the rights of the defence in infringement cases, are less likely to arise given that the hearing and subsequent determination of the case are carried out by the CC(CS) rather than the OC. On substantive matters, little can be drawn from the one Court of Appeal judgment dealing with substantive grounds and falling within the project scope as this did not involve complex competition law

214. *Supra* n. 7.

issues.[215] Thus, on substance, particularly if economic and technically complex considerations are involved, one can be less prophetic on the intensity of review, given that the Court of Appeal is not a specialist court. The CC(CS) itself, having only been allocated competition cases in 2019, may yet need to acquire more expertise and experience in substantive competition law. While the CC(CS) can fill the gap with the assistance of court-appointed experts, the CC(CS), both where it is acting as a competition authority and where it is acting as a review court, may be more inclined to lean towards the OC's position, the OC being perceived as the expert body on the matter, making it more onerous for the undertakings concerned or the complainants to prove their case. Conversely, it is expected that the CC(CS) will rigorously examine procedural grounds in the limited instances where the OC may take a decision.

5.5 Alignment with EU Law

On substantive matters, EU law and jurisprudence and Commission guidance have generally been referred to in the judgments, serving as an invaluable resource, particularly for the CFT and the CCAT, even where only the national provisions were invoked. With respect to procedural issues, reliance on EU sources has been less automatic. In its first partial judgment in *Mizzi*,[216] the OC claimed that the CCAT should follow the judgment of the Court of Justice in *VEBIC*[217] to determine the OC's role in the proceedings before the CCAT as the law stood before the 2011 amendments. The CCAT held that *VEBIC* would be given due importance as a source of interpretation as required under the CA, however, one first had to consider the legislator's will and whether Maltese law, without recourse to CJEU case law, provided a clear interpretation. While the CCAT noted that there was no obvious lacuna under Maltese law, so that it was able to reach a conclusion on the basis of the CA, the CCAT, nevertheless, still felt the need to comment that its conclusion was not incompatible with the judgment in *VEBIC*.

The CCAT continued to clarify its position in the second partial judgment in *Mizzi*,[218] which also concerned a procedural issue – the right of access to the file by the complainant. In arriving at its conclusion, the CCAT, after noting that the CA was silent on this matter, relied heavily on EU instruments[219] and case law. On the question of whether EU procedural law should prevail over Maltese law, the CCAT set the following hierarchy:

- where the CA provided for the matter under consideration, the CA would apply;

215. *See Hompesch* Court of Appeal judgment, *supra* n. 7.
216. *Supra* n. 4.
217. C-439/08, ECLI:EU:C:2010:739, 7 December 2010.
218. *Supra* n. 4.
219. *Supra* n. 189.

- where the CA is silent or unclear, the CA being a special law regulating special proceedings relating to a particular area of law, the CCAT would have recourse to EU competition law and jurisprudence as a source of interpretation;
- other national legislation, such as the COCP on disclosure of evidence, could be resorted to at the CCAT's discretion where further clarification was necessary but not at the cost of setting aside EU sources specifically providing for the matter at hand.[220]

In contrast to the use of EU law for interpretative guidance, the application of Articles 101 and 102 TFEU by the NCA has been sparse. It follows that appeal or judicial review cases have primarily involved national law. The findings show that no preliminary ruling from the CJEU has ever been sought by the reviewing tribunals and courts and there have not been many cases within the scope of the project where tensions between EU and national law have been raised. A case where the CFT was prepared to discuss Malta's obligations following EU accession is *Bargain Holidays*.[221] Without entering into the merits of whether there was an effect on trade, the CFT, drawing on the principle of sincere cooperation,[222] *Consorzio Industrie Fiammiferi (CIF) v. Autorità Garante della Concorrenza e del Mercato*[223] and the fact that EU law formed an integral part of Maltese law,[224] held that Malta could not adopt measures that could jeopardise the attainment of EU objectives, which include the objective that competition in the internal market must not be distorted.[225] It then went on to opine that a regulatory structure created by law, which enabled its board members (being undertakings on the market) to obtain an economic advantage to the detriment of competitors and consumers, could not be tolerated, calling for rectification of the problem.[226]

In the other cases where the question arose on whether the EU competition rules were applicable, it was decided that there was no effect on trade. In *Hompesch*, the CFT did not seem keen to engage in a detailed discussion and swiftly dismissed the claim that the conduct had an effect on trade.[227] In *Burdnara Bulk Cargo Group*,[228] the CCAT after making extensive reference to the Commission's *Guidelines on the effect on trade concept*[229] engaged in an explanation as to why there was no effect on trade, so that the sectoral EU BERs[230] relied upon by the undertakings concerned did not apply. The appellants further argued that notwithstanding the lack of an effect on trade, the BERs

220. At pp. 2, 8. *See also Liquigas* CCAT decision, *supra* n. 82, p. 8. On appeal, in *Liquigas*, *supra* n. 94, it was argued that the EU procedural provisions applicable in Commission investigations did not necessarily apply vis-à-vis the OFC's proceedings, but the Court of Appeal was able to decide the point without specifically addressing this issue (p. 10).
221. *Supra* n. 136.
222. Article 4(3) TEU.
223. Case C-198/01, ECLI:EU:C:2003:430, 9 September 2003.
224. The CFT referred to Article 3 of the European Union Act (Chapter 460 of the Laws of Malta).
225. At pp. 12-13.
226. At pp. 13-14.
227. *Supra* n. 7, Hompesch CFT decision, p. 16.
228. *See supra* n. 94.
229. [2004] OJ C 101/07.
230. *Supra* n. 167.

should still apply in line with the OC's practice of applying EU block exemption regulations even in a purely national context. The CCAT, however, rejected this argument. The CCAT's decisions were upheld on appeal.[231]

6 CONCLUDING REMARKS

Judicial control mechanisms aimed at ensuring respect for the undertakings' rights of defence and effective judicial protection in relation to the NCA's enforcement powers, were always available in terms of Maltese law and jurisprudence through judicial review, appeal or constitutional proceedings, as demonstrated in this report. The more challenging questions are to what extent judicial control has been exercised and how effective it has been.

The extent of judicial control ultimately depends on the number of NCA decisions. The OFC and OC suffered throughout the project timeline from lack of resources and the problem is still ongoing, resulting in few NCA decisions. The judicial model is likely to compound this problem as the time needed to reach a decision is likely to be more protracted given that the investigation and decision-making roles are split between two arms. Needless to say, the number of NCA decisions and subsequent judicial challenges have a direct impact on the effective development of competition law.

Where NCA decisions were challenged, different trends emerged vis-à-vis substantive and procedural issues with the reviewing tribunals and courts exercising careful scrutiny on procedural matters. This is probably attributed to the judges' strength on procedural questions across all areas of law, such as fair hearing. On substantive points, the evidence suggests that the reviewing tribunals and courts appeared more willing to confirm the NCA's or previous instance decision.

While *FEA* dealt with the nature of the deciding body and the scope of review by an independent court, and while the judicial model ensures that decision-making in infringement cases is institutionally separate and distinct from the investigatory role and guarantees full recourse before the Court of Appeal, the question as to whether the CC(CS) and the Court of Appeal, in practice, have the required expertise to handle intricate competition questions remains open and insufficiently tested. No doubt, if decision-making is to be genuinely fair and judicial scrutiny truly effective, the ability of the courts to carry out an in-depth assessment of the competition issues involved is *sine qua non*, and complementary to the impartiality requirement, especially where complex economic and legal considerations are involved and where the law provides for a full appeal. In the absence of sufficient expertise, the courts may be less willing to depart from the OC's position on substantive issues. In that case, the requirement of expert knowledge and adequate resources at the OC's level becomes even more important.

Time is also a relevant factor in assessing the effectiveness of judicial control. Over the project period, this was an issue where subsequent appeals at different

231. *Supra* n. 94.

instances were filed following an NCA decision. Going forward, challenges to infringement decisions have been restricted solely to the Court of Appeal. Hence, the length of time spent in litigation following a CC(CS) infringement decision should be less, compensating for the extra time required to reach an NCA decision under the judicial model. Further, the requirement for hearings before the Court of Appeal to be appointed within a set timeframe eliminates potential delays in the appointment of cases.

Finally, EU law has served as an important pillar in many cases, especially for the CFT and the CCAT, in interpreting and deciding competition issues, a trend that is likely to be pursued by the CC(CS) and the Court of Appeal. However, enforcement, and consequently appeals, based on the EU competition rules have been rare, although going forward this may change as the OC and the CC(CS) gain more confidence in applying the EU competition rules or as the OC embarks on cases more likely to involve an effect on trade.

CHAPTER 22

The Netherlands Report

Annalies Outhuijse

1 INTRODUCTION TO THE COMPETITION LAW ENFORCEMENT CONTEXT IN THE NETHERLANDS

Modern competition law enforcement based on the European model was established in the Netherlands in 1998 by the introduction of the Dutch Competition Act (*Mededingingswet 1998*). Prohibitions similar to those in Articles 101 and 102 of the Treaty on the Functioning of the European Union (TFEU) were introduced and the independent Dutch competition authority (*Nederlandse mededingingsautoriteit* (NMa)) was established to enforce the Competition Act, both of which came into force on 1 January 1998. Before that date, the Economic Competition Act applied in the Netherlands. That Act was based on what is known as the 'abuse system': cartels were allowed unless expressly prohibited. Because cartels were barely prohibited and enforced in the Netherlands, our country came to be known as the 'cartel paradise'. The lack of competition between companies in the Netherlands harmed the dynamics of the economy. Moreover, the Dutch abuse system clashed with the much stricter prohibition systems (cartels are prohibited unless they are expressly permitted) in the European Union (EU) and leading European countries. Transformation was therefore initiated.

The prohibition of anticompetitive agreements is enshrined in Article 6 of the Dutch Competition Act (and Article 101 TFEU) and the prohibition on the abuse of dominance in Article 24 of the Dutch Competition Act (and Article 102 TFEU). These rules are currently enforced by the *Autoriteit Consument en Markt* (Dutch Authority for Consumers and Markets (ACM)). It came into existence in 2013 through the merger of the NMa with two authorities enforcing consumer protection and telecommunications rules (*Consumentenautoriteit and Onafhankelijke Post en Telecommunicatie Autoriteit*). The ACM is authorised, among other things, to impose administrative fines on both companies and individuals and to impose other administrative sanctions and remedies.

The ACM public enforcement procedure consists of two phases: the investigation and the decision-making phase. The ACM's Competition Department conducts the investigation during the investigation phase. This phase concludes with an infringement report containing information on the procedure and the nature of the evidence, a review of the facts and circumstances of the case, a legal qualification of these facts (what is the alleged infringement, e.g., agreement, concerted practice or abuse of dominance), an assessment in light of the relevant legal provisions (Articles 6/24 of the Competition Act, Articles 101/102 TFEU), and the establishment of the undertakings' involvement. The infringement report is subsequently handed over to the Directorate of Legal Affairs (which is separate from the Competition Department) and it does not contain a draft sanctioning decision or other information about the fine or remedy to be imposed. It is also sent to the undertakings under investigation, which thereby receive the opportunity to review the information gathered by the ACM. They are subsequently invited to present their views on the report and explain them at a hearing.[1] At this stage, the undertakings can point out inaccuracies in the report and put forward exculpatory evidence. The Directorate of Legal Affairs decides within thirteen weeks of the date of the report whether a fine or other remedy should be imposed and drafts the infringement decision.[2] The undertaking may lodge an objection to this decision, which is a prerequisite for initiating court proceedings as described in the next section.

The ACM's Competition Department has broad discretion in the decision of whether to investigate a certain case and to impose a sanction.[3] The ACM may set priorities and is not obliged to investigate all alleged violations of competition law. The decision not to investigate a case can be appealed in court if the case was based on a complaint or enforcement request by a third party. The courts conduct only a marginal review in those kinds of cases, because of the ACM's discretion in these areas.

The ACM has a priority policy and publishes its focus areas every year. In practice, the ACM focused in the last twenty years on horizontal anti-competitive agreements, which were mainly sanctioned by fines.[4] This has changed lately, with

---

1. *See* about this and how this is done in practice: Beumer, A.E. (2016). *De publieke handhavingsprocedures van het mededingingsrecht in het licht van de mensenrechten.* Den Haag: Boom juridisch. Beumer provided insight into how often companies use the opportunity to submit a written view and explain it orally at the hearing. The study shows that by no means all companies that submit a written opinion also use the opportunity to explain it orally.
2. In practice, this deadline is often not met, and this usually has no consequences. *See* in this respect the ruling of the Rotterdam District Court of 25 August 2022 (ECLI:NL:RBROT:2022:7119) which confirms that the thirteen weeks are not a strict deadline. In this case, the defendant companies brought an action for failure to decide in time. This was granted, but the ACM was given until the end of the year to make a decision (almost nineteen weeks later).
3. *See* in more detail: K. Cseres & Outhuijse, A. (2017). Parallel Enforcement and Accountability: The Case of EU Competition Law. In M. Scholten, & M. Luchtman (eds), Law Enforcement by EU Authorities: Implications for Political and Judicial Accountability (pp. 82-114). Cheltenham: Edward Elgar.
4. Anne Beumer presented an overview of cartel cases that were enforced between 2004 and 2015 as an appendix to her thesis research. The studies show that within cartel fines, there are also certain types of offences that are most frequently fined, namely horizontal cartel agreements, and

more single-firm abuses and vertical restraints being investigated and sanctioned, also using wider remedies than simply a fine.[5] In relation to fines, it should be noted that as from 1 July 2016, the maximum amount of a fine was increased from EUR 450,000 to EUR 900,000, or 10% of the undertaking's annual turnover if the latter is higher.[6] If the infringement lasted longer than two, three or four years, the maximum fine was increased to EUR 1.8, 2.7 or 3.6 million, respectively, or to 20%, 30% or 40% of annual turnover. With the objective of increasing the deterrent effect of ACM competition fines, this amount was doubled for recidivists, to the maximum of either EUR 7.2 million or 80% of annual turnover - whichever is higher.

2 APPEAL PROCESS REGARDING ACM DECISIONS

As stated above, after receiving an infringement decision, the undertakings may lodge an objection with the ACM and request the decision to be reconsidered. This step is mandatory to allow for a subsequent appeal to the courts. This additional administrative procedure is designed as a procedure to solve disputes between citizens and the government so that lengthy, formal legal proceedings before the administrative courts can be avoided.[7] The ACM is required to review and reconsider its decision in its entirety during the objection procedure on the basis of the undertaking's objections, which may relate to all aspects of the decision, and the ACM has full discretion to uphold, modify or withdraw its decision. The ACM has several options if it decides to modify its decision, including adding additional evidence to its decision or improving the reasoning.

If the ACM decides to uphold the decision, with or without adjustments, the undertaking may apply for judicial review with two exclusively competent courts: the Rotterdam District Court as a first-instance court and the Trade and Industry Appeals Tribunal (TIAT) as a second and last instance court.[8] It is important to note that *reformatio in peius* is not permitted, meaning that the objection, appeal, and further appeal cannot result in the undertaking being in a worse position than it was before the

types of sectors where enforcement is frequent, namely the construction, healthcare, and agricultural sectors. Beumer 2016 (*supra* n. 1). These results are confirmed by this report.

5. *See* about the use of informal instruments: Lachnit, E. (2016). Alternative Enforcement of Competition Law. Eleven International Publishing; Brook, O. (2023). Do EU and U.K. Antitrust 'Bite'?: A Hard Look at 'Soft' Enforcement and Negotiated Penalty Settlements. The Antitrust Bulletin, 68(3), 477-518 DOI: 10.1177/0003603X231180245.
6. In various cases, the ACM ran up against the maximum penalty when calculating the fine. As a result, the amount of the fine was lower than it would have been without the maximum. For instance, in the cases of *Silver onions, Flour, Execution auctions, Laundries, Ship waste, First year onions and Taxi drivers,* the fines of some companies were lower because otherwise the statutory maximum of fines would have been exceeded.
7. Dutch research of administrative law cases other than competition law, in which the same objection procedure is used, has shown that in general the objection procedure is followed by judicial appeal proceedings in only 10% of cases. As will be explained, this trend is fundamentally different in cartel fine cases.
8. *See* on the establishment of these courts for competition law: Böcker, A., et al. (2010). *Specialisatie loont?! Ervaringen van grote ondernemingen met specialistische rechtspraakvoorzieningen.* Den Haag: Raad voor de rechtspraak.

objection (as a result, the fine imposed may not be increased during any of those procedures).

The Rotterdam District Court has exclusive jurisdiction in public competition law enforcement as the court of first instance. The comprehensive review conducted by the District Court includes a review of the establishment of the facts, the qualification of the facts (101/102 and type of infringements with qualification of 101/102), the evidence for the infringement, compliance with the relevant procedures, appropriateness of the sanction, (if applicable) the amount of the fine, and the interpretation of the law (*see also* section 5). The period for filing an appeal is six weeks after the ACM's objection decision and the fees currently (2023) amount to EUR 365.[9]

The TIAT is the highest administrative court specialising in the field of economic administrative law. Undertakings and the ACM may file a further appeal with the TIAT within six weeks after the District Court's judgment. The fee is also EUR 365 (2023). The TIAT not only reviews the lower court's judgment on legal grounds but, unlike some second-instance courts in other Member States, also completely reviews the factual grounds of the case. This comprises the establishment and qualification of the facts, evidence, compliance with the relevant procedures, appropriateness of the sanction, (if applicable) the amount of the fine, the interpretation of the law and the method and intensity of the judicial review by the District Court. The intensity of the review by the TIAT can in general be described as a comprehensive and intensive review (*see also* section 5). Like the District Court, the TIAT can substitute its findings for that of the ACM without limiting itself to the issue of whether the ACM could reasonably have reached a particular conclusion. In contrast, both courts review whether the ACM has reached the right decision.

As will be described in section 5, the Dutch courts are competent to review all the elements of a sanctioning decision (as stated above) and, indeed, they do so intensively if a fine is imposed. The courts even review intensively the elements that provide a margin of appreciation to the ACM (such as economic analysis). In contrast, the standard for judicial review for sanctions and remedies that are not fines – such as commitments – is more limited. The same applies to any review of an ACM decision not to investigate or sanction a case. The courts in these cases limit themselves to the issue of whether the ACM could reasonably have reached a particular conclusion. This is evidently a lower threshold for the ACM to meet than the issue of whether the ACM has reached the right decision.

Both the Rotterdam District Court and TIAT are specialised courts, being the exclusively competent courts for review of ACM competition law decisions. The complex and specialist nature of competition law and the small number of cases expected formed the rationale for the concentration of jurisdiction in these cases in particular courts.[10] According to the legislature, economic concepts such as 'relevant market' and 'restriction of competition' play an important role in competition law and their application requires specific expertise, which could be better achieved by concentrating judicial review in a single court. The combination of the Rotterdam

9. The fees slightly increase each year.
10. *See* Böcker et al. 2010 (*supra* n. 8).

District Court and TIAT as the exclusively competent courts was first introduced for competition law cases but was subsequently followed for the allocation of judicial review in other areas of economic administrative law, such as consumer protection, telecommunications, and energy, to stimulate coherence between the different areas of regulation and to make use of the expertise already gained.[11]

Both courts have considerable expertise in competition law, not only resulting from their exclusive competence but also because they have special teams dealing with competition law cases: only a limited number of judges and legal court assistants deal with such cases.[12] They are specially trained, accumulate expertise to rule on these cases and conduct internal discussions every six to eight weeks to consider legal developments, for example, European case law, academic literature, and other issues. Cases are dealt with by a chamber consisting of three judges and one legal assistant, with one substitute judge joining the chamber in some cases. Substitute judges may be called on because of their special expertise, for example, on the case law of the CJEU. Examples have included professors of Competition law, EU law or the Internal Market. Finally, courts are also authorised to appoint experts during the review procedure, for example, to bring in specialised economic knowledge, but this has never occurred to the best of my knowledge.

3 PRIOR RESEARCH

Previous studies analysing judicial review of competition law enforcement in the Netherlands are limited to cartel cases. The reason for that was that Article 102 TFEU sanctions were rarely imposed by the Dutch competition authority. The most complete analysis of judicial review in the Netherlands in relation to cartels is the PhD research by the author of this report.[13] The research was limited to cartel infringement fines,

11. In the final section, I will reflect on the fact that we almost lost the TIAT as the higher exclusive competent court. There was a merger planned with the general highest court in administrative law cases, but this legislative proposal was fortunately withdrawn.
12. *See* A. Outhuijse, Effective public enforcement of cartels: explaining the high percentages of litigation and successful litigation in the Netherlands (PhD Thesis), available via: https://research.rug.nl/nl/publications/effective-public-enforcement-of-cartels-explaining-the-high-perce.
13. *Ibid.* Other research worth mentioning includes research on convergence of Dutch jurisprudence with European competition law (A. Gerbrandy, *Convergentie in het mededingingsrecht* (The Hague: BJU 2009)), informal instruments by Eva Lachnit (E. Lachnit (*supra* n. 5)), research on the view procedure by Elsbeth Beumer (*supra* n. 1), research on use of commitments by ACM (Linssen, N.J. (2013). *Door toezegging geen boete ACM.* Juridisch up to date, 12; Elkerbout, R. & Wolbers, W. (2012). *Handhaving van het mededingingsrecht met toezeggingen.* NJB 2012/1100), sanctions for executives by Slotboom and Rosenboom (Slotboom, M.M. (2013)). *Sancties voor leidinggevenden in Nederlandse mededingingsrecht.* M&M, 4; Rosenboom, N. (2012). Career Development after Cartel Prosecution: Cartel Versus Non-cartel Managers. Journal of Competition Law and Economics, intensity and scope of review (Essens, O., et al., National Courts and the Standard of Review in Competition Law and Economic Regulation (European Law Publishing 2009)) and several annual chronicles by authors discussing individual rulings in *SEW* and *M&M*.

covering all cases since the establishment of the NMa in 1998, consisting of a total of fifty-two cartel cases. The chosen cut-off date was 1 January 2019.[14]

The research showed high percentages of litigation and successful litigation by the undertakings fined. Between 2003 and 2013, undertakings filed for appeal at the Rotterdam District Court in more than 70% of cases.[15] Since 2010, the ACM has imposed fines in twenty-two cartel cases, and at least one or more undertakings have filed an appeal in nineteen of the twenty-one cases, which represents 90% of cases.[16] This is much higher than in other administrative law cases in the Netherlands, also concerning fines imposed for other economic infringements. Appeals are also often followed by further appeals, which occurred in almost 70% of the cases brought before the District Court. Other deviations from 'the normal picture' demonstrated by this research were that the average percentage of annulled cartel fines was at least twice as high as is customary in administrative law. Regarding the latter, almost 60% of ACM fining decisions led to annulments by the Rotterdam District Court in the 2003–2013 period. This was even higher after 2013. In the research underlying this chapter, a broader focus is applied: it focuses on Articles 101 and 102 TFEU cases and also includes decisions other than fining decisions. It is also not only focused on explaining percentages of litigation and successful litigation but also includes a systematic insight into the judicial review in the Netherlands.

Finally, more general research was undertaken regarding the scope and intensity of the review applied by the Rotterdam District Court and the TIAT by Oda Essens and others.[17] A description of this was already given in the previous section.

14. That research started with the observation that the enforcement of the European and Dutch cartel prohibition was characterised by high rates of litigation and successful litigation; consequently the research sought to explain the high rates of (successful) litigation in Dutch anti-cartel enforcement via fines and thereby the factors influencing those high percentages. To determine the factors influencing the percentages, a comparative approach was adopted, looking at nine countries and four other Dutch market agencies. Data was obtained on the frequency and success of litigation in the case of fines for anti-competitive agreements through analysis of the fining decisions and court judgments for nine European countries - Belgium, Bulgaria, Croatia, Finland, France, Germany, Italy, Sweden, and the UK. The latter was also published separately in Outhuijse, A. (2019b). Effective Public Enforcement of Cartels: Rates of Challenged and Annulled Cartel Fines in Ten European Member States. World Competition, pp. 171-204.
15. *See* Outhuijse 2019a (*supra* n. 12).
16. At time of research, it was unknown whether appeal was filed for one cases. Therefore, the comparison is made with twenty-one cases instead of twenty-two cases.
17. Oda Essens et al. 2009 (*supra* n. 13); Outhuijse, A. (2020). The Effective Public Enforcement of the Prohibition of Anti-competitive Agreements: Which Factors Influence the High Percentage of Annulments of Dutch Cartel Fines? (March 2020) 8(1) Journal of Antitrust Enforcement 124-164, available at https://academic.oup.com/antitrust/advance-article/doi/10.1093/jaenfo/jnz020/5533078?guestAccessKey=a80bebc2-2b4a-42ee-b240-01fc7f85b55d.

4 QUANTITATIVE ANALYSIS

This section describes the findings resulting from a systematic analysis of judicial review of the public enforcement of EU and national competition laws by the NMa and ACM (collectively referred to below as the ACM) between May 2004 and April 2021.

4.1 Source of Information

Most competition law judgments of the relevant courts in the Netherlands are published on the national judiciary's website.[18] While there is no duty to publish all judgments, it is assumed that the analysis covers quite a comprehensive selection of the judgments during the relevant period.

4.2 Total Number of Cases

A total of 109 judgments were rendered during the relevant period: 57 by the Rotterdam District Court in the first instance and 52 by the TIAT in the second instance. Although it was difficult to establish the exact number of appealable decisions by the ACM and this is only an educated guess, a litigation rate of 52% was established (out of the 88 appealable actions from the ACM and its predecessor in the relevant period, 46 were appealed). The rate of appeal before the second-instance appeal court is 53%. These percentages of appeals are lower than found in previous research, which is not surprising, partly given that those were limited to review of cartel fines and the current study also includes other types of decisions.

The reason why the numbers are merely an educated guess is that, until a few years ago, the ACM and its predecessor (the NMa) did not publish a systematic overview of all decisions on their website. Moreover, the yearly reports of the competition authority are inconsistent in publishing numbers and in explaining what certain numbers entail, such as an explanation of which areas (Articles 101 and 102 TFEU, all competition law decisions or even other areas of regulation) and which types of decisions (fines, other administrative sanctions, decisions not to enforce) are included in these numbers. The numbers are determined based on the author's overview of the decisions published on the website, but not all decisions are published, and it is therefore unclear whether this reflects perfect accuracy.

18. www.rechtspraak.nl.

4.3 Total Number of Cases per Year

Figure 22.1 Number of Judgments According to Instances

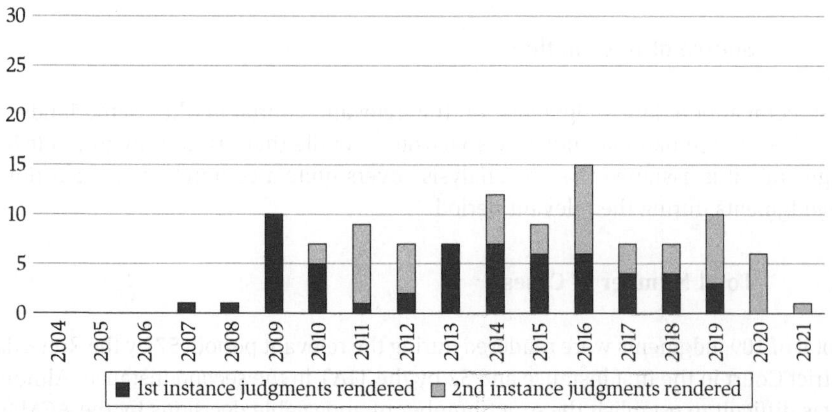

■ 1st instance judgments rendered ■ 2nd instance judgments rendered

The findings indicate that the changes in the number of judgments across the years can be explained by the number of NCA or previous instance decisions issued. For example, there were only a few ACM decisions in the 2017–2018 period, leading to a very low number of judgments at the Rotterdam District Court in the period since 2019.

Figure 22.2(a) highlights the number of District Court judgments in comparison to the number of ACM decisions appealed; Figure 22.2(b) shows the number of second-instance judgments in comparison to the number of District Court judgments. They demonstrate that in most cases appeals of ACM decisions or District Court judgments were examined collectively, in a single judgment.

Figure 22.2(a) First-Instance Judgments

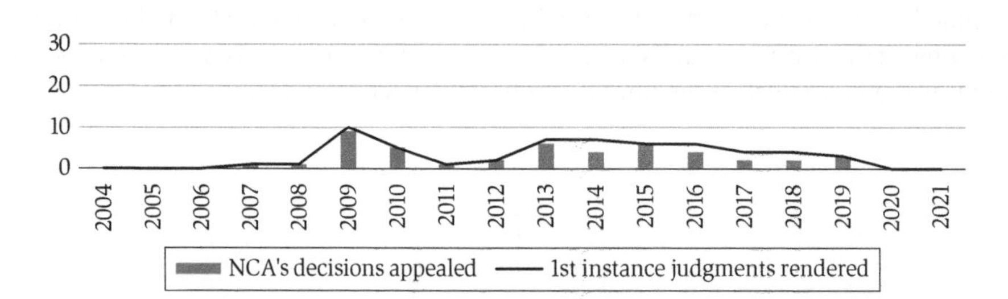

Figure 22.2(b) Second-Instance Judgments

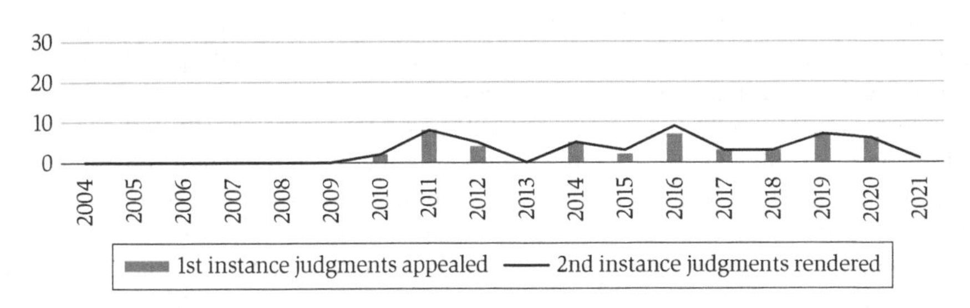

4.4 Success Rates and Outcomes

Figure 22.3 presents the success of appeals, across all instances. The success rates shown in the figure relate to the outcomes of all appeals, considering that separate appeals were aggregated if launched against a single NCA decision or previous instance judgment. That means that if an NCA decision was appealed by various parties in separate proceedings, the outcome of all those judgments will be counted as a single case for the purposes of this figure.

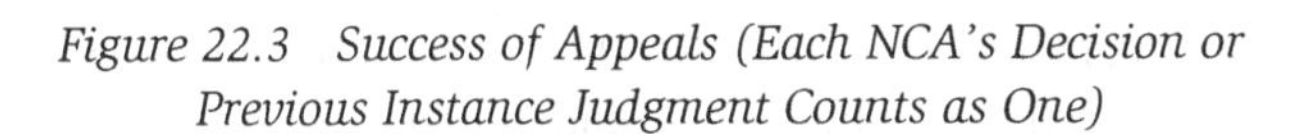

Figure 22.3 Success of Appeals (Each NCA's Decision or Previous Instance Judgment Counts as One)

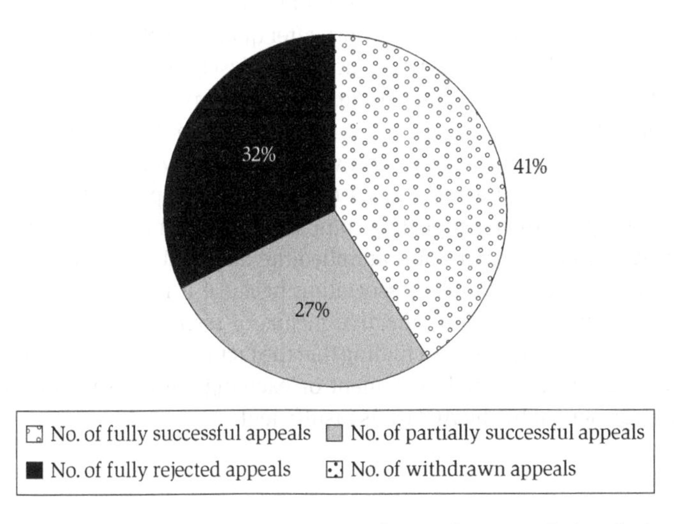

Figure 22.3 indicates a high success rate of appeals. Appeals in relation to 68% of NCA decisions were either partially or fully successful. The partially successful

category includes cases where either substantive aspects of the ACM decision were overturned or set aside (or there was success in some appeals but no other separate appeals in relation to the same ACM decision) and cases where the original penalty was reduced in some way (*see* discussion below). The fully rejected appeals entail all appeals against rejected complaints (*see* below).

Success rates are further elaborated in Figure 22.4, which identifies the outcome of the appeals. Unlike Figure 22.3, this figure examines each judgment separately and differs between the outcome of the appeal in separate instances. For both court instances, the judgments showed that cases are rarely deemed inadmissible.

Figure 22.4(a) shows that a ruling by the District Court led to modification of the ACM decision in 68 % of all cases (32 % complete rejection). This includes the 11 % of all judgments which amended the NCA decision only with respect to the level of the fines imposed. Other cases include judgments in which the District Court replaced the decision with its own decision, for example, by concluding that no fine could be imposed (e.g., because of insufficient factual evidence or insufficient economic analysis), or where it partly or fully annulled the ACM decision and ordered the ACM to adopt a new decision (e.g., insufficient reasoning). Insufficiently reasoned decisions included those in which the turnover used was insufficiently justified or the ACM insufficiently substantiated other aspects of the decision or insufficiently answered counterarguments brought forward by the parties involved. Examples of insufficient regard for the economic context included cases in which the District Court questioned the ACM's market definition, questioned whether the undertakings were in fact competitors or questioned whether the conduct was capable of restricting competition. An example is the *Taxi Driver* case, where the District Court, after qualifying the behaviour as a restriction by-object, ruled that the ACM's economic analysis, more particularly its market definition, was insufficient to demonstrate that the behaviour alleged was capable of restricting competition appreciably.[19] This resulted from a disagreement between the Rotterdam District Court and the ACM on whether the relevant market was limited to Rotterdam, as argued by the ACM in its decision, or comprised the entirety of the Netherlands, as argued by the appealing companies. Another example is the case *LHV*, in which the Rotterdam District Court annulled the fine of EUR 5.9 million imposed on the National General Practitioners Association because it ruled that its price recommendations did not constitute an effective means of restricting competition.[20] Insufficient evidence concerned the court finding that the factual evidence for the alleged facts (such as evidence for the cartel agreement or exchange of information between the undertakings) presented by the ACM was insufficient.

19. Rotterdam District Court 13 October 2016, ECLI:NL:RBROT:2016:7659-7664 (*Taxi drivers*).
20. Rotterdam District Court 17 December 2015, ECLI:NL:RBROT:2015:9352 (*LHV*).

Figure 22.4(a) First-Instance Outcome

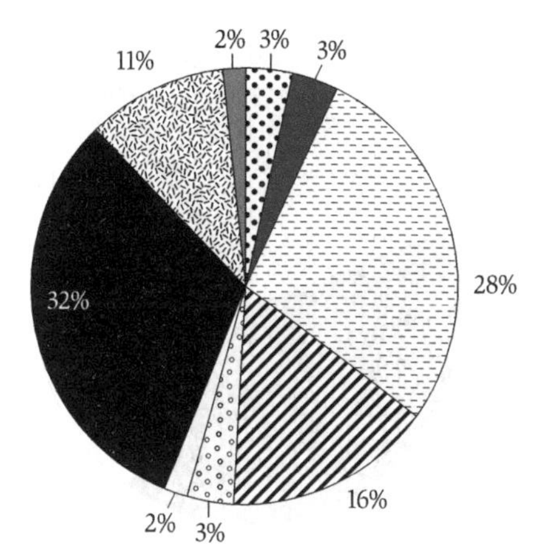

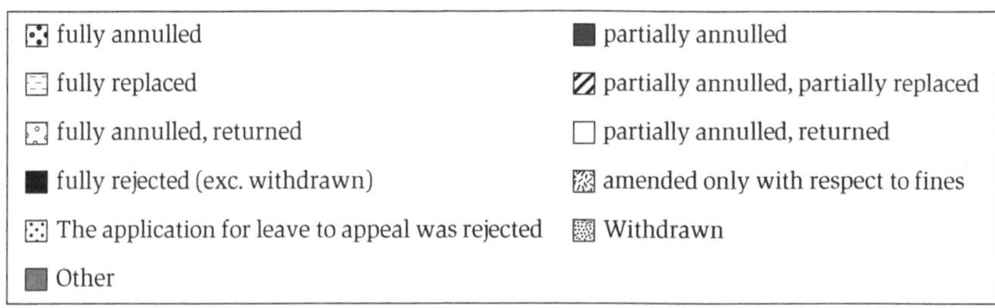

Figure 22.4(b) presents the outcome of cases after the TIAT judgment. The percentage of complete rejection of the appeal is 40%. In other words, the TIAT changed the District Court judgment in 60% of cases. Diverging views between the two court instances on the application of the competition law rules in specific cases concerned a wide variety of issues, such as insufficient evidence; insufficient economic analysis; lack of timely, adequate grounds; the limitation period; infringement of procedural rights, etc. In 17% of the cases, the adaption of the judgment only related to the level of the fine. It should also be noted that this also includes cases in which the annulment was the consequence of new arguments brought forward by the parties which were not reviewed by the District Court in the first-instance review. Several cases were sent back to the District Court, for example, to review the rest of the decision if the Rotterdam District Court only concluded that a specific type of evidence was not allowed and therefore the ACM was not entitled to impose a fine. Also, occasionally the ACM is ordered to take a new decision, but in general, the TIAT concludes a case as final as possible and will, if possible, replace the ACM decision with its judgment.

Figure 22.4(b) Second-Instance Outcome

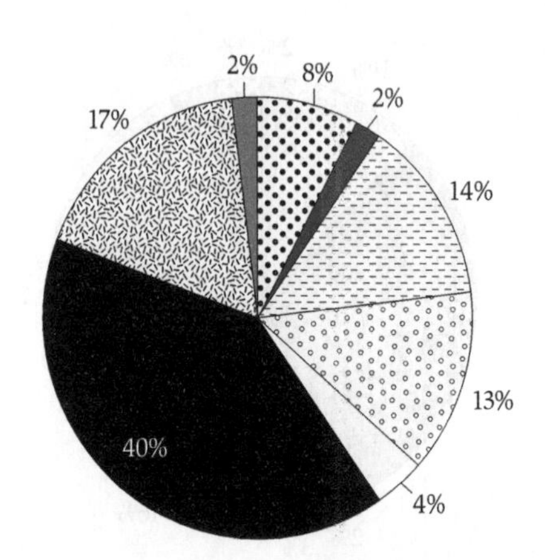

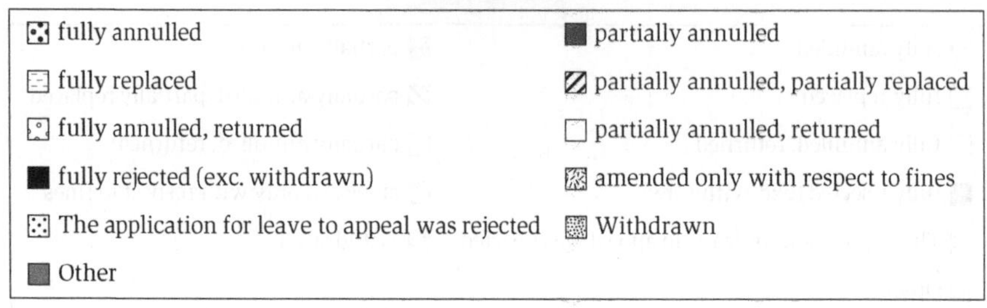

The numbers of annulments and an analysis of the second-instance rulings demonstrate there are some differences in approach between the TIAT and the Rotterdam District Court, although the relationship between the judgments of the District Court and the TIAT is not unambiguous: it cannot be inferred that the TIAT is generally more flexible or more stringent than the District Court in its review of the ACM's decisions.

There are clearly different approaches by the courts regarding certain elements of the decisions which become particularly clear in the case of fining decisions. This is especially evident on points of economic analysis and the severity factor (which is one of the elements of fine calculation). In recent years, the District Court has set a higher standard, for example, for the ACM's market analysis; it does not require that the effects of certain behaviour be proven, but it does demand a sufficient analysis of the relevant market and its functioning and the position of the undertakings on the market, in order to ascertain if all the undertakings operating in the market participated in the alleged behaviour. While the TIAT generally agreed with this line of jurisprudence of the District Court Rotterdam, and both courts emphasised the importance of satisfactory evidence by the ACM that behaviour is capable of amounting to a restriction of competition, the TIAT was less demanding than the District Court in what it required from the ACM in analysing the functioning of the market and the position of the undertakings on this market. An example is again the *Taxi Driver* case, in which the

District Court ruled that the ACM's economic analysis was insufficient to demonstrate that Rotterdam was the relevant market and therefore the behaviour alleged was capable of restricting competition appreciably.[21] The TIAT concluded however during further appeal that the economic analysis provided by the ACM was sufficient to assume that Rotterdam was the relevant market in this specific case. In contrast, the District Court seems less strict in relation to fine calculation. While the District Court confirmed the severity factor established by the ACM in several cases, the TIAT attached more weight to the consequences of the alleged behaviour for establishing the severity factor as well as to the proportionality principle and the fact that lower fines are in keeping with this principle resulting in a lower fine.[22] For example, in the *Wmo Friesland* case, the TIAT reduced the imposed fine by nearly EUR 1 million (from EUR 1,757,000 to EUR 767,000) by decreasing the severity multiplier from 1.5 to 0.5 based on these circumstances.[23] Other examples in which the TIAT lowered the severity multiplier, while the Rotterdam District Court found it appropriate or the TIAT opted for a lower multiplier than the District Court, include *First year onion plants* and *Demolition companies*.[24]

4.5 Type of NCA's Decisions Subject to Appeal

Most judgments concern cartel fines and, more specifically, horizontal restrictions (*see* Figures 7 and 9).[25] Naturally, this reflects the ACM practice in the period of review (May 2004–May 2021). Vertical cases and Article 102 TFEU infringements were not the ACM's priority and were rarely the subject of enforcement actions. This has changed in recent years: more vertical and 102 cases have been enforced and sanctioned by the ACM. In most cases (64%), the ACM relies both on Article 101 TFEU and the national equivalent, as Figures 22.5 and 22.6 show.

21. Rotterdam District Court 13 October 2016, ECLI:NL:RBROT:2016:7659-7664; TIAT 23 April 2019, ECLI:NL:CBB:2019:150-151 (*Taxi drivers*).
22. Also in the literature, there is much discussion about the correct severity factor in an individual case. While most authors find the factors excessive in some individual cases, others state that the factors are too low. *See, e.g.*, about the *Wmo Friesland* case: Cees Dekker et al., 'Kroniek Nederlands mededingingsrecht 2010' (2011) M&M 85; Claudia Bruins, CBb doet passende uitspraak in Friese kartelzaak thuiszorg, available at https://www.c-law.nl/nl/blog/cbbdoet-passende-uitspraak-in-friese-kartelzaak-thuiszorg/.
23. CBb 11 January 2017, ECLI:NL:CBB:2017:1 (*Wmo Friesland*).
24. Rotterdam District Court 24 July 2014, ECLI:NL:RBROT:2014:5930 (*First year onion plants*); CBb 6 October 2016, ECLI:NL:CBB:2016:272 (*First year onion plants*); District Court Rotterdam 26 November 2015, ECLI:NL:RBROT:2015:8610 (*Demolition companies*); CBb 12 October 2017, ECLI:NL:CBB:2017:325 (*Demolition companies*).
25. *See also* Beumer 2016 (*supra* n. 1).

Figure 22.5 Rule Being Appealed

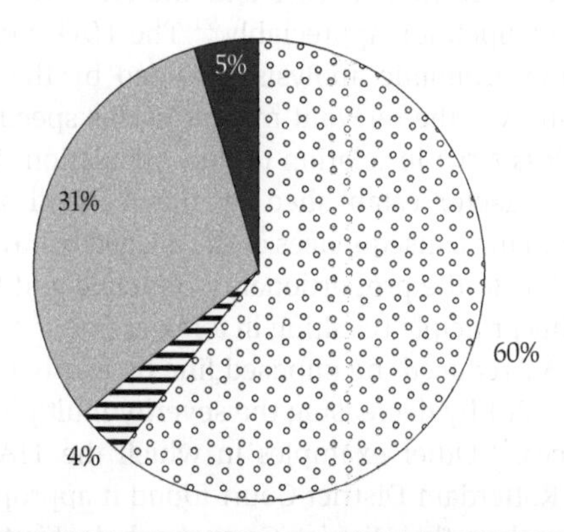

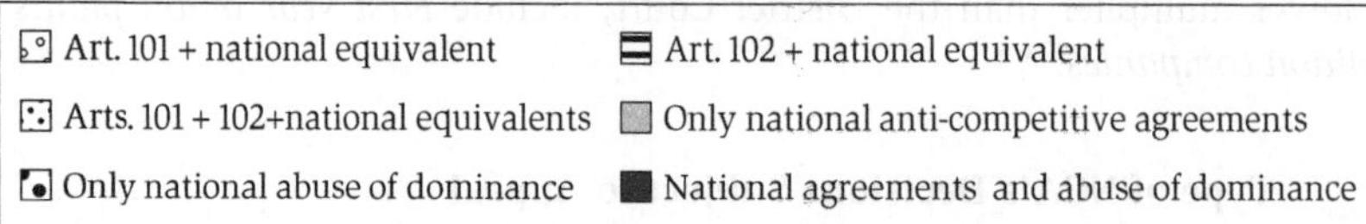

Figure 22.6 Rules Being Appealed According to Years (Each Judgment Counts as One)

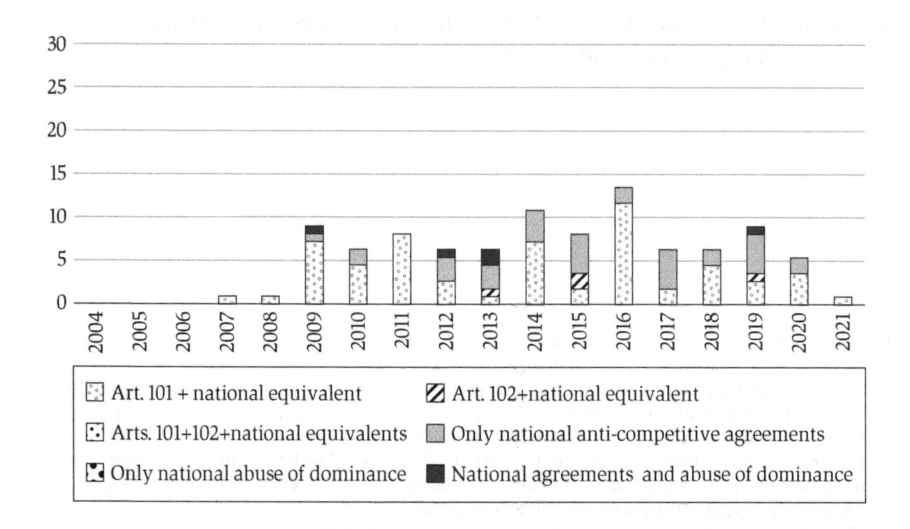

Figure 22.7 Types of Restrictions

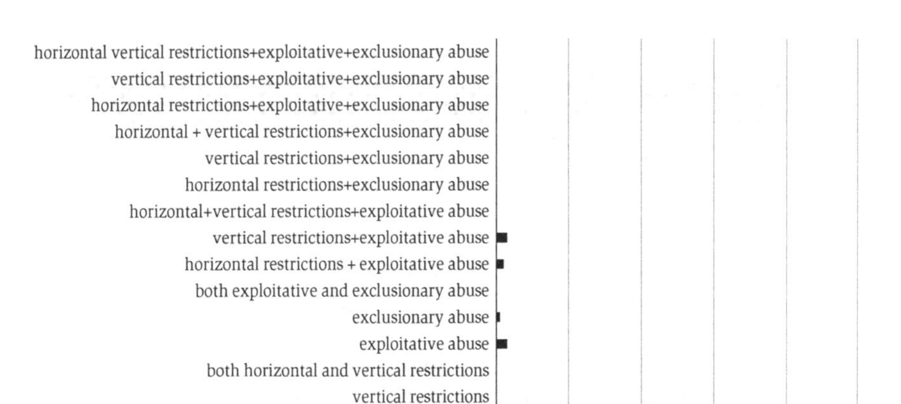

For Article 101 TFEU and the national equivalent, the ACM and its predecessor clearly focused on by-object restrictions (Figure 22.8). Although this figure only reflects the decisions that were appealed the NCA's decisions were always by-object decisions.

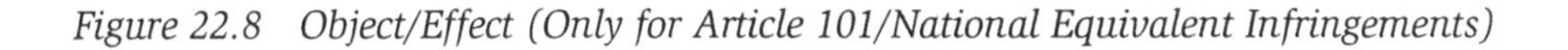

Figure 22.8 Object/Effect (Only for Article 101/National Equivalent Infringements)

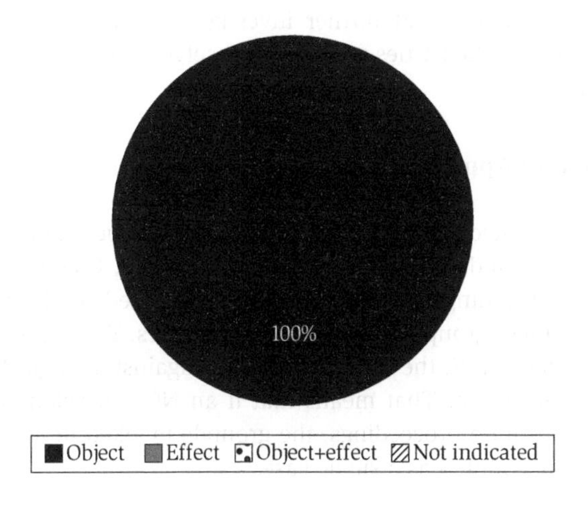

Figure 22.9 Competition Authority's Procedure

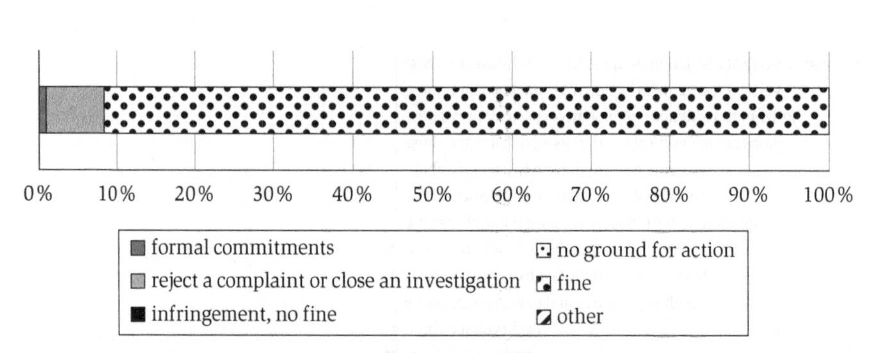

A few judgments concern the rejection of a complaint and the decision to close an investigation without enforcement actions. These ACM decisions are appealed in only a few cases, most often by the complainants themselves, such as competitors or purchasers. None of the cases was successful, which could be the reason why these decisions generally are not often appealed and definitely not further appealed. An example of an unsuccessful case is the District Court ruling of 2019 in which the court found that the ACM's decision to reject a complaint of possible infringement of Article 6 and/or 24 Competition Act based on its priority policy was reasonable.[26] The ACM had found that there were insufficient indications that the new conditions for the transmission of Fox Sports live football had a negative impact on consumers. The ACM therefore deemed further investigation into this subject unnecessary. According to the District Court Rotterdam, the ACM gave sufficient reasons why it was not evident that a breach had occurred and that further investigation into a possible breach was therefore not necessary. The parties resigned themselves to this ruling, thereby ending these proceedings.

4.6 Grounds of Appeal

This research distinguished between four main groups of appeals: procedural, substantive, level of the fine, and EU/national (*see* methodology, Chapter 2). Figure 22.10 reveals the empirical findings on which appeals were filed by the parties and their success rate within these groups across all court instances. This figure summarises the grounds and outcomes of all the appeals launched against a single NCA decision or previous instance judgment. That means that if an NCA decision was appealed by various parties in separate proceedings, the grounds invoked in all those judgments and their success are counted as a single case.

26. District Court Rotterdam 12 September 2019, ECLI:NL:RBROT:2019:7190.

Figure 22.10 Grounds of Appeal (Each NCA's Decision or Previous Instance Judgment Counts as One)

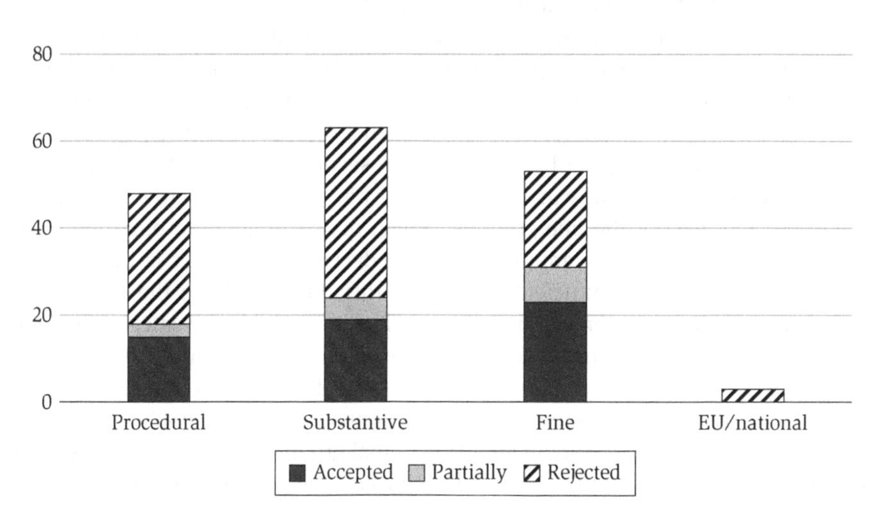

The judgment analysis further shows that the number of appeal grounds differs substantially per case. In some cases, there is one specific ground for appeal: the undertakings, for example, do not deny the infringement and only dispute the level of the fine. In other cases, no fewer than thirty-eight grounds were presented, and the undertakings sought to dispute all aspects of the decision.

As the figure shows, substantive arguments are most frequently brought forward in cases as grounds of appeal and EU/national only in a few cases. For some cases, there is an incomplete overview of the types of grounds of appeals raised because the courts start by discussing the procedural grounds first and, if this is successful, the substantive grounds and fine calculation grounds are not discussed. It is therefore difficult to assess in these cases if these grounds of appeal were raised. In some judgments, all grounds of appeal are mentioned before they are discussed one by one until one is successful, but that is not always the case.

In contrast to the District Court judgments which only concern the appeal grounds raised by the undertakings, the judgment of the second-instance court also relates to grounds of appeal brought forward by the ACM (there is hardly any third party participation in the appeals in the Netherlands, this applies equally to procedures at the Rotterdam District Court). In the years until 2013, the ACM most often filed an appeal in cases in which the Rotterdam District Court had lowered the fine. In other words, the ACM accepted the annulment and did not file for further appeal if the Rotterdam District Court found that there was insufficient evidence or economic analysis to impose a fine. This changed in later years when more appeals to the TIAT were lodged by the ACM in cases in which the District Court had found that there was insufficient evidence or insufficient economic analysis by the ACM.[27] In both situations, the ACM sought to have the judgment overturned by the TIAT and the grounds of appeal raised by the ACM focused on achieving this goal.

Figure 22.10 further shows that the successful procedural appeal grounds more often lead to a fully accepted appeal than with either substantive or fines-related grounds of appeal. This is understandable since a procedural mistake will often apply to the entire cartel, for example, if certain evidence was not allowed (e.g., leniency statements[28] or wiretaps given by the Public Prosecutors office to the ACM[29]), as a result of which no sanction can be imposed. This is not necessarily the case for substantive and level of the fine grounds, which may also apply to only one of the cartelists or lead to a partial annulment of the decision. The latter is the case, for example, if it concerns insufficient reasoning, this does not have the far-reaching consequence that no sanction can be imposed. The level of the fine category includes cases in which one of the fines is lowered because the wrong turnover of one of the cartelists was used. The substantive grounds rejected include all appeals against a rejected complaint which, as mentioned, were all unsuccessful.[30] Finally, it is notable that there are very few cases involving EU/national grounds, which may also explain the fact that no cases within the scope of the project were referred to the CJEU for a preliminary ruling.

Figures 22.8-22.10 demonstrates that most judgments include by-object cartel fines. These are regularly annulled by the courts. In recent years, the main grounds for annulments are insufficient evidence, insufficient economic analysis, and a fine reduction. The fine reductions by the courts can be extensive. The total percentage of cases in which the fine was reduced is 46% and the average fine reduction is 60%. For example, in the Limburg construction cases, the fine was reduced from EUR 3 million to EUR 463,000.[31]

4.7 Leniency and Settlements

As Figure 22.13 shows, half of the ACM decisions and previous instance judgments under appeal started with a leniency application.[32] If the ACM decision includes a statement by one of the cartelists confessing that the infringement occurred and who were involved, it may be assumed that this would probably have a positive influence on any subsequent review by an appeal court as to whether there was sufficient evidence. However, in some cases, it turned out otherwise and the leniency application itself was brought up for discussion by the parties. In *Clabbers*, for example, the District Court ruled that the two leniency statements on which the fine was based were

27. *See also* Outhuijse 2019a (*supra* n. 12).
28. Rotterdam District Court 3 April 2014, ECLI:NL:RBROT:2014:2273 (*Isolating double glass*).
29. Rotterdam District Court 13 June 2013, ECLI:NL:RBROT:2013:CA3079 (*Limburg construction* case).
30. Rotterdam District Court 12 September 2019, ECLI:NL:RBROT:2019:7190.
31. CBb 8 May 2018, ECLI:NL:CBB:2018:141 (*Limburg construction* cases).
32. Figures 22.11 and 22.12 were not included since they did not show trends which were worthy of discussion.

insufficient to prove Clabbers' involvement.[33] The District Court considered it unlikely that further investigation ten years after the facts would produce reliable information that could prove the infringement, and therefore replaced the fining decision with its own judgment ruling that no fine could be imposed by the ACM because of insufficient evidence. The ACM appealed that judgment and argued that the District Court had wrongly found that there was insufficient evidence to prove the undertaking's participation. The TIAT, however, confirmed the Court's judgment, ruling that evidence of the alleged offence was insufficient and that the ACM therefore was not entitled to find an infringement and impose a fine.[34]

Sometimes, though infrequently, the leniency applicant appeals. This was the case in *Vialis*, for example. The ACM granted a leniency discount of 80% rather than 100%, based on the argument that the leniency applicant organised an information meeting for the other cartel participants. The District Court ruled that the ACM had insufficiently substantiated why it reduced the leniency discount, as the ACM did not reduce leniency discounts of leniency applicants organizing similar meetings in other sectors.[35] According to the District Court, the ACM was unable to explain why meetings in other sectors should not also: (1) constitute a genuine risk that evidence would be destroyed; and (2) offer a forum to decide whether to lodge a leniency request in a concerted way. In the new decision, adopted after the judgment, the ACM granted a 100% reduction.

Figure 22.11 suggests that the involvement of a leniency application or the leniency applicant as one of the appealing parties has in general no significant influence on the general outcome of the case.[36]

33. Rotterdam District Court 1 October 2009, ECLI:NL:RBROT:2009:BJ9175 (*Clabbers*).
34. CBb 14 June 2012, ECLI:NL:CBB:2012:BW1393 (*Clabbers*).
35. Rotterdam District Court 5 March 2010, ECLI:NL:RBROT:2010:BL6819 (*Vialis*)
36. This confirms the outcome of previous research. *See*: Kai Hüschelrath and Florian Smuda, The Appeals Process in the European Commission's Cartel Cases: An Empirical Assessment (2016) 13 Journal of Empirical Legal Studies 330 DOI: 10.1111/jels.12117. Hüschelrath and Smuda analysed cartels fined imposed by the European Commission between 2000 and 2012 and reviewed whether specific characteristics of the parties, among other things whether leniency applicant was involved, were determinants for successful cases. They found that increased numbers of leniency applicants had no significant effect on the probability of a successful appeal. If the appeal is successful, the number of leniency applicants had a positive effect on the level of fine reduction granted. The authors suggest that if an error occurs, it is of a more severe nature, thereby justifying larger fine reductions. However, this does not imply that the leniency application does not influence the outcome in a specific case. It is possible that without the application, there was insufficient evidence, or on the other hand there would be no discussion and would lead to confirmation of the ACM decision.

Figure 22.11 Leniency

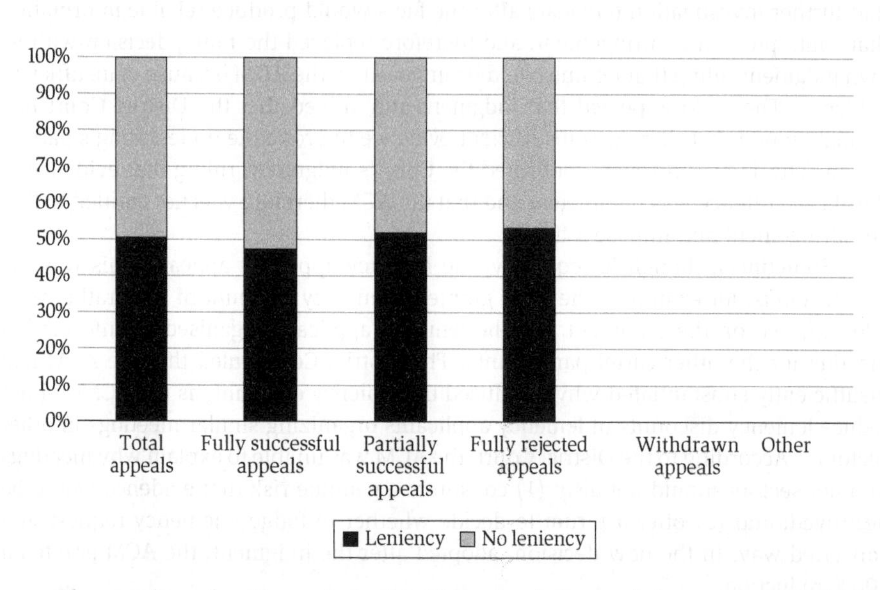

The number of settlements in the Netherlands is much lower compared with other Member States (30%).[37] These numbers include the construction fraud cases, which concern a type of settlement that will be explained. This case was a national price-fixing system involving 1,300 undertakings.[38] To simplify and accelerate the infringement process in relation to these undertakings, the ACM offered them an accelerated fine procedure. In exchange for a fine discount of 15%, the undertakings had to renounce their right to individual access to the file, the right to be heard individually and the right to object and appeal the facts and their qualifications. This procedure bears some similarity to a settlement but, unlike in the case of a settlement, the undertaking did not have to acknowledge its infringement of the cartel prohibition.[39]

The ACM has made more use of actual settlements since 2015.[40] In 2015, the ACM settled a case for the first time and another settlement followed on 23 March 2016. Since then, this instrument has been used more frequently. The examples at the EU level and in other Member States suggest that the use of settlements in the Netherlands might also lead to a decrease in court rulings.[41] The decrease in court rulings can

37. Outhuijse 2019a (*supra* n. 12).
38. G. Knoop-Rutten and J. Strijker-Reintjes, 'Schoon schip in de bouw: NMa blikt terug,' Tijdschrift Sanctierecht en Compliance, No. 3 (2012), 131-139.
39. Recognition of the infringement is one of the requirements for the settlement procedure in most Member States. This is a requirement in the United Kingdom and Germany, for example, but not in France. *See* A. Outhuijse, *Schikken met ACM: gewenste koers of rechtsomkeerd*, SEW, No. 12 (2016), 510-522.
40. Ibid.
41. The study of Hellwig et al. of 2016 showed a decrease in litigation in recent years and the relationship of this phenomenon with an increase in settlements. The Commission has settled in

probably be explained by the fact that the undertaking recognises the infringement and its involvement and accepts the amount of the fine in the settlement procedure.[42] Cooperation with the ACM significantly limits the grounds for an undertaking to file an appeal, and an appeal becomes less likely following an undertaking's past cooperation, especially if the undertaking does not want to dispute the settlement terms.

Figure 22.12 illustrates the number of settlements in relation to the outcome of the cases. The numbers suggest that the involvement of a settlement application has in general no significant influence on the general outcome of the case.

Figure 22.12 Settlements

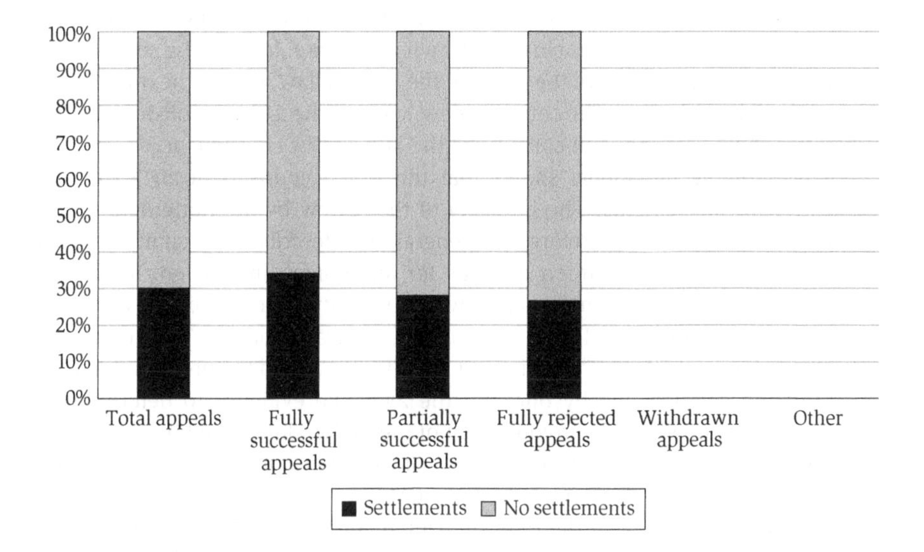

5 QUALITATIVE ANALYSIS

This section builds on the previously described quantitative analysis to highlight key dicta to assess the level of intensity of judicial review undertaken by both courts, their diverging views on competition law and the consequences involved for the effectiveness of judicial review and the extent to which they demonstrate a degree of judicial deference. In the final section of this report, I will discuss recent developments in Dutch competition law enforcement that influence judicial review by the courts.

almost 70% of cases since 2010 and, according to researchers, the use of settlements lowers the incidence of litigation up to 55%. M. Hellwig, K. Hüschelrath & U. Laitenberger, Settlements and Appeals in the European Commission's Cartel Cases: An Empirical Assessment, (2018) 52 Review of Industrial Organization 55-84 DOI: 10.1007/s11151-017-9572-1.

42. Outhuijse 2019a (*supra* n. 12).

5.1 Intensive Review

As the TIAT found in several cases, such as the *Flour* and *Foreclosure Auctions* rulings, the task for the courts when reviewing a decision to impose a fine for a violation of Article 6 of the Dutch Competition Act and/or Article 101 TFEU is to assess whether the ACM fulfilled its obligation to establish an infringement.[43] According to the TIAT's established case law, it is not only necessary to assess whether a decision was arrived at deliberately and based on sound justification but also whether the ACM correctly interpreted the legal concepts and made a plausible argument that the facts and circumstances meet the required legal conditions. In particular, the court should not only check the material accuracy of the evidence, its reliability and consistency but also whether those elements correspond to the relevant factual framework for assessment and whether they support the conclusions drawn from them. In sum, the courts do not rely on the ACM's explanation of the law and the EU case law, nor on the qualification of the facts in light of the law. The courts review whether the ACM established the facts and qualified them correctly and considered the law and its consequences.

Analysis of the judgments shows that the Dutch courts perform a thorough assessment of these elements. The intensity of the review by the Rotterdam District Court and the TIAT can therefore, in general, be described as comprehensive, particularly regarding the common grounds for annulment: insufficient factual evidence, insufficient economic analysis and wrong severity factor (which is one of the elements for fine calculation). The *Lymbouw* case illustrates that the TIAT carries out a thorough review of the facts.[44] In this case, the TIAT analysed the projects that could entail infringing conduct one by one and the available evidence to determine the number of projects in which the involvement of the undertaking could be proven. The *Taxi* case, referred to above, is an example of an intensive review of the market analysis and economic analysis made by the ACM.[45]

Regarding the amount of the fine, the Dutch courts state that they apply a full review based on national, EU and ECHR case law. As asserted in their respective judgments, the courts must consider whether the ACM applied the policy guidelines correctly, whether the maximum fine has not been exceeded, whether the relevant facts and circumstances have been considered and whether the fine is proportionate to the violation. These conditions in any event include the nature and seriousness of the violation, the extent to which it can be attributed to the individual undertaking, and the circumstances under which it was committed. Based on Dutch law, the court must reduce the fines if it finds that this standard has not been met.

The *Wmo Friesland* case is a good illustration of the abovementioned analysis.[46] The case illustrates that the TIAT reviews the functioning of the market intensively for the establishment of both the infringement and the severity factor to determine the

43. CBb 14 July 2016, ECLI:NL:CBB:2016:185 (*Flour*); CBb 3 July 2017, ECLI:NL:CBB:2017:204 (*Foreclosure Auctions*).
44. CBb 12 July 2012, ECLI:NL:CBB:2012:BX6386 (*Lymbouw*).
45. Rotterdam District Court 13 October 2016, ECLI:NL:RBROT:2016:7659-7664; TIAT 23 April 2019, ECLI:NL:CBB:2019:150-151 (*Taxi drivers*).
46. CBb 11 January 2017, ECLI:NL:CBB:2017:1 (*Wmo Friesland*).

amount of the fine. Based on a comprehensive analysis of the structure of the tenders (for example, the role of price in the tender) and competitive relationships (the fact that the appellant had by far the largest market share of current healthcare providers, that the competitive pressure from small providers was limited and, therefore, only a handful of relatively large suppliers were competitors), the TIAT found that the concerted practice affected competition to such an extent that it could be deemed to have an anti-competitive object. In assessing the level of the fine, the TIAT considered, among other things, the limited consequences of the behaviour for patients on the market, the restricted intensity of collaboration and the fact that the companies were deemed to make a change in an unrealistically short term from a government-funded foundation under the collective health insurance scheme to a commercial enterprise. Based on these circumstances, the TIAT reduced the fine by nearly EUR 1 million, from EUR 1,757,000 million to EUR 767,000 million, by decreasing the severity factor from 1.5 to 0.5.

The analysis of Dutch practice confirms the literature's account of older cases: both courts continue to engage in an intensive review of the fines in recent cases, in particular about evidence, economic analysis and the severity factor.[47]

5.2 Consequences for Effectiveness and Judicial Deference

The judgments also provide insight into the effectiveness of the judicial review and the absence of judicial deference.

The courts consider themselves sufficiently expert to correct the ACM on substantial points and do not apply deference. The judgments also show that the views of the various actors (TIAT; District Court Rotterdam and ACM) on certain competition concepts diverge. There are clearly different views between the courts and the ACM about certain elements of the fining decisions. This is especially evident on points of economic analysis and the severity factor. The courts demand a lot from the ACM regarding its market analysis; they do not require that the effects of certain behaviour be proven, but they do demand a sufficient analysis of the relevant market and its functioning and the position of the undertakings on the market if not all the undertakings operating in the market participated in the alleged behaviour. The courts emphasise the importance that behaviour is capable of amounting to a restriction of competition, which requires analysis of the functioning of the market and the position of the undertakings in this market. The ACM followed a more formalistic approach. This difference in approach offers some explanation for the number of decisions successfully challenged.

There is also a clear difference of perspectives between the ACM and the courts on the severity factor, and also between the two reviewing courts. While the Rotterdam District Court confirmed the ACM's severity factor in several cases, the TIAT has attached more weight to the consequences of the alleged behaviour for establishing the severity factor as well as on the proportionality principle and the fact that lower fines

47. Essens et al. 2009 (*supra* n. 13).

more often fall in line with this principle. The same cannot be said of the ACM, which has emphasised the importance of higher fines to achieve deterrence. This instrumental approach to fines is not surprising for an NCA. This difference in approach also offers some explanation for the number of decisions successfully challenged.

In sum, unlike the practice in other Member States, courts do not provide the ACM with a margin of appreciation in this regard - also not regarding economic analysis. What is described in older literature still counts in recent cases, namely that the courts in practice substitute their findings for those of the ACM and do not limit themselves to the question of whether the ACM could reasonably have reached a particular conclusion that positively affects effective judicial review and explains the absence of judicial deference.[48]

In the period researched, no preliminary references to the CJEU were made. Apparently, the Dutch courts did not consider the guidance of the EU courts to be necessary. However, the courts routinely refer to EU case law in their judgments to explain certain concepts, *inter alia*, to ensure the uniform application of the EU competition rules.

6 CONCLUDING REMARKS

The judicial review of public enforcement of competition law in the Netherlands has been addressed in this chapter. In short, the Dutch courts are competent to review all the elements of ACM decisions and review those elements intensively in the case of fines, including situations where the law provides a margin of appreciation to the ACM. The courts, for example, do not rely on the competition authority's assessment regarding the establishment of the facts, the qualification of the facts, the economic analysis or the interpretation of the law and case law. The intensity of review undertaken by the Rotterdam District Court and the TIAT can therefore, in general, be described as comprehensive. However, the standard for judicial review for sanctions and remedies which are not fines - such as commitments - is much more limited. The same applies to the review of any ACM decision not to investigate a case or to issue infringement decisions. The courts then limit themselves to the question of whether the ACM could reasonably have reached a particular conclusion. The intensive review partly explains the high number of appeals and further appeals, the number of ACM decisions annulled by the District Court and the number of District Court judgments annulled by the TIAT in the case of cartel fines. The main points of disagreement between the ACM, the District Court and the TIAT often relate to the evidence, both factual and economic, and the proportionality of the fine.

Several recent developments in Dutch competition law enforcement will influence future judicial review of ACM competition law decisions. First, as noted in the introduction, the ACM has been granted the possibility of imposing higher fines. As the amount of the fine is regularly a ground of appeal and the reason for partially annulling the decision, this is likely to influence judicial review and its outcome in practice.

48. *Ibid.*

Second, the ACM is increasingly resorting to settlements in its enforcement practice. Settlements have been used more frequently since 2015, but exact numbers are unknown since not all settlements are published. The increased use of settlements influences the number of court rulings and therefore the system of judicial review. The experience at the EU level and in other Member States suggests that the use of settlements in the Netherlands might also lead to a decrease in court rulings.[49] The decrease in court rulings can probably be explained by the fact that the undertaking accepts the infringement and its involvement and accepts the amount of the fine in the settlement procedure. Moreover, it is beneficial for companies if the infringement does not become publicly known, thereby limiting reputational damage and the likelihood of follow-on private damages claims. The increased use of settlements not only influences judicial review but is probably also the consequence of the strict judicial review as described in section 5.

Another development in the last years is the new enforcement strategy of the ACM. Since the ACM has a new chair, the ACM has adopted a strategy of imposing fines less frequently and making more use of other types of administrative remedies. These include so-called remedial sanctions, which are also subject to less intensive review by the competent courts. With remedial sanctions, the undertaking must adjust its behaviour. If it does not do so within a certain period, a 'fine' is imposed for each period (per week or per month) in which the infringement is not solved.[50] The ACM has announced its intention to use this instrument more often in future situations.

Finally, an interesting development in terms of judicial review was the legislative proposal to merge the two highest Dutch courts in administrative law (the TIAT and the Council of State).[51] The consequence of merging the highly specialised TIAT with the Council of State, which focuses on general administrative law, would be that the specialised judges of the TIAT would have been replaced by non-specialised judges. One criticism regarding this bill was that it would decrease the quality of judicial review, as judicial expertise is required when reviewing these cases. The bill was submitted to the Dutch House of Representatives but was withdrawn. Certainly, this would not have been good for the effectiveness of judicial review in the Dutch competition law enforcement.

49. Hellwig et al. (*supra* n. 41).
50. To give an example, Apple received a remedial sanction for an Article 102 TFEU infringement with a penalty of EUR 5 million for each week in which the infringement was not solved, subject to a maximum of EUR 50 million. Apple must change the conditions of access for dating app providers to the Dutch App Store. Dating app providers must be able to use other payment systems besides Apple's payment system in the App Store. In addition, dating app providers must be given the opportunity to refer in their app to payment options outside the app.
51. Outhuijse, A. (2017). Effective Public Enforcement of the Cartel Prohibition in the Netherlands: A Comparison of ACM Fining Decisions, District Court Judgments, and TIAT Judgments. In A. Looijestijn-Clearie, C.S. Rusu, & M. Veenbrink (eds), Boosting the Enforcement of EU Competition Law at the Domestic Level, Cambridge: Cambridge Scholars, pp. 26-52.

CHAPTER 23
Poland Report

Maciej Bernatt & Maciej Janik

1 INTRODUCTION TO THE COMPETITION LAW ENFORCEMENT CONTEXT IN POLAND

The establishment of modern competition law in Poland was part of the wider transformation from a centrally planned economic system to a market economy. The first competition statute dates back to 1987 when the (still-ruling) socialist party opted for a reform of the inefficient economic regime by adopting an act aimed at imposing limits on the use of economic power by state enterprises.[1] The enforcement under the 1987 Act was not impressive, with just nine decisions adopted,[2] but the experience gathered and lessons learned therefrom proved very useful once a new antimonopoly law was subsequently adopted in 1990,[3] (i.e., a few months after the collapse of communism in Poland).[4]

In its early days, the principal objective of the newly established Antimonopoly Office was to demonopolise the Polish economy rather than just eliminate anticompetitive practices.[5] However, as the economy gradually matured into a market economy, more and more decisions began targeting anticompetitive practices, in particular the unilateral practices of dominant state enterprises or the state-owned or privatised enterprises that succeeded them.[6] Interestingly, the 1990 Competition Act

1. Act of 28 January 1987 on Counteracting Monopolistic Practices in the National Economy (the 1987 Act).
2. Mateusz Błachucki, *Polish Competition Law: Commentary, Case Law and Texts* (UOKIK 2013) 13.
3. Act of 24 February 1990 on Counteracting Monopolistic Practices (the 1990 Competition Act).
4. Marek Martyniszyn and Maciej Bernatt, 'Implementing a Competition Law System—Three Decades of Polish Experience' (2020) 8 Journal of Antitrust Enforcement 165, 171.
5. Under the 1990 Competition Act, the Antimonopoly Office was entitled to dissolve undertakings. For the enforcement in the early 1990s in Poland *see* Tadeusz Skoczny, *Polish Antimonopoly Case Law* (ELIPSA 1995).
6. For an overview, *see* Martyniszyn and Bernatt (*supra* n. 4), 193-196.

contained original legal solutions not corresponding to the EU competition law template.[7] The 1990 Competition Act was subject to several amendments. They harmonised Polish competition law with the EU regime. This process of change culminated with the adoption of a new competition and consumer protection act in 2000.[8] Its substantive provisions, prohibiting anticompetitive agreements and abuses of dominant position, were modelled on Articles 81-82 TEC.

The Polish competition law regime was again amended in 2007 with the introduction of the currently applicable version of the Competition and Consumer Protection Act.[9] The 2007 Competition Act did not change the substance of competition law in Poland. The key change was procedural in nature. Formerly, antitrust proceedings could have been initiated by the Polish NCA (*Urząd Ochrony Konkurencji i Konsumentów,* UOKIK) not only *ex officio* but also by means of a complaint. In the latter case, a complainant enjoyed the status of a party to the proceedings. In 2007 that model was abandoned. Complaints became non-binding denunciations that the UOKIK could easily disregard. Moreover, complainants lost their status as parties to the proceedings. Access to the proceedings by third parties was also effectively eliminated. This was, *inter alia,* meant to change the impression that the antitrust procedure is of an adversarial nature, in which the UOKIK is expected to resolve a dispute between the complainant and the undertaking that harmed its interest through allegedly anticompetitive behaviour. Hence, the procedural change was to emphasise that the UOKIK acts solely in order to protect the public interest, and not the private interests of any market actor.[10]

Enforcement in the years 2000-2014 could generally be referred to as intense, particularly as regards abuses of dominance on national and local markets.[11] In the latter case, enforcement was in the hands (and still is until this day) of local offices of the UOKIK and in many cases of abuse of dominance the NCA imposed heavy fines. State-owned undertakings (hereinafter 'SOEs') were often fined. By contrast, the UOKIK did not manage to establish a good enforcement record against nation-wide hard-core cartels, focusing instead on vertical restraints, often simple RPMs.[12] After the Polish accession to the EU in 2004, the UOKIK used its power to adopt decisions under Articles 101-102 TFEU only in rare cases: most of the decisions, even those concerning the national market as a whole, were issued under national competition law provisions only.[13]

---

7. For example, the 1990 Competition Act allowed for an exemption of anticompetitive practices under the rule of reason, distinguished between a dominant and a monopolistic (i.e., super-dominant) position, which was reflected in listing separately abuse of dominance practices and monopolistic practices.
8. Act of 15 December 2000 on Competition and Consumer Protection (the 2000 Competition Act).
9. Act of 16 February 2007 on Competition and Consumer Protection (the 2007 Competition Act).
10. Marek Szydło, 'Nowa ustawa o ochronie konkurencji i konsumentów', (2007) 12 Monitor Prawniczy 645, 645-653.
11. Martyniszyn and Bernatt (*supra* n. 4) 193-195.
12. *Ibid.*, 196-199. *See also* Rajmund Molski, 'Polish Antitrust Law in Its Fight against Cartels, Awaiting a Breakthrough' (2009) 2 Yearbook of Antitrust and Regulatory Studies 49, 50.
13. *See* Marco Botta, Alexandr Svetlicinii and Maciej Bernatt, 'The Assessment of the Effect on Trade by the National Competition Authorities of the "New" Member States: Another Legal Partition of the Internal Market?' (2015) 52 CML Rev 1247.

The intensity of enforcement started to diminish in the 2010s and reached its all-time low in 2016-2019[14] after the political change that brought an illiberal party to power and resulted in significant personnel changes in the NCA.[15] In recent years UOKIK enforcement is obscured by controversies related to its de facto independence, in particular in merger cases, and broader concerns related to the rule of law decline in Poland.[16] The legal changes between 2015-2023 undermining the independence of the judiciary, including the judicial review of NCA decisions, are also relevant in this context.[17] Furthermore, the growing role of the state in the economy and the increasing market power of state-controlled enterprises such as PKN Orlen, Poland's largest oil company, has forced the NCA to navigate the complexities of the political and economic environment which is not in line with its mission of protecting merit-based competition.[18]

As far as the institutional organisation of enforcement in Poland is concerned, the powers are vested in the UOKIK (more specifically, the UOKIK President) as a central, administrative authority. In fulfilling their tasks, the UOKIK President is assisted by the central office in Warsaw and regional offices in major Polish cities. Still, in law, each decision is adopted individually by the UOKIK President.

The UOKIK is a multi-task authority. Since its establishment, the UOKIK's mandate has significantly expanded and today the protection of competition can hardly be seen as the authority's primary mission.[19] Its mandate covers also practices that infringe collective consumer interests, unfair contractual terms in standard contracts, surveillance over general product safety, trade inspection, and abuse of bargaining power in the agriculture market. It is also tasked with combatting payment gridlocks in the Polish economy. Arguably, the resources at the NCA's disposal for the protection of competition are not sufficient.[20]

14. In 2004, the number of infringement decisions adopted was seventy-one, in 2010: sixty-nine, in 2014: thirty-eight, in 2019: eleven, in 2021: ten and in 2022: eight. The number of infringement decisions issued by the UOKIK central office, which normally concern the practices covering the national geographic market, varied in recent years. Notably, in 2018 the central office did not adopt any decision. In 2019 it adopted two infringement decisions, in 2021 four infringement decisions (and two commitment decisions) and in 2022 two infringement decisions. Please note that the UOKIK in 2021 and 2022 conducted several dawn raids (seven in 2021 and nine in 2022) what may suggest that new decisions will be adopted in coming years. *Source*: the UOKIK annual reports.
15. *See* Maciej Bernatt, *Populism and Antitrust: The Illiberal Influence of Populist Government on the Competition Law* (Cambridge University Press 2022).
16. *See* Maciej Bernatt, 'The Double Helix of Rule of Law and EU Competition Law: An Appraisal' (2021) 27 European Law Journal 148, DOI: 10.1111/eulj.12422.
17. *See* Maciej Bernatt, 'Rule of Law Crisis, Judiciary and Competition Law' (2019) 46 Legal Issues of Economic Integration 345.
18. Bernatt (*supra* n. 15) 39-52.
19. Maciej Bernatt, 'Mandate of Competition Agency in Populist Times' in Nicolas Charbit and Sébastien Gachot (eds), *Eleanor M. Fox Liber Amicorum, Antitrust Ambassador to the World* (Concurrences 2021) 391-402.
20. Martyniszyn and Bernatt (*supra* n. 4), 178-185.

Recently, legal safeguards protecting the UOKIK's independence have been added as a result of the implementation of the ECN+ Directive[21] which entered into force on 20 May 2023. Currently, the UOKIK President is appointed by the Prime Minister for a five-year term in office, and can only be dismissed under defined circumstances.

The UOKIK is entitled to adopt infringement decisions and impose fines. It can also adopt commitment decisions or enter into settlements (in cartel cases). Moreover, it has the power to impose fines on individuals as far as various types of anticompetitive agreements are concerned (not just hard-core cartels).[22] Controversies continue to exist whether these broad powers are counterbalanced by sufficient due process safeguards.[23] Moreover, access to proceedings by third parties is very limited both by law and as a result of the NCA's practice, which deprives entities other than addressees of the original NCA decision from the possibility of challenging UOKIK decisions before the court.

2 REVIEW OF THE POLISH COMPETITION AUTHORITY'S DECISIONS

The judicial review of decisions issued by the Polish NCA takes place within what is usually referred to as a 'hybrid' procedural system. While the initial stage of a case is decided by a national administrative authority subject to the rules set out in the 2007 Competition Act and to the Polish code of administrative procedure, an appeal on any decision is exercised by a civil court[24] in *de novo*, contradictory judicial proceedings subject to the rules of civil procedure.[25] In other words, the completion of administrative proceedings conditions the possibility of litigation before a civil court.[26] Such a

---

21. Directive 2019/1 of the European Parliament and of the Council of 11 December 2018 to empower the competition authorities of the Member States to be more effective enforcers and to ensure the proper functioning of the internal market, OJ L 11/3.
22. Please note, though, that the Polish legal system does not provide for criminal liability of individuals for participating in a cartel.
23. It has been argued that the level of protection of defence rights in Poland is lower than in the case of the proceedings before the Commission, *see* Maciej Bernatt, Marco Botta and Alexandr Svetlicinii, 'The Right of Defense in the Decentralized System of EU Competition Law Enforcement: A Call for Harmonization from Central and Eastern Europe' (2018) 41 World Competition 309. For the description of some improvements introduced in 2015, *see* Maciej Bernatt, 'Catching-Up with EU Due Process Standards. A Case of Poland's Soft Law Guidelines' (2016) 3 European Competition Law Review 247.
24. This was also the case under the 2000 Competition Act and even the 1990 Competition Act. Before 2001, decisions issued by NCA were also appealed to a specialised general court, the Voivodeship Court of Warsaw – the Antimonopoly Court. The proceedings before the Court followed the rules of civil procedure code in commercial matters. Binding judgments of the Antimonopoly Court were subject to the review of the SCP in the course of 'extraordinary revision' (*rewizja nadzwyczajna*). *See* Mateusz Błachucki, *Polish Competition Law – Commentary, Case Law and Texts* (UOKIK 2013) 16.
25. Act of 17 November 1964 – Code of Civil Procedure (the Polish Code of Civil Procedure).
26. Dariusz Aziewicz, 'Due Process Rights in Polish Antitrust Proceedings. Case Comment to the Judgment of the Polish Supreme Court of 3 October 2013 – PKP Cargo S.A. v. President of the Office of Competition and Consumers Protection (Ref. No. III SK 67/12)' (2015) 8 Yearbook of Antitrust and Regulatory Studies 261, 263.

review model is significantly different from the cassatory, administrative model operating in EU competition law and different from the standard course of judicial redress for administrative action in Poland.[27] The latter is carried out by administrative courts in a cassatory procedure. As the law stands, the review in competition cases is full in all respects (facts and law, including fines). Therefore, the civil courts examining the appeal to the NCA's decision are not limited to the review of legality only as they have also considerable evidentiary powers and can make their own findings in relation to facts.[28]

It is worth pointing out that due to the changes introduced with the entry into force of the 2007 Competition Act, which gave proceedings before the NCA a uniquely inquisitorial character, only the addressees of the NCA decision can currently submit appeals to the CCCP. At later stages, the NCA can also file appeals against first-instance judgments siding with the original plaintiff's point of view. This will be discussed in further detail in sections 4.6 and 4.9 below.

2.1 Court of Competition and Consumer Protection (CCCP)

The court of first instance is the specialised Court of Competition and Consumer Protection (the XVII division of the District Court in Warsaw, the 'CCCP'). The CCCP may either dismiss the action brought against an NCA's decision and uphold the contested decision, or accept the action and decide on the merits by annulling or changing the NCA's decision (fully or in part). The first-instance court also states whether the decision under review was issued without legal basis or in gross violation of the law. However, the Polish lawmaker did not entrust the CCCP with universal jurisdiction over the entire activity of the NCA. While all the appeals against UOKIK's decisions will be heard by the CCCP,[29] there remain a number of matters that administrative courts will be competent to handle.[30] Despite the steady expansion of the CCCP's role in antimonopoly cases, there is a certain duality that may generate jurisdictional confusion, which in some situations may deprive a party of judicial

27. In the chapter we apply the distinction between reformatory and cassatory models of judicial review. While the former means full power for the judge, including the ability to change the appealed judgment or administrative act, the latter extends only to the annulment of the unlawful decision, when the case typically cannot be settled or closed by the court. *See, e.g.*, Zoltán Szente and Konrad Lachmayer, *The Principle of Effective Legal Protection in Administrative Law* (Routledge 2017).
28. Maciej Bernatt, 'Effectiveness of Judicial Review in the Polish Competition Law System and the Place for Judicial Deference' (2016) 9 Yearbook of Antitrust and Regulatory Studies 97.
29. In accordance with Article 81 sections 1 and 5 of the 2007 Competition Act.
30. For example, some forms of discontinuance of antimonopoly proceedings and – though this remains subject to debate – actions against the NCA for failure to act, e.g., due to the excessive prolonging of the explanatory proceedings and antimonopoly proceedings in anticompetitive practices cases. This stems from the fact that the 2007 Competition Act makes a general reference to the Code of Administrative Procedure in all matters not regulated in the act itself. None of those matters were coded for the purpose of the quantitative analysis presented in section 4 below.

protection, especially given the current legal framework in which administrative courts are not very eager to hear anti-monopoly cases.[31]

2.2 Court of Appeal (CoA)

Appeals against a CCCP judgment are heard by the Court of Appeal in Warsaw (the 'CoA'; currently, appeals in antitrust matters are examined by the VII Commercial and Intellectual Property Division of the CoA[32]). The appellate court can take a wide variety of decisions.[33] Due to the full extent of review in the civil judicial redress procedure, the law gives preference to rulings in which the case is decided on the merits. However, in certain situations, the CoA is obliged to remand the case back to the CCCP, including where there exists the need to conduct first-instance proceedings anew due to their previous invalidity, when a retrial is necessary due to the first-instance court's failure to examine the merits of the case, or when the evidentiary proceedings have to be repeated in their entirety.[34]

2.3 Supreme Court of Poland (SCP)

On the basis of an extraordinary cassation complaint, a case can reach the Supreme Court of Poland (the 'SCP'). Currently, cassations in antitrust matters are examined by the Chamber of Extraordinary Review and Public Affairs of the SCP. There are several rule of law-related controversies in relation to the Chamber. It came into existence as a result of the controversial 2017 law reforming the SCP.[35] It consists of those judges selected by the new National Judiciary Council of Poland (i.e., it is formed in the same way as the infamous Supreme Court's Disciplinary Chamber). The ECtHR held that the judicial panel of the Extraordinary Review Chamber lacks the attributes of a 'tribunal' which is 'lawful' for the purposes of Article 6(1) European Convention on Human Rights (the ECHR).[36]

Access to the SCP for cassation appellants is shaped at two stages, i.e., the admissibility of a complaint[37] and the acceptance thereof for examination.[38] These

31. Mateusz Błachucki gives the example of exercising judicial control over the transmission of appeal and case files to the CCCP. *See* Błachucki (*supra* n. 26) 31
32. By Order of the Minister of Justice of 15 September 2017 (OJ [Dz. Urz. MS] of 2017, item 201), as of 1 October 2017, the VII Commercial and Intellectual Property Division and took over antitrust matters from the VI Civil Division.
33. Article 386 of the Polish Code of Civil Procedure.
34. Article 386, § 2 and § 4 of the Polish Code of Civil Procedure.
35. Act of 8 December 2017 on the Supreme Court.
36. The ECtHR judgment in the case *Dolińska-Ficek and Ozimek v. Poland* App no 49868/19 and 57511/19 (ECtHR, 8 November 2021). The ECJ judgment in the Case C-487/19 *W.Z.* [2021] EU:C:2021:798, para. 152 leads to a similar conclusion which is relevant for Article 19(1) TEU safeguards. For the judicial reforms in Poland which are relevant for competition law cases *see* more Bernatt (*supra* n. 17).
37. Admissibility is based on the fulfilment a number of mostly formal requirements, which include the exhaustion of the course of the previous instances, the sueability of a judgment with a cassation complaint, which is inadmissible in specified types of matters (e.g., concerning lease or tenancy) or below a certain value of dispute in civil matters concerning property rights.

restrictions aim to ensure that the court will only examine cases of significant complexity and gravity so as to prevent an excessive number of cassation complaints from being filed.[39] Since antitrust and market regulatory cases often involve novel or not-yet-settled legal issues, the SCP is quite open to accepting cassation complaints and issuing judgments on the merits. Thus, it often provides interpretive guidance to lower-instance courts on both substantive law issues as well as procedural ones.[40]

Interestingly, the very character of the CCCP's review is not without controversies. Under earlier procedural rules (at that time when, e.g., there was no appeal against the CCCP's judgment to the CoA), it used to be a matter of heated dispute whether the CCCP was a first-instance court or a court merely reviewing the NCA's decisions.[41] Eventually, the Constitutional Court clearly ruled that the CCCP should be viewed as a first-instance court and an appeal from its judgment should be available. The provisions of the Code of Civil Procedure that excluded such a possibility were found to be unconstitutional.[42] Consequently, the Polish Code of Civil Procedure was amended on 2 July 2004.[43] As a result of these changes, the CCCP is empowered today not only to annul UOKIK decisions under its review but also to change the UOKIK decision on substance (full jurisdiction).

Another controversy concerns the scope and depth of the CCCP's judicial review in practice. Following various superficial and formalistic reviews of NCA decisions by the CCCP, the SCP ordered the first-instance court not to refrain from deciding on the merits of reviewed cases.[44] According to the SCP, it is the role of the CCCP, as the court of first instance, to deliver judgments pertaining to both facts and substantive legal questions. Moreover, given the *de novo*, contradictory character of the appeal proceedings before the CCCP, the SCP found in a 2009 judgment (in case III SK 5/09) that the court should not review the legality of the proceedings before the NCA but should judge the case on the merits, ignoring the procedural grounds of appeal related to the errors committed by the authority.[45] This approach reflects the belief that the submission of an appeal starts a new type of procedure in the form of a contradictory process of litigation between the parties (i.e., the undertaking that was party to the administrative

38. Admissible cassation complaints are then subject to the procedure of preliminary cassation acceptance (i.e., an equivalent of leave to appeal) in order to be accepted for consideration by the SCP. A cassation complainant submits an application for the acceptance of the cassation providing legal arguments proving that the complaint meets certain substantive requirements.
39. Zembrzuski, 'Access to the Supreme Court - Polish Approach' (*supra* n. 39) 234.
40. Bernatt (*supra* n. 30) 101.
41. *Ibid.*
42. The judgment of 12 June 2002, P 13/01.
43. The new provision allowing appellants to request the annulment of an UOKIK decision became effective as of 5 February 2005. Therefore, in a later judgment the Constitutional Court had to confirm that that the CCCP should also be entitled to repeal NCA decisions in proceedings taking place in the interim period between the Constitutional Court's judgment in the case P 13/01 and the entry into force of the new rules (*see* the Constitutional Court's judgment of 31 January 2005, SK 27/03).
44. *See* the SCP judgments of: 18 September 2003, I CK 81/02; 13 May 2004, III SK 44/04; 20 September 2005, III SZP 2/05. *See also* the SCP judgment of 17 March 2010, III SK 40/09 and the CoA judgment of 20 December 2006, VI ACa 620/06. For such a conclusion in market regulation cases see the judgment of the Supreme Court of 28 January 2015, III SK 29/14.
45. For example, as stated in the SCP judgment of 19 August 2009, III SK 5/09.

proceedings as the plaintiff and the NCA as the defendant), which is legally distinct from the previous proceedings of an administrative nature.[46] Of course, the CCCP is obliged to base its decision on evidence collected during the administrative phase of the proceedings. However, these should be reviewed and verified during the judicial proceedings.[47] Hence, if the CCCP found that such evidence did not prove the existence of an antitrust infringement, the NCA's decision should be changed. According to the SCP, because the first-instance court should, as a rule, issue a judgment on the merits, it must change the NCA's decision rather than revoke the decision if necessary evidence is lacking.[48] Curiously, in a few judgments, the CoA even went so far as to state that the CCCP is always obliged to decide a case *de novo* and that it is precluded from basing its judgments on the findings of the UOKIK.[49]

However, in a number of recent rulings, starting in 2011, the SCP held that the CCCP must verify a decision of the NCA, rather than adjudicate the case from the beginning.[50] The CCCP was thus held to be responsible for verifying the facts established by the NCA, and their legal assessment as to whether the conditions for identifying an anticompetitive practice have been fulfilled.[51] If the evidence collected during the administrative and judicial proceedings does not confirm that all the conditions for infringement decisions are satisfied, the court should overturn the NCA's decision or revoke it.[52] These recent judgments also confirm that judicial proceedings are conducted within the limits set by the scope of the NCA's original decision.[53] For this reason, the reviewing courts have to assess the practice in light of the charges formulated by the NCA in the original resolution on the opening of the competition proceedings.[54]

Recent jurisprudence also marks a change in the possibility of reviewing the NCA's proceedings from a procedural perspective.[55] Unlike the jurisprudence concerning the judicial review of decisions issued by regulatory authorities, the case law relating to antitrust matters long held that the aim of courts reviewing NCA decisions

---

46. Aziewicz (*supra* n. 28) 263.
47. The SCP judgment of 19 August 2009, III SK 5/09 and of 13 July 2012, III SK 44/11. *See also* the CoA judgments of 9 October 2009, VI ACa 86/09 and of 17 June 2015, VI ACa 1475/14.
48. *See* the SCP judgment of 10 April 2008, III SK 27/07. *See also* the SCP judgment of 5 November 2015, III SK 55/14 and of 5 November 2015, III SK 7/15.
49. The CoA judgment of 31 May 2011, VI ACa 1299/10. *See also* the CoA judgment of 20 March 2012, VI ACa 1038/11.
50. *See* the SCP judgments of: 16 April 2015, III SK 7/14; 6 May 2015, III SK 33/14; 4 March 2014, III SK 35/13; 21 June 2013, III SK 36/12; 18 May 2011, III SK 37/11; and the resolutions of the Supreme Court of: 20 February 2014, III SK 60/13; 14 January 2014, III SK 29/13; 3 October 2013, III SK 9/13; 13 August 2013, III SK 64/12. *See also* the CoA judgments of: 8 March 2012, VI ACa 1150/11; 17 June 2015, VI ACa 1475/14.
51. *See* the SCP judgments of: 12 April 2013, III SK 28/12 and 5 November 2015, III SK 7/15.
52. Interestingly, already very early in the development of the judicial redress system for antitrust matters, the SCP found that the antitrust court could not remand a case back to the NCA for renewed consideration and rectification of possible evidentiary insufficiencies.
53. *See also* the CoA judgment of 17 May 2016, VI ACa 630/15.
54. *See* the SCP judgment of 3 October 2013, III SK 67/12.
55. For example, the SCP judgment of 3 October 2013, III SK 67/12. The case concerned an infringement of the rules of administrative procedure by the NCA, where, during the course of on-going antitrust proceedings it amended its original resolution on the initiation of antimonopoly proceedings by, in fact, extending the resolution's initial scope.

is not to control the correctness of the administrative proceedings before the antitrust authority but to assess the matter anew on the merits. The SCP, however, eventually came to the conclusion that it was necessary to change that approach as there is no reason to ignore *a priori* all procedural claims raised by the appellants. This is justified especially when the NCA imposes a fine on an undertaking, a fact which should additionally increase the need to adhere to the highest procedural standards.[56] The fact that the appellant may and should invoke procedural grounds does not mean, however, that all the identified procedural infringements will result in the necessity to annul the defective decision. For example, the consequences of procedural defects relating to the collection of evidence may be rectified by the appellate courts as they themselves are capable of carrying out evidentiary proceedings.

The current role of the CCCP, to conclude, is to verify UOKIK decisions by providing a full review on the merits. This review concerns both factual and legal questions as well as fines. Still, this judicial review cannot be completely independent from the NCA's original findings.[57] In fact, it is correct for the CCCP to generally base its assessment of a case under review on the evidence gathered by the UOKIK during the administrative stage of the proceedings. This is inevitable given the fact that civil courts lack many powers that are available to the NCA, e.g., they may not inspect the premises of an undertaking or send information requests to undertakings that are not involved in the court proceedings initiated as a result of the appeal. Consequently, as eventually confirmed by the SCP, civil courts may also rule on certain procedural aspects of administrative proceedings as some procedural infringements would be impossible to remedy before civil courts.[58]

3 PRIOR RESEARCH

Judicial review of competition law cases has been subject to significant scholarly attention in Poland. Seven streams of debate can be distinguished.

First, is a historical debate, analysing judicial review in the context of the development in the 1990s. At the time when public access to courts' judgments was limited, publications by Gronowski, a judge of the Polish Antimonopoly Court (renamed later due to the expansion of its mandate on consumer cases as the CCCP) and a major figure in Polish antitrust, aimed at summarising the growing case law.[59] More recent publications look at the development of the Polish competition law system over the years.[60]

56. *See also* Aziewicz (*supra* n. 28) 265.
57. Bernatt (*supra* n. 30), 97, 103.
58. *See also* Aziewicz (*supra* n. 28) 267.
59. Stanisław Gronowski, *Ustawa Antymonopolowa w Orzecznictwie* (CH Beck 1996).
60. For example, Mateusz Błachucki describes the judicial review system in competition law cases from a historical perspective, *see* Mateusz Błachucki, *Sądownictwo antymonopolowe w Polsce – historia i ustrój* (UOKIK 2011). Martyniszyn and Bernatt studied various aspects related to the evolution of the Polish judicial system in the 1990s as part of their comprehensive study on the history and the development of competition law system in Poland, *see* Martyniszyn and Bernatt (*supra* n. 4) 202-209.

Second, there are studies focused on the hybrid model of judicial review in Poland.[61] On the one hand, several authors – including Błachucki, Stankiewicz, and Turno – criticise this model and call for a change to an administrative courts' system similar to the judicial review of other administrative actions in Poland.[62] On the other hand, Bernatt defends the existing model, arguing that it is in line with the Polish Constitution and, while imperfect in practice, offers a better venue for the review on the merits of the UOKIK decisions. Moreover, Bernatt argues that such a system is in line with the full review requirement of Article 6 ECHR.[63]

Third, there has been some discussion on whether the case law of the Polish Supreme Court and the CCCP's practice of excluding the judicial review of procedural violations are in line with the procedural fairness principle and Article 6 ECHR requirements.[64]

The fourth concerns the intensity of judicial review in Poland and its overall effectiveness. Bernatt addresses this problem from several perspectives, including the constitutional, comparative, and ECHR-related challenges.[65] He introduces the concept of judicial deference to Poland and analyses the extent to which Polish courts defer to the UOKIK expert assessment.[66] He examined the judicial review of fines imposed by the UOKIK and its fining guidelines,[67] as well as the insufficient expertise of Polish judges.[68]

Fifth, practical aspects related to the functioning of judicial review were addressed by Martyniszyn and Bernatt. They presented the statistics of the (significant)

61. For an authoritative characterisation in this respect *see* Zbigniew Kmieciak, 'Postępowanie w sprawach ochrony konkurencji a koncepcja procedury hybrydowej' (2002) 4 Państwo i Prawo 32. In this respect *see also* Stanisław Gronowski, 'Sądownictwo antymonopolowe w Polsce' in Małgorzata Krasnodębska-Tomkiel (ed.), *Zmiany w polityce konkurencji na przestrzeni ostatnich dwóch dekad* (UOKIK 2010) 456-459 and Aleksander Stawicki, 'Competence of Common Courts in Poland in Competition Matters' (2012) 5 Yearbook of Antitrust and Regulatory Studies 65. For a comparative study, *see* Tadeusz Skoczny, 'Instytucjonalne modele wdrazania reguł konkurencji na świecie – wnioski dla Polski' (2011) 2 Ruch Prawniczy, Ekonomiczny i Socjologiczny 77.
62. *See* Błachucki (*supra* n. 32) and Rafał Stankiewicz, 'Likwidacja procedur hybrydowych – krok w dobrym kierunku czy szkodliwy dogmatyzm' in Błachucki and Górzyńska (eds) *Aktualne problemy rozgraniczania* (*supra* n. 32); Bartosz Turno, 'Model Sądowej Kontroli Decyzji Prezesa Urzędu Ochrony Konkurencji i Konsumentów' (2012) 10 Państwo i Prawo 33.
63. Maciej Bernatt, 'W sprawie kontroli sądowej postępowania przed Prezesem UOKiK' (2013) 3 Państwo i Prawo 89.
64. *Ibid*., and Maciej Bernatt, 'The Control of Polish Courts over the Infringements of Procedural Rules by the National Competition Authority: Case Comment to the Judgment of the Supreme Court of 19 August 2009 – Marquard Media Polska (Ref. No. III SK 5/09)' (2010) 3 Yearbook of Antitrust and Regulatory Studies 300. *See also* Aziewicz (*supra* n. 28).
65. *See* among others: Bernatt (*supra* n. 30) and Maciej Bernatt, 'Konstytucyjne aspekty sądowej kontroli działalności administracji (między efektywnością a powściągliwością)' (2017) 1 Państwo i Prawo 34,
66. *Ibid*., Maciej Bernatt, 'Koncepcja powściągliwości sądowej w prawie ochrony konkurencji' (2017) 6 Państwo i Prawo 36. *See also* Maciej Bernatt, 'Transatlantic Perspective on Judicial Deference in Administrative Law' (2016) 22 Columbia Journal of European Law 275.
67. Maciej Bernatt, 'Między pełną kontrolą sądową a poszanowaniem polityki karania organu administracji – o sądowej kontroli kar nakładanych w sprawach konkurencji' (2016) 9 Europejski Przegląd Sądowy 18; Mateusz Błachucki, 'Judicial Control of Guidelines on Antimonopoly Fines in Poland' (2016) 25 Revista de Concorrência e Regulação 35.
68. Bernatt (*supra* n. 30).

length of duration of judicial proceedings in Poland and discussed expertise and resource constraints the CCCP faces.[69]

Finally, there is a stream of debate which critically analyses the implications of the post-2015 rule of law crisis in Poland.[70] In particular, it studies what were the consequences of the legal changes in Poland which undermined the safeguards of independence of the Polish judiciary for the Polish competition law system. Among others, the negative changes concerning judges' competition law-related expertise at the Supreme Court level are discussed. EU case law provides food for thought in this respect. In December 2022 a special issue of the Polish leading EU law journal, *Europejski Przegląd Sądowy* was dedicated to the General Court ruling in *Sped-Pro.*[71] A case comment to the *Sped-Pro* ruling has also been published in the Common Market Law Review.[72]

4 QUANTITATIVE ANALYSIS

This section examines the findings resulting from applying a systematic analysis of all judgments issued and made public between 1 May 2004 and 30 April 2021.

4.1 Source of Information

The full texts of the majority of the reviewed judgments were retrieved from paid online services aggregating Polish court and administrative decisions and relevant literature (monographs, journals and commentaries on laws),[73] and the official case law databases maintained by the Polish Ministry of Justice or the Supreme Court of Poland.[74] This stems from the fact that not all the judgments rendered by Polish courts on antitrust matters are published. The NCA maintains a database of its decisions,[75] which is meant to include all the relevant judgments linked to a given case. The database, though relatively comprehensive, is not complete. Most importantly, the scans of judgments attached to each NCA decision in the database contain only the conclusion part. They lack the justification necessary to fully understand the reasoning of the courts and the way they assess the arguments raised by the parties to the proceedings.[76] This was appropriately reflected in the database. Whenever we were

69. Martyniszyn and Bernatt (*supra* n. 4) 204-209.
70. Bernatt (*supra* n. 17) and Bernatt (*supra* n. 16).
71. Case T-791/19 *Sped-Pro v. Commission* [2022] EU:T:2022:67.
72. Maciej Bernatt, 'Economic Frontiers of the Rule of Law: *Sped Pro v. Commission*' (2023) 60(1) Common Market Law Review 199.
73. *See* <sip.legalis.pl> and <sip.lex.pl> provided, respectively, by publishers CH Beck and Wolters Kluwer.
74. *See*, respectively, <orzeczenia.ms.gov.pl> and <www.sn.pl/orzecznictwo/sitepages/baza_orzeczen.aspx>.
75. *See* <decyzje.uokik.gov.pl/bp/dec_prez.nsf>.
76. Out of the 1,196 judgments included in the database, 501 are shortened versions missing the justification or judgments which could not be analysed as explained in (*infra* n. 79).

unable to retrieve information on the arguments raised by the appellants and the courts during proceedings,[77] we indicated that such information was not available.

Consequently, some aspects of the quantitative analysis have been considerably affected by this missing data. This is especially visible regarding the grounds of appeal raised by the appellants and reviewed by the courts, which are unfortunately significantly underestimated.[78]

Moreover, we wanted the coding to be as accurate as possible, and therefore, we avoided relying on assumptions or guesses about the missing information. However, in exceptional cases, we did make certain estimations about the type of grounds raised by the appellants, or accepted/rejected by the courts. First, we always assumed that in decisions which fully rejected an appeal, the courts did not accept any of the grounds raised. Second, in judgments in which a court changed the decision under review, assumptions were sometimes made about which of the grounds invoked by the appellant(s) were the most probable reason for the court's decision. This was, however, done only in unequivocal cases.[79] Third, no such assumptions were made when the court decided to annul the reviewed decision, change it with regard to the amount of the fine, or remand the case back to a lower-instance court for renewed review. In such cases, it is rarely possible to identify the exact reason for the court's decision – e.g., an annulment or remanding is equally attributable to either procedural or substantive arguments.

4.2 Total Number of Judgments and the Ratio of Appeals

The database includes a total of 1,196 judgments and courts' decisions (for the sake of convenience, hereinafter jointly referred to as 'judgments' or 'rulings'[80]). Of those judgments – 714 were issued by the CCCP at first instance (pertaining to 506 relevant UOKIK decisions, thereby reflecting an appeal ratio of 36% of all the UOKIK's decisions issued in the reviewed 2004-2021 period), 373 by the CoA at second instance (pertaining to 352 CCCP's judgments and 25% of the UOKIK's decisions), and 109 by the SCP as the third (cassation) instance (8% of the UOKIK's decisions). This high rate of appeals against NCA decisions may be explained, *inter alia*, by the relatively low,

77. Either from the full version of a judgment or from the justification of a judgment issued by a higher-instance court reviewing the same case – e.g., a second-instance court is obliged to give account of the course of the proceedings before the lower-instance court and thus often cites all the grounds that were raised by the appellant during first-instance proceedings.
78. *See, e.g.*, Figure 23.9 below, which shows how often appellants either successfully or unsuccessfully invoked a given type of grounds of appeal. The numbers indicated refer only to the court judgments for which we could retrieve such information. Consequently, the numbers are significantly underestimated, which explains why the table indicates, e.g., that for the 1,196 judgments reviewed, substantive grounds were subject to examination in only 599 of them.
79. For example, when the court changed the reviewed NCA decision by finding that no antitrust infringement had in fact taken place. Given the scope of each category of grounds of appeal, the only reason for this change could be attributed to a successful substantive argument (as this is this type of grounds that relates to situations when either substantive legal issues or the facts of the reviewed case are challenged).
80. For example, when Polish civil courts dismiss an appeal due to formal inadmissibility (*odrzucenie apelacji*) they issue a decision (*postanowienie*).

fixed appeal fee, and the fact that courts are known to significantly decrease the amounts of fines imposed by UOKIK.

4.3 Judgments per Year

Figure 23.1 presents the number of judgments issued by Polish courts of various instances per year.

Figure 23.1 Number of Judgments According to Instances

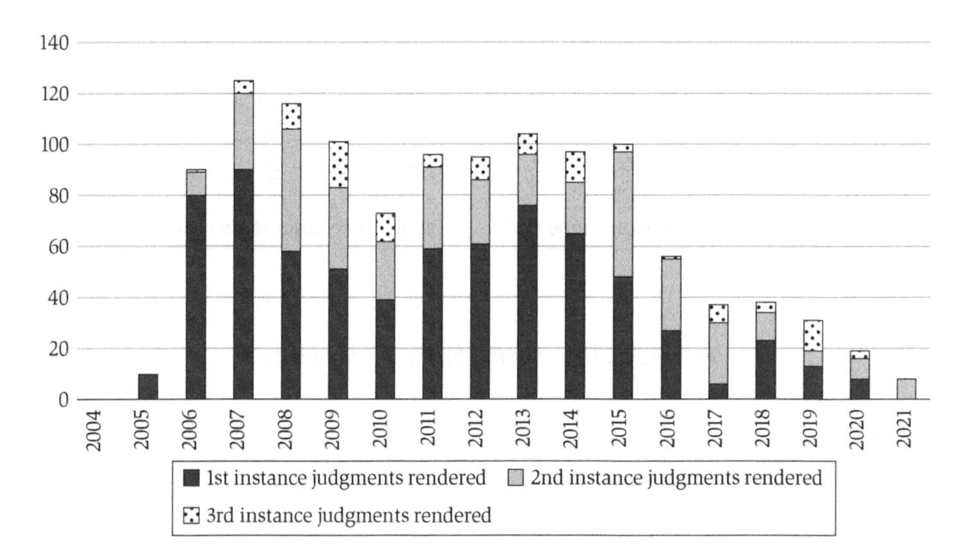

The visible decline in the number of rulings since 2015 is correlated with the considerable fall in the number of decisions issued by the NCA since 2014 (an average of 124.6 decisions per year during 2004-2013, in comparison to an average of 24.4 during 2014-2021).[81]

Figure 23.2(a) illustrates the comparison between the number of NCA decisions whose appeals were analysed in the study and the number of first-instance rulings rendered.[82] Similarly, Figure 23.2(b) shows the number of second-instance judgments in comparison with the number of CCCP rulings, while Figure 23.2(c) presents an analogous comparison between CoA and third-instance judgments.

81. Calculations based on official reports published by the UOKIK.
82. It is worth noting that one of the reasons for the apparent discrepancy between the number of NCA decisions issued in a given year that were subject to appeals and the number of CCCP judgments issued in the following year(s) is the fact that a single decision in multilateral conduct cases may give rise to several sets of simultaneous proceedings. Polish courts may decide to hear several appeals of different appellants in the course of one set of proceedings (under one docket number), or divide them into separate proceedings – as they see fit.

Figure 23.2(a) First-Instance Judgments

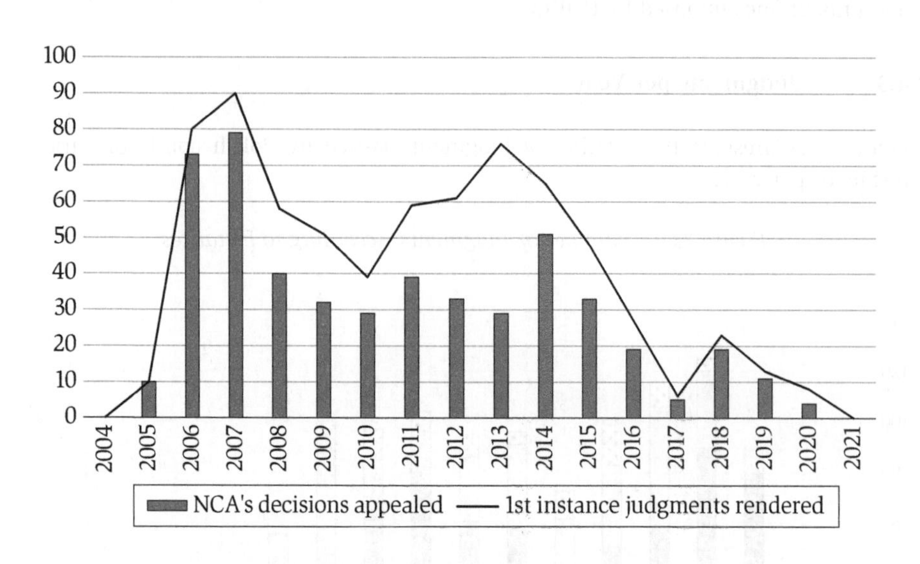

Figure 23.2(b) Second-Instance Judgments

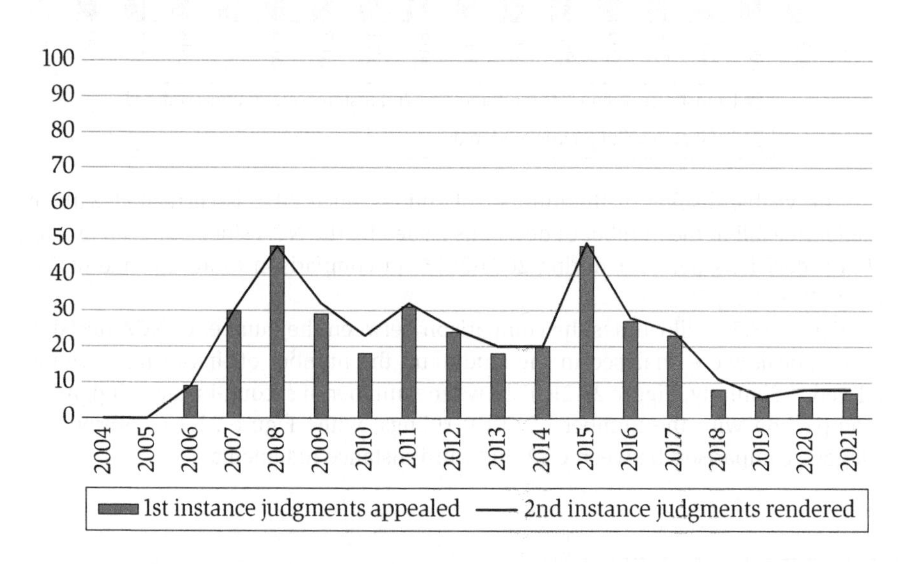

Figure 23.2(c) Third-Instance Judgments

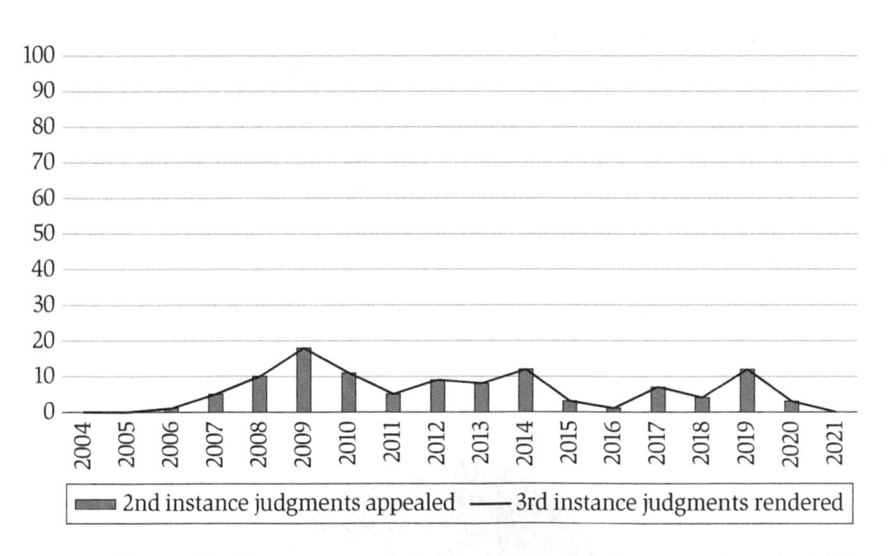

According to the figures presented above, 2007 was the year when the highest number of judgments in antitrust matters was rendered. This was mainly the result of the NCA's peak of enforcement activity in the years 2004-2006[83] when numerous decisions concerning practices of municipal services providers in local markets (water supply, waste disposal, sewage housing cooperatives or cemetery management) were issued. This includes, for example, CoA judgments in relation to UOKIK's decisions against the Katowice City Commune[84] and the Oborniki City Commune[85] for anti-competitive practices in the sector of municipal waste. Both of these cases were important as they eventually culminated in seminal SCP judgments concerning the applicability of the concept of undertaking,[86] and consequently the applicability of antitrust law rules, to the local government units' activity in the field of public utilities.[87] The low number of third-instance judgments by the SCP in 2018 followed by a sudden increase in the number of judgments issued by the SCP in 2019 is a result of institutional reform of the SCP which moved the antitrust cases to the new SCP chamber.[88]

83. During these three years, UOKIK issued around 34% of all the decisions handed down in 2004-2021.
84. The CoA judgment of 21 June 2007, VI ACa 1260/06.
85. The CoA judgment of 26 September 2007, VI ACa 439/07.
86. The SCP judgments of: 20 November 2008, III SK 12/08, and of 7 January 2009, III SK 17/08, respectively.
87. In the case of the Katowice City Commune, the SCP laid down the general rule that local government unit's may be considered an undertaking when carrying activity both in the *dominium* sphere (public administration as a provider of services) and the *imperium* sphere (public administration as public authority).
88. For the controversies in this respect and the broader impact of the reform *see* Bernatt (*supra* n. 17).

4.4 Success Rates and Outcomes

Figure 23.3 shows the success rate of the appeals across all instances. Hence, this data aggregates separate appeals launched against a single NCA decision and also further appeals against a given appellate court ruling. Consequently, if an NCA decision was appealed by various parties in separate proceedings, or, e.g., a first-instance ruling was the subject of two consecutive appeals to the CoA due to remanding the case for renewed consideration of the first-instance court, the outcome of all those judgments, despite their different docket numbers, will be counted as a single case for the purposes of this figure.

Figure 23.3 Success of Appeals (Each NCA's Decision or Previous Instance Judgment Counts as One)

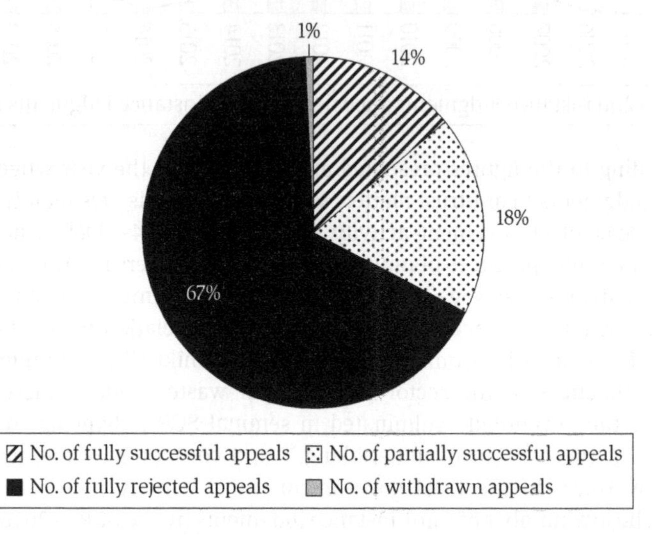

The figure shows that the success rate of appeals in the reviewed timeframe was relatively significant. In fact, 33 % of appeals resulted in either a full or partial success. The partially successful category includes cases where courts agreed with only some of the parties' arguments concerning the defects of the appealed decisions leading to changes in some of their substantive aspects (including the amount of the fine) or their partial overturning. Other partial successes comprised situations in which appeals launched by some of the parties were successful, while other separate appeals in relation to the same infringement were not.

The success rates are further elaborated by Figure 23.4, which identifies the outcome of the appeals. Unlike Figure 23.3, this figure examines each judgment separately and differs between the appeal's instances. This figure demonstrates that the rates of success (both full and partial) of the second and third-instance appeals were higher than the first instance (with a rejection rate of 63%, 68%, and 75%, respectively).

Figure 23.4(a) First-Instance Outcome

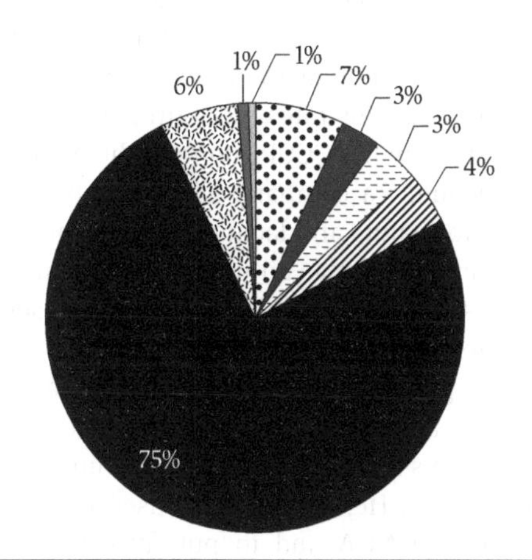

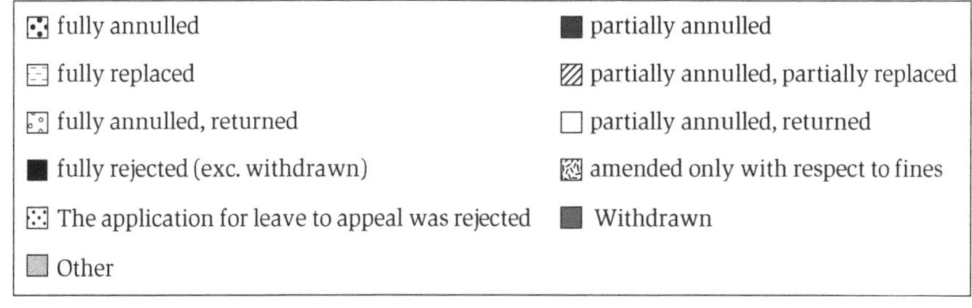

Figure 23.4(a) shows that 75% of the CCCP's judgments fully rejected the appellants' claims. However, only 67% of the judgments were rejections on the merits, and in 8% the court dismissed the appeal as formally inadmissible, due to, e.g.,

non-payment of the appeal fee. A third of the remainder of the first-instance judgments (with the exception of six appeals that were withdrawn and one appeal that was modified by invoking the correct legal basis for the identified infringement[89]) either fully or partially changed the findings made by NCA (approx. 7%). Another group of appeals resulted in the modification of the amount of the fine (approx. 6%).[90]

Three per cent of the CCCP's judgments annulled the NCA's decision partially, whereas only in the case of 7% there was a full annulment. The latter category includes, for example, the appeal against the NCA decision in the *Info-TV-FM Mobile TV* case,[91] which found no substance in the NCA's allegations against Poland's leading mobile phone operators of having formed a cartel to undercut the development of a new and innovative market for mobile TV services. In 3% of cases, the CCCP fully changed the NCA decision. This illustrates the court's wide power to revise the NCA's decisions. This is exemplified by the CCCP ruling in the appeal proceedings launched by Polskie Składy Budowlane,[92] a company alleged to have participated in vertical price fixing in the market for paints and lacquers.[93] The court challenged the authority's decision to qualify the appellant as an undertaking bearing full responsibility for antitrust infringements, as it was found that its activity resembled that of an agent acting on behalf of its members who are also shareholders. In principle, the entity functioned as a purchasing group whose aim was to negotiate prices for the undertakings holding its shares. The agreements signed by Polskie Składy Budowlane had no provisions obliging the group's members to apply the minimum resale prices imposed by the paint producer Śnieżka. Hence, the court used the power both to review the factual findings made by the NCA and to put forward its own interpretation of substantive provisions.

89. In the CCCP judgment of 10 May 2006, XVII AmA 8/05, the court changed the original decision and replaced the NCA's original qualification of the infringement, which was based on the provisions of the law in force since 2000, instead referring to the earlier antitrust statute.
90. For example, in the *Interchange fee* case (UOKIK decision no. DAR-15/2006) where the initial collective fine of PLN 164.8 million was reduced by PLN 120.46 million. The appeal proceedings against the original 2006 NCA decision are still ongoing, however. Another example is the *PGNiG S.A.* abuse of dominance case (UOKIK decision no. DOK-2/2012) in which the NCA's original fine of PLN 60 million was reduced by approx. PLN 5.5 million.
91. NCA decision no. DOK-8/2011.
92. The CCCP judgment of 29 January 2014, XVII AmA 121/10.
93. NCA decision no. RKT-43/2009.

Figure 23.4(b) Second-Instance Outcome

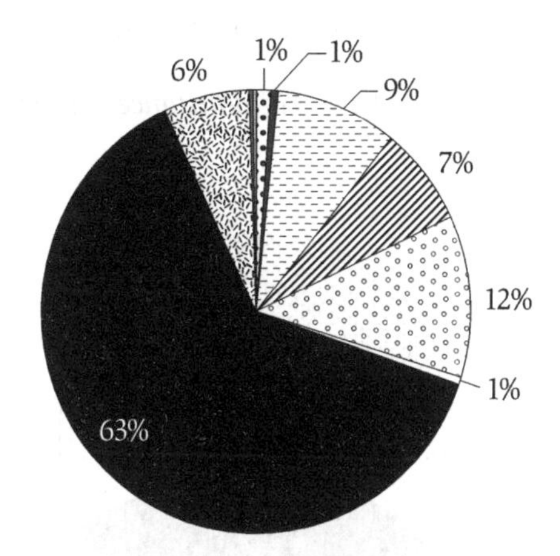

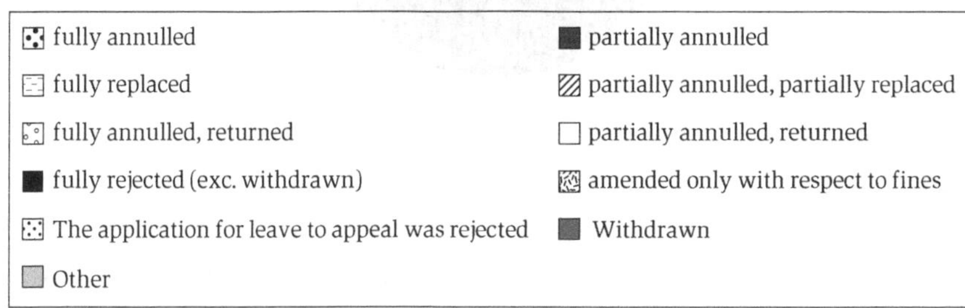

Figure 23.4(b) summarises the outcome of the cases in front of the CoA. As already mentioned, the results are more varied since the CoA, as a second-instance court, may issue more types of judgments than the CCCP. Moreover, the CoA reviews appeals made not only by the undertakings subject to the NCA's decision but also by the authority that issued the decision. As can be seen from the graph, the second most common type of decision taken in CoA rulings – the first being the full rejection of an appeal – was to remand the case back to the first-instance court (13%). Under Polish civil procedure, this can happen in several situations mentioned in section 2.2 above.

The first group of situations is relatively rare in judicial reviews in antitrust cases. An example of this is the CoA judgment issued in the *Termet S.A.* case, where the court had to remand the case back to the CCCP once it was established that one of the parties to the proceedings, undergoing bankruptcy proceedings, was dissolved and lost its capacity to be a party in court before the end of the first-instance proceedings, which in turn resulted in their invalidity.[94] In the vast majority of cases, however, the CoA remands the case back to the CCCP in order to rectify the defects concerning the first-instance court's review of the objections or evidence raised by the parties. For example, in the *Sfinks Polska S.A.* case, the CoA referred the case back to the CCCP for its failure to examine the merits of the case, which manifested, *inter alia*, in the court's

94. The CoA judgment of 30 October 2020, VII Aga 638/19.

neglect to analyse the possibility of applying an individual exemption to the agreement under review, and to scrutinise the actual functioning of the chain restaurants market by disregarding the undertaking's request for an expert opinion on this matter.[95]

Figure 23.4(c) Third-Instance Outcome

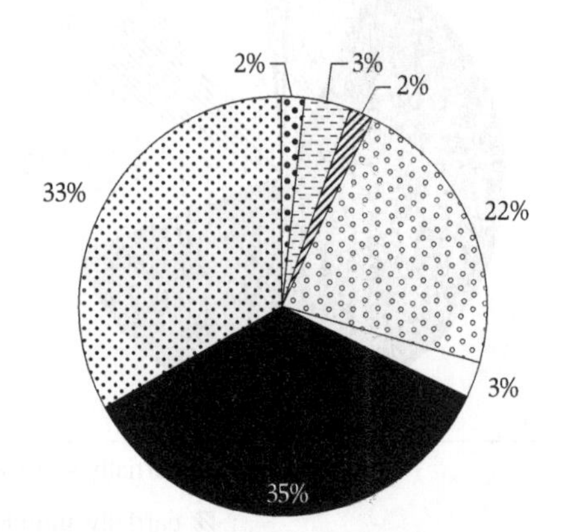

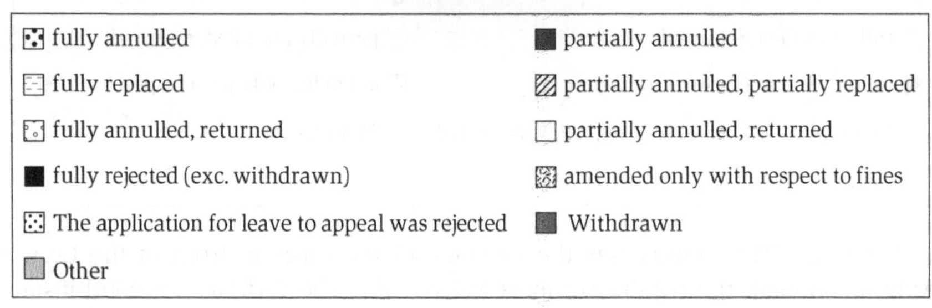

Figure 23.4(c), which summarises the outcomes of judgments by the Supreme Court, shows a similar picture regarding the number of antitrust proceedings that ended up rejected by the cassation court. Here, however, the total number of rejections (68%) is divided between rejections after an examination on the merits (35%) and a refusal of leave to appeal due to the non-fulfilment of cassation requirements set out under the rules of civil procedure (33%). A considerable part of the rulings comprises situations in which the SCP remanded the case in its entirety to the second- (or sometimes even first-) instance court (25%), whereas situations in which the cassation court changed the findings of the lower-instance court with its own conclusions comprise only approx. 5%.

An example of the latter is the judgment in the *Marquard Media Polska* case concerning the allegedly anticompetitive pricing policy of a sports newspaper publisher believed to hold a dominant position in the national market for sports dailies.[96] In fact, the case reached the SCP twice (in 2009 and 2013) and at first the court referred the

95. The CoA judgment of 16 December 2015, VI ACa 1799/14.
96. The SCP judgment of 12 April 2013, III SK 28/12.

case back to the CCCP for a more in-depth analysis of the facts of the case. In the later ruling, however, the cassation court found that, despite the re-evaluation and the guidelines received, both lower-instance courts were still unable to properly assess the case, notably failing to apply the instructions of the earlier SCP judgment. In particular, the superficial analysis of the content of the dailies under review was insufficient to substantiate the relevant market definition followed by the NCA. In consequence, the SCP changed the CoA judgment imposing a change to the CCCP judgment, thus repealing the original NCA decision altogether. The SCP found that Marquard Media could not have been considered to have abused a dominant position since the relevant market was not established correctly.[97]

4.5 Type of NCA's Decisions Subject to Appeal

The analysis shows a limited number of competition law rules being subject to review on appeal.

Figure 23.5 Rules Being Appealed

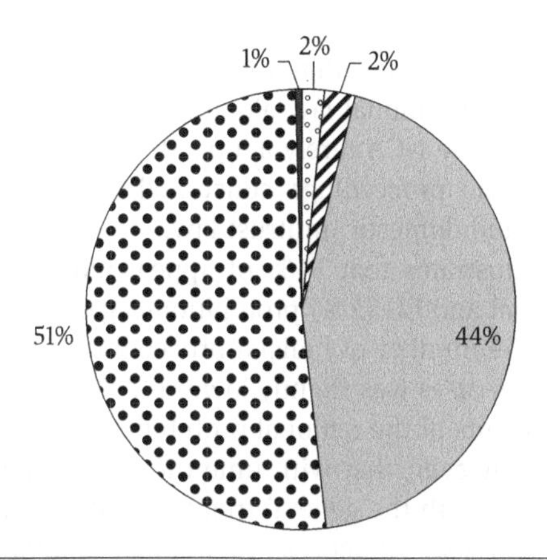

97. *See* Bernatt (*supra* n. 30) 110-112.

Figure 23.6 Rules Being Appealed According to Years (Each Judgment Counts as One)

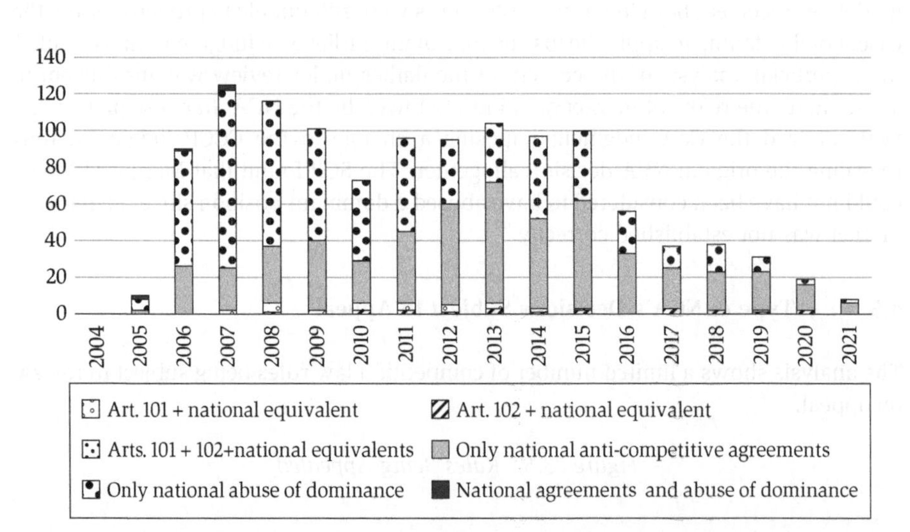

First, Figure 23.5 demonstrates that appeal judgments have predominately focused on the enforcement of national law alone (96%). This is in line with earlier research, demonstrating that the NCA rarely adopts decisions under Articles 101 and 102 TFEU.[98] The rest of the proceedings concerned a combination of practices prohibited both under EU and domestic antitrust law.

Second, the figure illustrates that 54% of appeal judgments pertained to the national (52%) and national and EU (2%) prohibitions against abuses of a dominant position. In comparison, the number of judicial proceedings related to the review of anti-competitive agreements cases was slightly lower (47% in total, out of which 45% concerned solely infringements of the national prohibition).

Figure 23.6 shows, however, that with time the focus on abuse of dominance reduced considerably in line with the general trend of UOKIK's diminishing enforcement activity in relation to abusive practices of dominant undertakings.

As a matter of fact, there was a significant number of early abuse cases between 2004 and 2011. During that time, an average of approx. 61% of the appeal judgments per year concerned the national and/or EU prohibition on abuse of dominance (sometimes in combination with anti-competitive agreements). Between 2012 and 2021, however, this has dropped to an average of approx. 34% appeal judgments per year.

The change in the competition rules subject to review could be related to a number of reasons, the most important being a special focus of the NCA on dominance abuses in the years following the economic transformation in Poland.[99] At the same time, one can explain the decrease in the number of dominance cases with the change

98. Botta, Svetlicinii and Bernatt (*supra* n. 13) 1262-1265.
99. *See* Martyniszyn and Bernatt (*supra* n. 4) 195.

of economic policy in Poland which today promotes SOEs.[100] Presently, as evidenced during the last three years, the authority does not issue more than one decision concerning abuses of dominance per year.

Third, in relation to the prohibition of anti-competitive agreements, appeals have involved only a limited range of issues (*see* Figure 23.7). From the 548 judgments related solely to anti-competitive agreements that were analysed in the study, 331 (60) concerned vertical agreements, 204 (37%) horizontal agreements, and 13 (2%) mixed horizontal-vertical matters. Remarkably, the NCA has classified *all* of those decisions as 'by-object' infringements (with the exception of ten cases - 1.8% - which did not indicate whether it was a 'by-object' or 'by-effect' infringement). There are several reasons for this, the most important being that the NCA's enforcement used to focus on easily identifiable, hard-core antitrust infringements. In more ambiguous cases, the authority was known to take a more lenient approach, sometimes even choosing so-called soft interventions instead of opening formal antitrust proceedings that would lead to a prohibition decision.[101]

This confirms the findings from earlier studies, which suggest that the authority was focused on pursuing the easier vertical (especially RPM) cases. In fact, during the EU accession process, Poland was repeatedly encouraged by the European Commission to start prioritising cartel enforcement.[102] It was also argued that the UOKIK failed to develop sufficient skills to proactively uncover and sanction cartel conduct. In fact, the NCA in its reports is known to have exaggerated the scale of its activities against cartels by applying a peculiar understanding of the term cartel by extending it also to hard-core vertical antitrust infringements, especially RPMs,[103] which are classified as 'by-object' collusions.[104]

Interestingly, 3% of the appealed NCA decisions involved cases where one or more of the parties successfully submitted a leniency application. This seems to confirm the prevalent approach that the functioning of the leniency program should be seen as a missed opportunity at best and a failure at worst.[105] Academics point to

100. *See* more *infra* section 5.1.
101. An example of such activity can be found in the case of Porozumienie Zielnogórskie (the Zielonagóra Accord), an association of healthcare employers who encouraged its members to stop concluding agreements with NFZ, the Polish national health fund, to gain leverage in negotiations for better contractual rates when providing public health services. The Polish NCA found that some of the actions could be anti-competitive by-effect but decided to make an official request to members of the association to rectify their behaviour instead of issuing a prohibition decision. *See* UOKIK press release of 12 March 2015. https://uokik.gov.pl/aktualnosci.php?news_id = 11515&news_page = 62&print = 1.
102. *See* Martyniszyn and Bernatt (*supra* n. 4) 38, 40.
103. For example, the OECD Glossary defines a price-fixing agreement as 'an agreement between sellers to raise or fix prices in order to restrict inter-firm competition and earn higher profits (...)'. *See further* OECD, Glossary of Industrial Organisation Economics and Competition Law (1993), 69. RPM does not fit under that definition. The NCA defines cartels as any agreements between firms aimed at limiting competition, noting that sometimes (sic!) in the scholarship the term 'cartel' is used to refer only to horizontal agreements, *see* UOKIK 2010 information brochure available under https://uokik.gov.pl/download.php?plik = 11127. *See* Martyniszyn and Bernatt (*supra* n. 4) 38.
104. *Ibid.*, 38.
105. *See* Martyniszyn and Bernatt (*supra* n. 4) 40, 43; Bartosz Turno, *Leniency. Program łagodzenia*

several reasons for this situation, indicating both issues related to the design of the leniency programme under Polish law (e.g., too broad substantive scope of the regulation covering not only cartels *per se* but also other types of horizontal as well as vertical agreements) and the actual suboptimal practices of the agency (e.g., lack of full transparency in relation to the total amounts of fines imposed on undertakings and their reductions under the leniency programme).[106] Moreover, issues concerning Poland's culture stemming from a historical, mainly post-communist, reluctance to cooperate with state authorities are also invoked in this context.[107]

At first sight, it may also seem very curious that none of the NCA decisions that were reviewed in the appellate-court rulings analysed in the study involved a successful settlement application. One has to remember, however, that the settlement procedure was only introduced into Polish competition law in 2015.[108] Only a relatively small number of UOKIK decisions, which pertained to anti-competitive agreements, issued after 2015 were reviewed in our analysis. Moreover, one of the conditions of a successful settlement, i.e., one resulting in a fine reduction, is for the benefiting undertaking to not appeal the decision.

By comparison, there was no greater divergence in the type of reviewed infringements of competition when it comes to the (EU and national) abuse of dominance cases. Hence, 45 % of the reviewed judgments regarding abuse of dominance related to exclusionary practices, and 42 % concerned exploitative practices. The rest were issued in cases of abuses of a mixed nature.

Figure 23.7 Types of Restrictions

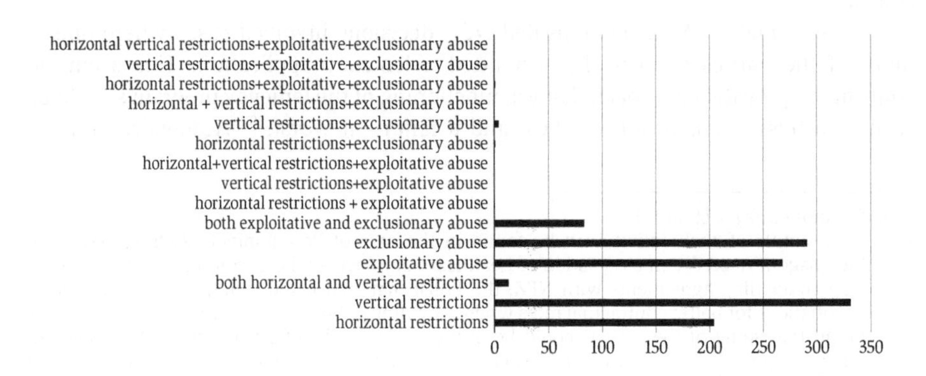

kar pieniężnych w polskim prawie ochrony konkurencji (Wolters Kluwer 2013) Ch. 7, section 3.3.

106. *See* Martyniszyn and Bernatt (*supra* n. 4) 43; Turno, (*supra* n. 107) Ch. 7, sections 3.2.7 and 3.2.8.
107. *See* Martyniszyn and Bernatt (*supra* n. 4) 42.
108. By means of the amendment of 10 June 2014 (Dz.U. of 2014, item 945).

4.6 Type of NCA's Procedure

Figure 23.8 summarises the types of NCA actions that were subject to appeal. Understandably, it indicates that 86% of first-instance judgments concerned decisions involving findings of infringements, together with the imposition of fines. Only 4% of the CCCP judgments reviewing NCA decisions involved findings of infringements with no fines.

It might be of interest to note, however, that almost 10% of these judgments related to either no grounds for action decisions or decisions to reject a complaint or close an investigation. All such decisions have been issued under the act in force before the current antitrust regulation. Following the reform to the rules of antitrust procedure in 2007, third parties making formal complaints about anticompetitive practices no longer have any legal status and rights in the ensuing proceedings. Even though complaints can still be filed with the NCA, the authority is not bound by them as currently antitrust proceedings are only initiated *ex officio*, solely at the discretion of the enforcer. The NCA is presently not even required to issue separate decisions to justify its choice not to pursue cases that were brought to its attention by third parties. This does not mean that the NCA does not issue decisions to close certain enquiries.[109] However, since currently only the authority and the addressees of a decision are parties to proceedings, such discontinuance decisions cannot be appealed.

The figure also shows that no commitments decisions were subject to the appeals.[110] The NCA's database does, however, indicate that there was one commitments decision in an abuse of dominance case against Tauron Sprzedaż Sp. z o.o., an electricity wholesaler, that was appealed against. The court ruling in this matter could not be identified as no docket number was provided. Nonetheless, commitments remedies, generally speaking, are not often used and when applied, given the nature of the commitments procedure, will not usually result in appeals since the addressee will not want to challenge decisions accepting commitments in lieu of a fine.

109. *See, e.g.*, the NCA decision no. DOK-1/2018.
110. There were, however, some infringement decisions imposing fines on undertakings, in which part of the allegations directed against the undertakings could not be sufficiently substantiated by the UOKIK during proceedings. *See, e.g.*, the CCCP judgment of 9 May 2014, XVII AmA 1/13 in the case of the Mint of Poland (decision no. RWR-29-2012).

Figure 23.8 The Competition Authority's Procedure

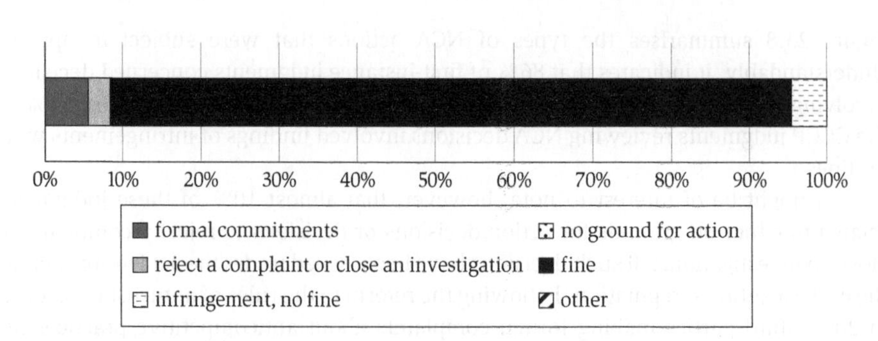

4.7 Grounds of Appeal

The empirical findings record the grounds which were raised by the parties' appeals and their success. To this effect, Figure 23.9 sets out the grounds of appeals across all instances. The data aggregates separate appeals launched against a single NCA decision and further appeals against a single ruling. Consequently, if an NCA decision was appealed by various parties in separate proceedings, or, e.g., a first-instance ruling was the subject of two consecutive appeals to the CoA due to remanding the case for renewed consideration of the first-instance court, the outcome of all those judgments will be counted as a single case for the purposes of this figure. It must also be borne in mind that more than one appeal ground has often been invoked in the same case.

Given the difficulties with accessing the full texts of all appeal rulings reviewed in the study (*see* section 4.1 above), the coding of the grounds of appeal cannot be seen as comprehensive. Efforts were made to provide the most complete picture of the arguments that were raised in the appeal proceedings and their evaluations by courts (e.g., on the basis of the descriptions in higher instance courts' judgments of previous procedural steps taken before lower instances). Nonetheless, it was not always possible to retrieve such information.

Figure 23.9 Grounds of Appeal (Each NCA's Decision or Previous Instance Judgment Counts as One)

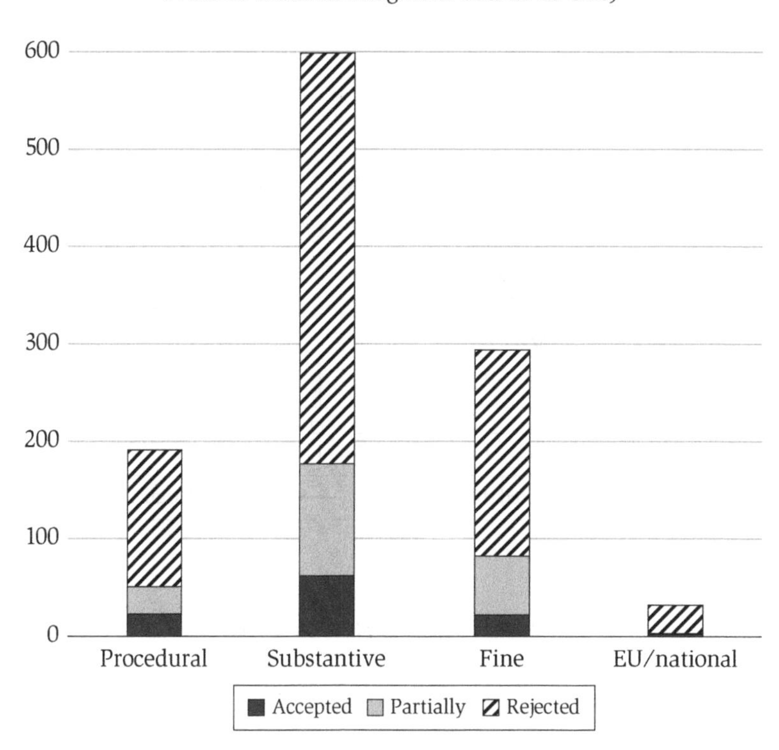

As can be seen from Figure 23.9, there were very few situations where higher-instance courts fully accepted the parties' arguments on any ground.[111] There are several possible reasons for that. First, the cases that go through second-instance appeals are more complex and their evaluation will usually require a more nuanced approach. Moreover, the prevalent litigation strategy consists of invoking as many arguments as possible in appeals, even if they are relatively weak. Since a court must review all of them anyway, this is seen as a way to maximise the chances of raising a point that will lead to changes in the decision or ruling under appeal. Since the study is designed to treat situations where only some of the arguments invoked by the parties are accepted by courts as 'partial successes', this will necessarily be reflected in results provided in Figure 23.9.

Figure 23.10 takes a different approach, focusing on the appeal grounds argued and accepted according to years, and counting each court ruling as a single judgment, irrespective of whether there were multiple separate appeals in relation to the same NCA decision or lower-instance court judgment.

111. The exception being, e.g., the full acceptance of grounds relating to the interplay between EU and national law in the *Tele2 Polska Sp. z o.o. See* the SCP judgment of 8 June 2011, III SK 2/09, and the CoA judgment of 20 February 2012, VI ACa 1304/11, rendered after CJEU's preliminary ruling in the case C-375/09 *Tele2 Polska*.

Figure 23.10(a) Procedural Grounds

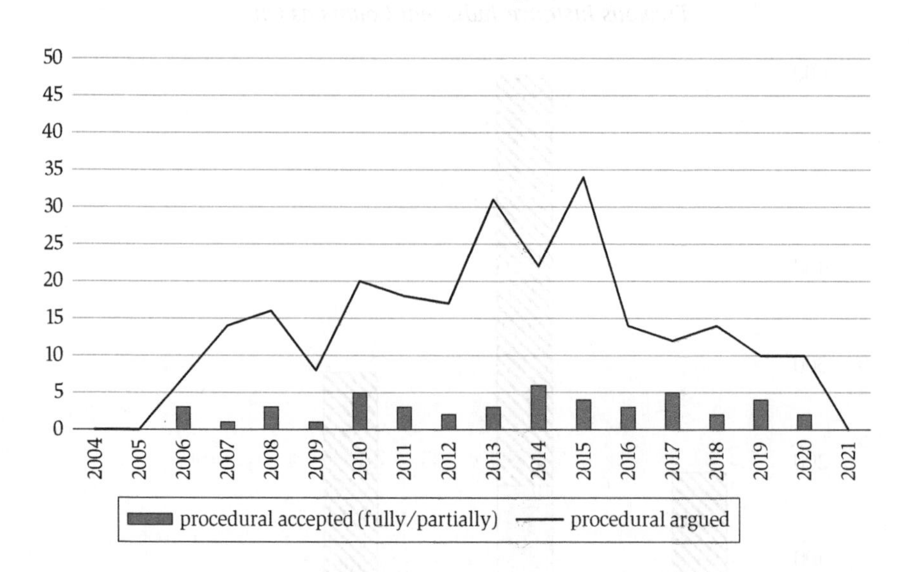

Figure 23.10(b) Substantive Grounds

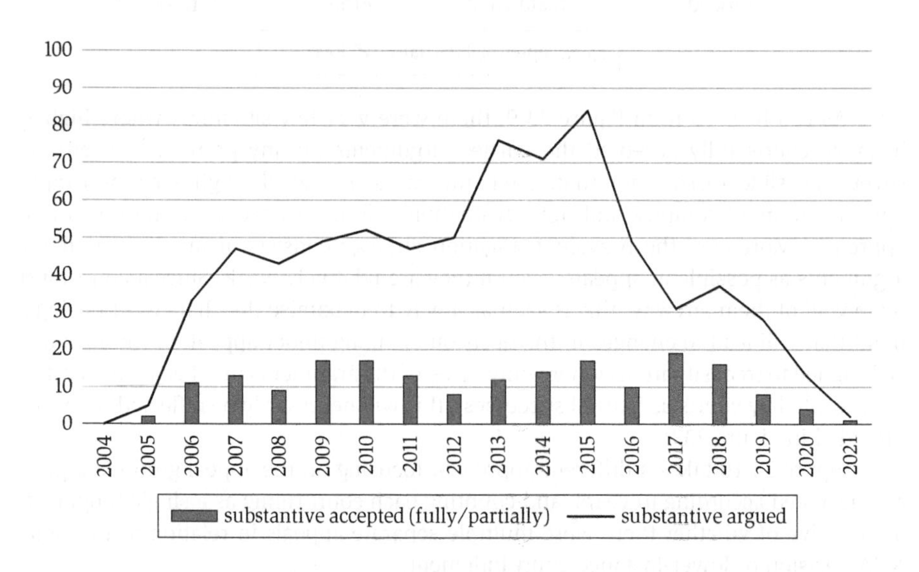

Figure 23.10(c) Fines-Related Grounds

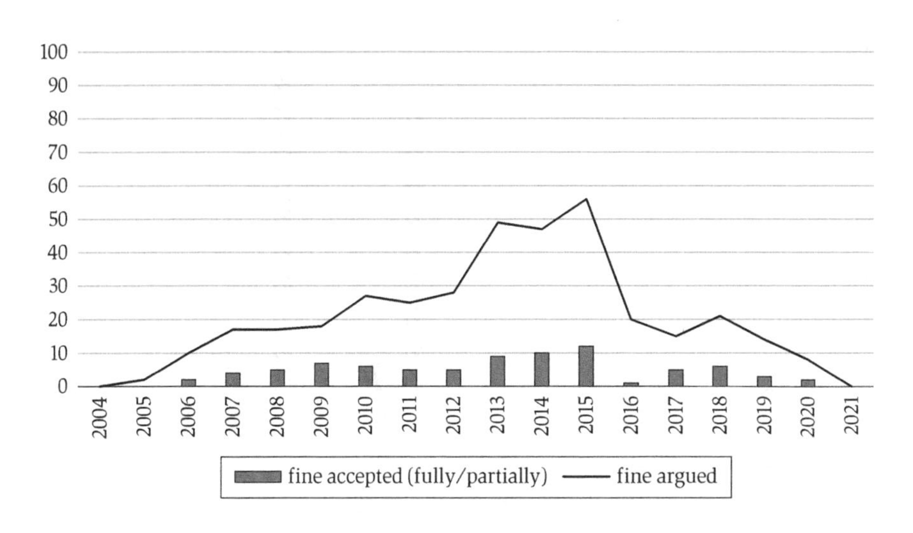

Figure 23.10(d) EU/National Grounds

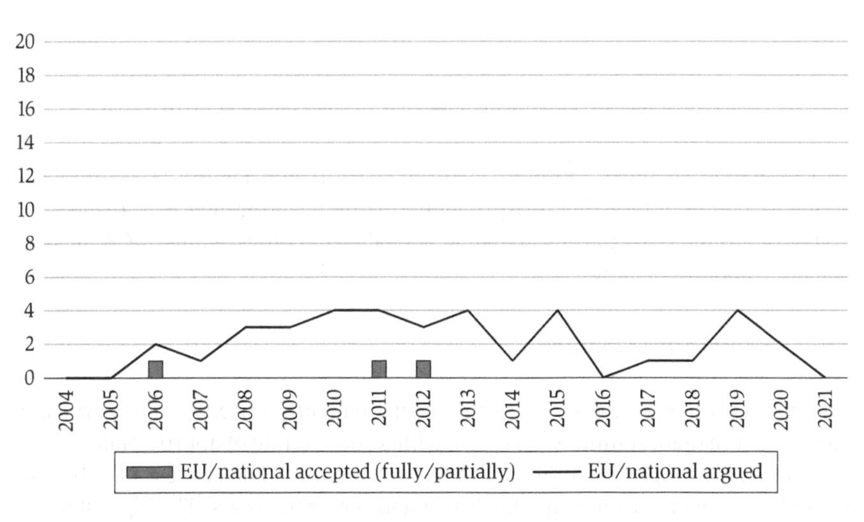

Figure 23.11 below breaks down the relationships between the types of restrictions targeted in the NCA decisions under appeal and the type and success rate of grounds invoked. The proportion of the types of arguments raised in appeals against decisions concerning practices classified as violations of Polish law only seems to be similar in the case of multilateral and unilateral infringements. The absolute amounts of different types of grounds argued are higher in the case of restrictive agreements, but mainly due to the much higher number of appeals lodged.

Figure 23.11 Types of Restrictions Versus Successful Grounds of Appeal

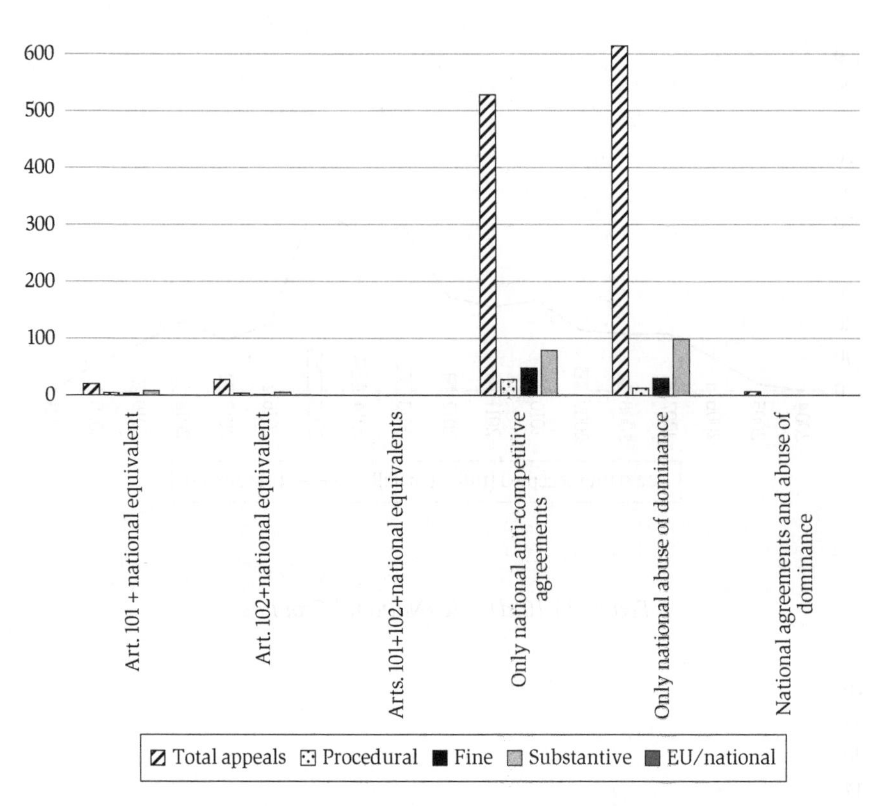

The graphs shown in Figures 23.10(a)-23.10(d) and Figure 23.11 provide an overview of certain interesting jurisprudential patterns and trends with respect to all the types of grounds that parties invoke in appeal proceedings against NCA decisions, which are elaborated below.

4.7.1 Substantive Grounds

Substantive grounds of appeal were the most frequently raised by the parties, and succeeded in the highest number of cases, with a success rate of approximately 27% in relation to all the judgments in which they were invoked. The success of substantive arguments, however, was not equally distributed across the years. The highest number of judgments where such grounds were successfully invoked come from 2009, 2010 and then 2015, 2017 and 2018. In the earlier period, this type of argument was invoked almost evenly in cases concerning both restrictive agreements and abuse of dominance (with a little advantage for dominance cases). However, with the already mentioned ongoing fall in enforcement actions against dominance abuses, in the later years most of the rulings, which accepted substantive arguments raised by the parties, were decided in cases relating to multilateral practices. It is also worth noting that in the period 2009-2011, the vast majority of the judgments of higher instance courts were handed down in favour of undertakings appealing against NCA decisions. In later years, especially in 2019, the SCP tended to side more often with the NCA's appeals against the rulings of the CoA.

In the end, the success of appeals will, nonetheless, always depend on the merits of a specific case. For example, a considerable part of the 2009-2011 appeal judgments, in which substantive grounds raised by the undertakings were accepted by the courts, were issued in proceedings challenging the apparently faulty decision of the NCA imposing fines on *Zakład Tworzyw Sztucznych Gamrat* and several of its distributors of gutter systems for their alleged involvement in vertical price fixing.[112]

4.7.2 *Fines-Related Grounds*

Grounds of appeal pertaining to imposed fines have also been frequent and prominent. The success rate of fine-related arguments was much more consistent throughout the years but slightly lower overall (22% of the judgments in which they were argued). In this context, it is worth noting that the reference to fine-related appeal grounds in Figure 23.10(c) only pertains to cases where the fining calculation process was challenged in itself. They do not include cases where the fine was reduced because the court accepted the substantive ground of appeal. In general, it is safe to say that more fine reductions took place as an outcome of accurately invoked substantive grounds. Nonetheless, there were several matters where a considerable fine reduction was achieved on the basis of arguments concerning solely improper fine calculations, e.g., the already mentioned abuse of dominance case against *PGNiG S.A.*, in which the initial fine of approx. PLN 60 million was reduced to PLN 5.5 million, or the vertical collusion case concerning sales of paints and lacquers of the producer Akzo Nobel Sp. z o.o., in which the combined fine was decreased from approx. PLN 54 million to PLN 8.9 million.

On a more general note, however, the findings of the study show that appeals against NCA's decisions had a relevant impact on the level of fines imposed. Accordingly, a review of the change in fines following appeal judgments - regardless of the ground of appeal - indicates that fine reductions took place in 19% of the judgments before the CCCP, 31% before the CoA and 26% before the SCP. The average fine reduction in those cases was 78% before the CCCP, 79% before the CoA, and 89% before the SCP.

4.7.3 *Procedural Grounds*

Figures 23.10(c) and 23.11 show that even though procedural grounds were invoked quite often, they were rarely successful (with a success rate of 19% of all the judgments issued in proceedings where such grounds were invoked). When accepted, they often concerned situations when the NCA went beyond the statute of limitations (e.g., the

112. *See* NCA decision no. RKR-32/2007.

abuse of dominance case against PZU S.A.[113]). In several cases, however, the courts also brought valuable clarification on procedural issues, which helped to better protect the undertakings' right of defence (e.g., the appeal judgment in a case against allegedly anti-competitive agreements concluded by the broadcaster Cyfrowy Polsat S.A., which stated that extending the scope of the initial decision on the commencement of antitrust proceedings in the course of proceedings was incompatible with the law in force and rendered the NCA's decision null and void).[114]

Our research confirms that courts are indeed slowly changing their approach as regards the assessment of procedural errors committed during the administrative phase of antitrust proceedings (as mentioned in section 2 of the Report). A good example can be found in the CCCP judgment in the *Anyro* case, in which the NCA identified the existence of an alleged vertical collusion between distributors and retailers of luxury watches.[115] The court found that the decision breached not only substantive provisions but also the distributors' right of defence by failing to indicate the other parties to the alleged agreement, which made it impossible for the plaintiffs to defend against the enforcer's allegations. The CCCP also found violations of procedural rules concerning the legality of the evidence acquired during the antitrust proceeding. The NCA supposedly used the evidence provided in the leniency application of one of the decision's addressees even though the NCA had known that the submission would not benefit from a fine reduction. The first-instance court considered this behaviour of the NCA as an alleged breach of the principle of trust towards public administration (as foreseen by the Polish code of administrative procedure) and the right to a fair trial (as foreseen in Article 6 ECHR). The CoA found the CCCP's interpretation to be overly expansive and far-fetched,[116] as the right to remain silent and the right not to incriminate oneself are not absolute rights, a view that has already been confirmed, e.g., in the jurisprudence of the CJEU.[117] The CCCP judgment, even though the appellate court did not confirm its reasoning in this respect, is a clear sign that courts are increasingly willing to engage in profound discussions concerning complex procedural matters.

Interestingly, Article 6 ECHR has also been found to generally apply to appeal proceedings against decisions of national sectoral market regulators imposing fines on undertakings.[118] The SCP repeatedly stated that even though these fines are not criminal sanctions *per se*, their application – due to their very high amount – cannot disregard the interpretations set out in the jurisprudence of the European Court of Human Rights. Given the duties stemming from participation in the ECHR, courts have to make sure that the judicial review in such cases is subject to requirements that apply

113. *See* the CCCP judgment of 31 July 2017, XVII AmA 11/17 upheld in full by both the CoA and the SCP.
114. *See* the CCCP judgment of 8 December 2014, XVII AmA 153/13, upheld in full by the CoA.
115. *See* the CCCP judgment of 24 June 2015, XVII AmA 84/14.
116. *See* the CoA judgment of 25 January 2017, VI ACa 1673/15.
117. Case T-112/98 *Mannesmannröhren-Werke AG v. Commission of the European Communities* [2001] ECLI:EU:T:2001:61.
118. *See also* Maciej Bernatt, 'Prawo do rzetelnego procesu w sprawach ochrony konkurencji i regulacji rynku (na tle art. 6 EKPC)' (2012) 1 Państwo i Prawo 51.

to courts issuing judgments in criminal matters.[119] It was also confirmed that this case law also applies to antitrust proceedings before the NCA.[120]

4.7.4 Grounds Related to the Tensions Between EU and National Competition Law

Figures 23.10(d) and 23.11 demonstrate that arguments related to the tensions between EU and national competition laws were rarely raised by the parties. Even when they were raised, they were almost never accepted. One of the most important exceptions to this rule is the appeal of Tele2 Polska Sp. z o.o. - a telecoms undertaking whose complaint started the NCA's proceedings into allegedly anti-competitive practices of former incumbent TP S.A. - against the NCA's decision finding no abuse of a dominant position.[121] These proceedings eventually led to the CJEU's preliminary judgment in the case C-375/09 *Tele2 Polska.*[122]

The above should come as no surprise given the fact that the NCA focuses almost exclusively on the enforcement of national antitrust provisions (96% of the cases) and very rarely adopts decisions under Articles 101 and 102 TFEU. There are several reasons for the limited application of EU law in national antitrust proceedings. Interestingly, national authorities when opening investigations often consider applying Articles 101 and 102 TFEU along with the corresponding national provisions. However, the final decisions issued in such proceedings may ultimately prove to be based only on national competition law. Some academics consider that this is caused by a lack of a unified approach to interpreting the effect on EU trade conditions. Moreover, some national enforcers may be confused about the application of Regulation 1/2003 and unsure whether they are authorised to adopt certain types of decisions under EU law.[123]

The question of the effect on trade criterion has been only briefly touched upon in the judgments that were analysed during the study. As a matter of fact, the courts will not tackle such questions on their own unless this has been invoked by the appealing party.[124] For example, in an appeal against a decision establishing the existence of an RPM agreement in the supposedly national wholesale market for bicycle parts and accessories, the CoA reproached the NCA for failing to consider the issue of the practice's effect on EU trade when defining the relevant market.[125] The court called for a broad approach to the application of the criterion in line with the

119. *See, e.g.*, the SCP judgments of: 5 January 2011, III SK 32/10; 14 April 2010, III SK 1/2010; 1 June 2010, III SK 5/10; 21 September 2010, III SK 8/2010; 4 November 2010, III SK 21/10.
120. *See, e.g.*, the SCP judgment of 29 January 2019, I NSK 6/18.
121. *See* the CCCP judgment of 29 October 2007, XVII Ama 122/06 (CCCP), the CoA judgment of 10 July 2008, VI ACa 8/08, the SCP judgment of 8 June 2011, III SK 2/09.
122. Case C-375/09 *Tele2 Polska* [2011] ECLI:EU:C:2011:270.
123. *See* more Alexandr Svetlicinii, Maciej Bernatt and Marco Botta, 'The Dark Matter in EU Competition Law: Non-infringement Decisions in the New EU Member States Before and After Tele2 Polska' (2018) 43(3) European Law Review 424.
124. Mariusz Minkiewicz, 'Pojęcie wpływu na handel i reguła konwergencji w praktyce stosowania prawa UE przez polskie sądy i Prezesa UOKiK' (2014) 3(3) Internetowy Kwartalnik Antymonopolowy i Regulacyjny 8, 17.
125. The CoA judgment of 13 July 2017, VI ACa 1142/15.

guidelines formulated by the Commission and the CJEU. However, this position found no support in the judgment of the SCP. The court remitted the case back to the CoA, indicating, *inter alia*, that it was excessive to require the NCA to conduct a detailed analysis of whether the reviewed agreement had an effect on EU trade in the circumstances of this specific case.[126] The first circumstance was that the decision concerned a correctly identified infringement by-object. The second was that the CoA took too much of an activist approach in that matter, given that it was not even questioned by the appealing undertaking. This position, however, seems to go against the generally held view – also among courts – that the NCA should always verify the effect on EU trade on its own initiative.[127]

The practice of courts in initiating preliminary reference proceedings in the field of antitrust is very scarce. Only two preliminary rulings have been issued by the CJEU since the accession in May 2004. Interestingly, both cases concerned the application of Article 102 TFEU and pertained to procedural and not substantive measures. In the C-375/09 *Tele2 Polska* case, the CJEU was asked to determine whether an NCA is precluded from issuing a decision declaring constitutively that a given practice does not restrict competition within the meaning of Article 102 TFEU if it establishes, after conducting its proceedings, that a dominant company had not infringed the prohibition. In C-617/17, the CJEU was asked whether the principle of *ne bis in idem*, enshrined in Article 50 of the Charter of Fundamental Rights of the European Union, did not preclude a national competition authority from fining an undertaking in a single decision for both an infringement of national competition law and an infringement of Article 82 TEC.

On a more positive note, even though the NCA may seem to insufficiently base its decisions on EU law provisions, both the Polish authority and the courts in their analyses very often refer to EU competition law and case law.[128] However, according to the prevalent view represented in the Polish jurisprudence, this 'factual' harmonisation should not be seen as stemming from a legal obligation to harmonise national with EU competition law. The SCP famously held that EU legal acts, the case law of the CJEU, and the Commission's decisions and guidelines may only constitute a source of inspiration in the application of national competition law.[129]

It is worth noting that the political situation in Poland between 2015 and 2023 was not conducive to reversing the existing reluctance to directly apply EU law in antitrust matters. However, we consider that the judgments that the CJEU issued in connection to the current 'rule of law crisis' in Poland should also be considered a national contribution to the development of case law on resolving the tensions between EU and national competition law. This applies especially to the findings of the General Court in the *Sped-Pro* case.

126. The SCP judgment of 15 October 2019, I NSK 72/18.
127. The CCCP judgment of 2 December 2019, XVII AmA 23/17.
128. Minkiewicz (*supra* n. 126) 16.
129. The SCP judgment of 9 August 2006, III SK 6/06.

4.8 Admissibility

Admissibility in appeals against judgments of courts in civil law proceedings (and hence also against the decisions of the NCA, due to its hybrid character) is analysed on the basis of several criteria of a predominantly formal character. Under the code of civil procedure, an appeal will be declared inadmissible, i.e., rejected by the court, *inter alia*, if it was filed too late, was not paid for, or suffered from formal deficiencies that were not remedied by the appellant. Inadmissibility can also be declared for reasons of a more substantive nature - most notably, when the court finds that the appealing party had no interest (gravamen) in making the appeal, as the contested judgment was not a source of harm, i.e., there was no disadvantageous difference between the claim made during the dispute and the court's resolution of the dispute.[130] Only 8% of the appeals were found to be (fully or partly) inadmissible by the CCCP and 2% by the CoA.

A more in-depth evaluation of admissibility is carried out in the proceedings before the SCP. The court analyses not only the formal admissibility described above but also engages in assessing whether leave to appeal against a contested judgment can actually be granted. As already mentioned in section 2.3, formally admissible cassation complaints further undergo a procedure of preliminary cassation acceptance before their full review by the SCP. A cassation complainant submits an application for the acceptance of the cassation providing legal arguments proving that the complaint meets certain substantive requirements. Under Polish law, a cassation complaint is accepted for consideration by the SCP in the following situations: (i) a significant legal issue exists; (ii) there is a need to interpret legal provisions which raise serious doubts or result in divergent court rulings; (iii) invalidity of the proceedings before lower-instance courts is found; or (iv) when the cassation complaint is clearly justified. Otherwise, the Court will refuse to accept the complaint.[131] Such refusal took place in 32% of the cases heard by the SCP.

4.9 Appellant Types and Third Parties' Participation

The 2007 amendment of the Polish antitrust law considerably reformed an important aspect of the proceedings before the UOKIK. Under the 2000 Competition Act, the following entities could request the UOKIK to initiate antitrust proceedings: undertakings with legal interest, local government authorities, state audit offices, consumer advocates, or consumer organisations.[132] The NCA was not obliged to act on such a request but the choice to decline the initiation of requested proceedings made it

130. An example of a purely formal rejection is the CoA judgment of 17 July 2008, VI ACa 1594/07, concerning the lease agreements concluded by Polskie Konsorcjum Gospodarcze S.A., the owner and lessor of the commercial part of the border crossing terminal in Koroszczyn at the Belarussian border.
131. This happened, for example, when the SCP decided to dismiss the appeal of Castorama (judgment of 3 October 2013, III SK 13/13) concerning the RPMs imposed by AkzoNobel on retailers selling its paints and lacquers.
132. Article 84 of the 2000 Competition Act.

necessary for the authority to issue a formal resolution that was appealable. If the request was successful, however, the complainants also became parties to the instigated proceedings and enjoyed all the rights that came with that status, including the right to file an appeal against the NCA's decision.[133] Moreover, the NCA had the possibility of allowing certain entities (e.g., an undertaking which could demonstrate harm stemming from the alleged infringement or who was party to an agreement covered by the proceedings) to participate in the proceedings as so-called interested entities who could submit evidence (statements, documents).

As of the entry into force of the 2007 Competition Act, however, the procedure before the NCA was reshaped to give it a uniquely inquisitorial character. Even though complaints can still be filed with the NCA, the authority is not bound by them as currently antitrust proceedings are only initiated *ex officio*, solely at the discretion of the enforcer. The NCA is presently not even required to issue separate decisions to justify its choice not to pursue cases that were brought to its attention by third parties. Even though other entities are formally allowed to submit statements to the NCA during the proceedings, the practical value of such submissions is very limited as such third parties do not have access to the case files and might not realise what the subject of such proceedings actually is. Consequently, the procedural changes introduced in 2007 are criticised as they represent a disadvantageous deviation from the procedural solutions available in the proceedings before the European Commission, which accommodates some degree of third party participation and access to file.[134]

As a result, only the addressees of an NCA decision can currently submit appeals to the CCCP. At later stages, also the NCA can file appeals against first-instance judgments siding with the original plaintiff's point of view. The variety of appellants is, hence, very limited at present.

However, as can be seen from our research, even under the 2000 Act, judicial review of NCA decisions that were initiated through appeals made by third party complainants was very rarely successful in practice (11 % of judgments in proceedings initiated by third parties alone). In most cases, the courts sided with the enforcer. One of the notable exceptions was the case initiated by Sped-Pro S.A., a transport undertaking and competitor of the dominant railway freight carrier, PKP Cargo S.A.[135] The NCA did find PKP Cargo responsible for a number of anti-competitive practices in the national market for railway cargo transports, e.g., applying discriminatory contractual provisions against some of its contractors. Nevertheless, the UOKIK found some of Sped-Pro's allegations, e.g., concerning the dominant undertaking's refusal to enter into an advantageous long-term agreement with the competitor, unfounded. Similarly, the NCA refused to make the decision against PKP Cargo immediately enforceable, which the complainant required due to the considered harm caused by the abusive practices. The CCCP agreed with some of the points raised in the appeal and changed

133. Article 86 of the 2000 Competition Act.
134. *See* Maciej Bernatt, *Sprawiedliwość proceduralna w postępowaniu przed organem ochrony konkurencji* (Wydawnictwo Naukowe WZ UW 2011) 157, 158.
135. The judgment of the CCCP of 12 July 2007, XVII AmA 72/05.

the original decision by adding the rigour of immediate enforceability regarding the infringements that had been identified by UOKIK.

5 QUALITATIVE ANALYSIS

5.1 Characteristics of the Case Law

Judicial review in 2004-2021 fits into broader trends characterizing competition law enforcement. The data collected shows a high number of judgments rendered between 2006 and 2015 and a significant decrease since 2016 with a record low point in 2021.[136] This reflects the period of intense enforcement by the UOKIK in the 2000s and first five years of 2010s when the UOKIK adopted many decisions in repetitive cases concerning abuse of dominance on local public utilities markets, and abuse of dominance decisions against the successors of former state enterprises holding dominant position in regulated sectors such as energy, telecommunication or railway transportation as well as in restrictive agreements RPM cases.[137] In addition, the UOKIK often sanctioned local cartels in particular in the taxi market.[138] Since the tendency is to appeal UOKIK decisions, this period of active enforcement translated into a high number of judgments rendered by the CCCP, the CoA and the SCP.

In turn, the significant drop in 2016 can be explained by new enforcement trends in Poland. First, the tendency to resolve the repetitive cases by means of informal guidance letters,[139] and second the drop in the number of abuses of dominance on local water supply markets due to the establishment of the regulator, Wody Polskie, which assumed enforcement responsibility in this sector from UOKIK. At the same time, the continued decline in the number of judgments since 2017 reflects the negative consequences of the illiberal shift in Poland's politics in 2015 which translated into the growing marginalisation of regulatory agencies in Poland and resource-related constraints in maintaining intense enforcement.[140] More limited actual independence, particularly as far as the SOEs are concerned, may also explain the diminishing enforcement.[141] While 2021 saw some reinvigoration in UOKIK enforcement,[142] the question remains if it is likely to be retained in the longer run and translate into a significant increase in the number of infringement decisions adopted by the UOKIK and consequently in an increase in judgments rendered by the courts.

136. *See supra* Figure 23.1.
137. Martyniszyn and Bernatt (*supra* n. 4) 193-200.
138. *Ibid.*
139. Please note also that some cases which faced intense enforcement in other Member States were dealt with by the UOKIK without adopting a formal decision. Importantly, this is the case of booking.com clauses and UBER transportation practices.
140. For possible explanations *see* Bernatt, (*supra* n. 15).
141. *Ibid.*
142. *See* Maciej Janik, Maciej Bernatt and Marta Sznajder, 'Main Developments in Competition Law and Policy 2021 – Poland' (Kluwer Competition Law Blog, 18 May 2022) http://competitionlawblog.kluwercompetitionlaw.com/2022/05/18/main-developments-in-competition-law-and-policy-2021-poland/, accessed 17 March 2023.

The data collected reflect also an interesting change that occurred in the substance of the UOKIK decisions: the diminishing ratio of infringement decisions in abuse of dominance cases.[143] In 2004-2007 more than half of the judgments concerned abuse of dominance cases. Since 2009 the number of abuse of dominance judgments diminished but they continued to exist. Since 2019, only two abuse of dominance decisions have been issued. Still, one also has to notice that many abuse of dominance judgments concerned practices which have rarely been subject to the European Commission's attention: many cases involve exploitative, or exploitative-exclusionary practices rather than simply exclusionary cases.[144] In particular, they often involved unfair contractual terms applied by the dominant firms vis-à-vis their customers.[145] Moreover, Polish experience involving unfair price cases has allowed the Supreme Court to establish parameters helping in the assessment of whether a given price is unfair or not.[146] There are also some interesting judgments concerning exclusionary practices, including predatory pricing.[147]

Another characteristic feature is that while the restrictive agreement judgments concern exclusively 'by-object' restrictions, a significant ratio of these 'by-object' cases involve vertical, and not horizontal agreements.[148] This is explained by the de facto prioritisation of RPM cases by UOKIK and the rejection by the SCP of the interpretation of these agreements as 'by-effect' restrictions despite the repetitive claims in this respect by the parties involved.

At the same time, while the statistics show that 'by-object' cases clearly dominate case law, it does not mean that the courts do not have a chance to explain the difference between 'by-object' and 'by-effect' restrictions. In particular, in its judgment in the interchange fee case, the Supreme Court distinguished between naked, hard-core price cartels and the agreements which while horizontal do not involve setting the price of the services at stake in a direct way.[149] Furthermore, the SCP confirmed a place for the analysis of pro-competitive characteristics of such agreements under Article 101(3) TFEU (and the national counterpart of this provision), in particular with respect to the question of whether consumers received a fair share of the benefits which materialised as a result of the implementation of the interchange fee agreement by the banks

143. *See supra* Figure 23.6.
144. Some of the exploitative cases have also exclusionary characteristics. *See* Maciej Gac and Maciej Bernatt, 'Rail Freight: How Does Poland Assesses Alleged Abuses by Dominant Firms' (2017) 8(6) Journal of European Competition Law & Practice 388.
145. This was the case of Dolnośląska Spółka Gazownictwa Sp. z o.o. (UOKIK decision no. RWR-1/2009).
146. An interesting example is the case of Stalexport. *See* Bernatt (*supra* n. 30) 114.
147. *See* Konrad Kohutek, 'Shall Selective, Above-Cost Price Cutting in the Newspaper Market Be Qualified as Anticompetitive Exclusion? Case Comment to the Judgment of the Supreme Court of 19 August 2009 – Marquard Media Polska (Ref. No. III SK 5/09)' (2010) 3(3) Yearbook of Antitrust and Regulatory Studies 294, 295-297.
148. Sixty per cent of all the analysed judgments relating to restrictive agreements concerned vertical agreements.
149. The SCP judgment of 25 October 2017, III SK 38/16.

involved. This judgment is also representative in terms of the influence that the CJEU case law has on the interpretation of national competition law.[150]

5.2 Unique Model of Judicial Review in Poland

As already discussed above, the model of judicial review in Poland reveals characteristics which distinguish it from the typical model of judicial review of administrative action in some other European countries. In particular, the review by the CCCP has a *de novo* character and the CCCP is empowered to overrule (change) the UOKIK decision in all respects (facts, law and fines). It goes beyond classic legality review as the CCCP, as a civil court, is competent to conduct fresh evidentiary proceedings to establish whether the infringement of competition law indeed took place rather than simply verifying the correctness of the UOKIK findings.

However, the existing studies demonstrated that, while different on paper, judicial review in Polish competition law is closer to the model known from EU law than one could expect. In practice, the CCCP acts as a review court and it aims to verify whether the NCA was correct on the merits in finding the infringement of competition law.[151] Clearly, it does not act as a typical civil, first-instance court establishing the facts of the case through broad evidentiary proceedings. The principal difference to the model known from cassatory-style jurisdictions is that, in the case of negative verification of the UOKIK decisions, the CCCP issues a judgment in which it overturns the UOKIK decision and declares the infringement not to exist. According to the SCP case law, such a resolution of the case should take place if the evidence collected does not support the UOKIK legal determination[152], or if the CCCP believes that UOKIK misinterpreted the law.[153] However, once the procedural irregularities concerning the UOKIK decision or the proceedings leading to its adoption are identified, the CCCP is competent to annul the UOKIK decision. The legal controversies in this respect discussed above[154] are now resolved and the CCCP is entitled to annul the NCA decision if a significant procedural error in the decision has been made, or if the procedural mistakes committed during the proceedings before the UOKIK affected the outcome of the UOKIK decision.[155]

The data collected for the purpose of this research (e.g., Figure 23.4(a)) demonstrate that the CCCP, even though it is very often confronted with substantive grounds of appeals, accepts them only occasionally. Moreover, in view of the fact that appeals against UOKIK decisions are in most of the cases unsuccessful, the above-mentioned tendency may be seen as a confirmation of the view that the CCCP is in practice more of a review court than a first-instance decision-maker, making an entirely new

150. The SCP relied on the CJEU ruling in case C-382/12 *MasterCard Inc. and Others v. European Commission* [2014] ECLI:EU:C:2014:2201.
151. *See supra* section 3. *See*, among others, the SCP judgments of 12 April 2013, III SK 28/12 and of 5 November 2015, III SK 7/15.
152. The SCP judgment of 7 March 2018, III SK 6/17.
153. *See, supra*, section 2.
154. *See, supra*, sections 2-3 and the literature invoked there.
155. *See, supra*, section 2.

assessment *ab initio*.[156] In theory, this was to be the role foreseen for the CCCP, which the more recent jurisprudence considers as a court that does not have to rely on the findings of the UOKIK. Therefore, it should, first of all, make its own assessment of the collected evidence, and where necessary supplement it. The practical extent of these evidentiary powers is, however, often disputed by academics as the CCCP does not possess such wide means of enquiry as UOKIK (e.g., dawn raids, requests for information, market studies).[157] As a result, though not limited to the facts established by the UOKIK, in practice, the CCCP normally does not conduct evidentiary proceedings, instead it contents itself with verifying whether the proof gathered by the UOKIK is sufficiently convincing and credible.[158]

Indeed, the CCCP is sometimes believed to marginalise not only the evidentiary duties attributed to it by the jurisprudence but also even those required by the law itself (e.g., the statement of reasons in CCCP judgment sometimes lacks the required discussion on how evidence was assessed). Consequently, the facts of the case provided in CCCP judgments tend to be identical to the facts established in the appealed UOKIK decision.[159]

5.3 Institutional Organisation of Judicial Review and Its Disadvantages

Another characteristic feature of judicial review in Poland is its multilevel structure. To start with, it is clear today,[160] that the CCCP is the first-instance court. In light of the actual way in which the judicial review by CCCP operates, this could be considered surprising, but it is well-grounded in the case law of the Constitutional Court and the SCP.[161] CCCP judgments are subject to an appeal before the Court of Appeal in Warsaw, and then, on an extraordinary basis, to cassatory complaint before the Supreme Court. If we take into account that, in practice, the SCP has been ready to accept these complaints and adjudicate on the merits of the case, we see that the decision-making in Poland in competition law cases takes place on four levels; clearly a very complex institutional model.

One could consider the multilevel structure of judicial review as an advantage since it provides many opportunities for errors to be corrected. However, such a system has several weaknesses as well. The first one relates to the length of judicial

156. *See* Bernatt (*supra* n. 30) 103; Marek Szydło, 'Sądowa kontrola decyzji Prezesa UOKiK w świetle prawa unijnego i prawa polskiego' (2015) 7 Europejski Przegląd Sądowy 13, 16.
157. Dariusz Aziewicz and Maciej Bernatt quoted in Radek Wasilewski, *Postępowanie dowodowe przed Prezesem Urzędu Ochrony Konkurencji i Konsumentów* (CH Beck 2020) 329-330.
158. Marek Szydło quoted in Wasilewski (*supra* n. 159) 329-330.
159. In fact, the CCCP after repeating the facts of the case, as established in the UOKIK's decision, sometimes provides a very terse explanation of the facts assessed during the appeal, which tends to be a variation of the following phrase: 'The above-mentioned facts of the case have been established on the basis of documents comprising the case file for the administrative part of the proceedings, and the court case file, which none of the parties questioned, while the court found no basis to doubt their veracity' (e.g., the CCCP judgments: of 20 August 2018, XVII AmA 48/16; of 7 September 2018, XVII AmA 45/15; 15 October 2018, XVII AmA 68/16).
160. For the legal controversies in the past *see*, *supra*, section 3.
161. *See*, *supra*, section 2.

proceedings. In complex cases, it takes several years for the UOKIK decision to become final. This is related not only to the mere fact that the proceedings before each court involved last for a long time[162] but also because cases can be remitted back to lower-instance courts, which means a judgment needs to be adopted again and may be subject to further appeal. Sometimes this can take the form of a veritable judicial 'ping-pong', where a case will 'travel' for several years between the CCCP, the CoA and the SCP. The second relates to the deterrence of competition law enforcement. In contrast with proceedings before the Commission or some of the other NCAs, fines imposed by UOKIK for competition law violations are not due until the decision is confirmed by the review courts.[163] Therefore, the multilevel character of judicial review prolongs, very often for several years, the point at which firms feel the actual consequences of their anticompetitive behaviour. This is further exacerbated by the fact that in some cases courts opt for a reduction of the fines imposed despite simultaneously upholding the UOKIK decision on the merits.[164]

In more general terms, such a multilevel structure makes sense if expertise related to competition law at all appeal instances is present and judges are open to confronting themselves with the complex nature of antitrust cases. The existing studies suggest that competition law-related expertise is a rare asset in the judiciary[165] and that in the new millennium, it used to characterise principally the SCP (up until 2018).[166] Such expertise within the CCCP used to vary and depend very much on the particular judge.[167] That era does not seem to be completely over but one could argue that today some of the judges at the CCCP are more open to undertaking in-depth scrutiny than they used to be in the past. This might not only be a matter of expertise but also personality, and therefore is very difficult to measure in an objective way. Still, in recent years there are examples of judgments and judicial proceedings before the CCCP in which judges became involved in a detailed analysis of the substance of UOKIK decisions.[168] Moreover, the recent judgment of the CCCP in the *Agora/Eurozet media merger* case also confirms that there are judges in the CCCP who are ready to conduct a profound review of UOKIK decisions, even despite the political nature of the case and the pressure that judges faced in Poland in recent years.[169]

162. For an explanation of various reasons in this respect *see* Martyniszyn and Bernatt (*supra* n. 4), 205-207.
163. In other words, the appeal against the UOKIK decision by its addressee suspends the obligation to pay a fine imposed in this decision.
164. *See* Bernatt (*supra* n. 69) 22-24.
165. Bernatt (*supra* n. 17) 357.
166. In 2017, the reform in the SCP took place and the adjudication in the competition law cases was moved to the new Chamber of Extraordinary Review and Public Affairs which was composed of newly appointed judges. *See* more, *ibid*.
167. Limited number of judge-assistants in courts leave individual judges often de facto alone with complex competition law cases.
168. *See*, for example, the CCCP judgment of 2 December 2019, XVII Ama 23/17.
169. *See* the CCCP judgment of 12 May 2022, XVII AmA 61/21.

5.4 Effectiveness and Intensity of Judicial Review

One of the key procedural questions in competition law relates to the intensity of judicial review and the scope of judicial deference. The studies conducted so far suggest that the challenge here lies in building a competition law system in a way that allows competition authorities to undertake their tasks efficiently while guaranteeing control over their activity. In other words, it is necessary for the courts to play their traditional role, namely to protect the lawfulness of administrative action and individual rights. However, the courts should not replace expert administrative authorities such as competition authorities in the fulfilment of the tasks delegated by the legislator.[170] The deferential style of judicial review of competition authorities' determinations based on their expert knowledge or on competition policy considerations should be considered permissible on the condition that administrative proceedings before the competition authority are fair, competent and impartial.[171] The final condition is that judicial review should be effective.[172] Only after courts exercise effective review, may they defer to the conclusions reached by the competition authority. In particular, before deferring to the competition authority's expert assessment the courts need to do their job by checking whether the law was interpreted and applied correctly by the competition authority and whether the evidence collected supports the conclusion reached by the competition authority.[173] Judicial review should also cover the NCA's economic assessment and the amount of fine. It is also crucial for the courts to review any alleged violations of a procedural nature by the competition authority.[174]

Against this backdrop, Poland's experience does not offer a clear picture. At the outset, statistics suggest that the CCCP tends to uphold the majority of UOKIK's decisions. This was the case with 67% of UOKIK's decisions in the reviewed period (May 2004-April 2021).[175] Still, the key question is whether UOKIK's decisions are upheld after an effective review by the CCCP, or whether the latter provides merely a formalistic and superficial review. The study conducted back in 2016 showed that in several cases the review by the CCCP was superficial and that the higher instance courts had to intervene to order the CCCP to re-consider the case under the appeal.[176] It has also been shown that, as already discussed, despite having clear powers in this respect, the CCCP tended not to review new evidence or to engage in active verification of the correctness of the UOKIK findings, for example, by hearing witnesses.[177]

170. *See* Bernatt (*supra* n. 68) 324-325.
171. *Ibid.*
172. *Ibid.*
173. *Ibid.*
174. Maciej Bernatt, 'Administrative Sanctions: Between Efficiency and Procedural Fairness' (2016) 9(1) Review of European Administrative Law 5, 31-32.
175. *See, supra,* Figure 23.3.
176. Bernatt (*supra* n. 30) 104-106.
177. For example, in the RPM case concerning a vertical agreement between the producer of paints and varnishes Polifarb Cieszyn and its distributors, in the judgment of 9 October 2009, VI ACa 86/09, the CoA accepted the use by the CCCP of presumptions of fact to prove the existence of the vertical agreement. Still, the CoA was not satisfied with the CCCP's review. It held that the

The research conducted was open-ended and not aimed at proving any preconceived hypothesis, e.g., whether the aforementioned, previously identified tendencies continue to exist. However, taking into consideration several judgments delivered after 2016 one is inclined to consider that it may still be the case. For example, in the interchange fee case mentioned above, the SCP, and subsequently also the CoA, sent the case back to the CCCP to establish whether the benefits originating from the banks' agreement in question were transferred to consumers. Clearly, this question has not been sufficiently analysed by the CCCP. The judgments in appeal cases are still subject to the careful scrutiny of higher instance courts in recent case law. However, it seems noticeable that in a majority of the cases from the last four years, in which judgments were remanded in order to rectify the lower-instance courts' errors, the SCP ruled in favour of UOKIK.[178] At the same time, there are cases in which the CCCP offers effective judicial review.[179] Ultimately, as mentioned above, the effectiveness of judicial review in the first instance may also to some extent be judge-related.

As far as the intensity of judicial review is concerned, the existing study showed that in practice courts tend not to defer to UOKIK complex economic assessments concerning the determination of the relevant market as well as with regard to its fining policy.[180] While the SCP in one of its judgments sent a signal that this could be possible, the UOKIK needs to actively defend its findings in the appeal proceedings rather than limiting itself to repeating what was established in its decision.[181] It is unclear regarding the position of new judges (so-called neo-judges due to political character and irregularities of their appointment process) of the SCP Chamber of Extraordinary Review and Public Affairs in this respect. Post-2018 case law does not address this question.

As far as fines are concerned, our studies confirm earlier findings[182] regarding the courts' readiness to reduce the amount of fines imposed by UOKIK. This phenomenon concerns both a relatively high ratio of cases in which fines were reduced (fine reductions took place in 19% of the cases before the CCCP, in 31% before the CoA and in 26% before the SCP) as well as a very high level of fine reductions (the average fine reduction in those cases was 78% before the CCCP, 79% before the CoA and 89% before the Supreme Court). This in turn, as was already mentioned above, has a negative impact on the deterrence of the competition law regime.

Regardless of the courts' actual readiness to accord judicial deference to UOKIK assessments, there were no changes in the organisation of the administrative phase of competition law proceedings before UOKIK in recent years which could serve as an

CCCP did not establish what role each of the firms concerned by the NCA decision played in the conclusion and realisation of the agreement, e.g., the first-instance court did not verify whether any evidence confirms the tacit acceptance of the pricing policy proposed by Polifarb Cieszyn.

178. For example, the CoA judgment of 2 October 2018, VII AGa 1161/18; the SCP judgments of: 15 February 2019, I NSK 10/18 and I NSK 11/18; 15 October 2019, I NSK 72/18; 5 December 2019, I NSK 1/19; 8 May 2020, I NSK 110/18.
179. The CCCP judgment of 2 December 2019, XVII Ama 23/17 and the CCCP judgment of 12 May 2022, XVII AmA 61/21.
180. Bernatt, (*supra* n. 30) 106-115.
181. *Ibid.*
182. Bernatt (*supra* n. 69) 22-24.

argument in favour of the introduction of greater judicial deference with respect to UOKIK expert or policy assessment. Crucially, the shortcomings concerning impartiality, expertise and due process safeguards in proceedings before the UOKIK continue to exist.[183] Furthermore, the actual independence of UOKIK is limited, which not only was demonstrated in recent research[184] but also brought to light, albeit indirectly, by the General Court in the *Sped Pro* case.[185] Hence, there are very few reasons to call for a more deferential style of judicial review. On the contrary, one should expect further improvements related to the effectiveness of judicial review, as well as reforms related to the administrative proceedings before UOKIK. The independence of UOKIK is also a key issue in this respect.

6 CONCLUDING REMARKS

Poland's experience with judicial review offers interesting lessons. In particular, the model of judicial review can be considered a point of reference for reforms in other countries. It sits well between two extremes: a cassatory, legality-focused model of judicial review, which tends to be formalistic and offers very limited space for the review of the substance of the competition authority's decision, and a very intrusive model of judicial review such as the one known from the UK, where the determinations made by the competition authority have in practice little or no weight in proceedings before the review body (such as the UK Competition Appeal Tribunal). This is not to say that judicial review has no scope for improvement. The list is relatively long and includes, among others, challenges such as the length of judicial proceedings, insufficient expertise of judges and courts' resources as well as the rule of law shortcomings, all of which affect the competition law system. Finally, a key question is how to safeguard full judicial review of UOKIK decisions while upholding the effective nature of competition law enforcement. In this context a three-level system of judicial review is far from perfect as it prolongs, very often for several years, the moment at which UOKIK's decisions become final.

183. Bernatt (*supra* n. 30). With respect to due process *see* Bernatt, (*supra* n. 136) 99-238.
184. Bernatt (*supra* n. 15) 66-79.
185. *See* Bernatt (*supra* n. 74) 213-215.

CHAPTER 24

Portugal Report

Miguel Sousa Ferro

1 INTRODUCTION TO THE COMPETITION LAW ENFORCEMENT CONTEXT IN PORTUGAL

Portuguese Competition Law is compiled in the Competition Act ('CA', Law 19/2012, of 8 May, as amended by Law 23/2018, of 5 June, by Decree-Law 108/2021, of 7 December, and by Law 17/2022, of 17 August). The most recent amendment transposes the ECN+ Directive.

Both substantive and procedural rules are largely harmonised with those of EU Competition Law. Article 101 TFEU corresponds to Articles 9 and 10 CA. Article 102 TFEU corresponds to Article 11 CA.

The only differences at the level of substantive competition rules are the addition of a prohibition of abuse of economic dependency (Article 12 CA), and the recent addition of one more example to the types of prohibited collective practices listed in Article 9(1) CA, concerning 'Most Favoured Nation' clauses in contracts with online platforms in the tourism/local housing sectors.

The Competition Act is enforced by the Portuguese Competition Authority ('AdC'). The AdC is an independent regulator, created in 2003, with a total staff of ninety-three workers. It seems fair to say that its human resources are limited for the tasks entrusted to it, namely in what concerns anticompetitive practices, and especially in light of the very high degree of litigiousness with which AdC Decisions are met.

The AdC's powers are very similar to those of the European Commission. It is empowered to adopt decisions declaring infringements and imposing fines up to 10% of the undertakings' turnover in the preceding year, to adopt commitment decisions, to impose provisional measures, to carry out dawn raids and order undertakings or any other person to provide it with documents, etc. The AdC may only carry out dawn raids if authorised to do so by judicial order (*see* below the discussion on whether this authorisation should be by the Public Prosecutor or by a judge), and within the limits defined therein. Inspections at some types of locations, or relating to certain types of evidence, require prior authorisation by a judge (and, in some cases, even the physical presence of a judge during the inspection).

The intensity of AdC activity has varied significantly during the mandates of different Boards. The Board in place from 2017 to 2023 was particularly active and adopted a comparatively high number of decisions during its mandate, imposing fines of larger amounts than tended to be imposed up to now.

A famous example is the so-called banking cartel, an investigation initiated in 2012, with a leniency application and dawn raids, and concluded in 2019 with the imposition of total fines of EUR 225 million. This decision is still being appealed, and it is sure to spark a complex discussion as to whether Portuguese law complied with EU Law (prior to ECN + Directive), as it allowed the time-barring of fines while an appeal of the AdC Decision was pending. Interestingly, the discussion could likely have been simpler if not for a discrepancy between the temporal scope of the ECN + Directive and its transposition in Portugal. A special (and unusual) temporal scope provision was included in the latter so that none of its rules apply to investigations initiated prior to the entry into force of the transposition. This prevented the new limitation period rule (no time-barring while appeals are pending) from applying, in the future, to pending cases, in an analogous application of the *Volvo DAF Trucks* (C-627/20) case law.

In the course of investigating an anti-competitive practice by a beer supplier, the AdC had access to documents which made it aware of other (apparent) widespread anticompetitive practices between large supermarket chains in Portugal and some of their suppliers. This became known as the Hub & Spoke group of cases. Seventeen investigations were opened, leading to ten Decisions being adopted. More than EUR 600 million in fines were imposed in the Hub & Spoke group of cases. Every one of these decisions has already been or is expected to be, appealed. A recent judgment of the Portuguese Constitutional Court has raised the prospect that all of these decisions may fall, under the fruit of the poisoned tree principle. From the beginning, it has been the systematic practice of the AdC, confirmed countless times by the courts, to carry out dawn raids with an order from the Public Prosecutor. The Constitutional Court has now stated that this is unconstitutional and that dawn raids can only be carried out with an order from a judge, and it did not limit the temporal effects of its ruling.

The leniency policy has played an important role in the initiation of AdC cases, but the majority of cases result from complaints submitted to the AdC or from its own initiative and investigations. In the period under assessment, Portugal did not see the same rate of use of its leniency policy as other Member States, including its neighbour Spain. More recently, however, it has seen a record number of leniency applications, and this despite the particularly active private enforcement scene in Portugal, namely as a result of consumer opt-out representative actions.

The AdC receives a high number of complaints per year and is required by law to respond, but it is free to prioritise cases and to decide not to pursue one, even if it believes there could be an infringement of competition law if it deems it not to fit within its current enforcement priorities. The AdC's enforcement priorities are defined by the AdC and published annually.

2 REVIEW OF THE COMPETITION AUTHORITY'S DECISIONS

Appeals of AdC Decisions are heard by the specialised Competition, Regulation and Supervision Court ('TCRS'), created in 2012. This is a court seated in Santarém (one hour north of Lisbon), which belongs to the Civil branch of the judiciary (not the Administrative one). Prior to the creation of the TCRS, these appeals went to the Lisbon Commercial Court.

The TCRS is competent to decide appeals of AdC decisions applying antitrust and merger control rules, but it does not centralise jurisdiction for every case against the AdC. Certain challenges raised in the context of dawn raids go before a criminal court. Actions for access to documents and actions invoking the liability of the AdC go before administrative courts.

The TCRS is also competent to hear appeals of decisions imposing fines adopted by Portuguese independent sectoral regulators (banking, securities, energy, water, health, etc.), and to decide antitrust private enforcement cases (as long as they are based exclusively on competition law). The Court's activity associated with AdC decisions takes up a minority of its total activity.

Competition Law in Portugal is deemed a branch of Misdemeanour Law, to which Criminal Law is applicable subsidiarily. This has numerous implications, both substantively and procedurally. One consequence of this is that courts deciding ordinary appeals of AdC decisions, at any stage of appeal, have the power of full review. They can amend (including increase) the fine.

Undertakings targeted by AdC Decisions had a non-extendable deadline of thirty working days (recently changed to sixty continuous days) to file their appeals, which are submitted to the AdC, who then forwards them to the TCRS. This is a frequently criticised aspect of the protection of the rights of the defence, as the deadline cannot be extended even if the AdC took months to write a Decision with several hundreds of pages and thousands of annexed documents. In the second stage of appeal, the deadline was even shorter. Parties wishing to appeal a ruling of the TCRS had only ten days to do so (now extended to thirty days).

The TCRS currently has four career judges and three Public Prosecutors. Public Prosecutors represent the State and usually argue alongside the AdC in court, but they are independent and have been known to argue for the annulment of an AdC Decision or for the reduction of fines. Judges who apply to the Competition Court must have at least ten years of experience as magistrates, but knowledge of competition or regulatory law is not a prerequisite, nor does it factor into the placement of candidates (only criteria are seniority and evaluations awarded by inspectors). As a result, typically, judges are not yet specialised in Competition Law when they begin their functions at the Court and must learn on the job. Together with a significant degree of turnover of judges, this has meant that the specialised nature of the TCRS has not been achieved in practice to the degree that was intended. But some of the judges have remained for several years at the Court, with one judge being there almost since its inception.

Each case is heard by an individual judge, with no possibility of a collective of judges for any type of case. The TCRS does not have economists or other technical experts of its own, but can and does, in individual cases, seek the assistance of external experts (notwithstanding difficulties frequently felt in identifying suitable experts).

TCRS judgments relating to AdC Decisions may (freely) be appealed to the Lisbon Appeal Court (TRL). The TRL is empowered to review both the facts and the law. Since the 2020s, all appeals relating to AdC Decisions (or in antitrust private enforcement actions) are heard by a specific chamber of the TRL, specialised in Antitrust Law, Regulatory Law and Intellectual Property Law. The number of judges in this specialised section currently has varied in time, from three to seven judges. As with the TCRS, these are all career magistrates, who arrive at the specialised section with potentially no specific training in Competition Law or experience applying it, learning on the job. While it is still too early to say, it is possible that the composition of this specialised chamber will be more stable than at the TCRS, with a smaller degree of turnover.

AdC Decisions have only two stages of ordinary appeal. A further appeal to the Portuguese Supreme Court is not possible (although there are exceptional circumstances in which the Supreme Court may be called on to make rulings in the context of AdC cases). Initially, this restriction was introduced to reduce the duration of judicial review, due to concerns that cases were becoming time-barred pending appeals. There are frequent calls (namely from the Supreme Court itself) to allow this further stage of appeal. The transposition of the ECN + Directive makes it impossible for AdC decisions to become time-barred pending judicial review, and this eliminates the original motivation for the exclusion of the Supreme Court from the review of AdC Decisions. But there have been no signs of an intention to allow an additional appeal to the Supreme Court. The Supreme Court's record in competition law, typically tackling such cases with civil law arguments or affirming interpretations in contradiction with CJEU case law, may explain some of the reluctance to add this additional step of judicial review for AdC Decisions.

After the Lisbon Appeal Court, AdC Decisions may still, if certain requisites are met, be appealed to the Portuguese Constitutional Court. This is allowed, in essence, when the appellant has raised issues of constitutionality, phrased in a specific manner, before the courts up to that point. The Constitutional Court is called on very frequently to rule on issues in the framework of appeals of AdC Decisions. Indeed, 27% of the coded judgments are Constitutional Court judgments.

While it was not always so, AdC Decisions are now almost always appealed. The increase in fines may be a contributing factor to this reality. But the decisive factor is probably the new reality of antitrust private enforcement, resulting from the transposition of the Damages Directive and the initiation of several follow-on opt-out representative actions on behalf of consumers. This has led to surprising situations, such as a beneficiary of immunity under the leniency policy appealing the AdC's decision to challenge the amount of the fine (which was not imposed on it), or a beneficiary of a 50% reduction of the fine under the leniency policy appealing the AdC's decision and challenging the existence of the infringement itself.

Within the period under assessment, AdC decisions were frequently unsuccessful (usually, for procedural reasons) before the Lisbon Commercial Court, or their fines were significantly reduced, but were subsequently almost never annulled by the TCRS. In April 2023, the TCRS annulled an AdC cartel decision, its first full annulment ever of an antitrust decision since the new Competition Act entered into force. On the other hand, the recent trend of TCRS rulings has shown a willingness not to reduce fines and, in practice, to increase them (e.g., keeping the same fine for an infringement with a narrower scope).

The number of judicial decisions falling within the scope of this study is relatively limited. However, first, this hides a much broader judicial activity of the TCRS and Lisbon Appeal Court. The CA has a procedural particularity. It allows autonomous appeals of interlocutory decisions of the AdC before the adoption of the final decision (e.g., challenges to the qualification of certain documents as non-confidential; challenges to the legality of information requests or to the validity of certain means of evidence; etc.). In other legal orders, these issues would typically be discussed in the appeal of the final decision. Especially in recent years, this type of case has become the large majority of the AdC-related cases heard by the TCRS. It seems to be a significant strain on the Court's resources, and also on those of the AdC. This part of the Court's activity is not reflected in the present report.

Second, in the period covered by the report, the AdC's activity was less intense (in terms of the number of Decisions adopted) than under the Board of 2017–2023. This relatively recent increase in the number of AdC Decisions, which will eventually be reflected in an increase in judgments, is not yet reflected in the period covered by this report.

Access to justice is relatively inexpensive in Portugal when compared to other Member States. Court costs for appeals are very low (usually between EUR 600 and EUR 1,000), and the losing side only has to pay adverse costs (e.g., the winning side's legal fees) up to half the amount of the court costs. However, companies targeted by AdC Decisions may still be required to invest significant amounts in lawyers, economists and other experts, in order to adequately defend their case.

3 PRIOR RESEARCH

There is a very limited amount of empirical research on appeals and judicial review of AdC decisions in Portugal.

A research project is currently underway, by CIDEEFF (a research centre of the Lisbon University Law School), to compile all competition law-related judicial decisions (public and private enforcement) in a single database. This is aimed at contributing to overcoming the difficulties of access to judicial decisions in Portugal, where first-instance rulings are not published, not all second and third-instance rulings and judgments are published, and requests for access to court case files or rulings (even to non-confidential versions) are not always granted. The AdC has a legal obligation, under the CA, to publish some judgments relating to its decisions, but it does not always comply – at least promptly – with this obligation, and it is not obliged to publish other types of judicial rulings in appeals relating to its Decisions. The lack of transparency in the Portuguese judicial system is not a problem specific to the competition law area. Very recently, the Portuguese Government has begun exploring the possibility of publishing all first-instance judgments online, and an initiative has been introduced in Parliament to that effect, but it is now known if and when such projects will bear fruit.

For additional information on the judicial review of AdC decisions in Portugal, and on the TCRS itself, *see*:

(a) Miguel Gorjão-Henriques (coord.), *Lei da Concorrência – Comentário Conimbricense*, 2nd edition, Almedina, 2017 – providing a more in-depth analysis of the applicable legal framework during the relevant period.
(b) Miguel Sousa Ferro, 'Tribunal da Concorrência, Regulação e Supervisão: uma análise jurídico-económica no seu 5.º aniversário', (2017) 30 *Revista de Concorrência e Regulação* 143 – providing empirical data on judicial review in the 1st 5 years of the TCRS's existence.
(c) Luís Miguel Caldas, 'Dez anos do Tribunal da Concorrência, Regulação e Supervisão – Algumas notas e propostas', (2022) 49 *Revista de Concorrência e Regulação* – providing an overview by the President of the Court of Santarém on the first ten years of existence of the TCRS, with an emphasis on challenges it has faced and issues to be addressed.

4 QUANTITATIVE ANALYSIS

4.1 Source of Information

Court rulings are not all published in Portugal. Although the AdC has a legal obligation to publish all of the judicial decisions appealing fines imposed by it, there is sometimes a significant time lapse between their adoption and their publication on the AdC website, and omissions may occur. Not all such delays or omissions are necessarily unintentional. In 2023, after the AdC failed to publish a judgment adopted almost a year earlier in the important '*banking cartel*' case (declaring the AdC's decision time-barred for one of the participating undertakings), even after it was asked to do so, a consumer association filed a popular action against the AdC, asking an administrative court to order the AdC to publish the ruling. Only after the court served this claim on the AdC did it finally publish the ruling.

The judgments included in this report were obtained from the AdC website[1] and from the DGSI website,[2] a Ministry of Justice-run website that makes available (some)

1. https://www.concorrencia.pt/.
2. http://www.dgsi.pt/.

judgments of higher courts. These limited sources were, in some cases, completed with direct requests to the Competition Court for access to certain rulings. The method used should ensure that the result is nearly complete, but potentially not exhaustive.

4.2 Total Number of Cases

A total of 100 judgments were identified within the temporal scope of this report, relating to the review of 28 NCA decisions. During this period, 37% of the NCA decisions were appealed. 82% of the NCA decisions that were appealed to the first instance were appealed to the second-instance court (and this figure is underestimated, due to some judgments falling outside the period of analysis).

As a further appeal to the Supreme Court is, in principle, not possible, the number of appeals to the third instance is marginal. But not so with the number of appeals to the Constitutional Court. There are almost as many rulings from the Constitutional Court (twenty-eight) in the database as rulings of first (thirty-four) and second-instance (thirty-five) courts.

These figures are mostly explained by the fact that a significant percentage of NCA decisions were settlements and commitment decisions. It seems fair to say that, as a rule, NCA antitrust decisions which were not commitment decisions and were not the subject of a settlement were appealed.

4.3 Total Number of Cases per Year

Figure 24.1 summarises the number of judgments per year, according to the instance of appeal. Within the scope of this report, from 2004 to April 2021:

(a) the number of NCA decisions appealed each year varied between zero and five, with an average of 1.5 decisions per year;
(b) there were thirty-four first-instance judgments, varying between zero and five each year, with an average of 1.9 judgments per year;
(c) there were thirty-six second-instance judgments, varying between zero and six each year, with an average of two judgments per year;
(d) there were twenty-seven Constitutional Court judgments, with an average of 1.5 judgments per year.

Figure 24.1 Number of Judgments According to Instances

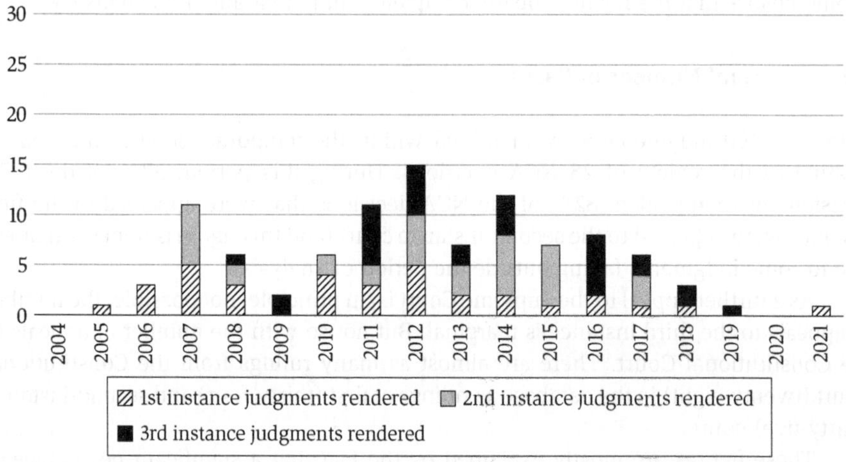

1st instance judgments rendered
2nd instance judgments rendered
3rd instance judgments rendered

No notable trends stand out during the period, which can be described as relatively stable.

Figure 24.2 indicates the number of judgments per year according to each instance (lines). It compares it with the number of NCA's decisions that were appealed in the first instance each year or the number of courts' judgments that were appealed in further instances (bars).

Figure 24.2(a) First-Instance Judgments

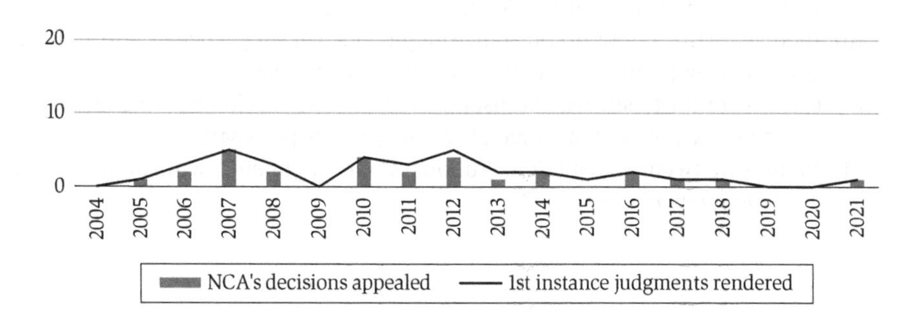

Figure 24.2(b) Second-Instance Judgments

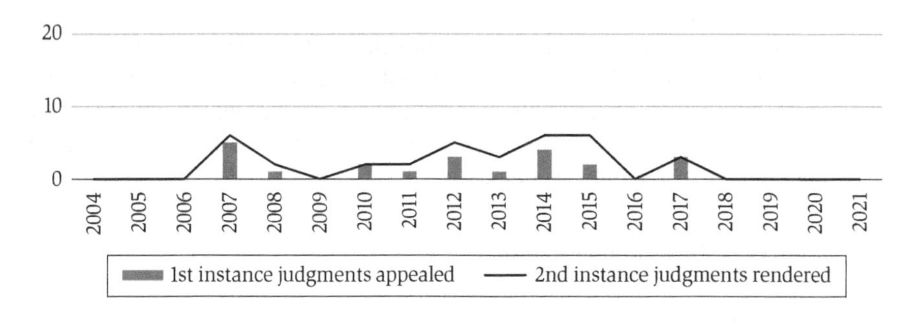

Figure 24.2(c) Third-Instance Judgments

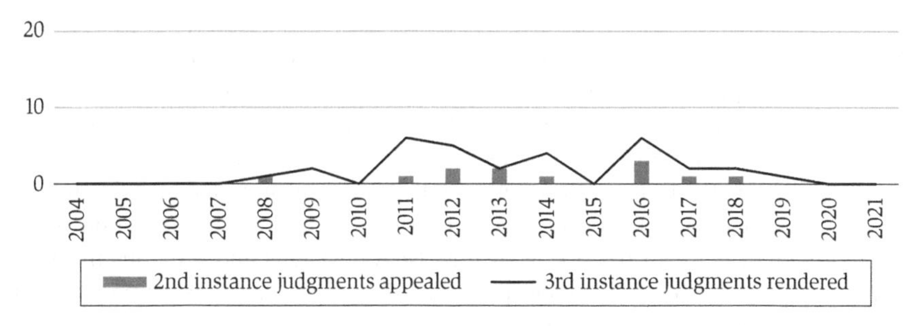

Figure 24.2 points to one feature of the Portuguese legal order, namely that procedural law is applied in such a way that frequently allows for two rulings to be issued at the same instance of appeal. For example, the second-instance court may issue a first ruling by a single judge, even though the defendant is then guaranteed a right to a second ruling from a collective panel of judges at the same court. Or there may be a ruling from a collective panel of judges, and Portuguese law allows the parties to request an amendment or a declaration of nullity of parts of that order. This explains why in so many cases a first ruling of the appeal or Constitutional court is followed by a second ruling of the same court just two or three months later.

The potentially surprising figure is the high number of Constitutional Court judgments in such cases (Figure 24.2(c)). Even more surprising when one considers that such appeals typically revolve around the repetition of the same issues. This is a reflection of the: (i) characteristics of the Portuguese legal order which grants a right of appeal to the Constitutional Court, even if the issue has already been decided many times before; (ii) very high litigiousness of undertakings in such proceedings; and (iii) sophistication of undertakings and their legal counsel, who are successful time and time again in having their appeals heard by a Court which rejects the vast majority of appeals it receives (generally) on highly formalistic grounds.

The fact that the relevant period ends in 2021 probably hides a more recent increase in judicial activity, as a result of the greater number of decisions adopted by the AdC in recent years.

It should be borne in mind that, in the statistics under analysis, a case is one or more appeals of the same AdC decision (all appeals are put together in the same case by the Court). As a result, a cartel with many members, each of which with their own appeal, counts as one case, just as an abuse of dominance case with a single appeal by a single undertaking also counts as one case.

4.4 Success Rates and Outcomes

Figure 24.3 summarises the success of appeals launched against either NCA's decisions or the previous instance's judgment. It demonstrates that only 10% of appeals against the NCA's decisions or previous instance's judgments were fully successful, leading to the annulment of the decision. Strikingly, while the Lisbon Commercial Court annulled several NCA decisions, the Competition Court has not once (during the period under analysis) annulled an NCA antitrust decision, since its inception. This may be said to reflect, at least in part, an evolution in the drafting of decisions by the NCA, and of its management of the procedure leading up to them. It also does not reflect an absence of control or 'rubber stamping' of decisions by the Competition Court.

In April 2023, the Competition Court for the first time annulled an NCA antitrust decision (insurance cartel), but an appeal is still pending before the Lisbon Appeal Court. Forty-eight per cent of appeals against NCA decisions and previous instance's judgments (16%) were entirely unsuccessful. In 42% of cases, at least some part of the decision was annulled or the fine was reduced.

In 84% of cases, undertakings were not fully successful in appealing an NCA decision, and this figure increased to 100% after the creation of the Competition Court (and until April 2023). Although this shows a contrast between the degrees of success of appellants, in the early phase, before the Lisbon Commercial Court and, subsequently, before the Competition Court, one shouldn't rush to the conclusion that the change of court wholly explains this. There were other variables during this same period of transition which could have had an impact, including a reform of the Competition Act and different types of cases and lessons learned by the NCA.

Within the framework mentioned in the previous point, outcomes vary significantly in the first instance. Figure 24.4 indicates the ratio of possible outcomes, according to each instance of appeal. In contrast with Figure 24.3, the data is presented from the perspective of each separate judgment. The greatest number of cases are those where the first-instance court partially annulled or partially replaced the decision and/or reduced the fine. Outcomes become much less varied in the second and third instances. The vast majority of appeals are unsuccessful, to the extent that, statistically, the odds are good that the outcome in the first instance will not change in subsequent appeals. Appeals to the Constitutional Court, in particular, were almost always – save once – unsuccessful (which hasn't stopped undertakings from routinely filing such appeals anyway).

Figure 24.3 Success of Appeals (Each NCA's Decision or Previous Instance Judgment Counts as One)

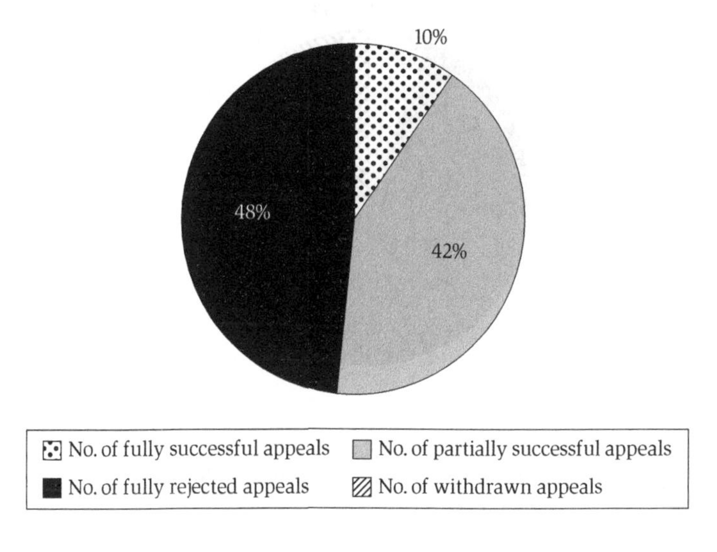

Figure 24.4(a) First-Instance Outcome

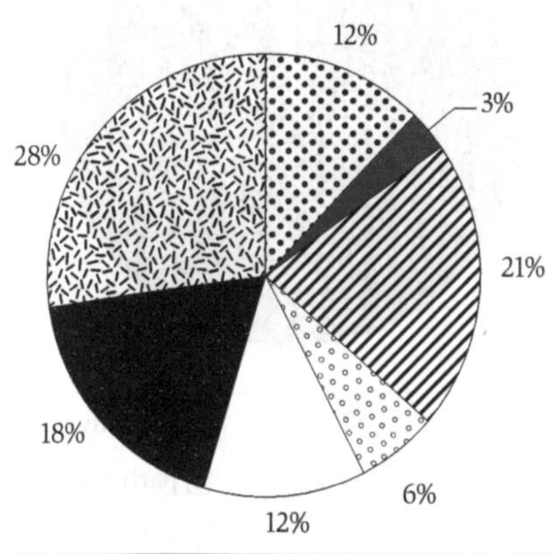

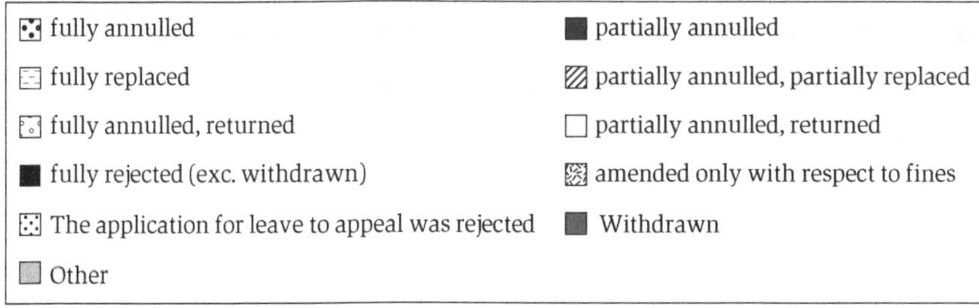

Figure 24.4(b) Second-Instance Outcome

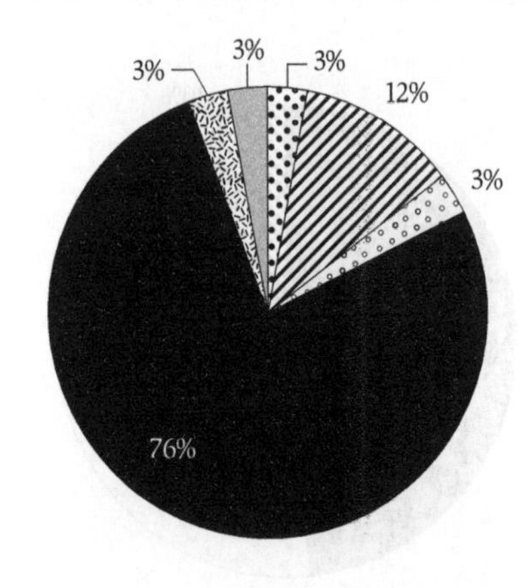

Figure 24.4(c) Third-Instance Outcome

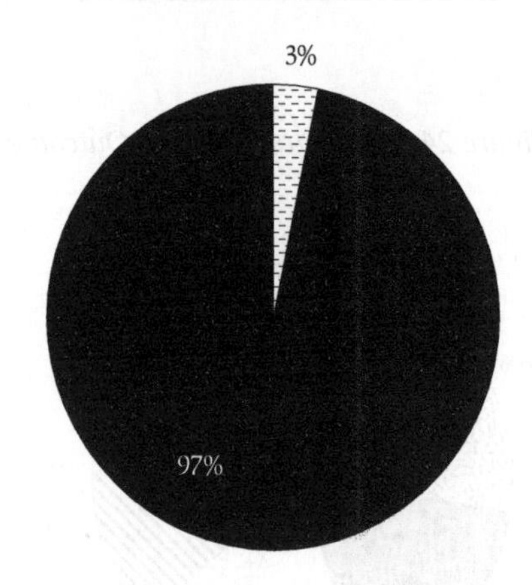

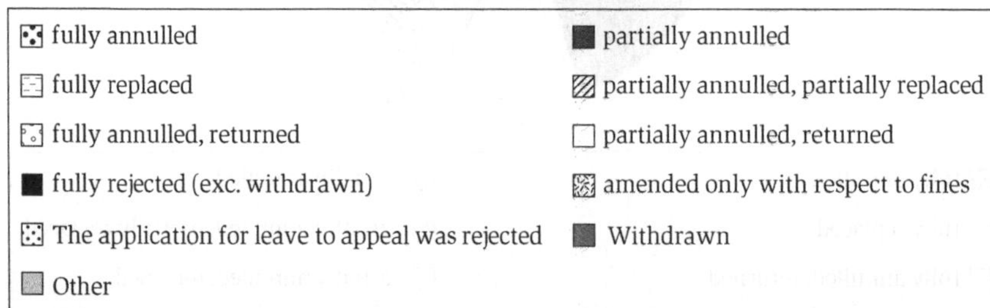

4.5 Type of NCA's Decisions Subject to Appeal

Figure 24.5 indicates the ratio of the different competition law prohibitions subject to the courts' review, across all instances of appeal. 84% of judgments concern appeals of Article 101 TFEU and/or its national equivalent. Thirteen per cent of judgments concerned Article 102 TFEU and its national equivalent. These figures are stable throughout the various instances and (proportionately) throughout the years of the relevant period (*see* Figure 24.6). They reflect a similar proportion of cases before the NCA. Fifty-six percent of judgments concern cases where only the national equivalent to Article 101 TFEU was in question, a figure which raises questions as to compliance with CJEU case law on the interpretation of the criterion of effect on trade between Member States. Particularly in an early phase of the case law, there was a tendency for courts to conclude an absence of effect on trade between MS in cases where, arguably, the CJEU case law would require at least a potential effect to be identified. Older approaches that refused to apply EU Law to agreements between Portuguese companies seem to have disappeared in more recent case law.

Figure 24.5 Rule Being Appealed

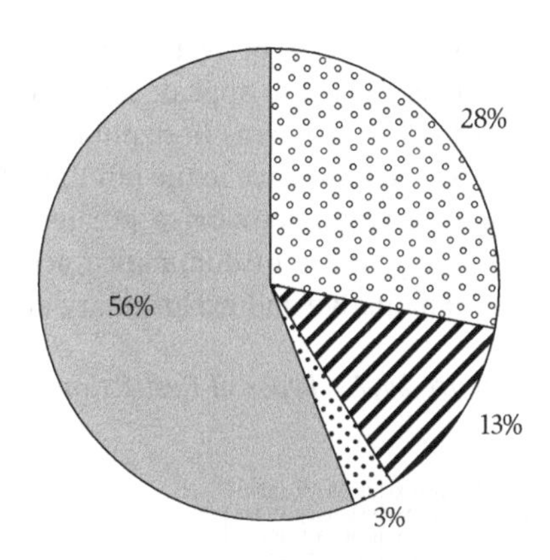

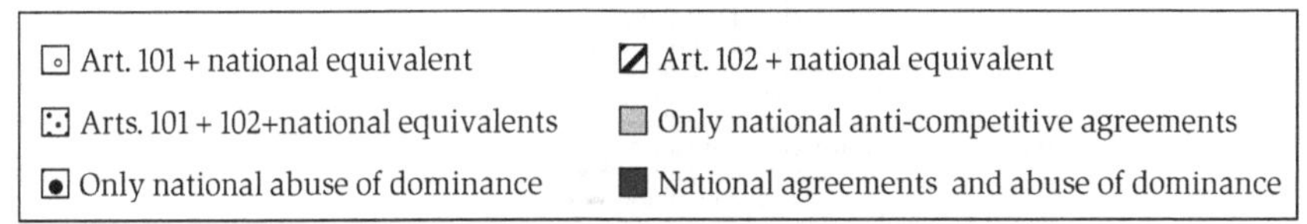

Figure 24.6 Rules Being Appealed According to Years (Each Judgment Counts as One)

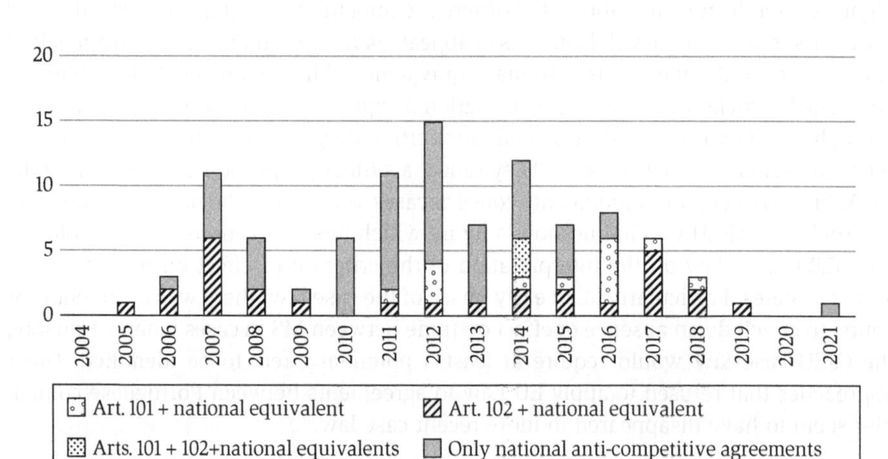

Figure 24.7 summarises the types of restrictions of competition that were examined in the NCA's decisions subject to appeal, across all instances of appeal. By far, the largest group of cases (75%) concerns horizontal restrictions. Vertical restrictions account for 10% of cases. The difference in the number of horizontal and vertical cases before the NCA is not as large, showing a greater tendency for appeals in horizontal than in vertical cases. Abuse of dominance accounts for 12% of cases, almost evenly split between exploitative and exclusionary abuses.

Figure 24.7 Types of Restrictions

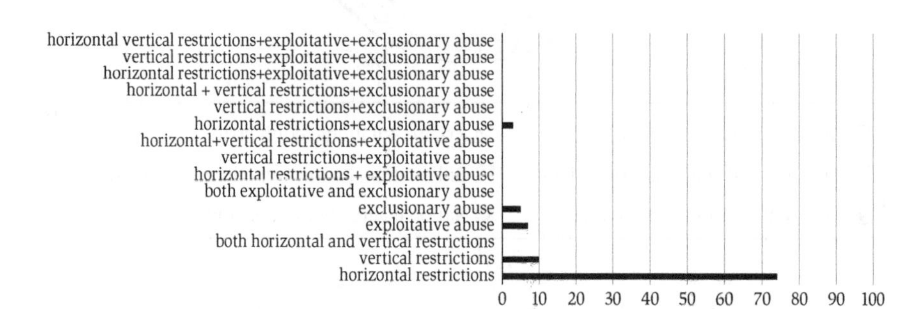

Figure 24.8 only examines appeals against NCA decisions where Article 101 TFEU and/or the national equivalent prohibition have been examined. It indicates the ratio of cases in which the NCA characterised or described the restriction of competition as by-object, by-effect, both by-object and by-effect, or left it unclassified. Within the infringements of Article 101 TFEU and its national equivalent, every single one was an

object restriction case. In 17% of cases, the NCA also tried to show restrictive effects, but it first argued for an object restriction.

Figure 24.8 Object/Effect (Only for Article 101/National Equivalent Infringements)

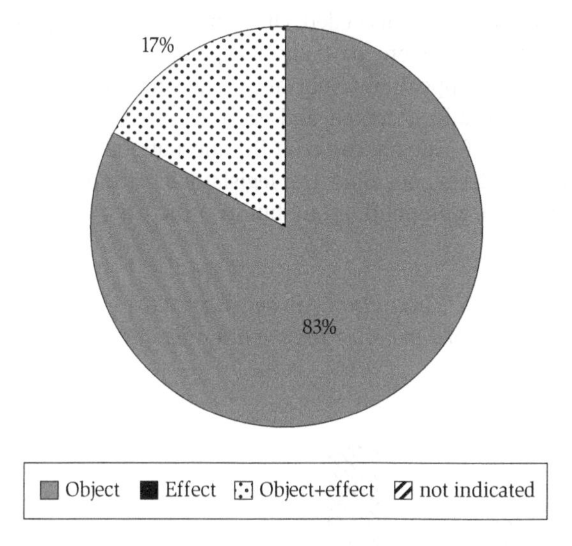

Figure 24.9 indicates the ratio of the type of NCA's procedures that were subject to judicial review, across all instances of appeal. Ninety-six percent of cases relate to NCA decisions declaring an infringement and imposing fines. One case related to a decision declaring an infringement but without a fine[3], one case related to commitments[4], and one to a finding of absence of grounds for action by the NCA[5].

Figure 24.9 Competition Authority's Procedure

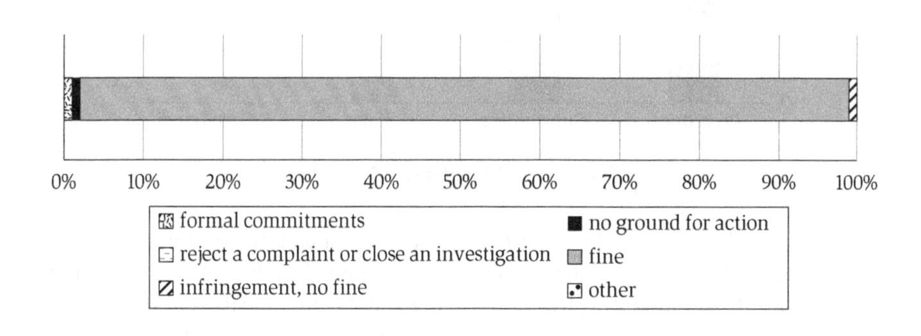

3. ANTRAM (412/09.4TYLSB).
4. Nestlé Portugal (766/06.4TYLSB).
5. GDA - Cooperativa de Gestão dos Direitos dos Artistas, Intérpretes ou Executantes (77/16.7YUSTR).

4.6 Grounds of Appeal

Figure 24.10 indicates the success of each ground of appeal launched by the parties to the procedure against an NCA's decision or on a previous instance's judgment. Appeals raising procedural grounds have been largely unsuccessful in full or in part. Only about 10% of such appeals have fully succeeded. Only one appeal seeking fine reduction was fully accepted,[6] while 41% were partially accepted and 56% were fully rejected. Similar figures apply to appeals on substantive grounds. Only four were fully accepted,[7] 17% were partially accepted and 75% were rejected. No cases could be identified where issues of primacy between EU and national law were raised, something which largely reflects, not only the legislator's harmonisation of Portuguese competition law with EU competition law but also the Courts' intention to interpret both harmoniously.

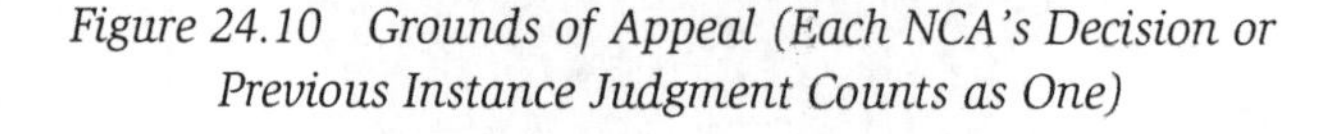

Figure 24.10 Grounds of Appeal (Each NCA's Decision or Previous Instance Judgment Counts as One)

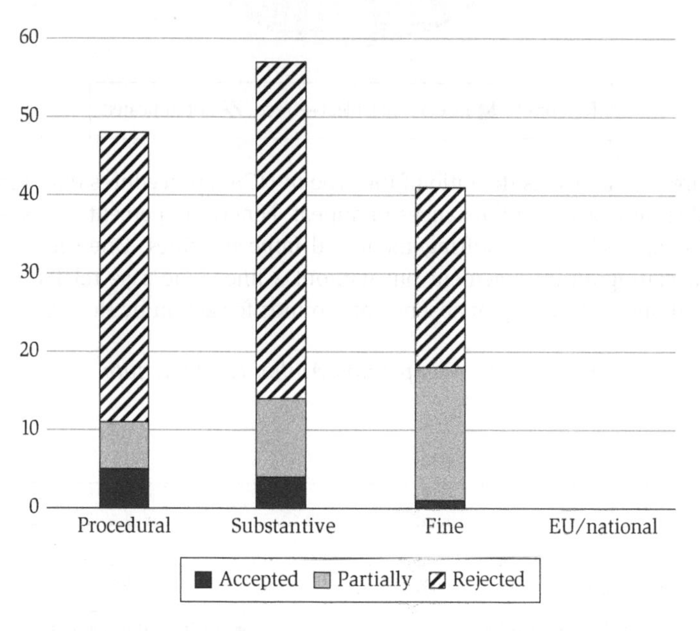

Figure 24.11 indicates the type of grounds of appeals raised by one or more parties against an NCA's decision or on a previous instance's judgment per year (lines). It also specifies the number of fully and partially successful appeals (bars). Unlike the previous figure, the data is presented from the perspective of each single appeal

6. PT Comunicações (1232/08.9TYLSB).
7. Aeronorte – Transportes Aéreos (48/08.7TYLSB); ANTRAM (412/09.4TYLSB); Portugal Telecom (1391/09.3TYLSB); PT Comunicações (1232/08.9TYLSB).

judgment (i.e., more than one judgment may be issued with respect to a single NCA decision). Figure 24.11 demonstrates that the argued grounds and their success rates are distributed yearly very proportionately. Nonetheless, these figures have changed in recent years, particularly after the period under analysis, with the Competition Court now showing itself less willing to reduce fines (even though the amount of the fines imposed by the NCA has increased).

Figure 24.11(a) Procedural Grounds

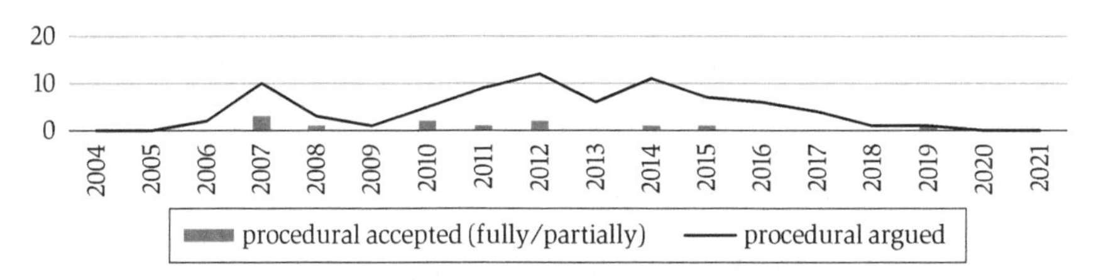

Figure 24.11(b) Substantive Grounds

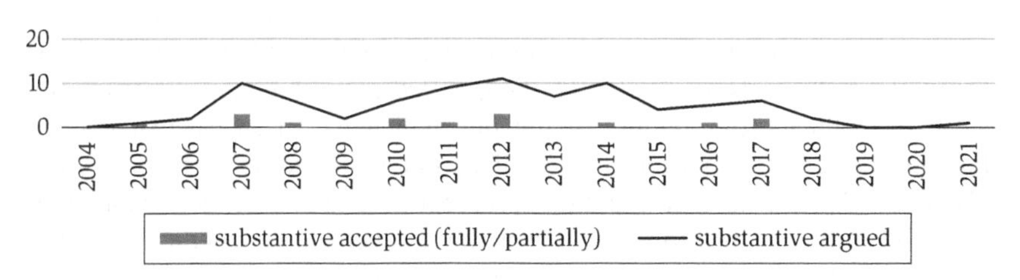

Figure 24.11(c) Fines-related Grounds

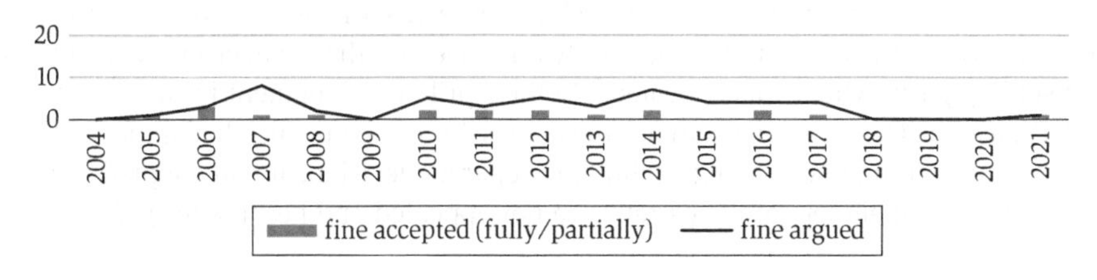

Figure 24.11(d) EU/National Grounds

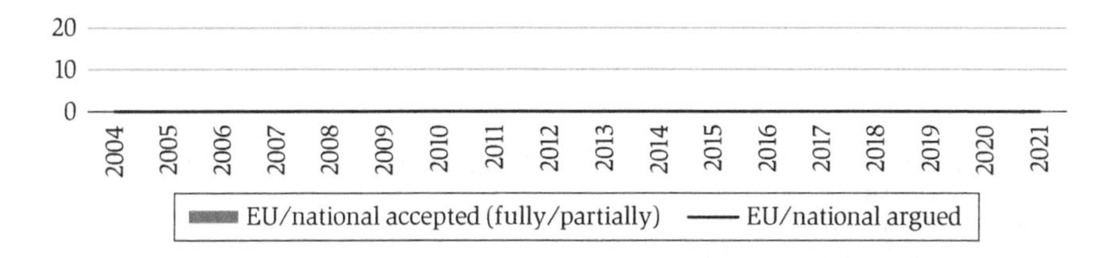

While full annulments of NCA decisions are very rare (and none after the creation of the Competition Court, within the relevant period), fine reductions were the norm during the relevant period. Fines were reduced in 85% of the cases (with no significant variation between first and second instances). On average, fines were reduced by 56%, with the greater degrees of reduction occurring in first instance.

Sixty-one percent of appeals of NCA decisions applying Article 101 TFEU, and 69% of those invoking Article 102 TFEU, were at least partially successful. However, appeals against decisions which applied only the national equivalent to Article 101 were at least partly successful only 37% of the time. The rate of success of challenges to the amount of the fine was slightly different, with a 32% success rate for Article 101 and a 23% success rate for Article 102. None of the (small number of) cases where Articles 101 and 102 TFEU were invoked in parallel were even partly successful.

4.7 Leniency and Settlements

Figure 24.12 examines the relationship between leniency and the success of appeals. In only 11% of NCA decisions which were appealed had there been an immunity recipient, under the leniency policy.[8] In the first instance, all those appeals were partially successful (reduction of fine). As previously mentioned, the increase of private enforcement in Portugal led to the bizarre situation of leniency beneficiaries appealing the NCA decision. In the '*banking cartel*' case, the recipient of immunity appealed to challenge the amount of the fine which had been calculated but not applied, on the grounds that the (non-applied) fine distorted its participation in the cartel and was detrimental to its reputation. A recipient of a 50% reduction for leniency appealed the finding of the infringement itself. It is not yet known whether this will lead to it losing the benefit of that 50% reduction (as the AdC argued), but the Public Prosecutor proposed that, not only should it not lose that reduction, but that the fine should be further reduced.

Figure 24.13 examines the relationship between settlements and the success of appeals. Within the relevant period, in only one case was there a decision with at least one settling party which was appealed.[9] In the April 2023 judgment in the '*insurance cartel*' case, the Competition Court annulled an NCA decision which had imposed fines on two non-settling undertakings, while the separate decisions it had adopted against the other three members of the cartel were not appealed and became *res judicata*.[10]

8. Eurest (Portugal) (262/10.5TYLSB; 88/12.1YUSTR); Contiforme (38/13.8YUSTR); Antalis Portugal (36/17.2YUSTR).
9. Antalis Portugal (36/17.2YUSTR).
10. Cartel dos seguros (229/18.5YUSTR-F).

Figure 24.12 Leniency

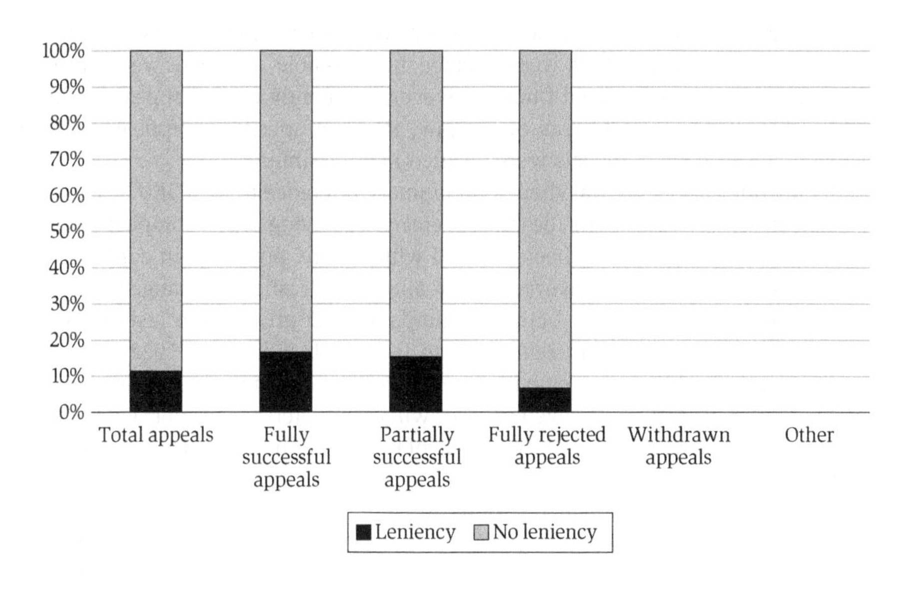

Figure 24.13 Settlements

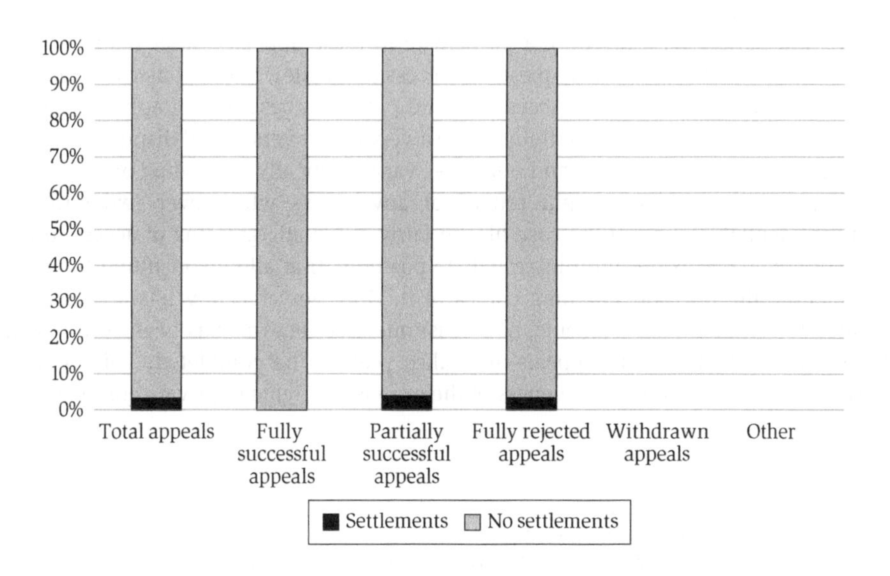

4.8 Other

With a single exception,[11] appeals were deemed admissible in the first instance. In the second instance, 17% of cases were deemed inadmissible, and 8% were partially inadmissible. The Constitutional Court, however, frequently rejects appeals as inadmissible (this is true for all areas of the law, it is not specific to appeals of NCA decisions) - 65% of such appeals were deemed inadmissible.

In only one case (1%) was there a preliminary reference to the CJEU.[12] This was so, particularly in the early years, despite several cases having raised complex issues of law and despite rulings having been reached which were, arguably, in contradiction with preexisting case law. However, this reality has drastically changed after the relevant period. More recently, both the Competition Court and the Lisbon Appeal Court have been quite frequent references to the CJEU. Indeed, in 2022 and 2023, referrals in such (public enforcement) cases have become the rule, rather than the exception.[13] Arguably, this is so even in cases where the referral does not seem to raise novel questions of law, or where the phrasing of the questions seems to leave room for only one answer.

In 92% of cases, the NCA decisions were appealed by undertakings, 8% by individuals and 1% by third parties (with one overlap). The example of an appeal by a third party was a situation where a very large undertaking, in the pursuit of its business interests, tried to push the NCA to impose a fine for an infringement which the NCA understood not to exist. That appeals were entirely dismissed, after a referral to the CJEU. As for appeals to the second instance, 71% of appeals were by undertakings, 9% by individuals, and 20% by the NCA.

Third parties typically do not participate in these appeals (other than through passive interventions, such as requests for access to the file). In only one case was any such participation identified.[14] Access by third parties to case files of appeals against NCA decisions has been and continues to be a very controversial and disputed issue in Portugal. Legal interpretations and outcomes vary drastically depending on the judge hearing the case, from outright refusal of any access whatsoever (even to the non-confidential version of the case file) to fairly automatic granting of access to the non-confidential version, with intermediate positions that allow consulting the non-confidential file but not obtaining copies of it. Only very recently has access been granted to confidential documents, in at least one case, but this has been surrounded by extensive litigation and appeals and takes years to be completed. This outlook creates tensions with the effectiveness of the exercise of rights in private enforcement.

11. Laboratórios Abbott (350/08.8TYLSB).
12. GDA - Cooperativa de Gestão dos Direitos dos Artistas, Intérpretes ou Executantes (77/16.7YUSTR).
13. *See, e.g.*, Super Bock Bebidas (C-211/22); Portuguese Banking Cartel (C-298/22); Imagens Médicas Integradas (C-258/23).
14. GDA - Cooperativa de Gestão dos Direitos dos Artistas, Intérpretes ou Executantes (77/16.7YUSTR).

5 QUALITATIVE ANALYSIS

5.1 The Standard of Review

In Portuguese Competition case law, discussions of the scope and intensity of judicial review are somewhat out of place. In Portugal, claw is a part of misdemeanour law, to which criminal Law is subsidiarily applicable. It is not administrative law. This drastically changes the parameters of the discussion. If it were administrative Law, one would need to discuss the degree to which the courts would have to respect the NCA's discretionary margin. But the applicability of criminal law principles means that, once there is an appeal, the NCA decision is formally considered an indictment, to be adjudicated upon by the court. Accordingly, the court is legally required to do a full and complete review, with no limitation of judicial review and no discretionary margin afforded to the NCA.

But one thing is the theory and principles, another is (or might be) the reality of judicial review. Defendants and defendants' counsel often point to the existence of a *de facto* excessive deference by the Competition Court to the NCA's decision-making. The fact that the Competition Court had – until April 2023 – never annulled an NCA decision may be pointed to in support of that position. However, the data gathered in this research does not support that conclusion, unless one assumes that the NCA was necessarily wrong in at least one of the decisions which has been appealed. There is no reason to make that assumption. The historical evolution of the NCA's decision-making (and the outcome of appeals in its earlier years, before the Commercial Court) suggests the learning of lessons from initial experiences and a significant qualitative improvement.

It is difficult and, ultimately, not useful to analyse the degree of deference or absence thereof, in each case, as this would require an in-depth assessment of all the details of the case and would, inevitably, boil down to subjective and manifestly debatable assessments, at least in what concerns the court's findings of fact. Indeed, any assessment of the quality of rulings is eminently subjective.

5.2 Institutional Reform and Its Impact

It seems fair to say that the quality of Portuguese judgments on appeals of NCA decisions evolved in time, in stages, and sometimes decreased. This is largely the inevitable result of the institutional reforms which were carried out (and the way in which they were carried out) and of the way judges are selected and appointed to decide these cases in the first and second instances. One of the judges of the Lisbon Commercial Court who decided appeals of NCA decisions, and who is currently a Judge at the General Court of the European Union, famously announced at public events that she would not have decided some of the legal issues in the same way, if she could go back to her earlier rulings. As explained in section 2, Portuguese judges start deciding appeals of NCA decisions at a time when they have not had any specific training in competition law and possibly may be required to study this branch of the law for the first time. Additionally, the same may be true for the other areas of the law (regulatory law, intellectual property) that they are called on to apply, meaning that they cannot dedicate their full attention to competition law. As a result, there is a learning curve of two to three years, which inevitably leads to an evolution in the quality of judicial decisions, for each individual judge. Some judges did not stay long enough in their position to get over that hump, and others left shortly thereafter. The high degree of turnover of judges at the Competition Court is, in itself, necessarily responsible for fluctuations in the quality of the rulings.

Additionally, institutional reforms were carried out in ways that were problematic for the enhanced quality of rulings. The decision to place the Competition Court in Santarém (a city one hour north of Lisbon) was, at the time, considered largely responsible for the judges of the Lisbon Commercial Court which by then had extensive experience in reviewing NCA decisions not transferring to the new Court. All the experience and knowledge acquired by the individual judges was lost at that time, and the process started from scratch. Unfortunately, for the reasons mentioned above, for the most part (with one exception) this institutional reform has not led to the long-term stabilisation of the judges who review NCA decisions in the first instance.

A second, more recent institutional reform, created conditions for greater specialisation of judges at the Lisbon Appeal Court, thanks to the introduction of the chamber for competition law, regulatory law and intellectual property law. Up to this time, NCA judicial reviews in the second instance were distributed among a much larger number of potential deciders. One of the visible impacts of this reform was that a much greater number of referrals to the CJEU are now being carried out, either by the Lisbon Appeal Court or by the Competition Court. As an example, in a recent ruling in the so-called *banking cartel*, a Competition Court judge justified the decision to refer questions to the CJEU, *inter alia*, with the argument that she fully expected the Lisbon Appeal Court's specialised chamber to make that referral, and so she preferred to seek that clarification of EU Law before ruling on the case herself.

5.3 Substantive and Procedural Grounds

Litigation in antitrust public enforcement cases in Portugal would likely look very strange to lawyers from some other jurisdictions, and it is important to understand those specificities. In their appeals, lawyers representing addressees of NCA decisions typically raise a very long list of procedural grounds, as a matter of course, almost as if applying a template. This is, in part, a reflection of the complete absence of consequences for invoking unsuccessful or even manifestly unmeritorious arguments. Courts typically give great leeway to the exercise of the rights of defence. As a result, public enforcement judgments, particularly at first instance, start with tens and tens of pages on procedural grounds, almost always rejecting every single one of those grounds. By the time they move on to substantive issues, some decision fatigue is inevitable, and courts tend to have less time to devote to the research of substantive issues as a result.

The absence of a rule of precedent means that the same legal issues tend to be litigated and re-discussed in every single case, even if they have always been decided in the same way by the courts. As an example, claimants always argue that the rules on fines are unconstitutional, or that the AdC cannot use emails to prove infringements. But this is not to say that invoking such arguments over and over can never lead to different results. A 2023 judgment of the Constitutional Court allowed this Court to answer, for the first time, a specific phrasing of a question concerning the manner in which the NCA was authorised to seize emails. For years, undertakings appealing NCA decisions had argued that an order from a Public Prosecutor was insufficient to seize emails because these are 'communications' and so can only be seized with a court order. The Competition Court and Lisbon Appeal Court had, countless times, rejected such arguments. But the Constitutional Court has now agreed with one of the appellants, stating that an order from a judge is required.

The almost complete absence of judgments overturning decisions on substantive grounds, after the creation of the Competition Court, is difficult to explain. But it should be noted that other (sectoral) regulators by no means enjoy the same track record of success before the Competition Court, suggesting that there is something specific to the NCA's decisions, or to the way the Court approaches these decisions, that leads to different outcomes.

It was not possible to identify any sign of *de facto* limitation of judicial review. The Court carries out extensive analysis of both the laws and the facts and often writes judgments consisting of hundreds of pages. It has also disagreed with the NCA on significant points of law on various occasions, even if this has not led to a decision being overturned.

Only when it comes to appeals of NCA merger control decisions, or of decisions rejecting complaints (which are governed by Administrative Law), does one see the Competition Court recognising a discretionary margin to the NCA in making certain assessments. However, this falls outside the scope of the present analysis.

5.4 Review of Fines

For most of its history, appeals of NCA decisions were almost certain to lead to reductions in fines. These reductions tended to be substantial, frequently reaching 50% to 70%, and tended to be achieved largely at the first-instance appeal court. There has been a manifest evolution of the attitude of both the NCA and the review courts to fines. Arguably, it would seem that both administrative and judicial authorities were persuaded that the levels of fines being imposed were not sufficiently dissuasive and that the very frequent reduction of fines was creating a culture of nearly systematic appeals of NCA decisions. In recent years, the NCA has started to very significantly increase the amount of its fines. At the same time, the Competition Court has drastically decreased the number of cases in which it decreases these fines. Indeed, in a succession of the most recent judgments, the Court has not only not reduced the fine, but it has increased the fine imposed on a relative basis. This is so, not because the amount of the fine itself was increased, but because the scope of the infringement was reduced (e.g., less time), and the original fine was maintained. So far, the Lisbon Appeal Court seems to (mostly) agree with this approach. It is, however, too early to tell if this will be a constant tendency. Especially because some cases are still to come before the Court that may stretch the willingness of the Court to accept particularly high levels of fines.

Given the specificities of Portuguese Misdemeanour Law, in its review of the amount of fines, the Courts are in no way bound by the NCA's position. The NCA has published guidelines on fining, but they are not, and could not be, binding, as the NCA must comply with the legal criteria for fines. These are the same criteria which are applied by the Courts. Consequently, the Court typically dismisses arguments concerning equality or disproportionality in comparison to other infringers or other cases. It arrives at its own conclusion concerning the adequacy of the fine in light of the legal criteria. These criteria are rather imprecise and leave a large margin of discretion, beyond the 10% turnover limit. As a result, unlike what happens with the more or less mathematical method applied by the European Commission, it is very difficult for undertakings to foresee the amount of fines which may come to be imposed on them by the NCA. Furthermore, particularly in recent years, the NCA has shown an apparent willingness to use potential settlements as a tool to close cases in exchange for drastic reductions in fines. Whereas a settlement would typically be expected to lead to a 10% reduction in the fine, there is anecdotal evidence that the NCA is willing to settle for amounts which are, sometimes, several times lower than the fine it ends up imposing if the undertaking decides not to settle. It has also shown itself willing to extend immunity to a cartel member which held a preponderant role in its promotion. It was precisely in such a case (*see* the '*insurance cartel*') that the Competition Court drew the line and ended up annulling the entire decision, on grounds that are largely connected to criticism of the leniency procedure itself and how it is applied by the NCA.

5.5 The Role of the Constitutional Court

During the relevant period, the Constitutional Court issued a disproportionately high number of rulings in competition law cases, compared to the scarcity of judgments issued by the same court in other areas of the law. These judgments have repeatedly tackled a small number of issues, and, until very recently, had been mostly inconsequential. Challenges to the constitutionality of rules on fines, or of certain powers of the Competition Authority, or to alleged infringements of the right not to incriminate oneself, were repeatedly rejected by the Constitutional Court. Only its very recent bombshell judgment according to which the NCA has not had the necessary authorisation from a judge (only from the Public Prosecutor), in order to seize emails, in every single one of its dawn raids in previous years, has potentially thrown a wrench into the works of antitrust public enforcement in Portugal. But it is still too early to tell how this will play out, as no conclusion has been arrived at in any specific case yet, as a result of that ruling.

5.6 Alignment with EU Law

As previously mentioned, one of the defining institutional features of antitrust judicial review in Portugal is the frequency of reforms and the frequent change in the judges hearing such cases. Taking into account their absence of prior knowledge of competition law, some judges have recognised the presence of a steep learning curve, that requires two to three years of on-the-job training before they are familiar with the complexities of this branch of the law. As a result, the case law of the Lisbon Commercial Court showed a manifest evolution in the quality of its rulings.

Some initial rulings were very tied to Portuguese misdemeanour law, disregarding the specificities of EU competition law. As an example, in the '*salt cartel*' case, the first-instance court refused to assign liability to a parent company for an infringement by a subsidiary, dismissing any relevance to the economic unit concept of competition law and applying principles of criminal law. Many years went by before the NCA considered that it could try this issue again. At that point, the Competition Court tried to find a solution to reach the same outcome within the confines of Portuguese Criminal Law (via liability for omissions), but the Lisbon Appeal Court rejected that approach and once again did not find the parent company liable, omitting to discuss the impact of competition law's concept of an undertaking.

Once the judges at the Lisbon Commercial Court were more familiar with competition law, the Competition Court was created, in Santarém, and none of those judges was willing to move to that Court. Accordingly, judicial review effectively started again from scratch. Once again, earlier rulings from new judges showed interpretations of EU law which would drastically change in their own subsequent decisions. A good example of this was the Court's approach to identifying an effect on trade between MS. This was often refused in early cases, whereas now it is almost always identified. The fact that judges in the Competition Court often change, with one notable exception, also makes it hard to retain this acquired knowledge. The situation at the Lisbon Appeal Court is not too dissimilar.

That being said, recent years have seen a very noticeable advance in the depth of analysis of CJEU case law by both the Competition Court and the Lisbon Appeal Court. Both Courts now often discuss the leading issues of EU competition law, quoting the most recent case law and raising novel or borderline issues, even leading them to submit references to the CJEU. Some of these referrals do not, perhaps, raise novel issues and could perhaps have been avoided. But they are nonetheless evidence of a drastic change in attitude from both Courts, who are not only willing to delve deeper into EU case law but are also more pre-disposed to engage in a dialogue with the CJEU to clarify the appropriate answer to legal issues placed before them. One result of this tendency is that Portuguese courts have become significant contributors to the development of EU competition law, via the CJEU. During the project timeframe, however, as noted above, there was only one referral to the CJEU from a Portuguese antitrust public enforcement case.

6 CONCLUDING REMARKS

During the relevant period for this study, there was a relatively small number of judgments in the context of the judicial review of NCA decisions. The temporal scope of the analysis ended more or less around the time when, arguably, we may be seeing a change in some of the statistics discussed in this report.

One change that is not debatable is the increase in the frequency of references to the CJEU. There are currently at least four referrals (with possibly two more which have not yet been published) pending before the CJEU, originating from NCA antitrust judicial review cases before the Competition Court and Lisbon Appeal Court: Case C-331/21 *EDP & Sonae*; Case C-211/22 *Super Bock Bebidas*; Case C-298/22 *Banco BPN/BIC et al*; and C-258/23 *Imagens Médicas Integradas*. This is a significant change. In the most recent appeals, we can observe references in the majority of NCA antitrust judicial review cases, whereas until recently there was only one referral in the entire history of judicial review of NCA decisions in Portugal. If the courts of other Member States behaved similarly, this would surely trigger an institutional judicial reform at the EU level.

There has also been a visible increase in the percentage of NCA decisions which are appealed. Except in small cases, it would seem that the NCA cannot adopt a decision now without it being appealed (and then reappealed to the second instance and probably to the Constitutional Court), even in cases with leniency and settlements. The main drivers for this seem to be: (i) Portuguese law still allows for fines (in investigations initiated prior to the transposition of the ECN+ Directive) to be time-barred while an appeal is pending so that companies have a chance of getting away with not paying the fine simply due to the passage of time; and (ii) the growth in private enforcement, particularly in relation to consumer opt-out representative actions.

That being said, this tendency may not last. Arguably, one may also be witnessing a change in the Competition Court's attitude to the review of the amount of fines, and to other ways in which it reacts to appeals. In two recent cases (*Super Bock* and *EDP*), even though the Competition Court annulled part of the decision (e.g., finding that the NCA had not proved one of the unlawful behaviours it had identified, or that the infringement covered a slightly smaller period of time), it confirmed the amount of the fine. This effectively means an increase in the relative level of the fine (the same fine for a smaller infringement). The Competition Court may be reacting to the aggressive degree of litigation by defendants, not only in terms of the number of appeals but particularly in terms of the number and type of issues raised in the often several hundred pages-long submissions. However, the AdC has also recently changed its fining policy (at least in practice), significantly increasing the amount of fines it imposes. This could counterbalance that tendency, if the Court believes that the new level of fines is becoming disproportionate.

Additionally, these first experiments with public enforcement judicial review in a brave new world of follow-on private enforcement may end up teaching lessons that encourage or discourage appeals. For example, in the *EDP* case, where a follow-on case was already pending before the Competition Court, not only did the Court confirm the

NCA Decision and maintain the fine, it ordered an independent economic study which quantified the damage caused by the infringement and then *ex officio* ordered its judgment to be added to the case file of the follow-on action. In the '*banking cartel*' case, the Court's 2000 pages judgment not only increased the transparency and knowledge of specific facts and means of evidence which were not clear in the NCA Decision, but it also included conclusions concerning the effects the cartel had on the market, and how the information exchanges were effectively used by the undertakings to determine their market behaviour (even though it was framed merely as an object restriction). On the flip side, the Competition Court is showing a tendency (although not always) to automatically suspend any follow-on case while the NCA decision is not yet *res judicata*, not even progressing with the discussion of issues which are independent of the outcome of the public enforcement review, which does create an incentive for undertakings to exhaust appeals so as to postpone the private enforcement case.

Cold statistics do provide some basis for the concern often raised by counsel for appellants of NCA decisions, that the Courts defer too much to the AdC's position and are too quick to confirm its positions. However, it was not possible to arrive at a definitive conclusion in this regard. The Courts have often taken legal positions both alongside and against those of the NCA. Their assessment of the facts of the cases is difficult to judge from the outside. Perhaps the reasons for the statistics we observe are not only a result of the Courts' approach but also of the appellants' strategy, which tends to dedicate the majority of the time to procedural issues and not to hesitate in raising substantive arguments which are not argued with particularly conviction nor backed up by serious attempts to provide evidence for them. This may be obscuring or leaving less time for in-depth factual discussions concerning the more relevant substance of the infringements. At least on a psychological level, when a court is confronted with the need to reject a dozen procedural arguments which are the same in most cases, and to reject many clearly unmeritorious substantive arguments, it is perhaps less willing to entertain the seriousness of substantive arguments which could be meritorious. Whether or not this psychological effect has an impact or is surpassed by the care and devotion of the courts is impossible to ascertain. The few successes appellants have achieved were based on procedural issues, limitation periods, constitutional issues, or different interpretations of what the adequate amount of the fine should be. At least in public enforcement (but not so in private enforcement), it is hard to find a case won by an appellant in relation to a substantive issue of competition law.

CHAPTER 25

Romania Report

Adriana Almăşan & Ştefan Bogrea[*]

1 COMPETITION LAW ENFORCEMENT IN ROMANIA

1.1 Historical Outline

The first competition legal provisions in Romania were adopted in 1990, shortly after the end of the communist regime. The initial legislation was included in a law that transformed the centralised economic system into a liberalised market by means of a complex process of several stages enabling the reorganisation of state economic units and further on through the privatisation process, creating the autonomous companies and state companies. Three articles (36-38) pertaining to competition were included in Law 15/1990 in a distinct Chapter 5 entitled 'Association and free competition', consisting of a combination of competition rules and fair-trading practices principles. In fact, this law was not apt to be enforced. As an epitome of the poor drafting of these provisions, the wording of Article 36 was an erroneous translation of Article 85 EEC, the entire chapter amalgamating incoherent concepts of antitrust and unfair competition. The legal texts were not able to be applied and they remained idle until the adoption of the Competition Law 21/1996, in the same year the national competition authority (the NCA) was also established: the Romanian Competition Council (RCC), the first Romanian agency having anti-trust law enforcement power.

Despite some defects of Law 21/1996, it was a huge step ahead from the legislative perspective, the law being abundantly inspired by the EC legislation at that

* The authors of the present report gratefully acknowledge the contribution provided in collecting and analysing the data by assistant researchers with the Centre for Competition Law Studies at the Faculty of Law, University of Bucharest: Carina Vermeşan, Andreea Enescu, Eduard Florea and Rareş Farcaş. Without their astute observations and extended efforts, this report would not have been possible.

time. There were some differences to the EC legislation that were corrected in time, and the provisions that were ineffective were repealed as well. Some amendments to Law 21/1996 aimed to mirror the EU legislation more accurately. For instance, prior versions of the Law explicitly prohibited bid riggings and boycotts as forms of anticompetitive agreements.

Other provisions were repealed due to the lack of procedural instruments for implementation. For instance, in the initial version of Law 21/1996, Article 7 granted the RCC the possibility to dissolve a dominant position, as a sanction for the abuse of a dominant position. This provision was never employed in practice, as the NCA was required to file an action in court in order to request the dissolution of the dominant position. As the history of the RCC displayed, the national authority never desires to put itself into the position of the claimant in a trial. Also, in the early years after its establishment (until the early 2000s, noting Romania was set to accede to the EU in 2007) there was very little antitrust case law and even fewer cases of investigations pertaining to abuse of a dominant position.

In other situations, the legislation adopted in this field was not compliant with the constitutional requirements. This was the case of the Government Emergency Ordinance 39/2017 transposing the Directive 2014/104/EU,[1] which was declared unconstitutional by the Romanian Constitutional Court Decision 239/2020 and subsequently rejected by Law 78/2022. The reasons why the Constitutional Court found the Government Emergency Ordinance to be unconstitutional pertained to procedural aspects, and not to the rules provided in the Ordinance – that is to say not to reasons relating to how it transposed Directive 2014/104/EU.

The secondary legislation also echoed the EU provisions in competition. In principle, the RCC follows the policies applied by the European Commission as regards the prioritisation of cases, adaptive solutions and avoiding the negative effect of the interpretation in the letter of law, and increasing the competition law awareness, especially in the judiciary, by offering training sessions for the specialised judges.

The establishment of the Romanian Competition Council, as an autonomous national authority in 1996, institutionalised the enforcement and supported the applicability of competition rules. Simultaneously, the Competition Office was established as a government body, later dissolved, that had the prerogative of the administrative application of unfair trading practices legislation. Currently, the Romanian Competition Council has the sole jurisdiction in all competition matters and unfair trading practices.

Until the accession of Romania to the European Union on 1 January 2007, both the administrative application and the judicial review of competition law were scarce. This was the result of various factors, the most significant including a lack of good command of competition law due to the poor selection of decision-makers at the national authority level. These shortcomings were being resolved in the pre-accession

1. Directive 2014/104/EU of the European Parliament and of the Council of 26 November 2014 on certain rules governing actions for damages under national law for infringements of the competition law provisions of the Member States and of the European Union Text with EEA relevance.

period (years 2005–2007) and in the few years after 2007. In fact, improving competition law enforcement is an ongoing process.

As regards judicial enforcement, even though in a few law faculties in Romania Competition Law has been taught from as early as 1994, most of the judges who were competent to solve cases involving competition infringements had not been trained in this specialised area, as they were senior in the judicial system and trained in law before 1989. According to the law applicable at the time, the NCA was required to publish its decisions in the Official Monitor, the legislative bulletin, but there was no deadline set for publication, so only on very rare occasions were decisions published.

After 2007, Romania's accession to the EU changed the circumstances, and the growing trend of application of EU law is consistent. Several amendments to the Competition Law assimilated the national legislation with the EU competition law rules. Also, improvements have been noticed in the practice of the NCA and the courts' competence to solve competition cases, even though a recent trend of lower-profile cases can be noticed.

An interesting facet of the enforcement practice in Romania is dawn raids. They are a prerogative of competition inspectors, with Article 38 of Law 21/1996 granting them the power to enter any and all premises and means of transportation that the respective undertaking uses, examine any documents he or she deems necessary, and even, in certain conditions, copy any of the said documents in order to further the investigation at hand.

Currently, dawn raids undertaken by the Romanian Competition Council's Investigators take place following judicial authorisation. The judicial authorisation process was introduced by a recent amendment brought to Law 21/1996. Before 2015, Competition Inspectors could, in certain situations, initiate inspections without judicial authorisation, which contradicted the European Court of Human Rights guarantees under Article 8, insofar as they applied to legal persons as well.

The scope of the work in this report is consequently limited to the period starting with 2007, as no relevant cases were identified for the years 2004–2006. As the duration of an investigation and the duration of a trial are each multiannual, the data is very scarce for the first few years after Romania's accession to the EU.

Table 25.1 Competition Laws in Romania

Period	*Competition Laws in Romania*
1990-1996	**Articles 36-38 of Law 15/1990 on the reorganisation of state economic units as autonomous companies and state companies, enacted on 7 August 1990**, as amended by Law 58/1991, Law 80/1991, Government Ordinance 15/1993, Government Ordinance 70/1994 (approved by Law 73/1996) and Law 21/1996, repealing the provisions in Law 15/1990 pertaining to competition. Law 15/1990 continues to be in force by the provisions not related to competition.

Period	*Competition Laws in Romania*
1996-current	**Law 21/1996 Competition Law, enacted on 10 April 1996**, as amended by Laws and Government Emergency Ordinances and republished on 16 August 2005, 03 April 2014, 29 February 2016 and amended by Government Emergency Ordinance 9/2017, Government Emergency Ordinance 39/2017 (rejected by Law 78/2022 and declared as unconstitutional by the Romanian Constitutional Court Decision 239/2020), Government Emergency Ordinance 25/2019, Government Emergency Ordinance 6/2020 (approved by Law 254/2020), Government Emergency Ordinance 160/2020, Government Emergency Ordinance 170/2020, Law 254/2020, Government Emergency Ordinance 23/2021, Government Emergency Ordinance 46/2022

1.2 Institutional Framework

The public enforcement of competition law is carried out by administrative measures, applied by the RCC, as well as the competent courts of the judicial system, which have the prerogative of judicial review. The Romanian Competition Council (RCC)[2] is the main institution responsible for enforcing Law 21 of 10 April 1996 ('Competition Law')[3] and Articles 101 and 102 TFEU[4] and the designated competition authority for Romania pursuant to Article 35 (1) of Regulation 1/2003.

Historically, in addition to the powers granted to the RCC, several national agencies had adjacent competences aimed at enhancing the market environment in specific sectors, such as the communications sector, or the energy sector, especially regarding access to infrastructure. These prerogatives have been continuously diminished to eliminate the juxtaposition of attributions, the national agencies including the National Authority for Energy Regulations ANRE and National Authority for Administration and Regulations in Communications ANCOM, both currently have rather a support role for RCC in competition matters.

The RCC is an autonomous administrative authority, holding regulatory and administrative enforcement powers for this purpose. The RCC:

- investigates and decides on the infringements to the provisions of Law 21/1996 and Articles 101 and 102 TFEU;
- withdraws, by decision, the benefit of the exemption for agreements, decisions of business associations or concerted practices to which the provisions of one of the European category exemption regulations apply, according to the provisions of Article 29 paragraph (2) of Council Regulation (EC) no. 1/2003;

2. http://www.consiliulconcurentei.ro/en/.
3. https://legislatie.just.ro/Public/DetaliiDocument/157060.
4. *See* Article 3 para. 2 of the Competition Law.

- ensures the effective application of its own decisions, including the monitoring of the ordered measures and the effects of economic concentrations conditionally authorised by decisions;
- carries out, *ex officio*, sector investigations, i.e., investigation regarding a certain economic sector or a certain type of agreement in different sectors, when price rigidity or other circumstances suggest the possibility of restricting or distorting market competition. Upon the conclusion of a sector investigation, the Competition Council may publish a report on the results of the investigation regarding certain sectors of the economy or certain agreements in different sectors and invite interested parties to formulate observations. Also, the RCC may decide in certain cases, in which the suspicion of an infringement of the law is sufficient, that further investigation is required, and may open a case investigation;
- notifies the Government of the existence of a monopoly situation or other cases provided by Law 21/1996 and proposes the adoption of the necessary measures to remedy the distortions found;
- addresses the courts of law on the cases in which they are competent;
- pursues the application of legal provisions and other normative acts and may recommend to the competent authorities the modification of normative acts that have or may have an anti-competitive impact;
- notifies the Government of cases of interference by central and local public administration bodies in the application of Law 21/1996;
- issues opinions or points of view for draft normative acts, draft public policy documents, which may have an impact anti-competitive, and may recommend their modification;
- makes recommendations to the Government and local public administration bodies for the adoption of measures to facilitate the development of the market and competition;
- proposes to the Government or local public administration bodies the taking of disciplinary measures against their subordinate staff, in case they do not comply with the mandatory provisions of the Competition Council;
- carries out studies and prepares reports on its field of activity and provides the Government, the public and specialised international organisations with information regarding this activity;
- represents Romania and promotes the exchange of information and experience in relations with relevant international organisations and institutions; as a national competition authority, the Competition Council is responsible for the relationship with the institutions of the European Union, according to the relevant provisions of European legislation, and cooperates with other competition authorities;
- ensures the application and compliance with the provisions of Regulation (EU) 2019/1.150 of the European Parliament and of the Council of 20 June 2019 on the promotion of fairness and transparency for businesses using online intermediation services, as well as any subsequent regulations;

- ensures the application and compliance with the provisions of Regulation (EU) 452/2019 of the European Parliament and of the Council of 19 March 2019 establishing a framework for the examination of foreign direct investments in the European Union.

The RCC's plenary is a collegial body consisting of a president, two vice-presidents and four competition councillors. The members of the RCC are named by the Romanian President, acting on a proposal of the RCC's Consultative College,[5] taking into account the Government's opinion and after all candidates are heard in the specialised Parliamentary Commission. Terms are five years long and they may be named again in the same position upon expiry of the term. The RCC's plenary:

- examines the investigative reports, with any objections raised therein and decides on the measures to be taken; the RCC plenary is the decisional body in investigations. More recent practice proves that RCC's plenary requests the investigation team not to make proposals to eliminate any interference in the decision-making process on the sanctions it applies, hence separating the investigation phase and the sanctioning phase of the procedure;
- analyses the authorisation of economic concentrations; the RCC's plenary also has full autonomy in deciding remedial measures;
- adopts the RCC's points of view, recommendations, and opinions; these documents are published on the RCC's website;
- adopts draft regulations proposed for adoption; RCC acts as a competition law filter for economic legislation having a competition impact. It works closely with the Ministry of Justice's legislation directorate;
- adopts the annual reports which ought to be made compliant with Romanian Law; besides the annual reports RCC's plenary adopts sectorial reports and other general reports;
- Decides whether breaches of Law 21/1996 have been committed; this is the epitome of the plenary's prerogatives and represents its principal activity;
- authorises direct foreign investments pursuant to EU Regulation 452/2019.

The RCC draws up its own draft budget, which is provided for separately in the state budget, and the RCC's financing is ensured from said budget, as well as from own revenues from various taxes imposed by Law 21/1996.

1.3 Judicial Authorisation of Inspections

To compensate for the practice of investigated companies taking advantage of the suspensive effect of challenging the snap inspection, the Competition Law was amended in 2014 so that judicial authorisation can be contested only after the Competition Council has issued a final decision (i.e., after it imposes fines or other

5. The Consultative College (Colegiu Consultativ) is a consultative body, deemed to recommend candidates for the panel of counsellors of the Competition Council.

measures, in merit). Consequently, investigated companies find out about the inspections the moment they occur, and the legality and proportionality of the inspection itself cannot be contested *post-factum*. This impossibility brings up important questions both under Article 6 and Article 8 ECHR, since, if the Competition Council finds that no breach has taken place, any abuse that took place during the actual inspection cannot be contested by the undertaking, which may violate both its right to privacy and its access to a court pursuant to Article 6 ECHR, in case the final decision does not apply measures in merit. Only in the case when the RCC applies measures in merit the access to recourse is availed to the undertaking that has been subjected to snap inspection.

1.4 Third Parties' Rights

According to the civil procedural rules that are generally applied in judicial procedures pertaining to the judicial review of RCC decisions, third parties are allowed to intervene in a judicial process under the condition they prove a legitimate personal interest to do so. They are not allowed though to appeal cases they have not been a party to in the first instance.

1.5 Sourcing of Evidence

Most of the evidence considered in judicial review proceedings is collected from the RCC investigation file. Some other evidence may come from the police or prosecutor's office, especially where cases are first instrumented by the authorities applying criminal law. There are some other sources of evidence that might be occasionally used, at the discretion of the RCC. In a case, the domestic courts concluded[6] that the evidence may be sourced from criminal law authorities (Directorate for Investigating Organised Crime and Terrorism). Given the general trend of Romanian courts in refraining from second-guessing the RCC's findings, where evidence is sourced directly from the investigative authority, such as the RCC, judicial interference in the original decision is even less likely. While this does not appear at first glance to have any connection to the standard of review, when evidence is sourced from criminal investigations, the standard of review drastically falls, since Romanian Courts specialising in competition law are much less likely to opine against the findings of the criminal investigation authorities.

2 JUDICIAL REVIEW OF COMPETITION DECISIONS

There is a single judicial system in Romania, across all fields of law. The relevant decisions of the RCC can be challenged in the litigation procedure for administrative acts at the specialised sections of the Bucharest Court of Appeal ('CA'): the administrative and fiscal sections of the court. The scope of the challenge is the annulment of

6. CA Case 596/2019.

the RCC decision. The judges of the administrative and fiscal sections hear the cases in a single-judge panel. They judge all administrative and fiscal procedures and acts issued by the competent authorities. Even though there is no specialisation of these judicial sections in competition law – given that all judges in Romania receive the same general education during their studies at the National Institute for Magistrates, an inherent de facto specialisation occurs further to exclusive attributions to judge competition law cases. There are less than two hundred judges appointed to deal with such cases in the specialised sections.

The procedural rules require a separate action to be lodged with the competent judicial court for the provisional suspension of the effects of a decision. Decisions are normally fully enforceable even if an action for annulment is lodged. Consequently, if a suspension was not requested by the undertaking or not granted by the court when it was requested, the action for annulment is judged independently of the settlement of the fine (if that is the case) for the infringement of competition rules. All the decisions of the RCC are enforceable upon the expiration of a term of thirty days that is calculated from the date the decision is conveyed to the undertaking. This entails that if the undertaking asks for annulment, but does not ask for suspension, the RCC's decision is enforced against the undertaking, which is why most undertakings also ask for a suspension in practice, even if they are granted extremely rarely. One must note that suspensions are not normally judged by the same judge/judges who will judge the action for annulment, and there are no special provisions regarding the suspension of RCC's decisions. Consequently, applicants must rely on the general text that governs suspensions of administrative decisions, pursuant to Articles 14 and 15 of Law 554/2004.

The court judgments rendered in the first instance may be appealed to a final appeal ('recurs') on points of law at the administrative and fiscal section of the highest judicial court, the High Court of Cassation and Justice ('HCCJ'). As above, while a de facto specialisation exists amongst such judges, one cannot speak of a legally provided requirement of competition law specialisation for such judges.

Consequently, there are no third-instance appeals in the Romanian judicial system. The appeals in front of the HCCJ are examined by a three-judge panel. It should be stressed however that the Romanian word 'recurs' is not the equivalent English word 'recourse': the grounds for appeal on points of law entail breaching or wrongly applying provisions of material law. The review of the first court's award is limited to the application of law, and it is not a full appeal, hence the HCCJ does not necessarily reassess the facts of the case at hand.

Both the CA and the HCCJ have absolute jurisdiction to revise any sanctions applied by the RCC in general (full review in substance), but, as the data presented below shows, the case law usually displays serious restraint in the judicial review undertaken – with procedural grounds often being more successful than substantial ones, as the figures show.

Generally, Article 6 of the ECHR is not formally considered in procedures pertaining to competition law in Romania – while competition law cases usually take a long period to reach a final decision at the HCCJ (an average of two years, usually the first hearing is set in around one year from the registration of the file). Nonetheless, there have been no complaints lodged with the ECtHR pertaining to this specific type of case.

The judicial fee for appealing the RCC's decisions and then for appealing the CA's sentence is mandatory, but insignificant in amount - given that it is half of the judicial fee for filing an action for annulment (circa 5 EUR, half of the original 10 EUR judicial fee). This can also explain the extraordinary rate of appeals, as the following figures will show below.

While the general provisions of the Romanian Code of Civil Procedure (Article 61 *et seq* of Law 134/2010 on the Code of Civil Procedure) permit third-party interventions into any type of administrative procedure, they are seldom used in competition law cases, as the data shows.

It should also be noted that there is no *amicus curiae* mechanism as such, and third-party interveners must establish a personal interest in the case, in order for their intervention to be admissible. Neither is there evidence of the two competent courts having asked for the opinion of the European Commission in any case, pursuant to Regulation 1/2003, nor of the Commission presenting its own observations.

3 PRIOR RESEARCH

The (scarce) academic literature published to date demonstrates a very limited review of the RCC's decisions by the competent judiciary.[7] When assessing a competition case, the Romanian judges tend to apply more general rules of law, than the specific competition rules. As we shall mention below, certain endemic challenges make such an analysis difficult.

4 QUANTITATIVE ANALYSIS

4.1 Source of Information

Several observations ought to be made at a preliminary level, as pertains to the data underlying the content and conclusions of this report. While extensive efforts were made, the judgments included in the database are, in all likelihood, incomplete. The factors which lead to such a conclusion are connected to the limited public availability of data and to the realities of the Romanian legal system:

First, there is no official centralised database of legal decisions recorded in Romania, and this relates to the jurisprudence of both the CA and the HCCJ. The court

---

7. *See* Botta, M., & Svetlicinii, A. (2015). The Right of Fair Trial in Competition Law Proceedings: Quo Vadis the Courts of the New EU Member States? In P. Nihoul, & T. Skoczny (eds), Procedural Fairness in Competition Proceedings (pp. 276-308); Bernatt, Maciej and Botta, Marco and Botta, Marco and Svetlicinii, Alexandr, The Right of Defense in the Decentralized System of EU Competition Law Enforcement: A Call for Harmonization from Central and Eastern Europe (1 July 2018). World Competition: Law and Economics Review, Vol. 41, No. 3, 2018, Available at SSRN: https://ssrn.com/abstract=3207709 or DOI: 10.2139/ssrn.3207709.

judgments are not consistently published (online or otherwise) to the extent that they are accessible to the public.

Second, there is a lack of transparency pertaining equally to closing and pending cases before the judiciary authorities. For the text of any judgment to be released, the court ought to observe the rules protecting the personal data of the parties in the trial and the awards are to be cleared of any such information prior to access being allowed. Redacting the text for anonymisation purposes is an operation for which the courts do not have any dedicated personnel or procedure. Consequently, logistical reasons considerably prevent access to the case law even for research reasons.

There are a few incipient databases of case law gathered by private services and a publicly funded project that is yet to be released. Also, in the past, several judges and even some courts used to publish anonymised collections of judgments (released as volumes of case law by publishing houses). This practice was however discontinued long before the timeframe of this project.

To overcome this endemic deficiency, the database used for the purpose of this report is based on all the available case law databases released by commercial services currently existing in Romania.[8] However, it must be stressed that such services are third-party sources that expressly refuse to guarantee that the text provided is authentic (they are not allowed to confirm authenticity by the law, in the absence of a specific mandate to publish on behalf of the judicial authority). While, in preparation of this report, certain data was retrieved from the RCC's Annual Reports and the RCC website, the latter is not especially suited to filtering search results by any criteria and does not mention whether the decision identified was ever appealed, whether the appeal was successful and, if so, its outcome.

Even when published, parts of the judgments identified are redacted (names of the parties and other personal data, as well as confidential and privileged information), although identification of a competition law case is possible by using a search tool with the name of the RCC as a party to the proceedings.

Moreover, one must note that the identity of the judge/s that issues a judgment is not available for publication and there is no possibility of linking a judicial decision to the judge that rendered it. This situation does not result from an explicit express prohibition in the relevant laws but is based rather on the de facto protection of the judges' identity stemming mostly from a very broad interpretation of the GDPR. In the absence of information issued by the courts, it is very difficult to identify how and whether a specific judge has a specific outlook on a specific issue. Certainly, this is an approach that is not without merit for the legal system (as it avoids 'judge shopping' as a specific type of 'forum shopping'), however, it made research on this point virtually impossible.

Although the dataset is unlikely to capture all existing judgments, we are confident that a sufficient number of judgments were identified to enable relevant conclusions which are confirmed by the empirical observations of the researchers and practitioners. In simpler terms, the results of the research are not surprising for one

8. Wolters Kluwer's Sintact (https://www.wolterskluwer.com/ro-ro/solutions/sintact); Indaco's lege5 (https://lege5.ro/).

familiar with the Romanian legal system, in general, and the Romanian competition law judicial proceedings, in particular, as highlighted in the final section of this report.

4.2 Total Number of Judgments and the Ratio of Appeals

Notwithstanding the challenges in locating the relevant judgments, we were able to identify and record 324 first and second-instance judgments against RCC's competition decisions rendered during the relevant period. The CA rendered 236 of these judgments, while the rest, 88 cases, were rendered by the HCCJ at a second instance.

This points to a very high ratio of appeal against the RCC decisions. This entails that 44% of the RCC decisions were appealed in the first instance, and 32% of the CA's judgments were appealed to the CA.

4.3 Judgments per Year

Figure 25.1 Number of Judgments According to Instances

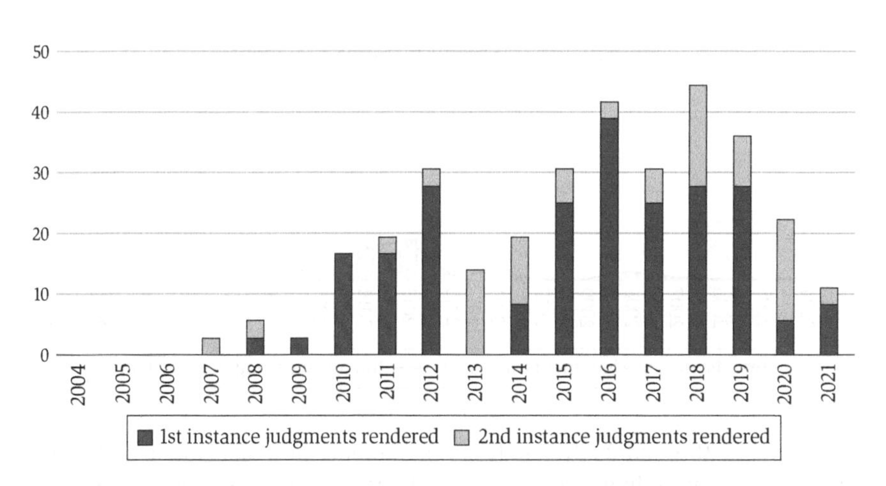

Figure 25.1 summarises the number of judgments issued per year by the two instances of Romanian courts, i.e., the CA and the HCCJ. As can be seen, the numbers appear to be stable, excluding the outlier years of 2008 and 2009 (when the judgments delivered all pertained to cases occurring before Romania's accession to the EU), and 2020 and 2021 (where the reduction can be attributed to a general reduction in Romanian court activity pertaining to the pandemic). The lack of delivered judgments in 2012 and 2013 at the CA level does not reflect that it had no activity, but rather that, despite the researchers' best efforts, their judgments could not be obtained. Nevertheless, the specific cases from those years are reflected in HCCJ decisions from subsequent years.

The number of judgments enables us to see the relationship between the years 2010 and 2011, on the one hand, when the number of judgments at first instance is prevalent, and the years 2012 and 2013 on the other hand, when the number of judgments on appeal at second instance is prevalent.

Figure 25.2(a) First-Instance Judgments

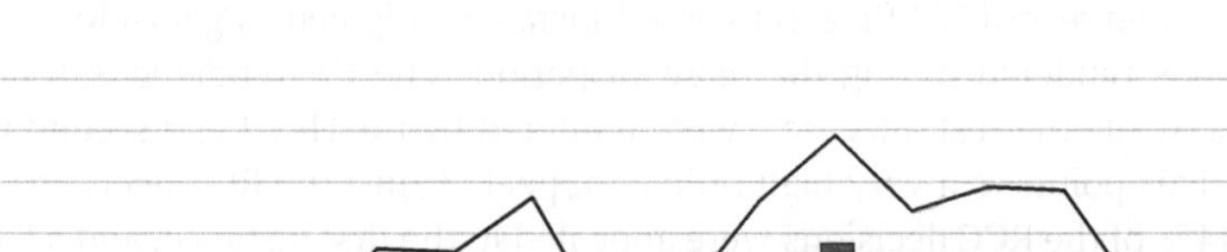

Figure 25.2(b) Second-Instance Judgments

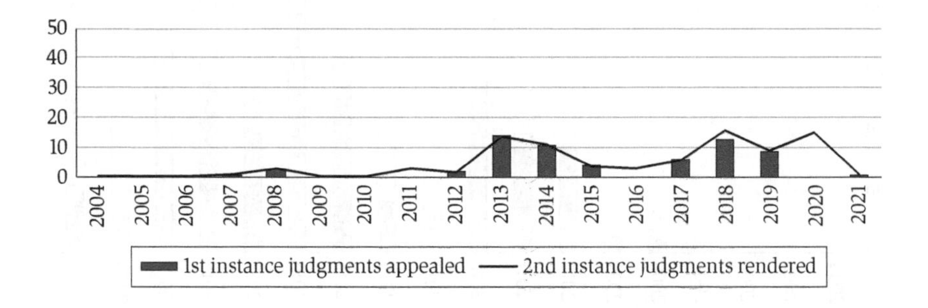

Figures 25.2(a) and 25.2(b) indicate the number of judgments included in the database per year according to each instance (lines). It compares it with the number of NCA's decisions that were appealed in the first instance each year or the number of courts' judgments that were appealed in further instances (bars). They demonstrate that in most cases, a single NCA decision was subject to multiple parallel appeals, each judged in a separate procedure and often by a different judge.

The procedural rules governing connected cases (Article 139 of the Code of Civil Procedure, cited above) require that each undertaking files a separate action – and joining cases is not mandatory, but left at the discretion of the judges. Appeals are never joined, which leads to a sort of sensible situation in which judges may expect their colleagues to reject an action for annulment, and as such judges may be apprehensive. On appeal, the cases remain separate.

4.4 Success Rates and Outcomes

Figure 25.3 Success of Appeals (Each NCA's Decision or Previous Instance Judgment Counts as One)

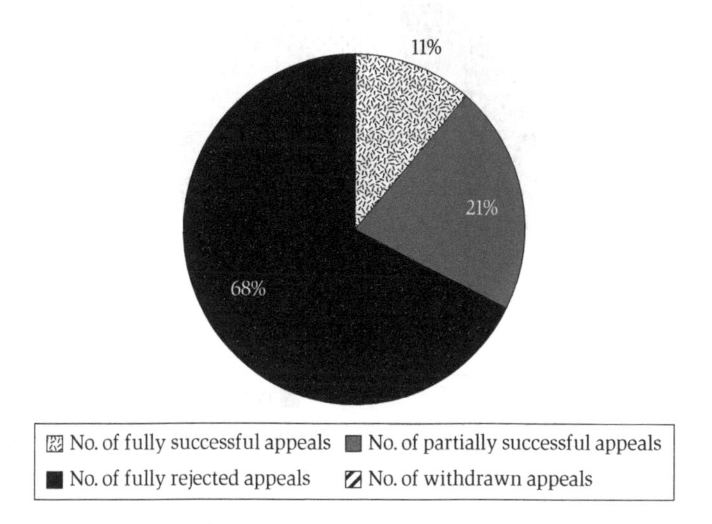

Figure 25.3 presents the success of appeals launched against NCA's decisions or on a previous instance's judgment, across all instances (the data is presented from the perspective of the NCA decision which has been appealed). It shows that the number of fully successful appeals across both instances is small – 11%. While little over a fifth – 21% of appeals are partially successful (usually reducing the fine), the overwhelming majority of appeals were fully rejected, 68%.

Figure 25.4(a) First-Instance Outcome

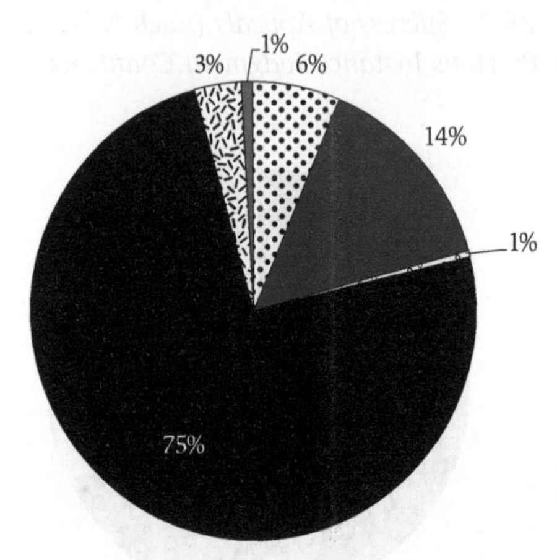

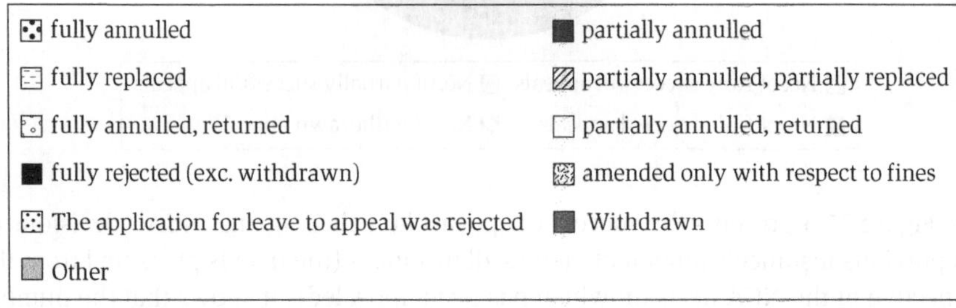

Figure 25.4 indicates the ratio of possible outcomes, according to each instance of appeal. In contrast with Figure 25.3, Figure 25.4 presents the data from the perspective of each single judgment. Figure 25.4(a) first shows the outcome at the CA level, at first instance. Here, 75% of appeals are fully rejected, with only 6% of appealed RCC decisions being fully annulled, 14% partially annulled and 3% amended only with respect to the fines that were appealed. These findings prove that, where an appeal is partially or fully accepted, in most cases the courts annul the RCC's decision, and where the domestic courts amend the first court judgment, they do so in regard to the fines applied.

Figure 25.4(b) Second-Instance Outcome

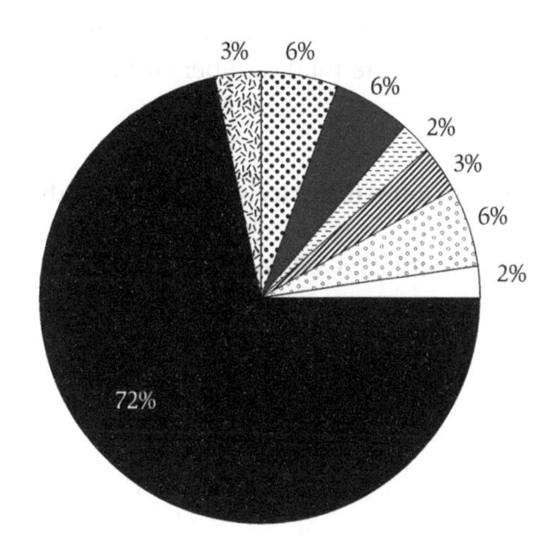

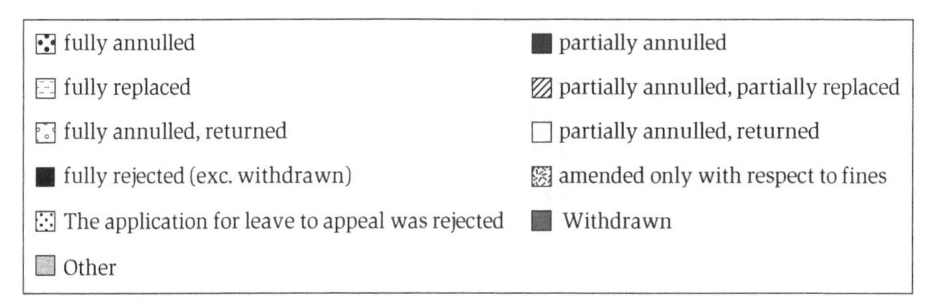

In the second instance, Figure 25.4(b) shows no significant difference in proportions: 72% of appeals on points of law are fully rejected: 3% were amended only regarding fines, 5% were fully annulled, 8% were partially annulled, 1.8% fully replaced, 2.7% partially annulled and partially replaced, 2.7% annulled and returned, and 1.8% partially annulled and returned, pursuant to the general rules governing appeals on points of law in the Romanian Code of Civil Procedure. The latter two figures can be explained on the basis that the HCCJ usually only returns cases to the CA on procedural grounds, all other grounds for appeal on points of law lead to a final decision on the merits by the HCCJ.

These percentages are not fully in line with the considerably lower success rates of appeals reported in the RCC's annual reports. The RCC publishes each year an annual report pertaining to its activity, which comprises data collected and interpreted by the institution. The data is not explained, and only raw figures are given, without detailing what types of cases the institution has accounted for (e.g., the data collected could include injunctions, procedural matters, provisional measures, legal privilege and so on). RCC uses vague language in these reports: for instance, the word 'favourable' is used without explaining whether the claim against the RCC was rejected in part or in full. The collective data presented in these RCC reports do not explain the types of cases taken into account, therefore they cannot be considered for comparison with the data found in the research for this report. The language used is ambiguous and this percentage might be interpreted otherwise (such as: '[t]he number of files in which RCC held the judicial capacity and had object competition matters in 2016 was 173. These files represented 92% of the total number of files involving the institution in court'[9]).

4.5 Type of Competition Authority's Decisions Subject to Appeal

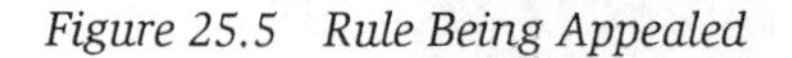

Figure 25.5 Rule Being Appealed

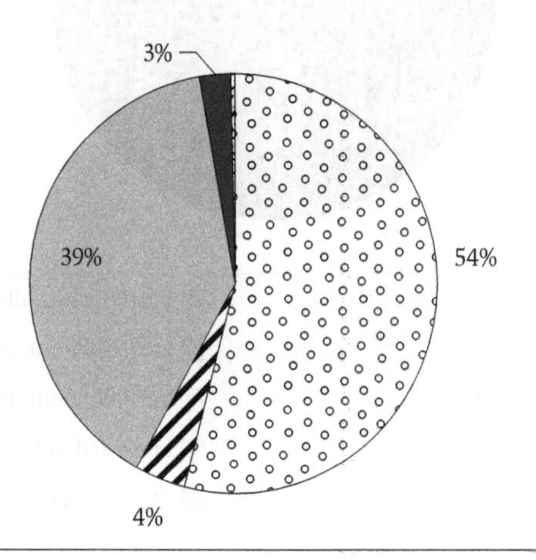

Art. 101 + national equivalent
Art. 102 + national equivalent
Arts. 101 + 102+national equivalents
Only national anti-competitive agreements
Only national abuse of dominance
National agreements and abuse of dominance

9. RCC Annual Report of 2016, p. 51. Moreover, according to the RCC Annual Report of 2014, the total percentage of fully rejected cases in appeal (final) on the merits was 96%, increasing from 93% in 2013, whereas 67% of the fines were maintained by the HCCJ, increasing from 64% in 2013 and 95% of fines maintained by the CA. *See* RCC Annual Report of 2014, p. 41. In another example, according to the RCC Annual Report of 2015, the total percentage of fully rejected cases in appeal (final) on the merits was 100%, increasing from 96% in 2014, whereas 82% of the fines were maintained by the HCCJ. *See* RCC Annual Report of 2015, p. 48. According to RCC Annual Report of 2016, the total percentage of fully rejected cases in appeal (final) on the merits was 100%, whereas 81% of the fines were maintained by the HCCJ. The same report states that 92% of the decisions were subject to challenge in court. *See* RCC Annual Report of 2016, p. 51. Also, according to RCC Annual Report of 2017, the total percentage of fully rejected cases on the merits was 100%, whereas 90% from the total cases solved by HCCJ in which RCC was a party were favorable to RCC. *See* RCC Annual Report of 2017, p. 39.

Figure 25.6 Rules Being Appealed According to Years (Each Judgment Count as One)

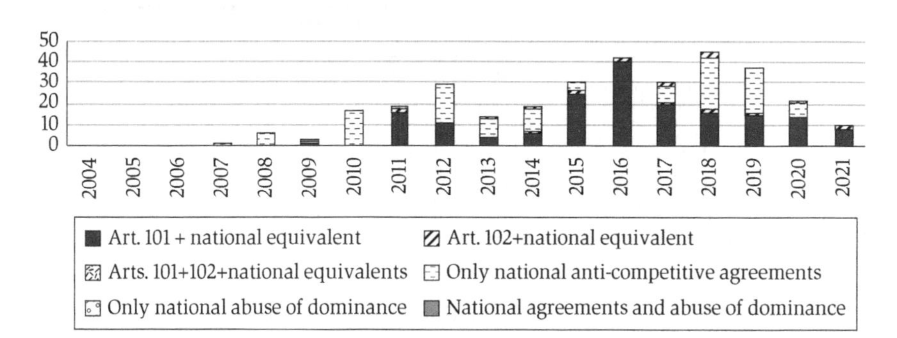

Figure 25.5 indicates the ratio of the rules subject to the courts' review, across all instances of appeal. Figure 25.6 further details this issue, by showing how these rules were applied in judgments delivered in the respective years. This leads to several conclusions:

First, Figure 25.5 shows that the majority of the RCC's decisions refer to applying Article 101 TFEU and the national equivalent or only the national equivalent – 55% and 39% respectively. In other words, the vast majority of judicial review in Romania (94%) focused on the prohibition against anti-competitive agreements. Very limited attention was given to the EU and national prohibitions against abuse of dominance. A single case examined both Articles 101 and 102 TFEU and their respective national equivalents.

Second, no discernible pattern exists as regards these types of cases. The general ratio seems to be constant over time and, consequently, one can say that it shows a preference for the RCC in the former type of investigation – Article 101 TFEU plus the national equivalent. It also means that most cases investigated by the RCC reflect a focus on Article 101 TFEU. Naturally, this is consequently reflected in the number of cases in judicial review, pursuant to the figures presented above.

The fluctuation might also result from the decline in the number of cases by the RCC, in recent years, with the number of cases as well as the aggregated number of fines continuing to descend in the past five years. It ought to be noted that the downward trend in 2019–2021 in Figure 25.6 reflects a reduction of cases of enforcement in the previous two to three years. Provided that the data collected for this report is not missing relevant cases and that the correspondence between the number of sanctioning decisions issued by the RCC and the number of cases referred to the judicial review by the undertakings is correct, the trend will continue for the foreseeable future, as the number of enforcement procedures has not increased.

Figure 25.7 Types of Restrictions

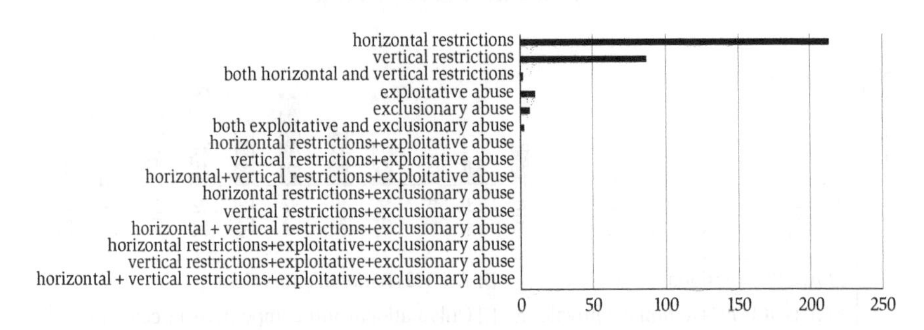

The vast majority of judgments relating to the prohibition on anti-competitive agreements (Articles 101 TFEU and the national equivalent) involved horizontal restrictions (213 out of the 302 judgments, and an additional two in combination with vertical restrictions). Judgments involving the prohibition on abuse of dominance (Article 102 TFEU and the national equivalent), pertained to both horizontal and vertical restrictions. The figures are more balanced in relation to exploitative abuse versus exclusionary abuse – eleven versus seven cases, respectively – with three cases featuring both such cases of abuse.

Finally, as regards judgments involving Article 101 TFEU and national equivalent provisions, Figure 25.8 indicates that the NCA has described 87% of the cases as by-object restrictions, with effect infringements only occupying 7% of cases. Only five cases boasted both object and effect infringements – 2%.

Figure 25.8 Object/Effect (Only for Article 101/National Equivalent Infringements)

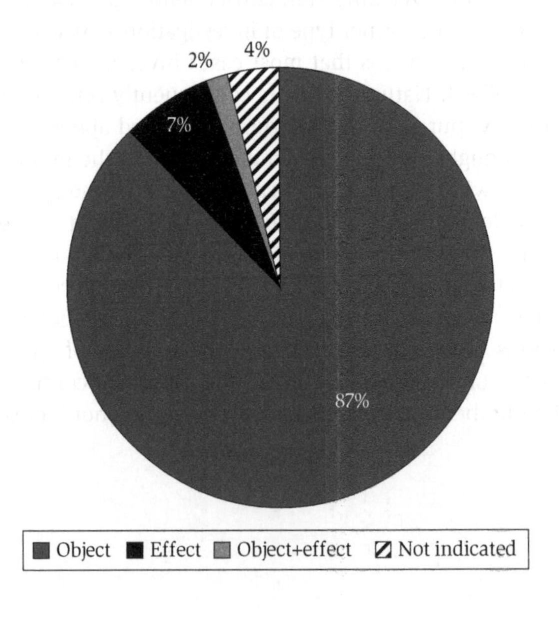

4.6 Type of NCA's Procedure

Figure 25.9 Competition Authority's Procedure

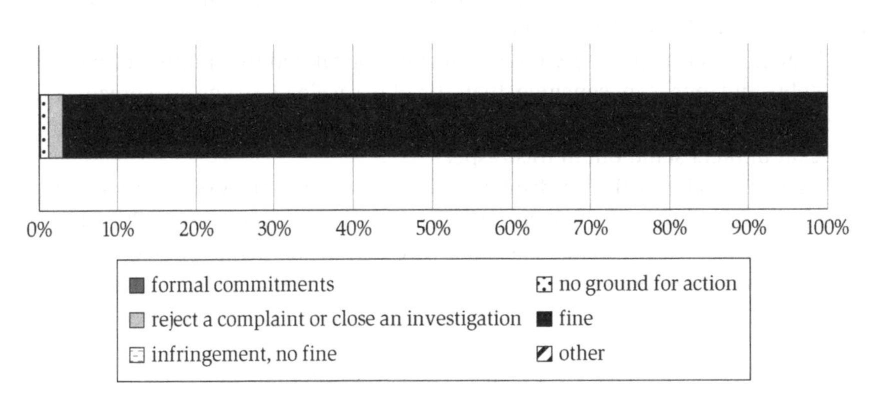

Figure 25.9 summarises the type of RCC decisions that were challenged, accounting for the procedure that took place. It shows that 97% of cases that went to court related to a fine which was imposed. This can be explained exclusively by reference to the relatively lower rate of success for grounds unrelated to the amount of the fine.

4.7 Grounds of Appeal

Figure 25.10 Grounds of Appeal (Each NCA's Decision or Previous Instance Judgment Counts as One)

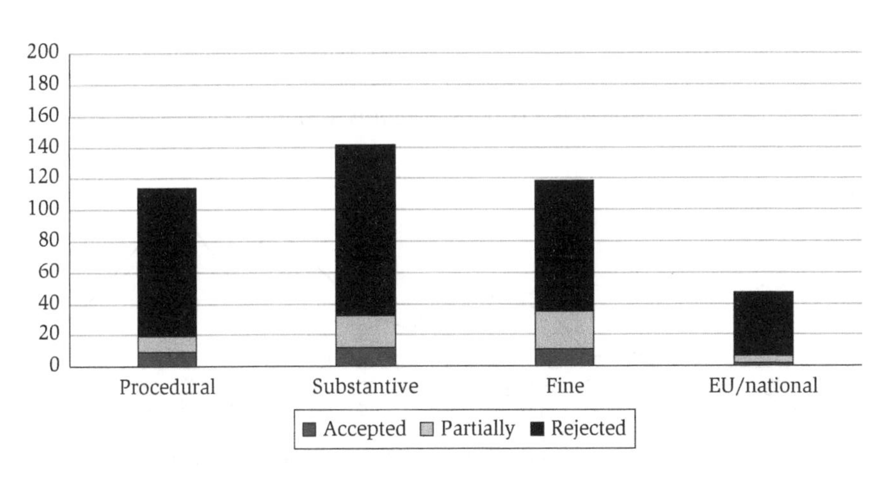

Figure 25.10 illustrates the grounds of appeal raised by the parties and their rate of success across both instances. The rates of success seem approximately equally

spread out. The most important grounds of appeal were substantive, pertaining to the fine, and procedural, without recording significant differences between these grounds. However, one must also note that such successful cases represent a small percentage overall. In fact, the procedural grounds are seldom successfully invoked by the claimants, especially in more recent years.

Figures 25.11(a)-(d) show the grounds of appeal and the number of judgments separately, and one can conclude that: (i) the caseload seems to spread equally amongst reasons throughout the years analysed (Figures 25.2(a)-(b)), and (ii) no significant outliers stand out in this respect.

Figures 25.11(a)-(d) also display a continued reluctance of the two courts to contradict the findings in RCC decisions, given that the proportion of RCC's decisions which are not overturned remains similar throughout the period subject to analysis. The Romanian courts tend to accept the assessments made in the RCC decisions, and this may be the simple rationale for the majority of appeal cases being rejected.

Figure 25.11(a) Procedural Grounds

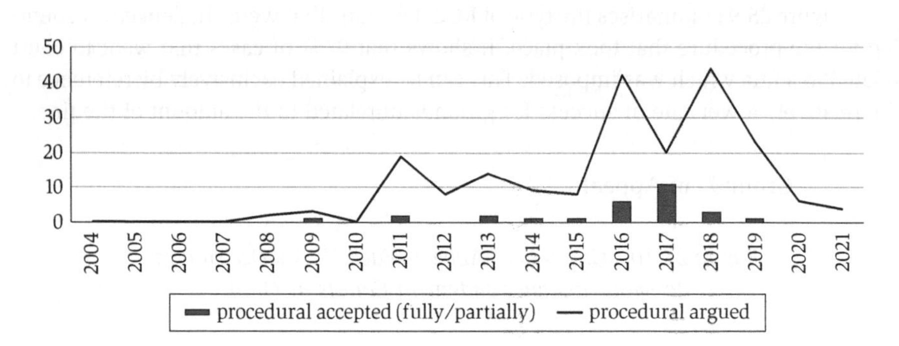

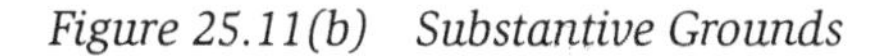

Figure 25.11(b) Substantive Grounds

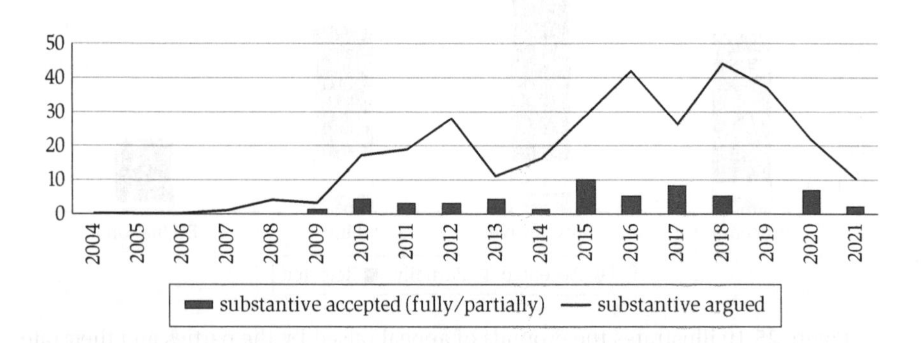

Figure 25.11(c) Fines-related Grounds

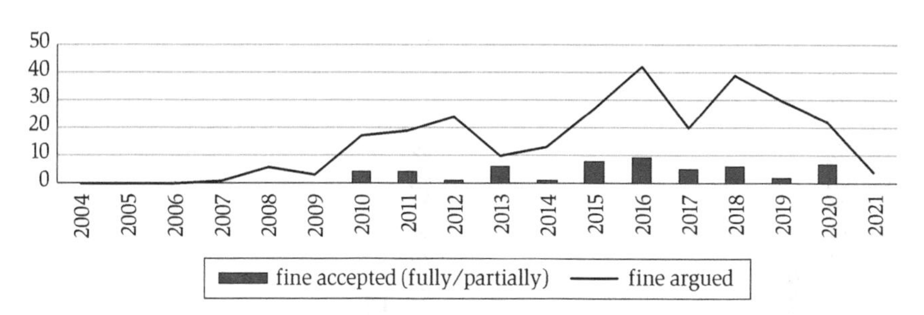

Figure 25.11(d) EU/National Grounds

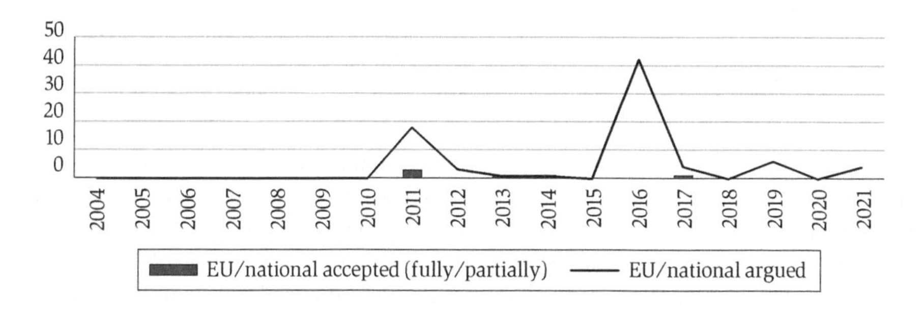

Figure 25.12 shows the success rate across the types of restrictions involved. This figure also sharply puts into perspective how few of the appeals filed, regardless of restriction, end up being successful. The trends in these figures show that parties most often raise all possible grounds they can reasonably raise, to bolster their chances of success. This is a staple of Romanian judicial culture, with parties often trying to raise arguments on the remote possibility that they are accepted, even if they appear without merit. The figures reflect the consistency of the domestic courts' practice, throughout the analysed period.

Figure 25.12 Types of Restrictions Versus Successful Grounds of Appeal

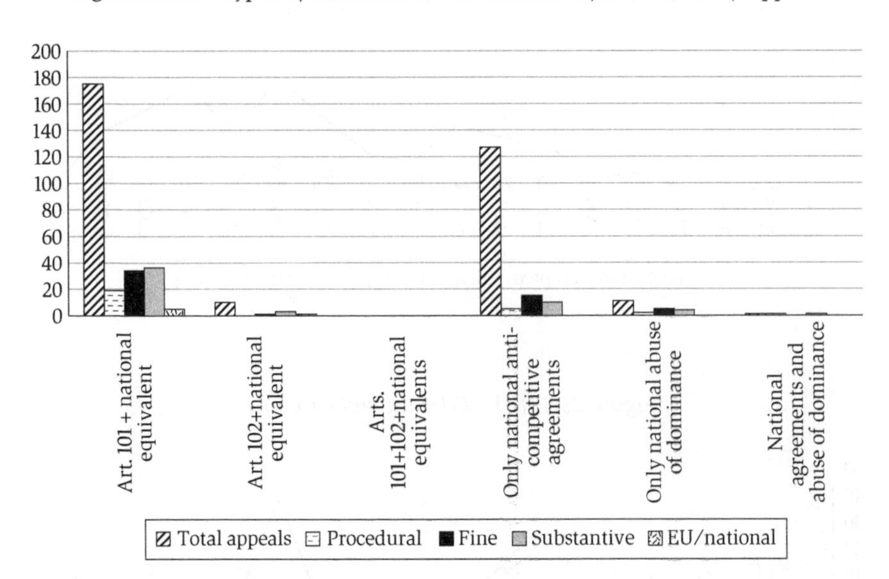

Nevertheless, in cases in which at least a partial reduction in fines exists (which amount to 21% of total cases), the average reduction of the fines was 87%, which suggests that undertakings which have been sanctioned have strong reasons to appeal - given the very small invariable judicial tax in place (currently EUR 10 for each annulment action, regardless of the value of the fine imposed, for example), there is little reason not to appeal and almost no risk in doing so. If the appeal is successful, it is likely to be successful in significantly reducing the fine, which in most cases may be the only key objective of the applicant. However, the reduction percentage cited above does not distinguish between different levels of fines. A more detailed analysis reveals that it is usually small fines which are significantly reduced, whereas appeals regarding large fines are very rarely reduced by the courts.

EU legislation or EU institutional reasons for appeal were least commonly used as a ground for appeal and constitute the least successful grounds raised in such proceedings. This can be attributed to a general apprehension by domestic courts in entering difficult EU competition law discussions on the one hand, and a possible higher scrutiny of the RCC in applying said rules in cases in which they are applicable, on the other hand. By invoking EU law in its decisions, it is less likely that undertakings will challenge an RCC decision, given the psychological impact the existence of an EU law infringement appears to produce for many undertakings. Very few appeals at any level are withdrawn by the parties, given the fact there is no incentive to withdraw.

In the earliest cases analysed (from Romania's accession in 2007 to approx. 2010), the data is scattered, and the small number of cases is insufficient for a proper aggregate assessment. Moreover, in this earliest phase, one must account for the fact that any judicial decisions only covered cases related to infringements under national equivalent provisions, given that they reflect infringements that took place before

Romania's accession to the EU. As a result, at this point, there is no case where issues related to the tension between EU and national competition laws were raised, and 2010 was the last year the research revealed only cases in which the national rules were grounds for decisions appealed.

Moreover, the applicable Romanian procedural rules require specific conditions for a third party to intervene, including the requirement that the third party should justify its own personal and direct interest, which explains the lack of *actio popularis* (that require impracticable conditions) and the rarity of third party interventions in the overall context of appeals.

Figure 25.13 Leniency

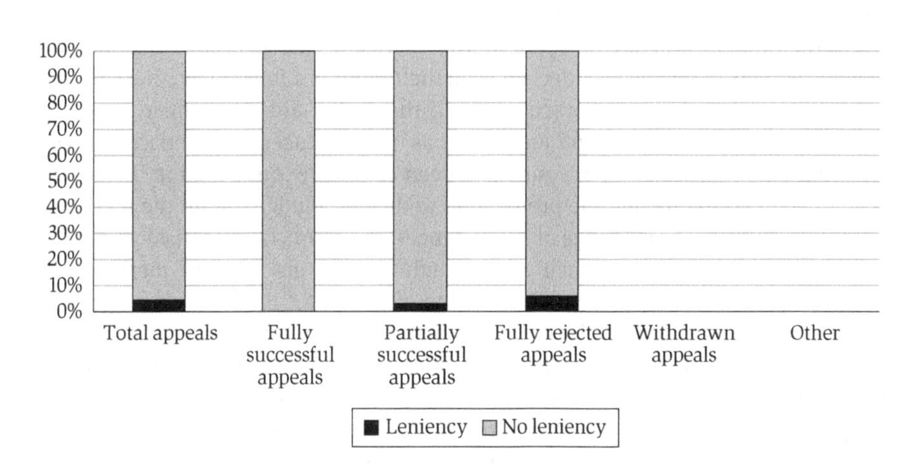

Figure 25.14 Settlements

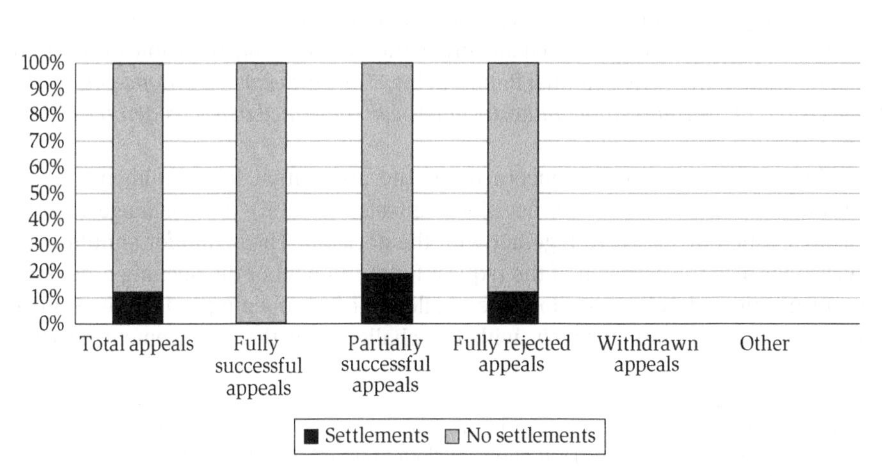

Figure 25.13 shows that leniency was seldom appealed when applied by the RCC. Figure 25.14 further demonstrates that the fact that settlements themselves are

appealed to the domestic courts can be explained by the procedure in force at the time. Undertakings could agree 'in blind', without having acknowledged the provisions of the decision, and then be unsatisfied by the concrete fine applied. The undertaking may admit the existence of wrongdoing, but not the specific illicit conduct, the market definition or some other substantive or even procedural issues in the decision.

5 QUALITATIVE ANALYSIS

5.1 Scope and Intensity of Judicial Review

At first glance, the rules under Romanian law provide the CA with the power to undertake a full review of any final decisions of the RCC, allowing it to consider procedural matters and an analysis of the merits of the decision. Despite these extensive powers to review RCC decisions on their merit in a full review, the data above reveal the paradox that, at a practical level, the courts are reluctant to exert their powers. In Romania, the *Menarini* judgment has not influenced the standard of review, as the margin of appreciation in courts has been constantly quite high in theory, with the competent courts having the prerogative to deliver a judgment on the merits.

Contrary to this broad range of competences, the courts rarely consider the merits of the case, leaving matters such as the definition of the relevant market or the economic analysis untouched, at the discretion of the NCA.[10] In Romania, competition law is perceived by all stakeholders, judges included, as a very technical field of law. This perception is reflected in the courts' practice, with many decisions refraining from tackling the most technical issues such as market definition, assessing the gravity of the infringement, evaluating the exemptions to the sanctioning, etc. For instance, the courts have never overruled the relevant market assessment made by the RCC.

Moreover, despite the NCA's exemplary record of non-reversed decisions in court, the empirical findings show that few cases did lead to reversals of its decisions.[11] Nonetheless, their record generated an aura of the RCC as being invincible in court, the usual formula in the NCA's Annual Report being '*The past years' experience shows that the decisions of the competition authority have been confirmed in a considerable ratio by justice.*'[12]

Judicial review mainly concerned: (i) the application for annulment of NCA decisions, (ii) the stay of NCA decisions' effects, and (iii) the challenge of other measures issued by the NCA, together with the decision. The action for annulment of a decision is also the occasion of the request for annulment of the opening order since the current procedural rules allow the challenge of an opening order (decision) of investigation only simultaneously with the challenge of the infringement decision.

10. *See*, e.g., the 'Distribution of central heating systems' case, 5141/2019 of the High Court of Cassation and Justice, or the 'Distribution of cloth trousers' case, 1180/2019 of the High Court of Cassation and Justice.
11. For a relevant example *see* case 5266/2011 of the Court of Appeal, in which it held that the undertaking in question had not participated in any illicit activity.
12. RCC Annual Report of 2014, p. 41.

There is only one exception to the simultaneity requirement, namely challenging the refusal of legal privilege by the RCC's president when he has ruled on this specific aspect.

To suspend decisions, applicants must simultaneously apply for the annulment of the said decision, and pay a significant bond. In practice, most of the suspension motions are dismissed. This is a clear sign that courts judging the suspension do not believe that there is a significant chance of an overturn of the RCC's decisions by the court judging the annulment of said decision. This is true even though: (i) the suspension motion is judged by a different instance, and (ii) the judge doesn't analyse the merits of the decision that is requested to be suspended.

As explained earlier, there is a larger number of cases grounded on Article 101 TFEU and, even if the entire case law on abuse is less significant than in relation to anticompetitive agreements, Article 102 TFEU is used significantly more frequently than its national equivalent in Romania. The main explanation for this trend resides in the fact that RCC bases its investigations on Articles 101 or 102 TFEU accordingly, the extensive application of Article 101 TFEU in RCC's practice most likely derives from the procedural particularities in case of application of the Treaty by a national competition authority but also from the deterrent effect for the challenging in front of a court decisions grounded on EU law.

5.2 Review of Fines

As was observed in Figure 25.4 only 3.2% of the first-instance judgments and 2.7% of the second-instance judgments were amended only with respect to the fines. These findings however do not include values, as most of the time, the fine is redacted in the publicly released version of the decision, as well as in the court awards, if available at all. These figures reflect the apprehension of the domestic courts when reviewing fines applied by the RCC, and that judicial interference of the assessment made in the RCC decision occurs only in exceptional situations.

5.3 Coherence with Substantive EU Competition Law and European Human Rights Law

The relationship between the European Union and national competition law is quite harmonious in Romania. There is no case law reflecting a conflicting application of national provisions against EU competition law or setting aside EU provisions in favour of national provisions. Moreover, the Romanian Courts make references to relevant EU Law cases, where applicable: they have, for example, referenced the *Aalborg Portland* case when holding that an undertaking cannot be exempted for participating in an anti-competitive agreement, even when not participating in all anti-competitive actions;[13] referencing the ECJ's *Sumitomo Metal Industries* case where informal anti-competitive meetings were concerned[14] and so on.

There is also a wide and more recent practice to sanction illicit competition conduct based not only on national provisions but also on TFEU provisions. The practice of enforcing national provisions and EU competition law in parallel has reached a point where the NCA includes infringements where the application of European Union law was not required, hence extending the application of EU law beyond its scope. This option of the RCC in extending the application of EU law has not been subject to any form of judicial consideration as of yet, but the possibility remains open for future developments.

Furthermore, cooperation between the Romanian NCA and the European Commission, including participation in dawn raids further to European Commission requests, further enhances the relationship between national and European law not only in substantive law, but also procedural law. The recent amendments to the Competition Law extended the collection of evidence to instruments relating to letters rogatory, furthering enhanced cooperation within the European Competition Network and with the European Commission.

Interestingly, the national courts find that the statute of limitation in Regulation 2988/1974 may be applicable to investigations initiated prior to Romania's accession to the EU, which is a prime example of a harmonious interpretation as early as 2009. In one of the most-debated solutions in Romanian practice, the HCCJ held that the requirement of a reasonable duration of an investigation is a principle that should be considered even for cases started before.[15]

5.4 Preliminary Rulings and Coherence with EU Law

Certainly, preliminary rulings are a method of ensuring the coherence of national enforcement with EU Law. There have been very few preliminary references made by the Romanian courts to the ECJ, as detailed below. Several preliminary references are notable in this context: C-172/14 - *ING Pensii*; C-308/19 - *Whiteland Import Export* and the most recent C-385/21 - *Zenith Media*. In *ING Pensii*, the question at hand pertained to interpreting Article 101(1) TFEU, and the Court of Justice held that 'Article 101(1) TFEU must be interpreted as meaning that agreements to share clients, such as those concluded between the private pensions funds in the main proceedings, constitute agreements with an anti-competitive object, the number of clients affected by such an agreement being irrelevant for the purpose of assessing the requirement relating to the restriction of competition within the internal market.'

In *Whiteland Import Export*, the main question was the limitation period in place in such cases and of the interpretation of Regulation (EC) No 1/2003, Article 4(3) TEU and 101 TFEU. The Court of Justice held that EU law must be interpreted as meaning

13. *See* judgment 3352/14.09.2010, of the CoA.
14. *See ibid.*
15. CA Case 2264/2009.

that national courts are not required to apply Article 25(3) of Council Regulation (EC) No 1/2003 of 16 December 2002 on the implementation of the rules on competition laid down in Articles [101 and 102 TFEU] to the time-barring of a national competition authority's powers to impose penalties for infringements of EU competition law.

Finally, in *Zenith Media Communications*, the Court of Justice held that Article 4(3) TEU and 101 TFEU 'must be interpreted as precluding national legislation or practice under which, for the purposes of calculating the fine imposed on an undertaking for infringement of Article 101 TFEU, the national competition authority is required, in all circumstances, to take into account the turnover of that undertaking as shown in its profit and loss account, without having the possibility of examining evidence put forward by that undertaking to show that that turnover does not reflect its real economic situation and that, consequently, another amount which reflects that situation should be taken into account as turnover, provided that that evidence is precise and documented.'

These valuable judgments of the Court in preliminary rulings pertaining to competition law and arising out of enforcement procedures prove that domestic courts should not be apprehensive in using the preliminary ruling mechanism in domestic competition law proceedings, although the limited number of cases in which this has been the case indicates the contrary.

6 CONCLUDING REMARKS

Various important conclusions can be drawn from the research undertaken and the data collected. Romania's EU accession process has clearly influenced the legislation on competition and its application.

The standard of judicial review, even though on the merits and not deferential, affords the NCA a vast margin of appreciation in fact, as the courts are reluctant to overturn the findings of the RCC (sometimes the courts refer to the RCC as the specialist agency that can best assess competition law matters). The important role of the NCA as the undisputed specialist authority in the field is reflected in the practice and outcomes of judicial review where very few decisions are overturned by the judiciary.

There are some endemic deficiencies in the Romanian judicial system making it impervious to research, notably the lack of transparency in publication of judicial determinations. These deficiencies of the system are vulnerable to critique. More accessibility, if not more transparency, should be warranted and free access to judicial decisions could be ensured while ensuring that data protection and privacy laws are respected. The same conclusions could be drawn with regard to the general quantitative analysis of the case law of Romanian courts.

Furthermore, there is no mechanism similar to the AG's role at the CJEU or for an *amicus curiae* in the procedure, even though the complexity and specificity of competition law litigation should warrant special assistance. The fact that third parties almost never participate in competition law cases can be explained through this procedural lens, as highlighted above. The implementation of the institution of *amicus curiae* would be however difficult, considering the absence of impartial, well-reputed persons or institutions that might fulfil the profile.

More specifically, the above figures show that generally, the RCC's decisions are often judicially reviewed. In principle, this is a welcome outcome, because it strengthens scrutiny of the RCC's activity. However, the existing data shows that a great majority of these challenges in front of the competent courts are unsuccessful, close to 70% (closer to 90% according to the RCC reports that cannot be verified), while partially successful appeals usually imply solely a reduction of applied fines – although these reductions might be substantial.

A worrying trend is that the tension between EU and national law is the least commonly used ground of appeal by applicants, and, when those EU grounds are actually used by the claimants, they are the least successful in courts. Claimants, when challenging RCC decisions, seldom raise EU rules directly applied in the decision. The language in the case law studied shows an apprehension to rely solely on substantial EU rules when deciding on competition law cases in Romania – a fact which is highlighted further by the very small number of preliminary rulings requested by the Romanian courts – only three such references in fifteen years.

Moreover, the fact that both the CA and the HCCJ appear to have a proportionally similar percentage of rejected appeals and appeals on points of law shows the difficulty in overturning the RCC's decision, once delivered. This trend, if continued, will probably lead to a much larger number of settled cases during the investigation procedure in the future, with applicants preferring to refrain from pursuing lengthy and expensive litigation involving very little chance of success.

CHAPTER 26

Slovakia Report

Ondrej Blažo

1 INTRODUCTION TO THE COMPETITION LAW ENFORCEMENT CONTEXT IN SLOVAKIA

1.1 Historical Outline

In the former Czechoslovakia, antitrust regulation was first introduced by Act No. 141/1933 Coll. on cartels and private monopolies (Cartel Law).[1] The Cartel Law of 1933 can, however, hardly be considered a true competition law. It did not prohibit cartels and made them subject to governmental control merely via mandatory registration[2] involving the power of the Government to prohibit enforcement of a cartel agreement if that agreement was unduly restricting entrepreneurial activity of the undertakings that were obliged to pay prices set by the cartel or were limited or restricted by the cartel. The application of the Cartel Law was terminated by the Czechoslovak Constitution of 1948 that prohibited monopolies and cartels.[3] It must be noted that the Constitution of 1948 did not prohibit cartels and monopolies in order to protect free market but partly to restrict private entrepreneurship as a whole, as part of wider nationalisation and the introduction of central planned economy.[4] Thus, any development of competition law in the Slovakian territory was interrupted until the Velvet Revolution in 1989 and the re-introduction of a market-oriented economy thereafter.

Act No. 103/1990 Coll.[5] was a temporary solution to amend the socialist Economic Code 1964[6] and to effect the transition of the character of the national

1. Zákon č. 141/1933 Sb. o kartelech a soukromých monopolech (kartelový zákon).
2. §§ 5 et seq. Cartel Law.
3. § 161 Constitution of 1948: Ustavní zákon č. 150/1948 Sb. Ústava Československé republiky.
4. § 146-§ 160 Constitution of 1948.
5. Zákon č. 103/1990 Zb. ktorým sa mení a dopĺňa Hospodársky zákonník.
6. Hospodársky zákonník č. 109/1964 Zb.

economy of then Czechoslovakia, changing the title of provisions §119 et seq. from 'Principles of cooperation of socialist organization' to 'Principles of economic competition'. Compared to Cartel Law 1933, Act No. 103/1990 Coll. contained general clauses resembling a more modern understanding of competition law. The act prohibited organisations'[7] '...abuse of economic position for achieving unjust or disproportionate benefits to the disadvantage to other organizations or consumers ...'[8] and also provided that 'Organisations shall not, alone or in agreement with other organisations, engage in conduct in their economic activities which, contrary to the interests of the national economy, restricts or otherwise adversely affects the activities of other organisations or is detrimental to consumers.'[9] This temporary solution was in force for less than one year and on 1 March 1991 the first competition act came into force: Act No. 63/1991 Coll. Protection of Economic Competition[10] (ZOHS 1991).[11] This federal law contained elements and notions resembling European competition law as well as concepts associated with the Cartel Law 1933. The wording of the prohibition of 'cartel agreements' was similar to the wording of Article 85 EEC Treaty but the individual exceptions and 'block' exemptions were subject to prior registration at the competition authority. Regarding abusive practices, ZOHS 1991 distinguished between a monopoly position[12] and a dominant position[13] and undertakings were obliged to notify their monopoly position or dominant position. The act considered a 30% market share as constituting a dominant position [§ 9(1) ZOHS 1991]. The abuse of monopoly or dominant position was prohibited [§ 9(13) ZOHS 1991]. Although the wording of the concepts related to anti-competitive behaviour in some aspects differed from EU law, the non-exhaustive list of practices were the same as they are in Article 85 and 86 EEC Treaty. The ZOHS 1991 remained in force in both republics after the split of Czechoslovakia in December 1992, and in Slovakia[14] was replaced in 1994 by Act No. 188/1994 Coll. (ZOHS 1994).[15] The new legislation brought slight changes in the substantive law and a significant strengthening of the powers of the competition authority (the Antimonopoly Office of the Slovak Republic – Protimonopolný úrad Slovenskej republiky) (PMÚ). Compared with ZOHS 1994, the maximum fine was raised from 5% of an undertaking's turnover to 10%. The wording of the notion of agreements restricting competition [§ 3(1) and (2) ZOHS 1994] copied Article 85 EEC Treaty and the prohibition of abuse of dominant position [§ 7(4) and (5) ZOHS 1994] followed Article 86 EEC Treaty. However, ZOHS 1994 contained a legal definition of the notion of dominant position and a rebuttable presumption of dominance (40% of

7. The act used the term 'organisation' for economic unit as it was merely accepting the notions of the Economic Code because socialist economy did not accept existence of private entrepreneurship,
8. § 119b(1) Economic Code.
9. § 119b(2) Economic Code.
10. Zákon č. 63/1991 Zb. o ochrane hospodárskej súťaže.
11. If there is well-established Slovak acronym for the title of act or name of institution, it is preferred.
12. Undertaking did not face any competition.
13. Undertaking did not face any significant competition.
14. In Czechia, ZOHS 1991 remained in force by 2001.
15. Zákon Národnej rady Slovenskej republiky č. 188/1994 Z.z. o ochrane hospodárskej súťaže.

market share). ZOHS 1994 was replaced again in 2001 by Act No. 163/2001[16] (ZOHS 2001) that remained in force for two decades until 2021 when it was replaced by Act No. 187/2021 (ZOHS 2021).[17] From the substantive point of view, ZOHS 2021 is codification of the repeatedly amended ZOHS 2001 and at the same time, it introduced minor changes in procedural law transposing the ECN+ Directive.[18]

Slovakia joined the European Union in 2004 and Slovak competition law was gradually approximated to EU law by subsequent changes to the competition legislation (the most extensive amendment of ZOHS 2001 was adopted in order to fulfil its duties in relation to EU competition law). Until ZOHS 2021, the main difference between Slovak competition law and EU law was in relation to the definition of 'undertaking'. Slovak law maintained a quite rigid concept of an undertaking as a person defined by the Commercial Code or other natural or legal person engaging in activity on the market [§ 3(2) ZOHS 2001]. This rigid concept was criticised by academics[19] and also led to practical difficulties in enforcement, e.g., in the GIS cartel, the European Commission imposed five separate fines on single companies and seven fines jointly and severally on groups of companies while the PMÚ imposed sixteen separate fines.[20] Thus the PMÚ had always identified the precise natural or legal person that engaged in anti-competitive behaviour rather than identifying an 'economic unit'. When the PMÚ was not strictly bound by the legal definitions provided by ZOHS 2001 (in particular, due to the non-existence of any definition of the notion in issue) it could successfully benefit from the parallel wording of the Slovak and EU substantive competition law rules and thereby 'transplant' concepts employed by EU law in order to fill gaps in Slovak law. The 'economic continuity test' was effectively introduced in

16. Zákon č. 136/2001 Z. z. o ochrane hospodárskej súťaže a o zmene a doplnení zákona Slovenskej národnej rady č. 347/1990 Zb. o organizácii ministerstiev a ostatných ústredných orgánov štátnej správy Slovenskej republiky v znení neskorších predpisov.
17. Zákon č. 187/2021 Z. z. o ochrane hospodárskej súťaže a o zmene a doplnení niektorých zákonov.
18. Directive (EU) 2019/1 of the European Parliament and of the Council of 11 December 2018 to empower the competition authorities of the Member States to be more effective enforcers and to ensure the proper functioning of the internal market (OJ L 11, 14.1.2019, pp. 3-33).
19. Katarína Kalesná and Mária T Patakyová, 'Subjects of Legal Regulation – Different Approaches of Competition, Public Procurement and Corporate Law', *Economic and social development* (Varazdin Development and Entrepreneurship Agency 2019); Katarína Kalesná, 'Je Podnik (Stále) Legislatívnou Výzvou?' (2017) 36 Acta Facultatis Iuridicae Universitatis Comenianae 122; Katarína Kalesná, 'Kto Môže Niesť' Zodpovednosť' Za Porušenie Súťažného Práva?' (2009) 92 Právny obzor 123; Ondrej Blažo, 'Definovanie Osobnej a Územnej Pôsobnosti Komunitárneho Kartelového Práva', *Debaty mladých právníků 2007* (Univerzita Palackého 2007); Ondrej Blažo, 'Twenty Years of Harmonisation and Still Divergent: Development of Slovak Competition Law' (2014) 7 Yearbook of Antitrust and Regulatory Studies 109 DOI: 10.2139/ssrn.2738387; Katarína Kalesná, 'Právnické Osoby v Konfrontácii s Ekonomickou Realitou Test Ekonomickej Kontinuity', *Pocta Milošovi Tomsovi k 80. narozeninám* (Aleš Čeněk 2006).
20. Decision of the PMÚ, No. 2009/KH/R/2/035 (14 August 2009).

the *Cargo* case[21] and confirmed on appeal.[22] The legal definition of abuse of an essential facility was another stumbling block under the ZOHS 2001[23] since it created a specific form of abuse of dominance and the general clause was not applicable in those cases.[24]

Summing up, the development of competition law in Slovakia is a story of gradual allegiance to the concepts of EU law (previously EEC) together with a transition from a socialist centrally planned economy to a modern market-economy within the EU. Initially, the legislation contained plenty of legal definitions but later, the concepts were 'purified' and broad general norms and definitions only remained. Thus, the regulation effectively benefited from copying EU law and its enforcement relies on concepts defined by EU case law even in purely national cases. The historic overview is also necessary for understanding how the PMÚ and the courts continuously adapt their practice to the new legal environment. Currently, § 4 ZOHS 2021 copies Article 101 TFEU and § 5 ZOHS 2021 Article 102 TFEU as did § 4 and § 8 ZOHS 2001. Slovak law also contained specific prohibited anti-competitive behaviour covering distortion of competition by administrative and self-governmental authorities (§ 6 ZOHS 2021 and § 39 ZOHS 2001) that has no parallel under EU law.

1.2 Enforcement Framework

The PMÚ is the sole authority empowered to protect economic competition within the meaning of Articles 101 and 102 TFEU. Sector regulators do not have powers to enforce competition rules and are purely confined to market regulation within specific sectoral and utilities laws (transposing the EU law): the Transport Authority for air, water and rail transport: the Regulatory Office for Network Industries for gas, water, electricity, heat and wastewater sectors: the Regulatory Authority for Electronic Communications and Postal Services for telecommunication sector and postal services. The powers of the PMÚ also extend to the field of coordination of state aid.[25] The PMÚ does not enforce public procurement rules, consumer protection or unfair trade practices in the agriculture and food sector.

From an institutional point of view, this enforcement framework has been relatively stable over time.[26] Slovakia followed the Czechoslovakian system of administrative enforcement by a non-ministerial body of central government (i.e., the PMÚ is

21. Decision of the PMÚ No. 2011/KH/1/1/055 (22 December 2011).
22. Judgment of the Regional Court in Bratislava No. 1S/27/2007-227 (6 December 2007), judgment of the Supreme Court of the Slovak Republic, No. 1Sžhpu/1/2011 (31 January 2012).
23. *See* for details Blažo, 'Twenty Years of Harmonisation and Still Divergent: Development of Slovak Competition Law' (*supra* n. 19) 119-120.
24. Decision of PMÚ No. 2005/ DZ/2/1/064 (25 May 2005); decision of the Council of the PMÚ No. 2005/DZ/R/2/143 (21 December 2005); judgment of the Regional Court in Bratislava No. 1S/31/2006 (27 September 2007); decision of the PMÚ No. 2008/DZ/2/1/066 (14 August 2008); decision of the Council of the PMÚ No. 2009/DZ/R/2/026 (15 May 2009); judgment of the Regional Court in Bratislava No. 4S/108/2009 (3 December 2010); judgment of the Supreme Court of the Slovak Republic No. 4Sžhpu/1/2011 (28 June 2011); decision of the Council of the PMÚ No. 2012/ZK/R/2/005 (27 January 2012).
25. Zákon č. 358/2015 Z. z. o úprave niektorých vzt'ahov v oblasti štátnej pomoci a minimálnej pomoci a o zmene a doplnení niektorých zákonov (zákon o štátnej pomoci).
26. The PMÚ was established in 1990 even before ZOHS 1991 came into force.

a body of central government, together with ministries, but is not headed by a minister, similarly to, e.g., the Office for Public Procurement). The main institutional change was introduced by an amendment to ZOHS 2001 in 2004 when the Council of the PMÚ was established as a collective appellate body to review decisions of the PMÚ.[27] The Council of the PMÚ still remained a collective body within the PMÚ and both administrative instances are handled by different organisational structures within the same institution. Thus, the PMÚ holds administrative investigation and decision-making powers, while the first-instance decisions of the PMÚ (in fact, decisions of the division or department of the PMÚ signed by the Vice President of the PMÚ) can be subject to review by the Council of the PMÚ (chaired by the President of the PMÚ).

Under the Administrative Code[28] the first-instance procedure and second-instance administrative proceedings form together a single administrative procedure and the appellate body (the Council) has the same powers as the first-instance body and can review the first-instance decision as a whole; thus the Council can not only confirm or annul the first-instance decision but can also repair defects in the first-instance proceedings and decision and adopt a completely new amended decision based on a second-instance proceeding (§59 Administrative Code). The administrative procedure of the PMÚ is governed by two sets of procedural rules: specific rules laid down by competition legislation, e.g., in relation to such issues as inspections, parties to proceedings, sanctions, settlement, leniency and commitment procedures: and general rules under the Administrative Code. Equally, the Council has competence to order an inspection, accept leniency, commitments or settle the case, and can also change the level of the fine (even raise the fine).

Since there is no general act on administrative sanctions in Slovakia covering all types of administrative infringements (minor offences, infringements by undertakings, natural or legal persons), the absence of precise rules and the practical consequences led to several cases being brought to the court to review the PMÚ's decisions. In particular, there are no general rules for the content of the operative part of administrative decisions, or in relation to the standard of proof and these lacunae were also reasons for judicial appeals (*see*, e.g., *Highway cartel* saga).[29]

A second-instance administrative decision, i.e., a decision of the Council of the PMÚ, can be subject to judicial review before the courts because court procedural rules allow courts to review only administrative decisions that cannot be appealed by an administrative appeal. If there is a two-instance administrative proceeding (such as proceedings in competition matters), a decision of an administrative appellate body can be reviewed by the courts. Due to the principle of the unity of the first and second-instance administrative proceedings, when the court reviews second-instance administrative decisions, it shall take into account the whole proceeding that led to

27. Before the change, the decisions of the PMÚ were reviewed by the President of the PMÚ alone. This model of two instances within the one governmental body is common among all central governmental bodies, except the Office for Public Procurement that followed the PMÚ's example.
28. Zákon č. 71/1967 Zb. o správnom konaní (správny poriadok).
29. O Blažo and S Šramelová, 'The First Bid Rigging Case in Slovakia after Years of Judicial Disputes' (2015) 8 Yearbook of Antitrust and Regulatory Studies 249.

such a decision, i.e., the investigation prior to launching formal administrative proceedings, the first-instance administrative proceedings, the first-instance administrative decision, the second-instance administrative proceedings and the second-instance administrative decision itself, as elements of the single administrative proceedings as a whole. This approach and the intensity of the first-instance administrative proceedings and administrative decision can vary depending on the character of the second-instance administrative decision: if the Council of the PMÚ confirms or merely partially amends the first-instance administrative decision, it is inevitable to read both administrative decisions together and review them together; if the Council of the PMÚ replaced the first-instance administrative decision by its own conclusions, it is obvious that there will be focus on the second-instance decision. As a result, the court may either reject an action, amend the second-instance administrative decision, annul solely the second-instance administrative decision or annul both the second-instance administrative decision as well as the first-instance decision of the administrative body, if the errors made in the first-instance administrative proceedings cannot be solved via the second-instance administrative proceedings then the proceedings shall start *de novo*.

1.3 Enforcement Practices and Priorities

In order to better understand enforcement practice and priorities it is useful to also look at the period before 2004 because when applying ZOHS 1994, the main focus and decision-making activity remained on 'negative attests', i.e., comfort letters for non-violation of the competition law. The combination of a newly appointed president (Danica Paroulková 2001-2011) and accession to the EU (2004) boosted optimism and led to assertive enforcement of competition by the PMÚ when the PMÚ handled several high-profile cases: in relation to abuses in the telecommunication sector (Slovak Telekom cases), rail transport (Cargo cases), and the highway cartel. Therefore, the beginning of the period under this study coincides with the higher activity of the PMÚ under Ms Paroulková's presidency and the accession of Slovakia to the EU.

After 2011, i.e., after the end of Ms Paroulková's term (the new president of the PMÚ was appointed for two five-year terms without any public hearing or selection procedure, apparently on a basis of some political agreement[30]), a gradual decline in its enforcement activities can be observed. In the period 2004-2011 the number of investigations in agreements cases was between twenty-eight and eighty-seven per year (average fifty-five per year), while after 2011 under the new leadership of the PMÚ, the numbers dropped, in particular in 2013-2015 when they were below thirty;

30. Close ties between Mr Tibor Menyhart and Most-Híd party (the member of government coalition) were questioned by journalist, e.g., Martin Turček, 'Kto ovláda Protimonopolný úrad? L'udia s väzbami na oligarchu spájaného so stranou Most-Híd', *Aktuality, 4 April 2019*, [online] https://www.aktuality.sk/clanok/660986/protimonopolny-urad-je-napojeny-na-oligarchov-okolo-bugara/; Dušan Mikušovič, 'Verejné vypočutia sú dobrý základ, vyradia nemehlá, no nezabránia politickým nominantom', *Dennik N*, 31 May 2017, [online] https://dennikn.sk/781309/verejne-vypocutia-su-dobry-zaklad-vyradia-nemehla-no-nezabrania-politickym-nominantom/.

while in abuse cases the decline in enforcement activities was even more apparent: in the period 2004-2011 the number of investigations was between forty-one and seventy-six, whereas after 2011 it dropped below twenty and, more precisely below ten per year after 2012. Consequently, the number of decisions adopted in enforcement actions dropped: there were ninety-one in the period 2004-2011 and only thirty-five in the even longer period 2012-2021, and the PMÚ adopted no decision on abuse of dominance in three consecutive years (2015-2017). These two periods of different levels of enforcement activity by the PMÚ have resulted in a different number of reviewed cases by the courts: thirty-eight cases involving a total amount of fines of EUR 137.9 million from the period 2004-2011 and twenty-three cases from the period after 2012 involving a total amount of fines of EUR 33.9 million. It can also be observed that the PMÚ, in recent years, turned its attention to bid-rigging cases, the majority of which involved collusion by small, localised firms. This prioritisation focus[31] also resulted in a lower level of fines[32].

Since the PMÚ is not obliged to issue a decision when rejecting a complaint, rejections are not subject to judicial review (the PMÚ simply does not launch administrative proceedings after a preliminary investigation). However, a decision involving the settlement procedure does not exclude the possibility of judicial review.

2 REVIEW OF THE COMPETITION AUTHORITY'S DECISIONS

The institutional framework and the setting of procedural rules, including the intensity and the scope of review, were reformed several times during the period that is within the scope of analysis.[33] By September 2004, decisions by the PMÚ were reviewed by the Supreme Court of the Slovak Republic (SC) in two instances of judicial appeal: from October 2004 to July 2021 by the Regional Court in Bratislava at first instance and by the SC at second instance; and from August 2021 *(de iure* from January 2021) the Supreme Administrative Court of the Slovak Republic (SAC) replaced the SC at second instance.

Moreover, the procedural codes applied by the courts were changed several times. By June 2016, the general Civil Procedural Code of 1963 (OSP)[34] also governed judicial review of administrative decisions. Under the reform of court procedural rules

31. For detailed tables and sources *see* Ondrej Blažo, 'Proper, Transparent and Just Prioritization Policy as a Challenge for National Competition Authorities and Prioritization of the Slovak NCA' (2020) 13 Yearbook of Antitrust and Regulatory Studies 117, 137-138.
32. For the overview of total and average fines in that period can be compared, e.g., O Blažo, 'More Than a Decade of the Slovak Settlement Regime in Antitrust Matters: From European Inspirations to National Inventions' (2023) 16 Yearbook of Antitrust and Regulatory Studies 9, pp. 36-39 DOI: 10.7172/1689-9024.yars.2023.16.27.1.
33. For more comprehensive historical overview of administrative judiciary *see* Jana Baricová, Marián Fečík and Anita Filová, '§ 1 [Predmet Zákona], § 2 [Právo Na Súdnu Ochranu]' in Jana Baricová, Marián Fečík and Marek Števček (eds), *Správny súdny poriadok* (C H Beck 2018); Marián Vrabko, 'Správne Súdnictvo v Slovenskej Republike (Historické, Politické a Právne Východiská)', *Pôsobnost' a organizácia správneho súdnictva v Slovenskej republike* (Právnická fakulta UK 2012).
34. Zákon č. 99/1963 Zb. Občiansky súdny poriadok.

effective from July 2016, judicial review of administrative decisions is handled under the specific Administrative Court Code (SSP).[35] Thus, for the purpose of coding of the judgments, the period within the scope of research was split into four periods and for the same purpose, even the same court was coded as a separate court for each period due to its different competence under each period: for example, the SC deciding at first instance, SC deciding on appeals against judgments of the SC, the SC deciding on appeals against judgments of the regional court, and, finally the SC deciding on cassation complaints, were all coded as separate courts due to its different competence and the differing scope of review of appeals.

2.1 Period with the OSP in Force: 2004-June 2016 (Appellate System)

The OSP was adopted in 1963, i.e., in the communist era and originally it did not contain comprehensive regulation of judicial review of administrative decision. After 1989, this code was not replaced but rather amended to adapt to new democratic conditions; in total, it was amended eighty-seven times, including forty-four times since 2004. However further analysis covers legislative changes related only to the review of decisions by administrative bodies. The judicial review of administrative decisions and other acts was included in the OSP by its amendment of 1991; however, it remained within the competence of courts of general jurisdiction: district courts, regional courts and the SC.[36] Review of decisions by the PMÚ as a body of the central government was covered by an amendment of the OSP in effect form October 2004.

2.1.1 Period until September 2004: The SC as the Only Competent Court for Review the PMÚ's Decisions

Until September 2004, the SC was the only competent court for review of decisions by the ministries and other bodies of the central government (therefore including the PMÚ) if special legislation did not provide otherwise (from October 2004 this provision was changed to the effect that the SC was competent at first instance only if special legislation provides so).[37] This institutional setting falls only partially within the scope of the study (several months only) and only two cases were handled under this framework.

The SC had competence to either reject the action for review, if the decision was in line with the law,[38] or to annul it if the decision was incorrect in law or the findings of facts on which the administrative decision was based were inconsistent with the contents of the administrative file or the findings of fact were inadequate to conclude the case.[39] If the court annulled the decision, it was always obliged to send it back to the administrative body for reconsideration, i.e., it could not close the case itself. In

35. Zákon č. 162/2015 Z. z. Správny súdny poriadok.
36. Vrabko (*supra* n. 33) 18-19.
37. § 246 (2)(a) OSP.
38. § 250j(1) OSP.
39. § 250j(2) OSP.

general, the court was bound by the facts established by the administrative body, but in the case of review of sanctions, the court was empowered to review the facts and on its own evidence gathering and examination to establish facts.[40] Regarding sanctions, the court had competence not only to reject an action or annul an administrative body's decision but also to decide 'otherwise' regarding the sanction and thus replace the decision of the administrative body to this extent.[41]

The OSP allowed an appeal against a first-instance judgment of the SC, but the scope varied depending on the grounds of the first-instance judgment. If the SC rejected the action, the applicant could appeal. The administrative body could appeal (i.e., its decision was annulled by the first-instance court's decision) only if the court decided that the administrative body erred in law or the conclusion on facts did not correspond with the content of the administrative file.[42] And finally, if the court changed the fine under § 250(5) OSP, both parties could appeal in full.

Since the SC was the first-instance court, appeals were heard by the same court, by a panel of different composition (at first instance, the case was heard by a three-member panel, and on appeal by a five-member panel).[43]

The SC was a court of general jurisdiction to hear appeals and extraordinary requests for review and there was no specialisation for competition cases, i.e., all judges were hearing cases reviewing all types of administrative decisions of all spheres of administrative decision-making.

2.1.2 Period 2004-2016: Two-Instance Appellate Regime

In 2004, the Fifth Part of the OSP on Administrative Judiciary was significantly amended.[44] First, in competition cases, this transferred the first-instance appeal to the Regional Court in Bratislava (RCB)[45] while only second-instance appeals were heard by the SC[46] (in both instances in three-member panels).[47]

In general, the court could review an administrative decision within the limits of the scope, reasons and content of the appeal (action against the PMÚ's decision)[48] and a decision could be annulled only for reasons stipulated in § 250j(2) OSP (similarly to pre-2004 law)[49] if they were invoked by the applicant. Notwithstanding the scope of the

40. §250i (2) OSP.
41. § 250j (5) OSP.
42. § 250j (4) OSP.
43. § 246b(3) OSP.
44. Zákon č. 428/2004 Z. .z., ktorým sa mení a dopĺňa zákon č. 99/1963 Zb. Občiansky súdny poriadok v znení neskorších predpisov a menia a dopĺňajú sa niektoré ďalšie zákony.
45. § 246(1) and § 246a(1) OSP.
46. § 246c OSP.
47. § 246b(1) OSP.
48. § 250j (1) and (2) OSP.
49. The court had to annul the decision, if, within the limits of the scope of the action, found that:
    (a) the decision of the administrative authority was based on an error of law;
    (b) the findings of fact on which the administrative decision was based are contrary to the content of the file;
    (c) the findings of fact are insufficient to determine the case;

claims, the court was obliged to annul an administrative decision if it was issued on the basis of an ineffective legal provision, if the decision was unreviewable for lack of clarity or reasons, or if the decision was unreviewable because the administrative authority's file was incomplete or because the file had not been submitted.[50] Broad interpretation of the concept of 'unreviewability for lack of clarity or reasons' actually enabled courts to annul administrative decisions for reasons raised by the court itself *ex officio*.

The concept of full jurisdiction to review the sanction was maintained from the pre-2004 period.[51]

Different grounds and different intensities of review were also reflected in relation to the admissibility of an appeal against first-instance judgments. Only judgments rejecting an action or annulling a decision of an administrative authority due to an error in law or because the findings of fact on which the administrative decision was based were contrary to the content of the file could be subject to appeal.[52] Thus, e.g., if the court annulled an administrative decision due to insufficient finding of facts, the judgment could not be subject to second-instance appeal, but, if the first-instance court found insufficient finding of facts together with an error in law, the administrative authority could appeal.

The second-instance appellate court could decide in three ways on the second-instance appeal: (1) confirm the first-instance judgment, (2) annul the first-instance judgment and send it back to the first-instance court, or (3) change the first-instance judgment[53] by annulling the administrative decision, if the first-instance appeal was originally rejected by the first-instance court,[54] or by rejecting the first-instance appeal,[55] if the administrative decision was originally annulled by the first-instance court. Due to this broad portfolio of outcomes, the SC could, in fact, decide the case on its own, notwithstanding the first-instance judgment, and therefore the SC became the focal point of the whole decision-making process in competition law.

2.2 Period from 2016: SSP and Cassation System

The adoption of the SSP was a part of the overall reform of Slovak civil procedural law. From the institutional point of view, this period can be split into the period when the SC acted as a cassation court (until 2021) and the period after when the newly

(d) the decision is unreviewable for lack of clarity or reasons or the decision is unreviewable because the administrative authority's file is incomplete or because the file has not been submitted;

(e) a defect has been found in the proceedings of the administrative authority which may have affected the lawfulness of the contested decision.

50. § 250j(3) OSP.
51. § 250i(2) and § 250j(5) OSP.
52. § 250ja(2) OSP.
53. Due to procedural economy of the procedure, the second-instance court was allowed to annul first-instance judgment only in the irreparable failures of the first-instance procedures stipulated in § 221 OSP. Thus, after October 2004 was annulment of the first-instance court judgment rare.
54. § 250ja(3) OSP.
55. § 250 OSP.

established SAC took the competence of the cassation court. However, no judgment of the SAC falls within the temporal scope of the study.

Although the rationale for the establishment of the SAC was to raise the quality of the decision-making process in the review of administrative decisions, the SAC remained a 'general' administrative court, similar to the administrative collegium of the SC. Equally, in this period the RCB remained the first-instance administrative court to hear cases against the PMÚ.[56]

For these reasons, it is not necessary to provide details on the scope and intensity of the judicial review for the period involving the SC and the period involving the SAC because the procedural rules established under the SSP applied equally to both. Accordingly, both the SC and SAC will be together identified as the 'cassation court'.[57]

The composition of three-member panels at first instance and also the cassation court was adopted under the SSP, similarly to the OSP, with a novelty introduced by the SSP – the possibility to refer the case to the grand chamber composed of seven judges.[58] The purpose of the grand chamber is to unify previous case law of the cassation court and also to shape the practice of administrative bodies in cases of continuous discontent with the legal opinions of administrative bodies and administrative courts.[59] To date, there has been no decision of the grand chamber of SAC/SC in competition cases.

Although the SSP followed the principle of binding the court by the limits of the scope of the administrative action[60] it significantly expanded the list of reasons to adopt a judgment *ultra petita* (i.e., judgment rendered notwithstanding the content and claims raised in the administrative action). For the review of the PMÚ's decision, some of the general grounds for the possibility of deciding *ultra petita*,[61] as well as the grounds applicable for administrative actions in relation to administrative sanctions are as follows:

---

56. §15 SSP.
57. In June 2023 (due to governmental crisis in Slovakia, the date was postponed), a new structure of the administrative courts will be established. Thereafter, the Administrative Court in Bratislava hears cases against the PMÚ. There is no specialisation to hear competition cases, except the Administrative Court in Bratislava is the only administrative court hearing competition cases (along with its all general agenda). Nevertheless, this reform is outside of the temporal scope of the study.
58. § 22 SPP.
59. The case is referred to the grand chamber if:
    (a) a panel of SAC (previously SC) has reached a different legal opinion from that already expressed in a decision of the SAC (SC) and has referred the case by order to the grand chamber for a decision;
    (b) a panel of the SAC (SC) has again reached a legal opinion in its decision which differs from the legal opinion of the public authority on the same legal question and has referred the case by order to the grand chamber for a decision;
    (c) the Prosecutor General so requests on the grounds of divergent decision-making by the administrative courts or persistent divergence in the decision-making of the administrative courts and the public authorities.
60. § 134(1) SSP.
61. § 134(2)(a) and (b) SSP: a decision of a public authority or a measure of a public authority has been taken on the basis of an ineffective legal provision, or the decision or measure was issued by an authority which was not authorised to do so by law.

(a) the findings of fact by the public authority were insufficient for a proper assessment of the matter or the facts on which the public authority based the contested decision or measure are contradicted by or unsupported by the administrative file;
(b) lapse of the limitation period;
(c) the basic principles of criminal procedure under the Code of Criminal Procedure are involved and are to be applied to administrative sanctions;
(d) compliance with the principles of sentencing under the Criminal Code, which must also be applied to the imposition of sanctions in the context of administrative sanctioning;
(e) assessment of whether the administrative body exceeded its margin of discretion in the imposition of sanction.[62]

The reasons for reviewing decisions *ultra petita* are interesting from the point of view that they include unwritten rules and concepts derived from another legal regime (criminal law), thereby requiring administrative bodies to consider principles of criminal law (substantial and procedural) when imposing sanctions, even if not directly required by administrative law. These provisions of the SSP, in fact, fill some gaps in the system of administrative law due to the absence of general administrative rules on administrative sanctioning. It must be noted that there is an ongoing debate as to whether the application of the principles of criminal law is automatic or applies only if it is necessary in considering the circumstances of the case.[63]

Compared to pre-2016, the court can reduce the sanction only if the applicant requests. The SSP strictly distinguishes between reviewing any excessive use of the administrative authority's discretion as a potential reason for annulment under § 191 SSP and in relation to moderation of a sanction that can be applied even in cases when the decision by an administrative body did not exceed its margin of discretion but the court considers it disproportionate to the character of the offence or can lead to the applicant's inability to pay.[64]

However, the SSP excluded some previous grounds for annulment that can be used *ultra petita*, in particular, if the decision is unreviewable for lack of clarity or reasons. Therefore, if the decision is clear enough for the administrative body as well as for the plaintiff, the court cannot annul it because it is unclear to the court.

The SSP maintained the list of the reasons for the annulment of an administrative decision; accordingly, the decision shall be annulled if:

(a) it was issued on the basis of an ineffective legal provision;
(b) it was issued by an authority which was not legally entitled to do so;
(c) is based on an error of law;

62. § 195 SSP.
63. Hana Kováčiková, 'Directive (EU) 2019/1 as Another Brick into Empowerment of Slovak Market Regulator' (2019) 12 Yearbook of Antitrust and Regulatory Studies 149 DOI: 10.7172/1689-9024.yars.2019.12.20.6.
64. § 198(1)(a) SSP.

(d) it is unreviewable on the grounds that it is incomprehensible or that it lacks reasons;
(e) the finding of the facts by the public authority was insufficient for a proper assessment of the case;
(f) the facts on which the public authority based the contested decision or measure are contradicted by or unsupported by the administrative file;
(g) there has been a substantial breach of the provisions relating to the procedure before the public authority which may have resulted in the adoption of an unlawful decision or measure on the substance.[65]

One of the aims of the reform established by the SSP was to change the appellate review system by OSP to a cassation review system. Therefore, compared to the OSP, judgments at first instance cannot be appealed (i.e., reviewed within the ordinary review regime that suspends the force of the judgment under review) and only the cassation complaint is available as an extraordinary measure for the review of a judgment by the administrative court. The SSP does not restrict the possibility of filing a cassation complaint regarding the content and grounds of the first-instance judgment, but restricts the grounds of the cassation complaint itself:

(a) grounds related to the first-instance proceeding: lack of competence of administrative court, lack of personality of the party to proceeding, impairment of *res iudicata* and *litis pendentia*, wrong composition of the court, violation of procedural rights of the party;[66]
(b) error in law;[67]
(c) deviation from the established case law of the cassation court or a previous opinion of the cassation court in the same case;[68]
(d) the action was unlawfully rejected as inadmissible.[69]

Although the cassation court is bound by the grounds of the cassation complaint, in cases when the first-instance court is not bound by the administrative action, neither is the cassation court bound by the scope of the cassation complaint.[70]

The cassation court can, based on its evaluation, reject a cassation complaint, annul the judgment of the first-instance court and send it back to the first-instance court for reconsideration or terminate the proceeding, or vary the first-instance judgment rejecting the administrative action or annulling the administrative decision.

Summing up, the move from an appellate system to a cassation system has not been complete and in practical terms, there is no significant change during a review. For example, in the *Chemkostav* case, the cassation court dealt with claims for wrong

65. § 191(1) SSP.
66. § 440(1)(a) to (f) SSP.
67. § 440(1)(g) SSP.
68. § 440(1)(h) and (i) SSP.
69. § 440(1)(j) SSP.
70. § 453(3) SSP.

evaluation of evidence as an error in law,[71] and in the *eD ´system Slovakia* case also dealt with claims for erroneous evaluation of a fine as an error in law.[72] Moreover, even though the cassation complaint does not have a suspensive effect on the first-instance judgment, in cases of administrative sanctioning this effect is granted.[73]

2.3 Constitutional Review

Judgments adopted by the SC can be subject to review by the Constitutional Court of the Slovak Republic (CC). Yet, submitting a complaint under Article 127 of the Constitution of the Slovak republic cannot be deemed as an appeal against the judgment of the second instance because the only CC provides protection to natural and legal persons against infringement of 'fundamental rights or freedoms, or human rights and fundamental freedoms resulting from the international treaty [...], save another court shall decide on protection of these rights and freedoms'. The CC constantly rejected acting as a third instance of the judiciary, reviewing the application of law by courts in general (except manifest arbitrariness), as well as unifying case law of courts.[74] In particular, it refused to review competition law judgments in the cases of *VAS,*[75] *VÚB,*[76] *ASBIS SK,*[77] *STRABAG(2),*[78] *ENVI-PAK,*[79] and *MARIANUM,*[80] while stating that the constitutional complaints were manifestly unfounded. Similarly, the CC found no violation of the constitutional rights of the individuals in *Slovnaft*[81] *and Siemens AG.*[82]

Given the character of the constitutional review and its limited scope, the orders and findings of the CC are not within the scope of the study on judicial review of the decision of the NCAs. Yet, it should be noted that in two cases, the CC encroached judicial review of the NCA's decision by the SC by annulment of the SC judgments in the *STRABAG(1)*[83] case and *Cargo* case (twice)[84] due to reshuffling the judges sitting in panels for the respective cases which constituted a violation of the right to be heard by judge established by law.

71. SC: 8Sžhk/1/2017 *Chemkostav et al.* (20 February 2020).
72. SC: 8Sžhk/1/2016 *eD ´system Slovakia* (26 October 2017).
73. § 446(2)(c) SSP.
74. Case law summarised in, e.g., CC: III. ÚS 541/2016 *MARIANUM* (17 August 2016), para. 29.
75. CC: III. ÚS 23/2016 *VAS* (19 January 2016).
76. CC: III. ÚS 470/2014 *VÚB* (6 August 2014).
77. CC: IV. ÚS 313/2018 *ASBIS SK* (16 May 2018).
78. CC: III. ÚS 459/2017 *STRABAG* (4 July 2017).
79. CC: II. ÚS 489/2014 *ENVI-PAK* (22 August 2014).
80. CC: III. ÚS 541/2016 *MARIANUM* (17 August 2016).
81. CC: III. ÚS 151/2014 Slovnaft (10 June 2014).
82. CC: I. ÚS 505/2015 Siemens AG (13 January 2016).
83. CC: II. ÚS 893/2014 *STRABAG* (17 June 2015).
84. CC: II. ÚS 170/2011 Železničná spoločnost' Cargo Slovakia (14 June 2011) and IV. ÚS 170/2014 Železničná spoločnost' Cargo Slovakia (1 July 2014).

3 PRIOR RESEARCH

To the best of the author's knowledge, there is no comprehensive study covering judicial review of the decisions of the Slovak NCA, from a qualitative or quantitative perspective. Several papers have analysed legal the framework of judicial review[85] decisions of the courts in specific periods,[86] and specific cases.[87] From a qualitative point of view, these papers analysed, and often criticised deviation from EU law and the practice of the CJ EU and the European Commission[88] or particular 'inventions' of the courts which may appear to be 'alien' to EU law practice (e.g., application of *nullum crimen sine lege, nulla poena sine lege* for annulment the decision/fine in cases without pre-existing precedent[89]). Nevertheless, there has been no comprehensive study of judicial review over any period of time.

4 QUANTITATIVE ANALYSIS

4.1 Source of Information

The database includes judgments rendered and published between May 2004 to April 2021 reviewing decisions of the competition authority in the same period. The database is presumed to be comprehensive.

During this period, the method of publication of judgments related to the PMÚ's decision varied. At the beginning of the period, all judgments were published on a webpage of the PMÚ.[90] The SC published its judgments on its webpage as well.[91] Although the RCB did not publish its judgments officially, they could be found on the webpage of the PMÚ. Due to §82a of Act No. 757/2004 Coll. on courts[92] introduced by an amendment in 2012 the courts are obliged to publish all final judgments within

85. For example, Kováčiková (*supra* n. 63); Ondrej Blažo, 'Administrative Competition Procedure and Judicial Review in the Slovak Republic' in Csongor István Nagy (ed.), *The Procedural Aspects of the Application of Competition Law: European Frameworks – Central European Perspectives* (Europa Law Publishing 2016).
86. For example, Silvia Šramelová and Andrea Šupáková, 'Development of the Judicial Review of the Decisions of the Antimonopoly Office of the Slovak Republic' (2012) 5 Yearbook of Antitrust and Regulatory Studies 105 DOI: 10.2139/ssrn.2296662; Zuzana Šabová, Katarína Fodorová and Daniela Lukáčová, 'Recent Developments in Slovak Competition Law – Legislation and Case Law Review' (2013) 6 Yearbook of Antitrust and Regulatory Studies 223 DOI: 10.2139/ssrn.22 96662.
87. Ondrej Blažo and Silvia Šramelová, 'The First Bid Rigging Case in Slovakia after Years of Judicial Disputes' (2015) 8 Yearbook of Antitrust and Regulatory Studies 249 DOI: 10.2139/ssrn.2741 673.
88. For example, Blažo, 'Twenty Years of Harmonisation and Still Divergent: Development of Slovak Competition Law' (*supra* n. 19).
89. For example, Katarína Kalesná, 'Zneužívanie Dominantného Postavenia v Teórii a v Aplikačnej Praxi' (2012) 95 Právny obzor 297; Zuzana Šabová, 'Zásada Nullum Crimen Sine Lege a Ukladanie Sankcií v Súťažnom Práve' (2013) 96 Právny obzor 105; Šabová, Fodorová and Lukáčová (*supra* n. 86); Blažo, 'Twenty Years of Harmonisation and Still Divergent: Development of Slovak Competition Law' (*supra* n. 19).
90. https://www.antimon.gov.sk.
91. https://www.nsud.sk/rozhodnutia/.
92. Zákon č. 757/2004 Z. z. o súdoch a o zmene a doplnení niektorých zákonov.

fifteen days after the date when they become final and the judgments are published on the webpage of the Ministry of Justice.[93]

4.2 Total Number of Cases

A total of 106 judgments were rendered during the relevant period, from which 58 were first-instance judgments and 48 second-instance judgments. Those judgments pertain to forty-two decisions of the PMÚ and forty-five judgments of the first-instance appeal court; this difference between the number of cases at the PMÚ level and reviewed first-instance judgments is caused by two procedural practices of the court: (1) in some cases actions of several undertakings challenging the same decision of the PMÚ were not joined in the one proceeding, and (2) one decision of the PMÚ could be reviewed several times due to judicial 'ping pong' between court instances and the PMÚ.

During the relevant time-period, the PMÚ issued 126 enforcement decisions under Articles 101 and 102 TFEU and the national equivalent provisions. However, only sixty-one of such decisions could be reviewable due to judicial procedural rules. An action for judicial review of an administrative decision is admissible only in case of exhausting administrative remedies by applicants in administrative proceedings (i.e., administrative appeal). The action can be filled by the parties of the administrative proceeding and at the same time, under ZOHS 2004, undertakings charged with an infringement of the competition rules are parties to the administrative proceeding before the PMÚ (i.e., complainants or the third parties have no formal position as a party to the administrative proceeding at the PMÚ). This construction leads to the situation that non-infringement decisions and commitment decisions are in fact unreviewable because they are never brought to the second instance of the administrative proceeding and it would also be illogical for undertakings as addressees of such decisions to challenge decisions rendered in their favour.

For this reason, for the purpose of this study, the number of enforcement actions based on the figures extracted from the annual reports of the PMÚ was adjusted to the number of the second-instance administrative decisions in which the Council of the PMÚ closed the case by imposing or confirming the sanctions. This leads to a very high appeal ratio of the PMÚ's decisions. 66% of the reviewable PMÚ's decisions have been appealed at first instance.[94] It must be noted, that of the sixty-one decisions reviewable PMÚ's decisions, twenty were adopted in 2004, of which only four were reviewed. The

93. https://www.justice.gov.sk/sudy-a-rozhodnutia/sudy/rozhodnutia/.
94. Two cases dismissed by the RCB due to lack of standing cannot be considered in this ratio because it challenged the decisions of the PMÚ that were also non-reviewable by the court, not even theoretically. If we take into account, in calculation of this ratio, the number of all reviewed decisions and the number of all decisions that were either reviewable or actually reviewed, there is no substantial difference (66.7%).

relatively high number of decisions in 2004 was caused by the series of decisions on a system of vertical agreements in which every agreement was handled in a separate proceeding. If we exclude data from 2004,[95] the ratio of reviewed decisions of the Council of the PMÚ raises to 88%, namely that after 2004 almost every reviewable decision was appealed. This ratio rises even further if we reflect ongoing review proceedings or judgments that were rendered outside the timeframe of the research.[96] We can observe a similarly high ratio of second-instance appeals. The second-instance court reviewed forty-five judgments of the first-instance courts, out of the total fifty-eight first-instance judgments rendered during the period (77%). it must be borne in mind, that the appeal ratio is likely to be even higher, as some appeals are still ongoing or judgments were published after the April 2021 cut-off date.[97]

The database includes two RCB orders rejecting actions as inadmissible because these actions were filed by parties with no standing in judicial review. In both cases, the applicants had no standing in the preceding administrative proceeding as well and therefore their appeals were utterly frivolous. The rules on standing of parties to the judicial review procedure are rigorously and exhaustively laid down by law, and the lawyers of the applicants in these two cases simply ignored them.

4.3 Total Number of Judgments per Year

Figure 26.1 summarises the number of judgments included in the database per year, according to the instance of appeal.[98] It shows some variation in the number of judgments per year, with lower numbers in 2005-2008 (4.5 per year on average), peaking through 2009-2017 (8.2 per year on average) and falling again afterwards (4.6 per year on average between 2018-2020).

95. It means that twenty reviewable decisions of the Council of the PMÚ and four judicial appeal linked to four cases of those twenty were excluded from this calculation.
96. Cases at RCB: 2S/166/2020 *Volkswagen distribution system (18 undertakings)* (19 June 2021), 2S/12/2020 *Železničná spoločnosť' Cargo Slovakia, a.s.* (29 September 2021), 2S/67/2020 *M.CUP, s.r.o. et al.* (20 October 2021).
97. Case at SAC: 6Asan/24/2019 *IMPA Bratislava, a.s.* (2 February 2022).
98. The style of numbering of the cases was not consisted throughout the analysed period. In general, the number of a case consisted of the number of a panel assigned to a case, number of case before that panel and year. Judicial clerks sometimes separated the elements of the case number by blank space sometimes by a slash symbol. For better readability and searchability, all number of cases in this chapter and in the accompanying database were 'normalised' and slash symbol is used as separator of elements of case number, notwithstanding, how the number of case is written in the particular judgment. For better readability page numbers in the file was also omitted when referring the number of a judicial decision (i.e., judgments and orders are identified by the number of file/case). Case No. 2S/102/2006 is the only exemption, since two judgments were rendered in the same proceeding after annulment of the first one by the SC.

Figure 26.1 Number of Judgments According to Instances

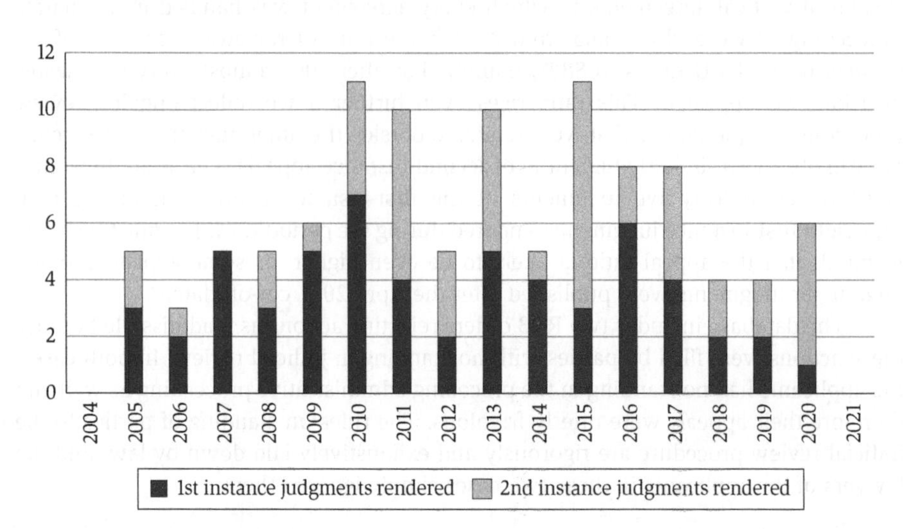

The higher number of judgments in 2009-2017 can be explained by the combination of a number of factors.

First, is the substantial delay between submitting an appeal to the delivery of the judgment; the most extreme example was the *Highway cartel* originating from the decision of the Council of the PMÚ of 2006 that was completed in 2016. Therefore, the higher number of judicial decisions in 2009-2017 have their origin in the higher number of PMÚ's decisions in the period 2004-2011 (Ms Paroulková's presidency) and the decline in the number of judgments in later periods corresponds to a lower number of decisions after 2011.

The second factor relates to the 'multiplication' of cases. Although court procedural rules within the period under study allowed connected proceedings to be joined,[99] the courts did not always apply this rule consistently. This leads to a higher number of appeal cases vis-à-vis an administrative decision. For example, the courts handled the *Highway cartel* as a single appeal involving all applicants together, while the *Banking cartel* was dealt with as three individual and separate cases (moreover, this separation led to different outcomes). For the purposes of the quantitative analysis, therefore the number of court cases and the number of reviewed decisions does not correspond. In this context, it shall be noted that the courts have been obliged to call all the other parties to the administrative proceedings as either third parties (§ 250(1) OSP) (until 2016) or as parties to the existing court proceedings (§ 32(3(a) SSP) (from 2016).

99. § 112 OSP, § 65 SSP.

However, the courts were not precise in applying this rule in coopetition cases in the period under the study. In the *Banking* case, for example, the court handled the appeals of every member of the cartel separately without the involvement of the other member of the cartel as a third party. These separate cases led to further fragmentation of the review and multiplication of cases because the court did not review the same objections against the existence of the cartel once in a single proceeding but in three separate reviews.

This multiplication is demonstrated in Figure 26.2, which indicates the number of judgments included in the database per year according to each instance (lines). It compares it with the number of NCA's decisions that were appealed in the first instance each year or the number of court judgments that were appealed in further instances (bars). Figure 26.2(a) confirms that while the first peak of the first-instance judgments in 2010 follows the higher number of PMÚ's decisions, the second peak (and the rest of the period 2010-2017) was influenced by the 'multiplication' of cases when the same decision was reviewed in different court proceedings.[100] Figure 26.2(b) shows that in second-instance proceedings, the numbers started to rise after 2010/2011, peaking in 2015. As mentioned, 80% of the first-instance judgments have already been reviewed and thus this trend follows the trend of the first-instance judgments with a certain time delay.

Moreover, the number of second-instance judgments is in some cases higher than the number of first-instance judgments, in particular, in the 2009-2017 period. This situation was caused by annulment of judgments of the SC by the Constitutional Court of the Slovak Republic where the SC was obliged to decide the case again, sometimes within the same panel under the same case number, and sometimes in a different panel under a different case number. In particular, the *Highway Cartel* case was decided for the first time under case number 1Sžhpu/1/2009 and the second time under case number 5Sžh/2/2015, even though the same first-instance judgment was reviewed. The *Železničná spoločnosť Cargo* case was subject to two annulments by the Constitutional Court and in the first two 'rounds' of review, it was handled by the same panel of the SC (but under different case numbers) and for the third time by another panel; that is why the review of the first-instance judgment was handled under three different case numbers at the SC: 1Sžhpu/2/2008, 1Sžhpu/1/2011 and 4Sžhpu/2/2014.

100. For example, in 2013, one case (the *GIS cartel*) was reviewed in five separate proceedings at the RCB: 4S/213/2009; 4S/230/2009; 4S/232/2009 *Toshiba Corporation et al.* (25 January 2012), 3S/231/2009 *Hitachi Ltd. et al.*(14 May 2013), 3S/230/2009 *Nuova Margini Galileo* S.p.A (14 May 2013), 3S/229/2009 VA Tech Transmission & Distribution GmbH & Co KEG (14 May 2013), 3S/228/2009 *Siemens AG* (28 May 2013).

Figure 26.2(a) First-Instance Judgments

NCA's decisions appealed — 1st instance judgments rendered

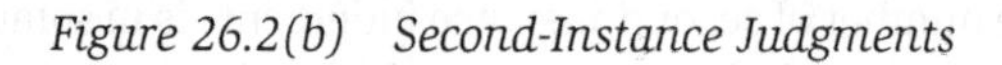

Figure 26.2(b) Second-Instance Judgments

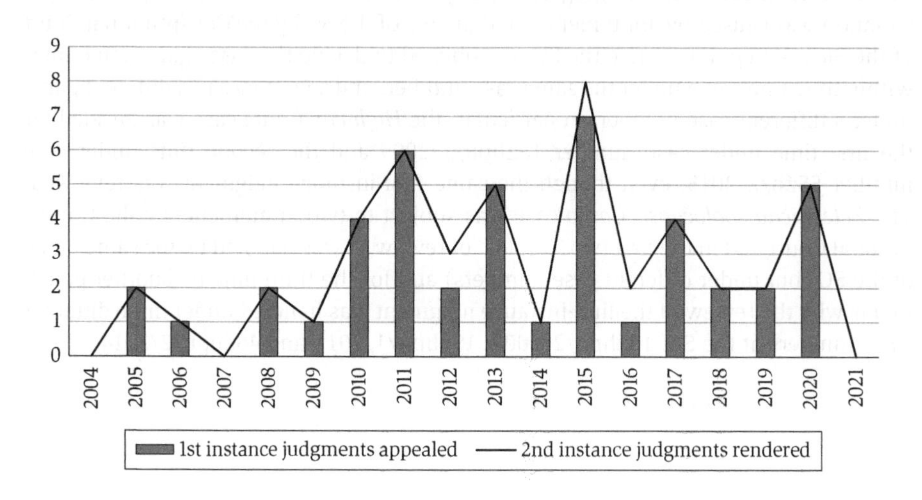

4.4 Success Rates and Outcomes

Figure 26.3 presents the success of appeals launched against either the NCA's decisions or a prior review court instance's judgment, across all instances. The success rates shown in Figure 26.3 relate to the outcomes of all appeals, considering that separate actions or appeals were aggregated and launched against a single NCA decision. That means that if a PMÚ decision was challenged by various parties in separate proceedings, the outcome of all those judgments will be counted as a single case for the purposes of this figure.

From Figure 26.3 it is apparent that in 55 % of actions/appeals, the court accepted at least one of the grounds for action/appeal (namely, fully or partially successful appeals).

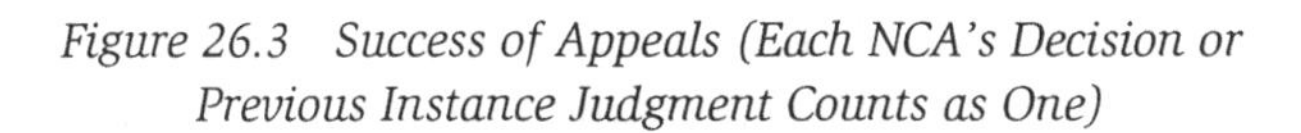

Figure 26.3 Success of Appeals (Each NCA's Decision or Previous Instance Judgment Counts as One)

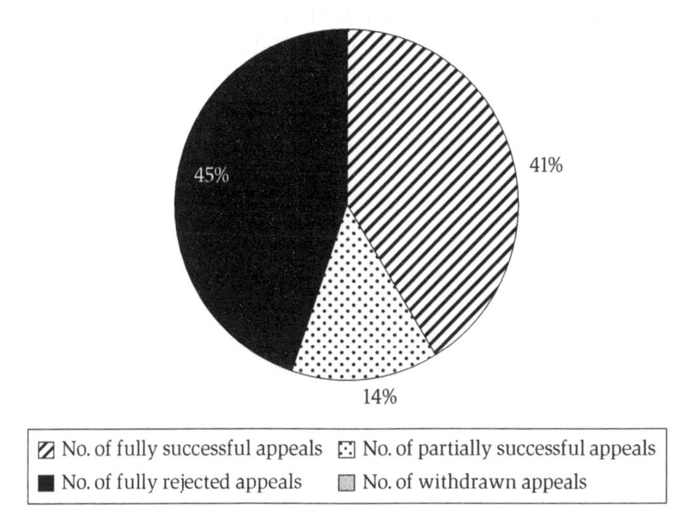

This is also demonstrated in Figures 26.4(a) and 26.4(b), which present the outcome of each judgment. The figures show that undertakings were fully or partially successful in 57 % of first-instance proceedings and that the second-instance court rejected 46 % of appeals against first-instance judgments (i.e., upholding first-instance judgments) while 17 % were fully annulled, in 4 % the amount of fine was changed and in 33 % cases the second-instance court changed first-instance judgment and replaced it by its own. In practice, this 'full replacement' means that: (1) the second-instance court rejected the appeal of an undertaking against the decisions of the PMÚ in cases where the first instance annulled the decision of the PMÚ, or (2) the second-instance court annulled the decision of the PMÚ in cases when the first-instance court rejected the appeal of an undertaking against the decision of the PMÚ.

Due to the pivotal character of decisions of the second-instance appeal court, it is interesting to observe the following:

(1) In thirty-eight cases[101] (70 %), the final court decision confirmed the imposition of the fine, at least partially, i.e., confirmed the sanction imposed by the PMÚ or decreased it; in two additional cases was.
(2) In fourteen cases, the final court judgment annulled the administrative decisions of the PMÚ.[102] This means, that in 26% of the judicial appellate proceedings, the undertaking was fully successful in escaping the fine imposed by the PMÚ. The success rate changed over time. In the first part of the period under the study, 2004-2011, the PMÚ lost eleven cases out of nineteen (the undertakings were completely successful in 58% of cases), while in the second part (2012-2021) the PMÚ lost only three cases out of thirty-three (the undertakings were fully successful in merely 9% of cases).

101. Every judicial proceeding counts as one case notwithstanding corresponding number of the PMÚ's decisions.
102. It means that the decision of the PMÚ was:

(1) either annulled and returned for recalculation by the first-instance judgment that:
    (a) was not subject to further appeal; or
    (b) was upheld by second-instance appellate court,
(2) or annulled by the second-instance court notwithstanding previous rejection of the appeal by the first-instance court.

Figure 26.4(a) First-Instance Outcome

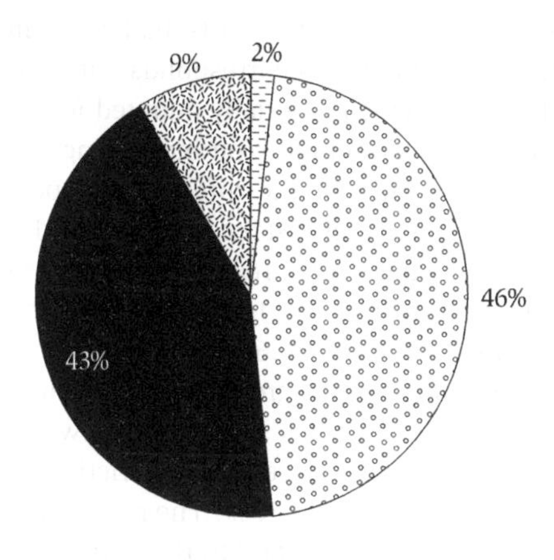

Figure 26.4(b) Second-Instance Outcome

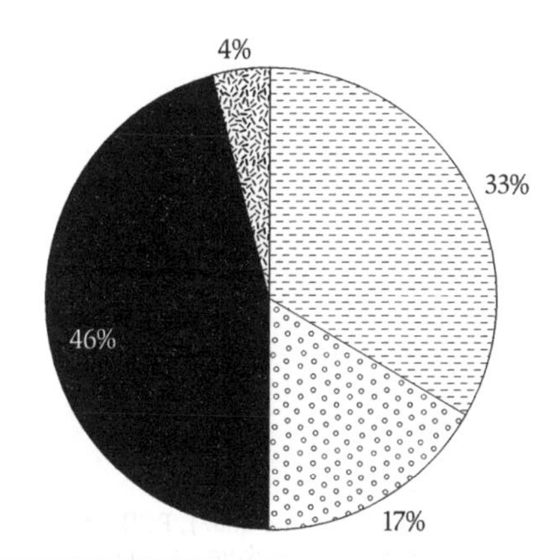

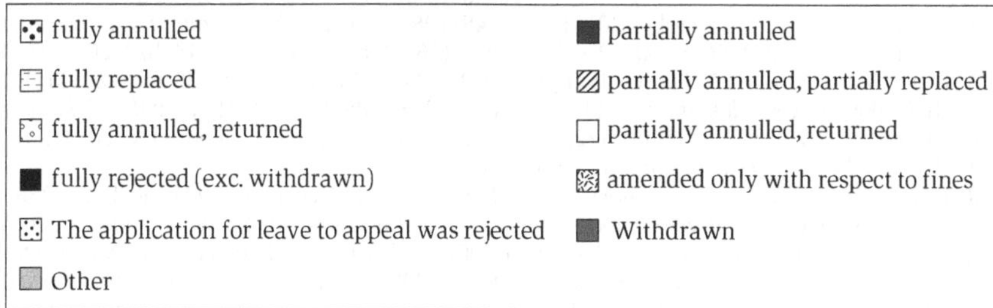

4.5 Type of NCA's Decisions Subject to Appeal

In the period covered by this study, the courts had to examine limited types of anti-competitive practices. Of course, this corresponds with the types of enforcement decisions rendered by the PMÚ which gradually adopted fewer decisions in abuse of dominance cases and focused predominantly on bid-rigging cases.

Figure 26.5 indicates the ratio of the different competition law prohibitions subject to the courts' review, across all instances of appeal. It demonstrates that the NCA decisions reviewed in Slovakia have predominately focused on the enforcement of national law alone and confirms that this trend has not changed even after a longer period of membership in the EU (Figure 26.6).

National rules on anti-competitive agreements restricting competition were the most frequently applied substantive rules in cases reviewed by the courts (42%). Overall the majority of cases dealt with agreements restricting competition (national or national together with Article 101 TFEU) - 56%. The ratio of cases dealing with abuse of dominance does not completely correspond to the number of cases handled by the PMÚ, but the number of appeal cases before courts was expanded due to the judicial 'ping pong' in *the Slovak Telekom* cases[103] and *Cargo* cases[104] and multiple reviews thereof.

103. RCB: 1S/424/06 *Slovak Telekom, a.s.* (21 June 2007), RCB: 2S/102/2006 *Slovak Telekom, a.s.* (18 September 2009), 3S/85/2009 *Slovak Telekom, a.s.* (10 August 2010), SC: 6Sžh/2/2009 *Slovak Telekom, a.s.* (26 October 2010), RCB: 4S/108/2009 *Slovak Telekom, a.s.* (3 December 2010), RCB: 2S/102/2006 *Slovak Telekom, a.s.* (18 March 2011), SC: 4Sžh/2/2010 *Slovak Telekom, a.s.* (28 June 2011), SC: 4Sžhpu/1/2011 *Slovak Telekom, a.s.* (28 June 2011), RCB: 2S/105/2009 *Slovak Telekom, a.s.* (11 January 2012), SC: 8Sžhpu/1/2011 *Slovak Telekom, a.s.* (30 October 2012), SC: 3Sžhpu/1/2012 *Slovak Telekom, a.s.* (11 February 2014), RCB: 2S/105/2009 *Slovak Telekom, a.s.* (21 June 2017).

104. RCB: 1S/42/05 *Železničná spoločnosť' Cargo Slovakia, a.s.* (8 December 2005), RCB: 2S/258/06 *Železničná spoločnosť' Cargo Slovakia, a.s,* (7 November 2007), RCB: 1S 27/2007 *Železničná spoločnosť' Cargo Slovakia, a.s,* (6 December 2007), RCB: 1S/263/2006 *Železničná spoločnosť' Cargo Slovakia, a.s,* (17 April 2008), SC: 8Sžhpu 1/2008 *Železničná spoločnosť' Cargo Slovakia, a.s,* (14 August 2008), SC: 2Sžhpu/4/2008 *Železničná spoločnosť' Cargo Slovakia, a.s,* (14 October 2008), SC: 1Sžhpu/2/2008 *Železničná spoločnosť' Cargo Slovakia, a.s,* (26 October 2010), SC: 1Sžhpu/1/2011 *Železničná spoločnosť' Cargo Slovakia, a.s,* (31 March 2015), SC: 4Sžhpu/2/2014 *Železničná spoločnosť' Cargo Slovakia, a.s,* (31 January 2012), RCB: 5S/30/2015 *Železničná spoločnosť' Cargo Slovakia, a.s.* (13 October 2015), SC: 8Sžh/3/2016 *Železničná spoločnosť' Cargo Slovakia, a.s.* (31 May 2018).

Figure 26.5 Rules Being Appealed

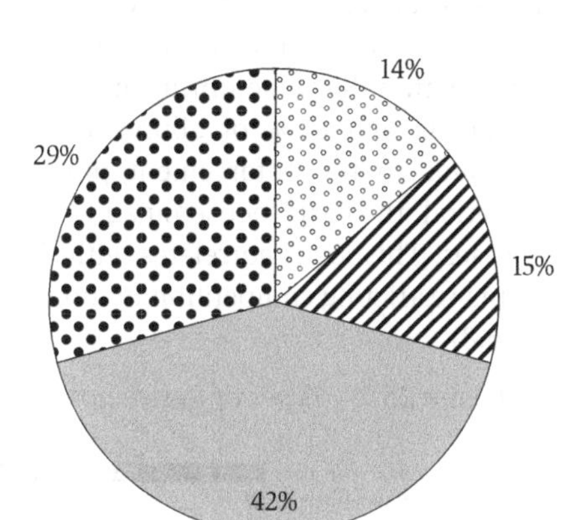

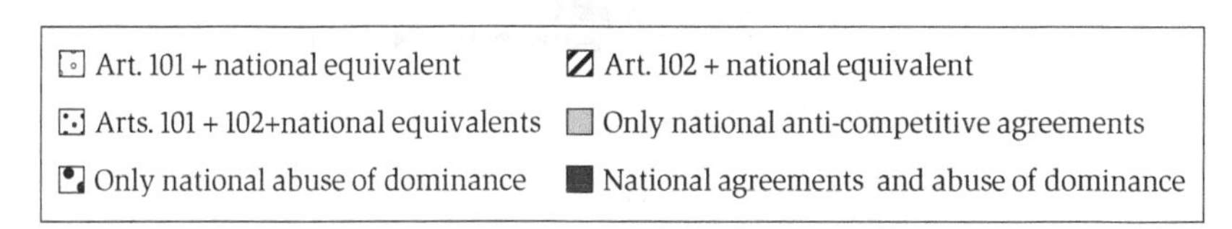

Figure 26.6 Rules Being Appealed According to Years (Each Judgment Counts as One)

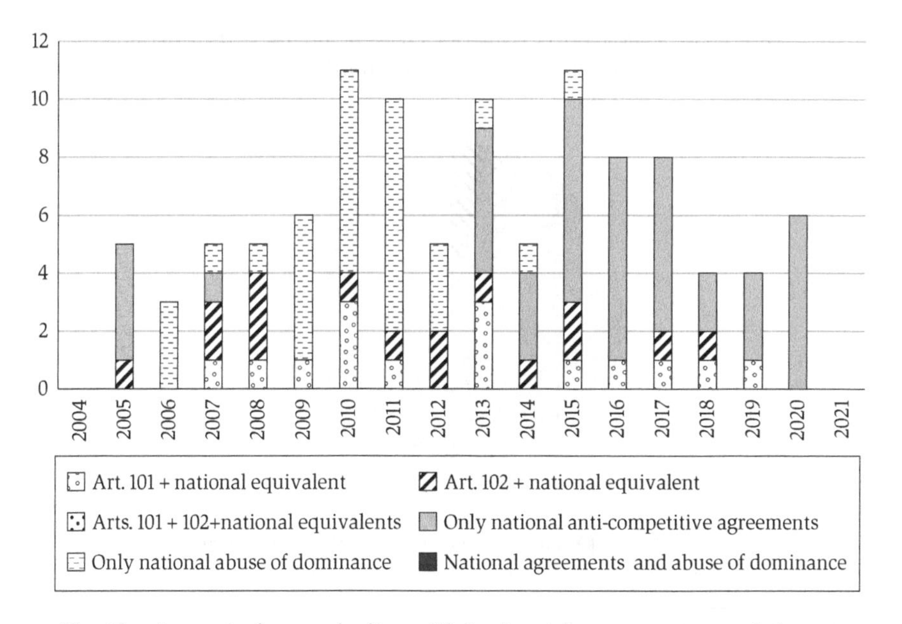

The 'dominance' of cases dealing with horizontal agreements restricting competition is followed by the data shown in Figure 26.7, summarising the types of restrictions of competition that were examined by the NCA's decisions subject to appeal, across all instances of appeal. The majority of dominance cases involved exclusionary abuses. With the reservation noted above, the types of infringements can be more precisely compared within the same infringement: 96% of agreements cases involved horizontal agreements and 82% of abuses cases involved exclusionary abuses. This fully corresponds to the enforcement practice of the PMÚ and its priorities;[105] in the recent period, the PMÚ focused mainly on bid-rigging cases with a limited number of abuse cases. This focus correlates with the absolute prevalence of cases prohibiting agreements restricting competition by-object – 93% object only, 4% object and effect (Figure 26.8).

Figure 26.7 Types of Restrictions

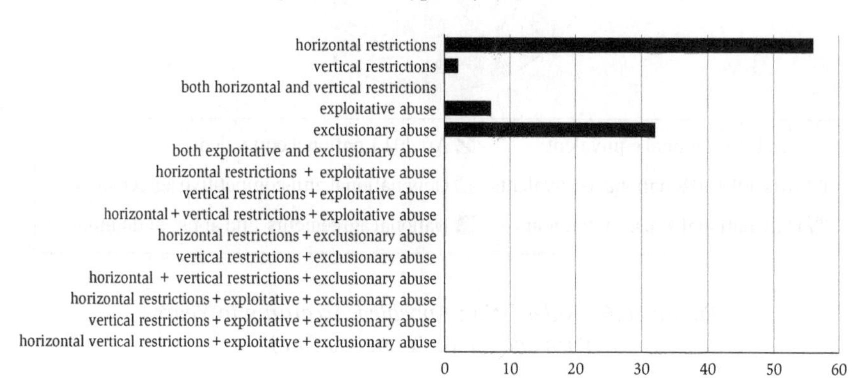

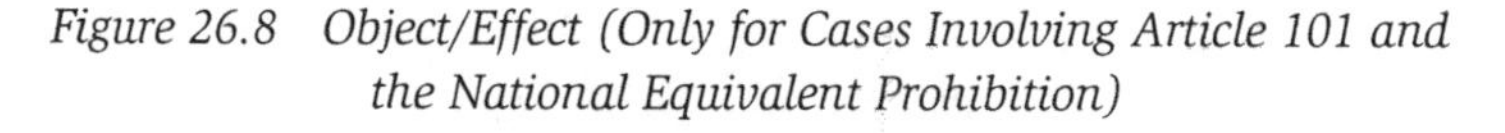

Figure 26.8 Object/Effect (Only for Cases Involving Article 101 and the National Equivalent Prohibition)

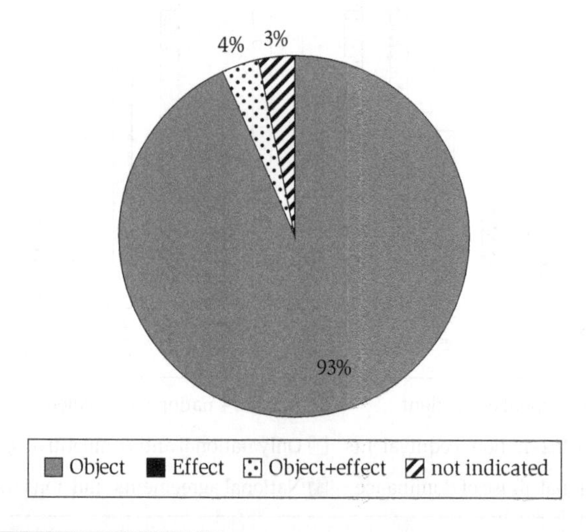

105. For more details and sources see following paper and sources cited therein: Blažo, 'Proper, Transparent and Just Prioritization Policy as a Challenge for National Competition Authorities and Prioritization of the Slovak NCA' (*supra* n. 31).

Figure 26.9 indicates the ratio of the type of NCA's procedures that were subject to judicial review, across all instances of appeal. As noted above, legally it is almost impossible to file an action against the Council of the PMÚ other than in relation to an infringement decision imposing a sanction and therefore all reviewed cases were infringement cases imposing a fine. In two cases, the applicants requested the setting aside of decisions by the Council of the PMÚ to terminate proceedings without imposing a fine or declaring an infringement of competition law. However, they filed the actions manifestly without any standing at administrative court proceedings and therefore the RCB dismissed the case without examining the appeal grounds.[106]

Figure 26.9 The Competition Authority's Procedure

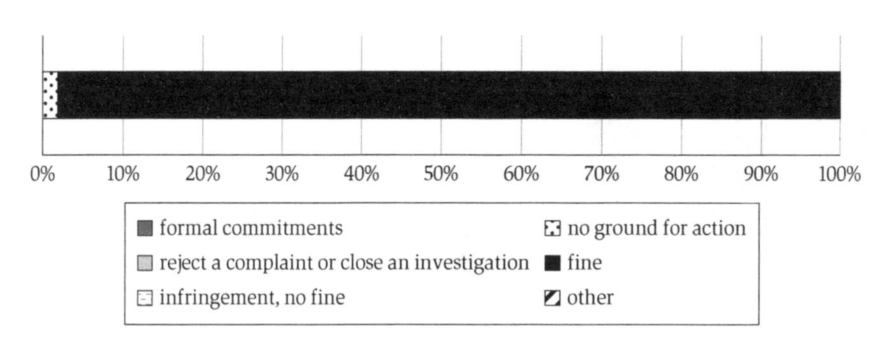

Although the data shows a fairly high ratio of appeals against the PMÚ's decisions in which one or more parties have successfully applied for leniency (15%) and settlements (5%), in the interpretation of this ratio, 'multiplication' caused by multiple separate reviews of the same decision of the PMÚ of cases has to be taken into account. In particular, only three leniency cases of the PMÚ (7% of all cases) were subject to judicial review (*GIS cartel,*[107] *J.P. Stav et al. cartel*[108] and *IMPA et al. cartel*[109]) and only two settlement cases (*J.P. Stav et al. cartel* and *IMPA et al. cartel*) were reviewed (4.7% of all cases). *J.P. Stav et al cartel* is an example of an unsuccessful hybrid settlement when undertakings that did not agree with the settlement raised various separate actions for annulment and those undertakings who agreed with the settlement were

106. Order of 16 April 2008, 2S/15/06 and order of 19 December 2007, 1S/331/05.
107. The RCB cases 4S/213/2009; 4S 230/2009; 4S/232/2009 *Toshiba Corporation et al.* (25 January 2012), 3S/231/2009 *Hitachi Ltd. et al.* (14 May 2013), 3S/230/2009 *Nuova Margini Galileo* S.p.A (14 May 2013), 3S/229/2009 *VA Tech Transmission & Distribution GmbH & Co KEG* (14 May 2013), 3S/228/2009 *Siemens AG* (28 May 2013), and the SC cases 2Sžhpu/1/2013 *VA Tech Transmission & Distribution GmbH & Co KEG* (25 February 2015), 8Sžhpu/4/2013 *Nuova Margini Galileo S.p.A* (26 February 2015), 8Sžhpu/1/2013 *Toshiba Corporation et al.* (26 February 2015), 7Sžhpu/1/2013 *Hitachi Ltd. et al.* (30 April 2015), 3Sžhpu/1/2013 *Siemens AG* (9 June 2015), 5Sžhpu/1/2014 *Siemens Aktiengesellschaft Osterreich* (28 April 2016), 2Sžhpu/3/2014 *Fuji Electric Co. et al.* (24 May 2017).
108. The RCB cases 1S/103/2015 *J.P. Stav* (16 June 2016), 5S/106/2015 *Vertikal – SOLID, s.r.o.* (15 November 2016) and the SC cases 4Sžhk/1/2016 *J.P. Stav* (6 February 2018), 2Sžhk/2/2017 *Vertikal – SOLID, s.r.o.* (25 November 2020).
109. RCB: 6S/139/2017 *IMPA Bratislava, a.s.* (7 February 2019).

dragged involuntarily through judicial proceedings, called as parties or third parties to the judicial proceedings.

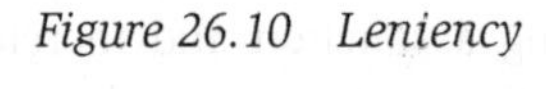

Figure 26.10 Leniency

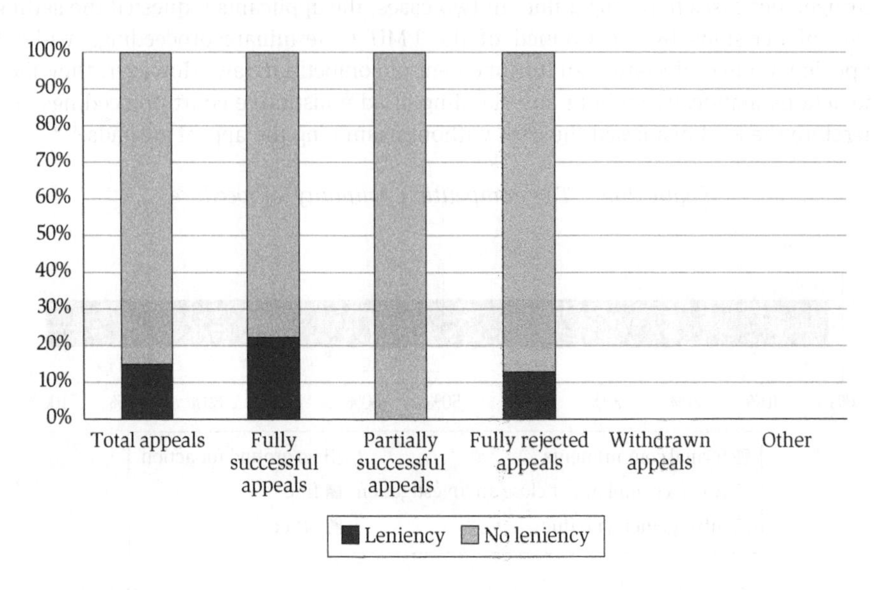

Figure 26.11 Settlements

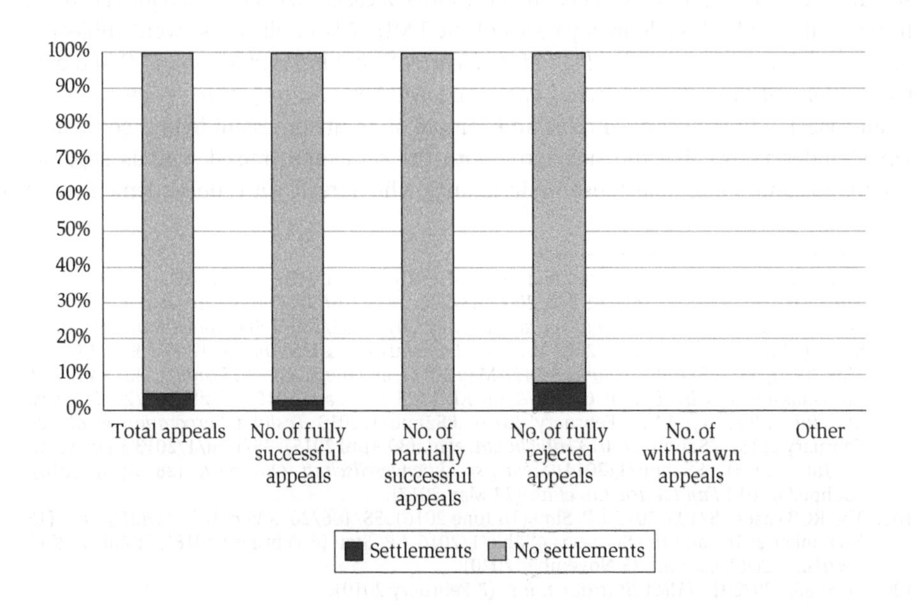

4.6 Grounds of Appeal

As described in section 2, the court procedural rules contain *nummerus clausus* of possible reasons for annulment of the administrative authority's decision as well as appeal against first-instance judgments. Although, they may look quite formal, within the notion of 'error in law' substantial and procedural errors can be included, as well as within the notion of 'lack of reasons'. Similarly, the facts and substance of the case can be challenged by claims that the fact-finding by the PMÚ was not sufficiently complete to close the case or that its conclusions were unrelated to the content of the file.

For the purposes of this study and its comparability across the EU27 + UK jurisdictions, the assessment of the grounds for appeal will not follow the statutory categorisation of the grounds for appeal and judgments. The grounds are, therefore, classified into four groups: (1) procedural, (2) substantive, (3) grounds related to imposition of fine, (4) competence to apply EU/national law (*see* Methodology Chapter).

The empirical findings presented in Figure 26.12 reveal the grounds on which an action/appeal was raised by the parties and their likelihood of success. Each PMÚ decision or previous instance judgment is counted as one, notwithstanding the number of judgments of the court. That means that if an NCA decision was appealed by various parties in separate proceedings, the grounds invoked in all of those judgments and their success will be counted as a single case.

Figure 26.12 Grounds of Appeal (Each NCA's Decision or Previous Instance Judgment Counts as One)

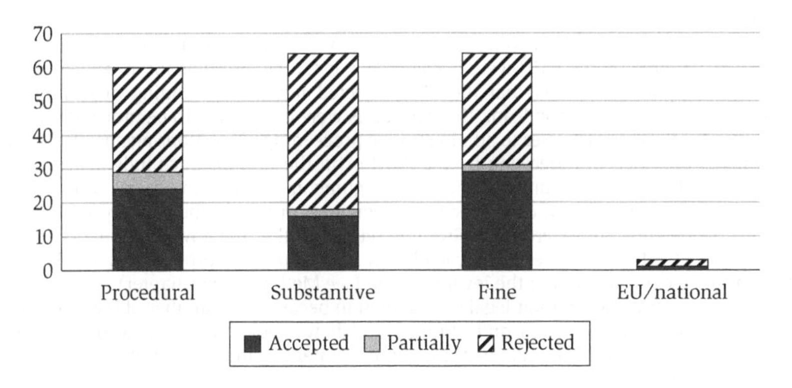

A closer look at the cases reveals that the substantive grounds are usually related to the question of the existence of anti-competitive behaviour, the responsibility of an undertaking for such behaviour, and the length of anti-competitive behaviour. The procedural grounds are usually related to the violation of procedural rights of the undertakings during the course of an investigation and to the administrative proceedings by the PMÚ or by the first-instance court (including *ex post* objections against inspections in the premises of an undertaking).[110]

The figure reveals that the most common grounds for appeals involved a mix of procedural and substantive grounds, as well as objections regarding the fine imposed. This parallel invoking of grounds has its source in the structure and conditions for judicial review as well as in the common three-prong strategy of undertakings in judicial review to raise:[111] (1) procedural grounds, in general, and procedural grounds related to insufficient fact-finding; if unsuccessful, (2) substantive grounds, that the evidence does not support the conclusion of existence of the infringement, and finally, if unsuccessful, (3) arguments that the fine is disproportionate to the infringement or is illegal because of the non-existence of an infringement.[112] This strategy allows and at the same time requires the court to review the case as a whole, in all its substantive, and procedural aspects and in relation to the level of fine as well. The data shows this strategy by undertakings to challenge all aspects of the decision and that the success rate (i.e., accepting at least one of the grounds for appeal) was the highest in those appeals based on substantive, procedural and fine-related grounds (62%).[113]

It must be stressed, that in appeals against administrative decisions imposing a fine (i.e., all of the NCA's decisions included within the scope of the study), the court is not bound by the scope and grounds of action filed by the appellant. Therefore, in practice, in some cases the courts raised grounds on their own motion: in *Československá obchodná banka, a.s.*, both procedural grounds and in relation to the inapplicability of EU law,[114] in *ENVI-PAK* regarding the inapplicability of EU law[115] and in

110. Some grounds lie on the borderline between substantive and procedural, in particular arguments that related to the body of evidence and its assessment. For instance, if a party claimed, merely, that existing evidence was incorrectly assessed, the grounds would be considered substantive for the purposes of the study. Similarly, arguments regarding a lack of evidence gathered by the PMÚ were considered substantive grounds for an appeal. However, where an applicant claimed that the PMÚ rejected further fact-finding or examination of evidence required by the applicant, these grounds were considered to be procedural, linked to the procedural rights of parties to administrative proceeding. Objections against the wording of arguments provided in a decision by the PMÚ or in the first-instance judgment are another example of borderline grounds: claims that arguments are missing at all were considered procedural grounds, while the incorrectness, vagueness or arbitrariness of any arguments were deemed to be substantive grounds. Grounds related to the fine cover arguments against the imposition of a fine, its level or its calculation and arguments provided by the PMÚ or the first-instance court to explain the level of a fine (*see* Methodology Chapter).
111. Including the strategies of their legal representation because the number of law firms focusing on competition law has been quite limited and if we look on the name of the law firms representing different undertakings throughout the period under research, we discover high number of repetitions.
112. In particular, 59% of the appeals launched by the undertakings against a decision of the PMÚ involved procedural, substantive and fine grounds that were invoked together, compared to 2% of the appeals involving only procedural grounds, 14% only substantive grounds, 5% substantive and procedural, 16% substantive and fine and 5% procedural and fine.
113. Comparing to 22% in appeals based on substantive and fine-related arguments and 33% in appeals based on procedural and fine-related arguments. The appeals based on grounds in the remaining combinations were not accepted.
114. RCB: 3S 57/2010 *Československá obchodná banka, a.s.* (28 September 2010).
115. RCB: 1S/249/2010 *ENVI-PAK* (1 December 2011).

MICRONIX spol. s.r.o., procedural grounds.[116] Moreover, in some cases, the court raises different grounds for setting aside or varying the previous decision or first-instance judgment than those invoked by the parties, although they fit within the same group of grounds (procedural/substantial/fine) as argued by the parties.

The empirical findings reveal that substantive grounds were the least accepted grounds of appeal in both judicial instances (72% rejected) compared to procedural and fines-based appeals (equally 52% rejected). The first-instance court rejected 47% procedural, 74% substantive and 54% grounds based on fines and the second-instance court rejected 57% procedural, 72% substantive and 48% fine reduction grounds. The success rate at the second-instance court proceedings must be divided between appeals initiated by an undertaking or by the NCA. The arguments of undertakings based on substantive grounds were the least successful (63% rejected) compared to arguments by the NCA (45% rejected). Overall, arguments of undertakings at the second instance were less successful compared to those of the NCA: in relation to procedural grounds there was a 64% rejection of arguments by undertakings compared to 45% rejection of arguments by the NCA and in arguments regarding the fine (including reduction of fine by the first-instance court) there was a 64% rejection of undertakings' arguments compared to 30% for rejected arguments raised by the NCA.

The success rate of the various grounds for review is not equally distributed across the years. To this end, Figure 26.13 indicates the type of grounds of appeals raised by one or more parties against an NCA's decision or a previous instance's judgment per year (lines), and the number of fully and partially successful appeals (bars). Unlike Figure 26.12, the data is presented from the perspective of each single appeal judgment. As Figure 26.13(a) shows, in the first part of the period, approximately until 2010, the success rate of procedural grounds was quite high (except for 2007 when it was between 66% and 100% per year). This period also corresponds to the period when the majority of appeals were fully or partially lost by the NCA (albeit some of them were in the later period revised by the second-instance court). In this period, the courts also developed strict theories on the content of the fining decision applying principles of criminal law, i.e., they required, inter alia, a fining decision to establish the precise time and place of cartel agreement[117] which was not, obviously, established in cases without a written or oral agreement. From 2010 until 2015, procedural grounds were still relatively successful, but the court started to shape enforcement of the competition law by providing their own opinion on substantive matters (Figure 26.13(b)), e.g., in *Slovnaft* case and the *Slovak Telekom* case.[118] The SC also started to accept arguments of the NCA and changed previous formalistic judgments based on procedural grounds adopted by the RCB, e.g., *Highway cartel*,[119] *ENVI-PAK* case.[120] Appeals on grounds related to fines maintained a high success rate throughout the whole period (Figure 26.13(c)) and after 2015 maintained its relevance

116. SC: 5Asan/19/2018 *MICRONIX spol. s.r.o.* (27 February 2020).
117. RCB: 2S/430/06 *Doprastav, a.s. et al.* (10 December 2008) (*Highway cartel*).
118. RCB: 1S/165/2011 *Slovnaft, a.s.* (22 March 2012), SC: 8Sžhpu/1/2011 *Slovak Telekom, a.s.* (30 October 2012).
119. SC: 1Sžhpu/1/2009, *Doprastav, a.s. et al.* (30 December 2013).
120. SC: 8Sžhpu/1/2012 *ENVI-PAK* (23 May 2013).

compared to the decline in success of other grounds. The EU/national) ground remained marginal throughout the whole period (Figure 26.13(d)).

As of 2010, the NCA started to be more successful in relation to procedural grounds (Figure 26.13a(bis))[121] changing the outcome of the case at the second instance of judicial review. Similarly, from 2013 the NCA started to be more successful in its substantive arguments (Figure 26.13b(bis)) and in relation to grounds based on fines (Figure 26.13c(bis)).

Figure 26.13(a) Procedural Grounds

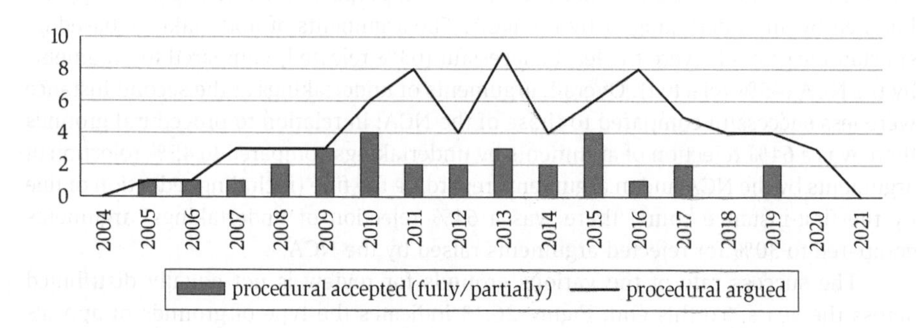

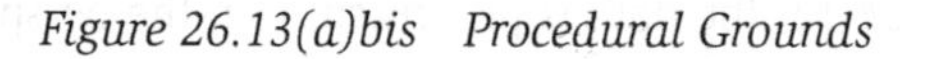
Figure 26.13(a)bis Procedural Grounds

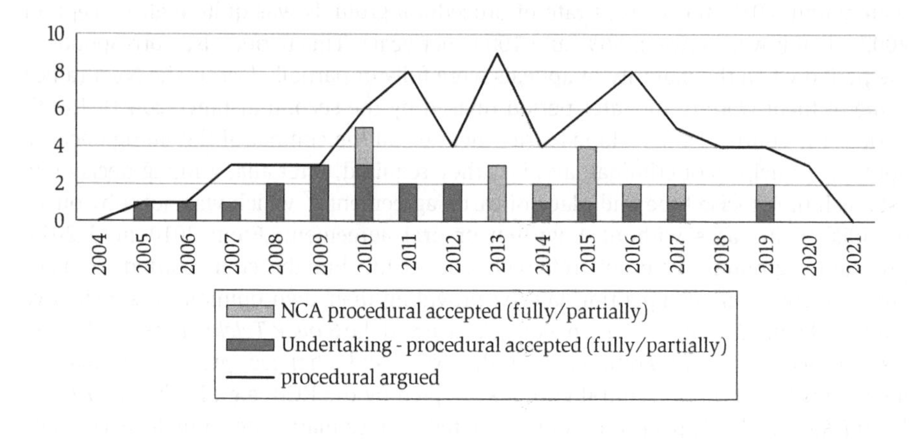

121. For Figures 11a(bis) to 11c(bis) the same methodology was used as for 11a to 11c and the only difference was made in splitting the number of grounds accepted depending on the appealing party, i.e., undertaking or NCA.

Figure 26.13(b) Substantive Grounds

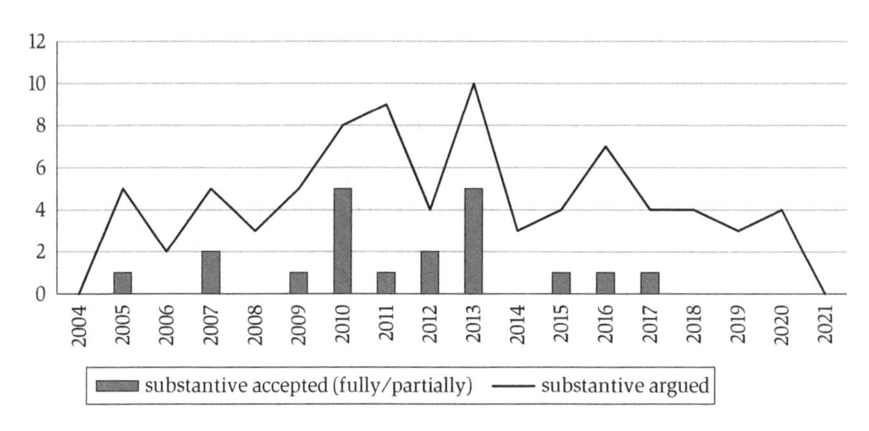

Figure 26.13(b)bis Substantive Grounds

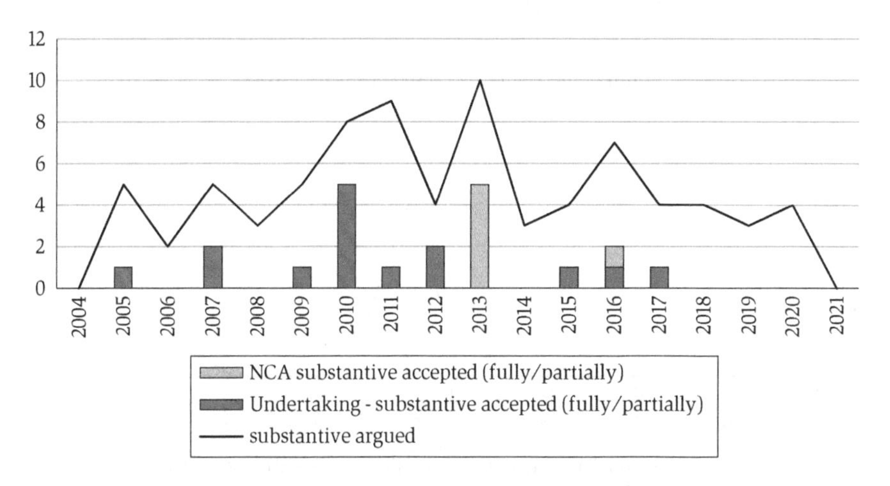

Figure 26.13(c) Fines-Related Grounds

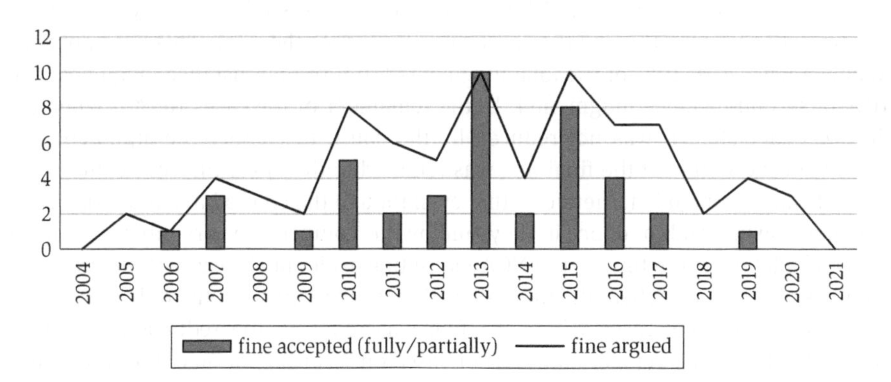

Figure 26.13(c)bis Fines-Related Grounds

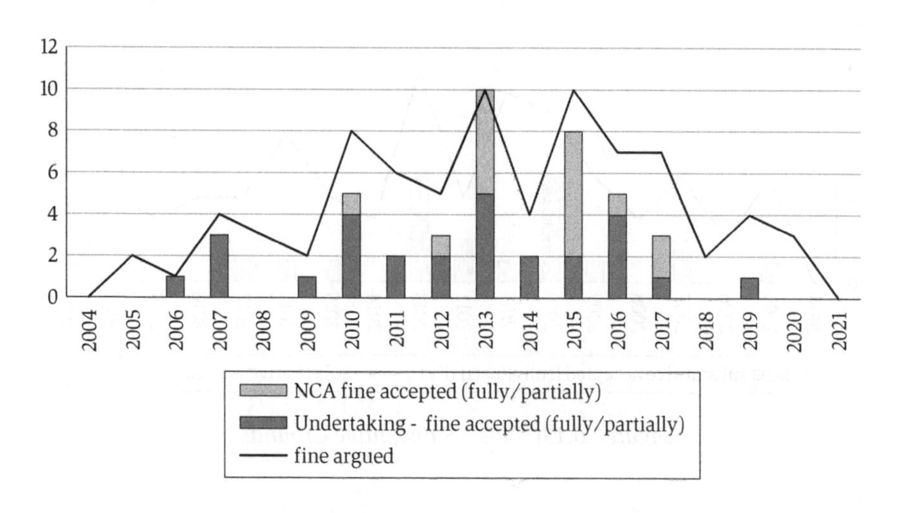

Figure 26.13(d) EU/National Grounds

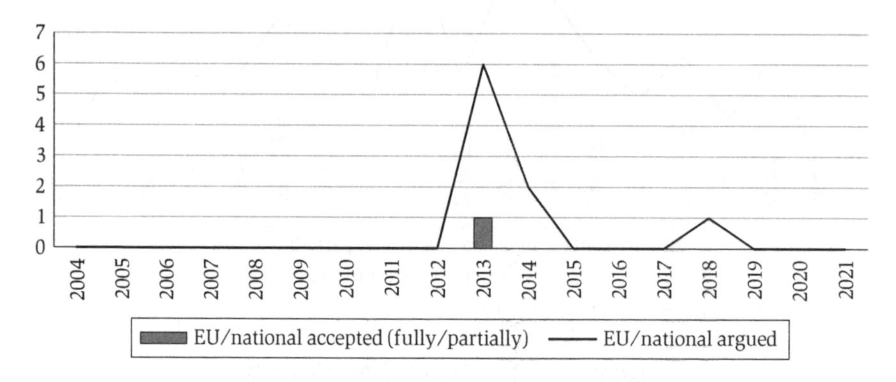

The fine imposed by the PMÚ has rarely been successfully challenged in judicial review (when varying the fine the court can only reduce the fine). This has happened in only a few cases, 10% of the total judgments (10% of first-instance judgments and 10% of second-instance judgments). In the remainder of the cases (63%), when the fine was contested, it was not reduced by the court, i.e., either the argument was rejected or the setting of the final fine was remitted to the lower-instance court or the NCA. It can be concluded, therefore, that even though the courts have full jurisdiction to review the fine and to reduce it, they employ this competence very rarely and prefer the recalculation of the fine by the NCA via setting aside the decision of the PMÚ as a whole (even in cases, where the fine calculation was identified as the only error in the decision). In the few cases where the fine was reduced, the reduction was quite substantial (73% on average) and was not based on reconsideration of the substantive scope of the decision. In the *Cargo* case, the RCB reduced the fine by approximately

86%[122] on the basis that the application of the economic continuity test was a mitigating factor in the calculation of the fine (upheld by the SC). In the case of *IT distributors*, the RCB decreased the fine by 90% due to the disproportionality of possible gains,[123] but, after a second-instance review, the fine was reduced by 50% only (in the case of one of the undertakings).[124] In the banking cartel, the RCB reduced the fine by approximately 50% due to the argument that it was a self-defence cartel.[125] And finally, in the *MARIANUM* case, the SC did not reduce the fine itself and sent it for recalculation by the NCA, but it concluded that it was not possible to impose a fine[126] (*see* further the analysis of *nullum crimen sine lege* dispute).

Figure 26.14 shows that the type of infringement does not seem to be decisive in terms of the success of the grounds of action/appeal. This figure examines only the fully or partially successful grounds, recording the relationship between the type of restriction of competition and the success of the appeal grounds. To put this number in context, the figure also specifies the total number of judgments concerning each type of restriction. The figure presents the data from the perspective of each single appeal judgment (noting that more than one judgment may be issued with respect to a single NCA decision).

Figure 26.14 Types of Restrictions Versus Successful Grounds of Appeal

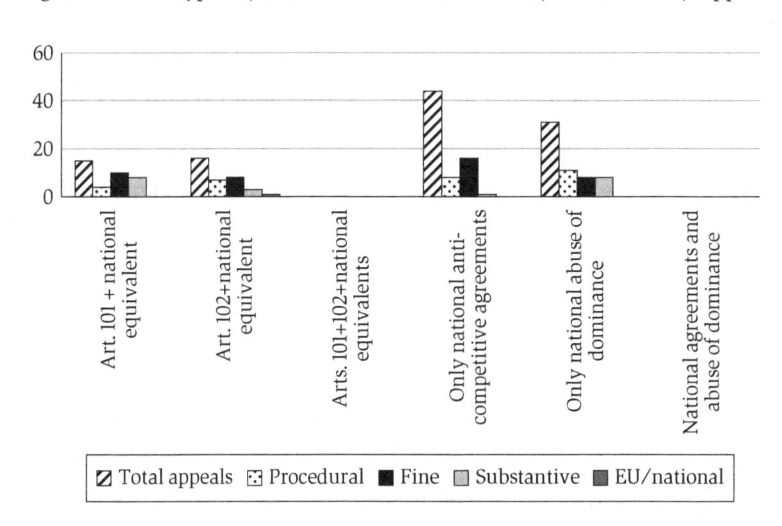

122. RCB: 2S/258/06 *Železničná spoločnosť' Cargo Slovakia, a.s.* (7 November 2007).
123. RCB: 1S/131/2015 ASBIS SK spol. s r.o., 1S/136/2015 eD´ system Slovakia, s.r.o., 1S/121/2015 SWS Distribution a.s.
124. SC: 3Sžh/2/2016 ASBIS SK spol. s r.o.
125. RCB: 2S/115/2014 Československá obchodná banka, a.s.
126. SC: 3Sžh/3/2010 MARIANUM - Pohrebníctvo mesta Bratislavy.

4.7 Appellants and the Involvement of Third Parties

As noted above in section 4.2, the court procedural rules do not allow third parties to initiate judicial review proceedings - this is only possible for an administrative body and parties to the administrative proceeding (or persons who claim that should have been parties to that proceeding). Therefore, almost in all cases, the addressee of the PMÚ's decision was the applicant in the first-instance appeal[127] and all subsequent appeals were lodged by the NCA, by the undertakings (depending on the outcome of the first-instance judgment), or by both (if the court reduced the fine only). Owing to the quite strict court procedural rules, there has only been one case when an appeal by the PMÚ was not admitted because the law did not allow any appeal against the first-instance judgment in issue.[128] Undertakings filed fifty-seven administrative actions and the NCA appealed in thirty-one cases and the undertaking subsequently appealed in twenty cases against the first-instance appeal judgment. From the practice of the NCA, it is apparent that it appealed against any judgment, whenever it was admissible if it lost at first-instance appeal.

The judicial rules do not provide for the participation of a complainant in the court review procedure,[129] but in the *Banking cartel*, the original complainant (AK-CENTA CZ) was admitted as a third party or an 'accessory participant'[130] (not a party to the proceeding).[131]

4.8 European Commission as *Amicus Curiae* and Preliminary References

The involvement of EU bodies in the judicial review process in Slovakia arose in three cases: in the *Cargo* case[132] and *ENVI-PAK* case[133] the European Commission submitted its comments as *amicus curiae* and in the *Banking cartel*, a preliminary question was submitted by the SC.[134]

127. Only two appeals were lodged by other parties than undertaking and both were dismissed inadmissible due to lack of standing of appellant.
128. SC: 2Sžhpu/4/2008 *Železničná spoločnosť' Cargo Slovakia, a.s.* (14 October 2008).
129. Complainants or the third parties have no formal position as a party to administrative proceeding at the PMÚ and therefore have no standing at the court proceeding.
130. RCB: 1S 18/2010, *Slovenská sporitel'ňa, a.s.* (23 September 2010), RCB: 3S 57/2010 *Československá obchodná banka, a.s.* (28 September 2010), RCB: 3S/56/2010 *Všeobecná úverová banka, a.s.* (28 September 2010), SC: 5Sžh/4/2010 *Československá obchodná banka, a.s.* (19 May 2011).
131. In that period, the OSP allowed participation of an 'accessory participant' to the court proceeding, i.e., a person who is not a party to the court proceeding (i.e., cannot file an action and can support one of the parties to the proceeding) but can have legal interest in the outcome of the proceeding.
132. SC: 1Sžhpu/2/2008 *Železničná spoločnosť' Cargo Slovakia, a.s.* (26 October 2010), SC: 1Sžhpu/1/2011 *Železničná spoločnosť' Cargo Slovakia, a.s.* (31 January 2012), SC: 4Sžhpu/2/2014 *Železničná spoločnosť' Cargo Slovakia, a.s.* (31 March 2015).
133. SC: 8Sžhpu/1/2012 *ENVI-PAK* (23 May 2013).
134. Judgment of 7 February 2013, *Slovenská sporitel'ňa*, C-68/12, EU:C:2013:71.

In the *Cargo* case.[135] the European Commission argued on the economic continuity test; and in the *ENVI-PAK* case, the European Commission contributed to the possibility of imposing a sanction for a violation of Article 102 TFEU in general, i.e., without referring to any form of abuse of the non-exhaustive list and on the possibility of the parallel application of EU law and national law. The arguments presented by the European Commission were accepted.[136]

In the *Banking cartel*, the court dealt with the case in three separate proceedings and the court refused to join them into a single proceeding even after the NCA's request. As a result, the RCB annulled the same decision three times (vis-à-vis each member of the cartel) and the case was subject to appeal at the SC, handled by three different panels of the SC. One panel of the SC quite swiftly confirmed the judgment, while another sent a preliminary reference to the CJEU (and the third panel waited on the outcome of the preliminary ruling). As a result of the CJEU's ruling, the SC varied the first-instance judgments and upheld the PMÚ's decision. The PMÚ had to continue proceedings against one party, as a single cartelist in its administrative proceedings. Moreover, this part of the case was under judicial scrutiny again and the RCB reduced the final fine due to the specific character of the case (the rest of the members of the cartel had to pay the original fine). Finally, the SC changed the outcome of the case by rejecting the reduction of the fine by the RCB and upholding the fine imposed by the PMÚ.[137]

5 QUALITATIVE ANALYSIS

From the statutory point of view, the courts have so-called full jurisdiction in cases reviewing administrative sanctions, as described in section 2. The court, at first and second instance, notwithstanding the legal framework of the 'appellate period' (by 2016) or the 'cassation period' (2016 onwards), in fact, fully reviewed the decisions of the PMU, albeit to differing levels of quality and intensity. For the purpose of further analysis, the analysed period will be split into three eras: (1) the beginning of judicial review (until 2006); (2) when courts were unprepared for judicial review (2006-2013); and (3) the period of consolidation (2013 onwards).

5.1 The Beginning of Judicial Review (until 2006)

Most of this era is outside the scope of the research, and this period ends with more complex cases involving EU law (and also the involvement of the RCB in these complex cases). This period was characterised by quite short court judgments and an expressed trust by the courts in the PMÚ's expertise[138]and deference to that expertise.[139]

135. In fact, a single case reviewed by the SC three times due to two annulments by the Constitutional Court.
136. Although the SC saw economic succession as a mitigating factor for reducing the fine.
137. SC: 3Sžh/1/2016 *Československá obchodná banka, a.s.* (23 November 2017).
138. For example, in SC: 2Sž/14/2004 *Slovak Telekom, a.s.* (28 February 2005): 'The notion of relevant market is not subject to a legal definition because its content is based on non-legal, in

It is hard to evaluate whether quite formal and short evaluation of the cases is a consequence of the court's attitude to the judicial review process or a consequence of less sophisticated cases and the lower quality of arguments by the undertakings.

5.2 Courts Unprepared for Judicial Review (2006-2013)

From 2006, the PMÚ started to issue decisions in more challenging cases in which legal and economic theories of EU law were introduced for the first time in Slovak practice:

- in the *Highway cartel*, EU and national competition law were applied in parallel and the authority sought to prove the existence of the cartel by parallel indices in prices among the bidders without any direct evidence of communication;
- the *Cargo case* where the *economic continuity* test was employed, albeit not included in Slovak competition law;
- the *GIS cartel*, a residuum of EU-wide cartel within the pre-accession period involved groups of undertakings and the PMÚ had difficulties in following the EU law concept of undertaking while describing participants to the cartel as individual legal persons, as has been required by the Slovak administrative law;
- in the *Slovak Telekom* case the PMÚ fined margin squeeze as an exclusionary practice.

In order to understand the quality of judicial review and the length of the proceedings (e.g., more than ten years in the *Highway* cartel), it is useful to note several peculiarities that have shaped the work of judges sitting in the panels reviewing the competition cases. First, many of the judges of the RCB and SC in the administrative collegia had no previous experience with competition law and administrative law and they were transferred from other collegia of that court (e.g., at RCB *Slovak Telekom* case was the first competition case heard by the administrative panel No. 1 presided by Judge Bakošová and the administrative panel No. 2 presided by Judge Pohančeník was assigned to *Cargo* case and *Highway cartel* together with two other competition cases in 2006 as one of the first competition cases dealt with by them).

particular economic, considerations, since, in its interpretation, this leaves room for the administrative authority's discretion, which undoubtedly also takes into account the dynamics of the development of the market itself.'

139. For example, in SC: 1Sžhpu/3/2008 *HYBRAV Nitra a.s. and 30 others* (23 July 2005): 'In this connection, it should be pointed out that it is neither the duty nor the right of the Supreme Court in the appeal proceedings to seek or to presume for the applicants the reasons and arguments supporting the success of the appeal. In these circumstances, the applicants cannot successfully argue that there has been an error of fact and law unless they adduce facts and evidence to support such a contention.'

Second, it appears that transfer to the administrative collegium served as a form of 'punishment'[140] by the President of the SC Mr Štefan Harabin[141] as the work in administrative panels was considered less prestigious compared to criminal, civil or commercial law. Consequently, judges with training and expertise in completely different areas sat in panels reviewing competition cases.

Along with a deterioration in the working atmosphere at the administrative collegium, the intrusion of Mr Harabin in the work of administrative panels of the SC has resulted in the annulment of various judgments of the SC by the Constitutional Court of the Slovak Republic due to the unconstitutional reshufflings of members of the panel deciding the case, for instance in the high-profile *Highway Cartel*[142] case and *Cargo* case.[143]

It is no surprise that the judges sought to avoid resolution of cases by finding procedural failures (real or alleged) of the PMÚ without providing conclusive opinions on the case. Another strategy was to decrease or eliminate the fine in order to 'have a cake and eat it', approach, i.e., comforting the PMÚ by confirming the substance of the case, yet at the same time ensuring the outcome was not overly harsh to an undertaking.

The unpreparedness of judges to handle competition cases was admitted by the SC itself directly in the reasoning of its judgment in the *Highway cartel* case referring to the necessity for knowledge of EU law and sources in foreign languages,[144] awareness of economic theory,[145] and the requirement overall for specialised judges.[146] Given the

140. For instance, transfer of a long-time criminal law specialist judge of the SC, Mr Paluda, or the transfer to administrative panel of other criticising judge, Mr Miroslav Gavalec (currently judge of the CJEU) together with his allocation to an office with unsuitable conditions Mr Harabin commented with words: '... he can do pensions, there he cannot cause any damage ..., since he is an engineer, he can work in boiler room ...'. *See, e.g.*, Jozef Majchrák, 'Harabinokracia' (*Časopis.týždeň*, 2009) https://www.tyzden.sk/casopis/5614/harabinokracia/, accessed 4 March 2023; SITA, 'Harabin Vraj Preložením Len Trestá Oponentov' (*SME*, 2010) https://domov.sme.sk/c/5574045/harabin-vraj-prelozenim-len-tresta-oponentov.html, accessed 4 March 2023; L'uboš Kostelanský, 'Paluda Už Nie Je Trestným Sudcom' (*Pravda*, 2010) https://spravy.pravda.sk/domace/clanok/168351-paluda-uz-nie-je-trestnym-sudcom/, accessed 4 March 2023.

141. President of the SC in 1998-2003 and 2009-2014 and Minister of Justice in 2006-2009. Mr Harabin was appointed as a representative of the party Vladimír Mečiar, whose autocratic methods as a Prime Minister almost disqualified Slovakia from the accession to the EU for details see Ondrej Blažo, 'Questions of Democracy and Rule of Law Process and Their Importance for the Association and Membership in the Light Od Experience of the Slovak Republic' in Naděžda Šišková (ed.), *From Eastern Partnership to the Association: A Legal and Political Analysis* (Cambridge Scholars Publishing 2014).

142. Constitutional Court of the Slovak Republic, Decision of 17 June 2015, II. ÚS 893/2014-175.

143. Constitutional Court of the Slovak Republic, Decision of 14 June 2011, III. ÚS 170/2011.

144. SC: 1Sžhpu/1/2009 (20 December 2013): '... the panel of the supreme court must note (...) that the case in issue falls into particularly specialized agenda that is quite new for the judges and that is due its character factually and legally substantially compacted and almost always connected to international element, legislatively stemming from communitarian regulation (primary and secondary one) that requires high level of knowledge of not only foreign-language scientific literature as well as decision-making activity of the Commission and of the CJ EU, which decisions are accessible in Slovak language for the judges of the Supreme Court of the Slovak republic only in limited extent.'

145. SC: 1Sžhpu/1/2009 (20 December 2013): 'Regarding aforementioned, one must note particular character of competition law which is exceptional not only by connecting objective law with

judges, even those of the SC, lack that knowledge and experience, the enforcement of EU competition law is endangered.[147]

If we read through the judgments we can observe that they are continuously longer, compared to the previous period, however, measuring on the basis of the extent of the presentation of own arguments, these parts are usually extremely short and, in some cases, there is no presentation of own opinion of the court; the court shortly states that there is either reason for setting aside the first-instance judgment or to confirm it or briefly refers that agrees with either of parties.[148] Indeed, there are also opposite examples when in *Doprastav, a.s et al.*,[149] the court turned the previous decision of the RCB by a 115-page judgment of which five pages reviewed evidence and twenty-five provided own legal assessment, or in *Slovak Telekom, a.s.*[150] the panel of the SC provided not only its own assessment but also guidance in the areas where the RCB remained silent when annulling the PMÚ's decision.[151]

In this period, certain controversial theories or 'inventions' by the Slovak courts were the most discussed competition law issues in Slovakia among practitioners and academia.[152] Not only because they showed the courts were more active in undertaking a judicial review in competition cases but also due to their apparent deviation from concepts and practice developed under the CJEU case law and enforcement by the European Commission, for instance in relation to: (1) the requirement to provide the

---

economic theory, but also by implanting economic notions into legal order which then become legal rules by long-term legal practice, while only few legal areas use economic institutes in such depth such as competition law. (...)'

146. SC: 1Sžhpu/1/2009 (20 December 2013): 'This character of agenda, showing also rising level of variability and flexibility of anti-competitive practices, undoubtedly requires high specialization of judges with rising accent on decision-making tier, necessity of their systematic and permanent education as well as professional capacity of judicial personal in this area, which is unfortunately still permanently missing in the conditions of the Slovak Republic.'
147. SC: 1Sžhpu/1/2009 (20 December 2013): 'Without deep and firm experience of judges, in this particular agenda, it is not possible due to Art 101 to 106 TFEU secure fulfilment of union competition rules by issuing broadly acceptable and authoritative judicial decisions.
     Therefore the panel agrees with complaints of the Commission that the Slovak judicial system does not show stability of panels trying competition agenda, and not even on such high level as the Supreme Court of the Slovak Republic, it is still not able unity of its decision-making activity in this area (...) what undoubtedly endangers competition on Slovak market.'
148. For example, in *Železničná spoločnosť Cargo Slovakia* the SC provided its own opinion on fine, that was reduced, on one-eighth page of twenty pages of judgment (4Sžhpu/2/2014, 31 March 2015), however, the dissenting opinion to this issue contained seven pages; similarly in ENVI-PAK (8Sžhpu/1/2012, 23 May 2013) the CS provided four pages of own assessment of the case and one-fourth of page on fines from total twenty-two-page decision. In this context, arguments of the RCB in *Železničná spoločnosť Cargo Slovakia* case (1S/27/2007, 6 December 2007) sound ludicrous because the RCB criticised the PMÚ that it gave reasons for calculation of fine within one half of page and afterwards, it gave reasons for reduction of fine from SKK 75 million to SKK 9 million, in fact, within one sentence precisely.
149. SC: 1Sžhpu 1/2009 *Doprastav, a.s et al.* (30 December 2013).
150. SC: 4Sžh/2/2010 *Slovak Telekom, a.s.* (28 June 2011).
151. Judge Hanzelová presiding that panel was one of the experienced judges who continued at SC and was also engaged in judicial review of the competition cases in the era before 2004.
152. For example, Kalesná, 'Právnické osoby v konfrontácii s ekonomickou realitou: test ekonomickej kontinuity' (*supra* n. 19); Kalesná, 'Zneužívanie dominantného postavenia v teórii a v aplikačnej praxi' (*supra* n. 89); Šabová, Fodorová and Lukáčová (*supra* n. 86); Šabová (*supra* n. 89); Blažo and Šramelová (*supra* n. 87); Blažo, 'Twenty Years of Harmonisation and Still Divergent: Development of Slovak Competition Law' (*supra* n. 19).

precise place, time and means of an infringement in the operative part of the decision, (2) the economic continuity test and its mitigating consequences, (3) the misapplication of *nullum crimen sine lege, nulla poena sine lege.* These issues will be explained further.

5.2.1 Requirement to Provide the Precise Place, Time and Means of Infringement in the Operative Part of the Decision

In the *Highway cartel* case, the RCB tried to apply the principles of criminal law when shaping the requirements for the operative part of the decision of the NCA.[153] The strict requirement for establishing the precise place, time and manner of committing the offence, as established by the RCB, would hinder the application of the competition rules, in particular relating to cartels or concerted practices, where illicit agreements are not written.

This opinion was hanging above the PMÚ as a Sword of Damocles until 2013 when was corrected by the SC (and finally in 2016).

5.2.2 Economic Continuity Test as Mitigating Factor?

In its judgment in the *Cargo* case[154] (4Sžhpu/2/2014) confirming the previous judgment of the RCB, the SC followed the argument relating to the lack of grounds for imposing the fine as well as the mitigating factor based on the transfer of liability under the economic continuity test. In order to demonstrate the low quality of arguments by the SC in terms of the fine, it is useful to present them in full: 'The Supreme Court agreed with the Regional Court's conclusion that the defendant's objections to the amount of the fine imposed were unfounded. It is not apparent from the reasoning of the defendant's decision on what turnover and for what accounting period the Council of the Authority based its decision on when imposing the fine. Also in the Supreme Court's view, the imposition of a fine of SKK 75 000 000 is not adequately justified in the defendant's decision and a fine of that amount is punitive in nature. The Supreme Court agrees with the Regional Court's conclusion that the court's power of moderation

153. RCB: 2S/430/06 *Doprastav et al.* (10 December 2008): 'In the Court's view, it follows from the foregoing that the administrative decisions under review do not contain such a specification of the particulars containing the description of the offence by indicating the place, time and manner of its commission so that that offence cannot be confused with another offence. (...) In this connection, it should be noted that the description (legend) of the alleged agreement is completely lacking in the present case, i.e. how, between whom and when it was to have been established and what at least the basic content of the agreement was (which could also be inferred from the communication platform, which, however, is incomplete and does not show contacts between all the applicants, owing to the insufficiently established factual situation). The operative part of the decision lacks a "timeline" which would make it clear during what period of time the alleged infringement should have lasted. (...) Thus, the administrative authorities did not thoroughly deal with the place, time or manner of the offence and did not sufficiently specify the description of the offence either in the operative part or in the reasoning of the decisions, and therefore the decisions in question must be regarded as unreviewable for lack of clarity from this point of view.'

154. SC: 4Sžhpu/2/2014 Železničná spoločnosť Cargo Slovakia, a.s. (31 March 2015).

under § 250i(2) in conjunction with § 250j(5) OSP must be exercised in the present case.'

5.2.3 Nullum crimen sine lege, nulla poena sine lege *Dispute*

One cannot object to the general principle of criminal law in a country governed by the rule of law: *nulla crimen sine lege, nulla poena sine lege*. However, within the judicial review of the PMÚ's decisions, the idea presented by Judge Rumana in the *MARIANUM* case[155] was the most bizarre controversy of the judicial review process in that period.

The RCB originally dismissed the appeal against the PMÚ's decision, rejecting the applicant's argument on the shortcomings of the NCA's decision consisting of its failure to indicate a precise qualification of the abuse of dominant position in issue as one of the forms of abuse of dominant position stipulated in the non-exhaustive list provided in subparagraphs § 8(2) (a) to (e) ZOHS 2011 (this non-exhaustive list corresponds to the wording of Article 102 TFEU).

Reviewing the first-instance judgment, the SC agreed with the opinion of the RCB,[156] but it provided an interpretation leading to the annulment of the imposition of the fine.

The SC upheld the decision of the PMÚ in part on the basis that the behaviour of an undertaking under scrutiny constituted an abuse of a dominant position was lawful and factually correct. In the opinion of the SC, the PMÚ was therefore allowed to declare an existence of an abuse of dominant position but could not impose a sanction for such an infringement. The rationale of the SC was, that the 'crime' under the law was established by the decision of the PMÚ and therefore any sanction could only be imposed for such behaviour in the future. The SC, thus, did not acknowledge the general prohibition of an abuse of dominant position enshrined in law as a definition of 'crime' for the purposes of the observation of the '*nullum crimen sine lege*' principle. At the same time, the SC attributed to the PMÚ the right to establish a definition of prohibited behaviour that would be subject to administrative fines in the future. Indeed, such power of an administrative body to establish the definition of punishable behaviour on a case-by-case principle is actually a violation of the principle '*nullum crimen sine lege*' and demonstrates the depth of misunderstanding in the application of competition law by the SC. In practice, the opinion of the SC, if applied, would have led to a situation whereby only behaviour that could fit within the definitions included in the non-exhaustive list of types of abuse of a dominant position could be subject to a

155. SC: 3Sžh/3/2010 *MARIANUM – Pohrebníctvo Mesta Bratislavy* (3 May 2011).
156. According to the SC, 'the so-called general clause is contained in Article 8(2) of Act No. 136/2001 Coll. by the use of the term "in particular". It is not possible to capture all the facts of the administrative offence of abuse of a dominant position in the Act and, in the event that a practice occurs which cannot be subsumed under any of the demonstratively listed facts, the Authority must base its assessment on the general clause relating to the abuse of a dominant position on the relevant market, but must respect the principles of administrative punishment based on the general clause and impose a sanction only if the undertaking does not respect the facts established by the decision. Consequently, it may sanction the undertaking for a period when the principle of nullum crimen has been satisfied.'

fine. Other abusive practices could be subject to fines only after a declaration that such a practice was an abuse of a dominant position by the PMÚ and undertakings engaged in the very same behaviour again (or continued its infringement).[157]

The RCB reacted immediately as in the *ENVI-PAK*[158] case it followed the arguments of the SC in the *MARIANUM* case and annulled the decision of the PMÚ based on the argument that the behaviour of the undertaking was not identified as falling within the non-exhaustive list of § 8(2) ZOHS 2011.

This line of interpretation was ended by the judgment of the SC in ENVI-PAK,[159] just two years and two weeks after the *MARIANUM* judgment.

5.3 Consolidation Period (2013 Onwards)

During the consolidation period, the SC started to vary or annul previous judgments with controversial content.

The SC also finally abandoned the strict requirements for the operative part of the administrative decision consisting of the precise setting of the place and time of conclusion of an agreement restricting competition by accepting the specific nature of competition infringements.[160]

It is quite hard to predict the development of the intensity and quality of the judicial review in the future and draw conclusions from the 'consolidation' period. First, within the consolidation period, the courts finished the 'old' cases and in the same period, the enforcement activity of the PMÚ declined albeit some of the PMÚ's cases from that period are still ongoing. Therefore, the number of judgments after the period of consolidation of 'old cases' is significantly lower. Second, there were only rulings in three groups of cases were available within the scope of the research: *IT Distributors* cartel where the level of fine was the crucial question; *Chemkostav et al* involved an alleged cartel where the PMÚ used wiretaps without legal permission (more precisely, transcripts of wiretaps that were damaged), and it is not surprising that the court nullified it; and series of minor bid rigging cartels whose evaluation was

157. SC: 3Sžh/3/2010 *MARIANUM – Pohrebníctvo Mesta Bratislavy* (3 May 2011): 'The principle of proportionality requires that if the competition authority has the power to formulate new definitions of prohibited behaviour of abuse of a dominant position on the basis of a general clause and a non-exhaustive definition of the law, on the other hand, the undertaking must be able to know the exact wording of the practice which is prohibited. Only after this point it can be sanctioned. The antitrust authority's activity should, therefore, be focused on identifying practices in the first place, than capturing their content in a decision, prohibiting them and only then sanctioning them when the principle of nullum crimen could be already fulfilled.'
158. RCB: 1S/249/2010 *ENVI-PAK* (1 December 2011).
159. SC: 8Sžhpu/1/2012 *ENVI-PAK* (May 2013).
160. For example, SC: 4Sžhk/1/2019 *VUMAT SK, s.r.o. et al.* (4 November 2020), para. 86 'The Supreme Court also finds, with particular reference to the text of the operative part of the contested decision, that the defendant included in it a description of the applicants' conduct which is unambiguously specific both as regards the elements and the manner in which the offence in question was committed. The cassation court agrees (...) that it is necessary to consider the differences arising from the nature of administrative offences in the field of protection of competition as well as the wording of the statutory provisions themselves (e.g., § 4 and § 8 of Act No. 136/2001 Coll.), which do not allow the specification of the acts in the same way as it is in the case of minor offences or criminal offences.'

shaped by the previous SC's guidance in the *Highway cartel*. Except for the consideration of fines, these cases provide little in the way of broader judicial 'policy setting'.

Nevertheless, in this period, the courts started to produce some judgments that have been useful for the future in relation to judicial deference, the standard of proof and the review of fines.

5.3.1 *Judicial Deference*

In the previous periods, the courts tended to merely copy the text of law without further analysis of the relevant competition law issue. The courts based their deference to the competition authority on the general concept of separation of powers rather than the derived from the expertise, independence of the PMÚ or its legitimacy.[161] The rationale and scope of judicial deference by the courts was rooted in the discretion of administrative bodies, such as PMÚ, and the absence of court powers to interfere with this administrative discretion, if the administrative body acted within the limits of the law provided reasoning for its decisions.[162] This approach by the courts is not specifically linked to the PMÚ or competition law but is part of the general framework for judicial review of decisions of administrative authorities.

However, aside from this formal deference, the practice of the courts showed that they were prepared to undertake a profound review of the factual circumstances of the case, the evidence, and the fine. From 2004 onwards, it can be observed that the courts usually undertook an intense review of the case, although in some cases this was undertaken in a rather formalistic way without providing guidance for further evaluation of the case and thus exposing the undertaking (the NCA as well) to a prolonged 'trial and error' method of decision-making.

In relation to judicial deference, it must be noted that by 2016 the courts had full jurisdiction to review the case *de novo* if sanction was imposed. This meant that the courts were not bound by facts established by the administrative authority and thus the court could either rely on those facts or re-examine evidence gathered by the administrative authority or find and establish evidence on its own.[163] Under this competence, the court could replace a decision of an administrative authority with its own

161. For different rationales *see, e.g.*, Maciej Bernatt, 'Transatlantic Perspective on Judicial Deference in Administrative Law' (2016) 22 Columbia Journal of European Law 275, 280; José Carlos Laguna de Paz, 'Understanding the Limits of Judicial Review in European Competition Law' (2014) 2 Journal of Antitrust Enforcement 203 DOI: 10.1093/jaenfo/jnt014.
162. For example, SC: 4Sžhk/1/2019 *VUMAT SK, s.r.o. et al.* (4 November 2020), para. 91: 'From the established case-law of the Constitutional Court of the Slovak Republic it can also be deduced that the decision on certain issues is subject to administrative discretion and therefore the court is not entitled to substitute its own discretion for that of the administrative authority, because it would unduly interfere with the competence of the executive authority, which does not belong to it. It is for the general courts to examine the administrative discretion from the point of view that it has not exceeded the limits and considerations laid down by law. If they find that it is in accordance with the rules of reasoning, if the conditions for such reasoning have been established by due process of law, then the courts may not draw different or even contrary conclusions from the same facts, for that would interfere with the administrative discretion of the administrative authority concerned.'
163. § 250i(2) OSP.

decision.[164] This competence of the court to establish facts on its own and replace the decision of administrative authorities was used in competition cases only in relation to fine reduction (i.e., no court decided to modify the assessment of a competition case on its own). This competence of the courts was modified in 2016 such that the courts may replace the decision of the administrative authority in competition cases in relation to the fine: either to reduce the fine or to decide not to impose any fine.[165] Therefore, notwithstanding substantial changes in court procedural rules in 2016, the practice of the courts remained unchanged.

5.3.2 *Revision of Fines*

As described in section 2, the court procedural rules provide 'full jurisdiction' for the courts to review cases of administrative sanctioning and with the power to reduce the fine. The courts reduced the fines in several cases even in the period between 2006 and 2013, but the court's reasoning in that period was inadequate, and the courts did not provide any guidance to allow for understanding of how they had calculated the reduced fine.

The approach of the courts in the period of 2013 onwards changed and the courts showed a certain deference.

The SC accepted the discretionary power of the PMÚ in setting the fine,[166] (it related the discretionary powers of the PMÚ and reviewed the competence of the courts to the relationship between the European Commission and the CJEU[167]), and also rejected its role as policymaker in fining policy in competition matters and left the decision-making to the NCA. The SC refused to provide any 'formal formula' to calculate fines in the future.[168] On the contrary, the SC accepted the Methodological Guidelines of the PMÚ on Setting Fines as 'a Euro-conform internal regulation, taking

164. § 250j(5) OSP.
165. § 198 SSP.
166. SC: 4Sžhk/1/2019 *VUMAT SK, s.r.o. et al.* (4 November 2020), para. 98: 'In this respect, the cassation court emphasises that, according to the established case-law (in particular the ruling of the Constitutional Court of the Slovak Republic, No. II ÚS 127/07-21, or the decisions of the Supreme Court, Case No. 6Sžo/84/2007, Case No. 6Sžo/98/2008, Case No. 1Sžo/33/2008, Case No. 2Sžo/5/2009, Case No. 2Sžo/5/2009, Case No. 8Sžo/547/2009) it is not the role of the court in the exercise of administrative justice to replace the activity of administrative authorities, but only to review the legality of their procedures and decisions, i.e. whether the authorised and competent administrative authorities have respected the relevant substantive and procedural law when dealing with specific issues defined by the scope of action.'
167. SC: 8Sžhk/1/2016 *eD' system Slovakia, s.r.o.* (26 October 2017): 'In this context the Supreme Court also refers to the case-law of the Court of Justice, which shows that the Commission also has discretion in determining the amount of any fine (...).'
168. SC: 8Sžhk/1/2016 *eD' system Slovakia, s.r.o.* (26 October 2017): 'The Supreme Court of the Slovak Republic considers it necessary to emphasise that the courts in the administrative justice system supervise the observance of legality of public administration bodies when issuing decisions, considering the specificity of individual cases, in compliance with the conditions required by law. This is particularly apparent in the assessment of the proportionality of the fines imposed, where the existence of both the circumstances of individual cases and mitigating circumstances precludes the courts from laying down a "formal formula" which should guide the defendant's practice in determining the level of fines to be imposed in the future.'

into account generally accepted and applied rules of the imposition of penalties for the type of administrative offences in question.'[169] Thus, in the review of fines, the SC employed a legality test (i.e., whether the fine is within the statutory limits) and proportionality test (i.e., whether the fine 'fulfils its purpose both from the point of view of general prevention and from the point of view of the requirement of a punitive nature, with the consequence that it should motivate the undertaking to comply with the legislation in future').[170]

A major fine reduction occurred in the *IT Distributors cartel* where the RCB reduced the fines by 90%. In cassation proceedings in this case,[171] the SC shaped judicial deference for the future by considering the margin of possible reduction of the fine by the court in competition cases. Reducing the fine to 0.1% of undertaking's annual turnover was found by the SC to be an error in law made by the RCB because, in the opinion of the SC, cartels must be viewed '...as one of the most dangerous forms of anti-competitive conduct which must be severely punished...'.[172] Moreover, the SC found it unreasonable to reduce the fine below 50% of its original level, if the conditions for leniency reduction are not met.[173] Similarly, another panel of the SC employed the same approach when it reduced the fine only by 50% whereas the RCB had reduced it by 90%.[174]

These judgments show that the SC maintained its broad competence for review, even in the cassation system, when the review of fines was included in the review of the legality of the judgment of the first-instance court.

5.3.3 Standard of Proof

The standard of proof is a constant matter of dispute within the judicial review system and this discussion can be split into two parts. The first deals with the level of the required standard of proof itself and the second covers assessment of indirect (circumstantial) evidence in proving cartels.

In the *Cargo* case, the RCB and SC provided a detailed insight into how they originally understood the standard of proof in competition matters. First, the RCB referred to the requirement of establishing the 'substantive truth', which it equated with proof of facts 'beyond any doubt'.[175] In its judicial review, the SC was not even sure which standard of proof was actually applied by the RCB, nevertheless, it upheld the decision of the RCB,[176]

169. SC: 2Sžhk/2/2018 *MAHRLO, s.r.o.* (8 December 2020), para. 47.
170. *Ibid.*
171. SC: 6Sžhk/1/2017 *SWS Distribution a.s.* (23 March 2019).
172. *Ibid.*, para. 85.
173. *Ibid.*, paras 84 and 85.
174. SC: 3Sžh/2/2016 *ASBIS SK spol. s r.o.* (23 November 2011).
175. RCB: 5S 30/2015 *Železničná spoločnosť' Cargo, a.s* (13 October 2015).
176. SC: 8Sžh/3/2016 *Železničná spoločnosť' Cargo, a.s.* (31 May 2018): 'the Regional Court applying to the case in issue the standards corresponding to the concept of "beyond any doubt" (...) did not exceeded the standards of criminal procedure, because the facts of the case, which are free from reasonable doubt, are sufficiently established only for the purposes of the preparatory proceedings (where, ultimately, the guilt and punishment of the offender are not

Furthermore, the SC stressed that even in cases involving the application of EU law, national rules for the standard of proof apply and thus if national rules require a higher standard of proof than the EU rules, the national rules shall apply.[177] The SC found the standard of proof as requiring 'sufficiently precise and coherent proof to justify the view, that there has been an infringement' (i.e., the standard of proof argued by the PMÚ based on CJEU case law), which is lower than the standard required by § 3(5) and § 32(1) Administrative Code. Therefore, in the opinion of the SC in the *Cargo* case, a decision of the administrative authority shall 'be based on a reliably ascertained state of affairs, the true state of affairs having to be ascertained accurately and completely. The Administrative Code is therefore based on the principle of substantive truth.'[178]

These arguments provided by the courts, on the standard of proof and their attempt to raise the standard of proof to the level required by criminal law standards, were incorrect. The Slovak Penal Proceeding Code (2005)[179] does not require 'beyond any doubt' standard of proof.[180] It is possible that the judges relied on an understanding of the standard of proof in penal law employed before the Velvet Revolution since the Penal Proceeding Code (1961)[181] actually required 'substantive truth' standard of proof.[182] However, this standard of proof has not been in force in Slovakia since October 1994.[183] It is clear that the Administrative Code uses similar wording for the standard of proof as in the Penal Proceeding Code (1961) prior to 1994[184] as the Administrative Code was adopted in 1967 and the provision on the standard of proof remained unaltered even after the modernisation of the Slovak legal order. This historical remnant, if wrongly and absolutely literally applied, can lead to a weakening in the administrative enforcement of law, because it would require a higher standard of proof in administrative matters than in criminal law.

This strict understanding of the standard of proof was later moderated by the SC in the *Highway cartel* case where the SC admitted that the application of the standard

decided), but not for the purposes of the criminal proceedings at the trial stage. (...) the Supreme Court is also of the view that the standard of proof requiring 'sufficiently precise and coherent evidence to justify the conclusion that a violation has occurred' was not met in the administrative proceedings before the defendant. In that connection, account must be taken, lastly, to the fact that the European judicial institutions have also, in their decisions, confirmed the conclusion that doubt in cases of infringement of competition rules must be interpreted in favour of the alleged infringer of those rules (...).'

177. SC: 8Sžh/3/2016 *Železničná spoločnosť Cargo, a.s.* (31 May 2018)
178. *Ibid.*
179. Zákon č. 301/2005 Z. z. Trestný poriadok.
180. § 2(10) Penal Proceeding Code (2005): 'The law enforcement authorities shall proceed in such a way as to establish the facts of the case beyond reasonable doubt to the extent necessary for their decision.'
181. Zákon č. 141/1961 Zb. o trestnom konaní súdnom (trestný poriadok).
182. § 2(5) Penal Proceeding Code (1961): 'The law enforcement authorities shall proceed in such a way as to ascertain the true state of the case and base their decision on it.'
183. Zákon č. 247/1994 Z. z., ktorým sa mení a dopĺňa Trestný poriadok.
184. § 32(1) Administrative Code: 'The administrative authority is obliged to ascertain accurately and completely the true state of the matter and, to that end, to obtain the necessary supporting documents for the decision.'

of proof shall depend on the peculiarities of substantive law applied by the administrative authority.[185] In terms of cartels, bid-rigging in particular, the SC accepted that the character of infringement 'makes it difficult, if not impossible, to use "classical" means of proof, which are the carriers of direct evidence, and, on the contrary, forces the enforcement authority to resort to indirect evidence. Indirect evidence, i.e. circumstantial evidence, and its probative force, then, derives primarily from the application of logical rules of reasoning (in particular, logical proof by argument), and demonstrates that the prerequisites that there should be an anticompetitive object are met.'[186]

The SC also made it clear that the standard of proof required by administrative law cannot be understood as a requirement for the PMÚ to discover and establish all facts and details possible, but only those that are decisive to establish the unlawfulness of the behaviour of the relevant undertakings.[187]

This approach was followed in cartel cases decided later and thus the line of authority established by the SC in the *Cargo* case was finally abandoned.

Relaxing the interpretation of the Administrative Code regarding the standard of proof and establishing more reasonable requirements for the level of the standard of proof, the SC in the *Highway cartel* also confirmed the acceptability of indirect evidence based on the similarity of bids as a sole source of knowledge and proof of the existence of a bid-rigging cartel. As the majority of the decisions by the PMÚ in the following period dealt with bid-rigging cartels, the courts were enabled to provide further guidance on understanding circumstantial evidence in bid-rigging cases.[188]

---

185. SC: 1Sžhpu/1/2009 *Doprastav, a.s. et al.* (30 December 2013): 'In connection with the legislator's requirement for correct fact-finding in administrative proceedings or in special proceedings before an administrative authority, it must be stressed that the scope of fact-finding in the process of application of law is defined by the applied legal norm. In the present case, the defendant has emphasised that the legal basis for the applicants' unlawful conduct is the formation of an agreement restricting competition.'
186. SC: 1Sžhpu/1/2009 *Doprastav, a.s. et al.* (30 December 2013).
187. *Ibid.*: 'The facts to be established consist of individual facts which enable not only the administrative court but also the parties to approximate and consequently to understand a real event or happening at a certain point in time (i.e., the act) which should be cognizable. From this framework, it is necessary to exclude facts that are not necessary (irrelevant) for the legal assessment of the act and, on the contrary, it is necessary to focus on the decisive facts, the framework of which is always individualized (predetermined) by the conduct of the participant, which is evaluated by the administrative authority as prohibited. It is quite clear that none of the officials of the competition authority deciding on the unlawfulness of the behaviour of the undertaking (competitor) was present at the place and time when the actual event occurred or the relevant events took place.'
188. For example, SC: 4Sžhk/1/2019 *VUMAT SK, s.r.o. et al.* (4 November 2020): 'the cassation court points to the special nature of competition law, where direct evidence is rare. Collusion in public procurement is carried out clandestinely, through various techniques or strategies, with cover bids, also known as formal bids, being one of its most common forms. The existence of an anticompetitive practice can also be demonstrated by a body of circumstantial evidence, derived from the market conduct or other manifestations of the undertaking, which, taken as a whole, may constitute evidence of an infringement of the competition rules, unless there is no other logical explanation for such conduct. All means which are capable of establishing and clarifying the facts of the case and which are compatible with the law may be used as evidence. The public authority shall evaluate the evidence according to its discretion, each piece of evidence individually and all the evidence in its context.'

The SC confirmed that it is possible to consider indirect evidence as proof of bid-rigging provided there is no other feasible explanation.[189] The undertakings can still provide their explanation for the similarities of bids[190] which does not, however, mean that the burden of proof has shifted. The court did not accept any shift in the burden of proof regarding the infringement itself but merely regarding the claims by undertakings that the collusive outcome, which had been precisely established by the PMÚ, was not a result of an agreement restricting competition.

In the context of the standard of proof, the SC also provided the test of admissibility of evidence in competition matters[191] providing guidance for retrieving evidence acquired by authorities other than the PMÚ, such as the prosecutor's office or police force.

6 CONCLUDING REMARKS

The starting point of the timeframe for this study coincides with the accession of Slovakia to the EU. Slovak competition law had already been approximated to EU law and the prohibitions under national law corresponded to the prohibitions under Articles 101 and 102 long before the accession of Slovakia to the EU. The beginning of the timeframe of the study also coincides with increasing enforcement activity by the PMÚ that later decreased, in particular after 2011. During the study period, only a few decisions of the PMÚ, which were potentially reviewable by the court, were not in fact scrutinised by the court.

It appears that the more intense activity of the PMÚ caught the Slovak judiciary unprepared and only a few competent judges were able to adapt to the more complex

---

189. SC: 2Sžhk/2/2018 *MAHRLO, s.r.o.* (8 December 2020), para. 36 'The analysis unveiled that the competitive bids of the individual bidders showed similarities which could not have arisen by chance but only on the basis of a coordinated process. There is no objective explanation for this coincidence other than that the undertakings had already exchanged information on the content of the individual bids in the process of preparing the bids, with the aim of enabling the pre-determined bidder to win. 37 (...) independent price fixing cannot lead to a matching of bid prices such as that which occurred in the tendering procedure in question.'
190. SC: 2Sžhk/2/2018 *MAHRLO, s.r.o.* (8 December 2020), para. 43: 'As to the proof of the existence of an agreement restricting competition, the Supreme Court states that it may also be inferred from the entirety of a number of circumstances and indicia which, taken together and considered in conjunction with each other, in the absence of plausible explanations, constitute evidence of an infringement. The parties to the proceedings had the burden of proving that they had a plausible explanation for the extraordinary coincidence in the price quotations within the framework of their procedural rights of defence.'
191. SC: 8Sžhk/1/2017 *Chemkostav, a.s. et al.* (20 February 2020), para. 66: 'that test, it should answer certain fundamental questions:

    (1) whether the evidence was already lawfully secured in the original proceedings,
    (2) whether the administrative authority has the evidence in such a form that enables its verification,
    (3) whether the administrative authority has legal possibility for verification of the legality and authenticity thereof,
    (4) whether the evidence can be lawfully used in administrative proceeding in issue, considering the subject-matter of the rule, which was allegedly infringed by the administrative offence.'

agenda involving review of competition law decisions. A key role was conferred on the RCB as the first-instance court and at the same time, the judges of the SC were under personal pressure by the Court's president.

Nevertheless, in the first part of the period under research, the number of appeal cases started to rise and there was substantial appeal success by appellant undertakings. After the peak of successful appeals in 2013, the NCA started to be more successful in its own submissions or in responding to actions filed by undertakings. At the same time, however, the number of cases started to drop due to the decreasing enforcement activity of the PMÚ.

The empirical data shows that the probability of success is almost precisely 50:50 at every instance of the appeal process and decisions by the PMÚ are constantly reviewed across almost all parameters: substance, procedure and fine. It has been noted, that by 2013, the review of substantive issues was quite formal and the court was willing to annul decisions by the PMÚ by relying on a formal assessment of the evidence and by establishing strict conditions for the standard of proof and a formal requirement for facts to be established precisely. By 2013, the courts adopted several controversial judgments that were contrary to standard European understandings of how to interpret and apply the competition rules.

After 2014, the SC established a series of rulings related to the standard of proof, fining policy and judicial deference that were followed in later judgments. However, in 2021, just after the end of the timeframe for this study, the competence of the second-instance judicial review was transferred to the SAC, and in June 2023 new administrative (regional) courts were created for first-instance judicial reviews (the Administrative Court in Bratislava is replacing the RCB as the competent for review of competition cases). Given the fact that the judges were not simply transferred to the SAC, it is hard to predict the future course of judicial review by the SAC. However, it is highly probable that the SAC will fully align with the accepted EU approaches to competition law since at least two judges were professionally involved in the application of competition law and all the judges are well-trained lawyers (e.g., currently two of them are university professors in law).

CHAPTER 27

Slovenia Report

Ana Vlahek

1 INTRODUCTION TO THE COMPETITION LAW ENFORCEMENT CONTEXT IN SLOVENIA

Today, competition Law in Slovenia is regulated by the Prevention of Restriction of Competition Act (hereinafter: 'PRCA-2' or 'PRCA-2 of 2022'),[1] which was adopted by the National Assembly of the Republic of Slovenia on 29 September 2022. The PRCA-2 entered into force on 26 October 2022 but only started to apply three months after its entry into force, i.e., on 26 January 2023. This is already the fourth competition law act enacted in the independent Republic of Slovenia since 1991 to further reform Slovenian competition law. In January 2024, the PRCA-2 was already amended for the first time.[2]

The prohibition of practices restricting competition in a manner contrary to the law is laid down in Article 74/3 of the Constitution of the Republic of Slovenia of 23 December 1991.[3] At that time, the drafting activities for the new competition act of the independent Republic of Slovenia were already underway, but the final text of the Protection of Competition Act was enacted only in 1993 (hereinafter: 'PCA' or 'PCA of 1993').[4] In the meantime, the relevant provisions of the Federal Yugoslav Commercial Act[5] still applied.[6]

---

1. Sl. *Zakon o preprečevanju omejevanja konkurence (ZPOmK-2)*, Official Journal of the RS, No. 130/22 of 11 October 2022.
2. PRCA-2A (Sl. *ZPOmK-2A*), Official Journal of the RS, No. 12/24.
3. Official Journal of the RS, Nos 33/91-I et seq. For further details on the relevant provisions of the Slovenian Constitution, *see* Zabel et al., Zakon o konkurenci s komentarjem, Zakon o trgovini s komentarjem, Gospodarski vestnik, Ljubljana 1993, pp. 12-15.
4. Sl. *Zakon o varstvu konkurence (ZVK)*, Official Journal of the RS, No. 18/93, entered into force on 24 April 1993. *See* Zabel et al., *supra*, pp. 12-15.
5. Official Journal of the SFRJ, No. 40/90.
6. *See* Zabel et al., *supra*, p. 139.

The PCA of 1993 laid down the rules on restrictive business practices (Articles 3-9 regulating separately cartels and other restrictive agreements, and Articles 10-11 regulating abuses of a dominant position),[7] concentrations, unfair competition, speculative practices, dumping and subsidisation, as well as regulatory restrictions of competition. On the one hand, the act was based on German competition law and thereby EU competition law, and thus set out modern rules on restrictive practices and concentrations, while on the other hand, it followed the provisions of the old Yugoslav Law of 1974 on Suppression of Unlawful Competition and Monopoly Agreements[8] and thus set out also the rules, e.g., on illegal speculation, dumping, and unfair competition.[9] In 1994, the Office of RS for the Protection of Competition (Sl. *Urad za varstvo konkurence*, hereinafter: 'UVK') was established under the PCA as a public body organised within the Ministry for Economic Relations and Development.[10] UVK's administrative proceedings were initiated *ex officio* by the UVK or at the request of an interested undertaking.[11] The PCA provided for a peculiar judicial review of the UVK's administrative decisions, i.e., by filing an action in civil proceedings, while lodging an appeal within administrative proceedings, or starting an administrative dispute was explicitly excluded.[12] Opting for judicial review in civil proceedings guaranteed three-stage judicial proceedings while in the case of administrative dispute proceedings, the review would have been more limited.[13] The PCA also set out sanctions for competition law-related commercial offences of undertakings, as well as sanctions for minor offences of natural persons, but the offences were determined and fines for them were set outside the UVK's proceedings.

During Slovenia's EU accession process, a new, modern Prevention of Restriction of Competition Act was adopted in 1999 (hereinafter: 'PRCA of 1999' or 'PRCA')[14] that was in force until 2008. It was amended twice – in 2004[15] and in 2007.[16] As opposed to

7. For further details, *see* Zabel et al., *supra*, pp. 24-64.
8. Sl. *Zakon o zatiranju nelojalne konkurence in monopolnih sporazumov*, Official Journal of the SFRJ, Nos 24/74 and 72/86.
9. For further details on the history of competition law on the Slovenian territory before its independence, *see* Zabel, Tržno pravo, Gospodarski vestnik, Ljubljana 1999, pp. 141-145; Fatur, Podobnik, Vlahek, Competition Law in Slovenia, Wolters Kluwer, Alphen aan den Rijn 2020, pp. 27-28.
10. Until the UVK was established (Article 35 of the PCA stated that it was to be established by 30 September 1993), its tasks were performed by the ministry itself. For further details on the functioning of the UVK and the critique of its status, *see* Fatur, Podobnik, Vlahek, *supra*, pp. 77-81; Zabel et al., *supra*, pp. 121-127.
11. If the UVK found that the undertaking infringed competition law, it issued a decision annulling the agreement or the decision in question (with either *ex tunc* or *ex nunc* effects), or prohibited the undertaking to further restrict competition. Zabel et al., *supra*, p. 126.
12. Articles 24-25 of the PCA of 1993. *See* Zabel et al., *supra*, pp. 123-129.
13. Zabel et al., *supra*, p. 128.
14. Sl. *Zakon o preprečevanju omejevanja konkurence (ZPOmK)*, Official Journal of the RS, Nos 56/99 et seq., entered into force on 14 July 1999.
15. PRCA-A (Sl. *ZPOmK-A*), Official Journal of the RS, No. 37/04. The changes were both substantive (such as the changes in the *de minimis* agreements definition and in the regulation of commitments and fines) and procedural (such as the abolishment of individual exemptions and notification of agreements to the UVK).
16. PRCA-B (Sl. *ZPOmK-B*), Official Journal of the RS, No. 40/07. Protection of the source and the right to access to documents were regulated and the rules on the fines were amended.

the PCA of 1993 that set out only some of the basic competition law concepts, the PRCA of 1999 regulated extensively both substantive and procedural issues relating to restrictive practices (both those of undertakings and those of the state) as well as concentrations of undertakings. The regulation of competition law was divided into two legal frameworks, where the new PRCA regulated restrictive practices (restrictive agreements were defined in Article 5 and abuses in Article 10 of PRCA), while the PCA of 1993 still regulated unfair competition.[17] According to the PRCA of 1999, the UVK determined infringements in administrative proceedings. Judicial review of its declaratory administrative decisions was performed by the Administrative Court of the Republic of Slovenia (hereinafter: 'Administrative Court') and the Supreme Court of the Republic of Slovenia (hereinafter: 'Supreme Court') in administrative dispute proceedings. Minor offences proceedings in which minor offences were determined and fines were set to undertakings and their responsible natural persons, however, took place only before the local courts on the initiative by the UVK.

On 1 May 2004, Slovenia entered the EU. On the same day, Regulation 1/2003[18] was applicable, and the UVK became the national competition authority within the meaning of the EU competition law enforcement regime. It was vested with the power to apply Articles 101 and 102 TFEU (Articles 81 and 82 TEC at the time).[19]

In 2008, a new Prevention of Restriction of Competition Act (hereinafter: 'PRCA-1' or 'PRCA-1 of 2008') was enacted.[20] It closely followed the concepts set forth in the EU competition law modernisation regulations (i.e., Regulation 1/2003 and Regulation 139/2004[21]) as well as in the Commission's soft-law, and sought to create and strengthen a new competition culture in Slovenia.[22] The PRCA-1 regulated restrictive practices, concentrations of undertakings, regulatory restrictions of competition and measures to prevent restrictive practices and concentrations, which significantly restrict effective competition, where they cause or might cause effects on the territory of the Republic of Slovenia. Provisions on restrictive agreements were set out in Article 6, and provisions on abuses in Article 9 of PRCA-1. Texts of both articles remained unchanged as already in the PRCA of 1999, they were in line with the prohibitions in Articles 81 and 82 TEC.

Although in principle, the PRCA-1 regulated only national antitrust and national law on concentrations, some of the provisions had been inserted into its text directly on the basis of the requirements set out in Regulation 1/2003 and Regulation 139/2004.

---

17. Additional parts of the PCA of 1993 had become obsolete with the enactment of modern Slovenian consumer protection legislation.
18. Council Regulation (EC) No. 1/2003 of 16 Dec. 2002 on the implementation of the rules on competition laid down in Articles 81 and 82 of the Treaty (Text with EEA relevance), OJ L 001, 4 January 2003 pp. 0001-0025.
19. For further details on this, *see* Fatur, Podobnik, Vlahek, *supra*, p. 77; Vlahek in Grilc et al., ZPOmK-1 s komentarjem, GV Založba, Ljubljana 2009, pp. 82-90.
20. Sl. *Zakon o preprečevanju omejevanja konkurence (ZPOmK-1)*, Official Journal of the RS, Nos 36/08 et seq., entered into force on 26 April 2008.
21. Council Regulation (EC) No. 139/2004 of 20 January 2004 on the control of concentrations between undertakings (the EC Merger Regulation) (Text with EEA relevance), OJ L 24, 29 January 2004, 1-22.
22. Fatur, Podobnik, Vlahek, *supra*, p. 30.

The PRCA-1 was thus to a certain extent also an implementing measure of the EU competition legislation.[23] The PRCA-1 was amended eight times, once in 2009,[24] twice in 2011,[25] once in 2012,[26] once in 2013,[27] once in 2014,[28] once in 2015,[29] and once in 2017. In 2009, provisions on the protection of confidential data and on disclosure of data, as well as provisions on leniency were amended. The 2011 and 2012 amendments established and regulated *a novo* the Public Agency of RS for the Protection of Competition (Sl. *Agencija za varstvo konkurence*, hereinafter: 'AVK') that replaced on 1 January 2013 the UVK that had been the Slovenian competition authority since 1994. In 2013, the amendments to the Courts Act restructured the system of judicial assessment of the AVK's decisions. As will be explained in more detail below, jurisdiction to review the authority's decisions was given from the Supreme Court back to the Administrative Court as was the regulation of the PRCA of 1999 prior to its revocation by the PRCA-1 in 2008. The 2014 amendments, which came into force in May 2014, followed the decision of the Constitutional Court of the Republic of Slovenia (hereinafter: 'Constitutional Court') a year earlier finding the AVK's dawn raid proceedings unconstitutional.[30] It established the requirement for a court order for an investigation to be undertaken by the AVK in the absence of the undertaking's consent. A duty of the AVK to publish on its website all national courts' decisions revisiting the AVK's decisions, save for confidential data, was also added to the PRCA-1. The 2015 amendment to the PRCA-1 transferred the remaining provisions of the PCA of 1993, i.e., those on unfair competition, into the PRCA-1 without giving the AVK any power within this field. Finally, the 2017 PRCA-1 amendments[31] took place as a consequence of transposing Directive 2014/104 on competition law damages actions.[32] Apart from implementing the directive, the law added new and amended some of the existent

23. *Ibid.*
24. PRCA-1A (Sl. *ZPOmK-1A*), Official Journal of the RS, No. 40/09, entered into force on 13 September 2009.
25. PRCA-1B (Sl. *ZPOmK-1B*), Official Journal of the RS, No. 26/11, entered into force on 23 April 2011, and PRCA-1C (Sl. *ZPOmK-1C*), Official Journal of the RS, No. 87/11, entered into force on 3 November 2011.
26. PRCA-1D (Sl. *ZPOmK-1D*), Official Journal of the RS, No. 57/12, entered into force on 28 July 2012.
27. Act amending the Courts Act (Sl. *ZS-K*), Official Journal of the RS, No. 63/13, entered into force on 10 August 2013.
28. PRCA-1E (Sl. *ZPOmK-1E*), Official Journal of the RS, No. 33/14, entered into force on 10 May 2014.
29. PRCA-1F (Sl. *ZPOmK-1F*), Official Journal of the RS, No. 76/15, entered into force on 24 October 2015.
30. Decision of the Constitutional Court No. U-I-40/12-31 of 11 April 2013.
31. PRCA-1G (Sl. *ZPOmK-1G*), Official Journal of the RS, No. 23/17, entered into force on 20 May 2017.
32. Directive 2014/104/EU of the European Parliament and of the Council of 26 November 2014 on certain rules governing actions for damages under national law for infringements of the competition law provisions of the Member States and of the European Union (Text with EEA Relevance), *OJ L 349, 5.12.2014, p. 1–19.* For further details as to the directive and its transposition in Slovenia, *see* Fatur, Podobnik, Vlahek, *supra*, pp. 107-125; Podobnik, Vlahek, Slovenia, in Piszcz (ed.), Implementation of the EU Damages Directive in Central and Eastern European Countries, University of Warsaw, Faculty of Management Press, Warsaw 2017, pp. 263-296.

definitions (e.g., the notion of the settlement application was introduced); deleted the provisions on the agency's duty to report to the Government and the National Assembly, and the Government's approval of the agency's working and financial programmes; and amended the existent rules on the cooperation between the Slovenian courts and the competition authorities.[33]

On 26 October 2022, a new competition law act – the PRCA-2 entered into force. It started to apply on 26 January 2023.[34] One of the main reasons for its adoption was the ECN+ Directive[35] whose transposition required that the act was drafted anew.

The other important set of amendments covers the way the proceedings before the AVK take place. Under the previous regime (in place from 1 January 2005 when the UVK was vested with the power to set fines for minor offences under the PRCA), two separate sets of proceedings with regard to the same restrictive practice had to take place with the UVK/AVK. In practice, they were performed successively. First, administrative proceedings for determining the infringement of competition law were performed by the UVK/AVK, and afterwards, separate minor offences proceedings for determining the minor offence and setting of fines for this offence upon undertakings and their responsible natural persons took place also before the UVK/AVK.[36] Such was the practice of the UVK/AVK although neither of the relevant acts laid down any detailed rules on the relationship between these two formally separate proceedings.[37] The rules on the administrative proceedings before the UVK/AVK were laid down in the PRCA-1 and the General Administrative Procedural Act (hereinafter: 'GAPA'),[38] while the determination of the offence and the setting of the fines by the UVK/AVK in minor offences proceedings was performed in accordance with the provisions of the PRCA-1 and the Minor Offences Act (hereinafter: 'MOA-1')[39] and was perceived as

33. Fatur, Podobnik, Vlahek, *supra*, pp. 31-32.
34. The new act applies only to proceedings initiated by the AVK after this date, while any already initiated administrative and minor offences proceedings are to be finalised under the PRCA-1 regime. Further, the new provisions on the administrative sanctioning of undertakings apply only to administrative offences taking place after 26 January 2023. Otherwise, the previously valid provisions of the PRCA-1 on the sanctioning of undertakings apply, save for those cases where the application of the novel PRCA-2 provisions on administrative sanctioning of undertakings are more lenient for the infringers than those set out in the previous act.
35. Directive 2019/1 of the European Parliament and of the Council of 11 December 2018 to empower the competition authorities of the Member States to be more effective enforcers and to ensure the proper functioning of the internal market (Text with EEA relevance), OJ L 11, 14.1.2019, 3-33. The directive should have been transposed into the Slovenian legal order already by 4 February 2021.
36. Fatur, Podobnik, Vlahek, *supra*, pp. 87-88.
37. *See also* Smiljanić, Rihtar, *supra*, pp. 73-74; Krašek, *supra*; High Court of Ljubljana in the minor offences proceedings of the *SAZAS* case (PRp 142/2016). *See also* Decision No. U-I-40/12-31 of 11 April 2013 of the Constitutional Court where the court explained that the two proceedings differ as to their legal nature, but cover the same factual questions, and that thus the data obtained on the basis of the investigation order, will thus be used in both proceedings.
38. For details on the rules on administrative decisions, *see* Krševan, Androjna, *Upravno procesno pravo*, GV Založba, Ljubljana 2017, pp. 304-342.
39. For further details, *see* Fatur, Podobnik, Vlahek, *supra*, pp. 90-99; Bratina in Grilc et al., *supra*, pp. 563-570.

being part of punitive law.[40] Different rules on who could initiate the proceedings applied. Different persons within the UVK/AVK performed the proceedings and issued the decisions. In both proceedings, the UVK/AVK had to examine the facts of the case and determine the infringement of competition law (in administrative proceedings) and the offence (in minor offences proceedings). The offence was committed if competition law was infringed. Different standards as to the contents of the operative parts of the two decisions (i.e., one administrative decision and one minor offences decision) applied, etc. As will be explained in fuller detail *infra*, as a consequence of the two-tier proceedings regime, UVK/AVK's decisions regarding the same restrictive agreement/abuse were assessed by different courts in different proceedings – administrative decisions finding competition law infringements were reviewed by the Administrative and/or Supreme Court in administrative dispute proceedings, while minor offences decisions finding the offences were reviewed by one of the local courts (as of 5 March 2008 exclusively by the Local Court of Ljubljana) in minor offences judicial proceedings.

This two-tier regime of finding and sanctioning the undertakings' infringements has been criticised both by theory and practice.[41] Under the new rules of the PRCA-2, single administrative proceedings take place within which any infringements of competition law (so-called administrative offences) are determined, and so-called administrative sanctions (in the form of payment of a one-time monetary sum or periodic monetary sums) for these administrative offences are imposed on the undertakings that infringed competition law intentionally or with gross negligence (as well as to their controlling undertaking or legal successor if that be the case).[42] Determination of the existence of any administrative offences is to be performed solely under the novel set of rules of the PRCA-2 without the application of the general rules of the MOA-1 on the minor offences proceedings.[43] The responsibility of natural persons in charge of the undertakings is, however, still being assessed in separate minor offences proceedings under the rules of the MOA-1.[44]

40. *See, e.g.*, the reasoning of the High Court of Ljubljana in the minor offences proceedings of the *SAZAS* case (PRp 142/2016).
41. *See, e.g.*, Zajc, Removing obstacles; The Competition Law Regime of Slovenia, in Gerbrandy, Berends (eds), Removing Obstacles: A Mutual Learning Experience Towards Good Practices in Competition Law Enforcement, Eleven International Publishing, The Hague 2012, pp. 186-187; Smiljanić, Rihtar, Institutional Design, Efficiency and Due Process in Competition Enforcement: Lessons from Slovenia and Serbia, YARS 2020, 13/(22), pp. 70, 72-77, 80.
42. *See* Articles 66, 69 and 70 of the PRCA-2.
43. *See* Articles 62-78 of the PRCA-2. The MOA-1 has in fact stated in its Article 2 already since 2016 that its rules do not apply to administrative sanctioning of legal persons as regulated by the rules of, *inter alia*, competition law. This rule had been, however, a dead letter until the enactment of the PRCA-2 that laid down the rules on administrative sanctioning of undertakings. At the time the MOA-1 was amended in this regard, the relevant amendments of the PRCA-1 were also already foreseen, but the legislative process was not finalised up until 2022 when the new PRCA-2 was enacted.
44. *See* Articles 136-140 of the PRCA-2.

On 30 January 2024, the new PRCA-2 was amended in order to set out the rules required by Regulation 2019/1150[45] and Regulation 2022/1925,[46] as well as to amend part of the procedural rules regarding concentrations.

2 DISCUSSION OF THE APPEAL/REVIEW PROCESS OF THE SLOVENIAN COMPETITION AUTHORITY'S DECISIONS

It should be stressed that during the relevant project period, judicial review of the competition authority's decisions in Slovenia started (and this is still so today) by filing an action (Sl. *tožba*) against the Republic of Slovenia/AVK[47] with the Administrative Court (in the case of administrative decisions) and/or the request for judicial review (Sl. *zahteva za sodno varstvo*) with the local court (in the case of minor offences decisions). Technically, these remedies are not called 'appeal' (Sl. *pritožba*) – the notion of 'appeal' is a different type of remedy under the Slovenian rules on administrative and judicial procedures. Where this report uses the term 'appeal' as the remedy of judicial review of the UVK/AVK's decisions, the action filed with the Administrative Court or the request for judicial review with the local court is being referred to (or any of the judicial proceedings before higher instances courts).

Further, administrative dispute proceedings before the Administrative Court are special judicial proceedings for the review of the administration and are not deemed first-instance judicial proceedings in the regular sense of the word.[48] It should be noted here that for the purposes of this project the term 'first-instance court' covers the Administrative Court (for cases before 2008 and after 2013) and the Supreme Court (for cases between 2008 and 2013) in administrative dispute proceedings, and the local court(s) in minor offences judicial proceedings, while the term 'second-instance court' covers the Supreme Court (for cases before 2008 and after 2013) in administrative dispute proceedings and the high court(s) in minor offences judicial proceedings. The term 'third-instance court' covers only the Supreme Court in minor offences judicial proceedings. As explained *infra*, the Constitutional Court is not deemed part of the ordinary judicial framework. Its decisions are therefore not covered in the project database and results.

45. Regulation (EU) 2019/1150 of the European Parliament and of the Council of 20 June 2019 on promoting fairness and transparency for business users of online intermediation services (Text with EEA relevance), OJ L 186, 11 July 2019, 57-79.
46. Regulation (EU) 2022/1925 of the European Parliament and of the Council of 14 September 2022 on contestable and fair markets in the digital sector and amending Directives (EU) 2019/1937 and (EU) 2020/1828 (Digital Markets Act) (Text with EEA relevance), OJ L 265, 12 October 2022, 1-66.
47. Before 1 January 2013, the action was filed against the 'Republic of Slovenia, Ministry of Economy – UVK' as the UVK was not an independent agency.
48. Kerševan in Kerševan (ed.), Zakon o upravnem sporu s komentarjem, Lexpera, GV Založba, Ljubljana 2019, p. 414. The ADA-1 itself, though, states explicitly that in the administrative dispute proceedings, the Administrative Court decides on the first instance unless stated otherwise, and uses this terminology in various parts of the act.

2.1 Judicial Review of UVK/AVK Decisions under the PRCA and PRCA-1 Regime (July 1999-January 2023)

Both under the PRCA regime in place from 14 July 1999 to 25 April 2008, and under the PRCA-1 regime in place from 26 April 2008 to 26 January 2023 (still applicable to proceedings initiated before this date), two separate proceedings before the UVK/AVK could be undertaken with regard to the same case: (i) administrative proceedings finding the infringement; and (ii) minor offences proceedings finding the minor offence and fining the undertaking and its responsible natural person(s). This resulted in two-tier judicial review proceedings: administrative decisions of the UVK/AVK would be reviewed in administrative dispute proceedings before the Administrative Court, while minor offences decisions of the UVK/AVK would be reviewed in separate judicial proceedings before a local court. These two sets of proceedings are analysed in detail in turn *infra*. All cases included in this project analysis (UVK/AVK decisions and their review decisions rendered from 1 May 2004 to 30 April 2021) are assessed under these sets of rules.

2.1.1 Judicial Review of Decisions Finding an Infringement Issued in Administrative Proceedings Before the AVK in the PRCA and PRCA-1 Regimes (July 1999-January 2023)

In proceedings initiated under the PRCA and the PRCA-1 regimes, administrative decisions of the UVK/AVK were issued in administrative proceedings as set out in the PRCA and later the PRCA-1. With regard to the questions not regulated in these competition law-specific acts, the GAPA applied.

The UVK/AVK's decisions could be challenged in judicial review proceedings before the Administrative Court at its seat in Ljubljana and thereafter the Supreme Court (also in Ljubljana) deciding on appeals (Sl. *pritožba*) and revisions (Sl. *revizija*) against the Administrative Court's judgments. No appeal against the UVK/AVK's decision was available to any administrative body (this is still so today), and any party seeking to challenge a decision by the UVK/AVK thus had to (and still has to) file a claim initiating administrative dispute proceedings directly with the Administrative Court.[49] Such a regime without any appeal available already within the administrative proceedings before a second-instance administrative body (as is typical in other administrative matters outside competition law) was not deemed unconstitutional by the Constitutional Court as long as the judicial remedy available (i.e., the administrative dispute proceedings before the courts, even if only before one court) is as efficient as would be the administrative appeal proceedings before a second-instance administrative body.[50]

During the relevant period, administrative judicial review proceedings in competition law cases were regulated under Articles 42 and 43 of the PRCA, and later in

49. Fatur, Podobnik, Vlahek, *supra*, p. 208.
50. *See, e.g.*, Decision of the Constitutional Court No. Up-2501/08 of 19 February 2009.

more detailed Articles 54-61a of the PRCA-1. These articles provided only for a couple of specific provisions as to the administrative dispute proceedings in competition law cases.

Article 42 of the PRCA stated only that judicial review of the UVK's decisions is guaranteed in administrative dispute proceedings, while Article 43 laid down rules on judicial review of the UVK's orders (review was available unless explicitly excluded; filing of the action did not suspend the order's enforcement; specific rules for order on inspections applied).

The PRCA-1 that applied as of 1 January 2008 provided for a broader set of competition law-specific rules on judicial review of the UVK/AVK's decisions (and, to some extent, orders). As a rule, the review court was to decide without a hearing in a closed session[51] (but could/had to decide to have a hearing if the circumstances of the case required so).[52] Cases subject to the judicial review procedure were to be considered urgent and were to be handled by the court with priority.[53] The plaintiff could not introduce new facts or present new evidence apart from that already presented before the UVK/AVK (the court itself could thus not take evidence).[54] The review court reviewed any decision of the UVK/AVK (in some cases also its orders)[55] only within the limits of the claim and within the limits of the grounds stated in the action and only considered *ex officio* any essential procedural infringements.[56] This meant, for example, that the correctness of the assessment of the facts gathered by the UVK/AVK could also be assessed by the court if this was claimed by the plaintiff. Although the court could not gather the evidence, it could determine the relevant facts on the basis of the given evidence differently from the UVK/AVK, and was not bound by the UVK/AVK's factual findings regarding the case – the court had to rely on the facts and the evidence put forward before the authority, but was not prevented from establishing a different factual state of the case on the basis of these facts and evidence.[57] Further, access to case file documents before the court was allowed under

51. Article 59 of the PRCA-1. This rule has been criticised. *See* Fatur, Podobnik, Vlahek, *supra*, p. 219; Kerševan in Grilc et al., *supra*, p. 480. The PRCA-2 does not contain it anymore and the general rules of the ADA-1 apply where the performance of a hearing is set as a rule in Article 51 (with exceptions laid down in Article 59 that were amended in 2023 (Sl. *Zakon o spremembah in dopolnitvah Zakona o upravnem sporu (ZUS-1C)*, Official Journal of the RS, No. 49/23)).
52. *See* the ECtHR decision in *Produkcija plus storitveno podjetje d. o. o. v. Slovenia*, No. 47072/15 of 23 October 2018 and Cases No. 32303/13 *Mirovni inštitut v. Slovenia* and No. 58512/16 *Cimperšek v. Slovenia*. *See also* Dekleva, Spor polne jurisdikcije, doktorska naloga, Univerza v Ljubljani, Pravna fakulteta, 2020, pp. 115-116. *See also* the reasoning of the Supreme Court in the *Alpetour et al. – long-distance public transport – 13* case (X Ips 15/2019) and the *Telekom – broadband access et al. SIOL – 3* case (X Ips 3/2019-6).
53. Article 55/5 of the PRCA-1.
54. Article 57 of the PRCA-1. *See* Kerševan in Grilc et al., *supra*, p. 476. *See also* the Supreme Court's critique of such rule in proceedings before the Constitutional Court, No. U-I-40/12-31 of 11 April 2013.
55. Article 55/2,3,4 of the PRCA-1.
56. Article 58 of the PRCA-1. *See* Kerševan in Grilc et al., *supra*, pp. 477-478.
57. Kerševan in Grilc et al., *supra*, pp. 476-477.

the same grounds as before the UVK/AVK.[58] As of May 2014, all review judgments must be published on the AVK's webpage.[59]

Administrative Dispute Act (hereinafter: 'ADA-1')[60] was to be applied *mutatis mutandis* with regard to all other procedural aspects of the administrative dispute (be it before the Administrative Court or the Supreme Court) that were not regulated already in the PRCA or the PRCA-1. As of 14 September 2017, the Civil Procedure Act (hereinafter: 'CPrA')[61] applies in case the ADA-1 itself does not provide for a certain procedural solution.[62]

The grounds for review, as set out in the ADA-1, consisted (and still consist) of: (i) errors in the application of substantive law; (ii) fundamental errors in procedure that resulted or could result in the illegality or the incorrectness of the decision; (iii) incorrect or incomplete determination of the factual state, or incorrect conclusions on the factual state on the basis of the established facts; and (iv) reasons for which administrative acts may be declared null.

The PRCA and the PRCA-1 did not provide for any rules on whether the administrative dispute proceedings before the Administrative Court are the so-called proceedings on the legality of the challenged act (Sl. *spor o zakonitosti*) where the court may merely set aside the challenged decision and return the case back to the UVK/AVK to decide on the merits of the case taking into account the review court's instructions (guidelines), or the so-called proceedings of full jurisdiction of the court (Sl. *spor polne jurisdikcije*) where the court changes the administrative decision of the UVK/AVK and itself decides on the merits of the case.[63] The general rules of the ADA-1 applied in that regard setting out strict prerequisites for administrative disputes to be disputes involving full jurisdiction.[64]

According to Article 65 of the ADA-1, the Administrative Court may (must if the action requires a decision on an individual's right, obligation or a legal benefit) set aside the administrative act and decide on the merits of the case itself with a judgment, if the nature of the case allows this and if the data of the procedure provide a reliable basis for this, or if the court itself established the facts of the case at the main hearing, especially (i) if the setting aside of the contested administrative act and the new procedure with the administrative authority would cause the plaintiff irreparable

58. Article 60 of the PRCA-1 referring to Article 18 of the PRCA-1 regulating the right of parties to review the authority's case file.
59. Article 61a of the PRCA-1.
60. Sl. *Zakon o upravnem sporu (ZUS-1)*, Official Journal of the RS, Nos 105/06 et seq., applicable as of 1 January 2007. Before the ADA-1, the Administrative Dispute Act (ADA, Sl. *Zakon o upravnem sporu (ZUS)*, Official Journal of the RS, Nos 50/97 et seq.) applied as of 1 January 1998. For further details, *see* Kerševan in Grilc et al., *supra*, pp. 462-475.
61. Sl. *Zakon o pravdnem postopku (ZPP)*, Official Journal of the RS, Nos 26/99 et seq.
62. Article 22 of the ADA-1. Since 2017, the rules of the CPrA no longer apply only 'as appropriate', but directly. Article 22 of the ADA-1 states which rules of the CPrA do not apply in administrative dispute proceedings. For further details, *see* Kerševan, Androjna, *supra*, p. 544.
63. Article 33 of the ADA-1. Kerševan in Grilc et al., *supra*, pp. 464-466; Dekleva, *supra*, p. vii. *See also* van den Berghe, Montesquieu and Judicial Review of Proportionality in Administrative Law: Rethinking the Separation of Powers in the Neoliberal Era, European Journal of Legal Studies, Vol. 10, No. 10, 2017.
64. Kerševan in Grilc et al., *supra*, pp. 465-466.

damage, or (ii) if after the administrative act has been set aside, the competent authority issues a new administrative act that contradicts the legal opinion of the court or its views relating to the procedure. The court may also decide on the merits of the case when the competent authority does not issue a new administrative act within thirty days after its administrative act was set aside (or within the time limit set by the court) and does not do so even at the special request of the party within another seven days, if the party requires the court to decide on a right, obligation or a legal benefit, and this is necessary due to the nature of the right or the protection of a constitutional right.

In the *Alfa et al. – driving schools – 2* case[65] where the claimant asked the Administrative Court to rule in full jurisdiction proceedings, the court explained that the prerequisites for such proceedings to be performed were not met in the case at hand. It stressed that the administrative dispute is primarily a dispute on the legality of the contested administrative act and that the constitutional principle of division of powers must be observed, according to which interference of the judicial branch into the decision-making of the executive branch must be limited. It added that judicial review of administrative decisions must not lead to an assumption of the role and function of the executive branch. It must be taken into account that competition law proceedings are primarily administrative and not judicial proceedings which is why the role of the courts is limited to *ex post* control of the legality of the agency's decisions. That is why the court must restrain itself when deciding whether to opt for full jurisdiction proceedings. Only when the court is of the opinion that such proceedings are necessary for the protection of the pursued right, it may resort to deciding in full jurisdiction proceedings. In the *Alfa et al. – driving schools – 2* case, the court deemed that was not the case and added that the claimant did not even put forward any arguments as to why this was the case. Similarly, the Administrative Court emphasised in the case *Alpetour et al. – long-distance public transport – 9*[66] that it made an assessment of the correctness and legality of the authority's decision, and that it does not have the power to overtake the role and the functions of the NCA being an independent body for the protection of competition.

Between 1999 and 2008 (i.e., as of entry into force of the PRCA of 1999 and up until the enactment of the PRCA-1 of 2008), judicial review in administrative dispute proceedings was performed by the Administrative Court,[67] while the Supreme Court reviewed the decisions of the Administrative Court. Between 2008 and 2013, however, the only available legal remedy against the decisions[68] of the UVK was the initiation of an administrative dispute directly before the Supreme Court that decided competition law cases in a panel of three judges.[69] The Supreme Court thus had sole jurisdiction to assess the UVK's decisions and orders meaning that no complaint, appeal, revision or

65. U 164/2019-10.
66. I U 930/2017-64.
67. Article 42 of the PRCA of 1999.
68. As well as against some of the orders issued by the SCPA. *See* Article 55/2,3,4 of the PRCA-1.
69. Articles 56 and 61 of the PRCA-1 that were repealed in 2013.

any other legal remedy was available against the decisions of the Supreme Court,[70] there was only one stage in these judicial review proceedings. The Administrative Court did not have any jurisdiction in these cases during that time. Perceiving such a system to be unconstitutional, the Supreme Court asked the Constitutional Court to assess whether the judicial review proceedings in force were in line with the Slovenian Constitution. It was the Supreme Court's position that the rules set out in Articles 54-61 of the PRCA-1 as valid at the time, were in breach of Article 23 of the Constitution guaranteeing the right to judicial protection.

On 25 January 2012, the Supreme Court stayed the judicial review proceedings in the *Ski tickets* cartel cases[71] (in which the UVK determined a breach of Article 6 of the PRCA-1 (Article 5 of the previous PRCA) as well as (from 2004 onwards) Article 101 TFEU (Article 81 TEC prior to 1 December 2009) in the form of (agreed or concerted) price fixing of daily skiing tickets for adults that has allegedly taken place since 2000 by the majority of Slovene skiing undertakings),[72] and asked the Constitutional Court for constitutional review of two sets of provisions of the PRCA-1[73] as in force at the time – first, the provisions enabling the UVK to perform inspections in undertakings and to examine communications without court orders,[74] and second, the provisions providing for one-stage judicial review of the UVK's decisions by the Supreme Court.[75] As the same questions had arisen also in the 'construction cartel' case pending before the Supreme Court at the initiation of major Slovene construction undertakings, taking, as substantiated by the UVK, part in the cartel (by way of sharing projects, bid rigging and exchanging information on bid prices before submission of bids),[76] the Supreme Court has stayed the proceedings in that case, too.[77] In fact, the Supreme Court decided to continue to assess those and all other competition law-related disputes only after the Constitutional Court would decide on the matter. That led to an approximately sixteen-month blockade in review of the UVK's decisions. Due to the lengthy deadlock situation that had emerged, many undertakings, their attorneys and other competition law professionals perceived such a decision of the Supreme Court (as well as the long-lasting assessment by the Constitutional Court) as having a negative and unnecessary impact on effective assessment of complex competition law related cases.[78]

The Constitutional Court issued the decision in April 2013.[79] It did not follow the reasoning of the Supreme Court and did not find the review system unconstitutional. The Slovenian legislator had nevertheless decided to amend the system so that the

70. While appeals were expressly excluded by Article 61 of the PRCA-1, the non-availability of a revision ensues from the following decisions of the Supreme Court: III Ips 111/2009, III Ips 117/2009, III Ips 118/2009, III Ips 116/2009, and III Ips 115/2009.
71. *See* Orders Nos G 23/2010 and G 18/2010, issued by the Supreme Court in the proceedings initiated by the skiing undertakings.
72. Decision No. 306-95/2009-62 of 11 May 2010, not available online.
73. It acted in accordance with Article 156 of the Constitution and Article 23/1 of the Constitutional Court Act (Sl. *Zakon o ustavnem sodišču (ZUstS)*, Official Journal of the RS, Nos 15/94 et seq.).
74. Articles 28 and 29 of the PRCA-1 as in force at the time.
75. Articles 54-61 of the PRCA-1 as in force at the time.
76. CPO's Decision No. 306-25/2010 of 23 March 2012.
77. *See* Orders Nos G 10/2011 and G 13/2011.
78. Fatur, Podobnik, Vlahek, *supra*, pp. 210-211.
79. Decision No. U-I/40-12-3 of 11 April 2013, published on 6 May 2013.

Administrative Court had regained jurisdiction in administrative judicial review proceedings, while the Supreme Court was again merely the court assessing the Administrative Court's decisions in appeal or revision proceedings (as is generally the case in other cases of judicial protection in administrative cases[80]).

Between 2008 (when the Supreme Court was vested with sole jurisdiction of judicial review of the UVK's decisions in administrative dispute proceedings) and 2012 (when the Supreme Court stayed all competition law-related cases until the decision of the Constitutional Court), the Supreme Court issued a very important substantive judgment (copy-pasted *mutatis mutandis* in other judgments dealing with the same UVK's decision) in the well-known so-called electricity cartel case where four electricity undertakings concerted their electricity prices.[81] After the Constitutional Court's decision of 11 April 2013, the Supreme Court continued assessing pending cases in which it stayed the proceedings pending the Constitutional Court's assessment of the PRCA-1 constitutionality.[82]

The legal remedies against the Administrative Court judgments were (and still are): (i) a limited appeal regulated in the ADA-1 and available only in specific circumstances of the decision-making before the Administrative Court, i.e., only if the Administrative Court itself determined the factual state differently than the administrative body, and amended the challenged administrative act; and (ii) an extraordinary remedy of revision on the ground of fundamental breaches of procedure before the Administrative Court, or on the ground of incorrect application of substantive law. Revision has been the most often used remedy before the Supreme Court in competition law cases, while the prerequisites for the appeal, as they are laid down in the ADA-1, are typically not met in competition law cases.[83] Until 2017, the remedy of revision was available under the following prerequisites set out in the ADA-1: (i) if the value of the challenged part of the final administrative act or final judgment, if the court has decided on the merits, exceeds EUR 20,000 in cases where the right or obligation of the party is expressed in monetary value; (ii) if the court is to decide on an important legal issue, or if the decision of the Administrative Court deviates from the jurisprudence of the Supreme Court regarding a legal issue that is essential for the decision, or if there is no uniformity in the jurisprudence of the Administrative Court on this legal issue, and the Supreme Court has not yet ruled on this; (iii) if the decision challenged in the administrative dispute proceedings has very serious consequences for the claimant. In 2017, however, these specific prerequisites for the filing of revision with the Supreme Court in administrative dispute proceedings were deleted from the ADA-1

80. *See* Article 12 of the ADA-1.
81. Cases Nos U 5/2008, 2/2008, U 9/2008, U 4/2008, and U 6/2008 of 30 June 2009, reviewing the CPO's Decision of 6 August 2008.
82. Fatur, Podobnik, Vlahek, *supra*, p. 212.
83. *See, e.g.*, the *LOG – funeral services – 2* case (I Up 719/2005-4) where appeal was lodged under the rules of the ADA of 1997 that listed a broader set of appeal grounds. Kerševan explains that revision against the Administrative Court's judgment is not allowed if an appeal is available the judgment (Kerševan in Kerševan (ed.), *supra*, p. 463).

and instead, the application of the general rules of the CPrA on the revision prerequisites started to apply also in administrative dispute proceedings.[84] According to Article 367 of the CPrA, a revision is allowed by the Supreme Court only if the decision of the Supreme Court can be expected to lead to a decision on a legal issue that is important for ensuring legal certainty, uniform application of the law or for the development of law through case law. The court may allow revision in particular in the following cases: (i) if it concerns a legal issue regarding which the decision of the court of previous instance departs from case law of the Supreme Court; or (ii) if it concerns a legal issue regarding which there is no case law of the Supreme Court, especially if the case law of the previous instance is not uniform; or (iii) if it concerns a legal issue regarding which case law of the Supreme Court is not uniform. The Supreme Court first decides on whether to allow the revision based on the party's proposal for revision. Only if the proposal is granted, does the Supreme Court proceed with the assessment of the case.[85]

2.1.2 Judicial Review of Decisions on Sanctions in Minor Offences Proceedings in the PRCA and PRCA-1 Regimes (July 1999-January 2023)

As has already been emphasised, under the PRCA and PRCA-1 regimes, a separate set of minor offences proceedings for imposing fines on undertakings and their responsible persons for committing the minor offences, i.e., infringements of competition law, took place with the UVK/AVK. The UVK/AVK started these proceedings either *ex officio* or on the basis of a written request by the victim of the offence, a public prosecutor, a state body or a local authority. In practice, the UVK/AVK started minor offences proceedings only after it had found in administrative proceedings that an undertaking infringed competition law. Although minor offences proceedings were separate from administrative proceedings and were organised under a different set of rules, such practice of performing the proceedings consecutively instead of simultaneously was the only reasonable way for the UVK/AVK to perform its tasks. This meant, however, that usually a lot of time had passed before the fines were set by the UVK/AVK. This posed a threat to efficient public enforcement due to the rules on limitation periods for starting and performing minor offences proceedings.[86] In practice, the UVK/AVK relied

84. For further details, *see* Krševan in Kerševan (ed.), *supra*, pp. 461-471.
85. *See, e.g.*, cases *Banks – ATMs – 6* (X Ips 114/2010) and *Telekom – Medinet ADSL – 2* (X Ips 111/2008) where the revision was not allowed. In the *Banks – ATMs – 6* case, one of the questions that was deemed as already clarified by the Supreme Court regarded the interpretation of the 'object or effect' part of Article 101 national equivalent. In the *Banks – ATMs – 7* case (X Ips 113/2010), the revision was allowed as the Supreme Court deemed that the question of economic entity was an important question not yet assessed by the Supreme Court. *See also* case *Alpetour et al. – long-distance public transport – 13* (X Ips 15/2019).
86. *See* Smiljanić, Rihtar, *supra*, pp. 73-74. According to Article 55 of the PRCA, a relative two-year and an absolute ten-year periods were set, while under Article 75 of the PRCA-1, the relative period was prolonged to five years. For further details, *see* Kerševan in Grilc et al., *supra*, pp. 578-579.

in minor offences proceedings on its evidence gathered for the purposes of administrative proceedings.[87]

The UVK/AVK's orders imposing fines were reviewed on a priority basis by local courts as the first-instance courts in minor offences judicial proceedings. Since 5 March 2008, the Local Court of Ljubljana has had exclusive jurisdiction in these cases[88] and also has to assess these cases with priority.[89] An appeal with a suspensory effect against the local court's decision was available with the High Court (as of 5 March 2008 only with the High Court of Ljubljana as the appeal court against the decisions of the Local Court of Ljubljana).[90] Extraordinary remedies, considerably limited in scope and standing, were available before the Supreme Court in minor offences judicial proceedings.[91] Neither of these courts are specialised in competition law. This is still the regime under the PRCA-2 with regard to the AVK's minor offences decisions against responsible natural persons. Both at the local court(s) and the high court(s) there has been a special minor offences department, but no special competition law department.

2.2 Judicial Review of AVK's Decisions under the New PRCA-2 Regime (since January 2023)

Under the new rules of the PRCA-2, single administrative proceedings take place with regard to a competition law infringement within which both the infringement of competition law (newly called 'administrative offence') and the fine for the undertakings (newly called 'administrative fine') are determined. The responsibility of natural persons in charge of the infringing undertakings is, however, still being assessed in minor offences proceedings.[92] The cases that have been analysed in this project fall outside the novel PRCA-2 regime that will for this reason not be analysed in any detail.

2.2.1 Judicial Review of AVK's Administrative Decisions under the New PRCA-2 Regime (since January 2023)

Review of the AVK's administrative decisions on finding an infringement (administrative offence) and setting administrative sanctions to undertakings first takes place before the Administrative Court, and before the Supreme Court upon an appeal or

87. Smiljanić, Rihtar, *supra*, p. 74.
88. Paragraph 5 was inserted anew into Article 214 of the MOA-1 by the MOA-1E (Sl. *ZP-1E*), Official Journal of the RS, No. 17/08.
89. Article 60/3 of the MOA-1.
90. For further details, *see* Bratina in Grilc et al., *supra*, pp. 565-566.
91. For further details, *see* Jenull in Čas et al., Zakon o prekrških s komentarjem, GV Založba, Ljubljana 2018, pp. 873-906. An extraordinary remedy called 'request for the protection of legality' can be filed with the Supreme Court by the State Attorney (*see* cases *SSNZ – Association of Slovenian Natural Spas – 4* (IV Ips 83/2010), *ZBS – Association of Slovenian Banks – 4* (IV Ips 129/2010), *Ski tickets – 10* (IV Ips 55/2015)).
92. *See* Articles 136-140 of the PRCA-2. The MOA-1 has in fact stated in its Article 2 already since 2016 that it does not apply to administrative sanctioning of legal persons within the field of competition law, but this has been a dead letter until the enactment of the PRCA-2 that brought about the highly anticipated change in procedure before the AVK.

revision against the Administrative Court's judgment. The rules of the ADA-1 on the administrative dispute proceedings apply *mutatis mutandis* next to the specific rules of the PRCA-2. The majority of these rules were copied from the PRCA-1 (not, however, for example, that according to which, as a rule, the review court was to decide without a hearing). There is still no specialisation in competition law cases in place at both of the courts.[93]

2.2.2 *Judicial Review of AVK's Decisions on Sanctions on Natural Persons in Minor Offences Proceedings under the PRCA-2 Regime (since January 2023)*

Review of the AVK's decisions issued to natural persons in charge of the infringing undertakings[94] in minor offences proceedings, still requires separate minor offences judicial proceedings before the Local Court of Ljubljana. The rules of the MOA-1 on minor offences proceedings, some of which are specifically tailored for proceedings in competition law cases, apply next to the specific rules of the PRCA-2.

2.3 Role of the Slovenian Constitutional Court in Judicial Review Proceedings

The Constitutional Court is not considered a part of the 'ordinary' judicial framework.[95] Its role in pending judicial proceedings before the 'ordinary' courts is twofold: first, it reviews the constitutionality of Slovenian legislation, and second, it decides on constitutional complaints in case of alleged violations of human rights and fundamental freedoms by the judgments of the 'ordinary' courts.

Slovenian 'ordinary' courts, including the Supreme Court, are not empowered to decide on the conformity of the laws with the Slovenian Constitution. This is reserved for the Constitutional Court to which the ordinary courts must refer the matter in the case they suspect that the law they are to apply is unconstitutional.[96] Some of the provisions of the PRCA-1 were under constitutional review in 2013, including the provision of 2008 that shifted the jurisdiction in competition law cases from the Administrative Court to the Supreme Court making the latter the only instance in competition law review proceedings. Although the Constitutional Court did not find such a provision unconstitutional, the legislator decided in 2013 to give jurisdiction back to the Administrative Court while the Supreme Court became again only a review court in administrative judicial proceedings. In one of the minor offences cases, the

93. For decades, there have been calls for instituting a specialised court or at least specialised departments or judges within the existent courts that would review the UVK/AVK's decisions. *See, e.g.*, Zabel et al., *supra*, p. 128; Fatur, Podobnik, Vlahek, *supra*, p. 219.
94. A novelty of the PRCA-2 as regards sanctioning of natural persons is that under certain circumstances the AVK does not impose sanctions on them if they were the responsible persons of the undertakings applying for leniency.
95. Galič, Civil Procedure in Slovenia, International Encyclopaedia of Laws, Wolters Kluwer, Alphen aan den Rijn 2014, General Introduction, § 1.
96. *Ibid.*

provisions of the MOA-1 were claimed to be unconstitutional, but the Constitutional Court did not accept this particular case as the party did not have a legal interest in pursuing the case.

In assessing violations of human rights and fundamental freedoms, too, the Constitutional Court is not deemed an appellate or any other instance within the judicial proceedings. That is why its decisions were not coded albeit they might be issued regarding competition law judicial review proceedings in which constitutional rights were (allegedly) violated. When the Constitutional Court decides on the constitutional complaint, it is not empowered to decide on the correctness of the application of the substantive or procedural law in question, or on the finding of the facts. It assesses only whether the ordinary court has interpreted the law in a way contravening a constitutional right.[97] A publicly accessible catalogue of competition law cases with filed constitutional complaints does not currently exist, but the search tool available on the website of the Constitutional Court reveals that there have been cases where this remedy has been made use of.[98] In this context, parties have claimed, *inter alia*, the violation of their right to a natural judge, the right to equal protection of rights, the right to a legal remedy, the right to a court, and the right to equality before the law. Sometimes, parties have been successful in showing violations of the Slovenian Constitution.[99]

3 PRIOR RESEARCH

No in-depth prior research on judicial review of the Slovenian competition authority's decisions has been made so far. This is thus the first full and in-depth research of Slovenian case law in judicial review proceedings.

Works on competition law in Slovenia have mostly only generally presented the legal framework for the judicial review proceedings in competition law cases (*see*, e.g., Fatur, Podobnik, Vlahek, Competition law in Slovenia, 2nd ed., Wolters Kluwer, Alphen aan den Rijn 2020; Grilc, Bratina, Galič, Kerševan, Kocmut, Podobnik, Vlahek, Zabel, Zakon o preprečevanju omejevanja konkurence s komentarjem, 1st ed., GV Založba, Ljubljana 2009). Rarely have they focused specifically on the design of judicial review of the authority's decisions and provided for a critical analysis of the rules (*see*, e.g., *Smiljanić, Rihtar, Institutional Design, Efficiency and Due Process in Competition Enforcement: Lessons from Slovenia and Serbia*, YARS 2020, 13(22), DOI: 10.7172/1689-9024.YARS.2020.13.22.3 where the authors explain the pitfalls of the two-tier administrative – minor offences proceedings before the Slovenian competition authority and the review courts, and present the ideas for a shift to a uniform administrative proceedings before the authority and the courts; *see* also the critique of

97. *Ibid. See also, e.g.*, Decisions of the Constitutional Court No. Up-81/04 of 18 October 2004 and No. Up-947/13 of 20 November 2014.
98. https://www.us-rs.si/decisions/?lang=en.
99. *See, e.g.*, Decisions of the Constitutional Court No. Up-947/13 of 20 November 2014, No. Up-2332/06 of 7 September 2006, No. Up-164/14 of 17 September 2015, Up-217/15 of 7 July 2016.

the two-tier system in *Krašek*, V varstvo konkurence prihaja enotni postopek sankcioniranja, Pravna praksa, 27(38), pp. 6-8; the Bar Association of Slovenia also discussed different aspects of judicial review regime in their comments to the proposals for the amendments to the competition law acts and other relevant procedural law acts;[100] the Administrative Court, too, submitted their comments on one of the drafts of the PRCA-1 amendments,[101] but the comments are unfortunately no longer available online; the Administrative Court unfortunately was also not available for discussions on the judicial review in competition law cases for the purposes of this project research).

4 QUANTITATIVE ANALYSIS

4.1 Source of Information

The judgments included in the database were gathered from different online sources.[102] The starting point was the webpage of the AVK (www.avk.si) where some of its decisions as well as some of the newer review decisions of the courts are published decisions issued by the courts in judicial review proceedings against the AVK decisions must be published on the agency's website, excluding confidential information, only as of 2014 onwards). As the AVK's publicly available information was not complete, the general website of the Slovenian judiciary was also searched (www.sodisce.si). There, too, not all judicial decisions are published - only some of the Supreme Court's, the higher courts' and the Administrative Court's judgments and decisions are included in the database, and it is not likely that this database is comprehensive. What is more, there is only a general search tool available on this webpage, and the cases have not been categorised *ex ante* into different categories where one could search for cases within a specific field of law. That is why it is doubtful that the search results obtained there covered all existent competition law review judicial decisions. Some older judicial decisions were obtained several years ago from the Administrative Court on the basis of the Public Information Access Act.[103]

Although Article 63 of the PRCA-1 requires the Slovenian courts to inform the UVK/AVK of each set of judicial proceedings relating to the application of national or EU competition law, no database with this information is publicly available either at the courts or the AVK. It is also possible that the European Commission have not been regularly informed of the outcomes of 101 and 102 TFEU cases as required by

100. *See* comments of 16 September 2016 to the PRCA-1G proposal, comments of 20 March 2019 to the PRCA-1H proposal, and comments of 5 March 2021 to the PRCA-2 proposal, published (in Slovenian only) on https://www.odv-zb.si/category/zakonodaja-pripombe-predlogi-ozs/.

101. *See* Krašek, *supra*.

102. I would like to thank my former students of University of Ljubljana, Faculty of Law Andrej Fatur and Žana Žabnikar for their invaluable initial search of the judgments as well as the analysis of part of the coded case law.

103. Sl. *Zakon o dostopu do informacij javnega značaja (ZDIJZ)*, Official Journal of the RS, Nos 24/03 et seq. Having regard to the requirements of Regulation 1/2003 and Article 63 of the PRCA-1, it is surprising that cases in which EU or/and national competition law is applied, have not been gathered in a specific (publicly available) database.

Regulation 1/2003 as its folder on Slovenian cases (when it was available online) was incomplete and was not being updated.

Given the above, I asked the AVK for their assistance in filling in the gaps in my project database. Their prompt and kind response by sending me their lists of the proceedings and their outcomes was of utmost importance for finalising my analysis. The latter has proven to be an extremely difficult task due to the complexity of both the proceedings before the Slovenian competition authority and the courts, as well as the lack of an all-encompassing, synchronised and easily searchable database of judicial decisions in this field. Some of the coded judicial decisions are not available, and their contents were (partially) established from other decisions. Despite best efforts to include all relevant decisions, the following caveat applies: it is possible that some relevant cases have not been coded, and it is possible that errors have been made in coding due to the complexity of the analysed proceedings. It should also be stressed that the coding results have to be read taking into account the complexity and many amendments of multiple sets of procedural rules in place during the period of time covered by the project.

In the seventeen years that are relevant as the period of assessment of the project (i.e., 1 May 2004 to 30 April 2021), a total of thirty-nine different bundles of cases were detected regarding thirty-nine different infringements in which the UVK/AVK initiated administrative and/or minor offences proceedings and issued decisions that were challenged before the courts. The database, however, contains 165 coded judgments as in some of these thirty-nine bundles of cases, multiple court judgments in relation to the same competition authority decision were issued. The reasons for that are as follows: there were multiple undertakings involved in a case, and each of them (or some of them) challenged the UVK/AVK's decision separately; several partial decisions each covering part of the alleged infringement were issued to the same undertaking(s) in the same UVK/AVK's case, and they were reviewed in separate judicial proceedings; several decisions were issued and challenged before the courts in the same case with regard to the same undertaking and the same infringement because the UVK/AVK's decision regarding that undertaking was (partially or fully) set aside by the court and returned back to it for assessment, followed by a decision issued in the new proceedings that was again challenged before the courts; in addition to administrative decisions, the UVK/AVK issued minor offences decisions in separate proceedings regarding the same case, and some of these minor offences decisions were separately challenged before local courts in minor offences proceedings (in some of these cases, the UVK/AVK's administrative decision was not challenged by the same undertaking, while in some of them, two parallel judicial proceedings (one administrative and one minor offences) with multiple stages took place with regard to the same infringement); two-stage administrative judicial proceedings and/or three-stage minor offences proceedings took place with regard to one or more undertakings with possible returning of the case for assessment back to a lower instance.

In two cases where the UVK/AVK issued a commitment decision, such decision was challenged by a competitor which later withdrew its action, and the court proceedings were stopped without any judicial assessment of the case.

In some of the cases, the database covers only the judgment reviewing the UVK/AVK's minor offences decision, in some only the judgment reviewing the UVK/AVK's administrative decision, while in others, both the administrative decision and the minor offences decision issued by the authority in the same case were reviewed.

The lack of full information also pertains to the statistics as to the number of the competition authority's decisions.[104] Not all of the cases in which the UVK/AVK initiated proceedings are included in the database as in some of them, no actions were filed with the courts either because the UVK/AVK stopped the proceedings (because it did not find the infringement or it deemed further proceedings purposeful, and the persons who had standing to attack such decisions did not do so[105]), or because the infringing undertaking did not opt for a judicial review that was available to it. I was able to detect only a small number of UVK/AVK decisions which were not challenged. This clearly shows that in the vast majority of the cases, undertakings challenge the NCA's decisions before the courts. The NCA issued commitments decisions which were not challenged in ten cases. The UVK/AVK's annual reports unfortunately do not serve as a good basis for calculating the number of all of their decisions issued in the researched timeframe, and for detecting to which cases the data covered in the reports actually refers.

It is to be noted that in some of the cases of multiple infringing undertakings, only one/some, and not all of the undertakings challenged the administrative and/or minor offences decisions. In relation to the remaining undertakings, i.e., those that had not challenged the decision, the decision became final. In some cases, this led to a different outcome for different undertakings in relation to the same decision of the UVK/AVK.[106]

4.2 Total Number of Judgments

The total number of judgments in the database is 165, of which 130 are judicial decisions in administrative dispute proceedings, and 35 are judicial decisions in minor offences proceedings. It should again be noted that these judgments relate to only 39 different bundles of cases (i.e., a series of cases dealing with the same infringement) as in many of these bundles of cases, there was either more than one undertaking that challenged the (same) UVK/AVK's decision in separate judicial proceedings (*see*, for

104. Rather good information is available in the AVK's annual reports for 2013-2021 published on http://www.varstvo-konkurence.si/aktivnosti-agencije/porocila-in-statistike/, while information for further back is scarcer and less detailed.
105. The rules on standing changed throughout time.
106. *See, e.g.*, the *SCT holding et al. – road construction and renovation* cases (G 27/2012, G 20/2012, G 13/2012, G 24/2012, G 12/2012, G 25/2012, G 14/2012, G 19/2012, G 26/2012, G 18/2012, G 17/2012, G 21/2012, G 23/2012, G 22/2012) where two of the undertakings did not attack the NCA decision, while the rest of the undertakings attacked it successfully. *See also* cases *IC Kranj – driving schools* (G 27/2011-10), *GH Holding* (I U 903/2015-17, I U 881/2015-23) and *Alfa et al. – driving schools* (I U 130/2019-11, U 164/2019-10, Sodba U 163/2019-9, X Dor 116/2020-3, X Dor 115/2020-3, X Dor 114/2020-3).

example, the *Ski tickets* cases[107] and the *Electricity undertakings* cases[108]), or there was more than one decision issued by the UVK/AVK in the course of the proceedings (when, for example, the case was returned back to the authority by the reviewing court, as, for example, in the *Banks – ATMs* cases[109]), or there were two judicial instances taking part in either administrative or minor offences judicial review proceedings, or both (*see*, for example, the *Electricity undertakings* cases and the *Banks – ATMs* cases[110]).

Only rarely have undertakings decided not to challenge the competition authority's decisions (be it the administrative decision or the minor offences decision). In the period from 1 May 2004 to 30 April 2021, only eight decisions could be detected where the UVK/AVK found an infringement in administrative proceedings, but the undertakings did not make use of the judicial remedies available to them in administrative dispute proceedings. In some of these cases, however, they did challenge the authority's decision(s) on fines issued in minor offences proceedings. In thirty-five out of the thirty-nine coded bundles of cases in which the authority determined the infringement in administrative proceedings, one or more undertakings challenged the authority's decision (in relation to twelve of these bundles of cases, the authority's decision on fines was also challenged), while in four of the coded bundles of cases, only the authority's decision on fines was challenged.

As far as the administrative decisions of the authority are concerned, in some of the cases (in the period between 2008 and 2013) the Supreme Court was the one and only instance of review, whereas in some of the cases (before 2008 and after 2013), a two-instance judicial review (first before the Administrative Court and then before the Supreme Court) was available. Where the Supreme Court was the only instance, there was no legal remedy available against its decisions.

In the case of challenged authority's minor offences decisions, the majority of the decisions were reviewed by a first-instance court or by both the court of first and the court of second instance, and only rarely by the court of third instance (as the available remedies before it are very limited).

4.3 Judgments per Year

The total number of all coded judgments in the relevant seventeen-year timeframe is 165. In 2009, 2013, 2014, 2015 and 2016, larger numbers of judgments were rendered (30, 19, 32, 14 and 11 respectively) because these judgments refer to the same decisions issued to many undertakings all or most of which challenged the UVK/AVK's decision. In other years, the number of judgments rendered varies from zero to eight. It should

107. G 19/2010, G 20/2010, G 23/2010, G 21/2010, G 22/2010, G 18/2010, G 24/2010, G 1/2015, ZSV 2991/2010-2424, PRp 410/2015, IV Ips 55/2015, ZSV 1404/2016, PRp 12/2019, ZSV 1409/2019.
108. U 5/2008-19, U 9/2008-13, U 4/2008-14, U 2/2008-35, U 6/2008-15, ZSV 4620/2008-2424, PRp 762/2011, III Ips 117/2009, III Ips 115/2009, III Ips 111/2009, III Ips 116/2009, III Ips 118/2009.
109. U 565/2007-28, U 582/2007-9, U 584/2007-21, U 581/2007-7, X Ips 70/2010, X Ips 114/2010, X Ips 113/2010, X Ips 126/2010-3, ZSV 2551/2009-2403.
110. *See supra* nn. 108 and 109.

be noted here that the second-instance judgments in a particular year do not necessarily cover the same cases as the first-instance judgments in the same year.

Figure 27.1(a) Number of Judgments According to Instances (Both Administrative and Minor Offences Judicial Proceedings)

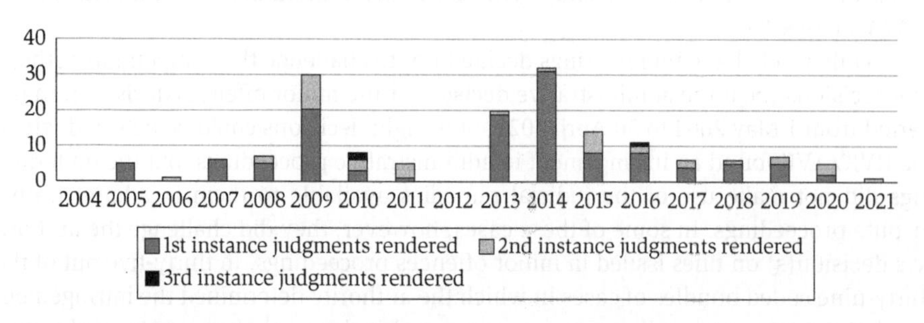

Out of 165 judgments, 102 judgments were rendered in administrative dispute proceedings by a first-instance court (be it the Administrative Court (66) or the Supreme Court (36)) and 28 by a second-instance court (i.e., the Supreme Court). From January 2012 to April 2013, the Supreme Court, being the only review court at the time, did not render any judgments as it stayed all its proceedings and waited for the Constitutional Court to decide on the (un)constitutionality of the system in place where the Supreme Court was the only review court under the PRCA-1 regime.

Figure 27.1(b) Number of Judgments According to Instances (Only Administrative Judicial Proceedings)

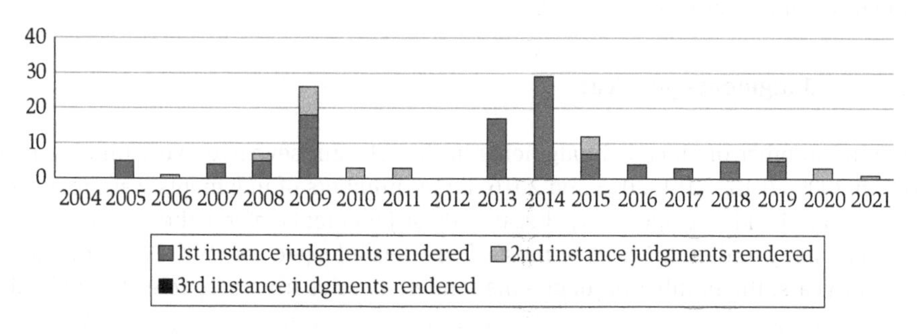

Thirty-five judgments were rendered in minor offences judicial proceedings (twenty by a first-instance local court, twelve by a second-instance (high) court, and three by the Supreme Court as the third instance).

Figure 27.1(c) Number of Judgments According to Instances (Only Minor Offences Judicial Proceedings)

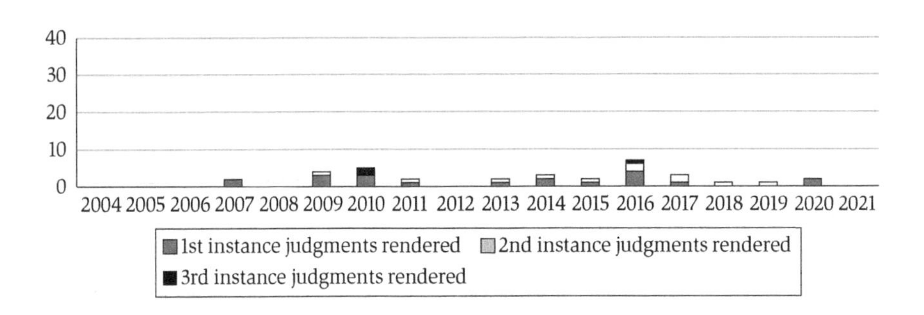

Figure 27.2(a) First-Instance Judgments (Both Administrative and Minor Offences Judicial Proceedings)

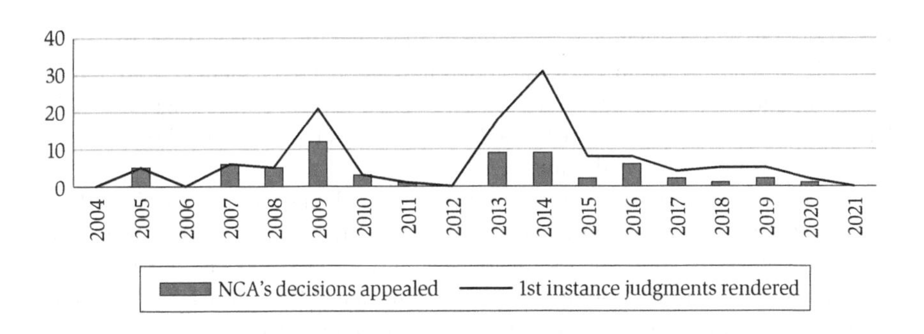

Figure 27.2(b) Second-Instance Judgments (Both Administrative and Minor Offences Judicial Proceedings)

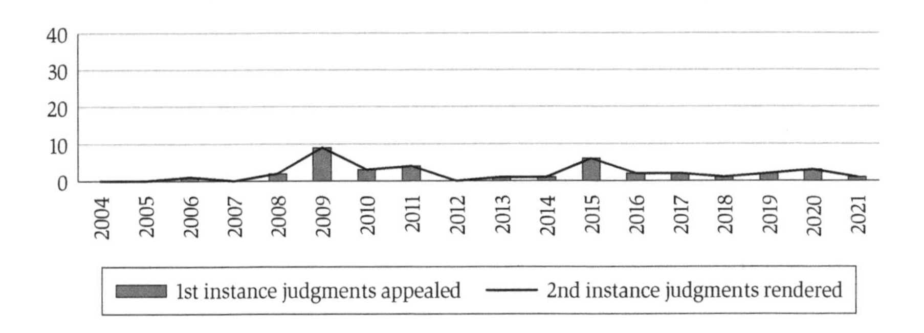

Figure 27.2(c) Third-Instance Judgments (Both Administrative and Minor Offences Judicial Proceedings)

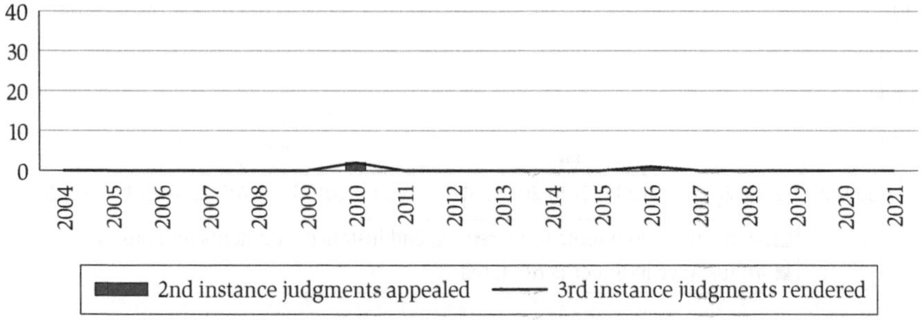

4.4 Success Rates and Outcomes

4.4.1 Success Rates

In 56 of the 130 coded judgments rendered in administrative proceedings, the appeals were fully rejected, while in 29 of the coded judgments the challenges were partially successful, and in 43 fully successful. In two coded review proceedings, the actions filed by competitors dissatisfied with the NCA's decision not to pursue the case against the alleged infringer were withdrawn.

Figure 27.3 summarises the success of appeals launched against either NCA's decision or a prior review court instance's judgment. It indicates the ratio of fully successful appeals, partially successful appeals, fully rejected appeals, and appeals that were withdrawn prior to adopting a judgment. The data in this figure is presented from the perspective of the NCA decision which has been appealed. For example, if three separate first-instance judgments were issued with respect to a single NCA decision, and the appeals were fully accepted in two court judgments, but rejected in the third, the figure will record this case as a single partially successful appeal. It demonstrates that appeals launched against 51 % of the NCA's administrative decisions were fully rejected, 24 % were partially successful, and 23 % were fully successful.

Figure 27.3(a) Success of Appeals (Each NCA's Decision or Previous Instance Judgment Counts as One)

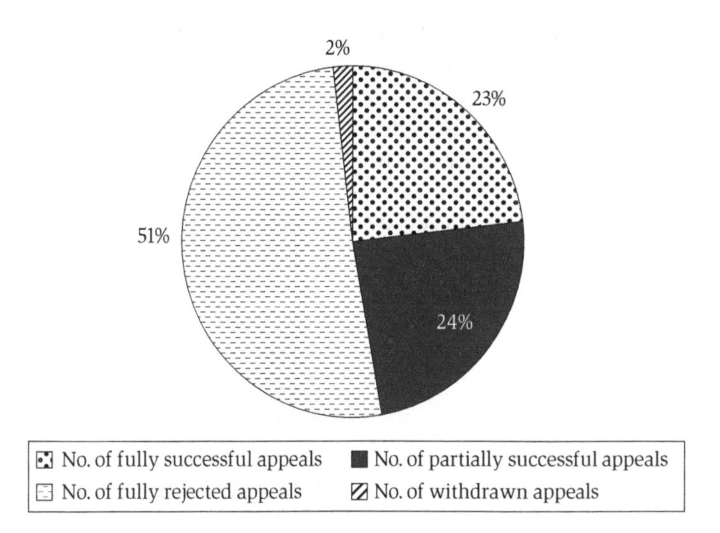

Figures 27.3(b)-(c) break down the success rates according to the type of procedure. Figure 27.3(b) presents the success of appeals on the NCA's administrative decision.

Figure 27.3(b) Success of Appeals on Administrative Decisions (Each NCA's Decision or Previous Instance Judgment Counts as One)

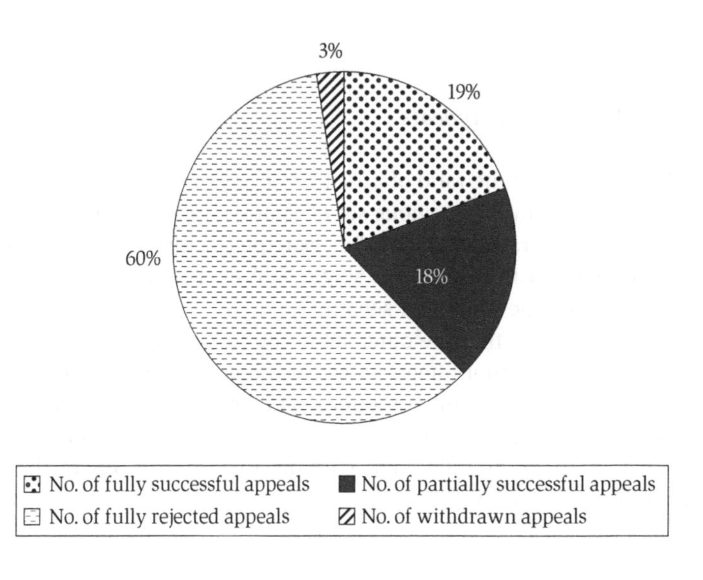

Next, Figure 27.3(c) examines the appeals launched against minor offences proceedings. It points to considerably higher success rates. From the thirty-four coded minor offences case court judgments (in one of the thirty-five coded minor offences cases, the remedy was inadmissible), twelve appeals were fully successful, nine were partially successful, and ten were fully rejected. In three judgments the outcome was coded as 'other' as it did not fit in one of the above categories. When aggregating all appeals against an NCA minor offences decision as one, this means that only 29% of the appeals launched against an NCA decision were fully unsuccessful and that 32% and 39% of the appeals were fully or partially successful, respectively.

Figure 27.3(c) Success of Appeals on Minor Offences Decisions (Each NCA's Decision or Previous Instance Judgment Counts as One)

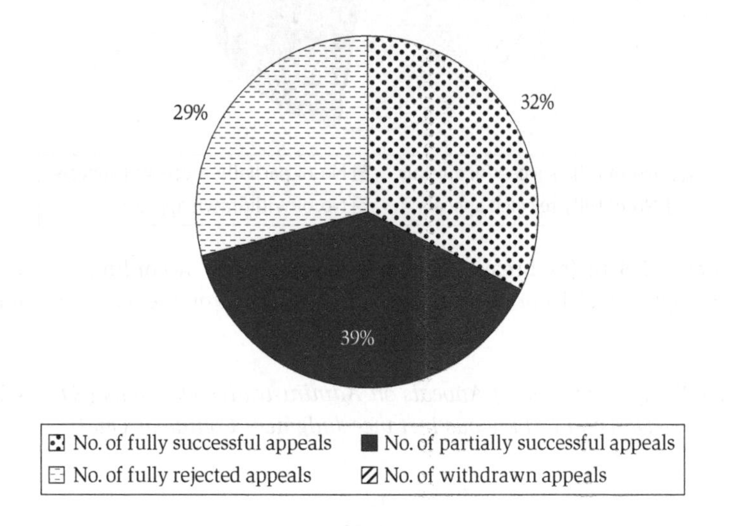

4.4.2 *The Outcomes of Appeals*

Figures 27.4(a)-(c) present the ratio of possible outcomes, according to each instance of appeal. In contrast with the previous set of figures, the data is presented from the perspective of each separate judgment. For example, if three separate first-instance judgments were issued with respect to a single NCA decision, the outcome of each of those three cases would be presented separately.

Figure 27.4(a) shows that the outcome of the first-instance review proceedings (both administrative and minor offences) was as follows: in 33% of the coded judicial proceedings, the decision was fully annulled and returned. In 13% it was partially annulled and returned. In 3% of the cases, the decision was fully annulled, and in 7% the decision was partially annulled and partially replaced. In 3% of the cases, the UVK/AVK's decision was fully replaced.

The outcome of the second-instance review proceedings (both administrative and minor offences) are summarised in Figure 27.4(b). In 15% of the cases, the judgment was fully annulled and returned, in 7% it was partially annulled and returned. In 5% of the cases, the outcome was coded as 'other'.

The outcome of the third-instance review proceedings (available only in minor offences judicial proceedings) is presented in Figure 27.4(c): one judgment partially annulled the decision, one fully replaced it, while one is coded as 'other'.

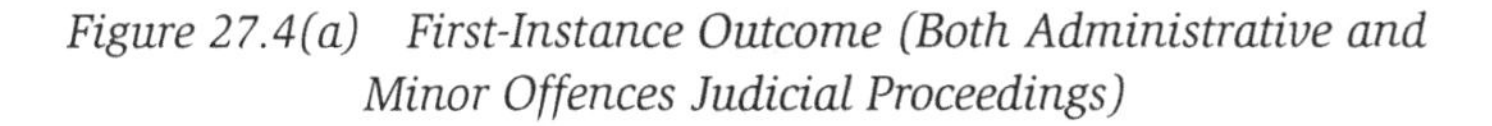

Figure 27.4(a) First-Instance Outcome (Both Administrative and Minor Offences Judicial Proceedings)

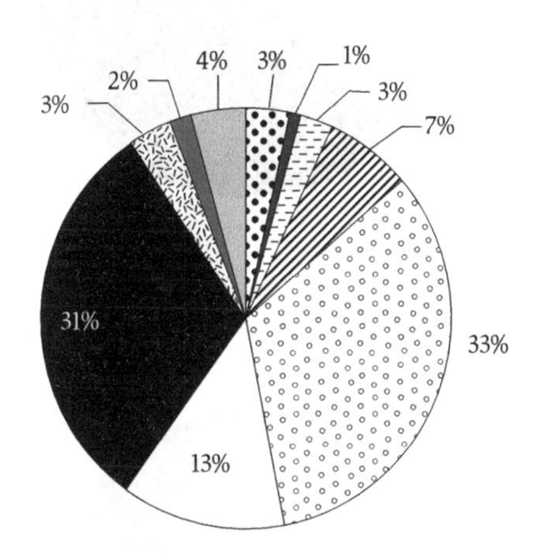

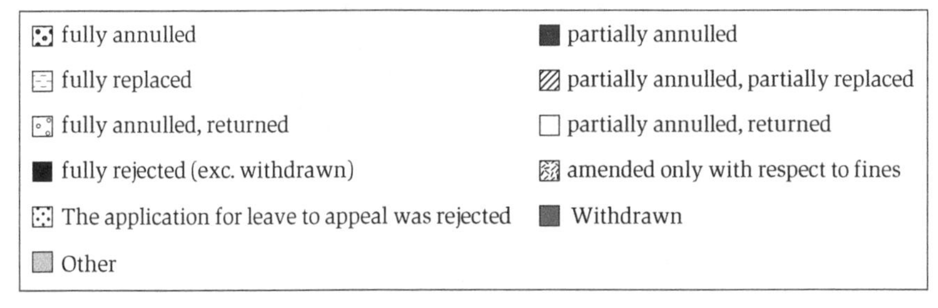

This set of figures indicates the ratio of possible outcomes, according to each instance of appeal. When an appeal was fully or partially accepted, the range of outcomes may include, for example, a full or partial annulment of the NCA's decision or previous instance judgment, replacement of the NCA's decision or previous instance judgment by that of the reviewing court, or an order returning the case to the NCA or previous instance court, or a combination of outcomes.

In contrast with the previous figure, the data is presented from the perspective of each separate judgment. For example, if three separate first-instance judgments were issued with respect to a single NCA decision, the outcome of each of those three cases would be presented separately.

Figure 27.4(b) Second-Instance Outcome (Both Administrative and Minor Offences Judicial Proceedings)

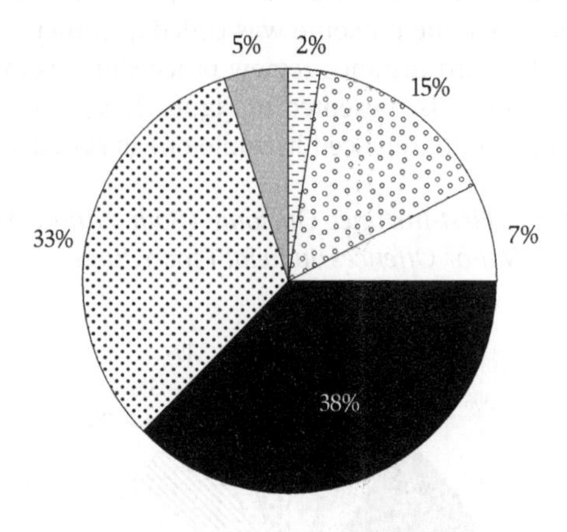

Figure 27.4(c) Third-Instance Outcome (Minor Offences Judicial Proceedings)

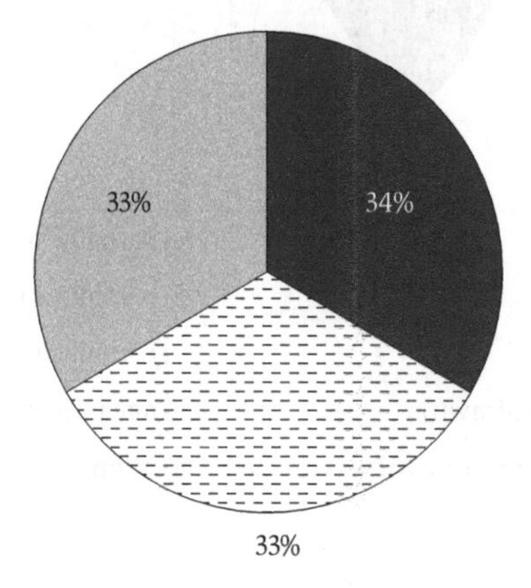

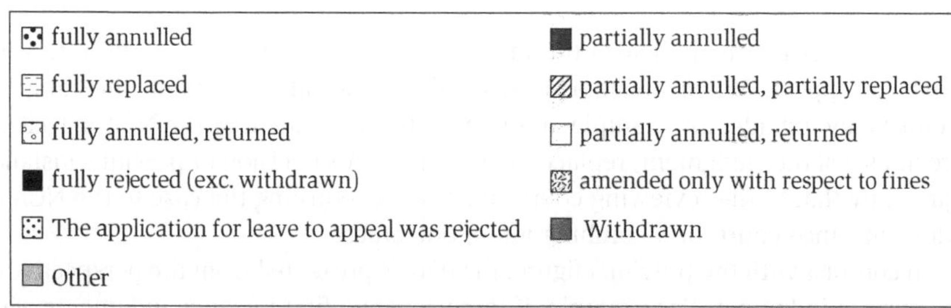

4.5 Type of NCA's Decisions Subject to Appeal

4.5.1 The Rules Being Appealed

Figure 27.5 indicates the ratio of the different competition law prohibitions subject to the courts' review, across all instances of appeal. It differentiates between the prohibition on anti-competitive agreements and abuse of dominance, and between cases in which both the EU and the national equivalent prohibitions have been applied and purely national cases in which only the national equivalent prohibitions have been applied due to the absence of an effect on trade between Member States.

Of the 165 coded judicial proceedings 121 concerned anti-competitive agreements, and 44 the abuse of dominance. It is clear that the percentage of Article 101 and national equivalent cases is higher as in these cases, there were typically multiple infringers that challenged the decisions in separately coded judicial proceedings. Looking at cases as bundled cases, the figures are as follows: twenty-one out of thirty-nine bundles of cases concerned anti-competitive agreements, concerted practices and decisions by associations of undertakings, while in only eighteen out of thirty-nine bundles of cases, abuse of a dominant position was being analysed. This means that approximately half of the bundles of cases dealt with abuses, and half with agreements.

In 76 out of the 121 coded judgments assessing anti-competitive agreements, both Article 101 TFEU and the national equivalent were applied, while in 44 of these coded judgments, only the national equivalent was applied (in one of the cases, the applicable rule was not stated). In 18 of the 44 coded judgments on abuses, both Article 102 TFEU and the national equivalent were applied, while in 26 of these 44 judgments, only the national equivalent was applied. Reflecting on the authority's decision-making work in bundled cases, the figures are as follows: in seven bundles of cases, both Article 101 TFEU and its national equivalent were applied, in 13 bundles of cases, only the national equivalent prohibiting anti-competitive agreements was applied, and in one case, the applicable rule was not stated. Further, in eight bundles of cases, Article 102 TFEU and its national equivalent were applied, while in 10 bundles of cases, only the national equivalent prohibiting abuse was applied. This means that in the authority's enforcement practice, it applied only the national equivalent in slightly more decisions than both Article 101/102 and their national equivalents.

Figure 27.5 Rule Being Appealed (Both Administrative and Minor Offences Judicial Proceedings)

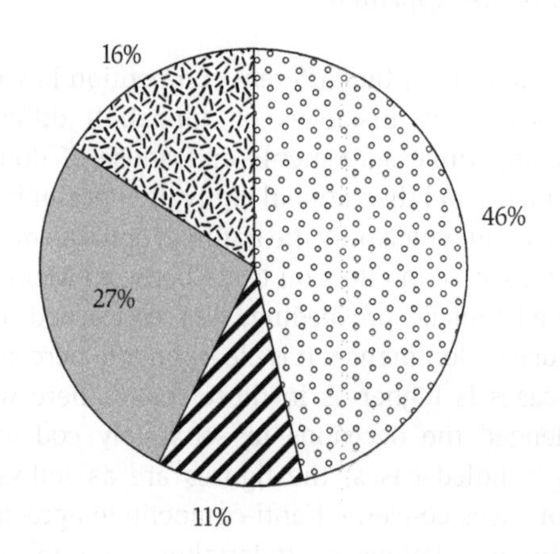

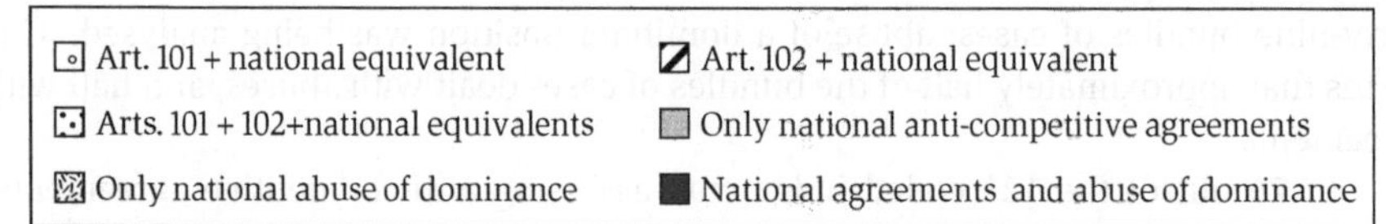

Figure 27.6 examines the rules being appealed according to years.

Figure 27.6 Rule Being Appealed According to Years (Each Judgment Counts as One) (Both Administrative and Minor Offences Judicial Proceedings)

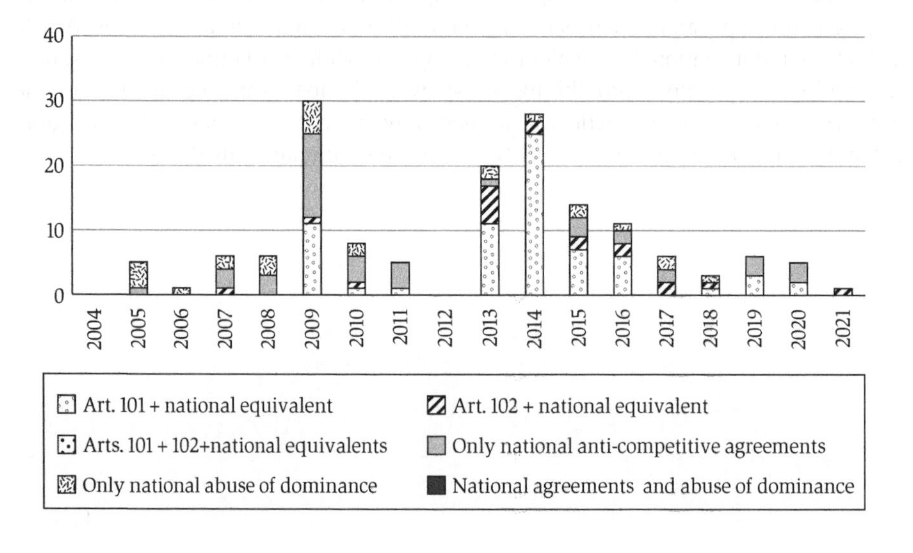

4.5.2 *The Restrictions Being Appealed*

Figure 27.7 summarises the types of restrictions of competition that were examined in the NCA's decisions subject to appeal, across all instances of appeal. It shows that the vast majority of the coded judgments dealt with horizontal restrictions (117, of these 73 were administrative dispute proceedings cases, and 34 were minor offences judicial proceedings cases) as in such cases multiple judicial proceedings usually take place because multiple undertakings challenge the decisions/judgments in separate judicial proceedings. Only four coded judgments (issued regarding the same infringement in four different administrative dispute proceedings) cover vertical restrictions.[111] The reason for a larger number of cases covering horizontal agreements both before the authority and consequently before the review courts probably lies in the fact that such agreements are more harmful, mostly relatively easy to detect, and thus also more intensively investigated. Given the structure of the market, the size of the economy, and also unfortunately the rather low-competition culture in Slovenia, horizontal agreements are probably also more frequent. Five bundles of cases dealt with an 'agreement'; four bundles of cases assessed 'agreement or concerted practice' without specifying which of the two actually took place; in three bundles of cases, a concerted practice was being analysed, while eight bundles of cases covered decisions by the association of undertakings. The cases mostly concerned price fixing and bid rigging and were scattered throughout different sectors (tourist agencies, pharmacies, health spas, printing houses, health centres, banks, electricity prices, sea traffic services, ski tickets, construction bid rigging, driving schools, stationary equipment, bus services, etc.).

The number of exclusionary abuse proceedings (eighteen; fourteen of these were administrative dispute proceedings cases, and four were minor offences judicial proceedings cases) and exploitative abuse proceedings (nineteen, thirteen of these were administrative dispute proceedings cases, and six were minor offences judicial proceedings cases) are roughly the same. In seven of the coded judgments, both exploitative and exclusionary abuses were considered (six of these were administrative dispute proceedings cases, and one was a minor offences judicial proceedings case). Here, too, the alleged infringements took place in different sectors (telecommunications, waste management, cinema screening of films, gas supply schemes, fire extinguishing equipment, access to port infrastructure, TV advertising, collective management of music IP rights, funeral services, etc.).

111. *See* the *Gen energija & GEN-I* electricity cases (G 33/2012-8, G 32/2012-11, I U 215/2015-12, I U 306/2015-10). I could find only four cases of vertical agreements assessed in the authority's decision in the period 2004-2021: one was the *Gen energija & GEN-I* case where the authority found the infringement but the proceedings were eventually terminated, one was the *GSK et al.* case (also finding the infringement but not coded as no judicial decision was rendered in the relevant period), while in two cases commitments were accepted by the AVK (cases also not coded).

Figure 27.7 Types of Restrictions

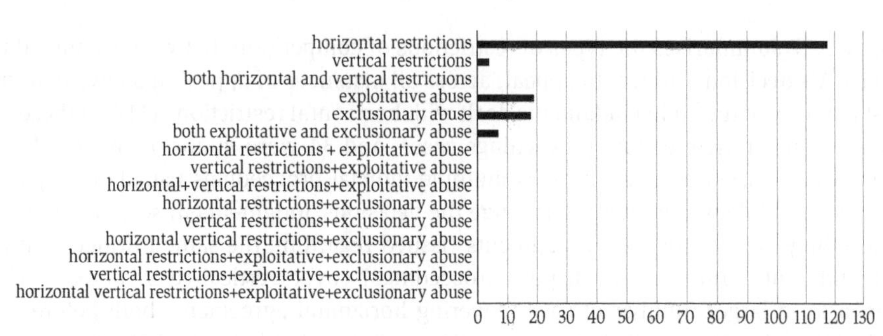

For the appeals against NCA decisions where Article 101 TFEU and/or the national equivalent prohibition have been examined, Figure 27.8 examines how the NCA classified the restriction. It demonstrates that in ninety-three (77%) of the coded judgments, the restrictions were classified as by-object, and in eleven (9%) as by-effect. In seventeen (14%) of the coded judgments, the restrictions were classified as by-object and effect.

In some judgments, the courts focused on the difference between determining restrictions by-object and restrictions by-effect. In doing that, the courts referred to the case law of the CJEU (also in cases where only national competition law was applicable) and gave the NCA guidance as to how to appropriately determine breaches by-object and breaches by-effect.[112]

Figure 27.8 Object/Effect (Only for Article 101/National Equivalent Infringements)

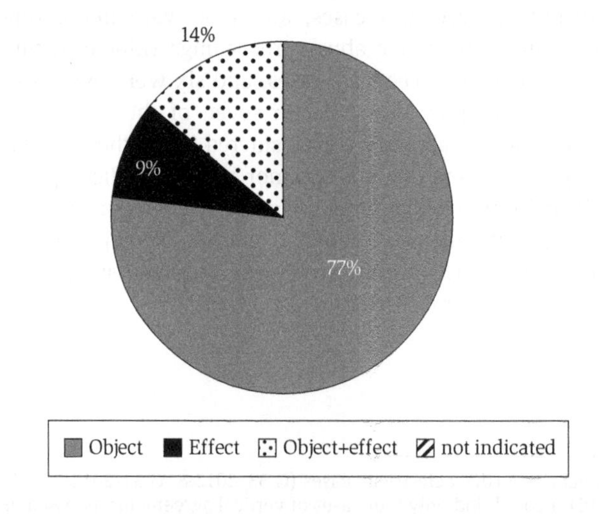

112. *See, e.g.*, cases *ZBS – Association of Slovenian Banks* (U 2780/2006-24, X Ips 45/2009), *Gen energija & GEN-I – electricity* (G 33/2012-8, G 32/2012-11, I U 215/2015-12, I U 306/2015-10), *DZS et al. – public tender for office supplies* (I U 1819/2014-16, I U 1823/2014-12, I U 1815/2014-11).

4.5.3 Type of Competition Authority's Procedure

In the analysed period there was a two-tier proceedings system in place in Slovenia according to which infringements were being determined by the competition authority in administrative proceedings, while fines were being imposed upon the infringing undertakings as well as their responsible natural persons by the competition authority in separate minor offences proceedings. The majority of the analysed judicial proceedings dealt with the authority's administrative decisions (130 out of 165, i.e., around 79%), while the minor offences decisions were assessed by the courts in 35 judgments, i.e., in around 21% of the coded judgments. In around 5% of the administrative judgments, the courts dealt with the UVK/AVK's decisions rejecting a complaint or closing the investigation.

Figure 27.9 The Competition Authority's Procedure

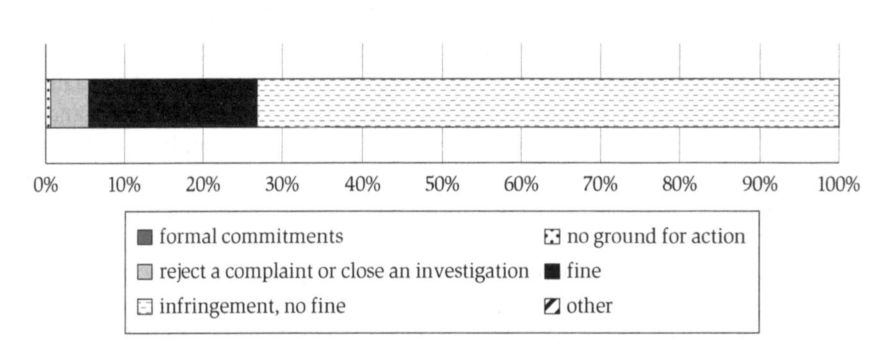

4.6 Grounds of Appeal

Figure 27.10 indicates the success of each ground of appeal launched by the parties to the procedure against an NCA's decision or on a previous instance judgment. For each type of ground - procedural, substantive, fine, or EU/national - the figure indicates whether this ground was fully accepted, partially accepted, or rejected. The data is presented from the perspective of the NCA decision which has been 'appealed'. For example, if three separate first-instance judgments have been issued with respect to a single NCA decision, and the procedural grounds were fully accepted in two court judgments but rejected in the third, the figure will record this case as a single partially successful procedural ground of appeal.

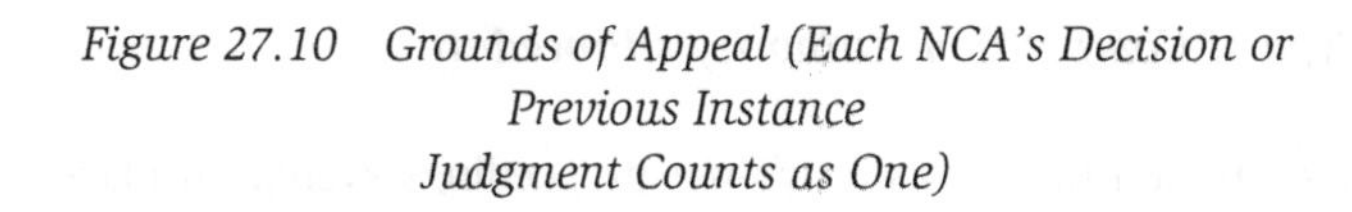

Figure 27.10 Grounds of Appeal (Each NCA's Decision or Previous Instance Judgment Counts as One)

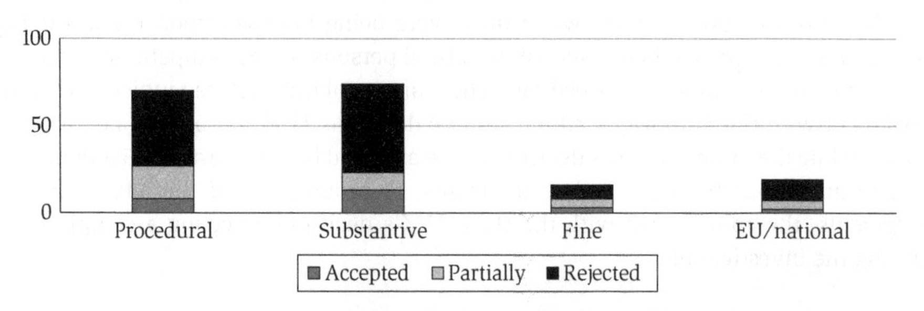

The figure demonstrates that substantive grounds were the most prominent ground of appeal. They were fully accepted in thirteen of the judgments, partially accepted in ten of the cases, and fully rejected in fifty-one cases. Procedural grounds were also often invoked. They were fully accepted in eight cases and partially in nineteen, and rejected in forty-three of the cases. Grounds related to the fines and the tension between EU and national law were considerably rarer. Grounds related to fines were accepted only in three cases fully and five partially. And grounds related to the tension between EU/national law were fully accepted in two cases, and partially in five cases.

Figures 27.11(a)-(b) indicate the type of grounds of 'appeals' raised by one or more parties against an NCA's decision or on a previous instance's judgment per year (lines). It also specifies the number of fully and partially successful appeals (bars). Unlike the previous figure, the data is presented from the perspective of each single appeal judgment (i.e., more than one judgment may be issued with respect to a single NCA decision).

The figures show that EU/national grounds were mostly argued in 2009, 2013 and 2014 in multiple judicial review proceedings regarding the same decisions involving multiple undertakings. Substantive and procedural grounds were most frequently argued in 2009, 2013, 2014 and 2015 as then, too, there were sets of judicial review proceedings involving multiple undertakings regarding the same infringement.

Figure 27.11(a) Procedural Grounds (Administrative and Minor Offences Judicial Proceedings)

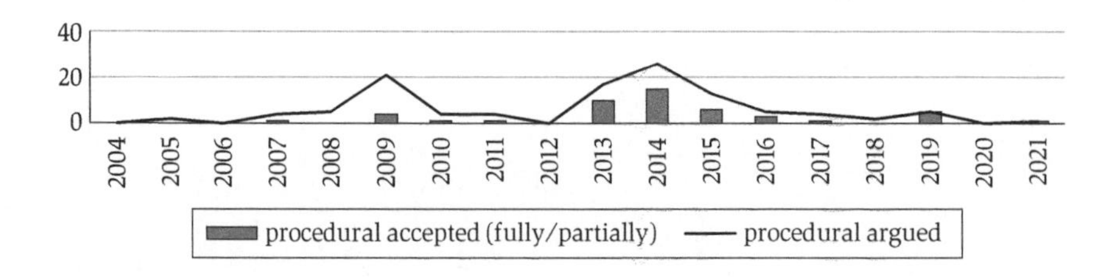

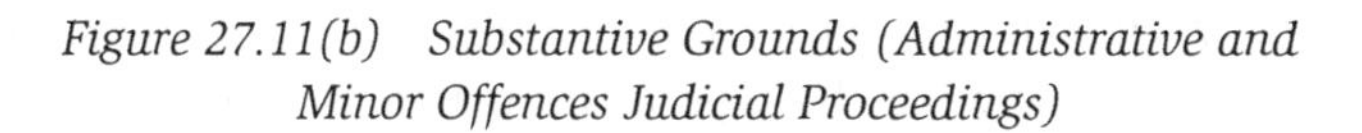

Figure 27.11(b) Substantive Grounds (Administrative and Minor Offences Judicial Proceedings)

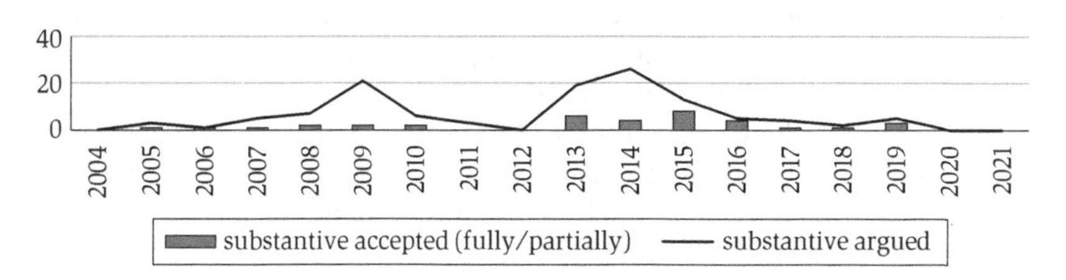

Figure 27.11(c) Fines-Related Grounds (Minor Offences Judicial Proceedings Only)

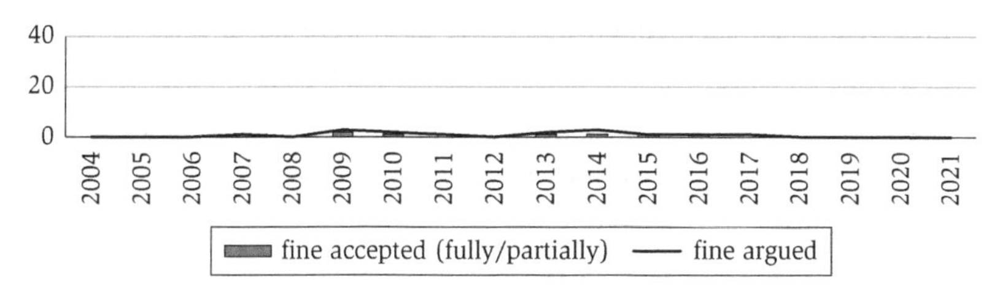

Figure 27.11(d) EU/National Grounds (Administrative and Minor Offences Judicial Proceedings)

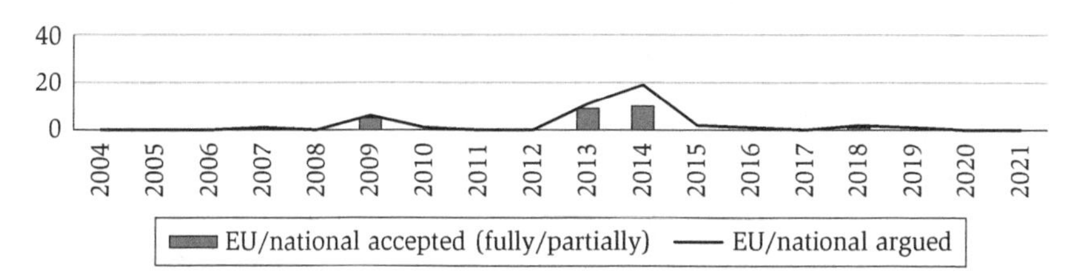

In fifteen of the thirty-five coded minor offences judgments, the fine was fully reduced by the court (the decision setting the fine was, for example, annulled or the court stopped the proceedings due to the running out of the limitation period). In eleven out of the thirty-five coded minor offences judicial proceedings, the fine was partially reduced, while in seven of the cases, it was not reduced. In two cases, recalculation was required. The average fine reduction was 85%.

In the *Electricity undertakings* case,[113] for example, the fines for the undertakings were lowered because the previous version of the act, setting lower fines than that version wrongly applied by the NCA, should have been applied. Additionally, the NCA erroneously assessed the mitigating and aggravating circumstances of the case.

113. ZSV 4620/2008-2424.

Finally, Figures 27.12(a)-(b) look closer at fully or partially successful grounds. They record the relationship between the type of restriction of competition (e.g., anti-competitive agreements/abuse of dominance and EU or national prohibitions) and the success of the procedural, substantive, fine, and EU/national grounds as defined above. To put this number in context, each figure also specifies the total number of judgments concerning each type of restriction.

Figure 27.12(a) shows that in the administrative judicial proceedings applying Article 101 TFEU and national equivalent rules, the procedural grounds were the most successful grounds of appeal followed by substantive grounds of appeal. In Article 102 TFEU and national equivalent rule proceedings, as well as in cases covering only national rules on anti-competitive agreements, the successful grounds were more dispersed. In cases covering only national rules on abuse of dominance, the successful appeal grounds were only substantive grounds. As fines were not set in administrative proceedings before the competition authority, they were not a relevant ground of appeal before the courts reviewing the authority's administrative decision.

Figure 27.12(a) Types of Restrictions Versus Successful Grounds of Appeal (Only Administrative Judicial Proceedings)

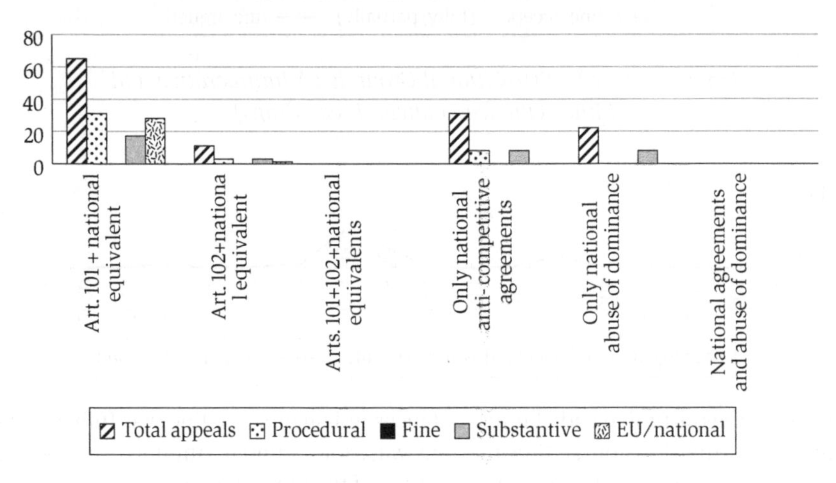

In minor offences judicial review proceedings, grounds of 'appeal' related also to fines set in the authority's minor offences decisions.

Figure 27.12(b) Types of Restrictions Versus Successful Grounds of Appeal (Only Minor Offences Judicial Proceedings)

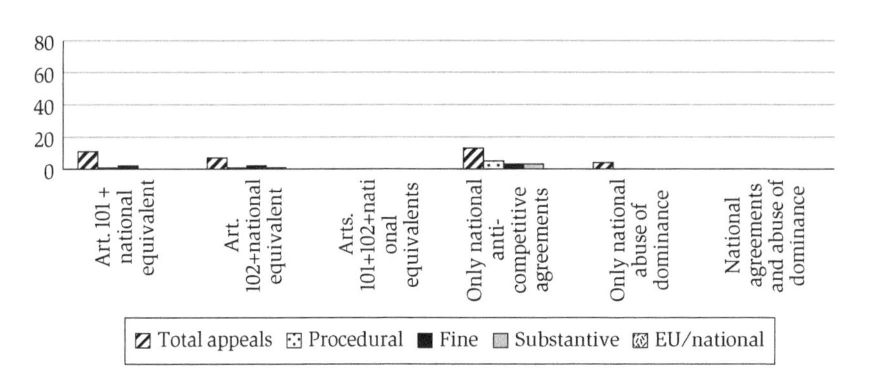

4.6.1 *Leniency and Settlements*

The settlement application mechanism was introduced in the PRCA-1 with the 2017 amendments. It is regulated in more detail by the PRCA-2 but is rarely used in practice. There were no settlement applications in the cases involved in the coded judgments.

Leniency was introduced already in 2008 with the adoption of the PRCA-1. During the relevant period, a leniency application was made in relation to fourteen judgments included in the database, all relating to the single bundle of *Alpetour et al. – long-distance public transport* case (Figure 27.13). In this case, three undertakings and their responsible natural persons successfully applied for leniency in front of the NCA and received full immunity from fines (almost EUR 1 million altogether). The remaining undertakings, which were not part of the leniency application, have challenged the NCA administrative decision. The first-instance court (i.e., the Administrative Court at the time) has accepted their challenge and returned the case back to the NCA. In the new proceedings before the NCA, the NCA stopped the proceedings against four undertakings and again found the infringement with regard to the remaining seven undertakings (three of those filed the leniency application). Four of these undertakings challenged unsuccessfully the new NCA decision before the Administrative Court, and one of them then challenged the Administrative Court's judgment before the Supreme Court. The latter returned the case back to the Administrative Court with regard to the undertaking concerned. The Administrative court rejected the claim (the latter case is not coded as it falls out of the project analysis time frame). One of the infringing undertakings challenged also the NCA's minor offences decision that set the fines. The minor offences proceedings were, however, eventually terminated by the first-instance court in minor offences judicial proceedings regarding all infringing undertakings due to the expiry of the limitation period (period for pursuing the case).[114]

114. ZSV 1380/2019.

Figure 27.13 Leniency

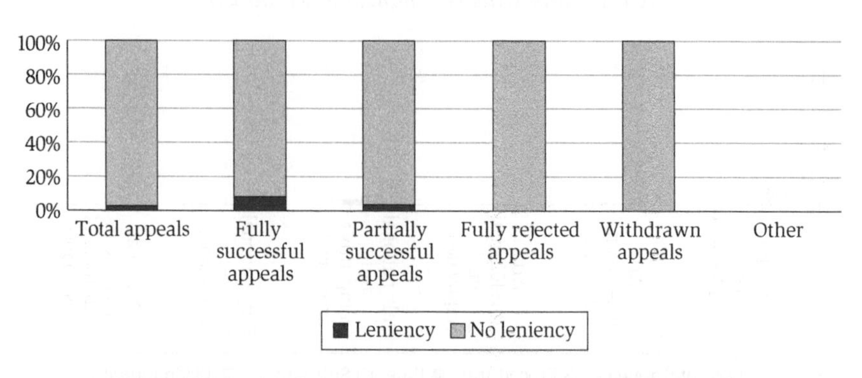

4.6.2 Admissibility

In eighteen of the coded judgments, the judicial review remedy was deemed fully inadmissible, and in one partially inadmissible. This represents a relatively small amount of all coded judgments (around 12%).

For example, in some of the *Alfa et al. – driving schools* cases,[115] the Supreme Court did not grant the authority the option to file the extraordinary remedy. The court emphasised that in the case the authority's decision was quashed and returned back to the authority that will issue a new decision that can be attacked again, it is not appropriate to allow parallel revision proceedings reviewing the Administrative Court's judgment that quashed the NCA decision that is yet to be taken anew. In the *Banks – ATMs* cases,[116] the extraordinary remedy of revision was deemed inadmissible by the Supreme Court as the questions posed were not important legal questions. The Supreme Court thus did not even assess the case and the claimant's arguments outside those relevant to its decision on whether to allow the extraordinary legal remedy or not. Further, in several *Electricity undertakings* cases,[117] the Supreme Court did not accept the extraordinary remedy of revision as it was not admissible – no remedy was available against the Supreme Court's first and final instance decision under the rules in place at the time according to which judicial review of the competition authority's decision could be undertaken only by the Supreme Court. In one of the minor offences judicial proceedings in the *Electricity undertakings* case,[118] the High Court of Ljubljana dismissed the appeal of one of the responsible natural persons of one of the undertakings: the appeal concerned the amount of the fine lowered by the first-instance local court (from EUR 21,000 EUR to 4,100) and was held inadmissible since no appeal is available in cases where the fine cannot be lower than that set by the first-instance court (i.e., the EUR 4,100).

115. X Dor 116/2020-3, X Dor 115/2020-3, X Dor 114/2020-3.
116. X Ips 114/2010, X Ips 126/2010-3.
117. III Ips 111/2009, III Ips 116/2009, III Ips 118/2009, III Ips 117/2009, III Ips 115/2009.
118. PRp 762/2011.

4.7 Preliminary References

No preliminary reference proceedings were initiated under Article 267 TFEU by the Slovenian courts in the cases analysed in the project. However, in some of the cases, the parties suggested that the court send question(s) on the interpretation of EU law to the Court of Justice, but the national courts refused to do so.

In multiple judicial proceedings regarding the case *SCT holding et al. – road construction and renovation*, the defendant asked the Supreme Court (that was the first and only instance court at the time) to send a preliminary reference to the Court of Justice regarding interpretation of the relevant market and the effect on trade, but the Supreme Court opined that at that point, the questions were not yet focal for the court to take the decision in the case at hand.[119]

In *Kemofarmacija et al. – medicine wholesalers-6*, too, the party asked the Administrative Court to send preliminary questions to the Court of Justice but the court rejected it stating that it was too soon in the proceedings to be able to do that (not even the facts were established at the time).[120] The claimant argued before the Supreme Court that the Administrative Court did not explain why it did not send preliminary questions under Article 267 TFEU to the Court of Justice. The Supreme Court answered that the Administrative Court was not even obliged to send them as it was not the last instance court, and moreover, the questions did not concern EU law, but only national law.

Similarly, in the *SODO-4* minor offences proceedings, the High Court of Ljubljana explained that Article 267 TFEU would not be utilised since the case did not require interpretation of EU law as only national antitrust was being applied.[121]

In the *SAZAS-3* case, the competition authority appealing the first-instance minor offences judgment asked the High Court of Ljubljana to send a preliminary reference to the Court of Justice. Here, too, the court rejected the proposal stating that the question involved national minor offences law, not interpretation of Article 102 TFEU and its national equivalent.[122] In the *Pro Plus* case, the High Court of Ljubljana denied the authority's request to send preliminary questions because the first-instance court whose judgment was being appealed, terminated the minor offence proceedings solely on the ground that the operative part of the NCA minor offences decision was not drafted in accordance with the minor offences rules which did not cover the application of EU law.[123]

4.8 Appellant Types

In the vast majority of the cases, undertakings challenged the authority's decision (almost 90% of the coded judgments) or the court's first-instance judgments (more

119. *See, e.g.*, G 14/2012.
120. I U 1789/2013.
121. PRp 395/2017.
122. PRp 142/2016.
123. PRp 504/2014.

than 70% of the coded judgments). Other applicants filing an action against the authority's decisions were individuals, third parties (a representative of public interest,[124] a competitor), or complainants before the authority, while other applicants challenging the lower courts' decisions were the authority, individuals and third persons. In some of the cases, information on the applicant was not available. Third-instance minor offences proceedings were initiated by a higher state attorney.

4.9 Third Parties' Participation

Third-party participation was very rare and comprised of complainants and the representatives of the public interest. Some cases also involved co-infringing undertakings in judicial proceedings initiated by one of them (*see*, e.g., the *Alpetour et al. – long-distance public transport* cases). In some of the cases, information on third-party participation was not available. European Commission and the NCAs did not make use of their *amicus curiae* or other types of participation available under Regulation 1/2003 and national law.

5 QUALITATIVE ANALYSIS

Over the seventeen-year timeframe of the research, the UVK/AVK had instituted proceedings with regard to (at least) 51 different infringements. In 39 of these 51 cases, the parties resorted to judicial review. At least 165 judicial review proceedings have taken place during this period with regard to these 39 infringements. The data shows that undertakings challenge almost every decision issued by the authority. This may tie in with the general distrust in administrative and judicial decisions, which is typical in the Slovenian legal environment, as well as with the fact that in Slovenia, parties tend to make use of all available legal remedies and refer to all possible grounds for review in pursuing their case.

In around half of the cases initiated by the competition authority in which judicial review was made use of (be it by one or more undertakings concerned), the claimants were eventually fully or partially successful, and in many cases, the renewed proceedings before the competition authority resulted in different outcomes than evidenced in their initial decisions.

As far as the quality of the application of Articles 101 and 102 TFEU and equivalent national provisions by the courts is concerned, the Slovenian review courts have shown rather good knowledge of the competition law concepts as established in EU law, including the relevant CJEU case law. At times, they referred also to (mostly Slovenian) literature on competition law. Different substantive issues have been raised in judicial review proceedings depending on the case and the parties' submissions (the court assesses only the claimant's submission as to procedural breaches, incomplete or

124. According to the ADA-1, state attorneys are representatives of public interest within the meaning of the ADA-1. At the request of the Government in an individual case, the state attorney's office must file a lawsuit for violation of the law to the detriment of the public interest.

incorrect determination of the facts or incorrect application of law whereas only material breaches of procedure are assessed *ex officio*. In relation to Article 101 TFEU and its national equivalent, notions such as 'undertaking', 'concerted practice', 'economic unit' 'restriction of competition by-object/effect', and 'appreciable effect on trade between the Member States' were most often analysed, while under Article 102 and its national equivalent, the courts most often dealt with the definition of the relevant market, determination of a dominant position, the difference between exclusionary and exploitative abuse, consumer harm,[125] and the nature of the abuse concept. The following trends in the quality of judicial review throughout the analysed years can be identified: the courts have intensified referencing to the CJEU case law, relevant EU regulations as well as the Commission soft law and practice; they have increased the references to the relevant competition law notions and their analysis, although the depth of the analysis could be intensified; and the courts are also giving more and more guidance to the competition authority on the relevant notions, when sending cases back to the authority.

The review courts regularly refer to the case law of the General Court and the Court of Justice. They do so even in cases where only national competition law is to be applied. The Administrative Court has emphasised in this regard that the CJEU case law may be used as an argument of persuasion in order to interpret the basically identical national provisions.[126] The Slovenian courts do not, however, make use of the preliminary ruling procedure under Article 267 TFEU in competition law cases. The reason behind this probably lies in the fact that in these cases they generally seldom deal with questions of the application of substantive law (including Articles 101 and 102 TFEU) in the context of which resort to the preliminary ruling procedure would be helpful/required. Instead, they are usually faced with the authority's insufficient or wrong factual determination or with procedural breaches and return the case back to the authority for another assessment.

What is clear from the project research is that the procedural rules applicable in competition law cases are complex and scattered in a set of different acts that are often being amended.

The analysis also shows that the two-tier system of administrative and minor offences proceedings in place during the research period was inefficient as it required two sets of different proceedings before the competition authority and two sets of different proceedings before the review courts to determine competition infringements

125. In the *Blitz-Kolosej-1* case (U 1853/2007-22), for example, the Administrative Court stated that consumer harm is irrelevant in the assessment of the existence of abuse as the relevant provision does not mention this notion.

126. *See* the *DZS et al. – public tender for office supplies – 3* case (I U 1815/2014-11), the *Alfa et al. – driving schools – 2* case (U 164/2019-10), and the *GH Holding – 2* case (I U 881/2015-23). An interesting question regarding the need to pay due regard to the CJEU case law arose in one of the telecommunications cases where the undertaking claimed that the review courts breached the Slovenian Constitution (its provision guaranteeing it equal protection of rights) by not explaining why they had deviated from the established case law of the CJEU. The Constitutional Court dismissed the argument as irrelevant as at the time of the facts of the case Slovenia had not yet joined the EU (Decision of the Constitutional Court, No. Up-282/09 of 24 November 2009).

and set fines for minor offences. This represented an unnecessary burden for decision-makers as well as a threat to legal certainty and prompt decision-making. As the statute of limitation for setting the fine had often already lapsed before the minor offences decision setting the fine became final, the two-tier system also minimised the deterrent effect of the public enforcement proceedings. The Bar Association of Slovenia has generally supported the introduction of the single proceedings for the administrative sanctioning of undertakings before the competition authority but has stressed that due regard must be paid to guaranteeing the parties in such proceedings proper protection of their constitutional rights. In the opinion of the Bar, the administrative sanctioning proceedings are of a criminal nature and the rules of criminal procedure should thus apply *mutatis mutandis*.[127]

It is also clear from the analysis of the case law that proceedings (both before the authority and the courts) often take considerable time before a final decision on the merits is reached. Years, sometimes even decades, pass before the case is finally resolved.[128] Although competition law cases subject to judicial review procedure are to be considered urgent and handled by the courts with priority, cases are assessed for at least a year or more, at one or two judicial instances, and then often returned back to the authority which launches another chain of administrative and possibly judicial review proceedings. A lengthy back-and-forth process from the authority to the courts is clearly inefficient and offers neither sufficient legal certainty nor deterrent effect.[129] Some proceedings even had to be terminated due to the expiry of the time period for infringements to be sanctioned by the authority, or because the infringements took place such a long time ago that the authority was not able to assess them efficiently or purposefully after the case was referred back to them by the reviewing courts.[130] The obvious solution to mitigate/prevent this is to ensure in the first place that the cases are assessed by the AVK in a timely manner and that the handling of the cases by the AVK is of the highest quality in terms of both substance and procedure. It is outrageous that after years or decades of 'pall mall' between the authority and the courts, the proceedings may be terminated because they are time barred or purposeless. In cases where there was no referral back to the NCA and the action was either dismissed by the court or the court itself amended the decision, the proceedings were much shorter but in some cases still required a couple of years.[131] A simple solution to reduce the timescale of judicial review proceedings (in addition to adherence to the existing rule that such cases are urgent and to be handled with priority – which sometimes does not seem to be followed given the lengthy proceedings before the Administrative Court)

127. Comments of 5 March 2021 to the PRCA-2 proposal, pp. 24-25.
128. *See, e.g.*, the timeframe of the *Alpetour et al. – long-distance public transport* cases.
129. *See, e.g.*, the timeframe of the *Telekom – ISDN ADSL* case.
130. *See* Article 40 of the PRCA-1 that enables the NCA to terminate the proceedings if special circumstances of the case show that advancing with it would not be purposeful. The equivalent provision of the new PRCA-2 does not require anymore that these circumstances be 'special'. *See* the following cases: *Gen energija & Gen I – electricity* cases, *Telekom – ABM* cases, *SCT holding et al. – road construction and renovation* cases, *Telekom – Itak Džabest* cases, *Kemofarmacija* cases, *Telekom – ISDN ADSL* cases and the *Telekom – Broadband access et al. SIOL* cases.
131. *See, e.g., Electricity undertakings* cases, and *GZS et al. – 1* case.

would be to abolish the two instance administrative dispute proceedings before the Administrative Court and the Supreme Court as was already the case between 2008 and 2013. Although that solution was not perceived to be unconstitutional, the two-instance review proceedings were reintroduced in 2013 as it was considered to be more appropriate. Reintroduction of one-instance judicial review proceedings is thus unlikely. In addition, there are generally more and more stringent rules on access to the Supreme Court to enable the Supreme Court to focus on important cases. Giving the Supreme Court sole jurisdiction to review the agency's decisions would not be in line with this goal of limiting access to the Supreme Court and would not address fully the challenges of the judicial review.

Another change that has been introduced by the new PRCA-2 is that there is no longer a specific PRCA-1 rule in place according to which the Administrative Court should, as a rule, decide without a hearing. Already under the PRCA-1 regime, the general rules of the ADA-1 on hearings were supposed to apply irrespective of this specific PRCA-1 rule, but in the majority of the cases, there was no hearing before the court. The general rules on the ADA-1 require the Administrative Court to perform a hearing and list the exceptions to this rule.

Analysis shows that in the vast majority of the cases, the Slovenian courts refer the case back to the competition authority either because of procedural breaches in the administrative procedure or because the facts have not been appropriately or fully established. In doing so, they tend to emphasise their constitutional role of reviewing (competition-related) administrative decisions, while providing the national competition authority with extensive guidance as to how to tackle the case in the novel proceedings. Although this is intended to protect the sovereignty of the competition authority and guarantee the division of powers in administrative matters, it seems that even the competition authority itself would prefer the courts to opt broadly for full jurisdiction proceedings and thus relieve the authority of the burden of performing novel administrative proceedings after a case is returned back to them from the reviewing court. During the process of drafting amendments to the PRCA-1, the agency expressed its angst at the practice of the courts in referring cases back to them instead of deciding on the cases on their own. They stated that where there is no settled case law, or there are deviations from the case law, the agency's right to access to court is not being guaranteed by this practice.[132] Informal discussions with competition law attorneys also reveal that they have been in favour of intensifying the full jurisdiction dispute before the review courts, and have for this reason even suggested the adoption of the Austrian system as it would require the courts to decide on the merits of the case. Resolving this Montesquivian knot[133] can probably not best be done by cutting it with a sword and implementing revolutionary solutions. Instead, it must be carefully addressed and, if deemed necessary, untied so as to strike the right (better) balance between proceedings on the legality of the administrative act and full jurisdiction proceedings. Guaranteeing the constitutional division of the administrative (executive)

---

132. *See* the comments of 20 March 2019 of the Bar Association of Slovenia to the PRCA-1H proposal, pp. 33-34, where the Bar expresses its confusion by the agency's position.
133. *See* van den Berghe, *supra*.

and judicial powers, and ensuring at the same time the most efficient protection of the individuals' rights by the courts is of great importance.

Another question to be addressed is whether the Administrative Court which has jurisdiction to assess a large variety of completely different administrative cases is well suited to perform judicial review of the competition authority's administrative decisions, or whether a specialised competition court (or at least a specialised panel or specialised judges with the Administrative Court taking into account a rather small number of antitrust cases before the authority and consequently the review courts) should instead be established. To some extent, specialisation has been attempted by giving jurisdiction in these cases only to the Administrative Court's unit in Ljubljana.[134] Additionally, the judges of this unit form three branches covering three major fields of administrative law (public finances; property relations and environment; protection of constitutional rights) meaning that possibly the judges of one of the branches (given the information on which judges involved in the coded judgments, this involved property relations and environment unit) would deal with all competition law cases.[135] Analysis of the case law actually shows that in the period from 1 May 2004 to 30 April 2021 (save from April 2008 to August 2013 when the Supreme Court had sole jurisdiction), there were around fifteen different judges of the Administrative Court in total dealing with competition law cases, but the vast majority of the cases were judged by three same judges (be it together in a panel of three judges or where two of them were in a panel with another judge).[136]

At the Supreme Court, it was either the Commercial Division or the Administrative Division that had jurisdiction in competition law matters (save the Criminal Division in the case of the minor offences proceedings). Here, too, there has been only a couple of judges determining competition law cases.[137] This means that there are in fact only a handful of judges in Slovenia who assess competition law matters. This undoubtedly fosters uniform application of competition law and enables a greater specialisation of the judges, but it must be stressed that these are still not judges specialised only in competition law assessing only competition law cases, but a wide range of administrative/commercial cases. Suggestions by competition law attorneys as to how to assure the highest quality of the judicial review in competition law cases have included, *inter alia*, the introduction of a specialised court with panels composed of one administrative, one commercial and one criminal judge. So far, no legislative proposals for a specialised competition law court (or at least a unit or a panel) dealing with only competition law cases have been drafted.

134. Article 9 of the ADA-1.

135. *See* https://www.sodisce.si/usrs/osnovne_informacije_o_sodiscu/organizacijske_enote/ (accessed on 23 May 2023). The analysed judgments refer to the 'Administrative Division' of the Administrative Court.

136. Petra Hočevar, Mira Dobravec Jalen, Miriam Temlin Krivic (*nota bene*: information on the judges are not available in all the analysed cases).

137. Dr Mile Dolenc, Dr Miodrag Đorđević, Franc Testen, Vladimir Balažic, Marko Prijatelj, Brigita Domjan Pavlin (*nota bene*: information on the judges are not available in all the analysed cases).

As from the end of June 2023, panel decision-making at the Administrative Court (and to some extent also at the Supreme Court[138]) is being replaced by sole judge decision-making.[139] As pointed out by the Bar Association of Slovenia, this could negatively affect the quality of decision-making at the Administrative Court and would limit the establishment of settled case law. In the opinion of the Bar, the abolition of panel decision-making would seriously encroach upon the right to a fair trial and other constitutional rights.[140] The new rules do, however, generally enable panel decision-making in cases where complex legal or factual questions arise or where the judicial decision is expected to resolve an important legal issue, especially if it is a legal issue regarding which there is no/no uniform case law. In such cases, the judge in a particular case would ask the court president to provide for panel decision-making.[141] It will be interesting to observe to what extent this option will be utilised in competition-law cases.

6 CONCLUDING REMARKS

The analysis clearly shows that the judicial review of the UVK/AVK's decisions has been largely made use of by the parties (mostly undertakings) and that in a rather large number of cases in which they have resorted to judicial review, the parties were fully or partially successful with their claims. Judicial review proceedings thus play a pivotal role in competition law enforcement in Slovenia. It is thus extremely important that they are efficient as well as proficient.

Analysis shows that the major problem of public enforcement of competition law in Slovenia is its inefficiency. Proceedings before the authority and the review courts have taken years, even decades before they have been finalised, they have often even been stopped solely because they would no longer be purposeful after years or decades of back-and-forth between the courts and the authority. This, coupled with low sanctions and no criminal liability cases for the infringing undertakings' responsible persons,[142] certainly does not have a deterrent effect. One step to more efficient decision-making is surely the recent abolition of the two-tier proceedings (i.e., separate administrative proceedings and minor offences proceedings) against undertakings

138. Relevant only for the remedy of appeal (that will be decided upon by a sole judge if the Administrative Court judgment will be rendered by a sole judge, and by a panel of three judges if the Administrative Court judgment will be rendered by a panel of three judges), whereas the number of Supreme Court judges in the case of revision is now the same as in cases of revision in civil judicial proceedings under the CPrA, i.e., three judges for deciding on whether to allow the revision, and five judges for deciding on the allowed revision. In the previous ADA-1 regime the Supreme Court decided on the appeals and the revisions in a panel of three judges.
139. *See* the 2023 amendments to the ADA-1 that started to apply on 29 June 2023. Before, panel decision making was set as a rule with some exceptions where the decisions were taken by individual judges.
140. Comments of the Bar Association of Slovenia of 25 March 2021 to the ADA-1 proposal, pp. 1-2.
141. Article 13 of the ADA-1.
142. The Slovenian Criminal Code (Sl. *Kazenski zakonik (KZ-1)*, Official Journal of the RS, Nos 55/08 et seq.) incriminates in Article 225 (that is rather poorly drafted) 'unlawful restriction of competition' as one of the crimes against economy. For further details, *see* Fatur, Podobnik, Vlahek, *supra*, pp. 131-139.

before the AVK and the review courts. The effects of the amended rules on hearings, the number of judges assessing cases before the Administrative Court, the limitation of the number and scope of the parties' submissions, and the grounds for the appeal and revision before the Supreme Court on the efficiency and the quality of the decision-making remain to be seen. A series of other complex issues relating to efficiency, quality and extent of the judicial review still have to be addressed and/or resolved in order to guarantee that the judicial review system enables the merits of cases to be decided upon by judges specialised in competition law in a timely, efficient manner in the most suitable type of proceedings guaranteeing the parties their constitutional rights. Given all the changes in the administrative dispute proceedings and the debates by theory and practice that have led to them or are proposing new ones, it is obvious that in Slovenia, there is an ongoing search for an optimal administrative judicial review regime, including (and particularly) the one in competition law cases.

CHAPTER 28
Spain Report

Francisco Marcos[*]

1 INTRODUCTION TO THE SPANISH COMPETITION LAW ENFORCEMENT SYSTEM

In order to properly understand the functioning of the judicial review of decisions of the Spanish competition authority, it is worth briefly explaining how the competition law enforcement system is organised, which institutions are entrusted with this task and which procedures are applied (*see infra* sections 1.1 and 1.3), pointing out the relevant changes introduced during the period of this research project. The wording of the Spanish national prohibitions of anti-competitive behaviour mirrors the wording of the prohibitions in the TFEU (*infra* section 1.2).

1.1 Institutional Framework

The first Spanish Competition Act was enacted in 1963. Following a beautifully crafted Preamble, it included the standard prohibitions of multilateral and unilateral anticompetitive behaviour and established a specialised administrative authority in charge of the enforcement of the prohibitions (*Tribunal de Defensa de la Competencia/TDC*).[1] Investigations of infringements were conducted by a unit of the Ministry of Economy (*Servicio de Defensa de la Competencia/SDC*). Fines were proposed by the *TDC* but had to be approved by the Government. While the 1963 Act was in force, enforcement was feeble. Not a single fine was imposed.

* Assistance by Ghizlane Larouej and Beyzanur Inal is gratefully acknowledged. Relevant comments and suggestions by Or Brook, Barry J. Rodger and Ainhoa Veiga have greatly improved the initial draft. No public or private support has been received for this project.

1. *See* Repression of Anticompetitive Practices Act of 110/1963 (*Ley de Represión de Prácticas Restrictivas de la Competencia*, BOE 175 of 23/7/1963).

After Spain joined the EC in 1985, new competition legislation was adopted.[2] Yet, the enforcement institutional system did not change significantly. It remained as an administrative bifurcated system, with limited independence from the government. Moreover, the TDC was empowered to impose fines and to enforce any infringements of the EC antitrust prohibitions.[3]

Thereafter, the competition legislation and the institutional enforcement settings of the Spanish System have experienced three major reforms:

(1) *Creation of regional competition authorities*. A 1999 judgment of the Constitutional Court acknowledging the region's competition law enforcement powers triggered a decentralisation of the domestic enforcement system.[4] Since then, several regional competition authorities have been created with enforcement powers in relation to the domestic competition prohibitions in their corresponding region.[5] Regional authorities do not have the power to enforce the EC competition rules.

(2) *Strengthening and modernisation of the institutional system*. The TDC and SDC were merged in 2007, creating a single independent administrative law authority in charge of the enforcement of both domestic and EU competition prohibitions: the *Comisión Nacional de la Competencia* (CNC).[6] The CNC was also empowered to enforce the prohibitions in sectors subject to sectoral regulation (energy and telecommunications), but there were some conflicts with the regulatory authorities (*Comisión Nacional de la Energía*/CNE in the electricity and hydrocarbons sectors and *Comisión del Mercado de las Telecomunicaciones*/CMT in the telecommunications sector) regarding the fulfilment of their tasks of monitoring and regulating the energy and telecommunications industries.[7]

---

2. *See* Defence Competition Act of 16/1989 (*Ley de Defensa de la Competencia*, BOE170 of 18/7/1989).
3. *See* Decree 1882/1986 of 29/8/1986 (BOE221 of 1/9/1986).
4. *See* Constitutional Court judgment 208/1999 of 11/11/1999 (Rapp. TS Vives, ES:TC:1999:208).
5. Currently there are nine Regional Competition Authorities: Autoridad Catalana de la Competencia, Comisión Gallega de la Competencia, Autoridad Vasca de la Competencia, Jurado de Defensa de la Competencia de Extremadura, Tribunal de Defensa de la Competencia de Aragón, Tribunal de Defensa de la Competencia de Castilla y León, Comisión de Defensa de la Competencia de la Comunidad Valenciana, Agencia de la Competencia y de la Regulación Económica de Andalucía and Consejo Canario de Competencia. Two Regional Competition Authorities were closed shortly after they were created (Tribunal de Defensa de la Competencia de la Comunidad de Madrid and Comisión Regional de Defensa de la Competencia de Castilla la Mancha), *see* Francisco Marcos 'Autoridades de Defensa de la Competencia en vías de extinción' *Revista de Administración Pública* 188 (2012) 337-363. Some of the Regional Competition Authorities are also empowered to enforce consumer protection law.
6. *See* Defense Competition Act of 15/2007 (*Ley de Defensa de la Competencia*, BOE 159 of 4/7/2007), translation into English available at the CNMC website.
7. The CNE and the CMT were mandated by the relevant legislation at that time to protect and promote competition in exercising their regulatory functions on the relevant industries, *see* Act 54/1997 on the Electric Sector (*Ley del Sector Eléctrico*, BOE285 of 28/11/1997), Act 34/1998 on the Hydrocarbons Sector (*Ley del Sector de Hidrocarburos*, BOE241 of 8/10/1998) and Act 12/1998 General Telecommunications (*Ley General de Telecomunicaciones*, BOE99 of 25/4/1998).

(3) *The CNC and several independent regulators were merged*: In 2013 the competition authority and five existing sectoral regulators[8] – and two that had not been created yet[9] – were consolidated in the *Comisión Nacional de los Mercados y de la Competencia* (CNMC).[10] The creation of the CNMC was justified on the basis of saving resources and preventing conflicts between the competition and regulatory authorities.[11] Given the breadth of powers of the CNMC, it operates as a multi-task authority with regulatory powers in many industries and wide enforcement powers in relation to the competition prohibitions across the economy.

Table 28.1 National Competition Laws and Authorities in Spain

Period	*Legislation*	*National Institutions*
1963-1989	Act 110/1963	Tribunal de Defensa de la Competencia Servicio de Defensa de la Competencia
1989-2007	Act 16/1989	
2007-2013	Act 15/2007	Comisión Nacional de la Competencia
2013-Current	Act 5/2013	Comisión Nacional de los Mercados y de la Competencia

1.2 Legal Framework: The Competition Prohibitions

Spanish domestic legislation prohibits anticompetitive agreements and abuses of dominance, since 1989 their phrasing has evolved to mirror the EU prohibitions.

Agreements, collective decisions, recommendations, and concerted and consciously parallel practices that have as their object, produce or may produce the effect of the prevention, restriction, or distortion of competition in all or part of the national market are prohibited.[12] They are unlawful and void unless they contribute to improving the production or commercialisation of goods and services or to promoting technical or economic progress as long as they: allow consumers a fair share of the benefits; do not impose restrictions on the undertakings concerned which are not

8. CMT, CNE, Comisión de Regulación Ferroviaria, Comisión Nacional del Sector Postal (CNSP) and Comisión Nacional del Juego.
9. Consejo Estatal de Medios Audiovisuales (CEMA) and Comisión de Regulación Económica Aeroportuaria (CREA).
10. *See* Act 3/13 creating the National Markets and Competition Commission, translation into English available at the CNMC website. *See* Francesc Trillas & Ramón Xifré 'Institutional Reforms to Integrate Regulation and International Perspectives, and the Case of the CNMC in Spain Competition Policy' *Utilities Policy* 40 (2016) 75-87.
11. *See, e.g.*, judgment of 20/6/2006 (*Telefónica v. TDC*, rapp. M Campos, ES:TS:2006:3887), annulling the EUR 8,414,200 fine imposed on Telefónica by TDC resolution of 8/3/2000 (Retevisión/Telefónica, rapp. M Comenge), regarding some promotions that had been sanctified by the CMT (resolution of 30/4/1998).
12. Article 1.1 of Act 16/1989 and Article 1.1 of Act 15/2007.

indispensable to the attainment of those objectives; and do not afford the participating undertakings the possibility of eliminating competition in respect of a substantial part of the products or services envisaged.[13]

Abuses of a dominant position by one or several undertakings are also prohibited.[14]

Spanish legislation also grants powers to the competition authority to probe violations of unfair competition laws that disrupt free competition and impact the public interest.[15] Decisions on these infringements are not covered by the project.

Aside from public enforcement of the competition prohibitions, it should be noted that private enforcement in Spain has surged in the last few years, mainly following some cartel decisions by the European Commission and the Spanish national competition authority.[16] Finally, although some of the conducts falling within the competition prohibitions could also be criminally prosecuted, there have been very few attempts to do so, and none have led to a conviction.[17]

1.3 Enforcement Framework: Institutions and Powers (Investigation/Adjudication)

Public enforcement of the competition prohibitions in Spain follows an administrative model, in which investigation and adjudication of infringements of the competition prohibitions are decided by administrative authorities. Enforcement for those infringements that solely affect the territory of regions with competition enforcement powers is conducted by Regional Competition Authorities.[18] Those decisions are not covered by the project.

---

13. Article 3.1 of Act 16/1989 and Article 1.3 of Act 15/2007. Article 3.2 of Act 16/1989 also provided an exemption to the extent justified by the general economic situation and the public interest.
14. Article 6 of Act 16/1989 and Article 2 of Act 15/2007. An amendment of Act 16/1989 in 1999 included as a competition prohibition the abuse of economic dependence (Article 6.1.b) of Act 16/1989 introduced by Article Act 52/1999, this prohibition ceased to be an antitrust violation in 2007 and is only contained in the Unfair Competition Act (article 16 of Act 2/1991 on Unfair Competition, *Ley de Competencia Desleal,* BOE 10 of 11/1/1991).
15. *See* Article 7 of Act 16/89 and Article 3 of Act 15/2007. *See OECD, Regulatory Reform in Spain. The Role of Competition Policy in Regulatory Reform,* 2001, 16.
16. *See* Francisco Marcos 'Antitrust damages' claims in Spain' in Rafael Amaro & Emmanuel Guinchard (ed.) *Private Enforcement of Competition Law in Europe. Directive 2014/104/UE and beyond,* 2021, 365-382
17. *See* Article 262 (Alteration of prices in public tenders and auctions) of the Organic Law 10/1995 Criminal Code (Código Penal, BOE 285 of 24/11/1995, an English translation available in the Ministry of Justice webpage) and María Gutiérrez & Íñigo Ortiz 'Conductas restrictivas de la competencia y derecho penal' in Antonio Robles (ed.) *La lucha contra las restricciones de la competencia: sanciones y remedios en el ordenamiento español,* 2017, 79-121.
18. *See* Coordination of Powers Act of the State and the Regions Act on antitrust matters of 2001 (*Ley de Competencias del Estado y las Comunidades Autónomas en materia de Defensa de la Competencia,* BOE 46 of 22/2/2002). Regional Competition Authorities decide 85% of the proceedings for infringements of the competition prohibitions, *see* Francisco Marcos 'Análisis sistemático de la aplicación pública del Derecho de la competencia por las autoridades nacionales en España 2003-2022' *Revista Derecho Competencia y Distribución/RDCD* 2023 §IV.1.

While the 1989 Act was in force, the investigations were carried out by the TDC, which also adopted the final administrative decisions.[19] Mirroring EC competition law enforcement prior to Regulation 1/2003, a system of individual notification and authorisation by the TDC for exemptions of anti-competitive agreements or other conduct with pro-competitive benefits was in place.

In 2007, the individual authorisation system was abrogated, trusting the affected undertakings with the self-assessment of the applicability of exemptions. The investigation and the adjudication of proceedings for infringements of the competition prohibitions were integrated within the same administrative agency (the CNC), further gaining independence from the Government.[20]

Finally, following a global trend of integrating competition law and sectoral regulatory enforcement,[21] the CNMC was established in 2013. Enforcement decisions on competition law infringement cases are now adopted by the Competition Chamber of the CNMC,[22] which also has a separate Regulation Chamber in charge of sectoral regulatory supervision in energy, telecom, railway and air transportation, postal and audiovisual markets.[23]

Potential infringements of the competition prohibitions are investigated by the Directorate of Competition, *ex officio* or following a complaint.[24] Since 2008, investigations of cartel infringements may also be initiated by a leniency application,[25] which as of 31/12/2022 led to the uncovering of thirty-seven cartels.[26]

The CNMC investigative and adjudication powers are in line with Article 5 of Regulation 1/2003 and the ECN+ Directive.[27] The CNMC has comparable powers as those of the European Commission. In the investigation of suspected infringements, its Directorate of Competition may conduct dawn raids,[28] request information[29] and

19. Until 2007 the SDC was empowered to decide not to start or to close investigations, but those decisions could be appealed before the TDC (Article 47 of Act 16/1989).
20. The SDC was a unit dependent of the Ministry of Economy.
21. *See* Frederic Jenny 'The Institutional Design of Competition Authorities: Debates and Trends' in Frederic Jenny & Yannis Katsoulacos (eds) *Competition Law Enforcement in the BRICS and in Developing Countries. Legal and Economic Aspects*, 2017, 17-21.
22. Article 14.1.a) of Decree 657/2013, approving the Organic Statute of CNMC (BOE209 de 31/8/2013).
23. When the infringements of the competition prohibitions occur in sectors subject to the supervision of the CNMC, joint action of the Competition Directorate with the rest of the sectorial Directorates of CNMC is possible and reports may be issued by the Regulatory Chamber, but it is apparent that the creation of the CNMC has led to subjugation of the enforcement of the competition prohibitions to the objectives of regulatory supervision.
24. Article 49.1 of Act 15/2007.
25. Articles 65 and 66 of Act 15/2007. The leniency programme was operative on 28/2/2008 when the Royal Decree 261/2008 entered into force (BOE 50 de 27/2/2008). *See* Joan R. Borrel, Juan L. Jiménez & José M. Ordóñez 'The Leniency Programme: Obstacles on the Way to Collude' *Journal of Antitrust Enforcement* 3/1 (2015) 149-172.
26. *See* Marcos *RDCD* 2023 §IV.3.
27. Directive of 2019/1 of 11/12/2018 to empower the competition authorities of the Member States to be more effective enforcers and to ensure the proper functioning of the internal market, ECN+ Directive (OJEU 11 of 14/1/2019). It was implemented in Spanish domestic law by Decree Law 7/2021 of 27/4/2021 (BOE101 de 28/4/2021).
28. Article 40 of Act 15/2007 and Article 27 of Act 3/2013.
29. Article 39 of Act 15/2007.

conduct interviews.[30] In the enforcement of the prohibitions, the CNMC can accept commitments[31] and impose interim measures;[32] adopt a decision finding an infringement or imposing remedies;[33] and impose fines for procedural and substantive law breaches, as well as for non-compliance with its decisions.[34] Many of the decisions adopted by the CNMC in conducting its proceedings can be challenged in court independent or separately of the final decision on the merits, yet such appeals are not covered by this project.[35]

Enforcement actions are carried out through administrative penalty proceedings, with separate investigation and resolution phases, following the steps and specific rules set out in Act 15/2007.[36] The principles and rights set out in the EU Charter of Fundamental Rights are respected.[37] The proceedings have a maximum duration of twenty-four months from the resolution of the Competition Directorate of the CNMC to initiate them.[38]

The CNMC may also conduct sector inquiries;[39] it may issue opinions on matters relating to its competition and regulation enforcement mandate, as well as on proposed or existing regulations.[40] It is also empowered to challenge in court any administrative action or regulation that creates obstacles to the maintenance of effective market competition.[41]

In the last two decades, the size and resources of the Spanish NCA[42] have grown exponentially: its budget has doubled, and it has a staff of over one hundred people in charge of competition law enforcement.[43] Intense competition advocacy work is

30. Article 39bis of Act 15/2007.
31. Article 52 of Act 15/2007.
32. Article 54 of Act 15/2007.
33. Articles 53 and 63 of Act 15/2007.
34. Article 41 of Act 15/2007.
35. Decisions of the Competition Directorate which cause defencelessness or irreparable harm to legitimate rights or interests of the undertakings investigated may be appealed before the Council of CNC/CNMC (Article 47.1 of Act 15/2007) and then the decision of the CNC/CNMC council may be challenged in court following the same procedure described *infra* section 2 (this occurs, e.g., on decisions on the legality of dawn-raids, decisions not to initiate commitment proceedings).
36. The legal rules governing common administrative proceedings (Act 39/2015, *Ley del Procedimiento Administrativo Común de las Administraciones Públicas*, BOE 236 of 2/10/2015) are suppletive to the specific rules on competition proceedings (*see* Articles 44 and 70 of Act 16/1989).
37. Article 45 of Act 15/2007.
38. The expiration period has been extended by Article 219 of Decree-Law 5/2023, which will apply only to those proceedings initiated after 30/6/2023 (Transitory Provision 9th); it should be noted that previously the maximum duration of proceedings was eighteen months (Articles 36.1 and 38.1 of Act 15/2007). *See infra* section 4.5.2.
39. Article 5.1.h) of Act 3/2013.
40. Article 5.2.a) of Act 3/2013.
41. *See* Article 5.4 of Act 3/2013 and Article 127bis and following of the Act 29/1998 governing the administrative jurisdiction (*Ley reguladora de la Jurisdicción contencioso-administrativa,* BOE 167 of 14/7/1998),
42. For simplicity and to avoid confusion, the various administrative authorities responsible for enforcing antitrust law over time (TDC, CNC and CNMC) will hereinafter be referred to as 'Spanish National Competition Authority' (Spanish NCA).
43. *See* MARCOS *RDCD* 2023 §IV.2.

carried out, in addition to an annual average of around fifty decisions (although since 2009 there has been a significant drop in the number of infringement proceedings started). Most of the investigations are reactive (81%), responding to complaints filed, but the leniency program established in 2008 has made it possible to investigate and sanction some thirty cartels. In the last twenty years, fines totalling EUR 3,207,374,930 have been imposed.[44]

Fifty per cent of the NCA decisions concern multilateral anticompetitive conduct, predominantly horizontal restraints (and half of those concluded with fines). A quarter of the NCA decisions examine single-firm abuses (roughly a third of them concluding in fines). Most fines were imposed on more than eighty cartels that had been detected since 2007.[45]

The initiation of punitive proceedings by the NCA is discretionary and governed by the principle of opportunity.[46] However, this does not allow the NCA to be arbitrary, since it must give reasons for its actions and decisions, which are subject to control by the courts.[47] The entire sanctioning procedure is scrupulously regulated and governed by the principle of legality.

When the Spanish NCA detects an infringement of the prohibitions and declares that an infringement has occurred, it always orders the cessation of the infringing conduct and may impose certain conditions or obligations, whether structural or behavioural on the infringer, but fines are the most used remedy.[48] Thus, administrative fines are the main instrument granted by the legislature to the Spanish NCA to punish competition law infringements, thereby dissuading the commission of new infringements. To this end, the amount of the fine must be sufficiently deterrent.[49] Since 1989, the Competition Act has set a maximum cap for fines of 10% of the sales volume of the infringing undertaking on the fiscal year immediately preceding the NCA

44. EUR 35,817,087 are fines for acts of unfair competition law violations that affect the public interest by distorting free competition (*see* Marcos *RDCD* 2023 §§V.51 and IV.6.6).
45. EUR 1,898,740,215. Almost every fine larger than EUR 50 million relates to horizontal restraints, the majority of those being cartels, *see* Marcos *RDCD* 2023 §IV.5.1 (Table 1).
46. *See* Alejandro Nieto *Derecho Administrativo Sancionador*, 5th ed., 2008, 100-101.
47. *Ibid.*, 103.
48. Article 51.1 and 2 of Act 15/2007. *See* Francisco Marcos 'Remedios y obligaciones impuestos por las autoridades de defensa de la competencia' *CDT* 10/1 (2018) 331-371. In practice most behavioural and structural remedies are included as part of commitment decisions, *see* Marcos *RDCD* 2023 §IV.5.4.When the offenders are legal entities, their legal representatives and members of their management bodies involved in the infringement may be fined up to EUR 60,000 (Article 63.2 of Act 15/2007). The CNMC has imposed these fines since 2016 in a dozen resolutions, all of them infringements of the prohibition of horizontal multilateral conduct, mainly cartels. In addition, serious infringements of the prohibitions on anticompetitive conduct can be accompanied by a ban on contracting with the public administration for up to three years (Article 71.1 b) of Act 9/2017 on Public Procurement, *Ley Contratos del Sector Público*, BOE272 of 9/11/2017). Since 2019, the CNMC has declared in twelve resolutions that the conditions for the application of the prohibition were present.
49. The guiding principle is that the fine should be fixed at an amount high enough to make it economically unwise to engage in the prohibited actions and, therefore, it should be higher for more severe breaches, *see* Article 29.2 of Act 40/2015 of the Public Sector Legal Regime (*Ley de Régimen Jurídico del Sector Público*, BOE236 of 2/10/2015): 'The imposition of pecuniary sanctions shall provide that the commission of the infringements typified shall not be more beneficial to the infringer than compliance with the rules infringed.'

decision,[50] although the current regime and criteria for setting fines (Competition Act 2007) distinguishes between different infringement depending on their gravity.[51]

The exercise of the fining power by the NCA is not entirely discretionary, there is some margin of discretion depending on the circumstances of the infringement and its consequences, but the NCA assessment must be made within the framework provided by the law. Determining the amount of the fine is not a mechanical process of automatic subsumption within the parameters set by law: there is room for manoeuvre for the gradation of sanctions within the framework set by the legislature. The fines levied by the Spanish NCA have shown a consistent upward trajectory starting from 2008. This trend coincides with the establishment of the CNC and the implementation of the leniency program.

Fining decisions by the NCA take effect immediately.[52] However, the infringing parties may request as an interim measure the suspension of the fine and of any other remedies imposed in the contested decision while the appeal is decided.[53] Requests for suspension of the fine are usually upheld when the appellant shows that complying with the contested decision would deprive an appeal of its legitimate interest or when it causes harm that is impossible or very difficult to repair (e.g., given its financial situation, considering the amount of the fine).[54]

---

50. Article 10 of Act 16/89 and Article 63.1.b) of Act 15/2007. Until 2007 the Competition Act included minimal rules on the amount of fines. The general rule was that the amount of the fines may be as large as EUR 901,518.16, but this amount may 'be increased up to 10% of the turnover of the offender corresponding to the financial year immediately prior to court decision' (Article 10 of Act 16/1989). However, there was no scale of the fines depending of the severity of the infringement, the TDC should consider the following factors in setting the amount of the fine: (a) the type and scope of the restriction upon competition; (b) the size of the affected market; (c) the market share of the corresponding undertaking; (d) the effect of the violation on the actual or potential competitors, the other parties in the economic process and the consumers and users; (e) the duration of the restriction upon competition; (f) the recidivism of the offender. The TDC was supposed to adequately reason the criteria and parameters followed in setting the amount of the fine in each case. At that time there was uncertainty about how the TDC calculated the amount of the fine, some even arguing the unconstitutionality of the Competition Act on this regard (Francisco Marcos, 'The Enforcement of Spanish Antitrust Law: A Critical Assessment of the Fines Setting Policy and of the Legal Framework for Private Enforcement Actions' in S. Prasad (ed.), *Antitrust Law – Emerging Trends*, ICFAI Press 2007, 154). For that reason, e.g., a fine imposed on the former SOE Telefónica was partially annulled (reduced), *see* Judgment of Supreme Court of 23/3/2005 (*Telefónica v. TDC & BT*, rapp. M Campos, ES:TS:2005:1817) reducing to EUR 1,803,036 the EUR 3,485,870 fine imposed by TDC resolution of 21/1/1999 (412/17 *BT/Telefónica*, rapp. J Hernández).
51. Article 63.1 of Act 15/2007.
52. Article 98.1 of Act 39/2015.
53. The NCA may also impose structural or behavioural remedies, but these are not so frequent (*see supra* n. 48).
54. *See* Article 130.1 of Act 29/1998. *See, e.g.*, order of High National Court of 26/9/2023 (*RSCE v. CNMC*, rapp. B Santillán, ES:AN:2023:9610A) suspending the remedy imposed (provide the export pedigree certificate to those who request it without being able to impose the obligatory prior registration in the RSCE source books) due to the irreparable harm that could be caused. Lately, if the prohibition of contracting with the Administration is included as an additional remedy for severe infringements of the competition act (*see* Article 71.1 b) of Act 9/2017 on Public Procurement, BOE272 of 9/11/2017), given the harm derived from the application of such measure consisting in the prohibition to contract can be serious (depending on the profile of the enterprise), both in the enterprise's relations with the public sector and the private sector, the Supreme Court has considered that suspension requests of such measures could be granted

If the fine is suspended, the appellant must provide the necessary security to guarantee that the amount of the fine will finally be made available if the judgment resolving the appeal upholds the validity of the infringement decision.[55] If the suspension is not granted, the authority is empowered to monitor the fulfilment and compliance with the remedies imposed.[56] Failure to comply with them is considered a very serious infringement, that may be punished with fines of up to 10% of the total turnover of the non-compliant undertaking the fiscal year prior to the imposition of the fine,[57] regardless of the imposition of coercive fines of up to EUR 12,000/day in order to force compliance with the remedies imposed in the decision.[58] Given that many NCA decisions are appealed, and suspension is generally requested, the NCA must wait until the court resolves on that matter before initiating monitoring proceedings for lack of compliance.[59]

2 JUDICIAL REVIEW OF NCA DECISIONS

NCA decisions can be appealed before the Courts.[60] In Spain, the Judicial System is divided into four specialised judicial orders: Civil (Private Law), Criminal, Administrative and Social (Labour Law/Social Security). The Administrative Order oversees the legality of actions of the Government and Public Administration.[61] Appeals against NCA decisions are examined by the Administrative Order.[62] Appellants file a petition seeking a declaration that the decision is not in accordance with the law and that it be annulled.[63] A separate appeal is available for the protection of fundamental rights if the appellants consider that the investigation and infringement proceedings violated their

based on the same reasoning that applies to the fine, *see* judgment of 14/12/2021 (*Autocares Lorca Bus*, ES:TS:2021:3366, rapp. D Córdoba).

55. Article 133 of Act 29/1998, such surety of the full amount of the fine may be provided in any of the forms permitted by law (bond or guaranty), to avoid possible losses to the Public Treasury that could result from the insolvency of the person or company obliged to pay the related debts in favour of the Public Treasury, *see* judgment of Supreme Court of 26/4/2018 (*Colegio Arquitectos Sevilla*, Rapp. AR Arozamena, ES:TS:2018:1720).
56. *See* Article 41 of Act 15/2007.
57. *See* Articles 62.4.c) and 64.a.b) of Act 15/2007.
58. *See* Article 67 of Act 15/2007. In the period covered by this project Spanish NCAs adopted several decisions imposing fines for lack of compliance, which may have also been appealed in court. The judgments deciding those appeals are out of the scope of this project (*see*, *e.g.*, one of the cases examined in n. 122).
59. *See* judgments of National High Court of 5/6/2000 (*Telefónica v. TDC*, rapp. CM Montero, ES:AN:2000:4720) and 25/4/2001 (*Tabacalera v. TDC & Mc Lane*, rapp. JMª del Riego, ES:AN:2001:2545) annulling coercive fines imposed by the competition authority before the decision could be deemed binding and enforceable.
60. Article 36.1 of Act 3/2013, Article 48.1 of Act 15/2007 and Article 49 of Act 16/1989. This also includes decisions in merger review proceedings, which are outside the scope of this project.
61. Courts and judges serving in the administrative jurisdiction are part of the Judicial Power as the rest of judges and courts in Spain, and despite their specialisation, their selection procedure is the same. It is wrong to assume that this implies that a lighter review of government and administrative action is foreseen in the Law.
62. Appeals against decisions of Regional Competition Authorities are heard before the High Court of Justice (*Tribunal Superior de Justicia*) of the corresponding Region.
63. Article 31.1 of Act 29/1998 governing the administrative jurisdiction (*Ley reguladora de la Jurisdicción contencioso-administrativa*, BOE167 of 14/7/1998). *See* Oriol Mir 'Administrative

fundamental rights (frequently, due process rights).[64] This special appeal is an express and fast procedure, which is handled separately from other appeals against the NCA decision and which leads to a separate judgment.[65] It has been used assiduously by some offenders.[66]

Ordinary appeal proceedings follow the rules set out in Act 29/1998 governing the administrative jurisdiction, which refers to the rules of the Civil Procedure for suppletive application.[67]

NCA decisions are subject to the full jurisdiction of the reviewing courts competent to hear challenges against them. They may be annulled for any infringement of the law pleaded by the parties, which normally base their appeals on both procedural and substantive pleas. Despite the complexity of the analysis on which some NCA decisions are grounded, their technical assessments can be challenged on appeal and may be overturned by reviewing courts based on the arguments and evidence presented by the appellants. Naturally, to the extent that the grounds of appeal on cassation to the Supreme Court are more limited, the scope of review by the Supreme Court is narrower.

2.1 Decisions Subject to Appeal

Although the law declares that NCA decisions can be appealed before the Courts, during the investigation proceedings, most decisions cannot be individually or separately challenged. Due process and defence rights of the investigated parties are assumed to be guaranteed through the availability of appeal against the final NCA decision (which includes a ruling on the substance of the infringement).[68]

Procedure and Judicial Review in Spain' (Chapter 13) in GIACINTO DELLA CANANEA & MADS ANDENAS (eds) *Judicial Review of Administration in Europe. Procedural Fairness and Propriety*, 2021.

64. Articles 114-122 of Act 29/1998. *See* FABIO PASCUA 'El procedimiento para la protección de los Derechos fundamentales: Evolución y disfunciones bajo la Ley 29/1998' *Revista de Administración Pública* 185 (2011) 113-162.
65. Almost all the cases registered here reviewing NCA decisions, when the appellant (always a fined company) filed a separate appeal for fundamental rights violation, it also filed ordinary proceedings against the decision. The undertakings challenged through this procedure thirteen decisions in the period (including one no-fine decision, *see* CNC resolution of 2/11/2009 (S/0051/08 UNESA), six of which were annulled.
66. The outcome has occasionally been favorable to them, e.g., REPSOL used it in challenging three decisions (CNC resolution of 30/7/2009, 652/07 *BP/Cepsa/Repsol*, rapp. P Sánchez) CNMC resolution 20/2/2015, S/474/13 *Precios Combustibles Automoción* and CNMC resolution of 2/7/2015, S/484/13 *Redes Abanderadas*), two of which were fully annulled by the courts.
67. First Final Disposition, Act 29/1998. *See* Civil Procedure Act 1/2000 (*Ley de Enjuiciamiento Civil*, BOE7 of 7/1/2000).
68. According to the Courts, this applies to decisions to initiate an investigation (or even before a preliminary investigation – *información reservada*), decisions enlarging the scope of the investigation (*see* Supreme Court Judgment of 21/11/2014, *Iberdrola v. CNC*, rapp. JM Bandrés, ES:TS:2014:4698) decisions denying interested party status, the SO or the proposal of a final decision, decisions not to initiate commitment proceedings, decisions denying or granting confidentiality to data or documents (either obtained in an inspection or in answering to a request of information by the authority), including confidentiality requests on communications benefiting from attorney client privilege. *See* Supreme Court Judgment of 21/9/2015 (*Balat v.*

However, as a matter of fact, it is possible to challenge also other decisions adopted by the NCA during the proceedings from which the investigated parties cannot defend themselves or that cause irreparable harm to their legitimate rights or interests.[69] Challenges to these 'qualified' procedural decisions (*actos de trámite cualificados*) follow the same process indicated below for appeals against final NCA decisions. Unsurprisingly, undertakings under investigation try to challenge procedural decisions as an 'anticipatory' appeal of the final decision.

Although outside the scope of this project, the relevance of these appeals against 'qualified' procedural decisions should not be underestimated, since the possible annulment of those decisions could lead to the final NCA decision being overturned.[70] For example, when the NCA introduced a correction in the SO that was material (regarding the duration of the infringement).[71] Many other appeals on qualified procedural decisions concentrated on NCA inspections of the sites of undertakings under investigation, challenging several aspects of how the dawn raids were conducted, including the order of inspection and the evidence therein obtained.[72]

2.2 First-Instance Appeals

Appeals against the NCA decisions are heard by the Administrative Chamber of the National High Court (*Audiencia Nacional/AN*).[73] The appeal is heard by magistrates

---

CNMC, fundamental rights proceedings, rapp. PMª L Murillo, ES:TS:2015:4209), confirming High National Court judgment of 11/6/2014 (rapp. AI Resa, ES:AN:2014:2598) and CNC resolution of 16/4/2014 (R/0157/13 *Balat 2-Abogado*, rapp. F Torremocha & B Valdés).

69. Article 47.1 of Act 15/2007.
70. Many appeals of NCA qualified procedural decisions led to the full annulment of the fine, *see infra* section 4.5.2.
71. *See* CNMC resolution of 31/7/2014 (R/AJ/00245/14 *Nestlé España*), annulled by High National Court judgment 11/7/2016 (*Nestlé v. CNMC*, rapp. F De la Peña, ES:AN:2016:3063), confirmed by Supreme Court of 24/7/2018 (rapp. Mª I. Perelló, ES:TS:2018:3007).
72. *See, e.g.*, Supreme Court Judgments of 27/4/2012 (*STANPA v. CNC*, rapp. NA Maurandi, ES:TS:2012:3887); 30/9/2013 (*Transnatur v. CNC*, rapp. M Campos, ES:TS:2013:4722) and 25/4/2016 (*Lactalis v. CNMC*, rapp. Mª I Perelló, ES:TS:2016:1846). Courts have ruled that an inspection order must specify, with minimum information on the possible infringements and their scope, what the competition authority is looking for, *see, e.g.*, Supreme Court judgment of 27/2/2015 (*Transmediterránea v. TDC*, ES:TS:2015:941 rapp. Mª I. Perelló) revoking judgment of High National Court of 7/2/2012 (rapp. MªA Salvo, ES:AN:2012:693), which had rejected the appeal against CNC resolution of 2/7/2010 (R/0046/10 *Transmediterranea*, P Sánchez). *See also* Supreme Court Judgment of 10/12/2014 (*UNESA v. CNC*, rapp. E. Calvo, ES:TS:2014:5266, dissenting JM Bandrés & PJ Yague) revoking judgment of High National Court of 2/6/2011 (rapp. M. Pedraz, ES:AN:2011:2836), which had rejected the appeal against CNC resolution of 1712/2009 (R/30/2009 UNESA, rapp. I. Gutiérrez).

    In case of discrepancy between the NCA inspection order or the court order, the latter prevails. *See* Judgment of 10/12/2014 (*Campezo v. CNC*, ES:TS:2014:5479, rapp. E Espín), annulling the High Court judgment of 20/5/2011 (rapp. CM Montero, ES:AN:2011:2528), which had confirmed CNC resolution of 28/12/2009 (R/25/09 *Campezo/Guipasa*, rapp. E Conde).
73. *See* Article 66 of Organic Act 6/1985 of the Judicial Power (*Ley del Poder Judicial*, BOE157 of 2/7/1985) and Additional Provision 4th, 3 of Act 29/1998 ('*in single instance*'). The High National Court was created in 1976 (succeeding the Franco's Public Order Courts and the Central Criminal Courts, Decree-Law 1/1977, BOE4 of 5/1/1977) with country-wide jurisdiction on criminal and administrative matters.

serving in the Administrative Chamber, who are specialised in various matters of administrative law.[74]

The Administrative Chamber is further divided into eight sections; among which cases are allocated depending on the Government Department or public entity challenged. Judicial review of public enforcement of the competition rules is conducted by the 6th section of the Administrative Chamber, composed of six magistrates.[75] The section is not specialised in competition law.[76] It is understood that specialisation in competition law will be acquired through the repeated performance of their work in the matters allocated to each section, given that it is common for judges to occupy the posts in each of the sections for a long period of time.[77]

2.3 Appeal of Cassation

The Administrative Chamber of the National High Court decides on challenges of NCA decisions as a 'single instance', i.e., this is the only ordinary appeal provided. However, on limited grounds, judgments issued by the High National Court can be further appealed in cassation to the Administrative Chamber of the Supreme Court (*Tribunal Supremo*).[78] The Chamber is divided into six sections and appeals against judgments of the 6th section of the High National Court (reviewing NCA decisions enforcing the competition prohibitions) are heard by the 3rd section. Magistrates in the administrative chamber are specialised in Administrative Law.

74. Administrative judges are selected through competitive examination of their specialisation in administrative law. The appointment of magistrates to the AN is made on a competitive basis, through restricted contests among the senior specialist judges of the lower courts with greatest seniority (Articles 326 and 330 of Organic Act 6/1985).
75. In the period covered by this project fourteen magistrates served in the 6th Section: Lucia Acín, Ramón Castillo, Francisco De la Peña, José Mª del Riego, José Guerrero, Miguel de los Santos Gandarillas, Javier E. López, Concepción M. Montero, Mercedes Pedraz, Ana I. Resa, Mª Asunción Salvo, Berta Santillán, Santiago P. Soldevila and Mª Jesús Vegas.
76. The 6th section of the Administrative Chamber of the National High Court also hears appeals against acts and decisions of the Ministries of Education and Vocational Training, Culture and Sport, Science and Innovation, Universities, Finance and Civil Service (only in matters of contraband and local and regional taxes), Justice (appeals against decisions on nationality by residence), Home Affairs (appeals against decisions on international protection deriving from the right to asylum and subsidiary protection and the statelessness status) and of the Universities Council. *See* Resolution of the Permanent Commission of the General Council of the Judiciary of 15/12/2022 (BOE 313 of 30/12/2022). In the period covered in this project, the jurisdiction of the 6th section has progressively been reduced, but it has always been the one overseeing challenges against decisions of national competition authorities, *see* resolution of the Permanent Commission of the General Council of the Judiciary of 24/7/2001 (BOE 217 of 10/9/2001). For a personal account of the complexities of deciding cases on so many different matters and the turmoil that can arise in the dynamics of a collegial body, *see* José Guerrero, *Memorias de un juez desencantado*, 2020, 124-126.
77. Magistrates serving in the National High Court have limited opportunities for promotion in their judicial career (as has happened with many of them or are promoted to the Supreme Court, f.e., Jose Mª del Riego), unless they switch to another section in the Court. During the period of this project most magistrates in the 6th section held the position for several years (*see supra* n. 75).
78. Article 86.1 of Organic Act 6/1985 and Article 12.2.a) of Act 29/1998.

The 3rd section of the Administrative Chamber of the Supreme Court is composed of five magistrates.[79] As with the court responsible for first-instance appeals, the 3rd section is not specialised in competition law but hears appeals on many other administrative disputes.[80] Yet, magistrates serving in the 3rd section are said to become specialised in competition law over time by performing their task of reviewing appeals regarding NCA decisions.[81] Magistrates serving in the Supreme Court have reached the top judicial echelon in Spain and they normally serve for long periods of time before retirement on the basis of old age.[82]

Decisions by the Supreme Court are final and are not subject to any additional appeal. However, an exceptional motion is available for the nullity of the proceedings based on a violation of fundamental rights against either the inadmissibility of cassation or the judgment of the Supreme Court addressing the appeal petitions.[83] This motion for nullity is based on the omissive incongruence or a defect of motivation (*in aliunde*) by the Supreme Court which amounts to an alleged infringement of the constitutional right to effective judicial protection established in Article 24.1 of the Spanish Constitution.[84]

The request for nullity of proceedings is not conceived as a new instance or as an ordinary or extraordinary appeal against Supreme Court judgments. Neither can it be interpreted as granting the parties a kind of appeal against the judgment that resolves the cassation appeal. It is a remedy aimed at correcting errors or omissions in the proceedings or in the judgment to avoid constitutional recourse (e.g., presumption of innocence). The motion for nullity of the proceedings would fully exhaust previous judicial appeals, which would be indispensable for a subsequent petition for protection (*amparo*) to the Constitutional Court.

Motions for nullity of proceedings are regularly filed by appellants against NCA decisions, although they have always been rejected. The Supreme Court has always considered that the appellant, under the invocation of the violation of the right for

79. The number increases to six if the president of the Administrative Chamber joins the Section in some case. In the period of the Study there has been ten different magistrates serving in the 3rd section: Angel R. Arozamena, Jose Manuel Bandrés, Eduardo Calvo, Manuel Campos, Diego Córdoba, Jose Mª del Riego, Jose Luis Delgado, Eduardo Espín, Oscar González, Mª Isabel Perelló and Pedro J. Yagüe.
80. The 3rd section of the Administrative Chamber of the Supreme Court is also in charge of appeals of cassation against acts and decisions of the Ministries of Economy and Finance, Home Affairs (including Foreigners' Affairs), Development; Industry, Tourism and Trade, Rural and Marine Affairs and Territorial Policy and Public Administration (also concerning public corporations or institutions linked to or dependent on one of them). *See* Resolution of the Permanent Commission of the General Council of the Judiciary of 29/12/2010 (BOE14 of 17/1/2011).
81. *See supra* n. 75.
82. Judges and magistrates in Spain must retire by 70 years old, although they may request a two-year extension (Article 386.1 of Organic Act 6/1985).
83. *See* Article 241.1 of Organic Act 6/1985 ('In general, incidents of nullity of proceedings shall not be admitted. However, exceptionally, those who are or should have been a legitimate party may request in writing that the nullity of the proceedings be declared on the grounds of proceedings based on any violation of a fundamental right of those referred to in Article 53.2 of the Constitution, provided that it has not been possible to denounce it before the decision that ends the proceedings is handed down and provided that said decision is not subject to ordinary or extraordinary appeal').
84. Spanish Constitution of 27/12/1978 (*Constitución Española*, BOE31 of 29/12/1978).

effective judicial protection or of other fundamental rights, sought to reopen the case discussion.

Claims for the protection of constitutional rights and freedoms, nevertheless, may be brought before the Constitutional Court that is not part of the judiciary. For the purpose of this study, therefore, they are not considered an additional level of judicial review. The Constitutional Court is very restrictive in admitting individual appeals for the protection of constitutional rights and it has only delivered one opinion in a handful of cases in relation to the judicial review of NCA decisions.[85]

2.4 Proceedings Before the National High Court

Appeals against NCA decisions follow the general rules in administrative proceedings on the rights of parties and the admissibility of evidence in court. The Court could also order *ex officio* the taking of evidence.[86] The application instituting the proceeding and the statement of defence are written, and so are the submissions to the court during the proceedings, including the closure motions. Hearings are not usually conducted, but the court is empowered to decide otherwise.[87]

As NCA decisions are administrative acts, their adoption and content must comply with the legally established provisions and procedures, and the infringement of any of them is the main reason for their challenge in court.[88] The appellant petitions the annulment of the decision based on different motives and supporting evidence. As observed below (*infra* section 4.5), many appeals are grounded on relevant procedural defects that harm the rights of defence of undertakings, ignoring the procedural safeguards set in the law and the right to due process, or when the assessment conducted by the NCA was mistaken.

2.5 Cassation Proceedings

Cassation appeals are limited to legal or procedural issues, and neither the facts nor the assessment of the evidence is examined by the Supreme Court.[89]

The rules governing such appeals, including the grounds of cassation, have changed in 2016 and in 2023. The previous cassation appeals for the unification of

85. Early on there was a judgment regarding the admissibility of a direct challenge to the Constitutional Court of an infringement decision by the TDC, *see* judgment 80/83 of 10/10/1984 (*Agrupación Vendedores Prensa Pontevedra*, Rapp. G Begué, ES:TC:1983:80); judgment 175/12 of 15/10/2012 (*Buque Bus España*, Rapp. R Rodriguez, ES:TC:2012:175) and judgment 71/22 of 13/6/2022 (*Bimética*, Rapp. E. Arnaldo, ES:TC:2022:71). In other cases, challenges grounded on the violation of fundamental rights by Bombas Capari, Barna Import Médica and Club de Variedades Vegetales (rec. 477/2018) were unadmitted.
86. Article 61 of Act 29/1998.
87. Articles 63 and 64 of Act 29/1998, that may occur, for example, when witness or expert evidence is presented, with the witnesses or experts being summoned to appear before the Court, so the parties and the magistrates can question them.
88. *See* Article 31 of Act 29/1998.
89. *See* Article 87 of Act 29/1998 ('the appeal in cassation before the Administrative Chamber of the Supreme Court is limited to questions of law, excluding questions of fact').

doctrine and in the interest of the law have been abolished, as well as the minimum amounts that were required in the past. The new rules are aimed to protect and preserve the law and its uniform interpretation (nomophylactic). Appellants need to invoke a specific infringement of the legal rules, whether procedural or substantive, or of the case law, and to demonstrate an objective interest in the formation of case law.[90]

Initially, all challenges of NCA decisions were presumed to have an objective public interest. However, mere arguments by the appellants alluding to the potential impact on multiple other cases are not enough (as potential applicability to other disputes must be inherent in the legal debate). Cassation appeals should rather focus on the divergence in the interpretation of the law, lack of case law, or High National Court judgments deliberately departing from existing and consolidated case law of the Supreme Court.[91]

2.6 Outcome of Judicial Review

When the Courts uphold an appeal, the judgment declares the NCA decision not to be in accordance with the Law and annul it in whole or in part.

Annulments in full may be due to procedural errors, wrong assessment of the evidence by the NCA or lack of evidence of the infringement.

Partial annulments generally affect the amount of the fine imposed, when it is deemed excessive and disproportionate by the reviewing court. Reviewing courts can determine and reduce the amount of the fine on appeal themselves, depending on the gravity of the infringement and the criteria for setting it, as established in the Competition Acts. Indeed, Courts have done that a few times in the cases examined here, especially in the early years.[92] However, in most cases reviewing courts consider that fine determination may not be such a straightforward exercise and accordingly they prefer to order the NCA to recalculate the fine. This has considerably impacted this study because appellants normally challenge the appropriateness and proportionality of the fine imposed and it is not unusual for the courts to uphold their appeals. This means that the NCA decision is annulled only in relation to the amount of the fine, which must be recalculated again by the NCA, and the new decision is also often appealed (this time with less likelihood of success). For the purposes of this study, there is considerable evidence of a multiplication of judgments reviewing the NCA decision and considerable delay for many decisions to become final (only with respect to the fine's amount).

90. Article 88 of Act 29/1998. *See* José Luis Azofra & Claudia López 'El acceso al (todavía) nuevo recurso de casación: análisis estadístico y sustantivo en el ámbito de la defensa de la competencia' (Chapter 19) of *Anuario de Derecho de la Competencia 2019*, 321-344.
91. Article 88.3 of Act 29/1998.
92. *See, e.g.*, the Supreme Court reduced almost in half the fine to Correos for an abuse of dominance in TDC resolution 15/9/2004 (568/03 *ASEMPRE/Correos*, rapp. J Pascual) *see* judgment of 8/6/2010 (*Correos v. TDC*, rapp. JM Bandrés, ES:TS:2010:3178), reducing the fine from EUR 15,000,000 to EUR 8,149,500. It did the same thing with the EUR 300,000 fine imposed to Federación Gremial de Panadería y Pastelería de la Provincia de Valencia by TDC resolution of 18/10/2006 (*598/05 Panaderías de Valencia*, rapp. F Torremocha), *see* judgment of 1/12/2010 (rapp. JM Bandrés, ES:TS:2010:6464).

If a fining decision is quashed, the undertaking can claim compensation for any costs experienced because of the infringement decision. The declaration of liability of the Administration will require the fulfilment of certain established legal requirements and proof of harm caused by the annulled decision.[93]

3 PRIOR RESEARCH

There have been several contributions analysing judicial review of specific decisions of the Spanish NCA.[94] Most papers focus on the judicial review of prominent decisions with large fines,[95] and some papers have pointed to trends observed in the judicial review of NCA decisions.[96] While some empirical analysis of judicial review of competition law enforcement has also been conducted, they have not undertaken a meaningful systematic analysis of judicial review of NCA decisions.[97]

The Spanish NCA regularly examines the judicial review of its decisions in its annual reports and reports to the OECD,[98] but it does not follow a systematic analysis of judicial review, and annual reports tend to make a partial and fragmentary analysis which tends to be biased and focused on the NCA's court successes rather than in its failures.[99] Instead of maintaining and consolidating institutional memory, annual reports have been considered by each serving president as proof of his/her legacy,

93. *See* Articles 32-34 of Act 40/15.
94. *See, e.g.*, Francisco Marcos 'The Enforcement of Spanish Antitrust Law: A Critical Assessment of the Fines Setting Policy and of the Legal Framework for Private Enforcement Actions' in S. Prasad (ed.), *Antitrust Law – Emerging Trends*, 2007, 155-156.
95. *See, e.g.*, Francisco Marcos 'Lecciones de la revisión judicial del cartel del seguro decenal' *Actas de Derecho Industrial y derecho de autor* 36 (2016) 173-196.
96. *See, e.g.*, Francisco Marcos 'Incontinencia Judicial en defensa de la competencia' *Diario La Ley* 8802 of 13/7/2016.
97. They either focus on assessing the scope of judicial review of competition and regulatory authorities, *see* Nuria Ruiz, *El control jurisdiccional de los organismos reguladores*, 2018, or aim at comparing judicial review between jurisdictions, *see* Luis E. Mejia, 'Judicial Review of Regulatory Decisions: Decoding the Contents of Appeals Against Agencies in Spain and the United States' *Regulatory Governance* 15/3 (2021) 760-784 DOI: 10.1111/rego.12302.
98. *See, e.g.*, 'Note by Spain: The Standard of Review by Courts in Competition Cases', OECD Working Party No. 3 on Co-operation and Enforcement, DAF/COMP/WP3/WD(2019)18, 21/5/2019, 3 ('Recently the CNMC has analysed the judicial review of its sanctioning decisions regarding articles 1 and 2 – which are equivalent to 101 and 102 of the TFEU – of the Spanish Competition Act. The study carried out for the period 2014-2017 shows that the Spanish National Court has confirmed on average 75% of the Competition Authority's sanctioning decisions. The percentage rises to 82.7% in the case of the Spanish Supreme Court').
99. *See* CNC, *Memoria 2010*, 6 (in words of the president Berenguer 'moreover, the vast majority of our actions have been endorsed by the courts, which, at least in the first instance, have so far upheld 83.3% of our decisions. This gives us confidence and indicates that we are on the right track'), including statistical review later from 2007-2011 (*ibid.*, 55-56).

which transpires in the need for self-assertion,[100] especially in comparison with his/her predecessors.[101]

4 QUANTITATIVE ANALYSIS

4.1 Sources of Information

All judgments handed down by Spanish courts hearing antitrust cases are published. The NCA maintains a database of its decisions, which is also meant to include all the relevant judgments linked to a given case.[102] The database, though fairly comprehensive, is not complete and some information is missing. The full texts of all the reviewed judgments could, nevertheless, be retrieved from the official case law databases maintained by the CENDOJ.[103]

During the period of this research project, the Spanish Competition Authorities (TDC, CNC and CNMC) adopted 769 decisions concerning potential infringements of Articles 101 and 102 TFEU and their domestic equivalents,[104] of which more than one-third were fining decisions.[105] From 1/5/2004 to 31/4/2021 total fines of an amount of EUR 2,611.88 million were imposed.[106]

100. *See* Andrés Betancor 'Control de las autoridades de defensa de la competencia: virtudes y límites. El caso de los poderes de investigación y sanción' in A. Betancor et al. (eds) *Defensa de la Competencia: innovación y control en el contexto de la tradición intervencionista*, 2020, 303 (considering self-centeredness one of the pathologies of the Spanish NCA).
101. *See* Marcos *RDCD* 2023 §3 *in fine*. NCA Annual reports generally give notice about those judgments delivered in judicial review every year, but given that the NCA is a party to many proceedings (i.e., not only proceedings concerning final decisions) and given the circumstances in which judicial review is performed, it is possible to twist the reality and use partial data to depict a positive view of the NCA's performance in court, with the objective of providing the right image of the institution under the reins of each President. *See* CNMC, *Memoria 2021*, 21 (extracting only the positive information and in a disjointed manner, there is no hesitation in drawing positive conclusions). Eventually, the CNMC is franker in its own assessment, *see Memoria 2020*, 42.
102. Accessible through the search form available at https://www.cnmc.es/acuerdos-y-decisiones (the NCA publicises and makes available the judgments it is notified as party in the appeal proceedings, they are organised as a link to the appealed decision).
103. Accessible through the search form available at https://www.poderjudicial.es/search/indexAN.jsp.
104. Nineteen resolutions ruling on infringements of unfair competition acts prohibited by Article 3 of Act 15/2007 (Article 7 of Act 16/89) were subject to judicial review in the period (out of seventy-nine resolutions, but they are excluded from the study only four of them are fining decisions), *see supra* n. 15.
105. Although some appeals against them were decided beyond the temporal scope of this Project (or are yet to be decided), up to 2019, three hundred and sixteen NCA decisions were appealed.
106. The highest fines in the history of the Spanish competition authorities were imposed in the period under review, with twenty decisions each involving fines exceeding EUR 50 million. These fines punish almost always for infringements of Article 101 TFEU (or domestic equivalent), cartels or other horizontal restraints (*see* Marcos *RDCD* 2023 §V.5.1.). Although the number of fining decisions since the peak in 2012 seems to be declining, this has not led to a reduction in the total amount of fines imposed (i.e., the CNMC imposes fewer fines, but their amounts are higher). This may be due, among other reasons, to the fact that in recent years the CNMC has increased the average penalty rate used to calculate fines.

Due to the delays in the process of judicial review, as at the end of the project period, all appeals have been resolved only in relation to NCA decisions adopted prior to the end of 2015.[107]

4.2 Total Number of Judgments

More than one-third of all NCA decisions on the application of the competition prohibitions were challenged in court (*see* Figure 28.1), leading to 1,384 judgments (1,054 by the High National Court and 330 by the Supreme Court). The appeal rate is 36% at first instance.

Figure 28.1 Number of Judgments According to Instances

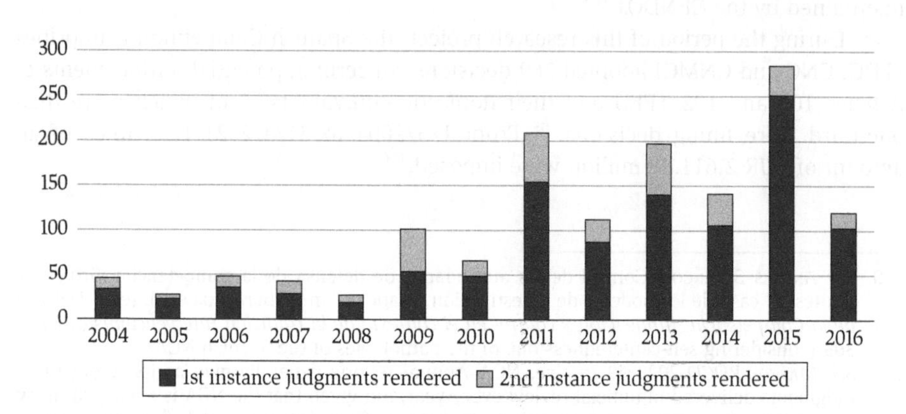

Note: In contrast with the other comparative reports in this project, here the accumulation of appeal judgments is anchored to the date of the decision, not to the date of the judgment (i.e., each year column represents all the judgments issued on review of all NCA decisions adopted that year).

The number of rulings resolving appeals grew throughout the period at a greater rate than the evolution in the number of NCA decisions adopted (which in fact have decreased). The exponential growth in appeals has been particularly pronounced since 2011, largely due to the judicial review of several cartels involving numerous participants (*see* Table 28.2, including all decisions that resulted in more than fifteen judgments on appeal, all relating to cartels).

107. Until 31/12/2015 there were 209 NCA fining decisions for infringements of 101 or 102 TFEU (or domestic equivalents), 92.8% were challenged in court by the undertakings fined (total amount EUR 1,697,153,916).

Table 28.2 NCA Decisions Leading to the Largest Number of Appeals (Judgments)

Date	*Case*	*Reference*	*Fine (EUR)*	*High National Court*	*Supreme Court*
28/5/15	Concesionarios Audi/Seat/VW	S/471/13	27,338,323	70	11
19/10/11	Licitaciones de Carreteras	S/226/10	44,033,240	53	24
8/1/15	Residuos	S/429/12	98,201,302	44	0
22/9/14	Palés	S/428/12	4,961,683.84	37	19
30/7/13	Coches de Alquiler	S/380/11	34,634,498	23	4
5/3/15	Concesionarios Opel	S/489/13	5,379,064	23	1
5/9/16	Cementos	S/525/14	29,380,936	21	0
23/5/13	Distribuidores Saneamiento	S/303/10	6,459,087	20	20
24/6/11	Bombas de fluidos	S/185/09	17,343,581	18	5
23/7/15	Fabricantes automóviles	S/482/13	92,007,346	18	14
18/6/14	Fabricantes de papel y cartón ondulado	S/469/13	57,686,188	17	0
6/9/16	Mudanzas internacionales	S/544/14	4,097,002	15	0

The large number of judgments reviewing the NCA decisions is explained by the right of each infringing party to challenge the sanctioning decision with respect to its specific participation in the infringement. As each alleged offender is presumed innocent, the judicial review process is tasked with scrutinising the NCA decision in the case. This review assesses whether the decision effectively rebuts this presumption by considering the available evidence of the individual's involvement in the alleged misconduct. Furthermore, it ensures that the evidence was gathered during an investigation and used in the decision while upholding procedural guarantees. Finally, the judicial review examines the coherence and adequacy of the final decision.

Although it is possible that parties may jointly appeal, they rarely do so, each of them filing an individual appeal (even when they belong to the same corporate group).[108] The National High Court could also decide *ex officio* to join the several appeals filed against the same NCA decision.[109] Reasons for efficiency and procedural

108. *See* Mejia *Regulatory Governance* 15/3 (2021) 772.
109. *See* Article 34.1 of Act 29/1998 ('Claims arising in connection with the same act, disposition or action may be joined in a proceeding'). In another context, regarding the decision of the High National Court ordering the claimants to lodge separate appeals (involving 15,000 litigants claiming compensation to the State for the closure of Spanish civil airspace on 3 and 4 December 2010), the Constitutional Court has ruled 'the joinder could not be ruled out without further explanation of the corresponding legal premises that link between the claims, in view of the similarity and homogeneity of the elements that outline them, in terms of their objective and causal links, even if there was no absolute identity in the pleadings in view of the different harm caused to each claimant.' *see* 4th legal ground of Constitutional Court judgment 8/2014 of 27/1/2014 (*AENA*, ES:TC:2014:8, Rapp. F Valdés).

economy would support a joinder of the appeals when the circumstances of the infringing conduct by various parties are substantially the same, but that has never occurred in the cases examined here.[110]

Given the collegiate nature of the reviewing bodies, for the sake of ensuring a degree of coherence in the judgments concerning the same NCA decision, there is often a form of coordinated processing of appeals, so that, although decided individually, they are decided around the same time.[111]

Naturally, coherence does not necessarily mean that all the rulings handed down on the same NCA decision coincide (that may often be the case). Given that it is possible that the motives, arguments, and evidence used by each offender are different, or that the review courts may make a different assessment from that of the NCA regarding the participation of each offender in the infringing conduct or on the adequacy or proportionality of the fine imposed, it may well be that the outcome of their appeals differs for each appellant.

Judicial review is a lengthy process. Judgments of the National High Court reviewing NCA decisions take two or three years to be issued, and cassation appeals by the Supreme Court are decided three or four years after that. Apparently, given the increase over the years in the workload of the reviewing courts (not only in competition law matters) the duration of judicial review has increased by one additional year or more in each court. Some NCA decisions only become final after even longer periods. The situation is even more dire in those cases in which the court partially annuls the fine imposed by the NCA and orders a recalculation, as this takes further time, and on many occasions, fines recalculated by the NCA are further appealed, generally without success, but lengthening the process again.

Obviously, this affects the analysis undertaken here, as only a few of the appeals against decisions adopted by the CNMC in 2016 were issued before 30 April 2021 (and when they were, some were only by the High National Court, with cassation appeals

110. The system of judicial productivity modules and variable remuneration can help to understand this trend, *see* GABRIEL DOMÉNECH 'La perniciosa influencia de las retribuciones variables de los jueces sobre el sentido de sus decisiones' *Indret* 3/2008, 44-56.

111. A recent amendment to the Act 29/1998 legally enshrines such a course of action (article 37.2 introduced by Decree-Law 5/2023, BOE154 of 29/6/2023): 'When a plurality of appeals with identical subject matter are pending before a judge or court, the court, if they have not been joined, will process one or more appeals on a preferential basis after hearing the parties for a common period of five days, suspending the course of the others, at the stage they are at, until a judgment is rendered in the first ones. In the event that this plurality of appeals with identical object could, in turn, be grouped by categories or groups that raise a substantially analogous controversy, the court, if they have not been accumulated, will process one or more of each group or category preferentially, after hearing the parties for a common period of five days, suspending the course of the others in the state in which they are until a judgment is rendered in those processed preferentially for each group or category'.

still pending). Indeed, judicial review proceedings of six of the twenty-four 2015 NCA decisions appealed were still ongoing at that date.[112]

Some disputes run for more than a decade,[113] especially in those cases in which, after the review of the case by the National High Court and the Supreme Court (and eventually also through the fundamental rights proceedings), the case is sent back to the NCA, and the new fining decision is appealed again, and the undertakings (mostly unsuccessfully) start the appeal process again.[114]

4.3 Success Rates and Outcomes

Figure 28.2 represents the success of appeals at the ends of the proceedings, i.e., final decision of the courts (either after the first instance and/or second instance). Contrary to the information of other reports in the Project, here the data refers to each NCA decision at the end of judicial review: 18% of appeals were fully successful, 30% partially successful and 52% were unsuccessful.

112. CNMC Resolutions of 20/2/2015 (S/474/13 *Precios Combustibles Automoción*); 16/7/2015 (S/490/13 *Acuerdos Telefónica/Yoigo*, dissenting opinions F Torremocha & B Valdés); 23/7/2015 (S/436/12 *DTS Distribuidora TV Digital*); 26/11/2015 (S/500/13 AGEDI/AIE Radio); 3/12/2015 (S/0481/13 *Construcciones Modulares*, dissenting opinion B Valdés); 12/12/2015 (S/299/10 *Consejo Colegios Odontólogos y Estomatólogos*).

113. For an extreme case, *see* TDC resolution of 10/5/2006 (588/05 *Distribuidores Cine*, rapp. J. Huerta), where after five judgments of High National Court, nine judgments of the Supreme Court and several new resolutions by the CNMC re-calculating the fines, the last ones dated 21/12/2021 (VS/588/05 Distribuidores Cine-Hispano Fox and VS/558/05 Distribuidores Cine-Warner), the undertakings have managed to reduce the fines roughly EUR 3 million (from EUR 12,900,000 to EUR 8,990,993.84).

114. A good snapshot is CNMC resolution of 26/2/2015 (S/425/12 *Industrias Lácteas 2*), which was annulled by judgment of the High Court of 11/7/2016 (*Nestlé v. CNMC*, rapp. F De la Peña, ES:AN:2016:3063), confirmed by Supreme Court judgment of 24/7/2018 (rapp. Mª I. Perelló, ES:TS:2018:3007) and subsequent judgments of the High Court of 20/9/2018 (*Nestlé v. CNMC*, rapp. SP Soldevila, ES:AN:2018:5373; *Lactalis v. CNMC*, rapp. SP Soldevila, ES:AN:2018:5301); 28/9/2018 (*AEG v. CNMC*, rapp. R. Castillo, ES:AN:2018:5302); 18/10/2018 (*Danone v. CNMC*, rapp. R. Castillo, ES:AN:2018:4039); 24/10/2018 (*Schreiber v. CNMC*, ES:AN:2018:3649; *Celega v. CNMC*, rapp. BMª Santillán, ES:AN:2018:4035 and *C.A.Peñasanta v. CNMC*, ES:AN:2018:4037); 25/10/2018 (*Gremio v. CNMC*, rapp. F De la Peña, ES:AN:2018:4036 and *Pascual v. CNMC*, rapp. F De la Peña, ES:AN:2018:4040); and 2/11/2018 (*CLAS v. CNMC*, rapp. SP Soldevila, ES:AN:2018:4193). The CNMC sanctioned the cartel again, with some variations in the scope of the infringement in resolution of 11/7/2019 (S/425/12 *Industrias Lácteas 2*). All the declared offenders appealed the new resolution, High National Court issued in February 2024 confirmed the fines imposed to most appellants, though the fine was fully annulled for one of them and it will need to be reduced by the NCA for another three appellants.

Figure 28.2 Success of Appeals (Each NCA's Decision Counts as One)

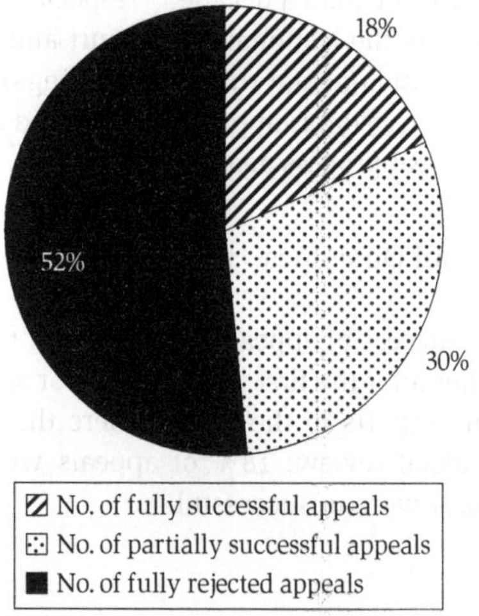

18%
52%
30%

No. of fully successful appeals
No. of partially successful appeals
No. of fully rejected appeals

4.4 Type of NCA Decisions Subject to Appeal

The rules and restraints subject to judicial review mirror the corresponding decisions issued by the NCA. Figure 28.3 indicates the ratio of the different competition law prohibitions subject to the courts' review, across all instances of appeal. It differentiates between the prohibition on anti-competitive agreements and abuse of dominance, and between cases in which both the EU and the national equivalent prohibitions have been applied and purely domestic cases in which only the national equivalent prohibitions have been applied due to the absence of an effect on trade between Member States. The effect on trade between Member States determines the applicability of EU law and this clause is interpreted broadly; when this occurs, the NCA also applies the TFEU prohibitions.[115]

Purely domestic infringements of the prohibition on anti-competitive agreements were the subject of 44% of appeals, while the same percentage of appeals concerned both Article 101 TFEU and Article 1 of the Competition Act infringements. The provisions on abuse of dominance were reviewed in 11% of the appeals. Reflecting the practice of the NCA, the rules being appealed are distributed evenly across years, with no discernible patterns.

115. Some 27% of the decisions adopted by the NCA in the last twenty years examine the application of both the provisions of the TFEU and national law. In the last decade, the simultaneous application of the prohibitions contained in national competition law and the TFEU is predominant. This has occurred in almost all proceedings initiated based on leniency applications and in a significant percentage of those concluding with a fine (43%). *See* MARCOS *RDCD* 2023 §IV. 6.

Figure 28.3 Rule Being Appealed

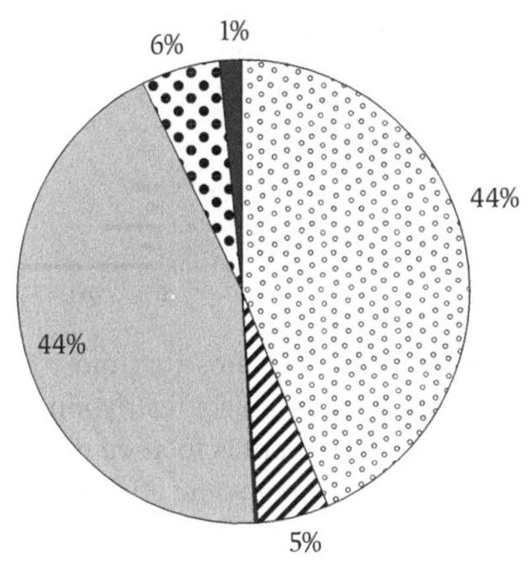

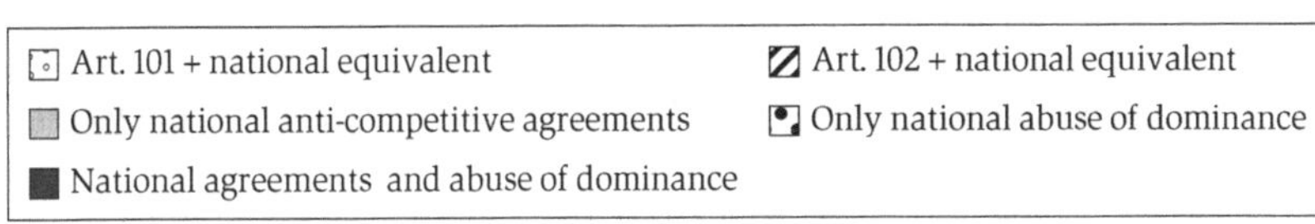

Next, Figure 28.4 summarises across all instances of appeal the types of restrictions of competition that were examined in the NCA's decisions subject to appeal. For cases in which the EU and/or domestic prohibitions on anti-competitive agreements have been applied, the figure differentiates between horizontal and vertical restrictions. For cases in which the EU and/or national prohibitions on abuse of dominance have been applied, it differentiates between exploitative and exclusionary abuses. It also records cases involving a combination of such restrictions. The figure presents the data from the perspective of each single appeal judgment (noting that more than one judgment may be issued with respect to a single NCA decision).

Most of the appeals are multilateral restraints cases (over 92%), with a few exclusionary and exploitative abuse cases (6%). There is a disproportionate concentration of challenges of NCA decisions on horizontal restrictions (73%), well above the 40% of total NCA decisions on restrictions in this area. Also significant is the high percentage of appeals on mixed multilateral restraints (11.7% of appeals). Finally, appeals against decisions on vertical restraints or abuses of dominance are well below the average number of NCA decisions on those matters in the period.[116]

116. *See* MARCOS *RDCD* 2023 §IV. 6.2 and 6.4, (4.2% versus 8.7% on vertical restraints; 9% versus 24% on abuses of dominance).

Figure 28.4 Types of Restrictions

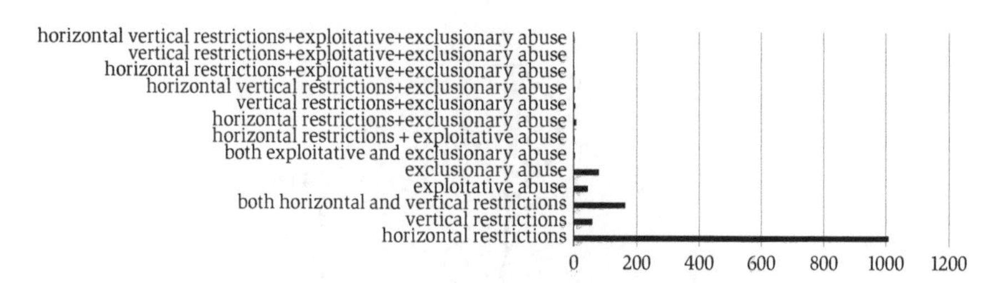

As Figure 28.5 shows the NCA declares that most of the infringements of the prohibition of multilateral restraints are object restrictions that have produced effects in the market. Most of the NCA assessment is focused on by-object infringements, but generally, the NCA adds as a complement some effects analysis.

Figure 28.5 Object/Effect (Only for Article 101/National Equivalent Infringements)

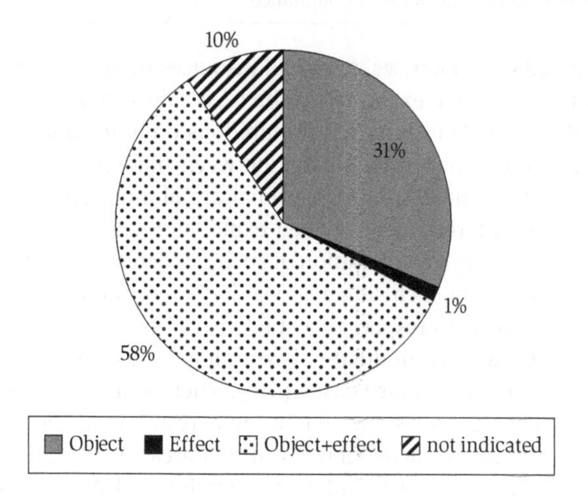

Figure 28.6 indicates the ratio of the type of NCA's procedures that were subject to judicial review, across all instances of appeal. It specifies the percentage of appeals on an NCA's finding of an infringement (distinguishing between cases where a fine was or was not imposed), or of no grounds for action findings, and decisions: to accept formal commitments, reject a complaint, or close an investigation.

Figure 28.6 Competition Authority's Procedure

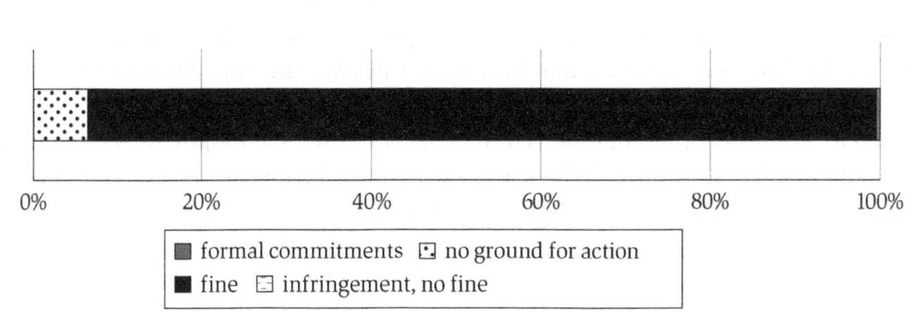

Note: The figure presents the data from the perspective of each single appeal judgment (noting that more than one judgment may be issued with respect to a single NCA decision).

Ninety-three per cent of the judgments concern fines, and in most of the fines that were not challenged in court their amount was very low (below EUR 10,000).[117] Slightly less than 6% of all appeals concerned NCA decisions declaring there to be no grounds of infringement, mostly involving challenges by the complainants that originally brought the case before the NCA (*see infra* section 4.6).

The NCA may declare an infringement, but not impose a fine. These decisions are very infrequent,[118] and two of those cases challenged before the courts relate to infringements by the public administration,[119] and in the remaining case, the investigating entity was found not responsible for the anti-competitive conduct.[120]

During the period of study, the NCA adopted forty-three commitment decisions, because the alleged infringers proposed commitments that resolved the effects on competition arising from the conduct that was the subject of the investigation and the public interest was sufficiently ensured.[121] Only one of them was challenged by a third party, unsuccessfully.[122]

117. The largest unchallenged fine was EUR 525,000 to DAMM for RPM, resolution of 19/2/2009 (*Distribuciones DAMM* 647/08, rapp. Mª J González).
118. *See* Marcos *RDCD* 2023 §IV.5.
119. *See* TDC resolution of 21/6/2004 (562/03 *Colegio Notarial de Bilbao*, rapp. F Torremocha, with his dissenting opinion) and CNC resolution of 14/4/2009 (639/08 Colegio farmacéuticos Castilla-La Mancha, rapp. J. Costas, dissenting opinion MªJ González), both were confirmed by courts. *See*, correspondingly, judgments of High National Court of 21/11/2006 (ES:AN:2006:6058, rapp. JMª Del Riego) and Supreme Court of 26/4/2010 (ES:TS:2010:2063, rapp. MªI Perelló), and judgments of High Court of 6/6/2012 (ES:AN:2012:2564, rapp. CM Montero) and Supreme Court of 9/3/2015 (ES:TS:2015:800, rapp. E Calvo).
120. *See* CNC resolution of 2/11/2009 (S/51/08 *UNESA*, rapp. E Conde), confirmed by High National Court judgment of 22/7/2010 (ES:AN:2010:3671, rapp. L Acín) and judgment of Supreme 14/12/2011 (ES:TS:2011:8851, rapp. J Díez).
121. Article 152 of Spanish Competition Act 15/2007. *See* Marcos *RDCD* 2023 §IV.5.3 (5% of the NCA decisions are commitment decisions).
122. CNMC resolution of 9/7/2015 (S/466/13 *SGAE Autores*) concerning a potential exploitative abuse (Article 102 TFEU and article 2 Spanish Competition Act), judgment of High National Court of 25/4/2019 (*RTVE v. CNMC & SGAE*, ES:AN:2019:1845, rapp. SP Soldevila). Appeals against decisions declaring the infringement of the commitment decision are out of the scope of the project, e.g., CNC resolution of 28/1/2010 (S/20/07 *Trio Plus*, rapp. F Torremocha), in which the undertakings entering the commitments successfully challenged follow-up decisions

During the relevant period, twenty-three of the decisions of the NCA in which one or more of the parties successfully applied for leniency have been challenged before the courts (6% of the total NCA's decision under appeal). Among these challenges, three appeals were fully successful, while in fourteen others, the appeals achieved partial success. Forty-three of the total number of challenges in court against NCA decisions, included a dissenting opinion, representing 15.6% of the total judgments issued in the relevant period.[123] Moreover, half of the challenges against decisions containing a dissenting opinion resulted in the full annulment of the decision (seventeen), and half of the rest resulted in a reduction of the fine (eight). Therefore, it seems clear that there is some correlation between dissenting opinions in the NCA decision and the likelihood of full or partial success of any subsequent appeals.

4.5 Outcomes of Appeals: Two Case Studies

Given the number of individual appeals in Spain and the large number of judgments issued with respect to each NCA decision, this section presents two case studies that illustrate the outcome of judicial review on the NCA's decisions imposing fines. Subsection 4.4.1 looks at the outcome of the review of all NCA fining decisions adopted in the period, while subsection 4.4.2 examines in-depth the individual judgments issued deciding the challenges against a single NCA fining decision imposing fines to a large number of infringers: resolution of 19/10/2011 (S/226/10 *Licitaciones de Carreteras*).

4.5.1 Outcome of Judicial Review of All Fining Decisions

Figure 28.7 illustrates the outcome of the challenges against all the NCA fines imposed in the period 2004-2015. After all judicial review has been completed, 38% of the NCA fining decisions challenged in court have been confirmed.[124] Notably, since 2006 there

---

of the CNC which had declared their breach. First, resolution of 15/9/2011 (VATC/0020 *Trio Plus*, rapp. J. Costas), *see* judgment of High National Court of 23/12/2013 (*Telefónica v. CNC*, ES:AN:2013:5555, rapp. SP Soldevila) confirmed by judgment of Supreme Court of 11/1/2017 (STS de 11/1/2017, ES:TS:2017:60, rapp. Mª I Perelló); judgment of 23/12/2013 (*DTS/Prisa TV v. CNC*, rapp. SP Soldevila, ES:AN:2013:5761) confirmed by judgment of Supreme Court if 11/1/2017 (ES:TS:2017:62, rapp. Mª I Perelló). Second, resolution of 23/1/2013 (SNC/16/11 *Digital + Mini*, rapp. L. Díez), *see* judgments of High National Court of 18/3/2014 (*Sogecable v. CNC*, rapp. JE López, ES:AN:2014:1461) and 24/3/2014 (*Telefónica v. CNC*, rapp. CM Montero, ES:AN:2014:1433).

123. *See* Marcos *RDCD* 2023 §V.4 (the average of dissenting opinions in all the NCA decisions is half that: 7.76%). As could be expected, the empirical data shows that decisions imposing a fine are more likely to have a dissenting opinion (mostly regarding infringements of Article 101 TFEU).

124. A CNMC study published in May 2019, *Revisión jurisdiccional en el período 2014_2018 de las declaraciones de infracción de la autoridad nacional de competencia*, probably drafted in reaction to news about the dire performance of the CNMC in the Courts and lack of control over the collection of fines (*see* Tribunal de Cuentas *Informe de fiscalización de la Comisión Nacional de los Mercados y la Competencia, ejercicio 2014, y del proceso de integración en ella de los organismos públicos declarados a extinguir por la Ley 3/2013*, 26/5/2016, 28), examining 536 judgments deciding challenges against decisions of the CNC and CNMC issued by the High

has been a decreasing trend in the confirmation rate of NCA fining decisions: annulment or fine reduction have been a more likely outcome of judicial review.

Figure 28.7 Final Outcome of Judicial Review (Each NCA Decision Counts as One)

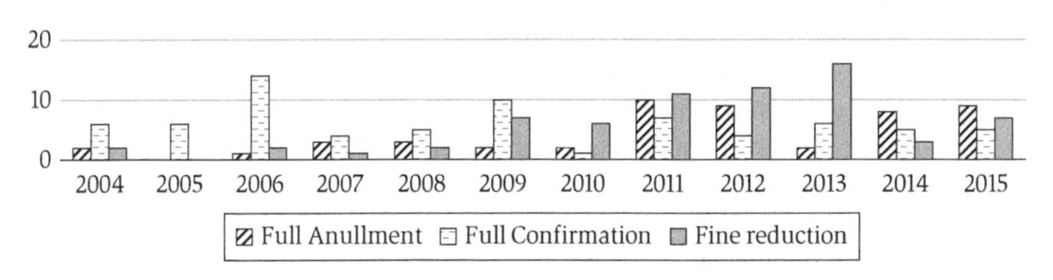

More than one-quarter of the NCA fines imposed from 2004-2015 were totally annulled by the Courts (26%).[125] Fifty-one decisions were fully quashed, with the peak of annulments relating to 2015 (almost half of the year decisions imposing fines in that year were annulled).[126] The figure includes two fines that were later reimposed by the NCA.[127]

Fining decisions are deemed to be fully annulled when the courts find the NCA decision to be unlawful, regardless of whether a few sanctioned undertakings did not challenge it, where it was annulled for all appellants.[128] They are also considered fully annulled when most of the fine has been quashed.

Full annulments normally occur when there is some common error or defect in the NCA decision that makes it invalid for all the undertakings. Most of the annulments were decided by the High National Court, many of them later confirmed by the Supreme Court, which occasionally changed the ground that led to the annulment by

National Court and the Supreme Court In the period 2014-2018 reports a 73.8% confirmation rate per decision (even higher - 83% - in the Supreme Court), but weirdly this study counts as confirmations those annulments of the decision that only concern the amount of the fine.

125. Naturally, this refers only to the project period. There were eight additional fining decisions adopted in 2016, 2017 and 2018 that had been annulled by judgments post 1/5/2021 on substantive grounds (S/DC/0503/14 *Fabricantes Turrón*; S/DC/0540/14 *ISTOBAL*;S/DC/0519/14 *Infraestructuras ferroviarias*; S/DC/0555/15 *Prosegur-Loomis*; S/DC/0545/15 *Hormigones Asturias*; SAMAD/06/2015 *ICAM-Justicia gratuita/Turno oficio*; SAMAD/12/2010 *Tanatorios Coslada*, and *Derivados Financieros* S/DC/579/16).

126. Within the project period until the end of 2015 (which is the last year fully reviewed by the courts), the total amount of fines imposed by the authorities amounted to EUR 1,697,153,916, of which around 40% were fully annulled by the Courts (EUR 723,270,118.30). That is 42.6% of the total fines imposed in the relevant period, the amount is a bit lower if EUR 88,258,813 fine imposed by CNMC resolution of 26/2/2015 (S/0425/12 *Industrias Lácteas 2*) and EUR 491,884 fine imposed by CNC resolution of 12/10/2017 (SAMAD12/10 Tanatorios Coslada) were excluded.

127. CNMC resolutions of 11/7/2019 (S/425/12 *Industrias Lácteas 2*) and of 12/10/2017 (SAMAD12/10 Tanatorios Coslada), though the later has already been fully annulled (High National Court judgment of 28/6/2023 (rapp. MDS Gandarillas, ES:AN:2023:3466).

128. Interestingly, in those cases, neither the NCA nor the courts extend any annulment to co-offenders that did not themselves appeal the fine when the decision was annulled for other undertakings (or was annulled based on other grounds). Likewise, the same applies when co-offenders requested an application to them of a reduction granted by the courts to a co-infringer.

the lower court.[129] Twenty-two NCA decisions annulled at first instance were not appealed in cassation and the appeals were inadmissible for four of them.

4.5.2 Outcome of Individual Challenges Against CNC Resolution of 19/10/2011 (S/226/10 **Licitaciones de Carreteras***)*

In many cases the outcome of judicial review may be different for some of the fined undertakings, so to illustrate the grounds and outcome of appeals in one of the cases with the largest number of appeals (*see supra* Table 28.2), all the challenges to one selected decision are examined. Given that each fined undertaking makes its own individual appeal, with different pleas and grounds of appeal, leading to a single judgment deciding upon each challenge, it is possible for there to be variations in the outcome of the different appeals, particularly regarding the absence of proof of the involvement of the undertaking in the infringement or in relation to the determination of the fine.

In this subsection we will focus on the review of one NCA decision, showcasing the typical review of a single fining decision adopted in the period analysed. This case concerned the infringement of Article 101 TFEU and Article 1 of the Spanish Competition Act, involving a cartel with forty-six co-offenders, sanctioned with a total fine of EUR 44,033,240 for coordinating their actions to alter the outcome of a roadworks public procurement.[130] The challenges against that single infringement decision gave way to a large number of judgments (seventy-seven in total): fifty-three first instance and twenty-four second instance.

All but two of the infringing companies challenged the decision before the High National Court, seven of them having the infringement decision annulled (for lack of evidence), and fifteen of the High National Court judgments were further challenged in cassation to the Supreme Court. For fourteen undertakings the High National Court ordered the NCA to re-calculate the fine, and the re-calculated fine was challenged again by eight of them, all of them (but one) being unsuccessful, three of them appealing in cassation to the Supreme Court. Figure 28.8 summarises the rate of success of appeals at both instances.

129. CNC resolution of 21/1/2010 (S/84/08 *Fabricantes Gel*) from substantive to both; TDC resolution of 7/7/2004 (552/02 *Empresas eléctricas*) from procedural to substantive.

130. CNC resolution of 19/10/2011 (S/226/10 *Licitaciones de Carreteras*, rapp. I Gutiérrez).

Figure 28.8 Success of Appeals Against Decision S/226/10 (Licitaciones de Carreteras)

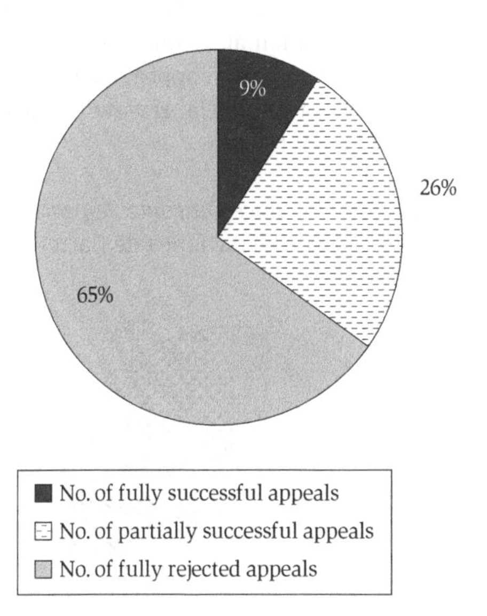

However, Figure 28.9 identifies the individual pleas and grounds used by each appellant and their degree of success. Substantive grounds followed by fine grounds were the more successful grounds of appeal. Appellants also complained about the conformity with EU Law of the system followed by the NCA for the calculation of the fine (regarding the turnover cap to the fines).

Figure 28.9 Grounds of Appeal Against Decision S/226/10 (Licitaciones de Carreteras)

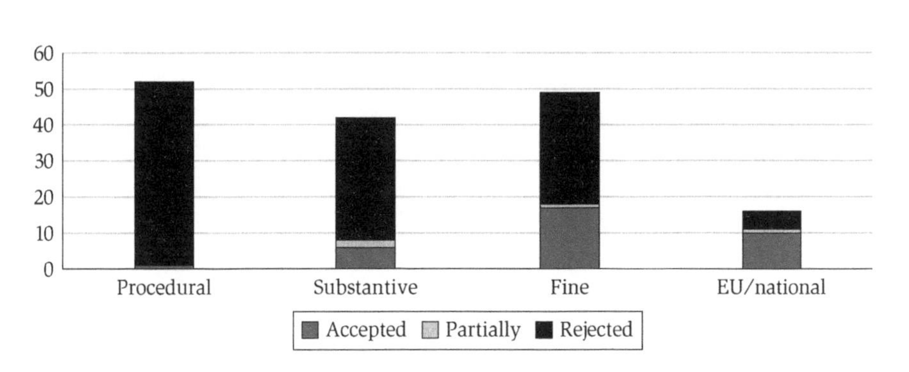

Finally, the next two figures look at the outcomes at first and second instances of all the appeals in this case. Full rejection of any appeal challenges was the most likely outcome both at first and second instances. Figures 28.10 and 28.11 show a larger variety of outcomes at first instance than at second instance, something that may be explained by the limited grounds of cassation appeal (*see supra* sections 2.3 and 2.5) and the progressive streamlining of the judicial review process following the earlier pronouncements of the High National Court.

*Figure 28.10 First-Instance Outcome Appeals Against Decision S/226/10 (*Licitaciones de Carreteras*)*

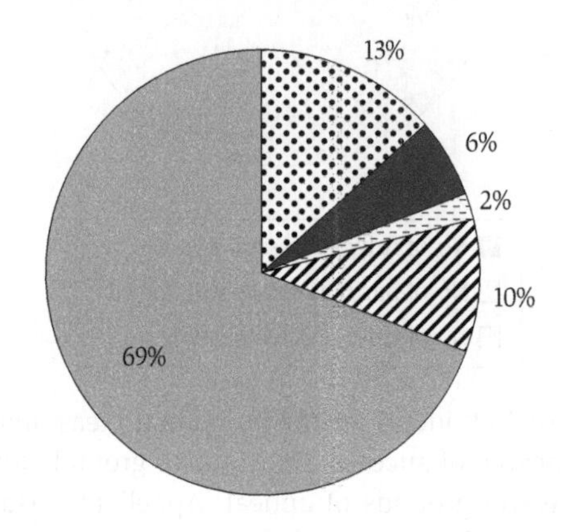

fully annulled	partially annulled, partially replaced
fully annulled, returned	partially annulled, returned
fully rejected (exc. withdrawn)	

Figure 28.11 Second-Instance Outcome Appeals Against Decision S/226/10 (Licitaciones de Carreteras)

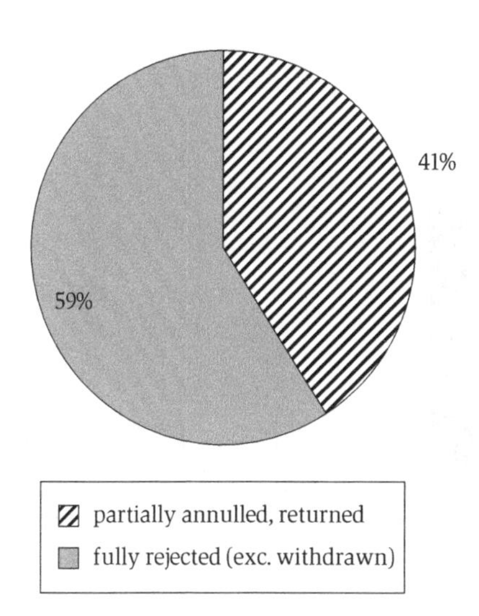

4.6 Grounds of Appeals: The Case Study of Appeals Against NCA Decisions Imposing Fines

Given the number of individual appeals in Spain and the large number of judgments issued with respect to each NCA decision, this section focuses on the grounds raised by the parties in judicial review against the NCA decisions imposing fines. As Figures 28.12 and 28.13 show the most frequent grounds leading to full annulment by the High National Court were substantive grounds (60%), and the percentage is even higher in the Supreme Court (67%).[131]

131. In very few cases, decisions were fully annulled both on substantive and procedural grounds, *see* Supreme Court judgments annulling CNC resolution of 21/1/2010 (S/84/08 *Fabricantes de Gel*) and High National Court judgments annulling CNC resolution of 24/11/2011 (S/232/10 *Prisa/Zeta*).

Figure 28.12 Grounds High National Court (Each NCA Decision Counts as One)

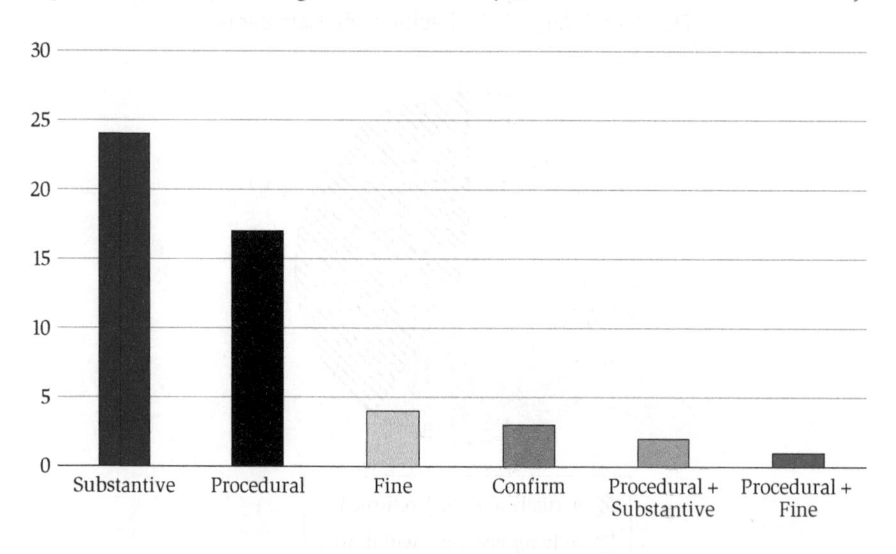

Figure 28.13 Grounds Supreme National Court (Each NCA Decision Counts as One)

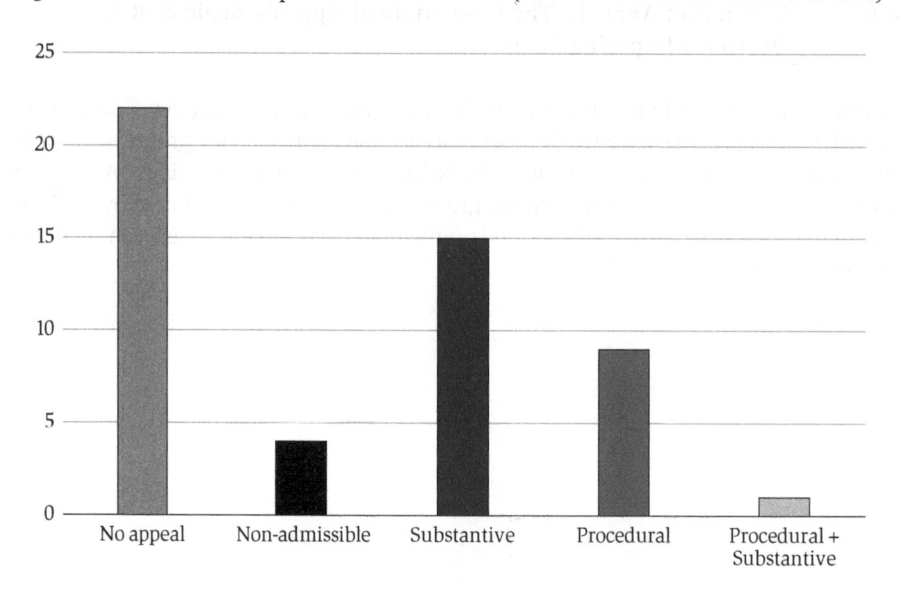

Note: The figures represent the information regarding the fifty-one NCA decisions overturned in their entirety at the end of the judicial review process.

4.6.1 *Substantive Grounds*

Substantive grounds of annulment are related to the lack of proof of the infringement or a mistaken assessment by the NCA. In these cases, the courts disagree with the NCA on the existence of infringement based on the available evidence. This has occurred both with infringements of Articles 101 TFEU and 102 TFEU (and/or their domestic equivalents). Courts have, for instance, disagreed with the NCA on market definition and the existence of dominance,[132] and on the anticompetitive features of joint ventures.[133] The absence of a single and continuous infringement has led to the annulment of several NCA decisions.[134] Lack of culpability or legitimate expectations arising from the involvement of the public administration in the infringing conduct is

132. Among the salient ones, *see, e.g.*, CNC resolution 19/10/2012 (S/248/10 Mensajes cortos, rapp. I Gutiérrez) which was quashed by the National High Court based on the questioning of the definition of relevant market (wholesale message termination market consisting exclusively of each operator's own network) and the alleged dominant positions of the three cellphone operators, *see* High National Court judgment of 4/9/2017 (*Telefónica Móviles España v. CNC*, rapp. B Santillán, ES:AN:2017:3556), confirmed by 20/12/2018 (rapp. D Córdoba, ES:TS:2018:4393), High National Court judgment of 1/9/2017 *Vodafone v. CNC*, rapp. SP Soldevila ES:AN:2017:3555), confirmed by Supreme Court Judgment of 8/1/2019 (rapp. E Espín, ES:TS:2019:253) and High national Court judgment of 1/9/2017 (*Orange v. CNC*, rapp. SP Soldevila, ES:AN:2017:3564), confirmed by Supreme Court Judgment of 21/12/2018 (rapp. A. Arozamena, ES:TS:2018:4566). *See also*, TDC Resolution 28/6/2007 (*613/06 Servicios funerarios La gomera*, rapp. I. Gutiérrez), annulled by High National Court judgment of 16/3/2009 (*MAPFRE Guanarteme v. TDC*, rapp. Mª A Salvo, ES:AN:2009:1415, with dissenting opinion CM Montero & JMª del Riego).

133. Two High National Court judgments annulled on substantive grounds CNC resolution of 15/10/2012 (S/318/10 *Exportación sobres papel*, rapp. MªJ González), judgment of 27/4/2017 (*PACSA v. CNC*, rapp. CM Montero, ES:AN:2014:3079, dissenting J Lopez, fine EUR 122,902) and judgment of 25/6/2014 (*SATMP v. CNC*, rapp. Mª A Salvo, ES:AN:2014:3201, fine EUR 274,028). Two others did the same, but they were later revoked by the Supreme Court, which ordered the CNMC to re-calculate the fine (same amount was imposed): High National Court judgment of 23/6/2014 (*Printeos v. CNC*, EUR 629,845 fine, rapp. S. Soldevila, ES:AN:2014:2921) revoked by Supreme Court judgment of 20/4/2017 (rapp. E Espín, ES:TS:2017:1593, the CNMC resolution of 20/7/2017 imposing a fine for the same amount) and High National Court judgment of 25/6/2014 (*Adveo v. CNC*, EUR 2,013,468 fine, rapp. MªA Salvo, ES:AN:2014:3207) revoked by Supreme Court judgment of 20/4/2017 (Rapp. JM Bandrés, ES:TS:2017:1528, the CNMC resolution of 24/4/2018 imposing a fine for the same amount).

    However, the EUR 5,650,483 fine imposed on four undertakings by CNMC resolution of 30/6/2016 (S/DC/519/14 *Infraestructuras ferroviarias*) was annulled by four High National Court judgments, the cassation appeals being unadmitted by the Supreme Court. *See* High National Court judgments of 27/12/2021 (*JEZ Sistemas Ferroviarios v. CNMC*. Rapp. MDS Gandarillas, ES:AN:2021:5847); 26/1/2022 (*Amurrio Ferrocarril v. CNMC*, rapp. F. de la Peña, ES:AN:2022:401) and 28/1/2022 (*Duro Felguera Rail v. CNMC*, rapp. BMª Santillán, ES:AN:2022:402; *Talleres Alegría v. CNMC*, ES:AN:2022:399).

134. *See* CNMC resolutions of 8/1/2015 (S/429/12 Residuos, EUR 98,201,302 fine), 11/2/2015 (S/464/13 *Puerto de Santander*, EUR 90,000 fine), 5/9/2016 (S/DC/525/14 Cementos, EUR 29,380,936 fine) and 12/9/7 (SAMAD/12/10 *Tanatorios Coslada*, EUR 141,884 fine).

the ground for annulment of some decisions.[135] Occasionally, there have been 'chain annulments' involving several decisions punishing similar anticompetitive conduct and they are all annulled sequentially as the courts revoked the substantive grounds in which the NCA supported its decisions.[136]

4.6.2 Procedural Grounds

Procedural grounds of annulment concern the handling of the investigation and proceedings by the NCA. As elaborated below, this can be due to the expiry of the deadline for the proceedings, for violation of the parties' right to due process, or for NCA excesses in conducting dawn raids.

Until 1997, the Competition Acts did not establish expiry deadlines for proceedings, but rather internal deadlines for the many procedures provided for therein.[137] Since then there has been a specific expiry date/deadline for investigations and proceedings by NCA (first it was thirty months, later twenty-four months, since 2007 it was eighteen months and now twenty-four months again).[138] The expiry date of the proceeding (*caducidad*) results in the closure of the proceeding due to its excessive duration (but still allowing the initiation of a new proceeding if the infringement is not time-barred).[139]

The law provides for the possible suspension of the deadline of the proceedings for specified causes, and in some cases, the appellants have been successful in challenging the validity of the suspension causes used by the NCA.[140] Several judgments have considered whether a request to the investigated undertakings to provide

135. *See* CNC resolutions of 20/1/2011 (S/196/09 *Colegio Notarial de Asturias*), 6/10/2011 (S/167/09 *Productores de Uva y Vinos de Jerez*) and 20/2/2013 (S/25/10 *Transcalit*).

136. Concerning abuses of dominant position in the electricity supply market, in the context of technical restrictions, *see* TDC/CNC resolutions of 7/7/2004 (552/02 Empresas eléctricas, rapp. Mª J. Muriel, dissenting A. Castañeda & M. Comenge) 28/12/2006 (602/05 Viesgo Generación, rapp. E. Conde), 14/2/2008 (624/07 *Iberdrola*, rapp. P. Nuñez) and 25/4/2008 (625/07 Gas Natural, rapp. MªJ González).

137. *See* judgment of Supreme Court of 31/3/2004 (*Caja Provincial de Ahorros de Tarragona, & Caja de Ahorros y Monte de Piedad de las Baleares v. TDC & Ausbanc*, rapp. E. Espín, ES:TS:2004:2228)

138. A maximum period for the proceedings is set to avoid the person concerned by the investigation being subjected to punitive proceedings and the associated legal uncertainty forever for reasons attributable to the NCA. Originally in Article 56 of Act 16/1989 (introduced by Act 66/1997, BOE 313 of 31/12/1987) it was 30 months (18 months in SDC and 12 Months in TDC), subsequently Act 52/1999 (BOE311 of 21/12/1999) reduced the duration to 12 months each, for a total of 24 months. Act 15/2007 reduced the expiry date to 18 months, in 2023 this period was extended to 24 months (Decree-Law 5/2023, BOE154 of 27/6/2023).

139. *See, e.g.*, CNMC resolution 17/7/2014 (S/345/11 *Criadores de Caballos*) sanctioning ANCCE with a EUR 152,833.32 fine, annulled by judgment of 13/11/2015 (*ANCCE v. CNMC*, rapp. JE López, ES:AN:2015:4121), but lead to a re-initiation of sanctioning proceedings, closed by CNMC resolution 21/11/2017 (S/DC/580/16 *Criadores de Caballos 2*) with a EUR 187,677 fine, confirmed by High National Court judgment of 8/9/2021 (*ANCCE v. CNMC*, rapp. F.de la Peña ES:AN:2021:3763), cassation appeal unadmitted by Order of 3/11/2022 (ES:TS:2022:15087A).

140. *See, e.g.*, judgment of the Supreme Court of 15/6/2015 (*Puig v. CNC*, rapp. MªI Perelló, ES:TS:2015:2797) that later led the High National Court to declare the expiration of those proceedings which had been suspended by the CNC once the ordinary (and initial) duration of

details of their previous year's turnover in order to establish the amount of the fine would allow the maximum time period of the proceedings to be extended.[141]

In the same vein, another infringement decision was annulled for abuse of the preliminary investigation phase (*information reservada*). The NCA had made an improper (unnecessary and unjustifiable) use of the confidential preliminary phase, with the consequence of postponing the date of initiation of the file and, thereby, artificially extending the limitations period.[142]

Several fining decisions have been annulled for due process violations (e.g., in relation to the NCA denial of a request for the taking of evidence,[143] or for a change in the qualification of the offence made by the investigating body without providing the accused with the right of defence).[144] Similarly, in two other cases, fines imposed on a leniency applicant were annulled because the decision which rejected the fine reduction that had been requested (and was proposed by the NCA Directorate of Competition in the SO and in the decision proposal) was made without a prior hearing being granted to the parties.[145]

---

the proceedings (eighteen months) had been exceeded, that led to annulment by the High National Court of most the fines imposed CNC resolution 23/5/2013 (S/303/10 *Distribuidores de Saneamiento*, rapp. I. Gutiérrez) and CNC resolution of 26/9/2013 (S/314/10 *Puerto de Valencia*, rapp. Mª J. González), the Supreme Court confirmed the full annulment of the first (but in two cases, *see* judgments of 26/7/2016, *Suministros Marval v. CNC*, Rapp. MªI Perelló, ES:TS:2016:3908; and of 3/4/2018, *Tubos y Hierros Industriales*, rapp. F Román, ES:TS:2018:1174, both ordering fine re-calculation), revoking the judgments annulling the second resolution, ordering instead the fine to be re-calculated by the CNMC.

141. *See* Antonio Creus 'Caducidad suspendida, se solicita volumen de negocios' *Anuario de Competencia ICO* 2019, 97-139.

142. *See* judgment of the High National Court of 23/12/2013 (*UAHE v. CNC*, rapp. SP Soldevila, ES:AN:2013:5772), annulling CNC resolution of 14/6/2012 (S/254/10 Hierros Extremadura, rapp. J. García, EUR 500,000 fine).The opening of the preliminary investigation is justified to the extent that it serves to corroborate the *notitia criminis*, which in the present case was completely unnecessary, since the CNC had full and absolute knowledge of the evidence founding its decision (e-mails and appellant's allegations regarding them), as they were both expressed within the CNC resolution of 17/5/2010 (S/106/08 *Almacenes de Hierro*, rapp. J Costas), in which the CNC had used them.

143. *See* judgment of 10/12/2009 (fundamental rights proceedings, *SOS Cuetara v. TDC*, rapp. J. Díaz, ES:TS:2009:7888), leading to three other Supreme Court judgments and four High National Court judgments annulling the decision for that reason.

144. Nine judgments of the High National Court annulled for that reason CNC resolution of 2/1/2014 (S/404/12 *Servicios Comerciales AENA*). Likewise, see n.71 and 114 concerning the annulment of CNC resolution of 26/2/2015 (S/4125/12 *Industrias Lácteas 2*).

 The High National Court had also annulled the decision fining the pallet cartel as the qualification of the infringement as a 'single and continuous' was done without hearing of the investigated undertakings. Twenty judgments of the High National Court annulled CNMC resolution of 22/9/2014 (S/428/12 Palés), mostly for that reason, the Supreme Court revoked most of them, ordering the fine to be re-calculated by the CNMC.

145. *See* Supreme Court Judgment of 30/10/2013 (*Wella v. CNC*, ES:TS:2013:6144, rapp. NA Maurandi) confirming the annulment by the High National Court of the EUR 12,032,000 fine imposed by the CNC resolution of 2/3/2011, S/86/08 *Peluquería Profesional*, rapp. MªJ González). *See also* Supreme Court judgment of 21/5/2014 (*Balearia Eurolíneas Marítimas v. CNC*, ES:TS:2014:2018, rapp. JL Díaz), confirming the annulment by the High National Court (judgment of 8/11/2012, rapp. Mª A. Salvo, ES:AN:2012:4494) of the EUR 15,214,402 fine imposed by the CNC resolution of 23/2/2012 (S/244/10 *Navieras Baleares*, rapp. P. Sánchez).

Finally, dawn raids allow the competition authorities to access the business domiciles of the investigated companies to search for evidence if they have a suspicion of the commission of an infringement.[146] Obviously, the inspection rules must have safeguards that prevent abuses and preserve the guarantees of the investigated undertakings.[147]

Correcting the excesses of the NCA in carrying out dawn raids, six fining decisions have been annulled as courts considered that they were adopted based on evidence which was obtained in a dawn raid conducted unlawfully. Most rulings concerning the legality of inspections by the competition authorities are founded on the rulings of the CJEU and the General Court on the matter (in relation to challenges against the European Commission's dawn raids).

146. Article 40 of Act 15/2007 and Article 27 of Act 13/2013.

147. *See supra* n. 72. Courts require the inspection activity to be duly justified in the investigation order, specifying the object and purpose of the inspection. *See* Supreme Court Judgment of 1/6/2015 (*Transmediterranea v. CNC*, rapp. E Espín, ES:TS:2015:2560) annulling the EUR 12,102,969 fine imposed on Transmediterranea by CNC resolution of 10/11/2011 (S/0241/10 Navieras Ceuta 2, rapp. J Costas); Supreme Court judgment of 1/6/2015 (*Transmediterranea v. CNC*, rapp. E Espín, ES:TS:2015:2559) annulling the EUR 36,110,800 fine imposed on Transmediterranea by CNC resolution of 23/1/2012 (S/244/10 Navieras Baleares, rapp. P Sánchez).

See High National Court judgments of 20/3/2015 (*Gas Natural v. CNC*, J. E. Lopez Candela, ES:AN:2015:876; Endesa v. CNC, rapp. CM Montero, ES:AN:2015:1070); 23/3/2015 (*Hidrocantábrico v. CNC*, rapp. S. Soldevila, ES:AN:2015:1069), 24/3/2015 (*E.ON España v. CNC*, rapp. JE López, ES:AN:2015:877) 25/3/2015 (*UNESA v. CNC*, rapp. AI Resa, ES:AN:2015:875; *Iberdrola v. CNC*, rapp. AI Resa, ES:AN:2015:874), annulling the EUR 52,400,000 fines imposed by CNC resolution of 14/5/2011 (S/0159/09 UNESA y asociados, rapp. I Gutiérrez).

Eleven of the fourteen undertakings fined by CNMC decision of 6/11/2014 (S/0430/12 Recogida de papel, with two dissenting opinions) successfully challenged it before the Supreme Court on the basis that the supporting evidence was found in the course of another investigation (S/0415/12 *ABH-ISMA*), *see* Supreme Court judgments of 18/2/2019 (*Alba Servicios Verdes v. CNMC*, rapp. JM Bandrés, ES:TS:2019:671, EUR 577,795), 25/2/2019 (*S. Solis v. CNMC*, rapp. E Calvo ES:TS:2019:583, EUR 432,232), 26/2/2019 (*Irmasol v. CNMC*, rapp. JMª del Riego, ES:TS:2019:670, EUR 603,685), 26/2/2019 (*Hijos de Demetrio Fernández v. CNMC*, rap. AR Arozamena, ES:TS:2019:585, EUR 465,372), 26/2/2019 (*UDER v. CNMC*, rapp. D Córdoba, ES:TS:2019:581, EUR 150,000), 4/3/2019 (*Ramón Vilella v. CNMC*, rapp. MªI Perelló, ES:TS:2019:1072, EUR 147,280), 12/3/2019 (*Destrudatos Confidencial v. CNMC*, MP: AR Arozamena, ES:TS:2019:812, EUR 10,000), 11/6/2019 (*Utramic v. CNMC*, rapp. JMª del Riego, ES:TS:2019:3256, EUR 285,830); Recio y Cabral v. CNMC, rapp. E Espín, ES:TS:2019:2005); 19/10/2019 (*Rua Papel Gestión v. CNMC*, rapp. E. Espín, ES:TS:2019:3411, EUR 354,888) and 20/5/2020 (*ISMA 2000 v. CNMC*, rapp. JMª del Riego, ES:TS:2020:1257, EUR 190,298).

The court order authorising the NCA inspection is not necessary, although the NCA must inform the company if it was requested, and it was rejected. *See* Supreme Court judgment of 15/6/2015 (*Montibello v. CNC*, rapp. Mª I Perelló, ES:TS:2015:2879), annulling for that reason the EUR 2,555,000 fine imposed to Montibello (Cosmetica Cobar) by CNC resolution (S/86/08 *Peluquería Profesional*, rapp. MªJ González). *See also* Supreme Court judgment of 17/9/2018 (*Repsol v. CNMC*, rapp. E Calvo, ES:TS:2018:3106) revoking High National Court judgment of 21/7/2016 (rapp. AI Resa, ES:AN:2016:3205), which had confirmed CNC resolution of 24/7/2013 (R/142/2013 *Repsol*).

4.6.3 *Grounds Relating to the Amount of the Fines*

The most successful ground of appeal concerns the amount of the fine, normally leading to the case being sent back to the NCA and the fine being re-calculated. More than half of the 2010-2013 NCA decisions challenged in court were partially annulled by courts because of the calculation of the fine, requiring the NCA to recalculate the fines. This trend seems to have decreased in the judicial review outcomes of the 2014-2015 decisions, although the courts also took a considerable chunk out of the fines imposed these last two years, via total annulments.[148] The Courts either reduced the fine (or ordered it to be recalculated by the NCA) in 38% of the NCA decisions challenged in court. The probability that the fine will be reduced after judicial review is the same as the probability that the fine will be upheld.

Of the total amount of fines imposed by the Spanish NCA in the period 2004-2015 (EUR 1,697,072,921), only 43% survived after judicial review (EUR 738,073,925), although the reduction in fines after judicial intervention varies over time, ranging from 100% confirmation of fines imposed in 2005 to reductions exceeding 70% of fines imposed in 2006, 2007 and 2009 (*see* Table 28.13).

Table 28.3 Fines/Surviving Fines/Confirmation Rate

	Fines (EUR)	*Survive after Review (EUR)*	*Confirmation Rate (%)*
2004	21,647,554.5	10,632,500	49.1
2005	9,588,000	9,588,000	100
2006	24,467,000	17,907,993.8	73.2
2007	70,316,064	50,660,849	72
2008	34,784,781	14,447,490.4	41.5
2009	204,201,665	154,253,486	75.5
2010	40,988,031	23,635,827.2	57.7
2011	224,498,636	104,489,812	46.5
2012	346,418,014	67,251,617.5	19.4
2013	185,951,102	106,311,849	57.2
2014	115,442,838	14,916,954	12.9
2015	418,769,235	163,976,916	39.1
TOTAL	1,697,072,921	738,073,295	43.5

Until 2010 the Courts rarely contested the amount of the fine imposed by the NCA. Since 2010, first the High National Court and later the Supreme Court have questioned the fines, annulling them, and urging their recalculation downwards, in many cases considering them not to be proportionate.[149] The judgments of the High

148. Apart from total annulments, fines have been reduced via partial annulments by EUR 336,539,389.3 in the relevant period.

149. A comprehensive empirical analysis of the High National Court judgments, in CARMEN LILLO 'La Audiencia Nacional ante las sanciones impuestas por la CNMC en aplicación de la Ley 15/2007, de Defensa de la Competencia' *RDCD* 15 (2014) 51-82.

National Court had as a corollary a judgment of the Supreme Court of 29/1/15.[150] According to the Supreme Court, the scheme followed for calculating the amount of the fine set in the NCA Guidelines on setting the amount of fines lacked an adequate legal basis.[151] For the Supreme Court, the initial point and framework for determining the level of fines under the 2007 Competition Act should follow the sliding scale set in Article 63.1. This approach should consistently guide the quantification techniques employed in the process. It emphasised that the legal framework cannot merely serve as an external boundary, as seen in the 2009 Guidelines on fines, to be applied once the fine amount is estimated using a specified methodology. While this method might be acceptable in EU Law per Article 23 of Regulation 1/2003 (which establishes the ultimate limit for fines) the Supreme Court disagreed that this was a suitable approach within Spanish Law. Authorities imposing sanctions must adhere to the fundamental principles and constraints of punitive law. This includes the legal predetermination of maximum and minimum fine amounts – whether they are fixed or percentage-based in relation to certain criteria – as a fundamental and unalterable principle of punitive law.[152] Since 2015, the NCA had to re-calculate many fines set according to the previous system, which was annulled on this point,[153] and it was required to stop following the Communication of fines in new cases, modifying the process and criteria for setting fines and their justifications, leading to confusion as to how fines should be calculated. Now, the concern that penalties should respect the principle of proportionality has led to a reduction in their amount, which may mean that they no longer provide a sufficient deterrent.[154]

One of the issues raised by the judicial review of fines imposed is that it affects how EU infringements have been punished by the Spanish NCA. EU Law does not require Member States to harmonise their fines.[155] Spanish law can follow a different

150. *BCN Aduanas y Transportes,* ES:TS:2015:112 (rapp. M Campos). *See* Francisco Marcos 'Blowing hot and cold: The last word of the Supreme Court on setting fines for competition infringements in Spain' *Revista de concorrência e regulação* 25 (2016) 17-34.

151. CNC, *Communication of 6/2/2009, on the quantification of fines for infringements of Articles 1, 2 and 3 of Act 15/2007, of July 3, 2007, on the Defense of Competition and Articles 81 and 82 of the Treaty of the European Community* (BOE36 of 11/2/2009). It combined features of the legal regime set out in the 2007 Competition Act with several extra-legal elements which, inspired in the 2006 Guidelines of the European Commission on the method of setting fines imposed pursuant to Article 23(2)(a) of Regulation N° 1/2003 (OJEU C2010 of 1/9/2006).

152. 'The legal predetermination of the maximum and minimum amount of fines –criminal and administrative (whether they are a fixed amount or a percentage on certain magnitudes)– in order to individualize their calculation may well be considered a common un-surmountable principle of punitive law' (5th Legal ground, ¶5 of Supreme Court judgment of 29/6/2015, *BCN Aduanas y Transportes,* ES:TS:2015:112, rapp. M Campos).

153. Given that the appeal is granted solely based on how the NCA interpreted and followed the criteria established in the Competition Act to set the amount of the fine, and the motivation given, it may well be that the amount of the fine imposed by infringement decision is the same. However, the new decision may still be further challenged in court on this same ground, albeit these second time appeals are almost always rejected.

154. *See* Ane M. Martín, Carlos Merino & Javier García 'Determinants of the Deterrence of Competition Fines in Spain (2015-2019)' *Journal of European Competition Law & Practice* 13/6 (2022) 401-412 (with reference to previous works arriving at the same conclusion).

155. Articles 13 to 15 of ECN + Directive have reduced the scope of autonomy of national legislators on this point but has not entailed any modification in Spanish legislation.

punitive path from that used in EU Regulation 1/2003, and when the NCA applies TFEU Articles 101 and 102, the approach employed for infringements of domestic prohibitions should be utilised.[156] Finally, as long as the fines imposed are effective, proportionate and have deterrent force, no objection can be raised against the fines imposed according to the domestic rules.

4.7 Undertakings and Third Parties' Appeals

Enforcement decisions in relation to the prohibitions adopted by the NCA can be challenged by anyone with legitimate rights and interests affected by them.[157] At first instance, most of the decisions are appealed by undertakings that are declared to have infringed the prohibitions, but appeals are also made by third parties (complainants).[158] *Amicus curiae* are not allowed in Spanish Procedure Law, but the European Commission may present written observations on appeals proceedings against NCA decisions when it considers it appropriate to ensure the coherent enforcement of Articles 101 or 102 TFEU.[159]

At first instance, 73% of NCA decisions are challenged by the undertakings, while 27% are appealed by third parties, generally against decisions finding no infringement.[160] In appeals before the National High Court, the NCA, as the entity responsible for the decision challenged, always acts as the defendant and other co-infringers may participate as well. No data is provided regarding second-instance appeals but given that often first-instance appeals are successful, the NCA is frequently the appellant on cassation to the Supreme Court.[161]

Third-party challenges were rejected in 83% of the cases, in which the courts have ratified the NCA's decision. In addition, 8% of the appeals were found inadmissible, as the appellant was found not to have standing. In the few cases in which third-party challenges were accepted (9%), the reviewing court generally sent the case

156. Article 5 of Regulation 1/2003.
157. Article 19.1.a) of Act 29/1998.
158. *See* Judgment of 26/6/2007 (*Grupo Godó & Prisa*, rapp. E Espín, ES:TS:2007:5173, dissents by M. Campos & O. González) annulling the TDC decision of 18/4/2001 (487/2000 *Radio Fórmula*, rapp. A Castañeda) declaring the infringement of article 1 of Act 16/1989 with no additional remedies.
159. Article 16 of regulation 1/2003 and article 15bis of Act 1/2000 on Civil Procedure. This seldom occurs but it did in six cassation appeals before the Supreme Court of the infringement decision on the decennial insurance (CNC Resolution of 12/11/2009 (S/0037/08 *Compañías de Seguro Decenal*, Rapp. J. Costas). An analysis of the catastrophic judicial review of such decision is made in Marcos *ADI* 36 (2016) 173-196.
160. The evolution of third parties' appeals in the period shows a clear decreasing trend, which runs parallel to the progressive reduction in the number of NCA non-fining decisions, *see* Marcos *RDCD* 2023 §IV.3.
161. NCA representation and legal assistance is carried out by State's legal counsels (*see* Additional Provision 9th of Act 15/2007; Act 52/1997 on legal assistance to the State and Public Institutions, BOE 285 of 27/11/1997; Additional provision 4th of Act 50/1998, BOE 313 of 31/12/1998; and Decree 649/23, BOE 172 of 20/7/2023). The CNMC entered successive agreements with the State Legal Service setting the terms of service (*see* agreement 6/6/2016; agreement 13/5/2018 and addendum 5/3/2020).

back to the NCA for a new investigation/decision,[162] leading to a new decision being adopted.

5 QUALITATIVE ANALYSIS

As the empirical evidence in the previous section shows, most of the challenges against the decisions of the NCAs are concentrated in fining decisions (95.5% of the decisions imposing fines were appealed).[163]

The fines imposed by the NCA generate unparalleled litigation. Undertakings appeal everything (not only the fine but also prior procedural decisions when feasible, and any subsequent decisions as well), and lawyers for the defendants/sanctioned parties take every chance to have the courts scrutinise the action of the NCA. Defence attorneys do not miss any opportunity to challenge the NCA's decisions whenever there is an opportunity to go to court, preferably several times (each and every time it is possible), and for every conceivable reason, without fear that it may harm any relationship with the NCA. Strikingly, they appeal against the fine even if its amount is less than the legal costs of processing the appeals and even if the chances of success of some of the motions filed are minimal.

Challenging the fines delays their final confirmation, but since the offenders must pay or guarantee the amount of the fine (*see supra* section 1.3), this delay is costly. Naturally, the increasing success of appeals filed against fining decisions adopted by the NCA since 2007 changes the incentives to challenge them. Even so, the volume of litigation related to NCA enforcement proceedings is exaggerated. It is difficult to find a plausible explanation for the above behaviour, although it is conceivable that the repetition of motions before the courts is a successful strategy that seeks to contribute to the creation of a momentum in which the courts accept some of the multiple pleas raised by the appellants.

In the case of multiple infringers, separate appeals are filed by each of them, which leads to individual judicial review for each infringer.[164] Although the appeals against each of the NCA decisions are heard by the reviewing courts around the same period, and there may be common issues raised by appellants, neither the High Court nor the Supreme Court consolidates or hears them jointly. Given that both courts are collegiate bodies, and even though the rapporteurs for each of the individual appeals may be different, there tends to be a consensus as to how appeals concerning each NCA

162. In one case, the Supreme Court quashed the dismissal decision of the NCA (TDC resolution of 30/10/2008, R734/08 *ASPA/Asepeyo*, rapp. M Cuerdo) proceeding itself to declare an infringement of article 7 of the Act 16/1989, *see* Supreme Court judgment of 4/3/2014 (*ASPA v. CNC*, rapp. M Campos, ES:TS:2014:784).

163. In other regulatory areas (financial regulation) the rates of appeal of fines are much lower, *see* Roy Gava 'Challenging the regulators: Enforcement and appeals in financial regulation' *Regulation & Governance* 16/4 (2022) 1274 (reporting a 38% rate of appeal against fined imposed by the CNMV and a 44% rate of appeal against fines imposed by the Bank of Spain),

164. Regularly, those found to be co-offenders appear in court even in other appeals regarding the same infringement decision, as co-defendants, as their rights and interests may be affected by the judgment. *See* Article 21.1.b) of Act 29/1998.

decision are resolved (although dissenting opinions are common).[165] One-off changes in the circumstances of each appellant, either regarding its involvement in the infringement or the legal arguments raised, explain potential divergences in the outcome of appeals for each of them.

As this report shows, Courts exercise a broad and intense review of NCA decisions.[166] Aside from the idiosyncratic procedural features of Spanish administrative procedure which explain the large number of judgments delivered, the courts fully scrutinise all questions of law and of fact, reviewing the assessment of the facts and the legality of the investigation/sanctioning proceedings. That helps to explain the large number of decisions quashed on substantive grounds (assessment of the potential infringing conduct by the NCAs) and on the basis of procedural improprieties.[167]

Judicial review of the substance of the infringements extends not only to the material accuracy of the evidence relied upon, its reliability and consistency but also to the relevance of the data and its adequacy to support the conclusions reached. This includes the definition of the relevant market and the assessment of the market position and the behaviour of the undertakings (including the alleged dominant position of one or more undertakings on that market in 102 TFEU cases). Thus, when the courts find that the NCA deductions made do not have a sufficient and reliable basis or that there is no logical correspondence between the decision reached and the data on which it is based, they annul the decision.[168]

As other empirical studies of administrative appeals before the Spanish courts show,[169] there is no pro-NCA bias on the part of the courts, on the contrary, there is no deference to the NCA's decision. Spanish Courts follow the CJEU's case law on the scope of judicial review of complex economic assessments in their review of NCA decisions.[170] Courts verify the rationality of the assessment reached by the competition authorities, including the reliability, accuracy and coherence of the data supporting the declaration of infringement. They do not afford the competition authorities any margin of appreciation with respect to complex economic assessments in the establishment of an infringement.

165. Mostly at the High National Court level, less frequently in the Supreme Court.
166. Precisely the opposite of what has been stated in a previous empirical study. *see* Mejia *Regulatory Governance* 15/3 (2021) 773 ('litigation against agencies in Spanish generalist courts allow a greater degree of deference to regulatory decisions concerning the technical discretion granted to regulators, and the scope of review is commonly limited to scrutinize procedural aspects of an agency decision (coded in this research as rule of law and individual rights principles').
167. Other empirical studies of judicial review of regulatory authorities' fines report lower annulment rates, *see* Ruiz *El control jurisdiccional de los organismos reguladores*, 2018, 206-297 (35% in telecommunications and 26% in energy).
168. *See, e.g.*, Supreme Court judgments of 20/12/2018 (*Telefónica v. CNMC*, rapp. D Córdoba, ES:TS:2018:4393) and 21/12/2018 (*Orange v. CNMC*, rapp. AR Arozamena, ES:TS:2018:4566) and 8/1/2019 (*Vodafone v. CNMC*, rapp. E. Espín, ES:TS:2019:253).
169. *See* Sofia Amaral-Garcia & Nuno Garoupa 'Do Administrative Courts Favour Government? Evidence from Medical Malpractice in Spain?' *Journal of European Tort Law* 6/3 (2015) 795-826 (365 medical malpractice cases decided by the Spanish Supreme Court in 2006-2010).
170. ¶54 of CJEU judgments 8/12/2011 (C-386/10P *Chalkor*, EU:C:2011:815) on collusion, and ¶54 of CJEU of 10/7/2014 (C-295/12 *Telefónica*, EU:C:2014:2062) on abuse of dominance.

6 CONCLUDING REMARKS

This report analyses the judicial review of Spanish NCA decisions on infringements of the prohibitions of Articles 101 and 102 TFEU (and their analogues in domestic legislation) between May 2004 and the end of April 2021. However, given the backlog in judicial review this only allowed an examination of data relating to the review of NCA decisions adopted until 2015. The high number of judgments issued in judicial review and the disparity in their content makes the information and data provided in this report stand apart from those followed for the rest of the jurisdictions examined in this project, nonetheless, empirical evidence on the judicial review of competition law enforcement in Spain between May 2004 to April 2021 presented in this report shows:

- In the period subject to this study, judicial review was complete for 274 NCA decisions, leading to 1,390 judgments.
- NCA decisions are regularly appealed, no matter their content.[171] However, as could be expected, an appeal is almost certain in the case of a fining decision, but an appeal cannot be ruled out if the decision is to close the case or not to initiate proceedings, although an appeal is very unlikely in commitment decisions.
- Challenges against NCA decisions were rejected in 51% of the judgments, appeals were successful in 19% of the judgments and partially successful in 30% of the judgments.
- There is a very low degree of acquiescence of those undertakings fined by the NCA: 95.5% of fining decisions are appealed. Thirty-eight percent of the NCA fines imposed from 2004 to 2015 were fully confirmed, but 26% of them were totally annulled by the Courts, and 38% of them were reduced. Of the total amount of fines imposed by the NCA in the period 2004-2015 (EUR 1,697,072,921), only 43% survived after judicial review (EUR 738,073,925).
- Logically, the degree of acquiescence is higher for complainants: 27% of NCA decisions to close an investigation without declaring an infringement or decision not to open an investigation are appealed (mostly unsuccessfully, in 91% of cases). Moreover, evidence shows that fewer and fewer of this type of decision are challenged and this trend is likely to continue as the NCA prioritisation measures are put into practice.

The extraordinary tendency to litigiousness is highlighted by the fact that investigated parties challenge not only the final NCA decision, until no more appeals are possible (and through all alternative proceedings available) but also a multitude of NCA procedural decisions. Every decision adopted by the NCA is appealed, and this

171. *See* Emilio Huerta 'Competencia, Innovación empresarial y productividad: el papel de la defensa de la competencia en la prosperidad de España' in A. Betancor et al (ed) *Defensa de la Competencia: innovación y control en el contexto de la tradición intervencionista*, F. Ramón Areces 2020, 166 ('*Controversial court rulings challenging previous investigations carried out by competition authorities are frequently observed*').

extreme trend is also demonstrated by evidence showing appeals being filed even against NCA advocacy reports.[172]

The prevalent litigation strategy consists of invoking as many arguments as possible in appeals, both substantive and procedural, even if they are relatively weak. Since a court must in any case review all of them, this is seen as a strategy to maximise the chances of raising a point that will lead to annulment or changes in the decision or ruling under appeal.

Practically all the fines imposed by the NCA are appealed in the confidence that it is highly probable that the judges will review the NCA's pronouncement at some point. This can be confirmed by the results set out in this report. Given that the probability of confirmation of the prior decision is lower than that of annulment or reduction, what is the point of acquiescence? In terms of judicial review, the Spanish NCA finds itself in a vicious circle that is difficult to escape.

Finally, contrary to what one might expect, and to what tends to happen in other jurisdictions, Spanish courts' judgments quashing NCA fines are not grounded on formal/procedural issues: more than half of the complete annulments of fines are for substantive reasons, although there are many decisions annulled for procedural reasons, including a dozen cases in which the authorities missed the deadline for the proceedings.

The previous sections clearly reveal the judicial bottleneck generated by appeals against NCA fines, which makes it difficult to perform an exhaustive analysis like that undertaken for the rest of the jurisdictions in this project. The Spanish experience tends to involve several companies that appeal simultaneously against the same decision, and subsequent court rulings that may vary in their outcome, depending on the appellant and the result of its appeal.

The backlog also affects the NCA itself, since the return of most of the decisions to the authority for the recalculation of the fine allows the undertakings to start the appeal process again (usually without success in that phase), which makes it not unusual for more than a decade to elapse from the initiation of the case until the outcome of the case (and appeal process) is final.

172. *See* judgment of 5/10/2015 (*Repsol YPF v. CNC*, rapp. E Calvo, ES:TS:2015:4096) confirming the High National Court judgment of 29/11/2012 (rapp. MªA Salvo, ES:AN:2012:4829), that rejected the challenge against CNC Follow-up report on the CNC's Automotive Fuels Report (*Informe de seguimiento del Informe de Carburantes para la Automoción de la CNC*).

CHAPTER 29
Sweden Report

Lars Henriksson

1 INTRODUCTION TO THE COMPETITION LAW ENFORCEMENT CONTEXT IN SWEDEN

In the 1800s, commercial trade was strictly regulated in Sweden and although policies changed in 1864 when Sweden introduced the general freedom to conduct business,[1] such liberalisation initiatives did not result in competition on markets being established automatically or working properly. Free competition was indeed an altogether new concept for many traders and companies in those early days compared to how markets work today.

In 1925, the first steps were taken to give authorities the power to investigate monopoly activities and restrictive agreements, although that law only had marginal significance.[2] A new Act on surveillance of anti-competitive agreements was enacted in 1946,[3] whereby a monopoly surveillance bureau was established within the National Board of Trade (*Kommerskollegium*) and a cartel register was set up, providing the surveillance authority with power only to monitor but not act against anti-competitive

1. The statutory guilds were abandoned in Sweden in 1846. The mandatory membership of city burghership, masteries and the mandatory membership of certain associations were discontinued in 1864. *See* SFS 1864:41 *Näringsfrihetsförordning* (commonly known as the 'Magna Carta' of business law in Sweden).
2. *See*, lagen den 18 juni 1925 om undersökning angående monopolistiska företag och sammanslutningar. The law gave HRH (in practice his government's authority) or one or more special experts the power to undertake investigations of a company or an association which could be assumed to be of a monopolistic nature. The investigating agency had extensive rights to obtain all the information required for the investigation. The law was applied only in a few cases, e.g., investigations concerning the milling companies, the yeast manufacturers, the sugar manufactures, the porcelain manufacturers and the fuel and lubricating oil companies.
3. Lag om övervakning av konkurrensbegränsning inom näringslivet (SFS nr 448). The law was later replaced and repealed by the introduction of the 1956 Information Disclosure Act (*uppgiftsskyldighetslagen*) concerning price and competitive conditions (SFS 1956:245).

agreements. The Surveillance Act was kept when the legislator in 1953 passed the first Act on harmful anti-competitive behaviour, criminalising vertical price restrictions and bidding cartels (The Anti-competitive Practices Act).[4] Central to that legislation was *the harmful effect of a restriction of competition*, which should be understood as restrictions of competition that in a general way improperly affected price formation, inhibited the effectiveness of the business world or made it difficult or hindered another undertaking's business practice.

These rules on competition were later updated in 1982. The substantive rules remained the same, whereas some changes were introduced to the criminalised behaviour. Alongside the possibility of curbing unwanted restrictions, the legislator also introduced the first national rules on merger control.[5] The national Swedish rules, therefore, developed unaligned with EEC rules and focused more on corrective measures rather than general prohibitions. As such, Swedish macroeconomic policies differed from the German competition laws (e.g., the *Wirtschaftspolitik* and *Wettbewerbsrecht*),[6] which in turn partly were the basis for Articles 85 and 86 of the Treaty of Rome 1957.

The older Swedish rules prior to 1993 were based on an ad hoc assessment of individual market behaviour with the view of rectifying the unwanted behaviour – primarily *in casu*. They did not contain any broad or general prohibitions on restrictive agreements or abuse of dominance, although some exceptions existed, e.g., criminalisation of bidding cartels. As such, the national rules were coordinated with rules on unfair marketing and consumer protection rules. Competition rules were embedded in a system of market regulation that covered also unfair trading practices, price regulation and considerable state intervention in individual agreements. This is also why several authorities worked in parallel to counteract unwanted market behaviour.

The Market Court, the Consumers' Ombudsman, the Office of the Competition Ombudsman (Näringsfrihetsombudsmannen, NO), the State's Price, and Cartel Authority (Statens pris- och kartellnämnd, from 1988: The Price and Competition Authority, Statens pris- och konkurrensverk) constituted the enforcement agencies until 1992.[7] The Market Court decided on cases related to the 1953 Anti-Competitive Practices Act, as the first and only forum for decision-making.[8] Appeals, in other words, were until 1993 not permissible.[9]

In addition, the macroeconomic policies of the 1970s and 1980s entailed a high degree of state market intervention and price control, which was administered by the

4. *See* Lagen den 25 september 1953 (nr 603) om motverkande i vissa fall av konkurrensbegränsning inom näringslivet m. m.; given Stockholms slott den 23 mars 1956.
5. 1982 Competition Act; Konkurrenslag, SFS 1982:729.
6. Cf. Gesetz gegen Wettbewerbsgeschränkungen (GWB), BGBI, I S. 1081, 27 July 1957.
7. A new competition authority was established 1 July 1992 and assumed all responsibilities from NO and SPK, Government Bill 1991/92:100 bil 13, p. 133, NU20, rskr 237. Pursuant to the introduction of the new EC-based competition rules in 1993, the duties of the of authority was changed.
8. *See* Näringsutskottets betänkande nr 41 år 1973, p. 7.
9. Before 1993, the Market Court had distinct a precedent-setting role. It was the first and last instance in the cases it handled and, therefore, its decision could not be appealed. *See* Government Bill 1992/93:56, p. 8.

old Competition Authority. An element of the previous competition policy that stands out is the Cartel Register, which essentially made cartels lawful if they were reported and registered. At its height, it covered more than 4,800 cartels.[10] The cartel register symbolises the enforcement context in general, as the competition policy revolved around making anti-competitive behaviour visible to the authorities and correcting harmful effects by 'fine-tuning' such business arrangements or more bluntly capping the negative effects thereof by simply regulating prices.[11]

In parallel to the older competition rules, the government applied the Price Regulation Act to control and curb high prices and combat inflation.[12] The rules stemmed from a period in the 1960s and 1970s when market law was in its infancy and characterised by self-regulation with less governmental interference in market behaviour in general. Unfair competition was therefore more concerned with correcting individual wrongdoings and less with that of the functioning of the market as such. It should be noted that national competition enforcement practice was more diverse in Western Europe during the 1970s compared with the situation today. European competition developed much later than the US antitrust rules and entailed initially both general prohibitions (e.g., in West Germany and France) and mixes of general prohibitions and rules on *in casu*-abusive behaviour. Alongside diverse national rules, the EEC (later EC and EU rules) later aligned these rules.[13] Sweden was one of the countries that much later embraced the prohibition principle in competition law.

The old enforcement agency from 1957 to 1992, Statens pris- och kartellnämnd (later renamed to Statens pris- och konkurrensverk, SPK), had few corrective instruments. The impact of the authority's decisions, moreover, was heavily reliant upon the indirect effects of publicity of its findings and the deterrent effect of conditional fines. Nonetheless, the enforcement system generated a considerable body of case law, contributing to a coherent stance on undesirable competitive market behaviour. However, in terms of substance, the older rules reflected the macro-economic policies of the time and in the late 1980s and early 1990s, these policies started to change considerably when Sweden prepared to join the European Economic Area (EEA) in 1993. Aiming to align national rules with EEA-rules and to mirror the shift in national

10. In 1946, following proposals laid down by the Post-WW2 Economic Planning Committee (SOU 1945:42), Parliament passed a special legislation on the monitoring of anti-competitive agreements (SFS 448). A national register for cartels was established and kept by the National Board of Trade (Sw. *Kommerskollegium*). Between 1947 until 1 July 1992, the cartel register comprised 4,777 cartels. *See* Näringsutskottets betänkande, NU 1973:41. *See also* the National Archive, Ref. No. SE/RA/420634/D7/80.

11. One could argue that this was a sort of micro-economic equivalent to parts of the Keynesian economic theory.

12. *See* General Price regulation Act, SFS 1956:236 (repealed) and Price Regulation Act, SFS 1989:978. In the wake of the accession to first the EEA and then the EU and the introduction of EC-based rules on competition, the price regulation activities were essentially reduced to nil, and repeal of the rules on general price regulation altogether was proposed, *see* Government enquiry, *En ny ransonerings- och prisregleringslag*, SOU 2009:69.

13. *See* Bernitz, U., *Marknadsrätt – En komparativ studie av marknadslagstiftningens utveckling och huvudlinjer*, Diss., Aronzon-Lundin, Stockholm, 1969; and *Svensk och internationell marknadsrätt*, Jurist- och samhällsvetareförbundet förlags AB, Stockholm 1971; and *Konkurrens och priser i Norden*, 1971. *See also* Grönfors, K., and Sundqvist, Å., *Konkurrensen, samhället och lagen*, Esselte, Göteborg 1973.

overall macroeconomic policies of the time, the substantive rules were changed on 1 January 1993. Older case law based upon now repealed competition rules was therefore scrapped, and as of 1 July 1993, Swedish competition law was explicitly based upon then Articles 85 and 86 EC and the case law of Court of Justice of the European Union (CJEU), marking a new era in Swedish competition law. Although the existing EU-based rules have been in place for almost thirty years, the current case law started to develop first in the late 1990s.

The role of the (1953-1992) repealed Näringsfrihetsombudsmannen, NO (Business freedom ombudsman) and the Market Court is of particular relevance for this study. The court decided on prohibitions after the ombudsman had brought an action before the court. If the ombudsman decided – for whatever reason – not to bring an action, a subsidiary claim for an injunction could instead be brought by an association of consumers, workers, or traders, or by a trader affected by the restriction of competition in question (a 'second bite' for those affected by the alleged restriction).[14] The venues for appeal of decisions and injunctions were very limited. In practice, the (now-old) Market Court decided in the first and last instance on infringements and its decisions could not be appealed.

Today, it may seem odd that the possibility to appeal was almost non-existent. This should, however, be viewed in the light of the modest sanctions associated with infringements. Essentially, purported wrongdoers did not risk much and in a worst-case scenario, they could face an injunction subject to conditional fines. Nowadays, however, the sanctions are quite substantial. The appeal system of the older period pre-1993 did, nonetheless, remain at least in part and followed into the new system in 1993 and until 2021 it only entailed a one-instance appeal system. Like the older rules, in that period 1993-2021, the Swedish Competition Authority had to bring actions before the Stockholm District Court unless there was a decision on injunction or the now repealed negative clearance.

The current substantive rules have remained the same since 1993, albeit some block exemptions and minor national rules for certain sectors have changed. The Swedish Competition Act (SCA) entered into force on 1 January 1993,[15] two years ahead of Sweden's accession to the EU. Procedural rules have, however, been modernised and revised. The enforcement agency, *Konkurrensverket, KKV* (Swedish National Competition Authority), was established on 1 July 1992, when it replaced the Statens pris- och konkurrensverk and Näringsfrihetsombudsmannen.[16] At first, it enforced the older competition rules from 1982, but shortly after its inception, it took on the statutory role of enforcement agency for competition law in Sweden In relation to the new substantive rules introduced in 1993.

At the outset in 1993, it was explicitly made clear by the legislator that the new rules marked a new epoch in Swedish competition law and the application and

14. Section 17 of the now repealed 1982 Competition Act.
15. Konkurrenslag, SFS 1993:20. The Act replaced the 1982 Competition Act, which was repealed in its entirety along with a sector specific law on competitive restraints related to agricultural products, lagen (1991:921) om förbud mot konkurrensbegränsning i fråga om jordbruksprodukter.
16. *See* Government Bill, 1881/82:100, bil. 13, p. 133, NU20, rskr. 237.

interpretation of the rules should be undertaken in accordance with the EC rules enshrined in Articles 85 and 86 (now Articles 101 and 102 TFEU) and the CJEU's case law.[17]

The current SCA entered into force on 1 November 2008.[18] The main substantive rules of 1993 remained unchanged, however, there were changes done to procedural matters such as joinder of claims, rules on the authority's examination, rules on the statutory limitation on fines, rules on litigation costs, and calculation of administrative fines. Also, the rules on merger control were more aligned with the EU rules from 2004. The Group exemptions in national law, mirroring the Commission's Regulations were elevated from the Government's ordinances to law (decided by the Parliament).

An oddity in Swedish law is the subsidiary claim for injunctions. It follows from Chapter 3, section 2 of the SCA that an aggrieved party can initiate a claim for injunction (not fines) with the Patent and Market Court. In practice, the aggrieved undertaking, or more formally, the undertaking affected by the alleged infringement, then assumes the role of the KKV before the Court, but still in the capacity of a private party. The peculiarity lies therein that it is a public enforcement instrument employed by a private party, who does not possess the investigatory powers of the KKV. At least in theory, the claimant also assumes the same burden of proof as the KKV, which should be challenging for the claimant. This onerous predicament has been alleviated to some extent by the Courts recognising this procedural shortcoming and in practice relaxed the burden of proof to demonstrate infringement, despite it being one and the same legal instrument that is employed. These procedural shortcomings can potentially result in deviating case law on substantive issues, not least how infringements are assessed. Regardless thereof, this instrument has been used several times by purported aggrieved undertakings. These cases are, however, outside the scope of this study.

2 REVIEW OF THE COMPETITION AUTHORITY'S DECISIONS

2.1 Overview of the Swedish Appeal System

Under the 2008 Act, the KKV was entrusted to issue so-called fine orders (Sw. *Avgiftsföreläggande*), but those decisions on fines could not be appealed at all and could be decided only in clear and undisputed cases, in practice only if the alleged infringer voluntarily consented to the fine. These fine orders were essentially modelled on the criminal summary imposition of a fine and breach-of-regulation fines, which due to their moderate sanctions and non-complexity do not warrant the right appeal as such.[19] In addition, the 2008 changes introduced permission to appeal requirements

17. Government Bill 1993/93:56, Ny konkurrenslagstiftning, pp. 18-22.
18. Swedish Competition Act, Konkurrenslag, SFS 2008:579.
19. Government Bill, prop. 2007/08:135, Ny konkurrenslag m.m., pp. 87-89. At the outset, it may seem hard to understand why any rational company would voluntarily accept fines imposed by the authority, but it still provided as an easy way out for the purported wrongdoers; first because the fines were relative low, and second, because the cases did not generate high legal costs. Still, the system could make smaller companies feel unduly pressured into settling the case, otherwise they would face a competent authority and difficult litigation. Very little research to that effect

when appealing decisions on, *inter alia*, administrative fines to the Market Court. Prior to 2008, it was not required to have leave of appeal before the Market Court.[20]

Cases not involving fines, but injunctions (Sw. *ålägganden*) and commitments (Sw. *åtaganden*) followed different procedural rules from the Court Matters Act.[21] Governed by the Swedish Code of Judicial Procedure, such matters are from a procedural point of view generally handled primarily in writing and do not require oral hearings. Despite the clear intention of the legislator to establish a more efficient handling of cases, it is doubtful whether this separation is justified.

Essentially, there has been a significant difference in the public enforcement process including appeals between competition cases (Sw. *konkurrensmål*) and competition matters (Sw. *konkurrensärenden*). The former cases relate to cases involving administrative fines, whereas the latter concern decisions on injunctions, e.g., a duty to supply goods or an order to desist from or to discontinue a certain market behaviour. An integral part of the latter (decisions on injunctions, etc.) is, however, the finding of an infringement. Nonetheless, there have been no cases adopting declaratory judgments on the existence of an infringement alone. All cases have therefore been related to some specific performance, be it payment of fines or any behavioural measures ordered. Further, there are no cases imposing structural remedies. In contrast to the current rules, prior to 1 March 2021, the KKV could not take declaratory decisions on infringements.

During the period of this study, the KKV could decide on injunctions or accept commitments in the first instance, later also combined with conditional fines to put weight behind such decisions and to ensure compliance. These decisions could be appealed to the Stockholm District Court/Patent and Market Court. Subject to leave of appeal the decisions could then be appealed to the Market Court/PMÖD, which until 2016 – in contrast to fines – was the first and last appellate instance. The introduction of the Patent and Market Courts in 2016 also entailed changes to the appeals insofar also decisions on injunctions should be appealed to Patent and Market Court (Patent- och marknadsdomstolen, PMD) instead of the Market Court/PMD. Therefore, PMÖD was until 2021 both the first and second appellate instance, depending on whether the case concerned fines or injunctions. From 2021, the PMÖD decides in the second and last instance only.

Noteworthy, regardless of whether the cases were handled under one or the other of the procedural rules, they both involve the appellate court's assessment of the existence of an infringement and are therefore included in the database.

It is notable that so far, there have been no appeals to the Supreme Court. This is because, until 2016 the Market Court was the last instance court but following the court reform entailing the introduction of specialised courts, the Patent and Market Court of Appeal nowadays has the possibility – but not duty – to allow an appeal to the Supreme

---

has however been done. *See* Henriksson, L., *Two Novelties in Competition Law: Fine Order and Trading Prohibition – A Critical Review*, in National Developments in the Intersection of IPR and Competition Law. From Maglite to Pirate Bay, Swedish Studies in European Law No. 3. Ed. Hans Henrik Lidgard.

20. *See* Government Bill, prop. 2007/08:135, Ny konkurrenslag m.m.
21. Lag (SFS 1996:242) om domstolsärenden.

court in issues involving important principles. Competition cases before the Supreme Court remain, however, scarce and there have been no cases to date involving administrative fines. Again, it should be underlined that within the framework of this analysis, appeals in Swedish until 2021 were based on judgments or decisions taken by the District Court/PMD in the first instance because until then the KKV had limited power to decide in the first instance in cases relevant to this study.

2.2 Reform of the Forum Rules in 2016

In 2016, the forum rules were changed whereby the Market Court was wound up and replaced by the Patent and Market Court of Appeal (Patent- och marknadsöverdomstolen, PMÖD) as a special court within the Svea Court of Appeal. Likewise, a special court was set up within the Stockholm District Court; the PMD, which nowadays acts as the first-instance court. Until March 2021, the old procedural rules remained unchanged insofar as the KKV had to bring actions for fines before the PMD and the PMD's judgments/decisions could be appealed to the PMÖD.

During the period covered by this study (May 2004–April 2021), the KKV did not have the authority to take decisions involving a finding of an infringement or to impose administrative fines. The authority had to bring an action before the Stockholm District Court (later the Patent and Market Court). The decisions relevant to this study, therefore, were adopted by the Court. Its judgment or decision could then be appealed to the Market Court (later Patent and Market Court of Appeal) as a single appellate instance. It is important to bear this in mind when comparing empirical results between jurisdictions analysed in this study and this is the main reason for the relatively few cases analysed.

In the preparatory works to the reform, the Government held that the older rules of judicial proceedings were fragmented, the cases were relatively few, and in need of better coordination. The complex nature of the cases and the fact that intellectual property, marketing law, and competition law cases were spread over several courts and the need to sustain technical, economic, and legal competence amongst judges and experts led the Government to propose the establishment of specialised courts handling, *inter alia*, competition law cases.[22] The reformed forum rules entered into force on 1 September 2016.

Under the older procedural rules, the Stockholm District Court and the Market Court were the exclusive forum, for claims by the KKV and appeals, respectively. However, civil cases on damages for infringement of the Competition Act could be tried by any of the forty-eight district courts in Sweden. The change in 2016 and 2021 now entails that all cases (damages included) are to be dealt with by the specialist courts.

22. *See* Government Bill, prop. 2015/16:57, *Patent- och marknadsdomstol*, pp. 127-129.

2.3 Reform of Judicial Proceedings in 2021

The appeal system and powers of the KKV changed considerably in 2021. In transposing the ECN + directive,[23] the mandate of the KKV underwent major reform on 1 March 2021. Previously, and as already mentioned, the KKV was *not* entrusted to take decisions on administrative fines in the first instance. Instead, and in line with older procedural tradition, the authority had to bring an action for fines before the Patent and Market Court. Recognising the shortcomings of this system and in order to establish a more efficient enforcement of competition law and reduce the overall handling time of cases and case matters, the court hierarchy was changed insofar that the KKV nowadays takes decisions in the first instance, and its decisions may be appealed to the Patent and Market Court (first appellate instance) and then to the Patent and Market Court of Appeal (second appellate instance).[24]

As of 1 March 2021, most decisions of the SCA may be appealed to the PMD except for certain procedural issues, acceptance of voluntary commitments, etc. In turn, the PMD's judgments may be appealed to the PMÖD. Leave of appeal is required with the PMÖD. The legislator envisaged the PMÖD would act as the second and final appeal instance in matters of competition law. The PMÖD has, in turn however, the possibility of *allowing an* appeal to the Supreme Court in matters which the court, in its discretion, views as important for adjudication.[25] In practice, therefore, the appellate court is to be regarded as a court against whose decisions there is no judicial remedy under national law, within the meaning of Article 267 TFEU. This entails, *inter alia*, a duty for the PMÖD to refer cases to CJEU when the criteria for a preliminary ruling are met.[26]

Pursuant to the procedural reform in 2021, matters that can be appealed to the specialised court are nowadays most notably, findings of infringements of Articles 101 and 102 TFEU and its national corresponding rules enshrined in the SCA,[27] decisions on administrative fines for infringements,[28] injunctions on cease and desist of infringements which are normally also subject to conditional fines,[29] decisions of revocation of accepted voluntary undertakings,[30] and decisions on fines for infringements of the duty

23. Directive (EU) 2019/1 of the European Parliament and of the Council of 11 December 2018 to empower the competition authorities of the Member States to be more effective enforcers and to ensure the proper functioning of the internal market, PE/42/2018/REV/1, OJ L 11, 14.1.2019, pp. 3-33.
24. Government Bill, prop. 2021/21: 51, *Konkurrensverkets befogenheter*, pp. 45-57.
25. Chapter 1, section 3 of the Patent and Market Court Act. This is commonly referred to as the 'valve' (Sw. *ventilprövning*), i.e., the PMÖD is at liberty to open the valve, but they are not required to. Upon allowing appeal to the Supreme Court, the claimant will still need to be granted leave of appeal by the Supreme Court, although that would likely be a low threshold to pass because the appellate court has thereby already indicated that the matter is of precedential importance.
26. To date, the PMÖD has referred nine cases to the CJEU for preliminary ruling, however none of these are competition cases, instead the requests to the CJEU concern marketing law, copyright, patents, trademarks and design rights.
27. Chapter 3, section 1a of the SCA.
28. Chapter 3, section 5 of the SCA.
29. Chapter 3, sections 1 and 3 of the SCA.
30. Chapter 3, section 4 of the SCA.

to submit particulars and give information.[31] Several new competences have been recently introduced in Swedish law and older appeals most frequently concern an appeal against a decision by the court of first instance in cases where the KKV had demanded fines. Moreover, appeals may concern decisions by the KKV on injunctions. Again, during the period of this study, the competences of the KKV were limited and there were no KKV findings of infringements alone (declaratory judgment). Fines were decided upon by the court. Only some injunctions (including interim injunctions) could be decided by the KKV.

2.4 Procedural Rules Concerning Competition Law

Until 2021 and during the time period covered by this study, the applicable procedural rules before the courts depend on the character and legal consequence of the decision by the KKV or the court. Cases were handled either as competition *cases* (Sw. *konkurrensmål*) when they involved the imposition of administrative fines or as competition *matters* (Sw. *konkurrensärenden*), e.g., injunctions on cease and desist, interim order, etc. Both types of cases presupposed a finding of an infringement. Yet, competition cases had to be adopted by the Court, whereas competition matters could be decided by the KKV.

In Swedish procedural law, there was therefore a procedural difference between competition cases, which were handled under the Code of Judicial Procedure (SFS 1942:740) and competition matters, for which the Court Matters Act (SFS 1996:242) were applicable. The latter legislation on court matters alleviates the procedure insofar as it is intended to be applied in cases where it is appropriate to proceed via a less formal and written procedure with the aim of making the process more efficient. However, the parties may still ask for a hearing, which in practice reduces the differences between court matters and cases under the judicial code on matters not amenable to settlement out of court.

The reason for having parallel procedural rules appears to be explained both by legal tradition, but equally important concerns associated with the criminal nature of competition law cases involving administrative fines, and the inherent complexity of antitrust infringements that may indeed require a more elaborate hearing instead of being reduced to a written submissions' procedure. The hearing of witnesses may indeed be decisive to the outcome of the case before the court, which, in turn, normally requires an oral hearing and possibly cross-examination, etc.[32] Central to both cases

---

31. Chapter 5, sections 1 and 21 of the SCA.
32. Cf. Ruling by the European Court of Human Rights, *A. Menarini Diagnostics s.r.l. v. Italy*, Case No. 43509/08, 27.9.2011. Originally, in making the choice of adequate procedural rules before the courts, the legislator was faced with the distinction between administration of justice (jurisdiction contentiosa) and voluntary justice (jurisdiction voluntaria) and the distinction could have implied a perceived necessity of formal rules under the Code of Judicial procedure. Over the years that difference has become unclear and focus has shifted towards to striking a balance between justice for the individual and efficiency of the court system. This implies that competition cases and matters are in practice not that different from one another in terms of procedure. In all cases, the question of infringement is by and large handled in the same way

and matters is naturally that the question of whether an infringement has been committed is properly assessed.

The Court Matters Act is influenced by the procedural rules before the administrative courts (Sw. *förvaltningsdomstolarna*), which adjudicate, *inter alia*, taxation cases, social security cases, public procurement, legality review of decisions by local municipalities, etc. decisions by municipalities on building permits, etc. Those cases are handled by the Administrative Court Procedures Act (*förvaltningsprocesslagen*, SFS 1971:291). The Court Matters Act largely mirrors that administrative procedure but applies only in the general courts.

In 2021, and after the period of this study, the procedural rules changed in Sweden. Nowadays, appeals on cases are handled entirely under the Court Matters Act instead of the Code of Judicial Procedure. The change was primarily made in order to enhance efficiency and shorten the total time of the process.[33] It remains to be seen what practical changes these changes will have for appealed cases. It is doubtful whether there have been or are any practical procedural differences between the two types of cases, despite the clear intention of the legislator to establish a more efficient handling and shorter process time of cases. Competition law cases remain complex and normally entail a considerable examination and comprehensive materials to be scrutinised by the Courts.

2.5 The Composition of the Courts in Competition Law Cases

Both the PMD and the PMÖD are composed of judges; legally trained judges (Sw. *lagfarna domare*), and lay judges (Sw. *nämndemän*), and economic experts. The presiding judge shall always be a legally trained judge. Competition law cases are normally tried by judges and economic experts, whereas the number of judges varies between different cases. In some cases, economic experts may, at the discretion of the court, be redundant due to the non-complexity of the case.[34]

In acknowledging the complexity of competition law cases, the legislator decided that economic experts should be appointed to the courts' handling of competition law cases. The main reason is ostensibly the inherent complexity of the economic aspects of competition cases. Basic legal education in Sweden provided very little training in that regard, although judges in general are not unfamiliar with complex assessments. Nonetheless, the economic effects and the motivation thereof of certain market behaviour, do necessitate special knowledge and competence within the fields of economics and accounting. Not all competition law cases entail complex economic

under both procedural rules. Nonetheless, little research has been done so far in relation to possible differences in findings of infringement under the Court Matters Act and the Code of Judicial Procedure. *See* Fitger, P., Eriksson, T., Hall, P, *Lagen om domstolsärenden*, 23 May 2022, JUNO ver. 3B, Commentary.

33. *See* Government Bill 2020/21:51, Konkurrensverkets befogenheter, pp. 48-57.
34. *See* Chapter 5, Law on Patent- and Market Courts, SFS 2016:188.

assessments, but when they do, economic experts have been deemed necessary to assist in adjudicating the case.[35]

For economic experts to undertake their tasks adequately, that special member (Sw. *särskild ledamot*) of the court should have the necessary expertise and thus be well acquainted with the technical (primarily patent law cases), economic (economic or accounting) or other issues that may arise in the case or matter. To be considered a special member, it is normally required that the person, based upon adequate education and professional experience, has acquired special knowledge in the subject relevant to the individual case. Furthermore, of course, it is required that the person is otherwise deemed *suitable* to act as a special member. Among other things, the person should not be connected to any actor in the case.[36]

Economic experts are appointed by the Judges Proposal Board (Sw. *Domarnämnden*), whereas ordinary judges are appointed by the Government based on the proposal of the Judges Proposal Board.[37]

3 PRIOR RESEARCH

To date, there has been little research nor publications on empirical research of competition appeal cases in Sweden. This may be partly because of the pending reforms and partly due to the small number of cases. Instead, and although the frequency of cases may be relevant, research is most commonly focused on qualitative scrutiny and analysis of case law in Sweden. Nonetheless, there is case law commentary in textbooks,[38] albeit not in a systematic way as here.

The new powers of the KKV, entailing competences of the competition authority to decide on fines in the first instance has, however, attracted attention in the academic literature. Some authors have voiced concerns about the necessary safeguards and need to 'Chinese walls' within the authority to accommodate the new mandate and ease concerns on Articles 6 ECHR and 47 of the Charter of Fundamental Rights.[39] Other authors have also expressed concerns about the possibility of inefficiency arising from the reformed powers, related to whether the KKV will adequately rise to the challenge and deliver decisions that will withstand the scrutiny of the courts.[40]

35. Government Bill 2015/16:57, Patent- och marknadsdomstol, pp. 256-257.
36. *Ibid.*, p. 259.
37. *See* Government Ordinance SFS 2013:391, förordning (SFS 2013:391) om Domarnämndens förordnande av särskilda ledamöter i allmän domstol och i allmän förvaltningsdomstol. *See also* lag (SFS 2010:1390) om utnämning av ordinarie domare.
38. *See* Karlsson, J., Osen Bergqvist, T., *Konkurrensrätt – En handbok*, Norstedts Juridik, 6th Ed. 2022; *see also* Bergman, M., Karlsson, K., *Konkurrenslagen – en kommentar* (1 May 2022, version 2G, Norstedts Juridik, and Bernitz, U., *Svensk och europeisk marknadsrätt 1 – Konkurrensrätten och marknadsekonomins rättsliga grundvalar*, 5th ed. 2019, Norstedts Juridik.
39. *See* Lagerlöf, E., *Should the Swedish Competition Authority Be Allowed to Adopt Legally Binding Decisions on Antitrust Fines? A Comment in the Perspective of Procedural Rights, the Role of the Commission and EU Law*, ERT 2016:2 pp. 265-280.
40. Mohseni, A., El Khatib, O., *Konkurrensverkets nya beslutanderätt och rätten till försvar – hur unionsrätten kan komma att påverka handläggningen av svenska konkurrensärenden*, ERT 2021:2, pp. 269-281.

Notwithstanding these concerns, the old system with only one instance of appeal and a quite cumbersome process for the KKV, was indeed rooted in a regulatory system that prevailed during the 1950s and was considered inefficient and out-of-date. Initiatives were therefore taken to allow for major reform.[41] A major breakthrough came with the Edwardsson report on proposals for a reform of the system.[42] Alongside the requirements laid down in the ECN+ directive, the findings of Edwardsson eventually led to the reform of the KKV's decisional powers that entered into force on 1 March 2021.[43]

4 QUANTITATIVE ANALYSIS

4.1 Source of Information

Court cases in Sweden are subject to the principle of free access to public records and judgments are made available online or upon request from the court or the KKV.[44] The judgments and decisions of the Patent and Market Court of Appeal are made available from the court's website.[45] The cases were identified primarily through the courts' and the SCA's websites, and the Juno database.[46] Hence, the database of this study is expected to be comprehensive.

Notably, the Stockholm District Court and PMD are not classified as appellate courts in the study, because they have taken decisions in the first instance. For the purpose of this study, they are equated with NCA decisions in other Member States. Rather, the old Market Court and the successor Patent and Market Court of Appeals are regarded for the purpose of comparability as the first-instance courts. It is important to note that the old Swedish appellate system that applied during the period of this study was different compared with the current procedural rules.

4.2 Total Number of Cases

The number of cases before the Swedish Courts was previously entirely dependent on whether the KKV – in its discretion – decided to pursue a claim for administrative fines with the Stockholm district court/Patent and Market Court, and all decisions on fines were therefore adopted by those courts (equated to an NCA decision for the purpose of the study). A total number of fourteen appeals were rendered during the relevant

41. *See* Public inquiry, SOU 2006:99, *En ny konkurrenslag*, pp. 312-332.
42. Edwardsson, E., *Domstolsprövning av marknadsrelaterad lagstiftning*, Report to the KKV, 2009-03-26. *See also* Norberg, S., *Konkurrenskrönika*, ERT 2009:4, pp. 763-771.
43. *See* Government Bill, 2020/21:51, *Konkurrensverkets befogenheter*.
44. Judgments and decisions by the Patent and Market Court (first instance) are normally provided on request or via commercial databases. The SCA regularly publish their decisions and the courts judgments on its website. *See* https://www.konkurrensverket.se/konkurrens/tillsyn-arenden-och-beslut/arendelista/.
45. *See* Patent och Markandsöverdomstolen vid Svea hovrätt, https://www.domstol.se/patent--och-marknadsoverdomstolen/.
46. A commercial online legal information database provided by Norstedts Juridik, https://juno.nj.se/b/areas/juno.

period of the study. Thirteen of those judgments were first-instance appeals, of which six were decided by the old Market Court, six by the Patent and Market Court of Appeal, and one by the Patent and Market Court. Only one judgment was subject to a second-instance appeal, in front of the Patent och Marknadsöverdomstolen and concerned an injunction. This reflects a relatively low ratio of appeal, according to which 13 % of the decisions/judgments enforcing competition law in Sweden were appealed in the first instance, and only 1 % in the second instance.

The relatively low number of cases could be explained first by the selection criteria and coding principles of this study to ensure comparability (*see* Methodology Chapter). This should not, however, be understood as public competition enforcement in Sweden being less vigilant than other Member States.[47] In addition to the identified cases, there are also six decisions by the KKV outside the scope of the study on the now repealed fine orders (Sw. *avgiftsföreläggande, see* above) which could not be appealed, although that instrument has been discontinued after the procedural changes in 2021.

4.3 Total Numbers of Cases per Year

Figure 29.1 summarises the number of judgments issued by the various instances of Swedish courts per year.

Figure 29.1 Number of Judgments According to Instances

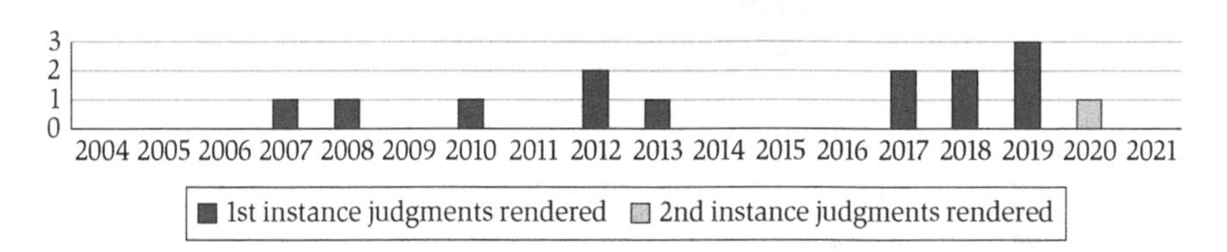

As mentioned, apart from the national procedure of fine orders (that were not subject to appeal), no decisions on fines could be taken by the KKV up until 2021, when the KKV received its mandate to decide on fines in the first instance.

The first-instance appeals in cases involving administrative fines were also the last instance. The number of cases is evenly distributed over the years and were brought before the Market Court in the past, and since 2016 – the PMÖD. There are no clear trends in terms of enforcement indicating any significant increase or decrease in

47. As a reference, during the time period, the KKV's own database indicates some 102 cases related to Articles 101 and 102 TFEU and its national corresponding rules. Twenty-three of those cases were decided by courts either by decision or judgment, eighteen cases concerned fines, whereas sixty-one cases were closed without any further action.

cases during the period. The effects on appeals of the 2021 reform, which entailed that the KKV nowadays takes the decision in the first instance, is yet to be seen. The 2021 reform has already generated one decision by the KKV which would fall within the substantive, albeit not the temporal scope of this study. Some backlog is expected as there were nine pending cases at the beginning of August 2022.

4.4 Success Rates and Outcomes

Figure 29.2 presents the success rate of the appeals, across all relevant instances.

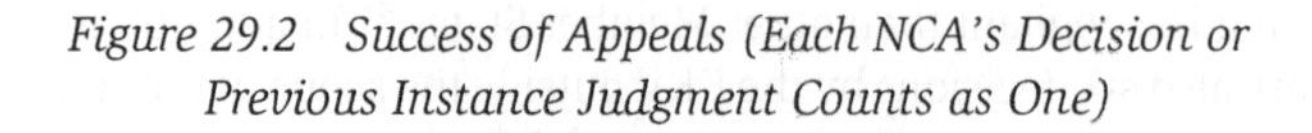

Figure 29.2 Success of Appeals (Each NCA's Decision or Previous Instance Judgment Counts as One)

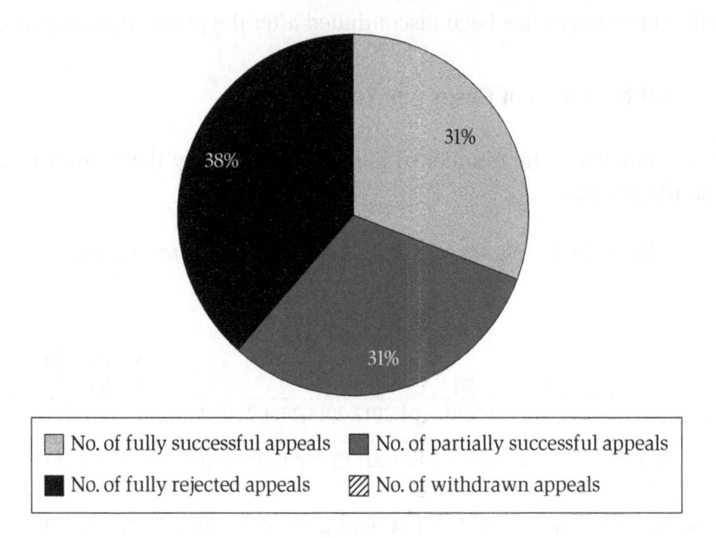

The figure indicates a relatively high success rate of appeals, irrespective of whether the appeal was brought by the undertaking or the competition authority. Of all appeals, 62% were either partially or fully successful. The partially successful category includes cases where either the substantive aspects of the infringement judgment were overturned or set aside and cases where the original administrative fine was reduced in some way.

The success rates are further elaborated by Figure 29.3, which identifies the outcome of the appeals.

Figure 29.3(a) First-Instance Outcome

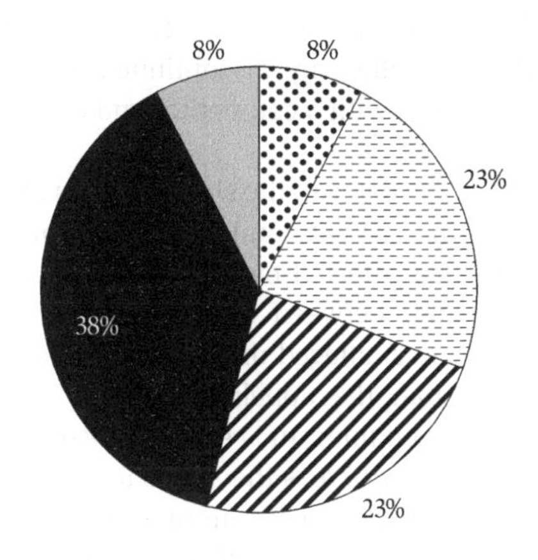

Figure 29.3(b) Second-Instance Outcome

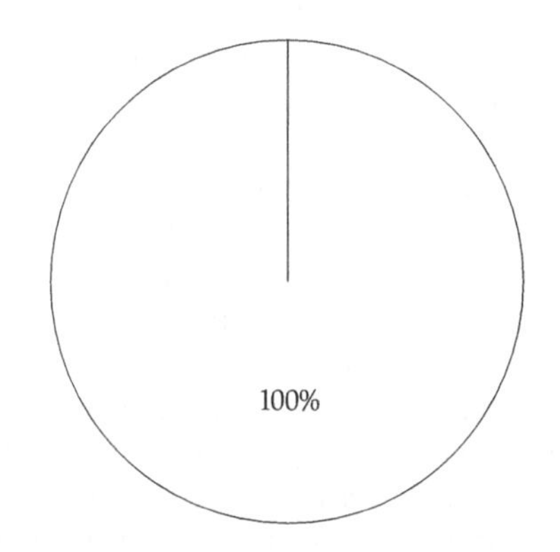

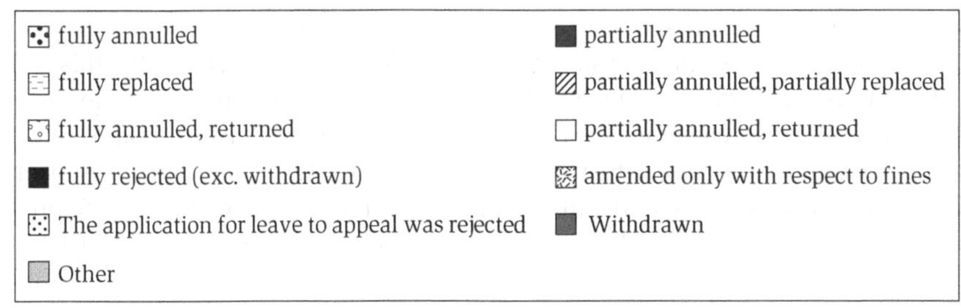

As mentioned, there is one case within the dataset that was appealed to the second instance; *FTI*,[48] whereas all other cases were decided only at the first instance of appeal. In *FTI*, the KKV's decision on injunctions related to a behaviour of a dominant undertaking that had allegedly discontinued a business relationship and thereafter refused further dealings with a competitor and denied continued access to a system of recycling bins.

Considering the cases in the dataset, the share of cases appealed that were raised by the competition authority, the KKV, amounted to 29 %, whereas the remainder were all appealed by the undertakings affected by the decision/judgment. There is a clear difference in terms of outcomes between cases involving injunctions (positive or negative measures directed against alleged unlawful behaviour) and those pertaining to fines. It appears evident that the appellate court was more likely to uphold injunctions compared to actions on fines. In *Svenska Hockeyligan*,[49] the court annulled the KKV's decision in its entirety, whereas the appellate court replaced the injunction decision in *Svenska Bilsportförbundet*[50] with more precise wording on the measures required by the addressee of the KKV's decision. The injunction relating to alleged discriminatory behaviour against certain taxi companies by the airport authority in *Luftfartsverket*[51] was unsuccessfully appealed by the airport authority. The court's reasoning was succinct and did not find any reasons to deviate from the KKV's assessment in substance, and the appeal was rejected.

Cases involving fines mark a more complex picture in terms of outcome. It is more common that the appellate court replaced the lower court's decision with its own findings and MD/PMÖD did not in any case affirm the lower court's reasoning. Instead, the appellate court regularly delivers its own reasoning and findings, even if that results in an affirmation of the lower court's conclusions. The Stockholm District Court/PMD tend to deliver elaborate and extensive reasoning, whereas it can often be difficult to back trace the appellate reasoning in relevant parts and whether the appellate court agrees on substantive aspects or not with the lower court. Therefore, the lack of such reasoning creates uncertainty in the law. Yet again, any omissions in that regard leave questions unanswered, especially in the light of the often well-articulated and extensively reasoned judgment by the lower court with extensive reference to CJEU case law. Following the court reform in 2016, the PMÖD has indeed taken on a more independent view of competition law cases, apparently unfettered by the extensive array of case law precedents developed by the old Market Court. Naturally, this is the prerogative of the PMÖD, but whether the changes are made by design or mistake/oversight or reluctance to state the reasons why the PMÖD does not refer to the Market Court's older precedents is still problematic. The Svea Court of Appeal is after all the second instance of the three-tier system in most other cases (the Supreme Court being the last instance). This apparently has set its mark on how the PMÖD drafts

48. Patent and Market Court of Appeal, case PMÖÄ 1519, *Svenska Förpacknings- och Tidningsinsamlingen AB v. KKV*, 2012-02-28.
49. Marknadsdomstolen, case MD A 2/12, *Svenska Hockeyligan v. KKV*, 2012-12-18.
50. Marknadsdomstolen, case MD 2012:16, *Svenska Bilsportförbundet v. KKV*, 2012-12-20.
51. Decision by Marknadsdomstolen, case MD 2010:5, *Luftfartsverket v. KKV*, 2010-02-05.

its judgments. Clarity of the state of law does, in my view, either require more elaborate reasoning or allow cases to be appealed to the Supreme Court. Preferably the PMÖD should heed the call of the legislator and more clearly assume the role of a final instance court delivering proper precedents.

Circa 44% of appeal judgments involving fines were appealed by the KKV. The KKV has, however, been largely unsuccessful upon appeals in these cases. In *Assistancekåren*[52] the KKV had originally unsuccessfully brought an action for fines of MSEK 1 and on appeal the Market Court did not find the KKV's investigation and body of evidence to support a finding of infringement. An appeal in the *AQM* case[53] is also significant. Originally, the case was depicted by the KKV as an outright cartel in the market for relocation services that attracted much media attention - not least spurred on by the authority in its active promotion of the matter. The case revolved around the potential restrictive nature of ancillary restraints to mergers.[54] Judging from the relative share of the companies' turnover, the claim for administrative fines indicated a severe violation of competition law by-object and at the very least by-effect. Unsuccessful in their claim before the PMD, the authority appealed to the PMÖD but based its appeal solely [sic!] on the existence of a restriction by-object. The PMÖD dismissed the appeal in its entirety. Also, in the *Nasdaq*[55] case, the KKV held that Nasdaq, the dominant provider of trading, clearing, exchange technology, listing, information, and public company services had abused its dominant position vis-à-vis a competitor, Burgundy. The KKV was unsuccessful both before the PMD and later upon appeal, where the PMÖD did not find the evidence to support a finding of infringement. In *Bilia*,[56] the appeal court did, however, affirm a finding on infringement for some of the undertakings involved in a horizontal anti-competitive behaviour, whereby the total fines were reduced from MSEK 157.5 to MSEK 21.2 on the substantive issue of infringement.

Cases involving fines and appealed by affected undertakings have on the other hand been more successful and only the case *Gothnet*[57] involved a complete rejection of an undertaking's appeal, albeit solely on procedural grounds. The undertaking was fined in an earlier case together with Telia Sverige AB. Telia appealed the PMD's

52. Marknadsdomstolen, case MD 2007:23, *KKV v. Assistancekåren Sweden AB, MRF-Bärgarna*, 2007-11-01.
53. Patent and Market Court of Appeal, case PMT 7498-16, *KKV v. Alfa Quality Moving AB, Vänrun AB (tidigare ICM Kungsholms AB) and NFB Transport Systems AB*, 2017-11-29.
54. Cf. Commission Notice on restrictions directly related and necessary to concentrations, OJ C 56, 5.3.2005, pp. 24-31.
55. Patent and Market Court of Appeal, case PMT 1443-18, *KKV v. Nasdaq AB, Nasdaq Clearing AB, Nasdaq Stockholm AB and Nasdaq Technology AB*, 2019-06-28.
56. Marknadsdomstolen, case MD 2008:12, *KKV, v. Aktiebolaget Bil-B.; Bil-M. i Skåne Aktiebolag; Göinge Bil Aktiebolag; J. A. Bil AB; Kristianstads Automobil Aktiebolag; Skånebil Personbilar AB; Bilia Personbilar AB; Bildeve Aktiebolag*, 2008-09-10.
57. Patent and Market Court of Appeal, case PMÖ 11973-18, *Göteborg Energi Gothnet AB v. KKV*, 2019-05-27.

judgment, but Gothnet abstained from appeal and the judgment in relation to Gothnet entered into legal force. Eventually, Telia was successful on appeal based upon a finding by the appellate court that there was no underlying infringement. Presumably, that finding should also have applied to Gothnet, but the only venue of appeal was to apply for a petition for a new trial (Sw. *resning*), which is an extraordinary remedy under Swedish procedural law. The appellate court did not find any grounds for a new trial, effectively rejecting the appeal. Undertakings were more successful in *Aleris*[58] and *Swedish Match*,[59] where the fines were reduced to zero based upon the appellate finding of no infringement in both cases, in stark contrast to the lower court's assessment of substance. In one case, *TeliaSonera*,[60] the dominant telecom company appealed a judgment on fines. A third party intervened against the dominant undertaking. The KKV was successful on the issue of infringement, but the fines were considerably reduced from MSEK 144 to MSEK 35 because the court did not agree on the relevant economic calculations on profitability in relation to the dominant firm.

4.5 Type of Competition Authority's Decisions Subject to Appeal

Figure 29.4 demonstrates that 43% of the appeal cases in Sweden concerned abuse of dominance and 57% were related to anti-competitive agreements. Most of the cases involved both the application of EU and national rules. The cases of *Assistancekåren*[61] and *Bilia*[62] concerned the national provisions alone, where only Chapter 2, section 1 of the SCA was applicable, i.e., no effect on trade between Member States was found. The *TeliaSonera*[63] and *Luftfartsverket*[64] cases also concerned national markets without any effect on trade between Member States. All other cases concerned relevant markets where trade between Member States was deemed to be affected, and therefore the EU competition law prohibitions were involved.

58. Patent and Market Court of Appeal, case PMT 7497-16, *Aleris Diagnosik AB, Capio S:t Görans sjukhus AB, Hjärtkärlgruppen i Sverige AB v. KKV*, 2017-04-28.
59. Patent and Market Court of Appeal, case PMT 1988-17, *Swedish Match North Europe AB v. KKV*, 2018-06-29.
60. Marknadsdomstolen, case MD 2013:5, *TeliaSonera AB v. KKV*, 2013-04-12.
61. Marknadsdomstolen, case MD 2007:23, *KKV v. Assistancekåren Sweden AB, MRF-Bärgarna*, 2007-11-01.
62. Marknadsdomstolen, case MD 2008:12, *KKV, v. Aktiebolaget Bil-B.; Bil-M. i Skåne Aktiebolag; Göinge Bil Aktiebolag; J. A. Bil AB; Kristianstads Automobil Aktiebolag; Skånebil Personbilar AB; Bilia Personbilar AB; Bildeve Aktiebolag*, 2008-09-10.
63. Marknadsdomstolen, case MD 2013:5, *TeliaSonera AB v. KKV*, 2013-04-12.
64. Marknadsdomstolen, case MD A 3/09, *Luftfartsverket v. KKV*, 2010-02-05.

Figure 29.4 Rule Being Appealed

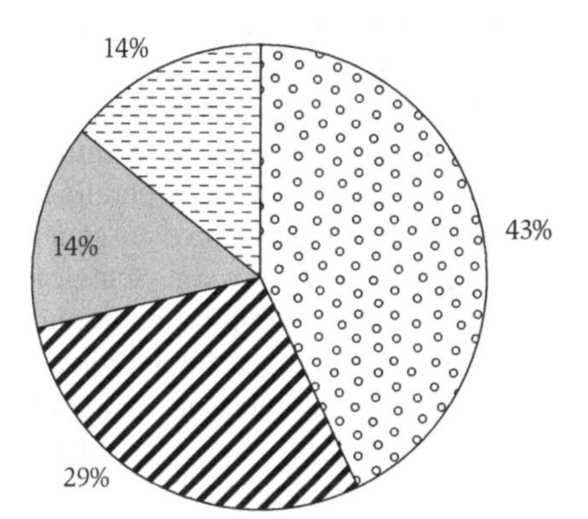

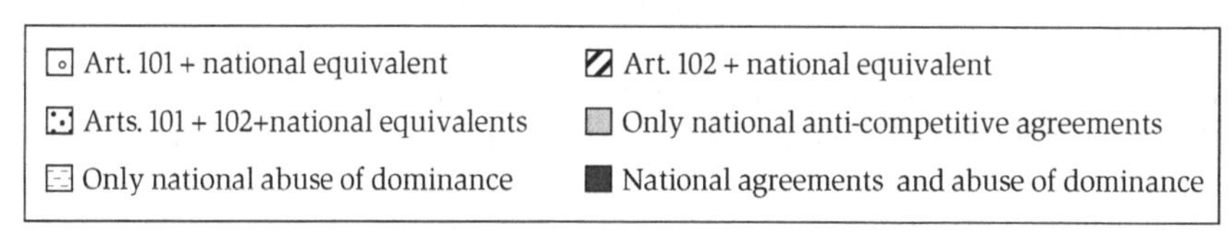

The Swedish economy is highly integrated with the European market and has traditionally been very oriented towards international trade, also outside the EU. Further, the Swedish market is quite small in terms of turnover compared to larger Member States. It is therefore commonplace that Articles 101 and 102 TFEU are applicable in parallel to the national rules in Sweden.

Figure 29.5 Rules Being Appealed According to Years (Each Judgment Counts as One)

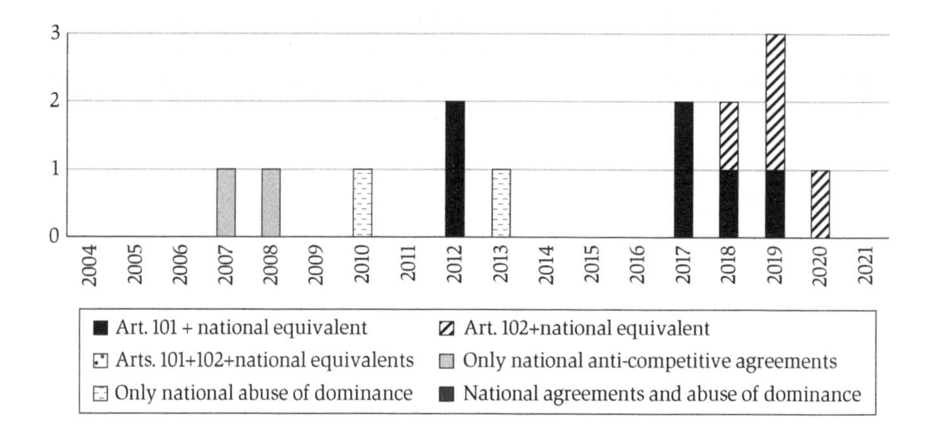

There is no clear trend relating to appeal cases concerning any differences between national or EU rules during the time period of the study. Nonetheless, it *appears* to be slightly more common for the EU prohibition rules to have been involved in judgments in more recent years as demonstrated by Figure 29.5. It does, however, remain unclear what the reasons are. Sweden is a relatively small economy on the world scene, but it has considerable foreign trade within the EU and third countries. Also, Sweden has relatively large undertakings operating on global markets. Those facts could explain why EU rules are concerned in general, but there are no clear reasons for the increase in case law in later years. Some cases – e.g., the *Gothnet* and *Aleris* cases – arose out of a prior national public procurement procedure subject to the thresholds of EU rules, but competition cases did not relate to the prior rules on public procurement. At the least the potential effect on trade between Member States is in those cases quite obvious – otherwise, the cases would have concerned matters below the EU public procurement thresholds.

The Swedish legislator explicitly made it clear already in the 1993 Competition Act that the national Swedish rules on anti-competitive agreement and abuse of dominance should substantively be interpreted and applied in accordance with the EC/EU rules. There is therefore very little difference – if any – between Swedish national rules and EU rules. Instead, there are different procedural rules that may indirectly affect the outcome of a case in terms of how comprehensive or thorough the assessment is. When the procedural rules changed from being handled under the Code of Judicial Procedure and instead being subject to the Court Matters Act, there is a risk that the primarily written procedure may not accord enough attention to complex economic matters of the cases under scrutiny. Whether that will materialise is yet unclear and will become more evident as the Courts in future hear cases decided by the KKV on appeal.

The appeals have involved a fairly limited subject matter. Figure 29.6 demonstrates that the cases in the dataset on anti-competitive behaviour pertain to horizontal restrictions and exclusionary abuse of dominance. Appeals in relation to cases concerning vertical restraints and exploitative practices remain very scarce. Presumably, these cases require the KKV to demonstrate anti-competitive effects and can rarely be categorised as restriction by-object or *per se*-violations, respectively and would also require extensive analysis of market effect to establish a convincing theory of harm.

Figure 29.6 Types of Restrictions

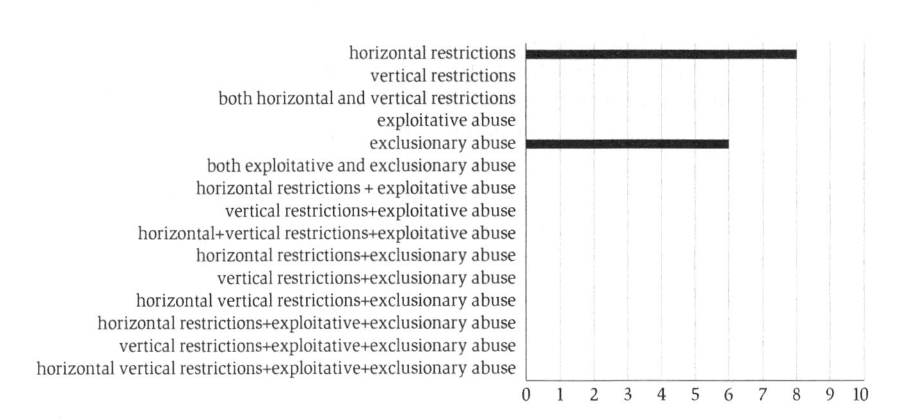

The choice to pursue cartels and exclusionary unilateral behaviour appear also to be consistent with the KKV's prioritisation policy for public enforcement. The KKV receives many complaints every year and they monitor several sectors continuously. At the same time, some restrictions and behaviours are deemed more harmful than others, and some have more direct consequences. Equally important for litigation, the KKV has had a limited budget and can only pursue a limited number of cases each year, which has a negative impact on the number of cases subject to appeal.[65]

Figure 29.7 Object/Effect (Only for Article 101/National Equivalent Infringements)

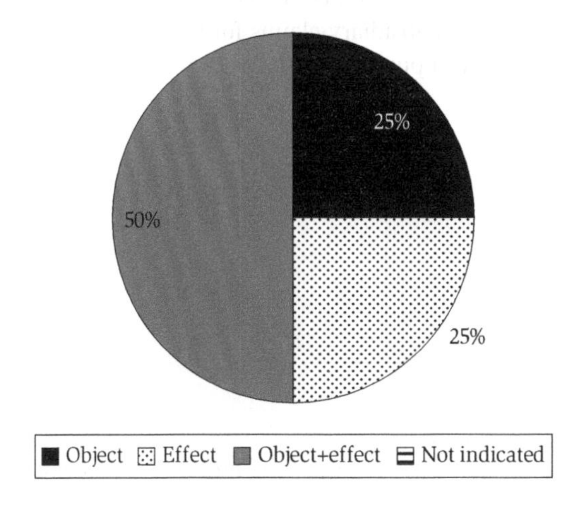

65. Konkurrensverket, *Konkurrensverkets prioriteringspolicy foör konkurrens- och upphandlingstill-synen*, dnr 6/2022, 2022-06-17.

In relation to appeals concerning anti-competitive agreements, Figure 29.7 summarises the type of restrictions that were subject to appeal. 50% of the cases were deemed by the KKV to involve restrictions by-object, 25% only restrictions by-effect and 25% both by-object and effect. Pursuant to the case law of CJEU, the criteria for restrictions by-object have, however, indeed been interpreted narrowly by the Courts in Sweden.[66] It was therefore unexpected that the KKV in *AQM* initially argued there was a restriction by-object *and* effect before the PMD, and thereafter upon appeal, focused entirely on the existence of a restriction by-object and dropped the arguments related to restriction by-effect. Arguably, this was a risky strategy since the only conceivable ground for success would have been demonstrating anti-competitive effects instead of the actions being restrictive by their very nature. As anticipated, the litigation strategy backfired considerably and the KKV's appeal was rejected on its merits.

Figure 29.8 summarises the type of enforcement decisions that were subject to appeal. About two-thirds of all appealed cases concerned a finding of infringement together with the imposition of administrative fines. The remaining one-third were cases involving injunctions based upon a finding of infringement. A finding of no infringement like a negative clearance does not exist under Swedish law, and neither was there earlier any declaratory judgments. This is because the declaratory judgment in general requires the criteria in Chapter 13, section 2 of the Code of Judicial Procedure to be met. Such judgments therefore require legal uncertainty, which is causing harm. Declaratory judgments are possible when there is an explicit statutory provision to that effect. Earlier, that was missing, but the legislator made such decisions or rulings possible in 2021.[67] In practice, therefore, there are no cases on appeal based on a decision that there are no grounds for action. This is also explained by the possibility for aggrieved parties to bring subsidiary claims for injunctions when the KKV decides – for whatever reason – not to pursue a case.

66. Cf. case C-67/13 P, *Groupement des cartes bancaires (CB) v. European Commission*, ECLI-:EU:C:2014:2204.
67. In implementing the ECN+ Directive, the legislator introduced in 2021 the possibility for declaratory decisions insofar the KKV is now empowered to decide on a finding of infringement alone (Chapter 3, section 1 a of the SCA). This was the missing piece of the puzzle for antitrust damages because a finding of infringement by the KKV that has entered into legal force has legal binding effect in follow-on antitrust damages (cf. Antitrust Damages Act (SFS 2016:964), Chapter 5, section 9). *See also* Government Bill 2020/21:51, *Konkurrensverkets befogenheter*, p. 100.

Figure 29.8 Competition Authority's Procedure

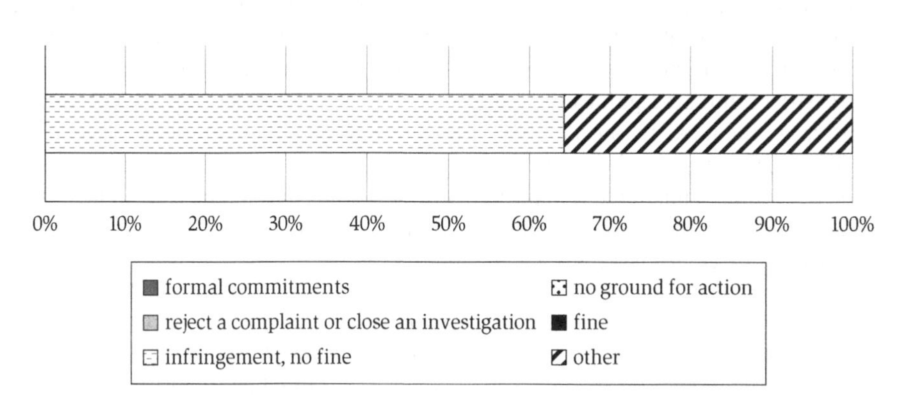

4.6 Grounds of Appeal

The empirical findings reveal the grounds on which appeals were raised by the parties and their likelihood of success. To this effect, Figure 29.9 sets out the grounds of appeal. This figure summarises the grounds and outcomes of all cases of the appeals launched against the rulings by the Stockholm District Court/PMD.

Figure 29.9 Grounds of Appeal (Each NCA's Decision or Previous Instance Judgment Counts as One)

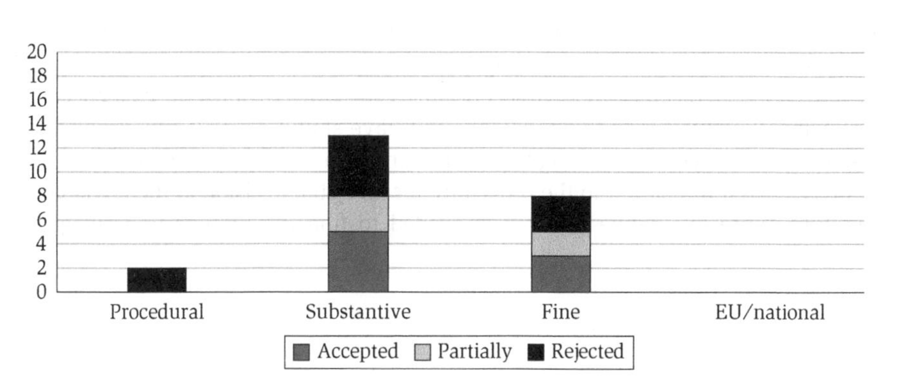

The grounds of appeal in the relevant case law have not varied significantly across the time period and relate almost exclusively to substantive grounds combined with fine grounds. It is common for the appeal grounds put forward to be made in the alternative, i.e., should the appellant be unsuccessful on the argument based on the infringement it will often also argue that the fines, notwithstanding, ought to be reduced on the basis of gravity, duration, etc. It should be noted that there are relatively few cases in which the appeal is founded upon procedural grounds. The success of motions by the undertakings in *Gothnet*[68] essentially hinged on whether the appellate court would accept the circumstances as sufficient to accept the petition for a new trial. In that case, the appellate court did not find any such ground to allow a new trial.

There is a trend in Sweden to the effect that any fines imposed by the PMD/District Court are significantly reduced on appeal by Market Court/PMÖD. In five of the cases included in the database, the fines were either annulled or reduced significantly. On average, the reduction rate across all cases was 92 %. Only in *Gothnet* did the fines remain unaltered, but primarily because the court did not rule in favour or a new trial, despite the fact that Gothnet's co-infringer was successful on its appeal in substance and the fines were reduced to zero.[69]

Again, it should be noted that the Swedish procedural rules entailed that the District Court/PMD decided on fines in the first instance after the KKV brought an action for fines. In three appealed cases (*Assistancekåren, AQM, Nasdaq*) the first court initially rejected the KKV's claims for fines, subsequent to which the KKV unsuccessfully appealed to the Market Court/PMÖD. Therefore, it is evident that the appellate courts have been quite restrictive in their approach to the existence of infringements and the level of fines deemed adequate when there was a finding of infringement. It therefore appears to be more difficult to demonstrate infringements before the appellate courts compared with the court of first instance. What merits this approach is not entirely clear and is most likely to be the result of a combination of reasons, suitable for further research.

There is no clear trend in Sweden indicating that the type of restrictions under scrutiny has had any influence on the success of appeals. As mentioned above, the general trend regarding the outcome of an appeal, regardless of the type of infringement, has so far clearly been in favour of undertakings. This also holds true irrespective of whether the KKV or the undertaking has been the appellant. Again, it is unclear if this reflects a general and excessive scepticism by the PMÖD against the existence of an infringement. Naturally, the undertakings can have skilful counsel and strong litigators, but if those were determining factors the same result would presumably also have manifested itself in relation to the procedure for an initial decision at the lower court. Therefore, more qualitative research is needed to find the reasons underlying this trend.

68. Patent and Market Court of Appeal, case PMÖ 11973-18, *Göteborg Energi Gothnet AB v. KKV*, 2019-05-27.
69. *Ibid.*

Figure 29.10 Types of Restrictions Versus Successful Grounds of Appeal

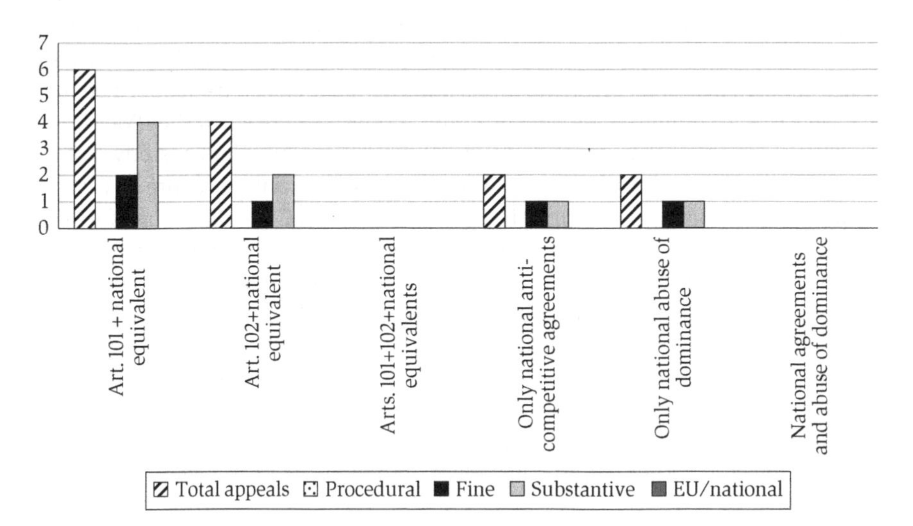

None of the cases included in the database involved either leniency or settlement applications. It should be noted that during the period of this study, it has not been possible to settle a case on fines in Sweden because of the governing procedural rules that do not allow settlement out of court. Instead, cases involving fines are subject to official examination (Sw. *officialprövning*), which does not entail any negotiations or settlement procedures. The now-repealed fine order, an instrument not subject to appeal, did however in practice entail some element of bargaining because fines could be accepted on a voluntary basis. Although there are no clear, verifiable drivers, the reasons why undertakings still accepted fines (six cases in total), may be explained by an undertaking's interest in avoiding an expensive and painstaking trial and perhaps to avoid any follow-on actions that could arise subsequent to a judgment. The offered fine route appears to have been considered less burdensome than the expected outcome of a full trial before the PMD. Nonetheless, the rationale for undertakings voluntarily accepting fine orders remains unclear.

5 QUALITATIVE ANALYSIS

The Swedish appeal system has undergone two major changes since the modernisation of EU competition law enforcement in 2004; one court reform in 2016 and a major reform of the KKV's mandate in 2021.

The Patent and Market Court is the exclusive forum for competition cases. Prior to 2021, the KKV could not take any decisions on fines in the first instance. Instead, it had in its discretion to bring an action for fines – based upon a finding of infringement – before the Stockholm District Court/Patent and Market Court, which decided on fines. Its judgment could then, and still can, be appealed to the Patent and Market Court of Appeals, the first and, in practice, last instance of appeal. Already before 2021, the

KKV was entrusted to take decisions on injunctions and to accept commitments and as mentioned above, the second change came at the very end of the period of this study. In 2021, the mandate for the KKV changed considerably, whereby the decisions on fines are nowadays taken in the first instance by the KKV. In May 2023, one decision on fines and two decisions involving injunctions by the KKV had been appealed to the PMD. No cases according to the new procedural rules have reached the PMÖD.

The older rules that applied during the time period of this study entailed procedure according to the rules in the Swedish Code of Judicial Procedure on cases not amenable to settlement out of court. The Stockholm District Court/PMD therefore ruled on fines (not stand-alone declaratory judgment on infringement) in the first instance. Appeals were possible to the Market Court (from 2016; the Patent and Market Court of Appeals). Although the appellate court could allow appeal to the Supreme Court, that did not happen in competition law cases. Sweden, therefore, had a one-instance appeal system in most of all cases. In theory, there were two instances but because the PMÖD had discretion on whether to allow an appeal, the appeal system was in practice reduced to a one-tier system. Injunctions could be decided by the KKV and were therefore subject to scrutiny in two instances, although such cases were very few on appeal.

It could be argued that the possibility of appeal was limited to only one instance and thereby this could raise concerns about adequate judicial review. Such concerns were, however, mitigated by the fact that the first-instance court (equated to an NCA for the purpose of the study) was truly independent of both parties and rendered impartial judgments after the KKV brought a claim before the court. Judicial review was therefore in practice undertaken in two instances, although appeal – properly so-called – was only available in one instance.

In 2021, the system changed and the KKV now has the power to decide on cases involving fines and even findings of infringements. Consequently, the PMD and PMÖD are nowadays appellate courts in the first and second instance, respectively. The roles before the first-instance appeal court are now reversed; the infringer pursuant to the KKV's decision is now the claimant/appellant and the KKV is the defendant. Whether this will bring about any major differences for litigation – especially in light of cases being considered under the Court Matters Act – remains to be seen. It is likely, though, that very few additional circumstances or arguments will be presented by the KKV on appeal. This is because the very purpose of procedural reform is to enhance efficiency.

Appealed cases involving administrative fines during the period of this study are relatively few and there is a clear trend of either rejecting a claim for fines in its entirety or significantly reducing the fine. The KKV's claim for fines in the protracted *TeliaSonera* case, which the District Court referred to the CJEU for a preliminary ruling, was affirmed and fines were set at MSEK 144. On appeal, however, and although the KKV was successful on the issue of infringement, the fine was reduced by almost 75 % based upon the unclear reasoning on profitability measurements. Also, in *Bilia*, the higher fines of MSEK 157,5 were reduced by 87%.[70] This was, however, explained by an adjustment by the KKV regarding the size of the geographical market, which led to a lower turnover of the infringers and thereby a lower fine. The appellate court did rule in favour of the KKV's adjusted claim. In *Swedish Match*, the original fine of MSEK 37,9 was reduced to zero by the appellate court.[71] The case involved an exclusionary practice and potentially an abuse of dominance and the Patent and Market Court of Appeal acknowledged the existence of the restrictive nature of the conduct under scrutiny but that it - contrary to the assessment of the lower court - should be deemed as objectively justified.

The reasoning of the Swedish Court is closely aligned with CJEU's reasoning and EU law in general both in relation to substantive issues of infringements and in setting fines. As such, the methods for calculating or adjusting fines are essentially based on the same principles Article 23(2)(a) of Regulation No. 1/2003 and the EU Commission's methods for setting fines.[72] The judgments do reveal which circumstances the Courts deem relevant or decisive and typically result in an all-embracing weighing of facts and circumstances leading to an overall finding. Although the Courts adhere to this method, the conclusions on fines appear to be more discretional than arithmetical, rendering it hard to back-trace the more exact components of the overall fine in relation to the individual circumstances and facts. The Courts tend to acknowledge that novel forms of infringements may be fined on a less stringent basis because it was difficult to foresee the illegality of the behaviour. This was argued in *TeliaSonera*, although dismissed by the Court. The reduction of fines in the appellate court typically mirrors either a different view on the infringement or the circumstances in relation to duration, seriousness, effects on the market, etc.

The *Telia Sverige* case[73] involved a purported cartel between Telia Sverige and Gothnet connected to a public procurement case on broadband services. The KKV was successful in the first instance and both Telia Sverige and Gothnet were fined MSEK 8 each. Gothnet decided not to appeal the judgment, whereas Telia Sverige appealed. The PMÖD ruled against the KKV on the matter of infringement as the appellate court did not find any restrictive behaviour neither by-object nor effect, whereby the fines were reduced to nil. The appellate court therefore disagreed with the PMD on the substantive issue and consequently, the fines were also annulled. There was considerable division amongst the judges, and the dissenting economic experts, both of whom argued for a finding of infringement - one of the experts even advocated for a

70. Marknadsdomstolen, case MD 2008:12, *KKV, v. Aktiebolaget Bil-B.; Bil-M. i Skåne Aktiebolag; Göinge Bil Aktiebolag; J. A. Bil AB; Kristianstads Automobil Aktiebolag; Skånebil Personbilar AB; Bilia Personbilar AB; Bildeve Aktiebolag*, 2008-09-10.
71. Patent and Market Court of Appeal, case PMT 1988-17, *Swedish Match North Europe AB v. KKV*, 2018-06-29.
72. *See also* Commission Guidelines on the method of setting fines imposed pursuant to Article 23(2)(a) of Regulation No. 1/2003, OJ C 210, 1.9.2006, pp. 2-5. *See also*, KKV, Metod för fastställande av konkurrensskadeavgiftens storlek, Ställningstagande 2021:1, dnr 21/2021.
73. Patent and Market Court of Appeal, case PMÖD 2018:4, PMT 761-17, *Telia Sverige AB v. KKV*, 2018-03-13.

restriction by-object. Spurred on by Telia's success on appeal, the purported co-infringer Gothnet also initiated procedures in the above-mentioned case *Gothnet*.[74] However, the original judgment had already entered into legal force and the standard venues for appeal were thereby not available. The appellate court dismissed the petition for a new trial and the original fine therefore remained unchanged for Gothnet. Although procedurally correct on appeal, the fact remains that the higher court's ruling that rejected a finding of infringement in substance left the affected alleged wrongdoers with two different outcomes, which appears unsatisfactory in relation to the consistent application of the law. If the original decision had been taken by the KKV it would probably have been possible to reverse or adjust that decision for all parties under the rules of administrative law in Sweden. The Patent and Market Court, cannot, however, unilaterally, and *ex officio* unravel a judgment that had entered into legal force. That is exactly what the petition for a new trial with the appellate court is designed for. This case therefore serves as a good example of a possible advantage of the new procedural rules.

Other cases concerned claims by the KKV for fines which were rejected by the Stockholm District Court/Patent and Market Court. Upon appeal by the KKV, in *Assistancekåren*,[75] *AQM*[76] and *Nasdaq* the appeal was rejected by the appellate court, who upheld the lower court's judgments in substance and no fines were decided upon. It can therefore be argued that the KKV has had considerable difficulties in their appeals, although the reasons underlying the different cases are different.

The first trend on appeal is that there appears to be a stricter view on the substantive matter of infringements in general. In *Assistancekåren*, the KKV argued for restriction by-object, however, both the court of first instance and the appellate court did not find an infringement. The case pre-dates the *Carte Bancaire* judgment by the CJEU[77] and is illustrative of the courts' general reluctance to affirm any finding of restriction by-object. In *AQM*, the infringement concerned an alleged cartel between undertakings active in relocation services abroad. However, the case did not actually amount to a clear-cut cartel case. Instead, the restriction under scrutiny concerned non-competition clauses agreed upon in connection with an acquisition of two separate business divisions, i.e., a question of ancillary restraints to a concentration. The KKV's claim was quashed in its entirety and on its merits by the Patent and Market Court, which conversely recognised the potential pro-competitive nature of such clauses.[78] On appeal, the KKV decided to only refer to a restriction by-object before the appellate

74. Patent and Market Court of Appeal, case PMÖ 11973-18, *Göteborg Energi Gothnet AB v. KKV*, 2019-05-27.
75. Marknadsdomstolen, case MD 2007:23, *KKV v. Assistancekåren Sweden AB, MRF-Bärgarna*, 2007-11-01.
76. Patent and Market Court of Appeal, case PMT 7498-16, *KKV v. Alfa Quality Moving AB, Vänrun AB (tidigare ICM Kungsholms AB) and NFB Transport Systems AB*, 2017-11-29.
77. Case C-67/13 P, *Groupement des cartes bancaires (CB) v. European Commission*, ECLI-:EU:C:2014:2204.
78. It is still unclear what motivated the KKV to pursue that case in the first place, bearing in mind how at odds the claim was in relation to even well-established guidance documents from the European Commission, *see* Commission Notice on restrictions directly related and necessary to concentrations, OJ C 56, 5.3.2005, pp. 24-31.

court. Predictably, the PMÖD rejected the appeal while adjusting the legal fees in favour of the defendant.

The *Nasdaq* case[79] concerned a novel form of exclusionary abuse, by means of which a dominant undertaking purportedly unduly interfered in a third party's contractual relationship with a view to ousting a competitor. The case was highly technical in nature and involved an extensive body of evidence relating to how the exclusion materialised and illustrative of how the appellate court was in line with its practice of requiring a firm body of evidence. Agreeing at least in principle with the potentially abusive nature of the practice as a result of actual or potential anti-competitive effects, the PMD and the PMÖD did not find convincing evidence to that effect. Decisive to the outcome on appeal was the lack of a firm body of evidence demonstrating at least potential anti-competitive effects. It is a clear illustration that the appellate court applies a high standard for proof in antitrust cases. There remain doubts about the requisite standard of proof, but after the 2016 reform, there appears to be a somewhat different and stricter approach to the issue of determination of infringements by PMÖD compared to its predecessor, the Market Court in relation to matters of evidence.

Cases on injunctions have been slightly more successful for the KKV compared with cases involving administrative fines. The *FTI* case[80] involved access to a national system of recycling bins for packaging materials (paper, cardboard, glass, plastics, etc.). The dominant undertaking decided to discontinue an existing business relationship with a competitor, whereby the competitor was cut off from using the bins and containers. The KKV held this to be an abuse of dominance whereby the dominant firm was ordered to rescind its cancellation of the existing agreement between the parties, and this was upheld on appeal by the Patent and Market Court. Upon appeal to the second instance, the PMÖD unexpectedly chose to view the behaviour as tantamount to a refusal to supply an essential facility, made direct references to the *Bronner*[81] criteria and concluded that the behaviour did not amount to an abuse. Arguably, the court's reasoning did not - regrettably - relate to the actual behaviour and therefore, this deviates considerably from EU case law.

Two cases from the sports sector have also been dealt with by the old Market court on appeal. In *Svenska Hockeyligan*,[82] the KKV decided to impose interim injunctions upon the Swedish Hockey League - a company that organises the top series ice hockey teams in Sweden. The KKV held it to be a horizontal restriction by the league not to allow short-term contracts of players from the National Hockey League (NHL)

---

79. Patent and Market Court of Appeal, case PMT 1443-18, *KKV v. Nasdaq AB, Nasdaq Clearing AB, Nasdaq Stockholm AB and Nasdaq Technology AB*, 2019-06-28. It cannot be argued that the KKV's actions were unwarranted and seemingly entailed a willingness to push the envelope and demonstrated that the KKV was not deterred by the mere fact that it would be difficult to litigate the case.

80. Patent and Market Court of Appeal, case PMÖÄ 1519, *Svenska Förpacknings- och Tidningsinsamlingen AB v. KKV*, 2012-02-28.

81. *See* case C-7/97, *Oscar Bronner GmbH & Co. KG v. Mediaprint Zeitungs- und Zeitschriftenverlag GmbH & Co. KG, Mediaprint Zeitungsvertriebsgesellschaft mbH & Co. KG and Mediaprint Anzeigengesellschaft mbH & Co. KG*, ECLI:EU:C:1998:569.

82. Marknadsdomstolen, case MD A 2/12, *Svenska Hockeyligan v. KKV*, 2012-12-18.

during a labour conflict in North America. On Appeal, the Market Court disagreed with the KKV, and that the restriction was necessary to attain justified objectives for the league. The *Svenska Bilsportförbundet* case[83] involved another type of horizontal restriction, targeted by an injunction by KKV in order to bring an infringement to an end. Essentially, the KKV's decision was upheld, but the court made the injunction order more precise.

A trend emerging from the court reform in 2016 is that the PMÖD does not make any references to older precedents from the Market Court. For instance, it can be noted from the cases referred to above that the new PMÖD is taking a different stance on certain substantive competition law issues compared to the old Market Court. This is naturally subject to further analysis, but some of the deviations have been addressed above. As indicated, the newly established case law may in some respect not entirely be in line with the CJEU's case law on substantive competition law issues.[84] Furthermore, there is a significant difference between the PMD's and PMÖD's judgments. The lower court appears to provide a well-reasoned and structured analysis, whereas there are seldom any similar arguments or reasoning put forward by the PMÖD. Being entrusted to be the court establishing the key substantive law rules and precedents in Swedish competition law should also entail a duty to lay down more articulated judgments clearly and systematically, or at the very least allow appeal to the Supreme Court. The occasionally limited and ambiguous reasoning is a shortcoming worthy of further academic attention.

6 CONCLUDING REMARKS

The Swedish appeal system has undergone key changes in 2016 and 2021. The major change came with the reform of the court system and forum rules in 2016 and the introduction of the Patent and Market Courts. Nowadays, the Patent and Markets Courts are exclusive fora in competition law cases in Sweden – also civil cases on, e.g., damages actions. The Patent and Market Court of Appeals (PMÖD) is in practice the main source of appeals and establishment of jurisprudence and precedent. Although there exists the possibility of appeal from the PMÖD to the Supreme Court, there have been no such appeals to date. Although the procedural rules have remained by and large the same during the period of this study, some substantial changes were introduced in 2021. Previously, infringement matters involving administrative fines were assessed according to the rules on cases not amenable to settlement out of court enshrined in the Code of Judicial Procedure. In order to, *inter alia*, make the appeal system more efficient, the rules changed in 2021 and appeals are now handled under the Court Matters Act, which should make oral hearings less comprehensive and emphasise the written procedure. It remains to be seen how the more simplified procedure will operate. It is therefore uncertain what effects the change in procedural rules will bring about – if any.

83. Marknadsdomstolen, case MD 2012:16, *Svenska Bilsportförbundet v. KKV*, 2012-12-20.
84. *See also*, Henriksson, L., *Sweden: Current Developments and Trends in Competition Law*, Concurrence No. 4-2021, pp. 196-206.

The national application of Swedish and European competition law is from a statutory point of view well-aligned with EU law. The Block Exemption laws directly refer to the Commission's respective block exemption regulations and in all other matters the case law of the CJEU is regarded as binding for the KKV and the courts. Substantive competition law is therefore on appeal overall adjudicated in accordance with EU law. Procedural law remains national, although heavily influenced by, e.g., the ECN+ directive. Albeit the Swedish and EU law in substances by design should be the same, in individual cases the procedural aspects play a significant role in the outcome of appeal – ranging from litigation proficiency, court tactics, rules on evidence and application thereof to the court procedure on oral or written hearings. The results and true impact of such variables are not so evident in hindsight when analysing the published judgments.

The introduction of the new decisional powers of the Swedish Competition Authority, Konkurrensverket (KKV) in 2021 constitute a major change in that the PMD is as of that date the first appellate court, whereas the PMÖD is the second, and in practice last, appellate instance (subject to potential appeal to the Supreme Court). During the full period of study, the KKV was not competent to take decisions on fines in the first instance and had to bring actions before the Stockholm district court/PMD on such cases. The judgments of that court could then be appealed to the Market Court/PMÖD. This effectively entailed a one-instance appeal system in Sweden, allowing for interesting comparisons with other jurisdictions.

The time period of this study involves appeal court judgments after the 2004 reform and before the 2021 reform. During that period Sweden had few appeal cases in terms of the limited focus of the study. Accordingly, there have been relatively few appeal judgments in Sweden, potentially explicable by various factors. First, competition law cases entail a complex economic and legal assessment, driving up legal costs to very high levels involving many experts and an extensive body of evidence and documents. Second, an appeal entails a full review of the court, which so far does not limit scrutiny of the appellate court and appeals therefore tend to entail extensive litigation. This may change because of the new procedural system, but it is too early to ascertain its potential impact. Third, the KKV has had a limited budget to bring actions for fines,[85] which significantly reduced the number of cases. Fourth, litigation tactics, including consideration of the level of fines, nature, and gravity of the infringement, etc. have played an important role in decisions on whether to appeal.

Based on the limited number of cases, it is difficult to draw any firm conclusions based on the limited statistical data available. Nonetheless, it appears to have been increasingly difficult for the KKV to prove infringements before the appellate courts and the success rate for the KKV both in terms level of fines and the existence of infringements is notably low in these cases. The low number of appeal cases may also be explained by other systematic factors, e.g., the KKV has used the now repealed system of voluntary fine orders in some minor cases. Those cases could not be appealed. In parallel to actual public enforcement, the subsidiary claims for injunctions

85. In 2021, the KKV was allocated SEK 137 million (≈ EUR 12.4 million) for the enforcement of competition rules. *See* KKV Annual Report 2021, p. 79.

have also been an effective venue for aggrieved undertakings to bring infringements to an end where the KKV has decided not to pursue a case.

References for preliminary rulings remain very limited from the appellate courts. During the time period of this study, no requests under Article 267 TFEU were made to the CJEU on competition law, save for one request in a case that was later withdrawn by the plaintiffs.[86]

The limited number of appeal cases may, in general, be a poor indicator of whether the Swedish competition rules are effective or functioning efficiently or its true impact on undertakings' market behaviour as a deterrent or corrective legal instrument. Although the ECN+ directive did not explicitly require any change in the decisional powers of the KKV and although acknowledged by the preparatory works that the old system did not entail any considerable obstacles for enforcement, the Government still emphasised the objective of making enforcement more efficient. The Government stressed that the underlying objective of the change in decisional powers of the KKV was to minimise all direct and indirect obstacles to effective cooperation between the competition authorities. rather than driven primarily by a concern with under-enforcement.[87]

The major reform in 2021, partly to transpose the ECN+ directive, will most certainly have a major impact on the scope for and number of appeals. The KKV is now entrusted to take decisions at first instance on administrative fines, both relating to competition law infringements and also fines for not complying with an investigation. To date, there have been two decisions on fines by the KKV, both of which were unsuccessfully appealed.[88] Also, there have been two orders of injunctions by the KKV and one of them was unsuccessfully appealed.[89]

86. The case started as a subsidiary claim for injunction after the complaint was rejected by the KKV. Pursuant to section 23 of the old Competition Act, media companies Kanal 5 and TV 4 brought an action against the Swedish collection society STIM before the Market Court. The court stayed the proceedings and asked for a preliminary ruling, *see* case C-52/07, *Kanal 5 Ltd and TV 4 AB v. Föreningen Svenska Tonsättares Internationella Musikbyrå (STIM) upa.*, ECLI:EU:C:2008:703. Later, the plaintiffs withdrew the action. Notably, although the Market Court was the appellate court, the old procedural system entailed no venues for appeal for subsidiary claims for injunctions. Hence, the case is outside the scope of this study. The Stockholm District court (here equated with an NCA for the purpose of the study) has made one request for preliminary ruling on competition matter – *see* C-52/09, *Konkurrensverket v. TeliaSonera Sverige AB*, ECLI:EU:C:2011:83.

87. Cf. Government Bill 2020/21:51, *Konkurrensverkets befogenheter*, pp. 48-57.

88. *See* KKV decision *Sanerings Companiet i Malmö AB och Sopkärlstvätt i Malmö AB*, dnr 121/2021 (on appeal: PMÄ 19173-22). The undertaking withdrew the appeal, and the Court wrote off the appeal. *See also* KKV decision *Taxi Beställningscentral i Ulricehamns kommun Aktiebolag och Väner Taxi AB*, dnr. 569/2020 (on appeal: PMÄ 17109-22). The claimant did not comply with the PMD's order to supplement the grounds of the claim. Absent this, the PMD ruled on the documents submitted and dismissed the appeal.

89. KKV decision *Nasdaq Stockholm Aktiebolag*, dnr 366/2022, the investigation was later terminated after the undertaking discontinued a practice deemed anti-competitive, and KKV decision in *Svensk Mäklarstatistik – statistik om bostadsförsäljningar*, dnr. 348/2021, 465/2021 (on appeal: PMÄ 11170-21). The PMD agreed in substance with the KKV but made some minor adjustments to the injunction.

CHAPTER 30

UK Report

Barry Rodger & Or Brook

1 INTRODUCTION TO THE COMPETITION LAW ENFORCEMENT CONTEXT IN THE UK

1.1 Historical Outline

The UK entered the then EEC in 1973, the same year the Fair Trading Act came into force. This statute however was not a response to membership of the EEC, but rather a consolidating piece of legislation. Further consolidating legislations were introduced in 1976, regulating anti-competitive agreements: the Restrictive Trade Practices Act 1976, the Restrictive Practices Court Act 1976 and the Resale Prices Act 1976.

Between the late 1980s and 1990s, there was a continuous debate on whether UK competition law should be reformed to mirror the European provisions.[1] The Competition Act 1998 ('CA98'), which came into force in March 2000, has radically altered UK competition law. New controls known as the Chapter I and Chapter II prohibitions were introduced, virtually identical to Articles 101 and 102 TFEU, respectively. Consistency of interpretation with EU law was ensured by section 60 of the Act, providing that the determination of any questions of interpretation regarding the prohibitions should be consistent with the treatment of corresponding questions arising under EU law. It is clear from the enforcement practice and, notably, from the judgments of the UK courts that EU case law has been routinely relied on as underpinning the interpretation of the domestic prohibitions.

1. Opening Markets: New Policy on Restrictive Trade Practices, Cm 727, 1989, following the earlier Green Paper, Review of Restrictive Trade Practices Policy, Cm 331, 1988; Abuse of Market Power, Cm 2100, 1992.

The Enterprise Act of 2002, further reformed procedural and institutional aspects of the UK competition law enforcement.[2] It created a specialist competition tribunal, the Competition Appeal Tribunal (CAT). As of 1 May 2004, a number of further procedural and institutional changes were made to mirror the changes introduced following modernisation of EU competition law.[3]

Further reforms took place in 2013. The Enterprise and Regulatory Reform Act of 2013 (ERRA13), which came into force in April 2014, merged the two existing competition authorities (the Office of Fair Trading - OFT and Competition Commission) into a single regulator - the Competition and Markets Authority (CMA). In addition, it introduced other procedural reforms aimed at making the competition regime more streamlined and efficient.[4] The Consumer Rights Act 2015 enhanced the role of the CAT by allowing it to hear stand-alone actions and grant injunctions, introducing an 'opt-out' collective action.

The UK's departure from the EU at the end of 2020 led to further changes. The CMA is now required to take on a significant number of antitrust and merger cases that were previously handled by the European Commission. Moreover, the post-Brexit replacement for section 60, the new section 60A, provides greater flexibility for the courts and authorities in interpreting and applying the UK prohibition. While the UK government appears committed to maintaining an effective competition law system, it is less clear whether that system will remain as aligned to the EU rules as before. However, it is important to stress that the high level of alignment was never required by EU law, it was a political choice of successive UK governments.

1.2 Enforcement Framework

As of 1 April 2014, as mentioned, the CMA took over the previous competition law responsibilities of both the OFT and the Competition Commission. The administrative model of public enforcement, where the CMA investigates and takes final decisions on infringements and sanctions, was retained. A far more radical proposed prosecutorial model of enforcement was rejected during the consultation phase leading up to the ERRA13.

The CMA exercise its powers concurrently with a variety of utility regulators: Office of Gas and Electricity Markets (OFGEM), Office of Communications (OFCOM), Office of Water Services (OFWAT), Office of Rail Regulation (ORR), Civil Aviation Authority (CAA), Financial Conduct Authority (FCA), Payment Services Regulator

2. The Act also reformed the UK merger control regime (which lies outside the scope of this project) by replacing the public interest test with a competition-focused test.
3. *See, generally*, the Competition Act 1998 and Other Enactments (Amendment) Regulations 2004, SI 2004/1261.
4. Department for Business, Innovation and Skills, 'Enterprise and Regulatory Reform Act 2013: A guide', June 2013, London: BIS.

(PSR), NHS Improvement (NHSI, formerly Monitor), and the Northern Ireland Authority For Utility Regulation (NIAUR).[5] The Competition Act 1998 (Concurrency) Regulations 2014[6] were introduced following the ERRA13 to enhance the effectiveness of the concurrency regime.

The CMA has a relatively high discretion to manage investigations. It decides which cases to investigate based on its Prioritisation Principles,[7] and has considerable powers to investigate potential infringements of the domestic prohibitions once a formal investigation has been opened.[8] The CMA has various options in dealing with a case. It can close the investigation on the grounds of administrative priorities or issue a no grounds for action decision. It has the power to accept binding commitments,[9] although the use of this remedy has not been as prevalent as by the European Commission under the EU competition rules.

Most importantly, the CMA can make a formal decision declaring that the rules have been infringed and order the parties in breach to cease the infringing conduct, as well as impose penalties under section 36 of the CA98. Section 36(8) provides that no penalty may be imposed which exceeds 10% of the turnover of an undertaking, calculated in accordance with the Competition Act 1998 (Determination of Turnover for Penalties) Order 2000.[10] Section 44 of the ERRA13 introduced a new section 36(7A) to the CA98, setting out statutory criteria to which the CMA must have regard when fixing the level of a fine for an infringement as follows: (a) the seriousness of the infringement concerned, and (b) the desirability of deterring both the undertaking on whom the penalty is imposed and others from infringing the prohibitions. These factors were already a central aspect of the CMA's Fines Guidance,[11] and the CAT, under section 38 of the CA98, is to have regard to the Fines Guidance in reviewing and setting fines imposed.

The CMA's leniency programme aims to enhance the deterrent effect of the legislation[12] and plays a key role in uncovering secret cartels. The CMA may also consider settlement for any case, provided the evidential standard for giving notice of its proposed infringement decision is met, and the reward for a business which settles

---

5. Section 54 CA98. *See*, for a detailed consideration of this issue, Niamh Dunne, 'Concurrency', in Barry Rodger et al (eds), *The UK Competition Regime: A Twenty-Year Retrospective* (OUP, 2021).
6. The Concurrency Regulations, SI 2014/536, under section 54 CA98, as amended by section 51 of the ERRA13. *See* CMA, 'Regulated Industries: Guidance on concurrent application of competition law to regulated industries', March 2014.
7. *See* CMA, 'Prioritisation principles for the CMA', January 2014.
8. *See* sections 25-29 generally as amended by paras 10-14 of Schedule 1 to the Competition Act 1998 and Other Enactments (Amendment) Regulations 2004, SI 2004/1261.
9. *See* para. 18 of Schedule 1 to the Competition Act 1998 and Other Enactments (Amendment) Regulations 2004, SI 2004/1261 and Schedule 6A to the Competition Act 1998. *See also*, OFT. 'Enforcement, incorporating the Office of Fair Trading's guidance as to the circumstances in which it may be appropriate to accept commitments', OFT 407.
10. SI 2000/309, as amended by the Competition Act 1998 (Determination of Turnover for Penalties) (Amendment) Order 2004, SI 2004/1259.
11. CMA Guidance as to the appropriate amount of a penalty, CMA 73, 18 April 2018.
12. Ibid. On the use of leniency and settlements in the UK, *see* Or Brook, 'Do EU and U.K. Antitrust "Bite"?: A Hard Look at "Soft" Enforcement and Negotiated Penalty Settlements' (2023) 68(3) *The Antitrust Bulletin* 477.

is a settlement discount which will be capped at 20% for settlement pre-Statement of Objections and 10% for settlement post-Statement of Objections.[13]

1.3 Enforcement Practices and Priorities

The CMA's predecessor, the OFT, was criticised for its relative inaction during the early 2000s and the limited level of fines imposed.[14] As elaborated below, even since, very few formal decisions have been issued by the OFT, CMA, and sector regulators enforcing EU and UK competition laws.

The most notable aspect, as evidenced by research on enforcement trends in the UK until 2019,[15] is the predominance of cases involving the EU and/or national prohibitions on anti-competitive agreements. The clear prioritisation of investigations relating to anti-competitive agreements may reflect various factors: the less discretionary nature of such investigations where leniency applications have been made; the perceived impact on consumers of anti-competitive harm from such arrangements; and the relative ease in establishing an infringement under this prohibition. There has also been a tendency for the CMA to focus on blatant but fairly small-scale localised horizontal cartel arrangements for which only relatively small fines could be imposed.

Most infringement cases in the UK have involved by-object anti-competitive agreements that are inevitably more straightforward cases for authorities to successfully establish an infringement. There has also been considerable focus on resale price arrangements generally, which were mostly handled by warning letters.[16] The CMA has more recently devoted considerable attention to online vertical competition concerns cases either directly involving online resale price maintenance or where limitations on online advertising were imposed to limit competitive pricing.

The statistics in relation to abuse cases appear to demonstrate a historical reluctance by the UK competition authority to take on abuse cases (or for complaints to be made) and the difficulties in pursuing a case through to an infringement finding. From 2000, and over a period of nineteen years, there were only six infringement decisions in cases in which the abuse prohibitions were applied,[17] albeit there is clear evidence of a renewed vigour in abuse case enforcement in recent years, particularly in relation to the pharmaceutical sector.

13. *See* CMA, Guidance on the CMA's investigation procedures in Competition Act 1998 cases', March 2014, at paras 14.1-14.33.
14. *See, e.g.*, The National Audit Office, 'Enforcing Competition in Markets', HC 593 Session 2005-06.
15. *See* Barry Rodger, 'Application of the domestic and EU antitrust prohibitions: an analysis of the UK competition authority's enforcement practice' (2020) 8(1) *Journal of Antitrust Enforcement and Practice* 86-123.
16. *See* Brook (n 12).
17. *See* Rodger (n 15).

2 REVIEW OF THE COMPETITION AUTHORITY'S DECISIONS

In the UK, there is a distinction between the notions of 'appeal' and 'judicial review'. Appeals refer to the merits of the case, allowing the court to substitute the decision of the primary decision-maker. Judicial review, by comparison, is linked to the validity of the decision and decision-making process rather than its merits,[18] and in a competition law context, such a level of review can take place in relation to mergers and market investigations (and commitments decisions, *see* below). For the purpose of this chapter, however, the judicial review of competition law enforcement by the CMA's and the utility regulators' will be collectively and interchangeably labelled as 'appeal' or 'review'.

2.1 First-Instance Appeal: The Competition Appeal Tribunal (CAT)

Decisions of the competition authorities and utility regulators can be appealed to the CAT, a 'hyper-specialised' appeal body.[19] The CAT can hear appeals against the substance of any decision taken by the CMA, including the level of any penalties imposed.[20]

The CAT may confirm, set aside, vary the CMA's decision, remit the matter to the CMA, or make any other decision that the CMA could have made. In relation to penalties, the CAT's primary task is to 'determine whether the overall figure for penalty was appropriate in the circumstances'.[21] Section 38 CA98 requires the CAT to have regard to the CMA's Fines Guidance in setting appropriate penalties. Accordingly, the CAT stressed in *Napp*[22] that it would make this assessment based on a 'broad brush' approach, and then carry out a 'cross check' to assess if it was within the parameters of the CMA's Finning Guidance. In *Replica Football Kit*, it held that it had the power to increase the penalty,[23] albeit this power 'should not be exercised lightly'.[24]

Detailed rules concerning the CAT procedure were adopted.[25] The Court of Appeal in England has recently tied these competencies to the *quasi*-criminal nature of the competition law proceedings, noting:[26]

> (i) (F)or a (non-judicial) administrative body lawfully to be able to impose quasi-criminal sanctions there must be a right of challenge; (ii) that right must

18. For a discussion *see*, Despoina Mantzari,. 'Judicial Scrutiny of Regulatory Decisions at the UK's Specialist Competition Appeal Tribunal.' in Jurgen De Poorter et al (eds.) *Judicial Review of Administrative Discretion in the Administrative State* (TMC Asser Press, 2019), 66.
19. *Ibid.*
20. Enterprise Act 2002, section 46(1).
21. *Argos Ltd and Littlewoods Ltd v. OFT* and *JJB Sports plc v. OFT* [2006] EWCA Civ 1318, at para. 194.
22. *See Napp, supra* n. 148, paras 497-503 and *Napp Pharmaceutical Holdings Ltd v. DGFT* [2002] EWCA Civ 796.
23. [2005] CAT 22 at paras 208-235.
24. *Ibid.*, at para. 218.
25. The Competition Appeal Tribunal Rules 2003, SI 2003/1372, applicable to proceedings commenced after 20 June 2003, replacing the 2000 Rules (SI 2000/261).
26. *See CMA v. Flynn Pharma Ltd and Pfizer Inc* [2020] EWCA Civ 339 per Green LJ (paras 135-147).

> offer guarantees of a type required by Article 6 {ECHR}; (iii) the subsequent review must be by a judicial body with 'full jurisdiction' (iv) the judicial body must have the power to quash the decision 'in all respects on questions of fact and law';(v) the judicial body must have the power to substitute its own appraisal for that of the decision maker;(vi) the judicial body must conduct its evaluation of the legality of the decision 'on the basis of the evidence adduced' by the appellant; and (vii) the existence of a margin of discretion accorded to a competition authority does not dispense with the requirement for an 'in depth review of the law and the facts' by the supervising judicial body.[27]

The types of appealable decisions were identified in *Bettercare v. DGFT.*[28] The CAT made clear that this is a matter of substance, based in particular on the position adopted on the complaint and the stage the investigation has reached.[29] Accordingly, an appeal may also be made where the CMA has not formally issued a decision, but, for instance, advised a complainant informally that it will not proceed with a complaint because it does not appear that either prohibition has been infringed.

The main party or parties against whom the CMA has made decisions can appeal, as can 'qualifying third parties' with a sufficient interest in the issue. The qualifying test allows interested consumers and organisations representing such consumers to appeal directly to the CAT.

Appeals in front of the CAT are heard by a Chairman, who is either the President or a member of the panel of Tribunal Chairmen, and two other appeal panel members.[30] The President must be a senior legally qualified person with appropriate experience and knowledge, whereas ordinary members need not be lawyers, and have varied expertise and background with legal and non-legal expertise in areas such as economics, business, and accountancy.

Although delivered prior to the time-frame studied in this project, some of the early appeal rulings by the CAT in relation to the UK and EU prohibitions were influential in terms of judicial pronouncements about the appeal context and intensity of review. It is necessary to recount this earlier period, to emphasise the degree of intensity of review undertaken by the CAT and the number of cases involving fully or partially successful appeals. It may be argued that its role here not only set out the wide parameters of the appeal process and potential scrutiny by the CAT but may also have had a dampening effect on the enforcement activity by the competition authorities, wary of subsequent judicial review of their enforcement decision-making.

The very first judgment by the CAT, the *Institute of Independent Insurance Brokers v. Director General of Fair Trading* of 2001,[31] quashed the competition authority's (at that stage the DGFT) finding that Chapter I prohibition did not apply to the Rules of the General Insurance Council, holding the rules were to be prohibited. In

27. *Ibid.*, para. 140.
28. *Bettercare v. DGFT* [2002] CAT 6. *See also, Freeserve.com v. DGFT* [2002] CAT 8; *Claymore/Express Dairies v. DGFT* [2003] CAT 3; and *Pernod Ricard SA and Campbell Distillers Ltd v. OFT* [2004] CAT 10.
29. *See* the fuller discussion in Alese Femi, 'The office burden: making a decision without a decision for a third party' [2003] ECLR 616.
30. EA2002, sections 12 and 14 and Schedule 2.
31. 1002/2/1/01 [2001] CAT 4.

the following year, in *BetterCare Group Limited v. Director General of Fair Trading*, the CAT overturned a decision finding that an NHS trust may be acting as an undertaking for the purposes of the Competition Act 1998.[32] In two consecutive rulings in 2002 and 2003 in the matter of *Aberdeen Journals Limited v. Director General of Fair Trading*, the CAT set aside the decision and remitted on the issue of the relevant market,[33] and upheld the decision on liability but reduced the penalty imposed by just under 25%.[34] In *NAPP*[35] the CAT upheld the substance of the Director's decision on the question of infringement but reduced the fine from GBP 3.21 million to GBP 2.2 million.[36] An appeal was also partially successful in *Freeserve.com PLC v. Director General of Telecommunications* of 2003 where the CAT found that the Director General had given inadequate reasons for rejecting one of the grounds of Freeserve's complaint about BT's actions.[37] The Tribunal set aside this aspect of the decision but dismissed the appeal in all other respects.

In *Genzyme Limited v. Office of Fair Trading* of 2004, the CAT upheld the OFT's decision that there was an abusive margin squeeze but overturned the decision in respect of an alleged abusive bundling and reduced the size of the penalty.[38] In the same year, in joined cases, *Allsports Limited v. Office of Fair Trading/JJB Sports PLC v. Office of Fair Trading*, the appeal on liability brought by Allsports was dismissed in its entirety and partly allowed in relation to JJB.[39] *Floe Telecom Limited (in liquidation) v. Office of Communications* involved an appeal against a decision of the Director General of Telecommunications that Vodafone Limited had not infringed the 1998 Act Chapter II prohibition in which the Director's decision was set aside and the matter remitted to OFCOM.[40] In *Argos Limited, Littlewoods Limited v. Office of Fair Trading*, the appeals on liability were dismissed[41] but in a later judgment on penalty, the fines were reduced.[42]

In related judgments in 2005, in the matter of *Apex Asphalt and Paving Co. Limited v. Office of Fair Trading* the appeal was dismissed,[43] and *in Richard W. Price (Roofing Contractors) Ltd v. Office of Fair Trading* the appeal was dismissed in relation to liability but allowed in relation to the penalty which was reduced from GBP 18,000 to GBP 9,000.[44] In joined cases in the matter of *Umbro Holdings Limited, Manchester United plc, Allsports Ltd and JJB Sports plc v. Office of Fair Trading*, the penalties were also reduced in relation to Umbro from GBP 6.641 million to GBP 5.3 million;[45] MU

32. 1006/2/1/01 [2002] CAT 7.
33. 1005/1/1/01 [2002] CAT 4.
34. Aberdeen journals [2003] CAT 8.
35. [2002] CAT 1.
36. *Ibid.*
37. 1007/2/3/02 [2003] CAT 5.
38. 1016/1/1/03 [2004] CAT 4
39. 1021/1/1/03 1022/1/1/03 [2004] CAT 17.
40. 1024/2/3/04 [2004] CAT 18.
41. 1014/1/1/03; 1015/1/1/03 [2004] CAT 24.
42. [2005] CAT 13, in Argos' case from GBP 17.28 million to GBP 15 million and in Littlewoods' case from GBP 5.37 million to GBP 4.5 million.
43. 1032/1/1/04 [2005] CAT 4.
44. 1033/1/1/04 [2005] CAT 5.
45. 1019/1/1/03, 1020/1/1/03, 1021/1/1/03 and 1022/1/1/03, respectively, [2005] CAT 22.

from GBP 1.652 million to GBP 1.5 million, and JJB Sports from GBP 8.373 million to GBP 6.7 million while the CAT increased the penalty for the first time in relation to Allsports from GBP 1.35 million to GBP 1.42 million.

In another group of joined cases in the matter of the *Racecourse Association and others v. Office of Fair Trading/The British Horseracing Board v. Office of Fair Trading* the CAT upheld the appeal and set aside the OFT's decision in relation to the relevant media rights,[46] and later in 2005 it also set aside the OFT's decision in Claymore Dairies Limited and *Arla Foods UK PLC v. Office of Fair Trading* due to serious doubts as to the adequacy of the OFT's investigation.[47] There were two later Court of Appeal rulings, both of which related to competition authority decisions prior to 1 May 2004. In joined cases *Argos Limited; Littlewoods Limited v. Office of Fair Trading/Sports PLC v. Office of Fair Trading*[48] the appeals from the CAT judgments were dismissed in relation to both liability and penalty. Finally, in *Floe Telecom Limited (in liquidation) v. Office of Communications*, a complicated process following an appeal by a complainant in relation to alleged abusive behaviour,[49] resulted in a minor success at appeal, and subsequent partial success at the Court of Appeal by the appellants OFCOM and the alleged infringer.[50] This dispute was particularly significant for the CAT ruling[51] and then the Court of Appeal judgment in 2006 on the scope of the CAT's jurisdiction in appeals.[52]

Overall, in this earlier period, aside from the interesting dicta, the CAT demonstrated the intensity of review on the merits which resulted in several partially and fully successful challenges to the authority's enforcement practice.

Andreangeli has stressed the importance of Article 6 ECHR for the UK public enforcement framework, and the existence of necessary judicial safeguards to ensure the right to a fair trial.[53] The CAT in *Napp* confirmed that it would ensure the authority established any infringement on the basis of a preponderance of probabilities, and 'strong and compelling' evidence was required by the authority due to the presumption of innocence.[54] Moreover, the CAT in *Napp* understood the ECHR requirement of full jurisdiction as requiring the widest possible scrutiny on all matters of fact and law on the merits.

46. 1035/1/1/04 1041/2/1/04 [2005] CAT 29.
47. 1008/2/1/02 [2005] CAT 30.
48. [2006] EWCA Civ 1318.
49. [2006] CAT 17.
50. [2009] EWCA Civ 47.
51. [2005] CAT 14.
52. [2006] EWCA Civ 768.
53. Arianna Andreangeli, 'Human Rights and the UK Competition Act: Public Enforcement and Due Process' in Rodger et al (eds.) *The UK Competition Regime, a Twenty Year Retrospective* (OUP, 2021).
54. Paragraphs 108-109.

2.2 Second-Instance Appeal: Court of Appeal in England and Wales, the Court of Session in Scotland, and the High Court in Northern Ireland

Decisions of the CAT can be appealed on a point of law to the Court of Appeal in England and Wales, the Court of Session in Scotland, or the High Court in Northern Ireland (together in this report – the Court of Appeal).[55] In undertaking its task, the Court of Appeal has expressed its deference to the specialist CAT as follows: 'it seems to us that it is right for the court to recognise that the Tribunal is an expert and specialised body, and that ... the court should hesitate before interfering with the Tribunal's assessment'.[56]

2.3 Third-Instance Appeal: Supreme Court

Further appeal to the Supreme Court is available on a point of law only. As demonstrated below, there have been no appeals at third instance in cases that fall within the time scope of the project.

3 PRIOR RESEARCH

Various studies have systematically examined the review of competition law enforcement in the UK.

Brook has systematically studied how the CMA and the reviewing courts have considered non-competition interests (efficiencies and public policy considerations) within the enforcement of Article 101 TFEU and the Section I equivalent (2004–2017). Her analysis found, in particular, that while many national courts have shown strong deference to the NCA's analysis of Article 101(3) TFEU and the national equivalent provisions, the CAT has accepted all of the appeals in which the undertakings raised concerns over the NCA's application of Article 101(3) TFEU during the relevant time period.[57]

Mantzari has explored the CAT's judicial scrutiny of regulatory decisions (that is, excluding competition law).[58] Her study demonstrates that the CAT's scrutiny of regulatory decisions is determined by a tripartite relationship between the expert regulators, the expert CAT, and the generalist Court of Appeal. This gives rise to a

55. CA1998, section 49. The requirement for resolution of a point of law limits the potential availability of appeal. *See*, for instance, *Napp Pharmaceutical Holdings Ltd v. DGFT (No 5)* [2002] EWCA Civ 796; [2002] 4 All ER 376.
56. *Argos, supra* n. 175, at para. 165. *See also* the CA ruling in *CMA v. Flynn Pharma,* [202] EWCA Civ 339.
57. Yet, those judgments were based on flaws in the assessment procedure, rather than on substantive scrutiny of the application of the Article's conditions. *See* Or Brook, *Non-Competition Interests in EU Antitrust Law: An Empirical Study of Article 101 TFEU* (CUP, 2022, 179-181.
58. Mantzari (n 18). Also *see* Despoina Mantzari,. *Courts, Regulators, and the Scrutiny of Economic Evidence* (OUP, 2022).

varying intensity of review better understood as a continuum: 'On the one end of the continuum lie judgments over primary facts reached following the evaluation of evidence, and discretionary decisions over which the tribunal will exercise a profound and rigorous scrutiny. On the other end of the continuum lie multifaceted policy considerations, which depend on inferences drawn from the evidence. In such cases the CAT is prepared to afford a margin of appreciation to the discretionary assessments of regulators.' Mantzari notes that the original limited review is the primary means to review any regulatory decisions, although this has itself subsequently accommodated ECHR issues via the Human Rights Act 1998.

However, it is also important to be aware that the appeal routes vary, and while there are different routes to the CAT, via judicial review and the Communications Act 2003, this project is focused on appeals under the 1998 Act, a specific, but not the only, role of the CAT, and that in the wider context inevitably the processes of review are inconsistent. She considers the CAT's institutional features, notably its membership and expertise and notes the different impact this has on the degree of deference afforded to discretionary assessments. She stresses that the tribunal has interpreted the reference to an appeal 'on the merits' to mean that it has 'full jurisdiction to find facts, make its own appraisals of economic issues, apply the law to those facts and appraisals, and determine the amount of any penalty'.[59]

Mejia studied judicial appeals by telecoms and competition regulators in Spain and the UK between 2000 and 2016, to assess the extent to which different legal traditions could lead to differences in the outcomes of judicial challenges to regulators' actions.[60] Similar findings by *Bernatt* concerning judicial review in Poland, suggest that judges with expertise in competition and EU law exercise more intense judicial review.[61]

4 QUANTITATIVE ANALYSIS

This section moves to examine the findings resulting from a systematic analysis of the review of competition law enforcement between May 2004 and April 2021.

4.1 Source of Information

All judgments of the relevant courts in the UK are published. Hence, it is anticipated that the UK appeal case law provides a comprehensive coverage of all relevant appeals

59. It has wide remedial powers *Aberdeen Journals Ltd v. DGFT* [2002] CAT 4, at para. 61. And its procedural powers allow it to undertake a detailed examination of findings by the authority/regulator, allowing cross-examination of witnesses and noting that a merits appeal 'provides…a right to call and cross examine witness[es]' per *VIP Communications Ltd v. OFCOM* [2007] CAT 3, at para. 43.
60. Luis E. Mejia 'Judicial review of regulatory decisions: Decoding the contents of appeals against agencies in Spain and the United Kingdom' (2021) 15(3) Regulation & Governance 760.
61. Maciej Bernatt, 'Effectiveness of Judicial Review in the Polish Competition Law System and the Place for Judicial Deference' (2016) 9(14) Yearbook of Antitrust and Regulatory Studies 97, available via https://ssrn.com/abstract=2896823.

during the relevant period. The judgments were identified primarily via the CAT's website, which provides details of all instances of appeals against decisions by the competition authority, and were cross-checked using the Westlaw database.

4.2 Total Numbers of Judgments and Ratio of Appeals

A total of forty-three judgments were rendered during the relevant period, thirty-seven in the first instance and six in the second instance. From the 107 appealable actions taken by the UK's competition authorities (OFT, CMA, and the sector regulators – together the 'competition authority') in the relevant period, only 26 decisions were appealed. The ratio of competition authority's decisions subject to appeal is therefore 24%.

This number of judgments is exceedingly low compared to many EU Member States, especially when one considers the size of the British economy, population, the relatively mature and developed system of competition law enforcement, and the large budget of the CMA and sector regulators. Ultimately, however, this can be primarily explained by the low number of competition authority's decisions.[62] This conclusion is also supported by comparison with the (relatively high) number of CAT's judgments relating to its other judicial capacities, notably in relation to private enforcement.[63]

Only 6% of the CAT judgments have been subsequently appealed to the Court of Appeal and no cases have been appealed to the Supreme Court.

4.3 Judgments per Year

Figure 30.1 summarises the number of judgments issued by the various instances of the UK courts per year.

Figure 30.1 Number of Judgments According to Instances

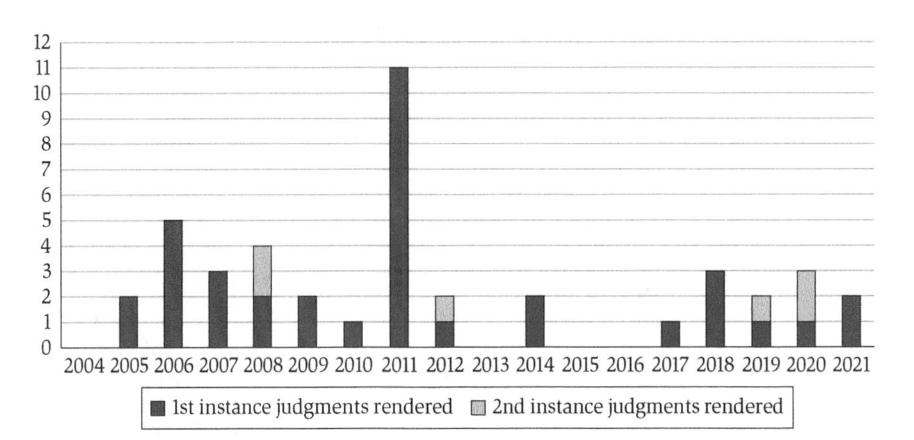

62. Rodger (n 15); Brook (n 12).
63. For a review of the number of CAT's private action judgments, *see* the 'Overall Case Activity' section of the CAT's Annual Report and Accounts, available via: https://www.catribunal.org.uk/about/publications.

The changes in the number of judgments across the years can be explained with reference to the number of the competition authority's decisions issued and the number of the CAT's judgments.

Figure 30.2(a) demonstrates that most of the competition authority's decisions that were appealed (bars) were examined within a single CAT judgment (lines), although in some exceptional cases, more than one appeal judgment was issued. Figure 30.2(b) confirms this is also true with respect to second-instance appeals reviewed by the Court of Appeal.

Figure 30.2(a) First-Instance Judgments

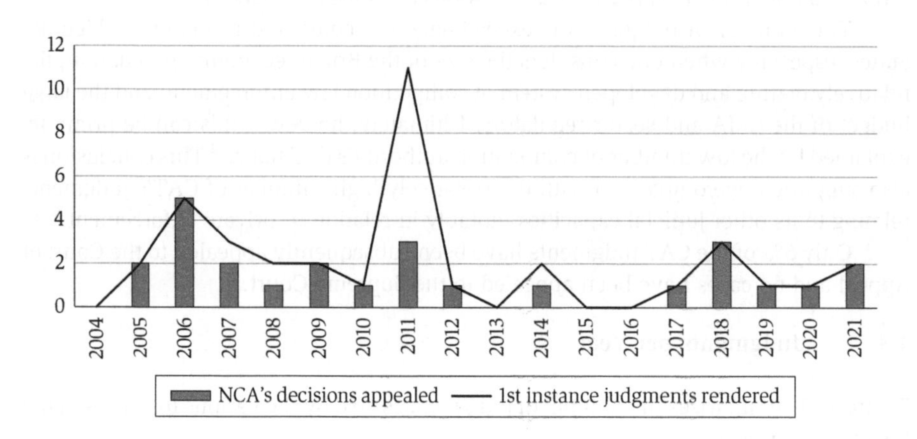

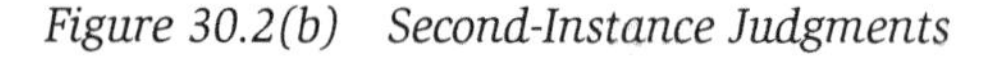

Figure 30.2(b) Second-Instance Judgments

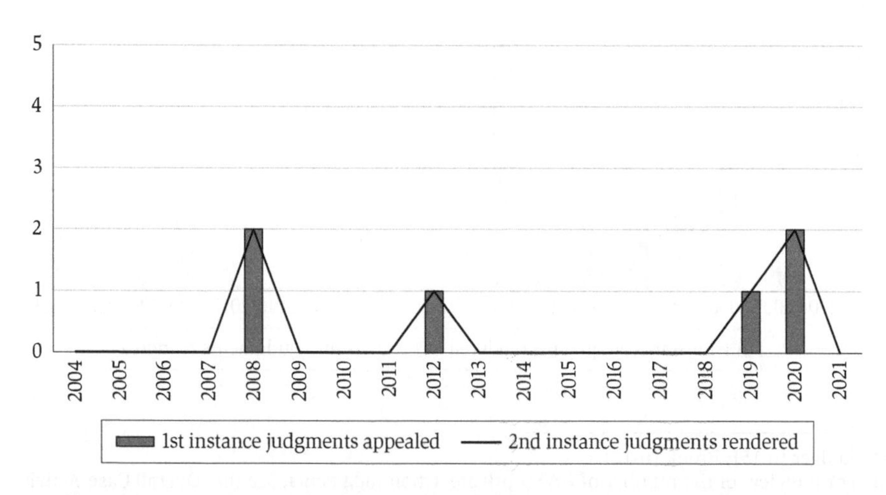

Figures 30.1 and 30.2(a) point out that 2011 was the peak year in terms of the number of judgments issued by the CAT. This, however, does not mark a substantive

trend but rather was the result of the OFT's *Construction Industry Bid-rigging* cases in 2010, in which 102 businesses were fined in relation to an England-wide infringement.

The two figures may suggest an additional trend of a growing number of second-instance appeals since 2019. There were three appeal rulings during 2019-2020 in the cases of *Balmoral Tanks Ltd v. CMA, Ping Europe Ltd v. CMA and Flynn Pharma Ltd, and Pfizer Inc. v. CMA*. These numbers are still far from decisive to point to a clear trend. Moreover, as those second-instance appeals were mostly unsuccessful (*see* next section), this may discourage appeals in the future.

4.4 Success Rates and Outcomes

Figure 30.3 presents the success of the appeals, across all instances. Those success rates are presented from the perspective of the competition authority's decision and the previous instance judgment which has been appealed, taking into account that separate appeals were aggregated where launched against a single decision of the competition authority or a previous instance judgment. That means that if a single decision was appealed by various parties in separate proceedings, the outcome of all those judgments will be counted as a single case for the purposes of this figure.

Figure 30.3 Success of Appeals (Each NCA's Decision or Previous Court Judgment Counts as One)

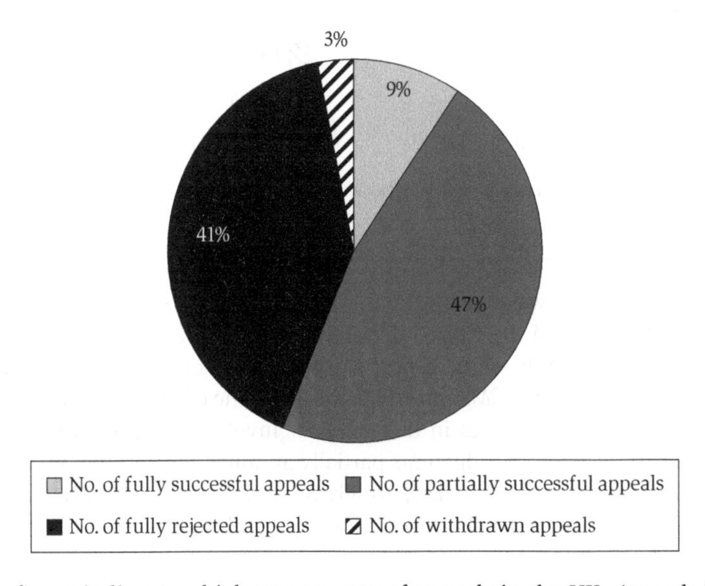

The figure indicates a high success rate of appeals in the UK. Appeals launched against 56% of the competition authority's decisions and the CAT's judgments were either partially or fully successful. The partially successful category includes cases where either the substantive aspects of the infringement decision were overturned or set aside (or there was a success in some appeals but not in other separate appeals in relation to the same infringement decision) and cases where the original penalty was reduced in some way (*see* section 4.6 below).

The success rates are further elaborated upon in Figure 30.4, which identifies the outcome of the appeals. Unlike Figure 30.3, this figure examines each judgment separately and differs between the appeal's instances.

Figure 30.4(a) First-Instance Outcome

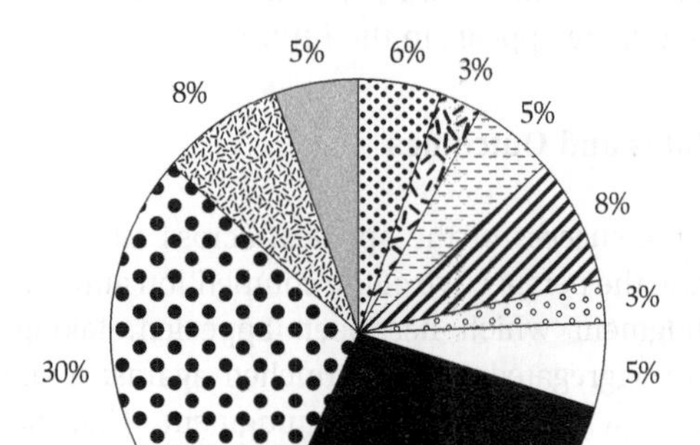

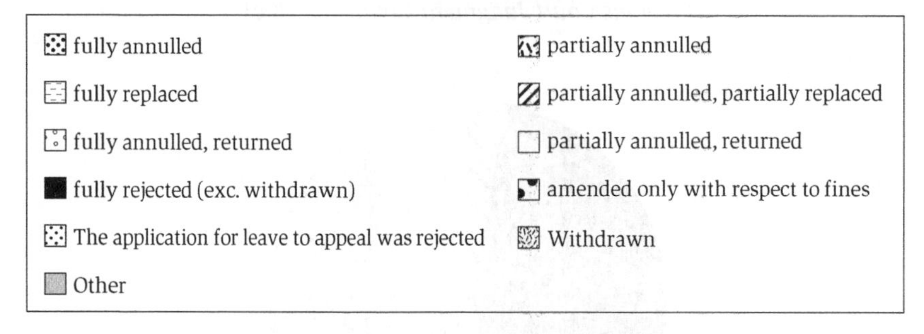

Figure 30.4(a) shows that in almost half of the CAT's judgments (46%), the tribunal partially changed the CMA's decision. This includes 30% of judgments that amended the decision only with respect to the fines, including *Terry Brannigan v. OFT*[64] and *Ping Europe Ltd v. CMA* (in which the CMA fine of £1.45 million was reduced by GBP 200 k).[65] All other cases in this category involved appeals in relation to the construction cartel.[66] 16% of judgments partially annulled the decision with respect to matters beyond the fines (including: partially annulled – 3%; partially annulled and partially replaced – 8%; partially annulled and partially returned to the competition authority – 5%).

64. [2007] CAT 23.
65. [2018] CAT 13.
66. For example, *G F Tomlinson Building Ltd and others v. OFT* [2011] CAT 7.

Only 8% of the CAT's judgments fully annulled the competition authority's decision. This includes *MasterCard UK Members Forum Limited v. OFT* (2006),[67] in which the OFT had already agreed to withdraw its decision. In an additional 5% of cases, the CAT fully replaced the decision. This illustrates the CAT's wide discretion and competencies. The two judgments in that category - *Burgess* (2005)[68] and *Albion Water* (2008)[69] - both examined the validity of the decisions to reject a complaint alleging abuse of dominance. In both cases, while the competition authority rejected the complainant's allegations of abuse, the CAT in its appeal ruling found an abusive infringement - emphasising that there is 'in principle no difference between an appeal against an infringement decision and an appeal against a non-infringement decision'.[70]

Figure 30.4(b) summarises the outcome of the cases in front of the Court of Appeal. As mentioned, out of the six cases, three were unsuccessful, and in one an application for appeal was rejected. In *Interclass Holdings Ltd v. OFT*, the second appeal was partially accepted with respect to the fine.[71] In *Flynn Pharma Ltd and Pfizer Inc. v. CMA*,[72] the Court of Appeal mostly upheld the CAT's decision to overturn the CMA's decision finding that the undertakings had charged excessive pricing. Nonetheless, the case was returned to the CMA for further consideration of the evidence and the level of economic value that should be attributed to the patient's benefit.

Figure 30.4(b) Second-Instance Outcome

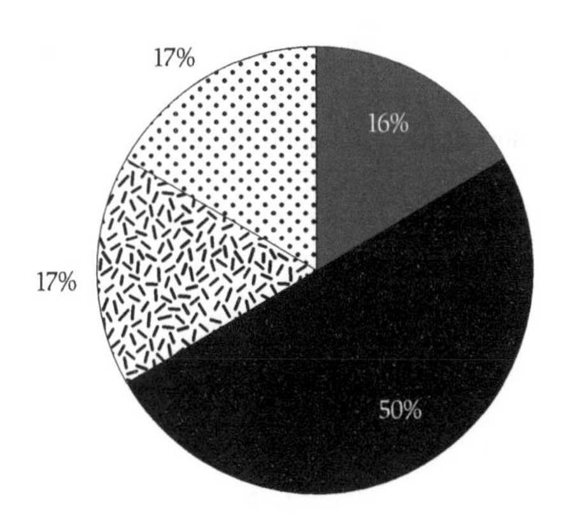

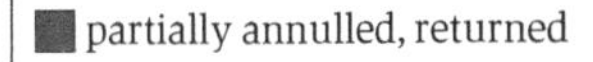

67. [2006] CAT 14.
68. *Burgess and Sons v. OFT* [2005] CAT 25.
69. *Albion Water Ltd v. Water Services Regulation Authority* [2008] CAT 31.
70. *Burgess and Sons v. OFT*, *supra*, para. 125.
71. *Interclass Holdings Limited v. OFT* [2012] EWCA Civ 1056.
72. *Flynn Pharma Ltd and Pfizer Inc. v. CMA* [2020] EWCA Civ 339.

4.5 Type of Competition Authority's Decisions Subject to Appeal

The empirical findings point out that only limited types of competition law rules are subject to review on appeal. This seems to correspond to a limited range of enforcement by the competition authority.[73] This may raise concerns as to the effectiveness of the appeal protection in the UK.

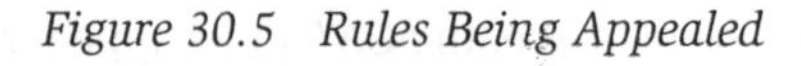

Figure 30.5 Rules Being Appealed

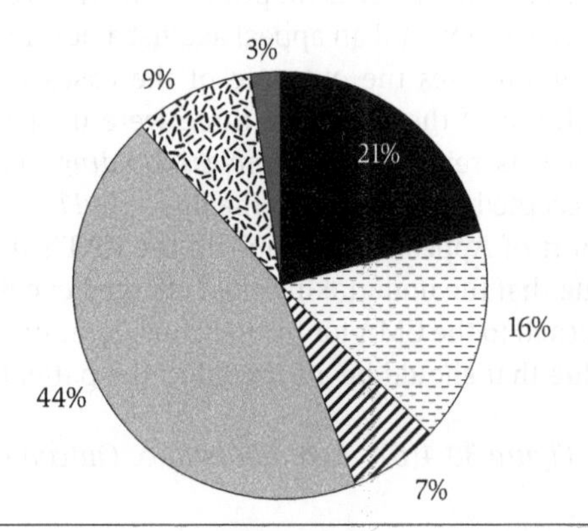

73. As previously reported by Rodger (n 15).

Figure 30.6 Rules Being Appealed According to Years (Each Judgment Counts as One)

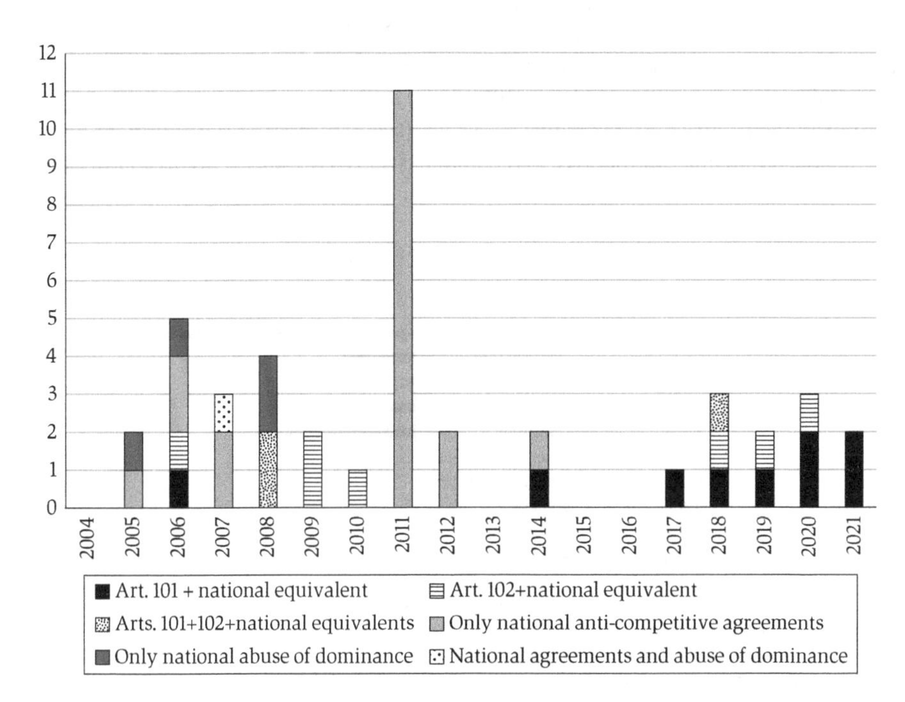

First, Figure 30.5 demonstrates that appeal judgments in the UK have predominately focused on enforcement of national law alone, even prior to Brexit. Indeed, 56% of appeals concerned the national rules alone. The rest of the proceedings involved a combination of both the EU and UK prohibitions. Nevertheless, Figure 30.6 shows that this trend had decreased between 2017 and 2021 where all appeals involved the EU prohibition.

Second, Figure 30.5 illustrates that 65% of appeal judgments pertained to the national (44%) and national and EU (21%) prohibitions on anti-competitive agreements alone. This trend is especially noticeable when examining the type of prohibitions according to years. Figure 30.6 demonstrates that while there were a significant number of early abuse cases between 2005 and 2010, these cases did not involve an appeal in relation to a finding that an abuse of dominance had occurred. Rather, they involved appeals launched by complainants against a decision not to pursue the case on the basis that there was no infringement.[74] After some years of exclusive focus on

74. 1044/2/1/04 *Burgess and Sons v. OFT*; 1024/2/3/04 *Floe Telecom Ltd v. Office of Communications*; 1046/2/4/04 *Albion Water ltd v. Water Services Regulation Authority*; C1/2007/0373 and C1/2007/0374 *Dwr Cymru Cyfyngedig v. Albion Water Ltd*; 1046/2/4/04 *Albion Water ltd v. Water Services Regulation Authority*; A3/2007/0658 and 2007/0665 *Floe Telecom Ltd v. Office of Communications*; 1099/1/02/08 *National Grid Plc v. Gas and Electricity Markets Authority*; C1/2009/1573 *National Grid Plc v. Gas and Electricity Markets Authority*.

Article 101 TFEU and Chapter I cases, the UK courts have again more recently dealt with cases involving abuse prohibitions. While the CAT and Court of Appeal judgments in the matter of *Flynn Pharma Ltd and Pfizer Inc. v. CMA* in 2018 and 2020 involved an earlier infringement decision, the appeal in *Royal Mail plc v. Office of Communications* in 2019 again concerned a decision to reject a complaint.[75]

Third, even in relation to the prohibition of anti-competitive agreements, appeals have examined only a limited range of issues (*see* Figure 30.7). Of the twenty-eight appeals related to anti-competitive agreements, twenty-two (82%) involved horizontal agreements.

Figure 30.7 Types of Restrictions

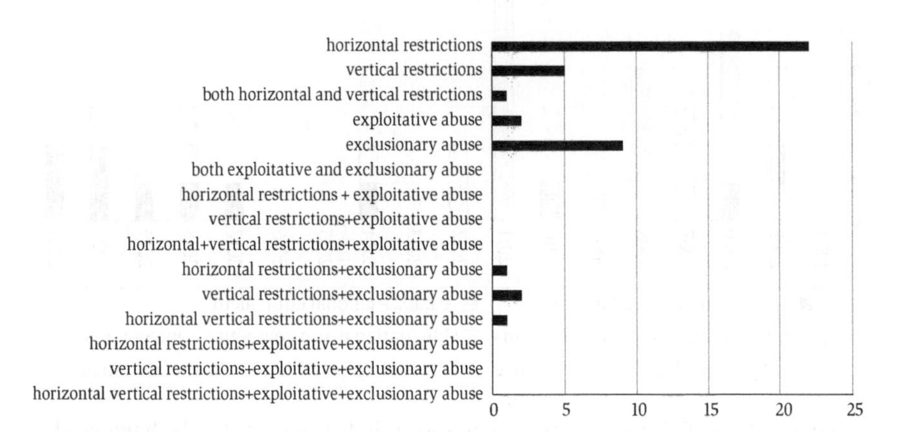

Figure 30.8 further points out that 91% of those decisions classified the restrictions as by-object (from which 3% were both by-object and by-effect). Moreover, interestingly, 31% of the NCA's decisions and CAT's judgments that were appealed involved one or more parties that had successfully submitted a leniency application, and 9% involved a successful settlement application. That means that the UK authorities (and consequently the appeal courts) have almost exclusively focused on enforcement against hard-core cartels, which are likely to raise only limited types of legal and economic challenges.

Fourth, nine out of the eleven review judgments concerning abuse of dominance (82%) related to exclusionary practices.

75. 1275-1276/1/12/17 *Flynn Pharma Ltd and Pfizer Inc. v. CMA*; C3/2018/1847 and 1874 *Flynn Pharma Ltd and Pfizer Inc. v. CMA*; 1200/1/3/18 *Royal Mail plc v. Office of Communications*.

Figure 30.8 Object/Effect (Only for Cases Involving Article 101 and the National Equivalent Prohibition)

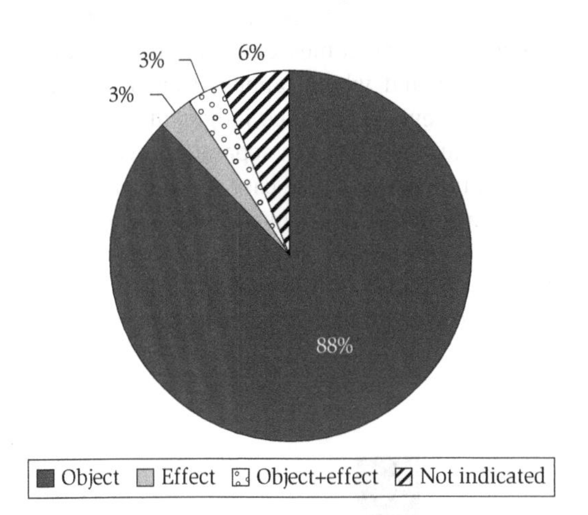

Figure 30.9 summarises the type of competition authority's actions that were subject to appeal. From all of those actions, 74% involved findings of infringements, together with the imposition of fines. Another 20% of the decisions were no grounds for action. These typically arose in the period to 2009 (e.g., *Burgess, Albion Water and Floe Telecom)* and involved appeals by complainants in relation to such no grounds for action decisions (normally in relation to the abuse of dominance).

The figure also shows that commitments were subject to appeal in the UK in only one case.[76] This corresponds to the limited resort of the commitments remedy by the competition authorities.[77] Appeals launched against commitments involve a different, lower, standard of review and scrutiny, as opposed to appeal on the merits.

Figure 30.9 The Competition Authority's Procedure

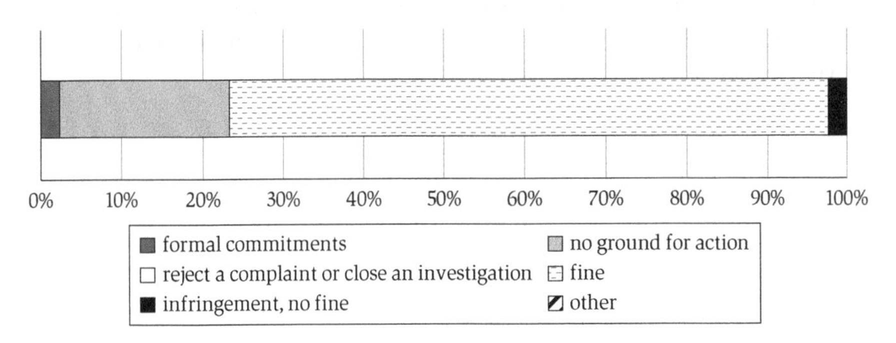

76. *Skyscanner ltd v. CMA* [2014] CAT 16.
77. Rodger, *supra* n 15.

4.6 Grounds of Appeal

Figure 30.10 sets out the grounds of appeals raised by the parties, across all instances. The success rates relate to the outcomes of all appeals, taking into account that separate appeals were aggregated where launched against a single decision of the competition authority or a previous instance judgment. That means that if a single decision was appealed by various parties in separate proceedings, the outcome of all those judgments will be counted as a single case for the purposes of this figure. More than one appeal ground has often been invoked in the same case.

Figure 30.10 Grounds of Appeal (Each NCA's Decision or Previous Court Judgment Counts as One)

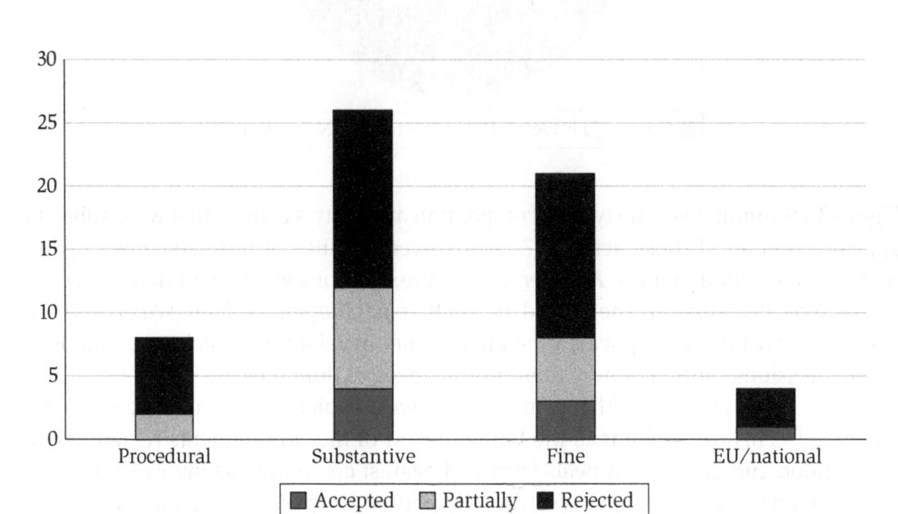

Figure 30.11 takes a different approach, focusing on the appeal grounds argued and accepted according to years, and counting each court judgment as a single decision, irrespective of whether there were multiple separate appeals in relation to the same competition authority's decision.[78]

78. Hence, the apparent inconsistency between Figure 30.10 and Figure 30.11(c) can be explained by the fact that many of the fine cases related to the one decision, on the construction cartel, and this accounts for the peak in 2011 in Figure 30.11(b) and Figure 30.11(c) in relation to the number of successful appeals on fines by multiple parties in different proceedings in relation to that infringement.

Figure 30.11(a) Procedural Grounds

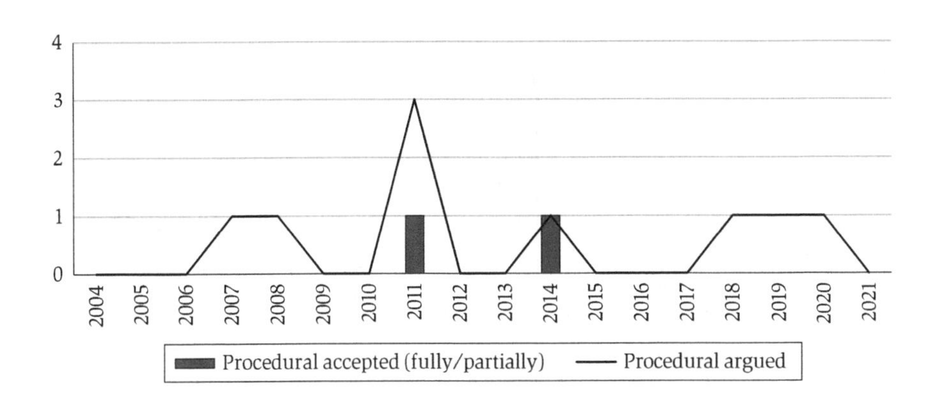

Figure 30.11(b) Substantive Grounds

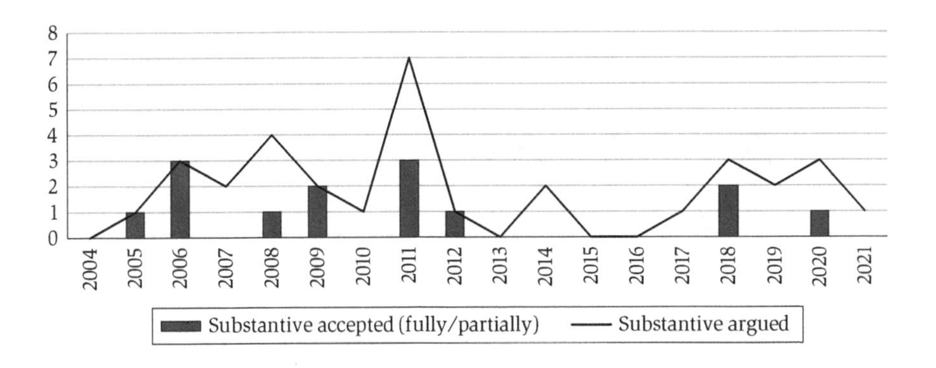

Figure 30.11(c) Fines-related Grounds

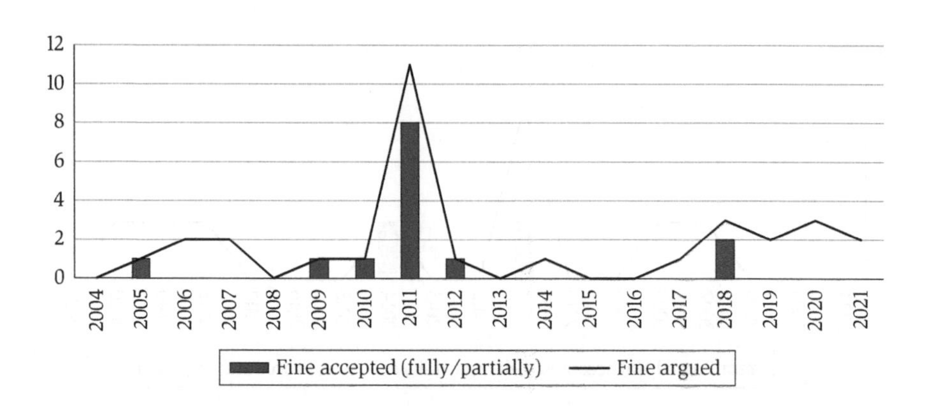

Figure 30.11(d) EU/National Grounds

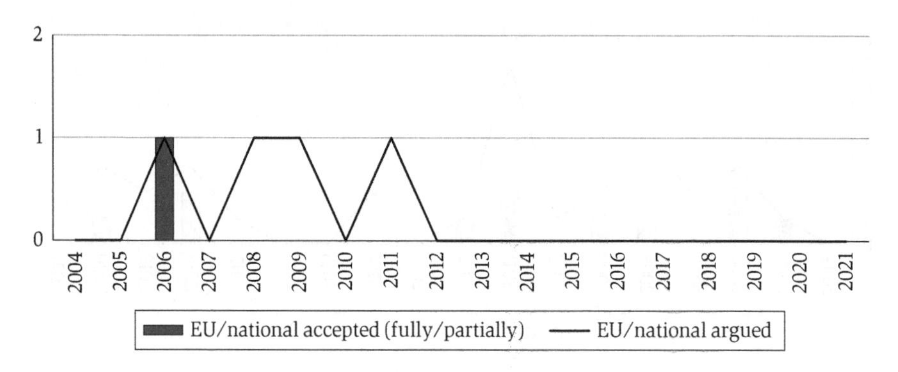

Various interesting trends emerge. First, substantive grounds of appeal were the most frequently raised ground by the parties, and the most likely to succeed. Their success rates, however, were not equally distributed across the years and were practically accepted by the courts between 2004 and 2012. Many of them involved complainants relating to the abuse prohibition and no grounds for action decisions, e.g., in *Burgess, Floe Telecom, Albion Water*. There have also been successful appeals on substance in two cases related to the construction cartel in 2011.[79] Some substantive grounds of appeal were partially successful in 2018 and 2020, in *Generics UK v. CMA* and *Flynn Pharma v. CMA* respectively, and both also relate to the abuse prohibition.

Second, grounds of appeal pertaining to the fines imposed have also been frequent and prominent. In addition to the multiple successful appeals on fines by multiple parties in relation to the Construction industry cartel in 2011, there are other

79. *Willis & sons ltd v. OFT* and *GMI Construction Ltd v. OFT, [2011] CAT 9.*

notable cases involving appeals on fine calculation, such as in *Ping Europe UK Ltd v. CMA* (CAT (2018) and CoA (2020)).[80]

Notably, the reference to the fines-related grounds of appeal in Figure 30.10 and Figure 30.11(c) only indicates cases where the fine calculation was challenged in itself. They do not include cases where the fine was reduced because the court accepted the substantive ground of appeal. A closer review of the empirical findings, therefore, reveals that the appeal rulings by the courts had a considerable impact on the level of fines imposed. Fines were reduced in 43% of the CAT's judgments and 33% of the Court of Appeal's judgments, and the average fine reduction in those cases was 72% for the CAT and 69% for the Court of Appeal. The fine was increased in a single case – that is the CAT's decision in *Roland (U.K.) Ltd and Roland Corporation v. CMA* of 2021.[81] The CAT decided that the fine should be calculated without the 20% settlement discount.

Third, Figure 30.11(a) shows that procedural grounds were seldom argued and rarely successfully. One notable exception was the Imperial *Tobacco Group v. OFT* ruling.[82]

Fourth, similarly, the only case where the issues related to the tension between EU and national competition laws raised by all parties were fully accepted was in *Floe Telecom Ltd v. Office of Communications* (2006), as will be elaborated in the following section.

4.7 Third Parties' Participation

A range of third parties participated in the appeals: in *Burgess* and *Albion Water* (CAT), the undertakings concerned intervened in an appeal submitted by a complainant; In *Floe Telecom*, interveners supported both the applicant and businesses. In *Albion Water* (Court of Appeal), OFWAT, OFT, and OFCOM joined the procedure.

In other cases, other related businesses intervened, for example, Siemens PLC in relation to *National Grid*, and in the *Skyscanner* commitments case the third party Skoosh International Ltd was granted permission to intervene in support of the undertakings (as were various other third parties, including Booking.Com BV in support of the CMA). In *Flynn Pharma* the European Commission intervened before the Court of Appeal and in *FP McCann* at the CAT, the interveners were directors, subject to ongoing director disqualification processes in the Northern Ireland High Court.

5 QUALITATIVE ANALYSIS

The nature of judicial scrutiny of the CMA's and utility regulators' enforcement is a distinctive feature of the UK competition law system. This section builds on the above quantitative analysis to highlight key dicta of the CAT and Court of Appeal and to

80. [2018] CAT 13 and [2020] EWCA Civ. 13 (with a fine reduction outcome).
81. *Roland (U.K.) Ltd and Roland Corporation v. CMA*, [2021] CAT 8.
82. Imperial *Tobacco Group v. OFT, [2011] CAT 41.*

explore how the courts have undertaken their appellate function. We will conclude this section with a discussion of recent proposals and consultation processes which have reflected on the enforcement practice and made suggestions for review and reform of the court review function in that context. Some of these proposals have suggested that the competition law court appeal system in the UK might have overstepped its appropriate role, in a manner that might hinder the effectiveness of its national competition law enforcement.

5.1 Substantive and Procedural Grounds

The high rate of successful appeals, and the focus on substantive grounds - can be explained by the CAT's standard of review (*see* Figures 30.3, 30.4, and 30.10 above) and its high level of expertise in competition law matters. The intensity of review of the CMA's (and its predecessor, the OFT) and utility regulators' competition law enforcement by the CAT is considerable. The CAT has the competence to review any error of law, fact, or discretion; to consider new evidence;[83] to review decisions finding a prohibition, non-prohibition, and the rejection of complaints;[84] and to replace the CMA's and utility regulators' decisions. In contrast to the marginal standard of review followed by the generalist EU Courts when it comes to 'complex economic assessment' by the European Commission, the CAT - as a specialist competition law tribunal - is deeply involved in the consideration of various aspects of the cases appealed.

The depth and intensity of review as set out in the statutory rules has been repeatedly confirmed and stressed by the CAT. In *Albion Water*, 2008, the CAT discussed at length the approach to the standard of review adopted on appeal:[85]

> The parties were unable to agree upon the correct standard of review in this case. Three approaches were canvassed. The first employs the principles of judicial review, which counsel for Dŵr Cymru argued the Tribunal should apply. He drew an analogy with the position under section 193 of the Communications Act 2003 ('the 2003 Act').
>
> The second approach, favoured by Albion, recognises that the reference to an appeal 'on the merits' in paragraph 3(1) of Schedule 8 means that the Tribunal's function is not limited to the review of the Report according to the principles of judicial review. In consequence the Tribunal should decide for itself whether the First Access Price is excessive and, if so, whether it is unfair and thus an abuse of a dominant position.
>
> ... third approach lies somewhere between the first two; here the Tribunal would treat the Report as evidence.
>
> ... [such an approach] would restrict the Tribunal's role to a limited form of judicial supervision which is inconsistent with the merits jurisdiction prescribed under the Act. We reject so restrictive an approach. The Tribunal's powers in

83. CAT in Makers Ltd [2007] CAT 11, para. 41. The position is more limited on appeal to the Court of Appeal, *see, e.g.*, *Independent Media Support Ltd v. Office of Communications*, [2008] EWCA Civ 1402. The right to adduce new evidence is now controlled under the CAT Rules by rule 9(4)(h) and the power of the CAT to exclude it: rule 21(2)(b)-(c).
84. [2008] CAT 31, paras 65-70; Freeserve [2003] CAT 5; [2007] CAT 23, para. 106.
85. [2008] CAT 31, paras 65-70.

> deciding this appeal are set out in paragraph 3(1) of Schedule 8 to the Act. That provision requires the Tribunal to decide the case 'on the merits' by reference to the grounds set out in the notice of appeal.
>
> The Tribunal has jurisdiction under paragraph 3(2)(e) of Schedule 8 to the Act to reach its own decision in respect of a matter forming part of the decision under appeal.

The scope of the CAT's powers on the merits, and in particular its power to take its own decisions on substantive grounds in cases involving non-infringement outcomes, was made evident by the CAT itself in *Burgess v. OFT*:[86]

> In deciding whether to take its own decision, the Tribunal is mindful of the fact that it is an appellate tribunal from an administrative decision and should not therefore turn itself into the primary decision-maker without good reason. On the other hand, as the Tribunal's recent judgment in Floe Telecomm v Office of Communications [2005] CAT 14 emphasises, the Tribunal's jurisdiction is a merits jurisdiction, and thus wider than a judicial review jurisdiction. The Tribunal referred, in particular, at paragraph 65 of that judgment, to the Ministerial statement of 18 June 1998 during the passage of the Competition Bill: 'It is our intention that the tribunal should be primarily concerned with the correctness or otherwise of the conclusions contained in the appealed decision and not with how the decision was reached or the reasoning expressed in it. That will apply unless defects in how the decision was reached or the reasoning make it impracticable for the tribunal fairly to determine the correctness or otherwise of the conclusions or of any directions contained in the decision. Wherever possible, we want the tribunal to decide a case on the facts before it, even where there has been a procedural error, and to avoid remitting the case to the director general. We intend to reflect that policy in the tribunal rules ...'.

The 2012 CAT ruling in *Tesco's* appeal in relation to the Dairy market infringements shows the number of witnesses involved and the detailed level of engagement with the facts and issues by the tribunal in upholding the appeal.[87] The CAT has linked its high level of involvement to the important public interest function embedded in competition law enforcement. In its 2018 ruling in *Flynn Pharma*, where the CMA had found an abuse of dominance based on unfair pricing, it noted:[88]

> Cases of pure unfair pricing are rare in competition law. Authorities find them difficult to bring and are, rightly, wary of casting themselves in the role of price regulators ... . In this case, there is much in the Decision with which we agree. However, we find the CMA's conclusions on abuse of dominance were in error.... The CMA did not correctly apply the legal test for finding that prices were unfair as laid down in the United Brands case ... . The importance of this case for the public interest makes it desirable to rectify the errors we have found. In a matter as important for government, for the public as patients and as taxpayers, as well as for the pharmaceutical industry itself, the law should be clear and any decisions made should be soundly based on proper evidence and analysis. It is important that there is a good legal foundation for any future action in this area.

86. [2005] CAT 25, para. 129.
87. [2012] CAT 31.
88. [2018] CAT 11, paras 462-464.

In other cases, the scope and intensity of the review were vindicated with reference to the protection of fundamental rights. In *Flynn Pharma Ltd*, for example, the CAT noted: 'The conferral of a merits jurisdiction upon the Tribunal flows from important legal considerations relating to the rights of defence and access to a court, under fundamental rights such as article 6 of the Convention.'[89]

At the same time, excessive intervention may also hamper the effectiveness of competition law enforcement. Indeed, the CAT had accepted some limits, to avoid transforming it from an appellate tribunal to a court of trial. In the 2011 '*tobacco*' case,[90] in which the OFT decisions were quashed, the CAT made interesting remarks regarding the authority's attempt to change its position during an appeal, and the inherent limits of an appeal process involving an authority's prior decision:

> In Aberdeen Journals Ltd v Director General of Fair Trading [2002] CAT 4, for example, the Tribunal said: '... such an approach could give rise to a tendency to transform this tribunal from an essentially appellate tribunal to a court of trial where matters of fact, or the meaning to be attributed to particular documents, are canvassed for the first time at the level of the tribunal when they could and should have been raised in the administrative procedure and dealt with in the decision. We do not think that such a development would be conducive to appropriate rigour in administrative decision making, or to a healthy and fair system of appeals under the [1998] Act.' The Court of Appeal in Office of Communications v Floe Telecom Ltd [2006] EWCA Civ 768 also stated that paragraph 3(1) makes clear that the appeal is on the merits and also 'limits the appeal to the points taken in the notice of appeal' (at paragraph 24). (...) In our judgement, the powers under paragraph 3(2) do not extend the scope of our jurisdiction under paragraph 3(1) and do not enable us to engage in an investigation, independent of the issues raised in the appeal, as to whether other infringements have been committed.

Such concerns were also voiced by the Court of Appeal. For example, in a relatively early case, the Court of Appeal was critical of the CAT for undertaking multiple and lengthy judgments in relation to the one appeal, albeit it was a particularly complicated context, in *Albion Water*.[91]

In recent appeals, the CAT has provided an updated and comprehensive account of its appellate function in relation to the prohibitions. For instance, in *Lexon UK Ltd v. CMA*, in 2021, after noting its broad competencies the CAT added that:[92]

> The Tribunal should interfere only if it concludes that the decision is wrong in a material respect. Whether an error is material will be a matter of judgment for the Tribunal. It is consistent with a merits appeal for the Tribunal, even having heard the evidence, to conclude that the approach taken by the CMA and its resultant findings are reasonable in all the circumstances and to refrain from interfering upon that basis. If the Tribunal considers that the findings of the CMA are reasonable it might be difficult to say that any findings at which it arrives, which differ from those of the CMA, are material (...) If the Tribunal annulled a decision

89. *Flynn Pharma Limited and Pfizer Inc. v. CMA* [2020] EWCA Civ 339, paras 141-145.
90. [2011] CAT 41, para. 136.
91. [2008] EWCA Civ 536.
92. [2021] CAT 5; *see also Roland (UK) Ltd v. CMA* [2021] CAT 8.

on the basis of an error that was very slight or de minimis and/or gave no reasoning to justify the annulment that might be considered an error of law.

In *Flynn Pharma Ltd,* Green LJ in the Court of Appeal, also provided guidance on the scope of the margin of appreciation to be afforded to the CMA, in particular, in relation to substantive liability and determinations of the existence of illegal, abusive behaviour. Green LJ indicated that 'materiality' should guide the exercise of the Tribunal's supervisory function:[93]

> Notwithstanding the above the jurisdiction of the Tribunal is not unfettered. ... The Tribunal should interfere only if it concludes that the decision is wrong in a material respect. ... First, materiality is not an exact science. The Tribunal might be able to do no more than conclude that an error might make a difference to the final outcome or to some significant component thereof; certainty might not be possible. Second, there is no fixed list of errors that the Tribunal might consider material. Case law indicates that the following might be relevant: failing to take account of relevant evidence; taking into account irrelevant evidence; failing properly to construe significant documents or evidence; drawing inferences of fact from evidence about relevant matters which are illogical or unjustified; failing adequately or sufficiently to investigate an issue that the Tribunal considers to be relevant or potentially relevant to the analysis.[94]

However, it should be noted that in relation to commitment decisions, as stressed by the CAT in *Skyscanner Ltd v. CMA*, the CAT exercises a different level of supervisory control based on judicial review rather than appeal on the merits, as emphasised in these key passages:[95]

> Bearing in mind that the commitments process is meant to provide a rapid solution and to look forward, rather than to make a condemnation of past conduct, the OFT (now CMA) must be allowed a fair degree of discretion in its assessment of the appropriateness of the commitments to meet the concerns it has expressed. Too heavy a degree of judicial scrutiny would have the effect of making the obtaining of commitments no more rapid and advantageous in terms of time and effort than a normal infringement decision, which would not be consistent with the purpose of the Act in this respect. This is perhaps why commitment decisions are subject under the Act to judicial review whilst infringement decisions are subject to full merits appeal. Nonetheless, the OFT (now CMA) clearly cannot be given a completely free hand to conclude any arrangement that it likes with alleged infringers merely to suit its own administrative convenience. In our view, the normal mechanism of judicial review, as explained above (*see* in particular paragraphs 31-33), is sufficient and appropriate to provide the necessary degree of scrutiny of commitment decisions.

93. *Flynn Pharma Limited and Pfizer Inc. v. CMA* [2020] EWCA Civ 339, paras 141-145.
94. *See also, e.g., Kier Group Plc and others v. OFT* [2011] CAT 3.
95. Where the decision was partially quashed, para. 158 as 'the OFT did not acquaint itself with the information needed to answer the statutory questions posed to it', [2014] CAT 16, paras 42-43.

5.2 Review of Fines

The CAT has also been highly involved in reviewing the fines imposed for competition law infringements. As mentioned, fines were reduced in 43% of the CAT's judgments and even increased in one judgment. There has been considerable discussion by the CAT about its appellate function and role in relation to the review of penalties- it can reject an appeal on the level of penalty, decrease or indeed increase the level of fine. A key issue guiding the Tribunal through its determination in relation to penalties is the principle of proportionality as stressed in *Kier Group v. OFT* in 2011, and reiterated in *Quarmby*:[96]

> In our view, the Appellants are correct to challenge the proportionality of the overall fine levied on them by the OFT in this case... . However, we also adopt and agree with the Tribunal's broader conclusions at paragraph 166 of the Kier Judgment, namely that there was a failure by the OFT to take a step back and ask itself whether in all the circumstances its proposed penalties were necessary and proportionate ... .

Like the scope and intensity of substantive and procedural grounds, the intervention in relation to fines was tied to its margin of appreciation argument. In *Eden Brown Ltd and others v. OFT*, it observed:

> 'Further, the Tribunal has recognised that the OFT enjoys a margin of appreciation, both as to the interpretation of the Guidance and as regards the level of fine the OFT considers appropriate for a particular infringement: Umbro Holdings Ltd v Office of Fair Trading ("Replica Kits") [2005] CAT 22, at [102]. That does not mean that the appellate scrutiny is of the lesser standard applied on an application for judicial review'.[97]
>
> 'In our view in those circumstances the Tribunal should focus primarily on whether the overall penalty imposed is appropriate for the infringements in question. In our view, provided that the OFT has remained within its margin of appreciation in applying the Guidance, the Tribunal's primary task is to assess the justice of the overall penalty, rather than to consider in minute detail the individual Steps applied by the OFT'.[98]

A good example of the 'rounded' approach to consideration of penalty assessment is in the CAT's 2018 ruling in *Ping Europe v. CMA* as follows:[99]

> Taking a step back from the detailed arguments on the step-by-step calculation of the fine, we now consider the overall fairness and proportionality of the fine imposed on Ping for this infringement. The Decision imposed on Ping a fine of £1.45 million. This equates to a fine of £290,000 per year of the infringement. In our view, this is within the correct ballpark figure for an infringement of this nature, taking into account the specific circumstances of the infringement ... In our view, however, the fine imposed is slightly too high and a further small reduction is therefore appropriate. Rather than mechanistically applying a 10% reduction to

96. [2011] CAT 3.
97. [2011] CAT 8, para. 34.
98. *Ibid.*, para. 106.
99. [2018] CAT 13, para. 254.

> the fine we will take a view in the round. On consideration, we consider that a fair and proportionate fine, taking into account that it was not an 'aggravated' infringement, should be £1.25 million. This equates to a fine of £250,000 in each year of the infringement.' The CAT noted it will 'have regard' to the CMA's Penalty Guidance when reviewing the fines imposed.

The CAT, interestingly, noted it will give regard to the CMA's Penalty Guidance, but will make its own assessment. This was demonstrated in the *FP McCann Ltd v. CMA* ruling, which gives an excellent overall appraisal of the CAT's appellate function:[100]

> The above authorities establish that: (1) an appellant is entitled to an appeal on the merits, which has been described as a full appeal; the jurisdiction of the Tribunal is not restricted to the jurisdiction which would be appropriate if this process were by way of judicial review; (2) it has been said that if the overall penalty is considered by the Tribunal to be appropriate, it will usually not be necessary to examine minutely the way in which the CMA interpreted and applied the Penalty Guidance at each specific step; (3) however, where an appellant makes specific complaints about particular steps taken by the CMA it will be necessary for the Tribunal to address the specific complaints which have been made; (4) it would not be right to ignore the conclusions and evaluations of the CMA but ultimately the Tribunal must make its own assessment as to the penalty which is appropriate in all the circumstances, having regard to the Penalty Guidance.

The Court of Appeal, by comparison, does not play a significant role in relation to penalty determinations. This is tied to the standard of review, whereby second appeals are limited to points of law alone and show deference to the expertise of the CAT in competition law matters. In *Tomlinson*, the earlier passage from Argos by the Court of Appeal was reiterated:[101]

> In the case of the Court of Appeal, it seems to us that it is right for the court to recognise that the tribunal is an expert and specialised body, and that, subject to any difference in the basis on which the infringements are to be considered as a result of any appeal on liability, the court should hesitate before interfering with the tribunal's assessment of the appropriate penalty.

The tribunal went on in *Tomlinson* to stress the deference accorded to the CAT in this context:

> Given the specialist nature of the tribunal and its obvious expertise in these matters, an appeal against penalty is unlikely to be successful unless it can be shown either that the CAT erred in principle (which can include a failure to take relevant matters into account) or that, looked at overall, the penalties imposed were clearly disproportionate or discriminatory so as to be unjustifiable by any of the matters which the CAT either did or should have taken into account.[102]

100. [2020] CAT 28.
101. *GF Tomlinson Building Ltd and Others v. OFT*, [2011] CAT 7, para. 165.
102. *Ibid.*, para. 59.

5.3 Third Parties' Rights

The UK review system provides noticeable rights for third parties, in particular allowing interested third parties to raise appeals under section 46 CA98 (as demonstrated by, for example, *Burgess v. OFT)*, and to intervene in proceedings. Third parties, moreover, may seek to review a commitments decision (e.g., *Skyscanner Ltd v. CMA)*.

5.4 Reflections on Effectiveness and Judicial Deference

Despite the expertise of the OFT/CMA and the UK sector regulators, the legal context and judicial dicta examined in this chapter have emphasised the full merits approach to the intensity of judicial review on appeal, with the exception of proceedings in relation to commitments. It is also notable that the Court of Appeal, at second instance, has demonstrated both in terms of judicial pronouncements and the data its greater deference to rulings by the CAT given the latter's specialist competition law expertise.

In relation to the intensity of review or judicial deference across the different types of appeal, Figures 30.10 and 30.11(a-d) show some clear trends in relation to the number of appeals and their judicial treatment. First, substantive grounds of appeal were those most frequently raised by the parties, and most likely to succeed. Many early cases between 2004 and 2012 involved complainants relating to the abuse prohibition and no grounds for action decisions, where the competition authority did not undertake a comprehensive economic and legal analysis and come to a fully reasoned decision. Nonetheless, there were also successful appeals on substance in two cases related to the construction cartel in 2011[103] and substantive grounds of appeal were partially successful in relation to the abuse prohibition in 2018 and 2020, in *Generics UK v. CMA* and *Flynn Pharma v. CMA* respectively.

Second, grounds of appeal challenging the fines imposed have also been frequent and prominent. In addition to the multiple successful appeals launched by multiple parties in relation to the Construction industry cartel in 2011, various other appeals have questioned the fine calculation and some were successful.[104] In addition to such cases which directly challenged the fine calculation (summarised in Figure 30.10 and Figure 30.11(c)), fines were reduced also where the courts have accepted the substantive ground of appeal raised by the parties. As a result, the courts have had a considerable impact on the level of fines imposed.

Third, the empirical findings indicated that procedural grounds were seldom argued in front of courts and rarely successfully. This may suggest a relatively high level of acceptance both by the party litigants and the courts as to the satisfaction of due process requirements by the competition authorities.

103. *Willis & sons ltd v. OFT* and *GMI Construction Ltd v. OFT*, [2011] CAT 9.
104. [2018] CAT 13 and [2020] EWCA Civ. 13.

5.5 Alignment with EU Law (Prior to Brexit)

Prior to Brexit, there was certainly a mixed story in relation to the role of the courts in ensuring the effectiveness of EU competition law and the alignment of the national practice with EU law. Figure 30.5 showed that appeals have focused primarily on enforcement of national law. Fifty-six percent of appeals concerned the national rules alone, and the remainder involved a combination of both the EU and domestic prohibitions. This trend had decreased since 2017, when all appeals involved the EU prohibitions. The Courts have also rarely considered the tension between EU and national law. From the entry into force of Regulation 1/2003 and until Brexit, the courts sought a preliminary ruling from the European Court of Justice (CJEU) only once in cases within the scope of this project - *Generics UK Ltd and others v. CMA* in 2018.[105] This may be reflective of a broader reticence by the judiciary to make preliminary rulings in cases involving EU law. In addition, the courts examined the relationship between EU and national competition laws only in four cases, and accepted it only in one case - *Floe Telecom Ltd v. Office of Communications*, involving the correct interpretation of national law in light of an EU Directive.

Nonetheless, EU competition law has played a key role. Reference to and reliance upon EU competition law jurisprudence established by the General Court and CJEU had been a cornerstone of the judicial practice of the Courts prior to Brexit, and notably the CAT. The CAT routinely sets out the relevant EU competition law principles through discussion of the relevant EU court case law. This was not only limited to judgments involving Articles 101 and 102 TFEU but also applied to cases concerning the national prohibitions alone. This was the result of the consistency of interpretation requirement established by section 60 of the Competition Act, at least until its replacement post-EU withdrawal by new section 60A of that Act.

5.6 Governmental Review of the Appeal Process

As the previous sections demonstrated, the CAT plays a regular and important role in competition law enforcement and does not shy away from intervention on matters of substance, procedure, and penalties. Various reviews of the UK judicial system have suggested that the CAT might have overstepped in its involvement, in a manner that might hinder the effectiveness of its national competition law enforcement.

In 2012, the government's responses to the pre-Enterprise and Regulatory Reform Act consultation[106] expressed its commitment to the existing appeal system. Yet, it encouraged the (then newly created) CMA to improve its internal procedures aiming to

105. Case C-307/18 *Generics (UK) and Others*, ECLI:EU:C:2020:52.
106. Department for Business, Innovation & Skills, 'Growth, Competition and the Competition Regime: Government Response to Consultation', March 2012 (hereafter 'The ERRA Consultation Response').

limit the number of appeals.[107] Soon after this, the government included appeals against competition decisions in its Regulatory Appeal Review,[108] but the response to its proposals to replace full merits appeals with judicial review (or a specific review system) for competition cases was negative and the proposals were dropped.[109] Nonetheless, the matter of appeals remains controversial. The minority view that the CMA is detracted from the performance of its tasks by the appeal system has nonetheless persisted.

Despite the considerably higher number of appeals in many other larger EU Member States, that minority viewpoint considered that a number of appeals was likely to create a chilling of enforcement activity, and in consequence less effective overall enforcement. In early 2019, the Chairman of the CMA, Andrew Tyrie, sent a letter to the then Secretary of State Greg Clark, requesting new powers to allow it to act quickly and with reduced oversight by the CAT.[110] The Tyrie letter refers to those accused of infringement using 'large teams of private sector lawyers' leading to 'often years of protracted dispute...far removed from the concerns of ordinary consumers'.[111] He also stated: 'The result is a more protracted and cumbersome appeal process than was originally intended for, and by, the CAT. Parties found by the CMA to have breached competition law can exploit this – leading to a situation where, as noted by the National Audit Office in its most recent report on the competition regime, many lawyers regard the UK as "the best jurisdiction in the world to defend a competition case".[112] This entails greater cost, delay and uncertainty than necessary'.[113] Moreover, he noted his concern at the 'second bite at the cherry' and preferred the need to move away from a full merits standard of appeal.[114] It should be stressed that there was widespread opposition to this viewpoint that the standard of review should be lowered in relation to antitrust enforcement cases in the UK. In light of this general consensus, no changes were subsequently implemented.

In 2021, the Penrose Report, Power to the People,[115] reflected on the UK competition law enforcement framework and recommended a task force to seek to

107. The OFT had already introduced some procedural improvements, including separate case decision groups, which were generally well received – *see* OFT, '*Review of OFT's Investigative procedures... Summary of Responses*'– OFT 1455 (2012).
108. Department for Business, Innovation & Skills, 'Streamlining Regulatory and Competition Appeals – Consultation on Options for Reform' (BIS 19 June 2013 – hereafter 'Regulatory Appeal Review').
109. It has re-emerged more recently – *see* the later discussion. An amendment to the standard of review in Communications Act cases was introduced by the Digital Economy Act 2017 2017 c. 30.
110. Letter from Andrew Tyrie to the Secretary of State for Business, Energy and Industrial Strategy, of 21 February 2019 (hereafter the 'Tyrie Letter'). Available via: https://www.gov.uk/government/publications/letter-from-andrew-tyrie-to-the-secretary-of-state-for-business-energy-and-industrial-strategy.
111. Ibid, p. 2.
112. National Audit Office report, 'The UK Competition Regime', February 2016, para. 2.15.
113. Tyrie Letter p. 35.
114. *Ibid.*, pp. 36-37.
115. John Penrose, 'Power to the People: Stronger Consumer Choice and Competition So Markets Work for People, Not The Other Way Around' (2021) (hereafter the 'Penrose Report').

effectively speed up the full process, along the way reviewing the merits appeal process, the ECHR justifications and refusing to recommend the introduction of a prosecutorial model of competition law enforcement. Nonetheless, the Report[116] did suggest that the revised merits to judicial review standard for review of certain decisions of the regulator OFCOM[117] could be used as a model for general appeals, despite the specific nature of the legislation and the problematic future status of retained EU law.

During 2021-2022, there was a further UK competition law review consultation process titled Reforming Competition and Consumer Policy Driving Growth and Delivering Competitive Markets that Work for Consumers,[118] which again reflected on the process and intensity of appeals before the CAT:

> 'However, in recent years there have been calls in the Furman Review, the Penrose Report, and Lord Tyrie's reform proposals for the standard of review in appeals against Competition Act investigations to be reviewed again.'[119] It noted 'It is also unclear whether or not the concerns that have been expressed about the level of scrutiny applied by the Tribunal are borne out in practice.'[120] And, subsequently: 'government welcomes views on the appropriate level of judicial scrutiny of the CMA's decisions in Competition Act investigations'.[121]

To date, there has been a clear rejection of the viewpoint that the current appeal process is too intensive and 'chills' the enforcement practice of the authorities by requiring them to undertake too many resources in preparing for appeals, and that the full merits approach should be reduced to a more standard judicial review approach, as is the case in relation to commitments. The CMA's submission to the Consultation process adopted a moderate line while urging further review.[122] The Consultation outcome, published in April 2022, did not propose any reforms to the appeal mechanisms in relation to the competition law prohibitions.[123]

Available via: https://assets.publishing.service.gov.uk/government/uploads/system/uploads/attachment_data/file/961665/penrose-report-final.pdf.

116. *See* the Penrose Report, p. 19.
117. Digital Economy Act 2017 2017 c. 30.
118. Department for Business, Energy & Industrial Strategy, 'Reforming Competition and Consumer Policy Driving Growth and Delivering Competitive Markets that Work for Consumers', July 2021 CP 488.
119. *Ibid.*, at para. 1.204.
120. *Ibid.*
121. *Ibid.*, at para. 1.207.
122. CMA, 'CMA Response to Consultation Reforming Competition and Consumer Policy Driving growth and delivering competitive markets that work for consumers' 4 October 2021, paras 2.84-2.86. Available via: https://www.gov.uk/government/publications/reforming-competition-and-consumer-policy-driving-growth-and-delivering-competitive-markets-that-work-for-consumers-cma-response-to-consultation
123. Department for Business, Energy & Industrial Strategy, 'Reforming competition and consumer policy: government response' April 2022. Available via: https://www.gov.uk/government/consultations/reforming-competition-and-consumer-policy/outcome/reforming-competition-and-consumer-policy-government-response, paras 1.164-1,167

6 CONCLUDING REMARKS

Since 1998, the UK has had a highly developed competition law system. Its competition law enforcement institutions, notably the CMA, have gained international recognition for their independence and robust decision-making processes. Moreover, the independent and specialist competition court, the CAT, plays an important part in the enforcement, especially given its broad competence.

Unlike many other jurisdictions, the CAT conducts a full 'on the merits' review, which examines both the facts and legal application (except in relation to commitments decisions). Appeals at second instance to the Court of Appeal are reviewed on the law alone. Yet, comparatively, the number of judgments is relatively very low. The primary reason appears to be the relative dearth of decisions by the competition authorities in relation to the prohibitions over the examined seventeen-year period.

Although there have been a number of cases rejecting appeals outright, overall appellants have frequently been successful, at least partially. The data on appeals reflects the prioritisation of the authorities on hard-core cartels. The most common outcome has been a fine reduction, although many of those cases in 2011 relate to the same construction cartel in 2010. A number of appeals were successful on the substance but indeed many of these coincide with the success (at least in the early period) of complainants regarding no grounds for action non-infringement decisions in relation to the abuse prohibitions, which were set aside by the CAT, and in some prominent cases replaced by an infringement finding by the CAT itself. Indeed, those cases in particular, exemplify both the depth and intensity of the review undertaken at the appeal level in the UK, and particularly in comparison with the role of the General Court in appeals at the EU level, the range of potential outcomes which are available to the CAT.

It should also be noted that there is limited deference to the competition authority's decision-making, although it appears to be greater in relation to the decision-making procedure and processes. There are conflicting trends in relation to ensuring the effectiveness of EU competition law in the period, with considerable reliance on EU jurisprudence in CAT (and CoA) rulings, yet enforcement - and consequently appeals - is predominately based on the national prohibitions. The judiciary's general reticence to make preliminary references is also reflected in the solitary reference and ruling within the scope of the project, albeit this may also mirror the limited level of EU enforcement action by the authority and the relatively mature level of EU jurisprudence already available to the CAT.

The role of the CAT and intensity of review is also evident from the in-depth analysis in this report of a range of judicial dicta from the CAT and the Court of Appeal over the years. Indeed, as noted, this has led to criticism and the perception that the CAT's role hinders the enforcement process. Nonetheless, despite this perception and recent reviews, the prevailing opposite view has led to the government rejecting calls to reform the appeals system, which remains unchanged. Moreover, despite international recognition of the UK competition law enforcement system, this research has demonstrated that at least on a relative basis, there are very few infringement decisions and consequently few appeals in relation to the competition law prohibitions in the UK.

PART III Comparative Analysis

CHAPTER 31

Comparative Report: National Judicial Review of Competition Law Enforcement in the EU and the UK

Or Brook & Barry Rodger

This chapter takes a bird's eye view, highlighting general trends and providing observations on the judicial review of competition law enforcement by national courts in the EU and the UK. Based on the data presented in the previous chapters of the book, we look at: (i) the structures of the national enforcement systems, (ii) the total number of judgments rendered in each jurisdiction, the ratio of appeals, success rates and the outcome of judicial review, (iii) the types of appellants, (iv) the competition rules subject to review, (v) the grounds of review, (vi) the use of preliminary references, (vii) leniency and settlements in appeals, and (viii) the role of third parties. The chapter also (ix) points to the lack of publication of judgments in many of the EU Member States and outlines a plea for greater transparency as a precondition for effective and uniform protection of competition law throughout the internal market. Finally, it (x) concludes by submitting that the current system of judicial review of EU and national competition law enforcement by national courts does not fully match the integration aims of EU law in general, and Regulation 1/2003 in particular.

We offer some comparative insights about the impact and functioning of the administrative and judicial enforcement systems including the role of specialist and non-specialist courts, across the above features of judicial review. In addition, we point to some commonalities in the judicial review institutional context and practical experience in the Central and Eastern European (CEE) Member States.

Unless indicated otherwise, the figures herein capture the period covered by this study, that is, from the entry into force of Regulation 1/2003 on 1 May 2004 and 30 April 2021.

1 STRUCTURE OF THE NATIONAL ENFORCEMENT SYSTEMS

The institutional design of competition law enforcement delineates the allocation of power between the body with primary jurisdiction over antitrust matters, on the one hand, and the reviewing courts or tribunals, on the other.[1] Yet, as was detailed in Chapter 1, EU law does not impose strict requirements on the institutional design of the NCAs or national courts. This section demonstrates that as a result, there is great divergence in terms of the institutional design of the NCAs (judicial or administrative model), the number of instances of appeal on the NCAs' decisions, the degree of specialisation of the reviewing courts in competition law matters, the standard and intensity of review, and the type of NCAs' decisions that could be subject to judicial review.

1.1 Institutional Design of the NCAs (The Administrative/Judicial Models)

There are two main institutional models for competition law enforcement systems in the EU.[2] Under the *administrative model*, one (the monist administrative model) or two (the dualist administrative model) administrative authorities investigate competition law infringements and make enforcement decisions. Such administrative bodies normally also have the power to impose fines. According to the *judicial model*, by comparison, after the administrative authority investigates a case, it must introduce proceedings before a court or a tribunal (or refer it to a prosecutor who brings it to court). The court or tribunal rules on matters of substance and has the power to impose fines. Scholars have pointed to different benefits and shortcomings related to each model.[3] They suggest that the judicial model rates highly in terms of accountability, independence, and transparency of decision-making as the administrative authorities' enforcement actions are always scrutinised, finalised and made effective by court rulings. The judicial scrutiny stage is designed to ensure protection for the procedural due process rights of the investigated parties. Yet, this comes at the price of expertise, as courts are typically less specialised and knowledgeable in matters related to competition law enforcement in comparison with competition authorities.[4] This model also often entails a longer duration for infringement proceedings. By comparison, the administrative model ensures a higher level of expertise. It focuses on protecting the substantive correctness of the competition law analysis in complex and technical

1. Javier Tapia and Santiago Montt. 'Judicial Scrutiny and Competition Authorities: The Institutional Limits of Antitrust' in Ioannis Lianos and Daniel Sokol (eds) *The Global Limits of Competition Law* (Stanford University Press, 2012), 141-157, 141.
2. European Competition Network, 'Decision-Making Powers Report' ECN Working Group Cooperation Issues and Due Process of 31 October 2012, available here: https://competition-policy.ec.europa.eu/document/download/b423e02b-d850-4c52-9dfa-95a4b5bcb3f7_en?filename=decision_making_powers_report_en.pdf, 5-3. Also *see* Michael J. Trebilcock and Edward M. Iacobucci 'Designing Competition Law Institutions' (2010) 25(3) *World Competition* 445.
3. *Ibid.*, 460-464.
4. *Ibid.*

matters, but it may provide, to varying extents, a lower degree of accountability, transparency, and procedural efficiency.[5]

Figure 31.1 demonstrates that while most of the Member States of the EU and the UK have followed the administrative model, Austria, Finland, Ireland,[6] Malta, and Sweden (until its 2021 reform) had an institutional structure based on the judicial model during all or part of the period covered by this study.

5. *Ibid.*
6. Following the cut-off date of the project, Ireland transformed its public enforcement structure. The Competition (Amendment) Act of 2022, introduces an administrative penalty mechanism for enforcing competition law.

Figure 31.1 Institutional Design of the NCAs

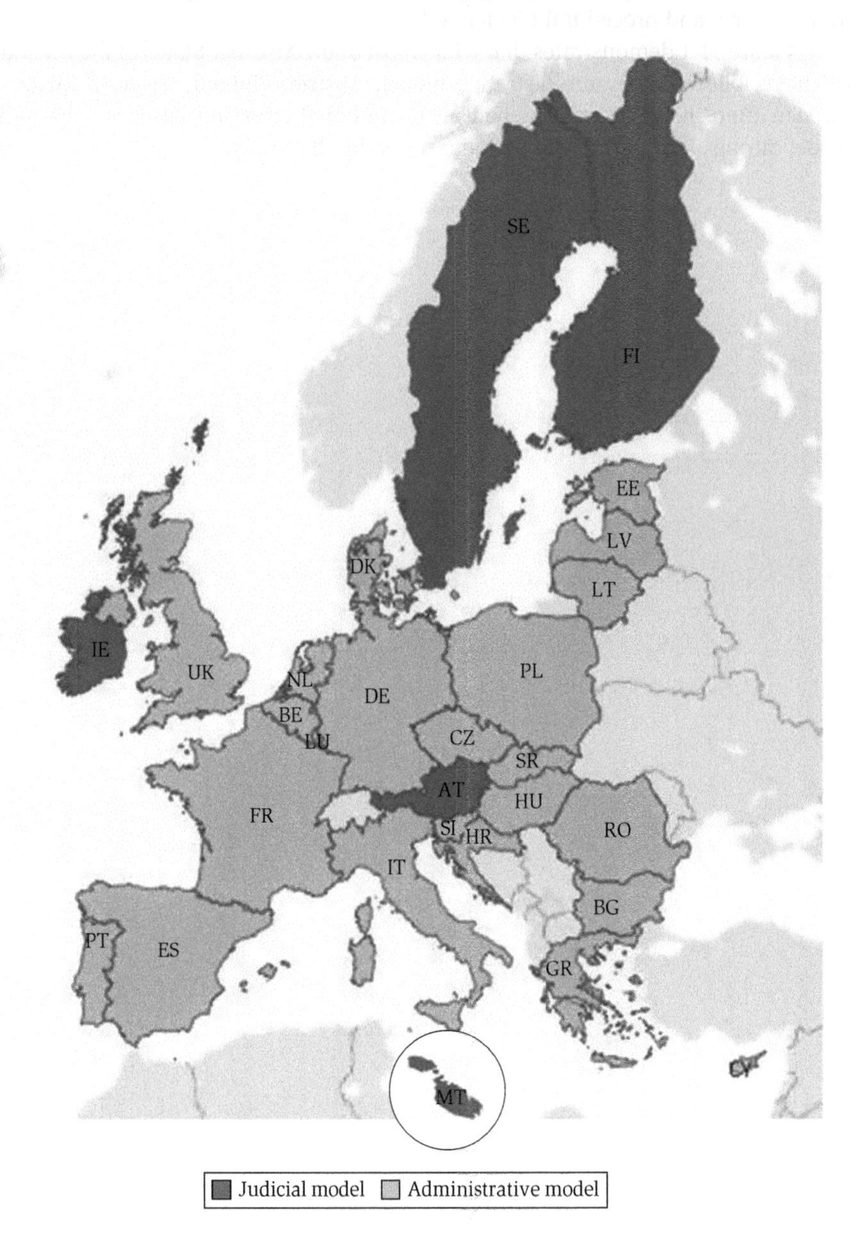

In some countries, including Belgium, Croatia, Denmark, Malta, and Sweden, there was a change in the enforcement model during the relevant period. Figure 31.1 thus refers to the situation at the end of the relevant period of this study (April 2021). Belgium, for example, shifted from a judicial enforcement to an administrative system in 2013, following the European Court of Justice's (ECJ) *Vebic* judgment.[7] While Croatia's enforcement framework is currently based on the administrative model, antitrust infringements were considered misdemeanour offences until 2009, meaning that the competition authority could only make findings of infringements, and the authority had to initiate separate proceedings in front of a misdemeanour court to impose a fine.[8] Until 2021, the Swedish NCA did not have the power to adopt infringement decisions or to impose fines, but rather had to bring an action before the Stockholm District Court (or after reforms, the Patent and Market Court). Nonetheless, it was transformed from a judicial to an administrative model as part of the transposition of the ECN+ Directive in 2021. As part of this reform, judicial review moved from a system involving a single instance of appeal to two instances of appeal.[9] Between 2011 and 2019, Malta had embraced the administrative enforcement model but following domestic jurisprudence it switched to the judicial model.[10]

As elaborated in the national reports, each NCA's institutional structure may have particularities, which means that even those which belong to the same model can differ. Greece, Hungary, Latvia, and the Netherlands, for example, follow the administrative model, yet their enforcement processes can be characterised as *quasi*-judicial proceedings, involving a fully-fledged oral hearing before the adjudicatory body of the NCA. In the relevant period, Slovenia also separated the decision-making within the NCA but on a different basis. The Slovenian NCA's enforcement consisted of two types of proceedings: first, the NCA had to initiate an administrative procedure aimed at bringing to an end an infringement of the competition rules. In practice, only after this decision was final, could the NCA have opened a separate minor offence procedure, where fines can be levied. Each of the procedures was subject to different rules, involved different teams within the NCA, and was subject to different judicial review rules and procedures.[11] Croatia also followed a similar system, which was abandoned in 2009.[12]

Other systems differ even more significantly. Denmark currently has an administrative model, whereby public enforcement of competition law is the responsibility of the Danish Competition and Consumer Authority (DCCA) and the Competition Council (CC). However, for the main period covered by the study, it was a hybrid

7. Belgium report, Chapter 4.
8. Ireland report, Chapter 16.
9. Sweden report, Chapter 29.
10. Malta report, Chapter 21.
11. Slovenia report, Chapter 27.
12. Croatia report, Chapter 6.

judicial/administrative model. The primary administrative tool was the power to stop an infringement by a formal decision, whereas the imposition of fines was a matter for the ordinary courts. This allocation of powers changed with the implementation of the ECN + Directive and it is now for the CC to impose civil fines on companies whereas fines on individuals (and possible imprisonment) are initiated by the public prosecutor and imposed by the courts. A complicated enforcement system also characterises Estonia. While, in principle, Estonia follows an administrative enforcement model, in practice, enforcement is performed through an intricate combination of four different types of procedures: criminal, misdemeanour, state supervision, and administrative procedures (in which no fines can be imposed, and in relation to which no actions were launched in the relevant project period). Estonia is currently, belatedly, transposing the ECN + Directive by reforming its competition law enforcement framework to a fully administrative system.[13]

The choice of enforcement model is sometimes a matter of national constitutional law. In Ireland, for example, the Competition (Amendment) Act 1996 did not grant the administrative competition agency either competence to make determinations on substantive infringements of competition law or to impose fines. Instead, during the period covered by this study, the authority only had investigation powers and had to initiate an action before a court seeking either a declaration that particular conduct violated competition law and/or an injunction. This institutional design derives from an interpretation of the national constitution to the effect that justice must be administered by courts.[14]

1.2 Number of Instances of Appeal

1.2.1 Tiers of Review

Figure 31.2 presents the number of possible instances of appeal in competition law matters (as of April 2021). It demonstrates that in most competition law enforcement systems examined by this study (nineteen out of the twenty-eight), the NCAs' decisions are subject to two levels of appeal. This, in particular, is characteristic of many of the systems which have adopted the judicial model. In eight of the jurisdictions, three instances of appeals were available (in addition, Hungary provided three levels of appeals until 2020). The figure represents the appeal system as of April 2021.

13. Estonia report, Chapter 10.
14. Ireland report Chapter 16.

Figure 31.2 Tiers of Review

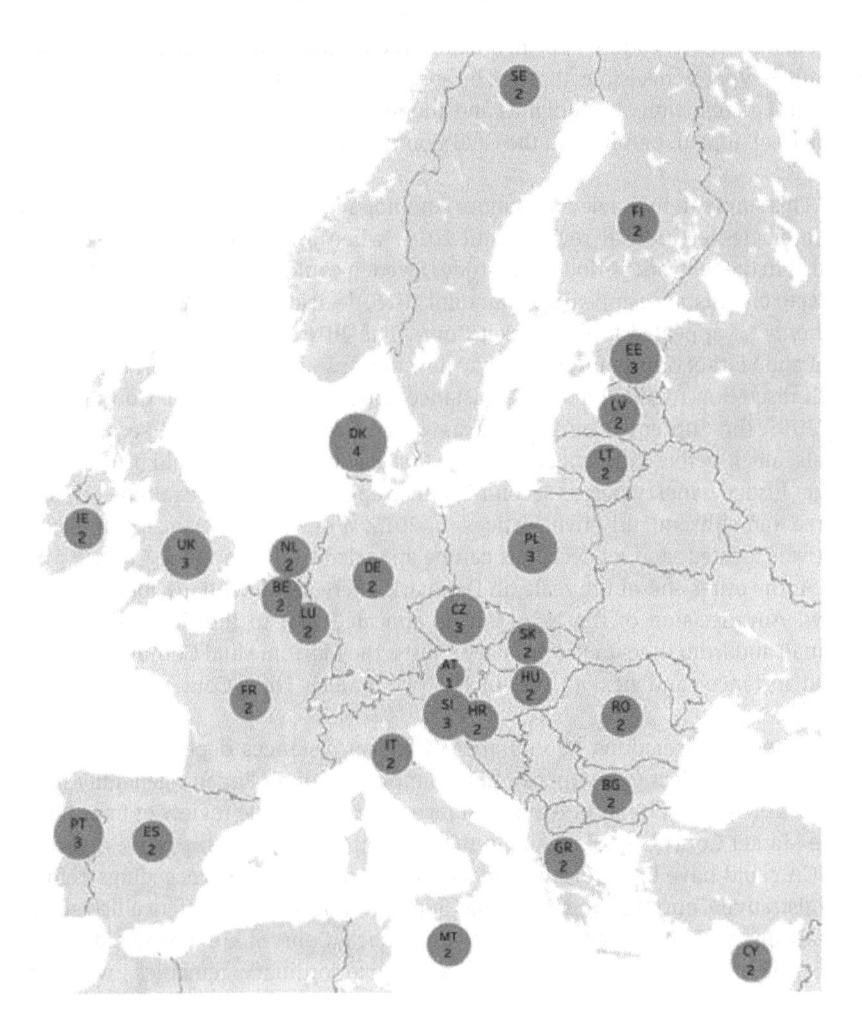

At one far end of the spectrum, Austria has a single instance of appeal. Adhering to the judicial model, a decision of the Cartel Court in Austria (the NCA in the meaning of Regulation 1/2003) can only be appealed before the Supreme Cartel Court on matters of law.

Other jurisdictions also have a limited number of appeal instances. In Croatia, there is normally a single-tier judicial review system, whereby an NCA decision may be challenged in 'administrative dispute' proceedings in front of the High Administrative Court, a review court for appeals in administrative matters. Yet, exceptionally, a request for an extraordinary review of the legality of a final judgment may be filed against such judgment before the Supreme Court (only a single judgment was recorded in the database in the relevant period).[15] There is also typically a single-tier judicial review system in Malta, whereby the decisions of the Civil Court (Commercial Section, acting as the NCA), can be appealed before the Court of Appeal alone. Nevertheless, the limited types of decisions that can be adopted directly by the Office for Competition in Malta (i.e., rejection of complaints and adoption of commitments), are subject to two instances of appeal, before both the Civil Court (Commercial Section) and the Court of Appeal.[16]

This single-tiered review was more common in the EU in the past. Ireland used to have a single-tier judicial review until 2014, when a new appeal court was established.[17] In the relevant period of the study, Sweden could also be categorised as having a de facto one-instance appeal system: until 2016, decisions on infringements and fines could only be appealed to the Market Court. The 2016 reform, which introduced the Patent and Market Court of Appeal as the new first-instance review court, also provided it with discretion to allow a second-instance appeal to the Supreme Court.[18] Finally, until 2015, the Supreme Court in Cyprus would hear both first and second-instance appeals, albeit before different panels. The first-instance appeal would be examined by a single Justice panel, whereas second-instance appeals would be examined by a panel of three and subsequently five Justices. In 2015, a new first-instance Administrative Court was formed, and its decisions can be appealed to the Supreme Court.[19]

At the other end of the scale, in Denmark, there are potentially four instances of review. Any decision of the NCA can be appealed first to the Competition Appeal Tribunal, and from there to the ordinary courts: the Maritime and Commercial Court at second instance, and next to one of the two Danish High Courts or the Supreme Court.[20]

In some jurisdictions, the number of appeal instances depends on the type of NCA decision subject to an appeal. For example, although Finland generally has two instances of appeals, it has only one instance of appeal for the review of fines imposed by the Market Court.[21] In Slovenia, in the relevant period, administrative decisions of the NCA could have been reviewed in 'administrative dispute' proceedings before the Administrative Court and thereafter the Supreme Court. Minor offence decisions, by comparison, could have been reviewed by the Local Court of Ljubljana, and thereafter by the High Court of Ljubljana, and some extraordinary remedies, which have

15. Croatia report, Chapter 6.
16. Malta report, Chapter 21.
17. Ireland report Chapter 16.
18. Sweden report Chapter 29. Yet, there were no such appeals in the relevant period, and more generally, appeals involving administrative fines are generally scarce.
19. Cyprus report, Chapter 7.
20. The appeal system has changed in 2021, upon the implementation of the ECN + Directive. When a case is appealed directly from the Maritime and Commercial Court to the Supreme Court, the Supreme Court must decide if the appeal should be heard by it, or rather referred to the High Court. If the case ends up in the High Court it can only be appealed further on to the Supreme Court, if permission is granted. *See* Denmark report, Chapter 9.
21. Finland report, Chapter 11.

considerable limitations in terms of scope and standing, could have been sought at a third-instance appeal before the Supreme Court.[22]

In Spain, the Administrative Chamber of the National High Court is in most cases the only instance of appeal against the NCA's decisions. Nonetheless, second-instance appeals to the Administrative Chamber of the Supreme Court are available on limited grounds.[23]

The national reports indicated that a greater number of review instances leads to the lengthening of the procedure, particularly where a second- or third-instance appeal can be remitted back to a lower-instance court (e.g., Spain).[24] This may also hinder deterrence, especially in systems where the fine for an infringement of the competition rules is not due until the appeal is final (e.g., Poland),[25] or is subject to initiation of a separate, consecutive procedure (e.g., Slovenia).[26]

1.2.2 Constitutional Review

Some countries have also adopted constitutional types of review, outside of the regular appeals system, focusing on the protection of fundamental rights and the rule of law. As elaborated in Chapter 2, the review of competition law decisions by constitutional courts was only included in the database of this study where the constitutional court examines appeals on the NCA's final decisions. The study does not cover constitutional complaints, alleging that the decision of the NCA or the judgments of the lower courts have violated human rights (e.g., in Croatia, Slovenia, and Spain). Such judgments were not included in the database but discussed within the national reports.

In Portugal, second-instance appeal judgments can be appealed to the Portuguese Constitutional Court if certain pre-requisites are met. This has been used very often, whereby 27% of the judgments in the relevant period were Constitutional Court judgments.[27] In Malta, while constitutional proceedings may be instituted where the parties believe that there has been a breach of their fundamental rights during the infringement procedure, this was used only in a single case following an NCA decision.[28]

1.2.3 Internal Review

Our study also highlights that in some jurisdictions, an NCA internal appeal-like review process must be completed before an appeal can be submitted to a court. In the Czech Republic, for example, decisions by the Vice-Chairman of the UOHS (known as the NCA's 'first-instance decisions') may be appealed to the Chairman of UOHS by the

22. Slovenia report, Chapter 27. The review system has changed in 2023, as detailed in the report.
23. Spain report, Chapter 28.
24. *Ibid.*
25. Poland report, Chapter 23.
26. Slovenia report, Chapter 27.
27. Portugal report, Chapter 24.
28. Malta report, Chapter 21.

parties to the proceedings. The Chairman has full jurisdiction to confirm, annul, or return any such decision to the Vice-Chairman for further investigation or to amend the decision. Only this 'second-instance decision' of the Chairman is subject to potentially three instances of appeal before the courts.[29] Similarly, in Slovakia, the Council of the PMÚ, which is chaired by the President of the PMÚ, acts as a collective appellate body to review any decisions of the PMÚ that are signed by the Vice-President. In contrast with the Czech system, however, decisions by the PMÚ and the Council are considered a single administrative procedure that is subject to review by the courts.[30]

In the Netherlands, an undertaking must lodge an objection with the NCA and request the decision to be reconsidered before submitting a subsequent appeal to the courts. The NCA must review and reconsider its decision in its entirety in light of the undertaking's objections, which may relate to all aspects of the decision. The NCA then has full discretion to uphold, modify or withdraw its decision. Only at that stage is an appeal available to the courts. This type of procedure is common in other types of administrative law enforcement in the Netherlands and is designed as a procedure to solve disputes between citizens and the government, to avoid lengthy, formal legal proceedings before the administrative courts.[31]

1.3 Degree of Specialisation

The existence, composition and functions allocated to a specialist competition court or tribunal are major factors in the institutional design of a legal system to deal with competition litigation, and there has been a proliferation of specialist competition courts and tribunals across jurisdictions worldwide over the last twenty-five years.[32] The main potential advantage of a specialist judicial body is that it may lead to better decision-making due to a greater appreciation of the complexities of the case law arising from its specialist knowledge and experience, resulting in more informed opinions.[33] Nonetheless, as *Roth* has stressed, the degree of specialisation required is partly dependent on the role and functions to be performed by the particular court or tribunal. Roth has suggested various additional advantages which may arise from the creation of a specialist court: it may assist in the process of judicial training; it can adapt

29. Czech Republic report, Chapter 8.
30. Slovakia report, Chapter 26.
31. The Netherlands report, Chapter 22.
32. *See* Barry Rodger, 'Introduction' in Barry Rodger (ed.), *Landmark Cases in Competition Law: Around the World in Fourteen Stories* (Kluwer Law International, 2011), 17; Despoina Mantzari, *Courts, Regulators, and the Scrutiny of Economic Evidence* (OUP 2022), 141.
33. D.S. Savrin 'Specialized Antitrust Courts: A Practitioner's Observations', Chapter 8, 116-117; P. Roth 'Specialized Antitrust Courts', Chapter 7, 105, both in B. Hawk (ed.), *Annual Proceedings of the Fordham Competition Law Institute* (Fordham Competition Law Institute, 2013). *See also* J. Rakoff, 'Lecture: Are Federal Judges Competent? Dilettantes in an Age of Economic Expertise', (2012) 17 Fordham Journal of Corporate and Financial law 4, 6; Michael R. Baye and Joshua D. Wright, 'Is Antitrust Too Complicated for Generalist Judges? The Impact of Economic Complexity and Judicial Training on Appeals' (2011) *Journal of Law & Economics*, 54/1, 1-24.

its processes and procedures to the specialist context; and it may be afforded a greater degree of deference by appeal courts.[34]

During the negotiations leading to the adoption of Regulation 1/2003, many stakeholders called for harmonised rules on the degree of specialisation of the relevant national appeal courts. The European Parliament,[35] its Committee of Economic and Monetary Affairs,[36] and the Economic and Social Committee,[37] for example, suggested that appeals against NCAs' decisions should only be heard by specialised courts dealing solely with competition law matters, or at least by special sections within a generalist court, to ensure consistency and legal certainty in the application of EU competition law.[38] Yet, these proposals were not adopted. Provisions on the nature of national courts were absent from Regulation 1/2003 and, consequently, a considerable degree of divergence in the extent of specialisation in the national courts persists.

Nonetheless, our study has confirmed that the classification of a reviewing court as a generalist or as a competition law specialist body is not binary, but rather a matter of degree. The range of legal systems studied demonstrate a wide variance in terms of the degree of specialisation, *de jure* and *de facto*, of the different instance appeal courts. Some systems have no specialist courts or panels at all; some systems have created panels within a generalist court, and in others, legislation has established a single first-instance specialist court or tribunal, with an onward appeal to generalist courts. *Tapia* and *Montt* suggested that specialisation is a comprehensive concept composed of three parts (according to which a generalist court would lack one or more components):[39] the judicial level of knowledge in the specific substantive area subject to consideration and judgments (competition law); the courts' experience, that is the accumulation of knowledge and skills over a sufficiently large number of decisions; and the object-specificity of the court, namely the choice of the legislature to establish a specialist court aimed at protecting the specific public policy. These authors also noted that the scope of judicial scrutiny would match the institutional characteristics of the reviewing body, namely, that non-specialist courts should pay greater deference to the NCAs' decisions on questions of policy, facts, and law.[40]

In some Member States, the courts are not specialised at all (e.g., Ireland, Croatia, Czech Republic, Hungary, and Greece). Other national courts are 'hyper-specialised'

---

34. *See* D. Bailey, 'Early Case-Law of the Competition Appeal Tribunal', in B. Rodger (ed.), *Ten Years of UK Competition Law Reform* (DUP, 2010), Ch. 2.
35. European Parliament resolution on the Commission White Paper on modernisation of the rules implementing Articles 85 and 86 of the EC Treaty (COM(1999) 101 - C5-0105/1999-1999/2108(COS)) of 18 January 2000, para. 18.
36. Committee on Economic and Monetary Affairs, Report on the proposal for a Council regulation on the implementation of the rules on competition laid down in Articles 81 and 82 of the Treaty and amending Regulations (EEC) No. 1017/68, (EEC) No. 2988/74, (EEC) No. 4056/86 and (EEC) No. 3975/87 (COM(2000) 582 ñ C5-0527/2000 ñ 2000/0243(CNS)) A5-0229/2001, 25-26.
37. Opinion of the Economic and Social Committee on the 'White Paper on modernisation of the rules implementing Articles 81 and 82 of the EC Treaty - Commission programme No 99/027' (2000/C 51/15), para. 2.3.2.8.
38. Also *see* DG COMP, White Paper on the Reform of Regulation 17-Summary of the Observations, 29 February 2000, para. 5.2.
39. Tapia and Montt (*supra* n. 1), 143.
40. *Ibid.*, 144.

appeal bodies, with wide competence to confirm, set aside, vary or remit the NCA's decision, and make any other decision that the competition authority could have made (e.g., the Competition Appeals Tribunals in the UK and Denmark).[41]

Courts which examine several areas in addition to competition law, reflect a medium level of specialisation. The Market Court in Finland is a specialist court that hears market law cases, competition cases and public procurement cases as well as cases regarding energy market regulation. There are also part-time expert members who participate in the consideration, inter alia, of competition cases. A part-time competition expert is added to the panel in the most significant cases. The Market Court annually decides on only a handful of competition law cases (normally one to three cases).[42]

Some Member States have a specialised chamber within a generalist court. In France, for example, a specialised chamber of four professional judges (as of January 2023), within the Paris Court of Appeal, rules on appeals against the NCA's decisions.[43] The only instance of appeal in Austria is to the Supreme Cartel Court, which is a specialised senate at the Supreme Court. The Supreme Cartel Court sits in panels of five judges, of which three must be professional judges and two must be expert lay judges.[44] In Belgium, specialisation has been enhanced since 2016, upon the establishment of a special section within the Brussels Court of Appeal, having exclusive power to hear appeals in competition cases at first instance.[45]

In some countries, only the first-instance court is specialised in competition law matters (e.g., Poland and the UK), while in the Netherlands, both the first-instance Rotterdam District Court and the second-instance Trade and Industry Appeals Tribunal are specialist courts, having exclusive competence to review the public enforcement of competition law. Their expertise is not only tied to their exclusive competence but also develops because only a limited number of judges and legal court assistants in each of the two courts deal with competition law cases. When needed, substitute judges (e.g., academics) may be called on because of their special expertise within the field. The two-tiered system of judicial expertise was justified by the Dutch legislator given the specific expertise needed to engage in economic notions when applying the rules.[46] Similarly, in Sweden, the Patent and Market Court is a specialist court, composed of legally trained judges, lay judges, and economic experts. The court has the discretion not to include economic experts when it believes the case does not involve complex economic questions. Following the shift to a two-tier appeal system in 2021, both the first and second-instance appeals in Sweden are dealt with by specialist courts.[47]

41. The UK report, Chapter 30; Denmark report, Chapter 9.
42. Finland report, Chapter 11.
43. France report, Chapter 12.
44. Austria report, Chapter 3. In the case of the need for a reinforced senate, the panel consists of seven professional judges and two expert lay judges. Judges serve both the panel on competition law matters (Supreme Cartel Court) as well as several panels dealing with other legal issues, meaning that their expertise is not exclusively focused on competition law
45. Belgium report, Chapter 4.
46. The Netherlands report, Chapter 22.
47. Sweden report, Chapter 29.

Some of the national reports revealed a gap between formal and *de facto* specialisation. In Poland, the Court of Competition and Consumer Protection, the first-instance court, has exclusive competence to deal with competition law matters. However, scholars have critiqued the level of competition law competence and knowledge of some of the judges, arguing that competition law expertise has rarely been evidenced in practice and depends on the particular judge.[48] Similarly, in Portugal, judges appointed to the Competition, Regulation, and Supervision Court do not have any prior knowledge or experience in competition law. This, together with the high turnover of judges, results in a lower level of specialisation in practice.[49]

A degree of specialisation can be achieved de facto by having a single court hearing competition law matters. In Italy, only the Regional Administrative Tribunal of Rome can hear appeals concerning decisions of the NCA. While it is not a body specialised in competition law matters, entrusting competence to hear appeals to a single Regional Administrative Tribunal is justified by the need to ensure coherence and uniformity in the judicial review of the competition rules.[50] Similarly, in Spain, first-instance appeals are heard by magistrates serving in the Administrative Chamber of the National High Court, reflecting the assumption that specialisation in competition law will be acquired through the repeated performance of their work in the matters allocated to them.

Likewise, in Romania, there is no competition law specialisation and all judges receive the same training. However, inherent *de facto* specialisation occurs since competition law cases have been exclusively assigned to a limited number of judges.[51] In Greece, a 2011 Law calling for the creation of specialised competition law chambers within the first-instance court has yet to be implemented, presumably in view of the low number of cases per year and most importantly the generalist character of the Greek Courts.[52]

In Germany, appeals against decisions of the NCA are examined by OLG Düsseldorf. Competition law-related appeals are concentrated in specialised cartel senates, with approximately fifteen judges dealing with competition law. Those judges do not necessarily have specific competition law expertise when starting their assignment, yet as they usually stay in the cartel senates for a long time, most judges become highly competent and experienced in evaluating and applying competition law. The same is true for the second-instance appeal. The Bundesgerichtshof has a specialised senate for competition law, the Cartel Senate, with around eight professional judges.[53]

Some scholars have suggested that specialist courts create incentives to enhance the scope of judicial discretion and show less deference to the NCA's assessment, leading such courts to revisit all aspects of the reviewed decision. According to this

48. Poland report, Chapter 23.
49. Portugal report, Chapter 24.
50. Italy report, Chapter 17.
51. Romania report, Chapter 25. This is also the case for Croatia, as detailed in the national report (*see* Chapter 6).
52. Greece report, Chapter 14. In practice, competition law cases are normally assigned to specific chambers, which allows for a certain degree of specialisation.
53. Germany report, Chapter 13.

argument, since specialist courts determine competition law disputes on a continuous basis, they are likely to feel more confident in their own capabilities when dealing with topics that in principle would appear to fall within the exclusive specialist remit of competition authorities - and hence they may be open to review technically complex matters.[54]

The degree of specialisation of the first-instance court might also inform the scope of subsequent judicial review. The non-specialised second-instance Court of Appeal in the UK, for instance, noted that it would afford deference to first-instance judgments by the Competition Appeal Tribunal given the latter's particular level of specialisation in competition law matters.[55]

Given the heterogeneity of the national judicial systems and the degree and nature of their specialisation, testing the hypothesis regarding the more intrusive role of specialist courts is not an easy task. Defining a more detailed metric for specialisation might be necessary. The empirical data on the success rates of first-instance courts presented in section 2.3 below, do not point to a strong correlation between the degree of specialisation and the success rates of appeals. While some highly specialist courts have often interfered in the NCA's judgment (e.g., in the UK and Poland), others have shown considerably greater deference (e.g., Denmark). Similarly, while some non-specialist courts have mostly confirmed the decisions of the NCA (e.g., Hungary and Croatia), others have often overturned the decisions of their NCAs (e.g., Ireland, Greece). Hence, other characteristics of both the NCA enforcement framework and judicial review system beyond the degree of court specialisation appear to have a greater influence on the issue of deference to NCA decisions.[56]

1.4 Standard and Intensity of Review

The concepts of the standard and intensity of review refer to the depth of investigation performed by an appeal court.

Each legal system has a different scope for review that is set by statute or precedent, making provision for the grounds for review, and the extent to which this may involve questions of law, fact, and/or procedure.[57] First-instance courts in almost all the examined countries were competent to exercise full review of matters relating to both facts and law. There are two notable exceptions. First, the single-instance Supreme Cartel Court in Austria may only review the Cartel Court's decisions on questions of law. While since 2017, appeals can also be launched where the files raise significant doubt as to the correctness of the relevant facts upon which the Cartel Court

54. Tapia and Montt (*supra* n. 1), 144. Also *see* discussion in Mantzari (*supra* n. 32), 141.
55. The UK Report, Chapter 30.
56. For a discussion of that wider context, *see*, for example, Maciej Bernatt, 'Transatlantic Perspective on Judicial Deference in Administrative Law', (2016) 22(2) Columbia Journal of European Law 275-325, 279; Annalies Outhuijse, 'The Effective Public Enforcement of the Prohibition of Anti-competitive Agreements: Which Factors Influence the High Percentage of Annulments of Dutch Cartel Fines?' (2020) 8(1) Journal of Antitrust Enforcement 124 DOI: 10.1093/jaenfo/jnz020.
57. Tapia and Montt (*supra* n. 1), 144.

based its decision, such appeals are limited to exceptional cases.[58] Second, the Administrative Court in Cyprus exercises only marginal review of administrative decisions, limited to testing their legality.[59]

Our study also discussed matters of intensity of review. Commentators use different terminology to describe the degree of intensity of review and the scope of judicial deference accorded by courts to the NCAs' decisions. However, most agree that intensity of review is a spectrum of control ranging from a more lenient test of whether an authority could have lawfully and reasonably arrived at a particular decision, to an intensive 'on the merits' review, including questions as to whether the decision was correct and appropriate in the specific case.[60] In Cyprus, although review of fines does not exist and review on substance is limited by law, the courts vigorously scrutinised the NCA's decisions on matters of procedure.[61] In Poland, the courts do not afford the NCA a noticeable margin of appreciation with respect to complex economic assessments.[62]

Our project also confirms that the intensity of review has sometimes evolved through judicial practice, rather than by law reform. In Italy, for example, whereas the court of first instance had historically taken a limited review approach, the Council of State held that administrative judges have the power to exercise an in-depth, full, and effective review, including on complex economic matters. This transformation was inspired both by the jurisprudence of the European Court of Human Rights (ECtHR) and the powers of EU Courts in competition law matters.[63] On the flipside, while the reviewing courts in Croatia and Romania have the legal power to undertake a full review of the NCA's decision, in practice, they have been reluctant to exert their powers.[64]

---

58. Austria report, Chapter 3.
59. Cyprus report, Chapter 7.
60. Tom Zwart, 'The Scope of Review of Administrative Action from a Comparative Perspective' in Oda Essens et al. (eds) *National Courts and the Standard of Review in Competition Law and Economic Regulation* (Europa Law Publishing 2009) 23; Cosmo Graham, 'Judicial Review of the Decisions of the Competition Authorities and the Economic Regulators in the UK' in Oda Essens et al., *National Courts and the Standard of Review in Competition Law and Economic Regulation* (Europa Law Publishing 2009). On the intensity of review also *see* Dubravka Aksamovic, 'Judicial Review in Competition Cases in Croatia and Comparative Jurisdictions' (2017) 67 Zbornik PFZ 405, 437; Damien Geradin and Nicolas Petit. 'Judicial Review in European Union Competition Law: A Quantitative and Qualitative Assessment' in Massimo Merola and Jacques Derenne (eds), *The Role of the Court of Justice of the European Union in Competition Law Cases* (Bruylant 2012); Bo Vesterdorf, 'Judicial Review in EC Competition Law: Reflections on the Role of the Community Courts in the EC System of Competition Law Enforcement' (2005) 1 Global Competition Policy 3-27, 9; Ioannis Lianos et al., 'Judicial Scrutiny of Financial Penalties in Competition Law: A Comparative Perspective', CLES Research Paper 3 (2014), available at: https://research.vu.nl/ws/portalfiles/portal/1244324/CLES2014%282%29.pdf; Bernatt (*supra* n. 56).
61. Cyprus report, Chapter 7.
62. Poland report, Chapter 23.
63. Italy report, Chapter 17.
64. Croatia report, Chapter 6; Romania report, Chapter 25.

1.5 The Types of NCA Decisions Subject to Review

EU law does not precisely prescribe which types of NCAs' decisions could be subject to judicial review. While infringement decisions imposing sanctions are subject to judicial review in all Member States,[65] Figure 31.3 illustrates that no ground for action findings and decisions to close investigations, reject complaints, or accept commitments could only be subject to review in some Member States. Moreover, in some legal systems, the type of NCAs' decisions that could be subject to an appeal changed over time.[66] The figure represents the law as of April 2021. The same is true when it comes to appeals launched against an NCA's decision involving leniency or settlements applications, as will be discussed later in section 4 below.

65. This is true for all jurisdictions where the NCAs can impose administrative fines for an infringement of the competition rules, that is, with the exclusion of Ireland and Estonia.
66. For example, while in the past all final decisions in infringement cases were subject to judicial review, following the 2006 Competition Act judicial review of decisions rejecting complaints was no longer available (*see* Belgium report, Chapter 4).

Figure 31.3 The Types of NCA Decisions Subject to Review

	Scope and standard of review		Types of NCAs' decisions subject to review						
	Law and facts	Full review	Infringement and fine	Infringement, no fine	No grounds for action	Rejecting complaints	Commitments	Leniency	Settlements
AT	■								
BE						■	■		■
BG									▒
CY		■							▒
CZ					■	■	■		
DE					■	■			
DK			▒				■	■	▒
EE			▒				▒	▒	▒
ES									▒
FI									
FR									
GR									
HR									
HU									
IE			▒			■		▒	▒
IT									
LT									
LU									▒
LV					■	■			
MT									■
NL									
PL									
PT									
RO									
SE					▒				▒
SI					▒	▒			▒
SK				■	■	■	■		
UK									

■ Not subject to judicial review □ Subject to judicial review ▒ NCA cannot adopt such decisions

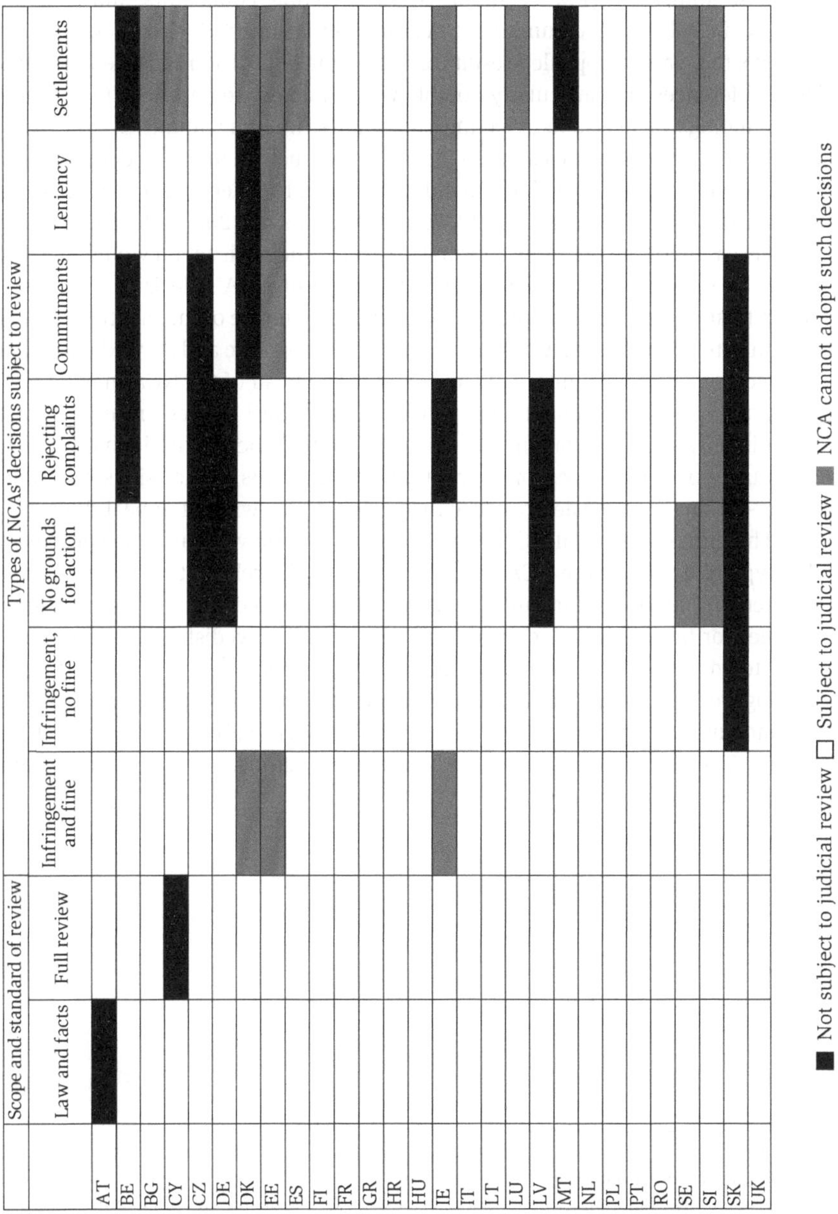

Some national systems explicitly declare that certain types of decisions are not subject to judicial review (e.g., decisions rejecting complaints and commitment decisions in Belgium,[67] commitment decisions in Denmark[68]). In others, the types of decisions that can be appealed result from the type of decisions adopted by the NCAs. These differences are particularly notable when it comes to appeals on no grounds for action findings or decisions rejecting complaints. In some countries, the NCA must adopt a formal - often reasoned - decision on such matters, and those decisions therefore will be generally subject to judicial review. In other countries (e.g., Germany, Latvia since 2016, Slovenia since 2008, and Poland since 2007), the NCA will simply close the case without adopting a formal measure, and such action would therefore not always be subject to judicial review.[69] The type of NCA's decisions that could be subject to an appeal is sometimes an indirect consequence of the institutional makeup of a domestic judicial review system. In the Czech Republic and Slovakia, for example, only decisions that were internally appealed to the head of the NCA may be reviewed by courts,[70] and complainants and other relevant third parties are not party to the proceedings. As a result, favourable decisions to the benefit of undertakings - such as no grounds for action, decisions accepting commitments, or decisions rejecting complaints - are never appealed because the undertakings will not appeal them.[71]

The different types of NCAs' decisions under review are also the consequence of what type of decisions the NCA can adopt. During the relevant period of the study or part thereof, the NCAs of Ireland, Denmark,[72] and Malta could not impose administrative fines for breach of the competition rules, and the Swedish NCA did not have the power to adopt grounds for action findings prior to 2021.[73]

Figure 31.4 moves from focusing on the rules to their operation in practise, by summarising the types of NCAs' decisions that were subject to an appeal in each country. The figure presents the proportions of first-instance judgments examining each type of NCAs' decisions.

67. *Ibid.*
68. Denmark report, Chapter 9.
69. For an empirical mapping of the national rules, *see* Or Brook and Katalin Cseres, 'Policy Report: Priority Setting in EU and National Competition Law Enforcement.' Available at SSRN 3930189 (2021) DOI: 10.2139/ssrn.3930189.
70. Text to *supra* n. 31.
71. Czech Republic report, Chapter 8; Slovakia report, Chapter 26.
72. This was changed following the implementation of the ECN+ Directive in March 2021. *See* Denmark report, Chapter 9.
73. Sweden report, Chapter 29.

Figure 31.4 Type of NCAs' Decisions Subject to First-Instance Appeals

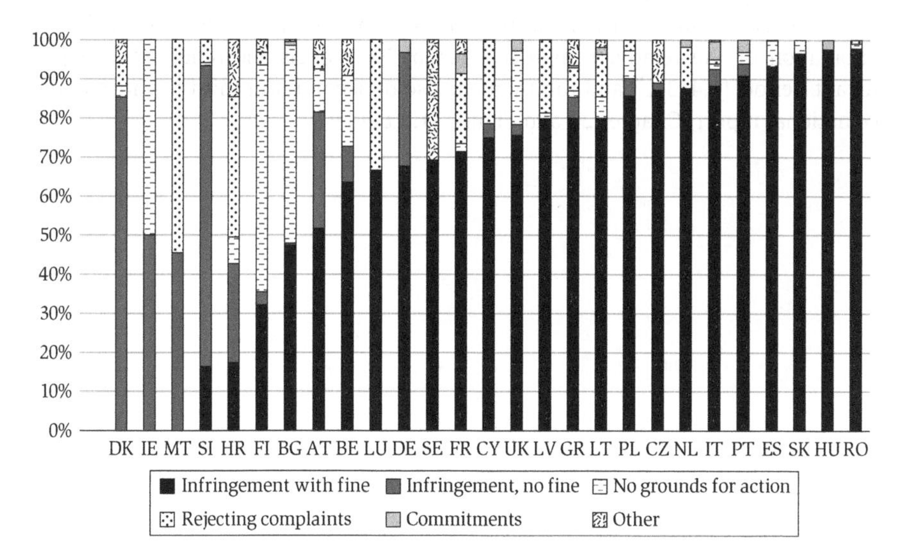

In most jurisdictions, infringement decisions imposing fines have been the focus of judicial review. In Denmark, Ireland, and Malta - in which the NCAs could not impose fines during all or part of the relevant period of the study - findings of infringements that were not accompanied by fines were also the focus of review. The practice of appealing decisions to reject complaints and no grounds for action findings, has been prominent only in a few jurisdictions and completely absent in some.

The figure also demonstrates that in most jurisdictions, commitment decisions are never or rarely appealed. Some notable exceptions are France (ten first-instance judgments, later subject to three second-instance appeals)[74] and Italy (thirteen first-instance judgments, later subject to twelve second-instance appeals).[75]

2 TOTAL NUMBER OF JUDGMENTS, RATIO OF APPEALS AND SUCCESS RATES

2.1 Total Number of Judgments

Figure 31.5 presents the total number of judgments included in the database in each jurisdiction, across all instances of appeal.

The figure reveals that there have been no appeals at all in Estonia and only two in Ireland, whereas the courts in Poland and Spain have issued the highest number of appeal judgments. Notably, the large number of appeals in those countries is not

74. France report, Chapter 12.
75. Italy report, Chapter 17. As elaborated in the national report, around 30% of the commitment decisions adopted by the Italian NCA during the relevant period have been subject to an appeal

explained by a particularly high ratio of appeals on such NCA's decisions. Rather, only 36% of the Polish and Spanish NCAs' decisions were subject to a first-instance appeal (*see* Figure 31.7 below). In Poland, the high number of appeals is explained by the combination of the relatively high number of NCA decisions rendered during the relevant period (1,413),[76] and the frequent use of second and third-instance appeals (*see* national report, Chapter 23 and Figure 31.8 below).

76. As indicated by the national report, the Polish NCA issued a particularly large number of decisions during the first ten years following the entry into force of Regulation 1/2003, which often related to repetitive and regional market practices.

Figure 31.5 Number of Judgments in the Database

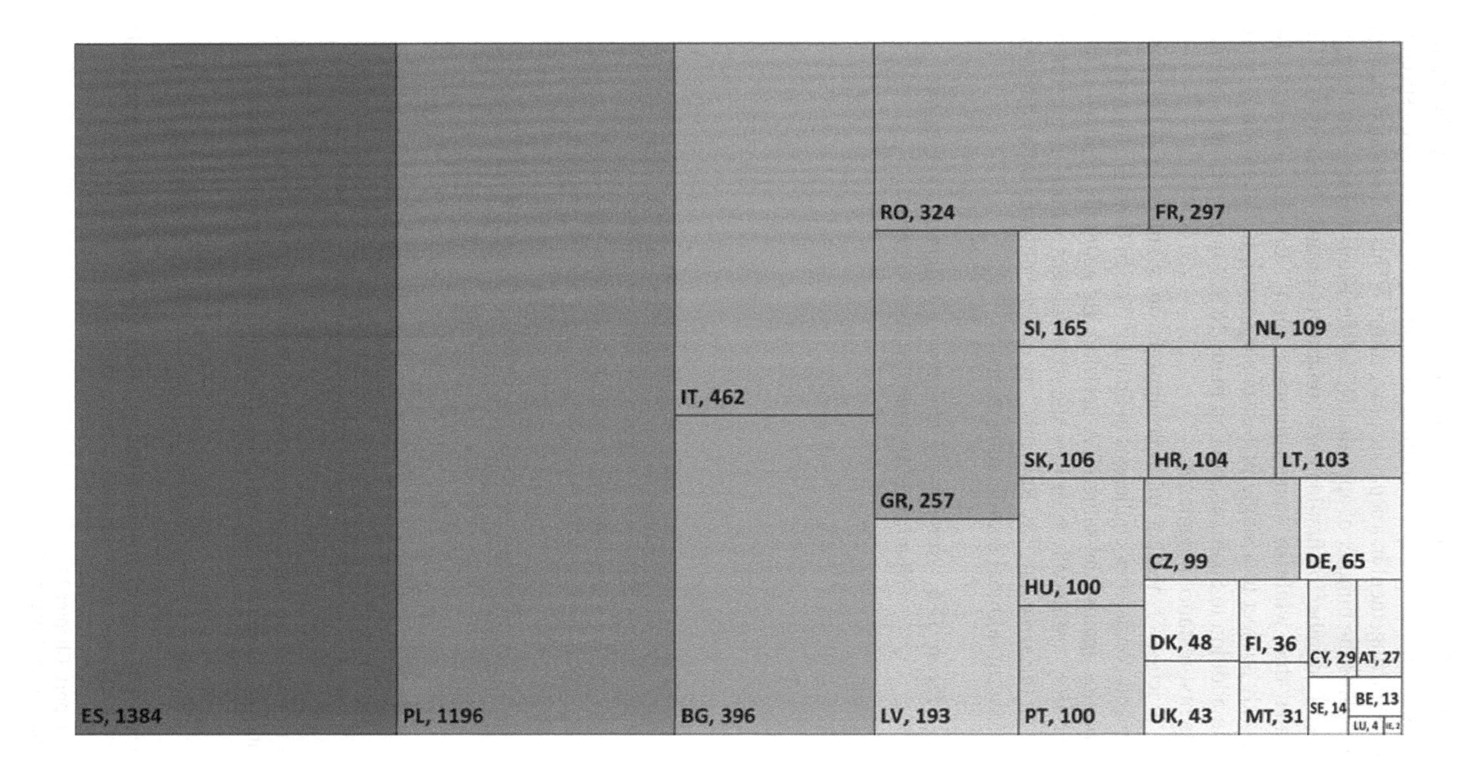

In Spain, the large number of judgments is explained by the right of each undertaking to challenge any sanctioning decision with respect to its specific participation in the infringement in a separate proceeding.[77] This is illustrated by Figure 31.6, which compares the number of appealed NCAs' decisions in each country (grey bars) to the overall number of first-instance judgments issued (black dots). The figure demonstrates that while in some countries, each NCA decision was always, or predominantly subject to a single first-instance appeal, in Poland, Italy, Greece, and Romania in addition to Spain, appeals on many NCAs' decisions have been reviewed in multiple first-instance judgments.

The practice of hearing multiple appeals on a single NCA decision created uniformity and consistency challenges in Spain.[78] Yet, in Greece, although appeals by multiple parties against the same NCA decision are generally dealt with in separate judgments, they are usually heard by the same judges whose judgments are often published on the same day.[79] In Romania, appeals are often heard by different judges, but some form of informal coordination exists.[80]

Figure 31.6 Number of First-Instance Judgments Versus the Number of Appealed NCAs' Decisions

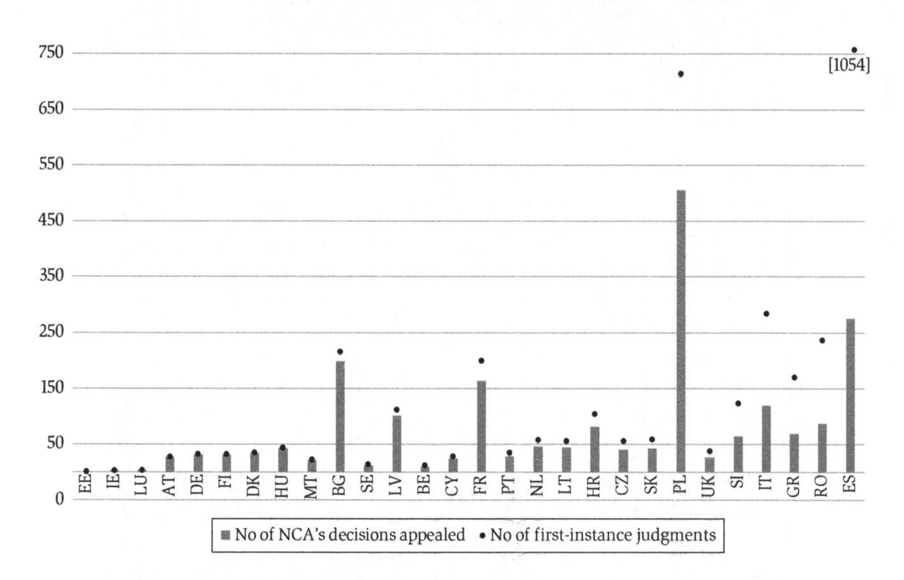

Note: The number of first-instance judgments in this figure includes cases where the second or third-instance courts returned the case for re-examination by the first-instance courts.

77. Spain report, Chapter 28. In some instances, as elaborated in the Spanish report, a single NCA decision was subject to seventy first-instance appeals.
78. *Ibid.*
79. Greece report, Chapter 14.
80. Romania report, Chapter 25.

2.2 Ratio of Appeals on NCAs' Decisions

Judicial review may also function as a tool for measuring and evaluating the effectiveness of competition law enforcement.[81] The ratio of appeals submitted against a competition authority's decisions is a common performance assessment indicator. At the same time, there is no 'perfect' ratio of appeals. On the one hand, '*quasi*-automatic appeals', where almost all decisions of a particular NCA are being appealed, may point to a low level of acceptance of the NCA's decisions by the undertakings concerned or to a flawed institutional structure. A very high appeal rate might thus be unsatisfactory from the point of view of public policy and good governance.[82] On the other hand, a low ratio of appeals may raise concerns that courts do not play a significant role in the overall competition law enforcement structure (e.g., that undertakings do not lodge appeals as they believe the courts would simply rubberstamp all of the NCA's decisions) or that there are undue obstacles to access to justice. Such a low ratio may also indicate a poor selection of enforcement targets by the NCA, for example, that the authority focuses on small and financially weak firms or seeks only minor concessions from infringing firms,[83] or overly relies on leniency and settlement applications or commitments.[84] Moreover, it has been suggested that decreasing rates of appeals can be associated with improvement in the quality of NCAs' enforcement action.[85]

Against this backdrop, Figure 31.7 presents the percentage of NCA's decisions in each jurisdiction that were appealed from the total number of NCA's decisions that could be subject to an appeal (the 'ratio of appeals'). The number of NCA's decisions that could be subject to appeal was generally calculated on the basis of the figures reported in their annual reports or from decisions that are publicly available. It corresponds to the types of NCAs' decisions that could be subject to an appeal in each of the examined jurisdiction (*see* section 1.5 above). This figure should be interpreted with caution: (i) since the total number of NCA decisions is mostly based on the NCA's calculations which might not always be fully accurate or adequately reflect the different types of decisions appealed, and when the NCA's calculations are not available - on external sources (e.g., France, Germany, Greece, Malta, the Netherlands, Romania, Slovenia, Spain); (ii) since not all NCA enforcement action and subsequent

81. Mats A. Bergman, 'Quis Custodiet Ipsos Custodes? Or Measuring and Evaluating the Effectiveness of Competition Enforcement' (2008) 56(4) De Economist 387-409, 389 DOI: 10.1007/s10645-008-9101-6.
82. Frank Montag, 'The Case for a Radical Reform of the Infringement Procedure under Regulation 17' 17(8) E.C.L.R. 17(8), 428-437, 428, 433 (1996); Annalies Outhuijse, 'Effective Public Enforcement of the Cartel Prohibition in the Netherlands: A Comparison of ACM Fining Decisions, District Court Judgments, and TIAT Judgments' in Anne Looijestijn-Clearie et al. (eds), *Boosting the Enforcement of EU Competition Law at the Domestic Level* (Cambridge Scholars 2017).
83. Bergman (*supra* n. 81), 390.
84. Or Brook, 'Do EU and UK Antitrust "Bite"? A Hard Look at "Soft" Enforcement and Negotiated Penalty Settlements.' (2023) 68(3) The Antitrust Bulletin 477-518 DOI: 10.1177/0003603x231180245. Also *see* section 7 below.
85. Svetlana Avdasheva et al., 'Distorting Effects of Competition Authority's Performance Measurement: The Case of Russia' (2016) 29(3) *International Journal of Public Sector Management* 288-306, 290 DOI: 10.1108/ijpsm-09-2015-0168.

appeal judgments are published (or were not published throughout the entire period of the study) in all jurisdictions (*see* section 9 below); (iii) given the time-lag between rendering and publishing judgments, which can amount to a few years in some jurisdictions. However, the figure might provide a rough estimate of the ratio of appeals in each jurisdiction, and some comparative insights.

Figure 31.7 Ratio of Appeals (Estimate)

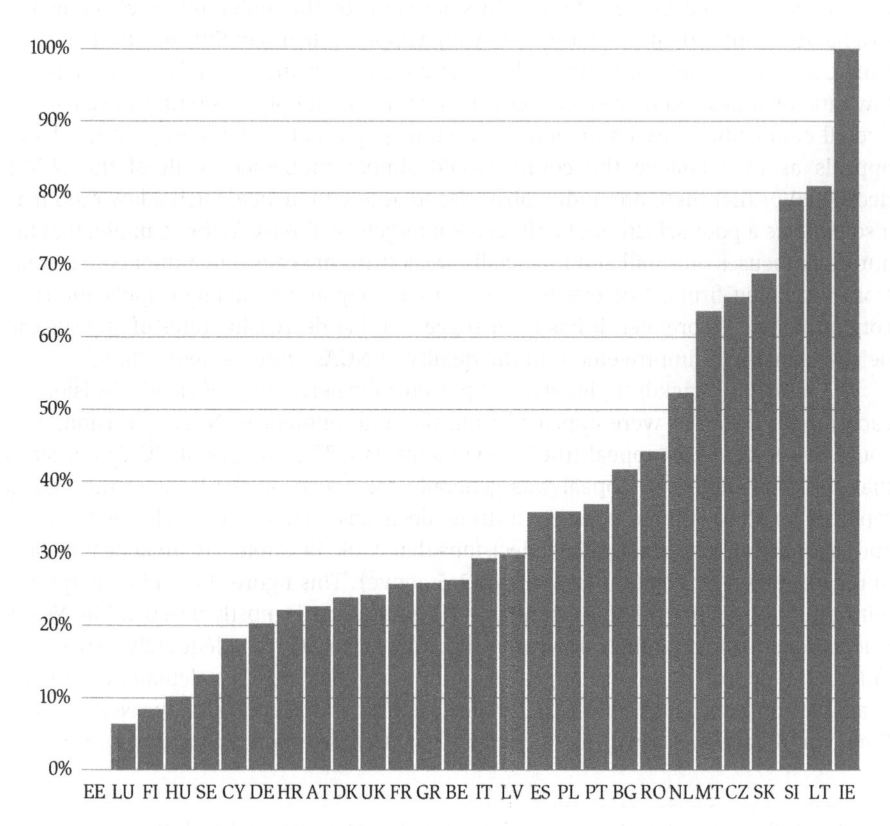

The figure points to a high heterogeneity in this regard. In eleven of the examined jurisdictions, less than 30% of the NCAs' decisions were appealed to the first-instance appeal court, of which there was an appeal ratio of no more than 10% in Luxemburg, Finland, and Hungary. In seven jurisdictions the appeal rate was higher than 50% (Czech Republic, the Netherlands, Malta, Slovakia, Slovenia, Lithuania, and Ireland). Ireland is an extreme case with 100% of decisions challenged, although as noted above, there were only two such decisions.

Most of the CEE jurisdictions are at the higher appeal rate end of the spectrum (with the exception of Hungary and Croatia). The high ratio of appeals in the CEE

Member States supports the hypothesis that jurisdictions having less experience in competition law enforcement are expected to demonstrate high rates of successful appeals.[86] Newly established NCAs spend at least a decade defending challenges in relation to almost every significant aspect of their authority, including the power to gather information, the application of the substantive mandate to challenge business behaviour, and the power to impose sanctions. It can easily take two decades or more to establish a sufficient strand of case law to 'either sustain the agency's efforts to exercise its legal mandate or make clear that further legislative reforms are necessary'.[87] Hence, it is to be anticipated that the initial operation of an NCA is likely to elicit challenges before the courts.

In the Czech Republic, 66% of the NCA's final decisions have been appealed. As noted in section 1.2.3 above, only findings of infringements that have been internally reviewed by the Chairman can be appealed to court. As mentioned in the national report, most of the Chairman's decisions that were not appealed concerned cases where the Chairman upheld the undertakings' challenge to the original NCA decision, as the parties to the proceedings have no incentive to challenge such a decision before the court. In Bulgaria, the ratio of CPC's decisions subject to appeal is 42%. One possible reason for the high rate of appeal is the relatively low cost of legal services and very low court fees to be borne by the appellants in administrative cases. Given the substantial amounts of fines imposed by the CPC, appealing the NCA's decision and any subsequent appeal of the first-instance judgment thus present an attractive option for undertakings targeted by the CPC's fines.[88]

A high level of second, third, and fourth-instance appeals raises concerns as to the effectiveness of the judicial system. Once again, Figure 31.8 reveals much divergence in the national practices. In Bulgaria, Spain, and Poland, for example, not only were a considerable number of the NCA decisions subject to a first-instance appeal, but subsequent second and third-instance appeals were also regularly launched. Portugal, Hungary, and Latvia also experienced frequent use of third-instance appeals. This inevitably leads to a considerably longer duration of those competition law proceedings and to high procedural economy costs. This has been observed in particular in Hungary and Spain.[89] Furthermore, the success rates of such appeals, as presented in the next section, reveal that in those jurisdictions, a significant rate of second- and third-instance appeals were fully or partially accepted.

86. William E. Kovacic and Marianela López-Galdós, 'Lifecycles of Competition Systems: Explaining Variation in the Implementation of New Regimes' (2016) 79 *Law & Contemp. Probs.* 85, 106-107.
87. *Ibid.*
88. Bulgaria report, Chapter 5.
89. Spain report, Chapter 28; Hungary report, Chapter 15.

Figure 31.8 Number of NCAs' Decisions Appealed and Subsequent Appeals

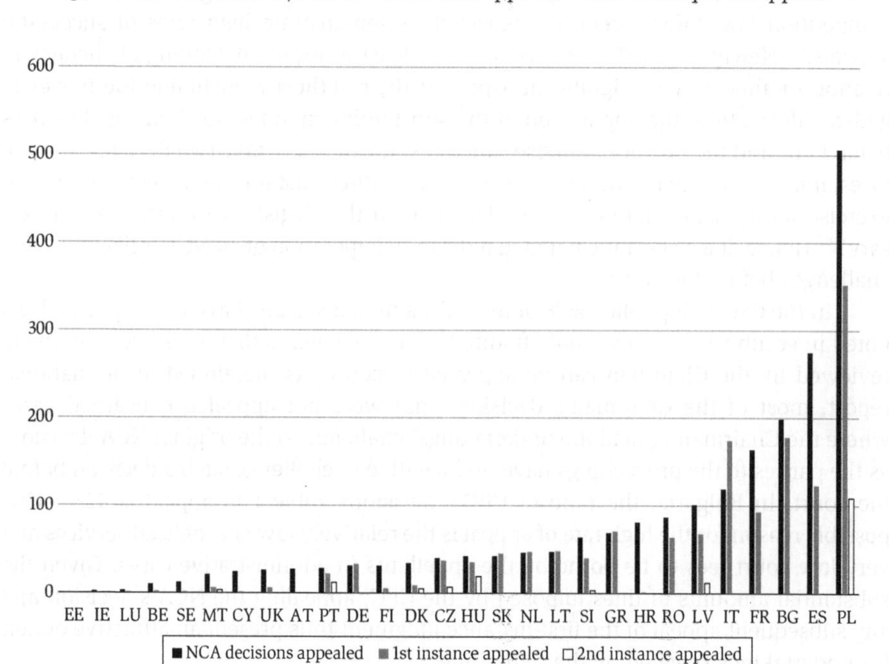

Notably, the figure does not point to a clear correlation between the choice of the administrative or judicial model and the success rates of appeal. Austria, Finland, and Sweden had low appeal rates, as expected from national systems following the judicial model because the decisions of the administrative authorities had to be confirmed by the courts. However, Ireland, which follows the judicial model, had a relatively high appeal rate (albeit it should be noted that this has not resulted in a large number of judgments in absolute terms, as the NCA issued few decisions during the project period).

2.3 Success Rates

The ratio of successful appeals is another popular performance assessment indicator of the operation and effectiveness of competition authorities.[90] This assessment indicator,

90. Avdasheva et al. (*supra* n. 85), 290; Yannis Katsoulacos, 'On the Choice of Legal Standards: A Positive Theory for Comparative Analysis' (2019) 48 *European Journal of Law and Economics* 125, 133-134 DOI: 10.1007/s10657-019-09616-7, 159; Bergman (*supra* n. 81), 389; Montag (*supra* n. 82).

like the ratio of appeals, has its limitations, and interpreting the meaning behind success rates is not a straightforward task. The application of the law is not a mechanical process, and no court operates quotas.[91] The expected (or 'optimal') success rates are expected to differ across jurisdictions having different legal systems, and it is not apparently clear how to interpret deviations.

Tridimas and Gari, for example, warned that a very high success rate for undertakings' appeals signals a serious value divergence between the branches of government and may be unsustainable at least in the medium to long term.[92] Yet, they suggested that despite the limitations of using success rates to evaluate the effectiveness of judicial review, success rates matter because: (i) they have a political significance (whether a court which has the ultimate authority to determine the outer bounds of political power trumps the government's choices frequently, sometimes, or rarely); (ii) statistical analysis of success rates in quantitative and qualitative terms can provide a measure of constitutionalism, namely the extent and degree to which the executive and the legislature comply with the constitution within a legal system; and (iii) the rate of success of judicial review reflects the constitutional equilibrium.

By comparison, others contend that high success rates in overturning decisions of the NCAs might indicate strong performance by the NCA and the national enforcement system.[93] In his seminal, albeit idealistic paper, *Shavell* argues that applicants only initiate proceedings against unlawful decisions. Hence, a welfare-enhancing judicial review system - one which eradicates all decisional errors - should reverse all challenged decisions.[94] Shavell argues that the optimal 100% annulment rate cannot be observed in practice, simply because annulment applicants often erroneously (or opportunistically) challenge lawful decisions. Shavell's article implies that a welfare-enhancing system of judicial review will at least quash a minimal number of negative decisions. A low rate of annulment judgments, therefore, would be viewed by some as problematic.[95]

A low success rate may also indicate that the legal system favours the competition authority or that the authority has a defensive litigation strategy.[96] An NCA can

91. P. Takis Tridimas and Gabriel Gari. 'Winners and Losers in Luxembourg: A Statistical Analysis of Judicial Review Before the ECJ and the CFI (2001-2005).' (2010) 2 *European Law Review* 133 DOI: 10.1023/a:1010645411771.
92. *Ibid.*, 133. Note that independent NCA's may not fit ideally within the branches of government framework depicted here.
93. Bergman (*supra* n. 81), 391.
94. Steven Shavell, 'The Appeals Process as a Means of Error Correction' (1995) 24(2) *The Journal of Legal Studies* 379. *See also* Geradin and Petit (*supra* n. 60), 63.
95. *Ibid.*, 61-62.
96. Bergman (*supra* n. 81), 391.

increase its success rate in court, for example, by only taking enforcement action against blatant violations of the law,[97] or focusing on negotiated penalty settlements.[98] This entails that the success rates of appeals might affect the selection of enforcement targets by the NCA. *Katsoulacos* has argued that competition authorities select their cases not only in a bid to maximise the expected benefits to competition, consumers, or society more generally but also on the basis of their public image or reputation.[99] As a result, authorities are more likely to pursue by-object infringements, especially in younger jurisdictions in which the competition authority is uncertain about the courts' choice of standards.[100]

Keeping these limitations in mind, Figure 31.9 presents the success rates of appeals in all jurisdictions,[101] across the first-, second-, and third- instances of appeal. The data is presented from the perspective of each NCA's decision subject to appeal or previous instance judgment. For example, NCAs' decisions that have been dealt with by multiple first- instance appeal judgments, are aggregated as one case in the figure (*see* section 2.1 above). Importantly, this figure captures the appeals submitted by all types of appellants (undertakings, NCAs, and third parties). The types of appellants will further be discussed in section 3 below.

97. *Ibid.*, 390.
98. *See* section 7 below.
99. Katsoulacos (*supra* n. 90), 127.
100. *Ibid.*, 159.
101. No data is available with respect to Spain, but the national report provides data on the success rates of judicial review of NCA fining decisions (*see* Chapter 28).

Figure 31.9 Success Rates

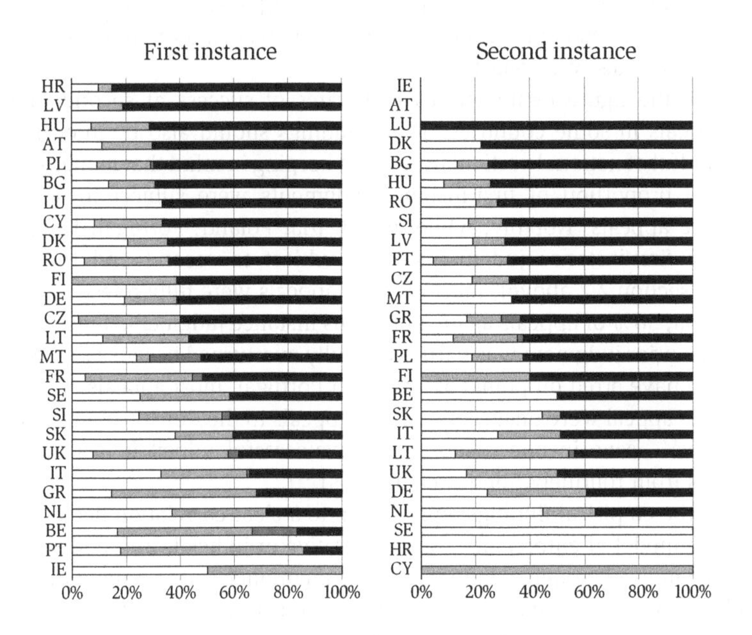

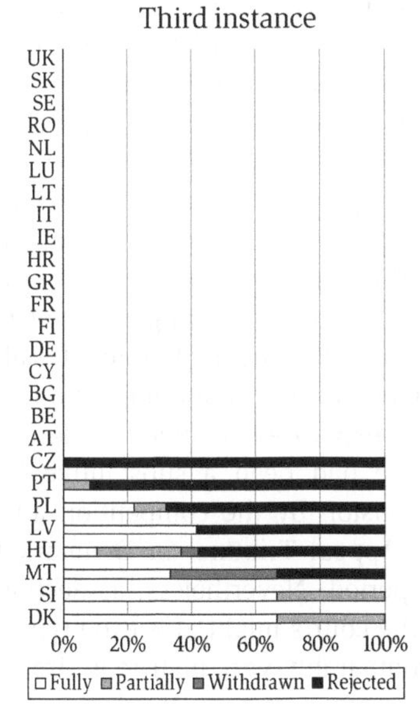

Several observations can be made. First, the empirical findings demonstrate that some first-instance courts have almost always accepted at least some of the claims of the applicants. In Portugal, Belgium, and the Netherlands, less than 30% of the first-instance appeals were fully rejected. In Ireland, 100% of the appeals were fully or partially accepted, but it should be stressed that there were only two appeal court judgments in total and accordingly these percentages should be interpreted with caution. At the other end of the scale, in Hungary, Latvia, and Croatia over 70% of the first- instance appeals were rejected.

Second, the figure demonstrates high rates of success at second- and third-instance appeals in some countries. These findings should also be interpreted with caution, mindful of national particularities, and keeping in mind that in many countries only a small proportion of first-instance judgments were subject to second- and third-instance appeals. Notably, while in Bulgaria, Poland, Portugal, Hungary, and Latvia many first-instance judgments were subject to second and third-instance appeals (*see* section 2.2 above), most of those appeals were fully rejected.

In Latvia, 56% of appeals against previous instance judgments failed: in most of those cases, a prior judgment was partially or fully overturned because the lower court was found to have erred on points of law.[102] In Portugal, most appeals at second and third-instance appeal were unsuccessful, and appeals to the Constitutional Court have almost always - save in one case - been unsuccessful (albeit it has not deterred undertakings from routinely filing such appeals).[103]

Third, the empirical findings do not point to a clear correlation between success rates and the model of enforcement, administrative or judicial. In the Member States following the judicial model of enforcement, as mentioned, infringement decisions are adopted by a court or tribunal following the administrative authority's investigation. Since a judicial body had already reviewed the administrative authority's decision, one might expect lower success rates on appeal.[104] This hypothesis was not confirmed by the empirical findings. Some of the first-instance courts in the Member States following the judicial model have regularly fully rejected any appeals (Austria), some to a similar extent as the EU-wide average (Sweden, Finland), and some have often accepted the appeals (Ireland). Similar findings are observed when breaking down the success rates according to the grounds of appeal, as elaborated in section 5 below.

Similarly, the empirical findings do not point to a clear trend of higher success rates in those legal systems where the reviewing courts were highly specialised. Such a trend was observed in the UK. The high rate of fully or partially successful first-instance appeals may have reflected the Competition Appeal Tribunal's standard of review and its high level of expertise in competition law matters, such that it would even consider whether there had been a substantive infringement of the rules, irrespective of an earlier decision by the competition authority to the contrary.[105] However, the Competition Appeal Tribunal in Denmark has rejected 65% of the appeals within the project period. Nevertheless, as Section 5 will demonstrate, the degree of specialisation of the courts might affect the type of grounds examined and accepted. Similarly, both comparably very high (e.g., Ireland, Greece) and very low

102. Latvia report, Chapter 18.
103. Portugal report, Chapter 24.
104. See section 1.1 above.
105. The UK report, Chapter 30.

(e.g., Hungary and Croatia) success states were reported in first-instance courts which are not specialised.

2.4 The Outcome of Judicial Review

Reflecting the EU principle of procedural autonomy, Member States have the power to determine the range of possible outcomes of successful appeals launched against NCAs' decisions. Many Member States have granted their national courts the power to issue a judgment that fully or partially replaces the decision of the NCA (sometimes known as a reformatory judgment). Other national courts only have the power to annul the decision, and others, to return the decision to the NCA or to the previous instance judgment court for re-examination. Figure 31.10 outlines the outcome of fully or partially successful appeals before the national courts, showing that many national systems allow a combination of those legal remedies. The figure presents the outcome from the perspective of each judgment rendered, across all instances of appeal in each jurisdiction.

Figure 31.10 Remedies in Fully or Partially Successful Appeals, Across All Instances

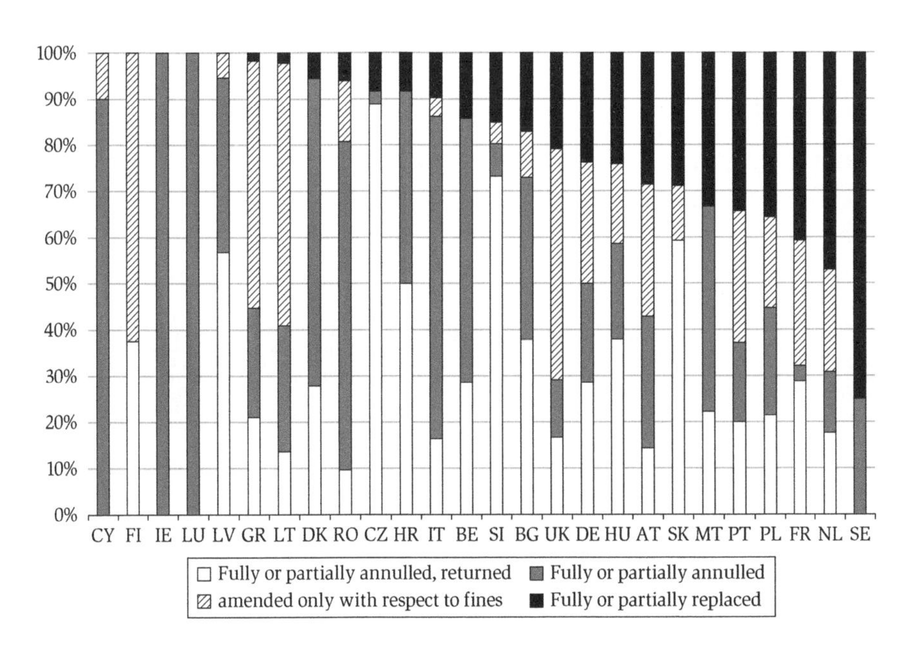

The figure demonstrates that many national systems allow reviewing courts to replace the NCA decision. These reformatory judgments were regularly used in Sweden (75% of the appeals) and are common also in the Netherlands and France (above 40% of the appeals). In other systems, upon accepting an appeal, the courts can only return the case for re-assessment by the NCA or the previous instance (e.g., Luxemburg and Cyprus). In Latvia, while the courts were initially regarded as competent to amend any fines imposed by the NCA, this later changed, and they cannot replace the NCA's decision with their judgment.[106]

3 TYPES OF APPELLANTS

Judicial review is aimed at protecting the rights of all stakeholders, the undertakings subject to infringement decisions, the public interest, and other third parties affected by the NCAs' decisions.[107] As in other areas of competition law enforcement, EU law does not determine the identity of the parties that can appeal against them. Consequently, the national systems differ in the type and range of possible appellants in relation to NCAs' decisions and court judgments.

106. Latvia Report, Chapter 18.
107. Geradin and Petit (*supra* n. 60), 58.

Figure 31.11 Appellants

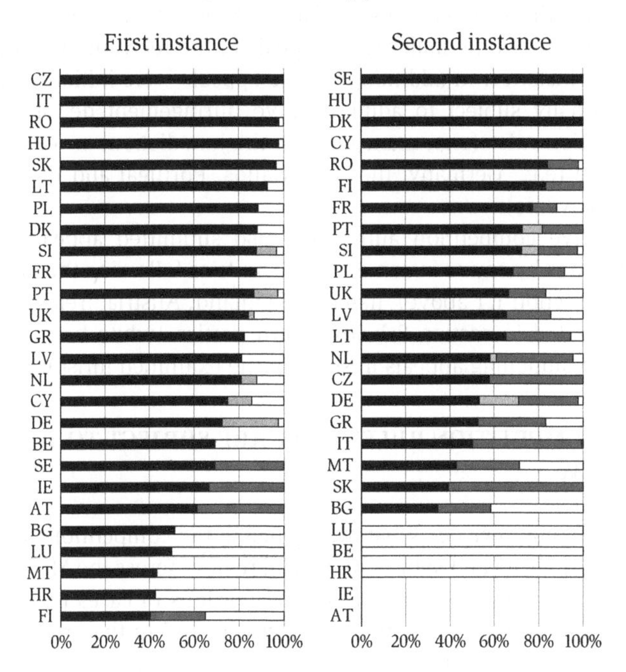

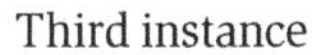

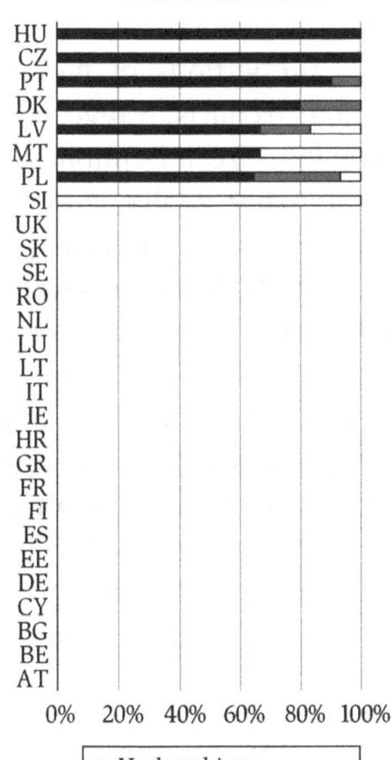

Figure 31.11 summarises the types of appellants for each judgment. Unsurprisingly, it reveals that those undertakings and associations of undertakings subject to the reviewed decision lodged the majority of appeals in the relevant period (black bars), especially at first instance. In addition, various appeals were initiated by individuals who were personally subject to administrative infringement decisions of EU and national competition rules (e.g., managers), in the jurisdictions where such proceedings are available (e.g., Germany, the Netherlands, Portugal and the minor offence proceedings in Slovenia).

Administrative competition authorities also submitted appeals following infringement decisions by courts in some of the countries following the judicial enforcement model (*see* section 1.1 above), namely in Finland, Austria, Ireland, and Sweden. As will be elaborated in section 8 below, third parties (white bars) have played a significant role in launching appeals in some of the examined jurisdictions.

4 THE COMPETITION RULES THAT ARE SUBJECT TO JUDICIAL REVIEW

The empirical mapping revealed great divergence in the competition law rules which were applied by the NCAs and subject to judicial review across the Member States and the UK. These differences relate both to the proportions of cases reviewing national and/or EU competition law prohibitions respectively and to the proportions of cases involving anti-competitive agreements or abuse of dominance. In many instances, these proportions mirror the focus of the enforcement efforts of the NCAs, as was indicated in the national reports.

Figure 31.12 examines the proportions of national and EU competition law prohibitions reviewed by first-instance courts. It reveals that many of the courts of CEE Member States (i.e., Bulgaria, Croatia, Czech Republic, Lithuania, Latvia, Poland, and Slovakia), as well as those of Germany, Malta, and Cyprus, have overwhelmingly reviewed decisions on the infringement of national competition laws alone (above 70% of all first-instance judgments rendered). By comparison, in Austria, Belgium, Ireland, Italy, and Luxemburg over 70% of the first-instance judgments rendered examined both EU and national competition laws. Earlier empirical research had already observed that the NCAs of some of the CEE Member States have mostly applied the national competition rules alone, and the authors suggested that this might result primarily from an inconsistent interpretation of the effect on trade test.[108]

The focus and classification of practices as solely infringing national competition laws entails that such NCAs' decisions and national courts' judgments escape the coordination and scrutiny mechanisms of Regulation 1/2003 that were examined in

108. Marco Botta et al., 'The Assessment of the Effect on Trade by the National Competition Authorities of the "New" Member States: Another Legal Partition of the Internal Market?' (2015) 52(5) Common Market Law Review 1. For an empirical study of the proportions of EU and national competition law enforcement in five Member States and interpretations of the effect on trade test, *see also* Or Brook, *Non-competition Interests in EU Antitrust Law: An Empirical Study of Article 101 TFEU* (CUP 2022), 356-359.

Chapter 1. It also means that the national courts that mostly reviewed purely national cases had played only a limited role when it came to safeguarding the effectiveness of EU law. This will be further examined in section 5.4 below.

Figure 31.12 EU/National Rules Reviewed

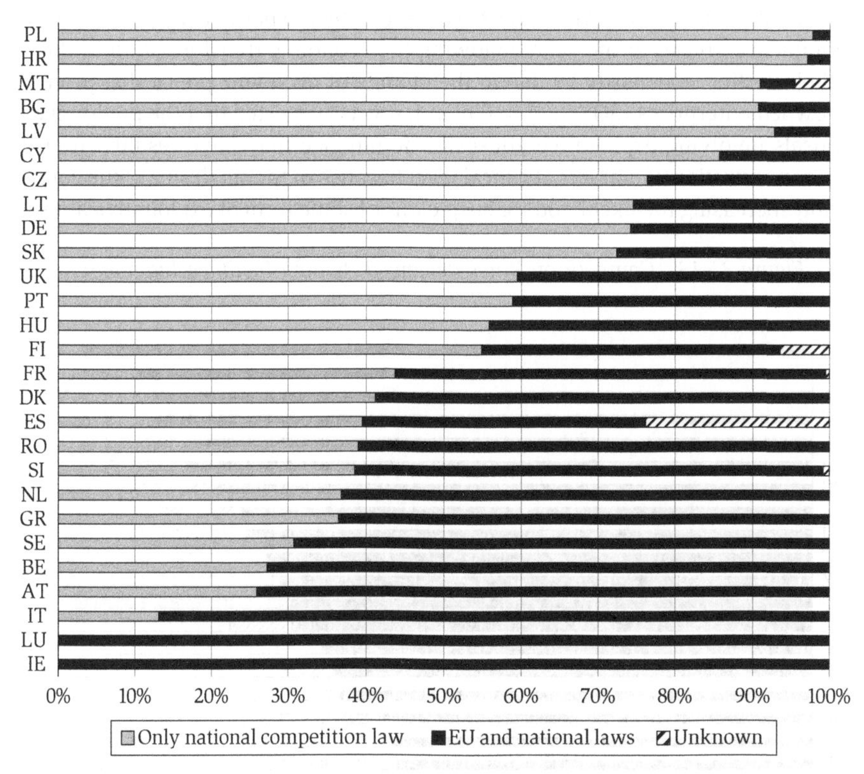

Figure 31.13 demonstrates that a similar divergence could be observed between national courts in relation to the proportion of first-instance judgments examining the prohibitions against anti-competitive agreements and abuse of dominance respectively. Although no general geographical trend was observed, the empirical findings indicate that the national first-instance courts of over a third of the examined jurisdictions have overwhelmingly dealt with the review of the application of the EU and national prohibitions against anti-competitive agreements. Accordingly, 70% or more of the first-instance courts' judgments in Austria, Greece, Germany, Hungary, Italy, Lithuania, the Netherlands, Portugal, Romania, and Slovenia examined the prohibitions on anti-competitive agreements alone.

In a small minority of (mainly CEE) States, the majority of appeals over the project period concerned the abuse of dominance prohibition(s). In Bulgaria, this was accounted for at least partly due to the competition authority's obligation to follow up on complaints, and similarly, in Croatia, a probable explanation for the disproportionately higher number of abuse of dominance appeals is that the majority of the authority's decisions rejecting a complaint related to an abuse of dominance situation.[109] In Poland, a significant number of early abuse cases between 2004 and 2011 constitute a clear majority of all appeals, although there was a notable decline in later years between 2012 and 2021 (from circa 64% to 34% of all appeal judgments). A potential rationale for the level of abuse cases may be the particular focus of the NCA on dominance abuses in the years following the economic transformation in Poland, and their decline may partly be due to the change of economic policy that promoted state-owned enterprises (SOEs).[110] In Finland, it was suggested that the predominance of appeals involving exploitative abuses of dominance may have resulted from the heavy concentration of markets at a local level because of the small size of the country, arguably increasing the likelihood (or suspicion) of some form of exploitative abuse.[111]

Figure 31.13 Competition Rules Reviewed By First-Instance Judgments

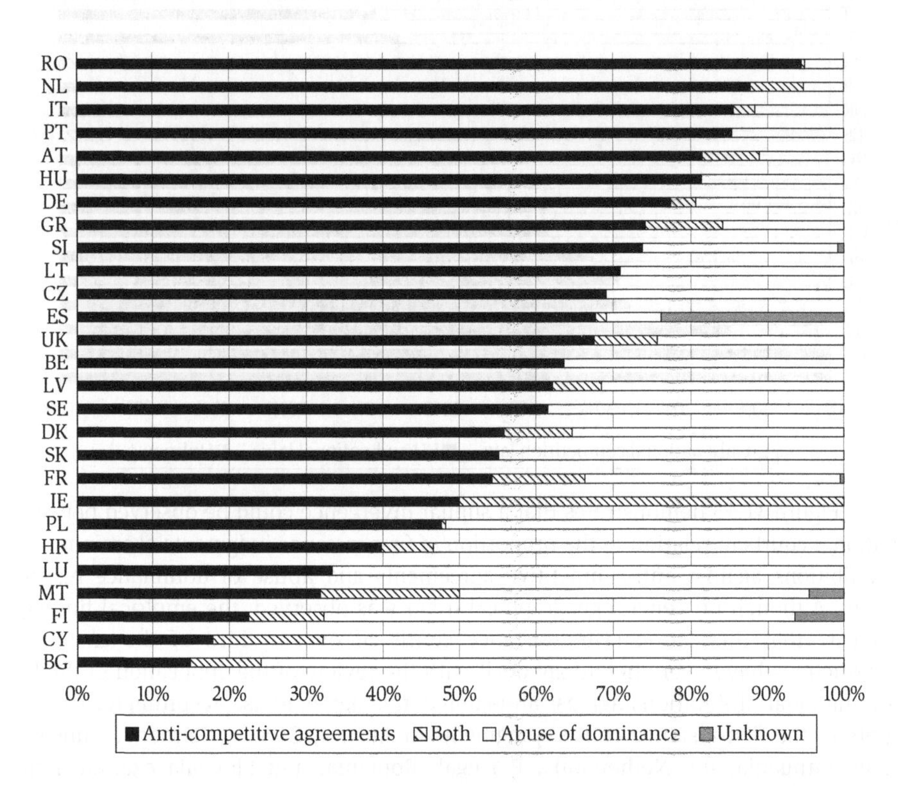

109. Bulgaria report, Chapter 5; Croatia report, Chapter 6. Similarly *see* in Cyprus, Chapter 7. Note that in Luxembourg, the rapporteur could not provide an explanation for the data that 75% of all appeals concerned abuse of dominance (*see* Chapter 20).
110. Poland report, Chapter 23.
111. Finland report, Chapter 11.

The selection of enforcement targets by some of the NCAs, therefore, has considerably constrained the opportunity of the national courts to examine the application and interpretation of those anti-competitive practices that were less frequently subject to review.

5 GROUNDS OF REVIEW

Our study seeks to capture the nature and scope of judicial review, in particular, by mapping out the appeal grounds raised by the parties across the Member States and the UK, and their success in each jurisdiction. The EU rules applicable to each category of appeal grounds and the significance of judicial review have been explored in Chapter 1. Moreover, as was elaborated in Chapter 2, one early finding of this study was that the European legal systems often classify similar grounds differently. For example, some jurisdictions regard limitation periods as a procedural matter, while in others they are viewed as substantive rules. To ensure a meaningful comparison, we have followed the comparative functional approach, where the classification of grounds was based on the function performed by the rules rather than their classification in accordance with the national legal framework. We believe that this approach is essential for studying multi-level governance networks such as those characterising EU competition law enforcement, in which the identical EU substantive rules are being applied by NCAs and national courts in a variety of national procedural rules and institutional settings.

It should be noted that the empirical findings presented in this section do not include Spain, on which such data was not collected for practical reasons,[112] and Estonia, where no administrative enforcement of competition law took place during the relevant period of this study.

5.1 Substantive Grounds

Judicial review is central to determining the direction and substantive evolution of EU and national competition laws.[113] EU and national competition laws are typically open-ended and do not define key terms, and consequently, various meanings may be attributed to those terms. As *Vickers* noted, '[t]he real substance of the law is fleshed out and evolves over time in the light of competition authority practice, and, above all,

112. The Spanish report, nevertheless, presents the grounds argued and accepted in a case study (*see* Chapter 28).
113. Cf. Pablo Ibáñez Colomo, 'Law, Policy, Expertise: Hallmarks of Effective Judicial Review in EU Competition Law' (2022) 24 *Cambridge Yearbook of European Legal Studies* 143-168, discussing the role of the EU Courts.

judicial precedent. The judicial interpretation of what a statute means in practical terms can change markedly over time in the light of experience and of legal and economic scholarship'.[114]

To this end, judicial review by the EU and national courts has two substantive aims: it is a mechanism for (i) correcting flawed decisions,[115] and (ii) establishing binding normative standards.[116] Especially given the complexity of competition law and the lack of conceptual homogeneity, competition law enforcement by the Commission and NCAs, in terms of the application of the substantive rules at least, may be prone to serious errors.[117] Judicial review can help to ensure that competition law is being enforced in the public interest,[118] and makes a significant contribution to shaping the substantive choices that define the boundaries of the competition law prohibitions.[119]

Figure 31.14 presents the percentage of judgments in which substantive grounds were raised by the parties, differentiating between the percentage of judgments in which those grounds were accepted (black bars) and rejected (grey bars). Substantive grounds were defined in our study as arguments based on or related to the definition of undertakings (e.g., state action, public/mix bodies, liability of parents/subsidiaries companies), the existence of agreements/concerted practices, restrictions by-object/effect, the application of Article 101(3) TFEU, BERs, and the national equivalent prohibitions, market definition, the existence of dominance, abuse of dominance, *de minimis*, any EU or national exemptions or exceptions to the competition rules, lack of sufficient evidence to support a fact (excluding the admissibility of evidence), and the burden of proof. The data is presented from the perspective of each NCA's decision or previous instance's judgment which has been appealed, entailing that multiple appeals submitted on a single decision or judgment will be aggregated.

114. John Vickers, 'Central Banks and Competition Authorities: Institutional Comparisons and New Concerns' (2010) BIS Working Paper No. 331 (No. 331), available here: https://papers.ssrn.com/sol3/papers.cfm?abstract_id = 1717809, 5.
115. *See also* Shavell (*supra* n. 94).
116. Geradin and Petit (*supra* n. 60), 24-25.
117. *Ibid.*, 32-36.
118. *Ibid.*, 37-39.
119. Cf. Colomo (*supra* n. 113), discussing the role of the EU Courts.

Figure 31.14 Substantive Grounds

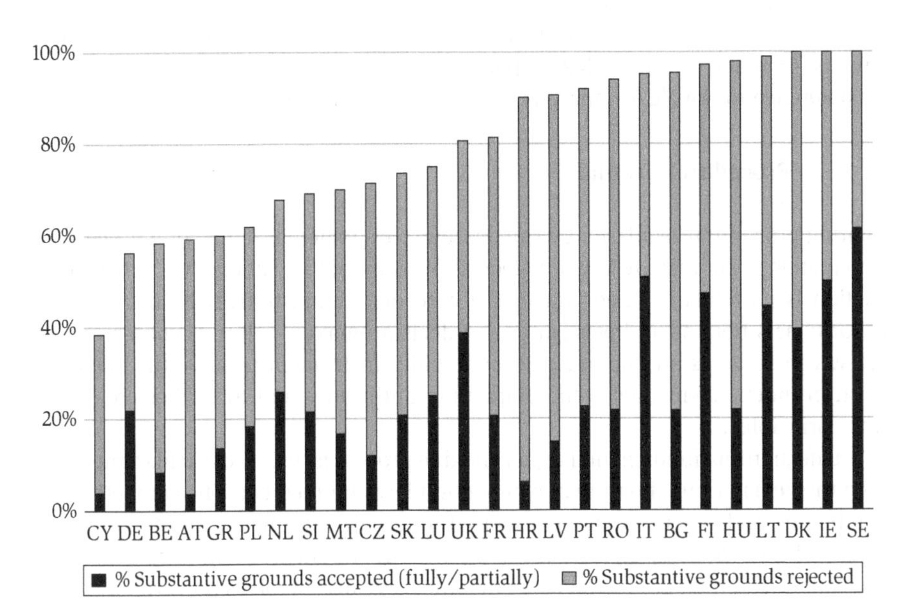

Our findings reveal that substantive grounds were the focus of most appeals in most jurisdictions, in comparison with the procedural, fines-related, and the EU/national grounds. Apart from Cyprus, substantive grounds were invoked in 56% or more of the appeals in front of all the examined jurisdictions, reaching over 95% in eight. This may suggest that despite the concerns voiced during the negotiations over Regulation 1/2003, fearing that national courts will not engage in substantive review of complex and technical competition law matters,[120] most national courts have contributed to the development of the competition rules.

The rates of successful acceptance of substantive grounds varied more significantly among the various countries, ranging from 10% or less in Austria, Croatia, and Cyprus to 50% or over in Ireland, Italy, and Sweden. The very limited consideration of substantive grounds in Cyprus and the low acceptance rates of those claims (38% of claims on substantive appeal grounds and 10% partially successful appeals) may be tied to the limited standard of review. As mentioned in section 1.4 above, the courts in Cyprus only exercise marginal review and do not have jurisdiction over issues of a technical nature, and matters pertaining to the substance of a decision or requiring specialised knowledge.[121] In Croatia, almost all of the fully or partially successful substantive grounds concerned anti-competitive agreements cases, whereas successful abuse appeals related primarily to matters of procedure.[122]

120. See Chapter 1, section 3.1.
121. Cyprus report, Chapter 7.
122. Croatia report, Chapter 6.

Highly specialist courts, such as the first-instance Competition Appeal Tribunals in the UK and Denmark, demonstrated both relatively high rates for invocation of substantive grounds (81% and 100%, respectively) and acceptance rates of those grounds (48% and 41%).[123] This supports the hypothesis that specialist courts will pay less deference to the NCAs' analysis in comparison with non-specialist courts.[124]

5.2 Procedural Grounds

Ensuring procedural regularity by safeguarding fundamental rights, due process, and participation is another well-acknowledged function of judicial review.[125] This review function is particularly important in the case of (administrative) NCAs, where the authority acts both as an investigator and decision-maker.[126] In this context, judicial review can serve as an important accountability instrument to solve the democratic deficit of independent unelected competition authorities and to further good governance principles.[127]

Safeguarding fundamental rights and due process is also of particular importance given the quasi-criminal nature of competition law enforcement. The competition law prohibitions and severe sanctions imposed inherently interfere with individual freedoms such as ownership rights, business freedom, and the freedom to contract and of association, and their enforcement is often intrusive and involves powerful inspection tools.[128] As recognised by the ECtHR jurisprudence, the high level of fines potentially imposed makes procedural regularity and due rights even more important in the competition law enforcement context.[129]

Figure 31.15 presents the percentage of judgments in which procedural grounds were raised by the parties, differentiating between the percentage of judgments in which those grounds were accepted (black bars) and rejected (grey bars). Procedural grounds were defined in our study as arguments based on or related to the right to be heard, rights of the defence, due reasoning, competence, admissibility of evidence

123. Note that these percentages reflect the invocation and success rates in front of the first-instance courts alone, and thus slightly differ from the ratios presented in Figure 31.14 above.
124. *See* section 1.3 above.
125. Geradin and Petit (*supra* n. 60), 26-28.
126. Cf. Colomo (*supra* n. 113), 144.
127. Geradin and Petit (*supra* n. 60), 29-30.
128. *Ibid.*, 36.
129. *See, e.g.*, ECHR 23 November 2006 *Jussila v. Finland* (Application no. 73053/01); ECHR 27 September 2011 *Menarini Diagnostics v. Italy* (Application no. 43509/08); Case C-272/09 *KME Germany and Others v. Commission EU*:C:2011:810; Case C-386/10 *P Chalkor AE Epexergasias Metallon v. European Commission EU*:C:2011:815, para. 51. *See* Wouter P.J. Wils, 'The Compatibility with Fundamental Rights of the EU Antitrust Enforcement System in Which the European Commission Acts Both as Investigator and as First-Instance Decision Maker' (2014) 37 World Competition 5-25 DOI: 10.54648/cola2012036; R. Nazzini, 'Administrative Enforcement, Judicial Review and Fundamental Rights in EU Competition Law: A Comparative Contextual-Functionalist Perspective' (2012) 49 Common Market Law Review 971-1006 DOI: 10.54648/cola2012036; M. Bernatt, 'Between Menarini and Delta Pekarny – Strasbourg View on Intensity of Judicial Review in Competition Law', in Csongor Nagy (ed.) *The Procedural Aspects of the Application of Competition Law: European Frameworks – Central European Perspectives* (Europa Law Publishing 2016).

(excluding lack of sufficient evidence to support a fact), legality of obtaining evidence, limitation periods, and *ne bis in idem*. They do *not* include pleas directly related to the imposition or calculation of fines. The data is presented from the perspective of each NCA's decision or previous instance's judgment which has been appealed, entailing that multiple appeals submitted on a single decision or judgment will be aggregated.

Figure 31.15 Procedural Grounds

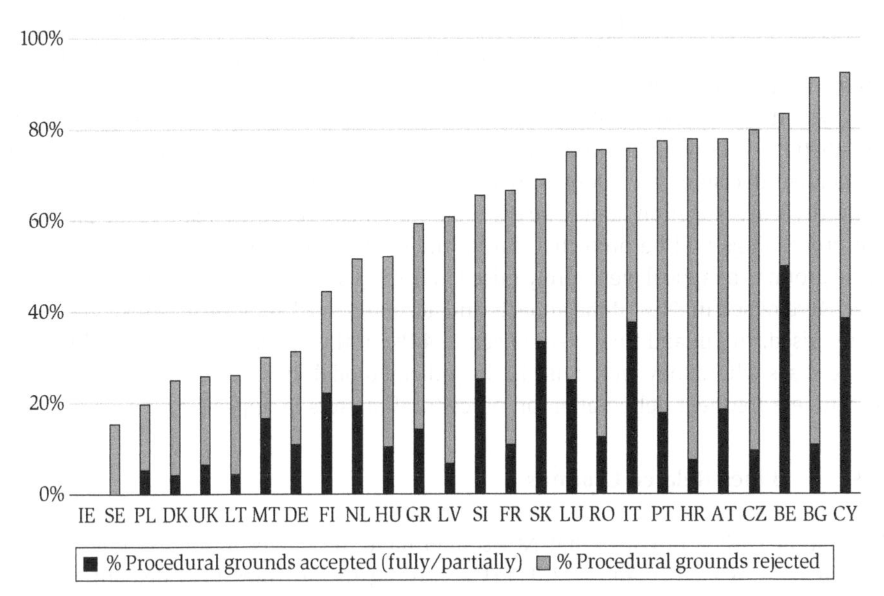

The figure reveals that in many CEE courts, procedural grounds were invoked in a very high proportion of review proceedings overall. This is evident, for example, in Bulgaria, Czech Republic, Croatia, and Romania (over 75% of the appeals), and to a lesser extent in Hungary, Latvia, Slovenia, and Slovakia (over 50% of the appeals). This may be explained by the relatively recent introduction of competition law in those jurisdictions. It is expected that in the early years of the establishment of particular competition law systems, courts will tend to focus closely on apparent deviations from procedural requirements established in the competition law or imposed by the jurisdiction's administrative procedure code.[130] Notably, the success rate of procedural grounds has varied considerably between those courts, meaning that high invocation rates of procedural grounds did not necessarily lead to their acceptance (e.g., relatively low acceptance rates in Croatia, Latvia, Bulgaria, Czech Republic, Romania, and Hungary). This finding is interesting when taken together with Figure 31.14, pointing to relatively low success rates of substantive grounds invoked in many of those jurisdictions.

130. Kovacic and López-Galdós (*supra* n. 86), 107.

The limited discussion of procedural grounds in Poland (20% of the appeals, and fully or partially accepted only in 27% of those appeals where argued), especially in comparison with other CEE countries, could be explained by the development of the national jurisprudence on the possibility of reviewing the NCA's proceedings from a procedural perspective. National case law emphasised that courts should not control the correctness of administrative proceedings before the NCA, but rather assess the matter anew on the merits. In more recent years, however, the Supreme Court held that there was no reason to ignore *a priori* all procedural claims raised by appellants. Scholars have also suggested that the old approach might not have been in line with the procedural fairness principle and Article 6 of the European Convention on Human Rights (ECHR) requirements.[131]

Another interesting observation relates to the role of procedural grounds in jurisdictions following the judicial model of enforcement. As mentioned, since infringement decisions are adopted by a court or tribunal following the administrative authority's investigation, it may be expected that the procedural rights of the parties to the proceedings will be protected during the enforcement process.[132] Indeed, procedural grounds of appeal were rarely raised in Ireland and Sweden. However, in Austria, they were raised in 78% of the appeals and accepted in 24% of those cases where they were raised. In Finland they were raised in 44% of the appeals, and accepted in 50% of the cases where they were raised. The judicial model, therefore, did not necessarily lead to less frequent deliberation on procedural matters in appeals.

5.3 Fines-Related Grounds

Regulation 1/2003 provides that NCAs shall have the power to impose fines for the breach of Articles 101 and 102 TFEU according to the rules provided for in their national laws.[133] In practice, however, as elaborated in the relevant national reports, no administrative fines were imposed for the infringement of competition law in Estonia, Denmark, Ireland, and Malta during the period covered by this project.

Regulation 1/2003 provides limited details on the way the Commission and NCAs should calculate the fines or what types of considerations should be taken into account in determining the appropriate level of a fine. Similarly, when it comes to judicial review, EU law provides only limited guidance on the review of the imposition of penalties. Some steps towards harmonisation of the legal regulation on the imposition of fines were introduced by the ECN+ Directive, stating, for example, that any fines imposed by NCAs for an infringement of the competition rules are expected to be effective, proportionate, and dissuasive.[134] It also provides that the maximum amount of the fine that is possible to be imposed for each infringement of Article 101 or 102 TFEU should be set at a level of not less than 10% of the total worldwide turnover of

131. Poland report, Chapter 23.
132. *See* section 1.1 above.
133. Regulation 1/2003, Articles 5 and 35.
134. ECN+ Directive, Preamble 40 and Article 13.

the undertaking concerned,[135] and details the parameters that should be taken into account to ensure that the fines reflect the economic significance of the infringement.[136] Given the cut-off date of this study, the effects of the ECN+ Directive are unlikely to be captured.

Figure 31.16 presents the percentage of judgments in which grounds related to the fines imposed were raised by the parties, differentiating between the percentage of judgments in which those grounds were accepted (black bars) and rejected (grey bars). Grounds related to fines were defined in this study as arguments against the amount of penalty imposed by the NCA. They do not include cases in which the fine was reduced as a direct result of accepting the other three categories of grounds. The data is presented from the perspective of each NCA's decision or previous instance's judgment which has been appealed, entailing that multiple appeals submitted on a single decision or judgment will be aggregated.

Figure 31.16 Fines-Related Grounds

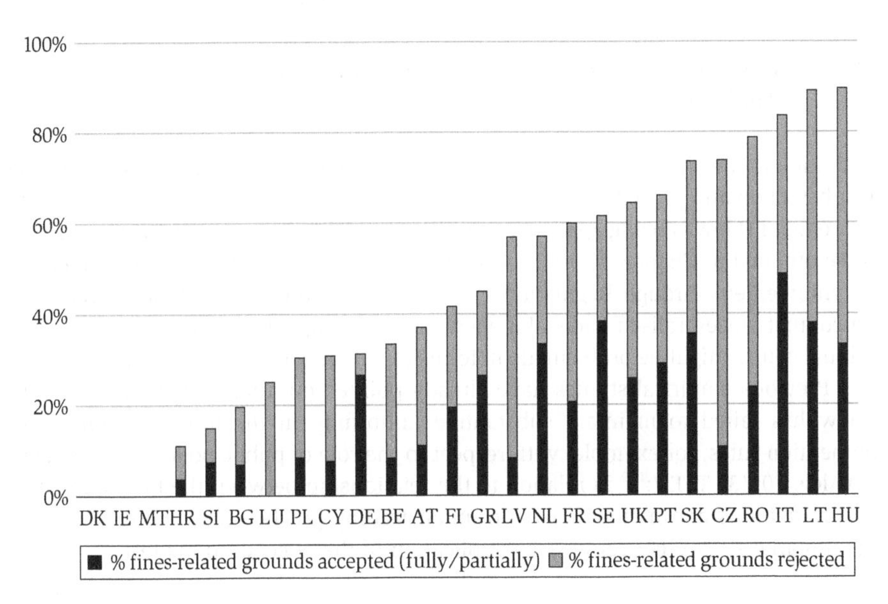

Considerable focus on fines-related grounds characterised many of the CEE countries. These grounds were raised in relation to 74% or more of the appealed NCAs' decisions and previous instance judgments in Hungary, Lithuania, Romania, Czech Republic, and Slovakia. The relatively high acceptance rates of fines-related grounds in Hungary (33%), Slovakia (36%), and Lithuania (38%) can be explained by the courts' inclination to reduce or even quash a fine rather than to overrule the substance of the

135. *Ibid*, Preamble 49 and Article 15.
136. *Ibid*, Preamble 47 and Article 14.

decision or to find procedural errors affecting the substance of the case.[137] The very low proportions of appeals involving the consideration of fines in other CEE countries – such as Croatia (11%) Slovenia (15%), and to some extent also Bulgaria (20%) – correspond with the types of NCA decisions that were subject to an appeal in those countries (*see* Figure 31.4 above). Since those NCAs have adopted only a limited number of infringement findings imposing a fine, these grounds were not relevant to many of the appeals. The high rates of discussion and acceptance of fines appeal grounds in Italy (84% and 49%, respectively) correspond with the Italian courts' similar outcomes in accepting procedural and substantive grounds, and therefore do not appear to point to a unique approach to the calculation of fines.

By comparison, an earlier empirical study found that the General Court (GC) had intervened quite frequently when reviewing fines imposed by the European Commission for infringements of Article 101 TFEU, reducing it in 45% of the judgments rendered between 2000 and 2010. The Commission enjoyed almost judicial immunity from fines imposed for infringements of Article 102 TFEU, which were reduced by the GC in only 18% of the cases where the fines were reviewed.[138]

5.4 Internal Market Grounds: Consistency and Uniformity of EU Law Application

In addition to the already complex task of judicial review of competition law decisions on substantive and procedural matters, national courts of the EU Member States must ensure that EU law is being applied in a consistent and uniform manner across the EU. As we outlined in Chapter 1, prior to the process of modernisation of EU competition law enforcement through Regulation 1/2003, some of the EU institutions were concerned that decentralised judicial review of EU competition law enforcement by national courts might be problematic in terms of ensuring consistency and uniformity.

Previous empirical studies have already pointed out that decentralised judicial review has failed to maintain substantive uniformity in the interpretation of the competition rules, for example, with respect to the role of public policy and the scope of Article 101(3) TFEU;[139] in relation to the relationship between the EU competition law prohibitions and national laws on unfair trading practices and the regulation of digital markets;[140] or concerning the application of the effect on trade test.[141]

137. Hungary report, Chapter 15; Lithuania report, Chapter 19; Slovakia report, Chapter 26.
138. Geradin and Petit (*supra* n. 60), 62. *See also* Jose Luis da Cruz Vilaca, 'The Intensity of Judicial Review in Complex Economic Matters – Recent Competition Law Judgments of the EU' (2018) 6 *Journal of Antitrust Enforcement* 173-188.
139. Or Brook, 'Struggling with Article 101 (3) TFEU: Diverging Approaches of the Commission, EU Courts, and Five Competition Authorities' (2029) 56(1) *Common Market Law Review* 121; Brook (*supra* n. 108).
140. Or Brook and Magali Eben. 'Article 3 of Regulation 1/2003: A Historical and Empirical Account of an Unworkable Compromise.' (2024) 12(1) *Journal of Antitrust Enforcement* 45.
141. Botta et al. (*supra* n. 108).

Figure 31.17 presents the percentage of judgments in which grounds related to the relationship between EU and national laws were raised by the parties, differentiating between the percentage of judgments in which those grounds were accepted (black bars) and rejected (grey bars). It shows that not only does such national divergence persist, but also that matters related to uniformity and consistency of the internal market or the tension between EU competition laws to national laws and policies have scarcely been raised before the national courts. The internal market grounds were defined in this study as arguments based on or related to the tension between EU and national competition laws. For example, they include matters related to the application of the effect on trade test, the interpretation of the obligations of Article 3 of Regulation 1/2003, and questions over the primacy of EU competition law or its uniform application. The data is presented from the perspective of each NCA's decision or previous instance's judgment which has been appealed, entailing that multiple appeals submitted on a single decision or judgment will be aggregated.

Figure 31.17 EU/National Grounds

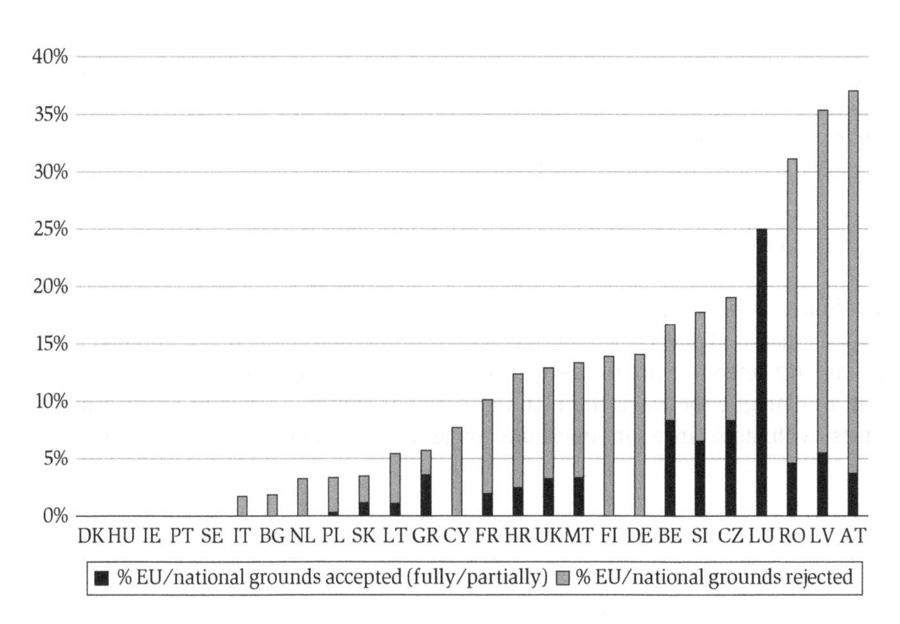

The figure demonstrates that no grounds related to the relationship between EU and national laws were ever raised in Denmark, Hungary, Ireland, Portugal, and Sweden. Such grounds were examined in 5% of the cases or less in Italy, Bulgaria, the

Netherlands, Poland, Slovakia, and Lithuania. Those grounds were more prominent only in a handful of jurisdictions (above 25% of the cases in Luxembourg, Romania, Latvia, and Austria).

The limited discussion of this type of appeal ground may be ascribed to soft convergence and relative alignment between EU and national competition laws in most of the Member States.[142] The relatively high percentage rate of appeals on EU/national grounds in Latvia, for example, was the result of classifying all anti-competitive agreements listed in the national provision equivalent to Article 101 TFEU as by-object restrictions, thereby diverging from the EU jurisprudence on the matter.[143] Similarly, the discussion of such grounds in Austria involved a series of cases raising questions on the interpretation of various EU competition law provisions.[144] Moreover, the limited appeals submitted regarding the relationship between EU and national laws might also be the result of the limited incentive for parties to the judicial dispute to contest the classification of their alleged infringement as based on EU or national competition laws.

The limited discussion over the relationship between EU and national laws is particularly striking when taken together with the findings on the highly limited application of EU competition law in some of the Member States, and particularly in most of the CEE countries (*see* discussion in section 4 above). In practice, this leads the national courts in those jurisdictions to have very limited opportunities to scrutinise the application of EU competition law by the NCAs and fulfil the important role envisioned for national courts by Regulation 1/2003.

6 PRELIMINARY REFERENCES

The limited attention paid to matters relating to the tension between EU competition law and national laws, as reported above, does not seem to be fulfilled by the preliminary reference procedure of Article 267 TFEU. This 'institutionalised mechanism of dialogue' between the ECJ and national courts,[145] aims to provide national courts with assistance on questions regarding the interpretation of EU law, to

142. Katalin Cseres, 'Relationship Between EU Competition Law and National Competition Laws' in Lianos and Geradin (eds), *Handbook on European Competition Law: Enforcement and Procedure* (Edward Elgar 2013), 578-583; Bogdan M. Chiriţoiu, 'Convergence Within the European Competition Network: Legislative Harmonization and Enforcement Priorities' in Adriana Almăşan and Peter Whelan (eds), *The Consistent Application of EU Competition Law: Substantive and Procedural Challenges* (2017 Springer), 3-22.
143. Latvia report, Chapter 18.
144. Austria report, Chapter 3.
145. Rafał Mańko, 'Preliminary reference procedure' European Parliamentary Research Service PE 608.628 (2017), available at: https://www.europarl.europa.eu/RegData/etudes/BRIE/2017/608628/EPRS_BRI(2017)608628_EN.pdf, 1.

contribute towards ensuring the uniform application of EU law across the Union.[146] Notably, in the field of competition law, preliminary references are aimed at ensuring the uniform application of EU competition law not only in terms of substance but also in matters related to the procedures followed by NCAs and national courts and the sanctions imposed.[147] Preliminary references can thus determine the limits of the procedural autonomy principle.

According to Article 267 TFEU, the decision on whether to submit a preliminary reference rests with the national court concerned. However, if it is a court of last instance and a question of interpretation of EU law or the validity of an act of the EU institutions is necessary to decide a question before it, that court must submit a question. In the field of competition law, the ECJ has established a relatively broad jurisdiction, declaring it has the jurisdiction to give preliminary rulings about the interpretation of national competition laws, where such national rules have been modelled on EU law.[148] Hence, at times it has issued preliminary rulings on the interpretation of the national equivalent prohibitions even in purely national cases.[149]

Nevertheless, Figure 31.18 points to a limited number of preliminary rulings issued in connection with the judgments included in the database, amounting to only thirty-five rulings in the relevant period. Very few rulings originated from CEE Member States, perhaps given their limited application of the EU prohibitions,[150] with five Member States (Greece, France, Italy, Latvia and Lithuania) being responsible for over half of the rulings issued.

146. *Ibid. See also* Paul Craig and Gráinne De Búrca, *EU Law: Text, Cases, and Materials UK Version* (Oxford University Press, USA, 2020), 496-497.
147. Jules Stuyck, 'The Role of Preliminary References in the Uniform Application of EU Competition Law' in Adriana Almăşan and Peter Whelan (eds) *The Consistent Application of EU Competition Law: Substantive and Procedural Challenges* (Springer 2017), 177-191, 187-188.
148. Joined Cases C-297/88 & 197/89, *Dzodzi*, EU:C:1990:360.
149. C-32/11 Allianz (2013), paras 20-23; C-413/13 FNV Kunsten Informatie en Media (2014), paras 17-20. Also *see* Stuyck (*supra* n. 147), 177-191.
150. See section 31.4 above.

Figure 31.18 Number of Preliminary Rulings

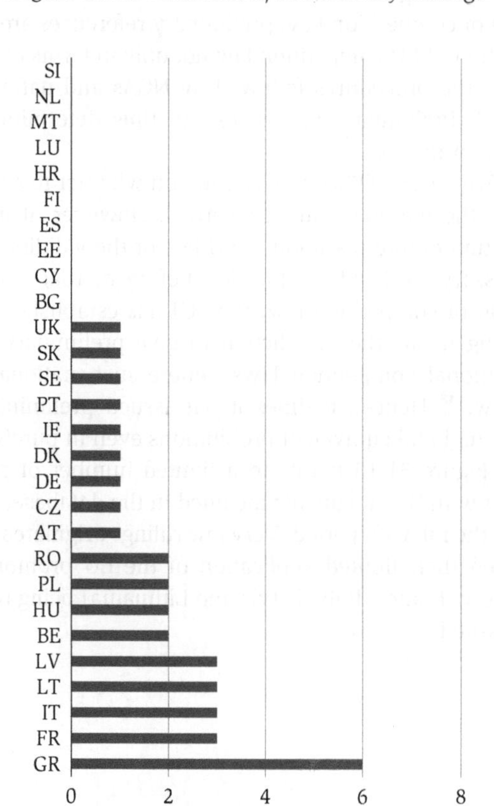

Notably, the figure only captured judgments that were issued after a preliminary ruling was issued. Given the length of the preliminary reference procedure and the re-initiation of national judicial procedures upon the delivery of such a ruling, it is possible that the figure does not capture preliminary rulings that were not issued or were not implemented by the national courts until the cut-off date of the study.

The limited use of the preliminary reference procedure in the decentralised public enforcement of EU competition law was already observed by earlier research.[151] When compared with the statistics on the total number of preliminary references across all fields of EU law,[152] there are surprisingly few references in the context of the public enforcement of the competition rules in the Member States, particularly in comparison

151. Alec Stone Sweet and Thomas L. Brunell. 'The European Court and the National Courts: A Statistical Analysis of Preliminary References, 1961-95' (1998) 5(1) *Journal of European Public Policy* 66-97 DOI: 10.1080/13501768880000041; Barry Rodger 'Competition Law Preliminary Rulings: A Quantitative and Qualitative Overview Post Regulation 1/2003' (2014) *Global Competition Litigation Review* 125-139; Brook (*supra* n. 108), 140, 192, 228, 264.
152. https://curia.europa.eu/jcms/upload/docs/application/pdf/2023-03/stats_cour_2022_en.pdf.

with references by courts dealing with competition law disputes by private parties.[153] Studies also indicated that despite the introduction of that decentralised enforcement system in the EU there were fewer preliminary rulings in competition cases in recent years to 2016, noting the potential impact of the settlements and commitments procedures.[154]

7 LENIENCY AND SETTLEMENTS

Leniency[155] and settlements[156] (together 'negotiated penalty settlements') offer undertakings a full or partial waiver of fines in exchange for admitting to the facts involved or to a violation of the competition rules and cooperation with the competition authority. The Commission adopted its own leniency and settlements programmes,[157] and most (yet not all) of the NCAs examined in this study have similar national programmes.[158]

The fine reduction in those programmes is likely to impact upon the deterrent effect of the competition law prohibitions, yet is often justified by procedural economy benefits, as leniency and settlement processes are assumed to help authorities quickly conclude their investigations and render their decisions.[159] For the purpose of this study, it is noteworthy that the procedural economy benefits were attributed, among others, to the avoidance of litigation costs. It is assumed that while both leniency and settlements are subject to judicial review before the EU and some of the national courts, in theory, undertakings benefitting from either leniency or settlement will have more

153. Rodger (*supra* n. 151).
154. *See* Jan Blockx, 'The Impact of the EU Antitrust Procedure on the Role of the EU Courts (1997-2016)' (2018) 9(2) *Journal of European Competition Law & Practice* 92-103 DOI: 10.1093/jeclap/lpy004.
155. According to the ECN+ Directive, Article 2(1)(16), a leniency programme is defined as 'a programme concerning the application of Article 101 TFEU or a corresponding provision under national competition law on the basis of which a participant in a secret cartel, independently of the other undertakings involved in the cartel, cooperates with an investigation of the competition authority, by voluntarily providing presentations regarding that participant's knowledge of, and role in, the cartel in return for which that participant receives, by decision or by a discontinuation of proceedings, immunity from, or a reduction of, fines for its involvement in the cartel'. In this project, we also included comparable national programmes that extend to all types of violations of Articles 101 and 102 TFEU and the national equivalent provisions, beyond secret cartels. It does not include criminal cartel immunity programmes.
156. According to the ECN+ Directive, Article 2(1)(18), settlement submission refer to voluntary presentations 'by, or on behalf of, an undertaking to a competition authority, describing the undertaking's acknowledgement of, or its renunciation to dispute, its participation in an infringement of Article 101 or 102 TFEU or national competition law and its responsibility for that infringement, which was drawn up specifically to enable the competition authority to apply a simplified or expedited procedure'.
157. *See*, for example, Eur. Comm'n, Notice on Immunity from Fines and Reduction of Fines in Cartel Cases, 2006 O.J. (C 298) 17, 3; Commission Regulation No. 622/2008 of June 30, 2008 Amending Regulation No. 773/2004, as regard the Conduct of Settlement Procedures in Cartel Cases, 2008 O.J. (L 171) 3, 1.
158. For a discussion of the diverging national programs see Eur. Comm'n Staff Working Paper, Impact Assessment accompanying the ECN+ Directive Proposal, SWD (2017) 114 final, 23-25 and Annex XII-XIII.
159. Brook (*supra* n. 84), 487-489.

limited incentives to appeal. At the EU level, for example, a reduction of 20% in the number of the Commission's decisions subject to appeal has been explained as a consequence of the introduction of the Commission's settlements programme.[160]

Figure 31.19 summarises the percentage of NCAs' decisions subject to appeal in which one or more of the undertakings have successfully submitted a leniency application. It should be noted that Ireland did not have a leniency programme during the period covered by this study, and that Malta introduced a leniency programme soon after the end of the relevant period covered by this study, following the implementation of the ECN+ Directive. Furthermore, infringement decisions based on a leniency application cannot be appealed in Denmark.

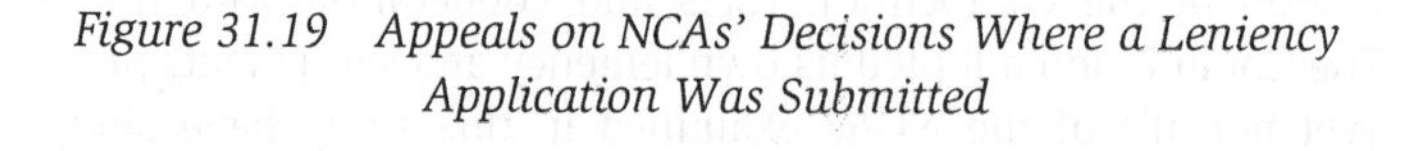

Figure 31.19 Appeals on NCAs' Decisions Where a Leniency Application Was Submitted

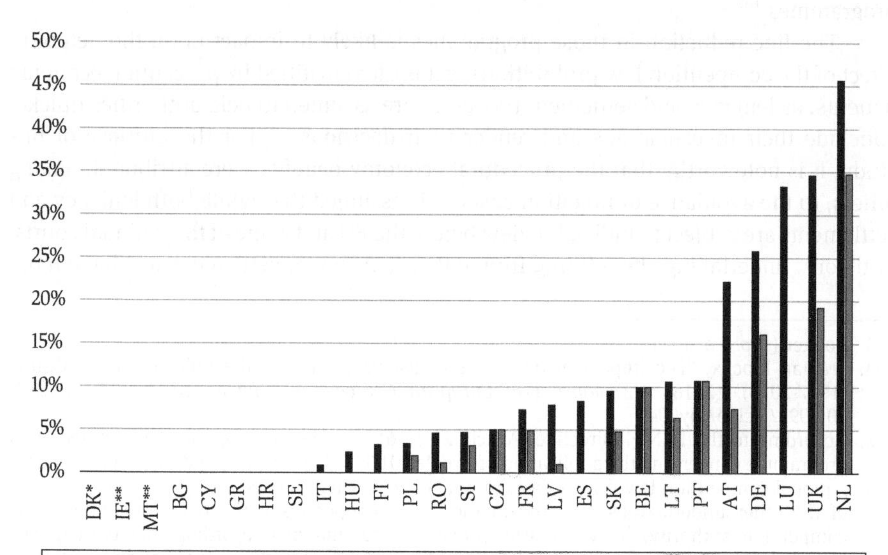

Note: For Spain, the figure does not include data on the acceptance rate of NCA's decisions where one or more of the parties have successfully applied for leniency.

* Jurisdictions in which infringement decisions based on leniency applications cannot be appealed

** Jurisdictions having no leniency programme during the relevant period of the study (April 2021)

160. Yannis Katsoulacos et al., 'Antitrust Enforcement in Europe in the Last 25 Years: Developments and Challenges' (2019) 55 *Review of Industrial Organization* 5-26, 19 DOI: 10.1007/s11151-019-09698-2.

Our findings question whether the assumption of the procedural economy benefits of leniency applications holds in all jurisdictions. The figures demonstrate that in nine jurisdictions, 10% or more of the NCA's decisions or previous instance's judgments subject to an appeal were adopted after one or more of the parties to the procedure have successfully applied for leniency (Slovakia, Belgium, Lithuania, Portugal), of which in five jurisdictions over 20% of the appealed decisions (Austria, Germany, Luxemburg, the UK and the Netherlands). This queries the extent to which the benefit resulting from those programmes can justify their detrimental impact upon deterrence.[161]

Almost half of the Dutch NCA's decisions and court judgments under appeal (46%) started with a leniency application, and 35% of such appeals were fully or partially successful. As elaborated in the national report, in some appeals, the effect of the leniency application itself was contested on appeal, such as the extent to which the application evidenced the role of an undertaking in the infringement. In a few cases, the leniency applicants themselves submitted an appeal, seeking a larger reduction in the fine.[162] In the UK, 35% of the decisions and judgments under appeal were adopted based on a leniency application. The appeals mostly contested the calculation of the fines and were fully or partially accepted in 19% of the cases.[163] In Austria, in which 22% of the appealed decisions were based on leniency applications, the appeal court often examined the application of the leniency instrument, and in some cases its compatibility with EU law.[164]

Similarly, Figure 31.20 depicts the percentage of NCA's decisions or previous instance's judgments subject to an appeal in which one or more of the undertakings had successfully negotiated a settlement with the NCA. Bulgaria, Cyprus, Denmark, Spain, Ireland, Luxemburg, Sweden and Slovenia[165] did not have a settlements programme during the period covered by the project, and in Croatia they were only introduced in April 2021. Infringement decisions based on a settlement cannot be appealed in Belgium. While such decisions can be appealed in Latvia, the grounds are limited to fraud, deceit, and duress.[166] In Malta, following the adoption of the judicial model in 2019, settlement decisions are delivered by the Civil Court (Commercial Section), following proceedings instituted by the administrative NCA. While all decisions of the NCA in Malta are subject to an appeal, the law requires that undertakings must waive their right to appeal or challenge settlement procedures.[167]

161. For a discussion *see* Brook (*supra* n. 84), 487-489.
162. The Netherlands report, Chapter 22.
163. The UK report, Chapter 30.
164. Austria report, Chapter 3.
165. Settlements were introduced in Slovenia in 2022, following the cut-off date of this study (*see* Chapter 27).
166. Latvia report, Chapter 18.
167. Malta report, Chapter 21.

Figure 31.20 Appeals on NCAs' Decisions Where a Settlement Application Was Submitted

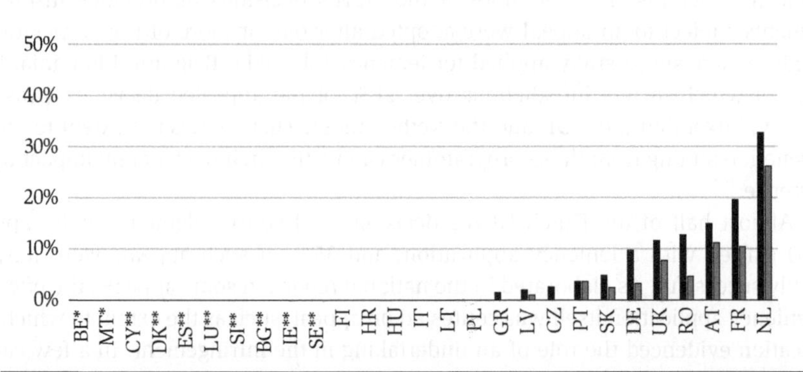

■ % of NCAs' decisions subject to appeal where one or more parties successfully applied for settlements

■ % of NCA's decision under appeal where one or more parties successfully applied for settlements, and were fully/partially accepted

Note:

* Jurisdictions in which infringement decisions based on settlement agreements cannot be appealed

** Jurisdictions having no settlements programme during the relevant period of the study (April 2021)

The figure reveals that in comparison with leniency, fewer appeals were submitted on decisions and judgments where a settlement application was accepted. Relatively high appeal rates in such cases are apparent in Austria (15%, from which 11% were fully or partially successful) and the Netherlands (33%, from which 26% were fully or partially successful), both of which also experienced high appeal rates in cases of leniency applications, as well as France (20%, from which 10% were fully or partially successful). In Austria, the three appealed decisions involving settlements concerned procedural and relatively minor questions, such as publication and costs.[168] In France, such appeals were lodged by undertakings that did not benefit from the settlement and by undertakings which had benefited from it but contested the method used to calculate the fine.[169]

8 THIRD PARTIES

Third parties' participation in competition law enforcement by NCAs and judicial review by national courts may support and complement judicial review. Granting participation rights to third parties provides them with the opportunity to contradict the decisions of the competition authorities, invoking errors, flaws, or mistakes that could

168. Austria report, Chapter 3.
169. France report, Chapter 12.

ultimately lead to the illegality of the final decision.[170] Third-party participation may increase the effectiveness of enforcement by providing valuable information necessary for the accurate representation of the factual situation, thereby enabling the competition authorities and courts to reach a decision that accurately represents both law and facts. They facilitate the administrative procedure by allowing them to gain greater information and they help to concretise the public interest.[171] Hence, appeals brought by third parties may be an indicator of the success of judicial review in protecting the rights of stakeholders in the process.[172]

The rules governing third parties' participation are determined according to national laws and vary considerably from one jurisdiction to another.[173] Third parties may have a double role in judicial review, either launching an appeal against an NCA decision (in particular decisions concerning the rejection of a complaint and in some jurisdictions decisions to close a case on priority grounds) or joining an appeal as an interested third party (often referred to as intervening).

The different involvement of third parties in lodging appeals is already illustrated in Figure 31.11. The figure revealed that in around a third of the examined jurisdictions, third parties played no role in launching first-instance appeals (Austria, Ireland, Sweden, Czech Republic) or a very limited role (3% or less in Italy, Romania, Hungary, Germany, Portugal, Slovenia, and Slovakia). By comparison, 27% of the first-instance appeals in Spain,[174] 49% of the first-instance appeals in Bulgaria, 50% of the first-instance appeals in Luxemburg, and 57% of the first-instance appeals in Malta and Croatia were initiated by third parties. The figure also reveals that in some countries, third parties were active in submitting second and third-instance appeals. All second-instance appeals in Belgium and Luxemburg were launched by third parties, as well as 41% of the second-instance appeals in Bulgaria, and 29% of the second-instance appeals and 33% of the third-instance appeals in Malta. The second-instance appeal in Croatia was initiated by the State Attorney Office and the third-instance appeals in Slovenia were initiated by the Higher State Attorney. By comparison, in relation to the EU Commission's decisions, third parties submitted 16% of the Article 101 TFEU annulment applications and 49% of the Article 102 TFEU annulment applications leading to judgments issued between 2000 and 2010.[175]

A similar trend is observed when it comes to the role of third parties in joining judicial proceedings as interested parties. As illustrated by Figure 31.21, the various judicial systems differ both in terms of the number of judgments where third parties have joined as third parties in the first-instance appeal, and in the characteristics of those third parties. The figure indicates where third parties to appeals were a national government agency or the government itself; a consumer organisation; the

170. Joana Mendes, *Participation Rights* (Oxford University Press 2011), 32.
171. *Ibid.*
172. Geradin and Petit (*supra* n. 60), 58.
173. For an empirical mapping on such rules, *see* Brook and Cseres (*supra* n. 69), 35-40.
174. This figure is based on a previous study by the Spanish rapporteur, which calculated this percentage from the perspective of each NCA's decision subject to an appeal (*see* Spain report, Chapter 28).
175. Geradin and Petit (*supra* n. 60), 58.

complainant in the NCA's decision subject to an appeal; undertakings and/or individuals that were part of the NCA's decision subject to an appeal but were not the applicants or the respondents in the appeal procedure; or other third parties not falling into any of the above categories. In relation to some judgments, more than one type of third party had joined the proceedings. The number of third parties joining first-instance appeals (bars) is compared to the total number of first-instance judgments (dots).[176]

Figure 31.21 Third Parties Joining First-Instance Appeals

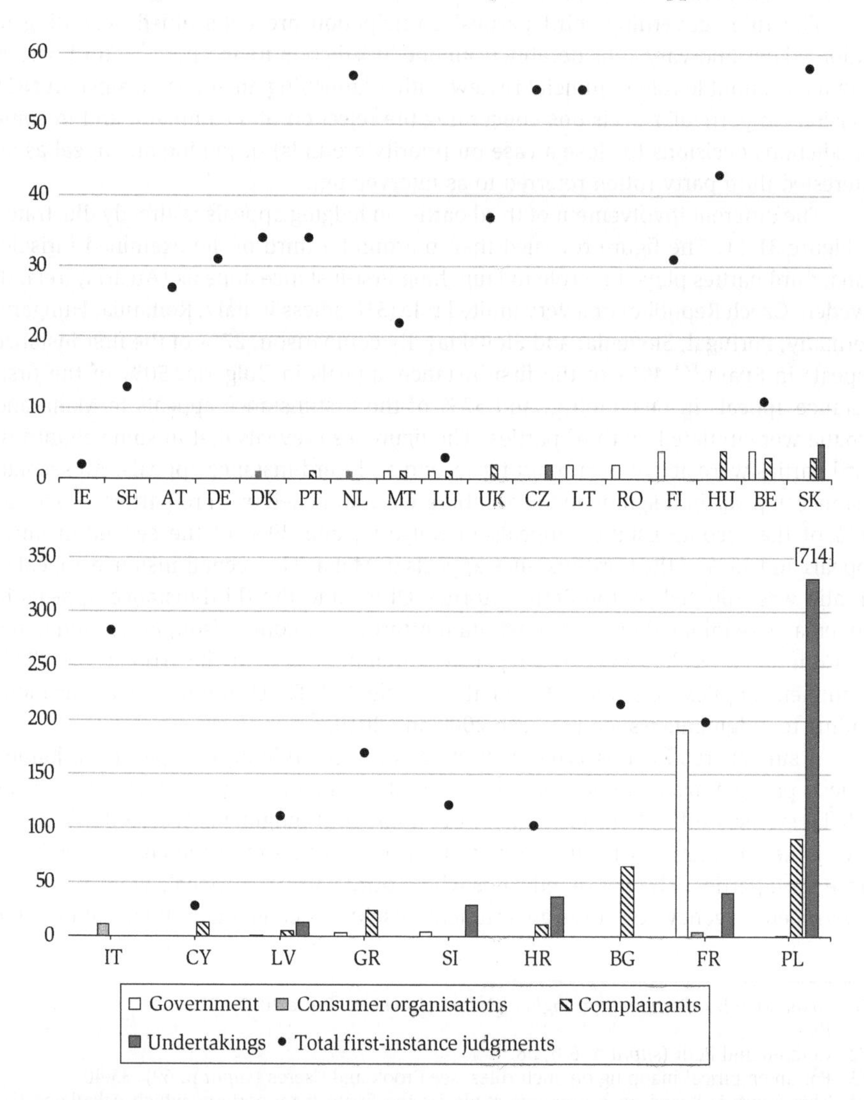

176. No data is available with respect to Spain.

The available empirical findings suggest that in many countries, third parties have never (Ireland, Sweden, Austria, Germany) or rarely (Denmark, Portugal, the Netherlands, the UK, Czech Republic, Lithuania, Romania, Finland, Hungary, and Malta) intervened in competition law appeals.

In other countries, third parties have been more active in joining appeals. For example, a high number of complainants joined the appeals in Bulgaria, Croatia, Cyprus, Greece, Luxemburg, and Latvia (prior to 2016). In those countries, unlike many others, a decision to reject a complaint or a finding of no grounds for action is subject to an appeal that may be lodged by a complainant (*see* section 1.5 above). In Poland, the very high involvement of complainants and undertakings that were not party to the NCA's decisions subject to appeal reflect the old legal rules, in force until 2007. In that period, undertakings with legal interest, local government authorities, state audit offices, consumer advocates, and consumer organisations had the right to call on the NCA to initiate infringement proceedings, and once proceedings were initiated, they would become a party to those proceedings and had the right to file and join an appeal. The 2007 reform stated that all NCA proceedings shall be initiated *ex officio*, solely at the discretion of the NCA. Although third parties are formally allowed to submit statements to the NCA during the proceedings, such submissions have a limited value, and third parties no longer have access to the case files. Moreover, only the addressees of the NCA's decision can submit an appeal.[177]

Figure 31.21 also illustrates that in some legal systems, branches of the government are involved in competition law appeals. This was most notable in France, where the Minister of the Economy has a right not only to lodge competition law appeals but also to intervene in the procedure by submitting oral and written observations.[178] The Minister of Economic Affairs also has the right to bring appeals in Belgium, yet made a more limited use of this power in practice in comparison with France.[179] In Greece, the government intervened only in a limited number of proceedings through public authorities, all concerning actions for annulment against the NCA's findings in the poultry farming cartel.[180] In Slovenia, the State Attorney's Office as the representative of the public interest has participated in four cases.[181] In Finland, governmental regulators acted as a third party in four appeals and included stakeholders such as the Finnish National Aviation Organisation, the National Telecommunications Regulator, and the National Post Office.[182]

Allowing branches of the government to intervene in competition law appeals may indirectly limit NCA independence, by allowing the government to make representations concerning the public interest and policy beyond competition law. Notably, while the ECN+ Directive prohibits the NCAs from seeking or taking instructions from the government or any other public or private entities when carrying out their duties

177. Poland report, Chapter 23.
178. France report, Chapter 12.
179. Belgium report, Chapter 4.
180. Greece report, Chapter 14.
181. Slovenia report, Chapter 27.
182. Finland report, Chapter 11.

and exercising their powers in the application of Articles 101 and 102 TFEU,[183] the Directive does not preclude Member States from making representations during judicial review.

9 A PLEA FOR GREATER TRANSPARENCY: THE (LACK OF) PUBLICATION OF JUDGMENTS

Publication of judgments is essential for both the public scrutiny of judges and courts and for public knowledge and awareness of the development of law.[184] A complete database of judgments is essential for the promotion of both a better understanding and critical analysis of competition law enforcement.[185] It is of particular value in the context of the enforcement regime of Regulation 1/2003, where undertakings must self-assess if and how they comply with the open-ended provisions of EU competition law.

At the EU level, competition law judgments by the ECJ and GC are published in accordance with the Rules of Procedure of the Court of Justice and the General Court.[186] Moreover, the EU Courts have acknowledged that publication of the Commission's competition law decisions may contribute to ensuring the observance of EU competition law. Their publication serves the public interest of providing greater transparency and awareness of the reasons behind the Commission's action while acknowledging the interests of economic operators in knowing the sort of behaviour that is likely to be punished. It supports the interests of anyone harmed by the infringement so that they can assert their rights, and it is also essential to the rights of the infringing undertaking to seek judicial review.[187] Publication of a Commission decision is the rule, and non-disclosure is the exception.[188]

Nonetheless, in relation to NCAs and national courts, there is no EU law requirement to publish decisions and judgments.[189] The diversity in the scope and nature of publication in different national legal systems was aptly demonstrated by a

183. ECN+ Directive, Article 4(2)(b).
184. Marc van Opijnen et al., 'On-line publication of court decisions in the EU: report of the policy group of the project "Building on the European Case Law Identifier"' *Available at SSRN 3088495* (2017), 7. Also *see* Zachary D. Clopton and Aziz Z. Huq, 'The Necessary and Proper Stewardship of Judicial Data' (2024) 76 Stan. L. Rev. (forthcoming).
185. Cf, Richard A. Posner, 'A Statistical Study of Antitrust Enforcement' (1970) 13(2) *The Journal of Law and Economics* 365, 417-418 DOI: 10.1086/466698; William E. Kovacic, 'Using Ex Post Evaluations to Improve the Performance of Competition Policy Authorities' (2005) 31 *Journal of Corporate Law* 503, 541.
186. Their publication is subject to confidentiality with respect to business secrets, *see* Charlotte Emin, 'Luxembourg Confidential: Keeping (Business) Secrets Before the General Court of the European Union' (2023) 14(1) *Journal of European Competition Law and Practice* 4 DOI: 10.1093/jeclap/lpac048.
187. C-189/02P, *Dansk Rørindustri and Others v. Commission* ECLI:EU:C:2005:408, 170; T-193/03 *Piro v. Commission* ECLI:EU:T:2005:164, 57, 69, 78; 41-69, 104; T-345/12 *Akzo Nobel and Others v. Commission* ECLI:EU:T:2015:50, 60.
188. Also *see* P. Iannuccelli and J. Nuijten, 'Article 30 Publication of Decisions: Commentary' in Luca Prete et al. (eds) *Regulation 1/2003 and EU Antitrust Enforcement* (Wolters Kluwer 2023), 665-666.
189. van Opijnen et al. (*supra* n. 184), 7.

comparative study of the EU Member States conducted by van *Opijnen et al.*[190] They show that publication requirements in some Member States apply only to certain courts, often those of higher instances,[191] and that even those Member States that have adopted legal or policy frameworks that require full or partial publication have not always complied with such rules.[192]

Rapporteurs for the various jurisdictions in our project faced vastly different degrees of difficulty in locating all of the relevant cases for the purpose of the case-law database. As the national reports have illustrated, during all or part of the relevant period, there was no obligation to publish all judgments concerning the public enforcement of competition law in the Czech Republic,[193] Germany, Estonia, Greece, Hungary, Latvia, the Netherlands, Poland, Romania, and Slovenia. In France, there has only been an obligation to publish online all courts and administrative authorities' decisions since 2016. Previously, French constitutional rules, Article 6(1) ECHR and various domestic rules only required that such decisions be 'public', meaning that they had to be accessible to anyone who requested them but not necessarily published online.[194]

At times, even the judgments that were published were considerably redacted or anonymised in a manner that hinders the opportunity to follow the 'trail' of appeals against a single NCA decision or to understand its outcome.[195] Accordingly, in Hungary, while judgments are freely available on the courts' website, they are anonymised and it is not possible to search for court cases on the basis of the case number of the administrative procedure and to link the anonymised judgments to the decision reviewed. In Poland, the NCA's website is relatively comprehensive, even if not complete, in terms of publication of appeal judgments on its decisions. However, the difficulty remains in evaluating appeal courts' analysis, as the website includes only the conclusion part of any judgment, and the court's reasoning is not always published.[196]

Although the Portuguese NCA is obliged to publish all court judgments in appeals on fines imposed by it, this obligation is not always respected, and there is often a significant delay in publication. As detailed in the national report, this has even resulted in litigation by a consumer association.[197]

In Germany, national law does not require administrative authorities or courts to publish their decisions and judgments and there is no public register indicating which cases have been decided. Publication decisions primarily lie in the hands of the judges, and even if published, may take time and may be heavily redacted.[198] Similar issues

190. *Ibid.*, 11-14.
191. *Ibid.*, 19.
192. *Ibid.*, 11-14.
193. While in the Czech Republic, only the judgments of 'top' courts are systematically published, the NCA publishes all judgments reviewing its final decisions (*see* Chapter 8).
194. France report, Chapter 12.
195. *See*, for example, Hungary report, Chapter 15 and Romania report, Chapter 25.
196. Poland report, Chapter 23.
197. Portugal report, Chapter 24.
198. Germany report, Chapter 13.

arise in Greece, where the judgments of Greek administrative courts are not consistently published online in a manner accessible to the public. While the courts publish online some of their judgments, their databases are not reliably searchable due to the ineffectiveness of the available filtering criteria. Even private databases of Greek case law suffer from similar shortcomings in terms of the comprehensive nature of search results.[199] In Latvia, while judgments of administrative courts are published, there is no reliable search tool which can assist in identifying all relevant competition law judgments. Moreover, it is not always possible to link the appealed NCA decision to those judgments dealing with its appeal.[200]

The lack of publication hinders not only the public and academic assessment of the effectiveness of competition law judicial review but also the ability of the Commission and EU institutions to capture the functioning of Regulation 1/2003. As was elaborated in Chapter 1, the Regulation's process for transmission of national judgments to the Commission[201] was not respected in practice, meaning that even the Commission has only limited information on the scope and nature of the national judicial review of EU competition law enforcement.

We believe that the lack of access to judgments considerably restricts the ability to assess the effectiveness of judicial review of EU and national competition law.

10 CONCLUSIONS: THE CURRENT NATIONAL JUDICIAL REVIEW SYSTEM FAILS TO MATCH THE INTEGRATION AIMS OF EU LAW

This project has created a new, open-access dataset of all judicial reviews of the public enforcement actions of Articles 101 and 102 TFEU and the national equivalent provisions, rendered by the national courts of the EU's twenty-seven Member States and the UK. The dataset covers a seventeen-year period from the decentralisation of the enforcement of EU competition law in May 2004 and ending in April 2021 covering all aspects of the judicial review of enforcement of the competition law prohibitions in line with the coding book, as outlined in Chapters 1 and 2 of Part I of this book.

Based on our findings, we submit that the current system of judicial review of EU and national competition law enforcement by national courts does not duly comply with the integration aims of EU law in general, and Regulation 1/2003 in particular. The evidence suggests that the existing EU and national rules on judicial review of the NCAs' enforcement do not ensure an effective, consistent, and uniform application of the competition rules by national courts in all Member States. In addition to the detailed findings presented in this chapter, we believe this conclusion is supported by two overarching outcomes emerging from the study: a conceptual and an empirical observation.

First, is the *lack of a shared, conceptual framework* to guide judicial review of competition law across the EU. There are no concrete EU law provisions that inform the operation of national courts, no harmonised terms and benchmarks with respect to

199. Greece report, Chapter 14.
200. Latvia report, Chapter 18.
201. Regulation 1/2003, Article 15(2).

fundamental matters such as the institutions and procedure, the standard of review and the degree of specialisation of the courts (section 1), the powers and remedies of courts upon accepting appeals (section 2.4), or the definition and focus of the grounds of appeal (Section 5). Moreover, there has been almost no attention afforded by policymakers and academics to foundational challenges associated with judicial review in a decentralised system, both at the EU and most of the national levels. In particular, very few systematic-empirical or EU-wide comparative studies have attempted, to date, to examine these questions (Chapter 1).

The lack of a conceptual framework not only hinders the study and review of the effectiveness and impact of judicial review but also complicates the gathering of empirical data. Judicial review, as we learn from this project, involves considerably divergent processes among the various Member States. One clear example arises in Member States following the judicial model, namely where a national court is the entity formally adopting infringement decisions in public enforcement proceedings (section 1.1). In that setting, according to Regulation 1/2003, such courts' decisions are considered part of the action of the NCAs rather than review by a court. Other differences relate to the type of decisions that can be appealed in each Member State (e.g., whether decisions to close an investigation or reject a complaint are subject to review, as well as commitment decisions and NCAs' decisions that were based on leniency and/or settlement applications, *see* sections 1.5 and 7), the number of instances of appeals and the different types of review (e.g., internal, judicial, or constitutional, *see* section 1.2), and the types of appellants and the role of third parties (sections 3 and 8). The considerably different national settings in which judicial review of EU competition law takes place, therefore, renders its comparative study and governance particularly complicated.

The second general finding of the project is an empirical one. It confirms that the above conceptual challenges were matched by *great diversity in terms of the practical experience of judicial review*. The empirical findings point to considerable disparity, for example, in relation to the number of judgments on competition law appeals issued in the relevant period. While over 1,300 judgments were rendered in Spain (with respect to approx. 300 NCA's decisions), over 1,190 in Poland (with respect to approx. 500 NCA's decisions), only approx. 40 judgments were rendered in the UK (with respect to approx. 25 NCA decisions) and 2 in Ireland (with respect to 2 NCA's decisions) (section 2.1). A similar high level of heterogeneity concerns the ratio of appeals, with most CEE countries being at the higher end of the range (section 2.2). Moreover, although the ratio of successful appeals has its limitations as a performance assessment indicator and interpreting the meaning behind success rates is not a straightforward task, our findings suggest for instance that they do not point to a clear correlation between success and either the administrative and judicial model of enforcement (section 2.2).

The findings also point to remarkable differences in the nature and type of NCAs' decisions subject to judicial review (section 4). In many jurisdictions, the overwhelming majority of appeals concerned hard-core restrictions, corresponding with the enforcement strategies adopted by the NCAs. Moreover, the infringement of national competition laws alone has been the focus of judicial review actions in various CEE Member States in particular.

The appeal success rates varied significantly among the countries, both in aggregated terms and when examined based on the grounds invoked (sections 2.3 and 5). Highly specialist courts, such as the first-instance courts in Denmark and the UK, had high rates of both substantive grounds appeals and their success, supporting the hypothesis that specialist courts are less likely to be deferential to the NCAs' analysis. As such, there is some evidence that those national courts have contributed to the substantive development of the EU competition rules. By comparison, in many CEE courts, procedural grounds were invoked in a very high proportion of appeals. The study also found that, contrary to initial expectations, the judicial model did not always lead to less frequent appeal deliberation on procedural matters. Similarly, there was considerable focus on appeal grounds related to fines in many of the CEE countries, and the empirical findings suggest that many of the national courts (especially first-instance appeals) are considerably more likely to intervene in the calculation of fines in comparison with the EU Courts.

Our findings also question whether the procedural economy benefits of leniency and settlements applications hold in all jurisdictions, given the high proportions of appeals submitted on decisions that were based on leniency, and to a lower extent on settlements applications, and the relatively high success rates of such appeals in some jurisdictions (section 7).

Finally, our empirical findings question the degree to which many of the national courts have fulfilled the important role envisioned for them by Regulation 1/2003, namely to ensure the effective, uniform and consistent application of EU competition law across the single market. In addition to the considerable divergence across substantive, procedural, and institutional aspects of judicial review, our project points to the limited deliberation over the relationship between EU and national laws before most of the national courts (section 5.4), the scant application of EU competition law in some of the NCAs and national courts (section 4), and the scarce resort to the preliminary reference procedure in most of the Member States (section 6). The reported diversity, found across the range of variables examined by the empirical study, does not appear to be associated with objective characteristics of the national markets. Therefore, it raises serious concerns as to the level playing field across the EU and the extent to which judicial review of EU competition law enforcement can be considered 'effective'.

The conceptual and empirical conclusions suggest that the few provisions of Regulation 1/2003, aimed at ensuring the substantive accuracy of the competition rules and their uniform and coherent applications by national courts, have failed at achieving their aims (*see* Chapter 1): Article 3 of the Regulation obliges the national courts (and NCAs) to apply Articles 101 and/or 102 TFEU when they apply their national competition law rules and establishes the primacy of the EU competition provisions. Yet, national courts have almost never questioned the classification of a case as purely national and the parties to an appeal seldom have the incentive to raise such questions on their own motion. Moreover, the cooperation mechanisms of Articles 15-16 of Regulation 1/2003, aiming at ensuring that the Commission and NCAs remain sufficiently well informed of proceedings before national courts, are mostly voluntary in nature and have only partially been respected in practice (Chapter 1).

As a result, there is no external monitoring of the overall operation of the national judicial review system nor scope for external challenges to the compatibility of national courts' appellate judgments with EU law.

Based on the insights gathered by this book on all aspects of the work of the national courts both individually and collectively on a comparative basis, we call for the procedural autonomy principle that has guided the EU decentralised enforcement system to be revised and recalibrated in favour of greater effectiveness, uniformity and transparency. First, we point to the value of enhancing access to competition law enforcement by ensuring full and timely publication of all NCAs' decisions and national courts' judgments applying the EU and the national equivalent competition law prohibitions, as was envisioned by Article 15 of Regulation 1/2003 (section 9). This, we believe, is imperative for greater accountability and oversight by the EU and national policymakers, stakeholders, and academic scholarship and would inform evidence-based policy reforms. Second, we advocate for the EU legislator, especially as part of the review of Regulation 1/2003, to consider ways to provide a more consistent and coherent framework for the judicial review of the NCAs' enforcement actions across the EU internal market, in terms of the substantive competition law rules, institutions, and procedures. While the ECN + Directive is a first step in the right direction, our empirical study has proven that further institutional, procedural, and substantive harmonisation and/or soft law coordination mechanisms are essential.

Index

O

P

R

S

INTERNATIONAL COMPETITION LAW SERIES

1. Ignacio De Leon, *Latin American Competition Law and Policy: A Policy in Search of Identity*, 2001 (ISBN 90-411-1542-0).
2. Wim Dejonghe & Wouter Van de Voorde (eds), *M & A in Belgium*, 2001 (ISBN 90-411-1594-3).
3. Yang-Ching Chao, Gee San, Changfa Lo & Jiming Ho (eds), *International and Comparative Competition Law and Policies*, 2001 (ISBN 90-411-1643-5).
4. Martin Mendelsohn & Stephen Rose, *Guide to the EC Block Exemption for Vertical Agreements*, 2002 (ISBN 90-411-9813-X).
5. Clifford A. Jones & Mitsuo Matsushita (eds), *Competition Policy in the Global Trading System: Perspectives from the EU, Japan and the USA*, 2002 (ISBN 90-411-1758-X).
6. Christian Koenig, Andreas Bartosch, Jens-Daniel Braun & Marion Romes (eds), *EC Competition and Telecommunications Law*, Second Edition, 2009 (ISBN 978-90-411-2564-4).
7. Jürgen Basedow (ed.), *Limits and Control of Competition with a View to International Harmonization*, 2002 (ISBN 90-411-1967-1).
8. Maureen Brunt, Economic Essays on Australian and New Zealand Competition Law, 2003 (ISBN 90-411-1991-4).
9. Ky P. Ewing, Jr., *Competition Rules for the 21st Century: Principles from America's Experience*, Second Edition, 2006 (ISBN 90-411-2477-2).
10. Joseph Wilson, *Globalization and the Limits of National Merger Control Laws*, 2003 (ISBN 90-411-1996-5).
11. Peter Verloop & Valérie Landes (eds), *Merger Control in Europe: EU, Member States and Accession States*, Fourth Edition, 2003 (ISBN 90-411-2056-4).
12. Themistoklis K. Giannakopoulos, *Safeguarding Companies' Rights in Competition and Anti-dumping/Anti-subsidies Proceedings*, Second Edition, 2011 (ISBN 978-90-411-3404-2).
13. Marjorie Holmes & Lesley Davey (eds), *A Practical Guide to National Competition Rules across Europe*, Second Edition, 2007 (ISBN 978-90- 411-2607-8).
14. Sigrid Stroux, *US and EU Oligopoly Control*, 2004 (ISBN 90-411-2296-6).
15. Tzong-Leh Hwang and Chiyuan Chen (eds), *The Future Development of Competition Framework*, 2004 (ISBN 90-411-2305-9).

16. Phedon Nicolaides, Mihalis Kekelekis and Maria Kleis, *State Aid Policy in the European Community: Principles and Practice,* Second Edition, 2008 (ISBN 978-90-411-2754-9).
17. Doris Hildebrand, *Economic Analyses of Vertical Agreements: A Self- Assessment,* 2005 (ISBN 90-411-2328-8).
18. Frauke Henning-Bodewig, *Unfair Competition Law: European Union and Member States,* 2005 (ISBN 90-411-2329-6).
19. Duarte Brito & Margarida Catalão-Lopes, *Mergers and Acquisitions: The Industrial Organization Perspective,* 2006 (ISBN 90-411-2451-9).
20. Nikos Th. Nikolinakos, *EU Competition Law and Regulation in the Converging Telecommunications, Media and IT Sectors,* 2006 (ISBN 90-411- 2469-1).
21. Mihalis Kekelekis, *The EC Merger Control Regulation: Rights of Defence. A Critical Analysis of DG COMP Practice and Community Courts' Jurisprudence,* 2006 (ISBN 90-411-2553-1).
22. Mark R. Joelson, *An International Antitrust Primer: A Guide to the Operation of United States, European Union and Other Key Competition Laws in the Global Economy,* Third Edition, 2006 (ISBN 90-411-2468-3).
23. Themistoklis K. Giannakopoulos, *A Concise Guide to the EU Anti-dumping/ Anti-subsidies Procedures,* 2006 (ISBN 90-411-2464-0).
24. George Cumming, Brad Spitz & Ruth Janal, *Civil Procedure Used for Enforcement of EC Competition Law by the English, French and German Civil Courts,* 2007 (ISBN 978-90-411-2471-5).
25. Jürgen Basedow (ed.), *Private Enforcement of EC Competition Law,* 2007 (ISBN 978-90-411-2613-9).
26. Jung Wook Cho, *Innovation and Competition in the Digital Network Economy: A Legal and Economic Assessment on Multi-tying Practices and Network Effects,* 2007 (ISBN 978-90-411-2574-3).
27. Akira Inoue, *Japanese Antitrust Law Manual: Law, Cases and Interpretation of the Japanese Antimonopoly Act,* 2007 (ISBN 978-90-411-2627-6).
28. René Barents, *Directory of EC Case Law on Competition,* 2007 (ISBN 978-90-411-2656-6).
29. Paul F. Nemitz (ed.), *The Effective Application of EU State Aid Procedures: The Role of National Law and Practice,* 2007 (ISBN 978-90-411-2657-3).
30. Jurian Langer, *Tying and Bundling as a Leveraging Concern under EC Competition Law,* 2007 (ISBN 978-90-411-2575-0).
31. Abel M. Mateus & Teresa Moreira (eds), *Competition Law and Economics – Advances in Competition Policy and Antitrust Enforcement,* 2007 (ISBN 978-90-411-2632-0).
32. Alberto Santa Maria, *Competition and State Aid: An Analysis of the EC Practice,* 2007 (ISBN 978-90-411-2617-7).
33. Barry J. Rodger (ed.), *Article 234 and Competition Law: An Analysis,* 2007 (ISBN 978-90-411-2605-4).

34. Alla Pozdnakova, *Liner Shipping and EU Competition Law*, 2008 (ISBN 978-90-411-2717-4).
35. Milena Stoyanova, *Competition Problems in Liberalized Telecommunications: Regulatory Solutions to Promote Effective Competition*, 2008 (ISBN 978-90-411-2736-5).
36. *EC State Aid Law/Le Droit des Aides d'Etat dans la CE. Liber Amicorum Francisco Santaolalla Gadea*, 2008 (ISBN 978-90-411-2774-7).
37. René Barents, *Directory of EU Case Law on State Aids*, Fourth Edition, 2022 (ISBN 978-94-035-4441-0).
38. Ignacio De Leon, *An Institutional Assessment of Antitrust Policy: The Latin American Experience*, 2009 (ISBN 978-90-411-2478-4).
39. Doris Hildebrand, *The Role of Economic Analysis in EU Competition Law: The European School*, Fourth Edition, 2016 (ISBN 978-90-411-6245-8).
40. Eugène Buttigieg, *Competition Law: Safeguarding the Consumer Interest. A Comparative Analysis of US Antitrust Law and EC Competition Law*, 2009 (ISBN 978-90-411-3119-5).
41. Ioannis Lianos & Ioannis Kokkoris (eds), *The Reform of EC Competition Law: New Challenges*, 2010 (ISBN 978-90-411-2692-4).
42. George Cumming & Mirjam Freudenthal, *Civil Procedure in EU Competition Cases before the English and Dutch Courts*, 2010 (ISBN 978-90-411-3192-8).
43. A.E. Rodriguez & Ashok Menon, *The Limits of Competition Policy: The Shortcomings of Antitrust in Developing and Reforming Economies*, 2010 (ISBN 978-90-411-3177-5).
44. Mika Oinonen, *Does EU Merger Control Discriminate against Small Market Companies? Diagnosing the Argument with Conclusions*, 2010 (ISBN 978-90-411-3261-1).
45. Eirik Østerud, *Identifying Exclusionary Abuses by Dominant Undertakings under EU Competition Law: The Spectrum of Tests*, 2010 (ISBN 978-90-411-3271-0).
46. Marco Botta, *Merger Control Regimes in Emerging Economies: A Case Study on Brazil and Argentina*, 2011 (ISBN 978-90-411-3402-8).
47. Jürgen Basedow & Wolfgang Wurmnest (eds), *Structure and Effects in EU Competition Law: Studies on Exclusionary Conduct and State Aid*, 2011 (ISBN 978-90-411-3174-4).
48. George Cumming (ed.), *Merger Decisions and the Rules of Procedure of the European Community Courts*, 2012 (ISBN 978-90-411-3671-8).
49. Eduardo Molan Gaban & Juliana Oliveira Domingues (eds), *Antitrust Law in Brazil: Fighting Cartels*, 2012 (ISBN 978-90-411-3670-1).
50. Giandonato Caggiano, Gabriella Muscolo & Marina Tavassi (eds), *Competition Law and Intellectual Property: A European Perspective*, 2012 (ISBN 978-90-411-3447-9).
51. Ben Van Rompuy, *Economic Efficiency: The Sole Concern of Modern Antitrust Policy? Non-efficiency Considerations under Article 101 TFEU*, 2012 (ISBN 978-90-411-3870-5).

52. Liyang Hou, *Competition Law and Regulation of the EU Electronic Communications Sector: A Comparative Legal Approach*, 2012 (ISBN 978-90-411-4047-0).
53. Barry Rodger, *Landmark Cases in Competition Law: Around the World in Fourteen Stories*, 2012 (ISBN 978-90-411-3843-9).
54. Andreas Scordamaglia-Tousis, *EU Cartel Enforcement: Reconciling Effective Public Enforcement with Fundamental Rights*, 2013 (ISBN 978-90-411-4758-5).
55. Bernardo Cortese (ed.), *EU Competition Law: Between Public and Private Enforcement*, 2014 (ISBN 978-90-411-4677-9).
56. Barry Rodger (ed.), *Competition Law: Comparative Private Enforcement and Collective Redress across the EU*, 2014 (ISBN 978-90-411-4559-8).
57. Nada Ina Pauer, *The Single Economic Entity Doctrine and Corporate Group Responsibility in European Antitrust Law*, 2014 (ISBN 978-90-411-5262-6).
58. Urška Petrovčič, *Competition Law and Standard Essential Patents: A Transatlantic Perspective*, 2014 (ISBN 978-90-411-4960-2).
59. David Telyas, *The Interface between Competition Law, Patents and Technical Standards*, 2014 (ISBN 978-90-411-5418-7).
60. Katerina Maniadaki, *EU Competition Law, Regulation and the Internet: The Case of Net Neutrality*, 2014 (ISBN 978-90-411-4140-8).
61. Horacio Vedia Jerez, *Competition Law Enforcement and Compliance across the World: A Comparative Review*, 2015 (ISBN 978-90-411-5815-4).
62. Kadir Baş, *The Substantive Appraisal of Joint Ventures under the EU Merger Control Regime*, 2015 (ISBN 978-90-411-5816-1).
63. Alberto Santa Maria, *Competition and State Aid: An Analysis of the EU Practice*, Second Edition, 2015 (ISBN 978-90-411-5818-5).
64. Lúcio Tomé Feteira, *The Interplay between European and National Competition Law after Regulation 1/2003: "United (Should) We Stand?"*, 2016 (ISBN 978-90-411-5663-1).
65. Giovanni Pitruzzella & Gabriella Muscolo (eds), *Competition and Patent Law in the Pharmaceutical Sector: An International Perspective*, 2016 (ISBN 978-90-411-5927-4).
66. Małgorzata Cyndecka, *The Market Economy Investor Test in EU State Aid Law: Applicability and Application*, 2016 (ISBN 978-90-411-6102-4).
67. Damiano Canapa, *Trademarks and Brands in Merger Control: An Analysis of the European and Swiss Legal Orders*, 2016 (ISBN 978-90-411-6717-0).
68. Inge Graef, *EU Competition Law, Data Protection and Online Platforms: Data as Essential Facility*, 2016 (ISBN 978-90-411-8324-8).
69. Anders Jessen, *Exclusionary Abuse after the* Post Danmark I *Case: The Role of the Effects-Based Approach under Article 102 TFEU*, 2017 (ISBN 978-90-411-8996-7).
70. Baskaran Balasingham, *The EU Leniency Policy: Reconciling Effectiveness and Fairness*, 2017 (ISBN 978-90-411-8479-5).
71. Eugene Stuart & Iana Roginska-Green, *Sixty Years of EU State Aid Law and Policy: Analysis and Assessment*, 2018 (ISBN 978-90-411-8869-4).

72. Anna Renata Pisarkiewicz, *Margin Squeeze in the Electronic Communications Sector: Critical Analysis of the Decisional Practice and Case Law*, 2018 (ISBN 978-90-411-6246-5).
73. Ploykaew Porananond, *Competition Law in the ASEAN Countries: Regional Law and National Systems*, 2018 (ISBN 978-90-411-9102-1).
74. Corinne Ruechardt, *EU State Aid Control of Infrastructure Funding*, 2018 (ISBN 978-90-411-9099-4).
75. Amalia Athanasiadou, *Patent Settlements in the Pharmaceutical Industry under US Antitrust and EU Competition Law*, 2018 (ISBN 978-94-035-0113-0).
76. Miroslava Marinova, *Fidelity Rebates in Competition Law: Application of the 'As Efficient Competitor' Test*, 2018 (ISBN 978-94-035-0570-1).
77. Gabriella Muscolo & Marina Tavassi, *The Interplay Between Competition Law and Intellectual Property: An International Perspective*, 2019 (ISBN 978-90-411-8687-4).
78. Fevzi Toksoy, Bahadir Balki & Hanna Stakheyeva, *Merger Control in the EU and Turkey: A Comparative Guide*, Second Edition, 2022 (ISBN 978-94-035-4303-1).
79. Paulo Burnier da Silveira & William Evan Kovacic (eds), *Global Competition Enforcement: New Players, New Challenges*, 2019 (ISBN 978-94-035-0283-0).
80. Giovanna Massarotto, *Antitrust Settlements: How a Simple Agreement Can Drive the Economy*, 2019 (ISBN 978-94-035-1133-7).
81. Marc Veenbrink, *Criminal Law Principles and the Enforcement of EU and National Competition Law: A Silent Takeover?*, 2020 (ISBN 978-94-035-1434-5).
82. Ferdinand Wollenschläger, Wolfgang Wurmnest & Thomas M.J. Möllers (eds), *Private Enforcement of European Competition and State Aid Law: Current Challenges and the Way Forward*, 2020 (ISBN 978-94-035-0281-6).
83. Jorge Marcos Ramos, *Firm Dominance in EU Competition Law: The Competitive Process and the Origins of Market Power*, 2020 (ISBN 978-94-035-2030-8).
84. Ingrid Margrethe Halvorsen Barlund, *Leniency in EU Competition Law*, 2020 (ISBN 978-94-035-1722-3).
85. Jan Blockx, Mens Rea *in EU Antitrust Law: When Intentions Matter*, 2020 (ISBN 978-94-035-2353-8).
86. Maria Wasastjerna, *Competition, Data and Privacy in the Digital Economy: Towards a Privacy Dimension in Competition Policy?*, 2020 (ISBN 978-94-035-2220-3).
87. Maria Fernanda Caporale Madi, *Regulating Vertical Agreements: A Comparative Law and Economics Review of the EU and Brazil*, 2020 (ISBN 978-94-035-2650-8).
88. Martin Gassler, *Information Exchange Between Competitors in EU Competition Law*, 2021 (ISBN 978-94-035-3183-0).

89. Andrea Biondi, Gabriella Muscolo & Renato Nazzini (eds), *After the Damages Directive: Policy and Practice in the EU Member States and the United Kingdom*, 2022 (ISBN 978-94-035-1302-7).
90. Angelika S. Murer, *Blocking Patents in European Competition Law: The Implications of the Concept of Abuse*, 2022 (ISBN 978-94-035-3814-3).
91. Barry Rodger and Or Brook, Maciej Bernatt, Francisco Marcos & Annalies Outhuijse, *Judicial Review of Competition Law Enforcement in the EU Member States and the UK*, 2024 (ISBN 978-94-035-0238-0)